QUARTERMASTER SUPPORT

OF THE ARMY

A History of the Corps

1775 - 19°°

by
Erna Risch

CENTER OF MILITARY HISTORY

UNITED STATES ARMY

WASHINGTON, D.C., 1989

Library of Congress Catalog Card Number: 62-60012

First Printed 1962—CMH Pub 70-35

Foreword

The study of logistics in war and peace is finally coming into its own. After decades of concentrating on strategy and tactics, military historians are increasingly turning to the role of logistics in operational art. It is well that they do so because, in truth, the historical profession has failed to keep pace with military planners and trainers. These officers understand the vital role that logistics — the supply of personnel and equipment for battle — plays in modern warfare and for that reason are anxious to know more about the logistical context of the nation's military past.

To encourage this new interest in logistical history, the Center of Military History is bringing back into print this important volume on the Quartermaster Corps, one of the oldest and most important supply agencies of the United States Army. This history provides a documented record of the origin and growth of the Corps and of the logistical support it gave the Army in war and peace. The story's 1939 ending was deliberately chosen to lead the reader into the comprehensive histories of logistics in the U.S. Army in World War II series. Similar studies are now underway for both the Korean and Vietnam conflicts.

Particularly during this "Year of Training" I commend this useful account of the pre-World War II Army not only to those officers and military students training for leadership positions in the combat support branches, but to all students of military history who wish to understand the contribution played by the logistician to victory on the field of battle.

Washington, D.C.
1 September 1988

WILLIAM A. STOFFT
Brigadier General, USA
Chief of Military History

iii

Preface to New Edition

This book was authorized by and first published under the auspices of the Office of The Quartermaster General (OQMG). On the eve of World War II, the Quartermaster Corps had long been one of the most important supply agencies of the United States Army, sustaining the troops when they took the field in active campaigns and supporting them in peacetime when they were stationed at posts and garrisons. In the course of its long existence, the Corps experienced many changes. Primarily responsible for the transportation of men and supplies when it was established in 1775, the Corps, by 1939, had become a supply service that procured and distributed clothing, rations, and equipment. An organization that originally was, to a large extent, civilian in character had evolved into a militarized Corps. The position of The Quartermaster General had changed from that of a G-4 who functioned as chief assistant to the Commanding General in the field, serving only during a war, to that of a bureau chief with permanent headquarters in Washington.

Fragmentary accounts of some of these developments had been written before this volume, but what was needed was a comprehensive, thoroughly documented account that would provide the continuity, hitherto lacking, for a history of the Corps. *Quartermaster Support of the Army* traces the growth and evolution of the Corps, the changes made in its responsibilities, and the methods and procedures it developed for executing its functions. Both the successes and the failures of the Corps are included.

The time span of the volume is from the appointment of the first Quartermaster General to Washington's Army in June 1775 to President Franklin D. Roosevelt's proclamation of limited emergency in September 1939. This terminal date was selected because the Corps' World War II operations are fully covered in four volumes in the United States Army in World War II series published by what is now the U.S. Army Center of Military History. This book, then, is the first in a sequence of volumes covering Quartermaster operations through World War II.

The limitations imposed by a one-volume history covering more than 150 years of Quartermaster developments prevented the inclusion of every facet of Quartermaster support in all theaters of operations in the wars from the American Revolution to World War II. Some activities receive only scanty treatment or are omitted entirely. In addition, a background of combat operations is not included for the war periods. It was assumed that the reader would have some familiarity with the battles and campaigns of those wars. In consequence, only some guidelines and a few sketch maps are offered; the emphasis is on analyzing Quartermaster wartime support operations.

The largest and most important collections of War Department and Quartermaster Corps records used in the preparation of this volume are deposited at the National Archives and Records Administration in Washington, D.C. Dr. Irvine Dallas, Chief Archivist, War Records Division of the National Archives, provided expert guidance to the various collections. The writer is also grateful to the late Dr. Carl Lokke for the suggestions he offered in using the Papers of the Continental Congress in his charge at the National Archives.

Various manuscript collections provided a considerable body of supplementary and enlightening material. The author wishes to acknowledge the help given by the staff of the Manuscripts Division, Library of Congress, and the courtesies extended by the directors and librarians of the American Philosophical Society Library, the New York Historical Society, the Pennsylvania Historical Society, the Chicago Historical Society, and the New York Public Library.

My debts of gratitude to the many individuals who read portions of this manuscript are too numerous to permit me to express my thanks publicly to each by name. Some contributions, however, merit particular mention. To Dr. Thomas M. Pitkin, a former chief of the Historical Branch, OQMG, the author owes a special debt for his sustained encouragement and for his constructive criticism of the entire manuscript. The then Chief Historian of the Department of the Army, the late Dr. Stetson Conn, provided sound advice and strong support in both the preparation and the publication of this volume. The author is particularly indebted to Mr. Detmar Finke for his assistance in obtaining permission from Mr. Henry I. Shaw, Jr., editor in chief of the Company of Military Collectors and Historians, to reproduce the excellent drawings of H. Charles McBarron, Jr., James Hutchins, and John Severin, and the delightful pen sketch by Col. H.S. Parker.

The author also wishes again to thank Houghton Mifflin Company for permission to quote from French's *The First Year of the American Revolution* and Arthur H. Clark Company for permission to quote from Bandel's *Frontier Life in the Army.*

Special thanks are also still due to Miss Mary E. Kennedy, chief of the Graphics Presentation Branch, OQMG, and her able staff who prepared the sketch maps. I also wish to thank the secretarial staff of the former OQMG Historical Office for the many hours of clerical and typing assistance provided at various stages in the preparation of this volume.

Responsibility for any deficiencies in this book is entirely mine.

Washington, D.C.   ERNA RISCH
1 September 1988

Contents

xiii

Charts

Maps

Illustrations

Credit for Illustrations

Illustrations, pp. 14, 50, 148, 165, 225, 252, 349, 501, 504, 712, are reproduced by permission of the editor in chief of the Company of Military Collectors and Historians. The drawings on pp. 14, 50, 148, 165, 225, 252, 349 are the work of H. Charles McBarron, Jr., those on pp. 501, 712 are the work of J. S. Hutchins and J. Severin, respectively, and Col. H. S. Parker did the sketch on p. 504.

The National Archives furnished the following illustrations from the Brady Collection: pp. 399, 400, 405, 418, 443, 448, 449. It also furnished, from Signal Corps files deposited at the Archives, the following illustrations: pp. 20, 33, 85, 90, 128, 293, 296, 320, 413, 421, 436, 474, 475, 477, 482, 483, 485, 526, 531, 532, 538, 552.

Illustrations, pp. 377, 385, 417, 442, 446, 447, 450, are furnished by the Prints and Photographs Division, Library of Congress.

All other illustrations are from Department of Defense files.

CHAPTER I

The Origins of Quartermaster Supply
1775 - 1778

"No body ever heard of a quarter Master, in History" lamented Maj. Gen. Nathanael Greene who, only out of patriotism and personal devotion to his commander-in-chief, General Washington, agreed to accept the post of Quartermaster General in the Continental Army.[1] For that matter little or nothing has ever been heard of any supply officer; military history, so voluminous in its recording of combat operations, has been, until recent years, strangely silent about the logistics of war.

Origin of the Supply Departments

The Quartermaster Corps, one of the oldest supply agencies of the United States Army, traces its origin to 16 June 1775. On that day, following Washington's address accepting command of the Army, the Second Continental Congress passed a resolution providing for "one quarter master general for the grand army, and a deputy, under him, for the separate army," who were to be paid, respectively, $80 and $40 a month.[2] It thereby adopted for American usage an agency that had long been established in the British army, and whose functions had become familiar to the colonists through their participation with British troops in the campaigns against the French and their Indian allies.

Congress on that same day also provided for a Commissary General of Stores and Purchases in whom it vested responsibility for feeding the troops. Later it established the office of Clothier General as well as other supply departments. Before the end of the Revolutionary War, however, Quartermaster General Timothy Pickering was to suggest that his Department absorb the duties of the Commissary General of Purchases. "Is there no man in the United States whose abilities can com-

---

[1] Washington Papers, vol. 104, f. 82 (To Washington, 24 Apr 1779). Manuscript Div., Library of Congress.

[2] Journals of the Continental Congress, ed. Worthington C. Ford and others (34 vols., Washington, 1904–37), II, 94.

prehend and execute the plans proposed," he queried.[3] That point remained undemonstrated because of Washington's objections to the proposal. Such a merger did not occur until 131 years later. On the other hand, 65 years after the formation of the Clothing Department, the Quartermaster's Department had gradually absorbed all of its duties. Because feeding and clothing the American soldier have become so thoroughly identified with the Quartermaster Corps today, early developments in these supply fields have been included in this history of the Corps despite the fact that separate agencies were at one time responsible for these functions.

In the years since 1775, the office of the Quartermaster General has evolved into that of a bureau chief who, administering a militarized corps and employing a large body of civilians, is primarily concerned with the supply of food and clothing and the performance of certain services that promote the health and welfare of the soldier. His functions bear little resemblance to those assigned to a Quartermaster General of an 18th century army. The latter was the right-hand man of the commanding general, in effect his chief of staff. As principal staff officer, he gathered information, assisted the commanding general in planning his marches, and distributed the march orders to the general officers. He thoroughly explored the field of operations, opened and repaired all roads on the line of advance and retreat, chose proper points for bridges, and examined fords. He laid out the camp and assigned quarters. In addition to such direct service to the army in the field, he was also responsible for the procurement of certain types of matériel. He and his assistants procured and furnished all camp equipment and tents and, when the army went into winter quarters, they provided the lumber and other articles needed for hutting the troops. He transported all men and all supplies. Accordingly, he furnished horses and pack animals and provided the forage for their maintenance. He supplied wagons when the army moved by land and boats when it resorted to water routes. In short, he took all measures to enable an army to march with ease and to encamp with convenience and safety. In contrast to the office of the modern Quartermaster General that operates in peace as well as in war, that of an 18th century Quartermaster General functioned only during war because it was held that the staff properly existed only at that time.[4]

---

[3] (1) RG 11, Papers of the Continental Congress, item 147, vol. VI, f. 453 (Pickering to Pres. of Congress, 21 Mar 1781). National Archives. (2) Octavius Pickering and Charles W. Upham, *The Life of Timothy Pickering* (4 vols., Boston, 1867–73), I, 287 (Pickering to S. Hodgdon, 22 Apr 1781).

[4] Thomas Simes, *The Military Guide for Young Officers* (2 vols., Philadelphia, 1776), I, 8–9. This was a British text, popular with the American colonists, and reprinted in Philadelphia in 1776.

When Washington arrived at Cambridge on 3 July 1775 to take command of the Army, he found a heterogeneous and undisciplined force of some 17,000 men assembled there, all of whom were enlisted for short periods—some only to 1 December, none beyond 1 January 1776. The Second Continental Congress had accepted these troops as the nucleus of an Army, but, desirous of creating a Continental Army with troops and principal general officers under its own authority, it had ordered certain troops raised in the pay of Congress. These consisted of ten companies of riflemen, six from Pennsylvania and two each from Maryland and Virginia, who were enlisted for one year and were "to join the army near Boston, to be there employed as light infantry, under the command of the chief Officer in that army." [5] This was the origin of the Continental Army. Gradually it was expanded, and enlistments were extended to two and three years and in some cases for the duration of the war. The states never filled their quotas of men, and throughout the war the Continental Army was always under strength. Militia, called out for short terms only, were used to build up strength during campaigns. Uncertainty as to Army strength contributed immeasurably to the difficulties of supply.

Although Washington had to cope with the problem of reorganizing the army, and in fact had the delicate task of replacing that army, within cannon shot of the enemy, with another army when enlistments expired at the end of 1775, his immediate problem was not a lack of men so much as a lack of supplies. His troops needed powder, lead, arms, tents, horses, carts, tools, and medical stores, though they had enough provisions. Joseph Trumbull, who had been appointed Commissary General of Stores and Purchases by Congress on 19 July, was meeting subsistence requirements of the Army by widening operations that he had been conducting as commissary for the Connecticut troops. [6] What Washington most urgently needed was a Quartermaster General, but he was reluctant to make so important an appointment without express authorization. His judgment was sound, for when Congress on 19 July authorized him to appoint his own Quartermaster General, as well as certain other officers of what now would be termed the general staff, John Adams thought that a major mistake had been made. In his view such officers ought to be a check on the commander-in-chief and their appointments ought to rest with Congress. [7]

Acting under the authority granted him, Washington on 14 August appointed a young Pennsylvanian, Maj. Thomas Mifflin as Quarter-

---

[5] *Journals of the Continental Congress*, II, 89 (14 Jun 1775).

[6] *Ibid.*, II, 190.

[7] *Letters of Members of the Continental Congress*, ed. Edmund C. Burnett (7 vols., Washington, 1921–36), I, 174, 177–78 (Adams to James Warren, 23 and 26 Jul 1775).

master General.[8]   Four months later Congress established the rank of his office as that of a colonel in the Continental Army.[9]   Mifflin, who held the office twice, was the first of four men who served as Quartermaster General during the Revolutionary War, his successors being Stephen Moylan, Nathanael Greene, and Timothy Pickering.   Each of these men served with the main Army under Washington.[10]   Congress itself appointed deputy quartermasters general to act with separate armies, fixing their rank as that of a colonel in the Army.[11]   In theory, a deputy quartermaster general of a separate army was under the direction and supervision of the Quartermaster General.   In actual practice, he generally functioned independently and was encouraged to do so, for his field of activity was usually so remote from the area where the main Continental Army was operating that the Quartermaster General was in no position even to advise him on a course of action.

Supervisory Controls

The Quartermaster General and the Commissary General, as well as their deputies, were responsible to the Continental Congress.   At the beginning of the war, Congress, burdened with many problems, offered no supervisory control of the supply agencies, nor was there an executive department to direct such supervision.   Standing committees in Congress handled executive duties, and special committees, sent to visit the Army, exercised such control of the supply departments as Congress provided. More often than not Congress dispatched such committees at periods of crisis, as, for example, after withdrawal of the Continental Army from Long Island in the summer of 1776, or during the encampment of the Army at Valley Forge in the winter of 1777–78.

Boards soon replaced standing committees in the course of the struggle to develop an executive department.[12]   When on 12 June 1776 Congress established a Board of War and Ordnance, it took the first step toward the creation of an administrative War Department.[13]   The Board's

---

[8] *The Writings of Washington,* ed. John C. Fitzpatrick (30 vols., Washington, 1931–39), III, 419 (GO, 14 Aug 1775).   Hereafter cited *Writings of Washington.*

[9] *Journals of the Continental Congress,* III, 445 (22 Dec 1775).

[10] Analysis of supply problems has of necessity been limited to those of the main Continental Army.   Only incidental mention has been made of either Northern or Southern Army operations.   For more information on supply problems encountered by the Southern Army, see Theodore Thayer, *Nathanael Greene Strategist of the American Revolution* (New York, 1960).

[11] See, for example, the appointment of Donald Campbell as deputy quartermaster general for the Northern Army.   *Journals of the Continental Congress,* II, 186 (17 Jul 1775).

[12] For a detailed analysis of this problem see Jennings B. Sanders, *Evolution of Executive Department of the Continental Congress* (Chapel Hill, 1935), 4 ff.

[13] *Journals of the Continental Congress,* V, 434.

membership underwent a number of changes, but its duties remained relatively constant.   Primarily it was concerned with keeping accounts of ordnance and supplies, laying before Congress estimates of military stores that were needed, and superintending the building of arsenals and foundries.   It was not until 25 November 1779 that the Quartermaster's Department was placed under the direction of the Board of War.[14]   Some 14 months later, however, Congress replaced the Board with a War Office, headed by a Secretary at War, but it was 30 October 1781 before Maj. Gen. Benjamin Lincoln was elected to fill that position.[15]   His duties, originally much the same as those formerly performed by the Board of War, were somewhat expanded the following April.   In any case, an executive department had finally been evolved, and the Quartermaster's Department, as well as all other military departments, were placed under its supervision.

In June 1775, however, not only was there no indication of the nature of the supervision to be exercised, but Congress in creating the offices of Quartermaster General and of Commissary General of Stores and Purchases defined neither their functions nor their bounds.   In time it did undertake to do so by enacting regulatory measures that became increasingly detailed, but in 1775 Congress permitted Mifflin and Trumbull to organize their departments as they saw fit.   While certain supply arrangements that had evolved before their appointments had to be drawn within their respective Departments, the field organization of the Commissary and Quartermaster's Departments necessarily had to conform to the troop arrangements of the Army in the Boston area.

Supply Organization

In the summer of 1775, the American Army confronted the British troops, located at Bunker Hill and Boston Neck, from an entrenched position that extended from Winter and Prospect Hills on the left to Roxbury on the right, with the central camp of the Army located at Cambridge.   Washington reorganized his Army into three divisions, each made up of two brigades, averaging six regiments each.   One division

---

[14] (1) *Ibid.*, XVII, 511–12.   (2) Originally, this Department was known as the Quartermaster General's Department, and in his correspondence General Washington uses that title.   Early in 1777, however, the Continental Congress began to refer to the Quartermaster's Department. (See *Journals of the Continental Congress*, VII, 191, 292, 355–59.)   There was no consistency in its use of the title.   The shortened version became the one most commonly used and in 1812 Congress officially designated the agency as the Quartermaster's Department.   (2 *Stat.* 696). For consistency's sake, the title of Quartermaster's Department is used in this volume throughout the years 1775 to 1812.

[15] Lincoln accepted the office approximately one month later on 26 November 1781. *Journals of the Continental Congress*, XXI, 1087, 1141.

on the right held the Roxbury lines under the command of Maj. Gen. Artemus Ward; Maj. Gen. Charles Lee commanded a second division on the left at Prospect and Winter Hills; and Maj. Gen. Israel Putnam commanded a third division, the center at Cambridge.

In the closing months of 1775 the Quartermaster's Department was also organized in three units. The largest of these, employing some 17 clerks and assistants, was located at Cambridge where Quartermaster General Mifflin was stationed. Four of these clerks kept accounts and records. Two clerks, assigned to an issuing store, distributed camp utensils and other equipment to the troops at Cambridge, while two other clerks received and delivered wood to them. The Department also operated a granary, a lumber yard, and stables. It employed two wagonmasters at Cambridge, one of whom, John Goddard, had been appointed "wagonmaster general to the Army of the twelve United Colonies" by Washington on 9 August.[16] Goddard was merely continuing the work he had been doing before the attack on Concord. From 8 March to 14 April 1775, various people under his direction had been carting casks of balls, barrels of linen, hogsheads of flints, loads of beef and rice, quantities of canteens, and other articles through the quiet country roads leading to Concord. At Cambridge, one man in the Quartermaster's Department superintended all the "smiths, armourers, and nailers in the Army," while another directed the work of 50 carpenters. In addition to the latter, an undesignated number of other carpenters in "Captain Ayers company" were constantly at work on the wagon trains that were used to haul supplies.

An assistant quartermaster general headed each of two smaller units of the Department. John Parke directed one office at Roxbury; John G. Frazer administered the second office, serving Winter and Prospect Hills. Each office employed one clerk and one wagonmaster. Roxbury, Winter Hill, and Prospect Hill each had also one clerk to receive and deliver the wood used by the troops in those areas.[17]

Trumbull's field organization for the Commissary Department was also made up three units. He used issuing stores, supervised by storekeepers, at Cambridge, Roxbury, and Prospect Hill to service the two brigades stationed in each of these areas. There was also an issuing store at Medford. A varying number of clerks assisted each storekeeper who also employed several laborers, one cooper, and sometimes a cook. Trumbull established storage places, so-called magazines, at Cambridge and Roxbury, at each of which three clerks or magazine helpers and one

[16] *Writings of Washington*, ed. Fitzpatrick, III, 411 (GO, 9 Aug 1775).
[17] Washington Papers, vol. 23, f. 36 (List of Personnel,—Jan 1776). Parke's appointment was announced in a General Order, 16 August, and Frazer's on 22 September 1775.

cooper were employed.   A number of deposit points located some 20 miles away on the roads leading to Cambridge and Roxbury backed up these two magazines.   They also employed a number of magazine helpers. Trumbull deposited flour at these points and there, too, he had cattle and hogs driven to be slaughtered, salted, and packed to meet Army demands.[18] The clerical help, storekeepers, artisans, and other personnel employed by Mifflin and Trumbull, and the issuing stores and other facilities that they established in the Boston area were to be duplicated by their successors wherever the Army moved.

In addition to their field organizations, both Mifflin and Trumbull made use of the services of merchants in various parts of the country to purchase subsistence for the Commissary Department and forage, tentage, canteens, and other articles for the Quartermaster's Department.   Unlike the personnel in the field organizations who were paid salaries and ration allowances fixed by Congress, these purchasing agents worked on a commission basis.   The Departments customarily paid them about 2 to $2\frac{1}{2}$ percent commission on the money they expended in making their purchases.

During the first 2 years of the war, the supply organization remained fluid, being adapted to changing operations.   Some additional personnel was required, but unfortunately in the Commissary Department Congress took care of that need in such a way as to threaten Trumbull's control of all commissary matters.   With characteristic lack of attention to overlapping jurisdictions, the Continental Congress promoted confusion by appointing a number of independent agents in Pennsylvania and New York to procure food for the troops in those areas.[19]   In New York, jealousy between New Englanders and New Yorkers further augmented the discord.   After several months of controversy between the commissaries, Congress resolved the problem by revoking its support of independent agents and sustaining the authority to procure subsistence for the Army that it had originally granted solely to Trumbull.[20]

Expansion of the Quartermaster's Department was effected without controversy.   When the Army moved to New York, a deputy quarter-

---

[18] *Ibid.*, vol. 22, f. 117 (List of Personnel, 20 Jan 1776); vol. 23, f. 3 (Trumbull to Pres. of Congress, 23 Jan 1776).

[19] *Journals of the Continental Congress*, II, 186 (17 Jul 1775); III, 419 (9 Dec 1775); IV, 159–60 (17 Feb 1776); 210 (16 Mar 1776).

[20] (1) *Ibid.*, V, 527 (8 Jul 1776); 752–53 (12 Sep 1776). (2) *American Archives*, ed. Peter Force (9 vols., 4th and 5th Series, Washington, 1837–53), 5th ser, I, 193 (Washington to Schuyler, 11 Jul 1776); II, 213–14 (Trumbull to Pres. of Congress, 7 Sep 1776); 348 (Pres. of Congress to Trumbull, 16 Sep 1776). (3) For elaboration on the New York controversy see Victor L. Johnson, *The Administration of the American Commissariat During the Revolutionary War* (Philadelphia, 1941), 121 ff.

master general was appointed at Boston to administer to the troops remaining in the Eastern Department. In New York, Mifflin found that the services of a local man, familiar with the resources of the state, would be desirable. Hugh Hughes, a former school teacher of New York City and then serving as commissary of stores, was appointed assistant quartermaster general in May 1776.[21] Upon him fell the main burden of carrying forward immediate Quartermaster preparations for the New York campaign, since shortly after his appointment Mifflin resigned as Quartermaster General when Congress promoted him to the rank of brigadier general of the Army.[22] As a result, Washington had to fill that important post before the impending battle in New York.

He turned to another member of his military family for his candidate, selecting Stephen Moylan, who since 11 August 1775 had been serving as Muster-Master-General to the Army and since 7 March 1776, also as aide-de-camp to Washington. Congress appointed him to the post on 5 June in the midst of active operations that demanded administrative skill to provide ample transportation and a steady flow of supplies.[23] Whether or not Moylan possessed such ability cannot be determined on the basis of present evidence, but Washington blamed his Department for the loss of heavy guns, ammunition, stores, provisions, and tents, left behind in the evacuation of New York City in September. That evacuation, like the one from Long Island after the disastrous battle in August, would have been effected without loss, the General maintained, "but for a defect in the department of the Quarter Master General's not providing teams enough." [24] In consequence, a congressional committee persuaded Moylan to resign less than 4 months after his appointment. To the great satisfaction of Congress and the Army, Mifflin reluctantly accepted reappointment to the office with the rank and pay of a brigadier general.[25] He was well acquainted with its business, William Ellery, member of Congress from Rhode Island, commented, and had "Spirit and Activity to execute it in a proper Manner." [26]

---

[21] *Writings of Washington,* ed. Fitzpatrick, V, 38 (GO, 11 May 1776).

[22] *Journals of the Continental Congress,* IV, 359 (16 May 1776).

[23] *Ibid.,* V. 419.

[24] (1) *Writings of Washington,* ed. Fitzpatrick, VI, 170 (To Sam. Washington, 5 Oct 1776). (2) The general found it convenient to attribute all blame to the Quartermaster General without admitting that in the evacuation from Long Island all the wagons, carts, and horses that had been sent there for the use of the Army had been lost. For the difficulties that Colonel Moylan encountered, see below p. 21.

[25] (1) Papers of the Continental Congress, item 78, vol. XV, f. 101–08 (Moylan to Pres. of Congress, 27 Sep 1776). (2) *Journals of the Continental Congress,* V, 838 (1 Oct 1776). (3) Mifflin's appointment, pending the action of Congress, was announced in GO, 28 September 1776. *Writings of Washington,* ed. Fitzpatrick, VI, 125–26.

[26] *Letters of Members of the Continental Congress,* ed. Burnett, II, 116 (To Gov. of Rhode Island, 5 Oct 1776); see also, 114 (Caesar Rodney to Tom Rodney, 2 Oct 1776).

Supplying Subsistence

During the first two years of the war, when details of organization were being evolved, supply procedures were also developing. No supply need was more immediately urgent in the summer of 1775 than feeding the hastily assembled troops at Boston. Congress ordered Washington "to victual at the Continental expense all such volunteers as have joined or shall join the united army." [27] Impressed with the way in which Trumbull had subsisted the Connecticut troops, Washington expected his Commissary General to make satisfactory provision for the Army. In this he was not disappointed, for Trumbull, in his efforts to supply the Connecticut troops, had built up a network of purchasing channels that, as Commissary General, he continued to use in order to bring to the Continental Army at Boston flour from New York, via Norwich, Conn., and vegetables, pork, and other subsistence items from various parts of the fertile Connecticut River valley.

When the war began each colony had its own established ration that it furnished its troops, but by 4 November 1775 Congress had agreed upon a uniform ration for all the soldiers of the Continental Army. It fixed the components as follows:

Resolved, That a ration consist of the following kind and quantity of provisions: 1 lb. beef, or ¾ lb. pork or 1 lb. salt fish, per day; 1 lb. bread or flour, per day; 3 pints of peas or beans per week, or vegetables equivalent, at one dollar per bushel for peas or beans; 1 pint of milk, per man per day, or at the rate of 1–72 of a dollar; 1 half pint of rice, or one pint of Indian meal, per man per week; 1 quart of spruce beer or cider per man per day, or nine gallons of mollasses, per company of 100 men per week; 3 lbs. candles to 100 men per week, for guards; 24 lbs. soft, or 8 lbs. hard soap, for 100 men per week. [28]

This was not a bad allowance and compared favorably with that issued the British soldier in the Revolutionary War, but the soap ration was certainly meager if the men were expected to keep both themselves and their clothes clean. [29]

As long as Trumbull remained Commissary General, he attempted to provide the troops of the Continental Army with a more generous allowance than that established by Congress. In the early months of the

---

[27] *Journals of the Continental Congress,* II, 100 (20 Jun 1775).

[28] (1) *Ibid.,* III, 323. (2) Spruce beer was a beverage made from spruce twigs and leaves boiled with molasses or sugar and fermented with yeast.

[29] In a typical contract of 1778–79, the British ration provided 1 lb. of flour per day; 1 lb. of beef per day or in lieu thereof slightly more than 9 ounces of pork; 3 pints of peas a week; ½ lb. of oatmeal a week and either 6 oz. of butter or 8 oz. of cheese per week. Edward E. Curtis, "Provisioning of the British Army in the Revolution," *The Magazine of History,* XVIII, 234.

war, he issued 8 more ounces of salted pork per man, per day, than the established ration called for. He also provided 6 ounces of butter per man, per week, and allowed 6 rather than 3 pounds of candles per 100 men, per week. In other details the two rations were identical. The inclusion of milk in the ration established by Congress, however, appears to have been an ideal; Trumbull did not provide it nor is there any evidence to indicate that any other commissary did. Spruce beer was not to be had in the Cambridge area, and Trumbull generally furnished molasses as part of the ration. On the other hand, when the troops moved to New York, he could not procure molasses and he issued spruce beer to the troops.[30]

After the Middle Atlantic area became the theater of operations, Trumbull and his successors found it increasingly difficult to procure rations. As the war went on, the Revolutionary soldiers were subsisted on a bread and meat diet. The Commissary Department was judged successful in its later operations if it provided sufficient quantities of flour and beef. Vegetables were usually lacking, and vinegar, later included in the ration for antiscorbutic purposes, was often omitted from issue by commissaries. Neither spruce beer and cider, nor rum and whiskey, subsequently authorized as part of the ration, were ever plentiful. Sutlers plied their trade, and Washington authorized markets at camp where farmers could sell their produce, but soldiers had little money to buy supplementary foods. Then, as in later wars, however, soldiers "seamed hearty in the Cause of Liberty of teaking what came in the way first to their hand." So when a patrol took up a sheep and two large turkeys, "not being able to give the countersign," Sergeant John Smith, a good soldier and good provider, recorded in his diary that "they was tryed by fire, and executed by the whole division of the free booters."[31] Despite such occasional feasts, an unrelieved diet of half-cooked meat and hard bread was responsible for much of the sickness that reduced the strength of the Army when it frequently was most needed.[32]

Trumbull was so successful in subsisting the troops during the Boston campaign that Washington later wrote, "Few Armies, if any, have been better and more plentifully supplied than the Troops under Mr. Trumbull's care."[33] The Commissary General deserved all the credit given him, but the Army was then encamped in the midst of a sympathetic people, the war was new, foodstuffs were generally plentiful, and prices

---

[30] Washington Papers, vol. 25, f. 77 (Trumbull to Washington, 19 Apr 1776).

[31] William Matthews and Dixon Wecter, *Our Soldiers Speak, 1775–1918* (Boston, 1943), 24.

[32] *Writings of Washington*, ed. Fitzpatrick. VIII, 441 (To Philip Livingston *et al.*, 19 Jul 1777).

[33] *Ibid.*, V, 192 (To Pres. of Congress, 28 Jun 1776).

had not yet skyrocketed to unheard of heights.   The real test of provisioning the Army was yet to come.

When the British evacuated Boston and Washington moved his Army to New York, Trumbull, for the first time, had to provision an ever-moving Army, and an Army whose strength changed repeatedly.   When Washington arrived in New York, it consisted of some 9,000 men; by June it had grown to about 19,000, most of the increase being raw recruits and militia; after the fall of Ft. Washington in November, the Army dwindled to 14,000, and kept decreasing as terms of enlistment expired and the contagion of desertion spread.[34]   Instead of transporting food to a stationary force, Trumbull now had to locate magazines at strategic points along the line of march.   He and his deputies drew ample stores of flour, beef, and pork from Connecticut, Pennsylvania, and the rich and readily accessible hinterland of New York City for the use of the troops on Manhattan and Long Island, but no sooner had they prepared well-stocked magazines than the Continental Army was forced to evacuate New York City, leaving behind large quantities of flour.   So constant was the movement of the Army in the autumn of 1776, involving retreat up the Hudson and across New Jersey, that it was impossible for Trumbull to develop permanent magazines.   The best he could do was to attempt to provide the soldiers with sufficient cooked rations to maintain 4 days' supply on hand.   He had to appeal to the New York Convention for assistance in accumulating flour.[35]

Even as Trumbull's commissaries strained to provide barrels of flour for the retreating troops and kept, in their rear, droves of cattle, to be killed or moved as occasion required, the Department also had to make preparations to supply the Army during the period of winter encampment and to build up reserves to support its active operations in the following year.[36]   Late fall and the early winter were the months when commissaries had to procure cattle and hogs, slaughter the animals, cure the meat, pack it in barrels, and deposit it in designated magazines. They also had to build up flour deposits.

About the middle of December 1776, Trumbull departed for Hartford to supervise personally these important preparations in New England, leaving a deputy, Carpenter Wharton, with the Army to supply its needs.   The latter was unsuccessful in provisioning the troops at the very time that Washington was attempting to capitalize on the advantage

[34] Christopher Ward, *The War of the Revolution* (2 vols., New York, 1952), I, 207, 275.

[35] *American Archives*, ed. Force, 5th ser, II, 699; 469 (Trumbull to N.Y. Convention, 16 and 23 Sep 1776); 1138–39 (Tench Tilghman to William Duer, 20 Oct 1776).

[36] (1) *Ibid.*, 5th ser, II, 372 (Trumbull to Pres. of Congress, 19 Sep 1776). (2) *Journals of the Continental Congress*, V, 825 (25 Sep 1776).

MERRY CHRISTMAS, 1776

gained at Trenton. The troops were unable to move for want of rations, and Washington charged that he was delayed for two days in crossing the Delaware and then had to permit the troops to "victual themselves where they could." [37] Wharton was further accused of profiteering, and so universal was the complaint against him that Washington called on Trumbull to return and regulate his Department.[38] Trumbull's supply procedures were effective in establishing well-stocked magazines in Massachusetts and Connecticut from which supplies were drawn for the troops during the winter of 1776–77. They did not suffer from a lack of flour or meat. On the other hand, the failure of the commissaries to provide vegetables, vinegar, and proper beverages led Elbridge Gerry to warn Trumbull that few men could subsist only upon bread, meat, and water.[39] Criticism of the Commissary Department mounted in 1777.

[37] *Writings of Washington*, ed. Fitzpatrick, VI, 457 (To Robert Morris, 30 Dec 1776); VII, 60–61 (To Robert Ogden, 24 Jan 1777).

[38] (1) *Ibid.*, VII, 160–61 (To Trumbull, 18 Feb 1777). (2) *Letters of Members of the Continental Congress*, ed. Burnett, II, 314–15 (R. Sherman to Trumbull, 18 Feb 1777).

[39] *Letters of Members of the Continental Congress*, ed. Burnett, II, 312 (Gerry to Trumbull, 26 Mar 1777).

Development of Quartermaster Supply Procedures

Quartermaster General Mifflin approached the duties of his office in 1775 without trepidation and, in fact, found opportunity to acquire temporary responsibility for clothing supply—a function not pertaining to his Department. Among the hastily assembled troops at Boston, uniformity in dress was nonexistent. The New England militia that formed the nucleus of Washington's Army came garbed in a variety of outfits. Some wore uniforms that had seen service in the French and Indian War; most of them were clothed in homespun, variously dyed and cut, and, since few of the men had brought any change of clothing, were beginning to be ragged as well. Washington wore the blue and buff of the Virginia militia. The ten companies of riflemen, having been instructed by Congress to find their own clothing, arrived at Cambridge in hunting shirts and round hats.[40] The hunting shirt, worn with long breeches or overalls, made of the same tow cloth, gaither-fashioned about the legs and held down by straps under the shoes, was a popular and acceptable uniform during the opening months of the Revolution.[41] Washington, knowing from experience its practical value, sought to have the hunting shirt adopted as a uniform, but Congress took no action. During most of the war, green and brown predominated as the color of the clothing worn by the troops rather than the "blue and buff" popularly associated with the dress of the Revolutionary soldier Blue was not adopted as the official color of the Army uniform until 2 October 1779.[42]

Replacing the motley garb of the troops with an acceptable uniform was an immediate supply problem difficult of solution since the colonies did not produce much cloth. Colonial women wove linen in their homes but wool and woolen cloth were scarce. At the beginning of the war, the supply of clothing and of blankets was dependent upon what could be obtained by canvassing all sources of supply within the states, even to the extent of making collections from house to house of all articles that could be spared. Congress supplemented this source by purchasing the importations of private adventurers and by utilizing the stocks of textiles, clothing, and blankets found in the cargoes of captured vessels. Though a considerable number of prizes were taken, this source of supply was too precarious to depend upon despite the boldness of privateers.

[40] James Thacher, *A Military Journal During the American Revolutionary War* (Boston, 1827), 40.

[41] *American Archives*, ed. Force, 4th ser, VI, 426 (GO, 6 May 1776); 5th ser, I, 677 (GO, 25 Jul 1776).

[42] (1) Washington Papers, vol. 108, f. 73 (Board of War estimate, 25 May 1779). (2) *Writings of Washington*, ed. Fitzpatrick, XVI, 387–88 (GO, 2 Oct 1779).

Officer and Privates of a Battalion Company

WEBB'S CONTINENTAL REGIMENT, 1777–1781

To meet the clothing deficiency, Congress had to turn to purchase abroad, and clothing and blankets were largely purchased on credit in France during the war.[43]   Even before any agent of the Continental Congress arrived in France, the French ministry had decided to offer secret assistance to the colonies.   A series of loans and subsidies from France and Spain provided much needed munitions of war.   This included tentage and clothing.   Such aid became increasingly important after 1777 when Continental currency depreciated rapidly and French supplies began to arrive in volume.   This supply was supplemented by a lively trade in the West Indies, centered particularly at St. Eustatius, and participated in by private American merchants and agents of both the state governments and of the Continental Congress.[44]

Accepting British army procedure as precedent, Congress directed that clothing for the Continental Army be provided at its expense and be paid for by the soldier at the rate of 1⅔ dollars per month deducted from his wages.[45]   Since Congress had not established any agency to handle clothing supply, it temporarily thrust that responsibility upon the Quartermaster General in the fall of 1775, largely, no doubt, because Mifflin had been actively promoting the procurement of clothing.[46]   As a result, Mifflin continued to stimulate the procurement of woolens and accepted delivery of captured cargoes of textiles and clothing sent to him for distribution to the troops.   He set Army tailors to work making clothing and directed its sale to the troops at a commission to himself of 5 percent for his trouble.   Despite these efforts, a congressional committee, probing the condition of the Army following its evacuation of New York City, had to report that clothing supply had been neglected "as well from the want of a proper Officer to superintend the Business as from the Scarcity of these Articles." [47]

The shortage of textiles also affected a basic function of the Quartermaster General, namely, providing shelter for the troops.   Canvas was at a premium, and, not only in 1775 but later, awnings and ships' sails were utilized to provide tents.   Shelter was as varied among the troops at Boston as uniforms were.   The Rev. William Emerson found it divert-

---

[43] *Journals of the Continental Congress*, IV, 24 (3 Jan 1776); VII, 92 (5 Feb 1777).

[44] (1) For more background and details of this aid, see Samuel F. Bemis, *The Diplomacy of the American Revolution* (Bloomington, 1957), passim.   (2) J. Franklin Jameson, "St. Eustatius in the American Revolution," *American Historical Review*, VIII (July 1903), 683–708.

[45] (1) *Journals of the Continental Congress*, III, 323–24 (4 Nov 1775).   (2) Deduction of a fixed sum for clothing in the British army dated from the days of Elizabeth if not still earlier times.   Sir John W. Fortescue, *A History of the British Army* (13 vols., London, 1899–1930), I, 284.

[46] *Journals of the Continental Congress*, III, 260 (23 Sep 1775); 471–73 (John Adams, "Notes of Debates").

[47] *Ibid.*, V, 844 (3 Oct 1776).

ing to walk among the camps in the Boston area, where every shelter, he thought, depicted the taste of the persons who encamped in it.

> Some are made of boards, some of sailcloth, and some partly of one and partly of the other. Others are made of stone and turf, and others again of Birch and other brush. Some are thrown up in a hurry and look as if they could not help it—mere necessity—others are curiously wrought with doors and windows done with wreaths and withes in the manner of a basket. Some are your proper tents and marquees, and look like the regular camp of the enemy. These are the Rhode-islanders, who are furnished with tent equipage from among ourselves and every thing in the most exact English taste.[48]

Tents, providing accommodation for six men, were intended to afford shelter for the troops during campaigns though there were seldom enough of them to meet all needs. On the march, wagons carrying baggage, kettles, and tents frequently failed to reach the troops when a halt was called for the night. In such a situation, Sergeant John Smith, retreating through mud and water from King's Ferry to Haverstraw in November 1776, found that he and his comrades were "obliged to make us huts with rails and covered with straw" to sleep under.[49] Once the campaign had ended, troops were lodged in barracks, provided they were stationed at posts. The Quartermaster's Department procured wood for the buildings and brick or stone and lime for chimneys and ovens. Under Quartermaster direction, carpenters erected the barracks, but in emergencies militiamen were sometimes called out on fatigue duty to build them.[50] When winter camp quarters were selected in the field at a suitable strategic location, the troops themselves built their own huts. Sometimes they utilized boards furnished by the Quartermaster's Department; more often they chopped down trees, building log houses that accommodated 12 men, with their bunks placed one above the other in tiers of three against each of the four walls.

Beginning with the first winter of 1775–76, it became established policy that as soon as the men moved into their barracks or huts, they delivered all tents to the Quartermaster General. Before the next campaign opened, he had them washed, repaired by artisans hired for the purpose, and stored until needed.[51] During the winter months the Quartermaster General not only directed the salvage of old tents but,

---

[48] Allen French, *The First Year of the American Revolution* (Boston, 1934), 300. (William Emerson to his wife, 17 Jul 1775).

[49] Matthews and Wecter, *Our Soldiers Speak*, 27.

[50] *American Archives*, ed. Force, 5th ser, II, 257 (T. Tilghman to Col. Moylan, 9 Sep 1776); 1254 (Mifflin to Duer, 28 Oct 1776); III, 302 (Resolution of N.Y. Committee of Safety, 8 Nov 1776).

[51] *Writings of Washington*, ed. Fitzpatrick, IV, 4 (GO, 22 Nov 1775); VI, 267–68 (To Mifflin, 10 Nov 1776).

utilizing all the duck that could be obtained, he had new tents manufactured. Replacements were always difficult to obtain and upon occasion that demand could only be satisfied at the expense of other needs. Following the loss of a large amount of tentage during the evacuation of New York City, for example, Congress insisted that "the soldiers should have Tents if they stripped the Yards of those Continental Frigates and Cruisers that had sails made up." As a result a committee of Congress reported, "we have now a parcell of fine vessells lying here useless at a time they might have been most advantageously employed." [52]

Repair of boats became a part of the Department's maintenance program after the first winter of the war. As soon as the Army was shifted to New York, the Hudson became a vital supply artery and boats of every description were much in demand. In addition to those hired to transport supplies, the Quartermaster's Department began building boats. In anticipation of the arrival of the British in the summer of 1776, Assistant Quartermaster General Hughes sent out orders for the procurement of ship timber, scantling, and oars for galleys and gondolas being built for the Army. He also shipped pitch, junk, and oakum up the Hudson to Albany where frigates were under construction. [53] Aware of the need to maintain an adequate number of boats ready for supply operations, Hughes, as the year 1776 drew to a close, proposed not only to repair Army boats on the Hudson but also to build additional ones if planks and boards could be obtained. [54] The care and maintenance of Army boats remained an important aspect of Quartermaster activities on the Hudson throughout the war.

In the winter of 1775–76, Army demands for forage for the animals and firewood for cooking and heating were filled by Mifflin's agents who purchased on a commission basis. Mifflin also had to transport ordnance stores and equip the soldiers. At the same time, he had to build up reserve stocks of all types of supplies for active operations. Unfortunately, that effort was complicated by the fact that militia, called out to strengthen the Army in an operation, seldom brought equipment with them, despite instructions to the state governments which were supposed initially to outfit their troops before they were sent into Continental service. For example, Quartermaster General Moylan, Mifflin's successor, complained that in the New York campaign, "the fluctuating state of

---

[52] *Letters of Members of the Continental Congress,* ed. Burnett, II, 109 (R. Morris to Maryland Council of Safety, 1 Oct 1776).

[53] (1) Hugh Hughes Letter Book (To Schuyler, 4 Jun 1776); (To Jacob Akerly, 7 Jun 1776); (To John Cambell, 12 Jul 1776). New York Historical Society. (2) Washington Papers, vol. 27, f. 106 (Return of stores shipped to Schuyler, 4 Jun 1776).

[54] *American Archives,* ed. Force, 5th ser, III, 1475–76 (To Washington, 29 Dec 1776).

the Militia, coming in destitute of every necessary, drained our stores." [55]
In such circumstances, criticism of supply shortages was certain to be
voiced long before replacements could be obtained.

Estimating the amount of supplies required in any campaign necessarily fell short of accuracy not only in 1775 but throughout the war.
In the procurement of Quartermaster items of supply, the procedures
followed in 1775 and 1776 remained the pattern throughout the war.
The Quartermaster General and his staff initiated preparations for the
coming campaign late in the year, or as soon as the troops had retired
to winter quarters. At that point, the deputy and assistant quartermasters general entered into contracts with master craftsmen for the
production by their workshops of a given number of articles wanted, such
as wooden canteens and pails. They set delivery usually for April or
May—in other words, for the opening of the campaign. Unfortunately,
lack of funds often delayed their arrangements so that supplies that
should have been ready when the campaign began were instead hurried
along in the midst of active operations.

The Quartermaster's Department procured and issued to the individual soldier wooden canteens and knapsacks. It also procured camp
kettles, one of which was issued to each company of men, and light axes,
spades, and other entrenching tools. It issued most of the latter only
as required, as, for example, when the troops were ordered to throw up
fortifications or to erect huts for themselves in winter quarters. Entrenching tools had a strange way of disappearing once they were issued. To
prevent what he called "embezzlement of the public tools," Washington
ordered the Quartermaster General to have each tool branded with the
mark "CXIII," meaning the Continent and the thirteen colonies. This
brand was later changed to "U.S." after independence had been declared.[56]
To make doubly sure that tools did not disappear, Washington incorporated the idea of property accountability in a general order published in
the summer of 1776. All officers commanding a party or detachment
from any regiment on the works were to be held accountable for the
tools they received and any lost under their care were to be paid for by
the officers. Any soldier who lost or destroyed a tool delivered to him
was to have the price of it deducted from his next pay and moreover be
punished "according to the nature of the offence." [57]

---

[55] Papers of the Continental Congress, item 78, vol. XV, f. 101–08 (Moylan to Pres. of
Congress, 27 Sep 1776).

[56] (1) *Writings of Washington*, ed. Fitzpatrick, V, 156 (GO, 18 Jun 1776); VII, 283 (To
Mifflin, 13 Mar 1777). (2) Col. John W. Wright, "Some Notes on the Continental Army,"
William and Mary College Quarterly Historical Magazine, XI, second series, No. 3 (July 1931),
188.

[57] *Writings of Washington*, ed. Fitzpatrick, V, 157 (GO, 18 Jun 1776).

The success or failure of a Quartermaster General was judged primarily by the ease with which he enabled an Army to take the field and by his ability to support that Army with a steady flow of supplies both during the campaign and after the troops had retired to winter quarters. The development of an adequate, smooth-functioning transportation system was never achieved during the Revolution. The vast extent of the country, its many broad tidal rivers, its forests and marshes, and its lack of roads all impeded transportation. With the British in control of the sea, supply was for the most part restricted to land transportation and subject to all its hazards during the war. It is difficult to appreciate the delays caused by natural obstacles, the hardships imposed by bad roads, and the time consumed in the slow, ponderous progress of ox teams, or the impossibility of effecting speedy replacement of losses sustained in battle or on the road, resulting from difficulties in transportation or the more familiar pilferage that has afflicted every supply line in every war.

In 1775, the Quartermaster General provided transportation both in the Army and on the supply lines by hiring teams and drivers. Washington instructed the wagonmaster general to maintain a sufficient number of wagons and teams to service each of the three divisions in the Boston area, but because of the scarcity of forage the Quartermaster's Department hired such teams with the understanding that the owners would provide the necessary feed and be paid accordingly.[58] Mifflin soon encountered difficulties in obtaining a sufficient number of wagons and teams to haul supplies. To relieve his distress, Washington suggested that the Massachusetts legislature adopt some expedient for drawing teams into service, or else invest the Quartermaster General with authority to impress them.[59] By the time the Army moved to fortify the heights of Dorchester in March, the move that finally forced the British to evacuate Boston, Mifflin's exertions had obtained the requisite number of ox teams and more than 300 carts. They made several trips during the night loaded with entrenching tools and with fascines and hay, screwed into large bundles of seven or eight hundred weight.[60]

Apparently in 1775, as later in the war, the Quartermaster's Department could not rely on teamsters to deliver supplies to a designated destination. It was not at all unusual for a teamster to drop his load on the road, possibly because he was disappointed in not receiving his pay or because he was lured by more attractive opportunities in hauling goods for sutlers or merchants. To prevent any loss of Quartermaster

[58] *American Archives*, ed. Force, 4th ser, III, 809–19 (Instructions to Wagonmaster General, 25 Sep 1775).
[59] *Writings of Washington*, ed. Fitzpatrick, IV, 60 (To Mass. legislature, 2 Nov 1775).
[60] Thacher, *Military Journal of the American Revolution*, 40.

TRANSPORTING CANNON FOR KNOX

stores when the Army moved from Boston to New York in the spring of
1776, the Department made an effort to hold each teamster accountable
for the load he received.   He was required to carry with him a copy of
the bill of lading that the receiver of the goods endorsed, thereby converting it into a certificate of delivery upon the presentation of which the
teamster was paid.   The wagons traveled by way of Norwich, Conn.,
the first of them carrying those articles—camp equipage, entrenching
tools, and cooking utensils—that the Army would need immediately
upon assembling at the general rendezvous point.[61]

Although Quartermaster stores went overland in wagons, the troops,
after marching as far as Norwich and New London, Conn., were transported by boat via Long Island Sound to New York.   In this first movement of men and their equipment from one theater to another, Washington dispatched his Quartermaster General on ahead to arrange for

<hr>

[61] *Writings of Washington*, ed. Fitzpatrick, IV, 465–67 (Orders to Parke, 3 Apr 1776).

the necessary boats.   When Mifflin had concerted his arrangements with
Generals William Heath and John Sullivan, he hastened to New York
to complete preparations there before the troops arrived.[62]

The Department found it easier to transport supplies in New York
than at Boston because the navigation of both the Hudson and East
Rivers was open, at least until the British arrived in mid-July.   Quartermaster General Moylan added a few wagons and horses, sufficient he
thought for all the exigencies of the Army.   Many of the wagons and
horses were sent to Long Island where a large part of the Army was
deployed.   Although in the brilliant withdrawal across the East River
to Manhattan on the night of 29 August the troops and their equipment
were saved, the wagons, carts, and horses could not be brought over.[63]
This was a serious loss for with the navigation of the Hudson hampered by
the presence of British vessels the Quartermaster's Department, "wanted
Waggons to do that duty, which boats were accustomed to do."   The
shortage of transportation was made even more acute by the immediate
necessity of removing stores from New York City to places of safety.
Despite the Department's impressment of all horses and wagons in the
town and the shipment of cargoes up the Hudson in boats, it had insufficient transportation available and Moylan's career as Quartermaster
General came to an abrupt end.

Dependence on hired and impressed teams to transport the Army's
baggage and equipment was bound to hamper movement and result in
losses.   Even before the retreat in New York, Maj. Gen. Charles Lee,
sent to counter the British threat to the southern states, was writing from
Charleston that Congress ought to make some "regular establishment for
wagons."   The purchase of at least one, if not two, wagons for each
company was necessary to permit expeditious movement.   "At present,
it is sometimes as much impossible to march an hundred miles, although
the fate of a Province depended upon it, as if the soldiers wanted legs,"
General Lee informed the Board of War.[64]

Thoroughly alarmed by what happened in New York, Congress
resolved to furnish Mifflin with $300,000 to enable him to procure the
supplies he had indicated to be necessary when he accepted reappointment
as Quartermaster General.[65]   Among these items Mifflin had listed
200 wagons with four horses each; 50 ox teams with two oxen each; and
50 drays with one horse each, besides 100 strong horses for the artillery

---

[62] *Ibid.,* IV, 429–30 (Orders to Mifflin, 24 Mar 1776).

[63] Papers of the Continental Congress, item 78, vol. XV. f. 101–08 (Moylan to Pres. of Congress, 27 Sep 1776).

[64] *American Archives,* ed. Force, 5th ser, I, 720 (To Richard Peters, 2 Aug 1776).

[65] *Journals of the Continental Congress,* V, 839–40 (2 Oct 1776).

and 50 for expresses and commissary.   He wanted and obtained a wagonmaster and a deputy as well as 20 conductors of wagons, one to be
allowed to each 10 wagons.   He proposed to detail soldiers from the line
as wagoners when sufficient teamsters could not be hired.   For this extra
duty, Congress authorized an allowance of one-eighth part of a dollar
over and above their regular pay.

A wagon service for the Army, with wagoners detailed from the line,
proved unsatisfactory and wasteful.   Before the end of the year, Assistant
Quartermaster General Hughes proposed changes because he was in a
better position to observe its workings than Mifflin who was in Pennsylvania recruiting troops at the request of Congress.   He suggested that it
would be advantageous to the service to enlist teamsters and wagoners
independent of the Army for a period of a year at least.   Such separate
enlistment, Hughes urged, would induce personnel to take better care
of their teams and wagons than under the existing system of detailing
men from the line.   As long as the latter knew they could return to their
regiments when they chose, they felt no responsibility for their teams.
In consequence, they neglected to give the teams proper care and the
usefulness of the animals to the Army diminished rapidly.[66]   His wise
suggestion stimulated no corrective action.

As soon as the troops were settled in quarters at Morristown during
the second winter of the war, Washington turned his attention to the
problem of transportation.   Convinced that the great losses of 1776 had
flowed from a want of teams, he had informed Congress, in the midst
of preparing his counter blow against the British in New Jersey, that he
intended to have Mifflin provide each regiment with a certain number
of wagons so that they might move "from place to place differently from
what we have done, or could do, this campaign." [67]   Ammunition carts
and carts for carrying entrenching tools ought to be provided.   Feeling
that "too much regard cannot be paid to the Waggons," he directed
Mifflin to provide as many as would serve all the purposes of each battalion
for their baggage, ammunition, and entrenching tools.   Then returning
to his idea of ammunition carts, he suggested the manufacture of light,
strong, covered "Chaises marine"—two-wheeled wagons—to carry artillery and regimental ammunition.   He did not want the Army encum-
bered with heavy and unwieldy wagons when the purpose could be better
served by light ones.[68]   By March, Mifflin could write that the ammunition wagons were coming in fast and production of other types was also

[66] *American Archives*, ed. Force, 5th ser, III, 1475–76 (Hughes to Washington, 29 Dec 1776).
[67] *Writings of Washington*, ed. Fitzpatrick, VI, 406 (To Pres. of Congress, 20 Dec 1776).
[68] *Ibid.*, VII, 83 (To Mifflin, 31 Jan 1777).

well under way.[69]   Preparations for the next campaign were in general moving along well despite the difficulty of obtaining funds.

Reform Measures

The long, disheartening retreat of the Army during the campaign of 1776, the threat to Philadelphia in December, the mounting criticism of the purchasing activities of the commissaries in the Middle Department, and investigation of supply failures produced a veritable "rage for reformation" in Congress by 1777.[70]   The first impetus in that direction came from a report of the congressional committee sent to inspect the Army and determine the best means of supplying its wants following the evacuation of New York City.[71]   Acting on the committee's findings that the failure of clothing supply was at least in part due to the lack of a proper supervisory officer, Congress passed a resolution calling for the appointment of a commissary of clothing for each of the armies.   It would be his duty to submit regimental clothing requirements to the states, receive and pay for the deliveries made by them, and then deliver the clothing to the regimental paymasters.   The latter would issue the clothing, deducting the costs from the soldiers' wages.   A week later Congress appointed George Measam to fill that post in the Northern Army and authorized Washington to appoint such a commissary for the Army under his immediate command.[72]

Preoccupied with the campaign, Washington did not get around to considering the matter until December when, thoroughly alarmed by the clothing shortage, he urged instead the appointment of a clothier general for the Army as a means of centralizing control of all clothing supply. One week later, Congress authorized him to make this appointment, though it enacted no regulatory measure for the department.[73]   James Mease, a Philadelphia merchant, promptly solicited the appointment and obtained the post on the basis of his experience in executing supply orders for Congress.[74]   Mease assumed his duties at camp by February.   By virtue of his commission he could appoint agents in each state to procure clothing on a commission basis, but Washington instructed him to work

[69] Washington Papers, vol. 42, f. 116 (Mifflin to Washington, 9 Mar 1777); vol. 40, f. 81 (Hughes to Washington, 3 Feb 1777).

[70] The Letters of Richard Henry Lee, ed. J. C. Ballagh (2 vols., New York, 1911), I, 352 (Lee to Washington, 20 Nov 1777)

[71] Journals of the Continental Congress, V, 844 (3 Oct 1776).

[72] Ibid., VI, 858, 859 (9 Oct 1776); 880–81 (16 Oct 1776).

[73] (1) Writings of Washington, ed. Fitzpatrick, VI, 404 (To Pres. of Congress, 20 Dec 1776). (2) Journals of the Continental Congress, VI, 1041 (27 Dec 1776).

[74] (1) Washington Papers, vol. 58, f. 123 (Mease to Washington, 6 Jan 1777). (2) Writings of Washington, ed. Fitzpatrick, VI, 492–93 (To Mease, 10 Jan 1777).

closely with agents already appointed by the states to purchase clothing for their respective regiments. Mease was to be allowed as many clerks and storekeepers as necessary to carry out his business. Washington advised him that, like other heads of supply agencies, he would have to be with the Army in order to execute his duties properly. Mease soon had purchasing agents in the field and added a deputy to his organization to assist him and remain with the Army when he was absent.

Clothier General Mease also became responsible for shoe procurement. Shoes were being bought under contract from local cobblers or imported from abroad, but the distress of the Army for want of shoes showed no improvement under Mease. Five months after his appointment, Washington complained that lack of shoes made some corps "almost entirely incapable of doing duty." Such shoes as Mease supplied were too small in size and therefore of little use. Imported shoes were "thin french pumps" that tore to pieces whenever they got wet.[75]

Apparently convinced that supervision and a close control of materials were the keys to improving supply, Congress resolved to establish a Hide Department under the direction of a commissary. Since the fall of 1776, the hides of the cattle that were slaughtered for Army use had been dried, cured, and held for the use of the Continental Congress, subject to its orders.[76] It now directed the Commissary of Hides to receive all raw hides belonging to the United States, exchange them for tanned leather or for shoes at the customary rates of exchange, and deliver the shoes to the Clothier General who would make distribution to the Army. If he could not make such exchanges on reasonable terms, Congress authorized the Commissary of Hides either to provide tanyards, materials, and workmen himself, or to contract with proper persons for converting the hides into tanned leather. It then placed the Hide Department under the supervision of the Board of War. At the Board's direction, the Commissary of Hides was also to make deliveries of leather to the Commissary of Military Stores who in addition to receiving and delivering all arms and ammunition also procured all types of accoutrements for the Army. Congress promptly selected a Commissary but when he declined to serve, 6 weeks passed before it was able to fill the office by appointing George Ewing.[77]

In the meantime, the Continental Congress also made some organizational changes in the Quartermaster's Department. Mifflin, who had been promoted to the rank of major general on 19 February 1777, had

---

[75] *Writings of Washington,* ed. Fitzpatrick, VIII, 292, 432–33 (To Mease, 23 Jun and 18 Jul 1777).
[76] *Journals of the Continental Congress,* VI, 973–74 (22 Nov 1776).
[77] *Ibid.,* VIII, 487–89; 607 (20 Jun and 5 Aug 1777).

been giving considerable thought to administrative reform in his Department. Washington approved of his ideas and submitted them to Congress. A committee to whom they were referred brought in a report that Congress adopted on 14 May.[78] The plan incorporated the essence of Quartermaster experience gained in the campaigns of 1775 and 1776 and for the first time set forth detailed regulations for the Department.

Congress provided for a more specialized division of duties by the creation of both a forage department and a wagon department within the Quartermaster's Department. In the forage department, it authorized the Quartermaster General to appoint a commissary of forage for the Army and one for each of the military departments, with as many forage masters as he thought necessary to receipt for deliveries of forage at magazines. The commissaries purchased all forage and stored it in magazines as directed by the Quartermaster General or his deputy in any military department. Congress also authorized the Quartermaster General to appoint a wagonmaster general for the wagon department and a wagonmaster for each military department. They received all horses, cattle, and carriages that the service required but neither purchased nor hired them without the express orders of the commanding general, the Quartermaster General, or one of his deputies.

Congress further authorized the Quartermaster General to appoint such assistants as he needed, transmitting to the Board of War the names of assistants, commissaries of forage, wagonmasters, forage masters, and clerks. It retained deputy quartermasters general for the military departments, but in addition it provided for the appointment of a deputy quartermaster general for each grand division of the Army and an assistant deputy quartermaster general for each brigade. Congress also set forth a system of returns to be made by the officers of the Departments, designated the forage allowances to officers, more or less codified orders previously issued to prevent the loss of tools, and enumerated details of rank and pay for personnel in the Department.

Mifflin was seldom at Headquarters in 1777 but in his absence his three subordinates supervised Departmental business. Joseph Thornsbury whom Washington appointed Wagonmaster General in May, directed the wagon department. Clement Biddle, appointed Commissary General of Forage on 1 July 1777, handled all matters pertaining to forage for the main Army. Mifflin's immediate deputy was Col. Henry Emanuel Lutterloh whom, at Washington's suggestion, he appointed

---

[78] (1) Washington Papers, vol. 42, f. 116 (Mifflin to Washington, 9 Mar 1777). (2) *Writings of Washington*, ed. Fitzpatrick, VI, 283–84 (13 Mar 1777). (3) *Journals of the Continental Congress*, VII, 191 (21 Mar); 272 (16 Apr); 292 (23 Apr); 355–59 (14 May 1777).

deputy quartermaster general with the main Army.[79]   Lutterloh had seen
Quartermaster service in the army of Brunswick and Washington thought
his experience would make him useful to the Department.   The Quartermaster office at Headquarters included some other personnel—three clerks
to keep the accounts, an assistant deputy quartermaster general to aid
Lutterloh, another assistant to supervise the Continental Yard with the
help of one clerk and four hostlers, and a second deputy to supervise
an issuing store, presided over by a storekeeper and one assistant.[80]

The rage for reformation expended itself most fully in reorganizing
the Commissary Department.   Investigation of Carpenter Wharton's
mismanagement of commissary affairs during the campaign of 1776
resulted in the formulation of a report by the Board of War in February
of the following year that proposed separation of the purchasing and
issuing functions of the Commissary General.   This development was in
agreement with organizational ideas entertained by Washington who had
long been of the opinion that the work of the Department had become
too extensive to be under the management of one man.[81]   Congress took
no action on that report but it pursued its inquiry into the conduct of
the commissaries in the Middle Department by appointing another committee for that purpose in March.   When that committee brought in a
report on abuses that developed from the use of agents paid on a percentage basis, and recommended that in the future Congress appoint the
commissaries and place them in designated districts under proper supervision and regulations, Congress immediately directed the committee to
prepare a draft of regulations to put their ideas into effect.[82]

Fully 12 months earlier Trumbull had sought regulations for his
Department, and now at the urging of Elbridge Gerry he hastened to
Philadelphia to give the committee the benefit of his ideas on the subject.
He was well pleased with the proposal to divide his office into two separate
departments, but he had definite opinions on compensation that were
diametrically opposed to the established mode of paying a fixed salary to
the Commissary General.   He had never been satisfied with that arrangement, and he reiterated a proposal made earlier that he be paid on a
commission basis—that is, ½ percent for himself on all monies passing

---

[79] (1) Washington Papers, vol. 47, f. 116–17 (Mifflin to Washington, 27 May 1777).   (2) Writings of Washington, ed. Fitzpatrick, VIII, 60 (GO, 14 May 1777); 327–28 (GO, 1 Jul 1777).
    [80] Papers of the Continental Congress, item 192, f. 159 (List of Jan 1778).
    [81] (1) Journals of the Continental Congress, VII, 119–20 (14 Feb 1777).   (2) See, for exam-
ple, Writings of Washington, ed. Fitzpatrick, VIII, 25–26 (To Brig. Gen. A. MacDougall, 7 May
1777).
    [82] Journals of the Continental Congress, VII, 266 (14 Apr 1777).

through his hands and $2\frac{1}{2}$ percent to the deputies purchasing sub-sistence.[83]

Assuming that he would be consulted from time to time about the preparation of the regulations, Trumbull remained in Philadelphia for 4 weeks but the committee never again called for his assistance and he finally returned to camp. There he found discontent rife among his assistants and the Department in such a demoralized state, as a result of congressional investigation, that he contemplated resigning on 15 June. "An Angel from Heaven could not go on long in my Situation," he wrote his friend Gerry. It was apparent that his deputies would leave him to a man if satisfactory arrangements were not made and in the existing uncertainties "they were not worth a farthing each." [84]

Although Trumbull had not yet been informed of the action, Con-gress on 10 June had adopted a regulation that was so minutely detailed— the text fills 15 pages of the *Journals*—that "if regulations could have furnished supplies, the army storehouses should have been bursting with a superabundance." [85]   The regulation established separate departments of purchases and issues, each headed by a commissary general. It pro-vided for congressional appointment of four deputies in the purchase field and three deputies to control issues. It authorized each deputy to appoint as many assistants as were necessary, and assigned each deputy commissary general of purchases to a specific area within which he was to make his purchases, delivering the provisions to the deputy commissary general of issues in that district. The organization provided was rela-tively simple, but the minutiae of detail in the regulation prescribing among others an elaborate record-keeping system, the branding of govern-ment animals, the recovery and tanning of hides, the monetary evaluation of the rations, and the establishment of gardens were such as to make effective administration of the measure an impossibility.[86]

In the course of the next 8 days Congress completed its arrangements. It resolved that the Commissary General of Purchases should maintain his office wherever Congress should be in session and that either he or his clerk would have to be in constant attendance.[87]   It then settled the question of compensation for commissary personnel. In lieu of com-missions, the use of which had become thoroughly discredited, Congress

[83] *Letters of Members of the Continental Congress,* ed. Burnett, II, 364 fn. (Trumbull to Wadsworth, 17 May 1777); 393–94 fn. (Trumbull to Hancock, 15 Jun 1777).

[84] *Ibid.,* II, 393–94 fn. (Drafts of letters that were apparently not sent to Hancock, Wash-ington, and Gerry, 15 Jun 1777).

[85] Edmund C. Burnett, *The Continental Congress* (New York, 1941), 273.

[86] *Journals of the Continental Congress,* VIII, 433–48 (10 Jun 1777).

[87] *Ibid.,* VIII, 452 (11 Jun 1777).

substituted fixed pay and rations for all personnel in the Commissary Department. This was the most disturbing feature of the new system from the viewpoint of the deputies, though the allowance of $8 per day and six rations to the Commissary General of Purchases was a more generous remuneration than had previously been granted. On 18 June 1777, Congress elected the officers needed to staff the new establishment. It continued Joseph Trumbull as Commissary General of Purchases, assisted by four deputies—William Aylett, William Buchanan, Jacob Cuyler, and Jeremiah Wadsworth. It designated Charles Stewart Commissary General of Issues. Three deputies assisted him—William Mumford, Matthew Irwin, and Elisha Avery. Until these appointees were prepared to assume direction of the business entrusted to them, Congress requested that Trumbull and his deputies continue supplying the Army as they had been doing.[88]

Trumbull himself apparently was not officially notified of his appointment until 5 July. Aware that Trumbull had said he would serve only if paid on a commission basis, Eliphalet Dyer wrote to urge him to accept the new appointment on patriotic grounds of service to his country and the Army.[89] But if Trumbull himself had been willing to reconsider, his assistants were not so disposed; in fact, no one seemed willing to act under the new regulations. During the next few weeks there followed a dismaying succession of resignations and new appointments.[90] Trumbull attempted to keep the Department functioning, but he had so few assistants that he himself had, on occasion, to stand at the scales to check the weight of provisions.[91] The effect of the confusion and the disorganization in the midst of the campaign of 1777 was such that Washington observed that almost every expedition he formed was "either frustrated or greatly impeded by the want of a regular supply of provisions." [92]

Efforts to get Congress to amend the regulation to make it more workable proved fruitless because so many members were so "fond of their New plan" that it was difficult to "make them attend to the Objections against" it.[93] The Continental Congress sent a committee to camp, but Trumbull soon learned that it was neither inclined to grant him

[88] *Ibid.*, VIII, 427 (18 Jun); 491 (23 Jun 1777).

[89] *Letters of Members of the Continental Congress*, ed. Burnett, II, 392, 407–08 (– Jun and 8 Jul 1777).

[90] *Journals of the Continental Congress*, VIII, 498 (26 Jun); 517 (1 Jul); 601 (4 Aug); 617 (6 Aug); 627 (9 Aug); 629–30 (11 Aug); 640 (14 Aug 1777).

[91] *Letters of Members of the Continental Congress*, ed. Burnett, II, 394 (James Lovell to Trumbull, 30 Jun 1777).

[92] Douglas S. Freeman, *George Washington* (5 vols., New York, 1948–51), IV, 441 n. (Timothy Pickering to Trumbull, 28 Jun 1777).

[93] *Letters of Members of the Continental Congress*, ed. Burnett, II, 414 (Dyer to Trumbull, 15 Jul 1777).

control of his deputies nor pay him on a commission basis, and he submitted his resignation on 19 July. Two weeks later he notified Congress that he would not consider himself obliged to perform the duties of his office beyond 20 August. On 5 August Congress appointed his successor, designating William Buchanan as Commissary General of Purchases.[94]

The wave of reform spent itself in a reorganization of the Board of War. Though Trumbull had resigned in July and Mifflin submitted his resignation in October 1777, Congress was reluctant to lose the services of the two men in the country most familiar with quartermaster and commissary problems. It appointed them members of the Board of War to lend the weight of their experience to the task of supervising the supply agencies.

Breakdown of Supply, 1777

Most of the members of Congress, lacking military knowledge, were nevertheless certain that the measures they had adopted were good. They fully expected that the Army would not only be better cared for but also more economically supplied than in the past. But improvements did not result from new organizations, new personnel, and in some cases new regulations. On the contrary, by the end of the year, with the Army encamped at Valley Forge, the supply system generally had broken down, key supply officers had submitted their resignations, and supply had deteriorated to such an extent that Congress, searching for ways to feed, clothe, and keep an Army in the field, willingly settled for any arrangements that promised to do so.

Mere appointment of supervisory officers—a Clothier General and a Commissary of Hides—could not of itself increase the amount of clothing and shoes sent to the Army, but a closer scrutiny of operations by them undoubtedly would have at least assured the troops full use of what was available. In 1776, the Army had hit upon the method of exchanging hides for shoes as a means of keeping the soldier fit for service. The Commissary Department obtained the hides from the cattle slaughtered to feed the Army and exchanged them with the owners of tanyards, farmers, and tradesmen at a designated ratio of so many pounds of hides for so many pounds of tanned leather or a specified number of shoes. In the fall of 1777, the recently appointed Commissary of Hides found that five pounds of hides could be exchanged for one pound of sole leather and eight pounds of hides for one of upper leather.[95] Washington rightly

---

[94] (1) Washington Papers, vol. 51, f. 96 (Trumbull to Washington, 19 Jul 1777). (2) Journals of the Continental Congress, VIII, 598 (2 Aug 1777); 607 (5 Aug 1777).
[95] Washington Papers, vol. 62, f. 90 (Ewing to Washington, 2 Dec 1777).

insisted that if all the hides of the cattle that were consumed by the Army were turned into leather, "they would much more than shoe the soldiers." [96]   Unfortunately, there was often a sharp discrepancy between the weight of the hides turned in and the amount of tanned leather or the number of shoes obtained in exchange.   The method lent itself to abuses by dishonest agents not only under Ewing but also later on in the war.   The Department also sustained losses through pilferage of hides from wagons in the course of transportation, since hides were a valuable asset in the market.

Clothier General Mease was plagued by a continuing shortage of textiles and clothing that could only be relieved by purchase abroad. Congress began importation on its account, but there was many a slip between placing an order and its delivery.   In the spring of 1777, a committee of Congress assured Mease that there was "a Moral Certainty of being plentifully furnished" with clothing in time for the next campaign, but its non-arrival in the fall was attributed to a variety of causes not the least of which was the effectiveness of the British cruisers in patrolling American shores.[97]   Even when deliveries were made, cargoes had to be landed at New England ports since New York and, for a time, Philadelphia were in the hands of the British.   Clothing had then to be hauled laboriously by wagons hundreds of miles to the Continental Army operating in New York, Pennsylvania, and New Jersey.

This long overland transportation provided opportunities for loss and misapplication of clothing.   Mease, whose abilities were mediocre, might have prevented losses en route by sending along conductors with the wagons to guard the clothing that was usually forwarded in small parcels.   He might also have introduced the use of a system of certificates of delivery to further safeguard the clothing.   Both devices were introduced with considerable success later.[98]   On the other hand, when state authorities stopped shipments en route from Massachusetts to camp and or when commanding officers at posts along the way felt free to plunder clothing parcels coming to the main Army in order to clothe their needy troops, Mease, lacking authority, could only appeal to Congress and to Washington for relief from such practices while the intended recipients continued wearing their tattered rags.[99]

[96] Writings of Washington, ed. Fitzpatrick, X, 45–46 (To Mease, 12 Nov 1777).

[97] (1) Washington Papers, vol. 47, f. 11 (Mease to Washington, 12 May 1777).   (2) Journals of the Continental Congress, IX, 883, 968–69 (10 and 26 Nov 1777).

[98] (1) Writings of Washington, ed. Fitzpatrick, XII, 445–48 (To Maj. Gen. William Heath, 14 Sep 1778).   (2) Washington Papers, vol. 85, f. 14 (Otis & Andrews to Washington, 19 Sep 1778).

[99] (1) Washington Papers, vol. 48, f. 74 (Mease to Washington 6 Jun 1777); vol. 51, f. 129 (Mease to Washington, 22 Jul 1777).   (2) Writings of Washington, ed. Fitzpatrick, VIII, 237–38 (To Mease, 13 Jun 1777); X, 41–42 (To Maj. Gen. Putnam, 14 Nov 1777).   (3) Journals of the Continental Congress, VIII, 473 (17 Jun 1777).

The supply of clothing and shoes grew steadily worse during the fall of 1777. The prolonged campaign of that year was particularly hard on clothing and shoes. To scarcity was added poor quality. Shoes made of green leather wore out faster than deliveries could be made. Sizes of both shoes and uniforms were generally too small. It was false economy, Washington argued, to be so sparing in the use of cloth; uniforms that were not large enough did not "wear out fairly, but tear to pieces."[100] Down through the years, criticism of sizes was to be a perennial complaint, and Mease's rebuttal was also to become only too familiar. It was not the sizes that were at fault but the fitting. Clothing was being made in three sizes but "in general so little pains is taken by the officers to fit the Men that I have often seen a large coat hanging like a sack on a little fellow, whilst you see at the same time a lusty fellow squeezed into a small one."[101] Stocks became so depleted that it was a wonder the Army could be kept in the field, and even the men in the hospitals were naked and had to stay there for lack of covering. Of the 9,000 men at Valley Forge, 2,898 were unfit for duty on 23 December 1777 because they were barefoot and naked. By that time Mease had submitted his resignation. He offered to continue in office until a successor could be found, but, pleading ill health, he stayed at Lancaster, refusing to stay with the Army.[102]

With food, the hardiest of the soldiers at Valley Forge could have survived despite the winter cold and the lack of clothing and blankets. But the supply of rations had become increasingly precarious during the campaign of 1777 and by December the threat of starvation stalked the camp. Washington was undecided whether these supply failures were attributable to "a fault" in the constitution of the Commissary Department or to "an unpardonable neglect in the Executive part," but Commissary General Buchanan was not neglectful of his duties. He was inexperienced and he did limit his activities too much to attending Congress and to attempting to reduce "the extravagance of the time" by carrying on a singlehanded campaign against spiraling prices.[103] Commissary support of Washington's Army as it moved to meet the British threat to Philadelphia he left to Ephraim Blaine, deputy commissary general for the Middle Department.

[100] *Writings of Washington*, ed. Fitzpatrick, VIII, 432–33 (To Mease, 18 Jul 1777).

[101] Washington Papers, vol. 51, f. 129 (To Washington, 22 Jul 1777).

[102] (1) *Writings of Washington*, ed. Fitzpatrick, X, 195 (To Pres. of Congress, 23 Dec 1777). (2) Washington Papers, vol. 63, f. 28 (Mease to Washington, 16 Dec 1777).

[103] (1) *Writings of Washington*, ed. Fitzpatrick, IX, 238 (To Pres. of Congress, 19 Sep 1777). (2) Ephraim Blaine Letter Book, 1777–78 (Blaine to A. Dunham, 11 Apr 1778). Manuscript Div., Library of Congress. (3) For a more detailed treatment, see Johnson, *The Administration of the American Commissariat During the Revolutionary War*.

Blaine worked energetically to obtain meat supplies to supplement the stores turned over when Trumbull resigned, but a variety of factors conspired to prevent procurement of adequate stocks. The British at Philadelphia dominated the area in the Middle Department where cattle raising was largely centered. The Army was also deprived of stocks of barreled pork and bacon that it had received from Virginia in the past because the enemy, in possession of the Delaware River, had thereby cut the line of communication with that State. Blaine had expected that an ample supply of beef would be forwarded from the Eastern Department. Unfortunately, meat purchases had been suspended from August to November by reason of the long delay in completing the organization of the department of the commissary general of purchases in that area.[104] Moreover, forwarding of supplies on hand in the Eastern Department was completely frustrated by the muddleheadness of Samuel Gray, the newly appointed deputy commissary general of issues, who failed wholly to understand instructions directing him to accept the transfer of subsistence stores from Trumbull.[105] In the meantime, militia reinforcements swelled ration requirements during the campaign of 1777 and "upwards of 800 head of Cattle per week" were being consumed in October and 400 barrels of flour a week were needed from Lancaster, Reading, and York but that quantity was not being delivered, largely because the farmers feared their wagons would be detained indefinitely at camp once deliveries were made.[106] Fall brought the season for curing and packing meats, but salt could not be hauled for want of transportation, and the lack of wagons also caused the commissaries to charge the quartermasters with responsibility for the failure to deliver flour.

In the early fall, advocates of the new commissary system had felt that sufficient time had not elapsed to permit a demonstration of its merits. By November, however, adversaries of the new organization were pronouncing it a failure.[107] Alarmed by the supply situation, Congress appointed committees to devise ways and means for providing a sufficient supply and to confer with the Pennsylvania assembly. These measures added little to the stock of food for the Army, the advance forces of which reached Valley Forge on 16 December 1777, with the main force under Washington arriving three days later to begin preparations for the

---

[104] (1) Ephraim Blaine Letter Book, 1777–78 (Blain to Colt, 18 Nov 1777). (2) Papers of the Continental Congress, item 78, vol. V, f. 411–16 (Colt to Hancock, 4 Oct 1777).

[105] Charles Stewart Correspondence, 1777–82 (Stewart to Gray, 8 Jul — should be Aug 1777).

[106] (1) Ephraim Blaine Letter Book, 1777–78 (Chaloner to Blaine, 3 Oct 1777); (Chaloner to Buchanan, 11 Oct 1777).

[107] *Letters of Members of the Continental Congress*, ed. Burnett, II, 544 (E. Dyer to Trumbull, 4 Nov 1777); 563–64 (R. H. Lee to Washington, 20 Nov 1777).

A SUPPLY TRAIN EN ROUTE THROUGH THE SNOW TO VALLY FORGE

winter encampment.   The troops were still in tents on Christmas Day, and the general cry of the soldiers was " 'No Meat! No Meat!' " [108]

The troops at Valley Forge were not starving and freezing because the states had been drained of all food and clothing.   Instead, a breakdown in transportation had made it impossible to haul these supplies from magazines and posts where they were deposited to the camp where they were so sorely needed.   Quartermasters maintained some government teams at various posts and magazines throughout the country which they used for hauling supplies.   But privately-owned wagons and their drivers, hired by deputy quartermasters general at a certain rate per day, conveyed the bulk of the provisions, forage, and stores along the various supply lines.   Customarily the owners furnished the necessary forage for the teams; whenever the Quartermaster's Department provided it, the cost was deducted from the amount due the owner.

[108] "Valley Forge, 1777–78: Diary of Surgeon Albigence Waldo, of the Continental Line," *Pennsylvania Magazine of History and Biography*, XXI, 309.

In 1777, the demand for wagons in Pennsylvania by both the State and the Continental Army was large and the cost of hiring them, in common with the prices of all other articles and services, rose rapidly. To check the advancing costs of transportation, Congress set 30 shillings per day as the price at which a quartermaster could hire a driver, a wagon, and four horses.   In view of the high costs of maintenance, wagon owners considered this price much too low, particularly since they could obtain £3 to £4 a day from private merchants.[109]   As a result, they did not willingly agree to employment of their wagons by the Quartermaster's Department.

But if the owners would not of their own accord permit the Department to hire their wagons, they were compelled to do so by impressment. Ever since 1776, the Army had drawn a large share of its wagons and teams from Pennsylvania.   With the campaign of 1777 centered in Pennsylvania, the burden of providing the Quartermaster's Department with transportation for hauling supplies fell heavily upon the inhabitants of that State.   For the most part, until late in 1777, wagons and teams were obtained by impressment not only by the quartermasters but also by personnel in the Commissary Department, the Clothing Department, and the Hide Department who, because of the failure of the Quartermaster's Department to supply transportation, were authorized to impress the wagons they needed.   Impressment, however, always aroused resentment; it lent itself readily to abuses; and it worked hardships on some who by reason of their proximity to the Army were repeatedly called upon to furnish wagons and teams while others, more distantly located, escaped this burden entirely.   Exasperated by repeated impressments, the inhabitants of Pennsylvania attempted to conceal their wagons when the Army sent out military press parties to bring supplies to Valley Forge.[110]

Late in December 1777, the Pennsylvania Executive Council sought to equalize the burden of impressment and make its impact uniformly felt by all its inhabitants.   It appointed a wagonmaster in each county who had the power to appoint in turn a deputy in each township.   The Council required each deputy to report the names of all wagon owners in each township and the number of wagons each owned.   Operating under orders of the state wagonmaster general, county wagonmasters called out wagons in rotation so that every person would be required to perform his tour of duty.[111]   To obtain wagons and teams, quartermasters of the Continental Army thereafter had to apply to the state

[109] *Pennsylvania Archives*, 1st ser, VI, 116–17 (Wharton to Delegates in Congress, 20 Dec 1777).

[110] Washington Papers, vol. 67, f. 71 (Greene to Washington, 15 Feb 1778).

[111] *Pennsylvania Archives*, 1st ser, VI, 124 (22 Dec 1777).

wagonmaster general for the number they needed, and they no longer had authority to obtain wagons through their own impressment efforts. Unfortunately, this process of applying for wagons often entailed delay, particularly if the county wagonmaster happened to be away at the time the order reached him.   It also happened that on occasion he was unable to get the constable to execute a warrant for bringing in some teams whose owners had been warned but who refused to serve with the Army.   There were instances, too, during the winter of 1777–78 when brigades of teams that were supposed to number twelve went to camp with only seven.[112]

Nor was there any certainty that the wagons called out would perform their duty.   In February 1778, for example, some 20 to 30 wagons came to camp from Northampton county in response to orders to the county wagonmaster.   They made one trip for provisions to the Head of Elk and then the wagoners deserted, losing several horses and drivers in their efforts to get away across the Schuylkill.   About the same time, a number of county wagons coming from Lancaster with flour "laid down their loads on the Horse Shoe road," and went home.[113]

Washington did not know whether it was the execution of the law or some other factor that hampered wagon supply, but, disappointed in getting wagons to transport supplies to camp, he sent Deputy Quartermaster General Lutterloh to confer with the Council in order that they might uncover the reason for "the great Delay and Backwardness of the People in forwarding Supplies and affording the Means of Transportation." [114]   The Pennsylvania Council maintained that it had always willingly cooperated with the Quartermaster's Department.   Transportation difficulties, it claimed, stemmed not from any fault in the law but from the failure of the Department to pay for the wagon service it obtained.   The Department made promises but when the time came for payment, the wagon owners received only certificates, paper promises of payment at some future date.   Moreover, the price set by Congress for the hire of a wagon was too low, and the Pennsylvania Council intimated that transportation would be improved if Congress raised the price allowed from 30 shillings to 45 or 50 shillings a day.[115]

Added to this were other difficulties.   The Deputy Quartermaster General at Lancaster reported that he was hampered in getting teams

---

[112] *Ibid.*, 1st ser, VI, 324–25 (George Ross, deputy quartermaster general to Col. Gibson, 2 Mar 1778).

[113] (1) *Ibid.*, 1st ser, VI, 320 (Chaloner to James Young, state wagonmaster general, 2 Mar 1778); 321–22 (Chaloner to Biddle, 26 Feb 1778).   (2) Washington Papers, vol. 68, f. 125 (Biddle to Lt. Col. John Laurens, 5 Mar 1778).

[114] *Writings of Washington*, ed. Fitzpatrick, XI, 45–48 (To Wharton, 7 Mar 1778).

[115] (1) *Pennsylvania Archives*, 1st ser, VI, 116–17 (Wharton to Delegates in Congress, 20 and 26 Dec 1777); 352–53 (Pa. Council to Lutterloh, 10 Mar 1778).   (2) Washington Papers, vol. 69, f. 43 (Lutterloh to Washington, 10 Mar 1778).

because so many were being employed by the militia. Even more damaging was the effect that the law governing militia service had upon his ability to get wagoners. The latter offered to furnish their teams and go out on a 2-month tour of duty with the Continental Army provided they could be excused from their militia service. Otherwise, if they failed to appear when called to duty they were subject to fines in the amount of their substitute money.[116]

Possibly if Mifflin had remained on duty and given the Department close supervision, transportation would not have failed so miserably. Ever since the winter of 1776–77, however, Mifflin had been in Philadelphia. At first he had been detained by congressional efforts to reorganize his Department and he had prolonged his stay to put the new plan into operation. Then, on the eve of the campaign, he had remained in Philadelphia at the request of Congress in order to stimulate recruitment as he had in the previous year. When he did return to camp, Washington, convinced that the British were about to move on Philadelphia, immediately sent him back to that city to remove stores and to "use his utmost endeavours to carry the designed opposition into effect." [117] Washington was torn between his desire to have his Quartermaster General at Headquarters and the need to utilize Mifflin's talent for recruiting troops. Since Mifflin in the early weeks of the campaign was obeying the orders of Washington and those of Congress, he could not be justifiably accused of neglecting his Quartermaster duties.

There is more reason to hold him accountable for the distress of the Army in the closing months of the campaign and during the winter encampment at Valley Forge. On 8 October, Mifflin, distressed by the defeats of the American Army, by British occupation of Philadelphia, and by the flight of the Continental Congress to York, pleaded ill health and submitted his resignation to Congress both as Quartermaster General and as a major general of the Army.[118] He sent no notice to Washington but retired to his home in Reading where society that winter was gay and agreeable even if the enemy was in possession of Philadelphia. There he remained, "a chief out of war, complaining, though not ill, considerably malcontent," brooding over his loss of favor at Headquarters and his failure to achieve his ambition of a separate command.[119]

Congress was as neglectful of the Quartermaster's Department and the Army as Mifflin was in the winter of 1777–78. For a month it took

---

[116] *Pennsylvania Archives*, 1st ser, VI, 69–70 (Ross to Col. Thos. Jones, 6 Dec 1777).

[117] *Writings of Washington*, ed. Fitzpatrick, VIII, 145 (To Mifflin, 31 May 1777); 293–95 (To Reed, 23 Jun 1777).

[118] Papers of the Continental Congress, item 161, f. 16–18 (Mifflin to Hancock).

[119] Alexander Graydon, *Memoirs of a Life* (Harrisburgh, 1811), 278; 282.

no action on his resignation.   Not until 7 November did it accept his resignation as Quartermaster General.   At the same time, however, since Mifflin's friends in Congress were averse to losing his valuable services, Congress appointed him to the Board of War, permitting him to retain his rank and commission though not his pay as major general.[120]   Much gratified by this action, Mifflin proposed waiting on Congress for orders as soon as it had made arrangements for the Quartermaster's Department so that he could leave Reading "without injury to the service." [121]

But on 8 November, Congress shunted consideration of the vital question of choosing a new Quartermaster General into the indefinite future by adopting a resolution that Mifflin, notwithstanding the acceptance of his resignation as Quartermaster General, should continue to carry out the functions of that office until a new appointee was named.[122] Four months passed before Congress made such an appointment.   Forgetting about "injury to the service," Mifflin did not attend to the duties of the Department; instead he let Lutterloh know that he could "now take the whole" upon himself.[123]   He had no funds to prepare for another campaign and he warned his deputy that he would have nothing to do with the Department except to settle his accounts.   Colonel Lutterloh and his subordinates at Headquarters tried to keep the Department functioning, but Washington was obliged to act as his own Quartermaster General as he often had during the campaign of 1777.[124]   Mifflin's neglect of Quartermaster duties and Congress' delay in taking action led to the gross confusion in the Quartermaster's Department that contributed to much of the suffering at Valley Forge in the winter of 1777–78.

[120] *Journals of the Continental Congress*, IX, 874.
[121] Richard H. Lee, *Memoir of the Life of Richard Henry Lee* (2 vols., Philadelphia, 1825), II, 174 (Mifflin to Lee, 12 Nov 1777).
[122] *Journals of the Continental Congress*, IX, 882.
[123] Papers of the Continental Congress, item 192, f. 217–19 (Anthony Butler to Lutterloh, 17 Jan 1778).
[124] George W. Greene, *The Life of Nathanael Green* (3 vols., New York, 1871), II, 49.

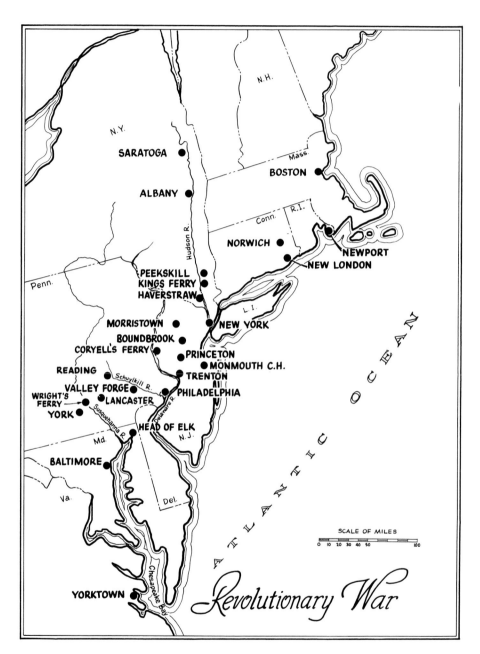

SARATOGA

BOSTON

ALBANY

NORWICH

NEWPORT
NEW LONDON

PEEKSKILL
KINGS FERRY
HAVERSTRAW

MORRISTOWN
BOUNDBROOK
CORYELL'S FERRY

NEW YORK

PRINCETON
MONMOUTH C.H.
READING
TRENTON
VALLEY FORGE
WRIGHT'S
FERRY
LANCASTER
PHILADELPHIA
YORK

HEAD OF ELK

BALTIMORE

YORKTOWN

SCALE OF MILES

0 10 20 30 40 50   100

Revolutionary War

MAP 1

CHAPTER II

The Impact of Inflation

Administrative Developments, 1778

"No Man, in my opinion," protested General Washington at Valley Forge, "ever had his measures more impeded than I have, by every department of the Army." [1]   After months of delay in attacking the problem of reorganizing the supply departments, Congress responded by sending a committee to camp early in January 1778.[2]   Two weeks later, the committee members informed Congress that unless the Quartermaster's Department was administered "by very superior abilities, but little can be expected from our Exertions during the next Campaign."   They at first suggested Maj. Gen. Philip Schuyler as a suitable chief for the Department, and, questioning the ability of William Buchanan as Commissary General of Purchases, they recommended his removal and the appointment of Jeremiah Wadsworth to that post.[3]

Meanwhile, Congress, sitting at York, had been listening to a favorable report by the Board of War on a plan submitted by Mifflin for a better organization of the Quartermaster's Department.   Out of his experience, he had proposed dividing the Department into military and civil branches, with the duties of the military branch being discharged by the Quartermaster General and those of the civil branch divided among three officers—a commissary of forage, a commissary for horses and wagons, and an agent for the purchase of tents, tools, and other supplies.   The estimates and orders of the Quartermaster General or the Board of War were to govern the purchases made by these three officers.   Congress adopted this plan on 5 February 1778.[4]

Almost a month had elapsed since the committee at camp had been appointed and its members, concluding that their letter of recommendations had miscarried, again wrote to Congress stressing the urgent need for action.   Although alarmed over the delay in bringing relief to the troops at Valley Forge, Congress waited another week after the receipt

[1] *Writings of Washington*, ed. Fitzpatrick, X, 194 (To Pres. of Congress, 23 Dec 1777).
[2] *Journals of the Continental Congress*, X, 39–40, 41 (10 and 12 Jan 1778).
[3] RG 11, Papers of the Continental Congress, item 33, f. 71, 75 (To Pres. of Congress, 28 and 29 Jan 1778).   National Archives.
[4] *Journals of the Continental Congress*, X, 102–03, 126–27.

of this letter before it directed the committee, acting with General Washington, to make the proper appointments in the Quartermaster's Department.[5]

By that time, the committee had received a copy of the plan adopted on 5 February. Analysis of the plan convinced the members that it would not work. They tactfully called attention to its shortcomings, particularly to the infinite confusion and controversies that would result from having so many co-ordinate and independent officers in one Department. In any case, success in the coming campaign, they held, would depend upon the character of the men appointed and not upon paper systems. They therefore discarded the plan of Congress and proposed instead the appointment of a Quartermaster General and two assistant quartermasters general.

By dint of much persuasion and appeals to patriotism, they had prevailed upon Maj. Gen. Nathanael Greene to head the Department and John Cox, an eminent Philadelphia merchant, and Charles Pettit, a lawyer and accountant who had been secretary to Governor Livingston of New Jersey, to accept appointment as his assistants if proffered by Congress. The committee at camp proposed that General Greene should perform the military duties of the Department and direct all purchases and issues; that Cox should make all purchases and examine all stores; and that Pettit should keep all accounts and all cash. To compensate them for their trouble, the committee allowed these three men one percent upon the money spent in the Department, to be divided as they agreed among themselves. Greene subsequently divided this commission equally, each man receiving one-third of one percent.[6]

---

[5] (1) *Ibid.*, X, 186 (21 Feb 1778). (2) Papers of the Continental Congress, item 33, f. 128–29 (Committee to Pres. of Congress, 12 Feb 1778).

[6] General Greene later remarked that the emoluments of his office were equal to his "utmost wishes," and these proceeds he invested in shipping, privateering, iron manufacturing, and real estate, the actual investments being handled by friends. Greene was not as scrupulous as Washington in avoiding anything that might provide a base for calumny, but he was discreet enough to clothe with secrecy his business operations, even to the extent of resorting to the use in 1779 of a code in corresponding with his business partners, Jeremiah Wadsworth and Barnabas Deane. Historians later speculated that the company they formed might have been created to sell supplies to the Army, but a more recent biographer of Greene, after exhaustive analysis of the records found that most of the company's capital was invested in shipping and privateering. Ventures in privateering in Revolutionary days were not unethical; they were in fact considered beneficial to the country as well as profitable to the individual. The favors Greene granted to his brother Jacob and his cousin Griffin, who were also his partners in business, are not easily dismissed even through Jacob Greene and Company received no more than the market price for standard quality goods sold to the Army, as far as the records reveal. (1) For a full analysis of Greene's business ventures while Quartermaster General, see Theodore Thayer, *Nathanael Greene, Strategist of the American Revolution.* (New York, 1960), pp. 229–38. (2) "Letters of General Nathanael Green to Colonel Jeremiah Wadsworth," *Pennsylvania Magazine of History and Biography*, XXII, pp. 211–16, provides an example of a coded letter.

The committee conceded that to pay such a commission was a temptation to speculation and should, in general, be avoided. It resorted to this method, however, because it was impossible to provide an adequate salary without creating fresh difficulties, since every other officer would expect a similar increase in pay. Only on the terms outlined and provided he was not deprived of his rank of major general in the line was General Greene willing to accept the burdensome and thankless appointment.[7] With time running out and preparation still to be made for the approaching campaign of 1778, Congress had no alternative but to adopt the arrangements proposed by its committee and it appointed the three men to office.[8]

Aside from the creation of the two assistantships to the Quartermaster General and the elimination of divisional deputy quartermasters general, there were no other changes in the Department's organization. The subordinate departments for handling forage and wagons were retained. Clement Biddle continued to head the forage department, but, Wagonmaster General Thornsbury having resigned about the same time as Mifflin, James Thompson had been temporarily appointed to that post on 22 December 1777. Greene permanently assigned him to that office when he became Quartermaster General. Greene had no intention of dismissing deputies who had worked for Mifflin. As long as their conduct manifested their fitness for employment, he proposed to continue them in their respective districts. Most of them remained at their posts, although Hugh Hughes refused to serve under him. Such continuity of personnel in the Department prevented the complete disruption of supply channels.

In view of Washington's assertion in December that the Army would have to "starve, dissolve, or disperse, in order to obtain subsistence," procurement of food for the troops at Valley Forge was the immediate need to which both Congress, through its Board of War, and the Pennsylvania assembly addressed their attention.[9] Their uncoordinated efforts promoted confusion, but gradually the supply situation improved. Quartermaster General Greene's administration of his Department was vigorous, and the response of the states to Washington's appeals assisted materially, as did the beginning of milder weather that permitted wagoners to drive their teams and wagons to camp fully loaded with provisions. By April, the Army was fairly well supplied with beef, bread, and flour.[10]

---

[7] Papers of the Continental Congress, item 33, f. 187–95 (To Pres. of Congress, 25 Feb 1778).
[8] *Journals of the Continental Congress*, X, 210–11 (2 Mar 1778).
[9] *Writings of Washington*, ed. Fitzpatrick, X, 192–93 (To Pres. of Congress, 23 Dec 1777).
[10] Ephraim Blaine Letter Book, 1777–78 (Chaloner to, Buchanan, 5 Apr 1778). Manuscript Div., Library of Congress.

By that time, too, Congress had effected a reorganization of the Commissary Department. The regulatory plan of 1777 had long been under attack, but it was not until the end of that year that its advocates finally gave up, "after distressing the Army, Congress, and the Continent with it for six or eight Months." [11] In January 1778, Congress appointed a Committee to revise the system. Though it contemplated no alteration of the Issuing Department, Congress was now ready to remove Buchanan and rescind the 1777 regulation governing the Purchasing Department. Buchanan saved the members the necessity of removing him by resigning on 20 March 1778.[12] Many would have preferred the reappointment of Joseph Trumbull, but, failing that, the committee endorsed Jeremiah Wadsworth for the office. Early in February, Congress invited him to attend that he might be consulted on proposed amendments.[13]

Unfortunately, that invitation apparently went astray for it was not until the end of March that Wadsworth came to York to consider the regulatory plan that Congress had in the meantime been drafting. As adopted on 14 April, the plan incorporated most of the suggestions that Trumbull had made in the summer of 1777. Congress vested full authority in the Commissary General of Purchases to appoint and remove any officer in his Department and to assign to the purchasing commissaries specfic districts to which they were confined in making their purchases. To make these posts attractive to competent men, Congress provided for a commission of 2 percent, payable to purchasing commissaries on all money they disbursed. It allowed a commission of ½ percent to the Commissary General of Purchases on all sums paid by him to his deputy commissaries in their respective districts. Though the Commissary General was no longer obliged to reside at the place where Congress was in session, he did maintain an office there and made periodic reports to Congress.[14]

Congress appointed Wadsworth to the office on 9 April 1778. With some satisfaction, James Lovell, delegate from Massachusetts, informed Samuel Adams:

We have got Col. Wadsworth at the Head of the Commissariate *unfettered* strictly so. Had the same steps as now been taken with Trumbull a year ago amazing Sums would have been saved . . . Let us look forward with hope.[15]

[11] *Letters of Members of the Continental Congress*, ed. Burnett, III, 76 (Gerry to Samuel Adams, 7 Feb 1778).
[12] Papers of the Continental Congress, item 78, II, f. 411 (Buchanan to Pres. of Congress, 20 Mar 1778).
[13] *Journals of the Continental Congress*, X, 51 (14 Jan 1778); 141 (9 Feb 1778).
[14] *Ibid.*, X, 344–48 (14 Apr 1778).
[15] (1) *Letters of Members of the Continental Congress*, ed. Burnett, III, 175 (19 Apr 1778).
(2) *Journals of the Continental Congress*, X, 327–28 (9 Apr 1778).

Wadsworth had a greater degree of control over his Department than had been granted to Buchanan, but, except for some adjustments in district boundaries, he made practically no change in organization or personnel. William Aylett remained deputy commissary general of purchases in the Southern Department as Ephraim Blaine did in the Middle Department. Jacob Cuyler continued to direct commissary purchases in the Northern Department, and Peter Colt and Henry Champion, who supervised cattle purchases in New England, were retained in the Eastern Department.

Having abandoned its previous measures for reorganizing these two supply departments, Congress was inclined, during most of 1778, to let Wadsworth and Greene work out the problems of their respective Departments without interference. Congress was also apparently willing to let the Clothing Department stumble along under the inept directions of Mease. It took no action to remove him despite Washington's demands for an investigation of the Department in April and his denunciation of Mease in August as unfit for the post he occupied.[16] Acting on the General's plea for a better regulation of the Clothing Department, a committee brought in a report recommending that the states in the future make provision for clothing their respective quotas of troops in the Continental Army, and that a court of inquiry investigate the conduct of Mease and his agents.[17] But with a leisureliness characteristic of the time, Congress postponed consideration of the report until the fall when it was referred to still another committee that submitted a slightly modified report.[18] There is no evidence that Congress ever acted upon it, and Mease reluctantly remained in office until a successor could be appointed.[19] The arrival of numerous cargoes of clothing in the spring of 1778, however, had prompted Congress to limit the Clothier General's power to purchase by directing a suspension of all further purchases of clothing on account of the United States by Mease or his agents. At the same time, it had directed that the states supply their respective quotas of troops with shoes, stockings, and shirts. Congress also directed the Board of War to purchase these items for the Continental Army until the Clothing Department was properly reorganized.[20] Because of the arrival of clothing from abroad and the initiative assumed by the Board of War, the clothing supply situation was much improved despite con-

---

[16] *Writings of Washington*, ed. Fitzpatrick, XI, 240; XII, 278–79 (To Pres. of Congress, 10 Apr and 4 Aug 1778).

[17] *Journals of the Continental Congress*, XI, 812–13 (19 Aug 1778).

[18] *Ibid.*, XI, 996–97 (9 Oct 1778).

[19] (1) *Ibid.*, XII, 937 (21 Sep 1778). (2) Papers of the Continental Congress, item 78, XV, f. 381 (Mease to Laurens, 19 Sep 1778).

[20] *Journals of the Continental Congress*, XI, 517, 545–46 (21 and 28 May 1778).

gressional delay in reorganizing the Clothing Department and appointing a new Clothier General.

Improvement in Supply

Fundamental to improvement in supply generally was the provision of adequate transportation facilities. Quartermaster General Greene immediately applied himself to this problem upon assuming the duties of his office on 23 March 1778. By that time it was becoming increasingly evident that the British intended to evacuate Philadelphia. In preparation for the reinforcements arriving at Valley Forge for the coming campaign—Washington had a large army of 11,000 to 12,000 men when the troops marched from Valley Forge—stores deposited in magazines had to be increased. Greene needed a large number of wagons, teams, and drivers to transport such supplies along the lines of communications. He also required a sufficient number of them to permit the Army to take the field with its baggage, ammunition, tools, equipment, and supplies. In addition, he had to provide an adequate supply of forage for the animals used in such transportation as well as for the artillery and riding horses.

To haul food and forage along the supply lines, Washington and Greene sent out appeals for wagons not only to Pennsylvania, where operations were centered, but also to Maryland and New Jersey. Greene directed the deputy quartermaster general stationed at the Head of Elk to purchase, hire, or impress teams in order that provisions might move from there to camp.[21] Greene developed no new procedures for procuring wagons and teams, but he sought relief from hampering restrictions. He visited the Pennsylvania legislature at Lancaster, proposing amendments to the state's wagon law. He also induced President Wharton to agree to instruct county lieutenants to exempt from militia fines such individuals as were employed by the Army and could produce certificates to that effect.[22] Pennsylvania authorities had occasionally used this procedure in the past. Greene also supplemented land transportation with water carriage on the Schuylkill until the water level fell so low in mid-May that navigation became obstructed.

To provide transportation organic to the Army, Greene built upon the foundation laid by Mifflin. The latter had established a wagon

---

[21] (1) *Pennsylvania Archives*, 1st ser, VI, 366–67 (Pettit to Vice Pres. Geo. Bryan, 17 Mar 1778). (2) *Writings of Washington*, ed. Fitzpatrick, XI, 123–24 (To Gov. Thomas Johnson, 21 Mar 1778). (3) Greene, *Life of Nathanael Greene*, II, 55–56 (To Washington, 26 Mar 1778); 61 (To Hollingsworth, 7 Apr 1778).

[22] (1) *Writings of Washington*, ed. Fitzpatrick, XI, 241–42 (To Pres. Thomas Wharton, 10 Apr 1778). (2) *Pennsylvania Archives*, 1st ser, VI, 416 (Wharton to Washington, 13 Apr 1778).

department, but failure to develop any regulation for it, lack of supervision, and the resignation of Thornsbury 6 months after his appointment as Wagonmaster General had resulted in a breakdown in such transportation. As a consequence, when the committee at camp arrived at Valley Forge, it had reported that "almost every species of camp transportation is now performed by men, who without a murmur, patiently yoke themselves to little carriages of their own making, or load their wood and provisions on their backs." [23] Deputy Quartermaster General Lutterloh had tried to direct the wagon service, but the neglect of teams and wagons exhibited by soldiers detailed from the line, as well as the utter carelessness of civilian wagoners, had led him to advocate enlistment of wagoners for the duration of the war.[24]

Greene undoubtedly appreciated the need for such enlistment, but his immediate objective, with the campaign only weeks away, was to procure new wagons, repair old ones, and enlist wagoners on the best terms that he could. His Wagonmaster General, James Thompson, was an able man who enlisted wagoners from various parts of the country, reduced the number of soldiers detailed from the line as wagoners, and in the course of the campaign made some progress in improving the care of horses and wagons. At the end of the campaign, he, too, recommended enlistment of wagoners for the duration of the war and, in addition, proposed granting them the same bounty offered to soldiers as an inducement to enlist. Greene was unsuccessful in his efforts to obtain favorable congressional action, and for the duration of the war short-term enlistments for wagoners remained the established policy. Yet so well had Greene succeeded in providing transportation during the campaign of 1778 that Washington praised him for the "great facility" with which he had enabled the Army and its baggage to move from Valley Forge in pursuit of the enemy and, after the battle of Monmouth, to march to the Highlands of the Hudson.[25]

His success must be attributed in large measure to the efficiency of Clement Biddle as Commissary General of Forage. Once again, Greene built upon a basis established by Mifflin. The latter had created a forage department but, by reason of his continued absence from camp, had

[23] Papers of the Continental Congress, item 33, f. 128–29 (To Pres. of Congress, 12 Feb 1778).

[24] Washington Papers, vol. 63, f. 117 (Lutterloh, Remarks on wagon department, 25 Dec 1777). Manuscript Div., Library of Congress.

[25] (1) Writings of Washington, ed. Fitzpatrick, XII, 277 (To Pres. of Congress, 3 Aug 1778). (2) Letters to and from Major-General Nathanael Greene, Quartermaster-General, IV, f. 100 (Thompson to Greene, 24 Feb 1779). American Philosophical Society. Hereafter briefly cited as Greene Letters. (3) Journals of the Continental Congress, XIII, 320–21 (16 Mar 1779); 467–68 (17 Apr 1779).

failed to develop it into an effective agency. Under Mifflin, Biddle's procurement activities had been strictly limited to the environs of Headquarters and he had established magazines as directed by the Quartermaster General. But since Mifflin resigned a few months after Biddle became Commissary General of Forage, the latter had received little or no direction from him. During the winter of 1777–78, Biddle had tried to exercise a greater degree of control but had failed because he had no authority over the many other purchasers of forage.

Ever since 1776, when the war shifted from New England to New York and the chief British base became located at New York City, the Continental Army, on the defensive, had been moving along a line extending from the Highlands of the Hudson through New Jersey to the Head of Elk on Chesapeake Bay. Early in 1778, Biddle proposed to establish a chain of forage magazines of varying sizes along that line of communications to sustain military operations.[26] He also suggested the amount of forage that would have to be accumulated, the personnel required to operate the magazines, and the records needed to afford a knowledge of stocks on hand. Greene studied the plan, approved it, and, in consultation with Washington, perfected the working of the lines of communications.

Within a week, after designating the general outline of the chain of magazines, he indicated that 200,000 bushels of grain would be required on the Delaware River; 200,000 at the Head of Elk and the intermediate posts to camp; 100,000 on the line of communications from the Susquehanna to the Schuylkill River, from Reading through Lancaster to Wright's Ferry; 100,000 from the Delaware to the North River; and 40,000 bushels around Trenton. These magazines were to be "tolerably high up" the river for security against British men-of-war.[27] Biddle, who was now to direct the purchase of all forage for the Army, lost no time in establishing magazines, in drafting instructions to his purchasing agents, and in issuing rules to govern forage masters at magazines in the receipt and issue of forage.[28] For the first time, a systematized procedure was introduced for supplying the Army with forage.

While Greene was improving the means of transportation, Wadsworth was infusing new vigor into the Commissary Department, and, in preparation for the Army's movement, Blaine, his deputy in the Middle Department, was storing provisions in magazines along the familiar route

[26] Papers of the Continental Congress, item 155, I, f. 373–77 (Plan, 9 Mar 1778).
[27] (1) Greene, *Life of Nathanael Greene*, II, 57–58 (Greene to Biddle, 30 Mar 1778). (2) *Writings of Washington*, ed. Fitzpatrick, XI, 177 (To Greene, 31 Mar 1778).
[28] Letter Books of Hugh Hughes (Biddle to Hughes and enclosures, 22 Apr 1778). New York Historical Society.

leading from Valley Forge via Coryell's Ferry, Boundbrook, and Morristown to the North River.[29] Wadsworth found it unnecessary to make any changes in the supply procedures originally developed in the Commissary Department by Joseph Trumbull. His problems were those of building up magazines, meeting sudden demands for provisions, and combating practices that led to competition in the procurement of subsistence.

The Newport expedition in the summer of 1778, for example, brought a sudden demand for large quantities of provisions for the land and sea forces of the American Army and the French fleet that were cooperating in that venture. It produced a temporary shortage of some commodities. Flour was especially scarce in the New England area, but Wadsworth's efforts to take advantage of the presence of the French fleet to ship flour from Virginia by sea were thwarted by congressional delays. By the time Congress got around to authorizing procurement, the Newport expedition had failed and the French fleet had sailed for Boston to refit. Wadsworth had to abandon the plan to ship flour by sailing vessels as too dangerous. Instead, he deposited flour at magazines on the inland line of communication from Fredericksburg, via New York City, to Boston, the supplies being transported there at far greater expense by wagons from Pennsylvania.[30]

This first joint allied operation at Newport produced results that were unfavorable to smooth commissary operations. The intendant of the French fleet, unwilling to depend upon the American Commissary Department for his supplies, entered into his own contractual arrangements. The higher prices he offered handicapped the American commissaries in their efforts to provision the allied force. Maj. Gen. John Sullivan, commanding the American forces, was equally guilty of hampering the commissaries for he, too, purchased supplies through his own agents because he feared sufficient provisions would not be made available.[31]

The net effect of these competitive practices was to send prices spiraling upwards. The arrival of the French fleet had helped unleash

[29] *Writings of Washington,* ed. Fitzpatrick, XI, 408 (To Blaine, 17 May 1778).

[30] (1) Papers of the Continental Congress, item 78, XXIII, f. 513 (Wadsworth to Blaine, 23 Jul 1778); f. 537 (Wadsworth to Laurens, 24 Aug 1778). (2) *Journals of the Continental Congress,* XI, 831 (24 Aug 1778). (3) *Writings of Washington,* ed Fitzpatrick, XII, 490 (To Pres. of Congress, 23 Sep 1778).

[31] (1) Johnson, *The Administration of the American Commissariat During the Revolutionary War,* 148–49. (2) *Writings of Washington,* ed. Fitzpatrick, XIII, 277–78 (To Sullivan, 18 Nov 1778). (3) O. G. Hammond, "Letters and Papers of Sullivan," *Collections of New Hampshire Historical Society,* XIV, vol. II, 423 (Peter Colt to Sullivan, 6 Nov 1778); 426–48 (Sullivan to Colt, 10 Nov 1778); 443–444; 446–447 (Sullivan to Washington, 23 and 27 Nov 1778). (4) Washington Papers, vol. 100, f. 87 (Wadsworth to Washington, 15 Mar 1779).

a wave of profiteering and everywhere Wadsworth found prices steadily rising. Throughout Virginia and Maryland, engrossers were busy buying flour, and, since they had ready money to pay for their purchases, no commissary could compete with them.[32] Despite the reluctance of farmers to exchange their products for a depreciating currency, Wadsworth's efforts made food available to the Army, and the winter of 1778–79 brought none of the extremes of hardship that had been suffered by the troops at Valley Forge.

Impact of Spiraling Prices

Preparations for the campaign of 1778 had required the expenditure of considerable sums of money, yet Greene had not been furnished with any sizable amount until May, and both the Commissary and Quartermaster's Departments had been compelled, much to their disadvantage, to operate on credit. By June, Greene had drawn upon the Treasury for almost four million dollars, yet it was "but a breakfast for the department, and hardly that."[33] As prices for supplies and services continued to rise, he became thoroughly alarmed. Upon a visit to Boston in the fall of 1778, he found hay brought $60 to $80 a ton; corn sold for $10 a bushel; oats were priced at $4 a bushel; and carting cost 9 shillings per mile by the ton, and even that price satisfied no one. If the extravagance of the people was not checked, he informed Washington, "there are no funds in the universe that will equal the expense."[34]

As prices soared and expenditures in the supply departments mounted, criticism of the Commissary and Quartermaster's Departments, that had subsided when Wadsworth and Greene were appointed early in 1778, began to grow in volume. Before the end of the year, Congress decided that more vigorous measures were necessary for their regulation, and it appointed a committee of three to superintend them. With some changes in personnel, that committee carried out its functions for a little more than a year when its duties were taken over by the Board of War.[35] Other committees were also appointed during 1779 to promote reform in one phase or another of the activities of the supply departments, for in that year there again was no dearth of reforming zeal.

---

[32] Papers of the Continental Congress, item 78, XXIII, f. 561, 569 (Wadsworth to Laurens, 6 and 29 Sep 1778).

[33] Greene, *Life of Nathanael Greene*, II, 82–83 (To Gouverneur Morris, 1 Jun 1778).

[34] *Ibid.*, II, 143 (16 Sep 1778).

[35] *Journals of the Continental Congress*, XII, 1114–15 (10 Nov 1778); XV, 1312 (25 Nov 1779).

Reorganization of Clothing Department

One result of that spirit was a tardy reorganization of the Clothing Department.   Late in 1778, Congress sent a committee to camp to confer with Washington on Army problems in general.   He seized that opportunity to review the problem of clothing supply and to reiterate views that he had been expressing for the past year.   Although Congress would have to decide on the method for effecting a regular and constant flow of clothing, Washington thought it could be best achieved by relying on governmental contracts with France because he believed that only the united funds and credit of the Continental Congress were sufficiently large for purchasing all the clothing needed.   If procurement was left to the states alone, they would depend on private mercantile contracts and the clothing supply would be inadequate.   But whether the Continental Congress or each of the states undertook to purchase clothing for the troops, Washington thought a definite organization, consisting of a clothier general, state clothiers, and regimental clothiers, was essential for handling distribution.[36]

The committee passed his ideas along to Congress.   When that body delayed acting for almost 2 months, Washington urged Congress to decide on a substitute measure if it could not approve his plan.   The Clothing Department would have to be reorganized, he insisted, since nothing but loss and discontent resulted under the existing management. Enlarging on his difficulties, he pointed out that, on the one hand, considerable quantities of clothing were being imported, of which the Army got no share because they fell into the hands of private buyers.   On the other, through inadequate supervision quantities of clothing were "wasting and rotting in different parts of the country," knowledge of which reached him only by chance.   Meanwhile, the Army remained, as always, half naked.[37]

On 23 March 1779, Congress enacted an ordinance for regulating the Clothing Department that followed Washington's ideas on organization. Congress appointed the Clothier General, who was subject to the orders of the Board of War and the commander-in-chief.   The states appointed state clothiers.   Handicapped by lack of funds, Congress made no provision for any centralized control of purchases but provided that all procurement was to be accomplished by the Board of War or by the states through their respective agents.   Both would buy for the account of the Continental Congress, the Board of War for the Army generally;

---

[36] *Writings of Washington,* ed. Fitzpatrick, XIV, 35–42 (To Committee of Conference, 23 Jan 1779).

[37] *Ibid.,* XIV, 244–45 (To Pres. of Congress, 15 Mar 1779).

CONTINENTAL INFANTRY, 1778–1783

the states for their respective troops.   All clothing imported from abroad, charged to the account of the Continental Congress, and all purchased by its agents in the United States was to be turned over to the Clothier General.   Of these supplies, each state clothier was to receive that proportion assigned for the use of the troops of his state, together with all clothing purchased by his state.[38]

Although Congress adopted the plan in March, its execution was delayed for 4 months because Congress failed to appoint a Clothier General immediately.   It was not until 24 July, after two other candidates had declined serving, that its third appointee, James Wilkinson, accepted the post.[39]   In instructing Wilkinson on preparations for the approaching winter months, Washington expressed the hope that the latter would soon "put matters in a proper train" and would spend as much time with the Army as was "consistent with the great Objects of your appointment." [40]   Alas for Washington's hopes; they died within 2 months.   By that time he was informing Maj. Gen. William Heath that "I am again reduced to the necessity of acting the part of Clothier General." [41]   Wilkinson was more often absent than present at Headquarters, though he did retain at camp, to supervise the issue of clothing to the Army, an assistant, John Moylan, brother of the former Quartermaster General.   The steady and regular flow of supplies that Washington had hoped to see established did not materialize because the states depended on the Continental Congress and the Continental Congress depended upon the states.

Wilkinson had also been made responsible for supervising the commissaries in the Hide Department.   In lieu of a single Commissary of Hides, the Board of War had recommended and Congress had adopted a plan for appointing a commissary in each state or group of states where the business of the Hide Department required one.   George Ewing having resigned as Commissary of Hides on 20 April 1779, the Board of War appointed under the new plan five commissaries of hides— William Henry, whose district included Pennsylvania, Maryland, and Delaware; John Mehelm for New Jersey; Moses Hatfield for New York; Robert Lamb for Massachusetts; and George Starr for Connecticut.[42] These commissaries were to be allowed as many assistants and clerks as the Board of War thought necessary to accomplish their business of

---

[38] *Journals of the Continental Congress,* XIII, 353–57 (23 Mar 1779).

[39] *Ibid.,* XIV, 844.

[40] *Writings of Washington,* ed. Fitzpatrick, XVI, 280–82 (To Wilkinson, 13 Sep 1779).

[41] *Ibid.,* XVII, 123 (18 Nov 1779).

[42] (1) *Journals of the Continental Congress,* XIV, 870–71 (23 Jul 1779).   (2) Washington Papers, vol. 116, f. 59 (Richard Peters to Washington, 3 Sep 1779).

receiving hides, converting them into tanned leather, and manufacturing shoes either in factories under their supervision or by contracting for the work. Wilkinson as Clothier General consolidated a quarterly return from those submitted by the commissaries and sent it to the Board of War. He also received and distributed all shoes to the Army. He had no authority, however, for removing a dishonest subordinate so that when he uncovered irregularities in the accounts of the Commissary of Hides for New York, he could do no more than call it to the attention of the Board of War.[43] Reorganization of the Hide Department brought little improvement either in the quantity or the quality of shoes made available to the troops.

Credit and Depreciated Currency

At the same time that Congress was attempting to improve the organization of the Clothing and Hide Departments, it also initiated measures for reorganizing the two major supply departments, though these efforts did not come to fruition until 1780. Faced with the difficult and perplexing problem of devising ways to restore credit, place Continental currency on a sound basis, and avert bankruptcy, the members of Congress, while recognizing other causes, were inclined to attribute mounting war expenditures and depreciation of the currency largely to the practices of quartermasters and commissaries. On the floor of Congress, Elbridge Gerry charged that the purchasing officers had been guilty of barefaced frauds—that, by inducing sellers to demand higher prices, they had deliberately enhanced prices in order to profit through larger commissions.[44] Of the ubiquitous commissaries and quartermasters William Shippen wrote:

Only think of a two penny Jack who never in his life was capable by any business he had been engaged in, of making a Shilling more than maintained his family and that but in a very so so manner shall now be making 40 or 50,000 pr. annum and that by lowering the value of our Money and raising the prices of every Article he purchases a truth acknowledged by all and yet the mischief suffered to go on and increase . . .[45]

By the end of 1779, the value of money had fallen to a point where $30 of Continental money had not the purchasing power of one specie dollar.

The supply departments attributed their woes to a lack of funds. Assistant Quartermaster General Pettit was beset on all sides by applications for money and not infrequently the deputy quartermasters general

---

[43] Washington Papers, vol. 124, f. 84–86 (Wilkinson to Board of War, 4 Jan 1780).
[44] Letters of Members of the Continental Congress, ed. Burnett, IV, 215 (Henry Laurens, Notes of Proceedings, 17 May 1779).
[45] Ibid., IV, 282 (To Richard Henry Lee, 22 Jun 1779).

kept messengers waiting in his office for weeks at a time until he had funds to give them. Pettit charged that the want of "timely supplies" of money had greatly retarded the preparations for the campaign of 1779, and that if they had been furnished "in due season," they could have been used more effectively and would have greatly lessened the indebtedness of the Department.[46] Commissary officers voiced the same views, for the universal lack of money in that Department made Wadsworth "despair of keeping the Army alive." [47]

However willing Congress might have been to grant the necessary funds, the Treasury was in no condition to furnish them in proportion to the demand, and there were interminable delays because money came into the Treasury so slowly. Pettit might, for example, receive an order for several million dollars, but the Treasury would be able to give him only one or two hundred thousand dollars of the amount, and that weeks after he had received the order. Nor could the Treasury even then inform him when he might receive the rest of the money. As a consequence, Pettit lamented that the money "moulders away in dribs," and that he was unable to send any deputy a sum adequate to his needs.[48]

Hard pressed by their creditors, the deputies were much in need of relief. Many of them had extended their credit to the utmost, having entered into contracts, the terms of which they could not discharge when due for lack of funds. "Twenty people have been with me this day," Colonel Mitchell at Philadelphia wrote, beseeching funds; "as many more will be at the Office before Night, and I have nothing to satisfy them." [49] Additional credit for the Quartermaster's Department could be obtained only on terms disadvantageous to the government, that is, by contracting to fix the prices of articles purchased at the time of payment, which made it to the interest of the sellers to raise prices more rapidly than they would otherwise have done. All of the deputies were greatly in debt; "we are out at the Elbows everywhere," Pettit informed Greene.[50]

Congress had granted large sums of money to both Greene and Wadsworth since they had assumed the duties of their respective offices. But Pettit maintained that these funds were only nominally large, for through depreciation of the currency they fell far short of the demands and were insufficient to "keep the machine in motion." [51] While some

---

[46] (1) Greene Letters, V, f. 28 (Pettit to Pres. of Treasury Board, 19 May 1779). (2) Papers of the Continental Congress, item 155, I, f. 257 (Pettit to Pres. of Congress, 17 Nov 1779).

[47] Papers of the Continental Congress, item 78, V, f. 425 (Chaloner and White to committee of Congress, 24 Nov 1779); XXIV, f. 129 (Wadsworth to Pres. of Congress, 24 Nov 1779).

[48] Greene Letters, VIII, f. 86 (Pettit to Greene, 30 Oct 1779).

[49] Ibid., IX, f. 102 (Mitchell to Pettit, 15 Nov 1779).

[50] Ibid., IX, f. 96 (5–9 Nov 1779).

[51] Papers of the Continental Congress, item 155, I, f. 257 (Pettit to Pres. of Congress, 17 Nov 1779).

members recognized the truth of Pettit's explanation, Congress was greatly alarmed by the spiraling costs.   The expenditures of both the Commissary and Quartermaster's Departments in 1776 had been $5,399,219; the following year they had increased to $9,272,534; and in 1778 they had more than quadrupled to $37,202,421.   By May 1779, the committee on the Treasury reported that unless measures were taken to put the country's finances on a better footing, expenditures for the two departments would amount to at least $200 million in that year.[52]   It was impracticable to carry on the war by paper emissions at the enormous rate of expenditures in the supply departments, and the Treasury Board recommended that they be put on "a different footing with regard to the expenditure of public money." [53]

Increased Criticism and Threatened Resignations

No one practice was suspected of contributing more to the cost of the war than the payment of commissions to purchasing agents.   Earlier efforts to eliminate such payments in the Commissary Department had proved unsuccessful, but the substitution of fixed salaries for commissions remained an attractive means of reducing expenses.   Even the terms under which the heads of the Commissary and Quartermaster's Departments served came under review early in January 1779.[54]   Greene was convinced that there were "measures taken to render the business of the quarter masters Department odious in the Eyes of the people." [55]   It can not be denied that some agents waxed wealthy on profits made by increasing prices to fatten their commissions, but the subject of commissions had undoubtedly, as Greene contended, "been improv'd into one great source of jealousy and discontent."   He maintained that it was a comparatively small evil since the greater part of the staff officers served upon a salary basis.[56]   Little was heard of the hardships suffered by salaried quartermaster personnel in the midst of inflation.   They were paid much less than were common laborers, and yet, Greene acknowledged, much was "due to their merit."   Their salaries had not been changed since they had been set by Congress in the summer of 1777. Unfortunately, the activity of the purchasing commissaries and quartermasters was much more evident to the public, and it was far easier to blame them for depreciation than for Congress to tackle the difficult

---

[52] *Journals of the Continental Congress,* XIV, 561–62 (7 May 1779).

[53] *Ibid.,* XIV, 662 (28 May 1779).

[54] Papers of the Continental Congress, item 173, IV, f. 119–21 (Greene to Pres. of Congress, 15 Feb 1779).

[55] Washington Papers, vol. 104 f. 55, 123 (Greene to Washington, 22 and 26 Apr 1779).

[56] Papers of the Continental Congress, item 173, II, 157–73 (Greene to Jay, 28 Jul 1779).

and complex problem of evolving effective measures for restoring the credit of the country's currency.

As a result of the "unmerited abuse and slander indiscriminately heaped on" the Commissary Department by every "petty scribbler," Wadsworth offered his resignation in June. Greene also had threatened 2 months earlier to "quit a business wherein I cannot please," but Congress had no intention of losing the services of either man.[57] It unanimously resolved that Congress had full confidence in the integrity and abilities of the Quartermaster General and the Commissary General. The resolution mollified both men and they continued in office.

Ever since the beginning of the year Greene had expected to hear of a new regulatory plan for his Department, but months had gone by without any news. It was July 1779 before a committee for regulating and retrenching the expenses of the Commissary and Quartermaster's Departments laid before Congress an elaborate, detailed plan, to which Congress evidently intended giving careful study since it ordered 60 copies printed.[58] But it was 18 October before a committee of the whole considered the plan, briefly debated it during some part of 2 days, and then laid it aside. It was not mentioned again until 4 December when Congress passed the plan over to a new committee.[59]

By that time, Greene, who had directed supply arrangements for two campaigns, was eager to resign. The continuing depreciation of the currency handicapped supply at every turn. Contracts could not be made nor could credit be obtained. More agents were required to collect supplies that would have been offered willingly if money had been stable. The increased number of agents only added to Departmental expenses and gave rise to suspicions that economy was not being practiced. Because the Treasury had no money, current expenses could not be met nor could past debts be discharged. As a result, creditors were beginning to sue purchasing quartermasters, but such suits, as Greene pointed out, served only to promote total loss of confidence in the Department's officers. When it was time to begin preparing for the campaign of 1780, Greene thought the moment opportune for requesting Congress to appoint a new Quartermaster General. Even if the emoluments were five times as large as they were supposed to be, he insisted, he would still wish to resign, and, in December 1779, he requested that Congress act promptly to fill his place.[60]

---

[57] *Ibid.*, item 155, I, f. 127–34 (Greene to James Duane, 16 Apr 1779); item 78, XXIV, f. 410 (Wadsworth to Pres. of Congress, 5 Jun 1779).

[58] *Journals of the Continental Congress*, XIV, 872–80 (23 Jul 1779).

[59] *Ibid.*, XV, 1186 (18 Oct); 1187 (19 Oct); 1349 (4 Dec 1779).

[60] Greene, *Life of Nathanael Greene*, II, 259–63 (To Pres. of Congress, 12 Dec 1779).

Two months earlier, Wadsworth had also submitted his resignation.[61] The Commissary Department, greatly in debt and always in need of funds, had been attempting to operate on a credit basis with increasingly poor results.   By the end of September 1779, the quantity of flour and bread available for the Army was so small and credit so nonexistent that Wadsworth had been compelled to evolve a plan for obtaining supplies from New York in exchange for salt, sugar, and other foreign commodities, greatly needed by the people of that State since they had been deprived of the use of their seaport for 3 years.[62]   The harvest of 1779 had been good, but, as the year drew to a close, supply streams were drying up and the magazines were being emptied because no farmer was willing to exchange his grain and livestock for a depreciating currency.

Long before the winter of 1779–80 brought a crisis in supply, Congress had realized that the issue of any more paper money would have to be halted.   In September it had resolved to limit the amount of bills of credit in circulation to $200 million, to emit no more on any account whatsoever, and to rely thereafter on state taxes and loans in order to prosecute the war.[63]   Unfortunately, the states were not prepared to tax themselves or to create funds outside of their control.   There was neither money nor credit to replenish empty magazines, yet in December the cry for money came from every supply department.   "Congress are at their wit's end," wrote William Ellery.[64]

Hardship at Morristown

While Greene and Wadsworth waited for replies to their resignations, the Army once again settled into winter quarters.   The troops were cantoned about Morristown, one brigade being left at Danbury, Conn., and four at West Point.   With the supply departments all but paralyzed, their sufferings exceeded those endured by the soldiers at Valley Forge, for to the distress experienced by the Army from want of food was added that resulting from the extreme severity of the weather in the winter of 1779–80.   "Those who have only been in Valley Forge and Middlebrook during the last two winters, but have not tasted the cruelties of this one," de Kalb wrote, "know not what it is to suffer." [65]   His division had left

[61] Papers of the Continental Congress, item 78, XXIV, f. 97 (To Pres. of Congress, 10 Oct 1779).

[62] (1) Journals of the Continental Congress, XV, 1130–32 (30 Sep 1779). (2) Letters of Members of the Continental Congress, ed. Burnett, IV, 476 (Jesse Root to Wadsworth, 6 Oct 1779).

[63] Journals of the Continental Congress, XIV, 1013 (1 Sep 1779); 1052 ff. (13 Sep 1779).

[64] Letters of Members of the Continental Congress, ed. Burnett, IV, 545 (To Gov. of Rhode Island, 21 Dec 1779).

[65] Fredrich Kapp, The Life of John Kalb (New York, 1884), 183.

West Point on 26 November. The march to the winter camp site took 6 days and "proved fatal to many of the soldiers, in consequence of the cold, the bad weather, the horrid roads, the necessity of spending the night in the open air, and our want of protection against snow and rain." [66]

Some 2 weeks later, James Thacher, a surgeon in the Army, marching from Danbury to Morristown, recorded: "The snow on the ground is about two feet deep and the weather extremely cold; the soldiers are destitute of both tents and blankets and some of them are actually barefooted and almost naked." [67] Arrived at camp, the troops lodged on the frozen ground until they could fell oak and walnut trees from which to build the shanties that afforded them shelter from the worst winter in the memory of the oldest inhabitant. Washington urged Wilkinson, who was absent from camp, to bring clothing, but lack of transportation delayed the supplies. Even when delivery of the woolen clothing was made, it was short of the amount required and had to be prorated among the troops.[68]

To piercing cold was added hunger. The roads became so obstructed by deep snow that cattle could not travel nor wagons move to bring badly needed provisions. In one 10-day period the troops received but two pounds of meat per man. Frequently, they were entirely without meat for 6 or 8 days and often lacked bread for a week at a time.[69] In their distress, the soldiers plundered the neighboring inhabitants, an evil that Washington deplored but insisted he would find increasingly difficult to control unless the local magistrates came to the Army's aid by collecting designated quantities of cattle and grain. His appeal obtained results sufficiently satisfactory so that by the last week in January he was able to inform Congress that the Army had been "for some days past, comfortable and easy on the score of provisions." [70] But this happy state of affairs did not long endure; melting snows turned roads into quagmires. Even though there was some grain at distant mills in New Jersey, it could not be transported to camp where in mid-March there was no more than 5 days' supply of bread on hand for about 10,000 troops. By a scanty and economical issue, Washington informed Congress, the meat supply might be made to last until about the end of April. Unfortunately, the situation was more desperate than he knew. The issuing commissary had miscalculated his supplies, basing his estimate on the number of

[66] *Ibid.*, 182.

[67] Thacher, *Military Journal of the American Revolution*, 180.

[68] *Writings of Washington*, ed. Fitzpatrick, XVII, 221, 287–88 (To Wilkinson, 6 and 19 Dec 1779).

[69] Thacher, *Military Journal of the American Revolution*, 181, 185.

[70] *Writings of Washington*, ed. Fitzpatrick, XVII, 459–60 (To Pres. of Congress, 27 Jan 1780); 362–65 (To Magistrates of New Jersey, 8 Jan 1780).

casks on hand instead of the amount of meat they actually contained. As a consequence, on 7 April there was only enough meat to afford a meager supply for 4 days.[71]   The pattern of subsistence supply through these months was one of acute shortages temporarily relieved by the timely arrival of small quantities of provisions.

Resort to System of Specific Supplies

Even when the supply situation looked the darkest, some one always could devise a plan that he believed would solve all difficulties.   If individuals could satisfy their wants without using money by resorting to a system of barter, as they were doing to a certain extent, why could not Congress eliminate the use of money in the supply process by devising a method whereby the states could furnish food and forage directly to the Army?   The resources of the country had not been depleted; only proper means were needed to draw supplies into public use.[72]

After some preliminary groping, Congress adopted the system of specific supplies—a system, the operation of which always kept the Army on the verge of starvation and the impact of which on supply brought changes in procedure and in organization.   The system of specific supplies was one of requisitions upon all the states with the promise that the specific supplies—beef, pork, flour, rum, salt, and forage—furnished by a state would be credited toward the quota of the money that it was called upon to raise by taxes for the United States.[73]   This initial general statement of the system had to be broken down into details—a complicated task that required extensive knowledge of existing and probable supplies in the states, the balancing of Army requirements against those supplies, and the proportionment of the burden equitably among the states.   The innumerable adjustments involved in working out these details afforded opportunities for endless discussion, and it was 25 February 1780 before Congress set specific quotas to be furnished by the states according to their resources.[74]

The adoption of the new system altered the former functions of the Commissary General in the procurement, storage, and forwarding of supplies and necessitated some changes in the organization of the Department.   State procurement of subsistence eliminated the need for

---

[71] *Ibid.,* XVIII, 121–22 (To Pres. of Congress, 17 Mar 1780); 127–28 (To Board of War, 7 Apr 1780).

[72] *Letters of Members of the Continental Congress,* ed. Burnett, V, 6 (Pres. of Congress to Gov. of Connecticut, 12 Jan 1780).

[73] *Journals of the Continental Congress,* XV, 1371–72 (11 Dec 1779); 1377-78 (14 Dec 1779).

[74] (1) *Ibid.,* XVI, 196–201 (25 Feb 1780).   (2) See Edmund C. Burnett, "Continental Congress and Agricultural Supplies," *Agricultural History,* II, No. 3 (Jul 1928), 111–28.

a deputy commissary general in each military department and for the horde of Continental commissaries who had purchased subsistence on a commission basis. Ephraim Blaine had been appointed Commissary General of Purchases on 2 December 1779 after Congress finally accepted the resignation of Wadsworth.[75] Under the new organization adopted for his Department in January 1780, Blaine had only one assistant commissary who resided at Headquarters and acted in his absence. In the event that any state failed to make provision for furnishing its quota of supplies, Congress authorized the Commissary General to appoint an assistant commissary for that state. Such commissaries were to be allowed 2 percent on the money they expended, but, as a control, Congress determined that the prices given were to be no more than twentyfold those paid for similar articles in 1774. In recognition of the uneasiness that the payment of commissions had excited, Congress reestablished a fixed salary for the Commissary General, setting his remuneration at $40,000 a year.[76] That generous salary was drastically cut late in November to $2,124 a year when Congress took cognizance of Blaine's reduced responsibilities. At that time, a deputy commissary general for the Southern Army was added to the Department's organization, and he and the Commissary General were each authorized to appoint one assistant commissary, one superintendent of livestock, two clerks, and as many butchers, coopers, drovers, and laborers as were necessary for conducting the business of the Department. In its efforts to reduce expenditures, Congress set the salaries of the clerks and assistants in the Department at such a low figure that Blaine complained he was left without a single person to assist him.[77]

Reorganization of the Quartermaster's Department

In the meantime, Quartermaster General Greene, who had submitted his resignation in December 1779, was still waiting for a reply in the summer of 1780. In the interim, he cooperated in the efforts being made to reorganize his Department, and after prolonged delay Congress adopted a new regulatory plan on 15 July 1780.[78] No sooner did Greene receive a copy of that plan than he resigned, despite the fact that his Department was in the midst of preparations for supporting the Continental Army in its proposed operations with the French forces. He had intended serving until the end of the campaign, but the introduction of

[75] *Journals of the Continental Congress*, XV, 1342–43 (2 Dec 1779).
[76] *Ibid.*, XVI, 5–7, 20–21 (1, 5, and 7 Jan 1780).
[77] (1) *Ibid.*, XVIII, 1109–11 (30 Nov 1780). (2) Papers of the Continental Congress, item 165, I, f. 341–44 (To Pres. of Congress, 25 Feb 1781.
[78] *Journals of the Continental Congress*, XVII, 615–35.

a new system in the midst of that campaign, the elimination of his two trusted assistants, Pettit and Cox, upon whom he depended for the conduct of the Department's business, and his apprehension that others would also leave made that impossible. Somewhat caustically he informed the President of Congress that:

Systems without Agents are useless things; and the probability of getting the one should be taken into consideration in framing the other. Administration seem to think it far less important to the public interest to have this department well filled, and properly arranged, than it really is, and as they will find it by future experience.[79]

This letter of resignation precipitated a storm in Congress that for a short time seemed likely to sweep Greene out of the Army entirely, but in the end wiser counsels prevailed. Congress accepted his resignation as Quartermaster General on 5 August 1780, and appointed Timothy Pickering, who had helped to frame the new regulatory plan. He was given the rank of colonel but the pay and rations of a brigadier general, over and above that allowed the Quartermaster General under the plan of 15 July.[80] At Washington's request, Greene continued to perform Quartermaster duties for the Army until Pickering's arrival at camp on 22 September, 7 weeks after his appointment. By that time, Quartermaster preparations for supporting a campaign in 1780 had, for all practical purposes, come to an end. Pickering was therefore not immediately involved in supplying active military operations.

Pickering's delay in arriving at camp was occasioned in part by the necessity to reorganize his Department and to appoint new officers. Basically, the organization of the Department remained unchanged but congressional efforts had been directed to reducing its personnel. Over the years, the Department had become a sprawling domain. In 1775 the Quartermaster General, his 2 assistants, and some 35 to 45 clerks, laborers, wagonmasters, and superintendents had handled the business of the Department. As military operations had widened, the number of Quartermaster personnel required to support the line had multiplied rapidly. By 1780, the Quartermaster General was aided by 2 assistant quartermasters general, 28 deputy quartermasters general, and 109 assistant deputy quartermasters general. The Department also included storekeepers, clerks, barrackmasters, express riders, laborers, and superintendents of government property, roads, stables, woodyards, and horse-yards. In the Department's forage branch there was not only a com-

---

[79] Papers of the Continental Congress, item 155, I, f. 399 (26 Jul 1780).

[80] *Journals of the Continental Congress,* XVII, 700. In the plan the salary of a Quarter-master General was set at $166 a month, or $1,992 a year in specie. A brigidier general got $125 a month, or $1,500 a year. Pickering's salary was thus $3,392 a year plus rations and forage for his horse.

missary general of forage and his assistant but also 25 deputies and 128 assistant deputy commissaries as well as clerks, forage masters, measurers, collectors, weighers, stackers, superintendents, and laborers.   The wagon branch employed, in addition to the wagonmaster general and 11 deputies, a large number of wagonmasters, wagoners, packhorse masters, and pack-horsemen.   Among personnel in the boat department were superin-tendents, masters of vessels, mates, and boatmen.   In 1780, the Quarter-master's Department employed almost 3,000 people at an estimated monthly payroll of $407,593, exclusive of the commissions paid to the Quartermaster General, the assistant quartermasters general, the commis-sary general of forage, and some, though not all, of their respective deputies.[81]

Under the plan of 15 July, Pickering was aided by only one assistant quartermaster general who was appointed by, and resided near, Congress to keep the accounts and make applications for money.   As in the past, there was a deputy quartermaster for the main Army and one for each separate army.   Congress further authorized the Quartermaster General to appoint one deputy for each state if he judged such appointment necessary.   In making these appointments, Pickering grouped states, where he could, under one deputy, with the result that he appointed only seven deputies.   These state deputy quartermasters were authorized to appoint as many assistants as they needed and as were approved by the Quartermaster General.   They employed all necessary clerks, conductors, artificers, and laborers, but, if any of them remained in service longer than 2 months, the conditions under which they served had to be approved by the Quartermaster General.   To remedy a deficiency in the system of specific supplies, the state deputy quartermasters were made responsible for transporting all public property in the state, for providing storehouses, and for appointing storekeepers to receive it, note deficien-cies, and reject all that was of improper quality.

With forage being procured by the states, personnel in the forage branch could also be sharply reduced.   It was necessary to retain only a commissary of forage with the main Army and a deputy for each separate army.   The appointment of forage masters was limited to the armies. It was no longer necessary to appoint them at issuing posts because the state deputy quartermaster issued all forage at posts.   Similarly, personnel in the wagon branch was limited to the Army.   Congress authorized the Quartermaster General to appoint one wagonmaster for the main Army and a deputy for each separate army and these appointments could be made specifically from the line of the Army.   The Quartermaster General

[81] Washington Papers, vol. 161, f. 77.

was to appoint only such assistants, clerks, and conductors as were required.[82]

Pickering was convinced that it was the need for economy that had given rise to the reorganization of the Quartermaster's Department in the summer of 1780 "after a four years wasteful profusion." As a result, he impressed upon his subordinates that it was their duty to find "superfluities" and "to lop them off."[83] He himself constantly sought to effect economies but it is doubtful whether these measures made any more funds available to the Department.

Effect of Continued Lack of Funds

Only large amounts of hard cash could have produced any improvement in the supply of clothing, equipment, provisions, and transportation for the Continental Army, but the Treasury could furnish little money. Early in 1780, the Board of War had pinned all of its hopes for clothing the troops on the supplies bought in France. In view of the lack of funds, the Board had thought it was "needless to involve either ourselves or the Officers under our directions in the persecution of being dunned for Debts it would have been impossible to pay."[84] Unfortunately, when the French fleet sailed for America a great part of the clothing that had been bought was left behind. Late in the year, with the Army facing another distressing winter encampment, it was no comfort to know that 10,000 complete suits remained in France because governmental agents could not agree whose business it was to ship them; nor that, for much the same reason, another quantity of clothing had been waiting in the West Indies for more than 18 months.[85] Appeals had to be made to the states but there was so much disparity in the provision made by them for their troops that it bred discontent. Washington was not sure that all the clothing available to the Army between Boston and Philadelphia would suffice for more than half the men who would be left in service after December 1780. But even the clothing that was available did not reach the troops. In November, for example, Washington was informed that 80 wagonloads of clothing had been lying in Springfield since the summer for want of transportation to forward it and the lack of care had resulted in large losses.[86]

---

[82] *Journals of the Continental Congress*, XVII, 615–35 (15 Jul 1780).

[83] Pickering Letters, vol. 123, f. 118 (To Lutterloh, 21 Nov 1780).

[84] Washington Papers, vol. 130, f. 90 (To Washington, 17 Mar 1780).

[85] *Writings of Washington*, ed. Fitzpatrick, XX, 462–63 (To Maj. Gen. Lincoln, 11 Dec 1780).

[86] *Washington Papers*, vol. 158, f. 25 (J. Trumbull to Washington, 21 Nov 1780); f. 41 (William Story to Washington, 22 Nov 1780).

Though the Quartermaster's Department was supposed to provide transportation on the lines of communications, it could not do so because it lacked funds to hire wagons and teams. During the winter of 1780–81 such transportation could be accomplished only by obtaining country teams. Applications to the justices for teams, however, frequently brought only excuses that the roads were bad, that their forage was exhausted, or that they did not have the money to bear the expenses of turning out the teams. Even when the justices instructed teams to report, the quartermaster could not rely on as many appearing as were ordered. Calls had gone out, for example, for teams to move a considerable quantity of flour from Ringwood, N.J., to camp. But of the 82 double teams requested, only 11 reported; and of the 75 single teams, only 17 arrived at Ringwood. If the flour was to be moved it would have to be done by military impress and Washington reluctantly agreed to the use of some dragoons.[87]

Lacking funds, some quartermasters resorted to whatever methods they could to move supplies to their destinations. When, for example, Deputy Quartermaster Hughes in New York was informed that no wagoner would transport provisions until part of the money due for the service was paid on picking up the load and the remainder assured on delivery, he sold some of the provisions to defray the cost of forwarding the rest in the spring of 1781. This was a method liable to abuse and was a wretched way of doing business. The Army needed the very provisions sold to pay for forwarding the remainder to camp. Washington himself, in desperation, diverted to the Quartermaster's Department funds turned over to him by the paymaster general of Massachusetts to pay the troops of that line in order that the Department might relieve the Army's distress by paying for the transportation to camp of flour from New Jersey and salt meat from Connecticut.[88]

Lack of funds had hampered the Quartermaster's Department in supplying transportation for the Army itself during the campaign of 1780. In preparing for the campaign, Greene had been dismayed because wagon manufacturers, seeing no prospect of payment, refused to complete orders. He had no funds with which to replace horses worn out in service. The appalling loss of animals could be attributed to the lack of forage supposed to be furnished by the states under the system of specific supplies. Such

[87] (1) *Ibid.*, vol. 169, f. 51 (DQM Platt to Lt. Col. D. Humphreys, 29 Mar 1781). (2) Pickering Letters, vol. 125, f. 89, 97 (Pickering to Humphreys, 6, 10 Apr 1781). (3) *Writings of Washington,* ed. Fitzpatrick, XII, 504–05 (To Pickering, 26 Apr 1781).

[88] (1) Papers of the Continental Congress, item 192, f. 57 (Pickering to Pres. of Congress, 30 Mar 1781). (2) Washington Papers, vol. 171, f. 23 (Pickering to Hughes, 17 Apr 1781). (3) *Writings of Washington,* ed. Fitzpatrick, XXII, 5 (To Pickering, 28 Apr 1781), 21-22 (To Pres. of Congress, 1 May 1781).

forage as the Army did obtain was impressed under the authority of Washington's warrant. Even the horses needed by the Army during the winter of 1780–81 had to be obtained by impressment.[89]

Breakdown of System of Specific Supplies

Analysis of the system of specific supplies early in 1780 had convinced competent supply officers that it would be a failure and the ensuing shortages in forage and provisions had promptly confirmed that prediction. For want of money, Blaine had been unable to keep up a temporary supply until the new system got into operation. Not only had the states been slow to put it into effect, but throughout the year they were often dilatory in responding to requisitions. Appeals to forward their quotas frequently went unanswered. In November 1780, for example, the Delaware assembly adjourned until some time in January without providing the supplies required in the requisition of that year.[90] On the other hand, some states, responding to urgent appeals, sent forward to camp such a large amount of supplies that a temporary over-abundance was produced, resulting in waste and loss. This method of provisioning the Army left supply fluctuating between want and over-abundance. In May 1780, at the very time that Lafayette brought news that a French naval and military force was being sent to aid the American cause, the troops were "pinch'd for Provisions" and "reduced to the very verge of famine." For days they had been entirely without meat and at best only on half or quarter allowances of rations. Their patience exhausted, mutiny had broken out and had threatened to spread.[91]

In this crisis, it was the patriotic merchants of Philadelphia who came to the relief of the Army by sending 500 barrels of flour to camp immediately. They then perfected a plan under which they proposed to subscribe a fund of £ 300,000 in hard money to be used to procure and transport 3 million rations and 300 hogsheads of rum to the Army, or enough to feed an Army of 40,000 men for 2 months. To carry out their plans, the associators, headed by Robert Morris, established a bank. Congress pledged the faith of the United States for its support and for the

---

[89] (1) Washington Papers, vol. 155, f. 22 (Greene to Washington, 11 May 1780). (2) Papers of the Continental Congress, item 192, f. 41 (Pickering to Pres. of Congress, 30 Oct 1780). (3) Pickering Letters, vol. 125, f. 49 (Pickering to Lafayette, 19 Feb 1781).

[90] Blaine Letter Book, 1780–83 (Blaine to Pres. of Congress, 12 Nov 1780).

[91] (1) Thacher, *Military Journal of the American Revolution*, 197. (2) *Writings of Washington*, ed. Fitzpatrick, XVIII, 413 (To Maj. Gen. Robert Howe, 25 May 1780); 427–28 (To Board of War, 27 May 1780).

security and indemnification of its subscribers.[92]   This was only a temporary relief.   The states continued to be dilatory in filling the requisitions made upon them, and by August Washington denounced this method of obtaining supplies as "the most uncertain, expensive, and injurious that could be devised."   To keep his Army from starving, he had to move his camp to another vicinity "with a view of attempting some relief from a forage." [93]

By that time, with the rest of the French fleet blockaded at Brest and unlikely to reach American waters before October, the fair hopes that Washington had entertained in May of an allied offensive in 1780 had vanished "like the Morning Dew." [94]   Washington still wanted to close the campaign "with some degree of eclat," but his plans had to be relinquished for lack of means.   The Army went into winter camps from West Point to Morristown, and it was with difficulty that the troops were moved to their places of cantonment.   Of necessity, Washington was compelled to dismiss the levies when the troops went into winter quarters.   "Want of clothing rendered them unfit for duty, and want of Flour would have disbanded the whole Army if I had not adopted this expedient," he wrote Greene, then commanding the Southern Army and equally desperate for provisions and clothing.   He suggested that "it would be well for the Troops, if like Chameleons, they could live upon Air, or like the Bear, suck their paws for subsistence during the rigour of the approaching season." [95]

The supply of food during the winter of 1780–81 remained as precarious as ever and the response of the states to requisitions was as dilatory as in the past.   An all too familiar pattern of scanty rations, inadequate clothing and shelter, and no pay exhausted the patience of the troops.   When enlistment grievances were added to these hardships, the troops of the Pennsylvania line mutinied at Morristown on 1 January 1781.   Their example was followed later in the month by three New Jersey regiments at Pompton.   "It is in vain to think an Army can be kept together much longer, under such a variety of sufferings as ours has experienced," wrote Washington in one more appeal to the New

[92] (1) *Letters of Members of the Continental Congress*, ed. Burnett, V, 224 (Schuyler to Washington, 18 Jun 1780); 235 (Madison to Jefferson, 23 Jun 1780); 280 (Pres. of Congress to Eastern States, 21 Jul 1780). (2) *Journals of the Continental Congress*, XVII, 549–50 (22 Jun 1780).

[93] *Writings of Washington*, ed. Fitzpatrick, XIV, 403, 437 (To Pres. of Congress, 20 and 24 Aug 1780).

[94] *Ibid.*, XIX, 482 (To Samuel Washington, 31 Aug 1780).

[95] *Ibid.*, XX, 470 (To Greene, 13 Dec 1780); 457–59 (To Gouverneur Morris, 10 Dec 1780).

England states.   Confronted with an empty Treasury, Congress, too, could only respond to Blaine's report of the supply situation with one more letter to the states urging them to fill their quotas.[96]

The supply departments for lack of funds could neither support the troops in winter quarters nor make timely preparations for another campaign.   For 2 years the Continental Army had been compelled to lie idle in the Highlands of the Hudson for want of supplies and inadequate strength.   Late in May 1781, prospects for applying enough force against the British at New York brightened immeasurably when dispatches arrived confirming that a large fleet under Admiral de Grasse was on its way to cooperate with Rochambeau's troops at Newport and the Continental forces.   Washington and Rochambeau met and concerted plans for moving against the British at New York.   When these became infeasible, they launched an alternative plan calling for a joint attack against Cornwallis in Virginia.   Unfortunately, the supply situation remained unpromising.   Only a few weeks before meeting with Rochambeau, Washington had recorded that:

> Instead of having Magazines filled with provisions, we have a scanty pittance scattered here and there in the different States.   Instead of having our Arsenals well supplied with Military Stores, they are all poorly provided, and the Workmen all leaving them.   Instead of having various articles of Field equipage in readiness to deliver, the Quarter Master General (as the dernier resort, according to his acct.) is but now applying to the several States to provide these things for the Troops respectively.   Instead of having a regular System of Transportation established upon credit—or funds in the Qr. Masters hands to defray the contingent expences of it we have neither the one nor the other and all that business, or a great part of it being done by Military Impress, we are daily and hourly oppressing the people—souring their tempers—and alienating their affections.[97]

Preparations for the Last Campaign

As he had so often in the past, Washington personally sought at that point to alleviate the distress of his troops.   He dispatched Maj. Gen. William Heath to New England to use his influence to persuade the states to send supplies.   By personal appeals to the state executives and assemblies, General Heath was to obtain a supply of cattle and to transport to camp all salt provisions in western Connecticut and Massachusetts in

---

[96] (1) *Writings of Washington*, ed. Fitzpatrick, XXI, 61 (Circular, 5 Jan 1781).   (2) Papers of the Continental Congress, item 165, I, f. 389 (Blaine to Pres. of Congress, 19 Jan 1781). (3) *Letters of Members of the Continental Congress*, ed. Burnett, V, 545 (Pres. of Congress to States from Pennsylvania to New Hampshire, 27 Jan 1781).

[97] *The Diaries of George Washington*, 1748–99, ed. John C. Fitzpatrick (4 vols., New York, 1925), II, 207–08 (1 May 1781).

order to relieve the immediate wants of the troops of the main Continental Army and those stationed at posts along the northern frontier. He was also to establish a regular, systematic, and effective plan for feeding the Army throughout the coming campaign.[98] General Heath was most successful in his efforts and when the Yorktown campaign got under way later in the summer of 1781, the New England states continued to forward cattle until Washington directed otherwise.

Shortly after Washington had initiated his measures to bring beef to the Army, Congress took steps to relieve the bread shortage. Those steps led to the adoption of a new system. Subsistence was to be furnished directly to the Army by private contractors with whom the government entered into arrangements for the procurement, delivery, and issue of rations instead of relying on the states to fill requisitions made on them or, where that failed, depending upon commissaries, attached to the Army, to purchase and issue the needed rations. Robert Morris, the newly appointed Superintendent of Finance, devised ways and means. He firmly believed that private contracting afforded the best means of husbanding the country's resources. Like Washington, he found the system of specific supplies inordinately extravagant and wasteful. He concluded that, in the interests of economy, it would be best to modify that system and return to a cash basis. At his request, Congress authorized him to dispose of specific supplies furnished by the states in any manner that he, with the advice of the commander-in-chief, judged best.[99] It was his idea to sell provisions deposited at distant locations and use the money so obtained to contract for supplies nearer to the Army. As the system of specific supplies had operated, however, no large quantities of provisions for disposal purposes had been accumulated anywhere.

In the meantime, Congress, having given consideration since mid-May to contracting for rations, specifically vested such power in the Superintendent of Finance in July.[100] Use of that power, however, depended on the revenues provided by the states, but in 1781 only Pennsylvania gave Morris money out of which to provide their specific supplies. Consequently, the only contracts he made to take effect that year were confined to that State. Out of the funds provided, he not only defrayed the cost of those contracts but also furnished flour to the Army on the Hudson and in Virginia.[101]

[98] (1) *Writings of Washington*, ed. Fitzpatrick, XXII, 58–59, 63–65 (To Heath, 8 and 9 May 1781). (2) See "Heath Papers" in Massachusetts Historical Society *Collections*, series 7, vol. V, 196–225, for correspondence covering the details of Heath's mission.

[99] *Journals of the Continental Congress*, XX, 597–98 (4 Jun 1781).

[100] *Ibid.*, XX, 734 (10 Jul 1781).

[101] Robert Morris Letter Book B, 245 (To Gen. N. Greene, 19 Dec 1781).

Obviously, after the election of Robert Morris to the post of Superintendent of Finance, that office had gradually absorbed the few remaining responsibilities formerly exercised by the Commissary General of Purchases. With no duties left to execute, Blaine submitted his resignation to Congress on 30 July.[102] No action was taken on his resignation but, since the Yorktown campaign opened shortly thereafter, Blaine continued to serve as Commissary General, carrying out the orders of Robert Morris, obtaining specific supplies from Delaware, Maryland, and Virginia, and supervising the establishment of magazines until the end of that campaign.

Despite his lack of funds, the Quartermaster General attempted to make preparations for the campaign of 1781 but was not too successful. He called upon the New England states for camp equipage in April. Only Massachusetts responded with any promise of tentage, knapsacks, and haversacks.[103] Although the need for boats was urgent, repairs of the public boats on the Hudson moved slowly. Pickering found the artificers employed there "dejected & discouraged." It could scarcely have been otherwise since most of them had families to support but had received no pay in 18 months. Wearied of serving unrewarded, some of the best hands had gone to the New England seaports to find more lucrative service and prompter pay. In June, when the boats should have been ready, Washington permitted a few artificers to be drawn from the line to speed repairs.[104]

Although horses and wagons were required for the campaign, adequate numbers were not in readiness when the Army began to move. On the basis of informal estimates of the number of Army horses being wintered in Pennsylvania, western Massachusetts and Connecticut, Pickering had concluded in January that he would have an ample supply. But when returns of the horses fit for service were actually made in May and June, the number had dwindled so alarmingly that Pickering ordered his deputies to hire teams. The deputies found it difficult to persuade owners of teams who remained unpaid for services rendered in the last campaign to agree to provide transportation in 1781. Since many of their wagons had been worn out in service, Pickering hit upon an inducement to offer them. The Army had spare wagons and he proposed that for each team of horses hired, the deputy quartermaster should offer to furnish the owner a wagon and harness, to be appraised and delivered as soon as the horses arrived. Depending on the appraised

---

[102] Blaine Letter Book, 1780–83 (To Thos. McKean, 30 Jul 1781).

[103] Washington Papers, vol. 176, f. 32 (Pickering to Lt. Col. D. Humphreys, 5 Jun 1781).

[104] (1) *Ibid.*, vol. 176, f. 80 (Pickering to Washington, 8 Jun 1781). (2) *Writings of Washington*, ed. Fitzpatrick, XXII, 196–97 (To Pickering, 10 Jun 1781).

value, this offer would, in effect, give the owner a month's wages in advance. Even with this inducement, the deputies doubted that enough teams could be hired. The lack of money either to hire teams or to forward public horses from winter quarters had a crippling effect on the ease with which the Army could move, so much so that when the Army marched to Peekskill the park of artillery was not able to do so for want of horses.[105] Pickering had to try to buy horses on credit, deferring payment for several months and allowing interest in the interim. To meet the payment when due he turned to Robert Morris for help. Until the purchase could be completed, he proposed and Washington authorized impressment of horses in New Jersey to satisfy the immediate needs of the artillery.[106]

It cannot now be determined whether it was the inadequacy of these preparations, Pickering's inexperience in meeting the demands of an active campaign, or the overriding importance of the expedition to be undertaken that raised doubts in Washington's mind as to the degree of reliance he could put upon his Quartermaster General and caused him to assume duties that officer should have directed. In any event, from the time that the allies turned to the alternative plan of attacking Cornwallis in Virginia, Washington gave close supervision and direction to the logistical support of the campaign. Wagon transportation was left to Pickering's direction as was supervision of the crossing of men and supplies at King's Ferry.[107] Washington, however, directed the preparation of water transportation on the Delaware; requested Morris to arrange for boats to take the men and supplies down the Chesapeake Bay; issued combat loading instructions to Maj. Gen. Benjamin Lincoln who supervised the forwarding of men and supplies at Head of Elk; laid out the overland route from Head of Elk to Williamsburg; directed the preparation of forage deposits; and called upon the Governors of Maryland and Virginia for additional supplies.[108] Through the cooperative efforts of the Quartermaster General, the state deputy quartermasters, and the Superintendent of Finance, Washington performed the prodigious feat of moving the allied forces from the Hudson southward 450 miles to the James River and defeating Cornwallis within the 2-month period between

[105] (1) Washington Papers, vol. 179, f. 97 (Pickering to Washington, 12 Jul 1781). (2) Pickering Letters, vol. 82, f. 1 (To Col. Neilson, 29 Jun 1781); f. 11 (To Col. Miles, 10 Jul 1781).

[106] Pickering Letters, vol. 82, f. 37 (To Robert Morris, 20 Jul 1781); f. 42 (To Dearborn, 20 Jul 1781).

[107] (1) *Ibid.*, vol. 127, f. 226 (To Col. Hughes, 18 Aug 1781); f. 217 (To Gen. Heath, 23 Aug 1781). (2) Pickering and Upham, *Life of Timothy Pickering*, I, 294.

[108] *Writings of Washington*, ed. Fitzpatrick, XXIII, 11, 40, 50–52 (To Robert Morris, 17, 24, and 27 Aug 1781); 54–55 (To Col. Miles, 27 Aug); 96-97 (Circular to Gentlemen on Eastern Shores of Maryland, 7 Sep 1781); 109–10 (To Peter Waggoner, 9 Sep 1781); 82–83 (To Rochambeau, 3 Sep 1781); 98–101 (To Maj. Gen. Lincoln, 7 Sep 1781).

14 August, when he received the news that Admiral de Grasse had sailed with a French fleet from the West Indies for the Chesapeake Bay, and 15 October 1781, the date set by the Admiral for the departure of the fleet.

Retrenchment

Ten days after the surrender of Cornwallis, the plans for the dispersal of the allied forces had been agreed upon. All arrangements for returning the American troops to the North were left to Pickering. Much of the captured British matériel was turned over to him for disposal. Along with some of the troops, part of that matériel was sent to support Greene's Southern Army. En route to the north, Pickering made arrangements to provide straw and wood for the sick and wounded in the hospitals at Williamsburgh and Hanover. Claims for damages and debts incurred in Virginia demanded settlement by the Department and during the winter of 1781–82 he was also much occupied in settling all transportation accounts arising out of the Yorktown expedition.[109]

From Yorktown until the formal close of the Revolutionary War was signaled by the signing of the treaty of peace on 30 September 1783, the dominant theme in supply activities was retrenchment. In view of the financial situation of the country and the necessity for consulting with the Superintendent of Finance on all expenditures, his office played an increasingly prominent role in supplying the Army. As early as 1781, Morris had become responsible for the purchase of clothing. In the summer of that year, Congress had adopted a new regulatory plan that suspended all state purchases on account of the Continental Congress. It further had provided that the Clothier General was to operate his department on the basis of an estimate of the clothing and disbursements required for a year, beginning with 1 November but submitted in June so that Congress would have time to furnish the funds and adopt the necessary measures for procuring them.[110] The Superintendent of Finance made all contracts for needed supplies and upon application of the Clothier General provided funds for paying the workmen who made clothing. By the time these new procedures had been adopted, John Moylan had succeeded Wilkinson as Clothier General.[111]

---

[109] (1) *Calendar of Virginia State Papers* (11 vols., Richmond, 1875–93), II, 589 (Pickering to Gov. Nelson, 8 Nov 1781). (2) Pickering Letters, vol. 82, f. 122 (To Lincoln, 20 Dec); f. 126, 136–39 (To Maj. Claiborne, 20 Nov, 7 Dec); f. 131 (To Greene, 23 Nov); f. 140 (To Yeates, 8 Dec); f. 152 (To Capt. Mitchell, 27 Dec); f. 158 (To conductors, 30 Dec); f. 221–24 (To Morris, 8 Dec 1781); vol. 83, f. 9–10 (To Maj. Cogswell, 5 Jan); f. 135–37 (To Yeates, 27 Feb 1782).

[110] *Journals of the Continental Congress*, XX, 662–67 (18 Jun 1781).

[111] (1) Papers of the Continental Congress, item 78, XXIV, f. 297–98 (Wilkinson to Pres. of Congress, 27 Mar 1781). (2) Washington Papers, vol. 166, f. 32 (Moylan to Washington, 18 Feb 1781).

He was more attentive to requisitions and more industrious in trying to meet Army needs than Wilkinson, but it did not necessarily follow that the Army was well supplied with clothing during the last years of the war. Considerable quantities of clothing, for example, had arrived from abroad in the spring of 1781, yet lack of funds prevented that clothing being made available to the troops during the Yorktown campaign. Moylan could not obtain money from the General Court of Massachusetts to enable him to transport the clothing supplies on Morris' order until late in October, and it was 3 November before he had 35 wagonloads on the way from Boston to Fishkill.[112]

The supply of clothing was dependent on what was obtained abroad, and though Morris was disposed to remove all complaints the straitened financial circumstances always kept inadequate the amount of clothing available to the troops. To function at all Morris had to sell such imported clothing as was unsuitable for military use in order to obtain funds to pay off Clothing Department debts, including sums due for work done by tailors.[113] By one means or another, however, Morris provided for the troops—not as fully as Washington desired but nevertheless more adequately than in earlier years of the war.

As the Superintendent of Finance broadened his direction of purchases in the various supply departments during the last 18 months of the war, procurement methods changed and supply departments underwent organizational changes. Once the Yorktown campaign was ended, the Office of the Commissary General of Purchases and the Office of the Commissary General of Issues passed out of existence. Both Blaine and Stewart relinquished the duties of their respective departments without waiting for any formal acceptance of resignations by Congress. As the year 1781 ended, Morris assumed complete direction of subsistence procurement, and, with the Treasury still hard pressed for funds, he again turned to his plan for reducing expenditures by contracting for the subsistence of the Army. Convinced that he would obtain funds from the middle and eastern states, he entered into contracts for supplying the Northern Army though a variety of factors deterred him from making similar arrangements for the Southern Army. He did empower General Greene to make such contracts whenever he had reason to believe that he could obtain sufficient money to fulfill his obligations.[114]

Morris entertained high hopes of the benefits that would flow from

---

[112] Washington Papers, vol. 184, f. 112 (To Moylan, 24 Sep 1781); vol. 182, f. 91 (Moylan to Washington, 3 Nov 1781).

[113] *Ibid.*, vol. 208, f. 97 (Morris to Washington, 15 Oct 1782).

[114] (1) Robert Morris Letter Book B, 245–52 (To Greene, 19 Dec 1781). (2) Washington Papers, vol. 188, f. 122 (Example of contract, 6 Dec 1781).

the use of the contract system to obtain rations. He was certain that it would provide a more effectual and punctual supply than had been obtained under the commissariat; that it would effect great savings by eliminating all purchasing and issuing commissaries; and that it would reduce transportation costs since the contractors would make delivery to the troops through issuing stores that they would operate. Unfortunately, these expectations were not satisfied. Within less than 6 months Army officers were criticizing the contractors whose avarice led them to restrict the number of issuing stores to such an extent that the troops were greatly inconvenienced and experienced much fatigue in obtaining their provisions. The Army soon accused the contractors of offering the troops tainted provisions and charged that supply failures occurred as frequently as they had under the commissariat.[115]

The contractors for their part became uneasy about the settlement of their accounts. They attributed all shortages and irregularity in supply to their failure to receive regular payments on their contracts.[116] Morris was having difficulty meeting his obligations, for his Department was adversely affected by peace rumors that brought a total stoppage of mercantile business. He was compelled to cancel one contract and make a new one at an advance in price for the rations furnished. Though disillusioned about the advantages of the system, Morris still considered it the only feasible method of subsisting the Army and the contract system was to be used for many years after the Revolutionary War.

The elimination of the commissariat made it possible to break up many posts, and, since Morris extended contracts to include delivery of forage and wood to the troops as well as subsistence, the services of many quartermasters became unnecessary. Pickering, who wholeheartedly approved of all economy measures, worked out a plan to reduce the total number of posts to 14 and to discharge all unnecessary personnel at the posts that were retained. In addition, he proposed, and the Secretary at War concurred in, the immediate discharge of all artificers and other personnel who were hired by the day or month at the posts. In the future, all work was to be contracted for and paid for by the piece.[117]

Before the end of 1782, Congress itself acted to effect other economies by reducing both the number of personnel and the salaries in the Quartermaster's Department. Pickering's staff was reduced to 10 officers

---

[115] *Writings of Washington,* ed. Fitzpatrick, XXIV, 158–59; 287–91; 348–51 (To Morris, 23 Apr, 17–25 May, 4 Jun 1782).
[116] Washington Papers, vol. 200, f. 30 (Sands to Washington, 17 Jun 1782); f. 34 (Sands & Livingston to Morris, 17 Jun 1782); vol. 202, f. 78 (Sands to Heath, 28 Jul 1782).
[117] Pickering Letters, vol. 83, f. 96–98 (To Morris, 19 Feb 1782).

—a deputy quartermaster in the main Army and one for the Southern Army; a wagonmaster and a deputy, and a commissary of forage and a deputy, respectively, for the main Army and the Southern Army; and a director and one sub-director of a company of artificers for each of these armies.[118]   Congress also authorized Pickering to appoint as many wagon conductors and assistants as both armies required.   It cut the Quartermaster General's salary to $2,000 a year and reduced the salaries of his staff so low that Pickering charged it would be impossible for him to retain men of ability and integrity.   He suspended making any appointments under the new plan because he expected it would be amended, but no action was taken before the war ended.   Meanwhile, a decreasing number of officers handled the dwindling Quartermaster activities.   By the end of 1782, the former state organization of the Department had virtually disappeared.   Only in New York and Pennsylvania were a few assistants retained to attend to Quartermaster duties.   In the closing months of the war, personnel in the Quartermaster's Department employed with the main Army numbered 42, including the Quartermaster General.[119]

In anticipation of peace, Pickering not only applied himself to reducing the expenses of his Department but he also began the task of settling accounts and of disposing of government property no longer needed by the Army.   He was impatient to be freed of his official duties but these demanded his attention for almost 2 years after the war.   By the summer of 1785, however, he recommended that the Secretary at War be charged with the remaining duties, and on 25 July 1785 Congress abolished the office of the Quartermaster General.[120]

---

[118] *Journals of the Continental Congress*, XXIII, 682–86; 693 (23 and 29 Oct 1782).

[119] (1) Papers of the Continental Congress, item 192, f. 125 (Pickering to Pres. of Congress, 4 Dec 1782).   (2) Pickering Letters, vol. 86, f. 60 (To Lincoln, 25 Feb 1783).   (3) RG 94, Estimates of Pay, vol. 103, f. 157 (Return, 25 Feb 1783).   National Archives.

[120] (1) Pickering and Upham, *Life of Timothy Pickering*, I, 516–17 (Pickering to King, 1 Jun 1785).   (2) *Journals of the Continental Congress*, XXIX, 574.

CHAPTER III

The Era of Civilian Ascendancy

"Standing armies in time of peace are inconsistent with the principles of republican governments, dangerous to the liberties of a free people, and generally converted into destructive engines for establishing despotism."[1] So Elbridge Gerry argued in the spring of 1784 as motion after motion to establish a standing army was brought forward only to be lost. To these popular arguments other members added that Congress had neither power under the Articles of Confederation to create a peacetime army nor funds to maintain such a military establishment.

Economy had dictated a rapid demobilization of the Continental Army, and by January 1784, Maj. Gen. Henry Knox, acting under instructions, had reduced its strength to one regiment of infantry, consisting of 500 rank and file, and one artillery battalion of 120 men.[2] Five months later the prolonged debate, occasioned by the need to raise troops to take possession of the western frontier posts, came to an end with the adoption of a resolution on 2 June directing the discharge of all the Continental troops in the service of the United States, except 25 privates to guard the stores at Fort Pitt, and 55 to guard those at West Point.[3]

It was nevertheless still necessary to raise other troops to garrison the western posts which were expected to be soon evacuated by the British. On the following day, Congress, adopted the only alternative open to it. It recommended that the states "most conveniently situated"—Connecticut, New York, New Jersey, and Pennsylvania—raise for this purpose 700 men from their militia to serve one year.[4] British delay in surrendering the western posts and the growing hostility of the Indians compelled Congress to call upon the same states in 1785 to raise 700 men for a 3-year term of service, reenlisting as many as possible of those recruited the previous year.[5] The full quota was never raised then nor

---

[1] *Journals of the Continental Congress*, XXVII, 433 (26 May 1784).

[2] (1) *Ibid.*, XXV, 606 (23 Sep 1783). (2) *Writings of Washington*, ed. Fitzpatrick, XXVII, 256–58 (To Knox, 3 Dec 1783); 278–80 (To Pres. of Congress, 21 Dec 1783). (3) RG 11, Papers of the Continental Congress, item 38, f. 375–95 (Knox to Pres. of Congress, 3 Jan 1784). National Archives.

[3] *Journals of the Continental Congress*, XXVII, 524 (2 Jun 1784).

[4] *Ibid.*, XXVII, 530–31; 538–39 (3 Jun 1784).

[5] *Ibid.*, XXVIII, 223–24; 239–41; 247–48 (1, 7, 12 Apr 1785).

in succeeding calls for troops made by Congress under the Articles of Confederation.

Obviously, an Army of such small proportions required no extensive field organization to supply its needs. Nor did such an organization exist; supply personnel of the Revolutionary War had either resigned or been discharged as rapidly as troops had been demobilized. Elimination of the Quartermaster General and his assistants was in accord with the theory of that day that the staff properly existed only in time of war. By mid-summer of 1785, neither the Quartermaster's Department nor any other of the staff agencies of the Revolutionary War remained in existence. Yet the troops on the frontier, whether stationed at posts or sent out on expeditions against the Indians, had to be provisioned, clothed, and equipped.

Civilian Control of Supply

Military supply was placed under civilian control in the post-Revolutionary War years, and such control persisted until the outbreak of the War of 1812. In this period, civilian ascendancy was carried to such an extent that even the Quartermasters General appointed to take the field during the campaigns against the Indians in the 1790's were civilians, granted the pay and allowances of a lieutenant colonel but not the military rank. Unlike their predecessors who served during the Revolutionary War, these Quartermasters General were little more than transportation agents. Procurement, storage, and issue of military supplies were functions that were now directed by the bureaus or agencies developing at the seat of government. Basically, control over supply throughout these years was divided between the Secretary of the War Office and the Secretary of the Treasury and their respective subordinate agencies. Supply was accomplished by extending the contract system, first applied by Robert Morris in 1781 to the procurement of subsistence.

When Congress abolished Timothy Pickering's position as Quartermaster General in July 1785, the Secretary at War, Henry Knox, took over the few duties still being performed by the Quartermaster's Department. His predecessor, Benjamin Lincoln, had retired as Secretary in mid-November 1783. For the next 17 months the whole management of the War Office had devolved upon his assistant, Joseph Carleton, who had hoped to succeed him. At Washington's suggestion, Henry Knox was appointed Secretary on 8 March, assuming the duties of his office on 25 April 1785. Congress did not adopt a proposal advanced by Washington and Knox for creating a post of master general of ordnance and combining its duties with those of the Secretary. A considerable part of the Secretary's duties did, however, involve the care and preservation of military stores, the maintenance of magazines and arsenals, and the supervision of various other ordnance matters, for the direction of which Knox, who had been Chief of Artillery during the Revolutionary War, was well qualified.[6]

Shortly before his appointment, Congress had directed that the Secretary was to keep exact records and returns of all military stores and supplies in the magazines; to accept all supplies turned over to him by officers in whose possession they had heretofore been; and to make estimates of all supplies needed by the troops and "for keeping up competent magazines." These estimates were to be submitted to the commissioners of the Treasury so that they might initiate procurement measures promptly. The Secretary was also to be responsible for the transportation, safe-keeping, and distribution of the supplies needed by the troops. Once a year he was to visit all magazines and deposits of public stores and report to Congress.[7]

Since the Secretary at War was expressly charged with the care of all military stores, a separate department to have charge of all arms, ammunition, and accoutrements was unnecessary, and Congress abolished the office of Commissary of Military Stores in the summer of 1785.[8] Presumably, Samuel Hodgdon, who began his career as a captain in the artillery corps under Knox in 1776 and had been serving in one capacity or another in the department of Commissary of Military Stores since 1777, was to be dismissed from office along with his assistants. Actually, Knox needed his services and apparently Hodgdon's tenure as Commissary of Military Stores at Philadelphia continued uninterrupted until 1800, though his title was later changed and his duties expanded.[9] Knox appointed additional storekeepers or deputy commissaries at other arsenals, though permanent magazines and arsenals were not to be established for some time. Newly acquired, as well as surplus military stores of the Revolutionary War generally, were deposited in various rented buildings. Such military stores included not only cannon, gunpowder, small arms, and accoutrements of the Ordnance Department, but also canteens, tools, equipment, and ironmongery of the Quartermaster's Department as well as military clothing.

[6] (1) *Ibid.*, XXV, 262n, 753 (29 Oct 1783); XXVIII, 121n (4 Mar 1785); 129 (8 Mar 1785); XXIX, 771 (9 Jun 1785). (2) Francis S. Drake, *Life and Correspondence of Major-General Henry Knox* (Boston, 1873), 85–86 (Knox to Washington, 17 Sep 1783, 3 Jan 1784; Washington to Knox, 2 Nov 1783). (3) *Writings of Washington,* ed. Fitzpatrick, XXVII, 339 (To Knox, 20 Feb 1784).

[7] *Journals of the Continental Congress*, XXVIII, 21–22 (27 Jan 1785).

[8] *Ibid.*, XXIX, 560–61 (20 Jul 1785).

[9] (1) *Ibid.*, XXXIV, 587–90 (2 Oct 1788). (2) RG 98, Post-Revolutionary War Records, vol. 80, Receipts, Samuel Hodgdon, Commissary General Military Stores, 18 Apr 1782–6 Nov 1789. National Archives.

The commissioners of the Treasury, to whom Knox sent his estimates of the supplies needed by the Army, had replaced the Superintendant of Finance. Robert Morris had submitted his resignation on 24 January 1783, but it was November of the following year before he actually retired from office.[10]   In the interim, Congress on 28 May 1784 adopted an ordinance creating a Board of Treasury to consist of three commissioners. They were to superintend the Treasury, manage the finances of the United States, and exercise all the powers formerly vested in the Superintendent of Finance, including that of contracting for food and clothing needed by the troops. It was January 1785 before Congress appointed the commissioners, and the Board of Treasury did not begin its administration until 21 April.[11]

The commissioners followed procedures established by Robert Morris in contracting for food. They advertised and awarded the contract to the lowest bidder, who made delivery of the rations at designated posts. Their first contract for provisioning the troops at the frontier posts of Fort Pitt, Fort McIntosh, and Fort Harmar in 1785 went to James O'Hara, who later served as Quartermaster General in the Army that Anthony Wayne led to victory in the Battle of Fallen Timbers.[12] The ration still provided a bread and meat diet, as it had during the Revolutionary War, but it had become even more austere in some of its allowances. The ration consisted of one pound of beef, or three-quarters of a pound of pork; one pound of bread or flour; and one gill of rum. For every one hundred rations the contractor also provided one quart of salt, two quarts of vinegar, two pounds of soap, and one pound of candles.[13] The soldiers supplemented this ration with the produce of gardens tended at the posts and the abundant game made available by hunters.

Contractor O'Hara, like his predecessors in the Revolutionary War, did not escape criticism for the manner in which he executed his contract. Col. Josiah Harmar, commanding the frontier troops, thought it was fortunate that there was such an abundance of fish readily available at Ft. McIntosh that summer since the contractor was failing to supply beef. On the whole, the contract was "performed tolerably well" in the opinion

---

[10] (1) *Journals of the Continental Congress,* XXIV, 151 (6 Feb 1783). (2) Papers of the Continental Congress, item 137, II, f. 115 (Morris to Pres. of Congress, 24 Jan 1783).

[11] *Journals of the Continental Congress,* XXVII, 469–71 (28 May 1784); XXVIII, 18 (25 Jan 1785), 223 (1 Apr 1785); XXIX, 582 (27 Jul 1785); XXXIV, 554 (30 Sep 1788).

[12] Fort McIntosh was located at the mouth of Beaver Creek, 29 miles from Fort Pitt; Fort Harmar was located in Ohio near Marietta.

[13] *Journals of the Continental Congress,* XXXIV, 585 (2 Oct 1788).

of a congressional committee; "the defects were perhaps inseparably connected with the state of the frontiers and of public affairs."[14]

The following year, Turnbull, Marmie & Co. of Philadelphia obtained the contract by offering a price considerably lower than that of 1785. The troops were greatly distressed for want of food in 1786 because the company failed to fulfill its contract. In extenuation of their shortcomings, the contractors argued that they had been unable to supply the troops adequately because they had been paid in the depreciated currency of Pennsylvania. The troops were better provisioned during the next 3 years when O'Hara again obtained the contract in 1787 and Elliot and Williams of Baltimore held it during the following 2 years. The cost of the ration steadily decreased at all the frontier posts during these years although the price quoted by contractors for the posts varied according to the distance delivery had to be made, the cost being higher, for example, at Vincennes than at Fort Pitt.[15]

The commissioners of the Treasury Board attempted to follow the same procedure in awarding clothing contracts. In the years following the Revolution, the troops were allowed one suit of clothing annually, payment for which was deducted from their pay as it had been in the war years.[16] Morris had not advertised for bids for clothing contracts, largely because it was so difficult to guard against impositions. If, for example, the clothing provided by the contractor was of such sleazy quality that it wore out rapidly, the soldiers nonetheless were compelled to wear those rags until a new issue was made the next year. Wishing to extend the system of public contracts, however, the Treasury Board advertised and awarded the clothing contract for 1785 to the lowest bidder, the firm of Thomas Lawrence and Jacob Morris of New York. As a protective feature, the contract made provision for inspection of the clothing and for arbitration in the case of disagreement over the rejection of any clothing.[17]

The Treasury Board received no official complaints of the clothing provided by Lawrence and Morris, but the commissioners nevertheless conceded that the low price at which the contract was taken must have prevented the contractors from furnishing clothing of the desired quality.

---

[14] (1) *Ibid.* (2) *Journal of Capt. Jonathan Heart,* ed. C. W. Butterfield (Albany, 1885), 75 (Ltr, Harmar to Col. Francis Johnson, 21 Jun 1785).

[15] *Journals of the Continental Congress,* XXXIV, 585–86 (2 Oct 1788).

[16] It consisted of 1 coat, 1 vest, 1 pair of woolen and 2 pairs of linen overalls, 1 pair of woolen breeches, 1 hat, 4 shirts, 2 pairs of socks, 2 pairs of hose, 4 pairs of shoes, 1 pair of shoe buckles, 1 stock and clasp, and 1 blanket. Papers of the Continental Congress, item 39, II, f. 144 (Contract, 16 Jun 1785).

[17] *Ibid.*

It was not on this ground that they justified their abandonment of the practice of advertising for bids on clothing contracts in 1786. It was the empty state of the Treasury that made it impossible for them either to promise payment in specie or set a precise time for making any payment, both essential points in all contracts proposed by advertisement. As a result, they settled on a method of payment that the Treasury Board could make by negotiating a contract with Turnbull, Marmie & Co. Lawrence and Morris protested the award of that contract to their competitors at a higher price than they had bid, but under the existing financial situation an investigating committee of Congress supported the Board's action.[18]

All clothing contracts specified the delivery point. In 1785, delivery was to be made at New York; in 1786 Turnbull, Marmie & Co. agreed to deliver at Philadelphia. There the clothing was inspected and subsequently, at the direction of the Secretary at War, the contractor transported the clothing to a designated destination point. He agreed to charge no more than the customary transportation costs and was allowed a 5 percent commission for superintending the delivery.[19]

By 1788, the troops that had enlisted in 1785 had received only two complete suits of clothing instead of the three to which they were entitled. Such was the financial stringency under which the Secretary at War operated that though provisions had been made for the third year's clothing supply, he had been compelled to divert it to the use of the recruiting service. Recruits could not otherwise have been enlisted except by offering them a suit of clothing as an inducement. He anticipated that the third suit of clothing due the soldiers would be furnished them by October 1789.[20]

The troops at the frontier posts also needed camp kettles, axes, canteens, tents, and other equipment—articles for the procurement of which the Quartermaster's Department had formerly been responsible. Such supply, according to a congressional committee, was now arranged on "principles highly Oeconomical and beneficial to the public." Instead of being provided by a Quartermaster General with "his train of attendants," subsistence contractors furnished such articles under contracts that they made with the Secretary at War. Such "indispensably necessary" articles were furnished only on a written order of the commanding officer of the troops, Colonel Harmar, or the commanding officer of a post. To compensate the contractors for this service, they were allowed

---

[18] (1) *Journals of the Continental Congress*, XXXI, 899–906 (5 Oct 1786), 912–14 (26 Oct 1786). (2) Papers of the Continental Congress, item 39, II, f. 145 (Contract, 2 Sep 1786), f. 149 (Lawrence and Morris to Pres. of Congress, 29 Sep 1786).

[19] See, for example, contract with Turnbull, Marmie & Co. in 1786. Papers of the Continental Congress, item 39, II, f. 145–46.

[20] *Journals of the Continental Congress*, XXXIV, 581 (2 Oct 1788).

5 percent on such expenditures when they settled their accounts every 6 months at the Treasury. On the other hand, the Secretary at War purchased, without benefit of any commission or charge to the government, all such Quartermaster items of supply furnished to the troops stationed within the states rather than at frontier posts.[21]

Handicapped by lack of funds, neither the commissioners of the Treasury Board nor Secretary Knox could make adequate provision for the troops. Ill-fed and ill-clothed, many of the soldiers on the frontier deserted because they were also unpaid.[22] The government was in no position to wage a vigorous campaign against the Indians, who were growing increasingly hostile as settlers began pushing across the Ohio. The only expedient that Knox could propose for meeting the Indian threat on the frontier was to post the few troops that he did have to the best advantage "to awe the savages" and to endeavor by treaties and presents "to incline them to peace." This was a policy that had been pursued since the end of the Revolutionary War. It had resulted in a number of treaties but had not brought lasting tranquility to the frontier.[23]

About the time Knox was making these proposals, the advocates of a stronger central government had succeeded in calling a convention that threw out the idea of simply revising the Articles of Confederation in favor of drafting a new constitution for a national government consisting of a legislature, executive, and judiciary. Their efforts resulted in the inauguration of a new government on 30 April 1789 when Washington took the oath of office as President of the United States.

As part of the executive branch of government, Congress now created a War Department. Washington continued Henry Knox in office as Secretary of War, a position he held until he resigned on 28 December 1794. His duties were now increased since he was made responsible for all matters that the President might assign to him relating to the army, navy, and Indian affairs. To him was also entrusted the duty of furnishing "warlike stores." [24] Congress also established a Treasury Department, headed by a Secretary of Treasury, to which post Washington appointed Alexander Hamilton. In assigning duties to the Secretary of the Treasury, Congress did not include the responsibility formerly vested

[21] *Ibid.,* XXXIV, 586–87 (2 Oct 1788).
[22] *Letters of Members of the Continental Congress,* ed. Burnett, VIII, 346 (Rufus King to Elbridge Gerry, 30 Apr 1786).
[23] Clarence E. Carter, *The Territorial Papers of the United States* (24 vols., Washington, 1934 —), II, 35 (Knox' report to Congress, 10 Jul 1787).
[24] (1) 1 *Stat.* 49–50 (Aug 7, 1789). (2) *Journal of the Executive Proceedings of the Senate,* I, 25, 26 (4, 12 Sep 1789). (3) Drake, *Life and Correspondence of Major-General Henry Knox,* 109, 110 (Knox to Washington, 29 Dec 1794 and reply, 30 Dec 1794).

in the Treasury Board for supplying the troops with clothing and subsistence.   Nevertheless, established procedures of the past persisted, and
during the first 3 years of the new government both the Secretary of War
and the Secretary of the Treasury executed contracts for Army clothing
and subsistence.[25]

In the spring of 1792, Congress clarified responsibility for supply
by directing that all purchases and contracts for providing the Army with
provisions, clothing, Quartermaster supplies, and military stores and for
furnishing the War Department with Indian goods, naval stores, and all
other supplies for its use were to be made by the Treasury Department.[26]
It thereby returned to the Treasury control over clothing and subsistence
contracts that it had possessed since 1781.   At the same time, it divested
the Secretary of War of the procurement authority he had exercised in
the purchase of quartermaster and ordnance stores since his office had
absorbed the duties of the Quartermaster's Department and of the office
of Commissary of Military Stores in 1785.

Under the new arrangement, the Secretary of War prepared estimates
of supplies that were wanted and furnished the Treasury Department
with standard samples or patterns of the articles to be purchased.   The
Treasury Department then made the contracts and arranged for inspection
of the items procured.   By the spring of 1794, the procurement of War
Department supplies had been placed in the hands of Tench Coxe,
Commissioner of Revenue in the Treasury Department.   Coxe found
this business so extensive that it interfered with the other duties of his
office.   When he requested that he be relieved of them, Hamilton proposed that an officer be specifically appointed in the Treasury Department
to direct procurement of all military supplies.   He considered that such
procurement had been properly vested in his Department because it had
more information on how to obtain supplies.   Moreover, during most
of the past decade, it had developed channels of communication with
contractors and procedures for handling contracts.   He further assumed
that the Treasury might be "expected to feel a more habitual solicitude
for economy" than any other department.   As a consequence, Congress
established the post of Purveyor of Public Supplies.   Under the direction
and supervision of the Secretary of the Treasury, the Purveyor procured
"all articles of supply requisite for the service of the United States." [27]

---

[25] (1) 1 *Stat.* 65 (Sep 2, 1789).   (2) See RG 217, GAO, Registrar's Office, Box 1–8, 27 Nov
1789–31 Dec 1789, for examples of contracts.   National Archives.

[26] 1 *Stat.* 279 (May 8, 1792).

[27] (1) 1 *Stat.* 419 (Feb 23, 1795).   (2) *American State Papers, Military Affairs*, I, 69 (Hamil-
ton to President, 2 Dec 1794).   (3) RG 75, Dept. of Interior, Coxe Letter Book, f. 1, 7 (Coxe to
Secretary of War, 14 Apr, 2 May 1795); f. 274–75 (Coxe circular to Treasury agents, 5 Jan 1795).
National Archives.

Tench Francis, who had been employed in the Treasury Department as a procurement agent for War Department supplies, became the first Purveyor of Public Supplies.[28]

Except for rations, delivery of which continued to be executed by the contractors directly to the posts or delivery points designated in the contracts, the Secretary of War directed the distribution of all military supplies. By 1794, experience had shown that it would be desirable to have one officer in the War Department who would be responsible for receiving, distributing, and superintending the issues of supplies. In response to President Washington's recommendation, Congress created the office of Superintendent of Military Stores in April 1794.[29] Washington appointed Samuel Hodgdon, still serving in Philadelphia as Commissary of Military Stores, to this newly created office.

Under directions from Secretary Knox and the Comptroller of the Treasury, Hodgdon organized his office to promote a more effective system of storage, a more adequate control of distribution, and a sounder knowledge of the stocks on hand. By Knox' orders all storekeepers at magazines and arsenals were brought under Hodgdon's control. The latter furnished them with instructions for separate storage of each type of article, for the proper care and preservation of stores, and for the preparation of quarterly returns. The storekeepers issued all matériel on orders of the Superintendent who acted on directions received from the Secretary of War. By personal inspection each year, he was to observe whether instructions were being carried out at the magazines and arsenals and whether the stores on hand compared with the returns being made. Unfortunately, Hodgdon later found that the demands of his office made an annual inspection tour impossible so that all the anticipated benefits did not materialize.[30]

By direction of the Comptroller of the Treasury Department, all contractors and purchasing agents deposited the supplies they purchased in the magazines or arsenals under Hodgdon's care, taking the storekeeper's receipt for them so that their accounts could be adjusted at the Treasury. In cases where from the nature of the business such deposits could not be made, the Purveyor furnished the Superintendent with statements indicating the stores purchased and the persons responsible for them. The Comptroller instructed Hodgdon on the forms to be used in keeping his accounts, proposing that all accounts of stores in the

[28] *Joural of the Executive Proceedings of the Senate,* I, 173, 174. His nomination on 24 February 1795 was confirmed the next day.

[29] (1) *American State Papers, Military Affairs,* I, 61 (Pres. to Senate, 7 Jan 1794). (2) 1 *Stat.* 352 (Apr 2, 1794).

[30] Instructions and Correspondence of Samuel Hodgdon, 1794–1800 (Knox to Hodgdon, 26 Jul 1794). Manuscript Div., Library of Congress.

Superintendent's office be kept according to the departments—Quartermaster, Ordnance, Navy, Indian, Clothing, Hospital, and Commissary—to which the stores belonged, with the stores of these respective departments subdivided into classes.[31]

In the summer of 1798, a threat of war with France brought some modification in the procurement arrangement. By that time, a separate Navy Department had been created, and apparently Congress intended to make the head of each Department responsible for the proper application of the funds advanced to him.[32] Congress therefore directed that all procurement of supplies for the military and naval services was to be under the direction of the heads of the War and Navy Departments. The Purveyor of Public Stores continued to execute all contracts except those for subsistence which were handled directly by the Secretary of War. The Purveyor procured supplies on orders received from the Secretary of War or the Secretary of the Navy. He rendered his accounts for such supplies to the accountants of the proper Departments for which the supplies were procured, but his accounts continued to be subject to the inspection and revision of the Treasury Department.[33] By this act, the War Department resumed the procurement authority that it had exercised so briefly in 1789. Until the War of 1812 brought changes in administrative organization, the Secretary of War directed the procurement and distribution of military supplies through the Purveyor of Public Supplies and the Superintendent of Military Stores, respectively.

Supplying the Harmar Expedition

During the years when these details for handling supply by bureaus were being worked out, the Army was involved in a series of Indian expeditions, in the course of which Quartermaster supply in the field progressed from administration by contractors to the re-establishment of a field organization under the direction of a Quartermaster General. As Governor of the Northwest Territory and Superintendent of the Northern Indian Department, Arthur St. Clair had been dispatched to the West under instructions to remove all causes of Indian discontent. Despite the conclusion of a new treaty at Fort Harmar on 9 January 1789, St. Clair's efforts to promote peace were futile. Indian raids continued against the small, scattered settlements in the Ohio Valley, and it was

---

[31] *Ibid.*, (Oliver Wolcott to Hodgdon, 2 Oct 1794).

[32] RG 107, Office of Secretary of War (OSW), Letters Received (John Steele, Comptroller, to James McHenry, Secretary of War, 24 Nov 1798). National Archives.

[33] 1 *Stat.* 610 (Jul 16, 1798).

FORT HARMAR

obvious that a militant policy would have to be pursued for their protection. It had become increasingly evident, too, that the Army's offensive
would have to be launched against the Indians living in the upper
Wabash and Maumee valleys. Their hostility to the tide of emigration
moving into the Northwest Territory was repeatedly fanned into new
attacks against the settlers by the intrigues of the Canadian fur traders,
operating under the covert protection of the nearby post of Detroit that
was still held by the British.

Having determined that peace could not be obtained without a show
of force, St. Clair met with Colonel Harmar in mid-July 1790 at Fort
Washington to plan an attack on the Indian villages in the Maumee
valley. In order that Harmar might know the supply situation, St. Clair
took with him to the meeting one of the contractors, Robert Elliot, of
the firm of Elliot and Williams, who in 1790 held the contract for
provisioning the troops on the frontier as it had since its first bid was
accepted by the Treasury Board in 1788. Elliot assured St. Clair and
Harmar that rations could be provided though corn might have to be
substituted for flour. The contractors agreed to supply, before the first
of October 180,000 rations of flour and 200,000 rations of meat. Since
at that time contractors were performing quartermaster duties as well as
furnishing rations, they also agreed to provide 868 artillery and pack-

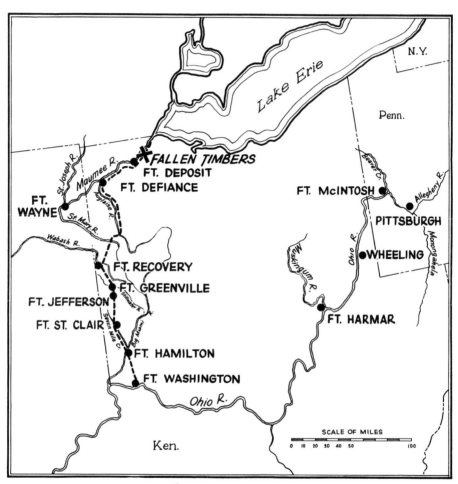

Indian Campaign of 1794

horses, the latter equipped with packsaddles, bags, and ropes. They were to furnish a horsemaster general, 18 horsemasters, and 130 packhorse drivers to supervise the transportation of supplies. Two months later, despite the short notice given them, the contractors reported that they had fulfilled the terms of their agreement.[34]

In the meantime, St. Clair had hurried to New York where, on 23 August, he laid his plans for the expedition before the War Department. Both Knox and the President approved them, and on the same day the Secretary of War took steps to support the expedition. He sent an estimate to the Treasury, detailing the funds required and the amount that ought to be advanced at once to enable the contractors "to execute the duties of the quartermaster's department." He immediately instructed Hodgdon, Commissary of Military Stores in Philadelphia, to forward, by way of Redstone and Wheeling, two tons of rifle and musket powder and four tons of lead bullets, cartridge paper, and case shot for $5\frac{1}{4}$-inch howitzers and for three and six pounders. Knox advised the contractors that sufficient funds had been advanced to their agent by the Treasury Department so that they would suffer no "want of pecuniary assistance" in making their preparations. He also informed Harmar of the measures he had taken and transmitted to him a thousand dollars for contingencies.[35]

To support the few regular troops, militia were called out from Pennsylvania and Kentucky. Knox suggested that it might be advisable for Harmar to persuade some of them to relinquish their rifles, which were not good for close fighting, for the spare muskets that were in store at Fort Washington. Knox did not foresee that instead of assembling fully armed and accoutered as they were supposed to do, the militiamen would arrive at the Fort between 15–25 September ill equipped with, and in many cases destitute of, camp kettles, axes, and arms. The best that Colonel Harmar could do in the few days before the departure of the expedition was to direct the issue of such arms as were available at the Fort and to order the repair of those that could be made fit for use.[36]

Harmar's combined force of 320 regulars and 1,133 militiamen moved northward on 3 October, returning to Fort Washington a month later. In the interim, they destroyed some abandoned Indian villages, located about 170 miles north of the Fort near the present site of

[34] *American State Papers, Indian Affairs*, I, 92 (St. Clair to Knox, 23 Aug 1790); 96 (Elliot and Williams to Knox, 14 Oct 1790).

[35] *Ibid.*, I, 98 (Knox to Secretary of the Treasury, 23 Aug 1790); 98–99 (Knox to St. Clair, 23 Aug 1790); 99 (Knox to Harmar, 24 Aug 1790); 99 (Knox to Elliot and Williams, 3 Sep 1790).

[36] (1) *Ibid.*, I, 99 (Knox to Harmar, 24 Aug 1790). (2) *American State Papers, Military Affairs*, I, 20 (Deposition of Maj. William Ferguson, 16 Sep 1791).

Ft. Wayne, Ind., and in two engagements with the Indians were routed because of the undisciplined, cowardly conduct of the militia. The losses were heavy; 183 of the 1,453 soldiers were killed.[37] The Indians had not been overawed by this show of force; rather they had been further infuriated by the burning of their villages and the destruction of their winter's supply of grain.

The expedition was also expensive in the loss of arms and equipment, in rations wasted, and in horses stolen or killed. The large number of horses lost was attributable to the negligence of sentinels and the connivance of the packhorse drivers and horsemasters. They were not only "ignorant of their duty, indolent and inactive," but by the terms under which horses and drivers were hired by the contractors it was to the advantage of the drivers, "who were chiefly parties in the business," to lose the animals instead of returning them to their owners. In that case, the owners were paid for the loss of the animals which were appraised at a high rate, and also collected the daily pay for their services until they were lost.[38]

The expedition afforded some supply lessons. It showed that contractor supervision of transportation would prove highly expensive. It demonstrated that an Army relying on packhorses to transport its supplies would not be able to conduct a march in Indian country after frost had destroyed the forage. It was also evident that either the federal government would have to equip the militia when they were called into service, or some measures would have to be taken to make certain that the states would maintain the militia fully equipped and ready to march when needed. Moreover, it was fully demonstrated that raw, untrained militia might be used to augment but could never strengthen the small, hard core of regular troops sent into the field. The lessons were clear enough but it did not follow that they would be applied in the next expedition.

Support of the St. Clair Expedition

The failure of the force under Harmar in 1790 made another expedition indispensably necessary in 1791. Winter imposed peace but spring would inevitably bring a renewal of frontier raids, for the Indians had won just enough of a victory to encourage them to renewed efforts against the white men. Speedy preparations were in no way characteristic of the St. Clair expedition either in planning or execution. Knox took so much time in making his report to Congress, and both houses debated

[37] *American State Papers, Indian Affairs,* I, 106 (Return, 4 Nov 1790).
[38] *American State Papers, Military Affairs,* I, 20, 24 (Depositions of Maj. William Ferguson and Lt. Ebenezer Denny, 16 Sep 1791).

so long about it, that it was generally doubted that men could be enlisted and march over the mountains "in season." [39]   It was late in January 1791 when Knox urged that at least 3,000 men be sent to establish a strong post at the Miami village, close to what is now the city of Ft. Wayne, Ind. Subordinate posts were to link it to Fort Washington, near the mouth of the Miami River.   Incurring such expense had not been considered wise as long as there had been hope of obtaining possession of Detroit, but that hope had vanished for the present, and erection of the post at the Miami village was the only alternative.

Arguing that their service would be more "efficacious" and economical, Knox proposed that, in lieu of militia, a corps of levies or volunteers be raised.   They would serve under officers selected by the federal government for the duration of the expedition which he thought would not last longer than 4 months.   He also urged an increase in the Regular Army by the addition of another regiment of infantry, bringing its strength to 2,128. [40]

On 3 March, Congress added the regiment of infantry and authorized the President to raise a corps of levies of no more than 2,000 men under federal control for a period of 6 months. [41]   Though before the passage of this act the authorized strength of the Army had been 1,216, in January 1791 only 820 privates and non-commissioned officers were actually in service. [42]   Anticipating therefore that the ranks of the authorized second regiment would not be filled in time for the expedition, Congress directed the President to make up any deficiencies by raising additional levies or calling militia into service.   On the following day, the President appointed Arthur St. Clair as major general in command of the expedition.

Never was an expedition so bungled in planning, preparation, and execution.   Knox expected that the regular troops and the levies would be recruited and rendezvous at Ft. Washington (later Cincinnati) by 10 July.   If at that date a peaceful settlement had not been made with the Indians, St. Clair, with a force of some 3,000 men, was to advance into the Indian country, building and garrisoning posts between Ft. Washington and the Miami village.   Actually, St. Clair did not arrive at Ft. Washington until late in May.   He might profitably have delayed his departure from Philadelphia until he had thoroughly reviewed the logistical support for his expedition, since at the time of his arrival the garrison consisted of only 75 men fit for duty.   Not until 15 July, 5 days

---

[39] William H. Smith, *The St. Clair Papers: The Life and Public Services of Anthony St. Clair* (2 vols., Cincinnati, 1882), II, 208 (Lt. Ebenezer Denny to Harmar, 9 Mar 1791).

[40] *American State Papers, Indian Affairs*, I, 112–13 (Knox to Pres. Washington, 22 Jan 1791).

[41] 1 *Stat.* 222–24 (Mar 3, 1791).

[42] *American State Papers, Indian Affairs*, I, 113 (Strength of Army, 22 Jan 1791).

FORT WASHINGTON IN 1789

after the original rendezvous date, did the first regiment—299 non-commissioned officers and privates—arrive at Fort Washington. It was September before all the troops had reported. St. Clair advanced into the Indian country 2 months behind schedule, and instead of the 3,000 men that Knox had advised him he would have, he had a little more than 2,000, including some Kentucky militia that had been called out. As in the previous Harmar expedition, the greater part of his force was untrained—a consequence that inevitably followed from the fact that Congress did not enact legislation for raising these troops until March. This was far too late in the year to permit recruiting and disciplining of an Army that was intended to move into action against the Indians in the summer of that same year.[43]

Before his departure from Philadelphia, St. Clair had briefly met with Knox to discuss supply arrangements. As in the past, food for the troops was to be procured and transported by a contractor—in this case, William Duer, who as long ago as the Revolutionary War had engaged in supplying the Army. Provisioning the troops of St. Clair's expedition

---

[43] (1) *Ibid.*, I, 171 (Knox instructions to St. Clair, 21 Mar 1791). (2) *American State Papers, Military Affairs*, I, 36–37 (Committee Rpt on St. Clair Expedition, 8 May 1792).

in 1791 formed only a small part of his business enterprises. It was impossible for Duer to devote due attention to subsisting the Army while at the same time promoting a large manufacturing company and engaging vigorously in stock speculations. The consequence was that the Army suffered.[44]

In 1791, Duer held two contracts for provisioning the troops, one of which he had obtained in an indirect manner from the original recipient, Theodosius Fowler, who had been granted the contract in October 1790 by the Secretary of the Treasury. Even before Congress authorized troops for the St. Clair expedition, Duer's agents were busy supplying the western posts.[45] It was not until the spring of 1791, however, that Duer informed Hamilton of the transfer of the Fowler contract and applied for certain advances of money that the Secretary of the Treasury agreed to make to Duer as the agent of Theodosius Fowler.

Meanwhile, the expedition had been determined upon and Congress provided that the levies and militia were to receive the same rations as the regular troops. The Secretary of War also contracted with William Duer, on 26 April 1791, to furnish provisions for the troops that were being recruited until their arrival at Fort Pitt. Duer entered into a $4,000 bond to execute this contract, but without any security. This was customary procedure in the execution of small amounts.[46]

Duer's problem was to provision the western posts and the troops en route to Fort Washington as well as to accumulate enough flour and cattle not only to support the expedition but also to enable him to deposit 6 months' supply of flour and salted meat at the posts to be built and garrisoned in the Indian country. The main deposit of provisions was required at Fort Washington because the plan originally called for the troops to proceed there immediately without being detained at Fort Pitt. Thereafter he was to forward provisions from post to post as the troops advanced into the Indian country and contructed them.

Between 22 March and 20 July 1791, Duer obtained advances of $70,000 on the contract made with the Secretary of the Treasury and a little more than $5,400 on the one made with the Secretary of War.[47] Since the contractor was so liberally provided with funds, Knox anticipated no deficiencies in the supply of provisions. Ration shortages, however, developed as soon as the first recruits assembled at the rendez-

[44] N.S.B. Gras and Henrietta M. Larson, *Casebook in American Business History* (New York, 1939), 277.

[45] Papers of William Duer, II, f. 299 (Laban Bronson to Duer, 17 Feb 1791; f. 231 (same to same, 17 Mar 1791). New York Historical Society.

[46] *American State Papers, Military Affairs*, I, 36, 42 (Committee Rpts, 8 May 1792; 15 Feb 1793).

[47] *Ibid.*

vous points of Carlisle, Pa., Winchester, Va., and Hagerstown, Md., largely because Duer failed to place funds in the hands of his contracting agents. To remedy the situation, Knox either advanced money to the agent on Duer's account or sent his own representative, furnished with enough funds to correct the deficiencies in supply.[48] By June, Maj. Gen. Richard Butler, second in command of the expedition, reported a beef shortage in the Fort Pitt area, much to Knox' surprise for Duer had assured him that supply would be adequate. In justice to the contractor, Knox recognized that the detention of troops at Fort Pitt, occasioned by War Department orders to Butler to use troops under his command for the protection of the settlements on the upper Ohio, "must occasion some change in the contractor's arrangements."[49] Meanwhile, the contractor was accumulating flour at Fort Washington and his agent, Israel Ludlow, had gone to Kentucky to purchase cattle for the expedition.

What troubled St. Clair was how the contractor intended transporting flour on the expedition. He was apparently unaware of Duer's proposal to use boats to ascend the Miami River. The contractor's plans called for the use of only a few hundred packhorses. Early in July, he directed his agent, John Wilkins, who in a few years was to become Quartermaster General, to buy 200 packhorses. With characteristic ineptness in long-range dealings, Duer not only misdirected these instructions but failed to notify Israel Ludlow, his agent at Fort Washington, of them. Ludlow could only inform St. Clair that he had received no instructions to provide for the transportation of provisions on the campaign. Before the purchase orders finally reached Wilkins, St. Clair, acting on Knox' repeated instructions that he was to take effective steps to supply any deficiencies, had ordered Ludlow to make a provisional agreement for 800 packhorses. This large number, so many more than the contractor had planned for, startled Knox, but he was sure St. Clair would order no more than necessary. Actually, Ludlow purchased about 600 horses, drawing bills on Duer for about $17,000. These the Treasury paid over Duer's protests.[50]

Despite St. Clair's action, it was the breakdown in transportation of provision that caused the troops on the expedition to be placed on one-half and one-quarter allowances of flour. Actually, there were more horses available for supply purposes than could be used. Ludlow could not employ all of those he did have because he lacked drivers. As a

[48] *American State Papers, Indian Affairs*, I, 186, 187 (Knox to Butler, 12 and 19 May 1791).

[49] *Ibid.*, I, 188–89 (Knox to Butler, 16 Jun 1791).

[50] (1) Papers of William Duer, II (Duer to John and Charles Wilkens, 3 Jul 1791; J. Wilkins to Duer, 6 Jul 1791 and 23 Sep 1791). (2) *American State Papers, Indian Affairs*, I, 180 (Knox to St. Clair, 4 Aug 1791). (3) Smith, *St. Clair Papers*, II, 230 (St. Clair to Ludlow, 6 Aug 1791). (4) *American State Papers, Military Affairs*, I, 38 (Committee Rpt, 8 May 1792).

consequence, the troops lived a hand-to-mouth existence and were kept from starvation only by the timely arrival of small quantities of flour and cattle forwarded by the contractor. Officers on the expedition charged that the contractor had no transportation system; that he could not be depended on for supplies; that in short, there was "unpardonable mismanagement in the provision department." [51]

The War Department directed all other preparations for the expedition, with results no less distressing than the efforts of the contractor. On Knox' recommendation that the business of the Quartermaster's Department—specifically the transportation of troops and all supplies, except subsistence—could be handled more economically by a Quartermaster than it had been by contractors, Congress authorized appointment of such an officer for the expedition in March 1791. He was to have the pay, rations, and forage of a lieutenant colonel commandant, but not the rank.[52] When Timothy Pickering refused the appointment, Knox turned to his trusted old friend and subordinate, Samuel Hodgdon, who was appointed on 4 March 1791.[53] The latter was flattered by the honor accorded him, but, realizing the assignment was temporary, he accepted only on condition that he be allowed to retain his position as Commissary of Military Stores at Philadelphia. He proposed that William Knox, youngest brother of the Secretary of War, who had been serving as a clerk in the War Department since 1786, should conduct the business of Commissary of Stores during his absence.[54]

Hodgdon was a competent businessman of great integrity, whose many years of experience as Commissary of Military Stores inclined him to be "exact in his Accounts, scrupulously tenacious of the public property." His critics generally agreed that he was indefatigable in the discharge of his duties, but that he did not comprehend the nature of the staff position he was now called upon to administer.[55] The task assigned

---

[51] (1) Smith, *St. Clair Papers*, II, 245ff. (Diary of Lt. Ebenezer Denny); 246–47 (St. Clair to Ludlow, 8 Oct 1791). (2) "Winthrop Sargent's Diary," *Ohio Archaeological and Historical Quarterly*, vol. 33, No. 3 (Jul 1924), pp. 245, 246, 248.

[52] (1) 1 *Stat.* 222–24 (Mar 3, 1791). (2) *American State Papers, Indian Affairs*, I, 120 (Estimate of 22 Jan 1791). The remuneration amounted to $1,126.80 a year, of which the pay at $60 a month came to $720, the rations at 6 per day or 2,190 a year at 12 cents accounted for $262.80, and the forage at $12 per month added $144 a year.

[53] (1) Pickering and Upham, *Life of Timothy Pickering*, II, 282–83 (Knox to Pickering, 25 Feb 1791). (2) *Executive Journal of the Senate*, I, 82–84.

[54] (1) RG 107, OSW, Letters Sent and Received, Box 3 (Hodgdon to Knox, 14 Mar 1792— should be 1791). National Archives. (2) Papers of the Continental Congress, item 150, I, f. 171 (Knox to Chairman David Ramsay, 4 May 1786). (3) William Knox was subject to occasional fits of derangement at this time and died about 1797. Drake, *Life and Correspondence of Major-General Henry Knox*, 101n.

[55] (1) Henry Knox Papers (Wilkinson to Clement Biddle, 13 Mar 1792). Massachusetts Historical Society. (2) Carter, *Territorial Papers of the United States*, II, 399 (W. Sargent to the Secretary of War, 9 Jul 1792).

him would have taxed the talents of a genius.   Hodgdon was burdened with heavy responsibilities for both quartermaster and ordnance supplies, but he had no adequate organization or staff of officers upon whom he could depend for the execution of his orders.   Aside from such few men as could be spared from the line, he acquired a few civilian assistants— William Knox at Philadelphia, Issac Craig at Fort Pitt, and Robert Buntin at Fort Washington.   He was St. Clair's most important staff officer but he was given no military rank, and consequently he had no authority over military personnel.   He could be and was subjected to abuse from line officers.   His place was with St. Clair as Quartermaster but he was compelled to combine the duties of a bureau chief at Philadelphia with those of a staff officer in the field for many weeks after his appointment.

In accepting his appointment, Hodgdon promised to exercise economy in the conduct of his business.   Economy was the watchword of the administration.   It was practiced to such an extent by both the Secretary of the Treasury and the Secretary of War that the quality of the supplies procured suffered as a result.   They awarded contracts to the lowest bidders even though the bids accepted were often so low as to permit only a bare margin of profit and necessarily must have induced contractors to resort to sharp practices to increase their earnings.   As a consequence, the troops on the St. Clair expedition received tents that afforded no protection from the rain, clothing that wore out before the levies reached Fort Washington, shoes that were "vile in the extreem," and powder that was so weak it would carry a ball only a short distance.[56]

Following his appointment, Hodgdon promptly settled his accounts as Commissary of Military Stores in expectation that he would shortly join St. Clair at Fort Washington to be present at the "General Rendezvous of Men & Stores."[57]   For 3 months, however, Knox detained him in Philadelphia not only to arrange for quartermaster supplies but also to direct the distribution of clothing and equipment to the levies.   In addition, Knox relied upon his knowledge as Commissary to procure and transport ordnance and military stores needed for the expedition.

Knox himself directed procurement of clothing while Hodgdon, as military storekeeper, receipted for the articles turned in by the contractors, gave them cursory inspection, and forwarded the clothing to the troops, employing the services of private wagoners to make delivery at rendezvous points.   Clothing for those who were enlisted in the regular Army offered no problem; for some years contracts had regularly been

[56] (1) Smith, *St. Clair Papers,* II, 289–91 (Testimony of General Harmar and Major Zeigler). (2) RG 107, OSW, Letters Sent and Received, Box 2 (Hodgdon to William Knox, 4 Aug 1791).
[57] RG 107, OSW, Letters Sent and Received, Box 3, (Hodgdon to Knox, 14 Mar 1791).

made for such clothing. Knox directed St. Clair to draw upon the surplus stocks that were deposited at Fort Washington to clothe the First Regiment.[58]

Clothing the levies was another matter. Knox had observed that many militia were soon rendered unfit for service by want of clothing. Upon his recommendation therefore, Congress provided that the levies were to receive a proportional share of the annual clothing supply allowed the regular troops, paying for it by a proportional deduction from their pay. Since the levies were enlisted for 6 months, this allowance amounted to one-half the annual supply of the regular troops, for which the levies paid one-half as much as they did, or 45 cents a month.[59] All of the clothing for the levies had to be contracted for and hurriedly manufactured. It could scarcely have been equal to the patterns the contractors were to follow. Except for overalls which were of good quality, the inspector of the Army later testified that the clothing of the levies was inferior to that of the regular troops. But even if it had been "ever so good," he asserted, it would not have lasted because they took no care of it.[60]

While clothing the levies at the rendezvous points and issuing arms, ammunition, and accoutrements to them on their arrival at Fort Pitt, Hodgdon was also forwarding there the quartermaster and ordnance supplies for shipment down the Ohio with the troops. Immediately following his appointment he had prepared a tentative estimate of the supplies that would be needed on the expedition. Neither that estimate nor the more specific one prepared by Knox a month later was adequate, particularly in respect to the tools needed to clear a road through the wilderness for artillery and to build posts. When the troops began to construct Fort Jefferson, for example, spades and mattocks were plentiful but the Quartermaster could furnish only 80 axes, and 13 of these were borrowed from the troops. There was but one saw and one frow, according to the Adjutant General. St. Clair, to whom the Hodgdon estimate had been shown before his departure for Fort Washington, approved of it without pointing out any of its deficiencies, though later, in the midst of a congressional investigation, he was critical of it and attributed the failure of his expedition to the shortcomings of the Quartermaster's Department.[61]

[58] *American State Papers, Indian Affairs*, I, 173 (Knox to St. Clair, 21 Mar 1791).

[59] (1) *Ibid.*, I, 124 (Estimate of expenses of levies, 22 Jan 1791). (2) 1 *Stat.* 22–24 (Mar 3, 1791).

[60] Smith, *St. Clair Papers*, II, 194 (Testimony of Col. Montgetz).

[61] (1) "Winthrop Sargent's Diary," *Ohio Archaeological and Historical Quarterly*, vol. 33, No. 3 (July 1924), p. 245. (2) RG 94, AGO, St. Clair Papers (Hodgdon estimate, 15 Mar 1791; Knox estimate, 17 Apr 1791). National Archives. (3) *Narration of the Manner in Which the*

The pursuit of economy and the failure to exercise close supervision of all planning details accounted for much of the difficulty encountered in the supply of military stores and accoutrements. Economy dictated the use, for example, of cartridge boxes that for years had been lying in storage without adequate attention being given to their maintenance. Refurbished in appearance, they were forwarded without scrutiny of their serviceability. As early as 17 March, Knox ordered Hodgdon to forward 200 shot and shells for each piece of artillery on the expedition. To promote economy by saving the costs of transportation, Hodgdon depended on obtaining them from a furnace at Fort Pitt owned by Turnbull & Marmie. This laudable objective unfortunately "turned out ill," for the furnace was unable to produce the shells required, though that fact did not become known until late in July when efforts had to be made to obtain the supply elsewhere. In the meantime, as late as the first week in July when according to original plans the expedition should have been ready to move against the Indians, St. Clair had to requisition additional supplies of powder, lead, 3-pound cannon balls, and 5½-inch shells for mortars. St. Clair's letters normally took at least a month to reach the War Department. Knox responded promptly in August by forwarding all the supplies requested, except the 5½-inch shells that could be obtained only at West Point. Obviously, delivery of them could not be made in time for the expedition though Knox apparently thought St. Clair had sufficient quantities on hand at Fort Washington for his immediate needs.[62]

No charges of shortages of military stores were made during the congressional investigation but there was much criticism of their quality. As early as June, Maj. William Ferguson, an artillery officer supervising military stores at Fort Washington, reported that powder casks were "very slight, and not properly secured; also the musket cartridge paper was not the proper sort, being too easily torn, and of course the cartridges made of it will not bear much carriage."[63] The inspector of the Army later testified that when he examined the arms and accoutrements of the troops on their arrival at Fort Washington he found many of the arms broken and unserviceable, "owing to the negligence of the men and accidents on the march." Some of the weapons were unfit for use because they were too old. Under the direction of Major Ferguson, about 32

Campaign Against the Indians . . . Was Conducted, Under the Command of Major General St. Clair . . . (Philadelphia, 1812), p. 114. Hereafter briefly cited St. Clair *Narrative.*

[62] (1) *American State Papers, Indian Affairs,* I, 180 (Knox to St. Clair, 4 Aug 1791); 195 (Knox to Hodgdon, 4 Aug 1791); 195 (William Knox to Hodgdon, 18 Aug 1791). (2) St. Clair *Narrative,* 89–90; 115.

[63] Smith, *St. Clair Papers,* II, 223 (Ferguson to St. Clair, 25 Jun 1791).

artificers were employed to repair arms, build new carriages and mountings for the cannon, and make 300 dozen cartridges.[64]

Hodgdon should have been at Fort Washington to supervise these preparations but it was 4 June before he left Philadelphia for Fort Pitt, under instructions to provide the necessary boats for shipping men and supplies down the Ohio. He was also directed to purchase 110 cavalry horses and 300 packhorses for transporting the baggage of the Army, the artillery, and the hospital stores. Even before his departure, Hodgdon had ordered the purchase of 40 flatboats to transport the Virginia and Maryland levies from Redstone to Pittsburgh.[65] Hodgdon arrived at Fort Pitt on 10 June, further instructed to take the advice on preparations of Maj. Gen. Richard Butler, second in command of the expedition. Subsequently, when St. Clair ordered Hodgdon to headquarters, General Butler thought he was more profitably employed at Fort Pitt and there the Quartermaster remained.[66]

He had many preparations to supervise at Fort Pitt. Camp kettles had to be manufactured from sheet iron that Hodgdon had forwarded in order that the kettles might not be damaged in shipment from Philadelphia. Knapsacks had to be strapped and painted. Packsaddles were being manufactured by Butler's orders to replace those Hodgdon had sent from Philadelphia. Though the Quartermaster had ordered them in various sizes and had taken the advice of supposedly good judges, the first deliveries to reach Fort Pitt were too large to be used on western horses. John Wilkins, who undoubtedly would have been pleased to furnish packsaddles at a profit to himself, derisively informed his friend, Brig. Gen. William Irvine:

> We have had an opportunity of seeing oeconomy & knowledge of this country displayed in sending on the packsaddles from Philadelphia for the expedition. It is said they have cost carriage and first cost four dollars, which I think the least they could have cost, for the carriage only was one Dollar, & when they are here they are not worth one farthing, for they would not fit on the largest Conestoga stallion in Lancaster County, they would even roll on a Hogshead . . .[67]

Viewing Butler's intervention in preparations, Hodgdon, with some exasperation reported that packsaddles were "now three times provided— and at last few will be wanted, as I shall generally hire the horses for

---

[64] *Ibid.*, II, 194–95 (Testimony of Col. Montgetz).

[65] (1) RG 107, OSW, Letters Sent and Received, Box 2 (Hodgdon to Col. James Marshall, 13 May 1791). (2) *American State Papers, Indian Affairs*, I, 193 (Knox to Hodgdon, 31 May 1791).

[66] *American State Papers, Indian Affairs*, I, 193 (Knox to Hodgdon, 3 Jun 1791).

[67] Papers of Brig. Gen. William Irvine, X, 88 (19 May 1791). Pennsylvania Historical Society.

that service, and they will be completely furnished as is usual in this country." [68]

In the midst of the bustle of preparations at Fort Pitt there was much confusion. Hodgdon could not tell what supplies had arrived at Fort Pitt because his assistant, William Knox, had failed to report what stores he had forwarded. Files, bells for the horses, shovels, spades, and grindstones were among the articles Hodgdon wanted William Knox to check upon. Two weeks later he was still waiting for a general return that apparently never arrived. Individual invoices sent along with boxes of articles often failed to correspond to the contents, and Hodgdon cautioned Knox to be careful. Without accurate knowledge of the supplies that had arrived, Hodgdon was nevertheless certain that many of the stores were still detained on the road. [69]

Obviously the caliber of wagon drivers showed no improvement in 1791 over those employed during the Revolutionary War. On 18 August, for example, Hodgdon was still waiting for the arrival of a load that had left Philadelphia a month earlier. Nor was he any more fortunate in other personnel hired for various duties. A conductor of military stores was sent back to Philadelphia from Fort Washington because he was drunk for weeks at a time. The conductor and forage master sent with 100 cavalry horses was so lacking in knowledge of how to care for the animals that 70 of them wandered away the first night after they were disembarked from the flatboats that had brought them down the river. [70]

By 21 July, Knox thought it "proper" that both Quartermaster Hodgdon and General Butler should be at headquarters as soon as possible. But it was 3 weeks later before Hodgdon wrote St. Clair that the last of the packhorses had gone forward and that he and the hospital stores, together with General Butler and the last detachment of the troops, would be on their way, possibly arriving at headquarters before his letter. [71] This optimistic forecast was not realized; some 2 weeks later Hodgdon was still at Pittsburgh. Knox, complaining that expenses exceeded estimates, hoped that the troops were not detained at Fort Pitt for want of boats. At Fort Washington, St. Clair was apprehensive that the state of the river would prevent Butler and Hodgdon from joining him. Indeed the lowness of the water made the river almost impassable

---

[68] RG 107, OSW, Letters Sent and Received, Box 2 (Hodgdon to William Knox, 24 Jun 1791).

[69] *Ibid.*, Box 2 (Hodgdon to William Knox, 14 Jun; 30 Jun; 14 Aug 1791).

[70] (1) *Ibid.*, Box 2 (Hodgdon to William Knox, 18 Aug; 18 Sep 1791). (2) St. Clair *Narrative*, 41–42.

[71] (1) *American State Papers, Indian Affairs*, I, 191 (Knox to Butler, 21 Jul 1791). (2) RG 107, OSW, Letters Sent and Received; Box 2 (Hodgdon to St. Clair, 12 Aug 1791).

in places, and necessitated the employment of more hands and more boats to transport all supplies since the flatboats could carry only half loads.[72]

Hodgdon, Butler, the last of the troops and the stores arrived at Fort Washington on 10 September. St. Clair could foresee no further delays to the expedition and expected to move forward by 25 September. But it was already too late to begin a march into the Indian country. In little more than a week, light frosts injured the pasturage upon which the cattle and horses depended, since no forage was carried with the expedition.[73] The Army slowly moved forward, averaging about 5 to 6 miles a day, stopping to build Fort Hamilton and then, 44 miles farther north, Fort Jefferson.

By then it was late in October and the subsistence supply had become so precarious that St. Clair dispatched Quartermaster Hodgdon back to Fort Washington to take the necessary measures to make good any deficiencies after ascertaining the resources of the contractor and the transportation he had available for sending rations forward. With forage entirely destroyed by frost, the horses failing and unable to keep up, transportation difficulties increased each day as the Army lengthened the distance from its base of supplies. It was obvious that with the season so far advanced, continuance of the campaign was impracticable.[74] Nevertheless, St. Clair pushed on to the inevitable denouement that occurred on the morning of 4 November when the Indians surprised the camp and routed the militia who fled through the ranks of the regular regiment, throwing the entire force into disorder. With the artillery silenced, all but one of the artillery officers killed, and more than half of the Army fallen, a precipitate retreat was made toward Fort Jefferson.[75] The troops abandoned wagons, horses, camp equipment, artillery, baggage, ammunition, and provisions. In their flight to safety, the greater part of the men threw away their arms and accoutrements. For miles the road was covered with "firelocks, cartridge boxes and regimentals." [76]

The shock of this disaster led to the appointment of a congressional

---

[72] (1) *American State Papers, Indian Affairs*, I, 195 (Knox to Hodgdon, 1 Sep 1791). (2) Smith, *St. Clair Papers*, II, 241 (Knox to President, 24 Sep 1791). (3) Papers of William Duer, II (John Nevill to Duer, 25 Aug 1791).

[73] Smith, *St. Clair Papers*, II, 240–41 (St. Clair to Knox, 18 Sep 1791); 254 (Denny Diary).

[74] (1) *Ibid.*, II, 248–49 (St. Clair to Hodgdon, 21 Oct 1791); 255 (Diary of Lt. E. Denny). (2) "Winthrop Sargent's Diary," *Ohio Archaeological and Historical Quarterly*, vol. 33, No. 3 (July 1924), p. 250.

[75] *American State Papers, Indian Affairs*, I, 137–38 (St. Clair to Knox, 9 Nov 1791).

[76] (1) *Ibid.* (2) Smith, *St. Clair Papers*, II, 261 (Diary of Lt. E. Denny). (3) For a list of Quartermaster supplies lost in this action see a return prepared by Assistant Quartermaster R. Buntin, RG 107, OSW, Letters Sent and Received, Box 2. (4) The value of the military stores, tools, and Quartermaster supplies lost was set at $32,810.78. RG 94, AGO, St. Clair Papers (Return, 1 Feb 1792).

committee of investigation. There was blame enough to go around. The committee confessed that congressional delay in enacting legislation for the protection of the frontier had not permitted sufficient time to recruit and discipline an Army for the expedition. It attributed the failure of that expedition to the want of discipline and experience in the troops, the lateness of the season at which the expedition was undertaken, and "the gross and various mismanagements and neglects in the Quartermaster's and contractors' departments." [77] The committee completely exonerated General St. Clair, but it is clear that he, too, must share some of the responsibility. He procrastinated as much as Knox; he profited in no way from the experience of the Harmar expedition; and he persisted in waging a winter campaign that some of his officers had, and he himself ought to have, acknowledged to be without hope of success.

Wayne's Expedition

St. Clair's defeat was also followed by the enactment of new legislation, on 5 March 1792, to make "more effectual provision for the protection of the frontiers of the United States." [78] Defense of the frontiers was no longer to be left to a few regular troops augmented upon occasion by militia or levies. Instead, the regular battalion of artillery and the two regiments of infantry, then in service, were to be brought up to strength. Congress also authorized three additional regiments of infantry, one of which was to consist of two battalions of infantry and a squadron of light dragoons, who, if occasion demanded, might be required to serve dismounted. These men were enlisted for 3 years but the three regiments might be discharged sooner if peace was made with the Indians. Washington appointed Maj. Gen. Anthony Wayne to the command of this Army.

Congress also provided for a Quartermaster and a deputy quartermaster who were to be paid, respectively, $100 and $50 a month. During the time the Army bill was being debated and passed by Congress, Samuel Hodgdon remained at Fort Washington under instructions to make every preparation that he could.[79] Issac Craig, his assistant at Pittsburgh, urged him to hurry to Philadelphia; his enemies were attempting to supersede him. But Craig's warning came too late, for on 19 April the Senate confirmed the appointment of James O'Hara as Quartermaster General. John Belli of Kentucky had already been appointed deputy quartermaster general on 16 April 1792.[80] Hodgdon did not return to

[77] *American State Papers, Military Affairs*, I, 38–39 (Committee Rpt, 8 May 1792).
[78] 1 *Stat*. 241–43.
[79] RG 107, OSW, Letters Sent and Received, Box 3 (Knox to Hodgdon, 4 Apr 1792).
[80] (1) *Ibid.*, Box 3 (Craig to Hodgdon, 22 Apr 1792). (2) *Executive Journal of the Senate,*

Philadelphia until the summer of 1792, at which time he resumed his duties as Commissary of Military Stores.

In appointing O'Hara, President Washington had turned to a businessman, intimately familiar with the problems of the West, whose career had been interrupted by service in the Revolutionary War, only to be resumed with more aggressive vigor at Pittsburgh when the war ended. The 40-year old O'Hara, like his predecessor, had no military rank as Quartermaster General, but he had a far better chance of being successful because of his familiarity with the frontier, because he performed no duties other than those of his Department, and because he had time to establish an effective organization.

Profiting from experience, the War Department had no intention of rushing another unprepared expedition into the field in the summer of 1792. Time was to be allowed to recruit troops as well as to train and discipline them. Both Wayne and O'Hara remained in Philadelphia for some time following their appointments, reviewing plans with Secretary Knox. Approximately a month after his appointment, Quartermaster General O'Hara submitted an estimate of the transportation, entrenching tools, artificers' tools, and other supplies his Department would require for the year 1792. His estimate bore little resemblance to the tentative one prepared by Hodgdon in the previous year, including as it did 1,000 felling axes and hundreds of other tools, 750 packhorses, 20,000 bushels of forage, 50 wagons to carry supplies to Fort Pitt, and 120 flatboats at Fort Pitt as well as 5 40-foot keelboats.[81] It was evident that he was not influenced by the spirit of economy that prevailed in government circles and that had dominated Hodgdon's preparations. All of O'Hara's estimates were on a generous scale. . There was seldom a noticeable relationship, however, between the estimates made and the supplies sent, and O'Hara, like his predecessor, suffered from matériel shortages.

By June 1792, General Wayne and his Quartermaster General were at Pittsburgh. The first load of supplies, including brass cannon and sheet iron for camp kettles, dispatched by William Knox, had arrived. The manufacture of camp kettles was well under way, but blacksmiths, carpenters, and wheelwrights were badly needed. They could not be

I, 117, 119, 120. Though the law provided for the office of Quartermaster and deputy quartermaster, President Washington nominated O'Hara and Belli as Quartermaster General and deputy quartermaster general respectively and Congress so confirmed them. (3) Under the act of March 5, 1792, the quartermaster, deputy quartermaster, and an adjutant general who also served as inspector constituted the General Staff of the Army. 1 *Stat.* 241.

[81] RG 98, Journal of Quartermaster General James O'Hara, f. 2–4 (O'Hara to Knox, 11 May 1792). National Archives.

hired for less than $15 to $20 a month and extra provisions, so O'Hara requested instructions on paying such high wages. He also discovered that Issac Craig would not continue as Quartermaster at Fort Pitt for the salary O'Hara could offer. Knox directed him to offer the artificers a monthly wage of $15 and extra provisions and to pay Craig the salary of a deputy quartermaster general; he was worth it.[82]

O'Hara soon met with many of the same difficulties as Hodgdon had in obtaining supplies from Philadelphia. Essential supplies mentioned in invoices failed to arrive. General Wayne thought there was "some very reprehensible conduct respecting the transportation of stores." O'Hara, too, condemned the existing mode of transportation that permitted wagoners to pass their loads along from one to the other with a resultant exorbitant price for their carriage. He himself had seen "lading pass to the fourth hand" before it reached Pittsburgh. He suggested that the only remedy was to reduce the price of carriage 12 percent by changing the method of computation from net to gross weight, and to require delivery between Philadelphia and Pittsburgh to be made in 25 days or suffer a penalty of $4 a day for each day's detention upon the road.[83] Though wagoners' receipts were scrutinized more carefully and transportation was more closely supervised, invoices checked against wagonloads that came from Philadelphia storehouses continued to reveal discrepancies, and Quartermaster Craig could only inquire whether the missing articles were lost or stolen.[84]

By the summer of 1792, O'Hara had the organization of his Department well established. To expedite Quartermaster business at Philadelphia, he appointed Hodgdon as his agent because his known integrity merited the Quartermaster General's confidence and because his industry and "knowledge of the mode of doing business in the public offices" made him the logical appointee. To him O'Hara gave his power of attorney so that Hodgdon might apply to the Treasury for the funds required by the Department and take charge of and submit Quartermaster accounts to the Treasury.[85]

O'Hara's field organization consisted of two deputy quartermasters general—Craig at Fort Pitt who supervised the forwarding of supplies that arrived from Philadelphia, and John Belli at Fort Washington who gave support to General Wilkinson's troops. In addition, there were six assistant quartermasters and clerks. To this initial organization, O'Hara

[82] (1) *Ibid.*, f. 8–9 (O'Hara to Knox, 20 Jun 1792). (2) Mary C. Darlington, *Fort Pitt and Letters from the Frontier* (Pittsburgh, 1892), 247–48 (Knox to O'Hara, 29 Jun 1792).

[83] (1) RG 107, OSW, Letters Sent and Received, Box 3 (Wayne to Knox, 3 Aug 1792). (2) RG 98, Journal of Quartermaster General James O'Hara, f. 12 (O'Hara to Knox, 17 Aug 1792).

[84] RG 107, OSW, Letters Sent and Received, Box 4 (Craig to Hodgdon, 9 Aug 1793).

[85] *Ibid.*, Box 3 (O'Hara to Hodgdon, 17 Aug 1792).

in the fall of 1792 added a commissary general of forage who contracted for and issued all forage required by the Army and upon occasion contracted for boats.   To transport the forage he had forage boats built, and O'Hara gave him specific instructions on how the forage was to be carried.[86]   O'Hara also appointed two assistant commissary generals of forage and four issuing commissaries.

In the fall of 1792, he estimated that the Army would require 500 tons of hay, 60,000 bushels of grain, and would need for its transportation 60 boats and 500 packhorses.   Even this number of horses would be insufficient unless sleds could be used for hauling forage to the posts in Ohio during the winter.   He admitted that a request for 60 more boats with so many already at Pittsburgh might seem extraordinary to the Secretary but those on hand were so flat and unwieldy in construction and navigation that he had to obtain boats nearer to the cargo to be picked up.

O'Hara planned to give mobility to Wayne's cavalry and pack trains by assuring them of an ample forage supply through the use of a system of forage boats.   These would move up the Monongahela as far as the Cheat River in present-day West Virginia, during the course of which the boats would be loaded with hay and grain contracted for in the area. They would then carry their cargoes to Legionville, the camp 27 miles below Fort Pitt on the Ohio, to which Wayne had removed his troops late in 1792, and to Fort Washington for distribution of the cargo to the chain of posts north of it.   O'Hara favored the use of keelboats, for too many supplies had been lost through the employment of "Kentucke Boats." [87]

To his organization O'Hara added a wagonmaster general to take charge of all public teams and drivers and a superintendent of packhorses.[88]   His instructions to the latter revealed some of the difficulties under which the packhorse system of transportation labored.   For one thing, receipts were to be taken from packhorse masters for all horses, saddles, bells, collars, lash ropes, bags, and other items of equipment for which they were to be held accountable.   Inspections were to be held at the end of each trip which would reveal not only what articles needed repair but all losses or damages due to carelessness or neglect for which the delinquent was to be punished.   To reduce the heavy loss of horses through negligence, he ordered the packhorse masters to drive their animals at a slow, constant pace, traveling no more than 23 miles a day,

[86] RG 98, O'Hara Journal, f. 15, 16–18 (O'Hara to Maj. Geo. McCully, 10 and 14 Oct 1792).

[87] Ibid., f. 20–21 (O'Hara to Knox, 19 Oct 1792); 16–18 (O'Hara to Geo. McCully, 14 Oct 1792); f. 39 (O'Hara to Belli, 26 Jan 1793).

[88] Ibid., f. 26–27 (To John Torrence, 5 Dec 1792); f. 78–80 (To Robert Benham, 26 Jun 1793).

and seeing that their animals were properly fed. He put an end to the destructive practice of riding packhorses, either loaded or empty, by dismissing packhorse masters who permitted it and by punishing any packhorseman guilty of it. At the same time, O'Hara also attempted to give better protection to the civilian personnel of this department. He directed that if military escorts offered any unprovoked insults or attempted any violence to personnel of the packhorse department, a report was to be made immediately to the proper office. If the commissary of provisions of the lines showed any discrimination in the issue of food to packhorse department personnel, a report to the commanding officer would bring justice to them.[89]

The Quartermaster's Department also employed 6 master boatmen, 120 boatmen, 46 artificers—saddlers, blacksmiths, carpenters, wheelwrights, tinmen, coppersmiths, ropemakers, and coopers—under a superintendent of artificers. The Department paid the artificers $15 a month plus 1½ rations and provided the tools and materials they used. It also paid for the services of several armorers, though they and the artillery artificers were under the direction of the commanding officer of artillery. The Quartermaster's Department transported all ordnance, arms, ammunition, accoutrements, but Knox appointed a conductor of military stores to receive, keep, and deliver all such supplies on orders of the commanding officer of artillery or the commander-in-chief.[90]

Except for its transportation, Knox relieved O'Hara of all further responsibility for clothing. Hodgdon as Commissary of Military Stores kept a record of the stock of clothing on hand. When the supply fell low, the Secretary of War applied to the Secretary of the Treasury who made contracts for additional supplies on the basis of patterns furnished by Hodgdon. Upon delivery by the contractors, Hodgdon receipted for the clothing which was inspected by an officer appointed for that purpose, though William Knox occasionally acted as inspector. A reputable shoe manufacturer of Philadelphia usually inspected the shoes. Paymasters received, distributed, and accounted for the clothing transported to the Army by the Quartermaster's Department.[91]

Inspection by no means guaranteed the receipt of good clothing by the Army. General Wayne complained of the very inferior quality of the hats and shoes his troops received. The hats when the least bit wet dropped over the ears and eyes of the men, losing their form entirely.

---

[89] *Ibid.*, f. 78–80 (To Robert Benham, 26 Jun 1793).

[90] (1) *Ibid.*, f. 77–78 (Knox to Samuel Henley, Conductor of Military Stores, 1 Aug 1792; 85–86 (O'Hara to Supt. of Artificers); 71 (O'Hara to Knox, 26 Apr 1793). (2) RG 107, OSW, Letters Sent and Received, Box 3 (Stagg to Hodgdon, 7 Dec 1792).

[91] RG 107, OSW, Letters Sent and Received, Box 3 (Stagg to Hodgdon, 12 Oct 1792; 29 Nov 1792; 8 Dec 1792); (Regulations, 8 Mar 1793).

As for the shoes, they went to pieces by the time a soldier had performed one tour of escort duty between Forts Washington and Greenville. If shoes were not provided at once, he wrote in the spring of 1794, the troops would be barefoot before the middle of June. So dissatisfied was he with the clothing provided that he suggested a substitute uniform. He thought that a well-made cocked hat in place of the flimsy round one, brown or blue woolen overalls instead of white ones, and a full coat in lieu of the coatee would much improve the uniforms for 1794. The long coats would give warmth in winter and provide patches for repairing clothing when they were shortened in the spring.[92] Wayne's criticisms of clothing were relayed to Hodgdon who justly commented:

> As long as these articles are furnished in the present mode, complaints may be expected. As things go, it is impossible to furnish a pair of shoes for a soldier for *seventy-five cents,* and more irrational to expect a suitable Hat for seventy three and a third cents—for though the contract is absolute, reference will be had, in the inspection to the price.[93]

Even if clothing of good quality was received from the contractor by the storekeeper in Philadelphia, the troops on the frontier were still quite likely to receive it in poor condition. Improper storage facilities almost guaranteed that result. Wool hats, for example, were liable to damage from moths, yet one inspector found them dumped in bulk on the floor of a storehouse. Clothing might also receive considerable damage in the course of transportation to the troops. About this time, the practice was instituted of appointing boards of officers to inspect shipments of clothing as they were received to determine the extent of the damage sustained.[94]

Wayne had spent the first winter training his troops at Legionville. With a view to moving to Fort Washington in the spring, O'Hara made the necessary preparations. Contracts were negotiated to provide 68 flatboats. Forty of these were to be covered boats to transport the troops and their baggage; 8 were provided for the transportation of the artillery, 12 for the horses and oxen, and 8 for wagons and Quartermaster stores. In addition, four keelboats were ordered to be procured and sent as soon as possible to Fort Washington loaded with corn.[95] The run of this large fleet of transports and forage boats was accomplished without loss

---

[92] Richard C. Knopf, "Wayne's Western Campaign: The Wayne-Knox Correspondence, 1793–94," *Pennsylvania Magazine of History and Biography,* vol. 78, No. 3, pp. 330–31 (Wayne to Knox, 10 Mar 1794).

[93] Wayne Manuscripts, vol. 34, f. 80 (Hodgdon to Knox, 2 May 1794). Pennsylvania Historical Society.

[94] RG 107, OSW, Letters Sent and Received, Box 4 (Rpt of Board of officers to Gen. Wayne, 23 Sep 1793).

[95] RG 98, O'Hara Journal, f. 46–47 (O'Hara to McCully, 15 Feb 1793).

or damage. Wayne arrived at Fort Washington on 7 May, setting up his camp and headquarters about a mile west of Fort Washington at a place he called Hobson's Choice. There the work of training the troops went on while federal commissioners continued their efforts to make peace with the Indians.

Supply preparations were stepped up by O'Hara. Forage deposits at Forts Jefferson and Hamilton were small but because his request for money to purchase horses had been rejected, the supply could not be increased. At Wayne's direction, he bought 300 packhorses and 20 teams in Kentucky.[96] Progress could then be made in transporting forage to the "outposts," but this was hampered by the lack of twilled bags ordered as long ago as February but still not received 4 months later. When still another month had gone by and neither the bags nor the 500 axes ordered in February had arrived, O'Hara tartly rebuked Craig for falling "into the fashionable error of thinking for the Army, at a very great distance." The axes he assured Craig were needed; there were only 274 on hand at Fort Washington on the day he had received an order to issue 400.[97]

When news of the failure of the peace efforts reached Wayne in September 1793, he prepared to move north. O'Hara estimated that the Army would need 573 packhorses, of which he had 273 on hand. He had ready for immediate service 20 teams of 4 horses each and 14 teams of 4 and 6 oxen each. He estimated that he needed an additional 32 draft horses.[98] Actually when the Army got ready to move and the packhorses had arrived from Kentucky, the superintendent was ordered to form them into brigades of 72 each, with 12 drivers and a packmaster in charge of each brigade. O'Hara instructed him that the drivers had to be proportioned to the horses at the rate of one man for each six horses, except in the case of horses for the artillery pieces. There the proportion was to be one man to each four horses. Of the seven brigades, numbering more than 500 horses, he allotted two for the transportation of ordnance and military stores, two for the baggage, one for Quartermaster and hospital stores, and two were loaded with forage.[99]

O'Hara also arranged for artificers to accompany the Army. He directed his superintendent of artificers to have ready to march with the Army 12 carpenters, 9 blacksmiths, 4 sawyers, 2 wheelwrights, 2 coopers, 8 saddlers, 2 harnessmakers, 2 nailers, 1 turner, and 1 tinman. For the transportation of their supplies, he directed the superintendent to use

[96] Ibid., f. 74 (O'Hara to Wayne, 17 May 1793); f. 76 (O'Hara to Hodgdon, 2 Jun 1793).
[97] Ibid., f. 83–85, 91 (O'Hara to Craig, 17 Jun, 11 Jul 1793).
[98] Ibid., f. 99–100 (O'Hara to Wayne, 13 Sep 1793).
[99] Ibid., 117–18 (O'Hara to Benham, 2 Oct 1793).

whatever ox teams and wagons were available. He provided three traveling forges for the troops, one of which was fitted up for the cavalry, and he ordered the superintendent to be prepared to erect and man three smith's hearths. The latter was to provide extra bellows and anvils; examine an invoice of tools recently delivered at Fort Jefferson to determine what additional ones would be required; and carry along on the march some bar iron, harness leather, rope, ax helves, horse shoes, nails, and other supplies that he might need to repair casualties on the march.[100]

On 7 October, the Army set out for Fort Jefferson, making their camp about a week later 6 miles beyond it. There, on 24 October, Wayne received a dispatch from Secretary Knox informing him the Army was to halt its advance and take up winter quarters. On no account would President Washington risk a defeat during a season when supplies and forage were difficult to obtain. That order was reinforced by the failure of the subsistence contractors, Elliot & Williams, to maintain an adequate supply of rations. In consequence, the Army went into winter quarters at Fort Greenville, which the troops built and Wayne named in honor of his friend, Gen. Nathanael Greene.

One of the greatest difficulties was to furnish a sufficient escort to protect the supply convoys. On 17 October 1793, a convoy was attacked by the Indians a short distance from Fort St. Clair, and about 70 horses were carried off though the wagons and stores were left standing in the road. The loss of the horses was particularly injurious since they were needed to assist the contractor in bringing provisions forward.[101] Wayne had not only ordered Elliot & Williams to furnish 3,000 complete rations for daily issue and provide supplies at the intermediate posts between the Army and Fort Washington but also to deposit, before the end of 1793, 270,000 rations in advance of the head of the line as it moved toward the Miami village. Elliot & Williams, however, supplied only enough to meet the Army's daily requirements. By great exertions, they deposited 70,000 rations at Fort Greenville; Wayne expected an additional 120,000 rations upon the arrival of a convoy late in October.[102] To supplement the contractor's means of transportation, Wayne ordered Quartermaster General O'Hara to purchase 250 packhorses and 40 pair of oxen or 60 wagon horses at the contractor's expense.[103]

The situation had a familiar ring to those who had been with St. Clair 2 years earlier, but supplies did arrive though never in the

[100] *Ibid.*, 107–08 (O'Hara to Superintendent of Artificers, 23 Sep 1793).

[101] (1) *American State Papers, Indian Affairs*, I, 361 (Wayne to Knox, 23 Oct 1793). (2) *Journal of Capt. Daniel Bradley*, ed. Frazer E. Wilson (Greenville, Ohio, 1935), 54.

[102] (1) Wayne Papers, XXX (Wayne to Elliot & Williams, 16 Oct 1793). (2) *American State Papers, Indian Affairs*, I, 361 (Wayne to Knox, 23 Oct 1793).

[103] RG 98, O'Hara Journal, 132–33 (O'Hara to Belli, 24 Oct 1793).

quantity ordered.[104]   Before the year closed, Wayne had erected another post, Fort Recovery, 23 miles from Fort Greenville on the site of St. Clair's defeat.   The subsistence contractors then bent all efforts toward accumulating supplies and completing preparations for the campaign of 1794. Elliot & Williams were still delinquent in their deliveries in April. Instead of a 90 days' supply, or 270,000 rations, on hand, exclusive of the daily issues, the contractors had only 19 days' supply of flour and 9 days of beef on 22 April.   Wayne demanded that they comply with his orders.[105]   The shortcomings of the contractors in providing adequate transportation to forward rations made Wayne affirm "the absolute necessity of some effectual & certain mode of supplying the Army than that of private Contract."   Avaricious individuals, he insisted, would always consult their own private interest in preference to that of the public. They would never part with enough money to purchase sufficient provisions or adequate means of transportation to make required deposits, preferring to supply the troops from hand to mouth, "whilst the principal part of the money advanced by the treasury may *profitably* be otherwise employed." [106]

Prodded by Wayne, the contractors delivered provisions.   When the Indians attacked in the summer, Wayne was prepared to move against them.   Before the middle of August 1794, his troops were building a post that he called Fort Defiance at the confluence of the Auglaize and Maumee Rivers.   On 20 August, they were victorious over the Indians in the Battle of Fallen Timbers.   After laying waste the Indian houses and cornfields, the troops returned to Fort Defiance to improve that fort, to destroy other Indian villages and cornfields in the area, and to build Fort Wayne.   During the building of that fort, completed on 21 October, and on the return march of the troops to Fort Greenville, the shortage of provisions kept the men on scant ration allowances, scarcely sufficient to keep body and soul together.

The difficulty of transporting provisions 200 miles through the wilderness, together with the death of Robert Elliot, the contractor, who was killed by Indians near Fort Hamilton, on 6 October 1794, caused the Army to be put on half allowance of flour.   What there was of flour was musty and the beef was poor.   The lack of salt proved disastrous for the cavalry and packhorses, which died at the rate of four or five a day in October.[107]   Wayne ordered O'Hara to supplement the efforts of the

[104] RG 107, OSW, Letters Sent and Received, Box 4 (Capt. Joseph Shaylor to Hodgdon, 24 Oct 1793).
[105] Wayne Papers, XXXIV (Wayne to Elliot & Williams, 22 Apr 1794).
[106] *Ibid.*, XXXIV (Wayne to Knox, 7 May 1794).
[107] (1) *Journal of Capt. Daniel Bradley*, ed. Wilson, 72–73.   (2) *Journal of Thomas Taylor Underwood* (Cincinnati, 1945), 19.

ROAD TO FALLEN TIMBERS

contractor. It must have been of considerable interest to the Army to learn later that Congress had granted the President discretionary power under special circumstances to increase the ration issued to the troops on the frontiers. These increases were not to exceed 4 ounces of beef, 2 ounces of flour, and half a gill of rum or whiskey to each ration, and half a pint of salt for each 100 rations.[108]

Wayne remained at Fort Greenville for about a year, administering the Army and negotiating with the Indians. His efforts were crowned with success, on 3 August 1795, when the Indians signed the Treaty of Greenville, under the terms of which they relinquished their claims to a considerable area of valuable land northwest of the Ohio River. Quartermaster General O'Hara was a signatory of the treaty. The Jay Treaty of 1794, which provided for British evacuation of the northwest posts, contributed to Indian acceptance of the Treaty of Greenville. With the Army occupying those posts in 1796, settlers in the area thereafter enjoyed real security.

O'Hara considered that his work was done when peace was estab-

[108] 1 *Stat.* 390 (Jun 7, 1794).

lished, and he was eager to return to the more profitable pursuits of business in the midst of a rapidly expanding frontier. He submitted his resignation, and, with the Army no longer engaged in active operations against the Indians, he believed no successor would be appointed to fill the office.[109] Many months were to pass before any action was taken on his resignation.

O'Hara's duties as Quartermaster General had been limited to providing logistical support for Wayne's army. He had no responsibility for supplying the handful of troops stationed at West Point or those at posts in Georgia and in the old Southwest Territory. Their support was directed by the War Department. The Superintendent of Military Stores, Samuel Hodgdon, forwarded their clothing, accoutrements, and military stores. He acted on orders received from the Secretary of War, drawing from stocks that had been procured by the Secretary of the Treasury. Contractors who had been successful in offering the lowest bids for a given area or group of Army posts furnished these troops with subsistence. In 1794, for example, Manning Wyckoff & Co. provisioned West Point.[110]

Whiskey Rebellion

The War Department also provided supplies for the militia army called out by President Washington to quell the Whiskey Rebellion. While Wayne had been pursuing the Indians in the Northwest Territory in the summer of 1794, rebellious citizens in western Pennsylvania were taking up arms against the imposition of a federal excise tax. It was Hodgdon who on orders furnished the stores, clothing, arms, accoutrements, camp equipage, and ammunition required by this militia army.[111] On the other hand, Ephraim Blaine of Carlisle, who had served as Commissary General of Purchases in the Revolutionary War, was appointed to provide transportation for the militia and to furnish them with forage, straw, and fuel. When a quartermaster general for this militia army, as well as a state quartermaster and his deputies in Pennsylvania began to operate in the field, Blaine wished to be relieved since his services were unnecessary, but he remained on duty to furnish transportation home for the troops.[112] In face of the prompt action taken by

[109] RG 107, OSW, Letters Sent and Received, Box 6 (Craig to Hodgdon, 23 Oct 1795).

[110] RG 107, OSW, Letters Sent and Received, Box 3 (John Habersham to Hodgdon, 28 May 1793); Box 4 (Stagg to Hodgdon, 14 Jun 1793); Box 5 (Melancton Smith to Hodgdon, 15 Jan 1794).

[111] *Ibid.*, Box 4 (Stagg to Hodgdon, 8 Sep 1794); Box 5 (Stagg to Hodgdon, 10 Sep 1794); (Invoice of supplies provided 11 Sep–30 Oct 1794).

[112] Henry Miller was quartermaster general for this militia army; Clement Biddle was quartermaster for the Pennsylvania militia. Blaine Papers, IV, No. 2424 (Hamilton to Blaine,

Washington, resistance had quickly collapsed. To provide protection against similar occurrences in the future, Congress enacted legislation for calling the militia into federal service to repel invasion or suppress insurrection. About the same time, it also provided for continuing the existing Military Establishment and bringing it up to authorized strength.[113]

No sooner had Wayne negotiated the Treaty of Greenville with the Indians than Timothy Pickering, who had succeeded Knox as Secretary of War on 2 January 1795, characteristically began to think of ways to economize. The transportation of provisions from the Ohio River to Fort Greenville "so prodigiously enhances the price," he wrote the President, that he proposed removing a considerable part of Wayne's troops to the banks of the Ohio. Washington, however, thought it best not to "build *too much*" on the peace treaty; "sufficiently respectable" garrisons had better be left at the posts. When James McHenry succeeded Pickering a few months later, he foresaw no possible savings in the Quartermaster's Department because the expenses of transportation to the western posts, whether by land or water, would remain large.[114]

Continuation of the Post of Quartermaster General

O'Hara was still serving as Quartermaster General for the frontier troops in the spring of 1796 when Congress, in legislating for the Military Establishment, decided to continue the general staff then in existence until 4 March 1797. As a matter of fact, even while action on O'Hara's resignation was pending, Congress had in 1795 re-established the grade of Quartermaster General and had included that officer, as well as a Paymaster General and an inspector, who also acted as Adjutant General, among those who constituted the general staff.[115] This congressional action in 1796, contradicting O'Hara's opinion that no new Quartermaster General would be appointed, showed an inclination to modify the heretofore accepted theory that a Quartermaster General served as a staff officer only in time of war. Obviously, with troops garrisoned at a number of posts on the frontier, some such officer was necessary at least to supervise

12 Sep 1794); No. 2437 (Miller to Blaine, 6 Oct); No. 2457 (Biddle to Blaine, 11 Oct); No. 2489 and 2525 (Blaine to Hamilton, 21 Oct and 13 Dec 1794).   Blaine was given the pay and allowances of a lieutenant colonel.

[113] 1 *Stat.* 424 (Feb 28, 1795); 430 (Mar 3, 1795).

[114] (1) Carter, *Territorial Papers of the United States*, II, 537–39 (Pickering to Washington, 2 Oct 1795).   (2) *Writings of Washington*, ed. Fitzpatrick, XXXIV, 330 (Washington to Pickering, 7 Oct 1795).   (3) Bernard C. Steiner, *Life and Correspondence of James McHenry* (Cleveland, 1907), 182 (Rpt to Senate, 14 Mar 1796).

[115] (1) 1 *Stat.* 463 (May 30, 1796).   (2) 1 *Stat.* 430 (Mar 3, 1795).

the transportation of men and supplies if not to plan logistical support
for a campaign.   Though given the title, he no longer performed the
military duties that had pertained to the office of Quartermaster General.

O'Hara's resignation was now accepted, and, on 1 June 1796, John
Wilkins, Jr., another Pittsburgh businessman, was appointed Quartermaster General of the Army, to have the same pay and emoluments as
his predecessor.[116]   His appointment carried no military rank.   A veteran
of the Revolutionary War who had served as a surgeon's mate while still
in his teens and a bold, energetic entrepreneur of the frontier since the
close of the war, Wilkins was only 35 years old when he became Quartermaster General.   For the next 6 years he administered the duties of
his office.

These were years of peace on the inland frontier, a time for negotiating new agreements with the Indians, particularly those south of the
Ohio; for building additional forts; and for hacking new roads through
the wilderness.   These were the tasks that occupied the Army and
changed the character of Quartermaster supply from logistical support
for campaigns to routine delivery of the annual supplies needed by the
small detachments of troops garrisoned at the frontier posts.   For
handling this supply, Wilkins made relatively few changes in the organization of the Quartermaster's Department.   Peacetime supply did not
require the services of a superintendent of packhorses, a wagonmaster
general, or a superintendent of artificers.   It did necessitate the employment of civilian assistants to carry out Quartermaster duties at the various
frontier posts.   Isaac Craig continued as deputy at Pittsburgh, and a
new deputy was stationed for a short time at Fort Washington, though the
importance of that post was dwindling.   As the number of frontier posts
increased, a greater number of assistant quartermasters were employed.
Lest this imply the existence of a formal organization, it should be
pointed out that these titles were used loosely.   The same individuals—
Craig at Pittsburgh, Matthew Ernest at Detroit, or Henry Glen who
directed the transportation of troops and supplies at Army posts in
New York—were also simply called agents.[117]   These men represented
the Department in the field.

Since Quartermaster General Wilkins also spent most of his time in
the field, attending the commanding general wherever his headquarters
might be located, it became desirable to have an agent of the Quartermaster General stationed at the seat of government to handle all accounts,

---

[116] *Executive Journal of the Senate*, I, 214.

[117] (1) RG 107, OSW, Letters Sent and Received, Box 8 (Wilkins to Hodgdon, 24 Aug 1797).
(2) *American State Papers, Miscellaneous*, I, 312 (Roll of agents in Quartermaster's Department,
17 Feb 1802).

to arrange all financial matters with the Treasury, and to direct the transportation of supplies issued by the Superintendent of Military Stores. In effect, the establishment of such an office represented a groping for the beginnings of a Quartermaster bureau at the seat of government, a development that was not to come to fruition until after the War of 1812.   At the beginning of his administration, Wilkins, like O'Hara, gave Hodgdon his power of attorney to act as his agent in Philadelphia.[118] By 1800, James Miller was acting as his agent in Philadelphia, the office having been separated from that of the Superintendent of Military Stores. In June of that year, the capital was moved to Washington, and Hodgdon informed Craig that he did not know whether an agent would be continued at Philadelphia but that one "must be at all times at the seat of Government." [119]   The Philadelphia office was closed in the summer of 1801.

Utilizing the services of his assistants, many of whom were thoroughly experienced men, Wilkins perfomed his duties as Quartermaster General satisfactorily.   In the beginning, his efforts were directed toward reducing expenditures, particularly in the well-established Pittsburgh area and among the posts immediately dependent upon it.   There, public artificers, boatmen, and wagoners were removed from the Department's payroll.   Freight could be hauled cheaper by hiring the services of commercial boatmen, fuel could be better supplied to the posts by contracts than by using public teams, and articles could be made or repaired more economically by contracting for the work to be done on the lowest terms.[120]   Throughout his term in office, Wilkins was chiefly occupied with directing the transportation of supplies to the garrisons stationed at the western posts.

[118] Hodgdon Letter Book, 1795–98 (Hodgdon to Secretary of Treasury, 29 Apr 1797). Manuscript Div., Library of Congress.
[119] RG 94, Hodgdon Letters, vol. 108, f. 3–4 (Hodgdon to McHenry, 28 Aug 1799); f. 378 (Hodgdon to Craig, 4 Jul 1800).
[120] RG 98, Book No. 11, Quartermaster General's Report of 1797, f. 7–8 (Wilkins to Wilkinson, 20 Apr 1797).

CHAPTER IV

Dominance of the Secretary of War

A precarious peace on the inland frontier followed the treaty of 1794 with the British and the treaties of 1795 with the Spanish and with the Indians, but new measures affecting the military establishment were soon evoked by a threat to the maritime frontier. The wars resulting from the French Revolution locked England and France in a struggle for empire and European domination, during the course of which both nations violated American shipping rights. By great efforts, President Washington averted war with England during his administration, and his successor, John Adams, was equally fortunate in settling differences with France peaceably. Commercial complications were no worse in 1812 than they had been for years, but the country went to war with Great Britain a second time, driven to it by the land hunger of the West and the aggressiveness of the War Hawks.[1]

During most of these years, the Army's strength remained well below 3,000 men and officers. The Army was ill-prepared for offensive action, except against the Indians. As long as England and France remained deadlocked and no external threat from land forces materialized, however, there was no compelling need for expansion of the Army. A large part of military expenditures was disbursed for Naval preparations. Each new war scare, however, caused Congress to authorize additional new regiments for the Army, but before troops could be recruited and the new regiments activated the threat of danger passed. Recruitment was then suspended and the legislation superseded by a new enactment. In 1798, for example, the possibility of war with France led to a flurry of legislation intended to afford better protection of the country's seacoast; to increase its stock of cannon, small arms, and military stores; and to strengthen the Army.[2] Had this last law been fully implemented, the military force would have been expanded to some 40,000 men. By 1800, however, the threat of war had disappeared and the enlistments and

---

[1] (1) See Julius W. Pratt, *Expansionists of 1812* (New York, 1925). (2) A challenge to the role that land hunger played in bringing on the war is to be found in Alfred L. Burt, *The United States, Great Britain and British North America from the Revolution to the Establishment of Peace After the War of 1812* (New Haven, 1940).

[2] 1 *Stat.* 554 (May 3); 555 (May 4); 558 (May 28); 569 (Jun 22); 604 (Jul 16, 1798); 725 (Mar 2, 1799).

appointments for the proposed expanded Army were suspended. Such officers and men as had been added to the Army were disbanded by the act of May 14, 1800, and the Army was reduced again to a little more than 5,000 men.

When the Democratic Republicans came into office in 1801, they further reduced the size of the Army. In his Inaugural Address, Jefferson referred to "a well-disciplined militia, our best reliance in peace and for the first moments of war, till regulars may relieve them." [3] He embodied more specific defense recommendations in his first annual message to Congress. Henry Dearborn, Secretary of War, estimated that no more than 20 companies each of artillery and infantry were necessary to garrison the various posts and stations. This was fewer than authorized, and Congress hastened to reduce the enlisted strength to 3,040, the minimum required to police the frontier and guard the arsenals.[4] Unimpressed with the use of a standing army for defense purposes, Jefferson kept the officers and troops busy at work that was not essentially military—treaty-making, roadbuilding, and exploration.

Toward the end of his administration, the *Chesapeake-Leopard* affair in June 1807 stirred the wrath of the people. As the danger of war with England increased, Congress again enacted a law in the spring of 1808 increasing the size of the Army.[5] Recruitment moved slowly and was suspended entirely the following year so that in 1810 the Army, exclusive of the staff, numbered only 2,765. Not until Harrison defeated the Indians in the battle of Tippecanoe in the fall of 1811 was interest in defense needs renewed.[6] Then Congress ordered the existing military establishment completed, but a month after war had been declared against Great Britain that goal had not been achieved.

Not only was the Army under strength and heterogeneously organized in the years from 1798 to 1812, but the troops—seldom more than company strength—were dispersed in small, isolated forts along the maritime and inland frontiers. As a consequence, their officers had little opportunity to learn the lessons either of command or of logistical support for large bodies of men. The small size of the Army made unnecessary the development of any organized system of staff departments that would be so essential to its supply in time of war.

[3] James D. Richardson, *Messages and Papers of the Presidents* (10 vols., Washington, 1876–99), I, 323.

[4] (1) *Ibid.*, I, 329. (2) *American State Papers, Military Affairs*, I, 155–56 (Dearborn to House Speaker, 23 Dec 1801). (3) 2 *Stat.* 132 (Mar 16, 1802).

[5] (1) *American State Papers, Military Affairs*, I, 227–28 (Jefferson to Senate and House, 25 Feb 1807). (2) 2 *Stat.* 481 (Apr 12, 1808).

[6] (1) *American State Papers, Military Affairs*, I, 250 (Army Return). (2) 2 *Stat.* 522 (Jun 28, 1809); 669 (Dec 24, 1811).

Supply became a wholly civilian-dominated operation between 1798 and 1812. It was controlled and directed by the Secretary of War, who discharged not only the duties of his office but also those of the Quartermaster General, Commissary General, Master of Ordnance, Indian Commissioner, Commissioner of Pensions, and Commissioner of Public Lands.[7] A large part of those responsibilities were transferred to his office in 1798 when the authority for the procurement of all Army supplies that had been vested in the Secretary of the Treasury was returned to the Secretary of War.[8] Thereafter, all food, clothing, equipment, ordnance, and hospital stores were procured on orders of the Secretary of War. He could not direct any purchases, however, before Congress passed the annual appropriation bill for the military establishment. Congress further provided that all supplies, except ordnance, were to be purchased on a yearly basis.[9]

Subsistence Contract System

Subsistence continued to be supplied under contract as it had been ever since 1781, the only difference being that after 1798 the Secretary of War executed the contracts. The procedure of soliciting bids by public advertisements and awarding contracts to the lowest bidder had become routine. There were more contractors in these years than in 1781 because expansion of settlement beyond the mountains increased the number of states and territories in which contracts were let for the supply of troops stationed at posts within their boundaries.[10]

The obligations of the contractor remained unchanged. He agreed to deliver and issue to the troops the authorized ration at the price fixed in the contract. He was obliged to have on hand sufficient rations to feed the troops at all times, providing subsistence for at least 6 months in advance at the more distant posts, such as Michilimackinac or Detroit, and usually for 3 months at all other posts. In the event the troops were moved from a post, the government paid for the transportation of the rations if their removal was considered desirable. It was a risk of the trade, however, for it sometimes happened that the War Department transferred troops without notice to the contractor, and he was left with unwanted rations on his hands.[11] As in the past, if a contractor failed to

[7] *Annals of Congress*, 12th Cong., 1st sess., vol. 2, pp. 1355, 1359, 1361–62.

[8] 1 *Stat.* 610 (Jul 16, 1798).

[9] *Ibid.*, I, 749 (Mar 3, 1799).

[10] (1) RG 107, Office of the Secretary of War (OSW), Military Book, vol. 1, pp. 102–05 (Advertisement, 18 Apr 1801). (2) RG 94, Orderly and Company Book, 1795–1813, pp. 98–103 (Contract with Hanson Kelly, 1 Jan 1801).

[11] RG 107, OSW, Letters Received, M–148 (5) (James Morrison to SW Eustis, 4 Jul 1810).

make delivery, the commanding officer had authority to supply any deficiency by purchase at the risk and on the account of the contractor. During this period, subsistence contracts also carried a provision requiring the contractor, when directed to do so, to furnish quarters as well as such quantities of fuel and straw as were allowed by War Department regulations at any recruiting rendezvous at which the contractor was required to supply rations.   He also provided the means of transportation when the recruits moved.   For these additional quartermaster services, the contractor was reimbursed for the money he spend and allowed a commission of 2½ percent.[12]

The ration provided was substantial but nutritionally as unbalanced as in the past, for it still continued to furnish the troops a meat and bread diet.   In 1798, the ration was increased over what it had been since 1790. It now consisted of the following allowances:

1¼ pounds of beef or ¾ pounds of pork,
18 ounces of bread or flour, and
1 gill of rum, brandy, or whisky.

For every 100 rations, the contractor also provided 2 quarts of salt, 4 quarts of vinegar, 4 pounds of soap, and 1½ pounds of candles.[13]   By arrangement between the contractor and the commanding officer it was possible to commute part of this ration for beans or other vegetables.[14] This same ration was supplied during the War of 1812.

The War Department made only one modification in the ration before the war.   In 1803, the Secretary of War tried an experiment at New Orleans.   He substituted malt liquor for spirits as being more beneficial to the health of the troops stationed in a warm climate.   The following year, malt liquor or light wines were made a component part of the ration to be supplied instead of rum, brandy, or whiskey at such posts and at such seasons of the year as the President deemed necessary to preserve the health of the troops.[15]   Difficulties soon developed; most wine had to be imported and could not be readily obtained.   Beer had to be manufactured locally and good brew masters were scarce.   In any case, the troops preferred hard liquor.   The experiment therefore proved unpopular and the Secretary soon abandoned it.

The quality of the ration showed no improvement during these

[12] (1) RG 107, OSW, Military Book, vol. 1A, pp. 64–65 (Regulations, 28 Apr 1801). (2) RG 94, Orderly and Company Book, 1795–1813, pp. 98–103 (Contract with Hanson Kelly, 1 Jan 1801).

[13] 1 *Stat.* 604 (Jul 16, 1798).   The ration was slightly altered the following year but the same allowances were restored in 1802 and repeated in January 1812. *Ibid.,* I, 734 (Mar 3, 1799); II, 132 (Mar 16, 1802); 671 (Jan 11, 1812).

[14] RG 107, OSW, Military Book, vol. 4, p. 293 (SW to James Morrison, 5 Mar 1810).

[15] (1) RG 107, OSW, Military Book, vol. 1A, pp. 459–60 (SW to Col. Constant Freemen, 17 Jun 1803). (2) 2 *Stat.* 290 (Mar 26, 1804).

years. Officers testified that the bread issued was often stale; that the flour was frequently moldy, "sometimes full of bugs and worms;" the pork rusty; and the beef not fit to be issued.[16] As long as the contractor system prevailed, the soldiers would continue to be poorly fed. The margin for profits on contracts that required rations to be furnished at prices ranging from 13 to 19 cents per ration were exceedingly narrow. To increase their gains, the more greedy contractors resorted to every dubious means. Opportunities for graft were innumerable, ranging from deliberate omission of the small articles of the ration, such as candles and soap—to effect savings for the contractor—to collusion with a commanding officer at a post, who might prevent a survey and rejection of poor, unwholesome subsistence and collect a reward sub rosa from the contractor for his official helpfulness. Some arrangement profitable to both is implied in the relations that existed between James Morrison, contractor in the New Orleans area, and Brig. Gen. James Wilkinson. "One thing I know with great Certainty, which is equally known to yourself," Morrison wrote Wilkinson in the summer of 1809, "and that is—that the Contract becoming ultimately profitable or otherwise depends on the *Commander in Chief.*" Fearing a survey would be demanded, the contractor suggested that Wilkinson order an examination of the flour only as a last resort. If part of the flour on hand became unfit for use, his agents had been ordered to purchase and mix sweet flour with it, Morrison advised the general, in order to make the whole palatable. The implication is plain enough when he added:

> Should I visit Orleans in winding up my Contract will make such arrange-
> ments on this head as will no doubt be satisfactory to you—On this subject
> dont have a moments uneasiness—Be as serviceable to me as you can, where you
> are; (keeping the public in view) and it may be in my power to be in some way
> Serviceable to you—[17]

The Secretary of War, informed of the bad rations issued at New Orleans, did nothing more than complain to the contractor.[18] Then, as at a later date, the War Department considered the contract system the most economical for subsisting the troops.

Clothing Supply

The procurement and distribution of all other supplies for the Army were centralized in Philadelphia. The orders of the Secretary of War

---

[16] *American State Papers, Military Affairs,* I, 281, 282 (Deposition of Maj. E. Backus; Capt. George Peter, 5 and 11 Apr 1810).

[17] Wilkinson Papers, vol. III, f. 81 (Morrison to Wilkinson, 28 Jul 1809). Chicago Historical Society.

[18] RG 107, OSW, Military Book, vol. 4, pp. 262, 273 (Eustis to Morrison, 18 Jan and 2 Feb 1810); vol. 6, p. 94 (SW to Morrison, 28 Mar 1811).

were executed by the Purveyor of Public Supplies of the Treasury Department, who contracted for all clothing, shoes, camp utensils, military stores, equipage, medicines, and hospital stores, and by the Superintendent of Military Stores, who stored and issued them. There were some exceptions; on orders of the Purveyor, agents procured hospital stores at Baltimore, New York, and New Orleans where they could be purchased on terms as reasonable as at Philadelphia and moreover saved the cost of transportation.[19] Purchases of clothing and equipment awaited passage of the annual Army appropriation bill.

By law, the soldier was annually supplied with a uniform that since 1790 had included a hat, coat, vest, two pairs of woolen and linen overalls, four pairs of shoes, four shirts, two pairs of socks, one stock and clasp, and one pair of buckles as well as one blanket. Underwear was not issued to the soldier. Congress slightly increased the amount of clothing furnished him in 1802. The issue of overalls was increased to two pairs of woolen and two of linen; two pairs of short stockings were added to the socks along with one pair of half gaiters. The soldier was also provided with one coarse linen frock and trousers for fatigue clothing.[20] He could draw from surplus stocks for any replacements of these articles that he needed, paying for them at their contract prices by deductions from his monthly pay. Deductions from his pay of 25 cents for each coat and 8 cents for each vest and pair of overalls were also made to cover the cost of altering such garments to obtain a better fit.[21]

These were the clothing items that had to be purchased after the appropriation bill was passed. Since passage of such legislation was usually not accomplished before February or March, the time allowed for purchase and the production of necessary articles was short. Shipments of clothing and such other annual supplies as stationary and hospital stores had to be ready to move from Albany and Pittsburgh no later than the end of May if the troops at the western posts were to receive their annual supplies before winter set in.[22] This time factor prevented the exercise of good management in the supply offices at Philadelphia because it precluded any deliberate operation. Instead, everything had to be hastily procured at a disadvantage to the government both in price and in quality. Medicines for the troops at southern posts should have been delivered by April, but, when appropriations were sometimes passed as late as March, it was impossible to procure and pack, let alone transport them, by that date.

---

[19] RG 92, Office of Purveyor of Public Supplies, Letters Sent, No. 249, p. 142 (Whelen to Lt. S. T. Dyson *et al.,* 18 Jun 1803). Hereafter cited Purveyor, Letters Sent.

[20] 1 *Stat.* 120 (Apr 30, 1790); II, 132 (Mar 16, 1802).

[21] *Ibid.,* I, 749 (Mar 3, 1799).

[22] RG 107, OSW, Military Book, vol. 2A, p. 66 (SW to T. Coxe, 18 Feb 1804).

As early as 1803 Israel Whelen, who had succeeded Tench Francis as Purveyor when the latter died in the midst of the campaign of 1800, attempted to ease the pressure on his office by taking advantage of existing conditions.[23]   Large quantities of cloth that had been purchased by his predecessor to provide uniforms for a proposed expanded Army in 1799 remained on hand when Congress cut back troop strength in 1800 and 1802.   Since Whelen had been using these stocks to prepare the annual clothing supplies after he became Purveyor, the annual clothing appropriations had not been used to any great extent.   The funds on hand therefore afforded a sufficient sum for putting into effect a plan he proposed—that of providing in advance at least a year's supply of clothing at the Arsenal.   Thereafter, he pointed out, the Purveyor would have a full year after the appropriation bill passed to prepare the annual supply for the troops.[24]   Whelen's sound suggestion evoked no action by the Secretary of War who apparently preferred to give the impression of economy in operation by requesting minimum clothing appropriations while using up the stocks on hand.[25]

Several years later, Tench Coxe, who became Purveyor when Whelen resigned in the summer of 1803, also offered a solution to this problem.[26] His proposal required the Secretary of War to seek a separate appropriation from Congress for the purpose of depositing at the Arsenal a stock of clothing and of hospital stores sufficient for 10,000 men.   After this appropriation, the annual grants would only have to be large enough to procure additions to the supply equal to the actual issues in the preceding year.[27]   Though the need was urgent, Coxe was no more successful than Whelen had been in effecting advance procurement of supplies.

Had procurement been correlated with actual needs, appropriated funds might also have been used to better purpose.   When the Secretary of War began to direct procurement in 1798, purchase orders for annual supplies were based on the authorized strength of the Army, though the regiments were usually under strength.   It was not until December 1807

---

[23] Whelen assumed the duties of his office on 22 May 1800. RG 92, Coxe and Irvine Papers, Box 24. (SW to Jonathan Williams, Jr., 12 May 1800).

[24] RG 92, Purveyor, Letters Sent, No. 249, pp. 116–18 (Whelen to SW, 19 Apr 1803).

[25] Clothing appropriations during these years ran as follows:

1799—$127,450	1802—$66,630
1800— 257,995	1803— 59,960
1801— 141,530	1804— 80,000

For each of the next four years the appropriation was $85,000. 1 *Stat.* 741; 2 *Stat.* 66, 108, 183, 227, 249, 315, 408, 412, 470.

[26] Israel Whelen submitted a letter of resignation on 9 July 1803. Tench Coxe assumed the duties of that office on 5 August. He served until the office was abolished and he was relieved from his duties on 1 June 1812. RG 92, Purveyor, Letters Sent, No. 449, p. 154 (Whelen to Secretary of Treasury, 9 Jul 1803); p. 175 (Coxe to Comptroller, 5 Aug 1803).

[27] RG 107, OSW, Letters Received, C-120 (5) (Coxe to Eustis, 12 May 1810).

that this system was changed.   At that time, the Secretary of War directed the commanding officers of companies to make annual returns to the War Department, showing the surplus clothing on hand from the previous year's annual supply and the quantities needed to complete the current year's supply.[28]   The Secretary then forwarded these returns to the Purveyor to govern him in his purchases, and to the Superintendent of Military Stores to guide him in packing the supplies.[29]

In addition to overpurchasing in the past, the War Department had developed no consistent procedure for utilizing surplus stocks on hand at the Arsenal.   Surpluses of clothing had accumulated for a number of reasons.   Changes made in the uniform left old-style clothing on hand. Over-ordering accounted for some of it, as did an unanticipated production of a larger number of clothing items from a specified amount of material.   Most important of all, according to Coxe, was the failure to deduct from purchase orders the quantity of garments on hand.[30]   To permit such deductions to be made, Coxe proposed that every room and loft of the Arsenal be numbered and inventoried and that thereafter storebooks be kept posted every day for every article that went into or was removed from each room.   Purchase orders would then be executed by the Purveyor only after deductions of the suitable articles already in the Arsenal had been made from the orders.   The military storekeeper approved of the plan and the Secretary of War ordered him to prepare such an inventory.[31]   Like so many plans, its execution was long delayed and apparently soon fell into disuse.

In his procurement of hats, shoes, clothing, camp equipage, and hospital stores, the Purveyor followed the procedure—established from the time Robert Morris first applied it to subsistence contracts—of advertising and awarding the contract to the lowest bidder.   The Purveyor introduced one innovation in procurement sometime in 1799. The impact of events at home and abroad brought changes in the practice of contracting for the clothing to be supplied to the troops.   Europe was at war and its armies required large amounts of clothing.   As the chief neutral carriers, American ships benefited by the European blockade, carrying materials to meet West Indian demands as well as the increased consumption that prosperity stimulated in the United States.   War demands abroad and increased consumption at home promoted a scarcity of textiles.   The shortage was made more acute by an increased demand

[28] William Duane, *Military Dictionary* (Philadelphia, 1810), 590 (Regulation, 1 Dec 1807).
[29] (1) RG 107, OSW, Military Book, vol. 3A, pp. 172–75 (SW to T. Coxe, 29 Jan 1808). (2) General James Wilkinson, *Memoirs of My Own Times* (3 vols., Philadelphia, 1816), II, 418.
[30] RG 92, Purveyor, Letters Sent, No. 251, pp. 241–43 (Coxe to SW, 25 Oct 1804).
[31] (1) *Ibid.* (2) RG 107, OSW, Military, Book, vol. 2A, p. 147 (SW to Geo. Ingels, 29 Oct 1804).

for military clothing for the American Army after Congress, fearing war with France, authorized twelve additional regiments of infantry and six troops of light dragoons in the summer of 1798. Apparently, the difficulty of obtaining sufficient cloth caused contractors to become delinquent on their uniform contracts and fail to make deliveries on time. To eliminate delays and prevent hardships to the troops, Purveyor Tench Francis began to purchase cloth for the government instead of contracting for finished clothing, giving rise to the first use of government-furnished materials in Army supply.[32]

When the cloth was delivered, the Purveyor had it deposited with the Superintendent of Military Stores. The Purveyor then contracted with master tailors in the Philadelphia area to make, in three sizes, a specified number of coats, vests, overalls, or complete suits of infantry or artillery clothing. He furnished each tailor with an order on the Superintendent for delivery to him of the necessary yardage of materials and trimmings required to complete his contract. Shirts were hand-sewn by seamstresses who also obtained the necessary thread and linen from the Superintendent. When garments were ready, master tailors and seamstresses delivered them to the Superintendent who had them inspected to see whether they conformed to patterns set as the standard for acceptance. If the garments passed inspection, the Purveyor paid the tailors and seamstresses for their work.[33] This plan of government-furnished materials was utilized for years until tailors and seamstresses were brought in to work at a factory operated at the Philadelphia Quartermaster Depot.

The supply system operating at Philadelphia in these years before the War of 1812 was one of centralized control. It ought to have been effective but personal animosities between the Purveyor and the Superintendent prevented harmonious functioning of the system. Nothing was productive of more disagreement between the two agencies than inspection. In the past, that had been a function of the Purveyor, who had entrusted inspection of hats, shoes, and clothing to workers skilled in the production of those articles. They were presumed to be the best judges of the quality and workmanship of the articles that were offered to the government by the contractors.[34] Within 10 months after he succeeded

---

[32] No statement of policy or procedure by either the Secretary or the Purveyor has been uncovered but casual references by others indicate this change was under way in 1799. Hamilton wrote of materials "procured at distant places" being brought to Philadelphia to be made up. (1) *Works of Alexander Hamilton*, ed. Henry C. Lodge (12 vols. New York, 1904). VII, 78–79 (To Washington, 3 May 1799). (2) See also RG 107, OSW, Letters Sent and Received, 1799–1801, Box 12 (Capt. James Bruff to Hodgdon, 9 Jun 1799).

[33] See Account Book of Purveyor's Office, 1802, for entries illustrative of procedures followed. Manuscript Collection, New York Public Library.

[34] RG 107, OSW, Military Book, vol. 1, pp. 49–50 (SW to Whelen, 17 Apr 1801).

Samuel Hodgdon as Superintendent, William Irvine became convinced that such inspectors were not doing their duty faithfully, and he informed Purveyor Whelen that he considered it his duty to inspect all articles "after the Inspectors." [35]

To prevent the impositions that had been practiced in the past, Secretary Dearborn offered William Irvine the position of inspector of clothing. He was to perform this duty in addition to his function as Superintendent of Military Stores, inspecting every article in person. For this service the Secretary suggested an allowance of 5 or 6 cents a suit, which would amount to $150 to $180 a year.[36] Though Irvine accepted the post, he did not do the inspecting himself but delegated the duty to one of his clerks who spent most of his time inspecting to the detriment of the clerical work that had to be done at the Arsenal.[37]

Shifting inspection from the Purveyor to the Superintendent did not still troop criticism of clothing. When the troops complained of some of the clothing they had received in 1803, Tench Coxe was quick to defend the Purveyor's office, though the articles criticized had been procured by his predecessor, Israel Whelen. Coxe was critical of the kind of inspection given by the office of the Superintendent of Military Stores. If the inspection was "duly attentive," he informed the Secretary of War, good items could be procured. But one clerk could scarcely possess "that quick eye, and that judicious eye to the qualities & making" of such a wide variety of articles as had to be inspected at the Arsenal. As a basis for comparison in making inspections, he proposed the use of samples or models of every item procured.[38] Commenting on the criticism to Irvine, Coxe informed him that a return to inspection by qualified workers would be acceptable to him, and he also suggested that it would be well to pay particular attention *"to the condition of goods at the moment of issue,* lest time, vermin, insects, &c may have occasioned them to be unfit for use." [39] Storage conditions undoubtedly warranted that thrust, and, though the troops had criticized the quality of the shoes and shirts sent them, they had also complained of the receipt of moth-eaten woolen articles.[40]

---

[35] (1) RG 92, OQMG Consolidated Correspondence File, Box 457 (Irvine to Whelen, 13 Jan 1802). (2) Hodgdon was removed from office when the Federalists went out of power in 1801. Irvine, who had risen to the rank of brigadier general in the Revolutionary War, was appointed on 13 March 1801 and served until his death on 29 July 1804. RG 107, OSW, Military Book, vol. 1, p. 75.

[36] RG 107, OSW, Military Book, vol. 1A, pp. 154–57 (22 Feb 1802).

[37] RG 92, OQMG Consolidated Correspondence File, Box 1006 (Geo. Ingels, acting Supt., to Dearborn, 5 Oct 1804).

[38] RG 92, Purveyor, Letters Sent, No. 251, pp. 9–11 (Coxe to SW, 16 Jan 1804).

[39] *Ibid.,* pp. 7–8 (16 Jan 1804).

[40] RG 107, OSW, Military Book, vol. 2, p. 158 (SW to Irvine, 24 Jan 1804).

The disagreement between Coxe and William Irvine widened to the proportions of a feud when Callender Irvine was appointed Superintendent following the death of his father in office.[41] Lack of hamony developed at every point of contact between the two offices. It occasionally happened that the Secretary directed a purchase order to the Superintendent who then called upon the Purveyor to execute it. To keep his accounts clear with the Treasury, Coxe insisted that he must have an abstract of the Secretary's letter as an authorization for the expenditure of funds for which he was accountable. The argument dragged on until, his patience exhausted, the Secretary ordered both men to furnish source, date, and import of an order to any officer whose cooperation was required to execute any War Department order.[42]

The threat of war with Great Britain led Congress to authorize expansion of the Army in the spring of 1808.[43] Providing clothing for the troops being recruited under this act was made more difficult by the impact of the Non-Importation and Embargo Acts upon the market. Imports dropped drastically as ships lay idle in the harbors. Cloth became increasingly scarce, and Coxe was compelled to purchase the best fabrics available even though they fell far below previously acceptable standards. Irvine refused to concede that good cloth could not be procured because of the embargo. "I doubt the fact. It is possible that Cloths are considerably enhanced, but will that circumstance justify the purchase of such, as will not last a Soldier six months with decency? I presume not." [44]

With rejections of garments submitted to Irvine for inspection running as high as one-third and frequently one-fourth of delivery, Coxe was unable to furnish clothing as rapidly as it was required. Ignoring textile shortages, Irvine thought supply could be better handled if the necessary materials were sent to the regiments to be made up by Army tailors.[45] The Secretary doubted the wisdom of adopting such a system while recruitment was under way.

As delays continued in the production of acceptable uniforms, Irvine

---

[41] Callender Irvine was appointed on 24 October 1804. *Ibid.*, vol. 2A, p. 145 (SW to C. Irvine). He served as Superintendent until the summer of 1812 when he was appointed Commissary General of Purchases on 8 August. He filled that office for the next 29 years until his death on 9 October 1841.

[42] (1) RG 92, Purveyor, Letters Sent, No. 250, pp. 115–16 (Coxe to Irvine, 2 Nov 1805). (2) RG 107, OSW, Letters Received, Box 14 (Coxe to Irvine, 9 Oct 1806). (3) RG 107, OSW, Military Book, vol. 2A, pp. 523–24 (SW to Irvine, 17 Oct 1806). (4) RG 92, OQMG Consolidated Correspondence File, Box 1203 (SW to Coxe, 17 Oct 1806).

[43] 2 *Stat.* 481 (Apr 12, 1808).

[44] RG 92, Supt. of Military Stores, Letters Sent, No. 398, pp. 261–62 (Irvine to SW, 20 Sept 1808).

[45] *Ibid.*, No. 398, pp. 150–53, 293–94 (Irvine to SW, 19 May and 22 Oct 1808).

attributed the trouble to the failure of Coxe to hold the contractors to delivery of complete uniforms at stated periods. He charged that, as a consequence, tailors often completed one article of clothing but made little progress on other parts of the uniform they were under contract to deliver. Irvine further claimed that if the tailors had private work, they felt no obligation to complete governmental contracts. He asserted that if Coxe had been willing to adopt his suggestion and had also offered better prices, there would have been no delay in delivery of clothing. He was certain the mere fact that he had made such a proposal was sufficient reason for the Purveyor to reject it.[46]

As the summer months waned and deliveries were still delayed, Coxe tried to get the Superintendent to adopt the practice of making partial shipments to the newly recruited troops of such clothing items as had been delivered and accepted instead of waiting until complete annual supplies could be shipped to them. Thus the soldier might at least have a blanket or a coat even if caps or overalls were not ready. Partial shipments, however, were only authorized to companies in the immediate vicinity of Philadelphia. In any case, Superintendent Irvine charged that the supplies Coxe urged him to forward existed only in the Purveyor's "fertile imagination." [47]

In time, Coxe suggested that to expedite clothing production Irvine might cooperate by examining parcels of cloth before he bought them, or after they were stored but before they were issued to the tailors and seamstresses and the garments cut out. Thus, rejection of the finished garments on the basis of quality of the fabric might be avoided. "If I go on to buy and expend all the funds upon the best I can get," Coxe informed the Secretary, "and an officer with unknown standards in his mind refuses to examine goods before I make them public property or afterwards, till they are cut and made, and then rejects, expence, delay, and embarrassment must follow." [48]

Once again the Secretary intervened to promote "harmonious intercourse" between the two offices. The Purveyor, he wrote, must exercise discretionary power in making his purchases. When he had made the best selections the markets permitted, even though they were not all that might be desired, he had performed his duty. The Secretary presumed

---

[46] *Ibid.*, No. 398, pp. 198–99 (Irvine to Coxe, 23 Jul 1808); pp. 295–97 (Irvine to SW, 22 Oct 1808).

[47] (1) RG 92, Purveyor, Letters Sent, No. 244, p. 271 (Coxe to Irvine, 16 Aug 1808); pp. 355–59 (Coxe to SW, 15 Oct 1808). (2) RG 92, Supt. of Military Stores, Letters Sent, No. 298, p. 223 (Irvine to Coxe, 17 Aug 1808).

[48] (1) RG 107, OSW, Letters Received, C-111 (5) (Coxe to SW, 4 May 1810). (2) RG 92, Purveyor, Letters Sent, No. 248, pp. 372–73 (Coxe to SW, 30 Mar 1810); pp. 395–96 (Coxe to Irvine, 25 and 26 Apr 1810); p. 399 (Coxe to SW, 30 Apr 1810).

that the inspector would make such allowances as circumstances, the public economy, and the public service required in performing his duty.[49] The controversy over inspection of cloth before it was used to produce finished garments continued. Irvine could see only some sinister plot in the kind of purchases the Purveyor was making. Irked by the inspection orders he received from the Secretary, he informed him that after the clothing for 1810 had been completed he would have nothing further to do with inspection.[50]

The Secretary of War thereupon made Coxe solely responsible for the procurement, production, and inspection of clothing.[51] By December, Coxe had assumed the duty of inspection and had returned to the former practice of utilizing as inspectors men skilled in the production of the articles they inspected.[52] He was still harrassed by textile shortages, and he turned to the task of stimulating domestic production of textiles needed by the Army. As long ago as 1803 Coxe had exhibited considerable interest in the efforts of certain Massachusetts manufacturers to produce acceptable linens.[53] Now with the need urgent, the Secretary of War in 1811 directed him to solicit bids for cloth of domestic production for Army clothing.[54] Coxe worked energetically and by November he reported optimistically that "the requisite supplies of woolen goods for any probable force may be obtained from our own manufacturers even for 1812." He added that "any requisite supply of substantial goods of flax and hemp seems to be perfectly within our capacity." [55]

These were the procedures followed in procuring clothing on the eve of the War of 1812. With slight modifications, they were used during the war itself though a new agency was created to take over the procurement of clothing and other supplies.

Transportation of Supplies

With procurement and storage centralized at Philadelphia, direction of the transportation of supplies to the Army was also centered there.

[49] RG 107, OSW, Military Book, vol. 4, p. 336 (SW to Coxe and Irvine, 3 May 1810).

[50] (1) RG 107, OSW, Letters Received, I-119 (5) (Irvine to Eustis, 7 Aug 1810). (2) RG 107, OSW, Military Book, vol. 4, p. 413 (Eustis to Irvine, 3 Aug 1810).

[51] RG 107, OSW, Military Book, vol. 4, p. 431 (To Coxe, 26 Aug 1810).

[52] (1) RG 92, Purveyor, Letters Sent, No. 243, p. 3 (Coxe to SW, 6 Dec 1810). (2) RG 92, OQMG Consolidated Correspondence File, Box 212 (Eustis to Coxe, 11 Dec 1810).

[53] RG 92, Purveyor, Letters Sent, No. 249, pp. 177–78 (Coxe to L. & T. Stibbins, 16 Aug 1803); pp. 206–07 (Coxe to James Burham, 4 Oct 1803).

[54] (1) RG 107, OSW, Military Book, vol. 5, pp. 138–39 (SW to Coxe, 24 May 1811). (2) RG 92, Commissary General of Purchases, Orders Received, No. 246, pp. 23–24 (Eustis to Coxe, 14 and 25 Jun 1811). (3) RG 92, Purveyor, Letters Sent, No. 243, p. 170 (Coxe to postmasters, 10 Jul 1811).

[55] RG 107, OSW, Letters Received, C-13 (6) (Coxe to Eustis, 7 Nov 1811).

RIVER TRANSPORTATION AT CINCINNATI, 1802

The clothing, shoes, equipment, stationary, and hospital stores from
Philadelphia were delivered to the troops stationed at the maritime posts
on coastal vessels, the owners of which contracted to carry the supplies.[56]
Those destined for troops stationed at western posts were sent by way of
two supply routes.   One was from Philadelphia to Pittsburgh, a 300-mile
overland route along which hired wagoners and carters transported supplies when the season permitted.   Only packhorses could bring supplies
though in the winter months.   At Pittsburgh, the Secretary of War ordered
flatboats constructed to transport both troops and supplies to the posts
on the Ohio and Mississippi Rivers.   Such boats were capable of carrying
twenty-five to thirty men and three to four tons of cargo.[57]   Transportation of supplies to posts on the Mississippi by this route was time-
consuming and expensive, so much so that it was more advantageous to
ship by sea to New Orleans.   Until 1803, use of this route was dependent,
however, upon the good will of Spain in granting the United States the
"right of deposit" or permission to pass Army supplies through New
Orleans without payment of duty.

The second route to the western posts ran from New York via
Albany, Schenectady, and Niagara, a route that combined both water
and land transportation for supplies destined for the posts on the Great
Lakes.   While the War Department employed private commercial facili-

---

[56] RG 92, QM Philadelphia, Letter Book, No. 525, p. 78 (Linnard to Dearborn, 11 Sep 1802).
[57] RG 107, OSW, Military Book, vol. 2, pp. 309–10 (SW to Lt. Moses Hook, 21 Mar 1805).

ties to transport supplies to Albany and the Lakes, it used government-owned boats, constructed for the purpose, to transport most supplies on the Lakes.   Two 24-foot yawls, provided with sails and oars, were built to ship supplies from Niagara to Detroit, Michilimackinac, Fort Wayne, and Fort Dearborn.   On the other hand, the government owned no public vessel on Lake Ontario where transportation was obtained by hiring private boats.[58]

At the beginning of this period, when the Secretary of War ordered supplies sent to the Army, the Superintendent of Military Stores arranged for their delivery to posts on the eastern seaboard while the Quartermaster General transported supplies in the west.   Although Quartermaster General John Wilkins was executing the duties assigned to him satisfactorily in 1798, his functions had little in common with those of a Quartermaster General of the Revolutionary War.   When conflict with France loomed as a possibility, the War Department, urged on by Washington and Hamilton, sought and Congress authorized the appointment of a Quartermaster General with the rank, pay, and emoluments of a major general.[59]   The law specifically excluded John Wilkins from appointment to the post, directing instead that he serve as a deputy quartermaster general with the rank of a lieutenant colonel in the event a Quartermaster General was named under the act.   Bearing in mind the qualifications needed in a wartime Quartermaster General, Hamilton wanted the appointment to go to Edward Carrington who had served as deputy quartermaster general to Greene's Southern Army during the Revolution. The President made no appointment under the act, however, and Hamilton was also unsuccessful in his efforts to prod Secretary of War, James McHenry, into developing a better supply organization.[60]   Wilkins continued in office, his status unchanged except that thereafter he apparently enjoyed the pay and emoluments of a major general.[61]

Introduction of Military Agents

More than 20 years had passed since the battle of Yorktown when Congress took under consideration the size of the military establishment

---

[58] *Ibid.*, vol. 1A, pp. 291–93; 300 (Dearborn to Gansevoort, 23 Sep, 5 Oct 1802); 2A, p. 261 (SW to Wm. Hull, 13 May 1805).

[59] (1) 1 *Stat.* 749 (Mar 3, 1799).   (2) *Works of Alexander Hamilton,* ed. Lodge, VII, 36 (Washington to McHenry, draft by Hamilton, 13 Dec 1798).   (3) *American State Papers, Military Affairs,* I, 124–27 (Adams to Congress, 31 Dec 1798, enclosing ltr, McHenry to Adams, 24 Dec 1798).

[60] (1) *Works of Alexander Hamilton,* ed. Lodge, VII, 70–75, 107–10, 125–32 (Hamilton to McHenry, 8 Apr, 19 Aug, 16 Sep 1799).   (2) Steiner, *Life and Correspondence of James McHenry,* 409–10 (McHenry to Hamilton, 29 Aug 1799).

[61] Based on a salary of $166 a month, that of a major general, shown in a report made by President Jefferson to Congress. *American State Papers, Miscellaneous,* I, 308 (17 Feb 1802).

in 1802.   If Congress saw no need to maintain and train more troops, it had even less appreciation of the necessity for staff officers.   An Army of less than 3,000 men required no elaborate supply organization, and in the interests of economy the line could in fact be called upon to do much of its own supply work.   As a consequence, while reducing the strength of the Army, Congress also eliminated the office of Quartermaster General. The Secretary ordered Wilkins to discharge, as soon after 1 April 1802 as possible, all personnel in his Department who did not belong to the line of the Army.   His own services were terminated on the last day of that month.[62]

In place of a Quartermaster General and his train of assistants, Congress provided a system of military agents.   It divided the country into three departments—a Middle, Southern, and Northern Department—each headed by a civilian who, as military agent, was granted a monthly salary of $76.   The President was to appoint at each post that required one an assistant military agent who was to be taken from the line and paid $8 in addition to his regular monthly pay.   Because Pittsburgh and Niagara were the gateways through which military supplies moved for shipment, either via the Ohio River or the Great Lakes, and the duties to be performed were in consequence heavy, the assistant military agents at these two posts were allowed $16 a month in addition to their pay in line.

The use of military agents was not unfamiliar to the War Department.   It had employed agents for the past few years to carry out supply duties in Tennessee and in New York.   Even personnel in the Quartermaster's Department under Wilkins had often been designated as agents rather than quartermasters.   When the capital was moved to Washington in the summer of 1800, the office of the Quartermaster General's agent in Philadelphia was closed.   It still was necessary, however, for the War Department to keep an agent in that city to direct the transportation of all military supplies prepared for distribution by the Superintendent of Military Stores.   Appointed by the Secretary of War, this transportation agent operated under the direction of the Superintendent, who was ordered to keep a record of such expenditures under the head of the Quartermaster's Department.   Upon the Superintendent's recommendation, the Secretary appointed William Linnard.[63]   For the next 34 years, Linnard performed quartermaster duties in Philadelphia for he was appointed military agent in the Middle Department on 5 May 1802 and

[62] (1) 2 *Stat.* 132 (Mar 16, 1802).   (2) RG 107, OSW, Military Book, vol. 1, pp. 161–62 (Dearborn to Wilkins, 18 Mar 1802).

[63] (1) RG 107, OSW, Military Book, vol. 1, p. 99 (SW to William Irvine, 30 Jun 1801). (2) Expenditures in QM and Naval Departments, 313 (Irvine's account, 4th Quarter, 1801). (3) RG 92, Purveyor, Letters Sent, No. 249, p. 29 (Dearborn to Purveyor, 1 Nov 1801).

was reappointed as quartermaster when the Quartermaster's Department was re-established in 1812, serving in that Department until his death in 1835.

The office of the military agent was considered as a substitute for that of a deputy quartermaster general. Of the three agents appointed, Linnard held the most important post. His Department included all posts on the seacoast from Norfolk, Va., to Portsmouth, N. H., inclusive, and from Fort McHenry on the Chesapeake Bay to Vincennes, Massac, Kaskaskia, Chickasaw Bluffs, Fort Adams, and Mobile in the Ohio and Mississippi Valleys. By reason of his location at Philadelphia, his office was in effect a central transportation bureau. He not only forwarded all military supplies to the posts in his Department but he transported all articles procured at Philadelphia for the Northern Department, which was under the direction of Peter Gansevoort, and to the Southern Department, headed by Abraham D. Abrahams. These two agents, because of their great distance from Philadelphia—Gansevoort was stationed at Albany, Abrahams at Savannah—were authorized to purchase supplies at the request of the Purveyor when these could be bought in the vicinity at less expense than they could be transported from Philadelphia. For the most part, such purchases were limited to camp kettles and hospital stores with the Purveyor furnishing the money for such transactions. In addition to transporting military supplies, the three military agents also forwarded all Indian goods intended as annuities, presents, or as articles of commerce. They provided transportation for detachments of troops moving through their departments. Except in cases of urgent necessity, when any repairs were required at posts or fortifications or articles were wanted for the use of the troops the amount of which exceeded $50, the agent had first to apply to the Secretary of War for instructions before taking action. All assistant military agents in their departments, though not appointed by them, were under their direction and accountable to one of the three military agents. For the performance of his duties, each military agent posted a bond of $10,000.[64]

Lieutenants of the line were appointed assistant military agents at the various posts to perform the duties of former quartermasters. Each took charge of the public property at his post and became responsible for disposing of all unnecessary horses or teams, for transporting all military stores and Indian goods to their destinations, for furnishing transportation for any recruits or detachments passing through his district, and for keeping accurate accounts of all expenses with vouchers so that settlement might be made at the office of the military agent. His

[64] RG 107, OSW, Military Book, vol. 1A, pp. 199–206 (SW to Abrahams, Linnard, Gansevoort, 5 May 1802).

purchases were local and limited to providing wood, straw, and forage for the garrison. Except in case of urgent necessity, he made no other purchases without the direction of the military agent within whose Department his post lay. Even wood contracts, at least for the winter months, were arranged at the direction of the military agent. Applications to purchase had to be accompanied with proper estimates, and any that involved sums larger than $50 had to be referred to the Secretary of War.[65]

When the system of military agents was first established in 1802, there were 15 assistant military agents in Linnard's Department, 4 in the Northern Department under Gansevoort, and 2 in the Southern Department under Abrahams. The following year, the United States purchased from France the Louisiana Territory. The Army, with American commissioners, moved into New Orleans and by 1804 the troops had taken over St. Louis and had relieved and replaced the garrisons of the posts in both the Orleans and Upper Louisiana territories. Though the strength of the Army was still below 3,000, the troops were even more widely dispersed than before at a greater number of posts. With troops stationed at New Orleans and at other posts in the area, it became necessary to send a military agent to direct the transportation of supplies to them. The Secretary of War therefore transferred Abrahams from Savannah to New Orleans. The Southern Department was rearranged to include all the posts in the Territory of Orleans and that part of the Mississippi Territory lying south of the 32d degree north latitude. The states of the southern Atlantic coast that had fomerly been under Abraham's control were transferred to Linnard and thereafter formed part of the Middle Department. The Northern Department continued to include as before all the posts in northern New York and on the Great Lakes and, in addition, Fort Wayne.[66]

The procedures utilized in the production of clothing and in the procurement and transportation of supplies continued to be applied with some modifications during the War of 1812, but with the impact of war the supply agencies had to be reorganized. Centralized control and direction of supply by the Secretary of War had one advantageous effect— it eliminated competition for supplies and kept prices low. On the other hand, any delays in the delivery of the annual supply of clothing, stationary, and hospital stores to the troops or any deficiency in the

[65] (1) *Ibid.*, pp. 206–07 (Circular to Asst. Military Agents, 6 May 1802). (2) RG 92, QM Phila., Letter Book, No. 525, pp. 8-9 (Linnard to Lt. J. Saunder, 29 May 1802); p. 63 (Linnard to Lt. Moses Sweitt, 27 Aug 1802).

[66] *American State Papers, Military Affairs*, I, 175-77 (Army Returns). (2) RG 107, OSW, Military Book, vol. 2A, p. 482 (SW to Abrahams, 21 May 1806); vol. 3, pp. 40-41 (SW to Abrahams, 1 Jul 1806), p. 74 (SW to Linnard, 15 Oct 1806).

rations supplied them necessarily meant hardships for the soldiers stationed at frontier posts.[67]   Lines of communication to Philadelphia and Washington were long and hazardous, and any corrective action was usually slow in making itself felt at the post.   As long as peace prevailed and the Army remained small in size, the Secretary of War could and did attend to the most minute details of supply.   He could hope, most of the time, to provision, clothe, and equip the troops satisfactorily, despite the fact that the War Department was vested with a variety of other responsibilities and lacked sufficient personnel to execute all its duties.   Unfortunately, the training of supply officers and the reform of supply organizations that should have been accomplished during these years of peace had to be hastily initiated on the eve of war.   The War Department itself had to be expanded and the supply agencies both in the field and at Philadelphia had not only to be reorganized in 1812 but further refined in 1813 after the country had muddled through the first year of the war.

[67] *American State Papers, Military Affairs*, I, 268 ff. Correspondence of the period and depositions taken in the course of a congressional investigation of the mortality in the troops at New Orleans are revelatory of supply failures and the life of the soldier.

CHAPTER V

Supply in the War of 1812

With the United States drifting into a war it was unprepared to conduct, Congress leisurely inaugurated a reformation of the supply agencies. As early as 1809, the Army and the War Department had accumulated enough experience to convince them that the system of military agents was unsatisfactory. Brig. Gen. James Wilkinson at New Orleans complained that commanding officers could not perform certain services that required expenditures of more than $50 because, except in extraordinary cases, the military agent was limited to that amount. But the commanding officer was not the judge of when a case was extraordinary; instead, the General complained, the military agent, "a man without rank, commission, or a single ray of military information, or experience" made that decision.[1]

Re-establishment of the Quartermaster's Department

Shortly after he became Secretary of War in March 1809, William Eustis suggested to Congress that a new arrangement was required for the conduct of Quartermaster business.[2] Some months later he elaborated more fully on the defects of the existing system and the burden it imposed on the Secretary. The chief defects were a lack of control and an inability to enforce accountability on the part of subordinate military agents that led to large property losses. These defects had originated in the law that provided for Presidential appointment of all military agents. As a result, the three military agents possessed no power over their assistant military agents and were unable to call them to account for malpractices or neglect of duty. Although Congress had also provided for brigade and regimental quartermasters in April 1808, they, too, were not under the control of the military agents. Brigade quartermasters were appointed by the brigadiers and regimental quartermasters by the colonels of the regiments. For lack of an officer to regulate and superintend the distribution of all supplies and to whom all subordinate

---

[1] Wilkinson, *Memoirs of My Own Times*, II, 353 (To SW, 12 May 1809).
[2] *American State Papers, Military Affairs*, I, 244 (Eustis to Chairman Joseph Anderson, 31 May 1809).

officers in his department were accountable, the Secretary of War had been obliged to perform the duties of a Quartermaster General.

In lieu of the system of military agents, Eustis proposed appointment of a Quartermaster General who should have military rank and be aided by an assistant quartermaster general, four deputy quartermasters general, and as many assistant deputy quartermasters as the service required. All of these officers were to be taken from the line. In support of his proposal, he pointed out that this system would provide more regular and rigid accountability, would be less expensive in the long run, and at the same time would instruct officers in a branch of service acknowledged by military men to be one of the first importance.[3]

A bill to establish a Quartermaster's Department died in committee in 1810. Eustis objected to another bill that was drafted the following year because it merged the duties of the clothing department with those of the Quartermaster General, and he thought the two were incompatible.[4] It was December of 1811 before any progress was discernible in the efforts to establish a Quartermaster's Department. Congress finally enacted a law on 28 March 1812, barely 3 months before the organization was to be tested by war.[5] In general, the Department was set up along the lines that the Secretary of War had outlined. At its head was a Quartermaster General with the rank, pay, and emoluments of a brigadier general. To assist him, the law provided for four deputy quartermasters, an additional four deputies if necessary, and as many assistant deputy quartermasters as the public service required.

Immediately upon the passage of the bill, the President appointed Morgan Lewis as Quartermaster General.[6] Lewis and James Madison had been friends since their college days. Lewis, at 57, was much older than any of his predecessors on assuming the duties of that office. Unlike most of them, too, his experience was not in the field of business but of law and politics. He was a lawyer who had served as judge, attorney general, legislator, chief justice of the supreme court of New York, and governor of that state. His military experience had been acquired in the Continental Army. He had served throughout the Revolutionary War, advancing to the rank of colonel. His administrative experience should have made him valuable in organizing the re-established Quartermaster's Department, but he was never much interested in its problems, had a limited view of its functions, preferred the prestige attached to

[3] *Ibid.*, I, 256–57 (Eustis to Chairman W. B. Giles, 1 Jan 1810). See also *ibid.*, I, 257 (Linnard to SW, 15 Sep 1809; 7 Dec 1809); 258 (Col. A. Parker to SW, 29 Nov 1809).

[4] (1) *Annals of Congress*, 11th Cong., 2d sess., vol. 2, pp. 1858, 1879. (2) RG 107, OSW, Reports to Congress, No. 1, p. 149 (SW to Michl. Leib, 2 Jan 1811). National Archives.

[5] 2 *Stat.* 696.

[6] AG 107, OSW, Military Book, vol. 5, pp. 327–28 (SW to Lewis, 4 Apr 1812).

commanding troops, and within a year had relinquished the post of Quartermaster General.[7]

Upon being notified of his appointment in the spring of 1812, Lewis hurried to Washington to consult with the Secretary of War before accepting the office.[8] He objected to some of the provisions of the law establishing the Department because they made the Quartermaster General accountable for all money and property administered by his subordinates without giving him the privilege of selecting them. At the request of the administration, Congress amended the law, relieving the Quartermaster General of accountability. It substituted instead a provision requiring every officer of the Department to post bond for "the faithful expenditure of all public moneys, and accounting for all public property" that might come into his hands. The amendments also provided for clerical help and office rental and repealed a section of the March law that had imposed numerous restrictions on the right of the Quartermaster General to be interested in trade or commerce, ownership of vessels, or purchase of public lands or property. On the other hand, Congress rejected proposals to appoint two assistant quartermasters general and to give the Quartermaster General command in the line according to rank when he was specially assigned for that purpose.[9]

The laws of March and May 1812 provided for other personnel necessary in any Quartermaster organization. They authorized the Quartermaster General to appoint a principal wagonmaster and as many wagonmasters as the service of the Army required, though there was to be no more than one for each brigade. The laws also provided for the appointment of one principal forage master and assistant forage masters, as well as a principal barrack master and deputy barrack masters. They further directed that a corps of artificers be attached to the Quartermaster's Department. It was to consist of a superintendent, 4 assistants, 12 master artisans, 77 artisans, and 24 laborers.[10]

Satisfied that appropriate action would be taken to meet the objections he had made to the law of March 28, 1812, Lewis accepted appointment as Quartermaster General and joined the commander of the Northern Department, Maj. Gen. Henry Dearborn, at his headquarters in Albany on 21 May 1812.[11] In the meantime, the Secretary

---

[7] Two months after he arrived at headquarters, he requested a command, and on 2 March 1813 he was promoted to major general. RG 107, OSW, Letters Received, L–199 (6) (Lewis to SW, 29 Jul 1812).

[8] *Ibid.,* L–78 (6) (Lewis to SW, 17 Apr 1812).

[9] (1) 2 *Stat.* 472 (May 22, 1812). (2) *Annals of Congress,* 12th Cong., 1st sess., vol. 2, pp. 1376, 1378 (May 1, 4, 1812).

[10] 2 *Stat.* 710 (Apr 23, 1812).

[11] RG 107, OSW, Register of Letters Received, vol. 5, p. 139 (Dearborn to SW, 21 May 1812).

of War reappointed the former military agents and assistant military agents as deputy and assistant deputy quartermasters, respectively.   In addition to William Linnard, who continued at Philadelphia as deputy quartermaster, Anthony Lamb became a deputy at Albany, Jacob Eustis at Boston, and William Swan at New Orleans.   The latter was soon replaced by Bartholemew Shaumburgh.   Until the Quartermaster's Department was fully organized and they received new instructions from the Quartermaster General, the Secretary directed these men to continue performing the duties they had executed as military agents.[12]

At Albany, Lewis gave thought to the organization of his Department. "To arrange a Department, Civil or Military," he informed the Secretary, "is a simple business, where you have the necessary officers," but at the end of May he was still waiting to learn what appointments had been made.   For administrative purposes, he proposed dividing the United States into six districts, each to be under the direction of a deputy.   He suggested that their offices be established at Boston, Albany, Trenton, Philadelphia, Washington, and the headquarters of the Western Army. He wished to make New Jersey a separate district, he confided to the Secretary, in order to induce Colonel Rhea, then quartermaster general of that state, to accept appointment in his Department as a deputy quartermaster.   Lewis had not been favorably impressed with Linnard's "talents and competence."   Moreover, he wanted to make that state "the grand Laboratory for the supply of Carriages for the Army." [13]

The Secretary of War accepted the idea of dividing the country into districts, but he expanded the number to eight to correspond with the number of deputies permitted under the law establishing the Department.[14]   He then went on to indicate that the deputies assigned to the first four districts, comprising all the states on the Atlantic seaboard from Virginia northward, would draw funds from, and be accountable to, the Quartermaster General; all the others would draw funds from, and account to, the War Department.   The deputies under the control of the Quartermaster General would establish their offices wherever he

---

[12] RG 107, OSW, Military Book, vol. 5, p. 332 (SW to Linnard *et al.*, 7 Apr 1812); p. 394 (SW to D. Baker *et al.*, 19 May 1812); p. 395 (SW to Col. B. Shaumburgh, 19 May 1812).

[13] RG 107, OSW, Letters Received, L–108 (6) (Lewis to SW, 29 May 1812).

[14] The districts were divided as follows:

1st —the four eastern states (Connecticut, Rhode Island, Massachusetts, and New Hampshire);
2d —New York and Vermont;
3d —New Jersey, Pennsylvana, and Delaware;
4th—Maryland, Virginia, and District of Columbia;
5th—North and South Carolina and Georgia;
6th—Ohio and Michigan Territory;
7th—Kentucky and Tennessee and Indiana, Illinois, and Louisiana Territories;
8th—Louisiana, Florida and Mississippi Territory.

designated; the others would be located by the general commanding the department. Under this arrangement, Lt. Samuel Champlain, for example, was appointed deputy quartermaster in the Southern Department, commanded by Maj. Gen. Thomas Pinckney, with headquarters at Charleston.[15] As Lewis pointed out later, his superintendence of the Quartermaster's Department thus became restricted to the armies north of the Potomac, the Secretary taking under his immediate charge those of the South and Northwest. He gave Lewis no notice of any of their movements nor of the appointment of a single officer.[16] At no time during the war did the Secretary divest his office of more than a part of the Quartermaster duties it had administered before the war.

Creation of Commissary General of Purchases

While these organizational details were being worked out, Congress reorganized other supply agencies. The same law that re-established the Quartermaster's Department abolished the office of the Purveyor of Public Supplies in the Treasury Department, replacing it with the office of the Commissary General of Purchases under the direction of the Secretary of War. Congressional debate indicated that the legislators were seeking precedents in the Revolutionary War. Such an officer had existed then but unfortunately no one now recalled that he had been the head of a Subsistence Department rather than of a Purchasing Department. The law authorized the President to appoint a Commissary General and as many deputy commissaries as the public service required, but the latter were not made subject to military law.

William Jones, a Philadelphia merchant, was appointed to the post on 4 April 1812.[17] After perusing the act, Jones refused the appointment; the salary offered—$3,000 a year—and the restrictions imposed in reference to any connections with trade made acceptance impossible.[18] While the Secretary searched for a man who would accept the office, Congress amended the law to eliminate some of the objectionable restrictive features. Purveyor Tench Coxe had solicited appointment before the bill had been adopted, but he was passed over and, under the terms of the law, went out of office on 1 June.[19] Someone had to direct the business of that office until a Commissary General could be appointed. Secretary Eustis therefore turned to Benjamin Mifflin who had been

---

[15] RG 107, OSW, Military Book, vol. 5, pp. 430-32 (SW to Lewis, 9 June 1812); vol. 6, pp. 85–86 (SW to Champlain, 18 Aug 1812).

[16] RG 107, OSW, Letters Received, L–20 (7) (Lewis to SW John Armstrong, 8 Feb 1813).

[17] RG 107, OSW, Military Book, vol. 5, p. 328 (SW to William Jones).

[18] RG 107, OSW, Letters Received, J–96 (6) (Jones to SW, 11 Apr 1812).

[19] *Ibid.*, C–217 (6) (Coxe to SW, 6 Mar 1812).

serving as chief clerk to Coxe.   Eustis appointed Mifflin a deputy commissary and instructed him to receive all public property transferred to him by Coxe as well as all goods delivered under contracts executed by the former Purveyor.[20]

As though the supply agencies at Philadelphia were not disorganized and demoralized enough, Eustis sent word to the Superintendent of Military Stores that it had been proposed that his office should be merged with the Quartermaster's Department.   Would it be "expedient to urge additional compensation," he queried.[21]   Irvine thought such a merger would result in many and serious disadvantages.   This was the first he had heard of the proposal and he was uncertain of the Secretary's meaning.

> Was it proposed, but afterwards, abandoned, that the office of Supt of Military Stores should be merged in the Q M Department—has it been lately proposed & is now under consideration; or am I to understand that the office is to be totally abolished? [22]

He wanted an immediate explanation to enable him to make suitable arrangements.   Whatver had been intended, nothing more was heard of that proposal.   In the meantime, Quartermaster General Lewis wrote that he hoped the system of the Superintendent and military storekeepers would be continued.   "It renders the Quarter Masters and Issuers an excellent Check on each other." [23]

While Mifflin directed purchases the search for a Commissary General continued.   On 3 July, Samuel Carswell of Philadelphia was appointed to the office.   He was absent from Philadelphia at the time the letter of appointment arrived and did not return until 31 July when he accepted the office.   Five days later, however, after talking to Mifflin and becoming acquainted with the duties of his office, Carswell wrote that he could not accept on account of his health.[24]

Seemingly as a last resort, the Secretary on 8 August offered the post to Callender Irvine, Superintendent of Military Stores.   Irvine accepted on condition that he be permitted to establish his office at Philadelphia.[25]   At Irvine's suggestion, William Linnard applied for the position of Superintendent, but his services as deputy quartermaster were badly

[20] (1) RG 107, OSW, Military Book, vol. 5, p. 407 (SW to Mifflin, 27 May 1812).   (2) RG 92, Commissary General of Purchases (CGP), Miscellaneous, No. 246, p. 59 (Eustis to Mifflin, 29 May 1812).   National Archives.

[21] RG 107, OSW, Military Book, vol. 5, p. 423 (4 June 1812).

[22] RG 107, OSW, Letters Received, I-156 (6) (Irvine to Eustis, 8 Jun 1812).

[23] *Ibid.,* L-128 (6) Enc. (Lewis to Eustis, 26 Jun 1812).

[24] RG 107, OSW, Military Book, vol. 6, p. 7 (SW to Carswell, 3 Jul 1812).   (2) RG 107, OSW, Letters Received, C-403 (6); C-404 (6); C-415 (6) (Carswell to Eustis, 25 Jul, 31 Jul, 5 Aug 1812).

[25] (1) RG 107, OSW, Military Book, vol. 6, p. 71 (SW to Irvine, 8 Aug 1812).   (2) RG 107, OSW, Letters Received, I-226 (6) (Irvine to Eustis, 13 Aug 1812).

needed and William Duncan was appointed instead.[26]   At long last the vacancies in the various supply agencies had been filled.   Congress had established a separate Ordnance Department on 14 May and on 15 July the office of Commissary General of Ordnance had also been filled by the appointment of Col. Decius Wadsworth.[27]

The war with Great Britain had been in progress for almost 2 months before the last of the staff appointments had been made.   Under the circumstances, it is not surprising that Quartermaster General Lewis, who had been promised reports of military stores issued, on hand, and under contract from both the Superintendent and Purveyor on which to base his operations, had received none by the end of May nor even by the middle of June.[28]   By August, when the office of Commissary General of Purchases was finally filled, supply arrangements had deteriorated to such an extent that Lewis complained to the Secretary.

Your Commissary Department embarrasses and paralizes every military operation.   (we know nothing of the state of their preparations; nor does any article, forwarded to this quarter, come accompanied with any thing like an invoice).   Of course we are compelled to unpack every thing at a great expence, and then to repack for their ultimate destination.   There is no remedy but confining that Department to the purchase of Cloathing alone and leave the residue (Hospital Stores, ordnance, Arms & ammunition excepted) exclusively to the Quarter Master Department.   We shall then provide what we want, at the nearest point where required, know at all times what we have, save much expense and more vexation.[29]

Not only were the laws establishing the supply departments enacted so late that their organization could not be completed before the war started, but they were also so poorly drawn that the functions of the agencies were not clearly delineated.   Irvine feared that without particular instructions defining the duties of the Quartermaster General, Commissary General of Ordnance, and Commissary General of Purchases, they would clash in the execution of their duties and retard the public service.[30]   These fears were well founded.

The law authorized the Quartermaster General and his subordinates, when directed by the Secretary of War, "to purchase military stores, camp equipage and other articles requisite for the troops," and, at the same time, ordered the Commissary General of Purchases "to conduct the

[26] (1) RG 107, OSW, Letters Received, L–162 (6) (Linnard to SW, 11 Aug 1812).   (2) RG 107, OSW, Military Book, vol. 6, p. 99 (SW to Duncan, 26 Aug 1812).
[27] (1) 2 *Stat.* 732.   (2) RG 107, OSW, Military Book, vol. 6, p. 28 (SW to Wadsworth, 15 Jul 1812).
[28] (1) RG 107, OSW, Military Book, vol. 5, pp. 377–78 (SW to Lewis, 8 May 1812).   (2) RG 107, OSW, Letters Received, L–108 (6); L–118 (6) Enc. (Lewis to SW, 29 May, 15 Jun 1812).
[29] RG 107, OSW, Letters Received, L–168 (6) (Lewis to SW, 7 Aug 1812).
[30] *Ibid.*, I–232 (6) (Irvine to SW, 20 Aug 1812).

procuring and providing of all arms, military stores, clothing, and generally all articles of supply requisite for the military service." [31]   Lewis, like Irvine, was at a loss to know what his functions were.   He found himself transacting the duties of every other department, even to the arming of vessels on Lake Champlain.[32]   The Secretary attempted to distinguish between the duties of commissaries and quartermasters.   In general, the commissaries were to make the purchases; the quartermasters were to receive and issue.   When the commissary could not make purchases on a reasonable basis because he was too far away or for any other reason, then the quartermaster was to purchase.[33]   In May, the Secretary had also instructed Lewis that in the course of service, losses and deficiencies might be experienced in the clothing and subsistence departments.   In that case, if the proper officer was not at hand, the Quartermaster General was authorized to procure the supplies necessary for "the accommodation and comfort of the Troops." [34]   The Secretary increased confusion when he issued a regulation in May covering the duties of the general staff.   The Quartermaster General found it was his function among other duties "to ensure a supply of provisions and a regular distribution thereof to the troops."   If, he inquired, this has not "crept in by accident, I wish to know, as the Army is supplied with provisions by contract (the worst of all possible modes) what it means." [35]

Lack of a Subsistence Department

The procurement of subsistence was not a function of the Quartermaster's Department.   Contractors supplied rations.   In legislating for the supply departments, neither the War Department nor Congress had given any thought to the establishment of a Subsistence Department. Taking no cognizance of all the criticism that had been leveled against subsistence contractors, they relied upon the contract system to supply the troops in war as it had in the years since 1781.   Before war was declared, the Secretary had executed contracts to supply the troops with rations for the year 1812.   For purposes of administration, the states and territories had been grouped into districts, and each contractor supplied a given district.   These districts, however, did not coincide with the military districts established later in 1813.   Despite the War Hawks' incessant cry of "Canada! Canada! Canada!," none of these contracts made provision

---

[31] 2 *Stat.* 690 (Mar 28, 1812).

[32] RG 107, OSW, Letters Received, L–181 (6) (Lewis to SW, 4 Sep 1812).

[33] RG 107, OSW, Military Book, vol. 5, pp. 430–32 (SW to Lewis, 9 Jun 1812).

[34] *Ibid.,* vol. 5, pp. 377–78 (SW to Lewis, 8 May 1812).

[35] (1) RG 107, OSW, Letters Received, L–181 (6) (Lewis to SW, 4 Sep 1812).   (2) RG 94, AGO, General Orders, 1812–17 (Regulation, 4 May 1812).

for supplying an Army that might invade the territory of the enemy if war occurred.

As in the past, the commanding officer could take matters into his own hands if the contractor failed to make deliveries. Obviously though, if the contractor failed to supply because food was scarce, transportation inadequate, or simply because he would lose money on the transaction, the agent appointed by the commanding officer to make good the deficiency would be able to do so only at enormous expense. "It is madness in the extreme to attempt to carry on war with such a system," wrote Lt. Col. Thomas S. Jesup, who within a few years was to become Quartermaster General. Either the contractors should be dismissed or made amenable to military law, and Jesup would have included not only the contractor's agent who accompanied the Army, "but the whole tribe from the principal, wheresoever he may reside, to the humblest bullock driver or scalesman." [36]

During the War of 1812, as in the Revolutionary War, the soldier and officer alike supplemented Army rations with such commodities as they could afford to buy from the sutler. The latter offered fresh vegetables, fruits, coffee, liquor, and tobacco at greatly enhanced prices. Such prices did not entirely result from his desire to gouge profits. Because the troops were paid irregularly, the sutler encouraged them to buy on credit, but he had no means of compelling payment of the debts contracted. The sutler often sustained heavy losses by the death or desertion of an indebted soldier. In consequence, his high prices covered that risk as well as the expense he incurred in purchasing his wares on long credit.[37] The War Department pursued no consistent policy of licensing sutlers but generally they were regulated by Army officers.

So much criticism of the contract system continued to be voiced that, in March 1813, Congress attempted to modify the system by authorizing the President to appoint special commissaries or to designate any officer of the Quartermaster's Department to procure and issue subsistence in all cases where deficiencies developed through the failure of the contractor to supply the troops. Such special commissaries were to be entitled to the pay and emoluments of a deputy quartermaster general.[38]

Before the end of the war, John C. Calhoun, then a member of the House of Representatives, offered resolutions directing an inquiry into the expediency of changing the system of subsisting the Army.[39] The

---

[36] Jesup Papers, Box 1 (Jesup to Col. ——, 8 Sep 1814). Manuscript Div., Library of Congress.

[37] *American State Papers, Military Affairs,* I, 806 (Rpt, Surgeon General Lovell to Calhoun, 16 Nov 1818).

[38] 2 *Stat.* 817 (Mar 3, 1813).

[39] *Annals of Congress,* 13th Cong., 3d sess., vol. 3, pp. 550–51 (Nov 10, 1814).

resolutions were adopted, and in response to an inquiry of the Committee on Military Affairs, James Monroe, Secretary of War, replied in favor of a commissariat. In support of his position, he forwarded the views of Maj. Gen. Winfield Scott, Maj. Gen. Edmund P. Gaines, and Col. John R. Fenwick. These were severely denunciatory of the contract system.[40] The House passed a bill providing for the establishment of a commissariat, and it was under consideration in the Senate when the end of the war caused its indefinite postponement.[41]

Supply of Clothing

Except for its transportation, supplying troops with clothing was not a function of the Quartermaster's Department. Clothing for an expanding Army on the eve of war was procured under contract by the Purveyor and, for the troops during the war, by his successor, the Commissary General of Purchases. When Congress expanded the size of the Army in January 1812, Secretary Eustis informed Tench Coxe that 20,000 uniforms would be required in addition to those for the existing military establishment. By great exertions, Coxe managed to complete these preparations in the usual 5-month period it had taken in the past to get the annual clothing supply ready for a smaller Army.[42] In February, Congress added another 25,000 men to the Army, and Secretary Eustis ordered Coxe to begin purchasing clothing for that number. He was to solicit bids through newspaper advertisements. Eustis also directed Coxe to distribute the purchases and the manufacture of the clothing in Pennsylvania, New York, Connecticut, and Massachusetts in order that preparations might be expedited and the finished clothing delivered at or near the places where it would be required by the recruits. He instructed Coxe to select proper representatives in these states to make the purchases.[43]

Coxe worked diligently, but he was seemingly unable to depart from the established routine of supply preparation at Philadelphia because he neither advertised in the newspapers nor appointed purchasing agents as directed. By 21 March, under War Department prodding, seven agencies of the Purveyor's office were set up at Exeter, N.H., Boston, Mass., Providence, R.I., Middletown, Conn., Baltimore, Md., and New York and Albany, N.Y., but Coxe still thought it would take at least

[40] American State Papers, Military Affairs, I, 599–601.

[41] Annals of Congress, 13th Cong., 3d sess., vol. 3, pp. 228–30, 232, 234, 236, 1101, 1131.

[42] (1) RG 107, OSW, Military Book, vol. 5, p. 262 (SW to Coxe, 15 Jan 1812). (2) RG 107, OSW, Letters Received, C–213 (6) (Coxe to Eustis, 18 Mar 1812).

[43] (1) RG 107, OSW, Military Book, vol. 5, pp. 273–74 (Eustis to Coxe, 14 Feb 1812). (2) RG 92, CGP, Miscellaneous, No. 246, p. 44 (Eustis to Coxe, 19 Feb 1812).

3 months to get most of the clothing ready and that the supply would not include woolens. The Secretary's expectations of an early and good supply of cloth, he thought, were "too sanguine." [44]

The Secretary sent Lt. Col. John Chrystie to Philadelphia to expedite the clothing supply. Late in March, he advised that nothing was ready for the new Army, but Coxe was not idle and within 3 weeks Chrystie was reporting that supplies were daily pouring into storage.[45] To the additional uniforms needed for an expanded regular Army, there was soon added the clothing required by the militia called into the service of the United States and by the volunteer corps whose service the President was authorized to accept. By law, the volunteers were to receive in lieu of clothing a sum of money equal to the cost of the clothing provided for noncommissioned officers and privates in the regular Army. In actual practice, both the militia and the volunteers received clothing provided by the Commissary General of Purchases, the cost of which was deducted from their pay.[46]

It is surprising that Coxe accomplished as much as he did for his organization was wholly inadequate to the demands made upon his office. He had only three clerks to help him yet he was responsible not only for the procurement of clothing but of all other Army supplies except subsistence. He employed some 5,000 tailors and seamstresses in making garments. As the supply poured into the Philadelphia Arsenal, Coxe lamented that there was but a single government cart to haul supplies to and from the Arsenal and that there were but two packing presses and only a few hands to pack clothing for shipment to the recruits.[47]

Under pressure to supply clothing rapidly and handicapped by lack of help, Coxe during these months must have been further harassed by the uncertainty of whether he would be retained in office. He sought appointment in the proposed Commissary Department. When Congress abolished the Purveyor's Office, however, the Secretary of War dismissed him with thanks for his "zeal and fidelity" barely 2 weeks before war was declared against Great Britain.[48]

[44] (1) RG 107, OSW, Military Book, vol. 5, pp. 291, 297–98 (Eustis to Coxe, 6 and 12 Mar 1812). (2) RG 107, OSW, Letters Received, C–213 (6) (Coxe to Eustis, 18 Mar 1812). (3) RG 92, Purveyor, Letters Sent, No. 243, p. 392 (Coxe to Eustis, 8 Mar 1812); pp. 414–15 (Coxe to Chrystie, 21 Mar 1812).

[45] RG 107, OSW, Letters Received, C–222 (6) C–245 (6) (Chrystie to SW, 23 Mar and 11 Apr 1812).

[46] (1) RG 107, OSW, Military Book, vol. 6, p. 251 (SW to Gen. Harrison, 16 Dec 1812); p. 252 (SW to Gov. of Penn., 16 Dec 1812). (2) The provision of clothing to the militia and to the volunteers was governed respectively by the act of 2 January 1795 and 6 February 1812. 1 Stat. 498; 2 Stat. 676.

[47] (1) RG 107, OSW, Letters Received, C–253 (6) (Coxe to Eustis, 14 Apr 1812). (2) RG 92, Purveyor, Letters Sent, No. 243, pp. 471–72 (Coxe to Lt. Col. Winder, 11 Apr 1812).

[48] RG 107, OSW, Military Book, vol. 5, p. 423 (Eustis to Coxe, 4 Jun 1812).

In the past, Coxe had obtained clothing by furnishing government-owned materials to master tailors who contracted to produce complete uniforms for one or more regiments. The master tailor not only used his own workmen but also employed the services of subcontractors to complete such a contract. In 1812 the Deputy Commissary General of Purchases, acting on the advice of Callender Irvine, introduced modifications that were followed for many years after the war. As long ago as 1808, Irvine had argued that it would be to the advantage of the government to have all Army clothing cut out at the Arsenal before it was issued to the tailors. Convinced that government-owned materials had in the past been stolen and that many thousand dollars annually would be saved "in a certain article termed by the Tailors *Cabbage*," Irvine was also certain that the new method would provide greater uniformity in cut and a better sizing of garments.[49]

When Irvine became Commissary General of Purchases, he concentrated both the cutting and inspection of clothing in a building he rented for that purpose in Philadelphia, carting the finished clothing to the more distant Arsenal only when it was ready to be packed for shipment. He thereby reduced expenses and brought the whole operation more closely under his supervision. He obtained the necessary rental money from the sale of the waste fabric left over after the uniforms had been cut.[50]

In the fall of 1812, Irvine tried to improve other phases of production. Clothing was botched in the making, he charged, because the contractors or master tailors pocketed a good round sum annually, but the poor who were employed in actually making the clothing were "pinched almost to death." Their necessities were such that they were compelled to make the clothing at whatever prices the contractors were disposed to grant. These, Irvine charged, were scarcely enough "to give them salt for their mush." The inspector ought to have rejected poorly made garments, but Irvine accused him of having a perfect understanding with the contractors. The result was that ill-made garments were sent to the troops. Irvine therefore requested the Secretary to remove the inspector and to approve his plan to eliminate the master tailors by employing two or three men to issue cut-out garments directly to those who made them and to give these makers a just price.[51] With the

[49] (1) RG 107, OSW, Letters Received, I–198 (6) (Irvine to SW, 15 Jul 1812). (2) RG 92, Supt. of Military Stores, Letters Sent, No. 398, pp. 318–19 (Irvine to Coxe, 15 Nov 1808). (3) Coxe had rejected the proposal because Purveyor Whelen had tried and abandoned the method several years earlier. RG 92, Purveyor, Letters Sent, No. 248, pp. 33–34 (Coxe to Irvine, 15 Nov 1808).

[50] (1) RG 92, CGP, Letters Sent, No. 381, p. 13 (Irvine to SW, 2 Sep 1812). (2) RG 92, CGP, Letters Received from SW, No. 190, p. 4 (Eustis to Irvine, 5 Sep 1812).

[51] For example, the contract of a master tailor gave him 65 cents for making a round jacket with sleeves, but he allowed the actual maker only 37 cents. By paying the issuer 5 cents a

Secretary's approval, he immediately put this system into effect. He appointed new inspectors and drafted regulations to govern the operations of the Philadelphia clothing establishment.[52]

In 1812, Irvine had a clothing establishment functioning at Philadelphia that was capable of turning out 2,000 to 3,000 suits per week. By the winter of the following year, he employed 3,000 to 4,000 people.[53] Deputy commissaries in other areas also procured considerable quantities of cloth and clothing. They had replaced the former purchasing agents of the Purveyor's office.[54] They purchased whatever cloth of domestic manufacture they could find that met their needs even to drab and mixed cloths, and they scoured the markets for any imported textiles. Unfortunately, the quality of the cloth and the clothing they procured by no means equalled the high standards that Irvine was attempting to set at Philadelphia, and there were numerous complaints from the troops.

Irvine attributed much of the difficulty to the law that allowed a commission of $2\frac{1}{2}$ percent on the money the deputy commissary disbursed, though limited the total sum to be paid him to no more than $2,000. Irvine feared that the "disposition to purchase largely & secure the commission" of $2,000 a year was so strong as to induce the commissaries to overlook the quality and the prices of the goods. He thought it highly desirable to give them fixed salaries, assign them to designated districts, and make them subject to military law so that they might be ordered to any part of their districts.[55] This particular reform, however, was not effected. By the spring of 1814, Irvine was promising to have the greater part of the clothing "made in future under my own Eye."[56] In an effort to improve the quality of the clothing, he determined to set

garment, the maker under Irvine's plan could be paid 60 cents, or enough to satisfy his hunger and enable him to do his work well. RG 107, OSW, Letters Received, I-365 (6) (Irvine to SW, 24 Nov 1812).

[52] (1) RG 107, OSW, Military Book, vol. 6, p. 239 (SW to Irvine, 25 Nov 1812). (2) RG 92, CGP, Letters Sent, No. 381, p. 226 (Irvine to Francis Brown, 5 Dec 1812), p. 284 (Irvine to Inspector Wm. McIlhenney, 12 Jan 1813).

[53] RG 92, CGP, Letters Sent, No. 381, p. 94 (Irvine to Eustis, 6 Oct 1812); No. 384, pp. 171–72 (Irvine to Wm. James, 22 Nov. 1814).

[54] Among the first deputies appointed were the following: John Langdon at Portsmouth, N.H., Elisha Tracy at Norwich, Conn., William Jarvis at Wethersfield, Vt., Amasa Stetson at Boston, Mass., Samuel Russell at New York, Hansom Kelly at Wiilmington, N.C., John Stith at Petersburg, Va., Benjamin Cudworth at Charleston, S.C., John Cummings at Savannah, Ga., Thomas Buford at Lexington, Ky., John McKinney at Washington, and Benjamin Morgan at New Orleans.

[55] (1) RG 107, OSW, Letters Received, I–370 (6) (Irvine to Eustis, 4 Dec 1812). (2) 2 *Stat.* 696 (Mar 28, 1812). (3) Jackson charged the deputy commissary general at New Orleans governed his purchases to make sure of his salary. See RG 92, Coxe and Irvine Papers, Box 34 (Robert Butler, AG at New Orleans, to Monroe, 17 Feb 1815).

[56] RG 92, CGP, Letters Sent, No. 383, pp. 319–20 (Irvine to SW Armstrong, 13 May 1814).

Musician, Company Officer and Private,
Winter Field Uniform

Sergeant,
Dress Uniform

18th U.S. Infantry, 1814–1815

up a clothing establishment at Albany similar to the one at Philadelphia. The war ended, however, before it could be put into operation.[57]

Despite the difficulties of procurement and production, Irvine was satisfied that he had furnished sufficient garments to clothe the troops in the winter of 1812–13. Yet frequent complaints were made that companies had not received their supply of clothing. In some cases, deliveries had gone astray as companies were moved to other stations. In other instances, the lack of clothing was attributable to the fine aesthetic sense of certain commanding officers that forbade their accepting for their regiments coats made of drab cloth; that is, brown coats faced with red. In mid-October, they apparently preferred to risk the health of their men by keeping them in linen jackets. Seeking the aid of General Dearborn, Irvine argued in terms reminiscent of those used by Tench Coxe—that color was of minor importance to the health of the men and besides "some allowance should be made for existing circumstances & some consideration had for the troops in other quarters." [58]

Like his predecessor, Tench Coxe, Commissary General Irvine discovered that separation of the procurement and the distribution of clothing and other military supplies had the effect of leaving him totally uninformed as to the state of the stores that he and his deputies had provided. It was indispensably necessary that storekeepers make monthly reports to his office, showing the receipt and issue of stores and stating from whom they were received, to whom issued, and by what authority.[59] Irvine complained that if he called for a statement of stores it was either incorrect or furnished so long after it had been requested that it was of little use to him. Early in 1813, he proposed that the Superintendent of Military Stores be relieved of directing the issue of supplies for the Army and that all storekeepers be ordered to make periodical reports to his office.[60] As a result, the Secretary of War made the Commissary General of Purchases responsible thereafter not only for providing supplies but also for their storage and distribution. The Superintendent of Military Stores and the military storekeepers were brought under his control, and all orders for the transportation of military stores by the Quartermaster's Department issued from his office.[61]

With the Quartermaster's Department in the process of being organized, it was undobutedly true that some transportation orders were not promptly executed. Irvine charged that clothing had been permitted

[57] *Ibid.*, No. 384, p. 200 (Irvine to Wm. James, 14 Dec 1814).

[58] *Ibid.*, No. 381, p. 118 (Irvine to Dearborn, 18 Oct 1812); p. 120 (Irvine to Adj. Gen. Cushing, 16 Oct 1812).

[59] *Ibid.*, No. 381, p. 99 (Irvine to Eustis, 8 Oct 1812).

[60] *Ibid.*, No. 38, pp. 283–84 (Irvine to SW Monroe, 18 Jan 1813).

[61] RG 107, OSW, Military Book, vol. 6, pp. 275–76 (SW to Irvine, 30 Jan 1813).

to remain at Albany, for example, instead of being forwarded to its destinations. Quartermasters, however, had found it somewhat difficult to forward supplies. Quartermaster General Lewis reported that there was too much inaccuracy in invoices, and that storekeepers followed no system of numbering invoices so that they could be identified with the parcels to which they belonged. The resultant confusion had serious consequences, such as tents being forwarded for clothing and camp kettles for cartouche boxes.[62] Deputy Quartermaster Linnard had received three sets of invoices requiring delivery of clothing for one company to be made at three different places many miles apart. Where, he inquired of the Superintendent of Military Stores, was the company stationed? It would make conveyance easier and less expensive, he suggested, if all clothing for recruits could be sent to the headquarters of the district and issued to the respective rendezvous in the military district by the commanding officers.[63]

Much clothing had been lost because it arrived at a recruiting district after the latter had been broken up. With no officer on hand to receive it, the wagoner, unauthorized to bring it back to the Philadelphia Arsenal, was likely to deposit the clothing with a private citizen at the delivery point. There it remained uncalled for and unused.[64] Moreover, in time, it became apparent that officers on recruiting service generally called for too much clothing. To furnish a recruit with a 6 months' to a year's supply of clothing and to give him arms and accoutrements while he was still at a recruiting rendezvous inevitably resulted in abuses and losses. Irvine later charged that the destruction of arms so issued was "beyond belief" and that the injudicious issue of clothing had caused the government a loss of between half a million and a million dollars.[65]

It was just this waste, the total lack of any system of accountability, the fact that clothing had been issued on the requisition of any officer—a subaltern officer could go into a public store and "turn it inside out"—that led Irvine to urge the appointment of issuing commissaries as early as the fall of 1812.[66] In addition, requisitions for clothing had been so loosely handled that Irvine charged that great waste had occurred. In one instance, three officers of the same regiment had made requisitions for the clothing of that regiment on three officers of the Commissary

[62] RG 92, CGP, Letters Sent, No. 381, pp. 108–09 (Irvine to Wm. Duncan, 12 Oct 1812).

[63] RG 92, QM Phila., Letter Book, 1812–13, No. 528, p. 321 (Linnard to Wm. Duncan, 2 Jan 1813).

[64] Ibid., No. 528, p. 233 (Linnard to Wm. Duncan, 5 Nov 1812).

[65] RG 92, CGP, Letters Sent, No. 384, pp. 265–66 (Irvine to Maj. R. H. Macpherson, 7 Feb 1815).

[66] Ibid., No. 381, pp. 99, 293 (Irvine to SW, 8 Oct 1812 and 22 Jan 1813).

Department.[67]   The lack of regularity in keeping clothing accounts had resulted in some troops receiving more than they were entitled to.   The consequence was that they "trafficked away the surplus."

In response to suggestions by the Secretary of War, Congress early in 1813 initiated action to provide greater accountability on the part of supply officers.   For this purpose, it abolished the office of Superintendent of Military Stores, the function of which had already been partially absorbed by the office of the Commissary General of Purchases, and created instead a Superintendent General of Military Supplies who was to reside at the seat of government.   He was not a staff officer but a civilian to whom was entrusted the duty of keeping proper accounts of all military stores and supplies purchased for the Army, the volunteers, and the militia.   He was to prescribe the forms of all the returns and accounts of the stores and supplies purchased, on hand, distributed, used, or sold that were to be rendered by the Commissary General of Purchases, the Quartermaster General, the Commissary General of Ordnance, the regimental quartermasters, the officers of the hospital and medical departments, and any other officer to whom supplies were entrusted.[68]   William Duncan, the former Superintendent of Military Stores, applied for the new office, but the appointment went to Richard Cutts on 5 April 1813.[69]

In the same law, Congress also authorized the President to appoint six assistant commissaries to receive clothing and other supplies from the deputy commissaries and distribute them to the regimental quartermasters for issue to the troops.   The law was passed in March, but it was July before the Secretary of War recurred to the need to appoint issuing commissaries, and it was 7 August before he instructed Irvine to appoint such officers at Niagara, Sackett's Harbor, Lake Champlain, and New Orleans, and with the troops under Generals Harrison and Pinckney.[70]   By the following month, Irvine had made some of these appointments.   He developed requisition forms and instructed issuing commissaries to make delivery only on the basis of actual strength.[71]

Compliance with the new procedures was difficult to obtain.   The system of issuing commissaries did check some of the abuses in clothing supply, but Irvine maintained that it did not go far enough.   In the fall of 1814, he outlined a system for the supply and issue of clothing

---

[67] *Ibid.*, No. 381, p. 362 (Irvine to Dearborn, 28 Feb 1813).

[68] 2 *Stat.* 816–17, Mar 3, 1813).

[69] (1) RG 107, OSW, Letters Received, D–79 (7) (Duncan to SW, 21 Mar 1813).   (2) RG 107, OSW, Military Book, vol. 6, p. 347 (SW to Cutts, 5 Apr 1813).

[70] RG 107, OSW, Military Book, vol. 7, pp. 23, 33 (SW to Irvine, 25 Jul and 7 Aug 1813).

[71] RG 92, CGP, Letters Sent, No. 382, pp. 280–281 (Irvine to SW, 2 Sep 1813); No. 383, pp. 1–2 (Irvine to James E. Herron *et al.*, 23 Oct 1813); pp. 199–200 (Irvine to Samuel Russell *et al.*, 28 Feb 1814).

under which the cost of an annual supply of clothing for each soldier
would be added to his pay.   Instead of encumbering the soldier with
half a year's clothing at a time, as had been the custom, Irvine proposed
placing issues on a monthly basis.   At each muster or monthly inspection,
the inspector would report to the paymaster the amount of clothing
required by each man.   The paymaster would direct it to be furnished
and deduct the costs of the clothing from the soldier's pay.   The clothing
would be obtained from a general depot of clothing that would be
established in each military district under an issuing commissary.[72]
Before any action could be taken on this proposal, however, the war ended.

Reorganization of the Quartermaster's Department

At the same time that Congress, early in 1813, was attempting to
introduce a greater degree of accountability among supply personnel, it
was also legislating to improve the organization of the general staff.
When John Armstrong became Secretary of War in January 1813, he
received numerous complaints on the shortcomings of the staff departments.   General Dearborn insisted that improvement in the Quartermaster's Department was an absolute necessity; otherwise it would be
"utterly impossible for an Army to perform an active campaign with
any probability of success." [73]   William Linnard felt that it was incumbent upon him to seek out the new Secretary and point out some of the
defects of the Quartermaster's Department.   The Quartermaster General
himself gave the Secretary the benefit of his ideas on the reforms required
in his Department.[74]   If the Quartermaster General was to perform field
duties, he argued, it was impossible for him to attend to more than one
grand army.   Lewis therefore proposed that each army have either a
principal Quartermaster officer attending it, or that the Quartermaster
General have an assistant, with suitable rank and powers, attached to
each army.

The result was that, on 3 March 1813, Congress passed an act for
the better organization of the general staff of the Army.[75]   It caused
radical changes in the organization of the Quartermaster's Department.
Under the new arrangement, the Department had a staff of 8 quartermasters general, 8 deputy quartermasters general, and 23 assistant deputy
quartermasters general.   The chief of the Department, attached to the
principal army, had the brevet rank and pay and emoluments of a

---

[72] *Ibid.*, No. 384, pp. 176–178 (Irvine to SW, 25 Nov 1814).

[73] RG 107, OSW, Letters Received, D–27 (7) (28 Jan 1813).

[74] (1) RG 92, QM Phila., Letter Book, 1812–13, No. 528, unpaged (Linnard to Lt. H. Johnson, 30 Jan 1813).   (2) RG 107, OSW, Letters Received, L–20 (7) (Lewis to SW, 8 Feb 1813).

[75] 2 *Stat.* 819.

brigadier general. All the other quartermasters general were granted the brevet rank and the pay and emoluments of colonels of infantry. The deputy and the assistant deputy quartermasters general had the brevet rank and the pay and emoluments of majors of cavalry and captains of infantry, respectively. The law authorized the President to take these officers from the line or not, as he thought expedient. The law retained the former provision for forage, wagon, and barrack masters, but they were to be appointed under the direction of the Secretary of War by each quartermaster general attached to a separate army, command, or one of the nine military districts into which the country was divided for administrative purposes. The latter were also to employ as many artificers, mechanics, and laborers as were required.[76]

Two and a half weeks after Congress had enacted this legislation, Robert Swartwout was appointed to succeed Morgan Lewis as head of the Quartermaster's Department.[77] Swartwout was a New York merchant whose business experience, it was hoped, would enable him to overcome some of the difficulties that had been encountered in supplying the troops. His military experience had been confined to militia service, and at the time of his appointment he was serving as a colonel in the New York militia. As head of the Department, he was stationed at Albany in the 9th military district, but he did not control the Quartermaster's Department any more than Lewis had before him. Except for the preparation of estimates that included all forces, his activities were restricted to Quartermaster support of the Army in the 9th District. Orders to the quartermasters general did not issue from his office but from that of the Secretary of War. Each quartermaster general operated independently of every other and consequently no greater degree of control or co-ordination was introduced in 1813 than had existed in 1812.

Like his predecessor, Swartwout assumed the duties of his office at a time when the Department was being reorganized, and he, too, was discouraged by his inability to obtain promptly from the War Department the names of the deputies and assistants appointed under the new law.[78] He was more fortunate than Lewis in receiving immediately upon his appointment a minutely detailed regulation covering the duties of his Department and clarifying its purchase responsibilities.[79] These duties

---

[76] For the personnel of the reorganized Department see *American State Papers, Military Affairs,* I, 389.

[77] RG 107, OSW, Military Book, vol. 6, p. 358 (SW to Swartwout, 21 Mar 1813).

[78] RG 107, OSW, Letters Received, S–169 (7) (Swartwout to SW, 27 Apr 1813).

[79] (1) Swartwout Papers, Box 1. Manuscript Collection, N.Y. Public Library. This regulation was appended to the letter of appointment dated 21 Mar 1813. (2) See also *American State Papers, Military Affairs,* I, 425 ff., for the rules and regulations of the Army, 1 May 1813, which includes the same regulation for the Quartermaster's Department.

apparently held no great interest for him for within a year Swartwout offered his resignation.[80]   Secretary of War Armstrong did not accept it, and Swartwout continued in office until the end of the war brought still another reorganization of the Department.

Transportation of Supplies

While the organization of the Department was altered and new appointments were made in the midst of the war, quartermasters carried out their basic function of transporting men and supplies, employing methods that differed in no way from those used in the Revolutionary War.   In the Army itself, supplies and baggage moved in wagons, manned by civilian teamsters or soldiers detailed from the line, under the direction of wagonmasters.   On the supply lines, clothing, equipment, medical supplies, and military stores were transported in wagons which quartermasters hired for the purpose.   To prevent loss, such supplies were usually placed under the care of conductors who accompanied the wagons. Where wagons could not be used, and particularly in the winter months, quartermasters hired packhorses and in some areas used sleds.   To save transportation costs, quartermasters moved supplies as much as possible by water routes.

As compared with the cost of water transportation, land freights were excessive.   When flour could be carried to Boston by boat in 1810, it cost 75 cents a barrel more than it did in New York City, but when British cruisers closed the Sound in 1813 and 1814, the difference was $5.03.[81]   Linnard regularly shipped supplies from Philadelphia to Albany by a commercial line that transported by land and water via Trenton and Amboy, keeping inside Staten Island to New York City.   There the assistant deputy quartermaster received the supplies and shipped them north on one of the Albany packets.[82]

War increased enormously the cost of the overland haul from Philadelphia to Pittsburgh.   At the latter place, the assistant quartermaster hired barges and keelboats to carry supplies down the Ohio and Mississippi.   Before the end of the war, the War Department entered into a contract with Robert Fulton to transport troops and munitions in steamboats on the Ohio and Mississippi.   A warrant for $40,000 under this contract was issued to Fulton in January 1815.   Though Fulton died about a month later, the Secretary requested Col. James Morrison to furnish him

[80] RG 94, AGO, Letters Received (Swartwout to Armstrong, 1 Apr 1814).

[81] Victor S. Clark, *History of Manufacturers in the United States* (Washington, 1916), pp. 335, 337–38.

[82] RG 92, QM Phila., Letters Sent, No. 531 (Linnard to Lewis, 30 Jan 1812).

a report on the time required for a steamboat trip from Pittsburgh to New Orleans, the number of troops a steamboat could carry, and, in general, the usefulness of such boats in transporting on the rivers. The Secretary directed the deputy quartermaster at New Orleans to utilize steamboats in all cases where their use would be more economical than the usual mode of transportation.[83] By that time, however, the war had ended, and there is no evidence that the Quartermaster's Department transported any supplies in steamboats during the War of 1812, even though some steamboats were in use on the Hudson and Fulton's competitor operated one on Lake Champlain during the war years.[84]

Preparation for Hull's Campaign

Quartermaster wartime supply operations could not wait either on the organization of the Quartermaster's Department in 1812 or its reorganization in 1813. War had in fact been declared against Great Britain on 18 June 1812 before the supply agencies required for the support of the Army were fully organized and staffed. War plans called for an invasion of Canada and the capture of Montreal, with the principal attack being launched by way of Lake Champlain from a base at Albany. Supporting movements were to be directed from Sackett's Harbor, Niagara, and Detroit.

The first events of the war developed in the West where the war spirit had long been running high. In response to President Madison's request, Return Jonathan Meigs, Governor of Ohio, called for 1,200 volunteers from the militia on 6 April, 2½ months before war was declared. More than the required number of men appeared at the rendezvous near Dayton before the end of the month. They were joined at Urbana by the 4th U.S. Infantry, that had been garrisoned at Vincennes. Governor William Hull of Michigan, a former Revolutionary War officer, was persuaded to take command of the troops and did so on 25 May. He appointed James Taylor his quartermaster general.

Taylor had been serving for some years as military agent in the state of Kentucky. When establishment of the office of Commissary General of Purchases was under debate early in 1812, Taylor solicited appointment in the Purchasing Department but the Secretary of War rejected his application.[85] In the meantime, he continued to carry out the

---

[83] (1) RG 107, OSW, Military Book, vol. 8, p. 17 (SW to Fulton, 11 Jan 1815); pp. 44–45 (SW to Morrison, 13 Feb 1815). (2) RG 107, OSW, Letters Sent to Quartermaster General and Purchasing Department, p. 31 (SW to Col. Simeon Knight, 13 Mar 1815).

[84] Seymour Dunbar, *A History of Travel in America* (New York, 1937), 382 ff.

[85] RG 107, OSW, Letters Received, T–71 (6) Enc. (Taylor to Eustis, 8 Feb 1812).

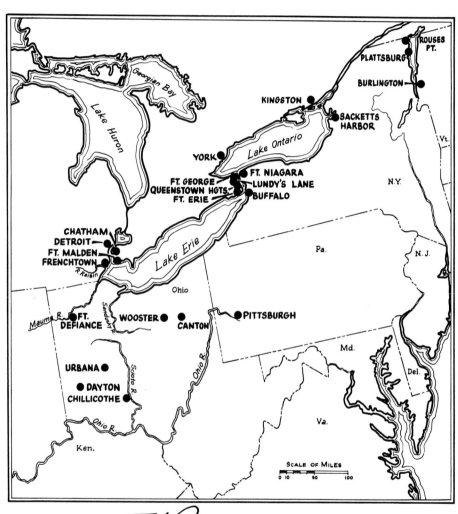

Georgian Bay

Lake Huron

Lake Ontario

ROUSES PT.

PLATTSBURG

BURLINGTON

KINGSTON

SACKETTS HARBOR

YORK

FT. NIAGARA

FT. GEORGE

LUNDY'S LANE

QUEENSTOWN HGTS.

FT. ERIE

BUFFALO

N.Y.

Vt.

CHATHAM

DETROIT

FT. MALDEN

FRENCHTOWN

R. Raisin

Lake Erie

Pa.

N.J.

Ohio

FT. DEFIANCE

Maume R.

Sandusky R.

WOOSTER

CANTON

PITTSBURGH

Md.

Del.

URBANA

Scioto R.

DAYTON

CHILLICOTHE

Ohio R.

Va.

Ohio R.

Ken.

SCALE OF MILES

0 10   50   100

War of 1812

MAP 3

Secretary's orders for providing transportation for men and supplies.[86] Considerable quantities of military stores on hand at the arsenal at Newport, Ky., were used for supplying Hull's troops. As soon as the Ohio volunteers began to assemble, they made demands upon Taylor for tents and camp equipage. The arsenal had some camp kettles but no tents. Taylor proposed having more kettles made and tents produced from country linen. He purchased powder on the orders of General Hull and the Secretary of War and soon prepared a second ammunition wagon for the troops. He advised Secretary Eustis that the cartridge boxes ought to be inspected since many had been delivered to the Ohio troops unfit for use. Many unserviceable arms, too, had been returned to the arsenal.[87]

Taylor's efforts to supply Hull's troops were supplemented by those of the assistant deputy quartermaster at Pittsburgh, appointed after the re-establishment of the Quartermaster's Department in March 1812. The latter forwarded to Newport supplies sent by the Superintendent of Military Stores from Philadelphia. He also executed the Secretary's orders for the purchase of axes, cartridge boxes, bayonet scabbards, belts, and other accoutrements at Pittsburgh, thereby saving the cost of transporting these supplies from Philadelphia.[88]

On 9 June, Taylor left Newport to join General Hull at headquarters and continue on to Detroit with the troops, leaving his nephew in charge of his agency during his absence.[89] At headquarters, Taylor soon found that the costs of transportation were going to be enormous. Baggage as well as contractor's provisions had to be transported through a wilderness of two to three hundred miles. He had some 120 teams hired by mid-June.[90]

Rations for Hull's troops were supposed to be supplied by the contractor, Augustus Porter, whose contract called for supplying all the troops stationed along the Great Lakes as far west and north as Michilimackinac and, of course, including Detroit. In mid-June, the Secretary of War directed him to place 14,000 rations at Sandusky and 366,000 at Detroit in addition to the usual deposits required under his contract.[91]

[86] *Ibid.*, 7-85 (6) (Taylor to Eustis, 29 Mar 1812).

[87] *Ibid.*, T-92 (6); T-102 (6) (Taylor to Eustis, 18 Apr and 24 May 1812).

[88] RG 107, OSW, Military Book, vol. 5, p. 456 (SW to Lt. Johnson, 23 Jun 1812); vol. 6, pp. 46-47 (SW to same, 25 Jul 1812; SW to Asst. Commissary T. Buford, 26 Jul 1812).

[89] RG 107, OSW, Letters Received, T-104 (6) (Taylor to Eustis, 6 Jun 1812). During his service with Hull's Army, that agency was abolished, and Lt. J. Bryson was appointed assistant deputy quartermaster at Newport, taking over the public property then in the hands of Taylor's agent. RG 107, OSW, Military Book, vol. 6, p. 94 (SW to Taylor, 22 Aug 1812).

[90] RG 107, OSW, Letters Received, T-111 (6) (Taylor to Eustis, 16 Jun 1812).

[91] (1) *Documentary History of the Campaign on the Niagara Frontier in 1812* (8 vols., Welland, Ont., 1896-1907), III, p. 68 (Eustis to Porter, 15 Jun 1812). (2) Porter's contract

But Porter failed to supply the troops, and, instead, on 2 July, just when Hull received word that war had been declared, Porter wrote his brother that the most important thing was to send an express to General Hull, "notifying him that provisions are on the lake but cannot be got up, and advise him to take his own measures to obtain supplies." [92]   A lack of boats and the threat of seizure posed by the British Navy prevented deliveries.   The contract system broke down as soon as the war began.

In consequence, it became necessary for Hull to appoint a special agent or commissary to provision his troops.   He selected John H. Piatt, a wealthy Cincinnati merchant, and ordered him to purchase 200,000 rations of flour and the same quantity of beef as well as 400 packhorses for transporting the rations.   He allowed Piatt 5 percent on his disbursements as payment.[93]   Piatt procured the necessary provisions and informed the Secretary, upon whom he drew for money, that he intended sending the rations forward under the protection of the troops that were to reinforce Hull.[94]   The Secretary of War requested Governor Meigs to call into service the necessary troops of the detached militia from Ohio to guard the supply route and to convey the provisions to Hull without delay.[95]   To make sure that the reinforcements coming from Kentucky should be provisioned, Eustis instructed the deputy commissary at Lexington, Thomas Buford, to purchase and issue to the troops on the march the necessary number of rations in the event the contractor failed to deliver.   He also directed him to purchase and send under the protection of these troops, or as soon after as practicable, 3 months' supply of provisions for 1,500 men.[96]

The Secretary had also arranged to have medical stores sent to Hull from Philadelphia via the lake route.   By orders of the Quartermaster General, those stores were detained at Buffalo when war was declared because Morgan Lewis was sure they could not get past the British at Fort Malden.[97]   A month later, Taylor reported that he could procure no surgical instruments either at Detroit or in Ohio and requested that

---

expired 31 May 1813.   For its terms and the prices at which he agreed to furnish rations at the various posts, see C. M. Robinson, "The Life of Judge Augustus Porter," *Publications of the Buffalo Historical Society*, VII, 247.

[92] *Documentary History of the Campaign on the Niagara Frontier in 1812*, III, p. 90 (To Gen. Peter B. Porter, 2 Jul 1812).

[93] Piatt Letter Book (Hull to Piatt, 9 Jul 1813).   Manuscript Div., Library of Congress.

[94] (1) RG 107, OSW, Military Book, vol. 6, pp. 34–35 (SW to Augustus Porter, 20 Jul 1812). (2) RG 107, OSW, Letters Received, P–210 (6) (Piatt to SW, 12 Aug 1812).

[95] RG 107, OSW, Military Book, vol. 6, pp. 47–48 (SW to Meigs, 26 Jul 1812).

[96] *Ibid.*, vol. 6, p. 53 (SW to Buford, 28 Jul 1812).

[97] RG 107, OSW, Letters Received, L–128 (6) Enc. (Lewis to SW, 26 Jun 1812).

supplies be sent to him. The Secretary thereupon ordered the assistant deputy quartermaster at Pittsburgh to fill that requisition.[98]

Before that order could be executed, General Hull had surrendered Detroit to the British. But the fort was not surrendered for lack of ammunition and provisions; on the contrary, it was believed to be amply supplied with both. It was reported that there were 600 rounds of fixed ammunition prepared for the 24 pounders, of which 200 were grape shot; the same quantity had been made ready for the 6 pounders and 200 rounds for the 4 pounders. There was a considerable quantity of shells on hand, and 75,000 cartridges had been made up in addition to the 24 rounds prepared for each man's cartridge box. The magazine held 60 barrels of powder and 150 tons of lead. There were at least 25 days' provisions in the contractor's stores and 150 horseloads of flour and 300 beeves were on their way from Ohio. Nearly 2,400 stand of arms were surrendered to the British, as well as 17 iron and 12 brass pieces of ordnance.[99]

Support of the Northwestern Army

Shocked by Hull's surrender, the Administration was determined to regain the ground lost, and Brig. Gen. William Henry Harrison, of Tippecanoe fame, was given command of the Northwestern Army. Secretary of War Eustis continued to direct procurement of supplies for military operations in the west. To ensure ample provisions for the Northwestern Army, he instructed Ebenezer Denny, a contractor supplying the troops in the Pittsburgh area, to purchase 1,098,000 rations for that Army in addition to his contract, and to provide the transportation for the flour, whiskey, and small parts of those rations as well as salt for packing the beef which would have to be purchased on the hoof and driven to the Army.[100]

General Harrison, convinced that provisions could be procured more economically in Ohio than transported from Pittsburgh, cut back that purchase order to 400,000 rations and directed Denny to deposit them at Wooster, Ohio.[101] He then called upon contractor James White in Ohio to build up ration storage points at Urbana and Wooster. White

[98] (1) *Ibid.*, T–133 (6) (Taylor to SW, 21 Jul 1812). (2) RG 107, OSW, Military Book, vol. 6, p. 69 (SW to Lt. Johnson, 7 Aug 1812).

[99] (1) Robert B. McAfee, *History of the Late War in the Western Country* (Lexington, 1816), 92–93. (2) *Documentary History of the Campaign on the Niagara in 1812*, III, 220 (John Lovett to A. VanVechten, 28 Aug 1813). (3) *Annals of Congress*, 13th Cong., 2d sess., vol. 2, p. 2533.

[100] RG 107, OSW, Military Book, vol. 6, p. 110 (SW to Denny, 1 Sep 1812).

[101] RG 107, OSW, Letters Received, H–385 (6) (Harrison to SW, 24 Sep 1812); D–196 (6) (Denny to SW, 11 Oct 1812).

held the contract for that section of the state of Ohio below the 41st parallel which included many of the recruiting stations. But White had neglected to sign his contract or post the necessary bond, and apparently intended to furnish supplies only when it suited his convenience. Harrison charged that White let his contract for the northwestern part of the state to a subcontractor at so low a rate that the latter was unable to furnish rations. White himself claimed he would make $100,000 by the contract.[102] As deputy commissary with the Northwestern Army, Harrison appointed John H. Piatt, who had served in the same capacity under Hull, and directed him to transport 300,000 rations to Fort Defiance, deposit 200,000 rations of flour and 500,000 of beef at Urbana, and purchase and store 500,000 rations at Wooster.[103] He planned to provision an army of 10,000 men.

With so many purchasing agents in the field, competition inevitably occurred. Denny, unable to obtain flour in Pennsylvania before November because lack of water prevented operation of the mills, sent his agent to Chillicothe, Ohio, to purchase in that area. His procurement activity deprived Commissary Piatt of flour that he might have obtained. Since Denny had engaged every mill from the Scioto River to Pittsburgh, Harrison in October revised his instructions and permitted that contractor to supply all the rations originally ordered by the Secretary. In December, he complained, however, that Denny and his agents had not "acquitted themselves as they might have done," for in 2 months they had forwarded only 1,800 barrels of flour.[104]

Subsistence was only one of the items of supply required for Harrison's campaign. The Secretary of War directed the assistant deputy quartermaster at Pittsburgh to expedite the shipment of ordnance stores and to furnish the necessary tents and camp equipage. To supplement his efforts, Eustis dispatched Maj. Amos Stoddard of the Artillery as a temporary deputy quartermaster to Pittsburgh to prepare and speed the shipment of arms, cannon, and ordnance stores to the Northwestern Army. The Secretary ordered entrenching tools forwarded by the Commissary General of Purchases at Philadelphia and instructed Thomas Buford, deputy commissary, and the assistant deputy quartermaster, at Newport, Ky., to furnish whatever General Harrison required. In

[102] Logan Essarey, "Messages and Letters of William Henry Harrison," *Indiana Historical Collections*, IX, 184 (Harrison to SW, 22 Oct 1812).

[103] (1) RG 107, OSW, Letters Received, P–266 (6) (Piatt to SW, 30 Sep 1812); H–384 (6) (Harrison to SW, 27 Sep 1812). (2) Piatt Letter Book (Harrison to Piatt, 21 Sep 1812).

[104] (1) RG 107, OSW, Letters Received, D–172 (6) (Denny to SW, 22 Sep 1812); D–213 (6) (Denny to SW, 22 Oct 1812, enclosing ltr, Harrison to Denny, 15 Oct 1812); H–459 (6) (Harrison to SW, 12 Dec 1812). (2) Essarey, "Messages and Letters of William Henry Harrison," *Indiana Historical Collections*, IX, 182 (Harrison to SW, 22 Oct 1812).

short, the Secretary alerted all agents concerned and set supplies flowing to the Northwestern Army. He gave General Harrison carte blanche in requisitioning supplies in order that he might be successful in recapturing Detroit.[105]

To direct Quartermaster supply in the field, Harrison selected James Morrison as deputy quartermaster general to the Army and on 18 September the War Department commissioned him a lieutenant colonel of volunteers.[106] Morrison had long been engaged as a contractor in provisioning the troops in the West. He saw no conflict of interest between the office he accepted and his private contracting business. He intended to conduct that business as usual. About a month after his appointment, he submitted a bid to provision the troops in Ohio that the War Department did not accept.[107] As a contractor, he was thoroughly familiar with the transportation problems confronting him. He pursued his quartermaster duties energetically and to the complete satisfaction of General Harrison who praised him warmly.

Morrison immediately consulted with the general, and advised the Secretary of War of the monetary arrangements that would be necessary for supporting a campaign in a wilderness where nothing would be available for the accommodation of the troops and all supplies would have to be transported from Kentucky and Ohio. Money, he warned, could not be raised by the sale of bills drawn on the Secretary; specie would have to be sent. He began by requesting $50,000 to $100,000, upon reflection doubled that amount, increased it to $500,000 before many weeks had passed, and by 1 November wrote that only $1,000,000 could be considered a sufficient sum.[108] The Secretary sent $400,000 in specie in mid-October, but before it arrived Morrison was compelled to borrow on his own credit to meet demands made upon him.[109] By December, the fund of $400,000 had been nearly exhausted and Morrison reported that the movement of the Army would be paralyzed in another month unless the Kentucky and Ohio banks consented to make advances.[110]

Morrison requisitioned supplies and forwarded woolen socks, mittens, and roundabout jackets donated by the state of Kentucky. But

[105] RG 107, OSW, Military Book, vol. 6, pp. 113, 117, 136–37 (SW to Stoddard, 1, 9, 11 Sep 1812); 134 (SW to Harrison, 10 Sep 1812).

[106] Ibid., vol. 6, pp. 143–44, 162 (SW to Morrison, 18 Sep 1812).

[107] RG 107, OSW, Letters Received, M–451 (6); M–476 (6) (Morrison to SW, 3 and 20 Oct 1812).

[108] Ibid., M–452 (6); M–498 (6) (Morrison to SW, 3 Oct, 1 Nov 1812).

[109] (1) RG 107, OSW, Military Book, vol. 6, p. 198 (SW to Stoddard, 17 Oct 1812). (2) RG 107, OSW, Letters Received, M–498 (7); M–509 (6) (Morrison to SW, 1 and 3 Nov 1812).

[110] RG 107, OSW, Letters Received, M–537 (6) (Morrison to SW, 13 Dec 1812).

woolen coats, overalls, and blankets could not be procured in the West, and he informed the Secretary that at least 10,000 of each ought to be sent without delay.   The militia, called out in the summer, were still wearing their thin, cotton clothing late in October and would have to be supplied.   Harrison diverted to the use of the troops all the woolens that the Secretary had sent for the Indians.[111]   It was almost the end of December before Harrison could report that shoes, blankets, and clothing for the militia were on their way up the Scioto River, although it was weeks later before those supplies reached the troops.[112]

Though there was a shortage of clothing, blankets, and tents in the West, there appeared to be no scarcity of provisions in Ohio, even though the troops were often on short rations.   Elias Darnell, with the Kentucky volunteers under Brig. Gen. James Winchester, recorded on 16 December that the troops had drawn no flour since the 10th and that the volunteers were threatening to go home if they were not supplied.   All the beef and pork had been issued that day but fortunately a drove of 300 hogs arrived on the following day.   On 22 December a little flour arrived. "Quarter-rations of that article were issued, which was welcomed by rejoicing throughout the camp." [113]

Transportation was the crux of the supply problem.   Moving supplies through a wilderness where roads and causeways had to be constructed for wagons and packhorses was a problem difficult to solve and a task costly to execute.   In northwestern Ohio, the Black Swamp stretched from the Sandusky River to the Maumee River, covering an area 120 miles long and 40 miles wide.   Except in winter, when the water was completely frozen, it was almost impassable.   Rivers in the area of operations could be used for transportation only when freshets provided enough water to make them navigable, or when winter's blast froze them solid enough for transportation by sleds.   Dependence on such means could result only in irregularity and delay in the flow of supplies.

Morrison hired wagons and teams of horses and oxen, and, upon occasion, the Army resorted to impressment.   Unfavorable reports

[111] Ibid., M–475 (6) (Morrison to SW, 20 Oct 1812); M–384 (6) (Harrison to SW, 27 Sep 1812).

[112] (1) Ibid., H–4 (7) (Harrison to SW, 21 Dec 1812).   (2) Late in October, General Winchester was assuring his troops that clothing has been shipped from Philadelphia on 9 September and there would be an early supply.   "Papers and Orderly Book of Brigadier General James Winchester," "Michigan Pioneer and Historical Society, Historical Collections, XXI, p. 279 (General Orders, 27 Oct 1812).   (3) Part of the clothing for the Kentucky troops arrived on 27 December and the rest of it came almost a month later on 25 January 1813. Elias Darnell, A Journal Containing An Accurate And Interesting Account of . . . Those Heroic Kentucky Volunteers and Regulars, Commanded by General Winchester (Philadelphia, 1854), pp. 41, 45.

[113] Darnell, A Journal, pp. 38–39.

brought back from Fort Defiance by wagoners who clamored for their pay made it impossible to hire others. Morrison decided to purchase packhorses in Kentucky as the only means of transporting supplies in the winter of 1812–13. It was the enormous cost of this overland transportation that led him steadily to increase his demands upon the Secretary for funds.[114] That cost included the supply of forage, the shortage of which in northern Ohio became so acute that the quartermaster was obliged to purchase corn below Chillicothe to make a deposit of forage 120 miles away at Upper Sandusky.[115]

Supply difficulties were further complicated by the strange course the Secretary of War pursued in assigning, less than 2 weeks after Morrison's appointment, a second deputy quartermaster general to the Northwestern Army with powers equal to those of Morrison. The Secretary sent Capt. William Piatt to Pittsburgh to furnish transportation for the troops assembling there. He was also to forward all the cannon and ordnance stores to the Rapids of the Miami where the three columns of Harrison's Army were to converge.[116] Capt. Joseph Wheaton, assigned to Piatt as assistant deputy quartermaster, was ordered to let nothing impede the transport of the ordnance and ordnance stores that he conducted from Pittsburgh by way of Canton and Wooster to Upper Sandusky. He was later accused of pocketing for his own use the greater part of the very large sums of money he obtained for the transportation of these stores.[117]

When, at the end of the year, both deputy quartermasters general were at headquarters with Harrison, confusion and difficulties over authority developed to such an extent that Harrison requested an immediate decision by the Secretary of War. The latter replied that when the two deputies were on duty together, Colonel Morrison, being the senior

---

[114] A calculation made by General Winchester in November 1812 provides more specific details. Packhorses traveled anywhere from 10 to 20 miles a day. Winchester estimated that 200 packhorses, operating between Piqua and Fort Winchester on the Auglaize, would each be able to carry 150 pounds of flour as well as 25 pounds of forage for their own supply. The flour carried by the horses would equal 26,666 rations, at 18 ounces to the ration. The trip would take 10 days—6 going and 4 returning. Allowing 6 days for resting the horses before starting another round trip, the 200 horses would transport every 16 days 26,666 rations. Many more rations than that had to be transported for the Northwestern Army besides clothing, equipment, and militay stores and, in addition to wagons, horses, and oxen, many more than 200 packhorses were used. Piatt Letter Book (Winchester to Piatt, 17 Nov 1812).

[115] RG 107, OSW, Letters Received, M–488 (6); M–497 (6) (Morrison to SW, 28 Oct 1812); H–20 (7) (Harrison to SW, 6 Jan 1813).

[116] RG 107, OSW, Military Book, vol. 6, p. 177 (SW to Capt. William Piatt, 30 Sep 1812).

[117] (1) Ibid., vol. 6, p. 176 (SW to Wheaton, 30 Sep 1812). (2) RG 107, OSW, Letters Received, G–133 (7) (Harrison to SW, 19 May 1813). (3) For the difficulties that Wheaton encountered in conducting these stores, see ibid., W–1 (7) (Wheaton to SW, 14 Dec 1812).

officer, would command.[118]   That decision must not have resolved the problem satisfactorily since Colonel Morrison insisted on resigning despite Harrison's reluctance to have him leave.   The general thought so highly of his deputy's services that he recommended his appointment to succeed Morgan Lewis as Quartermaster General when the latter was promoted to a major general.   He proposed that John C. Bartlett of Kentucky, then acting as field commissary, be appointed to succeed Morrison as deputy quartermaster general to the Northwestern Army.[119]

Large sums had been expended and tremendous efforts made to move men and supplies toward the frontier without achieving the goal of recapturing Detroit or taking Fort Malden.   Conditions had not changed much since Wayne had campaigned against the Indians in the same area. The roads were indescribably bad.   Men and animals slogged through an almost continuous swamp that mired wagons and rapidly wore out horses.   The fine teams that arrived on 10 December at Sandusky with the artillery were quickly worn out.   "Two trips from McArthurs block House (our nearest deposit to the Rapids)," Harrison informed the Secretary, "will completely destroy a Brigade of Pack Horses." [120]   River transportation could not be used until December because the water was too low.   When the opportunity was then seized to send out pirogues loaded with provisions, powder, and clothing, a sudden freeze held the boats icebound.   They had to be abandoned and the supplies hauled by sleds to their destination.[121]   It is not surprising that under these conditions supplies did not accumulate as rapidly as desired at deposit points. The winter operations in the West came to an end when troops under General Winchester were overwhelmed at Monroe, Mich., then known as Frenchtown, on the River Raisin.

Support of Campaigns on the Niagara and Northern Frontiers

Military operations in the East were no more successful than those in the West in 1812.   Supply preparations were initiated shortly after Congress enacted legislation increasing the size of the Army early in the year.   At the direction of the Secretary of War, the military agents at Philadelphia, Boston, and Albany purchased and had manufactured tents, knapsacks, canteens, cartridge boxes, and belts.   The military agent at Albany also took steps to provide barracks, storehouses, and a

---

[118] (1) RG 107, Register, SW, Letters Received, vol. 7, p. 178 (Harrison to SW, 20 Jan 1813). (2) RG 107, OSW, Military Book, vol. 6, p. 288 (SW to Harrison, 11 Feb 1813).
[119] RG 107, OSW, Letters Received, H–64 (7) (Harrison to SW, 12 Mar 1813).
[120] *Ibid.*, H–459 (6) (Harrison to SW, 12 Dec 1812).
[121] *Ibid.*, H–4 (7) Enc. (Thomas Bodley, Acting QM of left wing, to Harrison, 11 Dec 1812).

KENTUCKY MILITIA, AT THE RIVER RAISIN, JANUARY 1813

hospital near that city for the troops to be quartered there.[122] These same military agents—William Linnard at Philadelphia, Jacob Eustis at Boston, and Anthony Lamb at Albany—were reappointed deputy quartermasters general as soon as the Quartermaster's Department was established. At Linnard's suggestion, the Secretary appointed an assistant deputy quartermaster general for the harbor of New York. He not only speeded the transportation of supplies up the Hudson to Albany but also procured supplies in the New York area.

Tentage and camp equipment for the troops on the Niagara and northern frontiers were therefore drawn from Boston, New York, and Philadelphia, and funneled through Albany. At Philadelphia, Linnard also contracted for powder, for the production of which the Superintendent of Military Stores furnished the contractor with saltpeter and sulphur.[123] Some powder and shells were also obtained by contract at Albany. Clothing was drawn principally from Philadelphia where the Purveyor and subsequently the Commissary General of Purchases contracted for such supplies. Deputy commissaries also purchased clothing at New York, Norwich, and Boston. They also furnished tentage and camp equipment. The troops were supplied with arms from the Springfield and Philadelphia arsenals. This same flow of supplies occurred in all subsequent campaigns on the Niagara and Northern frontiers.

Soon after the war began, the subsistence contractors experienced difficulties in supplying rations on these frontiers. Augustus Porter, whose contract included Fort Niagara and its dependencies, became so uneasy about providing beef that he requested his brother, serving as quartermaster general of the state of New York, to contract for supplies even if he had to pay $3.50 per hundredweight.[124] Elbert Anderson, Jr., supplied rations to troops stationed anywhere else in the state of New York and in New Jersey and seems to have been called upon to subsist militia called into service. James Byers, a Vermont contractor, was also interested to some extent in provisioning troops in northern New York. As in the West, however, the system of contract supply failed early in the war. When reports were received that troops were literally starving for bread and that Fort Niagara would have to be evacuated if provisions were not supplied, the commanding general ordered the deputy quartermaster to purchase provisions.[125]

With the appointment of Morgan Lewis as Quartermaster General,

[122] RG 107, OSW, Military Book, vol. 5, pp. 304–05 (SW to J. Eustis and Anthony Lamb, 16 Mar 1812); p. 311 (SW to Eustis, 19 Mar 1812); p. 360 (SW to Linnard, 28 Apr 1812).

[123] *Ibid.*, vol. 5, pp. 364, 368 (SW to Linnard, 1 and 5 May 1812).

[124] *Documentary History of the Campaign on the Niagara Frontier in 1812*, III, 122 (11 Jul 1812).

[125] *American State Papers, Military Affairs*, I, 508–10.

Quartermaster supply support for operations in the East came under his direction. After a brief stop at Philadelphia en route from Washington, Lewis arrived at Albany to assume his duties on 21 May, barely a month before war was declared. He was at first preoccupied with the problem of organizing his Department. Uninformed concerning the appointments already made of subordinate officers, confused about his responsibilities, and, because other staff departments remained for some time without chiefs, called upon to perform the functions of commissary and ordnance officer as well as those of Quartermaster General, Lewis never did establish an effective organization. As previously noted, he preferred commanding troops to supplying their needs.

Early in July, Lewis made a tour of the posts on the northern frontier and reported that the troops were destitute of clothing, arms, and ammunition.[126] Neither the Office of the Commissary General of Purchases nor that of the Commissary General of Ordnance had as yet been filled, and Lewis was much concerned about supplies furnished by those departments. He also raised questions about supplying camp equipage and transportation to militia marching to the lines. Militia were supposed to arrive at rendezvous points fully armed and equipped.

By September, Lewis asserted that no amount of revenue raised would be adequate to support a war carried on by militia. The governor of New York, he informed the Secretary, ordered the militia to rendezvous by regiments at points often more than a hundred miles apart. There they waited, at the expense of the United States, to receive tents and camp equipage before they marched to their destinations. Even then they were unarmed, for the militiaman customarily arrived at camp without weapons, having left at home his musket and everything but the clothes he was wearing. Lewis warned that when their terms of service expired the government need not expect to have returned for further use anything that was furnished to them.[127] Supply expenses under these conditions soared to unexpected heights.

Lewis was frequently hampered by want of funds, but his lack of initiative was even more of a handicap in carrying out his functions and consequently he was not an effective Quartermaster General. He customarily acted only after consulting the Secretary of War and the commanding general. Providing adequate transportation facilities, for example, was a basic function of his office; yet he found it necessary to seek the advice of the Secretary when it became evident that use of portages and water transportation would reduce by half the expense of

---

[126] RG 107, OSW, Letters Received, L–137 (6) (Lewis to SW, 5 Jul 1812).

[127] (1) RG 107, OSW, Letters Received, L–181 (6) (Lewis to SW, 4 Sep 1812). (2) Dearborn Papers (Dearborn to Col. Clark, 3 Aug 1812). New York Historical Society.

moving supplies from Albany to White Hall at the entrance of Lake Champlain.   With some impatience, the Secretary cited the act establishing the Quartermaster's Department and suggested that he should consult with the commanding general when in doubt, adopting the means best suited to the public interest and the exigencies of the service.[128]

Lewis was harassed by the delays in organizing the other staff departments and filling vacancies in them, but subordinates in his own organization lamented the lack of written instructions from him.   "I am grovelling on in the Dark," Linnard wrote, sympathizing with the plight of the assistant deputy quartermaster general at New York who had received no word from Lewis.[129]   The Quartermaster General, after what could only have been a brief interview with Linnard, had expressed doubts as to his competency.   Linnard had accumulated a decade of experience in Quartermaster duties at Philadelphia by 1812 and had favorably impressed both his associates in the supply agencies at Philadelphia and the successive Secretaries of War at Washington.   Located at the most important center of supply, Linnard was a key figure in supplying the troops during the War of 1812, yet no close cooperation developed between the Quartermaster General and his deputy at Philadelphia.

Shortly after Lewis arrived at Albany, Maj. Gen. Henry Dearborn, appointed to the command of the Northern Department, left for Boston to attempt to raise troops in the New England states, an area that was hostile to the war.   During these weeks, Dearborn acted as his own quartermaster general, issuing orders to Jacob Eustis at Boston to furnish tents, camp kettles, knapsacks, wagons, saddles, and entrenching tools to the limited number of troops that he did raise.   He also instructed the deputy quartermaster general to have cloth on hand made up into uniforms.   Reflecting the confusion over staff functions, Dearborn decided that the duty of purchasing horses belonged to the Commissary Department, and therefore directed the deputy commissary general of purchases at Portsmouth not only to purchase horses for a company of dragoons but also to provide forage for the animals.[130]

Notwithstanding War Department plans for invading Canada, Dearborn lingered at Boston, concerned about the defense of New England. As late as 7 August he did not consider "any part of the borders of Upper Canada" as being within his command, despite War Department letters

---

[128] (1) RG 107, OSW, Letters Received, L–177 (6) (Lewis to SW, 30 Aug 1812).   (2) RG 107, OSW, Military Book, vol. 6, p. 120 (SW to Lewis, 5 Sep 1812).

[129] RG 92, QM Phila., Letter Book, No. 531 (Linnard to Van De Venter, 18 Jul 1812).

[130] Dearborn Papers (Dearborn to J. Eustis, 5, 10, 12 Jun, 6 Jul 1812); (To SW, 5 Jun 1812); (To John Langdon, 7, 10 Jul 1812).

to the contrary.[131]   He gave no orders to officers commanding at posts on the Niagara frontier before that time.   Such defense measures as were undertaken earlier had been directed by the governor of New York and his militia officers.

In mid-October, operations along the Niagara frontier got under way. A small number of troops under the command of Maj. Gen. Stephen Van Rensselaer of the New York militia crossed the Niagara River to take possession of Queenston Heights, only to lose it when the militia, standing upon their constitutional rights, refused to set foot on foreign soil.   General Van Rensselaer asked to be relieved.   He was succeeded by Brig. Gen. Alexander Smyth who issued bombastic proclamations, assembled troops, and then abandoned his plan to cross the Niagara at Buffalo.   Late in November, General Dearborn moved down Lake Champlain to Rouses Point on the state line, where the militia refused to advance into Canada.   Nothing was accomplished, winter was approaching, and Dearborn sent his troops into winter quarters at Burlington and Plattsburg.

The failure of the 1812 campaign on the Niagara frontier was attributable largely to poor leadership, to raw, inexperienced regular troops, and to undependable militia.   But if it was the unwillingness of the militia to invade Canada and not a lack of food that resulted in the miserable showing on the frontier, the inadequacies of the supply system contributed little to their morale.   Dearborn repeatedly complained of "a Great deficiency" in whatever related to the Quartermaster's Department.[132]   Horses starved for want of forage.   Obviously, an active deputy quartermaster general was needed with the troops on the Niagara frontier, but even after Capt. James Thomas had been appointed, it was charged that the soldiers, particularly the volunteers, could not get one-half of the articles to which they were entitled by law.[133]   When ample supplies of men and stores were finally forwarded to Van Rensselaer, Dearborn feared they would arrive too late, for "a strong fatality appears to have pervaded the whole arrangement." [134]   His apprehensions were well grounded.   Although some supplies arrived, in lieu of much needed musket cartridges, the Quartermaster General had to transport powder, lead, paper, and molds, and soldiers had to be detailed to make their own cartridges.   Dearborn suspected, too, that the powder might prove unfit for use and advised Van Rensselaer to have it inspected.[135]

    [131] *Ibid.*, (To SW, 7 Aug 1812).
    [132] *Ibid.*, (To SW, 29 Aug 1812; to Lewis, 26 Sep 1812).
    [133] *Documentary History of the Campaign on the Niagara Frontier in 1812*, IV, 342–43 (Baptist Irvine to General Porter, 6 Jan 1813).
    [134] Dearborn Papers (To Van Rensselaer, 26 Sep 1812).
    [135] *Ibid.*, (To Lewis, 8 Oct 1812); (To Van Rensselaer, 13 Oct 1812).

Inspection reports revealed that the quality of much that was supplied was exceedingly poor. Knapsacks and canteens were bad; arms were found to be in "infamously bad order;" the tents had never been any good and were so much abused on the march that they afforded little protection. Though it was October when the inspector made his report, troops of the 12th and 14th Regiments had not received any woolen clothing, and the men had to mount guard in cold, stormy weather clad in linen jackets and overalls. As noted before, this was not because clothing was unavailable, but because commanding officers refused to accept uniforms of drab and mixed cloth. The list of sick increased steadily not only because of inadequate protection against the elements but also because of the lack of provisions. A steady diet of fresh meat, invariably cooked by frying, was not conducive to good health.[136]

Though orders had been sent to Quartermaster General Lewis in September to construct winter quarters, not one barrack had been completed by December at Green Bush, Vt., nor were the troops adequately supplied with wood and straw. The situation was no better at Burlington and Plattsburg. In mid-December, Deputy Quartermaster General Lamb was directed to send tools so that the troops might complete their own shelters.[137]

Preparations for the Campaign of 1813

With the troops settled in winter quarters, the time had come to make plans for the next year's campaign. The Secretary called Lewis to Washington for consultation, but the latter questioned the wisdom of attending at that particular time. In addition to being Quartermaster General, Lewis was then also a member of the senate of the New York legislature. He thought his presence at a legislative session that was to open, in which "Questions of serious import to the general Administration will be agitated," would be more advantageous to the government than an immediate visit to Washington.[138]

General Dearborn, too, was giving thought to preparations for the coming campaign and to the need for improvements in the staff departments, especially in the Quartermaster's Department. For the benefit

---

[136] *Documentary History of the Campaign on the Niagara Frontier in 1812*, IV, p. 191 (J. W. Livingston to Gov. Tompkins, 9 Nov 1812); pp. 242–43 (Inspection Rpts, Cap. Wm. King, 5 Oct 1812).

[137] Dearborn Papers (To Lewis, 21, 22 Sep 1812;—Dec and 14 Dec 1812); (To Lamb, 15, 21 Dec 1812).

[138] (1) RG 107, OSW, Military Book, vol. 6, p. 254 (SW to Lewis, 19 Dec 1812). (2) RG 107, OSW, Letters Received, L–8 (7) (Lewis to SW, 8 Jan 1813).

of the new Secretary of War, John Armstrong, he outlined the qualifications of a competent Quartermaster General.

> It is indispensable that the Q.M.G. should be altogether a Man of business —In addition to talents General information & integrity he must be habitually industrious, perservering, energetic and prompt in the discharge of the important duties of the office, and should possess capacity for inspiring all those under him, with zeal & activity in the discharge of their respective duties. In short a Q.M.G. should anticipate every thing, see every thing, and be prepared at all times as far as human foresight is capable of for all emergencies.[139]

Obviously, Dearborn had long ago decided that Lewis did not possess these qualifications and he wished that Lewis could be transferred to the line.[140]

Secretary Armstrong assured Dearborn that a reorganization of the Quartermaster's Department was already under consideration.[141]   Early in March, Congress enacted the necessary legislation, and on 21 March Robert Swartwout was appointed chief of the Department.   In the meantime, Congress had also made provision for the appointment of six additional major generals, which permitted the promotion of Lewis.[142] The latter considered himself immediately removed from the office of Quartermaster General.   Until the new chief of the Department arrived, the Secretary of War placed funds at the disposal of General Dearborn so that preparations for the coming campaign might not be delayed, with the result that once again Dearborn was enmeshed in the performance of Quartermaster duties.[143]

Military plans in 1813 called for a campaign against upper Canada designed to take Kingston, where the British ships had been wintering, and to capture Forts George and Erie.   The Northwestern Army was to lend support by keeping the British alarmed for the safety of Fort Malden though no expedition for its capture was to be undertaken until control of the Great Lakes had been wrested from the British.   This was to be the primary objective in 1813.

These plans called for a concentration of supplies for supporting the troops under General Dearborn rather than for those of the Northwestern Army under Harrison, and the Secretary ordered a sharp cut in expenditures for that Army.   Since the troops of the Northwestern Army would, for the most part, be stationed at posts and the maintenance of

---

[139] (1) Dearborn Papers (To SW, —Jan 1813).   (2) See also RG 107, OSW, Letters Received, D-27 (7) (Dearborn to SW, 28 Jan 1813).

[140] (1) Dearborn Papers (To SW, —Jan 1813).   (2) RG 107, OSW, Letters Received, D-63 (7) (Dearborn to SW, 20 Feb 1813).

[141] (1) RG 107, OSW, Military Book, vol. 6, p. 293 (15 Feb 1813).   (2) See *ante*, pp. 152-53.

[142] 2 *Stat.* 801 (Feb 24, 1813).   Lewis was appointed on 2 March 1813).

[143] RG 107, OSW, Military Book, vol. 6, p. 302 (4 Mar 1813).

long supply lines through the wilderness would not be required, the Secretary directed Harrison to get rid of his heavy trains of horses and oxen.   He also instructed him to curtail sharply expenditures for any supplies to supplement those already on hand, to inform his special agents that their drafts on the War Department were to be limited to $20,000 a month, and to direct all supply officers to forward their accounts for settlement.   In short, Harrison no longer had carte blanche for requisitioning supplies.

Under the reorganization of the Quartermaster's Department, John C. Bartlett became Quartermaster General of the Northwestern Army, and the Secretary of War entered into a new contract with Benjamin Orr and Aaron Greely for the supply of its rations.[144]   To prepare for transportation that would be needed on Lake Erie, the Secretary of War informed Harrison that Capt. Thomas S. Jesup, of the 7th Infantry, had been temporarily detailed as deputy quartermaster general and charged with the construction of boats at Cleveland.   These would be capable of carrying from one destination to another on the lake 40 to 50 men with their baggage, arms, accoutrements, and provisions.   By May, Jesup had three boatyards established and in operation, and the Secretary advised Harrison that the boats would be particularly useful in navigating the lake between the chain of islands and the west shore.[145]

Meantime, opposite Kingston at Sackett's Harbor on Lake Ontario, further boatbuilding activity had been initiated under the supervision of another deputy quartermaster general.   Early in 1813, the Secretary had instructed him to hire boatbuilders at New York City, transport them to Sackett's Harbor, and there supervise the construction of 100 batteaux before 1 April.   Each boat was to be large enough to carry 40 men and their baggage and provisions.[146]   To avoid competition with the Navy, the deputy quartermaster general employed the same ship carpenter to supervise the building of these boats for the Army as Commodore Isaac Chauncey did for the Navy.[147]

To supervise the erection of huts and to provide wood and straw for the troops assembling at Sackett's Harbor, the Secretary had sent

---

[144] (1) RG 107, OSW, Military Book, vol. 6, pp. 325, 363 (SW to Harrison, 17 Mar, 3 Apr 1813).   (2) Piatt Letter Book (Harrison to Piatt, 27 Mar 1813).   (3) For the difficulties that developed with Orr and Greely see, *American State Papers, Military Affairs*, I, 644 ff.

[145] (1) RG 107, OSW, Military Book, vol. 6, p. 310 (SW to Jesup, 9 Mar 1813); p. 353 (SW to Harrison, 8 Apr 1813).   (2) RG 107, OSW, Letters Received, J–95 (7) and J–181 (Jesup to SW, 27 Mar and 24 May 1813).   (3) *American State Papers, Military Affairs*, I, 454 (SW to Harrison, 8 May 1813).

[146] RG 107, OSW, Military Book, vol. 6, p. 463 (SW to Dearborn, 10 Feb 1813); pp. 465–66 (SW to Van De Venter, 12 Feb 1813).

[147] RG 107, OSW, Letters Received, V–15 (7) (Van De Venter to SW, 16 Feb 1813).

Maj. William Swan as the commanding deputy quartermaster general.[148] While these preparations were being made at Sackett's Harbor, General Dearborn remained at Albany, complaining of the Quartermaster burdens imposed upon him and requesting to be relieved of the responsibility for handling Quartermaster funds. By 5 April, he reported that the affairs of the Quartermaster's Department had fallen into "a wretched state." He had not been able to join his troops at Sackett's Harbor because he was detained at Albany to perform Quartermaster duties. To continue moving men and stores without a Quartermaster General, a deputy, or funds, he warned the Secretary, would prove difficult, if not impracticable.[149]

Still awaiting the arrival of the new Quartermaster General weeks after his appointment, Dearborn wrote urging his prompt appearance at Headquarters. It was 18 April, however, before Swartwout came to Albany.[150] There he found the Department in great confusion—no person was available to give him information (General Lewis was then at Buffalo) and drafts to the amount of $100,000 were presented to him for payment of articles furnished and transportation provided by his predecessor. Until he received reports from the deputies, assistants, and storekeepers of his predecessor, he could not formulate an estimate of supplies that would be needed. To preserve the credit of the government and prevent delay, he notified the Secretary that at least $200,000 should be placed at the disposal of his Department.[151]

This information the Secretary received with some amazement since funds had been given to Lewis and his deputies to settle their accounts. "You ought not to entangle yourself with old Accounts," he advised Swartwout. He made $100,000 available, of which $60,000 was to be used by Swartwout and $40,000 by Col. Elisha Jenkins, who had replaced Lamb at Albany as quartermaster general in the 9th District under the reorganization of the Department in March 1813.[152] Obviously, the transfer of property from the old to the new Quartermaster organization was not accomplished smoothly or efficiently. Receiving no reports from subordinates, Jenkins could only set about collecting the property on

---

[148] RG 107, OSW, Military Book, vol. 6, p. 289 (To Lewis, 15 Feb 1813); p. 463 (To Dearborn, 10 Feb 1813).

[149] (1) Dearborn Papers (To SW, 21 Mar 1813; 5 Apr 1813; 14 Apr 1813). (2) RG 107, OSW, Letters Received, D–85 (7) (Dearborn to SW, 26 Mar 1813).

[150] (1) Dearborn Papers (To Swartwout, 12 Apr 1813). (2) RG 107, OSW, Letters Received, S–161 (7) (Swartwout to SW, 19 Apr 1813).

[151] RG 107, OSW, Letters Received, S–161 (7) (Swartwout to SW, 19 Apr 1813).

[152] RG 107, OSW, Military Book, vol. 6, p. 381 (To Swartwout, 25 Apr 1813); p. 379 (To Jenkins, 23 Apr 1813).

hand at various places, inventorying all he found, and depositing it in a storehouse hired for that purpose.[153]

Dearborn had ordered Swartwout to report to Headquarters at Sackett's Harbor by 15 May with ample funds for Quartermaster disbursements during the coming campaign. But since the general could not inform him what force would be employed, Swartwout had no basis for estimating needs. He could only hope that his funds would be adequate. The Secretary of War tartly observed that the general had "altogether lost sight of the State & usages of the Treasury." Only $1,400,000 per month could be drawn from the Treasury, and with that amount the Secretary had to "subsist, pay, equip, cloathe & move five or six Armies of Regulars & Militia." The Secretary assured Swartwout that he would be supplied from time to time as means were available, but he warned that "economy must be your alpha & omega as well as mine."[154] Preparations went forward with the cost of transporting supplies under the care of conductors absorbing the greater part of the funds made available to the Department.

A week after Swartwout arrived at Albany, the Canadian campaign began. With the Navy in temporary control of Lake Ontario, Dearborn's troops embarked on Commodore Chauncey's fleet. The batteaux and flatbottomed boats that had been constructed for the purpose of moving the troops could not be used to transport them safely.[155] The force sailed from Sackett's Harbor on 25 April 1813 to take possession of York (Toronto), following up that success by capturing Fort George at the mouth of the Niagara River. At this point, lack of naval support stalled operations.

The Northwestern Army fared better this year. Perry's naval victory at Put-in-Bay in September enabled Harrison to cross Lake Erie, defeat the British at Chatham where Tecumseh was killed, reoccupy Detroit, and regain control of the Northwest. This notable success was offset by a sad fiasco on the St. Lawrence. A two-pronged operation aimed at Montreal under Wilkinson, who had replaced Dearborn in the Northern Department, and Maj. Gén. Wade Hampton, with Secretary Armstrong lending his personal supervision to the attempt, proved a dismal failure. Winter put an end to military operations, and Quartermaster personnel in the 9th District shifted their attention from moving men and forwarding supplies to providing winter quarters for the troops.[156]

[153] RG 107, OSW, Letters Received, J–169 (8) (Jenkins to SW, 5 May 1813).

[154] (1) RG 107, OSW, Military Book, vol. 6, pp. 404–05 (4 May 1813). (2) RG 107, OSW, Letters Received, S–169 (7) (Swartwout to SW, 27 Apr 1813).

[155] American State Papers, Military Affairs, I, 442 (Dearborn to SW, 2 Apr 1813).

[156] RG 107, OSW, Military Book, vol. 7, p. 110 (SW to Jenkins, 20 Jan 1814).

Neglect of the Southern Department

Obviously, with Canada the objective of operations in 1812 and 1813, the Secretary of War could give little attention to troops stationed in the Southern Department. Their supply was neglected. It was late in September 1812, for example, before Eustis assured the commanding generals at New Orleans and Charleston that winter clothing would be sent immediately. He then ordered Linnard to forward supplies.[157] Meanwhile, the deputy quartermaster general at New Orleans, greatly hampered by the lack of funds, reported that the people employed in his department, unpaid for several months, were clamoring for their wages, and that owners of storehouses where government property was deposited were threatening to "turn the United States out of doors" if they were not paid.[158] The frequency and the large size of the deputy's drafts on the War Department caused the Secretary to suspect that "there was much indiscretion in the use of the credit," and that abuses existed in the Department at New Orleans. He therefore protested the deputy's bills and, upon the reorganization of the Quartermaster's Department, did not reappoint him. Instead, William Piatt was sent there as quartermaster general.[159]

Even when military operations were contemplated in the Southern Department, the Secretary directed no build-up of supplies for their support other than instructing the contractors of the area to furnish provisions. Following Hull's surrender of Detroit, the War Department feared that the British might attempt action against the Gulf ports. The Secretary therefore called for volunteers from Tennessee to reinforce Wilkinson, then commanding at New Orleans. Andrew Jackson responded immediately by marching two regiments of infantry and a corps of cavalry to Natchez. Instead of being ordered to advance, Jackson, in February 1813, received a letter from the Secretary countermanding the Florida venture. He had expected to receive Quartermaster supplies from the deputy quartermaster at New Orleans, but, as the head of a volunteer force, he experienced much trouble. He had at once encountered difficulty in obtaining forage for his mounted force. When the expedition was called off, he was left to lay out his own funds to get his men back to Nashville.[160] His troops fared no better in 1813 when he

[157] *Ibid.*, vol. 6, pp. 158–59 (To Wilkinson, 21 Sep 1812); pp. 158, 174 (To Linnard, 21 and 29 Sep 1812).

[158] RG 107, OSW, Letters Received, S–311 (7) (Shaumburgh to SW, 12 Aug 1812).

[159] (1) RG 107, OSW, Military Book, vol. 6 pp. 336–37 (To Shaumburgh, 25 Mar 1813); pp. 481–82 (To Piatt, 29 Jun 1813). (2) RG 107, OSW, Reports to Congress, I, 283 (SW to Chairman of Committee on Ways and Means, 24 Jul 1813).

[160] (1) *Correspondence of Andrew Jackson*, ed. John S. Bassett (2 vols., Washington, 1926), 1,275n, 286, 289–90 (2) RG 107, OSW, Letters Received, S146 (7) Enc. (Shamburgh to SW, 16 Mar 1813). (3) Marquis James, *The Life of Andrew Jackson* (New York, 1940), 148–50.

led an armed force against the Creeks. Only Jackson's untiring efforts kept them from starvation. He charged that the Creek war could have been terminated in a few weeks if the contractors had not failed to forward provisions.[161]

Final Campaign Preparations

Supply preparations for the final campaigns of the War of 1812 on the Niagara frontier and at New Orleans followed established patterns previously described. There were no further changes in organization to delay Quartermaster supply operations, but lack of funds hampered all quartermasters as well as commissaries.

As in previous years, the primary Quartermaster effort, supervised by Robert Swartwout and Elisha Jenkins in the 9th District, was directed toward transporting men and supplies to the Niagara frontier. There a vigorous campaign under Maj. Gen. Jacob Brown included the capture of Fort Erie, the victory at Chippewa, and the drawn battle of Lundy's Lane but produced no decisive results. With the repulse of the powerful British thrust at Plattsburg in September, active operations on the northern frontier came to an end.

The British raiding operations along the Atlantic Coast, culminating in the occupation of Washington, resulted in the removal of Armstrong from the cabinet. James Monroe assumed the duties of both Secretary of State and Secretary of War. When the British launched an attack at New Orleans, Monroe was able to place $100,000 at Jackson's disposal. Some 1,110 muskets were also sent to him, but Jackson obtained most of the supplies for his successful defense by ransacking the city of New Orleans for additional arms as well as entrenching tools, horses, and vehicles.[162]

The contract system of supplying provisions failed as miserably in the closing year of the war as it had in earlier campaigns.[163] Despite Callender Irvine's efforts to improve clothing supply, Maj. Gen. Jacob Brown still asserted late in 1814 that winter clothing rarely reached the troops before the middle of winter. The allowance, he conceded, was abundant "if the quality was only good," but it seldom was. Shoes were miserably put together, made of leather that did not deserve the name for it was "a Substance as porous as Sponge." Owing to the "wretched policy" that assumed a soldier could bear "all the vicissitudes of the

---

[161] *Correspondence of Andrew Jackson*, ed. Bassett, I, 256, 525–26 (To Armstrong, 20 Nov and 30 Dec 1813).

[162] James, *Life of Andrew Jackson*, pp. 215, 226.

[163] RG 107, OSW, Letters Received, J–2 (8) (Jenkins to SW, 2 Jun 1814); M–187 (8) (Brig. Gen. Duncan McArthur to SW, 10 Dec 1814).

climate and weather without requiring either quarters or covering," Brown charged, five men perished from disease to one that fell by the sword.[164]

Secretary Monroe found complaints universal as he sought to infuse new vigor into supply preparations in the winter of 1814–15. Fortunately, early in February, news of the peace treaty, signed on 24 December 1814, put an end to the extensive preparations that Swartwout had been authorized to make. The Secretary suspended purchases; he directed the commanding generals to discharge the militia at once; and he issued orders to preserve all arms, accoutrements, camp equipage, and military stores.[165]

Demobilization

The President submitted the treaty to the Senate on 15 February. Though in a special message 3 days later, he warned Congress against any immediate decrease in the size of the Army, motives of economy dictated that Congress lose no time in cutting expenses. On 3 March, it hurriedly reduced the size of the Army from its wartime peak of about 60,000 men to 10,000. At the same time, it abolished the existing Quartermaster's Department, substituting in its place four brigade quartermasters who were to be taken from the line.[166] All other officers in the Department were to be discharged. But demobilization problems— the safekeeping of government property, the disposal of surplus stores, and the payment of claims—permitted no such abrupt abolition of the Department. By Presidential authority, Swartwout and two deputy quartermasters general were provisionally retained in office. The Army having been reorganized into a division of the North and a division of the South under the command of Maj. Gen. Jacob Brown and Maj. Gen. Andrew Jackson, respectively, one of the deputy quartermasters general was assigned to each division.

The economy drive also had its effect upon the personnel of the Purchasing Department. Callender Irvine had long urged the desirability of placing all procurement responsibility in his hands, and upon his recommendation all deputy commissaries were discharged. Under Irvine's administration, supplies thereafter were largely procured and concentrated at Philadelphia. Their transportation, however, necessitated retention of a deputy quartermaster general at that city. In conse-

---

[164] Official Letter Book of Jacob Brown, No. 1, pp. 271–72 (To Monroe, 28 Nov 1814). Manuscript Div., Library of Congress.

[165] RG 107, OSW, Military Book, vol. 8, p. 45 (SW to Swartwout, 13 Feb 1815); pp. 47–48 (To COs of all military districts, 16 Feb 1815).

[166] 3 *Stat.* 224 (Mar 3, 1815).

quence, at Irvine's suggestion, the War Department also provisionally retained William Linnard as a deputy quartermaster general.[167] It permitted all other supply officers in the two departments to remain in service only long enough to settle their accounts.

The provisional character of these staff arrangements was unsatis-factory, and, by the end of the year, the Chairman of the House Military Committee raised the question of providing for such appointments by law.   In reply, William H. Crawford, who had become Secretary of War in August, wrote:

> The experience of the two first campaigns of the last war, which had fur-nished volumes of evidence upon this subject, had incontestably established not only the expediency, but the necessity of giving to the military establish-ment, in time of peace, the organization which it must have to render it efficient in a state of war.[168]

Since the "stationary staff of a military establishment" should be sub-stantially the same in peace and war, he recommended its organization provide for, among other officers, one Quartermaster General, who should be stationed in Washington.   This was a revolutionary proposal, for until that time the Quartermaster General had always been regarded as a field staff officer, appointed only in time of war and serving with the principal army.   Among this permanent staff, Crawford also included the Commissary General of Purchases who was to be stationed in Philadelphia.

Crawford argued that the organization of the division staff in the field should be regulated by the number of individual corps into which a military force was distributed.   Since the Army was then divided into two military divisions, and he saw no reason for change, he proposed that the staff at the divisional level include among its officers one quartermaster general and two deputy quartermasters general with regimental quarter-masters, as well as one deputy commissary general and two assistant commissaries of issue.

Unfortunately, when Congress enacted legislation in the spring of 1816, it ignored Crawford's suggestion for a permanent staff.   Instead, it simply provided for one quartermaster general and one deputy quartermaster general for each division of the Army, with an assistant quartermaster for each brigade, who superseded the existing brigade quartermaster and inspector.   The law also continued the office of the Commissary General of Purchases and provided in addition for one

---

[167] (1) RG 92, CGP, Letters Sent, No. 384, f. 377 (Irvine to Actg SW, 25 May 1815). (2) RG 107, OSW, Military Book, vol. 8, pp. 118, 142 (Actg SW to Linnard, 27 May, 3 Jun 1815); pp. 140–41 (Actg SW to Brown and Champlain, 2 Jun 1815).
[168] *American State Papers, Military Affairs*, I, 636 (27 Dec 1815).

deputy commissary for each division, for six assistant commissaries of issues, and as many military storekeepers as the service required.[169]

These arrangements proved to be of relatively short duration. During the 2 years they lasted, the Quartermaster's Department was headed by not one but two men, each of whom held the title of Quartermaster General and the rank of colonel. They shared equally the responsibilities of the office. General orders, issued from the Adjutant and Inspector General's office on 3 May 1816, announced that James R. Mullany of New York and George Gibson of Pennsylvania had been appointed Quartermasters General of the Divisions of the North and of the South, respectively, their appointments to date from 29 April 1816.

Both men had seen service during the War of 1812 and had been discharged in June of the previous year when the strength of the Army had been decreased. Only Gibson was called upon to support an active military operation—namely, Jackson's campaign against the Seminoles in West Florida, in which Gibson so effectively supplied the needs of the troops that Jackson had warm praise for his efforts.[170] For the most part, both men, during their short tours of duty as Quartermasters General, dealt with problems that were the aftermath of war—claims and disposal of surplus supplies. The condition of much of this matériel made it worthless to the Army, and the supplies were sold for whatever sums they would bring. Gibson, for example, after inspecting supplies on deposit at New Orleans, contemptuously dismissed them as "a great collection of trumpery"—broken tools of all kinds, worm-eaten saddles, and a variety of other articles, none of which were fit for issue and hardly worth repairing.[171] Settlement of claims was time-consuming but essential. Echoing arguments that were used by quartermasters in the Revolutionary War, Mullany urged prompt settlement so that those who dealt with the Army would no longer be compelled to charge extravagant prices for supplies and services in order to offset delays encountered in obtaining payment from the government.[172]

Concurrently with the settlement of these immediate problems, others, more enduring in character, were developing in relation to frontier supply. The close of the war opened a new era in American history. For the first time since the Americans had won their independence, they could turn their backs on Europe, concentrating their attention on domestic problems. Peace brought the necessity of extend-

[169] 3 *Stat.* 297 (Apr 24, 1816).

[170] (1) *Correspondence of Jackson*, ed. Bassett, II, 381 (Jackson to Calhoun, 2 Jan 1818). (2) RG 107, OSW, Letters Received, J–91 (11) (Jackson to Calhoun, undated).

[171] RG 107, OSW, Letters Received, G–63 (10) (Gibson to Jackson, 14 Apr 1817).

[172] *Ibid.*, M–417 (9) (Mullany to SW, 6 Dec 1816); M–352 (9) (Mullany to SW, 9 Aug 1816).

ing the military frontier in order to control the Indians, promote the fur trade, and exclude foreign traders. Construction of a chain of western posts was proposed. This program, with its problems of supply, was barely initiated, however, before a reorganization of the Department removed Quartermaster General Gibson and Mullany from office. The Department was reunited under the guidance of one Quartermaster General, Thomas S. Jesup, who, more than any other officer, was to give enduring form and character to the Quartermaster's Department.

CHAPTER VI

Jesup Shapes a Department

When Thomas Sidney Jesup was appointed Quartermaster General on 8 May 1818, the Army and the War Department were being thoroughly reorganized by John C. Calhoun. The latter had taken the oath of office as Secretary of War only 5 months earlier on 8 December 1817, but he quickly developed an appreciation of the problems confronting him. Foremost among these was the necessity of reorganizing the staff departments. He fully subscribed to the views expressed late in 1815 by his predecessor, William Crawford. Under Calhoun's vigorous and intelligent administration, a system of permanent staff supply agencies took form in Washington. Working with Senator John Williams of Tennessee, Chairman of the Military Affairs Committee, he drafted a bill that embodied his ideas.[1] The bill also benefited from the experience of high-ranking Army officers whom he consulted; from suggestions offered by his chief clerk, Maj. Christopher Van De Venter, who had served at various posts in the Quartermaster's Department; and from Calhoun's interest in the problem of provisioning the Army.[2]

Establishment of Supply Bureaus

Simplicity and efficiency of management would be promoted, Calhoun asserted, by placing the administration of the Quartermaster's Department under the control of a single, responsible chief. On 14 April, Congress enacted a law that retained the earlier provisions of the act of 1816 for the appointment of two deputy quartermasters general and four assistant deputy quartermasters general but eliminated the unsatisfactory arrangement that had called for administration by two co-equal heads. It substituted instead a single Quartermaster General for the Department who was to have the rank, pay, and emoluments of a brigadier general. The act also permitted the President to appoint

---

[1] (1) RG 107, OSW, Letters Received, W–35 (11) (Williams to Calhoun, 11 Feb 1818). (2) RG 107, OSW, Reports to Congress, I, 436, 439–40 (Calhoun to Williams, 5 and 16 Feb 1818). National Archives.

[2] Franklin J. Jameson, "Correspondence of John C. Calhoun," American Historical Association, *Annual Report for 1899*, vol. 2, pp. 791–92 (Virgil Maxcy to Calhoun, 2 Mar 1827).

12 additional assistant deputy quartermasters general. The law repealed earlier provisions for forage, wagon, and barrack masters.[3]

As organized in 1818, the Department consisted of 19 officers and it could also utilize the services of 18 regimental and battalion quartermasters. The Quartermaster General and one assistant quartermaster general, Capt. Trueman Cross, constituted the personnel of the Washington office. The remaining 15 assistant quartermasters general were stationed at various posts throughout the country, while one of the deputy quartermasters general was located in the Southern Division and the other, Maj. William Linnard, was continued at Philadelphia in the Northern Division.

At Calhoun's suggestion, Congress also abolished in 1818 the contract system of provisioning the Army that had been used since 1781, substituting in lieu of it a commissariat system. The latter had been advocated by Army personnel ever since the War of 1812, and Calhoun himself, while a member of the House of Representatives, had sponsored resolutions for that purpose in the fall of 1814.[4] For the first time since the Revolutionary War, a Subsistence Department was established. The new system was to be instituted as soon as existing contracts expired. The law authorized the President to appoint a Commissary General of Subsistence with the rank, pay, and emoluments of a colonel of ordnance. He was to be aided by as many assistants as the service required. They were to be taken from the subalterns of the line and allowed $20 a month in addition to their pay in the line for the services they performed. Like the Quartermaster General, the Commissary General of Subsistence was to maintain his office in Washington.[5] Viewing the establishment of the commissariat system as an experiment, Congress limited its life to 5 years. Not until 1835, and after the utility of the system had been fully demonstrated for 15 years, did Congress make it permanent.[6]

When Congress had under consideration a bill for regulating the staff departments in 1818, both George Gibson and James R. Mullany sought appointment as Quartermaster General.[7] The Secretary of War appointed neither. The War Department gave Mullany an honorable

---

[3] 3 *Stat.* 426.

[4] *Annals of Congress*, 13th Cong., 3d sess., vol. 3, pp. 550–51 (Nov 10, 1814).

[5] (1) 3 *Stat.* 426. (2) RG 107, OSW, Reports to Congress, I, 446–47 (Calhoun to Williams, –March 1818).

[6] (1) 4 *Stat.* 780 (Mar 3, 1835). See also 3 *Stat.* 721 (Jan 23, 1823); 4 *Stat.* 360 (Mar 2, 1819). (2) *American State Papers, Military Affairs*, V, 265–67 (Gibson to Chairman, House Military Committee, 21 Feb 1834).

[7] RG 94, AGO, Letters Received (Gibson file, ltrs, Pa. delegation to WD, –1818; Gaines to Calhoun, 7 May 1818); (Mullany file: ltrs, Daniel D. Tompkins to Pres. Monroe, 3 Apr 1818; Members of HR to Calhoun, 10 Apr 1818; Mullany to Calhoun, 11 Apr 1818). National Archives.

discharge from the Army. It designated Gibson to fill the newly created office of Commissary General of Subsistence on 18 April 1818, a position that he retained for the next 43 years until his death in 1861. Calhoun first offered the post of Quartermaster General to William Cumming of Georgia, who had served as Adjutant General during the last year of the War of 1812. When he declined to serve, Calhoun, by general order on 8 May 1818, appointed 29-year old Col. Thomas S. Jesup of the 3d U.S. Infantry, then Adjutant General of the Northern Division.[8]

Through some unaccountable delay in the mail, that order was 16 days on the road from Washington to Brownville, N.Y., where Jesup was stationed. Eight days later, the new Quartermaster General arrived at the capital but too late to consult with the Secretary before the latter left the city. Jesup was in sympathy with Calhoun's objectives and youthfully confident that he could master the difficulties of Quartermaster administration, though he was well aware "that some reputation is risqued in the attempt to give system to a Department, which has hitherto in our service, been in a state of confusion and disorganization." He was convinced that with Calhoun's support he could make it the first Department of the Army as it was in all European services. "I wish," he wrote the Secretary, "to give to it that character, and those features, which will render it efficient in time of war, and which, both in peace and in war, will insure a strict responsibility in all its branches." [9]

He considered his office "a military one," he advised Calhoun, and suggested the desirability of employing young, active, and intelligent subaltern officers to perform its duties. He was opposed to the use of professional clerks, who, although competent to cast accounts and copy letters, were wholly unversed in the details of military service. He believed that only men who had seen active service in the field and were familiar with military procedures could be useful in helping achieve the objectives which both he and Calhoun desired. He thought of his office as a school in which young officers might acquire habits of business and

---

[8] (1) RG 94, AGO, Letters Received 1813, No. 2670 (Cumming to Calhoun, 27 Apr 1818). (2) Jesup Papers, Box 1, Acc. 5276. Manuscript Div., Library of Congress. (3) Jesup's career in the Army began in 1808 when he was commissioned as a second lieutenant in the 7th Infantry. He served with distinction in the War of 1812, advancing to the rank of major in the Regular Army. For his gallant conduct and meritorious service in the battle of Chippewa and Lundy's Lane, in which he was severely wounded, he was brevetted lieutenant colonel and colonel, respectively. Though the strength of the Army was sharply reduced after the war, Jesup was among the officers retained, and he continued to serve in the Northern Division of the Army under Maj. Gen. Jacob Brown, becoming a colonel about 3 months before his appointment as Quartermaster General. Jesup was first a combat man and was to command troops in the Seminole War. This knowledge undoubtedly served him well as Quartermaster General.

[9] RG 107, OSW, Letters Received, J–134 (11) (To Calhoun, 5 Jun 1818).

educate themselves for the various duties of the staff. Officers thus trained in time of peace would provide a corps from which an efficient staff might be formed in the event of war.[10] Such ideas naturally won the approval of the Secretary of War.

The young men trained under Jesup's strict discipline were among the quartermasters who supplied the troops in the Mexican War and the Civil War as well, for Jesup served as Quartermaster General for 42 years until his death in 1860. His long tenure, together with the unbroken, lengthy span of service of some of his subordinate officers, gave a continuity to Quartermaster training, methods, and procedures that had been utterly lacking in the past.

Departmental Regulations

Jesup assumed the duties of his office on 15 June 1818, and about a month later he drafted a set of rules and regulations covering the nature and functions of the Quartermaster's Department and the duties of its officers. These were distilled from his own experience both in the staff and in the line, and from information obtained by studying, on the one hand, past administrative procedures in the American Army as revealed in the correspondence of Mifflin, Greene, and Pickering, Quartermasters General during the Revolutionary War, and on the other, the procedures followed in the French, Prussian, and British armies. Calhoun approved of his regulations.[11]

About this same time, Maj. Gen. Winfield Scott, on the basis of his experience and study of French and British authorities, was completing his draft of the first thoroughgoing regulatory code for the Army. This work he submitted to Calhoun on 2 September 1818. The similarity between its regulations for the Quartermaster's Department and those proposed by Jesup suggests that the two officers studied the same sources and that they undoubtedly benefited from a mutual exchange of ideas. When the code of regulations for the information and guidance of the Army was finally published in 1821, Jesup's regulations were incorporated in it.[12]

In his regulations, Jesup defined the three principal objectives of his Department. These were to insure an ample and efficient system

---

[10] RG 92, OQMG Letter Book, vol. 2, pp. 408–09 (To SW, 3 Feb 1821).

[11] *Ibid.*, vol. 1, pp. 13–16 (Jesup to Calhoun, 17 Jul 1818).

[12] (1) *American State Papers, Military Affairs*, II, 247–52 (Scott to Calhoun, 2 Sep 1818). (2) Scott's code, "General Regulations for the Army," was approved by Congress on 2 March 1821. 3 *Stat.* 615, sec. 14. (3) Before publication, the code underwent further alteration and clarification at the hands of a board of staff officers that included Jesup. RG 107, OSW, Military Book, vol. 11, 205 (GO, 19 May 1821). (4) *General Regulations for the Army, 1821*, p. 178 ff.

of supply, to give the utmost facility and effect to the movements and operations of the Army, and to enforce a strict accountability on the part of all officers and agents charged with monies or supplies. The rules and regulations he laid down in 1818 still govern in general the conduct of the office of the Quartermaster General.

Jesup emphasized the authority of the Quartermaster General by setting forth that he was to direct all correspondence of his Department. Under the direction of the Secretary of War, he was to have entire control of all subordinate officers acting in, or making disbursements on account of, the Department in all that related to the administrative part of their duties and to their accountability. The commanding officer would have military control. Except by order of the Secretary of War or of a general commanding a division, no Quartermaster officer was to be detailed or employed on duties other than those of the Department. No Quartermaster was to engage either directly or indirectly in trade. All officers of the Department were to furnish their accounts for settlement at prescribed times, and if any one of them failed to do so he was to be replaced.

Jesup felt himself competent to originate and put into operation a proper system of accountability for his Department. He therefore proposed that all monies for the Department should be drawn by the Quartermaster General and distributed by him, as the service required, to disbursing officers. Under his system, the receipts of those officers became his vouchers, and on producing them his accounts with the Treasury were closed and accounts opened with these subordinate officers. Whenever practicable, the senior quartermaster of each separate army or military department might be required to receive and account for all monies for that army or department. His accounts, both of money and property, were to be forwarded quarterly to the office of the Quartermaster General for examination and transmittal to the proper accounting office. In the event the accounting officer suspended or disallowed any voucher, it was to be returned to the Quartermaster General, accompanied by a written statement of the reasons for such action. The Quartermaster General then required a proper voucher or explanation from the quartermaster concerned.

Jesup made it clear that he had a military responsibility to compel the settlement of accounts and to enforce the performance of any other Quartermaster duty, but that his own pecuniary responsibility ceased when he produced the receipt of his subordinates for the money received.[13] He also proposed that all books and accounts of quartermasters be

---

[13] RG 92, OQMG Letter Book, vol. I, pp. 13, 16–17 (To Calhoun, 17 and 29 Jul 1818).

inspected whenever necessary, the inspection to include property as well as money. The books and accounts of the Quartermaster General were to be open to a similar inspection. These provisions for accountability were also incorporated in the regulations published in 1821.

By September, when printed forms became available, Jesup instructed his subordinates to submit quarterly abstracts showing all articles purchased by the officer, all expenditures and disbursements other than the articles purchased, and all monies received and expended during the period for which the accounts were rendered. If they made purchases at the direction of commanding officers that were not covered by the Quartermaster regulations, they had to obtain in each case a bill and receipt, accompanied with the authority on which the action was taken. All vouchers in proper form had to accompany the abstracts. In addition, at the end of every month each officer had to submit a summary statement showing the amount for which he was accountable and designating the bank in which that amount was deposited.[14]

From the days of the first organization of the Quartermaster's Department in the Revolutionary War, efforts had been made to enforce accountability for money, if not for property, and from time to time regulations had been formulated covering the duties of Quartermaster officers, but enforcement of such provisions had been gravely deficient. Confusion over duties had resulted in confusion in expenditures. Jesup consistently and persistently enforced regulations. He scrutinized vouchers closely and returned them to quartermasters for even minor corrections.[15] He examined abstracts for funds with equal care and corrected estimates by deleting from them supplies that regulations authorized other departments to procure. He instructed the assistant quartermaster general at New Orleans that the Purchase Department furnished military stores and he called his subordinate's attention to the precise paragraph of the regulations. No pretext existed, he advised the assistant quartermaster general at Boston, for calling on the Quartermaster's Department to furnish drums, fifes, and musical instruments. They properly came from the Ordnance Department, being a "species of accoutrement and a substitute for arms in the hands of the musicians." Though Jesup acknowledged that they had, in many cases, been furnished by the Purchases Department through the military storekeepers, he was determined to put an end to the irregularity of drawing supplies from one department that were provided by another.[16]

---

[14] *Ibid.,* vol. 1, pp. 57–59 (Circular to T. F. Hunt *et al.,* 9 Sep 1818).

[15] *Ibid.,* vol. 1, p. 113 (To Capt. T. F. Hunt, 21 Nov 1818).

[16] *Ibid.,* vol. 1, pp. 153–54 (To Capt. T. F. Hunt, 31 Dec 1818); 276–77 (To Capt. G. Bender, 13 May 1819).

Quartermasters often procured articles on orders of commanding officers, but the Washington office quickly spotted unauthorized items. Jesup, for example, recommended that Brig. Gens. E. P. Ripley and D. Bissell be held accountable for the pen knives and spy glasses procured on their orders by Captain Hunt, assistant quartermaster general at New Orleans.[17]   He acknowledged that a commanding officer was responsible for ordering the supplies necessary for his command, for he alone, and not the quartermaster, was the judge of what was needed. Jesup insisted that he would meet with no difficulty in obtaining supplies provided he applied to the proper department and followed the regulations.[18]   Experience in office only increased Jesup's faith in the efficiency of the system he had inaugurated in 1818.   Years later, after he had operated under those regulations in the field as a commander of troops during the Seminole War, he wrote:

> I had, under the most difficult circumstances, an opportunity of testing the high efficiency of the system—an efficiency which I had never before witnessed in the Department when serving in the field.   I never found the slightest difficulty from the working of the regulations; nor do I believe that any difficulty is occasioned by the regulations; all the difficulties I have observed since the system has been in operation, have resulted from Commanding officers forgetting their own high position and descending to, and interfering with, the minutest details of the duties of Quarter Masters—or in other words the difficulties have not resulted from the system, but from an unnecessary interference with it.[19]

Jesup obtained enforcement of the regulations, however, through persistent efforts.   Repeatedly, he called attention to the interference of line officers.   By diverting funds of the Department from the objects for which they were appropriated and applying them to those for which no appropriation had been made by Congress, they caused the development of large arrearages and aroused congressional dissatisfaction.   This was a practice that Jesup found less easy to bring under control at the more distant posts.[20]   In time, this difficulty was eliminated, but conflict between line and staff over their respective authorities was not so readily resolved.   For the first, but by no means the last time, a commanding officer charged that an attempt was under way to render certain branches of the staff independent of the proper military control.[21]   Conflicts

---

[17] *Ibid.*, vol. 1, p. 115 (To Calhoun, 23 Nov 1818).

[18] *Ibid.*, vol. 2, pp. 64–65 (To Maj. J. G. Crane, 28 Feb 1820).

[19] *Ibid.*, vol. 30, p. 106 (Jesup to Col. S. W. Kearney, 4 Jun 1840).

[20] *Ibid.*, vol. 3, p. 85 (To QM H. Stanton, 11 Jan 1821); p. 430 (To Maj. C. J. Nourse, 5 Mar 1822).

[21] (1) *Ibid.*, vol. 5, pp. 230–31 (To Col. J. Snelling, 1 Sep 1823); vol. 13, pp. 136–37 (To Maj. Gen. A. Macomb, 17 Jun 1829).   (2) For a specific example in the Purchases Department see, RG 92, Commissary General of Purchases (CGP), Letters Sent, No. 387, p. 50 (Irvine to Asst. Commissary E. B. Clemson, 12 Jun 1818); pp. 159–60 (Irvine to Calhoun, 16 Oct 1818).

between the line and staff were to materialize from time to time throughout the long history of the Quartermaster supply bureau.

Quartermaster Support of Expeditions

Jesup had been in office only 10 months when Calhoun ordered him
to St. Louis on 27 March 1819.[22]   He was to supervise supply preparations
for the support of troops who were being sent to execute Calhoun's
military policy for the inland frontier.   The policy was simply an extension of one that had been developed immediately following the War of
1812.   The necessity of extending the military frontier in order to
control the Indians, promote the fur trade, and exclude foreign traders
had dictated that the War Department build a chain of forts for these
purposes.[23]   At the time Calhoun became Secretary of War, the northern
military frontier was marked by posts that stretched from Michilimackinac
via Green Bay to Prairie du Chien.

By 1817, the thrust of westward expansion was rapidly outmoding
the effectiveness of that military frontier.   In that year an English
observer, Morris Birkbeck, wrote that "Old America seems to be breaking
up and moving westward." [24]   Settlement had crossed the Mississippi.
Missouri would establish a territorial government in 1819 and achieve
statehood 2 years yater.   Fur traders ranged to the Rockies and beyond.
The only course was to push the military frontier farther westward to
protect the settler and trader and to control the Indians.   Calhoun
therefore projected a new military frontier, and for that purpose the War
Department sent out two expeditions.   The main one was to move up
the Missouri River to the mouth of the Yellowstone River and erect
posts at Council Bluffs and the Mandan Village, near the present site of
Bismarck, N.Dak., the nearest point to the outpost on the Red River of
the Hudson's Bay Company.   The second expedition was to advance up
the Mississippi to the mouth of the St. Peter's River (the Minnesota River
of today) where it was to establish a strong post in what has since become
the metropolitan area of St. Paul.

On 16 March 1818, Calhoun instructed Brig. Gen. Thomas A. Smith,
commanding officer at St. Louis, to push a detachment of some 250
riflemen to the mouth of the Yellowstone River.[25]   With the staff departments then in process of reorganization, the supply of provisions and
of transportation was placed wholly under his control.   Calhoun antici-

[22] RG 107, OSW, Military Book, vol. 10, p. 290 (Calhoun to Jesup, 27 Mar 1819).
[23] *Ibid.*, vol. 8, pp. 106–09 (SW to Brown and to Jackson, 22 May 1815).
[24] *Notes on a Journey in America* (London, 1818), 31.
[25] RG 107, OSW, Military Book, vol. 10, pp. 33–34.

pated that the lateness of the season might prevent the detachment from reaching its destination during the summer, but he optimistically suggested that the troops might establish a post at some intermediate point, such as the Mandan Village, that would serve as a starting point for operations the following year. The Mandan Village was 1,540 miles from St. Louis, and Council Bluffs, considered a half-way point between St. Louis and the Mandan Village, was some 650 miles from the mouth of the Missouri River.[26] Calhoun ordered the Ordnance Department and the Commissary General of Purchases to provide the necessary military stores and clothing, but the preparations took far longer than he had anticipated. Col. Talbot Chambers, in charge of the troops, did not leave Belle Fontaine, about 20 miles west of St. Louis on the Missouri River, until late in August. Pushing up the Missouri in keelboats, the troops made slow progress. They did not reach the Mandan Village and, in fact, advanced only 400 miles up the river before they had to establish winter quarters.

By that time the reorganization of the staff departments had been accomplished, and supply preparations, in anticipation of spring operations, could be initiated in the winter of 1818–19. Since rations for the expedition had to be delivered before June 1819, when contracts could for the first time be executed by the newly created office of the Commissary General of Subsistence, the War Department had to depend upon existing contracts for the necessary supply of subsistence. In consequence, Calhoun ordered James Johnson of Kentucky, who held contracts for supplying the troops stationed at various posts in the West, to deposit 420,000 rations at Belle Fontaine by 21 March 1819. Later, the Commissary General requisitioned an additional 250,000 rations for delivery before 1 May.[27]

Having learned that Quartermaster General Jesup was then charged with all transportation of men and supplies for the expedition, Richard M. Johnson, brother of the aforementioned contractor and Chairman of the House Committee on Military Affairs, solicited a transportation contract in behalf of his brother.[28] Aware of the importance of military control and responsibility in such an expedition, Jesup was at first opposed to negotiating a contract. With some reluctance he entered into a transportation contract with James Johnson at Calhoun's orders. Johnson

---

[26] House *Ex. Doc.* No. 110, 16th Cong., 2d sess., pp. 223–24, 230.

[27] (1) RG 192, Commissary General of Subsistence (CGS), Letters Sent, I, 3 (Gibson to Calhoun, 20 Nov 1818). (2) House *Ex. Doc.* No. 110, 16th Cong., 2d sess., p. 226 (Gibson interrogation).

[28] House *Ex. Doc.* No. 110, 16th Cong., 2d sess., pp. 178–79 (R. M. Johnson to Jesup, 17 Nov 1818).

also held a third contract, under which he transported from Pittsburgh to St. Louis the clothing, ordnance, and medical stores for the expedition.[29]

As early as the summer of 1818, Johnson had proposed using steamboats to transport supplies up the Missouri River.[30] The transportation contract executed by Jesup on 2 December 1818 stipulated that Johnson was to furnish by 1 March 1819 two steamboats capable of navigating the Mississippi and its waters. They were to be placed subject to the orders of the Quartermaster General. One or more additional steamboats were to be provided if such transportation proved successful and if they were required. Johnson was obligated to furnish keelboats if the steamboats were not able to transport the provisions and supplies. Since no steamboat had ever navigated the Missouri and no rates were established, the government agreed to allow Johnson a reasonable compensation to be determined later.[31] Until it was ascertained whether steamboat transportation would be successful or not, Jesup advised his assistant quartermaster at St. Louis to retain all his keelboats and barges for possible use.[32]

While these measures were taken, the War Department ordered additional troops to St. Louis. These included the 6th Regiment of Infantry that moved from Plattsburg, via New York, Pittsburgh, and St. Louis, to Council Bluffs—a distance of 2,628 miles. It was the longest movement of an American expedition, aside from small exploring parties, undertaken to that time. The main body of the Mississippi expedition, consisting of a large detachment of the 5th Infantry, sailed from Detroit by way of the Great Lakes to Green Bay, traveling via the Fox and Wisconsin Rivers to Prairie du Chien, and then up the Mississippi to St. Peter's, a distance of 1,270 miles. Calhoun was well pleased with the expeditious movement of these troops directed by Jesup through his Quartermasters at Pittsburgh and Detroit.[33]

In December 1818, Johnson wrote that rations and every other article ordered would be ready to move in 30 days.[34] But returns of the military storekeeper at St. Louis later revealed that he failed to deliver subsistence stores at the time required. The steamboat *Expedition* did not arrive at Belle Fontaine with provisions until 18 May, but Johnson dared not land the cargo lest it and the steamboat as well be attached by

[29] *Ibid.,* pp. 242, 246 (Jesup statement).

[30] RG 107, OSW, Military Book, vol. 10, pp. 94–95 (C. Van De Venter to Johnson, 24 Jun 1818).

[31] House *Ex. Doc.* No. 110, 16th Cong., 2d sess., pp. 6–7 (Contract).

[32] RG 92, OQMG Letter Book, vol. 1, p. 154 (To J. McGunnegle, 31 Dec 1818).

[33] (1) *American State Papers, Military Affairs,* II, 31. (2) RG 92, OQMG Letter Book, vol. 1, p. 179 (Jesup to Stanton, 8 Feb 1819); p. 181 (To Atkinson, 11 Feb 1819); pp. 198–99 To H. Johnston, 3 Mar 1819). (3) Jameson, "Correspondence of John C. Calhoun," AHA *Annual Report for 1899,* vol. 2, p. 163 (Calhoun to Brown, 5 Sep 1819).

[34] House *Ex. Doc.* No. 110, 16th Cong., 2d sess., p. 181 (To Jesup, 27 Dec 1818).

the Missouri authorities in a civil suit that had been adjudged against him. In consequence, Johnson's boats fell downstream to the Illinois shore where he landed the provisions for inspection, resalting, and repacking.[35]

Obviously, if Johnson was using his steamboats in May to transport supplies, they were not made available to the Quartermaster General according to the terms of the transportation contract. Johnson did provide four rather than two steamboats—the *Expedition,* the *Johnson,* the *Jefferson,* and the *Calhoun.* The last, however, never reached St. Louis; it had insufficient power to ascend the Mississippi. Jesup reported that the boats were badly constructed and that their management was worse than their construction. Even with partial loads, they experienced difficulty in navigating the Missouri, and one by one they were abandoned for keelboats.[36]

As soon as he arrived in the West, Jesup found that the contractor's arrangements were not as far along as he had been led to expect. Jesup protested that "something more than idle professions and ostentatious boastings" by the contractor would be necessary to insure success. When the 5th Regiment arrived at St. Louis, the Quartermaster General would have taken transportation entirely out of the contractor's hands, inasmuch as Johnson had failed to meet the terms of his contract, but such large advances had been made to him that his services were retained.[37]

As was customary, Johnson had received advances on his contracts to enable him to execute them. On the subsistence contract, for example, these had amounted to $35,000 for each quarter. The contractor acknowledged that Calhoun's policy had been liberal "for ordinary years" but unfortunately 1819 was a year of panic.[38] Loans could not be obtained from banks or individuals. Settlement of debts were being demanded, and nothing could be bought on credit. The bubble of overexpansion following the War of 1812 had been pricked by the second Bank of the United States. Concerned for its own safety, it had demanded that the state banks redeem their obligations to it in specie. To preserve his own credit, Johnson had to obtain additional advances from the War Department. He flattered, cajoled, and wheedled Calhoun,

---

[35] (1) *Ibid.,* pp. 15–18 (Johnson to R. M. Johnson, 30 Sep 1819). (2) RG 107, OSW. Letters Received, C–26 (13) (Col. Chambers to General Bissell, 21 May 1819).

[36] (1) House *Ex. Doc.* No. 110, 16th Cong., 2d sess., pp. 221, 222. (2) RG 92, OQMG Letter Book, vol. 1, p. 461 (Jesup to Calhoun, 30 Aug 1821).

[37] (1) RG 92, OQMG Letter Book, vol. 1, pp. 495–96 (Jesup to Calhoun, 16 Dec 1819). (2) RG 107, OSW, Letters Received, J–30 (13) (Jesup to Calhoun, 26 Jun 1819); J–35 (13) (Jesup to Cross, 25 Jun 1819).

[38] RG 107, OSW, Letters Received, J–220 (12) Enc. (R. M. Johnson to Calhoun, 29 Mar 1819).

predicting disaster to the expedition if his pleas for funds were not heeded.[39]

Calhoun granted an advance of $50,000 on the transportation contract and accepted two drafts drawn by Johnson to meet payments for the purchase of an additional steamboat.[40]   Jesup was greatly surprised at this turn of events.   On his journey to St. Louis, he had passed through Kentucky and at Johnson's earnest solicitations had advanced him $10,000.   That advance, with those Johnson had already received, Jesup informed Calhoun, were more than the whole expenses of the expedition should have been for the year.[41]   Johnson's representation that the expedition would fail without that $50,000-advance was entirely incorrect. Jesup advised the Secretary that he had made provisional arrangements that would insure success independent of the Johnson brothers.[42]

Appeals to the Secretary of War, the Quartermaster General, and the Commissary General of Subsistence by no means exhausted the Johnson brothers' possibilities for obtaining advances.   Early in July, Calhoun received a letter from President Monroe, then on tour in Kentucky. The Johnson brothers had seized the opportunity to lay their problems before him and had been so persuasive that the President, to prevent failure of the expedition, directed Calhoun to advance the contractor $85,000 on his subsistence and transportation contracts.   He was also to grant Johnson an additional advance of $57,500 upon receipt of title to the four steamboats.   Johnson immediately drew against the advances Monroe had ordered.[43]

Calhoun was stunned.   The advances on the transportation contract had been large and those on the subsistence contract were within some $28,500 of all that would be due the contractor when he made his last delivery.   The War Department would be embarrassed for want of funds before the end of the year, and Calhoun begged Johnson to make no further drafts lest he be compelled to refuse payment.[44]

At St. Louis, Jesup, having refused to grant any further advances, charged that Johnson had furnished transportation for only four companies of men and about 350 tons of provisions and stores.[45]   Johnson insinuated that Jesup "this good man this gallant & faithful officer has

[39] *Ibid.*, (R. M. Johnson to Calhoun, 30 Mar, 3 Apr, 9 Apr 1819).

[40] (1) *Ibid.*, J–2 (13) (Johnson to Calhoun, 30 May 1819).   (2) RG 107, OSW, Military Book. vol. 10, p. 388 (Calhoun to Jesup, 3 May 1819).

[41] RG 107, OSW, Letters Received, J–11 (13) (Jesup to Calhoun, 12 Jun 1819).

[42] *Ibid.*, J–30 (13) (To Calhoun, 26 Jun 1819).

[43] *Ibid.*, P–40 (13) (Monroe to Calhoun, 5 Jul 1819); J–12 (13) (Johnson to Calhoun, 5 Jul 1819).

[44] *Ibid.*, P–40 (13) Enc. (Calhoun to Johnson, 20 Jul 1819).

[45] (1) *Ibid.*, J–36 (13) Jesup to Calhoun, 8 Jul 1819).   (2) RG 92, OQMG Letter Book, vol. 1, pp. 458–59 (Jesup to Johnson, 4 Jul 1819).

permitted his mind to be poisoned & operated upon" by Johnson's
enemies at St. Louis.[46]   Jesup reported that no reliance could be placed
on the contractor's "fair promises."   Some troops and stores had begun
moving in mid-June in keelboats furnished by the Quartermaster's
Department.   Jesup advised the Secretary that three companies of troops
under Col. Henry Leavenworth left Prairie du Chien on 6 August and
would arrive at the objective, St. Peter's River, that year.   On the other
hand, the Missouri expedition, headed by Col. Henry Atkinson, would
undoubtedly reach Council Bluffs by mid-October, but Johnson's failure
to comply with his contracts would prevent any troops reaching the
Mandan Village in 1819.[47]

Though preparations were begun in the winter of 1819–20 to carry
the Missouri expedition to the Mandan Village, congressional investigation aired charges of extravagance and prevented further appropriations
for the expedition.   The troops were halted at Council Bluffs and for a
time the policy of constructing forts on the northern inland frontier came
to an end.   War Department entanglement with the Johnson brothers,
however, was not yet ended.   Late in 1819 they presented a bill for their
services that included not only enormous charges for the use of their
steamboats and keelboats but claims for delays occasioned by the government.   Jesup rejected these claims, but, under the terms of the contract,
settlement was referred to arbitrators.   Much to the gratification of the
Johnson brothers, the arbitrators generously awarded them an allowance
of 16¼ cents per pound for all supplies shipped at the mouth of the
Missouri, St. Louis, or Belle Fontaine for Council Bluffs, either on board
steamboats or keelboats.   In effect, this amount was paid for all transportation the contractor performed as well as for all performed by the
Quartermaster's Department, for if a steamboat broke down, as the
Jefferson did after progressing only 144 miles up the Missouri, and the
Quartermaster's Department transported the cargo to Council Bluffs the
contractor was still paid the full price.[48]   A House committee investigating the contract and arbitration findings came to the conclusion that
the award ought to be set aside and recommended that the Attorney
General be directed to use all legal means not only to accomplish that
purpose but to recover for the United States whatever might be due from
James Johnson.[49]

---

[46] RG 107, OSW, Letters Received, P–40 (13) Enc. (Johnson to Calhoun, 26 Jul 1819).
[47] *Ibid.*, J–30 (13); J–68 (13) (Jesup to Calhoun, 26 Jun and 9 Sep 1819).
[48] RG 92, OQMG Letter Book, vol. 2, pp. 397–407 (Jesup's statement on case, Feb 1820);
pp. 167–68 (Cross to 3d auditor, 12 Jun 1820); vol. 8, pp. 220–21 (Jesup to Duff Green,
20 Sep 1825).
[49] *American State Papers, Military Affairs*, II, 324–25 (1 Mar 1821).

Economy Drive

At Calhoun's request, Jesup returned to Washington early in September 1819. The appropriation for his Department, the Secretary warned, was nearly exhausted, and while advances to Johnson were partly responsible, still the current disbursements of the Department appeared to be greater than they should have been.[50] Jesup was not surprised. The Department, he informed Calhoun, had been forced to furnish more than two-thirds of the transportation for the two expeditions despite the advances to Johnson; large sums had been applied to the services of the Ordnance Department; and Congress had made no provision for arrearages of the previous year.[51] Capt. Trueman Cross, who handled disbursements in the Washington office and had been acting as chief during Jesup's absence, raised still another pertinent point—the Department lacked control of its appropriation. Of $200,000 transferred to the Department in 1819, only $6,300 had been remitted on requisitions from the Quartermaster office; the rest, except for $32,000 remaining to its credit in October had been remitted on warrants issued at the War Office of which the chief of the Department had no knowledge. Thus the chain of responsibility was broken and the Quartermaster General could not be held accountable for the application of an appropriation that he did not control.[52] Obviously, retrenchment had to become the order of the day. Economy measures continued to be pursued with great care during the following year in the wake of congressional action that cut nearly $100,000 from Jesup's estimate of $526,500 needed for 1820.

The congressional economy drive was reflected in renewed efforts to reduce the size of the Army, both in the line and the staff. Calhoun had warded off earlier attempts, but in the spring of 1820 Congress directed him to report a plan for decreasing troop strength to 6,000 men.[53] Calhoun advocated little or no reduction of the staff in the plan he submitted in December 1820. He based his views on the principle that a peacetime establishment should be so formed that at the commencement of hostilities "there should be nothing either to new model or to create." The organization of the staff in a peacetime military establishment ought to be such, he argued, that every branch of it should be completely formed, with such extension as the number of troops and

---

[50] RG 107, OSW, Military Book, vol. 10, pp. 315–16 (Calhoun to Jesup, 19 Jul 1819). Jesup did not receive this letter until his return from Ft. Osage on 26 August.

[51] RG 107, OSW, Letters Received, J–63 (13) (Jesup to Calhoun, 31 Aug 1819).

[52] RG 92, OQMG Letter Book, vol. 1, pp. 416–17 (Cross to Calhoun, 1 Oct 1819).

[53] (1) *Annals of Congress*, 16th Cong., 1st sess., vol. 2, p. 2233 (May 11, 1820). (2) For Calhoun's earlier report see *American State Papers, Military Affairs*, I, 779 ff. (To House of Representatives, 11 Dec 1818).

posts occupied might render necessary.   So that the government might at all times be able to obtain a correct knowledge of the condition of the Army and also be able to introduce method, order, and economy in its disbursements, Calhoun believed that every branch of the staff should terminate in a responsible chief stationed at least in peacetime near the seat of government.   The bureau arrangement, first established in 1818, had been productive of economy, and further to perfect it the Secretary proposed that the office of the Commissary General of Purchases be established at Washington.   This Department was also to include an assistant commissary general and two storekeepers.   No change was recommended in the Quartermaster's Department, and the 19 officers then serving in the Quartermaster's Department were to be retained, except that the 16 assistant deputy quartermasters general were to be taken from the line.[54]

On 2 March 1821, Congress enacted legislation that reduced the Army from 12,664 to 6,183 officers and men.[55]   At the same time, it also decreased the number of staff officers.   Among other staff arrangements, the act provided for one Commissary of Purchases and two storekeepers in lieu of the former Commissary General of Purchases, two deputies, and six assistant commissaries of issue, with as many military storekeepers as the service required.   It cut the Quartermaster's Department from a total of 19 officers and 18 regimental and battalion quartermasters to 13 officers.   In addition to the Quartermaster General, the Department consisted of two quartermasters with the rank, pay, and emoluments of majors of cavalry, and ten assistant quartermasters taken from the line and paid an additional sum of not less than $10 nor more than $20.   The law eliminated the 18 regimental and battalion quartermasters.   The Subsistence Department remained unchanged with a Commissary General at its head.   The number of assistant commissaries, all taken from the line, was not to exceed 50.   They and the assistant quartermasters were, on orders of the Secretary of War, to be subject to duties in both Departments.   In enacting the law, Congress paid no attention to Calhoun's advice, discarded his recommendations, and attempted to make the staff efficient at the expense of the line.[56]

The law had intended to make up the limitation on the number of officers in the Quartermaster's Department by subjecting subsistence commissaries to the duties of quartermasters at stations where the latter

---

[54] *American State Papers, Military Affairs*, II, 188 ff. (Calhoun to House of Representatives, 12 Dec 1820).

[55] (1) *Ibid.*, II, 194, 452 (Organization of the Army, Dec 1820, 2 Mar 1821).   (2) 3 *Stat.* 615 ff.

[56] Bvt. Maj. Gen. Emory Upton, *The Military Policy of the United States* (3d edition, Washington, 1912), p. 152.

could not be located.   As soon as it was passed, therefore, Jesup requested that 33 assistant commissaries of subsistence be placed under his orders for duty in the Quartermaster's Department.[57]   While these commissaries might prove efficient auxiliaries in preserving public property and issuing supplies, they could not be used to advantage as disbursing agents. Before the end of the year and in response to a congressional query, Major Cross, again acting as the head of the Department during Jesup's absence, recommended that the law be amended by adding eight more assistant quartermasters to the Department to increase its efficiency.[58]

In annual reports submitted during the next 4 years, Jesup hammered at the need to expand the personnel of his Department.   The labors of the Department depended not upon the number of troops in service, but on the number and remoteness of the posts occupied, the extent of the frontiers, and the dispersed state of the military resources of the nation.   Moreover, the responsibilities of the Department had been increased.   The act of 1821, whether through oversight or intent, by reducing the Purchasing Department to a Commissary and two storekeepers, left that Department unable to execute its duties. The Secretary of War had to transfer responsibility for both the issue and preservation of clothing to the Quartermaster's Department.   By June 1, the Commissary General had turned over to Jesup clothing deposits at Detroit, Sackett's Harbor, New Orleans, Norfolk, Boston, New York, Charleston, Pittsburgh, and Carlisle.[59]   Of necessity, the Secretary of War also transferred the Purchasing Department's duties relative to the administration of, and accountability for, Army clothing to the Quartermaster's Department, thereby doubling its labors and responsibility at the same time that its personnel was reduced nearly two-thirds.[60]   By 1824, Congress began to consider the problems Jesup was raising, but it was not until 1826 that it enacted legislation increasing the staff of the Quartermaster's Department by two more quartermasters and ten assistant quartermasters, to be taken from the line of the Army.[61]

Between 1821, when the Department's personnel numbered 13, and 1826, when it was increased to 25, the Department, in order to carry out its duties, made use of the services of subsistence commissaries, lieu-

---

[57] RG 92, AGO, Letters Received, No. 12366 (Jesup to Calhoun, 28 May 1821).

[58] RG 107, OSW, Letters Received, C–69 (15) (To Calhoun, 24 Dec 1821).

[59] (1) RG 92, CGP, Letters Sent, No. 389, p. 19 (Irvine to Robert Irwin *et al.,* 18 May 1821). (2) RG 92, OQMG Letter Book, vol. 3, pp. 62–63 (Jesup to Capt. T. F. Hunt, 14 May 1821).

[60] *American State Papers, Military Affairs,* II, 559–60, 707; III, 100–101; 161–67 (Jesup to SW, 22 Nov 1823; 27 Nov 1824; 9 Feb 1824; 26 Dec 1825).

[61] (1) *Ibid.,* III, 100–102 (Committee on Military Affairs to Senate, 27 Dec 1824 and enclosures); pp. 161–65 (Committee on Military Affairs to House, 5 Jan 1826).   (2) 4 *Stat.* 173 ff. (May 18, 1826).

tenants detailed from the line to serve as acting assistant quartermasters, and military storekeepers. By this means, Jesup added between 25 to 30 officers to the staff of the Department.[62] After the Department's personnel was increased in 1826, its staff was restricted to the officers regularly appointed in the Department, and for the next 12 years the 25 officers, including the Quartermaster General, administered an ever-increasing burden of duties. As the Department's responsibilities increased, particularly in the construction of barracks, roads, and other projects assigned to it, the Department employed a large number of civilian artisans, at least on a temporary basis. Its employment rolls also showed masters, mates, and sailors employed to operate certain government-owned boats as well as agents hired to safeguard dismantled posts and military stores.[63] These civilians and most of the officers were stationed at posts in the field.

The Washington office remained small. In time, two other officers and a sergeant assisted Quartermaster General Jesup and Major Cross. In accordance with Jesup's ideas, only military personnel served in the office during the first 5 years of its existence. As paper work increased, however, he added two civilian clerks to the staff in the fall of 1824.[64] For many years thereafter, Jesup, assisted by two officers, one of whom was usually Maj. Trueman Cross, and a few clerks executed the duties of the Washington office.[65]

Neither the Black Hawk War in 1832 nor the campaigns against the Indians in Florida that began in 1836 produced any reorganization of the Quartermaster's Department. In the annual report for 1836, Major Cross, again serving as Acting Quartermaster General, recommended an increase in the Department's personnel. Experience had shown that 4 majors, 6 captains, and 14 lieutenants, drawn from the line, did not provide enough personnel to discharge the heavy duties of the Quartermaster's Department. It had been, both as to number and grades, barely sufficient to meet the demands of the service 10 years earlier. Maj. Thomas F. Hunt, who temporarily served as Acting Quartermaster General earlier in the year, expressed similar views.[66]

---

[62] RG 92, OQMG Letter Book, vol. 6, pp. 463–64; vol. 10, pp. 16–17 (Personnel Lists, 6 Aug 1824, 2 Sep 1826).

[63] Ibid., vol. 12, pp. 314–17; vol. 16, pp. 218–20 (Lists, 16 Oct 1829; 5 Oct 1831).

[64] (1) Ibid., vol. 6, p. 450 (Jesup to SW, 3 Aug 1824). (2) RG 92, OQMG, Estimates and Reports (1822–1826).

[65] RG 92, OQMG Letter Book, vol. 22, pp. 420–23 (Jesup to Chairman, House Military Affairs Committee, 21 Dec 1835).

[66] American State Papers, Military Affairs, VI, 831 (Annual Rpt, 22 Nov 1836); 186–87 (Cross to Senate, 29 Mar 1836); 785–86 (Hunt to SW, 24 May 1836); 987–91 (Cross to SW, 14 Jan 1837).

The Secretary of War forwarded these communications, with his approval, to Thomas H. Benton, Chairman of the Senate Committee on Military Affairs, but it was the summer of 1838 before Congress, spurred on by the threat of complications with Great Britain on the northeastern frontier, not only increased the staff of the Quartermaster's Department but also increased the size of the Army and mitigated some of the shortcomings that had been produced in it by the act of 1821.[67]

Largely in agreement with the recommendations that had been made by Major Cross, Congress increased the Department's personnel by 12 officers, making a total of 37. It corrected the disadvantages that had previously been created by the lack of a regular gradation of rank in the Department. Of the 12 new officers added, two were to be assistant quartermasters general, with the rank of colonel; two were to be deputy quartermasters general, with the rank of lieutenant colonel; and eight were to be assistant quartermasters, with the rank of captain. The assistant quartermasters already in service were given the same rank as the newly authorized officers of that grade. The pay and emoluments of the officers of the Department were the same as those allowed to officers of similar rank in the dragoon regiment. All appointments were to be made from the Army, and upon appointment officers were to relinquish their rank in the line and be separated from it. That provision was modified 2 days later to the extent that assistant quartermasters were not to be separated from the line.[68] For the first time since its establishment in 1818, the Department had a regular gradation of officers extending downward from the rank of brigadier general held by the Quartermaster General. The law also once again authorized the Quartermaster General to employ as many as 20 forage and wagonmasters, who were to be paid $40 a month, three rations per day, and forage for one horse. No further changes were made in the Army or the Quartermaster's Department until the War with Mexico began.

Changes in Clothing Supply

During the first decade of the Department's existence as a bureau, Jesup was not only concerned with increasing the strength of his staff and inculcating habits of responsibility and accountability in Quartermaster officers, but he was also absorbed in developing procedures for carrying out new responsibilities vested in his Department. In 1821, Quartermaster responsibility in supplying the Army with clothing was

---

[67] (1) 5 *Stat.* 256 (Jul 5, 1838). (2) Upton, *The Military Policy of the United States*, pp. 162–193.
[68] 5 *Stat.* 308 (Jul 7, 1838).

no longer restricted to its transportation.   By order of the Secretary of
War, the Quartermaster General also prescribed and enforced a system
of accountability for all supplies derived from the Purchasing Department.

Commissary General Irvine recommended the readoption of a
slightly modified system of accountability under Army paymasters and
inspectors that he had introduced in 1816 and 1817.[69]   In preparing
the Army regulatory code for publication in 1821, General Scott suggested that legislation would be required to make the change.   Irvine
considered it unnecessary and the War Department sought no congressional authority.[70]

Jesup was opposed to any re-introduction of Irvine's paymaster-
inspector system, and Calhoun did not adopt Irvine's proposal.   Jesup
viewed the recommendation as an attempt to introduce a part of the British clothing system.   "Its principles," he insisted, "though plausible in
theory, were found in practice like most of those borrowed from foreign
service, without regard to the difference of circumstances, to be entirely
inapplicable to the state of our army, dispersed as it was, in small detachments throughout the union."   The Quartermaster General pointed
out that it was impossible to have a paymaster at each post.   Moreover,
the system, Jesup argued, was wrong in most of its details, and although
some of its defects had been remedied in 1817, Army opposition had
caused its repeal.   Jesup made some improvements in accountability
under the regulations of 1821, but by 1824 the lack of legal authority prevented him from enforcing a system that, to be effectual, should have
contained authority to mulct delinquents.[71]

The provisions that he submitted to Calhoun as "indispensably
necessary" in February 1824 were incorporated in an act Congress passed
in May 1826.   This legislation provided that legal sanction that Jesup
required.   In compliance with the law, he drafted a system of regulations
and forms that became the basis of accountability for clothing and equipage until World War I.[72]

Under this system, every captain or commander of a company or
detachment opened an account book in which he entered against the
name of each individual in his command the clothing and equipment
issued to him.   He kept a separate account for extra issues and soldiers
settled for them at their next pay periods.   The officer also took dupli-

[69] RG 92, CGP, Letters Sent, No. 389, p. 18 (Irvine to Calhoun, 17 May 1821); pp. 31–32
(Irvine to William Lee, 26 May 1821).
[70] Ibid., pp. 105–06 (Irvine to Paymaster General D. Parker, 23 Jul 1821).
[71] (1) American State Papers, Military Affairs, II, 559–60 (To Calhoun, 22 Nov 1823).
(2) RG 107, OSW, Letters Received, Q–130 (17) (To Calhoun, 9 Feb 1824).
[72] RG 92, OQMG Letter Book, vol. 10, pp. 96–114 (To SW, 13 Oct 1826).

cate receipts of the issues made, one of which he transmitted as his voucher to the Treasury. The other he filed away with the company papers to be used as a check on the account books when the final certified statement of a soldier's clothing account was given to him at the time his term of service expired or he was discharged. The paymaster settled all clothing acounts.

The regular supply of clothing was distributed semi-annually in May and September or April and October, depending on the latitude where distribution occurred. All issues of clothing were made and receipted for in the presence of a commissioned officer. Camp equipage was not entered on returns as issued to the companies but had to be borne there as on hand, in use, and not dropped from the returns until it became unfit for service. It was then turned over to the quartermaster of the post for sale or other disposition as directed by the Quartermaster General.

When a quartermaster delivered clothing at a post, a board of officers made an immediate inspection of it. The board reported on any damage or deficiency, filing a copy of the report with the Quartermaster General and the quartermaster who furnished the clothing, or the Commissary General of Purchases if it was supplied direct from the Philadelphia depot. If clothing in the hands of company officers or in store became damaged or unfit for issue, a board of survey examined it and assessed the amount of damage. This was charged against the officer in whose hands the supplies became damaged unless he could show that it did not result from neglect. The officer turned over all condemned clothing and equipage to the quartermaster, who accepted the articles only if a survey had been made. The Quartermaster's Department further promoted uniformity in accountability by supplying clothing company books.[73]

When in 1821 Congress reduced the personnel in the Purchasing Department, the Secretary of War transferred to the Quartermaster's Department responsibility not only for the preservation and distribution of clothing but also for the preparation of estimates. Previously, the Commissary General of Purchases had prepared and laid before the Secretary for approval a consolidated report that was based on estimates submitted by the commanding officers of companies and detachments. These indicated the supplies of clothing and equipment needed during the ensuing year.

From 1821 until the Clothing Bureau was established in 1832, the commanding officers of regiments sent all annual clothing estimates to

---

[73] RG 92, OQMG Clothing Book, Letters Sent, I, 24 (Jesup to Maj. T. Cross, 7 Apr 1827).

the Quartermaster General on or before 1 July.   He scrutinized these estimates closely and modified them in the light of the clothing allowances permitted under the regulations.   With the approval of the Secretary of War, he sent the revised estimates to the Commissary General of Purchases whose Department furnished the supplies from the Arsenal, packed them, and turned them over to the Quartermaster's Department for shipment to the troops.   The Quartermaster General also used these same regimental estimates to prepare a detailed annual estimate of the clothing and equipment needed for the whole Army during the ensuing year.   When sanctioned by the Secretary of War, he transmitted that estimate to the Commissary General of Purchases and it became a guide for his future procurement and the basis of the monetary estimate the Commissary General prepared for submission to Congress in connection with the passage of the Army appropriation bill.[74]   Irvine made an attempt to secure a return of the estimating responsibility to his office in 1824, but the Secretary of War did not approve his proposal.[75]

Subscribing to the theory that Calhoun had put into practice—namely, that every branch ought to have a chief stationed in Washington—and feeling the need of an officer in his Department to whom he could submit all clothing problems, the Secretary of War in 1832 decided to establish a Clothing Bureau as an appendage to the War Office.[76] Irvine opposed its establishment but the Secretary appointed Maj. John Garland to head the bureau by 1 June 1823 and sent him to Philadelphia to confer with the Commissary General of Purchases.[77]   The Quartermaster's Department was still preparing the clothing estimates.   Fearful that the mixed jurisdictions set up for the control of Army clothing would result in misunderstandings, Jesup recommended, in March of the following year, that the preparation of estimates be transferred from his Department to the Clothing Bureau.[78]   In consequence, until the Secretary of War abolished the Clothing Bureau 8 years later in 1841, it prepared the clothing estimates.   The Commissary General of Purchases continued to submit the monetary estimates for clothing and equipment.

Throughout these years, Irvine made no basic changes in the method

[74] (1) RG 92, OQMG Letters Sent, vol. 6, pp. 132–35 (Jesup to editor of *Washington Gazette*, 20 Feb 1824).   (2) For examples of Quartermaster review of estimates from the field see *ibid.*, vol. 6, pp. 412–13 (To Col. T. Chambers, 21 Jul 1824); vol. 7, pp. 150–51 (To Col. M. K. Armistead, 19 Nov 1824).

[75] RG 92, CGP, Letters Sent, No. 390, pp. 195–196, 198–99 (Irvine to Calhoun, 2 and 14 Sep 1824).

[76] RG 107, OSW, Letters Sent, vol. 13, p. 163 (SW to Irvine, 14 Mar 1832).

[77] (1) *Ibid.*, vol. 13, p. 201 (SW to Garland, 1 Jun 1832).   (2) RG 92, CGP, Letters Sent, No. 392, p. 98 (T. Bangor to SW, 13 Feb 1832); pp. 113–17 (Irvine to SW, 2 Mar 1832).

[78] RG 92, OQMG Clothing Book, Letters Sent, IV, 332–33 (To SW, 9 Mar 1833).

of procurement or in the production of Army clothing.   The possibility
of returning to the contract method of obtaining clothing for the Army
was agitated from 1833 to 1835.   Commissary General Irvine professed
to have no predilection for any particular method, but he recalled at
length the disadvantages that the Army had labored under in obtaining
clothing before 1812.   To his relief and that of the War Department
generally, the prices quoted by contractors were so much higher than
those at which clothing was produced under the direction of the Clothing
Establishment at Philadelphia that the Secretary of War abandoned any
thought of returning to the contract method.[79]

Commissariat Subsistence System

Establishment of the Subsistence Department as a bureau in Washington in 1818 in no way altered the responsibility of the Quartermaster's
Department for transporting rations to the Army.   The shift from the
contract to the commissariat system, however, did greatly increase
Quartermaster expenditures for the transportation of subsistence stores.
Under the old system, the contractor provided rations at a stipulated
price and delivered them to designated posts in a given district.   Under
the commissariat system, the Commissary General of Subsistence still
purchased subsistence stores by contract on public notice, but the contractor delivered them in bulk to a given point or depot where a commissary made inspection.   The quartermaster distributed the subsistence
stores to the posts in the area, arranging for the transportation of the
rations and providing the necessary storehouses.   Assistant commissaries
issued the rations, requisitioning on the depots for their supplies.
Whether the posts were located on the inland frontier or the maritime
frontier, the Quartermaster's Department was required to provide a
greater amount of transportation than when the contractors had made
delivery to the posts.

After 1 June 1819, when the old subsistence contracts expired and
the commissariat system began to function, the new arrangement promoted economy.   Improvement in the ration was also made possible
by a provision of the act of 1818, incorporated at Calhoun's suggestion,
which authorized the President to make such alterations in the components of the ration as the health and comfort of the troops and as
economy might require.[80]   Previously, Congress had determined the

[79] RG 92, CGP, Letters Sent, No. 392, pp. 319–22; 336 (Irvine to SW, 22 Mar, 5 Apr 1833);
No. 393, p. 316 (Same to same, 6 Jan 1835); No. 394, pp. 11, 50 (Same to same, 21 Oct,
19 Dec 1835).

[80] (1) RG 107, OSW, Reports to Congress, I, 446–47 (Calhoun to Sen. John Williams,
–March 1818).   (2) 3 Stat. 426 (Apr 14, 1818).

components of the ration, but though the quantity of the ration Congress
had established in 1802 had been ample, it did not assure the health of
the troops.[81]

Considerable changes were made at once in the ration.   Of greatest
importance was the increase in the vegetable component.   Twice a week
a half allowance of meat, with a suitable quantity of peas or beans, was
issued.   Rice was introduced in the ration.   Fresh meat was substituted
twice a week for salted meat.   At southern posts, bacon and kiln-dried
Indian cornmeal were isued to a certain extent in lieu of pork and
wheat flour.   This last substitution was not successful.   Cornmeal was
generally disliked by the troops, and moreover it was far more perishable than flour.   Its use was tried for 3 years and then abandoned.[82]

At the same time, and coincidental with the first powerful temper-
ance movement in the United States, the Surgeon General of the Army
proposed to promote the health of the troops by eliminating the whiskey
ration.   The evils of intemperance in the Army were only too well
known.   By way of experiment, Commissary General Gibson, with
Calhoun's approval, initiated a program of volunteer relinquishment
of the whiskey ration in return for payment to the troops of the contract
price of the whiskey, the payment to be made either monthly or
quarterly.   The program met with little response and was soon abandoned because it proved ineffective.[83]   Another experiment at commutation was tried by the War Department in 1830.[84]   In the meantime,
Congress had shown considerable interest in the problem, but is was 1838
before Congress enacted legislation authorizing the issue of coffee and
sugar in lieu of whiskey and fixing the allowance at 6 pounds of coffee
and 12 pounds of sugar to every 100 rations.   Coffee and sugar were to
be issued weekly and when not available were to be paid for in money.[85]

Supplementing the efforts to introduce a better balanced ration
in 1818, the War Department issued an order requiring the troops at all
permanent posts where it could be done to cultivate vegetable gardens
so that they might be supplied with fresh vegetables.   At posts remote
from the settled parts of the country, the Department broadened the

[81] *American State Papers, Military Affairs*, I, 804–07 (Surgeon General Joseph Lovell to
Calhoun, 16 Nov 1818).

[82] (1) Jameson, "Correspondence of John C. Calhoun," AHA *Annual Report for 1899,*
vol. 2, p. 137 (Calhoun to Monroe, 22 Aug 1818). (2) *American State Papers, Military Affairs,*
I, 781 (Calhoun to House, 11 Dec 1818). (3) RG 192, CGS, Letters Sent, II, 503–04 (Gibson to
Calhoun, 11 Dec 1821).

[83] *American State Papers, Military Affairs*, IV, 248 (Gibson to SW, 6 Jan 1830).

[84] See GO 72.

[85] (1) 5 *Stat.* 256 (Jul 5, 1838). (2) *American State Papers, Military Affairs*, IV, 275–76
(Gibson to Chairman of House Military Committee, 2 Feb 1830; Committee to House, 8 Feb
1830).

order to include the cultivation of grain to provide forage for public teams and the raising of stock to add to the meat supply. At the same time, the produce of the gardens would at all times assure a supply of food within the posts themselves.[86] The troops' efforts to raise their own meat supply were not always successful; wolves devoured the hogs the soldiers tried to raise at Council Bluffs.[87] Proposals to supplement the ration by using buffalo meat at frontier posts met with Calhoun's approval.[88]

Obviously, the cultivation of vegetables in post gardens was not suggested for the purpose of meeting vitamin deficiencies, for knowledge of these aspects of food requirements was lacking. The main purpose was to add to available food supplies, to give some variety to the diet, and to reduce transportation expenditures. Within a few years, complaints were to be made about converting soldiers into farmers, but despite such criticism the cultivation of post gardens continued throughout this period.

Such cultivation by reducing transportation costs was of immediate interest to the Quartermaster's Department. In the beginning, the Department was concerned with avoiding any additional costs arising out of the program itself, and it cautioned quartermasters in the field that seeds and tools were furnished by the Subsistence and Ordnance Departments, respectively.[89] Later in the 1830's, after a regiment of dragoons had been added to the Army, Quartermaster interest in gardens was stimulated by the large amounts of forage that had to be provided for the cavalry. To diminish the cost of the dragoon service, cultivation of hay and grain was started at Ft. Leavenworth and the Acting Quartermaster General advised similar cultivation at Ft. Gibson on the Arkansas frontier. By that time, quartermasters contracted to to have the fields fenced and the first ploughing done. Where military duties prevented detailing troops to cultivate the fields, the quartermasters were authorized to hire the necessary laborers for the work.[90]

Transportation Procedures

Additional responsibilities were carried out by quartermasters but the basic function of the Department continued to be that of providing transportation. With troops stationed at posts on the maritime frontier

[86] *American State Papers, Military Affairs*, I, 781 (Calhoun to House, 11 Dec 1818).

[87] RG 192, CGS, Letters Sent, vol. 3, p. 111 (Gibson to Col. J. Snelling, 5 Sep 1822).

[88] Letter Book of Maj. Gen. Jacob Brown, No. 2, pp. 180–81 (SW to Col. Atkinson, 10 Apr 1820). Manuscript Div., Library of Congress.

[89] RG 92, OQMG Letter Book, vol. 2, p. 87 (To Linnard, 4 Apr 1820).

[90] *Ibid.*, vol. 25, p. 289 (Cross to Capt. Thomas Swords, 12 Oct 1837); vol. 26, pp. 137–38 (Cross to Lt. J. P. Davis, 26 Mar 1838).

and at widely dispersed posts on the inland frontiers, transportation costs were the largest part of Quartermaster expenditures, involving as they did not only the transportation of supplies but the movement of troops and their baggage.   For the most part, the Quartermaster's Department accomplished such transportation in privately owned conveyances, and it preferred to ship by water since land transportation cost more.

Actually, there had not been much change in the method of handling shipments by wagon since the days when William Linnard acted as military agent at Philadelphia in 1802.   Twenty-one years later Major Linnard was still performing the same duties as deputy quartermaster general, furnishing transportation for the annual supplies of clothing and equipment that the Commissary General of Purchases had packed at the Arsenal and turned over to him.   If the method of doing business was the same, its difficulties had increased as settlement grew beyond the Appalachians.   In the early years, merchants shipped their goods to the West only twice a year, in the spring and fall; for that matter, so did Linnard, for winter made roads impassable.   During the War of 1812, however, Army employment of transportation became constant through the whole year, and Linnard had enjoyed virtually a monopoly of all the best wagoners.   In the war years, wagoning was under the control of eight or ten master wagoners in Philadelphia.   They owned several fine teams and sometimes even kept a tavern for the accommodation of the wagoners.   The wagonmasters stayed in Philadelphia, collected the load-ings, sent out their wagons, and, because they knew the wagoners, made themselves responsible for the delivery of the loads.[91]

After the war, Army shipments fell off; hauling was no longer profit-able, so the wagonmasters sold their teams and engaged in other busi-nesses.   In the 1820's, wagons were individually owned and driven by the owner, or they were owned by merchants in the country who took in large quantities of produce, or by rich farmers who operated mills and consigned their supplies to merchants in Philadelphia.   Now the mer-chants had a complete monopoly of the wagons and wagoners.   As immigrants streamed westward and settlement grew, trade increased and the merchants shipped immense quantities of goods to the West.   By comparison, Army shipments were small, and Linnard found it exceed-ingly difficult to engage wagoners.   So much was this the case that in the spring of 1823, when supplies were packed for the troops at Council Bluffs and ready for hauling to Pittsburgh, Linnard applied to a wholesale grocer named Patterson for assistance in procuring wagons.[92]

[91] RG 92, CGP, Letter Book (Linnard), 1 May 1823–31 Dec 1825, unnumbered volume (Linnard to Capt. H. Johnson, 13 May 1823).

[92] Ibid., (Linnard to Johnson, 13 May 1823; Linnard to Jesup, 1 May 1823).

He made an agreement with Patterson, though not in writing. Other than the bill of lading, it was not customary to have a written contract in transporting goods by wagon or in shipping by boat. By his agreement, Linnard allowed Patterson $3.75 per 100 pounds and an additional 25 cents per 100 pounds for his trouble in obtaining the wagons, making out the bills of lading, signing the receipts, and holding himself responsible for the safe delivery of the stores. Since others asking the same price would not assume this responsibility, Linnard felt the terms were advantageous.[93]

In addition, to get supplies hauled it was necessary to come to terms on the weight of a wagonload, and Linnard agreed with Patterson that the standard weight for a full wagonload of light goods would be 40 hundred pounds. When goods were light—and public stores though bulky were often light in weight and did not pack well in the wagons— it was the practice to allow a given weight for a load at the market price equal to the general weight of heavier loads. That weight varied over the years. During the War of 1812, for example, wagons were smaller, there were few turnpikes, and the standard weight was calculated at 30 to 33 hundred pounds at the market price. By the 1820's, there were turnpikes, wagons had become larger, and the standard weight for the second class of wagons was then calculated at 40 hundred pounds and up, according to demand, and for the largest class, at 50 to 55 hundred pounds. Among the supplies Linnard sent off in the spring of 1823 was a wagon-load of boxes containing caps whose weight did not exceed 15 hundred pounds. When his arrangements were questioned, Linnard inquired: "Will any man acquainted with that business suppose that goods of that description could be got on at the real weight and market price especially when more profitable loads could be got." [94]

Wagon transportation of public stores was not only difficult to arrange but was subject to abuses in execution as it had been in the past. Wagoners charged that quartermasters were abusive and detained their wagons far longer than merchants did. Quartermasters, for their part, found wagoners unreliable and given to hauling private property at public expense.[95] Nevertheless, the bulk of Army supplies sent overland was transported in wagons during the first 20 years of the Department's existence as a bureau. In the 1830's, railroads began to be constructed and a number of short lines soon were in operation in the East. Quarter-

---

[93] *Ibid.*, (Linnard to Jesup, 29 Aug 1823).

[94] *Ibid.*, (Linnard to Johnson, 13 Jun 1823; Linnard to Jesup, 19 Jun 1823).

[95] (1) For a controversy that developed between Patterson and Capt. H. Johnson, military storekeeper at Pittsburgh, see RG 92, OQMG Letter Book, vol. 5, pp. 124, 214–15, 258–59, 273, 278–80, 281–82, 310. (2) RG 92, CGP, Letter Book (Linnard), 1 May 1823–31 Dec 1825, unnumbered volume (Linnard to Johnson, 6 Oct 1825).

masters immediately made use of this new means of transportation. As early as the fall of 1833, a bill of lading carried the information that certain Army supplies were to be sent across New Jersey by railroad.[96] Before the end of that decade, the Quartermaster at New Orleans was proposing with Jesup's approval to construct a short railroad line over government land that would connect the barracks area below New Orleans with a railroad then being built to join New Orleans with Lake Borgne.[97]

The Quartermaster's Department continued to prefer and use water routes when possible. Steamboats were in general use on the Great Lakes and on the rivers of the Mississippi Valley; packets plied the Erie Canal after 1825; and sailing ships and some steamboats carried coastal trade. Quartermasters employed all of them to transport troops and supplies. So many accidents befell steamboats on the Mississippi that frequently it was advisable to send supplies, despite the costs, via Pittsburgh rather than to New Orleans for transshipment up the river. The difference in cost was appreciable. Forty-four tierces of clothing intended for Council Bluffs and sent from Philadelphia to Pittsburgh, Linnard estimated, would fill four wagons and cost $400. The same amount shipped to New Orleans would cost $86.88.[98] In making their transportation arrangements, quartermasters always had to make sure that supplies sent by sailing ships to New Orleans arrived before the river fell so low as to impede steamboat navigation. They insured all goods shipped by sea.[99]

Other factors hampered delivery of supplies. If troops were stationed at posts not convenient to a seaport regularly visited by the sailing vessels, supplies were apt to be much delayed. Linnard, for example, had great difficulty in forwarding supplies to troops stationed at Pensacola, Fla. It was not yet a place of much trade in 1823, and few vessels sailed for that port alone. Usually vessels went to Mobile, since it was a greater market for cotton and other produce, and then also stopped at Pensacola. The amount of supplies shipped by the Army was too trifling for a merchant to send a special vessel there. Army supplies simply formed part of the cargo, and Linnard as shipper could not stipulate to which of the two ports the vessel should go first. He asserted that merchants were disposed to give the United States the preference if Army freight was of nearly equal value to private shipments, but if he

[96] RG 92, Coxe and Irvine Papers, Box 21.

[97] RG 92, OQMG Letter Book, vol. 29, p. 65 (Jesup to Maj. I. Clark, 21 Nov 1839).

[98] RG 92, CGP, Letter Book (Linnard), 1 May 1823–31 Dec 1825, unnumbered volume (Linnard to Jesup, 3 Mar 1824).

[99] Ibid., (Linnard to Jesup, 18 Mar 1824; To Capt. T. F. Hunt, 24 Mar 1824; To Insurance Co., 1 Mar 1825).

did not have a sufficient portion of the cargo to command a preference, "merchants will always send their vessels in a way most profitable to themselves." When the commanding officer at Pensacola therefore complained of delay and wished to punish the captain of the vessel delivering Army clothing by deducting a penalty from his freight charges, Linnard insisted that the captain could not be blamed under these circumstances.[100] The only alternative to using private shipping was the maintenance of an expensive army transport system, a development unlikely to be even considered in a Department hampered by lack of funds.

The Quartermaster's Department did own and operate some transports at various times. In the Southern Division, for example, in the 1820's it employed a government transport to move troops and military supplies between military posts extending from New Orleans to Tampa Bay on the west coast of Florida. Commercial intercourse between these points was too limited to be depended upon for the purpose.[101]

Troops moving to the western posts were usually sent by steamboat via the western rivers or the Great Lakes. Contract agreements sometimes stipulated a flat sum per man and baggage. At other times an entire vessel might be chartered. Capt. J. B. Brant, assistant quartermaster at Detroit, chartered the steamboat, *Walk-in-the-Water,* for $1,600 in 1821 to convey troops and their baggage from Buffalo to Detroit, Green Bay, and Mackinac. The contract stipulated that the provisions and stores sent along should equal in bulk 300 barrels.[102]

Regulations granted officers traveling on duty without troops a transportation allowance, computed on the distance they traveled, and required them to use the most direct mail route to their destination. When Jesup was appointed Quartermaster General, considerable confusion existed in regard to distances, particularly the mileage between frontier posts. To correct this situation, Jesup adopted a geographical authority as a uniform standard reference in computing allowances. He placed a copy of this work—Melish's *The Travellers Directory*—in the hands of each of his subordinates. It showed the distances on the principal roads of the United States. In addition, they also used the book of post roads published by direction of the Postmaster General, which gave the distance between Washington and all other post offices, as well as between the capitals of the states and the post towns in them.[103]

[100] (1) *Ibid.,* (To Jesup, 31 Jan 1824). (2) RG 92, Coxe and Irvine Papers, Box 27 (Linnard to Irvine, 21 Apr 1823).

[101] RG 92, OQMG Letter Book, vol. 8, p. 163 (To Secretary of Treasury, 22 Aug 1825); pp. 182–83 (To Capt. D. E. Burch, 1 Sep 1825).

[102] (1) *Ibid.,* vol. 4, p. 45 (Jesup to Pres. of Lake Erie Steamboat Co., 13 May 1822). (2) RG 92, OQMG Estimates and Reports, 1821–22.

[103] RG 92, OQMG Letter Book, vol. 7, p. 367 (Circular, 11 Apr 1825); vol. 9, pp. 335–54 (To Paymaster General, 6 Jul 1826).

The transportation of troops acquired considerable proportions during these years. Not only did settlement expand westward at a rapid pace, but the United States acquired additional territory. Ever since 1803, when Jefferson made the Louisiana Purchase and convinced himself that it included West Florida, the desire to obtain all of Florida had been growing with the years. It was satisfied in 1819 when Spain decided to sell Florida in exchange for assumption by the United States of claims of her citizens against Spain and relinquishment by the United States of claims to Texas. Occupation did not take place until 1821 after Congress finally ratified the treaty. In the spring of that year, the Quartermaster's Department was called upon to carry out one of the provisions of the treaty by transporting to Havana the Spanish troops and officers who had been garrisoned at the posts in Florida.[104] As the Spaniards were moved out, the Department arranged not only for the transportation of American troops to Florida but for quartering and supplying them at the newly acquired posts.[105]

In the meantime, extension of the military frontier westward imposed additional transportation burdens and expenditures on the Quartermaster's Department. By 1822, troops were garrisoned at a post 600 miles up the Arkansas River; they were 20 miles beyond Natchitoches on the Red River; they were located at Council Bluffs on the Missouri, at St. Peter's on the Mississippi, and had pushed 125 miles beyond Mackinac to maintain a post at the falls of St. Mary. Supply lines to some posts were well over 1,000 miles and transportation costs increased as distances lengthened.

Moreover, after 1821, the Army numbered little more than 6,000 men and officers. It was far too small to occupy all the points that required protection on the extended inland frontier. The government was therefore compelled to supply the want of numbers by frequent troop movements. But whether transportation was required by the transfer of troops at frontier posts, by the redistribution of Artillery regiments at the posts on the maritime frontier, or by the dispatch of troops to Florida, the quartermasters contracted for steamboat accommodations on the rivers and Great Lakes, utilized the advantages afforded by use of the Erie Canal after 1825, and hired sailing ships and some steamboats for coastal movements. Where these could not be depended upon, they used government transports in the Gulf of Mexico, and maintained keelboats and Mackinac boats on the inland waters to be used when the level of the rivers fell too low to permit steamboat navigation.

[104] *Ibid.*, vol. 3, pp. 16–17 (To DQMG Stanton, 21 May 1821); pp. 17, 32, 36 (To Maj. T. Cross, 22 Mar, 9 Apr, 13 Apr 1821).
[105] *Ibid.*, vol. 3, p. 185 (To SW, 31 Jul 1821).

Construction Responsibilities

The burden of executing other functions of the Department also increased as the country expanded.   The first two decades of the existence of the Quartermaster's Department as a bureau saw tremendous expansion of its responsibilities for constructing not only storehouses, barracks, and hospitals, but also miiltary roads and other projects that were assigned to it.   In an effort to place the United States in the best defensive position possible after the War of 1812, the War Department had projected plans for the establishment of posts along the northwestern frontier and an elaborate system of fortifications along the seacoast.   Construction of the coastal fortifications was a responsibility of the Engineer Department. The War Department also ruled that all barracks, quarters, and storehouses at such fortified places were to be erected by that Department and the expenses defrayed from the appropriations for fortifications.[106] Subsequently, it modified this interpretation to the extent of charging the Quartermaster's Department with responsibility for the construction and repair of all storehouses and sheds necessary to secure and preserve public property deposited at fortifications.[107]

On the other hand, responsibility for all construction at posts erected on the inland frontier was vested in the Quartermaster General.   The posts themselves, for example, those built on the upper Mississippi and Missouri Rivers between 1818 and 1820, were erected by the troops, who felled the trees and provided the necessary lumber.   The quartermasters furnished the nails and tools.   Since the beginning of the Army, this procedure had been followed and it continued to be the established routine as the military frontier was pushed westward.   Troops were expected to be able to "cover themselves comfortably wheresoever timber is to be found." [108]   Fort building on the northwestern frontier was temporarily halted in 1820 as Congress sought to reduce expenses, but within 5 years indispensable repairs had to be made at some of the posts.

Yearly thereafter the Quartermaster's Department engaged in making repairs or in erecting new barracks, storehouses, and hospitals.   In his annual reports, the Quartermaster General pointed out the projects that needed to be initiated—sometimes to eliminate the necessity of paying rentals, as at New Orleans where barracks and storehouses had been sold following the War of 1812; sometimes to maintain defensive positions, as at Mackinac, Crawford, and Green Bay.[109]   Jesup prepared estimates

---

[106] RG 92, OQMG Letter Book, vol. 2, p. 258 (QMG to Lt. Col. McRea, 6 Sep 1820).
[107] RG 107, OSW, Military Book, vol. 12, p. 27 (SW to QMG et al., 19 Feb 1824).
[108] RG 92, OQMG Letter Book, vol. 11, p. 302 (Jesup to Maj. J. M. Glassell, 16 Aug 1827).
[109] American State Papers, Military Affairs, III, 640–41 (Rpt, 31 Oct 1827); IV, 192–95; 747–49 (Rpt, 23 Nov 1829; 2 Nov 1831).

and Congress appropriated funds for approved works. Quartermasters supervised troop labor, made requisitions for materials and tools, and rendered accounts of the expenditures incurred. Troops could not always be spared from their military duties to attend to the construction of barracks. In such cases, the Quartermaster's Department hired civilians. For example, when the War Department decided to erect a new post on the western boundary of Arkansas in 1838, Major Cross directed Assistant Quartermaster Charles Thomas to visit the eastern cities for the purpose of raising a corps of artisans and laborers to take out to Arkansas. The government agreed to pay their passage and allow them rations and whatever fixed rate of wages were determined upon at the time of hiring them, the wages to begin after the men started work. For their part, the artisans and laborers agreed, under penalty, to serve for at least one year.[110]

Few of the barracks, storehouses, stables, and other facilities erected were more than simple wooden structures. Occasionally, as at Jefferson Barracks, where the War Department determined to erect an Infantry School in 1826, more elaborate plans were drafted because the Army had in mind permanent structures. At Jefferson Barracks, stone and brick were used. The officers' quarters, for instance, were to be a two-storied, brick structure built on a stone basement, the building to be 66 feet by 44 feet.[111]

Carpenters among the soldiers detailed to construct barracks made simple, plain-finished bunks, tables, and benches that constituted the furnishings of these barracks. Soon assistant quartermasters were inquiring whether they were permitted to provide furniture for officers' quarters. Unfortunately, no authority existed for such expenditures, though Jesup believed there was no logical reason why such articles should be furnished to the officers of the Navy and not to those of the Army. He was, however, unsuccessful in his requests for congressional appropriations.[112]

Candles furnished the light for barracks, but, since the amount allowed was small, men retired to sleep when darkness fell. Winter's chill was only partially dispelled by wood-burning fires on open hearths—the amount of wood rigidly controlled by regulations. In 1831, wood in the vicinity of some posts was becoming extremely scarce. For the first time and by way of experiment, the Secretary of War authorized the

---

[110] RG 92, OQMG Letter Book, vol. 26, pp. 273–74 (Cross to Thomas, 24 May 1838); vol. 29, p. 99 (Jesup to Messrs. G. W. and T. Jacques & Co., 4 Dec 1839).

[111] Ibid., vol. 9, pp. 392–93 (QMG to Capt. L. B. Brant, 31 Jul 1826); vol. 10, pp. 339–40 (QMG to Lt. G. Wharton, 25 Jan 1827); vol. 11, p. 373 (QMG to SW, 29 Dec 1827).

[112] (1) Ibid., vol. 12, p. 192 (Cross to AQM Harvey Brown); pp. 257–58 (Jesup to Brown, 28 Nov 1828); vol. 19, pp. 132–34 (QMG to AQM J. Engle, 20 Jun 1833). (2) American State Papers, Military Affairs, V. 184 (QMG Report to SW, 27 Nov 1833).

Quartermaster General to furnish six anthracite coal grates for the hospital at Fortress Monroe and six for use in officers' quarters.[113] Even at posts on the upper Mississippi and Missouri, it became increasingly difficult to procure an adequate supply of wood, and by the 1830's Franklin stoves were being used in barracks to overcome the waste of heat.[114] Obviously, the soldier of the Revolutionary Army would not have found too many improvements to make the barracks of the mid-1830's unfamiliar to him.

Internal Improvements

No government bureau was more vitally interested in the program of internal improvements that developed after the War of 1812 than the Quartermaster's Department. Since 1775, it had been responsible for opening and repairing roads needed for the movement of troops and supplies. The construction and maintenance of military roads to effect wartime supply and combat operations had been undertaken by troops during the Revolutionary War, the Indian wars of the 1790's, and the War of 1812. Some military roads had been built by the troops in the years of peace between Wayne's Indian campaign and the War of 1812, but Jesup reported that no details on troop labor or Departmental expenditures were available in reference to the construction of these roads.[115] In any case, no policy appears to have been formulated by the War Department until after the War of 1812.

The disasters of that war had fully demonstrated the impact of lack of roads on military operations and had led to the enunciation in 1816 of a policy to employ troops in opening military roads and in constructing new and repairing old fortifications to place the United States in the best defensive position possible. That policy, "believed to be no less necessary to the discipline, health, and preservation of the troops, than useful to the public interest." was communicated to the commanding generals of the Southern and Northern Divisions, Maj. Gen. Andrew Jackson and Maj. Gen. Jacob Brown, respectively.[116] In consequence, the troops began constructing roads that were designed to open essential communications on the southern, northern, and northwestern frontiers in the event of war.[117] Though Congress appropriated funds for the

---

[113] RG 92, OQMG Letter Book, vol. 16, p. 349 (Cross to QM H. Stanton, 29 Dec 1831).

[114] *Ibid.*, vol. 18, p. 357; vol. 19, pp. 415–16 (QMG to Maj. J. B. Brant, 11 Mar 1833; 28 Nov 1833).

[115] *American State Papers, Military Affairs*, IV, 262 (Jesup to SW, 7 Jan 1831).

[116] RG 107, OSW, Military Book, vol. 8, pp. 466–67 (SW to Jackson, 8 Mar 1816); pp. 485–86 (SW to Brown, 3 Apr 1816).

[117] Jackson's troops built a road from the Tennessee River near Muscle Shoals to Madisonville, La., between 1817 and 1820; troops under Maj. Gen. Alexander Macomb built a military

road Jackson's troops built, the others were constructed by executive direction with funds taken from the general Army appropriation. In this period, the role of the Quartermaster Department was restricted to providing the necessary tools and paying the sums due for extra pay to the soldiers employed in road contruction.[118]

Calhoun, a nationalist when he served as Secretary of War, thought that scarcely any road could be designated that was "highly useful for military operations, which is not equally required for the industry or political prosperity of the community." [119]   Calhoun had not yet become a proponent of states rights and strict construction of the Constitution. In view of the adverse effect of inadequate roads on Army operations in the War of 1812, he recognized the country's need for a good system of military roads.   President Monroe was a strict constructionist, but nevertheless, he was willing to approve acts appropriating funds for specific military roads as long as they included no broad approval of the principle of federal internal improvements.   Yet even he retreated from that position when he signed an act in 1824 calling for federal surveys of routes for roads and canals necessary for commercial, military, or postal purposes.[120]   By the terms of the law, this work was to be carried out under the direction of the Corps of Engineers.

Army regulations were accordingly amended in 1825 to indicate that the Corps of Engineers reconnoitered and surveyed for military purposes and for internal improvements, and that it superintended the construction of such internal improvements as Congress authorized and ordered the War Department to execute.[121]   Many of the roads built by the government under the internal improvements program were actually civil projects, but the topographical engineers surveyed and supervised their construction.   Almost any road built by the government came to be called a military road whether it served a military purpose or not.

Quartermaster responsibility for military road construction remained unchanged.   It continued to be the duty of the Department to direct the survey and to superintend the opening and repairing of roads and bridges

---

road from Detroit to Ft. Meigs; and a Plattsburgh to Sackett's Harbor road was begun by troops under General Brown but never completed. *American State Papers, Military Affairs,* IV, 626–29 (Jesup to SW, 7 Jan 1831).

[118] (1) RG 92, OQMG Letter Book, vol. 1, pp. 182–83 (Cross to Col. M. Arbuckle, 13 Feb 1819); vol. 1, p. 188 (Cross to ADQM Brant, 30 Jun 1820). (2) Letter Book of Maj. Gen. Jacob Brown, No. 2, p. 182 (Calhoun to Brown, 9 Jun 1820). Manuscript Div., Library of Congress.

[119] *American State Papers, Miscellaneous,* II, 536 (Calhoun to Speaker Clay, 7 Jan 1819).
[120] 4 *Stat.* 22–23 (Apr 30, 1824).
[121] *General Regulations for the Army of the United States, 1825* (Washington, 1825), p. 167.

that might be necessary to the movements of any part of the Army, or, as was specifically added after 1834, that might be needed as communications between the posts on the frontiers, and between those posts and the interior.[122] Because the War Department called upon Army engineers to build some of these roads and assigned to the Quartermaster's Department the duty of constructing some roads that were not strictly military in character, a certain amount of blurring of responsibilities for road construction developed between the two bureaus. In 1838, Congress created a separate Corps of Topographical Engineers.[123] The assignment to that bureau of responsibility for surveying and opening the roads authorized by Congress relieved the Quartermaster's Department of some of the duties it had been performing in executing the program of internal improvements. Roads that were strictly military in character, however, were not included in this reassignment of duties. They continued to be the responsibility of the Quartermaster's Department.[124] Discussion here is limited to military roads built by the troops or by hired laborers under Quartermaster supervision.

Between 1824 and 1828 Congress made provision for the construction of a number of military roads.[125] Most of the acts called for roads to be built in Florida and Arkansas, and that construction was administered by the Quartermaster's Department. A large share of the work was accomplished by troops detailed from the line under the supervision of a quartermaster. Since the Army was small, however, troop labor could not always be made available to build the roads, and consequently in some cases the Quartermaster's Department resorted to contracts or to the use of hired laborers.[126]

By 1828, Calhoun's concept that roads could be made to serve both the military and the economic needs of the country at large had been fully accepted by his successors. Secretary Peter B. Porter advised Congress that while a part of the Corps of Engineers was employed in constructing works of military defense, another part—the topographical engineers—"aided by scientific and enterprising officers detailed from the line of the army, is co-operating with our citizen engineers in develop-

---

[122] (1) *Ibid.*, p. 213; *ibid.*, 1841, p. 179.   (2) GO 59 (28 Aug 1834).

[123] 5 *Stat.* 256 (Jul 5, 1838).

[124] (1) Senate *Ex. Doc.* No. 1, 25th Cong., 3d sess., p. 141 (QMG Annual Rpt, 28 Nov 1838). (2) For the duties of the Corps of Topographical Engineers, see GO 15 (30 Mar 1840).

[125] (1) 4 *Stat.* 5 (Jan 31, 1824); pp. 5–6 (Feb 28, 1824); p. 135 (Mar 3, 1825); pp. 227–28 (Mar 2, 1827); p. 244 (Mar 3, 1827).   (2) For a more detailed account see Harold L. Nelson, "Military Roads for War and Peace–1781–1836," *Military Affairs*, XIX, No. 1, p. 7 ff.

[126] (1) *American State Papers, Military Affairs*, IV, 626 (Jesup to SW, 7 Jan 1831).   (2) RG 92, OQMG Letter Book, vol. 6, pp. 213–14 (Jesup to AQM Isaac Clark, 14 Apr 1824); vol. 8, pp. 87–88 (QMG to AQM D. B. Burch, 7 Oct 1824); vol. 12, pp. 269–70 (Jesup to SW, 5 Dec 1828).   (3) RG 107, OSW, Military Book, vol. 12, p. 280 (SW to QMG, 21 Mar 1827).

ing the capacities of the country for internal improvement, and in building up works which belong exclusively to the department of political economy." At the same time, the Quartermaster General, assisted by other officers and soldiers of the line, was "engaged not merely in military erections and accommodations for the troops, but in the construction of roads and bridges for the citizens at large." With enthusiasm, he concluded that the Army was being exhibited "as a body of military and civil engineers, artificers, and laborers, who probably contribute more than any other equal number of citizens, not only to the security of the country, but to the advancement of its useful arts." [127]

In 1825, Jesup had urged and built roads on the southwestern frontier to link up Natchitoches and Ft. Towson on the Red River with Ft. Gibson on the Arkansas as a defensive measure in the event of war.[128] By 1834, the growing political turmoil in northern Mexico that culminated in revolution and the achievement of independence by Texas 2 years later served to re-emphasize the need for additional roads in Arkansas Territory. At the same time, as the government pursued its policy of removing the Indians and resettling them on lands west of the Mississippi, the threat of Indian warfare grew. Not only was there danger of conflict between the newly settled Indians and the native tribes, but depredations on the white settlements were likely to occur as the buffalo and elk retreated westward, diminishing the Indians' means of support. In 1834, the troops under Quartermaster supervision built four roads in the Indian Territory beyond the western boundary of present Arkansas.[129] In that year, Congress also authorized four roads in Arkansas Territory and Jesup directed his principal officer in that area to initiate measures for surveying and opening these roads.[130] By 1835, a network of 13 military roads was in the process of being completed in Arkansas under Quartermaster supervision.

With the growing menace of the Indians on the western frontier, defense was more and more emphasized as the factor to be considered in military road construction. That development reached its height in the projection of the great military road of 1836. Plans for that road

---

[127] *American State Papers, Military Affairs*, IV, 2 (Annual Rpt, 24 Nov 1828).

[128] *Ibid.*, III, 117 (Jesup to SW, 26 Nov 1825).

[129] These were (1) from Ft. Towson to the False Washita River (now the Washita); (2) from Ft. Gibson to the Little Red River of Arkansas; (3) from Little Red River to the mouth of the False Washita; and (4) from Ft. Gibson to the north fork of the Canadian River. *Ibid.*, V, 384 (QMG Annual Rpt, 22 Nov 1834).

[130] These roads were (1) from Helena to the mouth of Cache River; (2) from Jackson, in Lawrence county, by Liberty and Fayettesville, in Washington county, to Ft. Smith; (3) from Strong's (a point on the military road from Memphis to Little Rock) by Litchfield to Batesville; and (4) from Columbia in Chicot county to Little Rock. *Ibid.*, V, 384 (QMG Annual Rpt, 22 Nov 1834).

precipitated a considerable amount of controversy over the tactics and strategy involved in handling the Indian problem. During the next 3 years, Quartermaster officers were divided in their views, some supporting the plan and others opposing it.

The plan stemmed from a letter that John Dougherty, Indian agent in Missouri, sent in December 1834 to Maj. J. B. Brant, quartermaster at St. Louis, who forwarded it to the Washington office.[131] Dougherty outlined his ideas on defense based on his many years of experience on the frontier. He suggested establishing a line of posts along the boundary between the white settlements and the Indians, extending from the Upper Mississippi River to the Red River in the south. He proposed to connect this cordon of posts by constructing a military road, along which dragoons, stationed at the posts, might patrol and keep the Indians under surveillance.

These proposaals fitted in very well with Jesup's ideas of defense for the inland frontier. Mounted Indians of the prairies could not be pursued by unmounted infantry, and as early as 1829 Jesup had been advocating putting at least a portion of the infantry on horseback. In 1832, Congress had authorized a battalion of mounted rangers, and 9 months later, with interest stimulated by the battles of the Regulars and militia with the Sac and Fox Indians under Black Hawk, it substituted a regiment of dragoons.[132] Building well-fortified posts, garrisoned in sufficient strength to resist sudden attacks, Jesup asserted, would promote peace. He strongly advocated the construction of good communicating roads between the posts and from them to the interior. The frequent movement of dragoons on the road would intimidate the Indians inclined to become hostile and inspire confidence in those disposed to be friendly. If war did occur the posts would constitute proper bases of operations. Since the authorized strength of the Army in 1836 was little more than 6,000, Jesup conceded that his views on defense bore little reference to the existing military establishment that experience had shown to be wholly inadequate.[133]

When the citizens of Clay County, Mo., endorsed Dougherty's proposal and petitioned Congress in 1835 for protection, Acting Quartermaster General Thomas F. Hunt, fully aware of Jesup's views, enthusiastically backed Secretary Lewis Cass in supporting congressional efforts

[131] *Ibid.*, VI, 14–15.

[132] (1)) *Ibid.*, IV, 611 (Annual Rpt, 23 Nov 1830). (2) 4 *Stat.* 533 (Jun 15, 1832); p. 652 (Mar 2, 1833).

[133] (1) *American State Papers, Military Affairs*, VI, 152–53 (Jesup to Cass, 15 Feb 1836). (2) Senate *Ex. Doc.* No. 1, 26th Cong., 1st sess., pp. 113–14 (Jesup to Poinsett, 29 Nov 1839).

to put the plan into effect.[134] Jesup estimated that by using troop labor
the plan could be executed for $100,000. On 2 July 1836, Congress
enacted the necessary legislation for erecting this "barrier" against the
Indians.[135]

Not all military men approved construction of the great military
road of 1836. Maj. Trueman Cross, serving as Acting Quartermaster
General in 1837 while Jesup took the field against the Indians in Florida,
questioned its effectiveness.

As a route of communication, it violates a fundamental principle of military science. The lines of communication should be diverging or perpendicu-
lar to the frontier, not parallel with it. The resources of an army are always
presumed to be in its rear, from whence it can draw its supplies and reinforcements under cover of its own protection and by lines of communications which
are secured from interruption by the enemy. It is clear that no army can
maintain its position long under any other circumstances. Roads between the
posts on the frontier might be found convenient for occasional passing and
repassing in times of peace; but as routes of communication they would be
wholly useless in time of war.[136]

Joel R. Poinsett, who had succeeded Cass as Secretary of War 8 months
after Congress enacted legislation for constructing the road, entertained
similar views. He opposed construction of the road but reported that
it would begin unless Congress, upon a deliberate review of the whole
matter, adopted some more suitable plan of defense.[137] Congress took
no such action. Jesup continued to support the construction of the great
military road upon his return to Washington, and, after some interruption, the road was completed under Quartermaster supervision by 1841,
except for a small northern section that Poinsett managed to eliminate.

In addition to road construction, quartermasters supervised river
and harbor improvements that were specifically assigned to the Department.[138] The most important of these was the construction of a breakwater at the mouth of the Delaware River. Originally that project had
been assigned to the Navy Department, but, in the spring of 1829, the
President re-assigned it to the War Department and the Secretary delegated responsibility for managing and superintending that construction

---

[134] *American State Papers, Military Affairs*, VI, 13–14 (Hunt to Cass, 8 Jan 1835); p. 12
(Committee resolution, 23 Dec 1835); V, 729–31 (Petition to Congress, 24 Dec 1835).

[135] (1) *Ibid.*, VI, 149 (Committee Rpt, 3 Mar 1836); pp. 149–52 (Cass to Chairman, 19 Feb
1836); pp. 152–53 (Jesup to Cass, 15 Feb 1836. (2) 9 *Stat.* 444.

[136] *American State Papers, Military Affairs*, VII, 783 (Cross to Poinsett, 7 Nov 1837);
see also pp. 778–81 for report of Chief of Engineers, Charles Gratiot, 31 Oct 1837.

[137] *Ibid.*, VII, 575 (Annual Rpt of SW, 2 Dec 1837); p. 777–78 (Poinsett to R. M. Johnson,
30 Dec 1837).

[138] For mention of such projects see, *American State Papers, Military Affairs*, IV, 193;
V, 644 (Annual Rpt, Jesup to SW, 23 Nov 1828; 6 Nov 1835).

project to the Quartermaster's Department.[139]   Administration of that public works required the services of two officers of the Quartermaster's Department for the next 7 years.

By 1836, the demands made upon the Department were so numerous and burdensome—there were but 25 officers including the Quartermaster General to attend to them—that it had to seek relief.   In addition to administering various construction projects and discharging their basic responsibility for transporting men and supplies, quartermasters were burdened with duties appertaining to other departments that involved much labor and heavy pecuniary responsibility.   Among these were the payment of Indian annuities and the purchase of supplies for the department of Indian Affairs.   In 1836, Major Cross reported the latter amounted to nearly $800,000.[140]   Quartermasters were often called upon "to make good the deficiencies in other branches of the staff."   By law, they were subjected, when necessary, to duty in the Subsistence Department.   When directed to do so by the Secretary of War, quartermasters in the field were also required to purchase camp equipage, medicines and hospital stores, and even occasionally arms and ammunition.[141]

Besides executing their regular peacetime duties in 1836, quartermasters were also being called upon to support the troops in their operations against the Seminoles in Florida.   Under these circumstances, the Acting Quartermaster General requested that the Department be relieved from the charge of constructing the Delaware Breakwater as well as the roads in Arkansas.[142]   The War Department transferred construction of the Breakwater to the Corps of Engineers, but responsibility for road construction continued to be vested in the Quartermaster's Department.   Lacking officers to supervise the building of roads in Arkansas, the Department was compelled to suspend that work during the next 2 years, and Quartermaster officers were assigned to the more urgent supply duties in Florida.

Supply Support in the Seminole War

The Seminole War afforded an opportunity for testing the effectiveness of the Department's regulations and the efficiency of its personnel. During the 7 years of that war, practically all officers of the Department were assigned to tours of duty in Florida, accumulating first-hand experi-

[139] RG 107, OSW, Military Book, vol. 12, p. 425 (SW to Jesup, 3 Apr 1829).

[140] *American State Papers, Military Affairs*, VI, 831 (Annual Rpt, 22 Nov 1836).

[141] See, for example, RG 92, OQMG Letter Book, vol. 24, pp. 177–78 (Cross to AQM M. M. Clarke, 11 Nov 1836).

[142] RG 107, OSW, Letters Received, Q–27 (39) (Hunt to Cass, 24 May 1836).

ALABAMA

GEORGIA

Chattahoochee R.

Apalachicola River

ST. MARKS

GAREY'S FERRY

Black Creek

St. Johns River

ST. AUGUSTINE

PICOLATA

APALACHICOLA

Suwannee

PALATKA

Drums Lake

Orange Lake

George Lake

Ocklawaha R.

CEDAR KEY

FORT KING

Monroe Lake

FORT BROOKE

Kissimmee
Lake

Kissimmee River

Indian River

TAMPA BAY

Peace River

Calloosahachee R.

Okeechobee
Lake

KEY WEST

Seminole War

MAP 4

ence in the difficulties of wartime supply operations. Florida was the training ground that provided an experienced cadre of quartermasters to man key supply posts during the Mexican War.

The Seminole War grew out of the effort of the government to remove the Indians from Florida and resettle them on lands west of the Mississippi River. A treaty for that purpose was repudiated by the Seminoles and their opposition to emigration flared into open resistance. When hostilities began late in December 1835, the small number of regular troops in Florida left the settlements at the mercy of the Indians. The troops posted at St. Augustine on the east coast, Fort Brooks at Tampa Bay on the west coast, Key West at the southern extremity of the state, and Fort King in the north-central section, near the present city of Ocala, consisted of 9 companies of artillery and 2 of infantry, comprising 510 men and 26 officers.[143] Arrayed against them, according to the best-informed estimates, were 1,200 to 2,000 Indian warriors.[144]

A large, experienced force would have been required to pursue and subdue the Indians who customarily assembled in force to strike a blow, and then scattered in small parties, disappearing into the swamps, leaving no track to guide soldiers to their hiding places. Congress did authorize a second regiment of dragoons and after 2 years of war increased the strength of the Army to 12,577, but when the Seminole War began the aggregate authorized strength of the Army was little more than 7,000. Of that number, only about 4,000 enlisted men were actually present for duty at all the posts scattered throughout the United States for the defense of the inland and maritime frontiers.[145] As a consequence, the War Department had to rely upon the support of volunteers and militia whose services were engaged for only 3-, 6-, and 12-month terms. The number of troops serving in Florida during the Seminole War were distributed as follows: [146]

Date	Regulars	Volunteers and militia	Indians	Total
30 Nov 1836........	1,757	1,713	750	4,220
30 Nov 1837........	4,552	4,046	178	8,776
30 Nov 1838........	3,300	371	...	3,671
30 Nov 1839........	3,031	793	...	3,824
30 Nov 1840........	4,191	1,843	...	6,034
30 Nov 1841........	3,801	...	...	3,801

[143] *American State Papers, Military Affairs*, VI, 57 (AG to SW, 9 Feb 1836).

[144] *Ibid.*, VII, 218 (Gov. C. K. Call to Jackson, 9 Jan 1836).

[145] (1) *Ibid.*, V, 633 (Rpt, Maj. Gen. A. Macomb, 30 Nov 1835). (2) Upton, *The Military Policy of the United States*, 162, 184.

[146] (1) Upton, *The Military Policy of the United States*, p. 190. (2) See also John T. Sprague, *The Origin, Progress, and Conclusion of the Florida War* (New York, 1848), 103–06.

Paying and equipping the volunteers and militia made the Seminole War expensive and it was protracted.[147]   Broadened to include operations against the Creeks, the war dragged on for 7 years under a succession of commanders, including General Jesup, who, relieved of his duties as Quartermaster General, was assigned as a brevet major general to the command of troops on 19 May 1836 and for 2 years directed operations in Florida.[148]   When the war was finally brought to a close in 1842, forcible emigration of the Seminoles had not been accomplished.

The first campaign against the Indians was characterized by the usual failure to make any advance preparations despite warnings that the Seminoles were unlikely to submit peaceably to removal from the land.[149] The supply agencies acted promptly but meager reserve stocks, lack of adequate lead time to produce new supplies, and the distance supplies had to be shipped all conspired to cause delay.

In anticipation of the demands that would be made on the Quartermaster's Department, Maj. Thomas F. Hunt, Acting Quartermaster General, immediately reassigned quartermasters to key positions in mid-January 1836.   He expected operations on the west coast of Florida to be supported by a general depot at Tampa Bay, drawing its supplies from the assistant quartermaster at New Orleans.   On the east coast, operations would be backed up by a depot on the St. John's River, obtaining its supplies from Charleston and Savannah.   In addition to assigning assistant quartermasters to these depots and ports and remitting funds for their operations, Major Hunt directed Capt. Samuel Shannon, assistant quartermaster at Pensacola, to report to General Scott's headquarters. All quartermasters in the field were placed under Shannon's direction. Before Maj. Gen. Winfield Scott, who had been ordered to take command of operations, left Washington, one-fourth of the Department's personnel had been assigned to support his troops.[150]

Without waiting for requisitions, Jesup ordered 5,000 bushels of corn, put up in bags of $2\frac{1}{2}$ bushels each, to be shipped from Baltimore to Savannah and directed the purchase and shipment of ten strong wagons with harness for six horses each.[151]   Despite this foresight, it was May before the last of the wagons arrived at Savannah, and they were "poor things, but ill suited to the service for which they were designed." Under the pressure of immediate need, Maj. Trueman Cross, in charge

[147] Upton, *The Military Policy of the United States,* pp. 192–93.
[148] *American State Papers, Military Affairs,* VII, 312–13 (SW to Jesup, 19 May 1836).
[149] *Ibid.,* VII, 307 (Brig. Gen. D. L. Clinch to Gen R. Jones, 8 Oct 1835).
[150] RG 92, OQMG Letter Book, vol. 22, p. 400 (Hunt to Clinch, 17 Dec 1835); pp. 455–56; 458–60 (Hunt to Engle, Dimmock, Shannon, 19 Jan 1836); pp. 467–69 (Hunt to Scott, 21 Jan 1836); p. 475 (Jesup to Shannon, 23 Jan 1836).
[151] *Ibid.,* vol. 22, pp. 476–77 (QMG to Maj. T. Cross, 26 Jan 1836).

of procurement, had been obliged to take what was available. He could find only four new wagons in the Baltimore market and picked up second-hand wagons to complete the order. Since the transportation of troops, provisions, and forage had top priority, wagons could be stowed on board the vessels bound for Savannah only when space was available. Two wagons arrived there on 7 February; six more came a month later; and the last two of the order arrived about 1 May. The assistant quartermaster at Savannah forwarded all to the depot established at Picolata on the St. John's River, including seven wagons that he procured on Scott's requisition and 216 horses.[152]

Not all means of transportation and forage for the campaign went to Picolata. Some went to an advance depot that was set up in March at Garey's Ferry, located where Black Creek emptied into the St. John's River; others were sent to the depot at Tampa Bay and to St. Augustine. The Acting Quartermaster General reported that between 15 January and 25 May 1836, the Quartermaster's Department supplied the Army in Florida with 75 wagons, 36 carts, 135 sets of harness, 98 packsaddles, 618 horses, and 69 mules. It also furnished 934,518 pounds of hay and fodder, 49,563 bushels of corn and oats, and 11,882 forage bags. From 1 January to 25 May 1836, the Department remitted to its quartermasters and agents $612,100 to enable them to comply with requisitions for supplies and meet demands made by the military operations in Florida.[153] The Department had not been remise in its efforts.

In the meantime, Scott at Augusta, Ga., had found a large number of muskets at the arsenal but neither accoutrements, cartridges, powder fit for service, nor knapsacks to equip his troops.[154] He wondered why the government took the trouble to build arsenals in the first place. Unfortunately for his needs, the supplies that had been stored at the Augusta arsenal had already been issued to Georgia volunteers called out to go to the relief of the beleaguered troops in Florida.[155] Reporting on the supply situation, Scott hoped that knapsacks and tents were on their way from Philadelphia.

Commissary General Irvine forwarded such supplies as were on hand, but his reserve stocks were scanty. His purchases for some years had been restricted to meeting the needs of the small Regular Army. He had, for example, 500 knapsacks then in the hands of the painters and a considerable number of others ready for delivery to them. In-

---

[152] *American State Papers, Military Affairs*, VII, 131–32 (Deposition of Dimmock, 5 Dec 1836).

[153] RG 92, OQMG Letter Book, vol. 24, pp. 195–200 (Cross to Recorder of Court of Inquiry, 23 Nov 1836).

[154] *American State Papers, Military Affairs*, VII, 244 (Scott to Jones, 31 Jan 1836).

[155] *Ibid.*, VII, 137 (Testimony of Col. William Linsay, 7 Dec 1836).

tended for the regular service in 1836, they were diverted to equip both the Regular troops and the Volunteers and militia in Florida.   In March, 5 weeks after Scott had hoped knapsacks were on the way, Irvine reported that he would have 2,000 additional ones made with the least possible delay.[156]

Irvine could supply only tents from stocks left on hand since the War of 1812, and by March 1836 such supplies were exhausted so that he had to begin contracting for wall and common tents.   The Philadelphia Arsenal, the main depot from which supplies could be drawn, had in stock only limited quantities of other equipment—800 camp kettles, 1,500 mess pans, and no canteens.   None of the latter had been purchased since 1814.[157]   With troops already in the field, preparations to equip them had first to be initiated.   Irvine was efficient and before the end of the year he had furnished 7,500 knapsacks, 9,000 haversacks, 397 wall tents, 1,355 common tents, 1,355 camp kettles, 2,608 mess pans, 1,205 axes, and 567 spades.[158]   Unfortunately, most of the articles reached the field too late for use in Scott's plan of campaign in Florida early in 1836.

Before leaving Washington, Scott and the Commissary General of Subsistence had agreed that rations of hard bread and bacon were more desirable than flour and pork on marches because of the weight factor. To preserve pork in warm weather it had to be pickled in brine.   Allowing for the brine and the wooden casks, the weight factor was about 51 percent in favor of bacon.   In other words, a wagon capable of carrying 2,000 pounds of pork could carry 3,000 pounds, or a little more, of bacon.   The difference in weight between a ration of 18 ounces of flour and one of 12 ounces of hard bread is evident.   Sufficient quantities of hard bread, however, were not made available and no bacon reached the depot at Picolata before 15 April.   Scott contended that to take with the columns on their marches nearly two-thirds of the subsistence in the heavier items of flour and pork "was the same thing as if a larger portion of our otherwise deficient means of transportation had been captured or destroyed." [159]

The supply situation obviously must have hampered Scott, but his operational plan was completely disrupted by the unauthorized action

---

[156] RG 92, CGP, Letters Sent, No. 394, p. 108 (Irvine to Maj. John Garland, 9 Mar 1836).

[157] *Ibid.*, No. 394, p. 133 (T. Bangor to Garland, 5 May 1836); pp. 130–31 (Irvine to Garland, 16 Apr 1836); p. 396 (Irvine to SW, 13 Apr 1837).

[158] RG 92, OQMG Consolidated Correspondence File, 1794–1915, Boxes 305–08 (Irvine to SW, 3 June 1841 and enclosures).

[159] *American State Papers, Military Affairs*, VII, 154, 195 (Testimony of assistant commissary of subsistence, 22 Dec 1836 and Scott Summary).

of Maj. Gen. Edmund P. Gaines, who, without co-ordinating his plans with Scott, brought a small force from New Orleans and moved inland to Fort King from Tampa Bay. Instead of helping, his troops only succeeded in eating up the rations accumulated there and intended for the support of Scott's force in its three-pronged operations against the Indians. Unable to use the Ocklawaha River to replace supplies, Scott found himself deficient in wagons. The campaign barely got under way when the terms of service of his troops, most of whom were 3-months' men, expired. There was no alternative but to discharge them and end his campaign against the Seminoles.

Subsequent campaigns profited from the experience gained and the greater length of time allowed for preparations. Callender Irvine, Commissary General of Purchases, now had time to procure duck for tents, and 2,288 common tents were made available to the troops in Florida in 1837. Large quantities of other camp and garrison equipage were procured in 1837 and during the subsequent years of the war.[160] Irvine continued to prepare the annual supply of clothing for the regular troops in Florida.[161] In addition, volunteers and militiamen called into the service of the United States were entitled, by law, to the same camp equipage and clothing, or money in lieu of it, as was issued to enlisted men in the Regular Army.[162] Irvine employed some 600 to 800 seam-

[160] Among the major items of camp and garrison equipage furnished the Army in Florida by the Purchasing Department between 25 January 1836 and 31 May 1841 were the following:

Item	1836	1837	1838	1839	1840	1841
Axes	1,205	1,308	...	...	....	...
Camp Kettles	1,355	1,672	...	...	344	...
Canteens, tin	....	....	...	500	1,000	...
Canteens, wood	....	9,100	...	...	....	...
Mess Pans	2,608	2,908	...	...	....	...
Saddles, Dragoon	....	200	400	300	300	250
Spades	567	872	...	...	....	...
Tents, Common	1,355	2,288	300	300	1,000	150
Tents, Hospital	....	38	20	...	30	...
Tents, Wall	397	395	100	100	225	50

RG 92, OQMG Consolidated Correspondence File, Box 305–08 (Irvine to SW, 3 Jan 1841 and enclosures).

[161] Distributed over a 3-year enlistment period, that supply for the infantryman included in each year 2 overalls made of wool and 3 of cotton, 2 cotton shirts and 2 flannel shirts, 1 cotton jacket, 3 pairs of boots, and 3 pairs of stockings. In the 3-year period he also received 1 forage cap, 2 wool jackets, 1 great coat, 3 pairs of drawers, and 2 uniform caps. (1) *General Regulations for the Army of the United States, 1835* (Washington, 1835), p. 209. (2) Compare with allowances in *War Department General Orders*, GO 26, 27 Apr 1837; GO 56, 4 Dec 1838.

[162] 5 *Stat.* 7 (Mar 19, 1836).

Colonel Brisbane's Regiment, South Carolina Militia, 1836

stresses in the Philadelphia area to produce the clothing items needed by the Army. In the course of the war, his Department procured, on the basis of estimates received from the Clothing Bureau, the following quantities of clothing and personal equipment for the troops in Florida: [163]

Item	1836	1837	1838	1839	1840	1841
Bootees, pr.	600	9,040	6,921	6,500	9,700	1,375
Caps, forage	....	1,590	1,762	2,100	7,600	800
Drawers, pr.	500	980	1,539	2,000	4,000	....
Jackets, cotton	....	....	2,056	1,300	2,500	....
Jackets, wool	450	3,090	3,675	2,300	4,268	1,000
Overalls, cotton	....	....	5,773	800	3,000	....
Overals, wool	500	3,936	6,318	4,200	5,536	1,000
Shirts, cotton	....	....	5,423	7,500	10,000	3,250
Shirts, flannel	500	5,080	2,994	800	4,000	....
Stockings, pr.	600	6,070	7,491	6,000	12,000	3,313
Blankets	600	990	1,562	....	.....	....
Haversacks	9,000	7,690	263	....	.....	....
Knapsacks	7,500	9,590	262	....	1,000	....

Depots not only of clothing but also of subsistence were built up on the east and west coasts of Florida. Difficulties at times compelled men to carry 5 to 6 days of rations with them, but there was no shortage of subsistence stores as in previous wars. The Subsistence Department functioned smoothly to sustain a steady flow of rations to the troops and even to modify the ration to promote the health of the soldiers. The components of the rations had remained unchanged since 1818, but under Presidential authority onions, potatoes, and other vegetables of an anti-scorbutic nature were occasionally substituted for beans. The Department issued low-priced French and Catalonia wines during the summer in lieu of hard liquor.[164] It also furnished coffee and sugar before the end of 1838.

The climate and the exposure of provisions resulting from the frequent movement of the troops with their supplies caused the destruction of much subsistence. Such losses undoubtedly contributed their share to the large expenditures of the Subsistence Department during the Seminole War. Gibson estimated that his Department spent $1,038,662 for rations during the war.[165] Subsisting the troops in Florida,

[163] RG 92, OQMG Consolidated Correspondence File, Boxes 305–08 (Irvine to SW, 3 Jan 1841 and enclosures). Data covers the period 25 January 1836 to 31 May 1841.

[164] (1) *American State Papers, Military Affairs*, VII, 614 (Gibson to SW, 20 Nov 1837). (2) RG 192, CGS, Letters Sent, vol. 14, p. 167 (Circular to assistant commissaries, 10 Nov 1837); p. 200 (Gibson to Cross, 27 Nov 1837). (3) RG 192, CGS, Letters Received, No. 2057 (Maj T. F. Hunt to Gibson, 2 Sep 1837).

[165] RG 192, CGS, Letters to SW, 1840–54, pp. 59–60 (6 Oct 1841).

however, was only part of his responsibility. Teamsters, steamboat hands, mechanics, and laborers employed by the Quartermaster's Department also had to be subsisted. The Subsistence Department provided rations for such Seminoles as emigrated to the lands west of the Mississippi, and, under congressional authorization, it issued rations to the unfortunate inhabitants of Florida who had been driven from their homes by the Indians and who were unable to provide for themselves.[166]

Intended as a temporary measure to succor the immediate needs of the distressed, the receipt of rations came to be looked upon as a right and the law was so liberally interpreted that the list of suffering inhabitants, it was charged, comprised some of the most opulent families.[167] The relief system threatened to jeopardize the military operations by diverting both subsistence and transportation intended for the Army to the relief program being supervised by Army officers. The Secretary of War ordered measures taken to divorce the program from the Army altogether and to employ agents to attend to it.[168] As a means of encouraging resettlement during the closing months of the war, the Secretary of War directed the Subsistence Department to issue rations to the settlers until their first crops were harvested. Including all of these expenditures, Gibson estimated that his Department had spent $1,155,585 from the beginning of the war until 30 September 1824.[169]

Much of Quartermaster support of the troops operating against the Seminoles was effected on a basis of anticipating demands rather than waiting for requisitions from the field. Major Cross, Acting Quartermaster General at Washington, thereby made certain that supplies would be available when campaigns were initiated. Quartermasters in the field often lacked early information on operational plans, and their requisitions therefore frequently came in too late to be filled in time for the intended use of the supplies at the opening of a military operation. Late in September 1836, for example, the assistant quartermaster of the depot at Garey's Ferry ordered 20 two-horse wagons for use the first week in October. But even if the wagons could have been purchased on the spot when the order reached the Department, it still took 20 days to transport them to Florida. With good reason, the Acting Quartermaster General doubted that these wagons would be available at the time they were wanted.[170] Preparing for the campaign in 1837, Major Cross

[166] 5 *Stat.* 131 (Feb 1, 1836).
[167] Sprague, *The Origin, Progress, and Conclusion of the Florida War*, p. 519.
[168] RG 107, OSW, Letters Sent, vol. 17, pp. 352–53 (Poinsett to Jesup, 3 Aug 1837).
[169] RG 192, CGS, Letters to SW, 1840–54, p. 96.
[170] RG 92, OQMG Letter Book, vol. 24, p. 113 (Cross to AQM Clark, 1 Oct 1836).

preferred to order supplies before General Jesup's requisitions arrived even if such action did involve the risk of some duplication.[171]

Information on mileage between depots and interior stations was soon acquired, and data for the organization of an efficient wagon train, upon which the success of any campaign depended, was passed along to depot quartermasters. The distance from the various depots on the St. John's River to the Withlacoochee River, where the Indians were concentrated in 1836, varied but, for purposes of illustration, Major Cross set it at 100 miles. A round trip, he advised depot quartermasters, might be accomplished in 12 days and the wagon train kept in constant motion by the use of a set of relief horses. A two-horse wagon could haul 6 barrels of flour or 1,332 pounds of supplies; a four-horse wagon could carry 7 barrels of pork, or 10 to 12 barrels of flour, or 2,100 pounds of supplies. The depot at Garey's Ferry had 20 two-horse wagons and 80 four-horse wagons that were capable of carrying a load of 194,640 pounds. Rations for the horses would have to be included in that amount. At 12 pounds a day per horse for 12 days for 360 horses the ration weight would amount to 51,840 pounds. To feed 3,000 men, the estimated force to be supplied, the depot quartermaster would have to estimate not on the basis of a complete ration that weighed $2\frac{3}{4}$ pounds, but on the basis of a meat and bread ration, equivalent to 2 pounds, including barrels. For 12 days, rations for the troops would amount to 72,000 pounds, from which some deduction could be made for beef cattle driven along with the train. The force to be supported also included 500 mounted men whose horses would have to be supplied. Allowing a half ration per horse, the wagons would have to haul 36,000 pounds of forage every 12 days. Deducting rations for the troops and forage for the animals, the wagon train would then be capable of hauling every 12 days 34,800 pounds of military stores and other supplies needed by the troops.[172]

At the beginning of the war, there was much diversity of opinion concerning the best type of wagon to be used in Florida. Preference ranged from one-horse carts to five-horse wagons. In this uncertainty, the Acting Quartermaster General decided it would be best to employ four-horse wagons for service between depots and the interior stations where roads could be built, and to use strong two-horse wagons, equipped with harness for four horses, for field service.[173]

In 1837, the Department also added, at Jesup's request, ponton wagons. These wagons, lined with India rubber cloth and capable of

[171] *Ibid.*, vol. 25, p. 207 (Cross to Jesup, 30 Aug 1837).

[172] *Ibid.*, vol. 24, pp. 170–71 (Cross to Clark and Dusenbery, 7 Nov 1836).

[173] *Ibid.*, vol. 26, p. 187 (Cross to Maj. J. B. Brant, 16 Apr 1838).

sustaining heavy loads afloat, were intended to afford ready means of passing rivers on the march.   In all other cases, they were to be considered and used as light transports.   Quartermaster Brant at Tampa Bay later complained that they were "wretched."   Inquiry soon revealed that the ponton wagons had not been utilized as intended but had been employed with the common wagin train in transporting supplies between the depot and the interior.[174]   It was therefore not surprising that they broke down in 6 weeks as Brant had charged.

The ponton wagon was only one of a number of items that had been under development using India rubber cloth in their construction. General experimentation with India rubber cloth had been initiated in the summer of 1835.[175]   When Jesup was ordered to the field a year later, he directed Lt. J. F. Lane, acting assistant quartermaster at Boston, who had been conducting the experiments to join him and bring along all the ponton equipment that he had completed in order that it might be fully tested in the field.   The test of the ponton equipment was completely successful and the bridge was enthusiastically recommended for use by the U.S. Army.[176]   Calls for such equipment were later to be made during the Mexican War.

Adequate supplies of wagons and carts were sent to Florida, but it soon became apparent that deficiencies would occur because returns sent to the Washington office showed a large number dropped as unserviceable. Major Cross inferred that wagons were being thrown aside too readily for want of repairs that could not be made without a supply of seasoned timber unavailable in Florida.   He therefore ordered the quartermasters at New York and Philadelphia to supply the depots on the east and west coasts of Florida with a small quantity of wheelwright timber suited to ordinary repairs as well as extra stokes, fellies, and axles.[177]

In the past, soldiers had been detailed from the line to make repairs,

[174] (1) *Ibid.*, vol. 26, pp. 75–77 (Cross to Brant, 26 Feb 1838); p. 90 (Cross to AQM McCrab, 7 Mar 1838); pp. 187–89 (Cross to Brant, 16 Apr 1838).   (2) The ponton wagon was an invention of Jesup's, but he gave all the rights to Lt. J. F. Lane who conducted experiments under his orders. Lane was later killed in Florida but though he had obtained patents for all inventions, Jesup had permission to use any of them for public purposes.   *Ibid.*, vol. 34, p. 499 (Jesup to Mackay, 5 Jun 1843).

[175] (1) *Ibid.*, vol. 22, p. 189 (Jesup to Lane, 28 Aug 1835).   (2) Experimental tents using India rubber cloth had also been made.   RG 92, CGP, Letters Sent, No. 394, p. 109 (Irvine to Garland, 9 Mar 1836).

[176] (1) RG 92, OQMG Letter Book, vol. 23, p. 221 (Jessup to Lane, 19 May 1836).   (2) Jesup Papers, Box 3 (Rpt, Bd of Examination on Bridge, 15–16 Sep 1836).   Manuscript Div., Library of Congress.   (3) The Army tested Lane's India rubber ponton bridge in September 1836 at Woolfork's Ferry on the Chattahoochie River.   Over a bridge 290 feet long and 13 feet wide, supported by 31 pontoons, 200 men of the Regular Army marched in full battle equipment.

[177] RG 92, OQMG Letter Book, vol. 25, pp. 185–86 (Cross to Stanton and Mackay, 23 Aug 1837).

drive wagons, and perform any other services the Army required. Jesup had been at his headquarters in Alabama only a few weeks before he requested the Secretary of War to authorize a corps of artificers and laborers. They were necessary, he asserted, because southern militia and volunteers could not be induced to labor at such tasks.[178] The Secretary approved a specific requisition for 20 mechanics and 50 laborers, and the quartermasters at Philadelphia and New York were directed to cooperate in engaging them. Though Jesup's requisition specified no distribution among the trades, the Acting Quartermaster General apportioned the artisans as follows: 4 blacksmiths, 2 wagon makers, 2 harness makers, and 12 carpenters.[179] In addition to the corps of 20 artisans, the Department organized a corps of 30 teamsters and 50 laborers. By 17 December, the vessel on which they had been embarked for Tampa Bay waited only on a fair wind to sail from New York.[180] The following year, the Department sent additional artisans to Tampa Bay and recruited a corps of artisans and laborers for the depot on the St. John's River. For the latter place, the corps included 6 wheelwrights and wagon makers, 4 blacksmiths, 4 saddlers, 2 boatbuilders, and 12 carpenters among the artisans, as well as 50 teamsters and 50 laborers.[181]

It was deemed essential that the teamsters hired be "acquainted with the nature of mules," for an increasing number of mules were employed on the wagon trains. At Jesup's request, the Department ordered a corps of muleteers, or packhorse drivers recruited at St. Louis from among the mountain fur traders for service in Florida for the duration of the 1837 campaign.[182] Existing legislation made no provision for wagon or forage masters, both essential to the conduct of active operations. To circumvent this omission, the Department hired agents until, on 5 July 1838, Congress legalized this practice by authorizing the appointment of no more than 20 wagon and forage masters.[183]

As the number of depots and subdepots increased during the war, the number of civilians supporting the military operations in Florida multiplied until a total of 1,063 persons were employed as of November

---

[178] (1) *American State Papers, Military Affairs,* VII, 325 (Jesup to Cass, 11 Jun 1836). (2) When in 1836 all work in the Quartermaster's Department in the field was brought to a standstill for want of teamsters, Jesup interpreted the law on payment for fatigue duty to permit him to employ Volunteers, paying them wages as teamsters and also as soldiers, since they were armed and compelled to serve as soldiers. RG 92, OQMG Letter Book, vol. 30, p. 140 (Jesup to 2d Comptroller, 13 Jun 1844).

[179] RG 92, OQMG Letter Book, vol. 24, p. 219 (Cross to Stanton and Mackay, 1 Dec 1836).

[180] *Ibid.,* vol. 24, p. 263 (Cross to Jesup, 23 Dec 1936).

[181] *Ibid.,* vol. 25, p. 155 (Cross to Mackay, 12 Aug 1837).

[182] *Ibid.,* vol. 25, p. 135 (Cross to Brant, 5 Aug 1837).

[183] (1) 5 *Stat.* 256, sec. 10. (2) RG 92, OQMG Letter Book, vol. 26, p. 352 (Cross to Clark, 14 Jul 1838); p. 457 (Stanton to Wagonmaster Shannon, 6 Sep 1838).

1840.[184] By that time, the principal depots were established at Palatka on the St. John's River; St. Augustine on the east coast; Tampa Bay and Cedar Key on the west coast; and St. Marks on the Gulf below Tallahassee. Except for St. Marks, soon abandoned in favor of a better location below it, all of these depots had extensive warehouse accommodations, wheelwright shops, smith shops, saddlers shops, stables, quarters for officers and men employed at the depots, well-built wharves, and at Cedar Key, even a rail-way and other facilities for repairing vessels and constructing boats.[185]

The Seminole War was the first war that required the Quartermaster's Department to furnish a considerable amount of water transportation both for operational maneuvers and supply support. The experience gained was put to good service later in the Mexican War. Regular troops transferred to duty in Florida and most of the forage, subsistence, clothing, equipment, and military stores procured for the Army's support were transported to Florida in ships chartered for the purpose by the Quartermaster's Department. In general, quartermasters at New York, Philadelphia, and Washington hired sailing ships to transport men and supplies to Florida. At these ports, there were few steamboats suited to navigation of the Atlantic. There were, for example, steamboats plying the North River and Long Island Sound, but they were not built and fitted for ocean service. The Sound steamboats were too lofty in structure and moreover burned wood. Called upon to send troops to Charleston quickly in the summer of 1836, Quartermaster Stanton could report only two steamboats suited for the purpose in New York harbor, namely, two Charleston steam packets.[186] On the other hand, quartermasters at Charleston and Savannah chartered a considerable number of steamboats to transport troops and supplies from these ports to Florida. Quartermasters also hired steamboats to transport supplies across the Gulf, though not without raising criticism of the exorbitant rates of hire and the consequent "frightful amount of money" wasted on them.[187] The Quartermaster's Department chartered some 40 steamboats during 1836 and 1837.[188]

[184] RG 92, OQMG Consolidated Correspondence File, Boxes 305–08 (Stanton to Jesup, 20 Jan 1841 and enclosures).

[185] *Ibid.*

[186] (1) RG 92, OQMG Consolidated Correspondence File, Box 1147 (Stanton to Hunt, 25 May 1836). (2) At Charleston, the assistant quartermaster was directed to arrange for the transportation of several companies of infantry and artillery by railroad to Augusta where wagons and teams were to be provided for the remainder of the journey to Fort Mitchell, Ala. RG 92, OQMG Letter Book, vol. 23, p. 198 (Hunt to Engle and Dimmock, 14 May 1836).

[187] RG 92, OQMG Letter Book, vol. 25, pp. 298–99 (Cross to Whiting, 22 Dec 1937).

[188] *American State Papers, Military Affairs,* VII, 994–97 (List of steamboats, 16 Feb 1838).

Transportation was hampered by lack of control over chartered ships. Civilian pilots made their own decisions on when they would take a ship out. Two companies of infantry were embarked on 5 June 1836, for example, but the late hour and threatening weather caused the pilot to refuse to leave New York harbor. The next morning the storm was worse, and 2 days later the commanding general waiting the arrival of the troops could only be informed that no conjecture could be made as to when the storm would cease and the pilot be willing to leave the harbor.[189]

Subsistence and forage accounted for the larger part of the cargo that the Department had to ship to Florida. Some idea of the scope of operations is apparent in a report made by Major Cross. In a 3-month period, he chartered and supplied the cargo for 20 brigs and schooners and for one transport owned by the United States that sailed from the District of Columbia to Jacksonville, Tampa Bay, and Garey's Ferry loaded with forage (72,707 bushels of oats, 21,350 bushels of corn, and 469,768 pounds of hay) and subsistence stores (605 barrels of flour, 3,664 barrels of hard bread, 162 barrels of bacon, 30 barrels of vinegar, and 353 barrels of potatoes).[190]

Ships sailing directly to the depot at Garey's Ferry on the St. John's River ran some risks since sand bars obstructed the entrance to that river. Ordinarily, wrecks were not too numerous, but storms exacted a heavy toll. The Department advised quartermasters to regulate their shipments to the depot by chartering only vessels of light draught since the depth of the water at the mouth of the river and at Garey's Ferry was not more than 8 feet.[191]

From the nature of the country, the Army used steamboats, barges, batteaux, and scows in military operations from the beginning of the war. In preparation for the extensive campaign projected by Jesup in 1837 that called for penetration of the Everglades via the St. John's, Indian, and Caloosahatchee Rivers, the Quartermaster's Department began construction of batteaux capable of carrying about 20 men each. Not too much was known about the navigation of these rivers but on the basis of one officer's experience in the country, these flat-bottomed boats, built with square bows and sterns, were to be 20 feet long, 6 feet wide, and draw no more than 9 to 12 inches of water when loaded. Each batteaux was to be provided with an awning stretched over a ridge pole and fastened to the gunwales so as to shelter the men from rain as well as

[189] RG 92, OQMG Letter Book, vol. 23, pp. 282–84 (Hunt to Jesup, 8 Jun 1836).
[190] Ibid., vol. 25, pp. 417–18 (Cross to Stanton, 2 Jan 1838).
[191] Ibid., vol. 25, p. 233 (Cross to Mackay, 4 Sep 1837); pp. 325–26 (Cross to Whiting, 2 Nov 1837).

sun.   Major Cross ordered 100 of these boats built at Charleston, Philadelphia, and New York, substituting on 50 of them a sharp for the square
bow, since he believed it would be best suited for penetrating streams
obstructed with grass.[192]   He expected to use steamboats to tow the
batteaux to their departure points.

The Department generally employed steamboats along the west coast
of Florida to forward supplies and transport troops to points at which
penetration of the Everglades was to be attempted.   It also used steamboats to forward supplies on the St. John's River and it was not uncommon to see a steamboat towing a schooner, both loaded with subsistence
and forage.[193]   As early as the first campaign, Scott had ordered the
steamer, *Essayon*, belonging to the Engineer Department, taken into the
service of the Quartermaster's Department on the St. John's River.[194]
At least two steamboats were purchased by the quartermaster at New
Orleans for service on the Chattahoochie against the Creeks in 1836.
Originally manned by seamen and commanded by naval officers operating
under the direction of General Jesup, these steamboats were later transferred to the control of the Quartermaster's Department, since the services
in which they were engaged were deemed not to be "professionally
rewarding" to the naval officers.[195]

Transportation available for the campaign of 1837 included two
government schooners and three steamboats on the west coast and one
government steamer and two chartered steamboats on the St. John's
River.   To expedite communication between the Army and Washington,
the Quartermaster's Department, on orders of the Secretary of War, also
purchased and put into operation a steamboat used as an express between
the St. John's River and Charleston where it connected with the regular
service from that port to Washington to provide 10-day mail service.[196]

The heavy expense to which the Department was subjected during
the war in the hire of steamboats resulted from the tremendous amount
of forage that had to be transported to feed the large number of horses
used by the Army in Florida.   In the fall of 1840, for example, there were
1,008 horses used as teams and saddle horses as well as 1,133 mules.   By
that time, the expense of steamboat hire had been somewhat reduced by
substituting steamboats owned by the United States for chartered boats,

---

[192] *Ibid.*, vol. 25, pp. 117–18 (Cross to Engle, 31 Jul 1837); pp. 160–61 (Cross to Mackay and
Stanton, 19 Aug 1837).

[193] *Ibid.*, vol. 24, pp. 167–68 (Cross to Jesup, 5 Nov 1836).

[194] *Ibid.*, vol. 25, p. 305 (Cross to Hunt, 23 Oct 1838).   The Department later reimbursed
the Engineer Department for the value of the boat.

[195] *Ibid.*, vol. 23, pp. 235–36 (Hunt to Clark and Jesup, 24 May 1836); vol. 25, p. 126 (Cross
to Vinton, 2 Aug 1837).

[196] RG 107, OSW, Letters Received, Q–86 (43) (Cross to Poinsett, 10 Aug 1837).

but there were still six hired boats employed in addition to the five government steamboats—all of them principally engaged, at an average monthly rate of about $2,500, in transporting forage.[197]

Enormous sums had been spent on a war that had been believed to be unimportant. It was no nearer conclusion in 1841 than in 1838 when Jesup wrote that "unless *immediate* emigration be abandoned, the war will continue for years to come, and at constantly accumulating expense."[198] Jesup had approved and supported the government's policy of Indian removal, but he argued that it ought not to be applied until the white population was in contact with the Indians.

In regard to the Seminoles, we have committed the error of attempting to remove them when their lands were not required for agricultural purposes; when they were not in the way of the white inhabitants; and when the greater portion of their country was an unexplored wilderness, of the interior of which we were as ignorant as of the interior of China. We exhibit in our present contest, the first instance, perhaps since the commencement of authentic history, of a nation employing an army to explore a country (for we can do little more than explore it), or attempting to remove a band of savages from one unexplored wilderness to another.[199]

He proposed letting the Seminoles remain in Florida, confined to the southern portion of the state, on condition that if they committed any depredations on the white inhabitants or passed the boundaries assigned to them, they would forfeit their right to the land.

Approval of his proposals would have saved the nation millions of dollars and the lives of many valuable citizens and military personnel. The Administration, however, was committed to the policy of forcible emigration of the Seminoles. By 1841, Col. S. W. Worth, the commanding officer in Florida, voiced much the same views as those of Jesup.[200] His proposals laid before a council of officers were rejected as neither politic, expedient, or judicious by all its members except Jesup. Preparations for continuing the war went on but every effort was made to reduce expenses. By May 1842, the government was at last willing to call a halt to operations and announce that the war would not be renewed unless provoked by new Indian aggressions. Retrenchment was now pursued more vigorously. Troops were gradually withdrawn until only customary garrisons were maintained in Florida. The Quartermaster's Department released steamboats and sailing vessels; broke up wagon trains; sold

---

[197] RG 92, OQMG Consolidated Correspondence File, Boxes 305–08 (Stanton to Jesup, 20 Jan 1841 and enclosures).

[198] Sprague, *The Origin, Progress, and Conclusion of the Florida War*, pp. 199–201 (Ltr, Jesup to SW, 11 Feb 1838).

[199] *Ibid.*

[200] *Ibid.*, pp. 441–44 (Ltr, Worth to Scott, 14 Feb 1841).

horses and mules; and discharged teamsters, mechanics, and laborers. Supply activities in Florida rapidly dwindled to those normally associated with sustaining garrisoned troops.

By 1842, Jesup had been directing operations of the Quartermaster's Department for almost a quarter of a century. He had molded and shaped it into an efficient supply agency. He had formulated its regulations; developed its methods of procedures; and trained a staff of officers who were thoroughly familiar with them. The Seminole War afforded an opportunity for testing these methods in practice and for evaluating the training given. Jesup found both sound, and the even more thorough testing to which the Department was shortly to be subjected only served to emphasize how well he had accomplished the goals he had established in 1818.

CHAPTER VII

Logistical Problems of the Mexican War

In the spring of 1846, the United States and Mexico drifted into war, and the Quartermaster's Department was called upon to apply the logistical lessons it had mastered during the 7 years of the Seminole War. So effectively did the Department contribute to the support of the armies in the field that the commanding generals achieved a series of brilliant victories. Unlike the disasters that overtook American arms in the War of 1812, every movement in the Mexican War was an "onward movement." Jesup proudly asserted that "with our depots farther from the sources of supply than Algiers is from Toulon or Marseilles, we accomplished more in the first six months of our operations in Mexico, than France, the first military power in Europe, has accomplished in Africa in seventeen years." [1] Supply failures in the Crimean War a few years later confirmed Jesup's conviction that the French army was far behind the American army in all administrative arrangements relating to the movement and supply of armies in the field. [2]

The success of Jesup's well-organized Department was achieved despite the handicaps imposed by unpreparedness for war. The sums required to accumulate reserve stocks of military supplies in the depots in the years immediately preceding the Mexican War were denied to Jesup by successive Congresses bent on economy. The country was not only unprepared in supplies but also in men. No sooner had hostilities with the Seminoles been officially declared at an end in the summer of 1842 than Congress immediately enacted legislation reducing the size of the Army from 12,539 officers and men to 8,613. [3] Through 1845, appropriations were limited to the wants of this small peacetime establishment. [4]

So drastically were funds cut that no repairs of barracks or other

---

[1] House *Ex. Doc.* No. 8, 30th Cong., 1st sess., p. 549 (QMG Annual Report, 1847).

[2] (1) RG 92, OQMG, Reports of QMG to SW and Heads of Departments, vol. 3, p. 629 (Jesup to Hon. John J. Mason, 25 Apr 1857). (2) RG 92, OQMG Letter Book, vol. 53, pp. 406–07 (Jesup to Maj. J. McKinstry, 6 Sep 1859).

[3] (1) 5 *Stat.* 512 (Aug 23, 1824). (2) Upton, *The Military Policy of the United States*, p. 193.

[4] The following table shows the funds appropriated in the spring of 1842, a few months

buildings, except such as were indispensable to their preservation, could be ordered during fiscal year 1844. No civilians could be hired; all dependence had to be placed on the troops to insure their own comfort. Only by order of the Secretary of War were the quartermasters at Philadelphia and at New Orleans each permitted to subscribe to one newspaper so that they might obtain shipping lists and current prices, knowledge of which was essential to the execution of their duties. The Washington office was allowed none—not even the newspaper that published the laws—and Jesup requested that the quartermaster at Philadelphia send him his newspaper "when you have done with it." Jesup harked back to the early days of his administration and advised that "to save the army we must come back to the economy which characterized Mr. Calhoun's administration of the War Department." [5] Not until 13 May 1846, 5 days after the battle of Palo Alto, did Congress enact the first appropriation bill passed with reference to a state of war. Until that time, the troops on the southwestern frontier had to be supported within the limited means at the disposal of the Quartermaster's Department. On 13 May it became the duty of the Department to provide immediately the supplies and means of transportation for three separate armies—the first concentrating on the lower Rio Grande, the second at San Antonio, Tex., and the third at Fort Leavenworth, on the Missouri.

There had been ample time for preparation. Ten years earlier, Texas had won its independence from Mexico. When it sought to join the United States in the 1840's, the Mexican government insisted that annexation would be equivalent to a declaration of war. Beyond concentrating some troops at Fort Jesup, La., as an Army of Observation under the command of Brig. Gen. Zachary Taylor in the spring of 1844,

before the Seminole War ended, for the fiscal year ending 30 Jun 1843, and in 1843, 1844, and 1845 for the ensuing fiscal year in each case.

Appropriation for fiscal year	1843	1844	1845	1846
Barracks	$135,000	105,000	140,000	170,000
Clothing and equipment	374,876	100,000	140,000	180,000
QM supplies	316,000	195,000	195,000	147,000
Transportation	242,000	170,000	170,000	140,000
Incidentals	127,000	115,000	90,000	90,000

5 Stat., passim.

[5] (1) RG 92, OQMG Letters from Maj. Gen. Thomas S. Jesup, 1839–1846, unnumbered box (Jesup to Brig. Gen. W. K. Armistead, 12 Jan 1844). (2) RG 92, OQMG Letter Book, vol. 34, p. 450 (Jesup to Cross, 13 May 1843); vol. 35, p. 65 (Jesup to AQM Ketchum, 18 Jul 1843); p. 344 (Jesup to Stanton, 24 Jan 1844).

when the first unsuccessful efforts at annexation were being made, the government initiated no preparatory measures for war. Shortly after Congress adopted a joint resolution of annexation on 1 March 1845, the War Department ordered Taylor to hold his troops in readiness to move if Texas accepted the terms of admission proposed. In June it directed him, on receipt of information of such acceptance, to proceed to such place on or near the Rio Grande as was adapted to repelling invasion.[6]

Early in June 1845, Taylor concentrated his forces at New Orleans preparatory to moving them later in that month to Corpus Christi on the Nueces River where he pursued a program of what at a later time was called "watchful waiting." Refusal of the Mexican government to receive the diplomatic representative of the United States, John Slidell, made rejection of this country's overtures for amicable settlement of all issues look almost certain. When news of the rejection reached Washington on 12 January 1846, Taylor was ordered to advance his forces to the Rio Grande. Communications being slow, the general received these instructions 3 weeks later, and it was not until 8 March that his troops began to move off on the road towards Matamoras, establishing a new base at Point Isabel on an inlet known as the Brazos de Santiago. Another month of "watchful waiting" followed until, on 25 April, a reconnoitering party of dragoons was attacked by Mexican forces, and Taylor reported to Washington on the following day that "hostilities may now be considered as commenced." [7]

Preliminary Quartermaster Preparations

What measures did the Quartermaster's Department take in the 13 months that elapsed between 1 March 1845, when Taylor was ordered to hold his troops in readiness to move from Fort Jesup, and 26 April 1846, when he reported that war had begun? Such measures as were taken were initiated by Col. Henry Stanton. He served as Acting Quartermaster General during the spring and summer of 1845 because Jesup had left Washington in April on an extensive inspection tour of the western posts from which he was not expected to return until autumn. Mindful of the demands that might be made upon the Department, however, Jesup, before departing, had discussed with Stanton a certain redistribution of personnel to strengthen the Quartermaster organization in the southwest.

In 1845, the personnel of the Department still totaled 37 officers as

---

[6] House *Ex. Doc.* No. 60, 30th Cong., 1st sess., pp. 79–82 (SW to Taylor, 28 May, 15 Jun 1845).

[7] *Ibid.*, p. 288 (Taylor to AG, 26 Apr 1846).

it had since 1838 when Congress had provided for 2 assistant quartermasters general, 2 deputy quartermasters general, 4 quartermasters, and 28 assistant quartermasters under a Quartermaster General. This was the authorized legal organization of the Quartermaster's Department but its actual strength was far less. On the eve of the Mexican War, there were six vacancies in the Department, one of quartermaster and five of assistant quartermaster. From the existing staff, one officer was permanently detached as superintendent of the clothing depot at Philadelphia and two served in the Washington office, one charged with the administration of affairs and the other with disbursements. Of the remaining officers, one was entirely disabled and two partially so. On the eve of the war, Jesup expressed the hope that Congress would increase the number of officers in his Department, and he urgently recommended that the Secretary of War at least fill the six vacancies immediately.[8]

The existing staff was small for performing the tasks that lay ahead, but its officers were thoroughly experienced. Most of them had seen service in the field during the Seminole War. Moreover, all the senior officers of the Department had, as young men, served in the line in the War of 1812. For more than a quarter of a century they had held important posts in the Department. Trueman Cross and Thomas F. Hunt had been among the first officers appointed by Jesup when he became Quartermaster General in 1818. Cross, Hunt, and Stanton had repeatedly been called upon to serve as Acting Quartermaster General during Jesup's absences from Washington. They had helped to shape the Department's organization, to formulate its regulations, and to develop its procedures.

The Department's strength was not increased until 10 months after the war began. Then Congress added four additional quartermasters and ten assistant quartermasters. It is to be understood that Congress authorized the appointment of additional regimental quartermasters, from subalterns of the line when it called the volunteers into service and when it increased the size of the Regular Army. It limited all of these appointments, however, to the duration of the war.[9]

Colonel Stanton began strengthening the Quartermaster organization in the southwest by transferring Lt. Col. Thomas F. Hunt to the key post of New Orleans. The deputy quartermaster general, then serving in Florida, was thoroughly familiar with the resources of the area and the duties of that post by reason of his many years of service at

[8] RG 92, OQMG Consolidated Correspondence File, Box 477 (Jesup to Marcy, 14 Apr 1846).

[9] 9 *Stat.* 17, 124, 126 (Jun 18, 1846 and Feb 11, 1847). The legislation limiting the service of the four quartermasters and 10 assistant quartermasters to the duration of the war was repealed by the act of July 19, 1848, but it provided, however, that no vacancy that might occur should be filled until authorized by subsequent legislation. 9 *Stat.* 201, 203.

New Orleans.   Capt. Osborn Cross, son of Col. Trueman Cross, was sent to take charge of Quartermaster duties at Fort Jesup, and Capt. George W. Crosman, on duty at Boston, was reassigned to Taylor's headquarters.[10]

Months earlier, Jesup had designated Col. Trueman Cross for service in the southwest, and in August the Secretary of War ordered the assistant quartermaster general, then on duty at New York, to General Taylor's headquarters, charging him with the immediate direction of affairs of the Department in Texas and its vicinity.   In addition to Captains Crosman and Cross, the Department sent two additional quarter-masters and four assistant quartermasters to Texas, and placed them, as well as Hunt at New Orleans, under the direction of Colonel Cross.[11] By the fall of 1845, 10 of the Department's roster of 37 officers were on duty in the area.   In the absence of provision for the service by Congress, Colonel Cross and Lieutenant Colonel Hunt were obliged to create the resources necessary to keep the Army in the field and, in Jesup's opinion, contributed largely to its early victories on the Rio Grande.[12]

Undoubtedly, it would have been of great advantage in 1845 to have had in readiness a wagon train of 300 to 400 wagons, all of them made from one established standard pattern, so that by freely interchang-ing parts, as Colonel Cross suggested, a complete wagon might have been made from two or three crippled ones.   Unfortunately, there were no wagons in readiness; in any emergency they had to be made in haste— "taken from the stump" in the graphic phrasing of Colonel Cross—after troops were ordered to the field.[13]   Under these circumstances and antici-pating that when Taylor's troops moved from Fort Jesup they would require additional means of transportation, Colonel Stanton, on 23 April 1845, ordered the quartermaster at Philadelphia to contract for the con-struction of 30 four-horse wagons of the type that had been used in Florida.   About a month later, these wagons with the necessary sets of harness were shipped to New Orleans to be held subject to Taylor's orders.[14]   By 17 August, Stanton had shipped an additional 30 wagons from Philadelphia and had ordered 20 more procured, though he stressed good workmanship rather than speed in ordering their construction.[15]

[10] RG 92, OQMG Letter Book, vol. 36, p. 439 (Stanton to Hunt, 29 Apr 1845); pp. 546–47 (Stanton to Taylor, 5 Jun 1845); pp. 564–65, 590–91 (Stanton to Crosman, 7 Jun, 2 Jul 1845).

[11] (1) *Ibid.*, vol. 37, p. 69 (Stanton to Cross, 18 Aug 1845). (2) House *Ex. Doc.* No. 119, 29th Cong., 2d sess., 279 (Stanton to Cross, 9 Sep 1845).

[12] RG 92, OQMG Reports of QMG to SW and Heads of Departments, I, 67 (Jesup to SW, 29 Jun 1849).

[13] House *Ex. Doc.* No. 60, p. 647 (Cross to QMG, 23 Nov 1845).

[14] RG 92, OQMG Letter Book, vol. 35, p. 481 (Stanton to Thomas, 23 Apr 1845); pp. 519, 547 (Stanton to Taylor, 17 May and 5 Jun 1845).

[15] *Ibid.*, vol. 36, pp. 605–06 (Stanton to Hunt and Thomas, 16 Jul 1845); vol. 37, pp. 66–67 (Stanton to Hunt and Thomas, 17 Aug 1845).

By that time, Taylor and part of his troops had arrived at Corpus Christi. Captain Crosman was attempting to organize an efficient wagon train, but he had only 30 wagons though the dragoons marching overland were expected to bring about 50 with them. In any case, he estimated that, if a movement was made to the Rio Grande, a train of at least 100 wagons would be required, and if the dragoon horses were to be foraged 40 miles in the interior, 50 more wagons would be needed.[16] Stanton at once ordered 50 additional wagons procured at Cincinnati.

Colonel Cross, who had been directing from New York the transportation of additional companies of Regulars to Texas, stopped at Washington before proceeding to Taylor's headquarters. Reviewing the available means of land transportation, he pronounced them inadequate. So far the Department had ordered 130 wagons, the last of which could not reach Corpus Christi before November. With 76 companies of Regulars either in or on their way to Texas, the baggage train alone for that number of men, he pointed out, would require 90 wagons. If the Army advanced to the Rio Grande, a line of operations would thereby be established 100 miles in length, over which all supplies including forage for dragoon and artillery horses would have to be transported. Cross estimated that a supply train of 175 wagons would be required for the purpose, making a total of 265 wagons. Allowing for the 130 wagons already ordered or delivered and the 50 the dragoons had with them, the Department would have to provide 85 additional wagons.[17] Drawing on his experience in the Seminole War, Colonel Cross also advised that to permit repair of wagons in Texas the Department ought to send out three good wheelwrights and three blacksmiths as well as a supply of 1,000 seasoned spokes, 500 fellies, 50 pairs of hounds, and 50 tongues.[18] Stanton immediately gave orders for the procurement at Philadelphia of the additional wagons and repair supplies and for the hire of the needed artisans.[19]

At Corpus Christi, Quartermaster officers were exerting every effort to obtain the necessary draft animals. For a time, a brisk trade in mules was carried on along the Mexican border. The failure to procure mules and horses in the area to the extent anticipated, however, compelled the quartermasters to turn to the use of oxen.[20] By January 1846, Colonel Cross had 592 oxen with the Army, of which 240 were daily at work

[16] House *Ex. Doc.* No. 119, pp. 334–35 (Crosman to Stanton, 26 Aug 1845).

[17] House *Ex. Doc.* No. 60, pp. 642–43 (Cross to Stanton, 10 Sep 1845).

[18] *Ibid.,* p. 643 (Cross to Stanton, 10 Sep 1845).

[19] House *Ex. Doc.* No. 119, p. 279 (Stanton to Thomas, 10 Sep 1845).

[20] *Ibid.,* pp. 334–35 (Crosman to Stanton, 25 Aug 1845); pp. 341–42 (Cross to QMG, 21 Nov 1845).

hauling grass for the animals and wood for the regiments and for the general purposes of the depot.[21]

Even more difficult to obtain than the animals were wagon drivers. In a frontier area, common laborers could scarcely be hired at any rate let alone experienced drivers. When drivers were brought in from New Orleans, Cross charged that they often were anything but what they professed to be. After incurring the expense of transporting them to Corpus Christi, the quartermasters found them to be incompetent, and they were either discharged or they left of their own accord without having rendered any service. What was needed, Cross suggested, was an efficient corps of enlisted train drivers, ready for service whenever the Army went into the field. The existing system, he maintained, could paralyze the Army's movements at any time, for these were dependent on a corps of hired drivers who might quit at their pleasure, or extort their own price by a general strike for higher wages. Such a strike had occurred in November and Cross had been compelled to yield to the drivers' terms.[22]

The Quartermaster organization at Corpus Christi worked strenuously to provide adequate transportation against the day when Taylor's forces moved to the Rio Grande. Colonel Cross assured Jesup that movement would not be delayed for want of transportation. Although the full number of wagons called for by his requisition in September 1845 had not arrived by February 1846, he reported that he would be able to muster a train of nearly 300 wagons—one for every ten marching men in the Army which he thought would not exceed 3,000. He had assigned 110 wagons for baggage and the hospital department and 190 for a supply train. The lack of Engineer reconnaissance to determine whether the roads were feasible for wagon trains had compelled Colonel Cross to gather his own data by sending out an experimental train toward Matamoras. He added further that he had received no line of instructions, or any order whatsoever from General Taylor respecting the means of transportation or other Quartermaster preparations.[23]

While the quartermasters with Taylor's forces coped with the problem of furnishing an adequate wagon train, upon Lieutenant Colonel Hunt fell the burden first of quartering the troops in New Orleans upon their arrival from Fort Jesup, then of providing for their transportation to the Nueces River, and finally of forwarding supplies sent via New Orleans. Hunt had been obliged to quarter the 3d Infantry Regiment in an empty cotton press at a high rental. Without knowing to which

[21] House *Ex. Doc.* No. 60, p. 649 (Cross to Jesup, 16 Jan 1846).

[22] *Ibid.*, pp. 646–48 (Cross to Jesup, 23 Nov 1845).

[23] *Ibid.*, pp. 649–50 (Cross to Jesup, 16 Feb 1846).

point in Texas Taylor would want transportation, Hunt solicited bids "being indefinite in regard to time and place." Under the circumstances he did not receive many. Use of schooners proved to be out of the question since there were no more than enough to transport half the command. River steamboats had to be rejected as unsafe to send to sea. There were only two Gulf steamers in port, but they drew too much water to enter any port between Galveston and the Rio Grande. Taylor preferred steamships and Hunt was finally able to charter suitable transports. Anticipating the need for lighterage, he also purchased one steam lighter and chartered a second.[24]

The troops were established temporarily on St. Joseph's Island until Taylor decided on a camp site at Corpus Christi on the west bank of the Nueces River. They then made a very rough passage of the bay in seven small fishing boats hired by the quartermaster for the purpose of transporting men and cargo. Supplies were landed with great difficulty, and under the supervision of Quartermaster Crosman a depot was established on the island.[25] He used a number of steamers to forward supplies from the depot to Corpus Christi. Captain Crosman also made preparations for handling the arrival of the additional companies of infantry and artillery, whose transportations to Texas from posts on the Canadian border and the Atlantic and Gulf coasts were arranged by the Quartermaster's Department. By mid-October 1845, the forces present at Corpus Christi numbered not quite 4,000—but this was almost half of the entire Army.[26]

The troops were encamped in tents, but there was considerable dissatisfaction. A board of survey inspecting certain tents used by the 7th Infantry Regiment pronounced the material from which they were made as unfit for use, being too thin to shed rain and, in many cases, so lacking in strength that it tore easily at the seams. Colonel Cross agreed with the report and requested an immediate shipment of some wall tents and common tents for at least 2,000 men. On 8 December, 110 wall tents and 333 common tents were ordered for the use of the Army in Texas.[27] In the event the troops remained for the winter season at Corpus Christi, Taylor saw no necessity for hutting them. Instead, he

[24] RG 92, OQMG Consolidated Correspondence File, Box 660 (Hunt to Stanton, 27 Jul 1845).
[25] (1) House *Ex. Doc.* No. 60, pp. 97–98; 99–100 (Taylor to Adj. Gen., 28 Jul, 15 Aug 1845). (2) Capt. William S. Henry, *Campaign Sketches of the War with Mexico* (New York, 1848), pp. 16–17. (3) Maj. Gen. Ethan Allen Hitchcock, *Fifty Years in Camp and Field* (New York, 1909), p. 194.
[26] House *Ex. Doc.* No. 60, pp. 110–11 (Taylor to AG, 15 Oct 1845).
[27] (1) RG 92, OQMG Consolidated Correspondence File, Box 659 (Cross to QMG, 16 Nov 1845). (2) RG 92, OQMG Letter Book, Clothing, vol. 9, p. 91 (Jesup to Cross, 6 Jan 1846).

proposed to use sheds with platforms on which to pitch the tents—a practice that had been extensively used in camps of position in Florida.[28]

However willing the Quartermaster's Department was to provide for the troops, its efforts were hampered by lack of funds. By mid-October 1845, Colonel Stanton warned Cross that "our appropriations will be hard run before they can be reinforced." [29] When a requisition came in from General Taylor for a complete set of ponton equipment, neither the Engineer Department nor the Quartermaster's Department had funds to procure the equipment estimated to cost from $15,000 to $20,000. The Acting Quartermaster General advised Captain Crosman that it could be provided only after Congress had made the necessary appropriation.[30] By the time the ponton equipment reached Taylor, it was no longer needed.

After Taylor had received instructions to advance to the Rio Grande on 4 February 1846, Quartermaster activities at camp hit a furious pace as supplies to be sent by water to the Brazos de Santiago were transferred from Corpus Christi to St. Joseph's Island to await shipment. The organization of the wagon trains required the exertion of every effort—formed as they were, according to Colonel Cross, "from the crudest materials:" 1,000 wild mules, "drawn by stealth from Mexico," (for the trade was contraband) and 600 half-broken oxen from the interior of Texas.[31]

The Army, carrying 20 days' subsistence and 16 days' grain for the animals, began its march, the first of the troops moving out on 8 March 1846. Its forces were not concentrated until they had crossed the Little Colorado River. A total of 1,900 horses and mules and 500 oxen moved with it. The entire train consisted of 307 wagons, of which 84 were drawn by ox teams. All were brought through with but few losses or casualties on the way—a creditable achievement, Cross reported, considering the distance by way of Point Isabel was 188 miles. An officer of the Department marched with each brigade of the Army. Quartermaster Charles Thomas remained at St. Joseph's Island to conduct the fleet of transports to the Brazos de Santiago and establish the new depot at Point Isabel. Both fleet and troops arrived there on 24 March. Then began the backbreaking work of getting the supplies ashore. Vessels drawing more than 4½ to 5 feet of water could not approach nearer than 5 miles to the landing. A double transshipment of every

---

[28] House *Ex. Doc.* No. 60, p. 112 (Taylor to AG, 7 Nov 1845).

[29] RG 92, OQMG Letter Book, vol. 37, pp. 160–61 (17 Oct 1845).

[30] (1) *Ibid.,* vol. 37, p. 161 (Stanton to Crosman, 17 Oct 1845). (2) House Ex. Doc. No. 119, pp. 335–36 (Crosman to Stanton, 4 Sep 1845 and indorsements).

[31] House *Ex. Doc.* No. 119, pp. 345–46 (Cross to Jesup, 17 Feb 1846).

cargo became necessary—first from the seagoing transports to the Department's light steamers, and then from the latter to flats and light boats. Colonel Cross hoped that much labor could be curtailed when a suitable wharf had been built from materials then on their way from New Orleans.[32] After taking up 10 days' subsistence and forage, the Army on 27 March moved to the Rio Grande to encamp opposite Matamoras and await events.

Cross reported that he would go with the Army and then return to regulate the depot at Point Isabel. But time was running out for Colonel Cross. Ambushed and killed by banditti outside the camp at Matamoras, he was accorded a military funeral 2 days before hostilities began.[33] Esteemed as an officer "of more than ordinary attainments," he had for 28 years worked closely with Jesup in developing a well-regulated and well-organized Department. The War Department, in May, temporarily appointed Maj. Charles Thomas chief of the Quartermaster's Department with the Army of Occupation, but it ordered him to remain at Point Isabel, supervising the establishment of the depot. The Department made Captain Crosman, the senior assistant quartermaster, responsible for the operations of the Quartermaster's Department with the marching force.[34] By 2 July 1846, Lt. Col. Henry Whiting, deputy quartermaster general, arrived at Point Isabel to take over the duties of chief quartermaster with Taylor's Army.[35]

Before Taylor's dispatch on the beginning of hostilities reached Washington on Saturday evening, 9 May 1846, the Regulars under his command had won the battles of Palo Alto and Resaca de la Palma. On receipt of the dispatch, Polk began to prepare his war message to be read in Congress the following Monday. With commendable speed, Congress 2 days later enacted legislation authorizing the President to accept 50,000 volunteers to serve for 12 months and appropriating $10,000,000 for war purposes.[36] On the same day, Congress also provided for expansion of the regular forces by authorizing the President to increase through volunteer enlistments the number of privates in each or any of the companies of dragoons, artillery, and infantry to not more than 100, that number to be reduced to 64 when the exigency requiring the increase should have ceased.[37]

[32] (1) *Ibid.*, p. 347 (Cross to Hunt, 6 Mar 1846). (2) RG 92, OQMG Consolidated Correspondence File, Box 660 (Cross to Jesup, 10 Mar, 26 Mar, 4 Apr 1846).

[33] Henry, *Campaign Sketches of the War with Mexico*, pp. 73, 75–76, 81–82.

[34] House *Ex. Doc.* No. 119, p. 197 (GO 58, 7 May 1846).

[35] (1) RG 92, OQMG Letter Book, vol. 37, pp. 443–44 (Jesup to Whiting, 3 Jun 1846). (2) RG 92, Whiting, Letters Sent, vol. I, p. 24.

[36] 9 *Stat.* 9 (May 13, 1846).

[37] 9 *Stat.* 11 (May 13, 1846).

The Secretary of War at once made requisitions upon the governors of Illinois, Indiana, Ohio, Kentucky, Missouri, Tennessee, Arkansas, Mississippi, Alabama, and Georgia for about 23,000 volunteers to be mustered into service immediately for a period of 12 months. The governors of the other states were asked to raise and enroll the rest of the volunteers, holding them in readiness to be called into service later at the discretion of the President. Such was the enthusiasm that a Kentucky regiment and a battalion from Baltimore and Washington were mustered into service as early as 30 May 1846. The other units were quickly filled during the summer.[38]

Subsistence Supply

The rapid movement of the volunteers to the Rio Grande called for an immediate supply of rations by the Subsistence Department. Like the Quartermaster's Department, the Subsistence Department was also understaffed. Its organization had remained unchanged since 1838. Headed by Col. George Gibson as Commissary General of Subsistence, it had a staff of five officers, of whom one was an assistant commissary general of subsistence and four were commissaries of subsistence. These officers procured the rations and administered the subsistence depots. Assistant commissaries, who were line officers with rank of lieutenant, handled issue to the troops. When Congress called out volunteers, it authorized the President to appoint for each brigade one commissary, with the rank of major, and for each regiment one assistant commissary, with the rank of captain. Their services were to continue as long as they were required.[39] These appointments proved unsatisfactory, and, when new troops were to be raised in 1847, the Department recommended that they be discharged and the Regular Army system be followed— namely, to allow the colonel of the regiment to select a subaltern for the duties of assistant commissary.[40]

It had become established practice to have procurement officers stationed at the principal provision markets at New York, Baltimore, New Orleans, and St. Louis. By law, the Department was required to procure rations by soliciting bids and making contracts from 6 to 18 months in advance, the subsistence being delivered for inspection in bulk at places designated in the contract. Ever since 1842, however, Colonel Gibson had been stressing the advantages of open-market purchases. The troop

---

[38] (1) House *Ex. Doc.* No. 4, 29th Cong., 2d sess., pp. 47, 54 (Rpt of SW). (2) Justin H. Smith, *The War with Mexico* (2 vols., New York, 1919), I, 192–93.

[39] 9 *Stat.* 17 (Jun 18, 1846).

[40] RG 192, CGS, Letters to SW, 1840–54, p. 182 (Acting CGS to Marcy, 13 May 1847).

movement to Texas in 1845 gave added force to his argument, for the movement took troops from posts where supplies were due under contract, and, except for the fact that the market price rose above the contract price, the government would have been compelled to receive provisions where they were not wanted or give a bonus to the contractors for surrendering their contracts.[41]   By direction of the Secretary of War, open-market purchases were permitted during the war, but at its termination the contract system was once again reinstated, much to the disgust of Colonel Gibson, who insisted the system was so objectionable that it ought to be abrogated altogether.[42]

Despite the rapid concentration of troops on the Rio Grande in the summer of 1846, Colonel Gibson reported that in general they were supplied with an abundance of wholesome provisions.   At distant points on the line of operation, however—and this was particularly true for the troops serving with Brig. Gen. Stephen W. Kearny—parts of the ration were necessarily omitted or reduced.[43]   As far as Scott's Army was concerned, once the troops had penetrated into the interior of Mexico beyond Jalapa, they were almost wholly supplied with subsistence from the country in the vicinity of their operations, the chief commissary with the Army purchasing the provisions.

The ration still consisted of much the same components as it had in the past.[44]   Potatoes were furnished for antiscorbutic purposes, but failure of the potato crop induced Gibson to recommend the use of dried apples.   On the other hand, he blocked all efforts to introduce a product called "extract of beef" in the ration.   This he found to be nothing more than an inferior quality of "portable soup" that had been tried during the Seminole War in the hope of lessening transportation costs and had been universally rejected by the troops.[45]

Although no official complaint of either the quality or the quantity of subsistence furnished to the armies was received by the Subsistence Department from any quarter, unofficial sources were not so reticent. William H. Richardson, a volunteer who marched under the command of Col. Alexander W. Doniphan, found his first meal in Indian territory was a supper of hard water crackers and mess pork.   He boiled the pork for nearly 2 hours, he recorded, but it was still so tough that it was "harder labor than I had been at all day to eat it."   A soup the men

[41] *Ibid.*, pp. 147–48 (Gibson to Marcy, 27 Oct 1845).

[42] *Ibid.*, p. 170 (CGS Rpt, 17 Nov 1846).

[43] *Ibid.*, p. 170 (CGS Rpt, 17 Nov 1846).

[44] (1) See *ante,* pp. 118, 203.   (2) Jonathan W. Buhoup, *Narrative of the Central Division* (Pittsburgh, 1847), p. 35.

[45] RG 192, CGS, Letters to SW, 1840–54, p. 176 (Gibson to Marcy, 20 Jan 1847); p. 186 (Same to same, 10 Aug 1847).

made out of pork, buffalo meat, and fish boiled together was "a rare mess, but we pronounced it first-rate." [46] Customarily, commissaries issued hard ship biscuit on the march, but when not available, the men drew flour.   On the march, there was only one way to cook it—the flour was mixed with water, poured into a pan in which pork-fat was frying, and cooked into "slap-jacks," as they were called on the Rio Grande. "This mixture called bread, with the meat, which was from cattle on the hoof, driven with the column and slaughtered at the evening's halt, laid the foundation for the discharge of many soldiers from the army," a Maryland volunteer confided.   "It took a strong man to stand it." [47] In the interior of Mexico, this mixture of flour and water earned the name "musquit bread" because there commissaries frequently issued Mexican flour in lieu of American flour.   It "reminded us of Dr. Franklin's celebrated sawdust pudding," wrote a volunteer who marched with Maj. Gen. John W. Wool from San Antonio.   But worse was yet to come.   Wool ordered nine ears of corn issued daily to each man and directed the troops to grind their own flour in steel mills that had been provided for the expedition (one for each company of the command). So great was the uproar against the "all-fired, infernal, flambusted, penetentiary instruments" called steel mills that the "corn laws" had to be rescinded. [48]

Fortunately, the troops were usually able to supplement their rations with more appetizing viands.   Wherever there were villages, the inhabitants offered vegetables, bread, eggs, cheese, fruits, chickens, and other provisions for sale.   Now and then a cow or goat was brought to be milked at the tent door. [49]   When the soldiers had no cash, they resorted to barter.   Two needles were exchanged for six ears of corn and some onions; buttons and a little tobacco were handed over for a few peaches. [50] Indian goods were carried along on the march to California for trade with the Indians en route.   Where prices were too exorbitant for the delicacies offered them, "some of the boys were compelled to adopt the old mode of mustering into service." [51]   Sutlers, too, had provisions for sale but at prices usually too high for the soldier's purse.

The sutler's price for liquor apparently proved no deterrent to sales.   Taylor tried to prevent the barter or sale of any liquor by sutlers in the Army or by private dealers.   He also prohibited the sale of liquor

[46] *Journal of William H. Richardson* (3d ed., New York, 1848), pp. 5, 15.

[47] John R. Kenly, *Memoirs of a Maryland Volunteer* (Philadelphia, 1873), p. 211.

[48] Buhoup, *Narrative of the Central Division*, pp. 67–72.

[49] (1) John T. Hughes, *Doniphan's Expedition* (Cincinnati, 1850), p. 76. (2) Kenly, *Memoirs of a Maryland Volunteer*, p. 153.

[50] *Journal of William H. Richardson*, pp. 29, 50.

[51] Buhoup, *Narrative of the Central Division*, p. 55.

in bars on steamboats plying the Rio Grande.[52]   Nevertheless, the soldiers managed to get muscal, brandy, aguardiente, or some other spiritous liquor.   Some of them even made a profitable business of buying it from the Mexicans and selling it to their comrades in arms.   "With a canteen on their sides, and a little cup in their pockets," they were ready, "when one raised his finger, to step round a corner, or into some courtyard, and pour them out a drink for a real or bit."   These "traveling groceries," as they were called, could be met in any street.[53]

Clothing and Equipping the Troops

The volunteers who answered the call of arms in the summer of 1846 had not only to be provided with rations but also equipped and transported to Mexico.   As soon as news of war reached Washington, Jesup immediately turned to the problem of procuring the Quartermaster supplies that would be needed by the Army.   For the first time, wartime procurement orders could be expedited by the use of the telegraph.   Only 2 years before the war, the government had financed an experimental line from Washington to Baltimore, and private enterprise had extended telegraph lines to New York and Philadelphia in 1845.   In less time than in the past, Jesup could order clothing and equipage from the Schuylkill Arsenal, arrange shipments from New York, or direct his quartermaster in Baltimore to speed up the procurement of wagons.   It became established procedure to supplement the telegraphed order by a follow-up letter the same day.

Even before Congress acted upon the war news, Jesup directed Colonel Stanton, assistant quartermaster general at Philadelphia, to ascertain the state of his supplies at the depot and "to strengthen yourself in such articles as you may not have an abundance on hand." [54]   A large quantity of camp and garrison equipment would be required at New Orleans for issue to the volunteers moving through that port.   By law, the government furnished them such equipment.   In accordance with General Scott's recommendations for the support of an Army of some 20,000 men, Jesup soon sent specific procurement orders to Stanton for 650 wall tents, 3,523 common tents, 800 spades, 1,760 axes, 4,082 hatches, 3,523 camp kettles, 7,045 mess pans, and 20,000 each of tin canteens, haversacks, and knapsacks.[55]

---

[52] (1) House *Ex. Doc.* No. 60, p. 497 (Order No. 94, 2 Aug 1846).   (2) Whiting, Letters Sent, I, 162 (Whiting to Capt. E. A. Ogden, 24 Jul 1846).

[53] George C. Furber, *The Twelve Months Volunteer* (Cincinnati, 1850), p. 419.

[54] RG 92, OQMG Letter Book, Clothing, vol. 9, p. 113 (10 May 1846).

[55] (1) *Ibid.*, vol. 9, p. 137 (17 May 1846).   (2) House *Ex. Doc.* No. 119, pp. 250–51 (Scott memoranda for chiefs of general staff of army at Washington, 15 May 1846.

Such articles of equipment and Army clothing had been procured in the past by the Office of the Commissary General of Purchases, but in 1846 a separate Purchasing Department no longer existed. Callendar Irvine, who had served as Commissary General of Purchases for 29 years, had died on 9 October 1841. For some years before his death, there had been a growing dissatisfaction with the operations of the Purchasing Department, and late in 1838 the Secretary of War had appointed a board to inquire into the system of furnishing clothing and camp equipage. The board had been instructed to report all defects and submit its views on improvements.[56] A conviction— unfounded according to Jesup—had developed among the members of Congress that certain sections of the country were favored in letting the contracts for supplies.[57] As a consequence, when the President gave J. Washington Tyson a recess appointment as Commissary General of Purchases a few days after Irvine's death, Congress had not only rejected Tyson's nomination upon reconvening but had also abolished the Office of Commissary General of Purchases on 23 August 1842. Despite the opposition of the Secretary of War, it had merged the duties of the former Purchasing Department in the Quartermaster's Department.[58] On 29 August, Tyson had handed over the office and its records to Col. Henry Stanton who had assumed direction of all Quartermaster activities in Philadelphia.

The Secretary of War had already abolished the Clothing Bureau in Washington in the fall of 1841, returning to the Quartermaster's Department the function of estimating clothing requirements that it had relinquished to that Bureau in 1832.[59] The Mexican War became the first war in which the Department was wholly responsible for the procurement, storage, and distribution of clothing to the Army.

The outbreak of war found the Schuylkill Arsenal with only the scantiest of clothing supplies on hand. Reduction of clothing appropriations in the years immediately preceding the war had permitted the Quartermaster's Department to do no more than provide the annual clothing supply for the small peacetime Army and to accumulate clothing stocks only to the extent of a half year's allowance to that small peacetime establishment. In the spring of 1846, the Arsenal was therefore in no position to furnish clothing to the volunteers and it was not called upon

---

[56] RG 107, OSW, Military Book, vol. 20, p. 45 (Poinsett to Stanton, et al., 19 Dec 1838).

[57] RG 92, OQMG Letter Book, Clothing, vol. 9, p. 170 (Jesup to Stanton, 13 Jul 1846).

[58] (1) RG 107, OSW, Military Book, vol. 24, p. 182 (SW to Tyson, 13 Oct 1841). (2) RG 107, OSW, Reports to Congress, vol. 5, pp. 172–73, 260–61 (SW to Chairman, Senate Military Affairs Committee, 25 Jan, 20 Jun 1942). (3) 5 Stat. 512 (Aug 23, 1842).

[59] (1) RG 107, OSW, Military Book, vol. 24, p. 238 (SW to QMG, 11 Nov 1841). (2) RG 92, Coxe and Irvine Papers, Metal tray No. 68 (Inventory of property in Clothing Bureau turned over to the Department, 30 Nov 1841).

3D U.S. INFANTRY REGIMENT, 1846–1851

to do so since Congress enacted legislation requiring the volunteers to furnish their own clothing. By law, each volunteer was allowed $3.50 per month for clothing during the time he was in service. To enable the volunteer to provide himself with good and sufficient clothing, the commutation allowance for 6 months—that is $21—was advanced to each volunteer after he was mustered into service.[60]

Even though the depot was not required to clothe the volunteers, the demands from the increased number of Regulars in the field put a tremendous pressure upon the clothing establishment at Philadelphia. The system of procurement and production instituted by Callendar Irvine still functioned in 1846 under Quartermaster direction. Cloth was purchased from manufacturers, cut into garments at the Arsenal by government cutters, and issued to seamstresses and tailors who returned the finished garments to the Arsenal for inspection and acceptance. The clothing establishment was capable of rapid expansion to meet the demands made upon it. "The spindles and looms of distant and neighboring manufactories were soon put in rapid motion;" the number of steamstresses and tailors was speedily increased from about 400 to 10 times that number; and within a few weeks clothing began to flow into the depot. Before the end of the war, the expanded clothing operation at Philadelphia insured delivery to the depot of over 85,000 assorted garments per month.[61]

To relieve some of the pressure upon the Schuylkill Arsenal, a branch of the clothing establishment was set up toward the end of 1846 at New York under the direction of Daniel Stinson, an experienced clerk who had served in the Department at that station for nearly a quarter of a century. Operations of the New York branch could also be enlarged to meet any emergency. By mid-January 1847, Colonel Stanton was certain that the Department would be able not only to meet the wants of the regular service but to fill the requisitions which might be made for destitute volunteers.[62]

By that time, many of the volunteers were indeed destitute. Commutation allowances had not been applied in every instance to the purchase of clothing, and even when they had, long marches were destructive of clothing and particularly of shoes. A Maryland volunteer recorded that "many of the men have made sandals from rawhide, which looks right well; on parade, there are a good many without jackets, yet they look soldierlike and trim with their cross- and waist-belts."[63] But

---

[60] (1) 9 *Stat.* 18 (Jun 18, 1846). (2) House *Ex. Doc.* No. 119, p. 191 (SW to Governors of states, –1846).

[61] RG 92, CGP, Letters Sent, No. 402, p. 523 (Stanton to Jesup, 22 Nov 1848).

[62] RG 92, OQMG Letter Book, Clothing, vol. 9, pp. 261–62 (Stanton to Jesup, 15 Jan 1847).

[63] Kenly, *Memoirs of a Maryland Volunteer*, p. 154.

the appearance of some of the volunteers led Lt. George B. McClellan to write that "Falstaff's company were regulars in comparison with these fellows—most of them without coats; some would have looked much better without *any pants* than with the parts of pants they wore; all had torn and dirty shirts." [64]

Colonel Stanton had good reason to believe that the clothing establishment would be called upon to provide for the volunteers as well as the regular forces in 1847. He had called their need to the attention of the Chairman of the Senate Military Affairs Committee. A resolution authorizing issue of clothing to volunteers was carried through the House but was not acted upon by the Senate before adjournment. It was not until 26 January 1848, a week before the treaty of peace was signed, that Congress made provision for furnishing the volunteers with clothing in kind. It failed, however, to make any appropriation for carrying the measure into effect, and made no money available until July.[65]

If clothing could not be issued to the volunteers in 1846, it could, by order of General Taylor, be made available to them for purchase in the field.[66] Despite the law, several thousand suits of clothing, sent to New Orleans and Mexico for the supply of the old Army under Scott, were issued not only to the new regiments raised under the act of 11 February 1847 but also to volunteers.[67] General Scott complained in December that his regiments had to remain naked or be supplied with very inferior garments procured locally because the small depot at Vera Cruz had been exhausted "by the troops under Generals Patterson, Butler and Marshall, respectively, all fresh from home or the Brazos, and as in the case of other arrivals, since June, without clothing!" [68]

But Jesup had placed thousands of forage caps, jackets, shirts, overalls, bootees, and blankets in the Vera Cruz depot, and in his defense noted that he had not a single cent that he could legally apply to the purchase of clothing for the volunteers. He maintained that the generals named by Scott had no right to take for their commands supplies placed at Vera Cruz for Scott's old regiments, and that they ought to be held accountable by the general. In any case, Jesup advised the Secretary

[64] *The Mexican War Diary of George B. McClellan,* ed. William Starr Myers (Princeton, 1917), p. 38.

[65] (1) RG 92, OQMG Letter Book, Clothing, vol. 9, p. 253 (Stanton to Maj. D. D. Tompkins, 14 Dec 1846); p. 285 (Stanton to Jesup, 22 Mar 1847). (2) 9 *Stat.* 210. (3) RG 92, OQMG Letter Book, vol. 40, p. 552 (Jesup to Stanton, 29 Jun 1848).

[66] RG 92, Whiting, Letters Sent, I, 560 (Whiting to Capt. G. Crosman, 26 Oct 1846).

[67] RG 92, OQMG Consolidated Correspondence File, Box 660 (Account of Clothing Issued to Volunteers at Vera Cruz, 6 Dec 1847).

[68] (1) House *Ex. Doc.* No. 60, p. 1047 (Scott to SW, 25 Dec 1847). See also pp. 1013, 1034 (Scott to SW, 25 Jul, 4 Dec 1847); p. 1224 (Scott to SW, 24 Feb 1848). (2) RG 107, OSW, Military Book, vol. 28, p. 216 (SW to Jesup, 28 Jan 1848).

of War that at the time Scott was making his complaint supplies at Vera Cruz had not been exhausted as the general charged.   Moreover, Capt. James R. Irwin, chief quartermaster with Scott's Army, had made a report on 27 September 1847 that warranted some delay in forwarding clothing:

I have now a thousand people engaged in making clothing; the quality of the material is not so good as our own, and the price, on the average, is fifty per cent. higher.   Still, supposing the road between this and Vera Cruz to be entirely open, I think the government will lose little, if anything, by purchasing here.   I shall be able to fill, in a very short time, every requisition which has been made on me, with clothing, which, though not exactly of our uniform, will be comfortable and good.[69]

By December, however, and in anticipation of favorable congressional action on providing clothing for the volunteers, Jesup ordered from Philadelphia a supply of clothing sufficient for the whole Army, Regulars and volunteers.   To do this, he applied, on his own responsibility, $368,000 of the Department's funds, appropriated for other purposes, to the purchase of clothing and authorized the use of credit in the expectation that Congress would make an appropriation that would enable him to meet the bills when they came due.[70]   By this means, Jesup gave practical application to the legal authorization for providing clothing in kind to the volunteers before the war ended.   The Department made every effort to furnish the annual supply of clothing to the Regulars during the war.   Except when lack of transportation hampered delivery or unlawful issue was permitted to be made to volunteers from stocks on hand, the Regulars suffered no shortages of clothing.   Where a deficiency did occur, as was the case among Scott's troops, the quartermaster took prompt measures to correct the supply situation.   Not only was there little or no complaint of clothing shortages, but on the basis of the very large quantity of supplies returned to the Schuylkill Arsenal from different points in Mexico at the close of the war, Colonel Stanton was justified in inferring that the Army had been abundantly provided for.[71]

Supply of clothing to the regular troops in the field at the beginning

---

[69] (1) RG 92, CGP Irwin, Letters Sent, No. 97, n.p.   Experience caused Irwin to change his views later on local procurement.   He had been able to supply clothing but the costs of production in Mexico were far higher than he had anticipated, and in December he recommended that all clothing be drawn from the United States.   *Ibid.,* (Irwin to Jesup, 8 Dec 1847). (2) House *Ex. Doc.* No. 60, pp. 1060–61 (Jesup to SW, 18 Feb 1848).   (3) RG 92, OQMG Letter Book, vol. 39, p. 583 (Jesup to Stanton, 25 Oct 1847).

[70] RG 92, OQMG Letter Book, vol. 40, p. 194 (Jesup to Capt. A. C. Myers, 22 Feb 1848). Myers succeeded Captain Irwin as assistant quartermaster at Mexico City upon the death of that officer.

[71] RG 92, CGP, Letters Sent, No. 402, p. 526 (Stanton to Jesup, 22 Nov 1848).

of the war followed the established procedure of forwarding annual supplies prepared in accordance with regimental estimates and drawn for accordingly. By October 1846, that system had been modified at Taylor's request to conform to the practice that had been followed during the Seminole War. In consequence, the Quartermaster's Department established a general depot of clothing for the regular troops at Point Isabel and at other depot points later. It deposited at the depot all clothing intended for specific regiments as a common supply. The military storekeeper in charge requisitioned directly on Philadelphia for clothing and camp equipage, determining the quantity and kind needed by reference to the strength of the Army and the supply on hand. He issued to officers on requisitions approved by regimental or battalion commanders, restricting all issues to undress clothing.[72]

During the Mexican War, a large part of the shoe production for the Army came to be centralized at Philadelphia. Unlike the system that had developed for the manufacture of Army clothing, Army shoes had always been obtained by contract. Known as bootees, they were still being procured exclusively by contract in the summer of 1847. By that time, the contract method had become productive of so much "delay, disappointment, imposition, and loss" that complete dependence on it could no longer be tolerated. To guard against deficiencies and to ensure a supply, the Quartermaster's Department set up a bootee-making establishment at the Schuylkill depot. By the end of the war, it was turning out 12,000 pairs a month in correct sizes and of such quality as to still complaints. The system was so successful that the War Department continued it after the war. It abandoned the contract method completely inasmuch as the bootee establishment could fill all demands of a peacetime Army.[73]

Even before bootees were made at the Schuylkill Arsenal, a tent-making establishment had been put into operation there. By the close of the war, its employees were turning out over 700 common, wall, and hospital tents per month. During fiscal year 1848, they made 6,664 common tents, 1,751 wall tents and flies, and 192 hospital tents and flies at a lower cost than the Department had been able to obtain in its most favorable contract. Only one tentmaker was hired on a monthly basis; the rest—there were 36 employed in 1847—were paid by the piece.[74]

[72] (1) House *Ex. Doc.* No. 119, p. 131 (Taylor to AG, 28 Aug 1846); p. 218 (Order No. 133, 18 Oct 1846). (2) RG 92, Whiting, Letters Sent, I, 531 (Whiting to military storekeeper, 19 Oct 1846); pp. 538–40 (Whiting to Stanton, 20 Oct 1846).

[73] (1) RG 92, CGP, Letters Sent, No. 402, p. 522 (Stanton to Jesup, 22 Nov 1848). (2) RG 92, Reports of QMG to SW and Heads of Departments, I, 468–69 (Jesup to SW, 28 Aug 1851).

[74] RG 92, CGP, Letters Sent, No. 402, p. 552 (Stanton to Jesup, 22 Nov 1848); p. 388–89 (List of Personnel, 30 Sep 1847).

Throughout the war, tents continued to be both procured under contract and manufactured at the depot.

As in past conflicts, an acute shortage of tents and of duck, out of which to make them, was immediately evident on the outbreak of war. Such tents as had been furnished to Taylor's troops at Corpus Christi had been selected from stock on hand at the Arsenal. From 1842 to 1846, Colonel Stanton had procured only 34 wall tents, 88 tent flies, and 8 hospital tents.[75] The appropriation for camp equipage that Jesup asked for in the spring of 1846 had been stricken out. Not a cent had been appropriated that could be legally applied to the purchase of camp equipage before May when Congress provided funds for the war. At that point, the Department had been obliged to procure whatever material could be obtained in Philadelphia, New York, Baltimore, or Boston. Tents equal to the old stock could not be furnished and in order to give the troops some kind of shelter, Jesup determined to use cotton canvas in lieu of the imported hemp canvas that was not available.[76]

Well aware of the country's lack of preparation for war but preferring to ignore it in making a case for his own defense, if that should become necessary, Taylor, then at Camargo, wrote that his "crying deficiency of camp equipage had been partially relieved by the issue of cotton tents of indifferent quality." [77] Jesup was willing to concede that much of the material used was probably of that quality but he thought that in the circumstances his officers deserved credit for their exertion rather than the censure they received. Recipients of the tents, however, found no shelter from the rain that turned the area around Camargo into a flooded quagmire. Criticism was voiced so universally that, in the fall of 1846, Jesup ordered Stanton to use raven duck in the production of tents, but there was still none to be found in the Philadelphia market.[78] Better tents could be made only as the market for duck improved.

While much of the procurement of clothing, shoes, and tents was centralized at Philadelphia, procurement of other items of equipment was spread to various parts of the country. The Department directed quartermasters at Pittsburgh and Cincinnati in particular to contract for knapsacks, canteens, and iron camp kettles and mess pans to be sent to New Orleans for the volunteers rapidly concentrating there.[79] It made

[75] RG 92, OQMG Letter Book, Clothing, vol. 9, p. 91 (Jesup to Cross, 6 Jan 1846).

[76] Ibid., vol. 9, pp. 142–43 (Jesup to Col. D. E. Twiggs, 20 May 1846); p. 158 (Jesup to AQM Dusenbery, 9 Jun 1846).

[77] House Ex. Doc. No. 60, p. 558 (Taylor to SW, 1 Sep 1846).

[78] (1) Ibid., p. 561 (Jesup to SW, 5 Dec 1846). (2) RG 92, OQMG Letter Book, vol. 38, p. 263 (Jesup to Stanton, 6 Nov 1946).

[79] (1) RG 92, OQMG Letter Book, Clothing, vol. 9, p. 157 (Jesup to Maj. D. D. Tompkins, 9 Jun 1846). (2) RG 92, OQMG Letter Book, vol. 37, pp. 428–29 (Jesup to Capt. Ed. Harding, 27 May 1846).

every effort to speed production. If India rubber cloth could be used instead of painting the cover of the knapsacks to make them waterproof, Jesup suggested, much time could be saved in equipping the volunteers. He urged Stanton to accept one firm's offer to make 500,000 knapsacks with India rubber covers.[80] Some regiments were furnished with India rubber bags, or canteens, to carry water. While their use permitted a quiet approach to the enemy, the water in them became warm as in tin canteens. Many a volunteer threw away his canteen, preferring to use a Mexican gourd instead because water in it remained cool through the hottest day.[81]

Transportation Problems

At the same time, the Quartermaster's Department was pushing production of clothing and equipment, it was exerting every effort to transport volunteers and to ship supplies to the Rio Grande. New Orleans was the chief point of assembly and embarkation for the volunteers. In 1846, most of them were drawn from the states of the Ohio and Mississippi valleys, and they began their long journey to Mexico on river steamboats.[82] Landing at New Orleans, the volunteers pitched their tents in the mud of the old battlefield below the city and waited impatiently for Colonel Hunt to arrange their transportation to Point Isabel.[83] He purchased sea vessels, at prices ranging from $3,000 for a small schooner to $85,000 for the steamship *Massachusetts*, and chartered others, usually paying about $7,000 for the service performed by each ship. The Department sent him other ships offered for its use, leaving it to the colonel to decide whether they were suitable. He also established a coal depot at New Orleans of sufficient size to meet all probable demands of transportation for an Army of from 20,000 to 25,000 men.[84]

His efforts were supplemented by those of Colonel Stanton at Philadelphia and Lieutenant Colonel Whiting at New York who were ascertaining on what terms sea steamers could either be chartered by the month or purchased at those ports. Jesup advised that no troops were to be sent in sea steamers without the sanction of their commanding officers.

---

[80] RG 92, OQMG Letter Book, vol. 9, p. 158 (1 Jun 1846).

[81] Furber, *The Twelve Months Volunteer*, p. 127.

[82] For announced arrivals of particular steamboats carrying volunteers, see *The Daily Picayune* of New Orleans, beginning 29 May 1846 and thereafter through the summer.

[83] See, for example, B. F. Scribner, *Camp Life of a Volunteer* (Philadelphia, 1847), pp. 11–15.

[84] (1) House *Ex. Doc.* No. 119, pp. 287–88 (Jesup to Hunt, 9 Jun 1846). (2) RG 92, OQMG Letter Book, vol. 37, p. 477 (Same to same, 17 Jun 1846). (3) See the columns of *The Daily Picayune*, New Orleans, for ships chartered and purchased.

If the latter objected, sailing ships were to be provided.[85]   Outlining the qualifications that such steamers must have for use by the Department in the Gulf of Mexico, Jesup suggested that they needed sufficient strength to withstand the stormy weather and the heavy sea common in the Gulf; their boilers and machinery had to be constructed for sea service; they should be provided with masts and sails to enable them to ride out a gale or make a harbor in the event of accident to their machinery; they must be able to carry at least 6 days' fuel besides cargo; they should be copper-bottomed if they were not made of iron; and their draft of water should never exceed 7 feet.[86]

There were not too many sea steamers available.   Americans, their eyes focused on westward expansion and the profits of inland transportation, had been content to concentrate on developing steamboats for use on the rivers of the Mississippi Valley, or on such inland or protected waters as the Chesapeake Bay or Long Island Sound, and to rely on their excellent sailing ships to carry their commerce on the seas.[87]   Their sea steamers were small, usually mere copies of river or sound craft though stouter built than such boats.   Their speed was no better than that of well-designed sail packet boats.   At the time of the Mexican War, they were frequently designated as steam schooners, steam brigs, and steamships to denote the particular rig of the sea-going craft.

In the summer of 1846, the Quartermaster's Department was able to charter a few steamships, such as the *Galveston* and the *John L. Day,* and to purchase a number of others, among them the *Massachusetts* and the *McKim,* to transport some of the volunteers to the Rio Grande.   It also purchased several sea steamers, some of which were of the sidewheel type and others were steam propellers.   The latter proved to be more satisfactory than the side-wheel steamers.   To meet the tremendous demands for transportation imposed by Scott's expedition against Vera Cruz in the following year, the Department purchased additional steamers.[88]

A considerable number of the ships purchased were acquired for the transportation of supplies.   For this purpose, the Department preferred the light-draft schooner.   In the fall of 1846, Jesup, then in the field, came to the conclusion that it would be necessary for the Department to have some flat-bottomed, light-draft schooners constructed.   Only by having a sufficient number of them available could it insure a constant

[85] RG 92, OQMG Letter Book, vol. 37, p. 400 (Jesup to Whiting, 11 May 1846); p. 434 (Jesup to Stanton, 30 May 1846); p. 440 (Jesup to AQM Vinton, 2 Jun 1846).

[86] *Ibid.,* vol. 37, p. 454 (Jesup to Vinton, 6 Jun 1846).

[87] See below for discussion of use of river steamboats during the war.

[88] (1) See Table, Government-owned Vessels of the Mexican War.   (2) For list of vessels employed in the expedition to Vera Cruz, see House *Ex. Doc.* No. 60, pp. 1256–59.   (3) Table compiled by author from the following sources: (a) RG 92, OQMG Consolidated Correspond-

Table—Government-Owned Vessels of the Mexican War

Ocean Vessels

| | Sail | | | Steam | |
	Name	Gross tons		Name	Gross tons
Types			**Types**		
Ships	AMERICAN	520	Screws	ASHLAND	182
	RHODE ISLAND	391		EDITH	407
	SAINT LOUIS	340		EUDORA	430
	SUVIAH	413		JAMES CAGE	115
				MCKIM	326
Bark	ROBERT MORRIS	240		MAJOR TOMPKINS	151
				MASSACHUSETTS	700
Brigs	ARCHITECT	149		OCEAN	191
	CRUSOE	115		SECRETARY MARCY	153
	JOHN POTTER	163		TRUMBULL	176
	MARY JANE	162		WASHINGTON	224
Schooners	ARISPE	119	Sidewheel	ALABAMA	676
	BELLE	43		ANSON	196
	BLANCHE E. SAYRE	167		COLONEL CROSS	160
	CAPTAIN LINCOLN	162		COLONEL HARNEY	132
	CAPTAIN MORRIS	130		COLONEL STANTON	138
	CAPTAIN PAGE	174		DE ROSSETT	186
	CAPTAIN WILLIAMS	143		FASHION	419
	COLONEL FANNING	138		GENERAL HAMER	168
	COLONEL YELL	165		MARIA BURT	366
	ENFANTA	170		MARY SUMMERS	125
	EQUITY	83		MENTORIA	108
	GENERAL			NEPTUNE	745
	PATTERSON	152		NEW ORLEANS	760
	HENRY LONG	88		TELEGRAPH	330
	HERVINE	73	Unknown	A. R. HETZEL	—
	INVINCIBLE	126		GENERAL BUTLER	370
	LOUISIANA	98		J. D. THOMPSON	160
	MAJOR H. BACHE	67		J. R. STEVENS	—
	MAJOR BARBOUR	143		JULIA	—
	MAJOR LEAR	115		MONMOUTH	235
	MAJOR VINTON	191		SECRETARY	
	MARY PHOEBE	147		BUCHANAN	—
	PIONEER	69		SECRETARY MASON	—
	SARAH			SECRETARY	
	CHURCHMAN	172		WALKER	—
	SARAH JANE	100		VIRGINIA	400
	SUSAN	—			
	T. F. HUNT	83			
	VELASCO	128			
	WHIG	89			
	WILLIAM H.				
	GATZNER	80			

River Steamboats

Types	Name	Gross tons	Types	Name	Gross tons
Sidewheel	BROWNSVILLE	99	Sternwheel	MAJOR BROWN	125
	COLONEL CLAY	257		TROY	92
	COLONEL YELL	233			
	CORVETTE	159			
	GENERAL JESUP	374			
	HATCHEE EAGLE ...	116			
	J. E. ROBERTS........	118	Unknown	ANN CHASE	—
	LITTLE YAZOO	46		COLONEL HUNT	214
	NEVA	141		COLONEL LONG	—
	ORELINE	61		DRAGON	—
	ROUGH AND			GOPHER	—
	READY	150		MCKEE	—
	UNDINE	197		PLANTER	147
	WHITEVILLE	102			
	WHITE WING	100			

flow of supplies for the troops at the different ports on the Gulf.[89] Lieutenant Colonel Hunt agreed with Jesup, for it had become increasingly difficult for him to hire such vessels on a freight basis.   In the past, he had preferred to avoid the risks of ownership, choosing to charter light-draft schooners in all cases possible and to ship his supplies at a contract price of so much per barrel.   Late in 1846, he, too, recommended ownership.[90]   In consequence, early in the following year, Colonel Stanton ordered 10 light-draft schooners built for the Department.[91]

During the course of the war, the Department acquired through purchase and construction a total of 38 sailing ships—4 ships, 1 bark, 4 brigs, and 29 schooners—and 35 steamships.   Wrecks, accidents, and deterioration through constant use reduced the size of the Quartermaster's fleet.   Though a total of 72 vessels were government-owned during the war, by 15 May 1848 the Department could count only 52.   Among these were 25 schooners, 2 ships, 1 bark, 7 steamships, and 15 sea steamers, of which 10 were steam propellers.[92]   Impressive as the Quartermaster fleet

ence File, Box 660 (Tompkins Rpt, 15 May 1848; Swords Rpt, 2 Jul and 22 Aug 1848).   (b) RG 92, Vessels Engaged in Mexican War and on Western Rivers during the Civil War.   (c) RG 92, OQMG Letter Books, *passim*.   (d) House *Ex. Doc.* No. 119, *passim*.   (e) RG 41, Vessels Bought from U.S.   (f) *Merchant Steam Vessels of the United States, 1807–1868*, ed. Forrest R. Holdcamper (Mystic, Conn., 1952).

[89] House *Ex. Doc.* No. 119, p. 435 (Jesup to Stanton, 15 Oct 1846).

[90] *Ibid.*, pp. 387–88 (Hunt to Stanton, 9 Dec 1846).

[91] RG 92, OQMG Letter Book, vol. 38, pp. 450–51 (Stanton to Jesup, 20 Feb 1847).

[92] (1) RG 92, OQMG Consolidated Correspondence File, Box 660 (Tompkins to Jesup, 15 May 1848).   (2) See Table, Government-owned Vessels of the Mexican War.

was in size, the Department chartered a far greater number of ships to transport both troops and supplies.

The use of water transportation posed problems. Less than 3 months after the war started, complaints began to be heard that the want of system in the discharge of cargoes from vessels at Point Isabel was resulting in demurrage that sometimes equalled $3,000 a day. The Army was too small to permit detailing soldiers for the purpose of unloading ships and laborers were difficult to hire. Nevertheless, Jesup thought that all transports, whether steam or sail, ought to be so regulated that not more than one or two at most should be in port at the same time. In his opinion, stevedores ought to be employed to unload all vessels as they arrived, placing the supplies on shore or in vessels used for storage purposes. In an effort to bring this transportation problem under control at the Brazos, Quartermaster Whiting appointed Capt. R. B. Lawton as superintendent of the harbor and put him in charge of unloading all cargo.[93]

In operating both government-owned ocean vessels and river craft during the war, it became the custom of the Department to pay the captain or master a fixed salary and to make it incumbent upon him to provide subsistence for himself and his officers.[94] In the case of a chartered vessel, there was no need to hire personnel. The owner manned and operated his ship, for the services of which the Department paid him a flat sum per trip, or so much per day over a period of time if the transportation involved troop movements, and a freight rate of so much per barrel if the ship was transporting Army supplies. The charter party might include the privilege of purchase by the government after the quality of the ship had been demonstrated in one delivery of troops or cargo. Customarily, the quartermaster who arranged the means of transportation for troops gave a copy of the charter party or lease of the vessel to the commanding officer. Until the latter handed over the charter party to the quartermaster at the destination point, the captain of the ship could not be paid his freight money.[95]

Whether troops were transported on government-owned or chartered steamships or sailing ships, they brought their own rations on board. Water, facilities for cooking, and deck accommodations were supposed to be provided for them but such arrangements were often neglected. Some 500 men of the battalion of Baltimore and Washington volunteers,

[93] (1) RG 92, OQMG Letter Book, vol. 37, p. 496 (Jesup to Whiting, 1 Jul 1846).   (2) RG 92, Whiting, Letters Sent, I, 80 (Whiting to QM at Brazos Island, 15 Jul 1846).

[94] (1) RG 92, OQMG Letter Book, vol. 50, p. 558 (Jesup to Crosman, 25 May 1847).   (2) For examples of such agreements see RG 92, OQMG Copies of Charter Parties and Names of Crews of Vessels, 1847.

[95] Kenly, Memoirs of a Maryland Volunteer, pp. 280–81.

for example, were crowded on the 700-ton steamer, *Massachusetts,* embarking at Fort Washington on the Potomac on 13 June 1846. Essentially, the *Massachusetts* was a sailing ship provided with auxiliary machinery for steam power that could be used only when the sea was smooth. Berths had been provided for only 200 men and carpenters had to be set to work after embarkation of the troops to construct additional bunks. Before the ship set sail, no fireplaces for cooking purposes had been provided, and those that were improvised afterwards were so insecure that the troops twice set the ship on fire. The blazing sun and the heat from the fiery furnace of the ship as it steamed across the Gulf made the men fearful that their dwindling water supply would be exhausted. Under the circumstances, it is not surprising that the sick list swelled rapidly. After 17 days' confinement in that "crowded pen," Brazos was sighted and a happy release from the ship was at last in prospect.[96]

The conditions described were in no way unusual but were duplicated on many another ship. An Indiana volunteer, who sailed on a chartered ship from New Orleans, found the quarters between decks "truly unenviable" and the heat and stench "almost insupportable." [97] Returning to the United States from Mexico, a Missouri volunteer was one of 250 men who, with their artillery and baggage, were stowed in a small brig that was beautiful in its exterior but "worse than a hog-pen" between decks. Only 100 bunks—a bunk being a slight elevation made of plank—were provided. So many soldiers crowded around the two small fires built for them to cook with that a long time elapsed before he could get any coffee. As a matter of convenience, the men, he recorded, were supplied with hard crackers and molasses, a diet that "only increased my disease." The ship running into a calm and the water becoming scarce, the allowance was reduced from a coffee pot full twice a day for coffee and a pint of drinking water for each man to a quart for each man. Well might this Missouri volunteer write after his first night on board the brig that "for suffering I have not experienced its equal in all my peregrinations through life." [98]

Supply of Taylor's Operations

Supply was complicated by many factors, not the least of which was a lack of knowledge of how many men would have to be fed, equipped, and transported. This was particularly true in the case of Taylor's forces. So quickly did the volunteers respond to the call to arms in

[96] *Ibid.,* pp. 23–35.
[97] Scribner, *Camp Life of a Volunteer,* p. 14.
[98] *Journal of William H. Richardson,* pp. 81–82.

May 1846 that Taylor and the supply departments were alike overwhelmed by the influx of volunteers at Point Isabel. That flood of
manpower resulted from a peculiar combination of good intentions,
instructions, and legislation. To begin with, Taylor, in accordance with
his instructions, called upon the governors of Texas and Louisiana for
nearly 5,000 men as soon as hostilities began in April. In advising the
War Department of his action, Taylor expressed the hope that the
necessary orders would be given to the staff departments for the supply
of this large additional force, but he made no specific requisitions.[99]

At the same time, he requested Maj. Gen. Edmund P. Gaines, commanding at New Orleans, to assist in organizing and supplying these
volunteer regiments. Gaines, on his own responsibility, extended the
call for volunteers to other states and accepted them without any limitation on numbers under terms of 6 months' enlistments. Consequently,
Taylor could not be certain how many men he would have to provide
for. More than 8,000 troops were sent by Gaines before he could be
stopped by being relieved from command.[100] These volunteers began
arriving about the time Taylor occupied Matamoras in May 1846 after
the immediate emergency had passed. Moreover, so hurriedly had they
been sent out that they landed at Point Isabel destitute of equipment and
the means of transportation, and Taylor reported that "this force will
embarrass rather than facilitate our operations."[101] The War Department held that Gaines' action was illegal. Since under the law of
13 May 1846 there was no place for these volunteers unless they re-enlisted
for a 12 months' term of service, the Quartermaster's Department returned
most of them home without their having performed any service.[102] In
the interim, their movement had absorbed a considerable amount of
much needed transportation, and during their idleness they had also to
be fed and sheltered.[103] Gaines' proceedings proved to be both embarrassing and expensive to the government.

Congress also had made provision for calling out volunteers on
13 May 1846, and so enthusiastic had the response been that some of
the 12-month volunteer regiments arrived on the Rio Grande during the

---

[99] House *Ex. Doc.* No. 119, p. 17 (Taylor to AG, 26 Apr 1846).

[100] (1) Upton, *The Military Policy of the United States,* p. 201. (2) House *Ex. Doc.* No. 60,
p. 299 (Taylor to AG, 20 May 1846).

[101] House *Ex. Doc.* No. 60, p. 306 (Taylor to AG, 3 Jun 1846).

[102] (1) *Ibid.,* p. 495 (Hq Army of Occupation, Order No. 91, 21 Jul 1846). (2) House *Ex.
Doc.* No. 119, pp. 36–37 (Gov. of La. to SW, 12 Jun 1846); pp. 37–41 (Marcy to Gov. of La.,
25 Jun 1846).

[103] Meade stated they ate up 240,000 rations and absorbed much of the river transportation
to get themselves to a shipping point—transportation that was badly needed to move supplies
and troops to Camargo. *The Life and Letters of George Gordon Meade,* ed. George G. Meade
(2 vols., New York, 1913), I, 115.

month of June, adding to the Quartermaster supply problem. Their number increased rapidly but, for want of transportation and uncertainty "in regard to the supplies that may be drawn from the theater of operations," Taylor took only a "moderate part" of the volunteer force with him when he moved from Camargo and began his march to Monterey. His army of little more than 6,000 was composed of two divisions of Regulars and a field division of volunteers. The rest of the volunteers were left at camp to drill and train.[104] The influx of 12-month volunteers, he wrote President Polk, "has even impeded my forward movement by engrossing all the resources of the Quartermaster's Department to land them and transport them to healthy positions." [105]

The general's plans for operating against Monterey called for establishing his principal depot at Camargo, some 350 to 400 miles from the mouth of the Rio Grande, using that river as the supply line. To get his supplies to Camargo and keep his wagon train free to move with the Army, he needed boats but there is no evidence to indicate that Taylor exercised any foresight in requisitioning them or even in determining the feasibility of using the Rio Grande though he had been encamped on its banks since March. Two months later he still was uncertain whether the river would serve his purpose, but he assured the War Department that he would lose no time in ascertaining its "practicability" for steamboats.[106] His plans were also made without any examination of the condition of the boats that the Quartermaster's Department had been using first at Corpus Christi and then at Point Isabel. The quartermaster there employed two government-owned steamers, the *Neva* and the *Monmouth,* and one chartered steamer to lighter cargoes from transports anchored inside the bar at the Brazos to the depot at Point Isabel. A fourth steamer, the *Colonel Long,* had been obtained by transfer from the Topographical Department, but both it and the *Neva* were so wormeaten as to be utterly useless.[107]

When Taylor found his operations paralyzed for want of steamboats, he denounced the government for sending a flood of volunteers without the means of transportation, decried "the extraordinary delay" shown by the Quartermaster's Department in getting boats, and expressed preposterous suspicions that "superior authority" had given orders to suspend the forwarding of means of transportation from New Orleans.[108] Obvi-

[104] House *Ex. Doc.* No. 119, p. 210 (Hq Army of Occupation, Order No. 108, 28 Aug 1846).
[105] *Ibid.,* p. 61 (1 Aug 1846).
[106] (1) *Ibid.,* p. 28 (Taylor to AG, 21 May 1846). (2) Hitchcock, *Fifty Years in Camp and Field,* p. 195.
[107] House *Ex. Doc.* No. 119, p. 388 (Thomas to Jesup, 15 May 1846).
[108] (1) House *Ex. Doc.* No. 60, p. 547 (Taylor to AG, 10 Jun 1846). (2) House *Ex. Doc.* No. 119, p. 381 (Taylor to same, 17 Jun 1846).

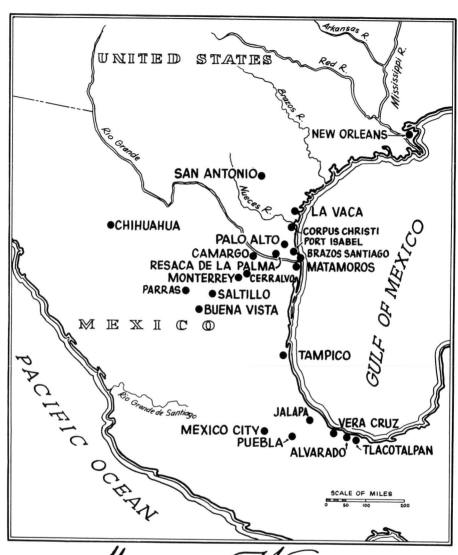

Mexican War

MAP 5

ously, if Taylor on the Rio Grande did not know what boats he would need or how much water they should draw, Jesup at Washington could not be expected to have the information. Maj. Charles Thomas, depot quartermaster at Point Isabel, had advised Jesup on 15 May of the condition of his boats and the need for one or two good river boats of moderate size. Three days later, on Taylor's orders, he requested Colonel Hunt to purchase and send a good, substantial river boat. About a week later, with the number of troops increasing daily, Taylor increased his requisition to four steamboats.[109]

These requisitions reached Colonel Hunt on 3 June and were the first notice he had "of the great and pressing demand for so many steamboats." [110] Meanwhile, General Taylor had called upon Col. John Winthrop, aide-de-camp to the governor of Louisiana, for help in chartering two or three light-draft but strong freight boats, for which he engaged to insure employment at a fair and reasonable compensation. Colonel Winthrop chartered two but at rates considered to be rather high.[111] To expedite the procurement of small steamboats, Taylor also sent Capt. John Sanders of the Engineers to New Orleans to assist Colonel Hunt.[112]

Steamboats of the type required on the Rio Grande were not so easily procured at New Orleans. To supplement his efforts there, Colonel Hunt sent Captain Sanders up the Mississippi and Ohio to canvas the river towns for suitable boats. He also thought that Taylor's requisition for four boats had better be doubled.[113] Jesup approved of this action and authorized a further increase, if necessary. Taylor's requisition was, in fact, almost quadrupled. To sustain Taylor and disabuse his mind of the idea that the Quartermaster's Department was not cordially supporting him, Jesup, on his own responsibility and without waiting to obtain authorization from the Secretary of War and Congress, applied large amounts of the balance on hand to the needs of the active service, transferring these funds from the specific items for which Congress had made the appropriation.[114] Hearing that certain light-draft steamboats were available at Cincinnati on the Ohio River and on the Chattahoochie in Georgia, Jesup directed his quartermasters

[109] House *Ex. Doc.* No. 119, p. 388 (Thomas to Jesup, 15 May 1846); p. 348 (Thomas to Hunt, 18 May 1846); pp. 349–50 (Bliss to Thomas, 24 May 1846); p. 350 (Thomas to Hunt, 31 May 1846).

[110] House *Ex. Doc.* No. 60, p. 654 (Hunt to Jesup, 4 Jun 1846).

[111] House *Ex. Doc.* No. 119, p. 337 (AQM Crosman to Winthrop, 26 May and 27 Jun 1846).

[112] *Ibid.*, p. 351 (Bliss to Sanders, 28 May 1846).

[113] *Ibid.*, p. 352 (Hunt to Sanders, 5 Jun 1846).

[114] House *Ex. Doc.* No. 60, p. 554 (Jesup to Sanders, 5 Jul 1846); p. 557 (Jesup to Marcy, 18 Feb 1847).

in those areas to examine and procure the boats if they were suitable.[115] They were not purchased, however, for Hunt and Sanders obtained a sufficient number of boats.[116]

By mid-June, Lieutenant Colonel Hunt began to dispatch steamboats to the Rio Grande. It was a perilous feat of seamanship to take these fragile, light-draft river boats from the Mississippi to the Rio Grande. A terrific gale, which delayed Colonel Whiting's arrival at Taylor's headquarters to assume his duties as chief quartermaster there, also prevented the early arrival of some of the steamboats, but by 3 July they were coming in fast in the wake of the calm weather following the storm.[117] On 23 July, 12 steamboats were at work on the Rio Grande conveying to Camargo the 300,000 rations that Taylor required there preparatory to his march on Monterey. The river was not deep and the current almost too swift for the weakly powered, small steamboats whose operations were further hampered by a scanty supply of dry wood for fuel as a result of the prolonged storm.[118]

Before Taylor set out for Cerralvo early in September, he reviewed the shortcomings of the Quartermaster's Department. He insisted that only by "repeated efforts" directed from his headquarters had suitable steamboats been procured and now that a part of the Army had been brought forward to Camargo, steamboats procured at Pittsburgh were just arriving. Unfortunately, these boats were the very ones procured by his own agent. "I hazard nothing in saying that, if proper foresight and energy had been displayed in sending out suitable steamers to navigate the Rio Grande," Taylor wrote the War Department, "our army woul long since have been in possession of Monterey"—a statement that might well be applied to the general himself.[119]

In regard to land transportation, Taylor charged that though his forces had increased five-fold his wagon train was less in size than when he left Corpus Christi. "I wish it distinctly understood," he warned, "that our ability to move is due wholly to means created here, and which could not have been reckoned upon with safety in Washington."[120] But Jesup did count upon it, and in a country abounding in mules—the means of transportation best adapted to the country and the only means

---

[115] (1) House *Ex. Doc.* No. 119, p. 289 (Jesup to Capt. M. M. Clark, 12 Jun 1846). (2) RG 92, OQMG Letter Book, vol. 37, p. 473 (Jesup to Maj. D. D. Tompkins, 16 Jun 1846).

[116] House *Ex. Doc.* No. 119, p. 351 (Hunt to Jesup, 11 Jun 1846); pp. 382–83 (Same to same, 4 Jul 1846); p. 421 (Sanders to Jesup, 28 Jun 1846).

[117] *Ibid.,* p. 364 (Whiting to Jesup, 3 Jul 1846)).

[118] *Ibid.,* p. 117 (Taylor to AG, 22 Jul 1846); pp. 366–67 (Whiting to Jesup, 23 Jul 1846).

[119] House *Ex. Doc.* No. 60, pp. 557–58 (Taylor to AG, 1 Sep 1846); pp. 559–60 (Jesup to Marcy, 5 Dec 1846)).

[120] *Ibid.,* pp. 557–58 (Taylor to AG, 1 Sep 1846).

used by the enemy—a general was expected to avail himself of the resources of the country in which he operated. Besides, Jesup also expected General Taylor to make use of the train of about 300 wagons that he had on hand.[121]   The Department, therefore, concentrated its efforts on furnishing sufficient wagons for the operations to be undertaken in the fall.

As soon as Congress enacted the first war measure in May, Jesup ordered the procurement of wagons.   During the next month, he directed quartermasters at Philadelphia, Cincinnati, and Pittsburgh to procure 700 wagons for mules and oxen with the necessary sets of harness, delivery to be made as soon as possible.[122]   Contracts had to be made with scores of wheelwrights in all parts of the country because most firms were small and produced only a few wagons at any one time.   The need was urgent and time was short.   Quartermasters therefore also went into the open market to purchase whatever wagons they could obtain that would be suitable for service in Mexico.   Hearing that a manufacturer at Pembroke, N.Y., had some wagons for sale, Jesup sent Capt. D. H. Vinton, assistant quartermaster at New York, to examine and purchase them on the best practicable terms.   The Georgia penitentiary at Milledgeville was supposed to produce great numbers of wagons.   "Ascertain whether the information is correct," Jesup wrote Assistant Quartermaster Wayne at Savannah, and "do the best you can, and in the shortest possible time." [123]   Hunt could procure few wagons at New Orleans and Capt. A. R. Hetzel found they were equally scarce at St. Louis.   He scoured the markets of Memphis, Vicksburg, and Natchez.   Wagons could be obtained in middle and east Tennessee, but their availability was of no use to the Department, he reported, because the waters of the Cumberland and Tennessee Rivers were so low as to preclude transportation of the wagons to New Orleans in any reasonable time.[124]

The Department waived specifications, and increased payments per wagon to stimulate greater production, but factors over which the Quartermaster General had no control hampered procurement.[125]   Only seasoned timber could be used in the construction of wagons, but large quantities of it were not available at Cincinnati.   Workmen were also scarce there.   So many had joined volunteer companies that production

---

[121] *Ibid.,* p. 560 (Jesup to Marcy, 5 Dec 1846).

[122] (1) RG 92, OQMG Letter Book, vol. 37, p. 425 (Jesup to Tompkins, 26 May 1846). (2) House *Ex. Doc.* No. 119, p. 285 (Stanton to Tompkins, 15 May 1846); p. 286 (Jesup to Harding, 2 Jun 1846).

[123] House *Ex. Doc.* No. 119, p. 303 (19 Jul 1846); p. 296 (Jesup to Vinton, 8 Jul 1846).

[124] *Ibid.,* p. 397 (Hetzel to Jesup, 28 Jul 1846).

[125] *Ibid.,* p. 288 (Jesup to Harding, 11 Jun 1846); p. 303 (Jesup to same, 20 Jul 1846); p. 405 (Clark to Jesup, 21 Jul 1846); p. 401 (Maj. H. Bache to Jesup, 21 Jul 1846)).

could not be increased by any inducement, and the approach of the harvest season threatened to reduce their number still further.[126]   Under the competition of other means of transportation, former centers of wagon production had almost disappeared.   York, Pa., for example, had formerly produced many of the wagons used during the Seminole War, but the operation of railroads had greatly diminished the wagon business in that part of the country.[127]

By August, wagons began to be delivered to the quartermasters in increasing numbers.   Some of them could be taken apart for shipment; others had to be placed intact on board the ships bound for Mexico. Use of steamers made it possible to deliver them at Brazos de Santiago in 15 days.[128]   By 20 August, Jesup called a halt to wagon procurement. Enough wagons had been obtained to meet immediate needs.   He advised that when a further supply was required in the autumn, proposals would be invited by notice in the newspapers.[129]

In the meantime, the forces on the Rio Grande were in need of land transportation, but General Taylor had been as indifferent to this problem of logistical support as he had been to that of water transportation.   Quartermaster Thomas made the first call for 50 mule wagons and 20 ox wagons with complete harness on 18 May 1846 though there is nothing to indicate that Taylor prompted that requisition.[130]   But even if he had, 70 wagons were a wholly inadequate addition to the train needed to support the force of 6,000 men with which Taylor intended to move against Monterey.   The Army on the Rio Grande was supposed to have had on hand some 300 wagons, but when Lieutenant Colonel Whiting reached headquarters he found the wagon train reduced to 175. To make up the deficiency, he sent Assistant Quartermaster Crosman out to hire or purchase pack mules with conductors and arrieros, paying them so much per day.   Later this mode was changed to payment by the cargo, that is, a mule load of 300 pounds.   Crosman was also to hire ox teams and Mexican carts.   By these means, Whiting hoped to be able to pack enough for the companies and use the train for the general purpose of hauling ammuntion and provisions and for transporting the sick.[131]   By authorizing Captain Crosman to requisition for animals upon the alcaldes or civil authorities, when he could not procure them

[126] *Ibid.*, p. 358 (Tompkins to Jesup, 7 Jun 1846).

[127] *Ibid.*, pp. 404–05 (Clark to Jesup, 20 Jul 1846); pp. 409–10 (Dusenbery to Jesup, 24 Jul 1846).

[128] RG 92, OQMG Letter Book, vol. 37, p. 584 (Jesup to Dusenbery, 1 Aug 1846).

[129] House *Ex. Doc.* No. 119, p. 321 (Jesup to Capt. Thistle and Capt. Clark, 20 Aug 1846).

[130] *Ibid.*, p. 390 (Thomas to Jesup, 18 May 1846).

[131] (1) *Ibid.*, p. 367 (Whiting to Jesup, 28 Jul 1846).   (2) RG 92, Whiting, Letters Sent, I, 447 (Whiting to Jesup, 29 Sep 1846).

with the consent of the owners, Whiting found little difficulty in obtaining mules.

During the time that rations were being forwarded by boat to Camargo and forage for 4,000 animals was being shipped up the river, the wagon train was retained at Brazos to haul the cargoes to the steamboats. On 4 August, Taylor went to Camargo, the remainder of the 10,000 troops having been ordered there at the end of July. At that point, the mule train had to be withdrawn from the Brazos and sent forward to Camargo. Only 40 or 50 ox teams were left at Brazos, a number inadequate to fill one quarter of the boats plying the Rio Grande. Wagons were beginning to come in from the United States, but until sufficient numbers arrived, Whiting hired all the Mexican ox-carts he could get and also called upon the alcaldes to deliver 500 mules for which a fair price would be paid. As soon as the mules came in, they were to be "put to the harness," and by this means Whiting expected to have a new mule train at Brazos in 2 or 3 weeks.[132] Although Mexican horses were too small to provide the dragoons with mounts or to be used for draft purposes, Mexican mules could be used for supply purposes and hundreds were bought at $18 to $20 each.

When Lieutenant Colonel Whiting arrived at Camargo on 23 August, Captain Crossman had the transportation situation fairly well in hand. Some 1,500 pack mules were with the Army, forwarding supplies to the temporary depot at Cerralvo where some troops were posted for its protection. With packs and drivers included the pack mules cost about 50 cents a day.[133] Ten days later, Taylor set out for Cerralvo. The number of hired pack mules had been increased to 1,900 and about 180 mule and horse wagons accompanied the Army.[134] By Taylor's orders, one pack mule was allowed to every eight noncommissioned officers and privates, three to company officers, and four to the headquarters of a regiment. Each brigade and each division headquarters was allowed one wagon, while three wagons were assigned to each regiment—one to transport water and two to carry such articles as could not be packed on mules. The Ordnance Department had fifty-three wagons, the Engineer Department one, and the Medical Director, four.[135]

After his arrival in Mexico, Whiting was certain that the country could furnish all the mules the Department would want. But back in Washington, Jesup had received no word throughout the summer on the

---

[132] House *Ex. Doc.* No. 119, pp. 369–70 (Whiting to Jesup, 6 Aug 1846).
[133] *Ibid.*, pp. 371–72 (Whiting to Jesup, 24 Aug 1846).
[134] House *Ex. Doc.* No. 60, pp. 680–81 (Whiting to Jesup, 3 Sep 1846).
[135] (1) House *Ex. Doc.* No. 119, p. 211 (Hq Army of Occupation, Order No. 109, 29 Aug 1846). (2) RG 92, Whiting, Letters Sent, I, 407 (Whiting to Crosman, 30 Aug 1846).

availability of mules and whether the Army intended using them.   He, too, was procuring and shipping mules and horses to the Rio Grande to insure mobility of the Army.[136]   Late in August, Whiting assured Jesup that pack mules might answer every purpose, "provided we could bring ourselves to make war as the enemy makes it."   But that was not likely to be the case, he admitted, voicing a sentiment that was to be reiterated in later wars.   "We have customs which neither the officers nor the soldiers will forego, excepting in cases of extremity.   Our camp equipage, so comfortable and yet so cumbrous, our rations, so full and bulky, all must be transported." [137]   In addition to the Army's preference for wagons as a more convenient mode of transportation than pack animals, the fact that only certain articles could be packed to advantage imposed a limitation on the number of pack animals that could be usefully employed.   Scarcely anything, either subsistence or quartermasters' stores, came to Mexico in shape for transportation by pack animals.   Consequently, a troublesome and expensive remodeling of nearly every package had to be made before it could be put on the back of a mule.[138]

The use of pack animals had to be continued, however, for wagons did not become available to Taylor's forces in time for the fall operations as had been anticipated.   Taylor called attention to the fact that the first wagons—only 125 in number—did not arrive in his headquarters until 2 November.   "The task of fighting and beating the enemy," he informed the War Department, "is among the least difficult that we encounter; the great question of supplies necessarily controls all the operations in a country like this." [139]   The Quartermaster's Department had not expected to have any wagons delivered at the Brazos before 1 September.   By that time, they did begin to arrive but the initial deliveries were needed at the depot, and it was not until 1 October that the first new train of 125 wagons left the Brazos.[140]   It took a month for it to reach Monterey.   Building up the depot at Monterery was accomplished by the use of pack mules, some 2,000 being employed to bring forward about 575,000 pounds of subsistence.   Some 300 wagons were also used to haul subsistence and quartermasters' stores.[141]

By the first week in December, there were about 1,200 wagons at

---

[136] See below.

[137] (1) House *Ex. Doc.* No. 119, p. 372 (Whiting to Jesup, 28 Aug 1846).   (2) See Henry, *Campaign Sketches of the War with Mexico*, pp. 162–64.

[138] House *Ex. Doc.* No. 60, p. 686 (Whiting to Jesup, 30 Nov 1846).

[139] *Ibid.*, p. 360 (Taylor to AG, 8 Nov 1846).

[140] (1) RG 92, Whiting, Letters Sent, II, 14–15 (Whiting to Stanton, 5 Nov 1846).   (2) House *Ex. Doc.* No. 119, p. 374 (Whiting to Jesup, 16 Sep 1846).

[141] House *Ex. Doc.* No. 119, p. 376 (Whiting to Stanton, 24 Nov 1846).

the Brazos with the necessary harness. Mules were also on hand, both procured in Mexico and sent in by Lieutenant Colonel Hunt.[142] The difficulty was that the Department lacked drivers. Whiting complained that those hired were dissipated and unstable and because the general objected none could be obtained by detailing soldiers from the Army. He saw only one remedy—to add one or two men to each company of the Army who should be enlisted as teamsters or hostlers and always be liable to be called on for service with teams and animals. When not wanted for this special service, they would serve as soldiers. He proposed that their pay be equivalent to that of an artificer. Efficiency and certainty, he maintained, would be doubled and the cost of transportation cut in half.[143] Jesup endorsed the idea and urged congressional action. On 3 March 1847, Congress did enact legislation but not to the extent that Whiting had recommended. It provided for one principal teamster, with the rank and compensation of quartermaster-sergeant, for each regiment and two teamsters, with the compensation of artificers, for each company of dragoons, artillery, and mounted riflemen in the Regular Army.[144]

Despite all difficulties, Taylor's forces moved with reasonable promptness, yet he complained repeatedly that he was hampered by lack of transportation. The means were available to him, and Jesup, who went to Mexico to expedite Quartermaster operations, reported that he had contracted for 2,000 mules in one day to be delivered at Matamoras and the Brazos in a month. "Ten thousand could have been obtained at any time since the army has been in Mexico," he advised the Secretary of War, "if proper measures had been adopted to obtain them."[145] It seems quite likely that Taylor's criticisms could only have been intended, as Brig. Gen. J. W. Worth intimated, to ward off responsibility in the event of failure and to augment his glory in case of success.[146]

Support of General Wool

At the same time that the Quartermaster's Department was supporting Taylor's Army of the Rio Grande, it was also hurrying supplies to San Antonio de Bexar where a force of Both Regulars and volunteers,

[142] RG 92, OQMG Consolidated Correspondence File, Box 659 (Hunt Rpt, 18 Apr 1846) shows that between 2 May 1846 and 7 July 1847 he sent 932 wagons for horses, 179 for mules, 2,139 horses and 1,570 mules to Brazos de Santiago. Of that number 11 wagons, 217 horses, and 371 mules were lost in shipment.

[148] House *Ex. Doc.* No. 119, p. 377 (Whiting to Stanton, 23 Nov 1846); p. 452 (Jesup to Stanton, 15 Jan 1847).

[144] 9 *Stat.* 184.

[145] House *Ex. Doc.* No. 60, p. 567 (Jesup to Marcy, 3 Dec 1846).

[146] Smith, *The War with Mexico*, I, 491, quoting ltr, Worth to Capt. S——, 5 Sep 1846).

coming from distant points, was assembling. Among the Regulars were two companies of the 1st Dragoons and two of the 6th Infantry drawn from Fort Gibson, Indian Territory, and Fort Smith, Ark., respectively, along with a company of light artillery that came overland from Carlisle Barracks, Pa. The volunteers included an Arkansas regiment of cavalry and two Illinois regiments, the latter journeying by steamboat to New Orleans, by ship to La Vaca, and then marching overland to San Antonio.[147] Under Brig. Gen. John E. Wool, assigned to command about the middle of June, this force was to operate against Chihuahua.[148]

As early as 22 May, Jesup advised Lieutenant Colonel Hunt that 3,000 or 4,000 men would be assembled at San Antonio de Bexar, and he ordered a 15- to 30-day supply of forage and subsistence to be placed there. To do this, a train would have to be organized and an entrepot established at the most convenient point on the Gulf. Jesup suggested La Vaca (now Port Lavaca on Matagorda Bay) as the site for the entrepot.[149] Two weeks later, he repeated his instructions on the formation of a train to Lt. Col. Henry Whiting when that officer was appointed chief quartermaster with Taylor's Army.[150] But at Matamoras, Whiting was too far away to supervise Quartermaster operations at La Vaca, news of which reached him only at long intervals via New Orleans. He reported that Hunt was sending supplies, and he assumed that Capt. J. R. Irwin, then assigned as assistant quartermaster to Texas, was getting them forwarded to San Antonio.[151] En route to Mexico, Whiting had assigned Maj. Charles Thomas as quartermaster in charge of Departmental operations with the division under Wool's command.

When more than a month passed without word of the formation of a wagon train at La Vaca, Jesup renewed and widened his orders to Hunt. He was to purchase and send forward all well-broken mules and all harness that could be obtained in Louisiana. Captain Irwin was to buy in Texas 200 ox, horse, and mule teams, with wagons, harness, and yokes. Captain Osborn Cross was also to be sent to Texas to purchase all the wagons, mules, and draft horses that he could obtain. Without waiting to accompany General Wool, Quartermaster Thomas, then at Memphis, Tenn., was ordered to proceed at once to San Antonio. Jesup instructed him to purchase all the horses, mules, and oxen necessary for the transportation of Wool's division.[152]

[147] House *Ex. Doc.* No. 60, pp. 454–55 (AG to Taylor, 16 Jun 1846).

[148] *Ibid.,* p. 328 (AG to Wool, 11 Jun 1846).

[149] RG 92, OQMG Letter Book, vol. 37, pp. 419–20 (Jesup to Hunt, 22 May 1846).

[150] *Ibid.,* vol. 37, pp. 443–44 (Jesup to Whiting, 3 Jun 1846).

[151] RG 92, Whiting, Letters Sent, I, 155 (Whiting to Jesup, 23 Jul 1846).

[152] House *Ex. Doc.* No. 119, pp. 298–99; 301–02 (Jesup to Hunt, 18 and 19 Jul 1846); p. 310 (Jesup to Tompkins, 10 and 23 Jul 1846).

Jesup had become increasingly alarmed about the means of transportation not only for Wool's division but also for Taylor's Army. Since the death of Colonel Cross in April, he had received no information as to whether Mexican horses and mules could be obtained and used by the Army. Requisitions had come in for replacements for Dragoon mounts lost in battle, and he feared that Taylor's Army needed artillery horses as well as draft animals. Subject to Taylor's approval, he early authorized Lieutenant Colonel Whiting to purchase in Mexico all the animals that were necessary.[153]

Even as he authorized quartermasters on the Rio Grande and in Texas to purchase, Jesup made doubly sure of the supply of animals by sending several assistant quartermasters and agents to procure mules and horses in the Mississippi Valley. The chief procurement officer was Capt. A. R. Hetzel, who, on orders of General Wool then en route to San Antonio from Louisville, procured 200 mules and 24 horses. These he sent to La Vaca late in July.[154] Hetzel and others were also purchasing for Taylor's Army, Jesup's orders having been increased during June and July to 1,000 mules and several hundred horses.[155] Shipment to the Rio Grande was accomplished by loading the animals on steamboats and sending them down the Mississippi to Hunt at New Orleans, who, if the need was considered urgent, could ship them by water to Point Isabel. Normally, however, animals were unloaded at some point on the river above New Orleans and driven overland, via Texas, to the Rio Grande under the care of conductors.

The use of this overland route made it possible in one instance to divert animals meant for Taylor's Army to Wool's division. Late in August 1846, the Department had ready for shipment a drove of some 400 mules and 400 horses. Though not requisitioned, the horses were intended for Taylor's artillery and the mules were to serve the immediate needs of the service resulting from the arrival of the mounted Kentucky and Tennessee regiments. The drove of animals and the mounted regiments were both supposed to arrive on the Rio Grande at the same time. Capt. S. H. Drum, assistant quartermaster in charge of the drove, landed the animals at Vidalia, La., and drove them 615 miles to San Antonio, making a stop there the first week in October. Quartermaster Thomas, without authority, appropriated them for Wool's division, much to Jesup's exasperation, and Wool refused to make any change in the disposition of the animals even after Thomas had been instructed as to

---

[153] *Ibid.*, pp. 301–02 (Jesup to Hunt, 19 Jul 1846); p. 291 (Jesup to Whiting, 17 Jul 1846).

[154] *Ibid.*, pp. 395–97 (Henzel to Jesup, 9 and 27 Jul 1846).

[155] *Ibid.*, pp. 290, 297, 299 (Jesup to Hetzel, 13 Jun, 17 and 18 Jul 1846); pp. 296, 306 (Jesup to Tompkins, 10 and 23 Jul 1846).

their proper destination. General Wool had also appropriated for his use, as he passed through New Orleans, some two or three hundred wagons that were on their way to the Brazos. Whiting later complained that the loss of the wagons and animals had greatly inconvenienced Taylor's movements.[156]

Condemning Major Thomas for his unauthorized action, Jesup maintained that "with proper energy, ox teams (the only means of transportation adapted to that country) could have been obtained in sufficient numbers for all necessary purposes." He informed the Secretary of War that he feared General Wool "has embarrassed himself with an unwieldy train of several hundred wagons among the mountains of Mexico." The large train, "gotten up at great expense," would be lost for it could neither reach Chihuahua, Jesup maintained, nor be sent back.[157] It was for the general, however, to decide the means and the amount of transportation required.

Unlike Taylor, Wool had been foresighted in ordering supplies while en route to San Antonio where he arrived in mid-August. Accumulating the necessary supplies of forage, subsistence, and ordnance was much hampered by the great distance from which they had to be drawn. Little or nothing could be obtained in the small town of San Antonio. All supplies were shipped from New Orleans to La Vaca and then transported by wagon train, about 160 miles, to San Antonio. When rains turned the road into bottomless mud, it took 2 weeks for loaded wagons to cover that distance. The amount of supplies required and the difficulty of forwarding them may be inferred from the fact that 1,112 wagonloads were taken from the depot at La Vaca to San Antonio, and 500 wagons were employed in the transportation of those supplies and the troops.[158] Preparations were in no way speeded by the shipment from New Orleans of parts of wagons from different lots so that Quartermaster Thomas was unable to assemble complete wagons until ships arrived bringing parts that had been left behind.[159] Despite delays, supplies were accumulated and when General Wool was ready to start for Chihuahua, he had more wagons with his column of less than 3,000 men than General Taylor had with all his forces.[160]

After a topographical party had studied routes and made inquiries

[156] (1) Ibid., pp. 423–26 (Drum to Jesup, 10 Sep and 13 Oct 1846); pp. 441–42 (Jesup to Whiting, 17 Nov 1846); p. 391 (Thomas to Jesup, 11 Oct and 4 Nov 1846). (2) House Ex. Doc. No. 60, p. 686 (Whiting to Jesup, 30 Nov 1846).

[157] House Ex. Doc. No. 119, p. 440 (Jesup to Stanton, 8 Nov 1846); pp. 269–70 (Jesup to SW, 3 Dec 1846).

[158] House Ex. Doc. No. 8, p. 545 (Rpt of QMG, 24 Nov 1847).

[159] House Ex. Doc. No. 60, p. 429 (Thomas to Wool, 9 Sep 1846).

[160] House Ex. Doc. No. 119, p. 378 (Whiting to Jesup, 30 Nov 1846).

about water, wood, and forage—the three essentials on any expedition—an advance section of Wool's forces of 1,244 men set out on 26 September with 175 wagons and provisions for 2 months.[161]   Assistant Quartermaster O. Cross accompanied this advance force.   Wool took a circuitous route, practicable for his wagons and artillery, to Monclova, and with great exertions he brought them through to that town on 29 October.   There the rest of his troops joined him, making a force of 2,688.   He never did go to Chihuahua.   At his suggestion and on Taylor's orders, he advanced his troops to Parras on 5 December, abandoning the long supply line to San Antonio and La Vaca in favor of a shorter line by way of the Rio Grande and Camargo.[162]   Wool had marched his force some 600 miles without firing a shot at the enemy.   Taylor pronounced the expedition to Chihuahua a failure, but when an urgent call came to Wool in mid-December to go to the aid of General Worth, threatened by Santa Anna, he was able to march immediately, taking with his troops 350 wagons, provisions for 60 days, 400,000 cartridges, and 200 rounds for his cannon.[163]

Supply of Kearny

In the summer of 1846, the Quartermaster's Department had to supply still a third armed force, assembling at Fort Leavenworth on the Missouri River, for operations against New Mexico and California. The War Department placed Col. Stephen W. Kearny in charge of the troops.   These included some 300 Regulars of the 1st Dragoons; 860 Missouri mounted volunteers under Col. Alexander W. Doniphan; 250 volunteers from two light artillery companies; a St. Louis company of mounted volunteers, numbering about 100, called the Laclede Rangers; and two small companies of infantry.   About 50 Indian scouts, a party of topographical engineers, and an interpreter were also attached to the expedition.   In all, this armed force number somewhat less than 1,700 men.   It moved out by detachments on 26 and 27 June 1846.

Kearny's reinforcements—about 1,200 men, most of them mounted volunteers under the command of Col. Sterling Price—followed him on the Santa Fe trail in mid-August.   This force also included a few Regulars in charge of a number of pieces of heavy artillery.   In addition, a Mormon Battalion of 500 was recruited from among the Mormons driven from Nauvoo, Ill., who had gathered at Council Bluffs with the intention of emigrating to California.

---

[161] Buhoup, *Narrative of the Central Division*, pp. 17, 19.

[162] House *Ex. Doc.* No. 60, pp. 361, 377 (Taylor to AG, 9 and 24 Nov 1846).

[163] (1) Smith, *War with Mexico*, I, 275. (2) Buhoup, *Narrative of the Central Division*, pp. 96–98.

All these troops had to be equipped and provided with rations and the means of transportation at Fort Leavenworth. The speed with which Kearny's expedition moved out precluded any timely shipment of stores from Philadelphia. In any case, they were more readily obtained in Missouri and the nearby states. As Quartermaster at St. Louis, Maj. Aeneas Mackay was under orders to procure and furnish camp kettles, mess pans, hatches, and all other equipment needed. Jesup directed him to procure by contract or otherwise 1,000 packsaddles, to be held subject to Kearny's requisitions. Jesup had intended sending tents from Philadelphia, but such was the shortage of tentage at the Schuylkill Arsenal that he soon had to advise Major Mackay that none could be sent.[164]

Supplies moved from St. Louis to Fort Leavenworth by steamboat. There, Captain McKissack, assistant quartermaster at the fort, took charge of the supplies until Capt. R. E. Clary relieved him in July. Jesup then sent McKissack and another assistant quartermaster, Capt. Robert Allen, to Santa Fe to take charge of Quartermaster duties at that post. At the same time, Jesup assigned Maj. Thomas Swords as Quartermaster to the Kearny expedition.[165] He not only supervised the preparations for the movement of the troops to Sante Fe but accompanied Kearny to California, though he did not join him at Santa Fe until mid-August, when he arrived with the mail and formal notice of Kearny's appointment as brigadier general.[166]

Meanwhile, Swords and McKissack had been busy at Fort Leavenworth, equipping the troops as they moved out and furnishing them with mules and wagons to haul their baggage and supplies. Wagons loaded with provisions had been sent ahead to Council Grove and the rendezvous point on the Arkansas below Fort Bent, 100 of them having been dispatched before the first detachment of Kearny's expedition left Fort Leavenworth the last week in June. Captain McKissack had worked energetically to purchase sufficient mules and ox teams to establish the wagon trains needed to maintain a flow of supplies to Santa Fe. Such wagon trains were sent on the road in groups of 25 or 30 wagons, each train under a wagonmaster and the wagoners all armed so that they could defend themselves without need of an escort.[167]

The line of operations extending to Santa Fe, a distance of almost

[164] RG 92, OQMG Letter Book, vol. 37, pp. 418–20 (Jesup to Mackay, 21 and 22 May 1846).

[165] *Ibid.*, p. 425 (Jesup to Swords, 26 May 1846); pp. 496–97 (Jesup to Allen, 1 Jul 1846); p. 503 (Jesup to Kearny, 2 Jul 1846).

[166] (1) Hughes, *Doniphan's Expedition*, p. 71. (2) House Ex. Doc. No. 60, pp. 153–55 (Marcy to Kearny, 3 Jun 1846).

[167] (1) Hughes, *Doniphan's Expedition*, pp. 29–30, 34, 41–42. (2) RG 92, CGP, McKissack Letters, No. 91, p. 1 (McKissack to Jesup, 1 Jun 1846).

900 miles, required vast transportation facilities to enable it to move and keep up its supplies.   Jesup later reported that for the transportation of Kearny's army and its reinforcements and supplies, the Quartermaster's Department had furnished 459 horses, 3,658 mules, 14,904 oxen, 1,556 wagons, and 516 packsaddles.[168]   Nevertheless, John T. Hughes, a Missouri volunteer, was extremely critical of the provision made for the expedition.

> Gen. Kearney's army was not well provisioned; nor was it furnished, in all its parts, with stout, able, and efficient teams, such as the difficult nature of the country over which it has to pass, required.   The commissary and quarter-master departments were wretchedly managed.   During much of the time, owing either to the neglect or incompetency of the heads of these departments, the general found it necessary to subsist his men on half rations.   It repeatedly happened that the wagons, particularly of the volunteer corps, were left so far behind during a day's march that they did not come into camp before mid-night.   Thus the men had to feast or famish by turns, owing to the gross and culpable neglect of government agents.   The volunteer troops were furnished with very sorry and indifferent wagons and teams, wholly inadequate for such an expedition, whilst the regulars were furnished in the very best manner.[169]

In the march across the plains, water was scant, wood nonexistent, and food became so scarce that rations were reduced to half and, during the last 10 days of the journey to Santa Fe, to one-third the allowance. Mired wagons had to be dragged out by troops; repairs were frequent. Often bridges had to be constructed, banks dug down, and roads built before the wagons could pass.   But Colonel Kearny kept the expedition moving, and after a tiresome march of almost 900 miles in less than 50 days, the whole command entered Santa Fe on 18 August 1846 to take possession of the province of New Mexico.[170]

A quick reconnaissance having convinced Kearny that quiet and peace prevailed in New Mexico, he proceeded to California, leaving Colonel Doniphan in charge until the reinforcements arrived.   At that time, Doniphan's Regiment of Missouri volunteers was to march to Chihuahua to join General Wool, while the Mormon Battalion followed Kearny to California.   On 25 September, General Kearny, 300 of the 1st Dragoons, and a small party of topographical engineers, having exchanged their horses for mules procured by Captain McKissack, left Santa Fe, taking about 65 days' provisions and their baggage in wagons drawn by eight mules each.[171]   About 150 miles from Santa Fe, an express

[168] House *Ex. Doc.* No. 8, p. 545 (QMG Annual Rpt, 24 Nov 1847).

[169] Hughes, *Doniphan's Expedition*, pp. 81–82.

[170] (1) *Ibid.,* pp. 43, 54, 66.   (2) House *Ex. Doc.* No. 60, p. 169 (Kearny to Brig. Gen. R. Jones, 24 Aug 1846).

[171] (1) Hughes, *Doniphan's Expedition*, pp. 204–05.   (2) RG 92, CGP, McKissack Letters, No. 91, p. 26 (McKissack to Jesup, 30 Sep 1846).

from the Pacific Coast brought word that California was in American hands, and Kearny, in consequence, decided to proceed with only 100 of the Dragoons, leaving the other 200 in New Mexico. He also discarded his wagons in favor of pack mules by which means he hoped to make quicker time, traveling 25 miles a day.[172] Instead of peace, Kearny and his men found counterrevolution in California, but after one engagement they arrived at San Diego on 12 December 1846.

When Quartermaster Swords left Fort Leavenworth, he had not been informed that Kearny's ultimate destination was California. In consequence, he had brought no packsaddles though there were many at the fort. Before the troops set out for California, therefore, Swords had to have packsaddles made at Taos, for no suitable timber could be obtained at Santa Fe. Despite all the care that could be taken of the animals, few of the mules that left Santa Fe managed to travel the 1,050 miles to San Diego. At San Diego, there were no supplies of any kind, except those belonging to the Navy, whose personnel were themselves on short allowance. Nothing but cattle could be procured in the country.

On Kearny's orders, Swords left for the Sandwich (Hawaiian) Islands, in a ship chartered by the Navy Department, to obtain funds and to procure the provisions necessary for both the Army and the Navy, as well as articles needed by the Quartermaster's and Medical Departments. No funds had arrived at Santa Fe before his departure and Swords had not been able to bring any to California. The expedition had carried articles of Indian trade with them that it used in bartering with the Indians for provisions en route. To pay for the articles he procured at Honolulu and also to cover the necessary expenses of the Army in California, Swords issued a proposal for an exchange for drafts which he drew upon Quartermaster General Jesup and the heads of the other supply departments in Washington.[173] The rate of exchange for bills was exorbitant; Swords obtained $1,100 at 18 percent and $4,500 at 20 percent. His voyage to the Sandwich Islands took 18 days and the return trip 25 days. He was then occupied in getting the stores he had purchased placed in the depot at San Diego. Later, he joined Kearny at Monterey where he erected a saw mill, furnished tools and materials for the construction of a field work by the Engineers, repaired the barracks, and superintended the landing of stores from ships dispatched by the Quartermaster's Department from New York in the fall of 1846.

---

[172] (1) RG 92, CGP, McKissack Letters, No. 91, p. 54 (McKissack to Mackay, 16 Nov 1846). (2) House *Ex. Doc.* No. 1, 30th Cong., 1st sess., p. 513 (Kearny to Brig. Gen. R. Jones, 12 Dec 1846).

[173] (1) RG 92, OQMG Consolidated Correspondence File, (Swords) (Swords to Jesup, 16 Jan and 27 Sep 1847). (2) *Report of SW, 1848–49,* p. 228 (Sword's Rpt, 8 Oct 1847).

On 1 June 1847, Kearny set out on his return journey to the East, Swords accompanying him.[174]

Lack of funds at Santa Fe also handicapped Captain McKissack in furnishing transportation for the men of the Mormon Battalion who were to follow Kearny to California under the command of Lt. Col. P. St. George Cooke. The mules the Battalion brought from Fort Leavenworth were broken down by the time they reached Santa Fe, but the replacements furnished by McKissack were not much better, supported as they had been on short rations. The Quartermaster calculated that he could furnish transportation only for a pound and a half for each man for 60 days. But the rations alone should have amounted nearly to that, and, in addition, baggage, equipage, ammunition, tools, pack-saddles, and other supplies also had to be transported. The last of the Battalion arrived at Santa Fe on 13 October, and 6 days later the Mormon Battalion started west, its aggregate strength 397. There were three mule wagons to each company besides six large ox wagons. There were four mule wagons for the field and staff, quartermaster's property, hospital department, and the paymaster, as well as four or five private wagons in the train. The expedition set out with 60 days' rations of flour, sugar, coffee, and salt; 30 of salt pork; and 20 of soap. After incredible hardships on the trail, Lieutenant Colonel Cooke brought some of his wagons and his gaunt men, half-naked and for the most part unshod, to San Diego by the end of January 1847.[175]

To the men who had toiled overland to California, President Polk, in the summer of 1846, decided to add a regiment of volunteers, about 800 strong, to be sent there by water and placed under Kearny's command on arrival in California. The Quartermaster's Department immediately initiated action to charter the necessary vessels and equip and supply the regiment. Under the command of Col. J. D. Stevenson, a part of the men sailed on three ships from New York in September, the rest following shortly thereafter in three more chartered ships, all of which carried ordnance stores, camp equipage, baggage, and subsistence. They arrived on the Pacific Coast during March and April 1847 to be mustered out in California, each man being under obligation to remain there and assist in colonizing the country.[176]

While General Kearny was marching to California, Colonel

---

[174] *Report of SW, 1848–49*, p. 229 (Swords' Rpt, 8 Oct 1847).

[175] Lt. Col. P. St. George Cooke, "Journal of the March of the Mormon Battalion," *passim*, in Senate *Ex. Doc.* No. 2, 31st Cong., Special Sess.

[176] (1) RG 92, OQMG Letter Book, vol. 37, pp. 497, 541, 543 (Jesup to Stanton, 1, 15, 17 Jul 1846); vol. 38, pp. 108–09, 133–34, 218–19 (Same to same, 4 Sep, 11 Sep, 15 Oct 1846). (2) House *Ex. Doc.* No. 60, pp. 159–62 (Marcy to Stevenson, 11 Sep 1846); pp. 162–63 (Marcy to Kearny, 12 Sep 1846).

Doniphan, at his orders and after the arrival of reinforcements at Santa Fe, set out for the Navajo country to negotiate a treaty. Quartermaster McKissack provided the necessary wagons, mules, and oxen.[177] By mid-December, this assignment had been completed and Doniphan, with 856 effective men, started from Valverda to join General Wool at Chihuahua. El Paso was taken without opposition, the enemy was defeated, and Doniphan's force took possession of Chihuahua on 1 March 1847. Wool, however, was at Saltillo. Doniphan's position was embarrassing. Most of his volunteers had been in service since 1 June and though their terms ·of service would expire in May, they had not received one cent of pay. Their marches had been hard and they were literally, Doniphan informed Wool, without horses, clothes, or money. Since his troops were not fit for garrison duty at Chihuahua, he requested that his force be allowed to join Wool before their term of service expired. After a 600-mile march through enemy territory, the troops reached General Wool's camp on 2 April. On orders of General Taylor, they then proceeded to Monterey and the Rio Grande, where they embarked for New Orleans to be discharged and receive their first pay after an incredible journey of more than 5,000 miles.[178]

From the time the first troops of the Army of the West arrived in Santa Fe, about mid-August 1846, that town became the deposit point for provisions and the depot for outfitting all expeditions setting out for California, other points in New Mexico, and Mexico itself. Santa Fe was alive with activity. Provision wagons came in daily from Fort Leavenworth during the fall of 1846. The commissaries and quartermasters were busy receiving and storing provisions and taking care of the stock. Quartermaster McKissack rented quarters for such troops and officers as were stationed in Santa Fe as well as buildings for hospitals and for storehouses. Exorbitant prices were charged and he proposed the construction of barracks if troops were to be stationed permanently in New Mexico. At Kearny's orders, he also set about building a saw mill that he hoped to complete before the end of the year, but he feared that "no calculations can be made of work performed by volunteers who only work when they please."

The country, he reported, was destitute of almost all materials needed for outfitting expeditions, and prices of most things had doubled since the arrival of the troops. The demand for packsaddles for the expedition had virtually drained the country, and to equip the Mormon

---

[177] RG 92, CGP, McKissack Letters, No. 91, p. 62 (McKissack to Jesup, 8 Dec 1846).
[178] (1) *Journal of William H. Richardson*, p. 46 ff. (2) House *Ex. Doc.* No. 60, pp. 1128–29 (Doniphan to Wool, 20 Mar 1847). (3) Senate *Ex. Doc.* No. 1, 30th Cong., 1st sess., pp. 497–502 (Doniphan to Brig. Gen. R. Jones, 4 Mar 1847).

Battalion he had made packsaddles out of broken wagons.   It was difficult to recruit broken down animals.   Grain was scarce; oats and hay
unobtainable.   He often had to purchase fresh oxen and send them to
the assistance of wagon trains that had broken down on the trail after
crossing the Arkansas.   As winter approached, the Indians below Bent's
Fort attacked more of the provision trains en route to Sante Fe.   Snow-
storms caught others and the expense of assisting them to reach Santa Fe
ran into thousands of dollars.   A considerable amount of that expense,
McKissack held, resulted from the gross carelessness of the teamsters,
for he found that private trains lost one ox to the government's thirty.
He resolved that when a wagon train lost over 100 oxen on the journey
from Fort Leavenworth to Santa Fe that the wagonmaster's pay and
rations would cease at once and his back pay be taken to compensate,
in part, for the loss.[179]

Much of the Department's troubles at Santa Fe stemmed from the
lack of funds and it was not until January 1847 that any cash arrived.
The post at Santa Fe required a quartermaster who could assume
responsibility without waiting for orders or directions from Washington.
The great distances and the poor means of communication meant that
for months the quartermaster was left to his own devices.   In mid-
February 1847, McKissack wrote Jesup that he had received no instructions since the Army had arrived at Santa Fe in August 1846.   On
5 July, he noted that it was now some 6 or 8 months since he had received
a letter from Washington.[180]

To the best of his ability, McKissack equipped Kearny's troops, the
Mormon Battalion, and Doniphan's Regiment, providing them with
transportation and provisions, and he supported the troops stationed at
Santa Fe and in its vicinity.   Obviously, once the expeditions were under
way there was no way of maintaining supply lines with Santa Fe and
quartermasters on those expeditions were as much on their own in providing fresh mules or provisions en route as Captain McKissack was at
Santa Fe.

Quartermaster Support of Scott

The operations of both Taylor's Army and the Army of the West
had been successful in bringing under American control a large part of
the territory belonging to Mexico.   They had not been successful in
terminating the war.   Confronted with the prospect of a war of unlimited

---

[179] RG 92, CGP, McKissack Letters, No. 91, pp. 26–29, 30–32, 48–51, 62–65 (McKissack to
Jesup, 30 Sep, 6 Oct, 11 Nov, 8 Dec 1846); p. 69 (McKissack to Capt. R. E. Clary, 30 Nov 1846).
[180] *Ibid.*, pp. 78–81; 131–33 (McKissack to Jesup, 9 Jan and 5 Jul 1847).

duration and expense, the government soon gave consideration to the proposal to compel Mexico to sue for peace by attacking Mexico City by way of Vera Cruz. It was 18 November 1846, however, before Polk reluctantly appointed Maj. Gen. Winfield Scott to the command of the expedition.

Scott had given much thought to the planning of such an expedition. He doubted whether the government ought to risk the attempt unless 12,000 to 15,000 men were assigned to the task. He considered a minimum force of 10,000 as indispensable, but sooner than delay his start and run the risk of exposing his men to the dangers of the black vomito that would be prevalent on the coast after mid-April, he thought the expedition ought to go forward with the first 8,000 men that might be embarked off Point Isabel. For operations into the interior, an additional 10,000 men would be required as reinforcements. To obtain the troops for the Vera Cruz expedition, Taylor's Army was cut almost in half and ordered to stand on the defensive at Monterey. From Taylor's forces, Scott called for Regulars—4,000 infantry, 500 cavalry, and 2 field batteries of light artillery—and volunteers—4,000 infantry and 500 cavalry—to be embarked from Tampico and the Brazos. Of the eight new regiments of foot volunteers to be sent from the United States, he expected to take three or four regiments, leaving the remainder for Taylor's command.[181]

Scott estimated that he would need 140 flatboats to put ashore at Vera Cruz, at once, 5,000 men with eight pieces of light artillery. About 1,000 horses for officers, cavalry, and artillery would be required as well as a ponton train to pass rivers. In the projets he submitted before his appointment to command, he recommended the immediate initiation of such preparatory measures. Ships to transport men and supplies ought also to be chartered, for the whole expedition should be afloat and beyond the Rio Grande by 15 January 1847, or, at the very latest, by 1 February to allow plenty of time for operations before the appearance of the yellow fever. Scott left Washington on 24 November, having made ample requisitions for ordnance, ordnance stores, and transportation facilities.

Almost 2 months earlier, Quartermaster General Jesup, with the approval of the Secretary of War, had left Washington for New Orleans to assume direction of Quartermaster affairs there and in Mexico so that any exigency might be promptly provided for, without the delay resulting from waiting for instructions from Washington. To eliminate

---

[181] House *Ex. Doc.* No. 60, pp. 839–40 (Scott to Taylor, 20 Dec 1846); pp. 851–53 (Scott to Butler, 3 Jan 1847); pp. 1268–70 (Scott projet, 27 Oct 1846); pp. 1270–73 (Scott projet, 12 Nov 1846); pp. 1274–75 (Scott to SW, 21 Nov 1846).

any opposition to his presence in the field—Jesup was the senior of every officer serving in Mexico—he had disclaimed any desire for a military command and had proposed to go in his capacity as an officer of the staff, ready to obey the orders of General Taylor or any other officer in command.[182] Jesup's inspection of Quartermaster operations in the field soon convinced him that the officers of his Department did not merit the criticism made of them. They had been obliged to guess what might be wanted and, as a result, risk an oversupply of some articles and an insufficiency of others. "No provident foresight," Jesup charged, had been exercised by any one in command.[183]

His inspection also resulted in unfavorable comment on the performance of both the Ordnance and Topographical Departments whose duties in the field, he charged, were being executed by quartermasters. He maintained that if a proper topographical survey had been made of the Rio Grande, and of the bays and harbors through which the supplies of the Army had to pass, much inconvenience and expense would have been saved. Jesup suggested that various works ought also to have been constructed during the summer, particularly a railroad from the mouth of the Rio Grande to Brazos. It would have saved at least half a million dollars during the present campaign, he informed the Secretary of War, conveniently forgetting that the Topographical Department had been as short of funds as the Quartermaster's Department.[184]

Jesup did not simply indulge in criticism; he took steps to improve supply. Since the forwarding of supplies by steamers from the depot at Point Isabel to the mouth of the Rio Grande had become hampered because so many vessels had been disabled and wrecked, and because the weather in the winter of 1846–47 was so bad as to obstruct navigation by the remaining boats, Jesup ordered the depot quartermaster to form a train of 200 wagons to keep up a direct communication by land. Use of the land route required the Department to build a bridge across a bayou, for although the distance was only about 10 miles the transporting of supplies would have been delayed by the necessity for ferrying wagons across the bayou.[185] Since all supplies landed at the Brazos had either to be reshipped or transported on wagon trains to a depot at the mouth of the Rio Grande, Jesup, to save both time and expense, also directed that all quartermaster stores, destined for the northern part of Mexico, be shipped directly to the depot at the mouth of the river, except when

[182] *Ibid.*, p. 562 (Jesup to Marcy, 26 Sep 1846); p. 563 (Marcy to Jesup, 1 Oct 1846).

[183] *Ibid.*, p. 566 (Jesup to Marcy, 27 Nov 1846).

[184] House *Ex. Doc.* No. 119, pp. 273–74 (Jesup to Marcy, 2 Jan 1847); p. 274 (Col. J. J. Abert to Marcy, 15 Jan 1847); p. 275 (Lt. Col. G. Talcott to Marcy, 22 Jan 1847).

[185] (1) *Ibid.*, pp. 273–74. (2) House *Ex. Doc.* No. 8, p. 546 (Rpt of QMG, 24 Nov 1847).

weather or the size of the ship required delivery of the cargo at the Brazos. Extensive storehouses and workshops were erected there as well as a dry dock to permit repair of steamboats and other vessels. He further suggested that the Commissary General of Subsistence also route his shipment of rations to the same depot.[186]

To expedite transportation in the field, he recommended changes in the packaging of ordnance and subsistence supplies. He urged the use of waterproof materials to protect the supplies sent to the Army and to decrease the heavy expense of replacement of damaged articles. He also proposed reduction in the size of packages to promote ease of handling. He recommended that the Secretary of War issue orders to that effect to both the Ordnance and Subsistence Departments.[187]

"Had we foreseen the nature of the navigation of the Mexican coasts and harbors, and of the Rio del Norte, and built suitable steamboats several months ago, a million dollars might have been saved by this time," Jesup lamented in November 1846.[188] Since the need had not been foreseen, he set about purchasing more ships and to expedite the lightering of cargoes at the Brazos he had Col. S. H. Long, of the Topographical Engineers at Louisville, Ky., build a steamer to specifications for use there.[189]

He found his Department deficient in personnel. He had little use for the newly appointed volunteer quartermasters. Not more than a fifth or a sixth of the quartermasters and assistants appointed from civil life, he declared, would make even tolerable wagon and forage masters. He feared that frauds had been committed, not with the concurrence of these officers but in spite of their "best exertions." To this charge of incapacity, Secretary Marcy slyly replied that Jesup surely could not be speaking wholly from personal knowledge since these appointments had been presented to the President "with the highest testimonials of qualifications."[190] To promote efficiency and economy, Jesup recommended and obtained the appointment of four additional majors and ten additional assistants from the Army.[191]

He was less successful in his efforts to obtain a militarized service corps to support the troops of the line. His greatest difficulty during the war was to obtain the mechanics, teamsters, and laborers required for carrying out the operations of his Department. The several armies

[186] RG 92, OQMG Consolidated Correspondence File, Box 477 (Jesup to Gibson, 30 Jan 1847).

[187] House *Ex. Doc.* No. 60, pp. 569–70 (Jesup to Marcy, 1 Jan 1847).

[188] *Ibid.*, p. 564 (Jesup to Marcy, 7 Nov 1846).

[189] House *Ex. Doc.* No. 119, pp. 444–45 (Jesup to Long, 24 Nov 1846).

[190] RG 107, OSW, Military Book, vol. 27, pp. 195–96 (Marcy to Jesup, 8 Feb 1847).

[191] RG 107, OSW, Reports to Congress, vol. 6, p. 26 (SW to Benton, 29 Jan 1847).

were too small for him to obtain assistance from them by detail of soldiers. Civilians had to be hired—several thousand of them at times—at high rates of wages and taken at heavy expense to the points where their labors were required. Few would engage for longer than 6 months; fewer still would re-engage. At the moment when they became qualified to render efficient service they claimed their discharge, often in the midst of the most critical and important operations and at places where it was impossible to replace them. The only solution, Jesup urged, was the organization of a corps to serve during the war, subject to the laws governing the Army and entitled to all the advantages given to the troops of the line.[192] His proposal brought no response, and, in fact, 65 years were to pass before Congress in 1912 enacted legislation bringing about this reform.

Jesup was in the field at the time preparations for the Vera Cruz expedition were undertaken. He met with General Scott at the Brazos to discuss the plan of campaign and its supply problems. He personally supervised the arrangements made for the transportation of the troops from New Orleans and Mobile and for the shipment of supplies from the Brazos, Tampico, and New Orleans. He accompanied the expedition to Vera Cruz, landing there with Maj. Gen. Robert Patterson's division of volunteers. During the course of the siege, he twice went to Tampico to hasten forward troops, supplies, and the means of transportation. Not until 31 March 1847, after Vera Cruz had been occupied, did he leave for Washington.[193]

While General Jesup gave "the utmost possible efficiency" to Quartermaster service in the field, Colonel Stanton directed preparations for the Vera Cruz expedition in Washington. One of the most difficult tasks imposed on the Department was the construction and dispatch within 30 days of the 140 surf boats required by Scott for landing his troops at Vera Cruz. Lacking personnel for all the duties to be attended to, Stanton hired Capt. Richard F. Loper, of the firm of Loper and Baird of Philadelphia, on a per diem basis as a special agent of the Department. To Loper he assigned the task of contracting at Atlantic Coast shipyards for the construction of the 140 barges, to be built in conformity with drawings and specifications furnished by the Navy. Lt. George M. Totten of the Navy was detailed to assist Loper.[194]

Each barge was intended to carry 50 to 80 men. To facilitate

---

[192] House *Ex. Doc.* No. 8, p. 548 (Rpt of QMG, 24 Nov 1847).

[193] RG 92, OQMG Letter Book, vol. 41, p. 256 (Jesup to C. M. Bagbee, 20 Oct 1848).

[194] (1) RG 92, OQMG Letter Book, vol. 38, pp. 302–03 (Stanton to Loper, 29 Nov 1846); pp. 343–44 (Stanton to Totten, 21 Dec 1846). (2) RG 92, OQMG Consolidated Correspondence File, Box 582 (Loper to Stanton, 5 Dec 1846).

shipment by permitting nesting of the boats, they were constructed in three lengths—40 feet, 37 feet 9 inches, and 35 feet 9 inches.[195]   It was almost as difficult to transport the barges as it was to construct them. There were few ships capable of carrying them on deck, and, in any case, Stanton found that they could not be sent as freight.   Consequently, he had to purchase a number of ships and cut the decks open to permit placing the barges in their holds and between decks.   When the ships sailed, Stanton sent along six experienced boatbuilders and ship carpenters to serve the Department in the field.[196]   The deadline of 1 January was met; the ships were promptly dispatched with their cargoes of barges, but bad weather frustrated the efforts of the Department to deliver them at Vera Cruz.   Only 65 of the 140 surf boats arrived in time to be used in landing the troops.

Before General Scott left Washington, he had urged the War Department to send out a number of large ships in ballast from the eastern ports because he feared that the expedition might be delayed.   It would be impossible to obtain a sufficient number of vessels at New Orleans and Mobile.   Scott had estimated that to transport 14,000 men with horses, artillery, stores, and surf boats, a total of 50 ships of from 500 to 750 tons each would be required.[197]   Two weeks later, the Secretary of War, much concerned at the exorbitant costs of transportation on the Atlantic Coast where freight rates were high, inquired of Jesup just what amount of transportation could be furnished at New Orleans and Mobile.   Replying on 27 December, Jesup, then at the Brazos, assured the Secretary that transportation for all the troops that might be drawn from Taylor's Army and for all supplies taken from the Brazos depot or New Orleans could be provided there by the Quartermaster's Department.   He estimated that the government-owned ships in the Gulf could carry 3,000 men, with all their supplies, and that if additional means of transportation were required they could be chartered at New Orleans on favorable terms.[198]

In the meantime, on 15 December, Secretary Marcy sent Jesup a detailed statement on the means of transportation that would be required. He proposed sending out the Massachusetts, New York, Virginia, and

[195] William G. Temple, *Memoir of the Landing of the United States Troops at Vera Cruz in 1847* (Philadelphia, 1896), pp. 60–62.

[196] RG 92, OQMG Letter Book, vol. 38, pp. 384–85, 404–05 (Stanton to Jesup, 14 and 22 Jan 1847).

[197] House *Ex. Doc.* No. 60, p. 1219 (Scott to SW, 24 Feb 1848); p. 1274 (Scott to SW, 16 Nov 1846).

[198] (1) RG 107, OSW, Military Book, vol. 27, pp. 95–96 (Marcy to Jesup, 11 Dec 1846). (2) House *Ex. Doc.* No. 119, pp. 270–71 (Jesup to Marcy, 27 Dec 1846).

North Carolina regiments from Boston, New York, Old Point Comfort, and Wilmington, respectively. The Pennsylvania, Mississippi, and Louisiana regiments would proceed via New Orleans while the South Carolina regiment would move out from Mobile. Each regiment with its ordnance and stores would require 3 ships so that the regiments leaving from the Atlantic Coast would need a total of 12 ships. The War Department estimated that an additional 5 ships would be required to transport the surf boats besides the 10 requested by Scott to be sent out in ballast, unless stores could be put on board. That left 14 ships to be provided by the Quartermaster's Department at New Orleans to make up a total of 41 ships for the expedition.[199] When Marcy received Jesup's assurances that transportation could be provided at New Orleans, he countermanded the order he had given Colonel Stanton for chartering the 10 ships to be sent out in ballast.

Scott later charged that the embarkation of the expedition at the Brazos and Tampico was delayed, in whole or in part, from 15 January to 9 March 1847, because the 10 ships on which he had confidently relied were not furnished.[200] Secretary Marcy was remiss in not notifying Scott and Jesup of his action, but the expedition was not delayed for want of ships. Jesup admitted that he had expected those 10 ships, for he thought they would be on their way before his letter of 27 December was received at the War Department. The weather had been so bad, however, that Jesup considered it unsafe to depend on their arrival, and he had made his arrangements without counting upon them and had so informed General Scott. Instead of the 27 vessels that it had been estimated would be needed for transportation of troops and supplies from the Atlantic Coast, Colonel Stanton had actually dispatched 53 ships, barques, brigs, and schooners, and, in place of the 14 ships, the Department had furnished 163 vessels at New Orleans, Brazos, and Tampico.[201]

Though want of ships caused no delay other factors did. Under the most favorable circumstances, it would have required time to organize so extensive a transport service, but because of drenching rains throughout the month of January, the ships chartered at New Orleans could not be prepared and sent to sea as rapidly as was desirable. Each transport was to carry enough fuel and water for 60 days and preferable for 90. Ships were detained at New Orleans first for want of extra water casks and then for lack of seamen. Supposed to leave New Orleans by 24 January and be at the Brazos by 1 February, they had put in no

[199] RG 107, OSW, Military Book, vol. 27, pp. 117–18 (Marcy to Jesup, 15 Dec 1846).
[200] House *Ex. Doc.* No. 60, pp. 1219–20 (Scott to Marcy, 24 Feb 1848).
[201] *Ibid.,* pp. 1253–55 (Jesup to SW, 17 Apr 1848).

appearance by 12 February, and Scott reported that the expedition was running a month behind the schedule he had set in November. [202]

Assembling the troops also ran behind schedule. Taylor's forces were dispersed at Parras, Saltillo, Monterey, Victoria, and Tampico, and the troops taken for service on the Vera Cruz expedition had to be drawn into Tampico and Brazos from distant places. As a consequence, Scott reported that Taylor's troops were not likely to arrive at the embarkation points before 25 January.[203] The January storms that prevented prompt departure of the ships from New Orleans also delayed the arrival at the rendezvous point of ships from the eastern ports carrying troops and supplies. Stanton had promptly chartered and dispatched the ships, yet, of the ordnance stores and the siege train requisitioned by Scott in November, only about one-half had arrived when the attack was made on Vera Cruz.[204]

During the last week in February, nearly all of the Regulars and large numbers of the volunteers arrived at the Lobos Islands, the rendezvous point for the expedition. On 2 March, the fleet of transports set off for Anton Lizardo, the next rendezvous point located about 200 miles from the Lobos anchorage, where the Navy squadron under Commodore David Conner was waiting to lend its assistance. Originally, Scott had intended to land his troops directly from the large transports on which he had expected them to sail. But the use of a large number of small vessels for transporting the troops made that plan impracticable. When Commodore Conner offered to transport the Army on the vessels of the squadron, Scott accepted and revised his arrangements. This first amphibious operation had been worked out in detail and was executed with smooth precision by the Army and Navy. Using the 65 surf boats, each of which was conducted by a naval officer and rowed by sailors of the squadron, Scott's Army of 10,000, each man carrying in his haversack bread and cooked meat for a 2 days' supply, landed on the beach unopposed and without accident.[205]

The surf boats were also used to land supplies. Horses and mules transported in small, light-draft vessels were brought as near the beach as the vessel could get, thrown overboard, and made to swim ashore. Those transported on large ships were first transferred to the Navy

[202] *Ibid.*, pp. 841, 855 (Scott to Brooke, 23 Dec 1846, 12 Jan 1848); p. 891 (Scott to Marcy, 12 Feb 1847); p. 893 (Scott to Patterson, 9 Feb 1847).

[203] *Ibid.*, p. 847 (Scott to Commodore D. Conner, 26 Dec 1846); p. 855 (Scott to Brooke, 12 Jan 1847).

[204] (1) *Ibid.*, pp. 1219–20 (Scott to SW, 24 Feb 1848). (2) RG 92, OQMG Letter Book, vol. 38, pp. 329–30 (Stanton to Vinton, 13 Dec 1846); pp. 437–38 (Stanton to Jesup, 16 Feb 1847).

[205] (1) Temple, *Memoir of the Landing of the United States Troops at Vera Cruz*, pp. 63–66. (2) House *Ex. Doc.* No. 8, pp. 216–17 (Scott to Marcy, 12–13 Mar 1847).

steamer *Petrita*, taken in as far as possible, and then made to swim ashore in tow of surf boats. In this way, nearly 500 got ashore in one day by a single division of boats consisting of 10 surf boats.[206]

Many animals were, however, lost. A storm interrupted operations and as many as 40 vessels were blown on the beach by the norther. Communication with the ships at anchor was disrupted until smooth seas made it possible to begin again the task of landing ammunition, heavy mortars, packsaddles, wagons, and rations. The beach, covered with piles of stores and crowded with men, looked like the levee of a vast commercial city.[207] While commissaries and quartermasters worked to get their stores under cover, the bombardment of Vera Cruz went on and, on 29 March, the Army occupied the city.

Observers believed that months would elapse after the capture of Vera Cruz before an army would be able to advance into the interior, but 10 days later a division of Regulars under Brig. Gen. D. E. Twiggs began a forced march to Jalapa in the hope of obtaining much-needed draft animals. Scott was handicapped by inadequate means of land transportation, and it was anticipated that mules as well as forage and subsistence could be more easily obtained at Jalapa than at Vera Cruz. Not a tenth part of the Army's needs in horses, mules, and oxen, Scott reported, could be supplied at Vera Cruz.

Supply plans had been formulated to meet the Army's need for land transportation. For his immediate needs, Scott had advised Capt. A. R. Hetzel, then senior quartermaster at the Brazos, that he would require 100 wagons and mule teams to follow closely on the heels of the expedition to furnish the necessary initial means of transportation.[208] Having attended to the transportation of troops and supplies from the Brazos, Hetzel, at Scott's orders, proceeded to Vera Cruz where he organized and, until his death from yellow fever, administered the Quartermaster depot he established there. Early in April, Hetzel had 180 wagons and teams ready for the move to Jalapa.

Far more land transportation was required for the Army as a whole and the need for such preparations had been called to Jesup's attention as early as January. For an army of 10,000 taking up the march into the interior of Mexico, Scott had later informed Jesup, he would need about 800 to 1,000 wagons with 5-mule teams, 2,000 to 3,000 pack mules, and 300 to 500 draft animals for the siege train.[209] Jesup had already ordered the Philadelphia quartermaster to have 400 wagons made with 2,000 sets

---

[206] Temple, *Memoir of the Landing of the United States Troops at Vera Cruz*, p. 69.
[207] Furber, *Twelve Months Volunteer*, pp. 505–13.
[208] House *Ex. Doc.* No. 60, p. 884 (Scott to Hetzel, 2 Feb 1847).
[209] *Ibid.*, pp. 912, 913 (Scott to Jesup, 11 Jan, 19 Mar 1847).

of mule harness, to be kept on hand subject to further orders. Early in April, there were some 300 wagons on board ships, but Hetzel feared many had been lost in the storms that plagued the expedition.[210]

Scott and Jesup had agreed before the expedition began that the Army would have to rely on the country about to become the theater of operations for two-thirds of the draft animals needed, and upon northern Mexico and the United States for the other third. According to Jesup, these expectations were well founded at the time since the country about Vera Cruz, Alvarado, and Tlacontalpan abounded in horses, mules, and cattle. On 30 March, Brig. Gen. J. A. Quitman, in a joint operation with Commodore M. C. Perry, was sent against Alvarado to neutralize the people of that section, acquire a harbor for Perry's small vessels, and open and secure the resources of the area. "An injudicious movement in anticipation of General Quitman," made by the commander of a Navy ship, resulted in the surrender of both Alvarado and Tlacotalpan, but without securing the resources behind them. That action defeated one of the prime objects of General Scott in sending out the expedition and also the expectations of the Quartermaster's Department. In consequence, the Department had to procure most of the draft animals required by the Army at New Orleans, Brazos Santiago, and Tampico.[211] Quartermaster General Jesup, then at Vera Cruz, had returned to these ports to hurry forward the land transportation that Scott required. Hunt at New Orleans reported that he sent a total of 336 wagons and 2,444 horses to Vera Cruz, while the assistant quartermaster at Tampico purchased and sent 548 wagons and 4,226 mules.[212]

The means of transportation slowly increased, and Capt. James R. Irwin, appointed chief quartermaster with Scott's Army, "showed great energy and powers of combination," Scott reported. By 20 April, there were 500 wagons on the road and 250 pack mules.[213] The hope of doubling the means of transportation by the forced move to Jalapa, however, was not realized. Contrary to expectation, subsistence, forage, and draft animals proved to be scarce there. Large supplies of animals could not be obtained in the enemy's country until after the fall of Puebla. Getting essential supplies—ammunition, clothing, salt, medi-

[210] (1) *Ibid.*, p. 908 (Scott to Marcy, 5 Apr 1847). (2) RG 92, OQMG Letter Book, vol. 38, pp. 415–46 (Stanton to Jesup, 29 Jan 1847). (3) RG 107, OSW, Military Book, vol. 27, p. 194 (SW to Jesup, 8 Feb 1847).

[211] (1) *Ibid.,* pp. 917–18 (Quitman to H. L. Scott, 7 Apr 1847). (2) House *Ex. Doc.* No. 8, p. 547 (Rpt of QMG, 24 Nov 1848).

[212] (1) RG 92, OQMG Consolidated Correspondence File, Box 659 (Hunt Rpt, 2 May 1846–7 July 1847). (2) *Rpt of SW, 1848–49*, p. 218 (Rpt of Tampico Operations).

[213] (1) House *Ex. Doc.* No. 60, pp. 928–29 (Scott to Marcy, 11 Apr 1847). (2) RG 92, CGP, Irwin, Letters Sent, No. 97 (Irwin to Jesup, 25 Apr 1847).

DEFENSE OF PACK TRAIN

cines, and hospital stores—forward to Jalapa was hampered by the deficient means of transportation. The heat, the sand on the road below Cerro Gordo, the danger of yellow fever, the threat of having trains attacked and destroyed by the Mexicans, and the consequent necessity of escorting them on the 70 miles between Vera Cruz and Jalapa added to the difficulties of getting the supplies forward.[214]

The greatest obstacle of all was the lack of efficient teamsters. To man the wagons, Irwin got permission to hire as teamsters volunteers whose services were about to expire. Dragoons and infantrymen were also detailed as teamsters, but not one in 10, Hetzel reported, was capable of driving a team.[215] Time worked no improvement in this situation, the inexperienced teamsters, driving teams, in many cases, unbroken

[214] House *Ex. Doc.* No. 60, pp. 946–47 (Scott to Col. H. Wilson, 23 Apr 1847); p. 948 (Scott to Worth, 23 Apr 1847); pp. 944–46 (Scott to Marcy, 28 Apr 1847).

[215] (1) RG 92, CGP, Irwin, Letters Sent, No. 97 (Irwin to Patterson, 25 Apr 1847). (2) RG 92, CGP, Hetzel, Letters Sent, No. 85 (Hetzel to Col. H. Wilson, 9 Jun 1847).

to harness, over rough roads resulted in such a high rate of wear and tear that Irwin was of the opinion that wagons, harness, and animals would have to be replaced every 4 months.[216]

Breadstuffs, beef, mutton, sugar, coffee, rice, beans, and forage, Scott hoped to find on the line of operations. The Army expected to pay for such supplies because, without the pursuit of such a policy, all provisions and forage would be withheld, concealed, or destroyed by the Mexicans, and all military operations would come to a halt while the troops spread out in search of food.[217] Both the Subsistence and the Quartermaster's Departments, however, were much hampered by a lack of funds. The Chief Commissary, Scott reported, had not received a dollar from the United States since the Army landed at Vera Cruz. By the end of July, he owed more than $200,000 and was obliged to operate on credit at a great disadvantage. Chief Quartermaster Irwin was equally hard pressed for funds. Both officers had sold drafts, though little could be obtained from them "this side of the capital," and both had borrowed so heavily from the paymaster that the troops had some 4 months' pay due them.[218]

The expenditures of the Quartermaster's Department were particularly heavy not only because of the outlay for animals and grain but also because it was furnishing supplies and making disbursements for the Medical and Engineer Departments.[219] On 30 April, Captain Irwin requested that $500,000 be placed to his credit at Vera Cruz. Only $300,000 arrived and Captain Hetzel retained $175,000 of that amount. Of the $125,000 forwarded to him by Hetzel, only $61,000 reached Irwin at Puebla in July, the difference having been spent on the road.[220] At that time, Captain Irwin protested against the use of the ruinous credit system. He could not raise $20,000 at Vera Cruz on a premium of 8 percent, he protested, and before he had received any part of the money requested in April, he had been reduced to the humiliating necessity of borrowing $500 at a time from a gambler to enable him to furnish fuel for cooking and forage to keep the animals alive.

Without the services of Louis S. Hargous, an American merchant at Vera Cruz who acted as General Scott's financial agent, the Army would

---

[216] (1) RG 92, CGP, Irwin, Letters Sent, No. 97 (Irwin to Hunt and to Jesup, 30 Apr 1847). (2) Compare the experiences of Col. J. S. McIntosh in attempting to bring a wagon train and reinforcements to Pueblo. House *Ex. Doc.* No. 8, appendix pp. 4–9 (McIntosh Rpt, 9 Jul 1847).

[217] House *Ex. Doc.* No. 60, pp. 944, 963 (Scott to Marcy, 28 Apr, 20 May 1847).

[218] *Ibid.*, pp. 994, 1012–13 (Scott to Marcy, 4 Jun, 25 Jul 1847).

[219] RG 92, CGP, Irwin, Letters Sent, No. 97 (Irwin to Hunt and to Jesup, 30 Apr 1847). Irwin later sought to be relieved of the necessity of continuing to make disbursements for the Engineer Department. (Irwin to Capt. H. L. Scott, 23 Jul 1847).

[220] *Ibid.*, (Irwin to Jesup and Hetzel, 18 Jul 1847).

have been even worse off for funds. At Vera Cruz, his firm took $90,000 of Irwin's drafts when there were no funds there to redeem them, and at Puebla he was the only resource of both the Quartermaster's and Subsistence Departments after the funds borrowed from the Pay Department had been exhausted. Without knowing how the Department's credit would stand when the Army reached Mexico City, Irwin had engaged at Puebla to take $450,000 from Hargous at par. His arrangements with Hargous terminated about the end of October. By that time, the Army had occupied the capital and drafts drawn by Irwin on the Quartermaster's offices at Washington, New York, or New Orleans were readily negotiated. In fact, they commanded a premium and if the old Mexico duty of 6 percent was kept upon the exportation of specie and bullion, Irwin reported, they would always command a premium of that amount. In consequence, although the War Department had made arrangements with August Belmont, the New York agent of the Rothschilds, to make funds available to any paymaster or quartermaster designated by Scott, Irwin made no immediate contract with Belmont since the latter required the payment of interest on drafts then worth a premium.[221] Irwin thought that he had served the Department to better advantage than the Secretary of War had in his contract with Belmont.

Scott had followed up the victory at Cerro Gordo by sending his troops on to Jalapa and then to Puebla. By mid-May, Puebla was occupied, but Scott's force was soon reduced to an effective strength of 5,820 men because, the service of the volunteer regiments being about to expire, Scott sent them home early enough to avoid the season of yellow fever at Vera Cruz. His force was now too small to keep open a line of communications with Vera Cruz, and consequently he decided to abandon Jalapa, concentrate his strength at Puebla, and await reinforcements there. By the first week in August, he was ready to begin his advance with about 11,000 men, the Chief Commissary and Quartermaster having used the interim to obtain funds by one means or another and to procure provisions, forage, and draft animals. Scott's drive carried him to the gates of Mexico City before the end of the month. When a temporary armistice failed to produce peace, the battle was resumed. Scott occupied Mexico City on 14 September 1847.

There, Captain Irwin set up a quartermaster depot in the custom house under a depot quartermaster, Capt. R. Allen, who was directed to lay in a supply of forage, horse shoes, and quartermaster stores. Capt. J. W. McKinstry was put in charge of the clothing depot.[222] On

[221] (1) *Ibid.*, (Irwin to Jesup, 26 Oct 1847). (2) Hitchcock, *Fifty Years in Camp and Field*, pp. 258, 289, 291, 292.

[222] RG 92, CGP, Irwin, Letters Sent, No. 97 (Order No. 17, 15 Sep 1847).

MARCH FROM PUEBLA

1 November, a train of 400 wagons left Mexico City for Vera Cruz to obtain supplies. Everything needed by the Army could be obtained at the capital, but at such increased prices as to make it expedient, when practicable, to transport supplies from the coast. Irwin had ample transportation available and only 250 loaded wagons were to return, the rest to be used by the troops between Puebla and Vera Cruz. The supplies to be obtained were principally clothing, some few subsistence items for the sick, and a small quantity of particular descriptions of ammunition. The Army had taken more ammunition in every instance than it had expended. The Army needed 300 good horses for the dragoons and artillery. A month later, Irwin had heard nothing from Vera Cruz, and he complained about his idle transportation at the capital. But with a garrison of only 6,000 effective men there, sufficient escorts could not be spared for trains.[223]

Demobilization

Peace negotiations had been delayed by internal political difficulties but, on 2 February 1848, a treaty was signed at Guadalupe Hidalgo. As soon as ratifications were exchanged on 30 May, the troops began

[223] *Ibid.,* (Irwin to Jesup, 26 Oct, 8 Dec 1847).

evacuating Mexico City. Captain Irwin had died on 10 January and Maj. Osborn Cross was appointed to succeed him. To him fell the task of returning the troops to Vera Cruz. When he called for transportation to rendezvous at Vera Cruz, Major Cross reported that 1,137 officers, 26,104 rank and file, and more than 5,000 mechanics, laborers, and teamsters would require transportation home.[224]

Once again the Quartermaster's Department had to charter and assemble a transport fleet to remove not only the troops at Vera Cruz but also at Tampico and at the Brazos. When confirmation of the treaty's ratification reached Washington, Jesup ordered Colonel Stanton to charter 20 ships, averaging 600 tons each, or an equivalent number of smaller vessels on the Atlantic Coast. Only about 14 ships from the east coast were used. At the same time, Maj. D. D. Tompkins, who had succeeded Hunt at New Orleans in July 1847, was directed to charter enough transports to carry 7,000 men. Sail vessels of not less than 300 tons were to be preferred, and calculating one man to each two tons' burden, some 45 ships would have been required at the minimum tonnage. On requisition from the depot quartermasters or the commanding officers of the troops, Tompkins was to charter additional ships. All ships were to carry a 60-day supply of water, allowing one gallon per man per day independent of the water required for the ship's officers and crew on the trip out and back. Charters were to be made for a designated sum per month, limited to the time they might be required by the Department.[225] Jesup estimated that a total force of 40,890 troops and civilian mechanics, laborers, and teamsters would have to be brought home at a cost of $800,000 to $1,000,000.[226]

To supervise the removal of the troops and civilians employed by the Army at Vera Cruz, Jesup sent Maj. Thomas Swords to act as general superintendent of embarkation. Swords arrived on 27 June, but the embarkation of troops had begun on 30 May, under the local quartermaster and, by 2 July, 65 vessels had carried 18,331 troops to New Orleans. A month later, the last transports departed carrying the civilian employees and the horses. Almost all the ships sailed for New Orleans, largely because it was impossible to provision them for a longer voyage from the supplies in the depot at Vera Cruz. Among the ships used in the first embarkation, 18 were chartered at Vera Cruz and 31 at New Orleans, while 16 were government-owned ships.[227]

[224] RG 92, OQMG Consolidated Correspondence File, Box 660 (Cross to Tompkins, 21 May 1848).
[225] RG 92, OQMG Letter Book, vol. 40, pp. 488–89; 490–91 (Jesup to Stanton and Tompkins, 8 Jun 1848).
[226] *Ibid.,* p. 502 (Jesup to Hon. James J. McKay, 10 Jun 1848).
[227] RG 92, OQMG Consolidated Correspondence File, Box 660 (Swords Rpts, 2 Jul, 22 Aug

There were considerable quantities of surplus property in the hands of quartermasters in Mexico when the war ended. All of them were instructed to sell such Quartermaster property as could not be conveniently moved from the country. Such instructions did not include animals and wagons. Jesup directed Major Cross to ship from Vera Cruz all good, serviceable wagons and all sound, well-broken mules and horses. He sent similar instructions to Maj. D. H. Vinton, quartermaster at Monterey, who had succeeded Colonel Whiting. Vinton did not ship the animals there, but sent 3,000 mules, 700 horses, and 400 wagons through the country to western Louisiana. Jesup then detailed a Quartermaster officer to arrange for the distribution of the best of them to the southwestern posts and for the sale of the remainder.[228] Jesup also instructed Assistant Quartermaster McKissack at Santa Fe to dispose of unfit articles but to retain all serviceable property for use at Santa Fe or at such other posts as might be permanently occupied by the Army in New Mexico.[229]

At New Orleans, Major Tompkins had to determine how many light-draft steamers would have to be retained for service on the Rio Grande by the Department, as well as the number of lighters required at Brazos and La Vaca, and the transportation requirements in the Gulf generally. If he could obtain fair prices, Jesup later instructed him to sell the public vessels, except for about a half dozen of the lightest-draft schooners and five designated steamers. He also suggested that three or four of the best brigs and barks might be useful on the Pacific.[230] By order of the Secretary of War, the steam propellers *Massachusetts* and *Edith* were sent to the Pacific with troops and stores, and four schooners were selected for service there. Most of the Quartermaster fleet was disposed of, some of the vessels being transferred to the Navy, and others turned over to the Topographical Department and to the Treasury Department for the coast survey. To avoid any criticism, Major Tompkins invited proposals in writing in the sale of vessels. The Department sold at auction all other property, but under specific contracts governing the compensation paid auctioneers.[231] By 1849, the

---

1848). A third report covering the period 2–18 July is missing and no similar reports were found covering any embarkation of troops or shipment of property from Tampico or the Brazos.

[228] RG 92, OQMG Letter Book, vol. 40, p. 470 (Jesup to Cross, 30 May 1848); p. 497 (Jesup to Vinton, 9 Jun 1848); vol. 41, pp. 131–32 (Jesup to Mackay, 8 Sep 1848).

[229] *Ibid.*, vol. 40, p. 511 (14 Jun 1848).

[230] *Ibid.*, vol. 40, pp. 611–12; 653 (Jesup to Tompkins, 19 Jul, 3 Aug 1848).

[231] (1) *Ibid.*, vol. 41, pp. 249–50 (Jesup to Tompkins, 18 Oct 1848). (2) *Report of SW, 1848–49*, p. 189 (QMG Rpt, 18 Nov 1848).

Edith having been lost at sea and the *Massachusetts* turned over to the Navy, the Quartermaster's Department retained under its control four sail ships on the Pacific Coast, five steamers in service on the Florida coast, three steamers operating on the Rio Grande, and three schooners used as transports on the Gulf of Mexico.[232]

Disposal of surplus property at the end of the war and, for that matter, supply operations during the war were not carried on without adverse criticism of the Quartermaster's Department.   It was rumored, for example, that the assistant quartermaster at Vera Cruz had allowed enormous compensation to the auctioneer selling surplus public property there.   Lieutenant Colonel Hunt at New Orleans was assailed for "enriching" himself and his relatives with the public money.[233]   Such charges were groundless because the system of accountability under which quartermasters functioned made impossible the frauds of an earlier day.[234]

Under the pressure of immediate needs, higher prices were undoubtedly paid at times for Quartermaster articles than would otherwise have been necessary.   Careless inspection permitted some poor horses to be sent to the Army.   Public transportation was used upon occasion to haul sutlers' stores and, at least in one instance, some circus people and their baggage.[235]   The Department was quick to take corrective action, however, and Jesup could take pride in its prompt support of the armies in the field and its clean record of accountability.   The organization, regulations, and procedures he had hammered out since 1818 had withstood the test of war.

[232] *Report of SW, 1848–49*, p. 194 (QMG Rpt, 18 Nov 1848).
[233] (1) RG 107, OSW, Letters Sent, vol. 28, p. 431 (SW to Jesup, 21 Oct 1848).   (2) RG 92, OQMG Letter Book, vol. 39, p. 375 (Jesup to Hunt, 4 Aug 1847).
[234] See *Report of SW, 1848–49*, p. 193 (QMG Rpt, 18 Nov 1849).
[235] RG 92, OQMG Letter Book, vol. 39, p. 382 (Jesup to Stanton, 5 Aug 1847); p. 207 (Jesup to Hetzel, 10 Jun 1847).

CHAPTER VIII

Supply on the New Frontier
1848–1860

During the years between the Mexican War and the Civil War, the Quartermaster's Department was primarily concerned with the problem of supporting the troops stationed in the new frontier area, most of which had been acquired as a result of the Army's victories in the Mexican War. By the end of that war, the present continental boundary lines of the United States had been established, except for a small strip of land in the southwest acquired by the Gadsden Purchase of 1853. The northern boundary had already been set at the 49th parallel by agreement with Great Britain in June of 1846. To maintain the peace throughout this vast frontier area, in which the fur trader, the miner, and the settler were pushing forward relentlessly, the Army spread its forces as widely as possible, though its reduced postwar strength permitted only the thinnest of coverage.

It was not a large Army that the Quartermaster's Department had to supply. In 1850, it had an aggregate strength of 10,763. Ten years later, after Congress had authorized increases, the Army's actual aggregate strength was still no more than 16,006. The distribution and position of the troops was of more significance to the Department than the mere size of the Army. According to a report of the Adjutant General's Office in 1850, there were 2,109 officers and men stationed at 33 posts east of the Mississippi and 6,385 officers and men at 67 posts west of the Mississippi. By 1860, the preponderance of troops located in the western frontier area was even more pronounced. Out of an actual strength of 16,006, the Adjutant General reported 929 men and officers stationed in the Department of the East and 13,143 in the Departments of the West, Texas, New Mexico, Utah, Oregon, and California.[1]

---

[1] (1) House *Ex. Doc.* No. 1, 31st Cong., 2d sess., Pt. 2, p. 116, s.n. 587. (2) Senate *Ex. Doc.* No. 1, 36th Cong., 2d sess., p. 189 ff, s.n. 1079 (AG Rpt, 20 Nov 1860). This total distribution figure of 14,072 does not include men at depots, the Military Academy, recruit rendezvous, and en route.

Clothing Changes

Territorial expansion and distribution of most of the troops at posts west of the Mississippi had a tremendous impact on the work of the Quartermaster's Department. The execution of its basic functions, except that of providing clothing for the Army, became more burdensome and much more expensive than in the past. The size of the Army rather than its distribution was the chief factor governing expenditures for clothing. The number of troops in service during these years was small. Moreover, so much clothing had been left on hand from the Mexican War that there was no need to procure any additional stocks for some years; the immediate problem was one of surplus disposal. That problem was made more difficult early in 1850 when the Secretary of War, yielding to the wishes of many officers, announced the adoption of a new and more practical uniform.[2] Developed out of experience in the Mexican War, the frock-coat style uniform adopted in 1850 was, with a few minor changes, to be worn by the Union soldier in the Civil War.

The general order announcing the new uniform was no sooner published than the Superintendent of the Recruiting Service requisitioned a supply, much to Jesup's exasperation. With more than a million dollars' worth of clothing on hand at the Schuylkill Arsenal and with a Congress bent on economy measures, the Quartermaster General considered it "injudicious and highly prejudicial to the interests of the Army" to request funds for new uniforms.[3] In fact, the Secretary of War soon directed the Department to continue issuing the old uniform until the supply was exhausted, and as late as 1855, though the stock had become insufficient for a year's supply for the whole Army, certain companies were still designated to wear the old uniform.[4] For some years no appropriations were made for clothing.

If service on the frontier had no effect upon either the procurement or the production of clothing at the Schuylkill Arsenal, it did result in demands for clothing items better suited to the needs of campaigning on the plains, as for example, felt hats, in lieu of caps, and buffalo overshoes. In the Mormon expedition, most of the soldiers on the sick report were rendered unfit for duty by frostbitten feet. Soldiers who stood guard or marched in snow shod only in leather bootees were soon incapacitated. From his headquarters at Camp Scott, Brig. Gen. Albert S. Johnston recommended that the government provide a pair of buffalo

---

[2] *War Department General Orders*, GO 2, 13 Feb 1850. Within a few months this order was suspended by GO 25, 23 August 1850.

[3] RG 92, OQMG, Clothing Letter Book, vol. 12, p. 91 (Jesup to Col. C. A. Waite, 22 Apr 1850).

[4] *Ibid.*, vol. 14, pp. 313–14 (Jesup to Col. P. St. George Cooke, 28 Apr 1855).

overshoes for each man serving in that climate, and he approved the admission of that item in the annual estimate of his chief quartermaster.[5] New items, however, had to be approved by the Secretary of War and it was not until the spring of 1859 that buffalo overshoes were shipped to Utah to be carried as organizational items of issue to guards and to troops on detached service.[6]

Since the government during these years did not furnish the troops with mittens, gloves, leggings, or other extra cold-weather garments, the soldiers made for themselves out of "old blankets, skins, pieces of old canvas and cast-off clothing, anything that necessity prompted them to invent for protection from the bitter cold." [7]   Private Eugene Bandel of the Sixth Infantry wrote his parents that hides, tanned by the Indians and finished by the soldiers, were made into warm clothing.   When he was above Fort Pierre in South Dakota, his winter outfit consisted of a coat of tanned deerskin, trousers of buffalo-calf leather with the fur inside, and a head covering of wolfskin with the fur outside.   Two pairs of mocassins replaced his shoes, one pair being made of deerskin, ornamented in Indian fashion, and the second, worn over them, of buffalo-calf leather with the fur inside.[8]

Not only in winter but also in summer the uniform issued to the troops tended to be worn at the post but was discarded on patrols or other service.   While on escort duty with a survey party in southern Kansas Bandel described the "prairie outfit" of the soldier.

Every man is wearing a broad-brimmed hat, each of a different color; white trousers of rough material; a woolen shirt of red, green, blue, or brown—in short, of any and every color, usually open in front and worn like a coat; the shoes (we still have shoes, though who knows how soon we may have to wear mocassins) with the uppers slashed wherever they might chafe in marching.[9]

Purchasing extra garments and adapting his clothing to his needs, the soldier in the field bore little resemblance to the smartly uniformed soldier at a post.

Frontier Construction

Unlike the provision of clothing, two other basic functions of the Quartermaster's Department—construction and transportation—were di-

[5] House *Ex. Doc.* No. 2, 35th Cong., 2d sess., pp. 34-35, s.n. 998 (Johnston to Army Hq. 7 Jan 1858).
[6] RG 92, OQMG Clothing Letter Book, vol. 16, p. 353 (Jesup to Thomas and to Crosman, 29 Jan 1859); vol. 17, p. 43 (Jesup to Crosman, 9 Apr 1859).
[7] Percival Lowe, *Five Years a Dragoon, 1849–1854* (Kansas City, 1926), p. 45.
[8] *Frontier Life in the Army, 1854–1861,* ed. Ralph P. Bieber (Glendale, Calif., 1932), pp. 221–22.
[9] *Ibid.,* p. 124.

rectly affected by the distribution of a majority of the troops in the newly acquired territories. The necessity of occupying numerous posts in the new area, and sometimes at points where construction of even the most temporary structure was attended with heavy expense, increased enormously Quartermaster expenditures for barracks, storehouses, and other military buildings. During fiscal year 1851, for example, Jesup reported that more than $451,000 had been spent for construction and repairs at posts in the new territories—about $73,000 on 19 posts in Texas, $58,000 on 13 posts in New Mexico, $242,000 on 11 or 12 posts in California, and about $78,000 on 2 or 3 posts in Oregon.[10] Less than a third of that amount had been appropriated for barracks and quarters in 1844. Permanent installations in the East also frequently required repairs and added to the overall expenditures.

The years brought no decrease in expenditures for construction and repairs of posts in the new frontier area. Because changes in the location of posts were frequent, only temporary structures were usually built, and these seemingly needed almost constant repairs. Moreover, both distance and the nature of the service that was required in areas, difficult of access and having so few resources that most supplies had to be purchased at high prices, put such expenditures beyond the control of the Department. During fiscal years 1856 and 1858, Congress appropriated $347,000 for construction and repairs in the Department of the Pacific, but that department spent $693,187. The discrepancy between appropriation and expenditure in the Department of the West was almost as great.[11]

Lengthening Supply Lines

To support troops stationed at distant posts on the frontier, supply lines had to be lengthened considerably. Transportation costs contributed even more than construction and repair costs to the increase of Quartermaster expenditures during 1850–60. As Jesup pointed out, western posts before the Mexican War had extended from the Gulf of Mexico to Lake Superior, with most of them either on or near navigable waters and therefore easy of access.[12] In consequence, the troops could be readily and cheaply supplied. Moreover, many of these posts were in well-populated and well-cultivated areas from which they could draw supplies. In contrast, the outposts in 1850 were on the Rio Grande, the Gila, the Pacific Coast, the Columbia River, and Puget's Sound, with

[10] Senate *Ex. Doc.* No. 1, 32d Cong., 1st sess., p. 219, s.n. 611 (QMG's Rpt, 22 Nov 1851).
[11] House *Ex Doc.* No. 2, 35th Cong., 2d sess., pp. 795–96, s.n. 999 (QMG's Rpt, 13 Nov 1858).
[12] See Map 6.

FRONTIER POSTS
AND LINES OF COMMUNICATION
★ Old Frontier Stations now
abandoned
○ Old Frontier Stations still
occupied
● New Frontier Stations
▬ ▬ Extreme Limit of Line of Frontier Stations in 1845
•••••• Lines of Land Transportation
━━━ Lines of River Transportation
▬▬▬ Lines of Ocean Transportation
━━ Boundary Lines
═══ Lines of Land Transportation anterior to War with Mexico

SCALE OF MILES
0 50 100   200   300

Reproduced from QMG's Report, 1851

MAP 6

long intermediate lines of posts between the former frontier and these new outposts. Agricultural resources in the new territories were, for the most part, only partially developed and Indian hostilities in some areas hampered further development. It was therefore inexpedient for the Subsistence Department to contract for subsistence in New Mexico, California, Oregon, and Texas, since in the event a contractor failed to make deliveries, the commissary would have found it impossible to purchase locally. Consequently, the Commissary General of Subsistence supplied troops stationed in the new frontier area by purchase in the open market of the older states, and the Quartermaster's Department transported the rations to the distant posts.[13] Not only rations but also most of the forage and nearly all other supplies, as well as all troop reinforcements, had to be transported from the older states, over long land and water routes, at an enormous expense. Although the authorized strength of the Army in 1850 has increased by little more than 50 percent over that of 1844, the cost of transportation had increased by more than 1,500 percent.[14]

These increased transportation costs resulted not only from the great distances the troops had to be transported in going to and from the various frontier posts but also from the frequency with which changes in station were made in order to utilize to best advantage the services of the small Army. In contrast to the period before the Mexican War, such movements were, for the most part, made by land. Even for the movement of a small number of men, the Quartermaster's Department had to provide a large amount of transportation, since not only the troops' baggage but also supplies of every kind, including subsistence, had to be carried with them. Other than grass upon which the animals might be foraged in the summer, the "uninhabited solitudes and sterile deserts" through which the troops marched yielded nothing for their support.[15]

Upon occasion, troops marched across the continent to the Pacific Coast, the most notable march being that of the Regiment of Mounted Rifles. With Maj. Osborn Cross serving as quartermaster, the regiment left Fort Leavenworth on 10 May 1848 and some 5 months later, after more than 2,000 miles of marching arrived in Oregon.[16] In addition to the 700 horses belonging to the regiment, the Quartermaster's Department provided 1,233 mules, 60 oxen, 41 horses, and 171 wagons. Most of the regiment's horses and a large number of the animals of the wagon

[13] House *Ex. Doc.* No. 1, 31st Cong., 2d sess., Pt. 2, p. 338, s.n. 587 (CGS' Rpt, 19 Oct 1850).
[14] *Ibid.,* pp. 121–22 (QMG's Rpt, 20 Nov 1850).
[15] House *Ex. Doc.* No. 2, 35th Cong., 2d sess., p. 3, s.n. 998 (SW's Rpt, 6 Dec 1858).
[16] House *Ex. Doc.* No. 1, 31st Cong., 2d sess., Pt. 2, pp. 128 ff, s.n. 587 (Cross' Rpt, 20 May 1850).

train were lost on that march, along with thousands of dollars worth of clothing and other supplies.[17]

For the most part, troops ordered to the Pacific Coast were sent from New York by one of two routes—by way of Cape Horn or by way of the Isthmus of Panama. The voyage around the Horn, in sailing ships chartered by the Quartermaster's Department, usually lasted over 5 months. By way of the Isthmus, troops could arrive at San Francisco in a month. The cost of transportation on that route was higher than by way of Cape Horn, for it included the use of first-class steamers on the Atlantic and Pacific Oceans and, until the construction of a railroad in 1855, passage across the Isthmus from Chagres to Panama was accomplished on muleback and by canoe. The use of sail ships on this route was too hazardous since they might be detained too long at Panama, thereby exposing the troops to the danger of cholera. The Department's contracts for the movement of troops by way of this sea and land route usually obliged the contractor to provide the subsistence required en route. In return, the Department paid the contractor an average of $225 for each commissioned officer and $150 for each enlisted soldier, as well as 15 cents per pound of extra baggage, each person being allowed 100 pounds on the steamer and 25 pounds across the Isthmus.[18]

The Department paid the owners a flat sum for ships chartered for the voyage around Cape Horn. Jesup preferred to charter the entire ship for Army use since annual supplies of medicines and subsistence were sent with the troops who were also permitted to take more than the usual amount of baggage with them. Such long-distance water transportation at times called for additional expenditures. On occasion, ships were wrecked at sea, necessitating payments for the work of rescue ships, for replacement of stores lost, and for the charter of still another ship. Sometimes, demurrage had to be paid, as for example, when a ship was detained at Panama during an outbreak of cholera among troops en route to California.[19]

On the Pacific Coast itself, the assistant quartermaster had to furnish transportation at San Francisco for troops ordered to Benecia, San Diego, Astoria, or Fort Vancouver. Early in this period, the Quartermaster's Department owned some transports, but the costs of operation were

[17] Senate *Ex. Doc.* No. 1, 32d Cong., 1st sess., p. 223, s.n. 611 (QMG's Rpt, 22 Nov 1851). In Oregon the regiment could be remounted only at enormous expense. Since most movements there were made by water and a mounted force was not required, the regiment was shortly transferred to Texas and furnished with horses there.

[18] RG 92, Reports of QMG to SW and Heads of Depts., vol. 3, pp. 81–83 (Jesup to SW, 16 Nov 1854). (2) RG 92, OQMG Letter Book, vol. 41, p. 530 (Jesup to Capt. J. L. Folsom, 6 Feb 1849).

[19] House *Ex. Doc.* No. 1, 33d Cong., 2d sess., Pt. 2, p. 73, s.n. 778 (QMG's Rpt, 14 Nov 1854).

extremely high.   The lure of the gold fields made it difficult to hire operating personnel.   No sailor would ship for less than $150 a month, Assistant Quartermaster Robert Allen reported to Jesup.   Captains of steamers in private employment were paid from $700 to $1,500 a month, and masters of sailing vessels, from $300 to $500.[20]   It was cheaper to hire vessels than to maintain government transports, and it became Jesup's policy to replace none of the latter when their services were lost to the Department.[21]

The cost of transporting supplies to sustain the troops at these distant posts also ran high.   Quartermasters sent supplies to the posts on the Pacific Coast by sea, but they were never shipped by way of the Isthmus of Panama; the cost was too prohibitive.   In 1854, it amounted to about $390 a ton, though it was expected that construction of a railroad across the Isthmus the following year would reduce the price of land carriage to a fourth of what it then was and bring the freight charges to $169 a ton for the whole distance.[22]   All supplies for the posts on the Pacific Coast were shipped via Cape Horn at so much per cubic foot. In 1854, for example, shippers charged 90 cents per cubic foot for subsistence stores and 60 cents for other packages, including ammunition.

To supply the posts on the western plains, the Quartermaster's Department depended upon land transportation.   Fort Leavenworth was the frontier depot for all posts on the Santa Fe Trail and the Oregon route.   All supplies were brought to Fort Leavenworth by water from St. Louis, 411 miles away.   Wagon trains then made the long overland hauls—310 miles to Fort Kearny, 637 miles to Fort Laramie, 728 miles to Fort Union, and 821 miles to Santa Fe.   Indianola on Matagorda Bay was the depot for the greater part of the posts in Texas and supported the interior depot at San Antonio.   From Indianola, itself, 540 miles by water from New Orleans, it was 420 miles by wagon to Fort Worth and 803 miles to El Paso.

Contract Freighting

During the Mexican War, the Quartermaster's Department had operated its own wagon trains on the Santa Fe Trail.   That experience had fully shown the disadvantages of using government-owned wagons. Quartermasters found it difficult to hire experienced wagonmasters and

---

[20] (1) Senate *Ex. Doc.* No. 1, 32d Cong., 1st sess., p. 306, s.n. 611 (Allen's Rpt, 30 Jun 1851). (2) RG 92, Reports of QMG to SW and Heads of Depts., vol. 1, pp. 592–95 (Jesup to SW, 15 Mar 1852).

[21] RG 92, OQMG Letter Book, vol. 54, p. 121 (Jesup to Lt. Col. S. Casey, 17 Feb 1860).

[22] RG 92, Reports of QMG to SW and Heads of Depts., vol. 3, p. 82 (Jesup to SW, 16 Nov 1854).

teamsters, and none of the pleas made by Jesup and other Quartermaster officers, then or later, induced Congress to enlist a service corps.   The cost of forage was high; wagons required repairs; equipment had to be replaced; extra animals had to be kept on hand to replace those worn out; and animals had also to be fed and cared for during the winter months when freighting was suspended.   During the winter of 1848–49, for example, Capt. L. C. Easton, assistant quartermaster at Fort Leavenworth, contracted to have a caretaker take charge of 3,862 oxen, 2,062 mules, and 195 horses at 86½ cents per month.   An additional 700 mules were wintered at a rate of 74¾ cents each per month.[23]   Jesup was soon convinced that the system of transporting military stores by government trains was not only more expensive but also more complicated and troublesome than hiring private wagons.

As early as May 1848, the Department resorted to the use of the contract system for overland transportation of some of the supplies destined for Santa Fe.   On 17 May, Captain Easton made a contract with James Brown, under the terms of which the latter transported 200,000 pounds of stores to Santa Fe at a rate of $11.75 per 100 pounds. The government disposed of some of its freighting equipment to Brown, who agreed to purchase 120 wagons at the price they cost the government, as well as such ox-yokes, chains, and other equipment as could be spared. He was to pay for them in specie, but apparently Brown encountered financial difficulties, for about 5 weeks later Easton agreed to deliver all the wagons that the contractor had not already paid for.   Brown was to discharge his indebtedness out of the first money due him on his contract for transporting supplies to Santa Fe.[24]

In 1850, contract freighting for the government was in full operation at Fort Leavenworth.   Contractors' wagons hauled more than five times the quantity of military supplies freighted in government wagons.   The assistant quartermaster at Fort Leavenworth sent out 266 government wagons in 1850.[25]   They carried 580,000 pounds of supplies or about 2,180 pounds per wagon.   In the same year, 658 heavy ox wagons, owned by contractors among whom were such freighters as Joseph Clymer, David Waldo, James Brown, and Brown, Russell & Co., carried military supplies to Santa Fe, Fort Scott in Kansas, to a new post in Arkansas, and to Forts Kearny, Laramie, and Hall on the Oregon Trail.   These contractors' trains, employing 6,600 oxen and 780 men, transported 3,174,783 pounds, averaging over 4,800 pounds per wagon.[26]

[23] Senate *Ex. Doc.* No. 26, 31st Cong., 1st Sess., p. 13, s.n. 554.

[24] *Ibid.*, pp. 12–13.

[25] Of these 10 went to Fort Kearny, 23 to Fort Laramie, 183 to Santa Fe, and 50 to a new post on the Arkansas.

[26] (1) RG 92, Reports of QMG to SW and Heads of Depts., vol. 1, pp. 600–601 (Jesup to

By 1855, William H. Russell, Alexander Majors, and William B. Waddell emerged as the chief freighters on the Santa Fe and Oregon Trails. The partners operated under the name of Majors and Russell, changing it 3 years later to Russell, Majors & Waddell. Since 1849, Russell, in partnership with various freighters, had been engaged in transporting supplies for the Army.[27] On the basis of their past experience, Russell & Waddell in 1855 offered certain inducements in exchange for a monopoly of all freighting of military supplies from Forts Leavenworth, Riley, Laramie, and Union, and the town of Kansas to posts or depots in Kansas and New Mexico, including El Paso and its vicinity, and Utah and Nebraska Territories. Instead of limiting their operations to the usual months of July to October, Russell & Waddell proposed to freight during all seasons of the year. The firm also offered to transport to any post within a large district instead of making deliveries, as had been customary, only to such posts as the Quartermaster's Department specifically designated in the contract. Thus, if troops were removed from one post to another, or if a new post was established, the Department would not be obliged to make a new contract. Moreover, Russell & Waddell did not propose to bind the Department to the delivery to them of any specified quantity of freight for transportation under penalty of being called upon to compensate the contractors if a lesser amount was shipped. Instead, they were to have the entire quantity of supplies the Department might have for transportation, which might vary from 50,000 to 2,500,000 pounds. The firm offered a schedule of rates based on a new method of computing the prices—a fixed sum per 100 pounds per 100 miles.[28] The rates were considered favorable and the advantages to the government were so attractive that the Quartermaster's Department signed a contract with Russell & Waddell on 27 March 1855 for that year and for 1856.[29] It signed other contracts with the firm in 1857, 1858, and 1860, the rates still based on a fixed sum per 100 pounds per

Chairman, House Committee on Military Affairs, 27 Jan 1851). (2) Senate *Ex. Doc.* No. 1, 32d Cong., 1st sess., p. 295, s.n. 611 (Rpt of Maj. E. A. Ogden, 4 Oct 1851).

[27] (1) House *Ex. Doc.* No. 38, 31st Cong., 1st sess., p. 24, s.n. 576. (2) RG 92, OQMG Consolidated Correspondence File, Box 948 (Maj. E. A. Ogden to John S. Jones and Wm. H. Russell, 15 May 1851); (same to Russell, Waddell & Co., 16 Jun 1853).

[28] The schedule was as follows:

To Ft. Union and intermediate posts...$1.14 to $2.00
From Ft. Union to any other post in New Mex.............................. 1.40 to 1.80
To Salt Lake City and intermediate points................................. 1.30 to 2.15
House *Ex. Doc.* No. 17, 34th Cong., 1st sess., pp. 9–10, s.n. 851.

[29] (1) RG 92, OQMG Consolidated Correspondence File, Box 949 (Ogden to Jesup, 24 Feb 1855). (2) RG 92, OQMG Letter Book, vol. 47, pp. 437–39 (Jesup to Maj. E. S. Sibley, 28 Feb 1855).

100 miles but adjusted to the month in which shipment was made, with the lowest rate in the summer months.

The system of contract freighting proved so much more economical than operating government wagon trains that the Quartermaster's Department wanted it used for the delivery of military supplies at all posts in the new frontier area. Most of the posts in Texas, supplied from Indianola or the main interior depot at San Antonio, had their stores delivered, for the most part, by government-owned wagon trains. Thus, in the fiscal year ending 30 June 1851, the assistant quartermaster at San Antonio sent out 752 government wagons and engaged the services of 99 ox-drawn wagons owned by contractors. The latter transported 255,085 pounds of supplies; the mule-drawn government wagons carried 1,930,207 pounds.[30]

The post at El Paso was an exception to the general rule of supply by government wagons in Texas; from the beginning of this period it was supplied by contractors. In 1850, a freighter contracted to transport 865,000 pounds at $12 per 100 pounds from San Antonio to El Paso and at $13.50 per 100 pounds from Indianola. But a military escort had to accompany the wagon train and the quartermaster also paid the contractor for carrying the rations of the escort so that the cost actually amounted to $22 per 100 pounds of military supplies. That was a prohibitive rate, and in an effort to determine whether the cost could not be reduced, the Department sent to El Paso, under Capt. S. G. French, assistant quartermaster, a government wagon train, loaded with subsistence to replace damaged rations that had been delivered by the contractor. The length and difficulties of the route made delivery of supplies, even by government wagons, cost $19 per 100 pounds. On the other hand, the long haul across Texas from San Antonio had the strategic advantage of showing the flag when troops escorted the wagons. It was counted upon to help check Indian activity in an area where the United States was bound by treaty to prevent raids into Mexican territory. In the meantime, the Quartermaster's Department had also let a contract in 1850 at Fort Leavenworth to deliver some supplies to El Paso, via the Santa Fe Trail, at $13.87½ per 100 pounds. Tests proved that El Paso could be supplied cheaper by way of the Santa Fe Trail than from Indianola and San Antonio, and reduction of expenditures outweighing strategic advantage, El Paso came to be included thereafter in the contracts for New Mexico made by the quartermaster at Fort Leavenworth.[31]

[30] Senate *Ex. Doc.* No. 1, 32d Cong., 1st sess., p. 255, s.n. 611 (Babbitt's Rpt, 30 Jun 1851).

[31] (1) *Ibid.,* pp. 211, 227 ff., 295 (Rpts of QMG, 22 Nov 1851; Capt. S. G. French, 2 Nov 1851; AQM Ogden, 4 Oct 1851). (2) RG 92, OQMG Letter Book, vol. 42, p. 600 (Jesup to Col. Wm. Gilpin, 22 Apr 1850); vol. 43, p. 216 (Jesup to Gibson, 30 Nov 1850).

In the summer of 1855, the Department recommended that the transportation of all regular Army supplies at the other posts in Texas be performed by contract.   The Secretary of War approved that proposal, and the assistant quartermaster at San Antonio executed a contract with George T. Howard on 17 November 1855.[32]   Howard continued to do a large share of the freighting in Texas until the Civil War as Russell, Majors & Waddell did on the Santa Fe and Oregon Trails.   By 1860, the system of contract freighting had been extended to the transportation of supplies to posts in Arkansas and California.[33]

During the 1850's, freighting on the western plains became a big business, employing large numbers of men, animals, and equipment that demanded a vast outlay of capital.[34]   In the early years, the wagons were not overly large, being drawn by eight oxen or mules.   But even by 1851, wagons with a carrying capacity of 5,000 pounds, drawn by 10 or 12 animals, began to be specified in contracts.[35]   In time, the mammouth wagons—the Murphy and the Espenshield made in St. Louis and the Studebaker of South Bend, Ind.—were loaded with three to five tons of freight.   The profits of the trade were attractive.   Russell & Waddell noted that a trip to Fort Union, made at the most favorable time of the year, that is May or June, yielded a return of a fraction over 10 percent. Where the risk was greater and only one trip could be made per season, as to Salt Lake City, the return was 18 percent.[36]

Unfortunately, with so much at stake, the pursuit of government business led to the use of questionable methods to obtain contracts.   Such developments were at least implied if not proved in the contracts obtained by William H. Russell for his firm from John B. Floyd, who became Secretary of War in 1857.   "One is forced to conclude that influence, favoritism, and possibly other factors which were never meant to receive publicity were involved in the Russell, Majors & Waddell contracts." [37]

Since 1851, the Quartermaster General had not been able to make or authorize any contract for supplies or services that exceeded $2,000 without the approval of the Secretary of War, a regulation that provided

[32] (1) RG 92, Reports of QMG to SW and Heads of Depts., vol. 3, pp. 203–06 (Actg QMG Thomas to SW, 15 Aug 1855). (2) House *Ex. Doc.* No. 17, 34th Cong., 1st sess., p. 24, s.n. 851; *ibid.,* No. 58, 35th Cong., 1st sess., pp. 17–18, s.n. 955; *ibid.,* No. 50, 35th Cong., 2d sess., pp. 11–12, s.n. 1006

[33] (1) House *Ex. Doc.* No. 50, 35th Cong., 2d sess., pp. 19–20, s.n. 1006.   (2) RG 92, OQMG Letter Book, vol. 54, p. 73 (Jesup to AQM A. Montgomery, 10 Jan 1860).

[34] For a detailed account of the operations of Russell, Majors & Waddell, see Raymond W. Settle and Mary Lund Settle, *Empire on Wheels* (Stanford University Press, 1940.)

[35] RG 92, OQMG Consolidated Correspondence File, Box 948 (Contract with Jones & Russell, 15 May 1851).

[36] *Ibid.,* Box 948 (Russell & Waddell to Col. Chas. Thomas, 19 Sep 1857).

[37] Settle and Settle, *Empire on Wheels,* p. 109.

that official an opportunity to show favoritism if such an inclination existed. When the War Department was unable to meet payments due to Russell, Majors & Waddell on its contract for 1857 and the firm was threatened with ruin, Secretary Floyd decided to permit Russell to draw drafts or acceptances on the Secretary of War in anticipation of the firm's earnings under its transportation contract for 1858.[38] As long ago as 1819, when the Johnson brothers had used drafts on the War Department to bolster their sinking business enterprises, Quartermaster General Jesup had learned that the use of drafts or acceptances was unwise. His objections to permitting their issue in 1858 were overruled by the Secretary of War, who also used his influence to help Russell obtain loans, using the acceptances as security.[39]

When the acceptances matured, and Russell, to prevent their being protested for non-payment, became a party to the embezzlement of Indian trust bonds, obtained from Mr. Bailey, a clerk in the Department of Interior, a House committee investigated the whole complicated transaction. It portrayed Russell, Majors & Waddell as "chiseling" contractors who "not only absorbed all the sums earned by them under their contracts, and sold all the bonds they received from Mr. Bailey, but also raised very large sums of money upon the acceptances issued by the Secretary of War."[40] While not holding Floyd responsible for the "fraudulent abstraction" of the Indian trust bonds, the committee unanimously declared the Secretary's issue of acceptances to be "unauthorized by law and fraudulent in character."[41] Though proof was lacking, the committee suspected that Floyd had profited generously from the contracts given to Russell, Majors & Waddell. Floyd, however, did not profit by the transactions with Army contractors.

Despite such developments, the use of the contractor system of freighting had definite advantages for the Quartermaster's Department. It obviated the necessity for maintaining large wagon trains at depots and permitted the disposal of all wagons and teams, except such as had to be retained to meet post requirements and emergency needs.[42] As the number of government wagon trains declined, the demand for teamsters, for mules, oxen, and horses, and for forage decreased, at least on the supply lines.

Competent, experienced drivers for government wagon trains had

[38] House *Rpt.* No. 78, 36th Cong., 2d sess., pp. 350–52, s.n. 1105 (Floyd to Speaker of HR, 27 Dec 1860).

[39] See, for example, his letter to A. Belmont, 15 February 1859, *ibid.*, p. 307.

[40] *Ibid.*, p. 17.

[41] *Ibid.*, pp. 19–20.

[42] RG 92, OQMG Letter Book, vol. 48, pp. 480–81 (Actg QMG Thomas to AQM Chapman, 27 Oct 1855); vol. 54, p. 73 (Jesup to AQM Montgomery, 10 Jan 1860).

never been readily available and certainly could not be hired at $15 per month, the wages offered in 1850. Major Cross found that teamsters hired at such wages were "totally ignorant of their duty," their one object in accompanying the Regiment of Mounted Rifles on its march across the continent was to reach the gold fields "with the least possible expense or trouble to themselves." Yet indifferent as these men were as teamsters, Assistant Quartermaster Cross had to depend on them, for soldiers could not be detailed for the duty. They were raw recruits—"some, not speaking the English language, were not capable of taking care of one horse, much less a team of six mules." [43]   Jesup again urged passage of a law authorizing the enlistment not only of all teamsters but of all mechanics, laborers, boatmen, farriers, and other personnel that the Department had to hire. He proposed enlisting such personnel for 2- or 3-year terms of service and making them subject to military law.[44] Despite Jesup's repeated recommendations, Congress enacted no law. Under these circumstances, it was much to the advantage of the Department to have private contractors furnish teamsters as well as wagons and to provide the mechanics and laborers needed to repair equipment and care for the animals.

Any decrease in the number of teams used by the Quartermaster's Department helped reduce the demands for forage. As supply lines lengthened and teams and pack animals increased in number, forage demands reached huge proportions. Demand plus scarcity in the immediate vicinity of the troops and the necessity of transporting the supply long distances increased enormously the cost of grain, hay, and fodder in the new territory. In 1845, when Fort Leavenworth was an outpost of the frontier, the cost of foraging a horse or mule throughout the year averaged less than $4 per month. In 1850, the cost per month averaged $19.82 in New Mexico, $27.72 at Fort Kearny, and $34.24 at Fort Laramie.[45]

For the most part, forage had to be brought in from the older, cultivated areas. In New Mexico, for example, the whole surplus products of that territory in 1850, after its inhabitants had been supplied, would hardly have been sufficient to meet the demands of the Army, if all of the surplus had been available for the Army's use. Much of it, however, necessarily went into the hands of emigrants moving to California by the route of the Gila. Only after the troops could be supplied

[43] House *Ex. Doc.* No. 1, 31st Cong., 2d sess., Pt. 2, pp. 129–30, s.n. 587 (Cross Rpt).

[44] (1) *Ibid.,* p. 8 (SW Rpt, 30 Nov 1850); p. 125 (QMG's Rpt, 20 Nov 1850). (2) House *Ex. Doc.* No. 5, 31st Cong., 1st sess., p. 195, s.n. 569 (QMG's Rpt, 10 Nov 1849).

[45] (1) RG 92, Reports of QMG to SW and Heads of Depts., vol. 1, p. 292 (Jesup to SW, 4 Nov 1850). (1) See also House *Ex. Doc.* No. 1, 31st Cong., 2d sess., Pt. 2, p. 110, s.n. 587 (SW Rpt, 30 Nov 1850).

by cultivation in the immediate vicinity of their posts could expenditures for the supply of forage be materially reduced.

For that purpose, the Department encouraged the cultivation of post farms. At Fort Leavenworth, farm culture by the troops had been practiced when it had been a frontier post. Troop farming at the post had long since given way to cultivation of the farm's 1,332 acres by hands hired for the purpose by the Quartermaster's Department. In 1851, about 30 hands were on the payroll, and the assistant quartermaster reported that the farm was expected to yield some 18,000 bushels of corn, 8,000 bushels of oats, 500 bushels of buckwheat, 600 bushels of barley, 528 tons of hay, besides straw, corn fodder, pumpkins, turnips, potatoes, and wheat.[46] The system of farm culture by the troops, as directed by general order, 8 January 1851, did not show successful results. In Texas, California, and Oregon, the Army undertook no cultivation in 1851 or 1852, for the troops were kept so constantly employed in pursuing Indians, establishing new posts to keep them in check, and protecting frontier settlements that they had no time for farming. The general-in-chief, Maj. Gen. Winfield Scott, reported that in New Mexico outlays for farm cultivation far exceeded the receipts. In any case, he maintained, troops could not be kept actively engaged in military duties and maintain discipline, if required to engage in cultivation beyond kitchen gardens. It might be wiser, he suggested, to discontinue the system and induce emigrants to settle near military stations by offering them a ready market for their surplus produce.[47]

Despite the shift from the use of government wagon trains to freighting by contractors, Quartermaster forage expenditures increased enormously during these years. Quartermasters at posts reduced the number of public teams to the minimum required for emergency operations, but they had to forage all the other animals employed by the Army—horses used on escort duty and for expresses, and the animals required to transport baggage, rations, and supplies on each transfer of troops to a new station and on each march against the Indians. Moreover, by 1851 the mounted troops of the Army had been nearly doubled in number since 1845 and were to be further increased before 1860. All the animals to be foraged by the Department increased from 847 in 1845 to almost 8,000 in 1851.[48] Had the mounted force been at its authorized strength, Jesup estimated that he would have been obliged

---

[46] Senate *Ex. Doc.* No. 1, 32d Cong., 1st sess., p. 292, s.n. 611 (Rpt of AQM Ogden 4 Oct 1851).

[47] Senate *Ex. Doc.* No. 1, 32d Cong., 2d sess., Pt. 2, p. 35, s.n. 612 (Scott's Rpt to SW, 22 Nov 1852).

[48] Senate *Ex. Doc.* No. 1, 32d Cong., 1st sess., p. 218, s.n. 611 (QMG's Rpt, 22 Nov 1851).

to provide forage for more than 10,000 animals in fiscal year 1851 at a cost of $2 million.[49]

The amount of forage to be supplied was governed by the allowance per animal. For most of this decade, the forage ration was 14 pounds of hay and 12 pounds of corn or oats. This was the maximum allowance which could be, and usually was, reduced by the commander in the field whenever circumstances dictated such a course.[50] Fortunately, too, the Department did not have to provide the full amount of the forage ration for all the Army's horses, mules, and oxen. At a few of the frontier posts in Texas and New Mexico, hay was furnished by troop labor or by hired hands of the Quartermaster's Department.[51] During the summer months, some of the animals could also be foraged on the grass of the prairies. Jesup always adjusted estimates for appropriations to cover the cost of foraging the Army's animals by including these supplies. Annual forage expenditures nonetheless hovered around the million-dollar mark.

Substitution of contractors' wagon trains for government wagon trains in the period 1848 to 1860 should have resulted in a saving in the procurement of animals by the Quartermaster's Department. It did mean that fewer draft animals had to be purchased for hauling wagon trains on the supply lines. It had no effect, however, on the number of draft animals used in the movement of troops. The increased use of mounted troops, moreover, required the purchase of more horses; nor was it only the initial mounting of these troops that was important. Service of the mounted troops was so severe that from one-fourth to one-third of their horses had to be replaced each year.[52] There is no data on replacement of mules and oxen used in the government wagon trains but the losses resulting from the careless handling of draft animals by incompetent drivers ran high.

The lack of care given the animals troubled Jesup. In 1853, he recommended the establishment of a veterinary corps, under the direction of the Surgeon General, thereby anticipating by 63 years the actual establishment of the corps. He proposed that the corps consist of a competent number of surgeons and assistant surgeons, who should be assigned to duty at depots, with mounted regiments, squadrons, detachments, cavalry, artillery schools of instruction, and trains. More was lost every year by the sacrifice of horses and mules, for want of proper veterinary aid, Jesup argued, than would support the expense of such a

[49] RG 92, Reports of QMG to SW and Heads of Depts., vol. 1, p. 296 (Jesup to SW, 4 Nov 1850).

[50] RG 92, OQMG Letter Book, vol. 50, pp. 368–69 (Jesup to M. K. Lawler, 3 Mar 1857).

[51] Senate *Ex. Doc.* No. 1, 32d Cong., 1st sess., p. 218, s.n. 611 (QMG's Rpt, 22 Nov 1851).

[52] RG 92, Reports of QMG to SW and Heads of Depts., vol. 1, p. 298 (Jesup to SW, 4 Nov 1850).

corps for 2 or 3 years.[53]   In 1856, he again urged the organization of such
a corps and the establishment of a veterinary school, where Dragoon
officers, mounted riflemen, and troops in the light artillery, as well as
candidates for the veterinary corps itself, might receive competent instruction in the care, management, and diseases of horses and mules.[54]   The
Secretary of War did not act upon Jesup's farsighted recommendations.
Meanwhile, though the law made no provision for veterinary surgeons,
the Quartermaster's Department hired such personnel, utilizing funds
appropriated for incidental expenses to pay for their services.

Transportation costs for the Army in this decade were high.   By
1855, they were about $2 million and expenditures so frequently exceeded
appropriations that deficiency appropriations were often necessary.   In
the 5-year period 1852–57, Jesup calculated that the average military force
in service numbered 13,600 rank and file, whose transportation had cost
more than $2 million a year.   By way of comparison, he noted that in
the 5-year period before the annexation of Texas, the average force in
service had consisted of 9,900 rank and file, transported at a cost of
$156,000 a year.[55]

Need for Internal Improvements

Jesup was well aware that the economy as well as the efficiency of
the service would be promoted by better means of communication with
the distant Army posts.   In 1850, there was no established steamboat
line that could be used beyond the Texas and Pacific coasts.   There
was not even an ordinary good turnpike in the new territories.   Supplies
had to be transported over routes that were long and entirely unimproved.
Jesup recommended the improvement of harbors and rivers in Texas so
that where possible water routes might be used.   He also urged construction of turnpikes on the principal routes to important points on the
frontier.[56]

Quartermasters in the field, however, soon learned that many rivers
in Texas and Arkansas were torrents in the rainy season and dry channels
at all other times, unsuitable for navigation.   The use of turnpikes for
the distances involved was too costly.   By 1852, Jesup concluded that
the only system of improvement, adapted to the country that had to be
traversed, was that of railroads.   He proposed the construction of a
central railroad from some point on the Mississippi through Arkansas to

[53] House *Ex. Doc.* No. 1, 33d Cong., 1st sess., pp. 134–35, s.n. 711 (QMG's Rpt, 22 Nov 1853).
[54] House *Ex. Doc.* No. 1, 34th Cong., 3d sess., p. 257, s.n. 894 (QMG's Rpt, 26 Nov 1856).
[55] House *Ex. Doc.* No. 2, 35th Cong., 2d sess., pp. 789–99, s.n. 999 (QMG's Rpt, 13 Nov 1858).
[56] House *Ex. Doc.* No. 1, 31st Cong., 2d sess., Pt. 2, p. 124, s.n. 587 (QMG's Rpt, 20 Nov
1850); Senate *Ex. Doc.* No. 1, 32d Cong., 1st sess., p. 226, s.n. 611 (QMG's Rpt, 22 Nov 1851).

the western frontier of Texas on the Rio Grande, with another road built through Texas to intersect it at some point. He suggested that a third road might be built from the frontier of Missouri, at least as far west as Fort Riley on the Kansas River. Other railroads, he added, might be started on the Pacific Coast, being built eastward to meet those projected westward from the Mississippi Valley.[57] Military considerations, not sectional economic rivalries, dictated Jesup's choice of railroad lines. Year after year in his annual reports, Jesup hammered at the need for railroads in the West and the benefits that could be derived from them in greater efficiency and economy of Army operations and in defense of the country.

Experience, Jesup insisted, had taught that in the transportation of its stores, the Quartermaster's Department was better advised to follow the lines of trade established by private mercantile enterprise than to lead or direct trade into new routes.[58] The Department had always used the tested, established routes of trade in transporting its supplies. In advocating construction of a transcontinental railroad, Jesup was not pioneering. In the decade before the Mexican War, John Plumbe, Asa Whitney, and others had by speeches and writings been arousing an interest in the building of transcontinental railroads that territorial expansion after the war made more keen and widespread.[59]

So great was the interest that, on 3 March 1853, Congress added funds to the Army appropriation bill to finance an extensive program of explorations and surveys. Military and scientific parties, working from both the Mississippi Valley and the Pacific Coast, were to determine the most practicable and economical route for the construction of a railroad to the coast. Under the direction of Engineer officers, these parties took the field, the Quartermaster's Department furnishing supplies and transportation.[60] They surveyed five routes, but though much geographical and scientific knowledge of the West was accumulated, no agreement as to the route of the railroad could be reached in the midst of the existing sectional rivalry. Not until the southern states seceded could a decision be made in favor of a central route that permitted construction of the Union Pacific Railroad to be started.

[57] Senate *Ex. Doc.* No. 1, 32d Cong., 2d sess., Pt. 2, p. 74, s.n. 612 (QMG's Rpt, 20 Nov 1852).

[58] RG 92, OQMG Letter Book, vol. 43, pp. 451–52 (Jesup to Levi Jones, 31 Mar 1851), vol. 52 (Jesup to Capt. J. G. Tod, 10 Jul 1858).

[59] See (1) M. L. Brown, "Asa Whitney and His Pacific Railroad Publicity Campaign," *Mississippi Valley Historical Review,* vol. 20 (Sep 1933), pp. 209–24. (2) John King, "John Plumbe, Originator of the Pacific Railroad," *Annals of Iowa,* vol. VI, 3d ser. (Jan 1904), pp. 289–96.

[60] (1) 10 *Stat.* 214. (2) RG 92, OQMG Letter Book, vol. 45, pp. 508, 510, 577–78 (Jesup to Vinton, 12 Apr; to Cross; 13 Apr; to Crosman, 24 May 1853).

Experiment With Camels

In the meantime, to reduce the heavy transportation costs of the Army, particularly in the arid regions of the Southwest, the War Department made an effort to introduce and use camels as carriers of military supplies. The possibility of using camels in the United States had first been broached in the late 1830's by George R. Glidden, who as U.S. Consul in the Mediterranean region, had written letters to the State Department on the subject. In the spring of 1843, Capt. George H. Crosman, then an assistant quartermaster, tried to interest the Quartermaster's Department in the use of camels as transporters of troops and supplies in the southwest. Jesup thought such projects might better be left to "enlightened private enterprise." In any case, the Treasury had no money, he informed Captain Crosman. He made much the same reply to Gales and Seaton, editors of the *National Intelligencer,* when they sent a letter on the same subject in the summer of 1849.[61]

In 1851, Jefferson Davis, then chairman of the Senate Military Affairs Committee, tried to get an amendment passed to the Army appropriation bill in order to provide funds for the purchase of about 50 camels. It failed of action and thereafter Jesup attempted to get private contractors to try the experiment of transporting Army supplies on camels, but nothing came of these efforts.[62] On 3 March 1855, however, Congress appropriated $30,000 for the purchase of a number of camels and dromedaries.

Jefferson Davis, then Secretary of War, lost no time in enlisting the services of the Navy Department to provide a ship for the transportation of the animals. He also obtained the services of Navy Lt. David D. Porter, and appointed Maj. Henry C. Wayne, assistant quartermaster, to go to the Levant, purchase the camels, and supervise their delivery to Indianola, Tex.[63]

In the course of two expeditions, 75 camels were imported into Texas.[64] Trial was then made of the camels as carriers of supplies. These experiments were successful in demonstrating the camel's ability

[61] RG 92, OQMG Letter Book, vol. 34, p. 431 (To Crosman, 6 May 1843); vol. 42, p. 229 (To Gales and Seaton, 9 Aug 1849).

[62] (1) RG 107, OSW, Rpts to Congress, vol. 6, pp. 445–46 (SW to J. Davis, 25 Feb 1851); vol. 7, pp. 164–66 (SW to James Shields, 5 May 1852). (2) RG 92, OQMG Letter Book, vol. 46, pp. 347–48 (Jesup to C. W. Webber, 30 Nov 1835); vol. 47, p. 439 (DQMG Thomas to Col. H. L. Kinney, 1 Jan 1855).

[63] RG 107, OSW, Military Book, vol. 36, p. 406 (Davis to Secy of Navy, 11 Apr 1855); vol. 37, pp. 12, 42–44 (SW to Porter, 4 and 16 May 1855); pp. 20–22 (SW to Wayne, 10 May 1855).

[64] For the correspondence relating to the importation of the camels see, Senate *Ex. Doc.* No. 62, 34th Cong., 3d sess., s.n. 881.

IMPORTATION OF CAMELS

to carry heavy loads, to subsist on what food could be obtained by grazing and on little water, and to make far longer marches each day than mules or horses. Unfortunately, their appearance on the roads stampeded wagon and pack trains. Both the public and the Army turned against them and the camel experiment ended in failure.[65]

Increased Expenditures

Apparently, there was little appreciation in the country either of the demands that would be made upon the Army by the acquisition of the new territory in the West or of the enormous expenditures that the supply departments would be called upon to make in supporting the troops stationed at western posts. At the end of the Mexican War,

[65] For a detailed account see Will C. Barnes, "Camels on Safari," *The Quartermaster Review,* vol. XVI (Jan–Feb 1937), p. 7 ff.

Congress was more concerned with returning the Army to its prewar status than with analyzing the new problems that would confront the troops. President Polk, in sympathy with this objective, reduced Jesup's estimate of expenditures for fiscal year 1850 by more than $900,000, despite the Quartermaster General's insistence that he had presented a minimum estimate. By April 1850, that appropriation was nearly exhausted, and Jesup reported that unless Congress provided additional funds the Department would be unable to meet the heavy drafts made upon it by assistant quartermasters in New Mexico and on the Pacific Coast.[66] No deficiency appropriation was passed and arrearages accumulated.

Jesup was apprehensive that it would be impossible to obtain appropriations "to carry on the service" in the face of mounting expenditures, and he called upon commanding officers to aid in reducing expenses in their departments.[67] His fears were well founded for the House Ways and Means Committee, misinformed on data submitted, cut his estimate for fiscal year 1852 in half on every item of expenditure.[68]

Aroused by what he considered unwarranted abuse, Jesup determined to set his Department right before Congress and the country in his next annual report. To show the growth of Quartermaster activities, he called for a full report from his principal subordinates in the field. At the same time, he also made every effort to reduce expenditures. He dispatched two of the Department's top-ranking officers to Texas and New Mexico to inquire into and correct all abuses or extravagances that might exist in those departments. He sent similar instructions to the chief quartermasters in California and Oregon.[69] These officers uncovered no abuses but did recommend certain economies. In consequence, Jesup issued instructions to dismiss civilian laborers and utilize troop labor to a greater extent. He also ruled that no agents were to be hired. He closely scrutinized transportation costs and suggested that these might be cut by reducing the weight of supplies shipped. As a result, the Clothing Branch at Philadelphia changed its packaging methods. Instead of packing the clothing intended for the troops stationed at

[66] (1) RG 92, OQMG Letter Book, vol. 42, p. 578 (Jesup to Lt. Col. B. Bragg, 5 Apr 1850). (2) RG 92, Reports of QMG to SW and Heads of Depts., vol. 1, pp. 237–39 (Jesup to SW, 3 May 1850).

[67] RG 92, OQMG Letter Book, vol. 43, pp. 334–35 (Jesup to Maj. Gen. D. E. Twiggs, 7 Feb 1851).

[68] (1) Compare estimate and appropriation in RG 92, Reports of QMG to SW and Heads of Depts., vol. 1, pp. 291–308 (Jesup to SW, 4 Nov 1850) and 9 *Stat.* 618 (Act of Mar 3, 1851). (2) Senate *Ex. Doc.* No. 1, 32d Cong., 1st sess., pp. 223–24, s.n. 611 (QMG's Rpt, 22 Nov 1851).

[69] (1) RG 92, OQMG Letter Book, vol. 43, p. 507 (Jesup to Maj. E. B. Babbitt, 23 Apr 1851). (2) Senate *Ex. Doc.* No. 1, 32d Cong., 1st sess., pp. 222–23, s.n. 611 (QMG's Rpt, 22 Nov 1851); p. 235 ff. (Appended Rpts of QM Swords and others).

western posts in wooden, iron-bound boxes and tierces, it baled these supplies. The Department sent a packing press and baling material to Fort Leavenworth to permit the quartermaster there to effect the same economy in shipping clothing from that depot.[70] Such measures did result in savings but they were necessarily minor in character. The major expenditures could not be reduced until distance was overcome by cheaper and quicker means of transportation or supplies could be obtained closer to the posts as settlements grew. Not fraud but the wide distribution of the Army and the growth of Quartermaster activities accounted for the increased expenditures of the Department, and so effectively did Jesup analyze the increase in rentals, construction costs, transportation costs for the troops and supplies, mileage for officers, and prices for forage and horses that he won the battle of appropriations for the rest of his administration.

Although the Army had been rapidly reduced to its prewar status in 1848, its operations during these years before the Civil War were not those of a peacetime establishment. Throughout this period, the troops were employed in the pursuit of one marauding party of Indians after another, and skirmishes with the Indians in the new frontier area followed one after the other almost without a break so that troop activities required considerable Quartermaster support.

Support of Operations Against the Mormons

The War Department initiated only one major operation during these years—the expedition against the Mormons—and it fully demonstrated the tremendous logistical problems involved in campaigning on the western plains. Ever since a territorial government had been established in Utah in 1851, the misunderstanding between the Mormons and the federal officials had engendered so much friction that by the spring of 1857 all but two of the latter had been forced to withdraw from Utah. The Mormons were not only challenging the sovereignty of the United States, but, it was charged, they were instigating the Indians to hostilities against its citizens. Under these circumstances, President Buchanan thought it advisable to send a body of troops with the civil officers newly appointed for the territory. The object was to establish them in their offices and to convert Utah into a geographical military department.[71]

---

[70] RG 92, OQMG Clothing, Letter Book, vol. 12, p. 268 (Jesup to Maj. Geo. H. Crosman, 17 Feb 1851). Freight from the tare of boxes and tierces sent from Fort Leavenworth in 1850 had amounted to almost $8,000.

[71] House *Ex. Doc.* No. 2, 35th Cong., 1st sess., p. 8, s.n. 943 (SW's Rpt, 5 Dec 1857).

About the end of May 1857, the War Department issued orders to assemble as soon as possible at Fort Leavenworth a force of some 2,500 men, consisting of the 5th and 10th Infantry, eight companies of the 2d Dragoons, and a battery of the 4th Artillery.[72] The Quartermaster's Department not only moved the troops to the rendezvous point by rail and steamboat but also concentrated wagons and animals at Fort Leavenworth to transport the baggage, clothing, ordnance stores, and other supplies that accompanied the expedition.[73] Telegraphed instructions set the wheels in motion.   In rapid order, Jesup called for the shipment of wagons on hand at Philadelphia and the manufacture of additional wagons, all now made with interchangeable parts; the delivery of several hundred kegs of mule and horse shoes; the procurement of 500 mules; and the purchase of 300 horses for the Dragoons.[74] Under orders from General Scott, the Department also procured 250 Sibley tents for the use of the troops in the event they could not hut themselves during the winter.   This circular tent, patented by Bvt. Maj. H. H. Sibley of the 2d Dragoons, had been under development since 1855 but had not yet been officially adopted for Army use.   The tent received its first test in the field on this expedition.[75]

While the Quartermaster's Department provided the wagons and animals to transport all the supplies needed by the command on its march, the contractors hauled all other material on the supply lines. Capt. Thomas L. Brent, assistant quartermaster at Fort Leavenworth, advised Majors & Russell that they would have to transport to Utah subsistence and other stores, amounting to 3 million pounds, in addition to the supplies already sent out to other points under the terms of their contract.[76] The expedition had to carry with it not only a supply of at least 3 months' subsistence that the troops and civilian laborers would consume in crossing the plains but also sufficient rations, clothing, ordnance stores, tools, and other supplies that the force might need until the following summer.   Not until then could it be resupplied from its depot over a thousand miles away.

Majors & Russell protested the demands made upon the firm.   Their

[72] House *Ex. Doc.* No. 71, 35th Cong., 1st sess., p. 4, s.n. 956 (Circular, 28 May 1857).

[73] RG 92, OQMG, Register of Contracts, 1852–59, vol. 12, pp. 385, 387, 394, 397.

[74] RG 92, OQMG Letter Book, vol. 50, pp. 573–74 (Jesup to Capt. T. L. Brent and Lt. Col. Geo. H. Crosman, 30 May 1857); pp. 594–95 (Jesup to Babbitt, 5 Jun 1857).

[75] (1) RG 92, Reports of QMG to SW and Heads of Depts., vol. 3, p. 605 (Jesup to SW, 30 Mar 1857).   (2) RG 92, OQMG Clothing, Letter Book, vol. 15, p. 326 (Jesup to Babbitt, 13 Apr 1857).   (3) The tent, 18 feet in diameter, was intended to accommodate 13 cavalry and 15 foot soldiers.

[76] (1) House *Ex. Doc.* No. 58, 35th Cong., 1st sess., p. 8, s.n. 955 (Contract, 27 Feb 1857). (2) RG 92, OQMG Letter Book, vol. 50, p. 573 (Jesup to Brent, 30 May 1857); p. 595 (Jesup to Thomas, 5 Jun 1857).

trains were already on the road with supplies for the various posts; the time was too short to assemble additional wagon trains; and to comply with the Department's demands would ruin them. Assured that the government would not allow the contractors to suffer, Majors & Russell yielded to the persuasions of Captain Brent and began to assemble their wagon trains. The expedition's demands had inflated prices so that the contractors had to pay 25 percent more for oxen and had to meet a 50 percent increase in wages demanded by the bullwhackers. Nevertheless, their wagons rolled toward Utah in the summer of 1857. A claim presented to Congress in 1860 showed that Majors & Russell had dispatched 41 wagon trains, carrying 4,525,913 pounds of supplies.[77] Under the name of Russell & Waddell, the contractors also made a contract with the Subsistence Department in June 1857 to deliver 2,000 head of cattle at Salt Lake City.[78]

Aware that it was late in the season to be sending an expedition across the plains, Jesup regretted that he had not had the spring months in which to prepare, and he impressed upon his quartermasters in the field that they must expedite all measures "to conquer time and distance."[79] Captain Brent at Fort Leavenworth and his immediate superior, Lt. Col. George H. Crosman, deputy quartermaster general at St. Louis, directed the preparations. Captains S. Van Vliet, W. S. Hancock, and J. H. Dickerson accompanied the expedition. To superintend all arrangements, Jesup sent Assistant Quartermaster General Charles Thomas to St. Louis and Fort Leavenworth to do for the commanding officer of the expedition what he had done for General Wool in 1846.[80]

To assure the Mormons that the troops would not molest or interfere with them and at the same time to arrange for the purchase from them of forage and lumber needed upon their arrival, Captain Van Vliet was sent ahead of the expedition to Salt Lake City. The Mormans, however, would sell no products to the Army, and Brigham Young declared the troops would not be allowed to enter Great Salt Lake Valley.[81]

As the troops approached Utah Territory, the Mormons attacked their trains on 4 October, destroying about 75 supply wagons carrying rations. In addition, a considerable quantity of tools, supplies for

---

[77] Settle and Settle, *Empire on Wheels*, p. 18.

[78] House *Ex. Doc.* No. 58, 35th Cong., 1st sess., p. 39, s.n. 955 (Contract, 26 Jun 1857).

[79] RG 92, OQMG Letter Book, vol. 50, p. 591 (Jesup to Brig. Gen. W. S. Harney, 5 Jun 1857).

[80] *Ibid.*, vol. 50, pp. 595–96 (Jesup to Thomas, 5 Jun 1857).

[81] House *Ex. Doc.* No. 2, 35th Cong., 1st sess., pp. 25–27, s.n. 943 (Capt. Van Vliet to Actg AG, 16 Sep 1857).

making wagon repairs, and other Quartermaster stores were destroyed.[82] The lateness of the season compelled Col. Albert S. Johnston, the commanding officer, to place his troops in winter quarters at nearby Fort Bridger. A terrific snowstorm that raged for days so hampered the movement of the force that it took 15 days to travel the 35 miles to Fort Bridger. Horses, mules, and oxen, unable to reach forage, died by the hundreds from starvation and cold. Lt. Col. Philip St. George Cooke, following with the 2d Dragoons, found the road for 30 miles nearly blocked with dead and frozen animals and with abandoned and shattered property, marking "perhaps, beyond example in history, the steps of an advancing army with the horrors of a disastrous retreat." [83]

By the time the command reached Fort Bridger, the expedition had lost on its journey from Fort Leavenworth 588 mules of some 2,400 provided by the Department, half the horses of the batteries, and two-thirds of the mounts of the Dragoons. Since many more animals would die during the winter for lack of forage, Chief Quartermaster Dickerson thought it would not be safe for Colonel Johnston to count on more than 500 serviceable mules and 40 battery horses by 1 May. Before any movement could be undertaken in the spring, a new outfit would be required, and he recommended sending a party to New Mexico to procure 400 horses and 800 mules. Capt. R. B. Marcy of the 5th Infantry, with 40 enlisted men and 25 mountain men, herders, packers, and guides, made a heroic winter's march to New Mexico for that purpose.[84]

Meantime, at Camp Scott, the expedition's winter quarters, the troops faced a winter of hardship. Despite the subsistence losses sustained in the destruction of wagon trains, the commissary had sufficient rations on hand to support the troops until June. To be on the safe side, however, he recommended that a reduced ration be issued.[85] A sufficient number of oxen, though poor, were saved to supply the meat portion of the ration 6 days in the week. Of this supply, a newspaper correspondent wrote

[82] (1) House *Ex. Doc.* No. 71, 35th Cong., 1st sess., pp. 30–32, s.n. 956 (Col. E. B. Alexander to AG, 9 Oct 1857); p. 63 (List of stores burnt). (2) RG 92, OQMG Letter Book, vol. 52, pp. 73–77 (Jesup to Bvt. Maj. Gen. P. F. Smith, 17 Apr 1858).

[83] (1) House *Ex. Doc.* No. 71, 35th Cong., 1st sess., p. 99, s.n. 956 (Cooke to AAG, 21 Nov 1857). (2) *Frontier Life in the Army 1854–1861*, ed. Bieber, pp. 221–22.

[84] (1) House *Ex. Doc.* No. 71, 35th Cong., 1st sess., pp. 101–03, s.n. 956 (Dickerson to AAG, 24 Nov 1857). (2) House *Ex. Doc.* No. 2, 35th Cong., 2d sess., p. 7–8, s.n. 998 (SW's Rpt, 6 Dec 1858). (3) RG 92, OQMG Letter Book, vol. 52, p. 77 (Jesup to Maj. Gen. P. F. Smith, 17 Apr 1858).

[85] The ration was to consist of 2 pounds of fresh beef and 12 ounces of flour, with beans to be issued three times in 10 days, rice, five times and desiccated vegetables twice in 10 days. Half rations of vinegar, candles, and soap were recommended. To each 100 rations he allowed one gallon of molasses and 10 pounds of dried peaches, the former to be issued twice and the dried peaches once in 15 days. House *Ex. Doc.* No. 71, 35th Cong., 1st sess., pp. 104–05, s.n. 956 (Capt. H. F. Clarke to AAG, 28 Nov 1857).

from Fort Bridger that the oxen were frequently shot down a few minutes before they died a natural death from starvation and cold. "I often got a piece of this beef, as tender as a piece of sole leather." [86]   Enough bacon was on hand to allow a supply for 1 day in the week for 7 months. In the ration provided for the expedition, tea might be issued in lieu of coffee, and, for the first time, the War Department introduced in the Army ration desiccated vegetables, long used in the Navy ration.   According to regulations, desiccated vegetables were to be issued once a week in lieu of beans or rice, but if a tendency to scurvy appeared among the troops the commanding officer might direct a more frequent issue.[87] Palatability of the meat and vegetables was not improved by the lack of salt.   The supply of that essential item had become exhausted in November.   A train of 30 mules, each loaded with 100 pounds of salt, was started from Ft. Laramie on 3 December.[88]

The troops at Camp Scott were not well supplied with clothing. They had left Fort Leavenworth with only a limited supply and by mid-October they were already reported as "nearly destitute."   Assistant Quartermaster Dickerson called for several wagonloads of socks, flannel drawers and shirts, shoes, and blankets to be brought forward.   A survey of the amount of clothing on hand at camp near the end of November showed 3,905 flannel shirts but only 723 blankets.[89]   Only 675 pairs of boots for mounted troops and 148 pairs of bootees for foot soldiers were on hand.   With no shoes to be had at any price, it was reported that "men are at work making a covering for the feet of beef hides." [90]   A large supply of clothing items had been sent from Fort Leavenworth in the supply trains, including 1,800 blankets, 4,660 pairs of bootees, and 1,280 pairs of boots.   Unfortunately, large stocks of clothing destined for the troops in Utah were still at Fort Laramie in December but there were no means available for sending them forward.[91]

As the troops of the Utah expedition waited for the long winter months to pass, the War Department ordered reinforcements to assemble at Fort Leavenworth.   A force of 3,018 officers and men were to march

[86] *Frontier Life in the Army,* ed Bieber, p. 53.

[87] (1) *War Department General Orders,* GO 9, 23 Jun 1857. (2) RG 192, Commissary General of Subsistence (CGS), Letters to SW, 1854–1866, p. 56 (Gibson to Floyd, 30 May 1857).

[88] (1) House *Ex. Doc.* No. 71, 35th Cong., 1st sess., p. 78, s.n. 956 (Johnston to AAG, 30 Nov 1857). (2) House *Ex. Doc.* No. 2, 35th Cong., 2d sess., p. 36, s.n. 998 (Maj. J. Lynde to AG, 2 Dec 1857).

[89] House *Ex. Doc.* No. 71, 35th Cong., 1st sess., p. 66, s.n. 956 (Dickerson to Col. C. F. Smith, 18 Oct 1857); pp. 106–07 (Dickerson to Jesup, 29 Nov 1857).

[90] *Frontier Life in the Army,* ed. Bieber, p. 53.

[91] (1) RG 92, OQMG Letter Book, vol. 52, pp. 89–91 (Jesup to Maj. Gen. P. F. Smith, 17 Apr 1858). (2) House *Ex. Doc.* No. 2, 35th Cong., 2d sess., pp. 49–52, s.n. 998 (Maj. J. Lynde to AG, 24 Dec 1857).)

as early in the spring as possible along with 850 recruits and 44 officers to bring the troops at Camp Scott up to the maximum standard.   The supply bureaus were called upon to provide for 3,912 men and officers on the march and an aggregate force of 5,606 when the whole army of Utah was united.[92]

On the march, the troops had to be supplied with 3 months' subsistence for consumption en route.   They were to carry with them a year's supply of rations for the entire army of Utah, and in addition the Subsistence Department was to throw forward to Fort Laramie an 8 months' reserve supply before winter set in.   Estimating that the force would also include 1,894 civilian employees, 300 servants, and 200 women, making a total of 8,000 to be subsisted, Commissary General Gibson reported that 4,880,000 rations would have to be provided for the year's supply and the depot reserve at a cost of $1,220,000.[93]   Before the end of March, most of the subsistence had been purchased and turned over to the Quartermaster's Department at St. Louis for transportation to Fort Leavenworth.   Contracts had also been made for beef cattle.[94]

In the meantime, the Quartermaster's Department made arrangements for the transportation of men and supplies.   For service with the operating columns, the Department furnished 988 baggage wagons as well as 29 light wagons, 6,447 mules, and 254 horses in addition to the horses provided for the mounted troops.[95]   The transportation of supplies to Utah and to the depots at Forts Kearny and Laramie from Fort Leavenworth required 3,908 wagons, 46,896 oxen, and 33 mules.[96]

Transportation of clothing, tents, wagons, and other supplies from the East could be handled in a different way than in former years.   For the first time, the Department could obtain railroad transportation from Philadelphia, New York, and Baltimore to St. Louis.   By December 1852, the Pennsylvania Railroad had opened regular service between Philadelphia and Pittsburgh, and one year later the Baltimore and Ohio Railroad reached Wheeling, but until lines were constructed in Ohio, Indiana, and Illinois no through service to St. Louis could be provided.   In May 1857, the Ohio and Mississippi Railroad began operating between Illinoistown, on the Mississippi opposite St. Louis, and Cincinnati, adding the last essential link to through transportation to St. Louis.

At Jesup's directions, quartermasters in Philadelphia, New York,

[92] House *Ex. Doc.* No. 2, 35th Cong., 2d sess., p. 31, s.n. 998 (Circular, 11 Jan 1858).

[93] House *Ex. Doc.* No. 33, 35th Cong., 1st sess., pp. 1–2, s.n. 955 (Floyd to Speaker HR, 15 Jan 1858).

[94] RG 192, CGS, Letters to SW, 1954–1866, pp. 75–78 78–80 (Actg CGS to SW, 22 Mar, 6 Apr 1858).

[95] House *Ex. Doc.* No.ʼ 2, 35th Cong., 2d sess., p. 797, s.n. 999 (QMG's Rpt, 13 Nov 1858).

[96] *Ibid.*

and Baltimore made inquiries of railroad agents to ascertain the lowest price at which the companies would transport military supplies from those cities to St. Louis. It soon became apparent that railroad policy had changed. Formerly, the Quartermaster's Department had advertised for bids from the railroads and awarded the contract for a definite shipment to the lowest bidder. In 1858, however, the railroads were all under an agreement to charge the same price for the same articles. They had fixed rates and classification of goods for civilian traffic. The Department thoroughly explored the problem of putting military items into the existing classifications. Colonel Thomas found that the railroad classification system placed Army wagons, clothing, and tents in the first class and that the Department would therefore be charged the highest rates. With Army wagons weighing nearly 1,900 pounds, the freight on them was 2½ times greater by rail than by sea via New Orleans.[97]

Further exchanges brought an agreement with the Pennsylvania Railroad rather than with the Baltimore and Ohio Railroad because the former was the first to entertain the idea of accepting emergency military orders and showed interest in classifying military stores into rate categories and at rates that would be more favorable to the Army than civilian rates. Moreover, Thomas came to the conclusion that the Pennsylvania was a safer road than the Baltimore and Ohio because there were fewer streams to cross and less handling of freight.[98] At the time, there were no railroad bridges across the Ohio at Wheeling or Parkersburg or across the Mississippi at St. Louis, and passengers and freight on the Baltimore and Ohio necessarily had to be ferried across the rivers in steamboats provided by the company. All freight was delivered to the terminal point of the Ohio and Mississippi Railroad opposite St. Louis, later known as East St. Louis.

One other contract completed the transportation arrangements west of the Mississippi. On 1 March 1858, the Department made a contract with the Pacific Railroad Company that operated 125 miles of road between St. Louis and Jefferson City, Mo., and was in the process of constructing the railroad westward to Kansas City. By agreement with Weldon & Able, the company also provided daily packet service on the Missouri River. The contract gave the company the exclusive right to transport, by railroad and steamboats, all the troops and military supplies, except such as might be transported in government steamers, from St. Louis to Fort Leavenworth, or such other points on the Missouri River as might be selected for temporary depots.[99]

---

[97] RG 92, OQMG Consolidated File, Box 869 (Thomas to Jesup, 30 Jan 1858).
[98] *Ibid.*, (Thomas to Jesup, 23 Feb 1858).
[99] (1) House *Ex. Doc.* No. 99, 35th Cong., 1st sess., p. 5, s.n. 958 (Jesup to Floyd, 6 Apr

Lack of funds considerably handicapped the preparations made by the Quartermaster's Department for supporting reinforcements sent to Utah. The Department had exhausted its appropriation for the fiscal year ending 30 June 1858 by January. Jesup reported that no Quartermaster supplies could be procured, no transportation arranged, and no cavalry and artillery horses purchased until Congress provided funds or the Secretary of War, under the authority vested in him, authorized the Department to purchase supplies by contract, to be paid for at a future time. To enable the reinforcements to move early in the spring and avoid the disaster that had overtaken the troops in 1857, the Secretary of War supplied funds from private sources and authorized the purchase of supplies by contracts to be paid for when Congress acted.[100] Congress passed a deficiency appropriation bill in May.

By that time, the second column of troops was on its march to Utah, the first emergency units having left Fort Leavenworth with part of the wagon train on 10 March. The first reinforcements of men and supplies arrived at Camp Scott between 8–10 June. About the same time, Captain Marcy arrived from New Mexico with horses and mules procured there. The Army of Utah, once again adequately equipped and provisioned, began its march to Salt Lake City on 13 June.[101] There was to be no fighting, however, because in June peace commissioners sent by President Buchanan obtained a promise from the Mormon leaders to obey the constitution and laws of the United States and to make no resistance to the Army. On receipt of this news, part of the troops en route were diverted to other places. Rations for their supply accompanied them. A one year's supply for the posts on the plains was taken from the Utah trains, and the rest continued on to Utah to provide a partial supply there for another year. Quartermaster stores, being nonperishable, were sent on to Utah to provide a store of supplies for the next 2 years. Horses, mules, and wagons that were not needed in the Department of Utah were diverted to other destinations.

1858). (2) The transportation rates were set at $12 for each officer and $6 for each enlisted man, with the current rates charged by steamers on the Missouri River at the time of shipment being applied to all supplies. The company agreed to deliver in either 5 or 7 days, depending on the destination point, under a forfeiture of 20 percent on the entire amount of freight that might be due on the shipment. RG 92, OQMG, Register of Contracts, 1852–59, vol. 12, pp. 442–43.

[100] (1) RG 92, Reports of QMG to SW and Heads of Depts., vol. 4, p. 206 (Jesup to Floyd, 17 Feb 1858). (2) House *Ex. Doc.* No. 2, 35th Cong., 2d sess., p. 8, s.n. 998 (SW's Rpt, 6 Dec 1858).

[101] House *Ex. Doc.* No. 2, 35th Cong., 2d sess., pp. 39–40, s.n. 998 (Col. W. Hoffman to AAG, 25 Feb 1858); pp. 105–06 (Brig. Gen. W. S. Harney to AAG, 27 May 1858); pp. 108–09 (Brig. Gen. A. S. Johnston to AAG, 11 Jun 1858).

Organization and Personnel

Though the dispersed state of the troops had increased enormously the burdens of the Quartermaster's Department during these years, its administrative organization remained unchanged.   In the Washington office, the Quartermaster General continued to be aided by one or two assistant quartermasters.   A chief clerk, five permanent clerks, and one messenger made up the office staff in 1849.[102]   These civilians gave continuity to office procedures by their long years of service in the office.   Two of the clerks had charge of the money accounts and the books in which they were entered; two kept the property accounts and were charged with all correspondence in connection with both property and money accounts; one clerk examined and recorded all contracts; and one analyzed and briefed the correspondence of the office and was responsible for bringing together all communications relating to any subject under consideration.[103]   Though Congress occasionally authorized the appointment of temporary clerks for particular duties, the inadequacy of his office staff led Jesup to appeal for more help, and, by 1858, Congress had increased the staff of permanent clerks to eleven, a number that was still modest for the records that had to be maintained.[104]

The number of officers that had to carry out the functions of the Quartermaster's Department and make its increasingly large disbursements was also small.   At the time of the Mormon expedition, the total number, including the Quartermaster General, was only 39.[105]   During the Mexican War, Congress had increased the personnel of the Department from 37 to 51 by providing for the appointment of 4 additional quartermasters and 10 assistant quartermasters.   When the war ended, none of these additional posts, under the provision of the law, could be filled when they fell vacant.   By 1860, the staff of the Department had returned to its basic authorized strength of 37 officers.   To take care of public property at the additional depots established during these years, Congress in 1857 did authorize the appointment of more military storekeepers, bringing the total number to eight.[106]   This staff was not large enough to perform all the duties required of it and, in addition to regimental quartermasters and such commissaries of subsistence as could be employed, the Department also used the services of more than 50 regimental officers either at posts or with marching detachments.[107]

[102] House Ex. Doc. No. 35, 1st Cong., 1st sess., p. 4, s.n. 576.
[103] RG 92, Reports to QMG to SW and Heads of Depts., vol. 2, pp. 143–46 (Jesup to Chairman, House Ways and Means Committee, 25 Jul 1852).
[104] Ibid., vol. 4, pp. 195–96 (Jesup to SW, 8 Feb 1858).
[105] See Army Registers for 1857 and 1858, House Ex. Doc. No. 66, 35th Cong., 1st sess., pp. 4–6, s.n. 955; No. 58, 35th Cong., 2d sess., pp. 4–6, s.n. 1006.
[106] 11 Stat. 200 (Mar 3, 1857).
[107] Senate Ex. Doc. No. 1, 32d Cong., 2d sess., Pt. 2, p. 73, s.n. 612 (QMG's Rpt, 20 Nov 1852).

Except for assignments to the offices at Philadelphia and New York, most Quartermaster officers were stationed west of the Mississippi. In general, too, the most important and responsible duties of the new frontier during much of this period devolved on the junior officers of the Department. This was providential because the experience they gained during these years enabled them to fill with competence many of the key supply posts of the Civil War. Capt. Robert Allen, who had immense responsibilities as chief quartermaster in California during these years, was well qualified to reorganize Quartermaster affairs at St. Louis in 1861 and supply the armies in the Mississippi Valley during the Civil War. Capt. Rufus Ingalls, who accompanied the Steptoe expedition that crossed the continent in 1854–55 and served as quartermaster in the Department of Oregon, distinguished himself as chief quartermaster to the Army of the Potomac. Capt. John H. Dickerson, chief quartermaster on the Mormon expedition, directed depot operations at Cincinnati during the Civil War. Capt. Daniel H. Rucker, assigned to duties in New Mexico during these years, established and directed supply from the Washington Depot during the Civil War.

The senior officers of the Department who should have been assigned to these important departments in the West were preoccupied after the Mexican War with the settlement of their accounts. They had accumulated large money and property accounts during that war, but delays in the Treasury Department prevented quick settlement of them. Those delays resulted from the fact that their accounts, unlike those of every other supply officer, had to be submitted to two auditors for settlement. That peculiarity had developed in the course of merging the Office of Commissary General of Purchases and the Quartermaster's Department. Different auditors had handled the accounts of the two departments. In consequence, after the consolidation, not only different vouchers in the same account but also different items in the same voucher had to go to different auditors in the Treasury.[108] Under such circumstances, the settlement of accounts often dragged on for years. Jesup repeatedly urged amendment of the settlement procedures so that all accounts and vouchers of the disbursing officers of the Department might be settled by one auditor of the Treasury Department, but this desirable reform was not enacted into law until 1857.[109]

Aside from settlement of accounts, the age and health of some of the senior officers of the Department precluded their appointment to the onerous duties of frontier posts. Many of these officers had seen service

---

[108] For example, a quantity of canvas used to repair a wagon cover would have to be accounted for to the 3d auditor, but a quantity of the same material taken from the same bale of canvas to repair a tent would have to be accounted for to the 2d auditor.

[109] (1) House *Ex. Doc.* No. 1, 31st Cong., 2d sess., Pt. 2, p. 125, s.n. 587 (QMG's Rpt,

in the War of 1812 over 35 years ago; some, and among them were a number of junior officers, had their health impaired in the Mexican War. Discussing assignments in 1853, Jesup observed that Assistant Quartermaster General Henry Stanton was unable to perform duty; Capt. Frederick H. Masten was so feeble that he was of no service to the Department; Maj. Samuel B. Dusenberry had performed no important duty since the Mexican War; and Capt. James G. Martin had but one arm, and the stump of the other gave him great pain.[110] There was no retirement program for disabilities or age in those years and quartermasters were carried on the rolls until death removed them.

In the 1850's, a number of the senior officers of the Department died; Col. Aeneas Mackay in 1850, Col. Henry Whiting in 1851, Major Dusenberry in 1855, Col. Henry Stanton and Col. Thomas F. Hunt in 1856. All but one of them—Dusenberry had been a cadet at the Military Academy in 1816—had served during the War of 1812. Colonel Whiting had been in the Army since 1808. Stanton and Hunt were the last of the small group of officers originally appointed when the Department was set up as a bureau in 1818.

Many a junior officer must have looked at Jesup with awe. He was still Quartermaster General as the decade of the 1850's ended, though his health was much impaired. During most of 1859, he conducted Quartermaster business from his home with the help of Deputy Quartermaster General Sibley. His administration of the Department, begun shortly after the War of 1812, lasted until almost the beginning of the Civil War. This period of tremendous territorial expansion, internal improvements, and industrial growth was reflected in Quartermaster operatitons. When Jesup became Quartermaster General in 1818, he felt that he was risking some reputation in trying to systematize a Department that had previously been so confused and disorganized. When his administration ended, he had converted the Department into an efficient supply bureau, developed a body of trained Quartermaster officers, created a satisfactory system of accountability, and evolved a set of regulations covering the functions of the Department and the duties of its officers that stood the test of time. After 52 years of continuous service in the Army, and 42 of those years as Quartermaster General, Jesup's long stewardship of the Quartermaster's Department came to an end with his death on 10 June 1860.

---

20 Nov 1850). Similar pleas were made in the annual reports of 1851, 1853, 1854, 1856. (2) RG 107, OSW, Military Book, vol. 35, pp. 41–44 (SW to Secy of Treasury, 9 Nov 1853). (3) 11 *Stat.* 200 (Mar 3, 1857).

[110] RG 92, OQMG Letter Book, vol. 46, p. 392 (Jesup to Hunt, 21 Dec 1853).

CHAPTER IX

Impact of Civil War

Jesup's death, in the midst of the tense political campaign of 1860, brought to a close a 42-year period in the history of the Quartermaster's Department, during which it was established as a supply bureau in Washington and its development was shaped by the control of one man. Within a few months the Buchanan administration was to end with the inauguration of Abraham Lincoln as president on 4 March 1861, but in June 1860 Buchanan was called upon to fill the vacant post of Quartermaster General. Promotion from within the Department would not have been unusual, but Col. Charles Thomas, assistant quartermaster general at Philadelphia and senior officer in the Department, was not considered.[1] Instead, Secretary of War John B. Floyd, who before the end of the year was to resign and later offer his services to the Confederacy, successfully carried through the appointment of a fellow-Virginian, Lt. Col. Joseph E. Johnston of the 1st U. S. Cavalry.[2] He was appointed Quartermaster General with the rank of brigadier general on 28 June 1860 and assumed the duties of his office on 2 July.

Impact of Secession on Personnel

Quartermaster General Johnston's administration of the Department was so brief—it lasted barely 10 months—that he left no imprint on developments. He tendered his resignation on 22 April 1861, 3 days after he learned that Virginia had passed an ordinance of secession on 17 April. President Lincoln immediately assigned as Acting Quartermaster General Maj. Ebenezer S. Sibley, an officer with 34 years of service

---

[1] It is probable that his age counted against him for he had been in service since 1819. The numerous deaths that had been occurring among officers who had been in the Army since the War of 1812 and the years immediately thereafter undoubtedly influenced the Secretary of War to go outside the Department in search of a younger man.

[2] The General in Chief of the Army, Winfield Scott, called upon to designate the officer best fitted in his opinion for the post, had instead submitted a list of four names—Bvt. Brig. Gen. Albert S. Johnston, Lt. Col. Joseph E. Johnston, Lt. Col. Robert E. Lee, and Lt. Col. Charles F. Smith. The choice soon narrowed down to the two Johnstons, with Floyd favoring Joseph E. Johnston and Jefferson Davis, who had been Secretary of War and was then senator from Mississippi and chairman of the Military Affairs Committee, advocating the appointment of Albert S. Johnston.

in the Army, 23 of them in the Quartermaster's Department.[3]   During the first 2 months of the war, Sibley was placed in the unenviable position of trying to execute the duties of the Department while the new Secretary of War, Simon Cameron, intent on patronage, ignored the legitimate supply agency of the Army and infringed upon its duties by appointing "irresponsible temporary agents, through whom a system of favoritism could be consummated," to purchase and forward supplies and transport troops.[4]

The southern states had threatened to secede if the "Black Republican" won the election of 1860, a threat that South Carolina promptly carried out in December.   By the following February, six southern states had joined her, but President Buchanan, troubled by constitutional scruples, took no steps nor did the new Lincoln administration, when it came into power, initiate any measures preparatory for war.   There was, in fact, no conviction among the people and their leaders that war was inevitable.   No unanimity of opinion existed in the North concerning even the action to be taken against the seceded states.   When Fort Sumter was attacked on 12 April, however, doubts and uncertainties were dispelled.   A war spirit was kindled that swept men into the Army faster than they could be clothed and equipped.

At that time, the Quartermaster's Department had an authorized staff of 37 officers, including the Quartermaster General, and 7 military storekeepers.[5]   Actually, on 12 April it had only 35 officers.   Capt. Henry Wayne of Georgia had resigned on 31 December 1860 and later served in the Confederate Army, while Capt. Abraham C. Myers of South Carolina, who was to become Quartermaster General of the Confederate Army, had resigned about a month after his native state passed an ordinance of secession.[6]   When Lincoln called out the militia, four more southern states seceded, and the Quartermaster's Department lost six more officers, including Quartermaster General Johnston.   Four officers of southern birth remained loyal to the Union and none of the military storekeepers resigned.   The Department thus lost nearly one-fourth of its personnel at the beginning of the war.

Its remaining staff was thoroughly experienced.   Approximately

---

[3] *The War of the Rebellion: Official Records of the Union and Confederate Armies* (130 vols., Washington, 1880–1901), ser. III, vol. I, p. 99 (SO 113, 22 Apr 1861).   Hereafter briefly cited as *OR.*

[4] "Government Contracts," House *Rpt.* No. 2, 37th Cong., 2d sess., p. 55, s.n. 1142.

[5] In addition to the Quartermaster General, the staff consisted of 2 assistant quartermasters general, 2 deputy quartermasters general, 4 quartermasters, and 28 assistant quartermasters, with the rank, respectively, of colonel, lieutenant colonel, major, and captain.

[6] RG 92, Rpts of QMG to SW and Heads of Dept., vol. 5, pp. 410–15 (List of Officers, 12 Apr 1861).

one-third of the officers had been in Quartermaster service since 1838. They had supplied the troops in the Mexican War, and in 1861 they filled the top positions in the Department.   At least half of the remaining personnel had from 12 to 15 years experience in the Department, and from among these younger officers came the quartermasters ultimately assigned to some of the key positions with the armies in the field and at supporting depots.

Months were to pass, however, before some of these experienced officers could be brought East and reassigned, for, like the greater part of the Regular Army, most quartermasters in the years before the war were assigned to duties on the frontier.   Some of them, stationed at southern posts, were captured at the beginning of the war and their services, at least temporarily, were lost to the Department.   In addition, valuable officers were also lost by appointment to combat commands. Obviously, the scope of Civil War operations called for the services of many more officers than were on the Department's roster in April 1861. The Department was soon seriously embarrassed by the lack of officers of experience and knowledge to execute its duties, and throughout the conflict it was greatly hampered by the small size of its staff.   The Department's regular staff organization was never expanded during the war to an extent commensurate with the volume of business it handled or the number of troops it supplied.   Only once during the war was the size of its staff increased.   On 3 August 1861, Congress raised the Department's authorized strength from 37 to 64.[7]

For approximately the first 2 months of the war, Quartermaster operations were severely handicapped by the lack of a duly appointed chief of the Department.   It was natural that some of the senior officers should advance their claims to recognition.   General Scott would have been willing to give the appointment to Col. Charles Thomas in order to promote the valuable officers below him.[8]   Such was the importance of the Quartermaster General's position that the office was much sought after by others outside the Department, and considerable maneuvering by interested parties occurred during these weeks.   Senator John Sherman and his friends tried to obtain the appointment for his brother, William T. Sherman.[9]   Secretary of State William Seward and Postmaster

---

[7] (1) Congress added one colonel, 2 lieutenant colonels, 4 majors, and 20 captains to the Department's staff. 12 *Stat*. 287. (2) By act of July 5, 1862, the number of military storekeepers in the Department was also increased from seven to a total of no more than twelve. 12 *Stat*. 505.

[8] (1) *The Lincoln Papers*, ed. David C. Mearns (2 vols., Garden City, N.Y., 1948), II, 630 (Scott to Lincoln, 5 Jun 1861). (2) *The Collected Works of Abraham Lincoln*, ed. Roy P. Basler (8 vols., Rutgers University Press, 1953), IV, 394, fn. 1.

[9] Lloyd Lewis, *Sherman Fighting Prophet* (New York, 1932), p. 162.

General Montgomery Blair backed a rival nominee, Capt. Montgomery C. Meigs of the Engineer Corps.

Meigs was well known in Washington as the designer and builder of the aqueduct that supplied the city with water. He had also super-intended the construction of the wings and dome of the United States Capitol. His excellent Army record was further enhanced in April 1861 by his part in the successful Fort Pickens expedition—that astonishing affair, secretly planned and executed not by the authorized military departments but by the Secretary of State and President Lincoln, assisted by Captain Meigs, Lt. Col. Erasmus D. Keyes, military secretary to General Scott, and Navy Lt. David D. Porter. For his part in that affair, Captain Meigs was appointed colonel of the 11th Regiment of Infantry on 14 May. With considerable reluctance, he gave up his more influen-tial position in the Engineer Corps and accepted the appointment only after it had been explained to him that it would be a stepping stone to an early advance to a brigadier generalship and the post of Quartermaster General. "They did not like to excite the jealousy of the army by so high a lift at once," he informed his father.[10]

His role in the Fort Pickens expedition had earned him the enmity of Secretary Cameron, who opposed his appointment as Quartermaster General. Lincoln, on the other hand, was favorably impressed with the 45-year old Meigs, who combined "the qualities of masculine intellect, learning and experience of the right sort, and physical power of labor and endurance," and he enlisted the influence of General Scott to remove Cameron's objections.[11] Scott was successful and on 12 June Meigs was appointed Quartermaster General.[12]

The following day, Meigs entered upon the duties of his new office. As Quartermaster General, he was the second most important officer in the Army, not in military rank but in actual real influence. He proudly pointed out to his father that a major general commanded a corps d'armée on a single line; a lieutenant general commanded the whole army; but the Quartermaster General supplied the means of moving that army and his command extended from the Atlantic to the Pacific, from the lakes to the Gulf.[13] It would have been difficult to find an abler

[10] (1) Meigs Papers, (21 May 1861). (2) Pocket Diaries of Meigs, (entries for 17, 18, 27 May; 8, 11, 13 Jun 1861). Manuscript Div., Library of Congress.

[11] (1) The Collected Works of Abraham Lincoln, ed. Basler, IV, 394–95 (Lincoln to Scott, 5 Jun 1861). (2) The Lincoln Papers, ed. Means, II, 630 (Scott to Lincoln, 5 Jun 1861).

[12] (1) Meigs Papers, (Appointment and letter of acceptance, 13 Jun 1861). (2) Originally, Meigs' rank of brigadier general was to date from 10 June. Subsequently, Lincoln renomi-nated Meigs with rank to date from 15 May in order to correct the error by which his rank was dated after that of other officers, while his appointment was actually of an earlier date. Executive Journal, XI, 543–44.

[13] Meigs Papers, (12 Jun 1861).

Quartermaster General.   He had every qualification for the post, General Scott conceded—"high genius, science, vigor & administrative capacities." [14]   He lacked special experience in Quartermaster business and, to function effectively, he had to win the cordial support of the principal officers of the Department.   He overcame both of these deficiencies within a short time, and after Edwin M. Stanton replaced Simon Cameron in January 1862 he had the solid support of the Secretary of War.

Office Organization

Administrative detail necessarily engaged a considerable part of Meigs' attention.   He soon found that the Department's clerical force in Washington was inadequate to examine the thousands of accounts and reports that had to be submitted by quartermasters.   Repeatedly during the war, Meigs called for more clerks, but although Congress authorized increases, the growth in Quartermaster operations was so extensive that its business continually outran the means provided by law to examine and adjust accounts in the Washington office.[15]   He found it difficult to retain experienced clerks in the face of rising costs in the city.   For the first time in its history, the Department employed women copyists.   Beginning modestly with three in 1862, the number rose to 29 by the end of 1864.   By that time, the male clerical staff numbered 184 and Meigs was calling for an additional 170.[16]

The accounts handled by the Washington office and the correspondence relating to them tended to fall into three categories—those relating to clothing and equipage, to transportation by land and water, and to regular and contingent supplies of the Department.   At the beginning of the war, only one of these categories was organized as a bureau in the office and that was the clothing bureau under the direction of Capt. Alexander J. Perry.   Such a bureau had been in existence since the early days of Jesup.   Gradually, under Meigs, other divisions of duties occurred.   Captain Perry continued to handle clothing and equipage accounts and correspondence, but by 1864 Colonel Thomas had been brought into the office to examine all contracts and superintend all money and property accounts.   Deputy Quartermaster General Sibley took care of all duties connected with quarters, hospitals, and estimates of funds. Col. Robert E. Clary had charge of water transportation, Capt. Benja-

---

[14] *The Lincoln Papers*, ed. Means, II, 630 (Scott to Lincoln, 5 Jun 1861).

[15] See *Annual Reports of the Quartermaster General, 1861–1865, passim.*

[16] (1) RG 92, OQMG Decision Book, No. 2, p. 207 (ASW Watson to QMD, 15 Oct 1862). (2) RG 92, OQMG Letter Book, vol. 64, p. 455 Meigs to Sen. T. Willey, 5 Dec 1862); vol. 81, pp. 405–09 (Col. J. J. Dana to J. Boyd, 5 Dec 1864).   National Archives.

mine C. Card handled claims, and Capt. George V. Rutherford examined reports from the field.[17]   In 1864, Meigs sought legal authorization for the division of duties that had developed in the office.   He proposed and Congress approved the establishment of nine divisions in the office of the Quartermaster General, each under the direction of a colonel.[18] This organization was limited to the duration of the war and for one year thereafter.

Supply Difficulties in 1861

While administrative developments grew increasingly important as the war progressed, supply was the prime consideration of the Quartermaster's Department in 1861 and throughout the war.   In April 1861, Quartermaster supplies on hand were barely sufficient for the wants of the small peacetime Regular Army.   The Schuylkill Arsenal was still the chief depository for clothing and equipage as it had been in the past. St. Louis, for example, was not a storage depot for supplies.   It was a point at which purchases were made under orders of the Quartermaster General to fill requisitions of officers at other western posts.   Accumulation of large reserve stocks of Quartermaster supplies was impossible since the funds Congress appropriated, for specific purposes and non-transferable, were usually sufficient to cover only immediate needs.

On the eve of the Civil War, the Quartermaster's Department like the Army generally, had long been hampered by lack of funds.   For years, it had been burdened with debts.   Its liabilities had usually been greater than the balance reported at the end of each fiscal year, largely because unforeseen expenditures were incurred as a result of actions taken to prevent or subdue Indian disturbances in the pre-Civil War years.[19] Congress initiated no measures to improve its situation or that of the military department generally.   Instead, in December 1860, the chairman of the Senate Military Affairs Committee had inquired whether expenses could not be further reduced without detriment to the public service.[20] Already hampered by lack of funds that had compelled the adoption of

---

[17] RG 92, OQMG Letter Book, vol. 74, pp. 536–37 (GO 10, 24 Feb 1864).

[18] (1) 13 *Stat.* 394–95 (Jul 4, 1864). (2) Briefly, the nine divisions were as follows: 1st (horses and mules) under Col. James A. Ekin; 2d (clothing and equipage) under Col. Alexander J. Perry; 3d (ocean transportation) under Col. George D. Wise; 4th (rail and river transportation) under Col. Lewis B. Parsons; 5th (forage) under Col. Samuel L. Brown; 6th (military buildings) under Col. Benjamin C. Card, who was also charged with the duties of the 9th division (records and correspondence); and 8th (inspection) under Col. George V. Rutherford.   RG 92, OQMG Letter Book, vol. 81, p. 405 (Col. Dana to J. Boyd, 5 Dec 1864).

[19] See, for example, Senate *Ex. Doc.* No. 1, 36th Cong., 2d sess., vol. II, pp. 233–36 (QMG's Rpt. 1860).

[20] RG 107, OSW, Letters Received, M–232 (97) (Jefferson Davis to Floyd, 13 Dec 1860).

policies of retrenchment, and by a reduction in its clerical staff that prevented execution of all its duties, the Quartermaster's Department was in no position to cut expenditures.[21]   Congress must share some of the responsibility for the inability of the Quartermaster's Department to meet the supply demands made upon it in April 1861.

When Fort Sumter was fired upon, Congress was not in session and Lincoln did not call it into special session until 4 July 1861.[22]   Not only had the appropriated funds of the Quartermaster's Department been dwindling rapidly even before the impact of war was felt, but Congress had provided that no contracts or purchases could be made unless under an appropriation adequate to its fullfillment.[23]   Contracts for clothing, subsistence, forage, fuel, quarters, or transportation in the War and Navy Departments were made an exception to this rule but purchases under such contracts were not to exceed the necessities of the current year. Such a provision hampered the accumulation of any reserve supply for the Regular Army and Congress had specifically appropriated no funds for supplying the Volunteers.

Procurement measures had nevertheless to be initiated immediately when on 15 April Lincoln called out 75,000 militia for 3 months of service.   It is one of the oddities of the war that General Johnston, who was to lead an army of the Confederacy, was Quartermaster General of the U.S. Army on that date and for a week thereafter.   He dispatched the first procurement directive of the war to Colonel Thomas at Philadelphia, instructing him to purchase sufficient knapsacks, canteens, and camp equipage to supply the 75,000 militia.   He followed this with an order to "direct all your energies to the preparation of fatigue clothing for Volunteers." [24]

Contracts had barely been let before supply demands were doubled by Lincoln's proclamation of 3 May.[25]   The President called for 42,034 volunteers to be enlisted for 3 years of service and expanded the Regular Army by an increase of 22,714 officers and enlisted men.   More than 91,000 men answered the April appeal.   By summer, nearly a quarter of a million men had rushed to arms in response to the various Presidential calls.   In the fall, Meigs estimated for an Army of 300,000, but

[21] (1) Senate *Ex. Doc.* No. 1, 36th Cong., 2d sess., vol. II, p. 236 (QMG's Rpt, 1860). (2) For examples of retrenchment see, RG 92, OQMG Letter Book, vol. 55, p. 195 (Johnston to Capt. S. Van Vliet, 17 Jan 1861); p. 236 (Same to Capt. R. E. Clary, 11 Feb 1861).

[22] *OR,* ser. III, vol. I, p. 68 (Proclamation, 15 Apr 1861).

[23] 12 *Stat.* 220 (Mar 2, 1861).

[24] (1) RG 92, OQMG Decision Book, vol. 2, p. 69 (Cameron to QMG, 16 Apr 1861). (2) RG 92, OQMG Letter Book, Clothing, vol. 17, p. 427 (Johnston to Thomas, 17 and 20 Apr 1861); p. 440 (Same to same, 20 Apr 1861).

[25] *OR,* ser. III, vol. I, p. 146.

even as Congress appropriated funds for that number it authorized the President to accept the services of 500,000 volunteers and increased the Regular Army to about 50,000.[26]

Under these circumstances, contracting could not be orderly, and in any event the small Quartermaster's Department of April 1861, geared to supply the Regular Army of 16,000 men, was wholly inadequate to meet the demands made by this rapidly expanding force. State governors clamored for arms and equipment to enable them to prepare their troops to take the field. Failing to obtain supplies from the War Department, they soon turned their attention to purchasing supplies to equip their regiments, and Cameron approved.[27] Colonels and quartermasters of these new volunteer regiments bought supplies. Lacking experience, they were often imposed upon by unscrupulous merchants who seized the opportunity to garner handsome profits. Not infrequently, these quartermasters shared in the profits.[28] Patriotic Union Defense Committees also quickly sprang into existence in the states to equip and forward troops. Thus, both federal and state agents were soon competing for supplies not only in the domestic market but also in foreign markets.

Secretary of War Cameron, inexperienced in Army matters, was hampered both by a lack of trained assistants and a well-organized War Department. Yet since his appointment he had done little to improve his Department. Political patronage had been of primary concern to him, so much so that even in the midst of the burdens imposed by war, clerkships in the Philadelphia Depot did not escape his attention. Colonel Thomas had to plead for the retention of his trained personnel lest he be unable to attend to all his duties.[29]

It is understandable that Cameron might not feel free to rely on his Quartermaster General for assistance with supply problems, since Johnston was torn between duty to his country and loyalty to his native state, but the services of other loyal, competent, and thoroughly experi-

[26] *Ibid.*, p. 866 (Meigs to Stanton, 28 Jan 1862).

[27] *Ibid.*, ser. III, vol. I, p. 73 (QMG of N.J. to Cameron, 16 Apr 1861); p. 89 (Gov. O. P. Morton to Cameron, 19 Apr 1861); pp. 115–16 (Cameron to Morton, 26 Apr 1861).)

[28] "Government Contracts," House *Rpt.* No. 2, 37th Cong., 2d sess., pp. 69–71, s.n. 1142.

[29] (1) RG 92, OQMG Letters Received, Box 78 (Telegram, Thomas to Sibley, 8 Jun 1861). (2) Rumors of impending changes had circulated as soon as the new Administration came into office but Colonel Thomas refused to give them credence. The depot commander had always had the selection of his clerks and assistants and his clerks had been with him for many years, serving through various Administrations of different politics. RG 92, AQMG Thomas, Letters Sent, 30 Jan–12 Apr 1861 (Thomas to Johnston, 12 Mar 1861). (3) The Commissary General of Subsistence was similarly distressed by Cameron's contemplated action and also made a plea for the retention of his office personnel. RG 192, Records of CGS, Letters to SW, 1854–66, p. 142 (23 Mar 1861).

enced Quartermaster officers were available to him. Major Sibley had often served as Acting Quartermaster General during General Jesup's absences. Colonel Tompkins at New York had handled complex transportation problems in the Mexican War, and Colonel Thomas, who had also served in that war, had long been purchasing clothing and equipment at Philadelphia. Assisted by additional agents, they might have been called upon to direct and supervise the equipping and forwarding of troops in April 1861.[30]

Instead, Secretary Cameron bypassed the Quartermaster's Department and appointed his staunch political friends and supporters as War Department agents to purchase and forward supplies and to direct the transportation of troops. This concentration of appointments among Pennsylvania Republicans of the Cameron school soon occasioned widespread criticism. The congressional committee investigating government contracts enlarged upon the harmful consequences resulting from the employment of such agents to purchase supplies and services.[31]

The appointment of Alexander Cummings was a case in point. Assistant Quartermaster General Tompkins and Maj. Amos B. Eaton of the Subsistence Department both were stationed at New York. But, when the Baltimore municipal authorities cut rail communications in that city on 19 April and isolated Washington, Cameron, 4 days later, appointed Alexander Cummings, one of his campaign managers in the national convention of 1860, to purchase and push forward supplies from New York and transport troops to Washington until such time as communications could be restored between the capital and New York.[32]

[30] It is said that the resignation of General Johnston left Cameron without a strong man in the Quartermaster's Department; only older and less aggressive officers remained to assist him. Bound by red tape, worn-out rules and regulations, they clung to the old ways as best. Samuel R. Kamm, *The Civil War Career of Thomas A. Scott* (Philadelphia, 1940), p. 22; A. Howard Meneely, *The War Department, 1861* (New York, 1928), pp. 108–09. It is true that the key posts were held by older officers whose actions were always governed by regulations, but there is nothing wrong with being governed by regulations. They are essential in operating any business, and the regulations of the Civil War years differed but little from those of the prewar years in the Quartermaster's Department. The older officers—men in their late fifties and early sixties, all but two of whom served throughout the war—possibly were not as aggressive as younger men might have been, but that was a characteristic necessary in the field. These men had the administrative and supervisory experience needed to keep the Quartermaster offices in New York, Philadelphia, and Washington operating. They knew the laws and the regulations that hemmed in their operations and protected the interests of the government, and it would have been definitely advantageous had all quartermasters during the Civil War known the regulations and applied them.

[31] One of the first acts of Congress upon being called into extra session was to appoint a committee on 8 July 1861 to investigate government contracts. Appointed by the Speaker of the House of Representatives, the committee under the chairmanship of Charles H. Van Wyck, held meetings in various parts of the country, submitting its findings in two voluminous volumes. See "Government Contracts," House *Rpt.* No. 2, 37th Cong., 2d sess., s.n. 1142 and 1143.

[32] Bridges on the Philadelphia, Wilmington & Baltimore Railroad between the Susque-

Cummings was to work with Gov. Edwin D. Morgan of New York. To cover expenditures for defense purposes, the Secretary of the Treasury, without requiring security, placed a fund of $2,000,000 in the hands of John A. Dix, Richard M. Blatchford, and George Opdyke, prominent members of the New York Defense Committee. Under Cameron's broad directive, this money was at the complete disposal of either Governor Morgan or Alexander Cummings, but, since the Governor was preoccupied with other duties, Cummings alone expended most of the funds.[33]

Business qualifications were certainly essential for this assignment, but Alexander Cummings gave little evidence of possessing these and, moreover, had no general acquaintance with business in New York. For 12 years he had been a Pennsylvania newspaper editor and in 1861 was a publisher of a New York newspaper. Operating without restrictions, he purchased supplies on an emergency basis, not in response to requisitions but based solely on his judgment of what was needed in Washington. The congressional committee investigating government contracts aired all the details of his shortcomings as a purchasing agent and but two examples are needed to illustrate them. Cummings spent over $21,000 in the purchase of linen pantaloons and straw hats because "hot weather was coming on" and he thought that they would be needed, though an inquiry at the Quartermaster office in New York would have revealed that regulations provided for the issue of neither article. Uninformed about business backgrounds, Cummings also purchased, without consulting Commissary Eaton, provisions and groceries from E. Corning & Co., a firm engaged in the hardware business at Albany, New York.[34]

Regulations setting forth the items of issue to the troops and requisitions indicating the quantities of such items required by the troops governed the procurement of supplies. Procedures for the purchase of supplies and services were based on laws enacted by Congress. Early in 1861, Congress had reiterated the basic policy that had long governed procurement. It had enacted legislation providing that all purchases and contracts for supplies and services in any governmental department were to be made by advertising for proposals, allowing a sufficient time for the submission of bids, and making the award to the lowest bidder. In any emergency demanding immediate delivery of articles or performance of the service needed, however, the law had authorized procurement by open purchase or contract.[35]

At the outbreak of the war, much procurement was necessarily and

hanna River and Baltimore and also on the Northern Central Railroad between Baltimore and the Pennsylvania state line were destroyed.

[33] "Government Contracts," House *Rpt*. No. 2, 37th Cong., 2d sess., pp. 55–58, s.n. 1142.

[34] *Ibid.*, pp. 59–60, s.n. 1142.

[35] 12 *Stat*. 220 (Mar 2, 1861).

rightly placed on an emergency basis. Unfortunately, the continued failure to invite competition, once the first emergency had passed, could not be justified. The congressional committee investigating government contracts concluded that the law on contract procedure was a dead letter, that the safeguards provided in the use of duly authorized public officers were disregarded by employing irresponsible agents, and that new and more precise legislation must be enacted to protect the interests of the government.[36] The committee condemned the irresponsible agents who sacrificed the public interests through lack of experience or integrity, but it praised the Regular Army quartermasters and commissaries as officers who, with a few exceptions, were men "of ample and equal capacity and fidelity," ever jealous for the public welfare.[37]

One such exception exposed by the committee was Maj. Justus McKinstry, quartermaster at St. Louis, who was responsible for supplying the troops of the Western Department, first under Brig. Gen. William S. Harney and then under Maj. Gen. John C. Fremont. St. Louis had not been a depot for Army supplies so that when volunteers crowded the city in response to Presidential calls, Quartermaster McKinstry had to procure supplies to equip them. He had no money with which to make purchases, and he later maintained that he could not depend upon the State government of Missouri for aid. Moreover, troop movements occurred before he could obtain supplies from eastern depots. He therefore resorted to open-market purchases and made use of middlemen who could afford to extend the necessary credit.[38] The trying circumstances under which McKinstry operated condoned emergency procurement at the start of the war, but the law on contracts continued to be disregarded thereafter. He procured large quantities of supplies on what was termed "requisition," that is an order to a firm to supply a given quantity of certain articles, all made of the best material, conforming to Army regulations and requirements. The cost of the material, manufacture, and transportation of the articles was to be furnished by the merchants to the quartermaster who then allowed them a fair profit. On the basis of such requisitions, one firm in St. Louis— Child, Pratt & Fox—furnished over $800,000 worth of supplies without the price of any of them being previously determined. As it worked out, the "fair mercantile profit" allowed by the quartermaster came to 40 percent.[39]

---

[36] "Government Contracts," House *Rpt.* No. 2, 37th Cong., 2d sess., p. 53, s.n. 1142.

[37] *Ibid.,* pp. 54–55.

[38] RG 92, OQMG Consolidated Correspondence File, Box 641 (McKinstry's vindication, 2 Jan 1862).

[39] "Government Contracts," House *Rpt.* No. 2, 37th Cong., 2d sess., pp. 53–54; 101–02; 104, s.n. 1142.

It is only too true that General Fremont's peremptory demands for supplies resulted in McKinstry's viewing every requisition as necessitating emergency action. The Quartermaster's Department furnished funds, but Fremont, busy building fortifications in St. Louis and arming and equipping his troops, appealed not only to the War Department for support but to Postmaster General Montgomery Blair and President Lincoln.[40] Meigs sought to reassure Fremont that he would be fully supported by his Department, but Fremont nevertheless appointed agents who operated outside the Quartermaster Department in making contracts and disbursements. He delegated to the Union Defense Committee of Chicago the power and duties of the Department in contracting for and providing clothing for the troops. Meigs doubted the propriety of placing Departmental funds under the control of a committee responsible only to public opinion.[41] The government was soon appalled by the costs that Fremont ran up in the Western Department.

As a result of investigations, Quartermaster McKinstry was arrested on 13 November 1861, brought before a general court martial, tried on charges of favoritism and corruption, convicted of some of these charges, and dismissed from the service.[42] Quartermaster Robert Allen was transferred from the Pacific Coast and assigned to St. Louis. He was on the job only a few days before he telegraphed the Quartermaster General that "unless the wanton, reckless expenditures in this command are arrested by a stronger arm than mine, the Quartermaster's Dept. will be wrecked in Missouri along with Gen. Fremont. The Army Regulations are a blank & the laws of Congress a contemptible farce." [43]

Yet congressional committees dealt kindly with Fremont, for his earnestness, zeal, honesty, and patriotism were above question and his political influence was great. Fremont, however, was poorly fitted for command of the Western Department. He made numerous irregular appointments; he was no judge of men; he had on his staff persons directly and indirectly concerned in furnishing supplies; and extravagance and fraud flourished as a result.[44]

All of Fremont's contracts for fortifications, supplies, food, arms, steamboats, wagons, and horses, it is estimated, totaled only about $12 million.[45] The wastefulness lay not in the amount expended but in the

[40] *OR*, ser. I, vol. III, pp. 409–10 (Fremont to M. Blair, 28 Jul 1861); vol. IV, pp. 416–17 (Fremont to Lincoln, 30 Jul 1861).

[41] RG 92, Rpts of QMG to SW and Heads of Depts., vol. 5, pp. 462–63 (Meigs to Cameron, 3 Sep 1861).

[42] AGO *War Department Orders*, GO 43, 13 Feb 1862.

[43] RG 92, OQMG Letters Received, Box 79 (8 Oct 1861).

[44] *OR*, ser. I, vol. IV, pp. 540–51 (Rpt, AG L. Thomas to Cameron, 21 Oct 1861).

[45] Allan Nevins, *Fremont* (2 vols., New York, 1928), II, 613.

fact that so much of the money went into the pockets of dishonest contractors at the expense of the troops. After Fremont had been relieved, Maj. Gen. H. W. Halleck, who took command late in the fall of 1861, reported complete chaos in the department. "The most astonishing orders and contracts for supplies of all kinds have been made and large amounts purport to have been received but there is nothing to show that they have ever been properly issued, and they cannot now be found." [46] Meantime, many of the troops at different points in the Western Department were reported to be without arms and suffering from the lack of clothing and blankets. Such were the fruits resulting from neglect of regulations and laws intended to safeguard public interests.

For every quartermaster in the Civil War willing to profit at the expense of the soldiers, there seem to have been at least two contractors eager to show him how it could be done with advantage to both. Many manufacturers and merchants who previously had enjoyed good reputations were revealed by the war to be rapacious seekers after profits. From the lowliest quartermaster to the Quartermaster General himself, all felt the force of the pressure that contractors, lobbyists, and speculators exerted to win a share of the lucrative government contracts. Of them de Trobriand wrote:

> These hurried to the assault on the treasury, like a cloud of locusts alighting down upon the capital to devour the substance of the country. They were everywhere; in the streets, in the hotels, in the offices, at the Capitol, and in the White House. They continually besieged the bureaus of administration, the doors of the Senate and House of Representatives, wherever there was a chance to gain something.[47]

Quartermaster General Meigs urged and Secretary Stanton acted to close the doors of the War Department at 3 P.M. to all but officers of the United States so that they might at least have a few hours in the day in which they could do something besides answer applicants for contracts.[48] Such was the business climate of the day, and businessmen of the Civil War years must shoulder a large share of the responsibility for the unsavory supply situation of that period.

Contract Procedures

Over the years, Congress had enacted legislation to protect the interests of the government. Well aware that war provided opportunities for swindling the government, Congress in the summer of 1861 proposed

[46] *OR*, ser. I, vol. VIII, pp. 389–90 (Halleck to McClellan, 28 Nov 1861).

[47] Regis de Trobriand, *Four Years with the Army of the Potomac,* trans. George K. Dauchy (Boston, 1889), p. 135.

[48] RG 92, OQMG Letter Book, vol. 56, p. 168 (Meigs to Chief Clerk, WD, 7 Aug 1861).

to enact new legislation that would prevent frauds by supply officers entrusted with the making of contracts. The conditions it proposed to impose—reduction of all contracts to writing and appearance before a magistrate to obtain affidavits—would not necessarily have prevented fraud but would have delayed and hampered supply. Meigs courageously fought this attempt to bind his Department with new regulations, insisting that the existing law was sufficient to protect public interests.[49]

For a time, Meigs' arguments prevailed, but the abuses exposed by the congressional committee investigating government contracts brought renewed interest in remedial legislation, and a year later Congress passed the act of June 2, 1862.[50] The provisions, applicable to all supply bureaus, were much the same as had been proposed the year before, and in addition the law required that a copy of the contract, together with all bids, offers, and proposals and a copy of the advertisement published, all numerically arranged, be sent to a record office to be established in the Department of the Interior. Having failed to prevent passage of the law, Meigs advised the Secretary of War that it would be impracticable to execute it. Quartermasters in the field made many purchases of supplies during active operations, and the only way in which they could observe the law's provisions would be to have magistrates attached to their offices as clerks. In addition, creating a separate record office in the Interior Department to which bids were sent, Meigs argued, would deprive the Quartermaster General of any opportunity to examine and control the award of contracts upon those bids. Meigs insisted that all that needed to be added to previously existing legislation were provisions imposing sufficient but reasonable penalties for fraud, with quick and efficient processes for enforcing them.[51]

Secretary Stanton thereupon ruled that in his opinion the law was to apply only to such contracts as had been required to be in writing under laws and regulations in force at the time of its passage. Any other interpretation would make the act impracticable of execution, and a general order to that effect was published on 16 June 1862.[52] A month later, Congress itself reconsidered its action and suspended the operation of the law until the first Monday of January 1863.[53] Meigs undoubtedly hoped that the law would be amended before that date, but despite his efforts to win members to his view, Congress adjourned without recon-

---

[49] OR, ser. III, vol. I, pp. 378–79 (Meigs to Sen. Henry Wilson, 2 Aug 1861).
[50] 12 Stat. 411–12.
[51] RG 92, Rpts and Ltrs from QMG to SW and Other Officials, vol. 2, pp. 433–36 (Meigs to Stanton, 13 Jun 1862).
[52] (1) RG 92, OQMG Letters Received, Box 93 (Stanton to bureau chiefs, 16 Jun 1862). (2) General Orders of the War Department, 1861–62, I, 298 (GO 69, 16 Jun 1862).
[53] 12 Stat. 596 (Jul 17, 1862).

sidering the law which automatically went into effect in January 1863. Stanton's general order of 16 June 1862 was once again put into effect during the remainder of the war.[54]

For the first 3 years of the war, Quartermaster supplies were procured by depot quartermasters or quartermasters in the field, either under contract or, in an emergency, by open-market purchase. When Congress reorganized the Quartermaster's Department in 1864, it provided for a more centralized control of contracts. Thereafter, the chiefs of the several divisions in the Quartermaster General's office contracted for all Quartermaster supplies. The bulk of the supplies they procured were sent to depots, but, when it was more economical or advantageous to do so, supplies could be sent direct to a quartermaster in the field. In either case, supplies were subjected to inspection, and payment for them was made at the direction of the division chief only on the receipt of inspectors' certificates. In an emergency, when supplies could not be obtained from a depot or through the chief of a division, the chief quartermaster of an army or detachment could procure supplies without advertisement on the order of the commanding officer.[55]

By 1864, Congress also enacted legislation bringing inspectors of Army supplies under control. In the summer of 1862, it had passed a law providing that any contractor found guilty by court martial of fraud or willful neglect of duty was to be punished by fine, imprisonment, or such other punishment as a court martial adjudged. The law further provided that anyone furnishing supplies to the Army was to be subject to the rules and regulations governing the Army. The provisions of that law were extended in 1864 to inspectors and to the agents of contractors.[56] Finally, a law passed in 1862, penalizing Congressmen who accepted compensation for services in connection with government contracts, was extended in 1864 to include department or bureau heads, clerks, or any officer of government.[57] Thus, by the last year of the war, all who might be considered influential in connection with contracts, contractors and their agents, inspectors, and quartermasters had been brought under the restrictions and penalties set forth in the laws passed by Congress. Actual enforcement of these laws appears, however, to have been limited.

Under the legislation governing contractual procedures, the Quartermaster's Department procured clothing, shoes, blankets, tents, knapsacks, haversacks, camp kettles, and canteens; it obtained ambulances, wagons, horses, mules, harness, and forage; and it purchased stationery, straw,

---

[54] RG 92, OQMG Letter Book, vol. 65, pp. 318–19 (Meigs to Sen. W. P. Fessenden, 9 Jan 1863); vol. 68, p. 201 (Meigs to Crosman, 23 Apr 1862).

[55] 13 *Stat.* 394 (Jul 4, 1864).

[56] 13 *Stat.* 596 (Jul 17, 1862); 13 *Stat.* 394 (Jul 4, 1864).

[57] 12 *Stat.* 577–78 (Jul 16, 1862); 13 *Stat.* 123 (Jun 15, 1864).

wood for fuel, as well as hundreds of items used in construction projects and repairs.   It chartered and purchased steamboats, tugs, barges, ferry boats, and gunboats; and it not only contracted for railroad transportation of troops and supplies during the Civil War but it also procured engines, cars, and items needed for repairing military railroads.   Each commodity field posed problems.

Clothing Procurement

During the Civil War, the Quartermaster's Department furnished the clothing needed by the troops either by contracting for the supply or manufacturing it in its own facilities.   In 1861, clothing for the Regular Army was still being manufactured at the Philadelphia clothing depot as it had been for more than half a century.   Cloth, purchased under contract from manufacturers, was received, cut into garments by government cutters, and issued to seamstresses and tailors who returned hand-finished garments to the Schuylkill Arsenal for inspection and acceptance.   Though the sewing machine had been invented by Elias Howe in the forties and improved later by Isaac Merrit Singer, it was not used in the production of clothing during the Civil War.   Hand-sewn garments were considered to be more durable.[58]   Remembering how the clothing establishment at Philadelphia had been expanded to meet the requirements of the Mexican War, Acting Quartermaster General Sibley had Reuben M. Potter, a military storekeeper of many years' experience and a parolee but recently returned from Texas, prepare a report describing the superiority of government production over procurement by contract and outlining a plan for expansion.   Sibley submitted this report to the Secretary of War with the recommendation that the proposed plan be adopted.[59]

Cameron approved and by July Sibley had established a clothing depot at New York.   The manufacture of Army clothing under Quartermaster direction was accomplished not only at the Philadelphia depot, where operations were expanded until 8,000 to 10,000 sewing women were employed, and at New York, but also at other clothing depots set up

[58] (1) RG 92, OQMG Consolidated Correspondence File, Box 1004 (Capt. Roger Jones to Meigs, 28 Jun 1861).   (2) RG 92, Phila. Depot, Letters to QMG, 1 Jul–15 Mar 1865, vol. E, pp. 59–61 (QM to Meigs, 30 Jul 1864).   (3) Machine sewing had been tried but its use had been abandoned for coats, trousers, jackets, and shirts.   Machines were only used for sewing caps and chevrons, articles that were not exposed to much hard usage.   RG 92, OQMG Letter Book, Clothing, vol. 17, pp. 29–31 (Jesup to Nechard & Co., 31 Mar 1859).

[59] (1) RG 92, OQMG Consolidated Correspondence File, Box 1004 (Potter to Sibley, 1 Jun 1861 and ind., Sibley to Cameron, 7 Jun 1861).   (2) RG 92, Personal Narrative Reports of Officers, QMD, for Fiscal Year Ending 30 June 1865, vol. N–W, pp. 181–83 (Potter Rpt).   Hereafter briefly cited Personal Narrative Rpts, F.Y. 1865.

36TH ILLINOIS INFANTRY REGIMENT, 1863

during the war at Cincinnati and St. Louis. These were the chief clothing depots of the war, but the Quartermaster's Department also carried on manufacturing in so-called "government halls" at several branch depots. In January 1862, it opened a government hall for the manufacture of clothing at Quincy, Ill., and the following year established another at Steubenville, Ohio. In March 1863, Military Storekeeper G. A. Hull initiated manufacturing operations at the Louisville clothing depot. Though their primary function was to assist in producing clothing needed by the western troops, the Department viewed such government halls partly as relief projects intended to give work to needy women whose menfolk were in service.[60] The Department also produced clothing at various times during the war at a number of other cities, among them Boston, Indianapolis, Detroit, Milwaukee, and Springfield, Ill.[61]

The branch depots did not contract for cloth but obtained their supply from the eastern depots. This was also largely true for the manufacturing operations at the government halls in St. Louis. The Cincinnati depot procured some of the material, but the Philadelphia and New York depots purchased the bulk of the textiles used by the Army since most of the country's mills were in the East.[62]

At the outbreak of the war, the stock of clothing on hand at the Philadelphia depot was small, the amount being sufficient to meet the needs only of the 16,000 men constituting the peacetime regular Army. Cameron's order to prepare fatigue clothing for issue to the 75,000 militia called out for 3 months' service must have been received with dismay by the depot commander. He followed this order with a directive to procure forage caps, infantry trousers, flannel sack coats and shirts, bootees, stockings, great coats, blankets, and such other articles as might be necessary to supply the wants of the troops of the different states.[63] Specific orders to issue clothing to the militia under the command of Maj. Gen. R. Patterson went out on 20 April 1861.[64]

Supplies that could be spared at the depot were limited in amount.

[60] (1) RG 92, OQMG Letter Book, Clothing, vol. 19, p. 16 (Meigs to E. P. Blair, 6 Jan 1862); vol. 20, p. 461 (Meigs to QM Allen, 3 Dec 1862); vol. 21, pp. 276–77 (Capt. N. Flagg to Meigs, 2 Mar 1862). (2) RG 92, Crosman, Letters Sent, 1 Sep–18 Nov 1863, p. 114 (Crosman to Capt. A. Conn, 18 Sep 1863). (3) RG 92, Personal Narrative Rpts, F.Y. 1863, II, pp. 260–61 (AQM Flagg Rpt); *ibid.*, F.Y. 1864, III, p. 342 (Hull's Rpt).

[61] *Annual Reports of the Quartermaster General, 1861–1865*, p. 17 (QMG's Rpt. 1862); p. 59 (Perry's Rpt, 19 Oct 1865, appended to QMG's Rpt, 1865).

[62] See *ibid.*, p. 92 (QMG's Rpt, 1865) Table 12 for a statement of the quantity of material purchased by these depots during the war.

[63] (1) RG 92, OQMG Letter Book, Clothing, vol. 17, p. 440 (Johnston to Thomas, 20 and 21 Apr 1861). (2) RG 107, OSW, Military Book, vol. 43, p. 263 (Cameron to QMG, 23 Apr 1861).

[64] RG 92, OQMG Letter Book, Clothing, vol. 17, p. 440 (Johnston to Thomas, 20 Apr 1861).

To manufacture clothing within the time for which the militia were mustered into service was difficult. Sibley therefore recommended that the militia provide their own clothing, the cost of which was not to exceed that of Army clothing and was to be paid for when Congress appropriated funds for that purpose. By mid-May 1861, with the Secretary's approval, he sent orders to that effect to Colonel Thomas at Philadelphia.[65] The action, however, gave no respite to operations at Philadelphia for even before it was taken the size of the Regular Army had been increased and 3 year-volunteers were being enlisted under the proclamation of 3 May 1861. Clothing for both would have to be made ready as quickly as possible.

Unfortunately, not only was it impossible to manufacture clothing at the depot within the time it was needed but also the mills of the country were not producing materials fast enough to clothe the troops. Only a small number of these were set up to produce the coarse and heavy woolens required by the Army, and it was going to take time to convert their machinery for such production. There was a scarcity of Army textiles of all types—for clothing, blankets, and tentage. When the Governor of Ohio ill-advisedly called for 22,000 overcoats in the midst of summer heat, Meigs informed him that "to cover nakedness and preserve health is as much as is now possible."[66] Troops would be comfortable, he assured him, with fatigue uniforms and blankets.

Since troops were being received through state authorities, the Secretary of War called upon the governors to aid the Department in clothing them. But still thousands waited for clothing in order to take the field in the summer of 1861. Regiments were ordered to Washington without clothing, and men went on guard duty, Meigs reported, in drawers for lack of pantaloons. Even regiments dispatched with clothing were soon ragged, owing to the bad quality of state supplies. Clothing wore out in 2 months of service.[67]

Obviously, the Department could not depend solely upon production in its own facilities. In any case, Meigs, having observed conditions after he became Quartermaster General and reviewed the situation, was not in favor of further expanding the government manufacturing establishment at Philadelphia. It ought to be kept up, he conceded, and worked to full capacity, serving as a source of supply and a model, but

---

[65] (1) RG 92, Rpts of QMG to SW and Heads of Depts., vol. 5, pp. 418–19 (Sibley to Cameron, 3 May 1861). (2) RG 92, OQMG Letter Book, Clothing, vol. 17, p. 467 (Sibley to Thomas, 15 May 1861). (3) *OR*, ser. III, vol. I, p. 213 (GO 22, 18 May 1861).

[66] RG 92, OQMG Letter Book, Clothing, vol. 18, p. 192 (Meigs to AQM Dickerson, 26 Jul 1861).

[67] *Ibid.*, vol. 18, pp. 80–81 (Meigs to Thomas, 20 Jun 1861); pp. 160, 185–86 (Meigs to Vinton, 15 and 21 Jul 1861).

to meet the demands created by the large force being called into service he thought it best to resort to the contract system. It would bring into use and give employment to many large, well-organized establishments whose business had been cut off by war and whose workers were suffering.[68]

It was his idea to furnish material procured and inspected by the Philadelphia depot to the large clothing houses which would then make it up into garments.[69] In effect, he was returning to a system that had been abandoned in 1812 by Callender Irvine as unsatisfactory. Contracts, however, were not restricted only to those in which the government furnished the material. They were also made with those manufacturers who were able to command their own supply of textiles. Within a short time, quartermasters and military storekeepers supervising manufacturing at clothing depots were repeating arguments used 50 years earlier to stress the advantage of government operation over contract supply. The garments they produced were superior to those sent by contractors; they were ample in cut and provided a better distribution of sizes; and their operations saved the government large sums of money. Too often contractors increased their profits by skimping on the material used in garments with the result that sizes ran small and additional garments in larger sizes had to be procured to provide a proper distribution of clothing. All contractors considered as a perquisite any government-furnished material left over after garments had been cut out. Sale of such "clippings" from thousands of garments added to the profit on their contract.[70]

As an engineer in charge of construction projects, Meigs had gained considerable experience with contracts, knowledge that as Quartermaster General he applied to contracting for Army clothing. He insisted that in no case were existing contracts to be simply extended but, instead, new bids were to be invited for each additional supply of articles required by the Army. Moreover, contracts were to be let only for certain specified quantities. Meigs disapproved of the practice of advertising for a certain quantity of articles with the privilege of doubling that quantity later. He contended that it raised suspicions that the contractor was managing to increase his delivery of profitable articles.[71] Meigs also determined to exercise a greater degree of control over clothing contracts than had been customary in the past. To enable the Quarter-

[68] *Ibid.*, vol. 18, p. 140 (Meigs to Thomas, 9 Jul 1861).

[69] *Ibid.*, vol. 18, pp. 80–81 (Meigs to Thomas, 20 Jun 1861).

[70] (1) RG 92, Personal Narrative Rpts, F.Y. 1863, III, 69–74 (Rpt of Capt. R. S. Hart); 342–43 (Rpt, MSK G. A. Hull). (2) RG 92, Crosman, Letters to QMG, 1 Jul 1864–15 Mar 1865, vol. E, pp. 59–61 (30 Jul 1864).

[71] RG 92, OQMG Letter Book, Clothing, vol. 18, pp. 121–23 (Meigs to Vinton, 5 Jul 1861).

master General "to speak by the book from actual knowledge" and to afford greater protection to the Department and its officers, Meigs relieved the assistant quartermaster general at Philadelphia of part of his heavy burden of responsibility by directing that, before contracts for large amounts were concluded, all bids with their analysis and comparison and the contract proposed were to be sent to the Washington office for examination and final action.[72]

One of the first instances of the application of this policy brought disagreement between Meigs and Colonel Thomas, then in charge at Philadelphia. Early in July 1861, John E. Hanford of the firm of Hanford and Browning of New York offered to supply 50,000 uniforms. The Quartermaster General, convinced that small orders and a wider distribution of them among clothing houses were more advantageous to the government, was unwilling to give him an order for more than 10,000 suits and then only at government prices published in 1859. In view of rising prices in the market of 1861, this last stipulation was unrealistic. Hanford was referred to Colonel Thomas at Philadelphia who was authorized to contract in whatever mode he considered most expedient and cheapest. Colonel Thomas had unfilled orders at the depot for thousands of garments. Having satisfied himself that the company had the backing of manufacturers who could supply the material Hanford and Browning would need and that the prices to be paid, though somewhat higher than those of 1859, would not be more than it would cost the depot itself to produce the garments, Colonel Thomas concluded a contract.

When Meigs found that the contract included more than 10,000 uniforms and, in fact, called for $1,200,000 worth of clothing at prices higher than he had stipulated, he disapproved the contract. He thought that Hanford and Browning had taken unfair advantage of Colonel Thomas and that, by forestalling the manufacture of the cloth for which he had directed Major Vinton at New York to issue advertisements, their contract embarrassed the Department. Colonel Thomas was much annoyed at this turn of events. Clothing was badly needed; Hanford and Browning was a reputable firm, able and willing to perform its contract; the price was lower than any he had received from other responsible or irresponsible persons; and he considered that he had been given full authority to act. Meigs reconsidered and, concluding that it was "better to be the victim of the trick than to delay the supplies," authorized Colonel Thomas to receive and issue the clothing from Hanford and Browning.[73]

[72] *Ibid.*, p. 65 (Meigs to Thomas, 14 Jun 1861); p. 123 (Meigs to Vinton, 5 Jul 1861).
[73] (1) *Ibid.*, pp. 121–23; 179–80 (Meigs to Vinton, 5 and 20 Jul 1861); pp. 178, 180–81, 185

Meigs soon learned that more large contracts would have to be made to prevent suffering by the troops in the coming winter. He learned, too, that distribution to numerous small houses entailed delays and complications and that turning over valuable material to irresponsible persons or houses of second-rate reputation involved great danger of fraud. He therefore directed that bids that appeared to be at rates involving "loss to the contractors, oppression to the working hands or stealing and cribbaging of materials" should be rejected. He advised Maj. David H. Vinton, who had been placed in charge of the New York clothing depot, that it would be well to employ two or three of the "most respectable houses in the trade" in New York to do the work at what experience at the Philadelphia clothing depot demonstrated to be firm rates.[74]

The Department paid in time for its unpreparedness. It took time for manufacturers to change their production lines and it took time to expand government facilities. Meanwhile, Meigs received daily appeals from regiments complaining that they were naked. Several Indiana regiments operating near Cheat Mountain pass in Virginia in the summer of 1861, when the temperature suddenly plummeted, sent word that they were suffering from lack of overcoats. Contract for the coats, Meigs ordered, and "save time if it costs money."[75] Rather than detain regiments in camp for want of clothing, he ordered the purchase of ready-made garments. "Slop shop clothing I did not wish to buy," Meigs confided, but so urgent was the need that he also directed Colonel Thomas and Major Vinton to buy any durable substantial cloth of any modest color— green, blue, or grey—and have it made into uniforms. Clothe and supply the regiments, he directed, so as to "secure the Dept. from just charge of inefficiency or of want of care for the comfort of the men."[76]

The clothing made of such materials was often inferior to the Army standard goods and did not wear well. Under the supply pressures that existed in 1861, Quartermaster officers were, in some cases, imposed upon by unscrupulous contractors who sold them worthless goods, and by unfaithful inspectors who passed such goods. Even more serious was the confusion promoted in the field by the use of varied colors, and where both Union and Confederate troops wore grey, it resulted in some

(Meigs to Thomas, 19, 20 and 22 Jul 1861).   (2) RG 92, Thomas, Letters Sent, 17 Jul–23 Aug 1861, pp. 2–4, 5–6, 27–30 (Thomas to Meigs, 19 and 21 Jul 1861).   (3) "Government Contracts," House *Rpt.* No. 2, 37th Cong., 2d sess., pp. 466–68, s.n. 1142.

[74] RG 92, OQMG Letter Book, Clothing, vol. 18, p. 407 (Meigs to Vinton, 9 Sep 1861).

[75] *Ibid.*, p. 290 (Meigs to Vinton, 19 Aug 1861).

[76] *Ibid.*, pp. 160, 179–80, 185–86 (Meigs to Vinton, 15, 20 and 21 Jul 1861); p. 183 (Meigs to Thomas, 22 Jul 1861).

instances of Union soldiers firing upon each other. Orders were thereupon issued forbidding the use of any color but the established uniform colors of light and dark blue. As fast as standard clothing could be obtained in 1862, irregular clothing was withdrawn from service. The Department was much criticized for its use of irregular materials but Meigs was of the opinion that anyone "who saw sentinels walking post about the capital of the United States in freezing weather in their drawers, without trousers or overcoats," would not blame the Quartermaster's Department for its effort to clothe them, even in materials that were not as durable as Army blue kersey.[77]

With winter approaching and production still lagging behind demand, the Quartermaster's Department turned to the foreign market. George P. Smith, a retired merchant of Pittsburgh, was sent to England to buy 1,200,000 yards of light and dark blue kersey, or the best substitute to be found. Except for payment of his expenses, Smith served without compensation. Colonel Thomas went with him as disbursing agent.[78] Newspaper accounts of the amount of money to be spent varied from $25 million to $60 million. Actually, the Department proposed spending only $800,000. The reports, however, were enough to cause the Boston Board of Trade to register a vigorous objection to foreign importations that would glut the American market, support the laborers of Europe rather than American workmen, and take specie out of the country instead of the government paying what it owed to American merchants.[79] The Board was certain that by 1 December 1861, the woolen machinery of the country would be producing at a rate sufficient to provide clothing for 400,000 men and to repeat this order every 6 weeks thereafter.

Meigs, dubious of the ability of the woolen industry to produce the quantity needed in time, opposed any move to revoke orders for foreign goods. If domestic manufacturers could supply the demand before the cloth could be imported, he reported that he would gladly purchase their fabric.[80] It was Meigs' intention not only to get a much needed supply of cloth from Europe promptly, but by turning to the foreign market bring domestic manufacturers and middlemen, "both of whom seemed to have gone crazy," to an understanding that the government would not submit to extortion and compel them to offer reasonable propositions. Apparently his move was effective for by December domestic prices were at least no higher than those in the foreign market and supply, he

---

[77] *Reports of the Quartermaster General, 1861–1865,* p. 17 (QMG's Rpt, 1862).

[78] RG 92, OQMG Letter Book, Clothing, vol. 18, pp. 532–33 (Meigs to Thomas, 14 Oct 1861); p. 534 (Meigs to Vinton, 14 Oct 1861).

[79] *OR,* ser. III, vol. I, pp. 583–86 (Special Committee, Boston Board of Trade, to Cameron, 18 Oct 1861).

[80] *Ibid.,* ser. III, vol. I, pp. 582–83 (Meigs to Cameron, 22 Oct 1861).

reported, "promises to be sufficient here."[81]   He thereupon called a halt to any more foreign purchase because, with prices at the same level at home and abroad, the government preferred purchasing at home.   Less than $380,000 had been expended for foreign textiles.[82]

By the end of 1861, the problem was not so much one of inadequate supply as of building up a reserve and maintaining a supply on hand at clothing depots.   By that time, the appropriation for clothing had long since been exhausted and the Quartermaster General was more immediately concerned with avoiding the accumulation of surpluses.[83]   Initial demands had been met and the troops had been re-outfitted after the losses sustained at the battle of Bull Run, where clothing and equipment had been thrown away in an effort to speed retreat.   Meigs therefore directed that no more contracts be made until the stock on hand had been reduced.[84]   In the summer oₗ 1862, the stock of clothing on hand amounted to a 6 months' supply for the Army.   About 3,200,000 yards of cloth were also in storage at the Schuylkill Arsenal.[85]

Co-ordinating supply and demand was not easy.   Because of the improvidence of inexperienced troops, the destruction, loss, and waste of overcoats and other articles of clothing were so large that the Department found it difficult to keep up the supply.   The rate of consumption for fiscal year 1862, Meigs reported, ran far beyond all allowances fixed by regulations from the experience of the Regular Army in time of peace.[86]   Then, in July 1862, the President called for 300,000 volunteers, followed in a month by a call for 300,000 militia.   The effect was to wipe out the surplus stocks, leaving nothing for the supply of the Army already in the field.   Meigs clothed the volunteers from the stocks of clothing on hand and used the material at the Arsenal to make clothing for the militia.   By agreement with the states, Meigs sent material and trimmings for coats and pantaloons either to the U.S. quartermaster stationed within the states or, if such quartermasters were not available, to the governors of the states.   They then made contracts for the manufacture of the clothes.   By distributing the work in the states, Meigs hoped that it might be done quickly and give satisfaction to the states and their soldiers.[87]

[81] RG 92, OQMG Letter Book, Clothing, vol. 18, p. 680 (Meigs to George P. Smith, 2 Dec 1861).

[82] OQMG Letter Book, vol. 59, p. 176 (Thomas to Meigs, 14 Feb 1862).   Thomas reported that he had spent £75,960.

[83] Ibid., vol. 57, p. 470 (Meigs to Col. Geo. H. Crosman, 24 Dec 1861).

[84] RG 92, OQMG Letter Book, Clothing, vol. 19, pp. 158–59 (Meigs to Crosman, 5 Feb 1862).

[85] OR, ser. III, vol. II, 371 (Meigs to Stanton, 13 Aug 1862).

[86] Annual Reports of the Quartermaster General, 1861–1865, p. 17 (Rpt, 1862).

[87] (1) OR, ser. II, vol. II, 372 (Meigs to Stanton, 13 Aug 1862).   (2) RG 92, OQMG Letter Book, Clothing, vol. 19, pp. 693–94 (Meigs to Vinton, 12 Aug 1862); pp. 709–10 (Meigs to Crosman, 13 Aug 1862).

To replace the stocks being used, Meigs ordered publication of advertisements inviting proposals at Philadelphia, New York, and Cincinnati. To avoid inflating prices by inviting bids for the whole amount at once, the advertisments announced that after 10 days the bids received to that time would be opened and contracts awarded, and that from time to time, as the service required, additional contracts would be given to the lowest bidder. In other words, the advertisements were published as standing invitations to manufacturers and were not withdrawn until January 1863.[88]

Meigs directed Colonel Crosman, who had succeeded Colonel Thomas at Philadelphia, to accumulate a surplus stock at his depot sufficient for the instant equipment of 100,000 men. He sent similar instructions to Major Vinton, depot quartermaster at New York. By 1863, with reserve stocks accumulated, the supply of clothing was well in hand and by the close of fiscal year 1864, Meigs could report that the supply was ample, the quality excellent, and the complaints few.[89]

Procurement of Blankets

The Department found it even more difficult to procure blankets for the troops than clothing. Under Army regulations, two blankets were issued to each soldier in a 5-year period, one in the first year and another in the third year.[90] An Army blanket was a grey, all-wool blanket that weighed 10 pounds a pair. Before the war, the quartermaster at Philadelphia procured blankets on contract for the Regular Army, but he had no large quantity in stock in April 1861.

Both state authorities and U.S. quartermasters were soon competing in the market for the supply needed to equip the troops. They promptly bought all available stocks of Army blankets and by August there were none to be had in the markets of New York or Philadelphia.[91] In the meantime, the mills had been set to work on orders from the Department. To meet immediate needs, however, Quartermasters purchased any blanket, of any color and of any weight of material, as long as it was made of wool and not of jute, cotton, or grass. To supplement domestic production, the Department sent agents to procure blankets in Canada and they purchased 200,000 of them in England to be delivered before the end of the year.[92]

[88] RG 92, OQMG Letter Book, Clothing, vol. 19, pp. 698–700 (Meigs to Crosman, 13 Aug 1862); vol. 21, p. 102 (Meigs to Crosman, 13 Jan 1863).

[89] *Annual Reports of the Quartermaster General, 1861–1865*, p. 12 (QMG's Rpt, 1864).

[90] *Revised Regulations for the Army of the United States, 1861*, p. 170.

[91] RG 92, OQMG Letter Book, Clothing, vol. 18, pp. 299, 333 (Meigs to C. C. Trowbridge, 20, 28 Aug 1861).

[92] *Ibid.*, vol. 18, p. 270 (Meigs to Johnston Townsend & Co., 14 Aug 1861); p. 399 (Meigs to Crosman and Vinton, 7 Sep 1861).

Despite inspection, the Department procured blankets of poor quality. Even those Meigs obtained from England were not up to the standard he had been led to expect. Old stocking yarn was used in the manufacture of the blankets, he learned later, and rival dealers pronounced the material shoddy.[93] They undoubtedly were familiar with shoddy, for the extent to which such fabric was palmed off on the government for the use of soldiers was inexcusable.[94] A journalist of the day vividly described shoddy as "a villainous compound, the refuse stuff and sweepings of the shop, pounded, rolled, glued, and smoothed to the external form and gloss of cloth, but no more like the genuine article than the shadow is to the substance." Soldiers, on the first day's march, or in the earliest storm, he reported, found their clothes, overcoats, and blankets, "scattering to the winds in rags, or dissolving into their primitive elements of dust under the pelting rain." [95]

In the existing state of shortages during the first year of the war, inferior blankets had nevertheless to be issued despite the objections of the troops to receiving them and actions by boards of survey in condemning them. Captain Turnley, assistant quartermaster at St. Louis who served on a board of survey, agreed that several bales of blankets received for issue to the troops were thin, light, and inferior in quality to the usual Army blankets, but he disagreed with other officers that they were therefore unfit for use. They were, he thought, as good an article as could be got at the price, and, depending on the weight of the blankets the soldier received, he recommended issue of them at the rate of two or three to a man.[96] Captain Turnley was realist enough to know that if such blankets were not issued, the soldier was likely to end up with none at all. In time, the supply situation did improve, but until the end of the war domestic production of blankets remained deficient and supplemental purchases had to be made in the foreign market.[97]

It is interesting to observe that efforts were made early in the war

[93] Shoddy was a trade term applied to fabrics made from remanufactured materials, that is from materials which had already been spun into yarn and woven into cloth and then were later ground up into a fibrous mass, respun, and rewoven. The clippings saved by clothing houses were used to produce shoddy.

[94] It was not uncommon for material rejected at one depot to be offered at another. For example, an inspector at the Philadelphia depot rejected a large amount of sky-blue kersey offered by a contractor. The latter thereupon disposed of it in the New York market. Colonel Crosman, hearing this, alerted the quartermasters at the New York and Cincinnati depots to be careful and not accept the inferior kersey, if offered to them. RG 92, Crosman, Letters Sent, 19 Mar–8 Jun 1863, p. 150 (9 Apr 1863).

[95] Robert Tomes, "The Fortunes of War," Harper's New Monthly Magazine, XXIX (June, 1864), pp. 227–28.

[96] "Government Contracts," House Rpt. No. 2, 37th Cong., 2d sess., pp. 120–21, s.n. 1142.

[97] RG 92, OQMG Letter Book, Clothing, vol. 23, p. 533 (Perry to Meigs, 30 Mar 1864); vol. 24, p. 64 (Capt. Robinson to Vinton, 16 May 1864).

by interested producers to introduce the use of waterproof blankets in the Army. In May 1861, the Quartermaster's Department had indicated that it had no intention of adding that item to supply, but some of the states equipped their troops with India rubber blankets, other troops soon requisitioned them, and, by September, Meigs requested a policy decision from the Secretary of War.[98]   Cameron directed the Quartermaster General to procure and issue waterproof blankets for use in camp, charging the soldiers with them as they were for articles of clothing. Meigs thereupon directed Colonel Crosman to procure blankets of several kinds of waterproof fabric.   At his orders, all were to be made with a straight slit and flap so that they might be used as ponchos, and also with grommet holes at 14-inch intervals around the edge so that by lacing the blankets together they might also be used as shelters in place of tents in bivouac.[99]   India rubber and gutta percha blankets were both used during the war, but reports from the field were so conflicting on their performance that the Department had decided on no single standard for waterproof blankets by the time the war ended.[100]

Tentage

No textile was in shorter supply during the Civil War than duck needed for the production of tents.   The supply of tents on hand at the depot in Philadelphia in April 1861 was soon exhausted.   For years the Army had utilized the common A or wedge tent, the wall tent, and for winter use, the Sibley tent.   These were the only large tents that had stood the test of actual service.   There was not enough material in the country, however, to provide such tents for all the troops being sent into the field although at the start of the war some troops were liberally supplied with tents.[101]   Except for hospital purposes, the use of large tents was not practical in campaigns.   To shelter the troops on active service, the Quartermaster's Department initiated procurement of tents made on the pattern of the d'Abri tent used by the French army.

---

[98] (1) RG 92, OQMG Letter Book, vol. 55, p. 353 (Sibley to M. J. Gibson, 4 May 1861). (2) RG 92, Letters and Rpts of QMG to SW and Heads of Depts, vol. 5, p. 472 (Meigs to Cameron, 25 Sep 1861).   (3) OR, ser. III, vol. I, p. 615 (Cameron to QMG, 1 Nov 1861).

[99] RG 92, OQMG Letter Book, Clothing, vol. 18, p. 677 (Meigs to Gov. E. D. Morgan, 4 Dec 1861).

[100] Ibid., vol. 25, pp. 304–05 (Meigs to Col. H. S. Olcott, 9 Feb 1865).

[101] Trobriand wrote of one regiment of 1,000 men that had 32 wall tents for its officers, 250 wedge tents for its non-commissioned officers and privates, and 2 hospital tents.   At the rate at which wedge tents were issued—one to every four men—that regiment had more than two and a half times the tentage it needed.   Four Years with the Army of the Potomac, p. 79.

The use of the shelter-half, so familiar to every American soldier since 1861, was thus introduced in the American Army.[102]

Shoe Procurement

No item issued to the soldier was more essential to his well-being than durable, comfortable shoes, and none gave rise to more criticism from the troops, especially during the first year of the war. From the Western Department, Major General Halleck reported that shoes and boots wore out in 3 to 4 days' march. Major General McClellan telegraphed from the Army of the Potomac that a march by Smith's and Porter's divisions had worn out the men's new shoes, the soles of which had been filled with chips.[103] Obviously, fraud in the production and inspection of shoes was as prevalent as in the manufacture and inspection of cloth. A so-called leather composition, that looked and smelled like leather but fell to pieces like paper when it became wet, was used as an inner sole, filling up the shoe between the welt and the outside sole.[104] Since the Mexican War, a bootee establishment had been in operation at the Schuylkill Arsenal producing bootees and boots for the Regular Army. In operating this establishment, the Quartermaster's Department purchased the leather, employed cutters in the Arsenal to cut out the shoes and boots, and then gave out the material to employees who lived and worked in the area outside the Arsenal. In June 1861, some 700 hands were employed in shoe production by the Arsenal. It was estimated that shoe production could be doubled by increasing the number of employees. About a year later, 15,000 pairs of bootees and boots per month were being manufactured at the Arsenal.[105] Many thousand more pairs of shoes were needed and, as in the case of clothing, the Department turned to contracting for its supply of shoes and boots. There was this difference; the Department did not furnish any material for production. All leather and findings were provided by the shoe contractor.

Army regulations called for all bootees and boots to be hand-sewn and made of oak-tanned leather. Demand at once raised the price of

---

[102] (1) RG 92, OQMG Letter Book, Clothing, vol. 19, p. 238 (Meigs to Crosman, 26 Feb 1862). (2) The small size of the shelter-half caused the soldiers to refer to them as dog-sized tents. It was not unusual for a soldier to stick his head out the tent opening and bark like a dog—hence the origin of the term "pup tent."

[103] (1) RG 92, OQMG Letter Book, Clothing, vol. 19, p. 354 (Meigs to Crosman, 3 Apr 1862). (2) RG 92, Rpts and Ltrs, QMG to SW & Other Officials, 1862, I, 94–98 (Meigs to Stanton, 2 Feb 1862).

[104] "Government Contracts," House Rpt. No. 2, 37th Cong., 2d sess., pp. 280, 282, s.n. 1143.

[105] (1) RG 92, OQMG Consolidated Correspondence File, Box 1004 (Capt. Roger Jones to Meigs, 28 Jun 1861). (2) RG 92, Crosman, Letters to QMG, 5 Apr 1862–12 Feb 1863, vol. B, p. 148 (Crosman to Meigs, 24 Jun 1862).

such leather in the market and in fact soon exhausted the supply. Contractors then substituted a less expensive hemlock-tanned leather at the price of oak-tanned, but, since even the most experienced tanners found difficulty in distinguishing between the two, most government inspectors passed it without a question. There was no appreciable difference in quality but, by its own specification, the Department was imposed upon and defrauded.

The Department also increased its expenditures by insisting upon hand-sewn boots and bootees which cost more than pegged shoes. Yet in the trade, sewed shoes had almost entirely disappeared from the market having been completely supplanted by pegged work. Shoemakers actually had to learn how to make sewed shoes when the government demand for them increased. The committee investigating government contracts believed that not one in ten of the soldiers ever had worn, in every day use, sewed shoes until after enlistment.[106]

The Department insisted upon purchasing hand-sewn shoes because the poor quality of the pegged shoes initially procured by quartermasters had served to confirm its conviction that all pegged work was unserviceable. Meigs had therefore directed that no pegged shoes were to be bought.[107] That order was later changed and both pegged and handsewn shoes were procured during the war. In addition, machine-sewn shoes were also introduced. Early in the war, Gordon McKay had improved and patented a machine for sewing the soles of shoes to the uppers. The first inspection report of such shoes was unfavorable, but sample shoes tested in the field were so well received that procurement of shoes sewn by machine was soon ordered.[108] Not only McKay but also other shoe manufacturers filled government orders, for McKay manufactured additional machines that he leased on a royalty basis to other shoe manufacturers.

The use of machines entailed the outlay of considerable capital but even in those cases where shoes were made by hand, large amounts of money had to be invested in leather. Few small cobblers—and they constituted the largest proportion of shoe producers—were in a position to lay out capital to that extent. In consequence, most shoe contracts were acquired by middlemen who handled the business with ample profit to themselves.

Rail Transportation of Men and Supplies

The profiteering of middlemen and contractors who supplied clothing and equipment was matched by that of shipbrokers and transportation

---

[106] "Government Contracts," House *Rpt.* No. 2, 37th Cong., 2d sess., pp. xlii–xlv, s.n. 1143.
[107] RG 92, OQMG Letter Book, Clothing, vol. 18, p. 375 (Meigs to Crosman, 3 Sep 1861).
[108] *Ibid.,* vol. 18, pp. 697, 737 (Meigs to Vinton, 12 and 28 Dec 1861).

agents. Since 1775, transportation of men and supplies had been a basic function of the Quartermaster's Department, but, in the crisis of April 1861, that responsibility was placed largely in the hands of Pennsylvanians whom Cameron appointed as War Department agents. The immediate transportation problem was to open communication between Washington and the East. There was no question of the ability of the men that Cameron called upon to co-ordinate and direct rail transportation of troops and supplies to Washington.[109] J. Edgar Thomson and Thomas A. Scott, president and vice-president, respectively, of the Pennsylvania Railroad, and Samuel M. Felton, president of the Philadelphia, Wilmington & Baltimore Railroad, were among the ablest railroad men in the country.

They were effective operators. Within 4 days after communications had been cut in Baltimore on 19 April, Thomson and Felton opened an alternative rail and water route to Washington over which troops and supplies from the New York and New England area moved for the next 3 weeks until passage via the Baltimore & Ohio Railroad could be restored. The route used the Philadelphia, Wilmington & Baltimore Railroad, open to Perryville at the mouth of the Susquehanna River. There, an old ferry boat and all available steamers at Philadelphia were pressed into service to transport men and supplies down the Chesapeake Bay to Annapolis where railroad connections to Washington were resumed via the Elk Ridge Railroad and the Washington branch of the Baltimore & Ohio Railroad.[110] Scott, who on 27 April 1861 was appointed by Cameron to take charge of the railways and telegraph lines between Washington and Annapolis, had tickets printed for a through trip on this rail and water route, establishing the rate for passengers at $6 each.[111] He directed traffic, repaired damaged tracks and bridges, and, by 14 May, had the line of communication reopened via Baltimore.[112]

Though troops moved over the alternative route promptly, the handling of supplies was not accomplished without some confusion. Acting Quartermaster General Sibley dispatched Capt. Asher R. Eddy to Perryville as disbursing quartermaster to receipt for and forward supplies. The latter soon reported that although large quantities of goods were arriving and being forwarded via steamers, he received no invoices. The entire business, he informed the Department, seemed to be in the hands of the railroad and steamboat companies whose representatives

[109] OR, ser. I, vol. LI, Pt. I, p. 327 (Cameron to Thomson, 17 Apr 1861); p. 330 (Cameron to Scott, 21 Apr 1861); ser. III, vol. I, p. 228 (Cameron to Scott, 23 May 1861).

[110] "Government Contracts," House Rpt. No. 2, 37th Cong., 2d sess., pp. 689–93, s.n. 1143.

[111] He fixed the fare between Washington and Annapolis at $1.75, and suggested a charge of $2.25 for steamer passage and $2 for the rail fare between Perryville and Philadelphia. RG 92, OQMG Consolidated Correspondence File, Box 869 (Scott to Felton, 27 Apr 1861).

[112] For a discussion of military railroads see pp. 394–404.

insisted that the contract governing such shipments had been made by the Secretary of War. But when Sibley took the matter up with Cameron, the latter professed no knowledge of such a contract and could only assume that shipments were being directed by the New York Defense Committee. The lack of system in forwarding supplies to Washington was so apparent that Sibley directed Captain Eddy to make certain that all stores arriving at Perryville were turned over to him and forwarded under regular bills of lading. He was to employ additional clerks, if needed, and he was to make certain that all agents and contractors employed in this transportation were governed by his orders.[113] It is doubtful that these objectives were achieved before shipment by way of the Baltimore and Ohio Railroad became feasible.

The promptness with which communication between Washington and the East was restored was admirable. What disturbed the critics of Cameron was that two of the men whom he had appointed were high ranking officials of the Pennsylvania Railroad and that one of them, Scott, still retained his post with that company, though he drew no pay, after he was appointed assistant secretary of war in August and at a time when he was contracting with that railroad for the transportation of troops and supplies. In addition, Cameron appeared to his critics to be more concerned with helping the Pennsylvania Railroad outstrip its competitor, the Baltimore & Ohio Railroad, than he was with speeding the war effort. The congressional committee investigating government contracts charged that Scott and Cameron increased the revenues of the Pennsylvania and Cameron's own road, the Northern Central Railroad, at the expense of the Baltimore & Ohio and of the government.[114]

It was the controversy over rates, however, that evoked most criticism. The rate problem first came to light in St. Louis. Ever since railroads had been used to transport Army supplies, it had been the practice of the Quartermaster's Department to solicit bids from the carriers and award contracts for definite shipments on the recommendation of the quartermaster concerned with the movement. The congressional committee investigating government contracts discovered that the practice of seeking competitive bids had been abandoned at St. Louis. There, Edward H. Castle had been placed in charge of railroad transportation in the Western Department by General Fremont and had put into effect a schedule of rates applicable to all roads. His testimony revealed that this schedule had originated with Thomas A. Scott. A copy had been sent from Wash-

---

[113] (1) RG 92, OQMG Letters Received, Box 75 (Eddy to QMG, 1 May 1861). (2) RG 92, OQMG Letter Book, vol. 55, pp. 355–56 (Sibley to Eddy, 4 May 1861).

[114] "Government Contracts," House *Rpt.* No. 2, 37th Cong., 2d sess., pp. xv, xix-xx, s.n. 1143.

ington, and Castle, with Fremont's approval, had issued a circular to the superintendents of railroads in the Western Department establishing the rates.[115]   In general, the schedule had provided for a rate of 2 cents per mile per man for transporting soldiers by railroad and a charge of local first-class freight rates for equipment and supplies accompanying a regiment.   All other government freight was to be charged local rates according to their regular classification.

A commission examining transportation claims at St. Louis was startled to learn from the claimants themselves that the freight rates allowed in the schedule were materially higher than their ordinary "through freight" charges and that the fare of 2 cents per mile per man was so profitable that there was great competition among the roads to obtain the transportation of troops.   Under these rates, unscrupulous railroad companies were in one case collecting as high as $20,000 in excess of a legitimate amount while in another the government was paying 80 percent more for the transportation of horses "per car" than were private customers of the road.[116]

An inquiry addressed to Cameron brought the reply that the circular on rates was not to be regarded as a contract but was only designed to fix the maximum rates beyond which no road would be allowed to charge.[117]   Scott testified to the same effect.   He had drafted a schedule of rates in July when called upon by the Quartermaster's Department for advice concerning rates to be allowed in settling claims with railroad companies for the use of their facilities.   His schedule was based on and conformed fairly closely with the agreement made by delegates from 21 railroads who met at Harrisburg, Pa., on 4 June 1861.   Neither Cameron's nor Scott's explanation was satisfactory.   Sibley, to whom the original schedule of rates had been sent, had not construed it as setting maximum rates.   In fact, Scott's instructions had directed him to "observe the following as a general basis."   Quartermasters to whom the circular was sent and all agents of the railroad companies accepted the circular as fixing a tariff rate, and no effort was made to bargain for lower rates.   When he asssumed office as Quartermaster General, Meigs testified that he was led to believe that the circular represented a "bargain with the roads at a reduction of 33⅓ percent." [118]

The insistence upon charging local rates, which were much the highest, for government freight rather than through rates increased

---

[115] (1) "Government Contracts," House *Rpt.* No. 2, 37th Cong., 2d sess., pp. 922, 929–30, s.n. 1142.   (2) *OR*, ser. III, vol. I, pp. 325–26 (Scott to Sibley, 12 Jul 1861).
[116] *OR*, ser. III, vol. I, p. 749 (Commissioners to Cameron, 17 Dec 1861).
[117] *Ibid.*, pp. 751–52 (20 Dec 1861).
[118] "Government Contracts," House *Rpt.* No. 2, 37th Cong., 2d sess., p. 490, s.n. 1143.

transportation costs enormously.   To avoid any doubt as to which rates were to apply, contracts for the shipment of beef cattle from the West provided for delivery at Harrisburg, Pa.   The effect was to make the freight local on the Pennsylvania Railroad from Pittsburgh to Harrisburg, and again local on the Northern Central Railroad from Harrisburg to Baltimore, whereas if the cattle had been shipped directly from Pittsburgh to Baltimore through rates would have applied.   This sharp practice was reflected in the increased earnings of these roads in 1861, though their prosperity was also heightened by the advantageous position they enjoyed in carrying government freight from the West as long as the Baltimore & Ohio Railroad remained closed.[119]

Following these revelations, Meigs on 29 January 1862 sent out a circular to his quartermasters, advising them that the former circular had been misunderstood; that they must seek to obtain lower rates from the railroads; and that they must pay no more than private individuals did in the transportation of freight.   The following month, Secretary Stanton called the Northern railroad managers together to discuss the rate problem and revise the existing schedule.   As a result of their deliberations, the schedule was altered.   Soldiers were still to be transported at 2 cents a mile but under the new schedule each was allowed to carry 80 pounds of baggage.   The military tariff for freight was to be 10 percent below the printed local and through freight tariffs of the railroads in force at the time of service, with maximum rates definitely fixed for certain classes of commodities.[120]   Though the congressional committee investigating government contracts continued to believe that transportation charges should be fixed by competitive bidding, Stanton felt that inasmuch as a definite schedule of rates had been arranged with the railroads, the government was obligated to support the arrangement as long as the roads placed their facilities at the disposal of the War Department for the prosecution of the war.[121]

By the beginning of 1862, Meigs reasserted and tightened his Department's control over railroad transportation.   Examination of transportation accounts had revealed that orders on railway companies for the transportation of troops and supplies had, in the initial rush to arms, been permitted to be given by officers of almost all grades.   This "pernicious practice", Meigs insisted, had to be eliminated if the Department was to exercise any control.   He therefore requested that a War Department order be issued requiring all contracts for transportation to

[119] *Ibid.*, pp. xix–xx; 633, 634.
[120] *Ibid.*, pp. xxx–xxxiii.
[121] Stanton Papers. Proceedings of the War Board, 13–27 Mar 1862, session of 14 Mar 1862. Manuscript Div., Library of Congress.

be made by officers of the Quartermaster's Department exclusively.[122] Thereafter, only quartermasters contracted for transportation of men and supplies via the nearest, cheapest and shortest route. By 3 March 1862, the more favorable schedule of rates had been furnished to them as a guide, and they were also instructed that in settling transportation claims before that date they were to allow no more than 2 cents a mile per man nor any charge on freight exceeding the rates of the printed local or through tariff of the roads to the public at the time of the service.

In the settlement of claims for transportation on railroads built by the grant of lands from the United States, a general policy was laid down by the War Department early in the war. In the laws granting land to States to aid in the construction of railroads, a clause had generally been inserted to the effect that such railroads should remain public highways for the use of the United States "free from tolls or other charges upon the transportation of any property or troops of the United States." Meigs, called upon to determine the rights of the government in the use of land grant railroads, interpreted the clause to give the government a clear right to use the roadway without compensation for the transportation of its troops and property, but the rate to be paid was to be a proper compensation for the motive power, cars, and other facilities incident to transportation. The rate set was 2 cents per mile for passenger travel, subject to a discount of 33⅓ percent due the government for charter privileges. In the transportation of supplies, payment was to be made on the basis of such reasonable rates as were allowed other railroad companies, subject to an abatement of 33⅓ percent.[123] Directing the movement of men and supplies by commercial railroad remained a responsibility of the Department, though Scott, to promote what he considered more effective management, proposed the establishment of a separate transportation bureau to include rail and water transportation and telegraphic operations.[124] No action was taken on this proposal.

Military Telegraph Office

Communications and railroad transportation were so closely related that when Thomas A. Scott had been called to Washington in 1861, he was placed in charge of the telegraph lines as well as the railroads appropriated for government use, though legal authorization for such

---

[122] RG 92, Rpts of QMG to SW and Heads of Depts, vol. 5, pp. 508–09 (Sibley to SW, 7 Nov 1861).

[123] RG 92, OQMG Letter Book, vol. 83, pp. 25–35 (Meigs to Sen. John Sherman, 14 Feb 1865).

[124] OR, ser. III, vol. I, pp. 807–08 (Scott to Stanton, 23 Jan 1862).

management was not granted until 31 January 1862. The first operators whom he brought to Washington were drawn from among the employees of the Pennsylvania Railroad. In the meantime, the governor of Ohio had requested Anson Stager, general superintendent of the Western Union Telegraph Company, located at Cleveland, Ohio, to take charge of the management of telegraph lines in southern Ohio. When about a month later George B. McClellan was appointed major general and assigned to the command of the Department of the Ohio, he appointed Stager superintendent of all military telegraph lines in his Department.[125]

Scott, preoccupied with railroad matters, could give little attention to communications. In the absence of centralized control from Washington, competition soon developed for telegraphic supplies. Stager was thereupon recommended to Cameron as the man best qualified to undertake the general management of all military telegraph lines. In the fall of 1861, the Secretary invited him to Washington to submit his views. Since Stager's suggestions called for payment by the Quartermaster's Department of all bills incurred, Meigs insisted that legally only assistant quartermasters could serve as disbursing officers, and Stager would have to be appointed an assistant quartermaster in his Department. On 11 November 1861, he was so appointed and detailed as general manager of government telegraphs.[126]

The organization that Captain Stager established was staffed with civilian assistants. Operating difficulties soon developed, however, because quartermasters had no legal authority for filling requisitions made on them by civilians. To overcome this difficulty, Stager sought and obtained military commissions for his civilian assistants. He himself was commissioned colonel on 20 February 1862 and attached as aide-de-camp to the Secretary of War. His chief assistant was commissioned a major and all the other assistant superintendents, assigned to the various military departments, became captains. All were appointed assistant quartermasters in the Quartermaster's Department. Telegraphers and other personnel employed in the organization remained civilians.

Essentially, this was a civilian organization responsible to the Secretary of War. The appointment of Stager and his supervisory officers as assistant quartermasters in the Quartermaster's Department was simply a device for legalizing the flow of funds and imposing monetary and property accountability on them. The Department used the services of the military telegraph, but Meigs gave no orders to Stager. At the

---

[125] William R. Plum, *The Military Telegraph During the Civil War in the United States* (2 vols., Chicago, 1882), I, 92–93.

[126] (1) *Ibid.*, I, 130–31. (2) RG 92, OQMG Letter Book, vol. 57, p. 263 (Meigs to Stager, 16 Nov 1861).

request of the Quartermaster General, Stager and his departmental superintendents submitted annual reports of their activities, expenditures, and property accountability.[127] The Quartermaster's Department furnished funds for the support of the military telegraph from its appropriations and they were disbursed under the direction of Colonel Stager. His chief purchasing officer, Capt. Samuel G. Lynch, procured telegraphic supplies. The Quartermaster's Department had no responsibilities for communications before the war, and, except for these financial arrangements and the provision of Quartermaster items of supply on requisition, the Department acquired none during the war.[128]

Ocean Transportation

The use of rail transportation by the Army was still so new as to justify the calling in of experts to direct operations in April 1861, but no such reason existed for ignoring the Department's long experience in employing all types of water transportation.[129] Secretary Cameron, however, chose to rely upon one of his Pennsylvania supporters. Following the riot in Baltimore, he urged John Tucker to come to Washington. Tucker, a former dry goods merchant and railroad president, arrived there on the first train that left Annapolis, and on 8 May 1861 Cameron appointed him general agent of transportation for the War Department.[130] He was authorized to purchase or charter all means of transportation necessary for the movement of troops or the forwarding of supplies. Since the making of railroad arrangements was among the first duties he performed, it is obvious that there was a certain amount of overlapping in the authority given to the various transportation agents that could have promoted conflict rather than co-ordination had not Tucker's activities been soon confined to ocean transportation. The Secretary of War directed the Quartermaster General and the chiefs of all other supply bureaus to inform Tucker of their transportation requirements and to give him such reasonable notice of their needs as circumstances allowed.[131]

The desirability of having a transportation agent in New York to work under Colonel Tompkins had been raised shortly after the first

---

[127] For reports of Maj. Thos. T. Eckert, Capt. Samuel Bruch et al., see RG 92, Personal Narrative Rpts, F.Y. 1863, 1864, 1865, passim.

[128] Meigs called attention to the fact that the duties of the officers of this organization brought them more directly under the notice of the Secretary of War than of the Quartermaster General. Annual Reports of the Quartermaster General, 1861–1865, p. 25 (Rpt for 1865).

[129] For discussion of transportation on western rivers, see below, pp. 405–15.

[130] OR, ser. III, vol. I, p. 175.

[131] RG 107, OSW, Letters Sent, vol. 44, p. 175 (10 May 1861).

call went out for militia.[132]   Later, Thomas A. Scott informed the investigating committee that Tucker was employed in order that one general agent, securing vessels at moderate rates, might eliminate competition among the quartermasters.[133]

Indeed, considerable confusion had already developed in the opening weeks of the war.   Assistant Quartermaster General Tompkins was the duly authorized representative of the government for handling transportation at New York, and he chartered a number of steamers during the first weeks of the war.[134]   Numerous other individuals, however, were also active in engaging vessels for government service.   The New York Defense Committee and General Wool, commanding officer in the Department of the East, took prompt measures to aid Washington when the capital was reported to be in imminent peril.   Ships were chartered and troops and supplies hurried off to Washington.[135]   Meanwhile, at Philadelphia, the president of the Pennsylvania Railroad, J. Edgar Thomson, "in accordance with the authority vested in me by the Secretary of War," appointed Richard F. Loper of Philadelphia as an assistant to act as a transportation agent in procuring vessels for use on the alternate rail and water route that he helped open to Washington.   From 20 April through 7 May 1861, Captain Loper chartered 24 steamers for government use before his services were terminated by the appointment of John Tucker.[136]

The intent of placing one person in control of water transportation to reduce confusion and eliminate competition was meritorious.   The ultimate end of reducing costs was not achieved by Tucker because he knew nothing about the business of chartering ocean vessels, and in addition he exercised no control over the agents he employed.   By his own admission he had never built, purchased, commanded, or operated a vessel in his life.[137]   As a result of his utter lack of experience, he paid excessive prices for vessels, some of which proved unseaworthy.

Acting Quartermaster General Sibley assumed that Tucker would be a subordinate in Colonel Tompkins' office and accordingly advised him that Tucker "will act as your adjunct and under your directions," but in fact he operated independently in executing the Secretary's orders and in carrying out the purchase directives given later by the Quarter-

---

[132] RG 92, OQMG Letter Book, vol. 55, p. 335 (Johnston to Col. Tompkins, 19 Apr 1861).

[133] "Government Contracts," House *Rpt.* No. 2, 37th Cong., 2d sess., p. 567, s.n. 1143.

[134] Senate *Ex. Doc.* No. 37, 37th Cong., 2d sess., pp. 2, 14–15, s.n. 1122.

[135] *OR*, ser. III, vol. I, pp. 179–81 (Wool to Cameron, 9 May 1861).

[136] (1) Senate *Rep. Com.* No. 84, 37th Cong., 3d sess., p. 274, s.n. 1151.   (2) Senate *Ex. Doc.* No. 37, 37th Cong., 2d sess., p. 2, s.n. 1122.   (3) This was the same Captain Loper employed by the Quartermaster's Department in the Mexican War.   See above, p. 287.

[137] "Government Contracts," House *Rpt.* No. 2, 37th Cong., 2d sess., pp. 310–11, s.n. 1143.

master General.[138]   Two days after Meigs assumed the duties of Quartermaster General, he wrote Colonel Tompkins that "by the personal attention and experience he brings to the business," Tucker could render valuable assistance in the shipment of stores, and he directed the assistant quartermaster general to consult the transport agent in making shipments. "He will enable you to make considerable reduction in cost," he informed Colonel Tompkins, naively assuming that Cameron's appointee must be well qualified.[139]   Queried later by the congressional committee investigating government contracts as to why the Department's responsibility for water transportation should have been taken out of its hands and delegated to Tucker, Meigs could only reply that the Secretary of War "exercised his own discretion."   He was not bound to give reasons. When Meigs became Quartermaster General, he found Tucker employed as transport agent, and though he talked to the Secretary several times about the matter he was told that Tucker was to perform that particular duty.   If the matter had been left to him, Meigs would have preferred to have the regular officers of his Department charter or purchase vessels, calling in the best advice and assistance they could get.[140]

Customarily, shipowners employed shipbrokers or mercantile agents who were paid a commission to buy or sell ships, procure cargoes, and generally transact such business as related to insurance and the issuance of bills of lading.   During the Civil War, public exigency made possible the extortion of enormous profits by shipbrokers and middlemen.   The isolation of Washington in April 1861, for example, created an immediate need for two light-draught steamers to transport troops and supplies between Perryville and Annapolis.   On General Wool's orders, Colonel Tompkins chartered the steamer *Cataline* on 25 April 1861.   The congressional committee later brought out the fact that this 18-year old vessel had been purchased with notes given by four men, one of whom was Thurlow Weed.   They paid $18,000 for the vessel and then chartered it to the government for 3 months at $10,000 a month, with a guarantee of $50,000 in case it should sink.[141]

That same emergency led to great activity on the part of Captain Loper to charter vessels at Philadelphia.   Then and for many months thereafter, Captain Loper was busily engaged in amassing commissions. He asserted later that he had "neglected everything since the war broke out but to attend to and try to assist the government and serve his country as much as in him lay."   He apparently did work hard and he won

[138] RG 92, OQMG Letter Book, vol. 55, p. 375 (16 May 1861).
[139] *Ibid.*, pp. 445-46 (17 Jun 1861).
[140] "Government Contracts," House *Rpt.* No. 2, 37th Cong., 2d sess., pp. 470–71, s.n. 1143.
[141] *Ibid.*, pp. 58–65, s.n. 1142.

praise from Brig. Gen. Ambrose E. Burnside for his "constant and untiring" zeal and from Lt. Col. Rufus E. Ingalls for his "generous aid" in procuring vessels for their respective needs.[142] His aid, however, came high. He charged 5 percent commission on every vessel obtained through his agency and these were chartered at extremely profitable daily or monthly rates. Anthony Reybold of Delaware City, who claimed his principal occupation was farming, chartered his fleet of vessels to the government through Captain Loper. His receipts ran about $1,100 per day, or at the rate of $401,500 per year. Captain Loper's commissions on these boats alone could not have been less than $20,000 a year, and in the opinion of the investigating committee it would have been cheaper for the government to have bought the vessels outright.

Like many another businessman of that period, Captain Loper enjoyed a good reputation. His patriotism, however, was never permitted to come in conflict with his pursuit of material gain. A shipbuilder and owner of many vessels, he was also president of the Philadelphia Steam Propeller Company. Naturally his own vessels found employment by the government and so profitable were his exertions in behalf of the Philadelphia Steam Propeller Company that he was able to increase its dividends from 10 to 50 percent a year in 1862 and in addition save a large surplus.[143]

As is evident, Captain Loper's services in behalf of the government did not end on 7 May 1861. John Tucker was an old and valued friend who availed himself of the "practical knowledge and enlarged experience" of the captain not only during his term as general agent of transportation but also while he served as assistant secretary of war—a post Tucker held until 21 January 1863.[144] The new Secretary of War, Edwin M. Stanton, who made Tucker his assistant, dismissed as unfounded the imputations being made against him in the winter of 1861–62. But Loper and a host of other greedy agents and subagents were employed by Tucker who chartered the vessels for General Burnside's expedition to North Carolina, for General McClellan's expedition to the Peninsula in March 1862 and the return of his army in August, and for General Banks' expedition when he relieved General Butler at New Orleans.[145] There was no evidence to indicate that Tucker profited in any way, but he did nothing to prevent the impositions practiced by his agents. The Senate Select Committee

[142] Senate *Rep. Com.* No. 84, 37th Cong., 3d sess., pp. 273–74; 275, s.n. 1141.

[143] *Ibid.*, pp. 13–19.

[144] (1) *Ibid.*, pp. 325–27. (2) Stanton Papers, vol. 2 (Stanton to H. Hamlin, 27 Jan 1862).

[145] See the voluminous testimony assembled in "Government Contracts," House *Rpt.* No. 2, 37th Cong., 2d sess., s.n. 1142 and 1143; and Senate *Rep. Com.* No. 84, 37th Cong., 3d sess., s.n. 1151.

concluded that he "had more or less connection with these gigantic and shameless frauds on the government."

Before the Civil War, the Quartermaster's Department had been accustomed to advertise for the vessels it required, taking the lowest bid offered. During the first year of the war, requisitions for transportation were urgent and in outfitting expeditions time was not allowed for public competition. Under Tucker, that procedure was abandoned in favor of making contracts through the agency of brokers. During Tucker's tenure in office, Quartermaster duties in relation to water transportation were reduced to the clerical function of signing the contracts so that they might have the official sanction of the Quartermaster's Department. As Meigs pointed out, the duties of an assistant secretary of war were not clearly defined, but as the representative of the Secretary, he was the superior officer and necessarily had authority over any assistant quartermaster detailed to assist him.[146] The power to fix the rate of charter, to determine the character of vessels to be employed, to inspect, and to charter were responsibilities carried out by Tucker and his agents.

The findings of the Select Committee of the Senate, whose probings in the winter of 1863 uncovered further abuses in the system of water transportation, were made known to the quartermasters at the chief ports. Meigs instructed them to annul charters tainted with fraud and to take steps to restore to the Treasury all sums that had been extorted by agents or fraudulently obtained. Settlements of some of the most extravagant claims were made at greatly reduced rates, and in some cases vessels were taken possession of and further compensation refused when the amount already paid far exceeded the value of the ship. Meigs also advised his quartermasters to compare tonnage stated in charter parties with the register at the custom house, since the government had paid out considerable sums on falsely reported tonnage.[147] The Department introduced a clause in all charters that gave the United States the right to purchase a chartered vessel at any time during its service on paying a reasonable percentage upon the original valuation of the vessel and the cost of her maintenance. Thus, should chartered rates be too high, the result was that the vessel soon became the property of the United States. Meigs' efforts at reform also led to a more adequate inspection system, with officers of the Navy detailed to inspect and appraise vessels offered for charter or purchase.[148] After Tucker had resigned and control once

---

[146] Senate *Ex. Doc.* No. 84, 37th Cong., 3d sess., pp. 24–26, s.n. 1151 (Meigs to Grimes, 4 Feb 1863).

[147] RG 92, OQMG Letter Book, vol. 67, pp. 29–30 (Meigs to Maj. S. Van Vliet *et al.*, 2 Mar 1863; p. 55 (Meigs to Capt. W. W. McKim *et al.*, 4 Mar 1863).

[148] *Ibid.*, pp. 201–03 (SO 3, 10 Mar 1863); vol. 75, pp. 175–77 (SO 4, 25 Jan 1864).

more rested fully with the Quartermaster's Department, it was by such measures that Meigs checked the irregularities formerly practiced in the coastal transportation of men and supplies.

Procurement of Wagons and Ambulances

Responsibility for the land transportation used by the Army—wagons, horses, mules, and the forage necessary for the support of the animals—continued to be vested in the Quartermaster's Department as it had been since its origin. The wagons and harness used had long ago been perfected as a result of Army experience on the western plains. The wheels, axles, and other principal parts were made to standard measurements to permit interchangeability of parts. After the close of the Mexican War, production of Army wagons had again become centered in Philadelphia, procurement being handled by contracts made by the depot quartermaster. The first orders for Army wagons in the Civil War were filled at Philadelphia in May 1861. Within a few weeks, it was obvious that Philadelphia could not be permitted to monopolize the manufacture of Army wagons.[149] Production had to be distributed among many places along the East Coast and the Ohio valley.

As troops assembled at Washington and a forward movement was planned, not only wagons but ambulances of both two- and four-wheel types and transport carts were needed. Orders to speed production went to the quartermasters at Philadelphia and New York, and Assistant Quartermaster Morris S. Miller was sent out to aid them by "a judicious distribution" of contracts among carriage makers at Rahway and Newark, N.J., New Haven, Conn., Pittsburg, Pa., Wheeling, W. Va., and other points.[150]

Whenever time permitted, quartermasters advertised for bids, but Army demands often were sudden and urgent. Unlike clothing, wagons could not be stored at arsenals to permit the Department to fill from reserve stocks the emergency requirements created by losses sustained through capture on the battlefield or through wreckage of shipments sent by sea. Such emergency requisitions had to be filled by open-market purchases from well-known carriage makers who kept on hand large supplies of the parts required—"some finished, some half put together, some not fitted or put together."[151]

Though at the beginning of the war orderly procurement was

[149] *Ibid.*, vol. 55, pp. 426–27 (Sibley to Maj. M. S. Miller, 10 Jun 1861).
[150] *Ibid.*, pp. 415-16 (Sibley to Tompkins, 5 Jun 1861); p. 422 (Sibley to Thomas, 7 Jun 1861); pp. 426–27 (Sibley to Miller, 10 Jun 1861); p. 439 (Meigs to Miller, 14 Jun 1861).
[151] *Ibid.*, vol. 77, pp. 396–97 (Meigs to M. R. Hazard Wagon Factory, 17 Jun 1864).

hampered by lack of knowledge of how many troops would be involved and how much wagon transportation they would need, procurement of wagons and ambulances subsequently caused no difficulty.[152] Only the most careful scrutiny by reliable inspectors, however, could prevent impositions. It was not uncommon for inspectors to find panels in wagon bodies with knotholes broken out and puttied up; axles not welded soundly; poplar hubs and even poplar tongues that snapped at the gentlest pressure; and various unsatisfactory substitutes used for the well-seasoned white oak called for in specifications.[153] Some inferior wagons were sent to the field because inspectors could be bribed. Complaints were few, however, largely because spare parts, materials for repair, portable forges, and boxes of smiths', wheelwrights', carpenters', and saddlers' tools were carried with all the large divisions of the Army trains in the field. Ordinary repairs could be made during the night halt, and it was seldom necessary to abandon a wagon on the march.[154]

Procurement of Animals

Nowhere was more trickery practiced than in the sale and purchase of horses and mules. Large numbers of them were needed for the Cavalry, Artillery, wagon trains, and ambulance trains. Because mules were hardy animals, capable of bearing the irregular care and hard treatment of a campaign better than horses, they were used to a great extent in the trains. Horses, however, had to be provided for the Cavalry and Artillery. The Army used pack trains only to a limited extent in the Civil War. Keeping up regularly organized pack trains was expensive. Instead, each corps carried 200 packsaddles in its wagon train, and where rough terrain made necessary the use of pack trains, they were made up temporarily by taking mules from the wagons.[155]

[152] The efforts of Deputy Quartermaster General Crosman to equip the 3 months' men serving under General Patterson in May 1861 was illustrative of the difficulty. To the latter was assigned the task of preventing the enemy's forces in the Shenandoah Valley from making a junction with their main body at Manassas when General McDowell moved toward the battle of Bull Run. Crosman had difficulty learning the size of the force he was to supply. His first instructions called upon him to furnish 100 wagons; shortly afterwards, another 100; and after a lapse of 2 or 3 weeks, in quick succession, 200 more, repeated four times at intervals of a few days to make a total of 1,000 wagons, with 4,500 or 4,600 animals for them and the batteries. Plaintively, Crosman wrote that an administrative officer must know something of the aggregate force before he could properly provide for its equipment. RG 92, Crosman, Letter Book, 13 May–24 Aug 1861, No. 335 (Crosman to Patterson, 10 Aug 1861).

[153] (1) RG 92, OQMG Letters.Received, Box 75 (Inspector Henry Dunlop to Crosman, 15 Oct 1861). (2) RG 92, OQMG Letter Book, vol. 58, p. 266 (Meigs to QM Dickerson, 24 Feb 1862). (3) RG 107, OSW Military Book, vol. 53 C, p. 154 (ASW Watson to Meigs, 12 Mar 1864).

[154] Annual Reports of the Quartermaster General, 1861–1865, p. 14 (QMG's Rpt, 1864).

[155] Henry G. Sharpe, The Act of Supplying Armies in the Field as Exemplified During the Civil War (n.p., n.d.), p. 78.

There was no centralized procurement of horses and mules at the beginning of the Civil War. It was the policy of the government and of the Quartermaster's Department "to distribute disbursements as much as possible so as to equalize the compensation for the burdens of this war."[156] In addition to purchases made by some of the regular staff officers of the Department, governors of states, mustering officers, and quartermasters of regiments were authorized and encouraged to purchase horses in the districts in which regiments were raised. Numerous agents and subagents also participated in the procurement of horses and mules. Inevitably, agents came into competition with each other. Purchases were made subject to inspection. At some places, inspection was accomplished by the local quartermaster; at others, by civilian agents whom he hired for the purpose. In at least one instance, an agent both purchased and inspected the horses he bought. That agent was John E. Reeside, appointed by General Fremont as inspector of horses in the Western Department and allowed a commission of $2\frac{1}{2}$ percent for his services.[157]

In some cases, impositions resulted from lack of knowledge, but in many others, regimental officers were exposed by the committee investigating government contracts as participants in the shameless defrauding of the government.[158] Departmental quartermasters were also involved. The committee was convinced that Quartermaster McKinstry at St. Louis was himself in collusion with unprincipled men to swindle the government as was Quartermaster Hatch at Cairo, Ill.

Purchases were often made in the open market to meet emergencies, but even when bids were solicited by public advertisement contracts fell into the hands of middlemen. The difference between what the owner received for his horse or mule and the price paid by the government went into the pocket of the middleman.[159] The government was defrauded not only in the large sums paid to these middlemen but in the quality of the horses and mules it obtained. Broken-down wagon and dray horses and mules were acquired by contractors and sold to the government at maximum prices. By criminal collusion between government inspectors and civilian contractors, horses were accepted and forwarded to the Army that were under and over age, spavined, blind, stifled, and afflicted with ringbone, sweeny, and every other disease known to horses.[160]

[156] RG 92, OQMG Letter Book, vol. 55, p. 460 (Meigs to McClellan, 20 Jun 1861); vol. 56, p. 284 (Meigs to Col. F. M. Kellogg, 26 Aug 1861).
[157] "Government Contracts," House Rpt. No. 2, 37th Cong., 2d sess., pp. xxxv–xxxvi; 749–62, s.n. 1143. For further testimony illustrating how this system of purchase and inspection operated see pp. 528–36 and passim.
[158] Ibid., pp. 69–71, s.n. 1142.
[159] Ibid., pp. 83–84.
[160] Ibid., pp. 78–82, s.n. 1143.

Not all of the thousands of animals procured in the opening months of the war were worthless.[161]   Many sound animals were obtained but none superior to the minimum specifications set by the Department. Moreover, though the quality of the horses offered by contractors might differ considerably, the law required that the contract be given to the lowest bidder.   Standards were further affected by the number of horses and mules required in a given time.   When emergencies were pressing, standards undoubtedly were permitted to fall too low.   Such an emergency existed at the time preparations were being pushed for the movement that culminated in the battle of Bull Run.   When dealers complained that the inspection of horses for Maj. Gen. Robert Patterson's troops was too severe, Meigs advised Quartermaster A. R. Eddy that although inspections should be efficient, a military movement should not be delayed in order to get first-class horses—"a horse that will do a month's work, may in certain cases be worth his weight in silver." [162]

It is not surprising that complaints came from the field.   By 1863, the chief quartermaster of the Army of the Potomac, Lt. Col. Rufus Ingalls, charged that the Cavalry and Artillery arms had been kept less efficient because of the inferior quality of the animals they had received under the existing laws and system of purchase and inspection.[163]   He called for reform and endorsed remedial measures that had been advocated by Col. Daniel H. Rucker, the commanding officer of the Washington Depot.

Colonel Rucker had long thought that the system could be improved by detailing experienced cavalry officers to do the purchasing directly from the owners in the stockraising parts of the country, leaving the purchasing agents free to bargain for sound animals at prices below a fair maximum one fixed by the Quartermaster General.   Thus, with a number of cavalry officers purchasing and shipping in small lots, depots would be supplied with sufficient animals to meet any ordinary wants of the service, more time would be allowed to make selections by reliable persons, purchases would, in most instances, be made directly from the stockraisers, and both the standards used in selecting the animals and the efficiency of the mounted service would necessarily be raised.[164]

---

[161] According to the Department's records 109,789 horses and 83,620 mules were procured during the fiscal year ending 30 June 1862.   This is not a complete figure for reports were not sent in by many inexperienced officers purchasing in the field.   No accurate statistical data is available on the number of animals procured during the Civil War.   For fragmentary reports see *Annual Reports of the Quartermaster General, 1861–1865, passim.*

[162] RG 92, OQMG Letter Book, vol. 56, p. 69 (15 Jul 1861).

[163] RG 92, OQMG Letters Received, Box 115 (Ingalls to Adj. Gen. Seth Williams, 1 Apr 1863).

[164] *Ibid.* (Rucker to Meigs, 22 Apr 1863).

THE ARMY BLACKSMITH

Along with these proposals, Colonel Rucker also called attention to the need to reduce the waste of animals in the Army. Thousands of horses and mules had been rendered unfit for service by "harsh and injudicious treatment" and by failure of the troops to give them ordinary care.

In consequence of the complaints of cavalry officers, a Cavalry Bureau was established, on 28 July 1863, under a chief charged with responsibility for organizing and equipping the cavalry forces and providing their mounts and remounts. He was to establish depots for the reception, organization, and discipline of cavalry recruits and regiments, and for the collection, care, and training of cavalry horses. As a result, a depot was established at Giesboro in the District of Columbia that became the principal remount depot for the supply of the armies in the East, as St. Louis and Nashville were in the Mississippi Valley. Quartermaster officers still purchased cavalry horses but under the direction of the chief of the Cavalry Bureau, and all horses for its service were to be inspected by cavalry officers. Quartermaster officers assigned to duty in the bureau made their reports and returns of money and property to the Quartermaster General, and all estimates for funds were submitted to the bureau

chief before being finally acted upon by the Quartermaster General.[165]
The basis for reform was laid, and under the able direction of Col.
James A. Ekin, detailed to the Cavalry Bureau as chief quartermaster,
the quality of the horses selected for the Cavalry was improved.[166]

In the spring of the following year, these arrangements were modified. The Cavalry Bureau was placed under the command of the Chief
of Army Staff who performed all the duties formerly assigned to the
Chief of the Bureau. All duties in relation to both the purchase and
inspection of horses, their subsistence, and their transportation were
performed by Quartermaster officers especially assigned to the duty.
Colonel Ekin continued as chief quartermaster of the bureau.[167] Later
in the year, when the Quartermaster's Department was reorganized, he
also was appointed chief of the First Division in the Quartermaster
General's office. As such, he had charge of the purchase and disposition
of all horses and mules used by the Army. The purchase of animals
could thereafter be made only on authority received from the Quartermaster General's office. By law, inspectors were made liable to punishment by fine and imprisonment by sentence of court martial or military
commission for any corruption, wilful neglect, or fraud in the performance of their duties. Any contractor who sought to influence an inspector
was to forfeit the full amount of his contract with the United States and
his offense was to be given full publicity throughout the country. The
Quartermaster's Department published rules and regulations to govern
the purchase and disposition of horses and mules, and also prepared forms
to be used in making reports to the First Division.[168] As a result of
these measures, a more regular system and better control of supply was
established and greater uniformity and greater skill was introduced in
the inspection of horses and mules for Army use.

So much did the system of procurement and inspection improve that
in forwarding the estimate of public animals needed by the armies of
the Potomac and James for December 1864, Chief Quartermaster Ingalls
commented: "The supply is already very good, and it is proper to state
that the artillery and cavalry horses sent to these armies during the past
three months have been the best we have received during the war." [169]
Much to the gratification of the Department, similar comments came

[165] War Department General Orders, 1863, vol. 2, pp. 289–91 (GO 236 and 237, 28 Jul 1863).
[166] Colonel Ekin took charge on 27 December 1863, relieving Col. C. G. Sawtelle who
temporarily filled the post the first 5 months after the bureau was established. RG 92,
Personal Narrative Rpts, F.Y. 1864, II, pp. 78–79.
[167] War Department General Orders, 1864 (GO 162, 14 Apr 1864).
[168] General Orders, Quartermaster General's Office, 1864–1865 (GO 43, 23 Sep 1864).
[169] Annual Reports of the Quartermaster General, 1861–1865 (Ekin's Rpt to QMG, 17 Oct
1865, p. 46.

from other armies in the field. By the last year of the war, an efficient system for the purchase, inspection, and disposition of horses and mules had finally evolved.

Procurement of Forage

The great loss of horses and mules in the Union armies can not be attributed solely to hard usage and lack of care. In many instances, lack of feed brought much suffering and great loss among the animals when the armies went into winter quarters. Maintenance of an adequate supply of forage was at all times a difficult task because the amount to be supplied was so enormous. Each horse had to be supplied daily with 14 pounds of hay and 12 pounds of oats, corn, or barley; each mule's ration consisted of the same amount of hay and 9 pounds of oats, corn, or barley. In the winter of 1861–62, the Army of the Potomac required about 400 tons of forage daily.[170] A certain amount of forage was also consumed by the animals of the wagon trains bringing the forage supply forward to the army.

At the beginning of the war, procurement of forage was completely decentralized. Chief quartermasters in the various geographical departments, depot quartermasters, and chief quartermasters with armies in the field were all procuring forage. Competition among them in the same markets resulted in higher prices for grain. By the fall of 1862, Colonel Tompkins at New York was having so much difficulty in procuring forage shipments for southern stations in competition with the procuring agents of the Army of the Potomac and the Washington Depot that he suggested the desirability of vesting all responsibility for forage procurement in New York City in one competent agent.[171] Nothing came of the proposal at that time.

The exceedingly high price of oats in the fall of 1862 led to an effort to economize that opened the door to fraud. Maj. S. Van Vliet, then serving as quartermaster at New York, proposed the use of a mixture of one-third corn to two-thirds oats in feeding the Army's horses and mules. His proposal was approved, and Capts. C. B. Ferguson and William Stoddard, assistant quartermasters at the depot at Alexandria, Va., supporting the Army of the Potomac, began purchasing mixed feed from contractors.[172]

The following summer, Lt. Col. James L. Donaldson, who was then quartermaster at Baltimore, began to hear rumors about the profits to

---

[170] RG 92, Personal Narrative Rpts, F.Y. 1863, V, 544 (Van Vliet's Rpt, 3 Oct 1863).
[171] RG 92, OQMG Letter Book, vol. 63, pp. 174–75 (To Meigs, 23 Sep 1862).
[172] *Ibid.*, vol. 64, pp. 270–71 (Sibley to Ingalls, 21 Nov 1862).

be made out of selling mixed grain to the Army. He directed the Department's attention to the possibility of fraud inherent in a dishonest mixture of oats and corn. With oats weighing 32 pounds to the bushel, and corn, 56 pounds, the lighter the oats the greater the fraud. Because of the difference in the weight and price of the grains, contractors were able to make a considerable profit on each bushel. Meigs requested a report from the chief quartermaster of the Army of the Potomac. Captain Stoddard in charge of the forage department at the Alexandria Depot explained that only the most reliable contractors furnished this mixture to the depot, and that to prevent fraud he always tested the proportions of grain used by separating and weighing each component. If any deficiency existed, he made a proportionate deduction from the agreed price. Ingalls was satisfied that all necessary safeguards were being taken and so informed Meigs.[173]

The explanation, however, did not halt the investigation that was now pressed by Peter H. Watson, Assistant Secretary of War. The depot quartermasters involved were ordered to purchase no more mixed grain, and in December both Capts. C. B. Ferguson, in charge of the Alexandria depot, and Stoddard were placed under arrest. Secretary Watson also had arrested the contractors directly involved in the swindle. Since they were politically important in Pennsylvania, great pressure was brought to bear to effect their release but to no avail. The fraud was fully investigated and future swindles of that kind made impossible.[174]

The Quartermaster's Department now instituted in the East a certain amount of control to avoid competition and high prices. It assigned responsibility to General Rucker for superintending the purchase of all forage required by the depots at Washington, Alexandria, Fortress Monroe, Baltimore, and the cavalry depot at Giesboro, and for all troops and transportation dependent on these points. The Department directed him to ascertain the amount of forage on hand and the number of animals to be supported from each depot, and to contract for the necessary supply. Any existing shortages might be handled on an emergency basis and supplied through open-market purchases until supply by contract could be established.[175]

Because a monopolistic combine had control of the available supply of oats and corn, the Department experienced great difficulty in procuring forage for the Army of the Potomac. In consequence, it sent Capt.

[173] Ibid., vol. 71, pp. 22–26 (Donaldson to Meigs, 10 Jun, 4 Aug 1863); (Ingalls to Meigs, 25 Jun 1863); (Meigs to Donaldson, 8 Aug 1863).

[174] Charles A. Dana, Recollections of the Civil War (New York, 1902), pp. 162–64.

[175] RG 92, OQMG Letter Book, vol. 73, pp. 188–89 (Actg QMG Thomas to Rucker, 7 Dec 1863).

Samuel L. Brown to New York as the sole purchaser of forage for the troops in the East. He had been in charge of the forage department of the Washington Depot and had also assumed the forage duties of Captains Ferguson and Stoddard when they were arrested. By "judicious purchases and drawing supplies from the interior," he was able to break the monopoly.[176]

Though Captain Brown purchased large quantities of forage in the winter of 1863–64, supplies still failed to reach the Army of the Potomac, and Chief Quartermaster Ingalls complained bitterly that his animals were likely to starve to death.[177] The trouble was that the Potomac, the small streams and harbors at the northern end of the Chesapeake Bay, and the Delaware and Chesapeake Canal were all frozen over. With shipments by water made impossible by ice, the Department appealed to the railroads to forward the forage purchased on their lines.[178] Because of the ice and a shortage of railroad cars, forage trickled slowly to Washington and the Army of the Potomac, the full daily ration for which amounted to 37,000 bushels of grain and 1,150 tons of hay.[179]

Early in 1864, Congress, seeking to promote reform by centralizing control of contracts in the office of the Quartermaster General at Washington, incorporated such ideas in the reorganization act that it passed for the Department in July. Meigs was dismayed; he feared that such centralization would require too many contracts to be made at "this centre of political influence and intrigue." [180] In the past, he had tried to mitigate the evil of dealing too much with large contractors by establishing as many depots as he could for contracting for supplies. Under the reorganization act, a Fifth Division, handling forage, was set up in the office of the Quartermaster General, and Quartermaster Brown, now promoted to a colonel, was placed in charge of it on 7 September 1864. Because he was then supplying forage for all the armies of the East and for the depots along the Atlantic and Gulf seacoast, Colonel Brown was permitted to remain in New York supervising shipments until 1 January 1865.[181]

Forage for the armies in the West had largely been supplied through

---

[176] RG 92, Personal Narrative Rpts, F.Y. 1864, I, pp. 353--57 (Brown's Rpt, 10 Jul 1864).
[177] RG 92, OQMG Letters Received, Box 131 (Ingalls to Actg QMG Thomas 6 Jan 1864).
[178] (1) *Ibid.*, box 129 (Rucker to Thomas, 7 Jan 1864). (2) RG 92, OQMG Letter Book, vol. 75, p. 67 (Meigs to Vanderbilt, 1 Mar 1864). (3) Meigs reported the railroads were "jealous of the government's going into the market, purchasing in the country, and calling upon them to transport the forage, a bulky and troublesome commodity at rates less than they receive from individuals." *Ibid.*, p. 120 (To Brown, 4 Mar 1864).
[179] RG 92, OQMG Letter Book, vol. 74, p. 155 (Thomas to Van Vliet, 20 Jan 1864).
[180] *Ibid.*, p. 546 (Meigs to Hon. Henry Wilson, 20 Feb 1864).
[181] RG 92, Personal Narrative Rpts, F.Y. 1865, vol. A–F, pp. 267–70 (Brown's Rpt, 17 Oct 1865).

the forage department of the St. Louis Depot. When Colonel Brown assumed his duties in Washington, he wished to extend his control, eliminate competition, and save the government large sums of money in procuring the vast quantity of forage required for both the East and the West, amounting to approximately 2,500,000 bushels of grain and 50,000 tons of hay per month. He recommended that suitable officers be stationed at the sources of supply who, under his direction, would have charge of purchases of all forage needed in the different sections of the country. Meigs approved of forage officers but not under Brown's immediate direction. The chain of military command, responsibility, and oversight ought not to be broken, he advised Brown. Since most depots already had an officer especially charged with the purchase of forage, Brown's instructions to them ought to go through their immediate chiefs at the depots. Meigs also warned Colonel Brown that the transportation of grain in large quantities from Chicago and other western markets to eastern ports was in violation of the spirit of the agreement with the railroad companies. The Quartermaster General had assured the latter that supplies would not be brought in from distant markets for the purpose of compelling them to transport at reduced rates. Only when necessity compelled such purchases did the Department insist upon the government rate being paid for transportation.[182] Within these limits, Brown was free to extend his authority, but further efforts to promote co-ordination and centralized control of forage procurement were shortly made unnecessary by the end of the war.

Subsisting the Troops

Supplying the troops with rations was not a function of the Quartermaster's Department during the Civil War. That responsibility continued to be vested in a separate supply bureau headed by a Commissary General of Subsistence. Like the Quartermaster's Department, the Subsistence Department, since its establishment as a bureau in 1818, had been administered by the same chief—Col. George Gibson. The latter had been a confirmed invalid for some years, the duties of his Department being executed when the war began by Lt. Col. Joseph P. Taylor as Acting Commissary General of Subsistence. Upon Gibson's death late in September 1861, Taylor was appointed Commissary General of Subsistence. He served until he died on 29 June 1864, when, by promotion from within the Department, Amos B. Eaton succeeded him.[183]

---

[182] RG 92, OQMG Letter Book, vol. 82, pp. 496–99 (Brown to Actg QMG Thomas, 23 Jan 1865); pp. 500–502 (Meigs to Brown, 3 Feb 1865).
[183] (1) *General Orders of the War Department, 1861–62*, I 164–65 (GO 84, 30 Sep 1861).

Despite the appointment of successive Commissary Generals of Subsistence during the war, the Department enjoyed the advantage of continued experienced leadership. It was greatly handicapped, however, in April 1861, by the small size of its staff and the losses that secession brought to its ranks. Including the chief, the Department's authorized strength was only 12. At the beginning of the war, 4 officers resigned, 3 of whom joined the Confederate Army. Obviously, 8 officers could not hope to provision an army of the size then being called into the field. On 3 August, Congress enacted legislation that added another 12 commissaries to the Department's staff, to be taken from the line of the Army, either of the Volunteer or Regular Army.[184] Four of these commissaries were to have the rank, pay, and emoluments of majors of cavalry and eight, of captains of cavalry. With the Commissary General of Subsistence holding the rank of colonel and a lieutenant colonel designated as assistant, the staff of the Department now totaled 24 officers. About a year and a half later, Congress, to promote the efficiency of the Department, increased the rank of its chief to that of brigadier general and added five commissaries so that the staff for the rest of the war numbered 29 officers.[185] These officers were the chief purchasing agents of the Department, commanded the general subsistence depots, and served as chief commissaries with the armies in the field.

For many years the Subsistence Department had been procuring rations by awarding contracts to those who submitted the lowest bids in response to the Department's public advertisements for proposals. This method of procurement was continued during the war. The legislation enacted by Congress to protect the interests of the government was as applicable to procurement by commissaries as by quartermasters.[186] While the Subsistence Department procured most rations by contract, Taylor early in the war advised Cameron that wartime needs would also have to be filled by open-market purchases. Possibly to forestall any proposed changes, he added that the experience of the Florida and Mexican Wars had proved that the bulk of subsistence supplies were best procured in the large cities by officers who also superintended their packing.[187]

---

(2) Taylor had joined the Army in 1813 and at the time of his appointment as Commissary General of Subsistence had served for 32 years in the Subsistence Department. His successor, Amos B. Eaton, a graduate of West Point, had been an officer of the Department for 26 years.

[184] 12 *Stat.* 287.

[185] 12 *Stat.* 648 (Feb 9, 1863). The staff now consisted of the Commissary General of Subsistence, one colonel and one lieutenant colonel, both designated as assistant commissary generals, and eight majors and 18 captains appointed as commissaries.

[186] See above, pp. 345–48.

[187] RG 192, Records of CGS, Letters to SW, 1864–66, p. 146 (7 May 1861).

The crisis of April 1861 made it possible for contractors to wring profitable contracts from the Department. The annual supply of rations for the troops stationed at the western posts had already been procured by contract and was then in transit. Since most of the Army until that time was stationed on he frontier, the Department possessed few subsistence stores on the Atlantic Coast to meet any emergency. The large force that collected at Washington and the isolation of the city in April made it necessary for the Department to procure beef without delay. Failing to obtain bids, the Department contracted with A. H. Sibley, Thomas Dyer, George W. Lawman, and H. Tyler for 2,000 to 10,000 head of cattle to be delivered at Washington at 8 cents per pound gross and at some point in Pennsylvania at $5\frac{3}{4}$ cents per pound gross.

Subsequently, the congressional committee investigating contracts uncovered the fact that these men were not dealers in cattle and that they sublet their contract to certain New York dealers, Joseph H. Williams and David and Archibald M. Allerton, who furnished the cattle at $6\frac{1}{2}$ cents per pound gross weight in Washington and 5 cents in Pennsylvania. The latter still made a profit but the original contractors secured an even greater profit as middlemen. Disregarding the supply and transportation situation at the time the contract was made, the committee condemned the manner in which it was awarded and charged "gross mismanagement, a total disregard of the interests of the government, and a total recklessness in the expenditure of the funds of the government." [188]   The rapid restoration of communications between Washington and the East shortly altered the supply situation, and the Subsistence Department promptly cancelled the contract. According to the Commissary General of Subsistence, only 2,000 head of cattle were delivered, of which a little more than 500 were received in Washington and the remainder at Harrisburg, Pa.[189]   The Department executed additional contracts at St. Louis and elsewhere during the early months of the war.

The Subsistence Department purchased subsistence supplies in the markets of Boston, New York, Philadelphia, Baltimore, Washington, Cincinnati, Louisville, Chicago, and St. Louis during the war.   In each of these cities, commissaries in charge of the subsistence depot procured and received supplies in bulk, subject to inspection.   After the supplies were packed, the Quartermaster's Department transported them to the depots in the field. Flour and beef were exceptions to this procedure. Commissaries procured flour under contract but usually at points near the armies.   Commissaries also procured fresh beef for the troops by

[188] "Government Contracts," House *Rpt.* No. 2, 37th Cong., 2d sess., pp. 67–68, s.n. 1142. See also testimony, pp. 160–69.
[189] *OR*, ser. III, vol. I, pp. 676–77 (Taylor to Cameron, 26 Nov 1861).

BEEF ON THE HOOF

purchasing cattle under contract, receiving them from the contractors at convenient delivery points, and then driving them to and with the armies in the numbers required.[190] As the war progressed, the Department supplied rations not only to the several large armies occupying widely different fields of operations and to the troops garrisoned at posts throughout the country, but also to prisoners of war and to contrabands.

During the opening months of the war, a considerable amount of confusion hampered the Department's operations. It failed to get reports from the armies and knew little of the subsistence support being given to troops outside of the Washington area. It learned that the troops at Cairo were being well supplied, but the army in West Virginia had suffered not only because of the difficulty of transporting rations over mountain roads, but because its officers had not known the proper depot from which to draw rations. The total ignorance of their duties exhibited by many brigade commissaries appointed from civil life resulted

[190] RG 192, Records of CGS, Letters to SW, 1864–66, p. 293 (Annual Rpt, Taylor to Stanton, 29 Oct 1863); p. 362 (Annual Rpt, Eaton to Stanton, 14 Oct 1864).

in numerous irregularities in accounts and increased the work of the staff in the Washington office.[191] Time and experience corrected these difficulties. Despite speculative dealers and the attempts of some associated houses to monopolize and control the prices of particular subsistence items, the Subsistence Department supplied the troops with abundant rations. In the course of military operations, temporary scarcities did exist but the Commissary General of Subsistence could take pride in asserting that no campaign, contemplated movement, or expedition failed because the Department did not supply subsistence.[192]

Obviously, the impact of war in April 1861 on the supply departments was overwhelming. They were called upon to provide for a force many times the size of the small prewar Army, without the cushion afforded by ample reserve stocks. Under the demands of the emergency, the procurement efforts of the small staff of the Quartermaster's Department were supplemented by those of state authorities, regimental officers, and federal agents. Unfortunately, though patriotism ran high, ignorance of regulations and laws protecting the government's interests, loose procedures, and inexperience provided a basis for procurement blunders and impositions. When coupled with cupidity, both in and out of the Army, they resulted in the scandals that marked the opening months of the Civil War.

Under the able administration of General Meigs, control over Quartermaster responsibilities was reasserted, first in the procurement of clothing and equipment, and, by 1863, in the transportation of men and supplies. Procurement tended to become centralized in the Washington office, and, as will become evident in a review of field operations, greater regularity and control of Quartermaster funds was brought about in the field. In consequence, the opportunities for fraud became more limited, while, at the same time, the increased experience gained by Volunteer quartermasters reduced the possibilities for imposition.

Despite the record of scandals in the early months of the war, the majority of the Volunteer quartermasters were honest men, some of whom filling positions of heavy responsibility, were brevetted for their services. With few exceptions, the Departmental quartermasters holding appointments in the Regular Army won praise, in the midst of the scandals exposed by congressional investigating committees, for their fidelity and capacity. The efforts of Meigs were, in fact, ably supported by the work of such outstanding and experienced Departmental quartermasters in the field as Rufus Ingalls, Chief Quartermaster of the Army of the

---

[191] *Ibid.*, pp. 175–76 (Taylor to SW, 26 Nov 1861).
[192] *OR,* ser. III, vol. V, p. 146 (Annual Rpt, 20 Oct 1865).

Potomac; Daniel H. Rucker, Chief Quartermaster of the Washington Depot; Robert Allen, Chief Quartermaster of the Mississippi Valley; James L. Donaldson, Chief Quartermaster of the Department of the Cumberland; and Langdon C. Easton, Chief Quartermaster of Sherman's Army, all of whom were brevetted major generals for their faithful and meritorious service during the war.

CHAPTER X

Quartermaster Field Operations in the Civil War

The Quartermaster organization in the field absorbed the greater part of the Department personnel. Except for the few officers who directed the work of the divisions in the office of the Quartermaster General in Washington, all quartermasters were assigned to posts in the field. Some of them held key positions to carry out Quartermaster responsibilities in the military departments, but the great majority of them during the war were assigned to support the tactical units of the Army.

Field Organization

For administrative purposes, the states and territories of the United States were grouped in geographical areas called military departments. Quartermaster duties had to be executed not only in those constituting immediate theaters of operations but also in areas remote from them, such as the Pacific Coast. It had been customary for the Quartermaster General to assign a chief quartermaster to each military department in the years of peace, but, in view of the shortage of personnel during the war, it was not unusual to group two or three military departments under one chief quartermaster. On the basis of troop strength, the latter prepared estimates of supplies and funds needed in his department, submitting them to the Quartermaster General through the departmental commander.[1] The chief quartermaster also closely examined all vouchers for supplies purchased in his department and through his hands passed the funds for their payment. He filled requisitions made upon him by troops stationed at posts in his geographical area as well as by an army operating in the field. Normally, he had little direct contact with combat operations, though on occasion he might go forward to an advance area to eliminate confusion and delays occurring in supply operations.

The military department was the basic organizational unit for administrative purposes. During the war, the number of such military

---

[1] For later modification see pp. 392–93.

departments tended to increase and repeated changes were made in their geographical boundaries.   In some cases, a department was divided to form two military departments, in others, a part of a department was set up as a military district.   On the other hand, this tendency was offset to a certain degree by a move toward consolidation.   In some few instances, several military departments were grouped together to form a single geographical division, as for example, the Military Division of the Mississippi, which, under Sherman in the spring of 1864, included the Departments of the Ohio, Cumberland, Tennessee, and Arkansas.

In addition to this Quartermaster administrative organization in the military departments, there was also a Quartermaster field organization that supported the tactical units of the Army.   It expanded in direct proportion to the increase in the size of the Army.   When Congress enacted legislation authorizing the President to accept the services of volunteers, it directed that they were to be formed into regiments, brigades, and divisions.   At the same time, Congress provided that each Volunteer regiment raised was to have a quartermaster-sergeant and a quartermaster, and each brigade, an assistant quartermaster as in the Regular Army.[2]   Unfortunately, volunteers appointed to such posts were, for the most part, inexperienced.   Their ignorance of regulations and of their duties and responsibilities as quartermasters promoted confusion in supply and irregularity in accounting for the public property placed in their charge.   It took several months for them to acquire the rudimentary knowledge needed to perform their duties, but if they had integrity and some business ability they could become satisfactory quartermasters.   Until time provided the experience they needed, the regular quartermasters were overworked and calls poured into the Washington office from harassed quartermasters in the field for assignment to them of additional assistant quartermasters.[3]

The colonel of a regiment appointed the quartermaster-sergeant and the regimental quartermaster, the latter holding the rank of lieutenant. The quartermaster-sergeant issued supplies to the troops and, in general, assisted the regimental quartermaster who had charge of the property of the Quartermaster's Department with the regiment—that is, the tents and equipage belonging to the regiment, and of the wagons, harness, and animals of the regimental train.   He also requisitioned for the supplies

---

[2] (1) 12 *Stat.* 269, 270 (Jul 22, 1861).   (2) The Quartermaster field organization was further expanded by the addition of more brigade, regimental, and battalion quartermasters and quartermaster-sergeants when Congress enacted legislation enlarging the size of the Regular Army a week later.   12 *Stat.* 280 (Jul 28, 1861).

[3] (1) RG 92, Crosman, Letter Book, 14 May–24 Aug 1861, No. 177 (Crosman to Meigs, 20 Jun, 18 Jul 1861).   (2) RG 92, OQMG Consolidated Correspondence File, Box 944 (Rpt of Brig. Gen. D. H. Rucker, 22 Jul 1863).   National Archives.

needed by the regiment and received and issued to the proper officers the clothing, forage, and other supplies furnished by the Department for the use of the regiment.

Two or more regiments constituted a brigade, and to each brigade the President appointed an assistant quartermaster with the rank of captain. Usually called a brigade quartermaster, he received and transferred to the proper officer all property and supplies furnished for the use of the brigade. He also had charge of the brigade train, its material, and animals.[4]

Two or more brigades formed a division. There was no division without its quartermaster, for he performed duties for the division similar to those executed at brigade level by the brigade quartermaster. Division quartermasters were indispensably necessary officers, but for the first 3 years of the war, though they were recognized in general orders, they had no legal position in the Army. It was not until the summer of 1864 that Congress provided for the appointment of division quartermasters with the temporary rank of major while so assigned.[5]

In addition to these regularly appointed officers, the Department made use of the services of hundreds of acting quartermasters during the war. Quartermaster General Meigs tried to get authority for the commanding general in the field to confer acting appointments as captains and assistant or brigade quartermasters upon officers of the Army, with the understanding that they would be nominated to the Senate by the President on the basis of the commanding general's recommendation. Meigs was induced to take this step by his inability to supply enough experienced quartermasters to the Army of the Potomac in 1862. Unfortunately, the pressure exerted by Congressmen in favor of their constituents who sought such posts made it difficult for the President and the Secretary of War to grant such authorization.[6] Acting appointments continued to be conferred, but the recipients were not always confirmed in office by the Senate.

Regular and Volunteer troops were organized at first in armies, but from the beginning of the war the idea of the army corps had prevailed. It was not until 17 July 1862, however, that Congress passed an act legalizing them and authorizing the President to appoint a chief quartermaster with the rank of lieutenant colonel to the staff of the army corps commander. Either Regular or Volunteer officers of the Quartermaster's

---

[4] *Annual Reports of the Quartermaster General, 1861–1865,* p. 20 (Rpt, 1864).

[5] (1) 13 *Stat.* 394 (Jul 4, 1864). (2) RG 92, Personal Narrative Reports of Officers, QMD, for Fiscal Year Ending 30 June 1863, vol. VI, 931–32 (Capt. J. F. Rusling's Rpt, 20 Sep 1863). Hereafter briefly cited as Personal Narrative Rpts, F.Y. 1863. (3) RG 92, OQMG Letter Book, vol. 75, p. 206 (Meigs to Hon. R. C. Schenck, 11 Mar 1864).

[6] *OR,* ser. I, vol. XI, 111–12 (Meigs to Maj. Gen. George B. McClellan, 19 Apr 1862).

Department could be designated by the Quartermaster General for such assignment, but both rank and pay were temporary, ending with reassignment of the officer to other duty or with the close of the war.[7]

When several corps were united into an army, a chief quartermaster of the army was designated with the rank of colonel. His duties were administrative and supervisory. He served as the chief disbursing agent, providing all funds for his subordinates in the army, as for example, funds needed by corps quartermasters to meet the payrolls for all persons employed in the Quartermaster's Department in their several commands. He required monthly and semi-monthly reports from all officers in his department on the condition of all property—wagons, animals, clothing, and other supplies—in their charge, and the amounts they needed to complete the equipment of their troops. He caused supplies to be brought forward from the depots under his control for distribution to the troops. He consolidated estimates of additional supplies needed and not available in the depots, and he also prepared estimates of funds required.

At the beginning of the war, all such estimates went to the Quartermaster General. By 1863, to reduce the number of disbursing agents and bring about greater regularity and control over Quartermaster funds, Meigs designated senior and supervising quartermasters. There were two at that date in the Mississippi and Ohio valleys—Brig. Gen. Robert Allen at St. Louis, who acted as senior and supervising quartermaster for the Departments of the Northwest, Missouri, Tennessee, and Kansas, and Colonel Thomas Swords, stationed sometimes at Louisville and at other times at Cincinnati, who performed the same function for the Departments of the Ohio and the Cumberland.

Not only the chief quartermasters of the military departments but the chief quartermasters of armies in the field in those areas forwarded their consolidated estimates for funds and for supplies to the senior and supervising quartermaster who supplied the funds or advised Washington of the best mode of sending any required, either by transfer from the office of the supervising quartermaster or by direct remittance to the chief quartermaster of the army. The supervising quartermaster also forwarded supply estimates to the Quartermaster General with letters of advice to guide the Department in the action to be taken. Thus, when Maj. Langdon C. Easton served as Chief Quartermaster with Sherman's

---

[7] (1) 12 *Stat.* 598–99. (2) In the past such officers had moved with the corps commander when he was reassigned. Under this law the officer, once assigned, remained permanently attached to the corps, without regard to the movement of the corps commander, until reassigned by the President. *General Orders of the War Department 1861–1862*, I, 471 (GO 212, 23 Dec 1862).

army in its march to Atlanta in 1864, his estimates for supplies went back to the depot at Nashville and his estimates for funds were sent to Lt. Col. James L. Donaldson, then senior and supervising quartermaster stationed there as Chief Quartermaster of the Department of the Cumberland. On the other hand, this system was not applied in the military departments in the East or on the Gulf, chief quartermasters of which continued to send their estimates directly to the Quartermaster General. The Army of the Potomac also formed an exception; its Chief Quartermaster, Brig. Gen. Rufus Ingalls, sent his estimates directly to the Quartermaster General.[8]

Each officer, from regimental quartermaster to chief quartermaster of an army, exercised a general supervision over the officers and agents subordinate to him and within his command. Each took his orders and instructions from the commander of the body of troops to which he was attached and also from his immediate superior in the Quartermaster's Department. A corps quartermaster, for example, obeyed the orders of the corps commander and the chief quartermaster of the army. The chief quartermaster of a military department took his orders from the Quartermaster General and also from the commanding general of the military department. This last-named officer was also usually the commanding general of the department's mobile forces, the latter being named the army of the military department.

It was 1864 before the final details of this field organization were enacted into law by Congress. The system had existed from the beginning of the war but complete gradations in rank had not been established. During the first 3 years of the war, the Volunteer quartermaster organization in the field had only three grades—lieutenant for regimental quartermasters, captain for brigade quartermasters, and lieutenant colonel for corps quartermasters. Quartermasters assigned to depots usually were assistant quartermasters, with the rank and meager pay of captains, yet in some instances they conducted a business that amounted to millions of dollars a year.

Early in the war, the low status of certain key quartermasters was improved by assigning them to the staff of the commanding general as additional or acting aides-de-camp, with the rank of lieutenant colonel or colonel. For example, Lewis B. Parsons, an expert on transportation in civilian life, was appointed an assistant quartermaster with the rank of captain. Assigned to St. Louis under Chief Quartermaster Robert Allen, Parsons supervised all river transportation first on the Mississippi and subsequently on the Tennessee and Cumberland Rivers as well. To give rank commensurate with his responsibilities, he was appointed an

[8] *General Orders of the Quartermaster General, 1862–1865* (GO 21, 8 Oct 1863).

additional aide-de-camp on the staff of Maj. Gen. Henry W. Halleck, with the rank of colonel. Not all quartermasters could be so accommodated. Assistant Quartermaster James J. Dana, for example, was in charge of the receipt and issue of all means of land transportation— horses, mules, wagons, ambulances, harness, and forage—used in the service of the Washington Depot during fiscal year 1863, as well as all that were issued to the Army of the Potomac and other troops serving in Virginia. He had over 1,000 teams in use; employed, in any given month, 4,000 to 7,000 men; and expended millions of dollars, yet his rank remained that of captain. Because rank and pay were not given in proportion to the importance of the responsibilities carried by Quartermaster officers, dissatisfaction grew to such an extent that by the end of 1863 the Department was threatened with the loss of many of its most experienced officers by resignation.[9]

Meigs solicited the support of commanding generals in the field and worked hard to convince Congress that the need for gradation in rank was urgent. He secured recognition for his field officers in the reorganization act of 1864, though not to the extent that he had hoped to obtain. Congress extended the gradation of rank from lieutenant through colonel, and gave to quartermasters at principal depots the rank of colonel. It made all rank temporary, however, to last during assignment to the designated post or to the end of the war.[10] By the close of the fiscal year ending 30 June 1864, the War Department gave additional recognition for their valuable services to some Quartermaster officers who held important and responsible positions. It commissioned them as brigadier generals of Volunteers or as brevet brigadier generals.[11]

Military Railroads

The transportation of men and supplies was one of the most important functions executed by Quartermasters in the field. This entailed

[9] RG 92, OQMG Letter Book, vol. 75, pp. 236–38, 396–98 (Meigs to Chairman of Senate Military Committee, 12 and 28 Mar 1864); pp. 438–39 (Meigs to Brig. Gen. Robert Allen, 31 Mar 1864).

[10] 13 *Stat*. 394 (Jul 4, 1864).

[11] Among those so recognized were the following: Chief Quartermaster of the Army of the Potomac, Rufus Ingalls, who was commissioned a brigadier general of Volunteers in 1863, Langdon C. Easton, Chief Quartermaster to Sherman's army, and James L. Donaldson and Robert Allen, who supplied that army from Nashville and Louisville, respectively, were brevetted brigadier generals in 1864 for distinguished service. All of these officers were brevetted major generals in 1865. For a list of Quartermaster officers brevetted during the war, see *Annual Reports of the Quartermaster General, 1861–1865*, pp. 390–93 (QMG's Rpt, 1865).

the provision and management of wagon trains, the employment of all forms of water transportation, and the use of military railroads.

The Civil War saw the first large-scale use of railroads by the Army and marked the first infringement since 1775 of the transportation responsibility of the Quartermaster's Department. The first extension of government authority over the railroads occurred in April 1861 when Brig. Gen. Benjamin F. Butler, without official authorization, took possession of the Annapolis and Elk Ridge Railroad, the tracks of which had been torn up for several miles, and began making repairs to enable him to move his troops to Washington. Before the end of the war, the government operated more than 2,000 miles of road in Rebel territory.[12] Butler's action was soon followed by the temporary extension of government control over the Washington branch of the Baltimore and Ohio Railroad between Relay House and Annapolis Junction. Within less than a month, Cameron, who had appointed Thomas A. Scott to take charge of the railways and telegraphs between Washington and Annapolis, gave him jurisdiction over all such facilities appropriated for government use.[13] All instructions relating to the extension of such roads and their operation on government account had to emanate from Scott's office.

For the first time, a transportation and communications office was established in the War Department, and for the first time the broad responsibility of the Quartermaster's Department for transportation was limited. The Department was to have nothing to do with the operation of military railroads. On the other hand, it was called upon to support railroad reconstruction. Even before Scott took over, the Secretary of War had directed the Department to supply the necessary means for repairing and keeping in order the railroad from Annapolis to Washington.[14] When Scott assumed control, he was bonded as a disbursing agent and the Department's duties were restricted to signing requisitions upon his estimates.[15] Scott's efforts and those of Capt. R. F. Morley, whom Scott selected to serve as general manager under his authority, were directed primarily to reopening communication via the Baltimore and Ohio Railroad and extending that road through Washington into northern Virginia where, at Alexandria, connections could be made with a

---

[12] House *Ex. Doc.* No. 1, 39th Cong., 1st sess., pp. 9, 28, 37, s.n. 1251 (Rpt of Bvt Brig. Gen. D. C. McCallum).

[13] *OR*, ser. I, vol. II, 603 (Cameron to Whom It May Concern, 27 Apr 1861); ser. III, vol. I, 228 (Cameron to Scott, 23 May 1861).

[14] RG 107, OSW, Military Book, vol. 43, pp. 301–02 (Cameron to Sibley, 7 May 1861).

[15] (1) *Ibid.*, vol. 45, p. 66 (Cameron to Meigs, 15 Jul 1861). (2) RG 92, OQMG Letter Book, vol. 56, p. 125 (Meigs to 2d Comptroller, 26 Jul 1861). (3) RG 92, Rpts and Ltrs from QMG to SW and Heads of Depts., I, 270 (Meigs to Stanton, 28 Feb 1862).

branch of the Alexandria, Loudon and Hampshire Railroad and the Orange and Alexandria line.

These initial arrangements were changed early in 1862. Edwin M. Stanton succeeded Simon Cameron as Secretary of War on 15 January, and about 2 weeks later Congress provided a legal basis for the seizure of railroads and telegraph lines by the government. In authorizing the President to take military possession of the country's railroads, Congress conferred upon the Secretary of War, and such agents as he might appoint, the power to control and supervise all railroad transportation of troops, munitions, military property, and supplies.[16] The law was broad in scope, but there was no need to exercise that power in the loyal states, where the managers and superintendents of the railroads fully supported the war effort. When the armies advanced into the insurgent states, it became necessary for the government to take possession of, repair, and operate railways abandoned by their owners and stripped of their equipment or partially destroyed by the Confederate forces. That policy did not apply to such roads as the Baltimore and Ohio or the Louisville and Nashville Railroads whose lines lay partly in enemy territory. To a large extent, they made their own repairs and the government paid for their services. Because these lines were important to military plans, the government did assist in their reconstruction and provided track protection through the use of troops.

In exercising the powers conferred upon him, Stanton eased Scott out of his supervisory position by sending him to the West on an inspection trip. On 11 February 1862, he appointed Daniel C. McCallum as his military director and superintendent of railroads in the United States. McCallum was responsible to the War Department and reported directly to Stanton.[17] The Secretary conferred full authority upon McCallum—

to enter upon, take possession of, hold and use all railroads, engines, cars, locomotives, equipments, appendages, and appurtenances, that may be required for the transport of troops, arms, ammunition, and military supplies of the United States, and to do and perform all acts and things that may be necessary and proper to be done for the safe and speedy transport aforesaid.[18]

---

[16] 12 *Stat.* 334–35 (Jan 31, 1862).

[17] (1) House *Ex. Doc.* No. 1, 39th Cong., 1st sess., p. 5, s.n. 1251 (McCallum Rpt, 26 May 1866). (2) Meigs observed that there was "a little confusion" in McCallum's position. Though the Secretary of War appointed him, he informed Meigs that McCallum would be under his orders. Stanton, however, was apt to give McCallum instructions direct, and the latter enjoyed a quasi-independence and did communicate directly with the Secretary. Meigs considered the military railroad agency to be under his direction, and it was he who ordered McCallum to the West to take charge of the railroad operations on the Nashville and Chattanooga line. RG 92, OQMG Letter Book, 1880–D, General and Miscellaneous, pp. 2060–61.

[18] *Ibid.*, p. 5.

Stanton indicated, however, that he wanted all procurement con-ducted through officers of the Quartermaster's Department. In effect, the Department became the procurement agency for the Office of the Director and General Manager of the Military Railroads.[19] McCallum arranged for his sources of supply, and Meigs approved the requisitions he submitted for locomotives, cars, equipment, and railroad supplies. As soon as the initial demands of the service had been met, however, Meigs insisted that his Department "should be more particularly advised in regard to the operations of that branch of the service which calls upon it so largely for money and supplies for Rail Road use." In consequence, McCallum also submitted reports to Meigs.[20]

Under Meigs' orders, quartermasters executed contracts for the rail-road equipment and supplies that McCallum required. Thus, in the spring and summer of 1862, McClellan in northern Virginia and Burnside in North Carolina requested locomotives and cars. McCallum directed a survey of the rolling stock that was excess to the needs of the railroads in the Northeast and, under Meigs' orders, Colonel Crosman and his assistant quartermaster, Captain Boyd, at Philadelphia, and another as-sistant quartermaster in the New England area purchased surplus loco-motives, flatcars, and boxcars.[21] To expedite the Quartermaster business of the Office of the Director of Military Railroads, Meigs assigned an assistant quartermaster, Capt. H. R. Robinson, to that office. He served in that post throughout the war and made numerous trips to New York and the New England area to purchase and direct the shipment of equip-ment and supplies needed by the military railroad service as well as to sell by auction scrap iron collected along the routes of the military railroads in Virginia.[22]

McCallum's appointment would appear to have conferred upon him all-inclusive authority, but while he was still preoccupied with the or-ganization of his office, Stanton reduced his jurisdiction at least tem-porarily. He called in Herman Haupt, an outstanding railroad construc-tion engineer, in April 1862 to reconstruct and open a military railroad between Fredericksburg and Aquia Creek to be used by Maj. Gen. Irvin McDowell as his supply line.[23] Subsequently, to clarify Haupt's position,

[19] RG 92, OQMG Letter Book, vol. 58, p. 459 (Meigs to Tompkins, 26 Mar 1862).

[20] (1) *Ibid.*, vol. 60, p. 503 (Meigs to McCallum, 25 Feb 1863). (2) See, for example, RG 92, Report of Genl. D. C. McCallum, 30 Jun 1864, U.S.M.R.R.

[21] (1) RG 92, OQMG Letter Book, vol. 60, pp. 228–31 (McCallum to Meigs, 21 May 1862). (2) RG 92, USMRR, Military Railroad Telegram Book, (July–August 1862), *passim.*

[22] RG 92, Annual Reports of QM Officers, Box 16 (Robinson's Rpts, 12 Sep 1863, 28 Nov 1864, 28 Oct 1865).

[23] General Herman Haupt, *Reminiscences* (Milwaukee, 1901), pp. 44–47.

Stanton named him Chief of Construction and Transportation in the Department of the Rappahannock. He authorized him to use whatever means were necessary to open all military railroads in that Department; prescribe rules and regulations; appoint assistants, define their duties, and fix their compensation; requisition details of men for purposes of construction or protection; and purchase all machinery, rolling stock, and supplies required for the operation of the railroads, certifying the same to the Quartermaster General, who was to make payment for them. In addition, he authorized Haupt to form a permanent corps of artificers, equipped as he ordered; supplied with rations, tools, and implements, obtained by making requisitions upon the proper supply departments; paid such rates of compensation as he deemed expedient; and governed by rules and regulations he prescribed.[24]

This authorization was the basis for the organization of the Construction Corps, which not only built railroad bridges and laid and repaired track but also constructed wharves and, when not otherwise occupied, erected storehouses, offices, and hospital facilities at depots, as, for example, at City Point, Va.[25] The personnel of this Corps received rations from the Subsistence Department and were clothed, equipped, supplied with materials for reconstruction purposes, and were paid by the Quartermaster's Department. From a few hundred men, the Corps expanded to nearly 10,000 before the war ended.

Haupt insisted on civilian operation of military railroads by qualified trained personnel—an objective not achieved without considerable opposition from commanding officers as well as quartermasters. When Maj. Gen. John Pope took over command of the newly created Army of Virginia in June 1862, he tried operating the military railroads without Haupt. He thought that since the railroads were used to transport army supplies they should be under the control of the Quartermaster's Department, a viewpoint with which a number of quartermasters in the field agreed. Since few Army officers understood railroad management or the strategic use of railroads, Pope soon found the roads blocked, few trains moving, and the confusion so great as to hamper supply of his army. Haupt was recalled after this expensive experiment.[26]

Early in June 1862, Haupt had published regulations aimed at eliminating interference with railroad transportation by Army officers. All orders in regard to the movement of trains had to be given by the superintendent or his local representatives, the dispatchers at stations. Nor

---

[24] *OR*, ser. I, vol. XII, Pt. III, 274–75 (Stanton to Haupt, 28 May 1862).
[25] RG 92, OQMG Consolidated Correspondence File, Box 159 (Ingalls to Meigs, 24 Jun 1865).
[26] Haupt, *Reminiscences*, p. 270.

QUARTERMASTER DEPOT, CITY POINT, VA.

could orders from any other source be obeyed if they were in conflict
with instructions, unless issued by the commanding general or the chief
of transportation.   No quartermaster, commissary, or any other officer
had the right to detain a train or order it to run in advance of its scheduled time.[27] On 25 June, he published additional orders, positively
forbidding assistant quartermasters and commissaries to load cars with
any freight that was not properly included among the stores of their
respective Departments.   This provision excluded the shipment of articles
intended for the private use of officers, individuals, or sutlers.   The
latter could transport goods only on the basis of a permit obtained from
the Quartermaster General.[28]

Application of such regulations restored regularity to the railway
service in Virginia, but it took persistent efforts to overcome the confusion
resulting from detention of trains beyond schedule time and the delays
that occurred in unloading cars.[29]   When the theater of operations

[27] *OR,* ser. III, vol. II, 102–03 (2 Jun 1862).
[28] Haupt, *Reminiscences,* pp. 67–68.
[29] For an example of the controversy that developed between quartermasters in the field
and transportation agents on the military railroads, see *OR,* ser. I, vol. XIX, Pt. II, 558–61;
564–67.

ENGINE AND CARS OF U.S. MILITARY ORANGE AND ALEXANDRIA R.R.

shifted from Virginia to Maryland in the fall of 1862, Haupt insisted that with proper management supply should present no difficulty. On the basis of causes that Haupt outlined as being productive of blockades and irregularities in the railway service, Meigs issued orders that were to be followed by all officers and agents of his Department. On no account were they to detain trains beyond their regular starting time. If the sick and wounded were not ready for movement, or if supplies had not been prepared for shipment at the designated time, quarter-masters were to call for extra trains rather than delay scheduled trains. Quartermasters also were cautioned not to forward supplies to advanced terminals of the military railroads until they were really needed. Nor were they to detain cars for use as storehouses but to unload and return them immediately.[30] Continued application of these regulations brought an effective military railroad system into operation in the East.

Developments in the western theaters of operations followed a differ-

[30] (1) Haupt, *Reminiscences*, p. 143. (2) *OR*, ser. I, vol. LI, Pt, I, pp. 867–70 (Haupt to Halleck, 27 Sep 1862). (3) *General Orders of the Quartermaster General, 1862–1865* (Circular, 1 Oct 1862).

ent course.   McCallum's authority was not extended to these theaters until 1864, and the wise regulations introduced by Haupt to put the military railroads in Virginia on an efficient operating basis were not applied in the West, though experienced railroadmen serving there, both in and out of the Army, were in complete agreement with his views and attempted to enforce similar regulations of their own.   Until 1864, railroad transportation in the western theaters was under the military control of the various commanding generals.   Thus, after the capture of Corinth in the fall of 1862, General Halleck appointed Brig. Gen. James B. McPherson of his staff as superintendent of all railroads coming under government control by capture.   To Brig. Gen. Grenville M. Dodge, an experienced railroad builder turned soldier, he assigned in June 1862 the task of rebuilding and holding the line of the Mobile and Ohio Railroad between Columbus and Corinth.   Dodge organized a pioneer corps of men from the troops under his command to reconstruct the road.[31]

Subsequently, Col. Joseph D. Webster of Grant's staff succeeded McPherson, controlling all roads in western Tennessee.   In the meantime, when Sherman was in command of the forces in Kentucky at the beginning of the war, he appointed J. B. Anderson, formerly superintendent of the Louisville and Nashville Railroad, as his confidential agent to look after and guard that road.   When Buell succeeded Sherman and was intrusted with operations in central and eastern Tennessee, he continued Anderson in charge of railroads.   The same course was followed by Rosecrans when he replaced Buell in October 1862.

Quartermasters in the western theaters had no more responsibility for railroad operations than those in the East had.   None of the railroad appointees of commanding generals reported to the chief quartermaster in the area concerned—that is, to Allen at St. Louis or Swords at Louisville—but, as in the eastern theaters, the Quartermaster's Department defrayed the costs of operation.   On the orders of Halleck and Grant, Chief Quartermaster Allen bought rolling stock amounting to over $292,000 by the summer of 1863.   Swords also paid bills for engines and cars.[32]

Commanding officers usually made requisitions for rolling stock on short notice.   Colonel Parsons, who as transportation officer at St. Louis had to fill such requisitions, was highly critical of the lack of plans for securing a constant supply of equipment to be used on the roads acquired

[31] (1) *Personal Memoirs of U. S. Grant* (2 vols., New York, 1885–86), II, 48.   (2) Jacob Randolph Perkins, *Trails, Rails and War* (Indianapolis, 1929), pp. 87, 89–92.

[32] (1) RG 92, OQMG Letter Book, vol. 70, pp. 423–24 (Meigs to Allen, 28 Jul 1863); vol. 71, pp. 172–73; 175–76 (Meigs to Haupt, 19 Aug 1862).   (2) RG 92, Letters Issued, AQMG Office, Louisville, 18 Feb–16 Jun 1862, pp. 170–71; 174–75 (Swords to Halleck, Anderson, Meigs, 10, 11, 13 Jun 1862, respectively).

as the armies advanced.   Compelled to obtain engines and cars quickly, Parsons had to deprive some roads of their own rolling stock, equipment that they needed for effective operations.   Annoying to the railroads, this method of procurement was also more costly and more productive of delays, Parsons argued, than if a supply of railroad equipment was kept on hand to meet emergency needs.[33]   No stockpiling of railroad supplies and equipment was effected in the Civil War.

In addition to rolling stock, quartermasters in the western theaters had to furnish a wide variety of railroad supplies, such as cross ties, brake shoes, and innumerable types of tools.   Markets for the purchase of these supplies were at Cincinnati, St. Louis, Chicago, and some of the eastern manufacturing towns.   The local disbursing quartermasters in the field procured such supplies.   In some cases, they also opened and operated machine shops, as, for example, at Columbus, Ky., and Corinth, Miss.[34]

As indicated, pioneer brigades carried out some of the reconstruction work in the western theaters.   Such brigades were composed of mechanics and engineers who called for various supplies needed in their repair work. An assistant quartermaster in such a brigade was responsible for furnishing Quartermaster supplies, but, with his duties not precisely defined, he found great difficulty in distinguishing between supplies required to be furnished by his own Department and those by the Engineers.[35]

In some instances, local quartermasters in the West also had to undertake railroad repair work.   Thus, on 1 October 1863, Capt. A. M. Tucker reported to the chief quartermaster at Louisville and was assigned to take charge of railroad construction in that city.   Carrying out orders from Thomas A. Scott, he altered within 11 days the gauge of the tracks of the Louisville and Frankfort and the Lexington and Frankfort Railroads (some 95 miles in all) from 4 feet 8½ inches to 5 feet.   Cars and engines were made to conform.   As a result, supplies could be loaded at Covington, Ky., and run through to the Army south of Nashville without transfer of freight at Louisville.   At the same time, Assistant Quartermaster Tucker also constructed an extension of the Louisville and Nashville Railroad from its terminal to the banks of the Ohio River. On orders, he then extended the railroad track on the opposite shore from the terminus of the Jeffersonville Railroad at Jeffersonville to the river. By the end of November, it was possible to transfer 20 cars and 2 engines per day from the Jeffersonville Depot to the Louisville and Nashville Railroad terminus whereas before these extensions were constructed on

---

[33] RG 92, Personal Narrative Rpts, F.Y. 1863, IV, 558–61 (Parson's Rpt, 6 Oct 1863).
[34] *Ibid.*, II, 273–78 (Capt. C. Dutton, 16 Jan 1864).
[35] *Ibid.*, V, 307–08 (Rpt of Capt. John Stewart, 6 Oct 1863).

the Kentucky and Indiana sides of the river it had taken 2 weeks.[36] These improvements had an important bearing on the ability of the Quartermaster's Department to supply the army at Chattanooga and Sherman's force in its campaign against Atlanta.

Civilian laborers as well as troops were employed in the reconstruction of railroads in the western theaters and they were also hired for the operation of the roads. The disbursing quartermaster attached to the military railroads paid all wages due such employees. Capt. C. Dutton, assigned as assistant quartermaster at Columbus, Ky., when the Army with the Department of the Tennessee took over the Mobile and Ohio Railroad and the Mississippi Central, reported that an average of some 1,100 men were employed on those roads and paid by him during fiscal year 1863.[37]

A crisis in railroad transportation in the West developed in the fall of 1863 when Rosecrans, defeated by Bragg at Chickamauga and then besieged at Chattanooga, required men, munitions, rations, and supplies at once to enable him to hold on. Months earlier the War Department had become concerned about railroad transportation in the western theaters as rumors of corruption reached the Secretary of War. As a result, Stanton had sent an investigator, F. H. Forbes, who recommended that operation of the railroads by military authorities be abandoned.[38] About the time Forbes submitted his findings, Stanton was obliged to meet the threat at Chattanooga by sending reinforcements at once. Under the direction of McCallum, ably assisted by the managers of the railway lines involved and the skillful direction of Scott at Louisville, the Eleventh and Twelfth Corps, with their arms and equipment were transferred from the line of the Rappahannock to the Tennessee, achieving what has been called "the accomplishment par excellence in Civil War logistics." [39]

Stanton sent Quartermaster General Meigs to Chattanooga to unsnarl the supply tangle. At Meigs' orders, Allen shifted his headquarters from St. Louis to Louisville as the most convenient point for controlling supply intended for the army concentrating on the Tennessee River. The Quartermaster General transferred Lt. Col. James L. Donaldson from Baltimore to take charge of Quartermaster activities at Nashville, the advance base of operations. He relieved Maj. Langdon C. Easton of duty at Ft. Leavenworth and assigned him as Chief Quartermaster of the Army of the Cumberland in the field near Chattanooga. To supplement

---

[36] *Ibid.*, F.Y. 1864, IV, 533–38 (Rpt of Capt. Tucker, 30 Jun 1864).

[37] *Ibid.*, F.Y. 1863, II, 300 (Dutton's Rpt, 16 Jan 1864).

[38] See RG 92, OQMG Consolidated Correspondence File, Box 577, for Forbes Report.

[39] Festus P. Summers, *The Baltimore and Ohio in the Civil War* (New York, 1939), p. 165.

movement of supplies by rail, he made Colonel Parsons responsible for all transportation of supplies on the western rivers. This concentrated attack on the supply problem, ably supplemented by Grant's actions to secure a line of supplies, soon relieved the Army at Chattanooga from its distress.[40]

In the meantime, a move toward civilian operation of military railroads in the West was also being made. On Stanton's orders, J. B. Anderson was appointed general manager of all railways in the possession of the government or that might be taken in the Departments of the Cumberland, Ohio, and the Tennessee.[41] The appointment and powers conferred on Anderson, however, were subject to Meigs' control. Stanton authorized the Quartermaster General to change, alter, or revoke them if Anderson failed in or neglected his duty. He also authorized Meigs to do everything proper to increase the efficiency of transportation.[42] Meigs directed his quartermasters to accumulate supplies at Nashville and, at his orders, Anderson soon had construction parties making repairs.

After the victories at Lookout Mountain and Missionary Ridge had given the army "room to operate," as Meigs expressed it, he directed McCallum to hire a large number of men and send them with their tools and equipment to operate as a Construction Corps in the West. Meigs ordered McCallum, himself, to report to him at Chattanooga.[43] Anderson, unequal to the demands made upon him, was replaced by McCallum on 4 February 1864 as general manager. Thereafter, the system of civilian operation and maintenance of military railroads and Quartermaster procurement of railroad supplies and disbursement of funds that had been developed in the East was applied in the western theaters. So effective was the system that, in the Atlanta campaign, Sherman's forces were amply supplied although operating hundreds of miles from their base at Nashville and dependent on a single line of railroad in the heart of the enemy's country. So closely did the construction parties follow on the heels of the Army that, according to Sherman, "the locomotive whistle was heard in our advanced camps almost before the echo of the skirmish fire had ceased." [44]

---

[40] (1) *Annual Reports of the Quartermaster General, 1861–1865,* pp. 6–7 (QMG's Rpt, 1864). (2) *Personal Memoirs of U. S. Grant,* II, 32–40.

[41] He was appointed by Special Order on 19 Oct 1863. *General Orders of the Quartermaster General, 1862–1865* (GO 52, 25 Nov 1864).

[42] *OR,* XXXI, Pt. III, pp. 190–91 (Stanton to Meigs, 19 Nov 1863).

[43] (1) *OR,* XII, Pt. III, pp. 422–23 (Meigs to McCallum, 16 Dec 1863). (2) House *Ex. Doc.* No. 1, 39th Cong., 1st sess., p. 12 (McCallum's Rpt, 26 May 1866).

[44] (1) *OR,* ser. I, vol. XXXVIII, Pt. I, 83 (To Halleck, 15 Sep 1864). (2) RG 92, Inspection Reports to Bvt. Brig. Gen. Jas. F. Rusling, 1864–65, I, 11–18 (Rusling to Donaldson, 21 Aug 1864).

TRANSPORT STEAMER MISSIONARY ON TENNESSEE RIVER

Role of River Transportation

Although railroads played a primary role in the transportation of troops and supplies during the Civil War, river steamboats were as important as railroads in the western theater of operations, where the Mississippi, Cumberland, and Tennessee Rivers afforded passage into the heart of the belligerent South. The means of transportation on the Ohio and Mississippi and their tributaries were all of the same type, and generally available and adaptable to service at any point. River steamboats were so constructed as to make them well suited to the transportation of troops and supplies. They had a further advantage; they could be tied up almost anywhere along the river bank and unloaded without the necessity of constructing wharves or emptying lighters as had to be done on the Atlantic coast, where the vessels employed were of such draught as to compel the use of these facilities.

Enemy action did not stop river navigation, though guerrillas and some rebel shore batteries fired at the steamboats. Such firing had to be most skillfully directed, however, to obstruct passage. Unlike the railroads, there were no rails to tear up or bridges to destroy and thereby cut supply lines. When there were rumors of unusual guerrilla activity, quartermasters requested a gunboat escort for troop transports or steamboats carrying supplies. Thus, in the winter of 1862–63, when guerrillas were reported to be infesting the Cumberland River, the transportation quartermaster at Louisville requested a convoy of gunboats to meet his fleet of 11 steamboats at the mouth of that river and escort it to the depot at Nashville.[45] Lower costs and the unlimited carrying capacity of river transportation gave it a decided advantage over railroads, particularly so if the road was a single-track line with accommodations for only a limited number of trains daily. A commissary officer estimated that an ordinary Ohio River steamer of 500 tons capacity could in one trip carry enough supplies to sustain for about 2 days a force of 40,000 men and 18,000 animals requiring about 260 tons daily.[46]

On the other hand, river transportation labored under certain handicaps that did not affect railroad transportation. Ice in winter and seasonal low water were disadvantageous factors that had to be taken cognizance of in planning campaigns and executing supply operations depending on the use of river steamboats. In addition, the management of river transportation was far more difficult than in the case of railroads. The latter were large, established corporations, operating under the direction of able businessmen with whom the government could make an agreement for the transportation of troops and supplies at prices below the ordinary rates. But among steamboat owners, however able they were as individuals, their interests were as numerous and varying as the boats they operated, and it was impossible for the government to negotiate with any group of them.[47]

The War Department provided no focal point for management either because there was no one individual directing the use and employment of river boats for the government in 1861. Local quartermasters customarily arranged for the shipment of supplies and the transportation of troops. There were as many quartermasters chartering steamboats on the western rivers as there were posts located on the Ohio and Mississippi. Since each quartermaster was independent of the other, each made his own rules, regulations, and contracts. It inevitably followed that there was great variation in the rates allowed owners of boats chartered

---

[45] For criticism of the delays caused by the use of gunboats in convoying steamboats, see RG 92, Quartermaster General Annual Reports, Box 14 (Rpt of Capt. John H. Ferry to Parsons, 11 May 1863).

[46] Sharpe, *The Art of Supplying Armies in the Field*, p. 63.

[47] *Annual Reports of the Quartermaster General, 1861–1865*, pp. 146–47 (Parson's Rpt, 15 Oct 1865, appended to QMG's Rpt, 1865).

by quartermasters at Cincinnati, Louisvile, Cairo, and St. Louis. Since few quartermasters knew anything about the operation of steamboats or their fitness for special purposes, the opportunities for defrauding the government were numerous. Through ignorance and indifference as well as intentional connivance, some quartermasters allowed such extravagant rates that owners of every old boat, Colonel Parsons charged, saw, and "too often found, a fortune in its rotten ribs." [48]

Before November 1862, a small steamboat of 173 tons was chartered at St. Louis for a period of 18 months, first at $90 per day, the owner paying all expenses including fuel, and later at $80, the government furnishing fuel. A certified statement of the owners admitted that these rates yielded a fair compensation. In November, they sold the boat for $7,000, and the new owner, after making repairs costing $1,000, chartered his boat in another military department at a rate of $175 per day, the government furnishing the fuel. In 7 months, he cleared $14,752.38 after all expenses had been paid and still claimed $2,000 more because of repairs. Still another boat valued at $22,000 was paid at the rate of $73,000 per year. These were by no means isolated examples but were only two of the many sent to Washington by critics of the system.[49] Colonel Parsons charged that "most boats in government employment, have paid their owners, net, more than their value, by a single year's service, while many have done it twice or three times over." [50]

Because there was no centralized supervision of river transportation, millions of dollars were wasted in unnecessary detention of boats. Even more important was the serious injury to the service that such detention might cause in an emergency. In other words, transports might be unnecessarily detained at a time when the principal point of supply for an army was dangerously short of transportation. For example, on 2 October 1863, General Banks had sent an officer to St. Louis to hurry forward his requisitions lest his movements be seriously delayed, and General Sherman, hastening to the support of General Rosecrans, was equally urgent in demanding his supplies. On that date, the St. Louis transportation office had requisitions for the immediate transportation of over 6,500 mules, horses, and cattle, 600 wagons, and about 1,000 tons of other freight to General Banks' command at New Orleans, 1,200 miles distant. At the same time, over 4,000 animals and 3,000 tons of commissary and quartermaster stores and coal had to be sent to Memphis, Vicksburg, and Little Rock. Colonel Parsons estimated that there were

[48] RG 92, Personal Narrative Rpts, F.Y. 1863, IV, 565 (Parson's Rpt, 6 Oct 1863).
[49] (1) *Ibid.*, pp. 565–67. (2) RG 92, OQMG Letter Book, vol. 59, p. 165 (AQM Wm. J. Kountz to SW, 19 Mar 1862). (3) Stanton Papers, vol. 3 (Scott to Stanton, 12 Feb 1862).
[50] RG 92, Personal Narrative Rpts, F.Y. 1863, IV. 569 (Parson's Rpt, 6 Oct 1863).

75 to 100 boats on the river below St. Louis, many detained unnecessarily. To transport the supplies requisitioned would require 40 to 50 boats, but on 2 October there were no more than five at St. Louis that could properly be used for the service.[51]

At the beginning of the war, demands for the movement of troops and supplies came at a moment's notice. Quartermasters took steamboats where they could be found and at prices hastily agreed upon with the owners. Since their destination was often changed, it was convenient to pay each boat by the day for its services and so the charter system came into existence. Abuses of that system soon became evident, however, and, as early as mid-December 1861, Capt. William J. Kountz offered plans for the reform and reorganization of river transportation. A prominent steamboat owner of Pittsburg, he had served as civilian superintendent of river transportation on the Ohio and Kanawha for his friend, Maj. Gen. George B. McClellan, when the latter was commanding the Department of the Ohio and operating against the Confederates in what later became the State of West Virginia.[52] Commissioned a captain and assistant quartermaster in November 1861, Kountz was ordered to Cairo by Chief Quartermaster Allen, to whose department he had been assigned. Kountz had a positive gift for ferreting out rascality and a crusading fervor that led him to denounce fraud wherever he uncovered it, but he threw about "charges of infidelity," Meigs confided, "as though he was the only honest man in the West."[53] The Quartermaster General found merit in his suggestions for establishing uniform charter rates and eliminating duplication, but, since his plan was predicated on the assumption that he was the only person with the knowledge and experience necessary for directing a centralized bureau for river transportation, Meigs was noncommittal about putting it into effect. "While it is certain that a one man power, if the one man is perfect, is best," he wrote Kountz, "all mankind agree that too much power in one hand is dangerous."[54]

There was plenty of wrongdoing to be uncovered in Cairo where Capt. R. B. Hatch, Fremont-appointed assistant quartermaster at the post, had practiced a regular system of defrauding the government until he was arrested in January 1862. Cairo had been an important post since the beginning of the war. A concentration point for Illinois troops, it was also the place at which supplies were being accumulated for the down-river expedition to be launched by Grant. Moreover, it was the

[51] *Ibid.*, IV, 571–72.

[52] See Theodore R. Parker, "William J. Kountz, Superintendent of River Transportation Under McClellan, 1861–62," *The Western Pennsylvania Historical Magazine*, XXI, 237–54.

[53] RG 92, Records of Volunteer Officers, QMD, III, 552–53.

[54] RG 92, OQMG Letter Book, vol. 57, pp. 476–77 (26 Dec 1861).

base for the gunboat flotilla being fitted out by Capt. Andrew H. Foote of the Navy. All these activities heightened its attraction for profiteers. When Thomas A. Scott visited Cairo early in 1862 on an inspection tour, he recommended a thorough reorganization of the whole post, except for the naval and commissary branches. He suggested that the government hire steamboats with everything provided by the owners by the day, by the mile run, or by the number of tons and passengers per mile carried. It would be preferable, he urged, for the government to purchase and operate its own steamboats and sell them when they were no longer needed.[55]

Meantime, Col. Lewis B. Parsons, who had been placed in charge of river and rail transportation at St. Louis, instituted reforms. Under Fremont, transportation had been obtained by chartering boats and hiring officers, allowing them 60 cents per day for rations instead of the ordinary rate of $12\frac{1}{2}$ cents. Parsons did not favor the operation of a government fleet either by charter or through purchase. Boats ought to be purchased or chartered, he maintained, only for special or post service. Believing that private enterprise would always be able to transport cheaper than the government could, Parsons abandoned the charter system at St. Louis and turned to contracting for transportation by the piece or hundred pounds. He solicited bids and awarded contracts to the lowest bidders. In the winter of 1862, his river transportation to Paducah (250 miles) and New Madrid (275 miles) cost $\frac{1}{2}$ cent per mile for each soldier with the usual deck accommodations and 1 cent for each officer with cabin quarters. Horses and mules were shipped at 1 cent, wagons at $1\frac{1}{4}$ cents for each wagon, and freight at 7 cents for each 100 pounds for each 100 miles. Even toward the close of the war, when prices generally had advanced, Parsons was transporting troops under contract at an average price of about $\frac{1}{3}$ cent per man per mile.[56]

His reduction of transportation costs was not accomplished without considerable complaints, since transportation agents in other departments allowed higher rates. Rates on the Ohio, he informed Meigs, were generally 25 percent higher than those he allowed on the Mississippi. He therefore recommended that there should be one officer, located at a central point, who, subject to the chief quartermaster of that military department, should have the general superintendence of all steamboat transportation on the Mississippi and its tributaries regardless of depart-

[55] Stanton Papers, vol. 3 (Scott to Stanton, 12 Feb 1862).

[56] (1) RG 92, OQMG Letters Received, Box 84 (Parsons to Meigs, 18 Apr 1862). (2) RG 92, Personal Narrative Rpts, F.Y. 1863, IV, 575 (Parson's Rpt, 6 Oct 1863). (2) *Annual Reports of the Quartermaster General, 1861–65*, p. 139 (Parson's Rpt, 15 Oct, appended to QMG's Rpt of 1865).

mental lines.[57]   As a result, in the midst of the supply crisis at Chattanooga, Meigs assigned Parsons to duty as Chief Quartermaster of Western
River Transportation, with headquarters at St. Louis, and placed him
under the orders of Brig. Gen. Robert Allen, Senior Quartermaster on the
Mississippi.[58]   All quartermasters in charge of river transportation on
the Mississippi and its tributaries thereafter made reports to, and acted
on instructions from Parsons.

Parsons at once applied the contract system to the Cumberland and
Ohio Rivers, effectively combating the steamboat interests who fought
against the loss of the lucrative charter trade.   Transportation became
far more efficient because boats under contract carried twice the cargo
that chartered steamboats had transported and discharged it in less time.
Whereas it had taken 123 steamers on the Cumberland to supply General
Rosecrans' army in the winter of 1862–63, it required only 66 to supply
not only that army but those of Grant and Sherman as well in the winter
of 1863–64.   It was estimated that in the Department of the Cumberland
alone a saving of from $2 million to $3 million was made by the change
from the charter to the contract system.[59]

In addition to the ordinary transportation of soldiers, their munitions, and supplies, large expeditions had to be moved, frequently on
short notice.   In such cases, quartermasters used boats that they had
under contract, but they also chartered and commandeered boats to meet
the emergency need.   On 11 December 1862, for example, Parsons received orders from General Allen, based on a telegraphic dispatch from
Grant, to provide sufficient transportation to be at Memphis 1 week later
to move Sherman's army of about 40,000 men, including cavalry, artillery,
and land transportation, for an attack on Vicksburg.   It being mid-
winter, there were no more than six or eight suitable boats at St. Louis,
the rest being engaged in ordinary business and scattered in all directions
on the rivers.   In addition, low water had resulted in a scarcity of coal
deliveries.   By seizing privately owned coal as it came in to St. Louis on
wagons, Parsons obtained a sufficient supply; and by taking all boats
arriving at Cairo, he was able to reach Memphis, 450 miles from St. Louis,
on 19 December with nearly 60 boats.   This was 1 day later than that
fixed for embarkation, but since the expedition was delayed anyhow for
other reasons, it was not detained for lack of transportation.   Parsons
personally supervised the loading of army divisions at Memphis on
20 December and, 6 days later and some 475 miles down the river, they

[57] RG 92, Personal Narrative Rpts, F.Y. 1863, IV, 574 (Parson's Rpt, 6 Oct 1863).
[58] *General Orders, Quartermaster General, 1862–1865* (GO 22½, 9 Dec 1863).
[59] *Annual Reports of the Quartermaster General, 1861–1865*, pp. 138–39 (Parson's Rpt,
15 Oct 1865, appended to QMG's Rpt, 1865).

disembarked at Chickasaw bayou, on the Yazoo River, 5 miles in the rear of Vicksburg.[60]

Quartermasters transported many other expeditions on the western rivers during the war, but one of the more spectacular transportation achievements, using both water and rail facilities, was the transfer of the 23d Army Corps, Major General Schofield commanding, from Clifton on the Tennessee River to the Potomac to participate in Grant's operations against Richmond.[61] The decision to attempt this mid-winter transfer was not made until 11 January 1865 when Colonel Parsons, then chief of the Rail and River Transportation Division of the Quartermaster General's office in Washington, left the city to supervise this movement. The Department wanted the troops transported by boat as far as Parkersburg and sent forward from there by the Baltimore and Ohio Railroad. Knowing the extreme uncertainties of winter navigation on the Ohio, Parsons arranged with managers of the western railroads to have cars on hand so that on 12 to 24 hours' notice, transportation facilities would be available at Cairo, Evansville, Louisville, or Cincinnati for moving the troops eastward. At the same time, assistant quartermasters at Cairo, Cincinnati, and other river ports were obtaining and dispatching steamboats to the mouth of the Tennessee. There were only enough boats at Clifton on the Tennessee River to bring down about half of Schofield's command. Boats were required for at least 10,000 more men, and Parsons started up the Tennessee with a fleet of about 25 boats to accommodate the troops.

The first troops left Paducah at the mouth of the Tennessee on 18 January. The coldest weather of the winter set in, filling the river with floating ice, and arousing fears that the steamboats would not be able to reach Cincinnati. Quartermasters sent them forward, however, from Louisville, and the first troops arriving at Cincinnati on the 21st were disembarked, loaded on cars of the Little Miami Railroad, and started eastward. A dense fog halted further river operations at Cincinnati for 30 hours. On the strength of favorable reports on river navigation received from Wheeling and Parkersburg, Parsons prepared to send the rest of the troops on by boat. Bad weather again closed river navigation, and one steamboat that had already departed had to be recalled. The troops were then loaded on cars, but even railroad transportation was dangerous for the uncommon severities of the weather broke rails, causing cars to be thrown from the track, and disasters were averted by only the narrowest of margins. At Wheeling, the troops were

<hr>

[60] RG 92, OQMG Letters Received, Box 108 (Parsons to Meigs, 29 Dec 1862).

[61] For other illustrations of expeditions see, *Annual Reports of the Quartermaster General, 1861–1865*, pp. 141–44 (Parson's Rpt, 15 Oct 1865, appended to QMG's Rpt, 1865).

loaded on cars of the Baltimore and Ohio Railroad for the journey to the Potomac, 700 cars being required for their movement. Parsons had taken especial pains to provide for the comfort of the men by having stoves put in the cars to warm them and by arranging with the Subsistence Department to have hot coffee served to supplement rations at designated points en route. Despite snow, ice, and fog, a corps of 20,000 men, with all its artillery, and over 1,000 animals were transferred a distance of 1,400 miles from the Tennessee to the Potomac in less than 17 days, though it had been anticipated that the attempt might take from 40 to 60 days.[62]

Quartermasters on the western rivers were not only concerned with the purchase, charter, and commandeering of steamboats, but they also build steamboats and gave assistance to such projects. One of the earliest of these projects was the construction of the western gunboat flotilla. In anticipation of sending an expedition down the Mississippi, Lt. Gen. Winfield Scott requested, and the Secretary of War approved, the construction of a gunboat flotilla to protect the troop transports. Execution of this project was assigned to the Quartermaster's Department. It made a beginning by taking over three small steamboats converted into gunboats on orders of General McClellan, then commanding in the Department of the Ohio.[63] Having solicited proposals under an appropriation provided by Congress, Meigs negotiated a contract with James B. Eads to construct seven gunboats.[64] In time, this flotilla was expanded to include 10 ironclad steam gunboats, 11 wooden gunboats, 22 steam rams, and 13 steam tugs. In addition, there were other vessels serving as ammunition ships, dispatch boats, and transports. The flotilla included a commissary store ship and a hospital ship. To this fleet the Department added 38 mortar boats, originally ordered constructed by General Fremont when he was commanding the Western Department.[65]

The Quartermaster's Department built and paid for the greater part of the vesseels, though the Ordnance Department and the Navy furnished their armament and ordnance. Originally, Capt. John Rodgers of the

[62] (1) *Annual Reports of the Quartermaster General, 1861–1865*, pp. 132–36 (Parson's Rpt, 2 Feb 1865, appended to QMG's Rpt, 1865). (2) RG 92, Quartermaster Annual Reports, Box 14 (Parson's Journal, Telegrams, Letters sent in regard to movement of 23rd Army Corps).

[63] Meigs Papers: Letters at the Beginning of the Rebellion, pp. 93–96 (Meigs to McClellan, 17 Jun 1861).

[64] (1) RG 92, OQMG Letter Book, vol. 55, p. 445 (Meigs to *Washington Star et al.*, 17 Jun 1861). (2) Capt. James B. Eads, "Recollections of Foote and the Gun-Boats," *Battles and Leaders of the Civil War* (4 vols., New York, 1956), I, 338–39.

[65] (1) RG 92, Letters and Rpts to SW and Heads of Other Depts., V, 554 (Meigs to Secy of Navy, 5 Dec 1861). (2) RG 92, Personal Narrative Rpts, F.Y. 1863, V, 901–02 (Wise' Rpt, 14 Sep 1863). (3) *Annual Reports of the Quartermaster General, 1861–1865*, p. 7 (QMG's Rpt, 1862).

GUNBOAT OF THE EADS CLASS

Navy was detailed to superintend the construction of the gunboats, but command of the fleet was later transferred to Capt. Andrew H. Foote. The Navy furnished the commanding officers of the gunboats and parts of the crews, but other crew members were detailed from the Volunteer army. The Quartermaster's Department employed the commanders and officers of the transports and of some other vessels. The Department paid for the expenditures of the gunboat flotilla, and assigned an assistant quartermaster, Capt. George D. Wise, to the flotilla to handle funds, process requisitions, audit accounts of acting assistant paymasters on the gunboats, and perform the duties not only of an army quartermaster but of a navy paymaster, storekeeper, and commissary.[66]

The gunboats performed effectively at Fort Henry and later at Memphis and Vicksburg. In the meantime, control of the fleet was shifted from the Army to the Navy. With the Navy Department determined to build gunboats, Meigs recommended that the War Department relinquish all responsibility for such construction. Stanton approved his suggestion and, on 16 July 1862, Congress authorized the transfer,

[66] (1) RG 92, OQMG Letter Book, vol. 56, p. 475 (Meigs to Wise, 2 Oct 1861). (2) RG 92, Personal Narrative Rpts, F.Y. 1863, V, 897–910 (Wise' Rpt, 14 Sep 1863).

though it was 1 December before Assistant Quartermaster Wise was relieved from duty.[67]

In 1863, it became necessary to provide steamboat transportation and gunboat protection on the upper Tennessee River. Late in the summer, General Rosecrans ordered Capt. Arthur Edwards, assistant quartermaster, to determine the most practicable way of procuring steamboat transportation on that part of the river. Since boats could not ascend the river above Muscle Shoals, Edwards recommended that they be constructed at Bridgeport, Ala., where he established his headquarters. His first efforts resulted in the building of a small steamer that was of great service in carrying supplies to Kelly's Ford, 8 miles below Chattanooga where the Union forces were being besieged by the Confederates. At Rankin's Ferry, Lt. Col. William G. Le Duc reported that the starving troops of General Cruft's division met the boat.

Their joy at seeing the little Steamboat and scows afloat and loaded with rations can be faintly imagined—hardly described; they shouted and danced on the bank of the river like crazy men. Hurrahed for the Steamboat, for the Captain, for the Crew, for full rations once more, and when the bows of the barge touched the shore, they boarded her with a rush . . . carried off the rations, and walked into them like starved men, as they were.[68]

After the battles about Chattanooga, Captain Edwards opened a boatyard at Bridgeport, on Meigs' orders, and in 9 months rapidly built 13 steamers, 4 of which were gunboats. The latter were placed at the disposal of the Navy Department to be used in patroling the Tennessee from Muscle Shoals to Knoxville. In addition, he also built skiffs, barges, and scows. When Edwards began operations, Bridgeport was a city of tents; not a building, except a sawmill, had been left standing by the Confederates when they departed. Around this sawmill, he built his boatyard, erecting 18 houses for the workmen and a machine shop. All the engines, machinery, nails, paints, and every other material, except lumber, used in the construction of these steamboats had to be brought from the Ohio Valley and transported 600 to 800 miles over military roads already greatly overtaxed. Under these circumstances, the construction of this fleet in such a short time was a remarkable achievement.[69]

In the fall of 1864, when Parsons went to Washington as chief of the Rail and River Transportation Division in the office of the Quarter-

[67] (1) Stanton Papers, Proceedings of the War Board, 1862 (Meeting, 25 Mar 1862). (2) *General Orders of the War Department, 1861–62*, I, 406 (GO 150, 2 Oct 1862).
[68] (1) RG 92, Personal Narrative Rpts, F.Y. 1864, III, 327–28 (Le Duc's Rpt, 25 Sep 1864). (2) William G. Le Duc, "The Little Steamboat That Opened the 'Cracker Line'," *Battles and Leaders of the Civil War*, vol. III, Pt. II, pp. 676–78. (3) RG, 92, Personal Narrative Rpts, F.Y. 1864, II, 67–69 (Edwards' Rpt, 11 Jan 1865).
[69] RG 92, Personal Narrative Rpts, F.Y. 1864, II, 61–74 (Edwards' Rpt, 11 Jan 1865).

master General, he availed himself of Edwards' experience by having him appointed general superintendent for the purchase, repairs, and maintenance of steamers and other means of transportation on the Mississippi and its tributaries. In the closing months of the war, a centralized control over repairs and maintenance was developing with repair stations being proposed at such points as St. Louis, Cairo, and New Orleans.[70]

The Quartermaster's Department acquired a considerable fleet of river steamboats and other vessels upon the Mississippi and its tributaries in the course of the war by purchase, construction, and through capture. Colonel Parsons listed as being owned by the Department during the war 599 boats, of which 91 were steamers, 352 were barges of different types, and the rest were wharfboats, coal boats, yawls, and other small boats.[71] The Quartermaster's Department built a total of 38 vessels on the western rivers during the war, of which 24 were steamboats. In the course of the war, the Department also chartered, hired, and pressed into service 822 vessels, of which 633 were steamers.[72]

Ocean Transportation

The Quartermaster's Department also employed and purchased a large fleet of vessels for ocean transportation. During the Civil War, it chartered or hired 753 ocean steamers, 1,080 sailing vessels, and 847 barges. The Department also purchased and built 183 ocean steamers, 43 sailing vessels, and 86 barges.[73] The Department made most of these purchases after the first 2 years of the war, when investigations had exposed irregularities and when Meigs had regained control of ocean transportation and had adopted remedial measures.[74] Among the latter was the insertion of a clause in all charters which allowed the government to take possession of a vessel by paying 33 percent profit on the valuation, and the running expenses and repairs, the government being credited with the amount paid for the charter. One or more officers of the Navy Department, detailed for the purpose, fixed the valuation. By this

[70] RG 92, OQMG, Western River Transportation, Letter Book, I, 24 (Parsons to Edwards, 22 Nov 1864).

[71] (1) *Annual Reports of the Quartermaster General, 1861–1865*, pp. 116–125 (Parsons' Rpt, —Aug 1865, appended to QMG's Rpt, 1865). (2) The accuracy of these figures is open to question. About 3 years later when another listing was prepared for the House, 85 steamers and 726 barges, wharfboats, floats, and other vessels were reported as having been purchased. House *Ex. Doc.* No. 337, 40th Cong., 2d sess., pp. 118–139. (Since this report covered acquisitions through 1867, purchases made after the close of the war must be deducted to arrive at wartime purchases.)

[72] House *Ex. Doc.* No. 337, 40th Cong., 2d sess., pp. 160–227.

[73] *Ibid.,* pp. 4–113; 140–157.

[74] See *ante,* pp. 372–73.

means, the Department purchased a large proportion of the ocean vessels that it acquired.[75]

The Army made heavy demands for ocean transportation during the first year of the war, and quartermasters as well as agents fitted out numerous expeditions. Among the first of these expeditions was one under the command of Brig. Gen. Thomas W. Sherman that resulted in the capture of Port Royal, providing a base of operations along the southeastern coast. Capt. Rufus Saxton, serving as chief quartermaster, chartered most of the vessels engaged for this expedition. It then became necessary to provide vessels for General Burnside's expedition to the North Carolina sounds and for General Butler's to New Orleans. In the spring of 1862, when McClellan had decided on the Peninsular campaign, a large number of vessels had to be obtained to transport his army from the lines in front of Washington to the lower Chesapeake Bay. Stanton directed Assistant Secretary of War John Tucker to obtain the necessary transportation and detailed Capt. Henry C. Hodges, assistant quartermaster, to help him charter vessels. In 37 days from the time he received the order in Washington, Tucker had engaged 113 steamers, 188 schooners, and 88 barges. An Army of 121,500 men, with all its artillery, cavalry, ammunition, wagons, baggage, and supplies, was embarked at Perryville, Alexandria, and Washington.[76] However remiss Tucker was in controlling his agents, he did not fail to supply the Army's transportation needs.

Requisitions for ocean transportation were usually urgent, and permitted no time for the solicitation of bids during the early days of the war. In any case, since the government employed nearly all available steamers, there was little or no chance for competition. Many unsuitable vessels were chartered at exorbitant prices because of the inexperience of quartermasters, the unfaithfulness of agents, and the pursuit of profits by shipowners. Generally, quartermasters and agents chartered vessels for a limited period, with the right granted the government to keep them as long as needed. To cover the expenses of outfitting vessels for a short-term service, owners set charter rates at a high level. Frequently, the government retained vessels in service far beyond the time originally scheduled in the charter. Such detention of vessels sent to the Chesapeake laden with supplies, Assistant Quartermaster General Tompkins charged in 1862, caused the Department to pay as much for demurrage as for freight. Moreover, he found it increasingly difficult to obtain the

---

[75] *Annual Reports of the Quartermaster General, 1861–1865,* pp. 99–100 (Rpt of Col. Geo. D. Wise, 31 Aug 1865, appended to QMG's Rpt, 1865).

[76] Senate *Rep. Com.* No. 84, 37th Cong., 3d sess., pp. 328–29, s.n. 1151 (Tucker to Stanton, 5 Apr 1862).

LANDING SUPPLIES ON THE APPOMATOX, BELOW
PETERSBURG. NOTE PONTON BRIDGE.

transportation he needed at New York, where his average daily shipment of subsistence stores alone amounted to about 7,000 barrels bulk.[77]

Military necessities, however, often compelled retention of vessels. The McClellan Peninsular campaign was a case in point. To transfer the Army of the Potomac down the Chesapeake and furnish it with supplies during the campaign, the Quartermaster's Department provided 405 vessels with a total tonnage of 86,278 tons.[78] Although it discharged many of these vessels after the transfer of the Army to the Peninsula, the greater number of them had to be retained because it was necessary to keep the Army's supplies afloat to follow its advance up the Peninsula.[79]

Water transportation was needed not only to move expeditions to their destinations and to maintain a steady flow of supplies to the troops, but, upon occasion, huge fleets were also required to evacuate troops and supplies. When McClellan abandoned his depot at White House and retreated from the Chickahominy to the James River and a new base at

[77] RG 92, OQMG Letter Book, vol. 60, p. 329 (Tompkins to Meigs, 30 May 1862).

[78] Of the 405 vessels, 71 were side-wheel steamers of 29,070 tons; 57 propellers of 9,824 tons; 187 schooners, brigs, and barks of 36,634 tons; and 90 barges of 10,749 tons. *OR*, ser. I, vol. XI, Pt. I, p. 158 (Chief Quartermaster Van Vliet's Rpt, 2 Aug 1862).

[79] *Ibid.*, ser. I, vol. XI, Pt. III, p. 149 (Van Vliet to Meigs, 7 May 1862).

TRANSPORTS IN MOUTH OF THE PAMUNKEY RIVER,
WHITE-HOUSE LANDING, VA.

Harrison's Landing in the summer of 1862, Quartermaster Ingalls skill-fully withdrew all supplies and property at White House without loss. Some 400 vessels laden with supplies moved out from the narrow and tortuous Pamunkey River to arrive most opportunely for supplying the troops as they reached the James.[80]

Troop movements at times made use of all available steamers on the coast. Early in August 1862, when the Army of the Potomac abandoned operations on the Peninsula, Meigs assured Ingalls that he had at his command all the steamboats of the coast that could be procured for the rapid withdrawal of that Army. No additional vessels could be obtained without breaking up the great ferries and routes by which the new levies were to be brought to the front. The 30 steamers he already had at Harrison's Landing, Meigs estimated, could carry 20,000 to 25,000 men on a single trip. To supplement these, Meigs ordered all vessels, both steam and sail, used to transport Burnside's troops to Aquia Creek re-turned to Harrison's Landing for Ingalls' use. He further directed that all transports carrying the sick to New York and Philadelphia to hasten

---

[80] (1) *Ibid.*, ser. I, vol. XI, Pt. III, pp. 273–74 (Ingalls to Meigs, 29 Jun 1862).   (2) RG 92, Personal Narrative Rpts, F.Y. 1863, III, 380 (Ingalls' Rpt, 29 Sep 1863).

back to Harrison's Landing as quickly as possible. Meigs ordered his quartermasters to send to Fort Monroe all schooners to be found at Baltimore and Philadelphia fit for transporting troops, and he directed Tompkins at New York to obtain, if he could, 200 additional sailing vessels. Meigs pointed out that almost as much transportation could be made available by sacrificing the deckloads of hay kept afloat on the very large fleet of supply vessels at Fort Monroe and on the James.[81] Horses, wagons, and ambulances would have to be shipped later. Bad weather and delays in returning transports to Fort Monroe prolonged the transportation of such equipment through the first week in September.[82]

Unnecessary detention of vessels was again stressed when Sherman's Army arrived on the Atlantic Coast late in 1864. Quartermaster Van Vliet, then stationed at New York, suggested that all quartermasters along the coast be reminded of the importance of ordering to New York all sea steamers as soon as they could be spared.[83] In anticipation of the arrival of Sherman on the coast, Meigs had ordered Van Vliet to prepare to ship clothing and equipment to refit 30,000 men (later changed to 60,000) and grain for 35,000 animals. In addition, the Department also had to get ready a large amount of Quartermaster stores, including 200,000 pounds of horse and mule shoes.

To provide for Sherman's troops in the event their path northward was blocked, Meigs sent a few vessels laden with supplies to Pensacola to await orders. Meanwhile, the Quartermaster's Department collected a great fleet of transports to carry the bulk of supplies needed to refit Sherman's army after its march to the sea, and held it in readiness at Port Royal, S.C., until Sherman established his base of supplies.[84] When Fort McAllister fell on 13 December, Meigs ordered the transport fleet to the mouths of the Ogeechee and Savannah Rivers, and quartermasters discharged the first cargoes at the dilapidated wharves of Savannah. In January, Sherman's forces moved northward and the Department ordered the fleet and supplies transferred to Beaufort, N.C. When Meigs arrived at Beaufort to see that supply was properly handled, he found 117 vessels loaded with supplies in the harbor.[85] Military operations were never hampered or delayed for want of water transportation.

[81] *OR*, ser. *I*, vol. XI, Pt. III, pp. 317–18 (Meigs to Ingalls, 12 Jul 1862); pp. 371–72 (Meigs to McClellan, 12 Aug 1862).

[82] (1) *Ibid.*, ser. I, vol. LIX, p. 173 (Tucker to Meigs, 3 Sep 1862). (2) RG 92, Personal Narrative Rpts, F.Y. 1863, V, 2–3 (Rpt of Lt. Col. C. G. Sawtelle, 29 Oct 1863, who superintended the transportation from Fort Monroe).

[83] RG 92, Van Vliet Letters to the QMG, p. 133 (6 Jan 1865).

[84] RG 92, OQMG Letter Book, vol. 81, pp. 9–10 (Meigs to Van Vliet, 3 Nov 1864); pp. 417–19 (Same to same, 6 Dec 1864); vol. 82, p. 106 (Meigs to Col. S. L. Brown, 20 Dec 1864); pp. 123–24 (Meigs to Easton, 31 Dec 1864).

[85] Meigs Papers: Letter Book, 1865–66 (Meigs to his father, 29 Mar 1865).

Wagon Trains

The use of steamboats, steamships, and railroads increased enormously the mobility of armies. While corps of an army not engaged in active operations could be transferred to another army hundreds of miles away in a few weeks. Supplies, too, could be shipped faster than ever before. Armies in the field, however, also required another type of transportation. Wagon trains not only had to accompany troops on active operations but supply trains also had to be employed to distribute stores brought in bulk to railway terminals and steamer wharves. As in the past, such transportation remained under Quartermaster control, with wagonmasters appointed to direct the work of teamsters. The Department employed civilians as teamsters, but their lack of subordination soon caused large numbers of enlisted men to be detailed for this task. Recommendations that a corps of enlisted teamsters be established, however, received no more favorable consideration in the Civil War than they had in the Mexican War.[86]

The Army wagon had been perfected by long years of experience and operation on the western plains, and Meigs thought that its regulation pattern and harness probably could not be improved. Early in the war, the Department procured both horses and mules for use with trains, but experience soon convinced quartermasters that mules were much superior to horses for such service. By the last year of the war, horses had disappeared almost entirely from the trains. In 1864, Chief Quartermaster Ingalls expressed the views of quartermasters generally when he reported that "the common six-mule wagon has proved to be the most economical and durable for years past of any ever tested." [87]

An Army wagon, drawn by four horses, over good roads, could carry 2,800 pounds. A good six-mule team, in the best season of the year, could haul 3,730 pounds plus its own forage of 270 pounds, or a total of 4,000 pounds.[88] In practice, wagons seldom hauled such loads during the war because roads generally were not good and operations were not limited to the best season of the year. Six-mule teams arriving at City

[86] (1) RG 92, Personal Narrative Rpts, F.Y. 1863, I, 1056-57 (Cross' Rpt, 14 Sep 1863); *ibid.*, F.Y. 1864, IV, 21 (Ransom's Rpt, 24 Aug 1864). (2) John D. Billings, *Hardtack and Coffee* (Boston, 1888), p. 366.
[87] *Annual Reports of the Quartermaster General, 1861–1865*, p. 35 (Ingalls' Rpt, 28 Aug 1864, appended to QMG's Rpt, 1864); p. 32 (QMG's Rpt, 1865).
[88] (1) Nathaniel S. Dodge, *Hints on Army Transportation* (Albany, 1863), p. 7. (2) Col. S. B. Holabird qualified the carrying capacity of a six-mule team. On a good solid road, that is macadamized, a six-mule team could haul from 4,000 to 4,500 pounds; on a solid dirt road 3,000 to 3,500 pounds; and in wild country districts, 1,800 to 2,500 pounds and from 5 to 10 days' grain for themselves. RG 92, Personal Narrative Rpts, F.Y. 1864, II, 764 (Holabird Rpt, 21 Feb 1867).

LANDING SUPPLIES ON THE JAMES RIVER, DESTINED FOR CITY
POINT, VA.

Point after a long, arduous, and difficult march from Culpeper, for
example, carried 2,000 pounds of baggage, or 3,000 pounds of forage, or
2,600 pounds of ammunition or hospital stores.[89]

The wagon trains of an army consisted of the headquarters, the regimental, and the general supply trains. The supply trains operated
between the principal base depots, to which points quartermasters transferred clothing, rations, and other stores by rail and water, and the
temporary, smaller depots established in immediate proximity to an army,
where authorized supply officers drew needed supplies and issued them
to the troops. The number of wagons in a supply train could not be
fixed by regulation. The number necessarily increased as the army's
distance from its base depot of supplies increased.

The headquarters and regimental trains transported baggage and
such supplies as always had to be with the Army. In the early months

[89] RG 92, Personal Narrative Rpts, F.Y. 1864, III, 1864 (Owens' Rpt, 13 Aug 1866).

of the war, such trains were generally larger than necessary, and their size induced troops and officers to carry too much useless baggage with them. Even privates frequently carried carpetbags and boxes in regimental wagons. General Sherman described the troops he saw about Washington in 1861 as being so loaded down with haversacks, knapsacks, tents, and baggage that it took "from twenty-five to fifty wagons to move the camp of a regiment from one place to another, and some of the camps had bakeries and cooking establishments that would have done credit to Delmonico." [90] Sutlers' goods, too, were often transported in such wagons in the guise of commissary stores.

In 1861, no regulation fixed the allowance of transportation in the field. Some generals commanding active troops set the allowance at 15 wagons to a regiment; others marched with 6. Capt. Nathaniel S. Dodge, mustered into service in July 1862 as regimental quartermaster, reported the 119th N.Y. Volunteers, 1,000 strong, had 6 teams.[91] Regiments frequently were under strength, yet each was still allowed a minimum of 6 wagons and some had 8 and even 9. Brigade headquarters, Captain Dodge charged, considered 7 wagons insufficient for field and staff purposes, while the Medical Department of every regiment claimed one wagon besides the ambulances, though the gross weight of surgical, medical, and hospital supplies required during a march or on a field of battle for an infantry regiment of 1,000 men was less than 320 pounds.[92] The excessive amount of wagon transportation allowed brought general criticism from quartermasters in the field.[93]

"Ah, the freshness and flavor of those early war days come back to me," wrote John D. Billings, who served with the Army of the Potomac. That was the time when tent-floors were transported, when the shelter tent had not yet replaced the larger varieties, when stoves had not yet

---

[90] *Personal Memoirs of Gen. W. T. Sherman* (2 vols., 4th ed., revised, New York, 1891), I, 206.

[91] The 6 wagons of a regiment at that time were usually employed as follows:

wagon number one		carried	medical stores;
wagon	" two	"	wall tents and personal luggage of field and staff officers;
wagon	" three	"	personal luggage of line officers;
wagon	" four	"	kettles and pans of 10 companies;
wagon	" five ⎫	"	commissary stores and forage (2 days' rations
	six ⎭		for the men and 5 days' forage for animals).

[92](1) RG 92, Personal Narrative Rpts, F.Y. 1863, II, 121–26 (Dodge's Rpt. –Aug 1863). (2) Dodge wrote and published a pamphlet, *Hints on Army Transportation*, that Meigs circulated to the field. RG 92, OQMG Miscellaneous Letter Book, 10–27 Apr 1863, vol. 31 (Meigs to Lt. Col. J. Dunlop *et al.*, 18 Apr 1863).

[93] See the comments of Col. Samuel B. Holabird who served as chief quartermaster of Banks' Army of the Shenadoah in 1862. RG 92, Personel Narrative Rpts, F.Y. 1864, II, 740–41 (Holabird Rpt, 21 Feb 1867).

given way to camp fires, and when the men still had their big knapsacks, which they were always ready to ride with or toss into a wagon when the regiment moved.[94] Mobility, however, was being sacrificed. On good roads, a four-horse team averaged 2½ miles per hour. Captain Dodge found that even with his animals in prime condition and the roads good, it took 6 days to march from Centreville to Falmouth, Va., averaging less than 14 miles a day. Victories gained did not produce the usual results, General Halleck explained in the fall of 1862, because "the defeated foe was not followed from the battle-field, and even when a pursuit was attempted, it almost invariably failed to effect the capture or destruction of any part of the retreating army." Halleck added that if the success of an army depended on its "arms and its legs," the Union armies had shown themselves deficient in these essential requisites, a defeat he attributed to their enormous baggage and supply trains.[95]

Meigs was as concerned as Halleck about this problem not only because military operations had been less successful as a result of armies being too profusely equipped with wagons, but also because the costs imposed a serious drain on his Department and the Treasury. Large trains were difficult to guard and the loss of wagons, horses, and mules had been very great. Every rapid retreat had resulted in the abandonment of some trains.[96] Meigs directed his efforts toward obtaining a regulation that would fix the wagon allowances for army trains and baggage in the field.[97] The provisions of the regulation, published in October 1862, were taken with little change from a general order issued by McClellan on 10 August.[98]

A month before McClellan's order came out, Lt. Col. Rufus Ingalls had been announced as chief quartermaster of the Army of the Potomac, succeeding General Van Vliet. Ingalls was primarily responsible for bringing about a reduction of transportation in that Army and a better organization of its trains. The order of 10 August reduced the number of baggage wagons by cutting down on the amount of baggage and tentage that could be carried. Although it still allowed six wagons for each full regiment of infantry, the order prescribed that allowances were to be reduced to correspond as nearly as practicable to the number of officers and men actually present. By 1864, the regimental wagons had been

---

[94] Billings, *Hardtack and Coffee*, pp. 354–55.
[95] *OR*, ser. I, vol. XIX, Pt. I, p. 6 (Halleck's Rpt to Stanton, 25 Nov 1862).
[96] *Ibid.*, ser. III, vol. II, pp. 654–55 (Meigs to Stanton, 9 Oct 1862).
[97] (1) RG 92, OQMG Letter Book, vol. 62, p. 441 (Meigs to Halleck, 13 Sep 1862). (2) *OR*, ser. III, vol. II, p. 544 (WD GO 130, 14 Sep 1862); pp. 654–55 (Meigs to Stanton, 9 Oct 1862). (3) *War Department General Orders, 1861–62*, I, 409–10 (GO 160, 18 Oct 1862).
[98] *OR*, ser. I, vol. XI, Pt. III, 365–66 (GO 153).

reduced to two and hauled only baggage and camp equipage.[99]   The August order further directed that all supplies in bulk—quartermaster stores, subsistence, hospital stores, and ammunition—were to be transported in special trains, thus outlining the beginning of supply trains.

In the course of the Maryland campaign that followed, Ingalls worked out much more specific details and applied his system of relating the number of wagons to the number of men to be supplied.   He introduced further refinements by 1863, particularly in providing forage wagons for the Cavalry and horse batteries and in separating the ammunition train from other supplies.[100]   Following the issue of these transportation orders, the Army of the Potomac turned in all its excess wagons to Quartermaster depots.   It took repeated orders, however, to reduce transportation allowances in all armies and to maintain them at the levels set.[101]   Once accustomed to a certain amount of transportation, an army was unwilling to do without the luxuries that it supplied in the field. Sherman, leaving Chattanooga for the advance against Atlanta, reduced transportation for a regiment to one baggage wagon and one ambulance. He limited each headquarters to one wall tent, and set the example himself by using only a tent-fly that was pitched over saplings or fence rails. But his orders were not strictly obeyed; General Thomas could not give up his tent and Sherman recalled that he "had a big wagon which could be converted into an office, and this we used to call 'Thomas's circus'." [102] Persistent efforts throughout the war did bring results, and under quartermaster management the size of the trains employed decreased in each successive campaign.[103]

It was Chief Quartermaster Ingalls who introduced in the Army of the Potomac the system of marking each wagon with the corps badge, division color, and the number of the brigade so that the particular brigade to which each wagon belonged could readily be discerned.   He also caused all wagons to be marked to indicate their contents, and, as soon as a wagon of the supply train was unloaded, it was sent to the base depot to obtain another load of the same item of supply.[104]

Not only did the size of the wagon train hamper movement at the beginning of the war, but its management was also at fault.   Experience

[99] Annual Reports of the Quartermaster General, 1861–1865, pp. 36–39 (Special Orders No. 44, Hq. Armies of U.S., 28 Jun 1864, appended to QMG's Rpt, 1864).

[100] (1) Ibid., p. 43 (Ingalls' Rpt, 28 Sep 1863, appended to QMG's Rpt, 1864).   (2) RG 92, OQMG Letters Received, Box 120 (Ingalls to Meigs, 17 Jul 1863).

[101] Despite orders, extra wagons were smuggled along in the Army of the Potomac. Billings, Hardtack and Coffee, p. 362.

[102] (1) Sherman, Memoirs, II, 22.   (2) See also OR, ser. I, vol. XXXVIII, pp. 507–08 (Sherman to Grant, 18 Jun 1864).

[103] See Sharpe, The Art of Supplying Armies in the Field, pp. 78–79.

[104] Personal Memoirs of U.S. Grant, II, 188–90.

had not then taught the value of organization and the importance on a march of moving a train of a division or even of a corps in one body and under one director.   At that time, the division quartermaster troubled himself very little about the movement of his brigade trains, the corps quartermaster not at all.   Brigade trains generally moved as units, without connection with other brigades of the same division.   In the same corps, therefore, there would be nine distinct and independent trains instead of one.   Conflicting orders and conflicting interests produced an awesome confusion.

No movement was more illustrative of the want of organization and control than that which occurred when the Army of the Potomac shifted its base to Harrison's Landing in the summer of 1862.   No order of march was issued.   "Each quartermaster acted on his own responsibility and according to the best of his judgment," reported Lt. Col. William H. Owen, "unenlightened by any knowledge of the roads, the position of the enemy, or the intended future movements of our own troops." [105]   With no officer present with authority to prescribe the route that the trains should take or the order of march, each train struggled for the lead.   At all narrow places or crossroads where other trains came in, there was conflict, "cutting in," and breaking up of the trains that at times degenerated into personal conflicts between officers, teamsters, and wagonmasters and resulted often in the breaking of wagons and the maiming of animals.

The weaknesses of train management having been glaringly revealed, Ingalls, upon assuming the duties of Chief Quartermaster, introduced remedial measures in the course of the Maryland campaign.   No longer were quartermasters left to shift for themselves, but orders as to movements were clear and explicit, and the "law of the road" became so well understood that few disputes occurred in subsequent campaigns.   Thereafter on the march, brigades and regimental quartermasters were distributed equally among the train, each having charge of a given number of wagons.   Moreover, they were required to remain with their trains, both on the march and in camp.   In a forward movement, Ingalls explained to Meigs, the trains of the Army of the Potomac were never in the way of the troops; each corps had its train that followed it on the march, forming its "indispensable, movable magazine of supplies." Wagon trains, he insisted, should never be permitted to approach within the range of battlefields—a principle he applied at Fredericksburg, Chancellorsville, Gettysburg, and on all subsequent battlefields of the

---

[105] *OR*, ser. I, vol. LI, Pt. I, p. 105 (Rpt to Meigs, 19 Sep 1863).   Owen at that time was assistant quartermaster with the Second Brigade, First Division, Third Army Corps, Army of the Potomac.   See also RG 22, Personal Narrative Rpts, F.Y. 1863, III, 683 ff. (Rpt of Lt. Col. Wm. G. LeDuc, 25 Sep 1864).

Army of the Potomac. When the battle of Gettysburg began, for example, he had the wagon trains assembled at Westminster, about 25 miles in the rear of the Army. He allowed no baggage in front. Officers and men went forward without tents and with only a short supply of food. Quartermasters brought up to the immediate rear of the Union lines only part of the ammunition wagons and ambulances. This arrangement, always made in the Army of the Potomac, on the eve of battle and marches in the presence of the enemy, enabled experienced officers to supply their command without risking the loss of trains, or obstructing roads over which columns marched. Empty wagons could be sent to the rear and loaded ones brought up during the night, or at such times and places as would not interfere with the movement of troops.[106] In the battles of the Wilderness, the empty wagons were also used to carry wounded soldiers from the field hospital to the depots, the Medical Department having no more ambulances than were absolutely necessary on the immediate fields of battle. The wagons then returned laden with forage and subsistence.

Sherman's march to the sea posed a different management problem. While train management varied in the different corps, Chief Quartermaster Easton thought the best arrangement was that in which the train of the corps followed immediately after the troops with a strong rear guard. At the head were the baggage wagons of the corps, division, brigade, and regimental headquarters, followed by empty wagons to be loaded with forage and other supplies taken from the country. Then in order came the ammunition train, the ambulance train, and the general supply train. As the empty wagons reached points where supplies could be obtained, a sufficient number were turned off the road. Generally they had to go but a short distance from the line of march to obtain supplies, and by the time the general supply train came up, the empty wagons were loaded. They then fell into their proper place at the rear of the general supply train without retarding the march.[107] The details of train management varied at different times and in different armies, but it is obvious that the war was more than half over before commanding generals and their field quartermasters brought into effect a satisfactory system of train operation.

---

[106] (1) *Annual Reports of the Quartermaster General, 1861–1865*, p. 28 (Ingalls' Rpt, 28 Aug 1864); pp. 43–44 (Ingalls' Rpt, 28 Sep 1863, appended to QMG's Rpt, 1864). (2) See also RG 92, Personal Narrative Rpts, F.Y. 1864, III, 3, 862–64 (Owen Rpt, 13 Aug 1866).
[107] *Annual Reports of the Quartermaster General, 1861–1865*, p. 554 (Easton's Rpt, 18 Aug 1865, appended to QMG's Rpt, 1865).

Depot System

From repeated references already made to depots, it should be clear that the Union armies of the Civil War were supplied through a depot system. That system had been gradually developing since the time of the Seminole War. By the end of the Civil War, the system included general, advance, and temporary depots. In the years immediately before the Civil War, the large depots of both the Subsistence and Quartermaster's Departments, which supplied different parts of the Army, had been designated as general depots. Such depots—those at New York, St. Louis, Fort Leavenworth, and San Francisco, for example—were under the general direction of the heads of the respective staff departments, but commanders of the geographical departments in which they were located also had authority over them for all the purposes of their commands.[108] The number of these depots was increased during the Civil War by the establishment of general depots at such places at Chicago, Indianapolis, Pittsburgh, and Detroit, among others.[109] There were also other small depots within a military department, drawing supplies from the nearest general depot but under the control of the commanding officer of the military department. On the other hand, clothing depots, such as those at New York, Philadelphia, and Cincinnati, remained directly under the authority of the Quartermaster General.[110] All of these depots were located in the rear area, remote from theaters of operation.

Some of the principal depots of the war—St. Louis, Louisville, Cincinnati, Washington, and Baltimore—served not only as general depots but also became the primary base depots from which the armies in the field drew their supplies. None was more important than St. Louis, and no chief quartermaster carried a heavier burden of responsibility than Maj. (later Bvt. Maj. Gen.) Robert Allen who served as Chief Quartermaster of the Department of the Missouri from October 1861 to November 1863 and thereafter, as Chief Quartermaster of the Mississippi Valley. Included under his supervision were the Division of the Mississippi and the Departments of the Northwest, Kansas, Missouri, and Arkansas. To write a full history of his transactions between 1861 and 1865 would be in effect to write a history of the war in the West and the Southwest.

Out of the disorganized department that he took over at St. Louis in October 1861, Allen built a powerful machine that supported far-flung operations. He was ably assisted by two officers—Col. William

---

[108] *General Orders, AGO, 1857–1860*, vol. 3 (GO 13, 17 Jun 1859).
[109] RG 92, OQMG Letter Book, vol. 71, pp. 248–49 (Meigs to Swords, 24 Aug 1863).
[110] *Ibid.*, vol. 57, p. 341 (Meigs to Gen. L. Thomas, 26 Nov 1861).

Myers and Col. Lewis B. Parsons.   He assigned Myers as his chief assistant to purchase all Quartermaster stores and to fill all requisitions made on the St. Louis Depot; he placed Parsons in charge of river and railroad transportation.   The purchase, manufacture, and transportation of clothing and equipment formed a separate department under an assistant quartermaster, as did the forage department.   By the fall of 1863, when Allen established his headquarters at Louisville, the pattern of organization had been set.   At both St. Louis and Louisville, one officer administered each depot for quartermaster stores, and separate assistant quartermasters were assigned responsibility for river and railroad transportation, quarters and fuel, clothing and equipment, forage, animals and corrals, and repair shop operations.[111]

Chief Quartermaster Allen was a man of tremendous organizational ability and administrative skill, capable of directing both the purchase and shipment of immense quantities of supplies to advance depots and the return to the base depot of vast amounts of unserviceable material for repair and large numbers of broken-down animals for recuperation.   At the same time, he not only supervised the transportation to the front of recruits and reinforcements but also the return of the sick and wounded to the hospitals in the rear.

Operating from St. Louis, he began his career as one of the great quartermasters of the Civil War by re-equipping the destitute force under General Fremont in the fall of 1861.   He then furnished supplies and transported troops on the Tennessee and Cumberland Rivers in movements that resulted in the capture of Forts Henry and Donelson, and he supported General Halleck in his Corinth campaign.   At the same time, he was supplying Maj. Gen. Samuel R. Curtis in his arduous campaign through Missouri and Arkansas against the Confederate Generals Price and Van Dorn.   Allen continued to provide supplies for the armies of Grant and Sherman in their operations along the Mississippi River which culminated in the fall of Vicksburg in the summer of 1863.   Following a brief lull, he soon was transporting the command of Sherman to Memphis and was foresighted enough to have steamers in readiness at Eastport on the Tennessee to permit Sherman's troops to cross without delay and reach Chattanooga in time to take part in the battle of Missionary Ridge.

In the fall of 1863, on Meigs' orders, Allen moved his headquarters to Louisville without relinquishing his responsibilities at St. Louis.   His

---

[111] (1) *Annual Reports of the Quartermaster General, 1861–1865,* p. 508 (Allen's Rpt, 1 Jul 1865, appended to QMG's Rpt of 1865).   (2) See also reports of his subordinate officers —Col. William Myers, Col. Lewis B. Parsons, Capts. Geo. W. Ford, J. L. Woods, R. S. Hart, Charles Parsons—in RG 92, Personal Narrative Rpts. F.Y. 1863, 1864, 1865. *passim.*

task was first to supply Chattanooga and later to equip and supply the consolidated forces under Sherman in his proposed campaign against Atlanta. Drawing upon the resources of the entire northwest, the officers serving under Allen procured the principal stores that were deposited at the advance depot established at Nashville.

It was a herculean task to collect, transfer and concentrate at one point horses and mules by the hundreds of thousands, corn and oats by the millions of bushels, hay by the tens of thousands of tons, wagons and ambulances by the tens of thousands, fitted out with harness, subsistence stores by the hundreds of thousands of tons, and miscellaneous articles, in the aggregate, proportionably large. [112]

In addition, immense trains of railroad stock, engines, and cars were brought from the East, ferried over the Ohio at Louisville, and sent forward to transfer stores from the Nashville Depot to the front. The shipment of clothing, equipment, ordnance, and medical supplies, and the transportation of troops added to the burden this campaign imposed. So essential were Allen's services as Chief Quartermaster of the Valley of the Mississippi that the Secretary of War denied Sherman's request to have him assigned as chief quartermaster to his command.[113]

As though his responsibilities were not burdensome enough, Allen, as part of his duties, also furnished transportation and supplies to the troops in New Mexico and on the plains. He fitted out several Indian expeditions, and although the troops engaged were not numerous, the lines of supply were extended and hazardous.

Even partial statistics make more graphic the scope of his activities. In the period from 1 October 1861 to 30 June 1865, General Allen received and expended $106,694,657.24. At the same time, his depot quartermaster at St. Louis, Colonel Myers, expended $90,799,435.88, making an aggregate expenditure of $197,494,093.12. When his accounts were settled, the Treasury Department disallowed not one penny of Allen's huge disbursements. By comparison, the total disbursements of the Quartermaster's Department for 1860 were only about $6,000,000. The total amount of supplies Allen purchased in those years cannot be enumerated, but a sampling fully illustrates the vast amounts involved. Under Allen's direction, his officers purchased 8,864,173 bushels of corn, 26,234,423 bushels of oats, 377,518 tons of hay, 6,638 wagons, 1,269 ambulances, 60,854 sets of harness, 100,364 horses, and 75,329 mules.[114]

---

[112] *Annual Reports of the Quartermaster General, 1861–1865*, p. 506 (Allen's Rpt, 1 Jul 1865, appended to QMG's Rpt, 1865).

[113] (1) *OR*, ser. I, vol. XXXII, Pt. III, 270 (Sherman to Meigs, 6 Apr 1864). (2) RG 92, OQMG Letter Book, vol. 76, pp. 273–74 (Meigs to Allen, 29 Apr 1864).

[114] (1) *Annual Reports of the Quartermaster General, 1861–1865*, pp. 505–08 (Allen's Rpt, 1 Jul 1865, appended to QMG's Rpt, 1865). (2) James F. Rusling, *Men and Things I Saw in Civil War Days* (New York, 1899), pp. 174–89.

In the East, the Washington Depot became the great depot through which a large part of the supplies passed for the armies before Richmond and on the Atlantic Coast. Unlike the St. Louis Depot, it never was placed under the authority of a chief quartermaster of a military department. Instead, a chief quartermaster of the depot, who reported directly to Meigs, directed its operation. Throughout the war, Maj. (later Bvt. Maj. Gen.) Daniel H. Rucker filled this post. His efforts to supply the troops were hampered in 1861 not only by the necessity of building a depot where none existed before, but also by uncertainty as to where it should be located. When Rucker arrived in Washington in April 1861, there not only was no depot organization but neither was there a wagon, animal, or article of camp or garrison equipage on hand for issue to the 3-months' militia pouring into the city. Moreover, wholly ignorant of every detail of military life, they not only had to be equipped by Rucker but also instructed "upon almost every conceivable subject connected with their new position." [115] Nevertheless, with the aid of four assistant quartermasters, Rucker equipped the troops who fought the first Battle of Bull Run.

The disastrous result of that battle and the necessity of refitting that army as well as supplying the additional forces assembling at Washington brought a crystallization of depot policy. Depot operations had not been systematized because, until 21 July 1861, no one had expected to establish a main depot for the Army at Washington. It had been anticipated that the advance of the Union forces would result in the capture of Richmond and the location of a permanent depot at that city to sustain operations further south. After Bull Run, the Quartermaster's Department leased buildings, erected storehouses, and built stables for the protection of animals and stores, and perfected the organization of the Washington Depot.

As Meigs assigned additional assistant quartermasters to Rucker, the latter divided depot functions among them in much the same pattern as occurred at the St. Louis Depot and for that matter at all other general and base depots. Functions varied slightly from time to time as changes were made in the depot's responsibilities. For example, after the establishment of the Cavalry Depot at Giesboro in the District of Columbia, Rucker no longer had to assign an assistant quartermaster at the Washington Depot to receive and issue horses and mules. An assistant quartermaster continued to be responsible for all transportation by wagon and ambulance and all repairs to such equipment. In contrast to St. Louis, Rucker assigned no over-all director of rail and water transportation. Instead, he subdivided that function among four assistant quartermasters.

[115] RG 92, OQMG Consolidated Correspondence File, Box 944 (Rucker Rpt, 22 Jul 1863).

One furnished railroad transportation to officers, troops in movement, furloughed soldiers, government officials, and employees; a second receipted and paid the freights on supplies shipped by river and ocean; a third chartered and paid for chartered vessels; and a fourth contracted for the victualling of government-owned or operated vessels.   In addition, separate assistant quartermasters had charge of forage, of clothing and equipment, of the receipt and forwarding of ordnance stores, and of the construction and hiring of hospitals, quarters, offices, and wharves.   The duties of the officer responsible for the purchase of Quartermaster stores and the operation of repair shops at the Washington Depot were considerably broadened by the assignment of new responsibilities to the Quartermaster's Department early in the war.   In the fall of 1861, the Secretary of War ordered the Quartermaster General to provide forms for preserving burial records at Army hospitals and materials for manufacturing headboards for soldiers' graves.   The following summer, Congress inaugurated the policy of establishing national cemeteries as burial sites for soldiers who died in the service of their country.[116]   Thereafter, the assistant quartermaster at the Washington Depot responsible for purchases and repair shop operations was also charged with the manufacture of coffins and headboards, the interment of deceased soldiers, and the care of the cemeteries at Soldiers' Home, Arlington, and Ft. Stevens.[117]

Quartermasters also established advance and temporary or movable depots to sustain armies in the field.   When the line of communication between an army and its base depot became too long and it was desirable to ease the transportation of supplies, quartermasters established an advance depot.   Such a depot contained a sufficient stock of stores and provided a variety of services that permitted an army to continue operations even if enemy action temporarily cut its line of communication to the base depot.   Advance depots were located at points readily accessible by means of rail or water transportation.   Supplies accumulated at such a depot were brought forward from a base depot and supplemented, when possible, by local procurement.

Advance depots frequently took on the proportions of secondary base depots.   The Nashville Depot, for example, served as the advance depot for supplying Sherman's troops in the campaign that terminated with the capture of Atlanta.   Lt. Col. James L. Donaldson, who was assigned as Chief Quartermaster of the Department of the Cumberland

---

[116] 12 *Stat.* 596 (Jul 17, 1862).

[117] (1) *Annual Reports of the Quartermaster General, 1861–1865*, p. 542 (Rucker's Rpt, 31 Aug 1865, appended to QMG's Rpt, 1865). (2) For duties of individual officers assigned to Washington Depot, see reports of Capts. James M. Moore, Edward S. Allen, Ben Burton, Chas. H. Tompkins, E. E. Camp, and E. L. Hartz in RG 92, Personal Narrative Rpts, F.Y. 1863, 1864, 1865, *passim*.

and senior and supervising quartermaster in October 1863, reorganized that depot. His assignment occurred at a time when the Union forces, barefooted, ragged, and on short rations, were hemmed in at Chattanooga by the Confederates. Donaldson's immediate duty was therefore to supply Chattanooga, a laborious assignment until the battles of Lookout Mountain and Missionary Ridge secured that stronghold late in November.

During the winter, he hurried along preparations for the proposed campaign against Atlanta. Donaldson then found the Armies of the Tennessee and the Ohio, as well as the Army of the Cumberland, looking to the Nashville Depot for supplies. Yet he could get no estimates from those two armies and in fact had no authority to call for them. In anticipation of the demands to be made upon Nashville, however, Donaldson sent large estimates for the spring campaign to Chief Quartermaster Allen at Louisville, estimating on the basis of supplies needed for 60,000 animals and 150,000 men to last as a 6-months' supply from and after 1 May 1864. He termed the response from Allen "magnificent." The Louisville and Nashville Railroad brought enormous quantities of supplies to Nashville, and Colonel Parsons, directing river transportation from St. Louis, crowded the Cumberland with steamers and barges. The Nashville Depot, Donaldson reported, was taxed to the utmost to handle the stores sent.

> For weeks together, my Levee thronged with transports of all sorts, and a force at least three thousand (3,000) men, and from four (4) to five hundred (500) teams were kept constantly at work, day and night, Sundays, and week days, in transferring the supplies to my various depots, and Store houses. My estimate is that, for three (3) months, or more together, I received, and handled daily, an average of from two (2) to three (3) thousand tons of Freight, exclusive of the amount arriving here by Railroad.[118]

When Donaldson took charge of the Depot, there were only two levees at which river freight could be landed. One accommodated 20 boats by crowding and the other, 12. The total accommodation was inadequate to care for the number arriving at Nashville and Capt. C. H. Irvin, an assistant quartermaster at the Depot, built a third levee. He also conceived of a plan for handling the vast influx of stores at Nashville. All available warehouses were in use at Nashville but it was obvious that they would be insufficient to store all supplies. With Donaldson's approval, Captain Irvin constructed three additional large warehouses, locating them on the railroad lines. He built one called the Forage House on the line of the Northwestern Railroad.[119] Two others, the

---

[118] RG 92, Personal Narrative Rpts, F.Y. 1864, I, 991 (Donaldson's Rpt, 15 Sep 1864).
[119] Its size was 1,709 feet long by 140 feet wide.

Bread Shed or Eaton Depot and the Taylor Depot, Irvin built on the line of the Tennessee and Alabama Railroad, and Donaldson assigned them to the Subsistence Department to be used for the storage of beef, pork, vinegar, and whiskey.[120]   Even with these additional warehouses, a considerable amount of forage had to be stored outdoors on raised platforms and covered with paulins.   This is scarcely susprising in view of the fact that Donaldson, in estimating for forage for 60,000 animals for 6 months, called for 108,000,000 pounds of forage, the bulk of which Allen forwarded to him by 1 May.

That amount of forage by no means oversupplied Sherman's armies; in fact a shortage developed.   When Sherman moved in May, the Nashville Depot began forwarding to Chattanooga an average of from 40 to 60 cars of grain daily, keeping this supply flowing until early in August when grain began to run short because the forage was being used to feed about 75,000 animals rather than the 60,000 for which Donaldson had estimated.   The supply at Nashville had to be replenished, and fortunately Allen was able to procure sufficient stocks from the new crop of oats then being harvested.   An alarming crisis, however, developed in transporting it to Nashville.   The railroads could not carry sufficient amounts and the Cumberland River had fallen to 10 or 12 inches of water on Harpeth Shoals, halting navigation to Nashville.   The quartermaster overcame this problem by introducing a novel feature in river navigation. Donaldson organized a fleet of light-draught steamers to come up the Cumberland to the shoals where he stationed 100 yoke of oxen to meet and tow them over the shallows into deep water from where they could make their way under their own power to Nashville.   This method provided 500 additional tons of freight every day, and was used for 2 weeks until heavy rains again made the Cumberland navigable at that point.

When Sherman was ready to begin his campaign, all the necessary supplies were on hand at the Nashville Depot except a sufficient number of horses for the Cavalry.   To provide this essential supply, Chief Quartermaster Donaldson was, in the end, compelled to procure an order for a general impressment of all horses at Nashville and within a radius of 20 miles.   By this means he mounted 1,000 men more than he would otherwise have been able to do.   Sherman was well into his campaign before horses in any large numbers were received at the Depot.[121]

Donaldson estimated that from the time Sherman began his movement, he never had less than 60,000 animals and 125,000 men to provide

---

[120] The Eaton Depot was 600 feet long by 112 feet wide and the Taylor Depot 517 feet long by 190 feet wide.   Both were one-story buildings.   RG 92, Personal Narrative Rpts, F.Y. 1864, I, 1010–1011 (Rpt, Donaldson to Maj. Gen. Geo. H. Thomas, 12 Oct 1864).

[121] Ibid., I, 997 (Donaldson Rpt, 15 Sep 1864).

for south of the Tennessee River and at least 15,000 animals and 40,000 men, including Quartermaster employees, north of it. When Sherman began his march, he had told Donaldson that he had no orders to give him; "only supply my Army," he warned him, "or I will eat your mules." [122] With pride, Donaldson informed Meigs that the Nashville Depot had not failed; Sherman's army never suffered for lack of any supplies. Sherman himself reported that, from 1 May to 15 September 1864, stores had been brought forward "in wonderful abundance, with a surplus that has enabled me to feed the army well during the whole period of time." [123]

To achieve this, Donaldson had converted Nashville into one vast storehouse and corral, "with warehouses covering whole blocks, one of them over a quarter of a mile long," and with corrals and stables "by the ten and twenty acres each." [124] His quartermasters maintained boatyards and vast repair shops to facilitate the repair of river steamers on the one hand and wagons and ambulances on the other. In addition, extensive machine and car shops were established at Nashville to keep in repair and operation the engines and railroad cars upon which Sherman's army depended. These were under the direction of Col. Daniel C. McCallum in charge of military railroads, but an assistant quartermaster under Donaldson handled all disbursements. To care for the sick and wounded soldiers and to maintain the health of his Quartermaster employees, Donaldson erected hospitals. He provided fuel so that the city water works could supply the large quantities of water needed by the hospitals, barracks, offices, and shops. He organized a fire department for the protection of the public stores. Having taken possession of the Methodist Printing House, he operated it to provide the stationery, forms, ledger books, and similar supplies needed by the army in the field and the Department of the Cumberland.

His disbursements amounted to over $5 million per month. He employed over 12,000 laborers, mechanics, and clerks. More than a dozen assistant quartermasters were on duty at Nashville, among whom were divided the duties of the Department.[125] This distribution of duties at an advance depot was much the same as that described at a general or base depot. Assistant quartermasters, assigned to that duty by Chief Quartermaster Donaldson, each handled responsibilities for river transportation, railroad disbursements, clothing and equipment, forage, and repairs and construction.

---

[122] (1) Rusling, *Men and Things I Saw in Civil War Days*, p. 111. (2) Sherman, *Memoirs*, II, 272.
[123] *OR*, ser. I, vol. XXXVIII, Pt. I, p. 62 (Sherman to Halleck, 15 Sep 1864).
[124] Rusling, *Men and Things I Saw in Civil War Days*, p. 185.
[125] *Ibid.*, p. 322.

Few advance depots were as large as the Nashville Depot but the one erected at City Point Va., the headquarters of Lieutenant General Grant, directing the operations against Richmond, was its equivalent in the East.   The principal depot at City Point was located on the James River, at the mouth of the Appomattox after the armies had crossed the James and begun the siege of Petersburg.   Until 7 November 1864, Col. P. P. Pitkin was chief quartermaster of the depot and was succeeded by Col. George W. Bradley.   The chief quartermaster of the depot retained direct charge of water transportation on the James River, but all other duties—forage, clothing, railroad transportation, and the like—were in charge of assistant quartermasters, subject to his supervision.   He reported to General Ingalls, the Chief Quartermaster of the armies operating before Richmond.

An average of 40 steamboats, 75 sail vessels, and 100 barges daily in the James River engaged in the transportation of supplies from northern ports.   A daily line of boats also ran between City Point and Washington to provide mail and passenger service.[126]   Wharves had to be constructed and storehouses erected to accommodate the daily supplies required by the armies as well as to hold in depot 20 days' supply of forage and at least 30 days' of subsistence, besides large quantities of clothing, ordnance, and hospital stores.   The daily consumption of supplies was enormous. In the matter of forage alone, the Army's animals required 600 tons of grain and hay daily.[127]   Although carpenters employed in the repair depot at City Point, under the direction of Bvt. Lt. Col. E. J. Strang, built some storehouses, stables, barracks for Quartermaster and Subsistence employees, and hospitals, the U.S. Military Railroad Construction Corps erected most of such buildings and constructed the wharves for ordnance stores, railroad supplies, forage, mail, coal, commissary supplies, clothing, and quartermaster stores at the direction of the depot quartermaster.[128]   The hospital buildings alone numbered 110 at City Point, and in addition there were also offices for the provost marshal, the harbormaster, depot quartermaster, commissary, and the assistant quartermasters in charge of specific supplies; repair shops, bakeries, kitchens; and stables and corrals.[129]   Colonel Strang employed a force of about 1,600 wheelwrights, carpenters, blacksmiths, saddlers, teamsters, laborers, and clerks,

[126] *Annual Reports of the Quartermaster General, 1861–1865,* p. 509 (Ingalls' Rpt, 28 Sep 1865, appended to QMG's Rpt, 1865).

[127] RG 92, OQMG Consolidated· Correspondence File, Box 159 (Ingalls' Rpt to Meigs, 24 Jun 1865).

[128] (1) *Ibid.* (2) *Annual Reports of the Quartermaster General, 1861–1865,* p. 741. (Strang's Rpt, 22 Sep 1865, appended to QMG's Rpt, 1865).

[129] See sketch of City Point.

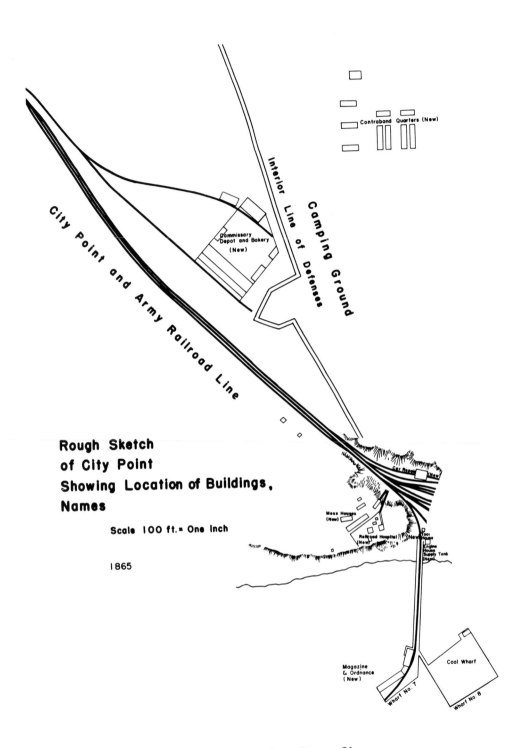

Contraband Quarters (New)

Interior Line of Defenses

Camping Ground

Commissary
Depot and Bakery
(New)

City Point and Army Railroad Line

Rough Sketch
of City Point
Showing Location of Buildings,
Names

Scale 100 ft.= One Inch

1865

Car Repair (New)

Mess Houses
(New)

Railroad Hospital
(New)

New House

Tool
House

Engine
House
Supply Tank
Depot

Magazine
& Ordnance
(New)

Wharf No. 7

Coal Wharf

Wharf No. 8

SKETCH OF CITY POINT, VA.

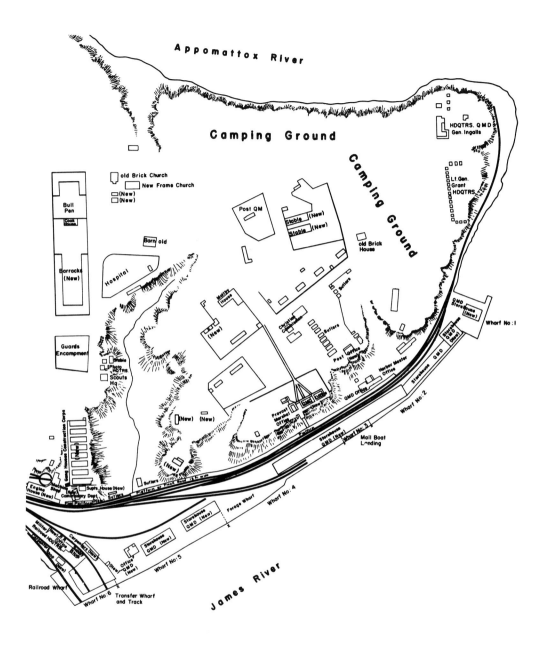

SKETCH OF CITY POINT, VA.

and the number of men employed monthly in the Construction Corps averaged from 2,000 to 3,000.

The depots at City Point and Nashville were extremely large advance depots. In the course of the Civil War, many smaller advance depots were established, as for example, at Belle Plain in Virginia on the Potomac River, and at Memphis, Tenn. Regardless of size, however, they conformed to the pattern described. All duties were divided among a number of assistant quartermasters, each being selected for his peculiar fitness for the assignment. All such depots included repair shops and a varying force of mechanics and laborers.

Immediately in the rear of the troops, assistant quartermasters established small depots, only large enough to provide for the daily wants of the troops. These temporary depots usually existed at any location only for a few days, the depot quartermasters making a forward or retrograde movement with their supplies in accordance with the movement of the army and upon the orders of its chief quartermaster. The workings of this depot system, brought to perfection as the war progressed, were nevertheless evident from the beginning.

In the Peninsular campaign undertaken by Maj. Gen. George B. McClellan in the spring of 1862, the base depots of the Army of the Potomac were located at Washington and Alexandria. An immense depot of clothing and equipment had been established in Washington, and transports for moving the Army of the Potomac from Washington to its new base at Fort Monroe, rendezvoused at Alexandria in mid-March. A depot of land transportation had been established in the previous summer at Perryville, at the mouth of the Susquehanna River, where assistant quartermasters accumulated wagons, horses, and mules because of the difficulty of subsisting the animals in the Washington area, limited as it was to transportation via the Baltimore and Ohio Railroad. Perryville, on the other hand, could be reached by both rail and water. As the Army moved into Virginia, the Quartermaster's Department broke up the Perryville Depot and sent its means of transportation to Fort Monroe. It forwarded and kept afloat at Fort Monroe huge stocks of forage purchased and stored earlier in New York on the orders of Chief Quartermaster Stephen Van Vliet. The depot established there became the main or advance depot for the Peninsular campaign.

By 6 April, assistant quartermasters established temporary depots at Cheeseman's Creek, primarily for forage, and at nearby Ship's Point, at the mouth of the Poquosin River below Yorktown, for subsistence. When the Enemy evacuated Yorktown, they broke up those depots and transferred the supplies to Yorktown. Thereafter, as the Army advanced up the Peninsula, quartermasters successively changed depots from one location to another until on 20 May the temporary depot was at White House on the Pamunkey River, where the railroad from West Point to Richmond crossed. As soon as that railroad was put into working order, supplies were moved over it to the front. When it became necessary late in June for the Army to fall back to the James River, the depot at White House was broken up, and the supplies were moved to Harrison's Landing on the James River. Thus, in accordance with the movement of the Army of the Potomac, assistant quartermasters moved supplies at the Temporary depots from place to place by transports, always keeping these depots within each reach of the wagon supply trains of the Army.[130]

In other campaigns, railroads formed a line of supply for depots. When the Army of the Potomac entered upon the Gettysburg campaign in the summer of 1863, its base of supply was at Baltimore. Chief Quartermaster Ingalls set up depots for the issue of supplies at Westminster and Frederick in western Maryland, the clothing, forage, and food being brought forward to Frederick on the Baltimore and Ohio Railroad and to Westminster on the "Branch road." Following the battle, the Confederate Army moved into northern Virginia and the Army of the Potomac concentrated near Harper's Ferry. At Ingalls' direction, temporary depots were established at Berlin, Harper's Ferry, and nearby Sandy Hook, and on 16 July the Army was ordered to replenish its supplies at these depots. The lines of supply then were the Chesapeake and Ohio Canal and the Baltimore and Ohio Railroad. Depot quartermasters supplied clothing, fresh horses, and mules. The troops were to be prepared to march with 3 days' cooked rations in their haversacks, 3 days' hard bread and small rations in their regimental wagons, and, in addition, 2 days' salt meat and 7 days' hard bread and small rations in the wagons of the supply train.

As the Army of the Potomac followed Lee into Virginia, these rations were expected to supply the Army until it reached Gainesville on the Manassas Gap Railroad and Warrenton on the Warrenton Branch. While the Army took up its march, the depot quartermasters moved their supplies via Alexandria, and Chief Quartermaster Ingalls went to Washington to arrange for the forwarding of supplies via the Orange and Alexandria Railroad. The campaign ended a little more than a week later with the Army taking up a line across that railroad near the Rappahannock River. Assistant quartermasters established depots for supplying the troops at Warrenton Junction, Warrenton, and Bealton.[131]

---

[130] RG 92, Personal Narrative Rpts, F.Y. 1863, V, 541–555 (Van Vliet's Rpt, 2 Aug 1862).

[131] (1) *Annual Reports of the Quartermaster General, 1861–1865*, pp. 28–30 (Rpt of Ingalls, 28 Aug 1864, appended to QMG's Rpt, 1864). (2) RG 92, Personal Narrative Rpts, F.Y. 1864, III, 1019–1021 (Rpt, Capt. P. P. Pitkin, 20 Sep 1864).

Quartermasters of temporary depots ordinarily made use of whatever buildings they found available for the protection of their stores, but frequently there were none. Such was the situation when Assistant Quartermaster Pitkin set up a temporary depot for the supply of the Army of the Potomac at Berlin, Md., in mid-July 1863, and later at Warrenton Junction, Va. He used canvas to protect his stores and issues were made in the open field.[132] Assistant quartermasters establishing temporary depots at various river points in the course of McClellan's Peninsular campaign occasionally found old wharves, as at Harrison's Landing, that they could use to accommodate commissary, ordnance, quartermaster, and hospital stores. Usually, however, they constructed temporary wharves by throwing ashore at high tide barges and canal boats and bridging them over.[133]

Operating through a depot system, quartermasters distributed supplies to the troops in the field with increasing efficiency during the war. There were few complaints of shortages after the first few months.[134] Requisitioning through the depot chain, supply officers obtained and issued rations to the men, forage for the animals, replaced worn-out or lost items of equipment, clothing, and shoes, built hospitals for the sick and wounded, erected facilities for the protection of animals and stores, and occasionally furnished shelter for troops and civilian employees.

Construction of Barracks and Other Facilities

All barracks and other buildings erected during the Civil War were considered temporary structures and consequently were built by the Quartermaster's Department.[135] The rush to arms in April 1861 allowed no time for the erection of barracks. The regiments pouring into Wash-

[132] RG 92, Personal Narrative Rpts, F.Y. 1864, III, 1021 (Pitkin Rpt, 20 Sep 1864).

[133] (1) *Annual Reports of the Quartermaster General, 1861–1865*, p. 39 (Ingalls' Rpt, 28 Sep 1863, appended to QMG's Rpt, 1864). (2) RG 92, Personal Narrative Rpts, F.Y. 1863, V, 549 (Van Vliet's Rpt, 2 Aug 1862).

[134] An exception may be found in the charges made by McClellan in the fall of 1862. Ordered to pursue and attack the enemy following the battle of Antietam, McClellan claimed that he was unable to do so because his Cavalry lacked horses and his troops were in want of blankets, shoes, and clothing. His claims could not be sustained in Halleck's opinion. Meigs refuted any charge of failure in his Department, while the Chief Quartermaster of the Army of the Potomac denied any suffering had occurred because of lack of clothing, though supplies had been delayed in transit. *OR*, ser. I, vol. XIX, Pt. I, pp. 12–13; 16–17 (McClellan to Halleck, 11, 12, 18 Oct 1862); pp. 7–9 (Halleck to Stanton, 28 Oct 1862); Pt. II, pp. 491–93 (Ingalls to Meigs, 26 Oct 1862).

[135] Under regulations, all quarters for officers and soldiers at permanent fortifications were built by the Engineer Department, but no such permanent structures were built during the war. (1) *War Department General Orders*, GO 41, 1 Mar 1860. (2) *Revised Regulations for the Army of the United States, 1861*, p. 369.

ington for its defense were temporarily sheltered in public buildings—
the Capitol and the Patent Office—and in the halls of Georgetown
College.   State authorities also resorted to the use of empty stores, halls,
and courthouses.   The 1st Massachusetts Infantry Regiment was quartered for a week in Faneuil Hall in Boston, then moved to its first camp
in an old icehouse that the State had partially fitted up for barracks.[136]
Some troops were fortunate enough to be quartered in nearby forts, but
most volunteers were quartered at small camps that sprang up throughout
the northern states.

The first troops to arrive at such a camp built the barracks they
occupied.   This was standard procedure; the Regular Army had always
been called upon to erect its temporary quarters in the field.   The
quartermaster furnished the tools, lumber, and other material required,
and the men did the work.[137]   Under these circumstances, the design had
to be simple, and generally such a barracks was a long, one-storied, gabled
building, having an entrance at one end, a broad aisle running through
the center, and a double row of bunks, one above the other on either
side.   Such a barracks was intended to hold one company of 100 men.[138]

By the spring of 1864, plans had been standardized for barracks and
were provided for the guidance of quartermasters directed to construct
them.   In these plans, the barracks, 24 feet by 128 feet in length, was a
two-storied structure, with provision for better ventilation in summer and
heating in winter.   The first floor provided quarters for officers, kitchens,
and storerooms; the second floor offered a dormitory for troops, the bunks
being arranged in three tiers down the length of the two side walls.[139]
Hospitals were built to the specifications and plans of the Surgeon
General's Office, but essentially they were much the same as a barracks,
except that only one row of bunks was provided at either side of the
aisle, and attendants' rooms, dispensary, and kitchen were included.

When the troops left the training camps for active service in the
theater, they depended for protection in summer on the shelter tent,
issued to them by the Quartermaster's Department, after the first few
months of the war, in lieu of the large Sibley and wall tents that had been
in use, and in winter, on the huts they built when the army went into
quarters.   Hutting had afforded winter protecton ever since the Revolutionary War.   The troops usually took up quarters in a well-timbered

---

[136] Billings, *Hardtack and Coffee*, p. 45.

[137] This practice was not confined to the beginning of the war.   When more draftees
arrived in the fall of 1863 than could be accommodated in the barracks at Rock Island, Ill.,
they were called upon to build additional barracks for their use.   RG 92, OQMG Letter Book,
vol. 72, p. 527 (Actg QMG Thomas to G. A. Reynolds, 18 Nov 1863).

[138] Billings, *Hardtack and Coffee*, pp. 45–46.

[139] *Orders, Quartermaster General, 1862–1865* GO 17, 28 Apr 1864.

CAMP OF 8TH N.J. VOLUNTEERS, MARCH, 1862

area, and it was the work of a few days only before a city of log cabins was built. The only difference in the Civil War was that the hut was usually covered with the shelter tent.[140] In winter quarters, quartermasters, using troop labor when necessary, but usually employing the large number of mechanics and laborers attached to the repair shops that accompanied all armies in the field, built sheds and platforms for the protection of supplies, stables for the animals, guardhouses, quarters for officers, and any other facilities required.[141]

Construction at depots was under the direction of quartermasters who furnished the required materials and supervised the work of hired civilians. Most general depots had an assistant quartermaster in charge of both construction and rentals, who hired mechanics and laborers to construct and keep in repair the warehouses, guardhouses, shops, stables,

---

[140] RG 92, Personal Narrative Rpts, F.Y. 1864, IV, 248 (Lt. Col. G. A. Shallenberger's Rpt, —Nov 1864).

[141] *Ibid.*, p. 249; *ibid.*, F.Y. 1863, II, 434–35 (Chief QM J. G. Farnsworth, 31 Aug 1863); *ibid.*, F.Y. 1864, III, 1025 (QM P. P. Pitkin, 3 Dec 1863).

WINTER HUTS AND CORDUROY ROADS

barracks, hospitals, and other buildings under the depot's control. In addition to an unknown number of artisans and laborers, Capt. E. E. Camp, attached to the Washington Depot, also employed the services of an architect, a draftsman, and a foreman. Some eight hospitals were under his charge, including Lincoln Hospital, consisting of 36 buildings with accommodations for 1,200 patients, and Harewood Hospital, with 26 buildings and space for 900 patients.[142] At advance depots, quartermasters used the services of the numerous skilled craftsmen brought from urban centers to work in the repair shops. A large proportion of laborers at all types of depots were so-called "contrabands," that is negroes who were employed not only in construction work, but also as teamsters, cooks, and stevedores to unload cargoes at depot wharves, and as handlers of forage at forage depots.[143]

---

[142] *Ibid.*, F.Y. 1863, I, 641–52.

[143] (1) Congress, in an act approved July 17, 1862, fixed their compensation at "ten dollars per month and one ration, three dollars of which monthly may be in clothing." *Orders, Quartermaster General, 1862*, Circular, 23 Sep 1862. (2) *Annual Reports of the Quartermaster General, 1861–1865*, pp. 19–20 (QMG's Rpt, 1863); p. 44 (Ingalls' Rpt, 1863, appended).

GOVERNMENT HORSESHOEING SHOP

Clothing the Troops

Although the troops were usually required to build their barracks and huts, officers of the Quartermaster's and Subsistence Departments, respectively, supplied them their clothing and rations. Volunteers received their initial issue of clothing and equipment from their respective states, for many companies and regiments were raised and equipped under state authority. Quartermasters at camps of rendezvous established in the different northern states issued their initial supply to other recruits. Such camps were supplied by United States quartermasters who were generally in charge of the general depot in the rear area, or were chief quartermasters of the military department in which the camps were located. For example, Capt. H. Dickerson, assistant quartermaster in charge of the Cincinnati depot, supplied all the camps in Ohio in 1862.[144] Replacements of clothing in the field were made by company supply officers on requisitions of the regimental quartermasters.

By law, the Volunteer Army received the same clothing allowance as the Regular Army. Under regulations, an infantryman received two caps and one hat, one overcoat, two dress coats, three pairs of trousers,

[144] *OR*, ser. III, vol. II, pp. 482–84 (GO 121, 29 Aug 1862).

three flannel shirts, three pairs of flannel drawers, four pairs of stockings, four pairs of bootees, and one blanket. An artilleryman or cavalryman received the same allowance except that a jacket was issued in lieu of the dress coat and boots were given instead of bootees.[145] This constituted a year's issue of clothing, except that the overcoat was expected to give service for 5 years and the blanket for 3 years. In active operations, this clothing allowance did not last the time for which it was intended. Wear and tear and losses necessitated frequent replacements. For items lost in battle, new articles were provided, the quartermaster being required to certify to that effect before new issues could be made. Any replacement for other losses were charged against the soldier's clothing account—it amounted to $42 a year—and were deducted from his pay at the end of the year, the system of accountability being the same as that originally introduced by Quartermaster General Jesup. The soldier's knapsack, haversack, canteen, and shelter tent were government property that were issued for his use but turned in at the end of his term of service. The big knapsack, well-stuffed by the soldier at the beginning of his service, was soon a casualty of war. Always dropped in battle, knapsacks were also discarded by weary soldiers on marches. In the Chancellorsville campaign, Ingalls reported, the loss of knapsacks of those actually engaged was at least 25 percent.[146] In time, the knapsack was seldom used by veterans. The blanket roll, slung over the shoulder, took its place.

Lack of discipline by commanding officers and carelessness on the part of the troops combined to produce heavy losses of clothing and equipment both on the march and in battle. Loaded down with musket and 40 to 60 rounds of ammunition, shelter tent, blanket or overcoat, and extra clothing in his knapsack as well as 3 days' cooked rations in his haversack, a soldier on the march lightened his burden by throwing away all but the most essential items.[147] In battle, the soldiers piled their knapsacks and threw away their blankets, overcoats, and other articles of clothing. Whether victorious or defeated, Meigs reported, the regiments seemed seldom to recover the property thus laid aside.[148] In the Chancellorsville campaign, the weather suddenly turned hot and the soldiers threw away overcoats and blankets "enough to carpet the roads they

[145] The clothing allowance was set up on a 5-year basis of issue. *Revised Regulations for the Army of the United States, 1861*, p. 170.

[146] (1) Billings, *Hardtack and Coffee*, p. 319. (2) *Annual Reports of the Quartermaster General, 1861–1865*, p. 35 (Ingalls' Rpt, 28 Aug 1864, appended to QMG's Rpt, 1864).

[147] (1) Billings, *Hardtack and Coffee*, p. 317. (2) Ingalls reported the soldier's load in the Chancellorsville campaign was 45 pounds, though the reports of different corps quartermasters varied. *Annual Reports of the Quartermaster General, 1861–1865*, p. 47 (Ingalls' Rpt, 29 May 1863, appended to QMG's Rpt, 1864). (3) See also RG 92, Personal Narrative Rpts, F.Y. 1863, V, 468 (Lt. Col. C. W. Tolles, 1 Sep 1863).

[148] *Annual Reports of the Quartermaster General, 1861–1865*, p. 18 (QMG's Rpt, 1862).

FALL IN FOR SOUP

travelled over," Quartermaster Le Duc informed Meigs. In the woods where the 5th Corps had bivouacked, the troops left wagonloads of blankets, coats, and pants. Some had been torn in strips but many were good and "the negroes and women of the country were busy in securing the plunder."[149] Quartermasters repeatedly commented on the fact that the troops were generally overloaded.[150]

The effect of such wastefulness was to increase the problem of supply by quartermasters in the field and procurement by the Department. The consumption rate for clothing and equipment was greater than necessary, and appropriations made upon estimates based on the regulation allowance provided for soldiers in the Regular Army proved insufficient to clothe and equip the soldier of the Volunteer Army. In consequence, large deficiency appropriations were necessary.[151]

[149] RG 92, Personal Narrative Rpts, F.Y. 1863, III, 743 (Rpt, Lt. Col. Wm. G. Le Duc, 25 Sep 1864).
[150] (1) Annual Reports of the Quartermaster General 1861–1865, p. 36 (Ingalls' Rpt, 28 Aug 1864, appended to QMG's Rpt, 1864). (2) See also RG 92, Personal Narrative Rpts, F.Y. 1863, III, 769 (Capt. J. G. C. Lee's Rpt, 20 Aug 1863).
[151] OR, ser. III, vol. II, p. 733 (Meigs to Stanton, 3 Nov 1862).

THANKSGIVING IN CAMP, 1861

Subsisting the Troops

The armies of the Civil War were as improvident of rations as of clothing and equipment. The ration allowed the troops had changed but little over the years. For the most part, it still provided a meat and bread diet as it had in the past.[152] On 3 August 1861, Congress generously increased the bread ration so that the soldier received 22 instead of 18 ounces of soft bread or flour, or 16 instead of 12 ounces of hard bread. It directed that fresh beef in place of salt meat was to be issued when practicable as often as the commanding officer of any detachment or regiment required it. Twenty ounces of fresh mutton might be issued in lieu of salt beef, and issues of dried, pickled, or fresh fish might be made.

---

[152] At the beginning of the war, the components of the ration consisted of the following: 12 ounces of pork or bacon, or 20 ounces of fresh or salt beef; 18 ounces of bread or flour, or 12 ounces of hard bread, or 20 ounces of cornmeal; and to every 100 rations there was also included for issue 8 quarts of beans, or 10 pounds of rice, or twice a week 150 ounces of desiccated potatoes and 100 ounces of desiccated mixed vegetables; 10 pounds of coffee, or 1½ pounds of tea; 15 pounds of sugar; 4 quarts of vinegar; 1 pound of sperm candles, or 1¼ pounds of adamantine candles, or 1¼ pounds of tallow candles; 4 pounds of soap; and 2 quarts of salt. *Revised Regulations for the Army of the United States, 1861*, p. 243.

COOKS AT WORK

If practicable, one pound of potatoes per man was to be issued at least three times a week, and hominy, peas, onions, or canned tomatoes were added to the vegetable list.   Molasses and syrup were also included.[153] In 1863, pepper in the proportion of 4 ounces to every 100 rations was added to the ration.   Whiskey formed no part of the regular ration but one gill was allowed daily in case of excessive fatigue and exposure.[154]

The original ration of 1861 had been ample in quantity, however lacking in variety and unpalatable it seemed to the volunteers.   A year's experience showed that the additional allowance of flour led only to waste and increased procurement and transportation costs.   The Commissary General of Subsistence therefore recommended a reduction in

[153] (1) *Ibid.*, p. 243.   (2) 12 *Stat.* 287.
[154] (1) *Revised Regulations for the Army of the United States, 1861,* p. 244.   (2) 12 *Stat.* 743 (Mar 3, 1863).   (3) Henry Symonds, *Report of a Commissary of Subsistence, 1861–65* (Sing Sing, N. Y., 1888), pp. 142, 148 gives data on amount of whiskey procured for Sherman's campaign.

DRESSED BEEF AT REGIMENTAL COMMISSARY

the amount of the ration, but it was not until 1864 that Congress eliminated the flour increase.[155]

The above-mentioned components of the ration were issued in camp. On the march, the soldier received one pound of hard bread; three-fourths of a pound of salt pork, or one and one-fourth pounds of fresh meat; sugar, coffee, and salt. Fresh meat was obtained from the herds of beef cattle driven along with the army by special drivers under the orders of the chief commissary of the army. Butchers connected with the brigade organization slaughtered the animals at night and the meat was then cooked. On the march, fresh meat was issued to the troops either at night or early in the morning so that it could be carried in the haversack.[156] To prevent scurvy, potatoes, onions, dried apples or peaches, pickles, and kraut were occasionally issued in small quantities.

[155] (1) 13 *Stat.* 144 (Jun 20, 1864). (2) RG 192, CGS, Letters to SW, 1854–1866, p. 242 (Taylor to Stanton, 28 Nov 1862). (3) *War Department General Orders, 1864*, GO 226, 8 Jul 1864.
[156] (1) Sharpe, *The Art of Supplying Armies in the Field*, p. 83. (2) Billings, *Hardtack and Coffee*, p. 321.

COMMISSARY DEPARTMENT AT HEADQUARTERS, ARMY OF THE POTOMAC

Condensed milk had been developed by Gail Borden, but the Subsistence Department did not include it in the regular ration. Sherman recorded that during the Atlanta campaign his Army was supplied with all sorts of patent compounds, including the derisively named "desecrated vegetables and consecrated milk," but in the Army of the Potomac condensed milk could be bought only from the sutler.[157] Canned foods were available but they were little used in the Civil War. The Subsistence Department purchased canned foods for sale to officers and for hospital use. Maj. Henry Symonds, commissary at Louisville, for example, provided canned fruits and canned tomatoes for officers serving with Sherman on the Atlanta campaign.[158]

Purchasing commissaries of the Subsistence Department procured in the markets of the North the components of the ration issued to the troops, the subsistence items provided for sale to officers, and the special foods required at hospitals. Such purchasing and depot commissaries were the key field officers in the supporting area of the rear. Maj. Amos Beckwith, who was chief commissary of the Washington Depot from 1861 to 1864, and Maj. Henry Symonds, who served at the Louisville Depot throughout the Civil War, were among the more important purchasing commissaries. Such depot commissaries also built and operated bakeries that produced fresh bread and hardtack, pork-packing plants that turned out salt pork, hams, lard, and grease, and pickle plants that yielded barrels of kraut and pickles. They also built large corrals at which cattle were received and inspected. The corral at Louisville, for example, could accommodate 40,000 head of cattle.[159]

---

[157] (1) Joe B. Frantz, *Gail Borden, Dairyman to a Nation* (Norman, 1951), p. 258. (2) Sherman, *Memoirs,* II, 391. (3) Billings, *Hardtack and Coffee,* p. 125.

[158] Symonds, *Report of a Commissary of Subsistence,* p. 156.

[159] *Ibid.,* pp. 105–06, 150–51, 155, 198–99, 203–07.

Subsistence Department

Unlike the Quartermaster's Department, which assigned a chief quartermaster to each military department, the Subsistence Department had only a few officers designated as chief commissaries of military departments. One was Capt. Thomas J. Haines, appointed chief commissary of the Department of the Missouri in 1861. His authority later was extended to include the Departments of the Tennessee and the Northwest. Such appointments appeared to be without legal foundation, for it was almost the end of the war before Congress authorized the Secretary of War to appoint, when necessary, chief commissaries to each geographical military division and military department.[160] While so assigned, the officer had the temporary rank, pay, and emoluments of a colonel of the Subsistence Department. Similar temporary rank was bestowed on the chief commissaries of the principal depots.

Like the Quartermaster's Department, the Subsistence Department also had a field organization that supported the tactical units of the Army. It consisted of both regularly appointed officers and a host of acting commissaries. At the beginning of the war, legislation provided for the appointment of regimental commissaries and commissary sergeants. Frequently, no commissary was appointed and the quartermaster sergeant executed commissary as well as quartermaster duties. Legislation also provided for the appointment by the President of brigade commissaries and commissaries for army corps who were given the rank of lieutenant colonel.[161]

Chief commissaries of armies were as essential as chief quartermasters and they were appointed from the beginning of the war. Thus, Col. Henry F. Clarke was appointed Chief Commissary of the Army of the Potomac and served until 1864. Maj. Robert Macfeely served as Chief Commissary of the Army of the Tennessee during the Vicksburg campaign, and Col. Amos Beckwith accompanied Sherman as his Chief Commissary in the campaign against Atlanta. Such appointments were not legally recognized until Congress enacted legislation, in March 1865, providing for the appointment of a chief commissary of an army with the rank of colonel. At the same time, it also recognized the need for still another group of commissaries who had been serving during the war, namely, division commissaries who were granted the rank, pay, and emoluments of a major of the Subsistence Department. All such rank was temporary, lasting only while the officer was assigned to the designated post.[162]

[160] 13 *Stat.* 513 (Mar 3, 1865).
[161] 12 *Stat.* 268 (Jul 22, 1861); p. 597 (Jul 11, 1862).
[162] 13 *Stat.* 513 (Mar 3, 1865).

It was the regimental, brigade, division, and corps commissaries and the chief commissaries of the armies who were responsible for requisitioning and issuing rations to the troops. They called for supplies from the purchasing depots, established the advance and temporary depots that moved with the armies, supervised the herds of beef cattle that accompanied the armies, and, when necessary, directed the building and operating of bakeries to provide fresh bread for the troops in the field.[163]

Summary

The Civil War wrought great changes in the supply departments. The Quartermaster's Department expanded, as Meigs later recalled, till "leavened by the knowledge and spirit and integrity of the small body of officers who composed it early in 1861, it showed itself competent to take care of the supplies and transportation of a great army during four years of most active warfare." [164] It collected a large fleet of vessels on the rivers and along the coast. It constructed and equipped a squadron of river ironclads that played an important part in the operations of the Army in the West. It supplied the Army both during its initial stages of organization and during active campaigns over long routes of communication by wagon, rail, river, and sea. It organized and operated an effective depot system, and, at the war's end, it returned to their homes over a million men.

In the course of the war, there were only two occasions when the Union Army suffered for want of supplies. The first occurred in 1863 when General Rosecran's army, checked at Chickamauga, fell back to, and was besieged at, Chattanooga. Having lost control of its long line of communication, the troops lived for a time on scant rations, and many horses and mules of the Cavalry, the Artillery, and the wagon trains perished. The second occurred when General Sherman captured Savannah in December 1864 but found it impossible to open the river to navigation at once. In consequence, some animals perished from lack of forage and the troops were short of supplies despite the presence of a heavily laden Quartermaster fleet waiting at the mouth of the river. It was detained a few days until the channel could be cleared by vessels and machines provided by the Department. General Meigs took quiet satisfaction in the fact that on both these occasions of want, he was with the troops, shared their hardships, and personally took action to relieve their distress.

---

[163] See Billings, *Hardtack and Coffee*, pp. 120–21.

[164] Henry L. Abbot, "Memoir of Montgomery C. Meigs, 1816–92" (Address before National Academy, April 1893) in *Civil War Pamphlets* (n.p., n.d.) quoting Meigs' farewell address upon his retirement as Quartermaster General.

CHAPTER XI

Post-Civil War Developments

Demobilization Operations

"Reduce! Reduce!! Reduce!!!" So Quartermaster General Meigs communicated his orders in April 1865 to Brevet Maj. Gen. James L. Donaldson, Chief Quartermaster of the Military Division of the Tennessee. Similar orders went out to other departmental and depot quartermasters.[1] Four years of bitter fighting had ended in Virginia at Appomattox, but the cessation of combat operation brought no immediate diminution of Quartermaster activities. Over a million volunteers were impatient to be mustered out of service. The rapid demobilization of the Civil War armies and the disposal of surplus supplies imposed upon Quartermaster officers tasks that were as burdensome as any encountered in the transportation of troops and supplies during the war.

The cost of the Civil War in men and resources had been enormous. During the war years, Congress had appropriated, in regular bills for fiscal-year expenditures and in deficiency bills, over one billion dollars for disbursements by the Quartermaster's Department alone.[2] Expenditures for clothing and equipment in fiscal year 1863 were over 40 times as much as they had been in 1861. The cost of transporting troops and supplies in the former year was almost $39 million as compared to a little over $3 million in fiscal year 1861, and by 1864 and 1865 it had risen to over $87 million and $80 million, respectively.[3] Expenditures in the other supply departments had increased at a similar rate. In consequence, when the war ended, Congress and the people of the country were keenly interested in a reduction of War Department expenditures. For the next 30 years, retrenchment was to be the dominating and controlling factor in Army life.

A rapid deduction of the Army to a peacetime basis was preliminary to any economy move, and the decision to discharge the Volunteer Army

---

[1] RG 92, OQMG Consolidated Correspondence File, Box 947 (Donaldson to Maj. Gen. Geo. H. Thomas, 15 Mar 1866). National Archives.

[2] *Annual Reports of the Quartermaster General, 1861–1865*, p. 45 (QMG's Rpt, 1865).

[3] These amounts were ascertained from only such accounts as had passed the required administrative examination of the Quartermaster General's office, and they are by no means definitive. See *ibid., passim*.

promptly was the first step in that direction. The prospect of early demobilization was most agreeable to the volunteer, whose one wish was to return to his civilian pursuits as quickly as possible after Lee's surrender. Execution of troop demobilization, however, brought no immediate reduction in transportation costs to the Quartermaster's Department. On the contrary, its transportation expenditures were exceedingly heavy until fiscal year 1868.[4]

Actually, the developments in Mexico, the Fenian invasion of Canada, the turbulent conditions in the West, and the necessity of maintaining troops in the southern states until the newly reconstituted governments could be re-admitted to the Union compelled the United States to retain some volunteers in the Army until their terms of service expired. Demobilization of the Volunteer Army that could have been accomplished in 3 months was spread over 18. The War Department carried out troop demobilization so quietly that the passage of the soldiers from the Army to civil life was scarcely known, "save by the welcome to their homes received by them."[5] Immediately following the review of the troops in Washington, the Armies of the Potomac and of the Tennessee were demobilized and, by 15 November, over 800,000 men had been mustered out of service. The ordinary process was to muster out the regiments in the field, or wherever they might be, transport them as organizations to the states from which they came, and there pay them off and discharge them from service.[6] The Quartermaster's Department furnished all transportation for troops returning home, whether by land or water.[7]

The Department's transportation activities were by no means limited to the movement of troops being demobilized. It transported volunteers retained in service to the Gulf and south Atlantic coast to take the place of those being discharged. The Department moved a large force of Cavalry to the western plains. It provided transportation for 60,000 war prisoners, released and sent to their homes in the southern states.[8] By the end of 1866, the Regular Army had been reorganized and the Department transported the troops to their posts. Once again, a large part of

---

[4] In fiscal year 1866, the Department examined and passed accounts for the transportation of troops and supplies amounting to a little over $85,500,000; in fiscal year 1867 these expenditures which included much of the cost of returning the volunteers to their homes, totaled almost $129 million. House *Ex. Doc.* No. 1, 39th and 40th Cong., 2d sess., pp. 69, 528 (QMG's Rpt, 1866, 1867).

[5] *OR*, ser. III, vol. V, 126 (Grant to Stanton, 20 Oct 1865).

[6] (1) *Ibid.*, ser. III, vol. V, 20–23 (GO 94, 15 May 1865). (2) House *Ex. Doc.* No. 1, 39th Cong., 2d sess., p. 1 (SW's Rpt, 14 Nov 1866).

[7] *Annual Reports of the Quartermaster General, 1861–1865*, pp. 155–58 (QMG's Rpt, 1865, gives instructions and routes used in returning the troops to their homes).

[8] *Ibid.*, p. 8 (QMG's Rpt, 1865).

the Regular Army was stationed on the frontier to restore order, the troops being distributed in small units at widely scattered posts. In addition to troop movements, the Department also transported, for purposes of concentration and storage, large quantities of war matériel. There was as much transportation activity at the close of hostilities as at any time during the war.

The concentration of serviceable Quartermaster items at a few main depots and the disposal of unserviceable and surplus stocks offered further means of reducing expenditures. As soon as Lee's forces surrendered in April, Meigs issued orders halting all procurement of horses, mules, wagons, harness, clothing and equipment.[9] Supplying large armies during 4 years of war had necessarily led to an accumulation of stores of all sorts. Large stocks were on deposit at the depots. In addition, vast quantities of equipment in the hands of the troops were turned in at the depots when the men were mustered out of service. The troops that served under Grant and Sherman in the Armies of the Potomac and the Tennessee were transported to their several states under arrangements made by the Washington Depot. Their horses, mules, ambulances, wagons, Quartermaster stores, surplus clothing, and camp and garrison equipage were turned in at that depot. In consequence, all available storage space in Washington, Georgetown, and Alexandria was crammed to capacity.[10] This situation was duplicated at most of the general and major base depots.

Procedures for the disposal of unserviceable property had long since been set forth in Army Regulations.[11] To dispose of unserviceable animals and other property, Meigs authorized the chief quartermasters of the military departments to sell at public auction to the highest bidder after due advertisement of the sale.[12] Such disposition was also to be made of articles that the government would find more economical to sell than to ship to other points. On the other hand, if the supplies were serviceable or could be made so—if wagons, harness, or equipment, for example, could be repaired and made useful for issue to the troops during

---

[9] (1) RG 92, OQMG Letter Book, vol. 84, pp. 84–85 (Meigs to Thomas, 12 Apr 1865); p. 230 (Meigs to Col. C. W. Moulton, 29 Apr 1865). (2) RG 92, OQMG Clothing Letter Book, vol. 25, p. 576 (Perry to Col. McKim, 12 Apr 1865).

[10] RG 92, Personal Narrative Reports of Officers, QMD, for Fiscal Year Ending 30 June 1866, pp. 736–77 (Rucker's Rpt, 3 Sep 1866). Hereafter briefly cited as Personal Narrative Rpts, F.Y. 1866.

[11] See *Revised U.S. Army Regulations of 1861*, pp. 152–53.

[12] (1) RG 92, OQMG Letter Book, vol. 84, p. 307 (GO 28, 8 May 1865). (2) This order was subsequently changed so that sales could be made only after invoices of the property was sent to the Quartermaster General for approval and submitted to the Secretary of War for his orders. *War Department General Orders, 1865*, GO 113, 15 Jun 1865.

the next 10 years—they were retained and concentrated at designated storage points.

Quartermasters disposed of the surplus Civil War stores of the Department at public auctions. Although the prices received were, for the most part, below the cost of the items being sold, the Department nevertheless realized large sums of money from the sales. These amounted to over $30 million, of which half was realized from the sale of surplus horses, mules, and oxen during the first year after the war. At the close of hostilities, the Department was heavily in debt, and on Meigs' representation that it would be for the advantage of the service, funds derived from the sale of surplus Quartermaster property were used to pay off vouchers for supplies and services held by creditors against the Department. By June 1866, the use of such funds for this purpose was no longer necessary, and thereafter the money was deposited in the Treasury to the credit of the Department, to be drawn out again upon requisition.[13]

In the course of concentrating supplies at the main depots, smaller depots and posts in the military departments were broken up. Thus, supplies in the depots at Knoxville and Chattanooga were shipped to the Nashville Depot for disposal. In the Virginia area, though the depot at City Point was retained for a short time, supplies were soon concentrated at Fort Monroe and the Washington Depot. Disposal activities, together with the filling of requisitions from supplies on hand at these concentration points, eventually contracted operations to such an extent that they too could be closed out. The Nashville Depot, for example, was liquidated after the last of its surplus serviceable stores were sent to the Jeffersonville Depot in the fall of 1866.[14] In preparation for curtailing its operations, the Washington Depot in November 1867 sent to the Jeffersonville Depot over 840 tons of Quartermaster stores, 500 army wagons, 100 ambulances, and 13 traveling forges. At the same time, the Washington Depot shipped over 946 tons of Quartermaster stores, 970 army wagons, and 40 traveling forges to Fort Leavenworth.[15]

About all that was left at the Washington Depot was a considerable stock of clothing and equipage. For some years, a clothing depot continued to be maintained at Washington, largely because there was no room to store any more of such items at the Schuylkill Arsenal, the principal depository in the East for clothing and equipage. Most of the clothing depots of the Civil War were liquidated promptly. In 1866, the Quartermaster's Department transferred the textiles, clothing and

---

[13] (1) RG 107, OSW, Military Book, vol. 56 C, p. 145 (Stanton to Meigs, 19 Jul 1865). (2) House *Ex. Doc.* No. 1, 39th Cong., 2d sess., pp. 47, 83 (QMG's Rpt, —Oct 1866).

[14] RG 92, Personal Narrative Rpts, F.Y. 1866, p. 261 (Donaldson Rpt, 8 Oct 1866).

[15] *Ibid.,* F.Y. 1868, n.p. (McFerran Rpt, 1 Jul 1868).

equipage maintained at the Cincinnati Depot to the Jeffersonville Depot. During the following year, such supplies as the Department did not sell at the New York clothing depot, it shipped to the Schuylkill Arsenal. It also discontinued the St. Louis clothing depot, its stocks being sent to Fort Leavenworth for storage and issue at that depot. The Department also discontinued all of the minor clothing depots.[16] Shortly after the Civil War, the great arsenals of supply in the East and West were located at Philadelphia and at Jeffersonville.

By 1869, only four depots were designated as general depots, reporting directly to the Quartermaster General. These four were New York, Philadelphia, Washington, and Jeffersonville. New York was a general depot only in the sense that the city being a great port and storehouse, the depot quartermaster could readily purchase and ship supplies to all parts of the United States. He kept no large stock of supplies on hand. From these depots, quartermasters drew supplies for the Army generally on orders of the War Department, though the depot quartermasters also operated under instructions to supply such stores as might be called for by the local commanders of the military divisions and departments within which the depots were located. All other depots were local and under the command of the commanding general of the divisions and departments, or districts in which they were situated.[17] Subsequently, general depots were also designated at San Francisco and St. Louis.

The sale of unserviceable property immediately after the war and the concentration of serviceable items at depots where the government owned storage facilities made possible the release of considerable numbers of rented warehouses, sheds, and other storerooms that the Department had been using. During the war, the Department had also constructed many temporary structures—barracks, officers' quarters, sheds, stables, and warehouses. Some of these, for example, the government buildings at City Point Depot, were turned over to the Freedmen's Bureau at the close of the war, but most of these surplus buildings were sold on orders of the Quartermaster General, approved by the Secretary of War. Except upon special request, all construction of buildings was halted when the war ended.

To reduce expenditures further, large numbers of civilian laborers, mechanics, clerks, and agents, employed at depots and posts in the military department, were discharged from the Quartermaster payroll. The suspension of all repair work and construction and the contraction of

[16] (1) RG 92, Personal Narrative Rpts, F.Y. 1867, p. 331 ff. (Rpt, MSK Capt. G. A. Hull, 30 Jun 1867); FY 1868, p. 203 ff. (Rpt, MSK Capt. Wm. H. Gill, 31 Aug 1868). (2) *Report of the Quartermaster General to the Secretary of War, 1868*, p. 69.

[17] (1) *Annual Report of the Quartermaster General, 1868*, pp. 18–19. (2) *War Department General Orders, 1869*, GO 32, 8 Apr 1869.

depot operations made possible sharp reductions in civilian employment. The use of troop labor at depots furthered this objective. As a consequence, Chief Quartermaster Rucker could report that civilian employment at the Washington Depot had dropped from 9,251 on 30 June 1865 to 1,380 a year later, and that number included the working parties engaged in cemeterial operations in Virginia.[18]

Believing that the sooner the United States retired from the communications and transportation business the better it would be for the government, Meigs was determined to dispose promptly of all government-owned and operated facilities in those fields and thereby reduce expenditures in his Department. During the Civil War, the U.S. Military Telegraphs, under the direction of Bvt. Brig. Gen. Anson Stager, had constructed over 15,000 miles of military telegraph lines, expending over $2,500,000 for their construction, maintenance, and operation.[19] Application of the principle of retrenchment to the Office of Military Telegraphs had to be delayed because at the close of the war its control was expanded by taking possession of some 5,000 miles of commercial telegraph lines in the southern states. The southern telegraph companies were required to repair their lines and furnish all labor and material. Stager's office kept an account of all government business passing over the lines in the months following the end of the war for possible future settlement.[20] On 1 December 1865, by order of the Secretary of War, the southern commercial telegraph lines were restored to the companies claiming ownership, though the government still considered it expedient to retain in certain localities expert telegraphers as cipherers in order to maintain at all times a reliable and rapid means of communication with its officers.

Two months later, by order of the Quartermaster General, all the U.S. military telegraph lines in the states south of the Ohio were turned over to the telegraph companies owning the "telegraph patent right" in the territory through which the lines passed. In return, the companies relinquished all claims against the United States for the use of their lines before they were restored to them and for all losses that they sustained by the exclusion of commercial business during the time the lines were in the possession of the United States.[21] At the same time, the Quartermaster General ordered the sale of all military telegraph lines in opera-

        [18] RG 92, Personal Narrative Rpts, F.Y. 1866, pp. 746–47 (Rucker Rpt, 3 Sep 1866).
        [19] House *Ex. Doc.* No. 1, 39th Cong., 2d sess., pp. 300–301 (Stager's Rpt, appended to QMG's Rpt, 1866).
        [20] *Reports of the Quartermaster General, 1861–1865*, p. 419 (Stager's Rpt, appended to QMG's Rpt, 1865).
        [21] House *Ex. Doc.* No. 1, 39th Cong., 3d sess., p. 299 (Stager's Rpt, appended to QMG's Rpt, 1866).

tion north of the Ohio River to commercial companies owning lines in the states in which such lines had been constructed. Disposal of the military telegraph lines was thereafter quickly accomplished. By the close of fiscal year 1866, the personnel employed in the U.S. Military Telegraphs had been reduced to 318 from 1,437 at the close of the previous year.[22] By that date, all but two officers of the agency—Stager, who continued to be stationed at Cleveland as chief, and Bvt. Brig. Gen. Thomas T. Eckert, on duty in the War Department at Washington— had been mustered out of service. Eckert was out of the agency in July though he continued to serve in the War Department until 28 February 1867. General Stager was mustered out on 1 September 1866, and the operation of the U.S. Military Telegraphs came to a close.

The Quartermaster's Department reduced transportation expenditures as rapidly as demobilization of troops and matériel permitted. Meigs began by ordering the discharge of all chartered ocean transports and river steamboats not required to bring home troops. He directed that troops were to be transported, as much as possible, in government-owned steamers. Munitions, supplies, and stores no longer required for operations in the southern states he ordered returned to the depots of New York and Washington in sailing vessels, or in such steamers as might be returning without troops.[23]

Discharge of chartered vessels was followed by sale of the government-owned fleet. All steamboats and barges owned on the western rivers were sold during the first year after the war. Some delay occurred in the program for disposing of government-owned ocean vessels, since it was necessary to retain some in the Department of the Gulf to support the armed force sent to Texas and to transport home later large numbers of Volunteer troops mustered out in the southwest. This involved heavy expenditures, but by the summer of 1866 the necessary sea service required by the Quartermaster's Department was being done, with some few exceptions, by commercial lines.[24]

Meigs was as much interested in getting the government out of railroad operations as he was in removing it from the steamboat business. Such a course would relieve the government of the heavy expenditures incurred in the maintenance and operation of the military railroads, and, it was hoped, would promote the resumption of trade. In the course of the war, the government had operated 50 railroads as military lines, having an aggregate length of 2,603½ miles. Repairs, equipment, and

---

[22] *Ibid.*, p. 58.

[23] (1) *Orders of the Quartermaster General, 1862–1865* (GO 24, 29 Apr 1865). (2) RG 92, OQMG Letter Book, vol. 84, pp. 230–31 (Meigs to Van Vliet, 29 Apr 1865).

[24] House *Ex. Doc.* No. 1, 39th Cong., 2d sess., pp. 54–55 (QMG's Rpt, 1866).

operation had resulted in an expenditure during the war of over $45 million.[25]   As of April 1865, the number of civilians employed in the military railroad department totaled 23,538.[26]   Among the first orders Meigs issued at the close of the war was one directing the suspension of all military railroad construction and repairs, except such as were needed on lines by which troops were still being supplied.   With this action went the discharge of all unnecessary laborers, the intention being to reduce and disband the Railroad Construction Corps as soon as possible.[27]

In May, Meigs formulated certain principles to govern the Department and the military authorities in disposing of the military railroads. He proposed that the roads be turned over to the parties asking to receive them who had the best claims to the railroads and were able to operate them.   If a state had a board of public works willing to take charge, the railroads were to be given to this board, leaving settlement of all questions of property rights between rival groups to the state authorities and judicial tribunals.   Meigs proposed to assess no charge for any improvements made while the railroad was in the hands of the military authorities. Moreover, he would have permitted all materials for permanent way, used in the repair and construction of the road, and all damaged material left along the route, to be considered as part of the railroad and given up with it.   On the other hand, he would allow no payment or credit to a road for its occupation or use by the United States.   He proposed to sell at auction to the highest bidder all movable property, including rolling stock, owned by the United States States, but all such property owned by the railroads and captured by the Army he would place at the disposal of the roads originally owning it.

Meigs proposed that southern railroads not taken over by the military authorities be left in the hands of their owners, who were to continue or resume operations, subject only to the removal of any individual who had not taken the oath of allegiance to the United States.   If anyone refused to take such an oath, the Treasury Department was to appoint a receiver who would administer the railroad.[28]

In the opinion of Assistant Secretary of War C. A. Dana, to whom Stanton referred these proposals, Meigs erred on the side of generosity, but with some slight amendment the principles formulated by him were applied in the disposal of the military railroads.[29]   At Dana's suggestion, iron and other materials deposited along the road for repair purposes

---

[25] *Ibid.*, p. 56.

[26] *Annual Reports of the Quartermaster General, 1861–1865*, p. 130 (QMG's Rpt, 1865).

[27] (1) *Orders of the Quartermaster General, 1862–1865* (GO 24, 29 Apr 1865). (2) RG 92, OQMG Letter Book, vol. 84, pp. 418–19; 420–21 (Meigs to Halleck, 17 and 18 May 1865).

[28] *OR*, ser. III, vol. V, 26–28 (Meigs to Stanton, 19 May 1865).

[29] *Ibid.*, pp. 40–42 (Dana to Stanton, 29 May 1865).

but not used, as well as all such material in depots, were to be sold to the railroad companies at a fair valuation. At Dana's insistence, too, the government was protected by clarifying one of Meigs' proposals to include the fact that not only would the United States allow no payment or credit for the use of any military railroad, but it would pay no damages done to any road in the prosecution of active hostilities.

By the end of June 1865, some of the railroads in Virginia and North Carolina had already been returned to their owners or to boards of public works. Most of the rolling stock and movable machinery collected in the states along the Atlantic Coast had also been disposed of at public auction, either for cash or in payment of debts for transportation due the railroads by the Quartermaster's Department.[30]

Before the end of fiscal year 1866, all military railroads had been returned to their owners, but in the southwest the roads were too impoverished to purchase for cash the rolling stock and machinery that had cost the Quartermaster's Department millions of dollars. Since the reconstruction and operation of these railroads was of great importance to the pacification and prosperity of the country, the President prescribed in executive orders a method by which the southwestern railroad companies could obtain the rolling stock and other property, in proportion to their needs, either for cash or on a credit basis.[31] By 30 June 1866, all but a small amount of military railroad property had also been disposed of.

Disposal was accomplished promptly, but collection of the debts incurred by the southern railway companies continued to plague the Department for more than 20 years. In January 1868, collection of this indebtedness was centralized in the Quartermaster General's office.[32] By 1870, all of the southern railway companies on the Atlantic Coast had met their obligations, much of the debt having been paid for in services, that is, the transportation of troops, military stores, and mails, the cost of which was credited to the companies when their accounts were rendered. In that year, however, 28 southern roads still owed over $4,500,000 to the United States and, though the government had been most lenient, it now instituted suits.[33]

The defaulting roads appealed to Congress for relief and the following year Congress enacted legislation authorizing the Secretary of War to compromise, adjust, and settle the suits pending against the roads.[34]

[30] *Annual Reports of the Quartermaster General, 1861–1865*, p. 24 (QMG's Rpt, 8 Nov 1865).

[31] For executive orders, 8 August and 14 October 1865, see *ibid.*, pp. 405–07 (QMG's Rpt, 1865).

[32] *Annual Report of the Quartermaster General, 1868*, p. 21 (Dana's Rpt, 10 Oct 1868, appended).

[33] *Ibid.*, 1870, pp. 9–10.

[34] 16 *Stat.* 473 (Mar 3, 1871).

A number of settlements were made under the law, but some roads still continued to contest payment. By 1883, 46 of the 50 roads originally indebted to the United States had settled their debts. Since the Department had neither the means nor the facilities for collecting disputed debts, the Quartermaster General recommended that his Department be relieved of the business, but 4 years passed before Congress authorized the Secretary of War and the Attorney General to settle the remaining cases, thereby relieving the Department of further responsibility.[35]

When the United States released its control of the military railroads in the South, the Quartermaster's Department once again relied for its transportation of troops and supplies on the privately-owned railroad lines of the country, and it was at once confronted with a new rate problem. Throughout the war, the government had enjoyed, as a result of an agreement made with the roads in March 1862, the benefit of much lower freight and passenger rates than the railroads granted the public. Shortly after the war was over, some of the railroads objected to continuing this rate agreement, and the President's proclamation of 20 August 1866, terminating the Civil War, made enforcement of it impracticable. The War Department thereupon determined to relinquish the uniform rate agreement, and, after 1 March 1867, the Quartermaster's Department paid the railroad companies the rates of their respective tariffs, unless lower ones were agreed upon.[36]

Care of the Dead

While most quartermasters were bending all their efforts towards contracting operations and reducing expenditures, the execution of one responsibility, legally vested in the Department during the war, required increasing appropriations in the postwar years. That responsibility was the care of deceased military personnel and the maintenance and supervision of national cemeteries. The delegation of those functions to the Department during the Civil War was natural. Ever since 1775 the Department had assumed certain duties in caring for the dead. In line with its responsibility for construction, repair, and maintenance at Army posts, quartermasters had long administered post burial grounds. They had always furnished the material for coffins and headboards and paid the expenses of burial. If the soldier died at a garrison and interment was made in a post cemetery, no expense was incurred for the grave. If

---

[35] *Annual Report of the Quartermaster General, 1883*, p. 14; *ibid., 1887*, pp. 11–12.
[36] (1) House *Ex. Doc.* No. 1, 40th Cong., 2d sess., p. 533 (QMG's Rpt, 1867). (2) *General Orders and Circulars of the Quartermaster General's Office, 1863–67*, GO 9, 22 Feb 1867.

the post had no burial grounds and interment was made in a nearby church plot or private cemetery, the Department paid the charges for the grave.[87]

Congress had always made a small appropriation every year for the funeral expenses of noncommissioned officers and soldiers, but before the Civil War it had not provided a cent toward the burial expenses of officers.[38] When an officer died, his burial expenses were paid from his estate, but if it proved insufficient for that purpose the Secretary of War customarily allowed a small sum from the fund for Army contingencies. If this fund was exhausted—and that occurred upon occasion—his fellow officers were expected to defray the costs of his burial.[39]

By the time of the Seminole war, certain precedents were being established that, many years later, helped support adoption of a policy providing for the return of the remains of deceased military personnel to their native soil. During the campaign against the Indians in Florida, relatives often made application to the Quartermaster's Department for aid in recovering the body of an officer killed in action. It became customary for the Department to advise the applicant that if he provided a leaden coffin and had it delivered to a designated quartermaster at a port, the Department would have it forwarded free of charge to a quarter-master operating in the field closest to the area of burial. The latter would cause the body to be disinterred and shipped to the applicant, utilizing whatever public shipping space he might have available.[40] This policy of affording every assistance that the Department could give in returning the remains of an officer for family burial continued to be applied in the Mexican War and later in the Indian campaigns on the western frontier.[41] In no case, however, could the Department incur any expense in giving this aid to bereaved families, since the laws sanctioned no payments for that purpose, though Quartermaster General Jesup sought, without success, to obtain congressional action amending the law.[42] The return of the remains of deceased officers was an exception

---

[87] RG 92, OQMG Letter Book, vol. 6, p. 3 (Jesup to SW, 15 Dec 1823); vol. 13, p. 274 (Jesup to Acting AQM John D. Scott, 10 Sep 1829); vol. 40, p. 581 (Jesup to Capt. J. A. Ogden, 8 Jul 1848).

[38] RG 92, Reports of QMG to SW and Heads of Depts., vol. 2, pp. 310–11 (Jesup to SW, 16 Mar 1853).

[39] RG 92, OQMG Letter Book, vol. 20, p. 121 (Jesup to Brig. Gen. H. Atkinson, 17 Mar 1834).

[40] 40 *Ibid.*, vol. 31, pp. 210–11 (Jesup to Maj. E. Mackay, 27 Jan 1841); vol. 32, p. 99 (Jesup to Capt. E. A. Ogden, 12 Jul 1841).

[41] See for example, *ibid.*, vol. 37, p. 456 (Jesup to Capt. G. F. Kane, 8 Jun 1846); vol. 38, p. 270 (AQMG Stanton to Col. H. Whiting, 12 Nov 1846); pp. 548–49 (Jesup to Miss M. East-man, 2 Apr 1847); vol. 42, pp. 478–79 (Jesup to Maj. S. B. Dusenbery, 15 Jan 1850); vol: 54, p. 162 (Jesup to Lt. Col. G. Crosman, 17 Mar 1860).

[42] RG 107, SW, Reports to Congress, vol. 6, p. 70 (SW to Chairman, House Committee on Military Affairs, 7 Mar 1848).

to the general practice followed in campaigns. Most officers and all enlisted personnel who died in battle were buried where they fell. For the most part, too, burial sites went unmarked and no records were kept other than the report of those killed in action.

The Civil War forced changes in the traditional policies governing burial and records. Recognizing that the War Department would be called upon to answer an increasing number of inquiries concerning the fate of individual volunteers, the Secretary of War took steps to preserve records. His first action, taken in September 1861, was aimed at the maintenance of records at Army hospitals.[43] To preserve accurate and permanent records of soldiers who died at Army hospitals, he directed the Quartermaster General to place blank books and forms for such record purposes at every general and post hospital of the Army. He also ordered him to furnish headboards for soldiers' graves. Proper execution of the forms provided became the duty of the commanding officer of the military corps or department in which the individual died. Each adjutant, acting adjutant, or commander of a military post or company, receiving a copy of any mortuary records from a military company, was ordered to transmit it to the Adjutant General at Washington.

Even before the Secretary's order reached him, Capt. E. L. Hartz, chief assistant to the quartermaster at the Washington Depot, had already begun to collect all the information possible on the military personnel who died in the Washington area. He later claimed that he had originated at the depot the system of burial and mortuary records adopted by the Quartermaster General for the Department generally.[44] When he was transferred to the Army of the Cumberland at the end of 1863, Capt. James M. Moore, who later supervised the establishment of the national cemetery at Arlington, carried on the burial and record program begun by Captain Hartz in the Washington area.

In April 1862, the burial and record program was extended to the theater. Under War Department order, commanding generals were required to give decent interment to those who had fallen in battle, "so far as possible," by laying off lots of ground in some suitable spot near every battlefield "so soon as it may be in their power." They were to cause the remains of those killed to be interred, with headboards to the graves bearing numbers, and "when practicable," the names of the persons buried in them. A register of each burial ground was to be preserved, in which all the data inscribed on the headboards would be recorded.[45]

The language of this order deprived it of the force of a command.

[43] *General Orders of the War Department, 1861–1862,* I, 158 (GO 75, 11 Sep 1861).
[44] RG 92, Personal Narrative Rpts, F.Y. 1863, III, 113–15; 128 ff.; F.Y. 1864, II, 570.
[45] *General Orders of the War Department, 1861–1862,* I, 248 (GO 33, 3 Apr 1862).

Since burials had to be made by fatigue parties detailed from the line, few battlefield interments were recorded in accordance with this directive, the deaths being reported by the commanding generals in the lists of those killed in battle. Most of the records kept during the war were of those who died in hospitals, camps, and barracks, and for whose burial there was time to make orderly provision.[46] Such burials were handled by a local undertaker, whose services were contracted for by the quartermaster.

The tremendous increase in the military force in 1861 and the higher mortality rate made inadequate most burial grounds at established posts serving as troop concentration centers. More burial sites were required but the law prohibited their purchase. Meigs suggested overcoming the difficulty by taking up long leases of 50 or 99 years, and paying for lease and right to bury.[47] In Washington, the Board of Governors of the Old Soldiers' Home agreed to permit a portion of their land to be used as a cemetery. Elsewhere, cemeterial associations patriotically offered small plots of ground for burial of the soldier dead. Some of these plots were maintained by the cemetery associations; others were deeded outright to the government.

Such measures offered a partial solution until Congress could take action. By 1862, the need was growing urgent, particularly in Washington. The capital was becoming the hospital center for the neighboring battlefields and military encampments in the area. On 17 July 1862, Congress authorized the President to establish national cemeteries "for the soldiers who shall die in the service of the country." [48]

No War Department policy was formulated during the war to implement this congressional action. Generally, such national cemeteries as were established were laid out to meet emergency needs. Most of them, created by the Quartermaster's Department, were located at troop concentration points, where mortalities in Army general hospitals accented the need for them. A few were laid out on battlefields as memorials to those who gave their lives in battle, the responsibility for such action being vested in the commanding general. But since the establishment of battlefield cemeteries depended upon a lull in active operations and the availability of troops who could be detailed for burial duties, only five were laid out during the war, and two of these—Antietam and Gettysburg— were created by the joint action of states whose troops had participated in the battles.[49]

[46] *Annual Reports of the Quartermaster General, 1861–1865*, p. 30 (QMG's Rpt, 1865).

[47] RG 92, OQMG Letter Book, vol. 57, p. 107 (Meigs to Maj. James Belger, 18 Oct 1861).

[48] 12 *Stat.* 596.

[49] The other battlefield cemeteries were Chattanooga, Stones River, and Knoxville, the first two established under the direction of Maj. Gen. George H. Thomas, and the third by order

Shortly after the guns were stilled at Appomattox, Meigs called for reports from his officers on the number of interments registered during the war.[50] From the returns made—101,736 out of a total fatality list of more than three times that number—it was evident that before interment in national cemeteries could be completed, a search, recovery, and reinterment program would have to be initiated for about two-thirds of the war dead.[51]

With analysis of reports and all correspondence relative to cemeterial work centralized in a Cemeterial Branch established in the office of the Quartermaster General in Washington, the task of concentrating remains and maintaining records was conducted under the direction of the chief quartermasters of the military departments and divisions. By 1870, the collection and reinterment program was virtually completed when the remains of 299,696 Union soldiers were buried in 73 national cemeteries.[52]

In the meantime, other phases of the work under quartermaster direction—maintenance and improvement of the national cemeteries, validation of land titles, and marking of graves—were also executed with vigor. In the course of concentrating the war dead in national cemeteries, a considerable number of battlefield cemeteries were established in the postwar years, most of them in the former Confederate States on lands appropriated for the purpose. The acquisition of valid titles to the land was essential, and, in 1867, Congress authorized the Secretary of War to acquire title in fee simple to land wanted for cemeterial purposes at a price mutually agreed to by the owner and the Secretary, or, if agreement was impossible, by a process of appraisement.[53] Three years later, the Quartermaster's Department had obtained valid titles to the land occupied for national cemeteries.[54]

In the same law of 1867, Congress also made provision for a continuing program of care and maintenance of national cemeteries. The Secretary of War was directed to detail an officer to inspect all cemeteries annually. On the basis of his report and the Secretary's estimate, Congress appropriated funds enabling the Quartermaster's Department to

---

of Maj. Gen. Ambrose E. Burnside. The work was not necessarily directed by a quartermaster in the field. On the orders of General Thomas, Chaplains T. B. Horn and William Earnshaw supervised the establishment of the Chattanooga and the Stones River National Cemeteries, respectively.

[50] General Orders and Circulars of the Quartermaster General's Office, 1863–1867 (GO 40, 3 Jul 1865).

[51] Annual Reports of the Quartermaster General, 1861–1865, pp. 176–77 (QMG's Rpt, 1865).

[52] Annual Report of the Quartermaster General, 1870 (Washington, 1870), pp. 68, 84.

[53] 14 Stat. 399 (Feb 22, 1867).

[54] For a tabular record of titles see, Annual Report of the Quartermaster General, 1870, pp. 86–87.

make repairs and improvements. In that same legislation, Congress directed the Secretary of War to mark each grave with a small headstone. The necessity of replacing the rapidly decaying wooden headboards of the war period with more durable markers had led Meigs to suggest, with economy in mind, the erection of a small cast-iron monument, coated with zinc to prevent rust. Bvt. Brig. Gen. James J. Dana, in charge of cemeterial operations in the Washington office, more correctly interpreted the sentiment of the nation when he thought that it would "sustain the expense of marble or other permanent memorials." [55]   The Secretary of War made no final decision until 1873, when Congress having appro- priated $1 million for headstones, he decided in favor of marble or durable stone and selected the design, slightly modified later but still in use today.[56]   Before the end of the year, the Quartermaster's Department had let contracts and the work of placing the headstones in the national cemeteries was begun.   Six years later, as a result of agitation, Congress authorized the Secretary of War to furnish the same type of headstones for the graves of Civil War veterans buried in private cemeteries.[57]

As the postwar years passed, Quartermaster cemeterial operations showed no signs of diminishing; on the contrary they expanded.   Before the last Union soldier had been reinterred in national cemeteries, inquiries had already been made concerning the burial rights in those cemeteries of ex-soldiers of the war.   The Secretary of War supported Meigs' strict interpretation of the law, and for the time being veterans were denied burial in them.[58]   Under pressure of interested groups, however, Con- gress in 1873 granted burial rights in national cemeteries to all honorably discharged veterans of the Civil War.[59]

The extension of burial rights in 1873 necessarily brought about a further expansion of the national cemeterial system.   Ten years later, the need to acquire additional land, either contiguous to established national cemeteries or nearby, was becoming acute at those cemeteries located near large cities, among whose population were many veterans, a certain percentage of whom would eventually exercise their burial

[55] (1) RG 92, OQMG Letter Book, vol. 92, pp. 107–09 (Meigs to Edward Clark, 5 Jun 1866). (2) House *Ex. Doc.* No. 1, 39th Cong., 2d sess., p. 61 (QMG's Rpt, 1866); p. 325 (Dana's Rpt, appended).

[56] (1) RG 107, OSW, Letters Sent, vol. 73, pp. 694–97 (Belknap to Meigs, 25 Jun 1873). (2) 17 *Stat.* 345 (Jun 8, 1872); p. 545 (Mar 3, 1873).

[57] 20 *Stat.* 281 (Feb 3, 1879).

[58] (1) *Annual Report of the Quartermaster General, 1869,* pp. 177–180. (2) RG 92, OQMG Letter Book, vol. 102, p. 319 (Meigs to Ingalls, 1 Jun 1869).

[59] (1) 17 *Stat.* 605 (Mar 3, 1873).   (2) In the previous year Congress had attempted to restrict the right to destitute veterans only, but the furor this legislation raised had compelled Congress to grant the right of burial to all honorably discharged veterans. 17 *Stat.* 202 (Jun 1, 1872).

rights in national cemeteries. In consequence, the Quartermaster's Department urged and obtained action to correct this situation at New York, Philadelphia, and Baltimore.[60]

Even before expansion in the East began, the Department established additional national cemeteries in the West, necessitated by the abandonment of military posts on the old emigrant routes as settlement progressed westward. Such abandonment entailed the removal of remains from the post cemeteries and reinterment in national cemeteries, for this course was less expensive than providing for the continued care and maintenance of the post cemeteries. Thus, in 1873, when Forts Kearny, Nebr., and Sedgwick, Colo., were abandoned, the Quartermaster's Department established a national cemetery at Fort McPherson, Nebr., to which the quartermaster removed the remains of those who had been buried in the cemeteries of the two abandoned posts.[61] It later established national cemeteries at Santa Fe and San Francisco, to serve the same purpose in other frontier areas. The establishment of the national cemeterial system, begun in the Civil War by the Quartermaster's Department, was to find even further expansion in consequence of subsequent wars.

Review of Supply at Western Posts

Demobilization and cemeterial operations were not the only problems to which Quartermaster General Meigs gave his attention in the spring of 1865. When field armies no longer needed to be supplied, Meigs, for the first time, could turn to an examination of Quartermaster operations in an area that, perforce, he had neglected during the war. That area was the region west of the Mississippi. Texas, Louisiana, and Arkansas had joined the Confederate States, but the rest of the trans-Mississippi region had remained in Union hands. Though there had been some local operations against Confederate forces in the area during the war, the major defense problem had been posed by the Indians, who, taking advantage of the withdrawal of the regular troops from the western posts, had ravaged the western settlements. Volunteer forces had engaged in some successful operations against the Indians, but the task of reestablishing control and making the West safe for the emigrant awaited the end of the Civil War and the return of the Regulars.[62]

Following the attack on Fort Sumter, most of the regular quartermasters of the Department, who had been stationed at western posts, had

[60] *Annual Report of the Quartermaster General 1882,* p. 194; *ibid., 1883,* p. 171.
[61] *Ibid., 1873,* pp. 22–23.
[62] No analysis is made of Quartermaster support of the various Indian campaigns in the post-Civil War years. The methods used showed no variation from those of the past.

also been called East, though Meigs assigned some experienced quarter-masters as replacements at a few key positions. Thus, he appointed Capt. J. C. McFerran, who had seen a decade of service in the Department of New Mexico, as its chief quartermaster when he called Maj. James L. Donaldson East, and he designated Deputy Quartermaster General Edwin B. Babbitt, serving as chief quartermaster of the Department of Oregon in 1861, to relieve Maj. Robert Allen as chief quartermaster of the Department of the Pacific. Generally, the subordinates of these two officers and, in fact, most of the assistant quartermasters appointed to western posts during the war were drawn from the Volunteer Army.

Many of them proved sound businessmen and able quartermasters, but some were as venal as any quartermasters to be found with the armies in the field east of the Mississippi. The latter group, under the increasingly close supervision exercised, were soon dismissed, but, unfortunately, adequate supervision of Volunteer quartermasters stationed at western posts was not achieved during the war. On the Pacific Coast, for example, where Colonel Babbitt supervised some 45 posts, "widely extended over an area of 1,500 by 600 miles," he found it impossible to visit any of the outposts of the department.[63] Nor could any of the chief quartermasters of the western military departments depend upon the local commanding officer to exercise supervision, because he too was a Volunteer officer, usually as inexperienced as his quartermaster, and sometimes as willing to share in any profits to be made.

Charges of widespread fraud in forage and wood contracts, of speculation in government vouchers, and of misuse of government materials and labor in post repair shops were being made to such an extent in 1865 that Meigs cautioned his chief quartermaster at St. Louis not to pay forage contractors until he received instructions.[64] Earlier unfavorable reports on the activities of the assistant quartermaster at Fort Scott, Kansas, had led Meigs to refuse to allow funds to be remitted to him, but the officer had continued to be employed because he had the confidence and favor of the military commanders in Missouri and Kansas.[65]

Postwar investigations revealed that fraudulent practices of contractors and Army personnel had been even more prevalent than the War Department had suspected. Meigs sent Bvt. Brig. Gen. James F. Rusling on an extended inspection tour from Fort Leavenworth to the Pacific

---

[63] *Annual Reports of the Quartermaster General, 1861–1865*, p. 622 (Rpt, Babbitt to Meigs, 16 Aug 1865, appended to QMG's Rpt, 1865).

[64] RG 92, OQMG Letter Book, vol. 88, pp. 84; 147–48 (Meigs to Easton, 17 May, 20 Nov 1865).

[65] *Ibid.*, vol. 86, pp. 241–42 (Meigs to Sherman, 28 Aug 1865).

Coast in 1866.[66]   He reported a "general looseness of ideas" as to government property on the Plains; nobody hesitated to swindle the United
States.   He learned that the cavalrymen who had served in the West
during the war had swapped horses with the settlers, "for a consideration"
before being mustered out of service, and in consequence had turned
in only refuse stock.   Rusling found that large numbers of government
animals, picked up when astray, stolen, or bought of those who had
stolen them, were being used openly in private teams and trains, and he
recommended seizure unless lawful title could be shown.[67]

Convinced that there had been reckless or ignorant management on
the part of many officers, Rusling informed Meigs that the contracts
made in fiscal year 1865, in the main, "smell to heaven." [68]   At Fort
Sedgwick, Colorado Territory, wood, for example, had been supplied
at $105 per cord in contrast to the $46 being paid in 1866.   While
acknowledging that falling postwar prices were having an effect on costs,
Rusling affirmed that the drastic reductions being made in contracts
resulted from assigning an experienced quartermaster to the post.   Moreover, the latter's changes were being made despite the opposition of
commanding officers who viewed him as an interloper having no business
to interfere with existing arrangements.[69]

The distant posts of the Pacific Coast and Arizona provided as
fruitful opportunities for mismanagement as any on the Plains.   Perhaps
no part of his investigation so aroused Rusling's ire as his inspection of
Drum Barracks, a post that by the "genius and audacity" of Phineas
Banning, general government contractor for southern California and
Arizona, had become "a huge opprobrium & scandal" to the Quartermaster's Department.[70]   Drum Barracks, located in the town of Wilmington, on the southern California coast some 18 miles south of Los Angeles,
was established in January 1862.   To encourage construction of this post
and depot that would bring government business to Wilmington where
the interests of Banning & Co. were located, Banning and a partner deeded
two parcels of land to the United States.   A post, originally maintained
at San Diego, had been abandoned, Rusling was informed, because of its
proximity to the border and the presence of Maxmilian in Mexico.   But
that explanation failed to satisfy Rusling's astonishment at the lavish

    [66] (1) *Ibid.*, vol. 92, pp. 362–63 (Meigs to Rusling, 10 Jul 1866).   (2) Rusling traveled more
than 15,000 miles, sent back innumerable letters, and 30 lengthy reports that covered every
aspect of Quartermaster operations.   These pointed out shortcomings and offered recommendations.   See RG 92, Rusling, Reports of Inspections in QMD.
    [67] RG 92, Rusling, Reports of Inspection in QMD, I, 1–2 (Denver Rpt, 12 Sep 1866).
    [68] *Ibid.*, pp. 7–8.
    [69] *Ibid.*, I, 3 (Ft. Sedgwick Rpt, 30 Aug 1866).
    [70] *Ibid.*, I, 1–2 (San Francisco Rpt, 6 May 1867).

waste of public funds at Wilmington where there was no harbor, where troops and supplies had to be taken from the roadstead at San Pedro to Wilmington by Banning's steam tugs at rates favorable to him, and where the distance to Fort Yuma, Ariz., destination point for troops and supplies for that territory, was almost twice that from San Diego and half of it across desert.

Despite these disadvantages, a complete depot and post for five companies had nevertheless been erected at Drum Barracks, and Banning had been successful in obtaining the contract for supplying the troops stationed there. He had also secured contracts for supplying other camps in southern California that an alert quartermaster, Rusling charged, could have provided for at a much lower rate by way of the Colorado River. Popular opinion held that Banning profited largely not only from these contracts but also in other ways. When it was alleged that the post had an insufficient supply of water, a ditch and flume, 12 miles long, that ran through the lands of Banning and others, had been erected in 1864 to bring water from the San Gabriel River to Drum Barracks. Built by troop labor with materials largely furnished by the government, this ditch, it was locally believed, was only ostensibly intended to benefit Drum Barracks, but in reality was to supply the town of Wilmington with water. It had brought an abundance of water to the post for a few months and the surplus supply, Rusling was informed, had been used to irrigate Banning's barley fields. When most of the troops were withdrawn in 1865–66, the ditch was no longer used or maintained in good repair. Rusling estimated that over one million dollars had gone into the permanent improvements made at Drum Barracks and Wilmington Depot, for which there was no longer any use, except as temporary accommodations for troops moving to Arizona. He recommended disposal of the ditch and sale of the depot and post buildings.[71]

Undoubtedly, part of the irregularities uncovered in the course of inspection tours could be attributed to the Volunteer officers' ignorance of the rules. On the other hand, inspection officers investigated many cases of malfeasance on the part of quartermasters and commissaries as well as commanding officers, who had entered into collusion with them to ensure profits to themselves. Yet the War Department initiated no prosecutions; the guilty parties had been mustered out of service before adequate evidence could be accumulated.

Long before the last of Rusling's reports had been sent to Washington, Meigs had concluded that it would be necessary to change all the

---

[71] (1) *Ibid.*, I, 1–53 (San Francisco Rpt, 6 May 1867). (2) For the subsequent problems involved in disposal, see RG 92, OQMG Consolidated Correspondence File, 1794–1915, Box 268.

post quartermasters on the Plains.[72]   The War Department, in fact, instituted changes in both the staff and the line as soon as possible after the war ended.   With the existing field armies broken up, it placed the troops once again under the control of commanding officers of military departments as they had been before the war.   In the fall of 1865, there were 19 military departments grouped under 5 military divisions, of which two, the Military Division of the Pacific, under Maj. Gen. H. W. Halleck, and the Military Division of the Mississippi, under Maj. Gen. W. T. Sherman, embraced all of the states and territories west of the Mississippi, except Texas and Louisiana.[73]

When Sherman went to St. Louis to assume command in 1865, Meigs assigned Deputy Quartermaster General L. C. Easton, who had served as his chief quartermaster in the campaign against Atlanta and on the march to the sea, as senior and supervising quartermaster of the Military Division and chief quartermaster of the Military Department of the Missouri.   Subsequently, in the fall of 1866, when demobilization of matériel was well in hand, Assistant Quartermaster General J. L. Donaldson, who had supervised Sherman's support at Nashville, relieved Easton as chief quartermaster at St. Louis.   The latter continued as chief quartermaster of the Department of the Missouri, taking up his headquarters at Fort Leavenworth, the chief supply depot for the posts on the Plains.   At about the same time, Meigs sent Assistant Quartermaster General Robert Allen, who had so brilliantly supplied the armies of the Mississippi Valley during the war, to the Pacific Coast as Halleck's chief quartermaster.   With experienced commanding officers taking charge, assisted by able, experienced chief quartermasters, Meigs hoped that abuses would be corrected and expenses reduced.[74]

Sherman, making a tour of the posts in his command in the summer of 1866, was not surprised that the Quartermaster General was shocked "at the terrible bills and contracts that turn up for this quarter."   But he wrote Grant's chief of staff, "we have no business to put men out here unless we give them food and shelter and all things but sand and water must be hauled from one to four hundred miles." [75]   Meigs, certain

      [72] RG 92, OQMG Letter Book, vol. 88, p. 147 (Meigs to Easton, 20 Nov 1865).

      [73] The Military Division of the Pacific included the Department of the Columbia (Oregon and the territories of Washington and Idaho) and the Department of California (California, Nevada, and the territories of New Mexico and Arizona).   The Military Division of the Mississippi included the Department of the Ohio (embracing all the states of the Old Northwest), the Department of Arkansas (including that state and Indian Territory), and the Department of the Missouri (embracing the states of Minnesota, Iowa, Missouri, and Kansas and the territories of Colorado, Utah, Nebraska, Dakota, New Mexico, and Montana).

      [74] RG 92, OQMG Letter Book, vol. 94, p. 103 (Meigs to Halleck, 17 Dec 1866).

      [75] House Ex. Doc. No. 23, 39th Cong., 2d sess., p. 7 (Ltr, Sherman to Gen. J. A. Rawlins, 24 Aug 1866).

to be confronted with reduced appropriations and dedicated to a program of retrenchment, could not be so philosophical. Estimates in 1866, he informed his chief subordinates in the West, were at the rate of $5 million a year for the Departments of the Platte and of the Dakota; those from the Military Division of the Pacific were running over $8 million per year.[76] He called attention to the fact that expenditures for a French soldier were no more than $200 a year. Before the Civil War, it had cost about $1,000 per man per year for all expenses in the United States Army, but on the Pacific Coast he estimated that the costs had doubled in 1866. "Surely," he pleaded, "it will be possible by stationing troops in favorable localities—by not moving them much from place to place and by enforcing rigid economy and responsibility upon disbursing officers and local commanders to bring down the rate of expenditures." [77]

Allen gently reminded Meigs that quartermasters had no control over troop movements or selection of stations, but he reported that he had reviewed expenditures with General Halleck as soon as he had arrived at San Francisco in December 1866. His first estimate showed a reduction of expenditures, and he promised further reductions if the Department made funds available to pay for articles as they were purchased, thereby putting an end to "the mischievous and wasteful system of discounting vouchers," of which his predecessor, General Babbit, had also complained.[78]

True economy, Allen pointed out, could be effectively promoted only by reducing transportation costs. It was transportation, not the original purchase price, that determined the cost of the item supplied. Barley, for example, was worth an average of 1 cent per pound where it was bought, but delivered at Camp Lyon, Idaho, it cost over 10 cents. In the Military Division of the Pacific, transportation, no matter how judiciously managed, would appear excessive in comparison with other military departments, he warned, for the posts supplied were widely scattered, and most of them were not only remote from the source of supply, but

[76] RG 92, OQMG Letter Book, vol. 94, p. 3 (Meigs to Allen, 10 Oct 1866); p. 233 (Meigs to Donaldson, 9 Nov 1866).

[77] *Ibid.*, vol. 94, p. 4 (Meigs to Allen, 10 Oct 1866).

[78] (1) RG 92, Personal Narrative Rpts, F.Y. 1867, p. 13 (Allen's Rpt, 17 Jan 1867). See also *ibid.*, F.Y. 1866, p. 37 (Babbit's Rpt, 25 Jul 1866). (2) On a western inspection tour, General Ingalls also called attention to this problem and its effect. At Fort Yuma, for example, he found the prices of articles purchased and labor hired were based on the value of "certified vouchers." If an employee was paid $100 in currency, he was obliged to exchange it for $65 in coin at the sutler's store or other broker's establishment. If he was paid by a "certified voucher" of $100, which might not be cashed in currency for a year to come, he was compelled to sell it for $45 in coin. The inevitable result was to cause suffering to the employee, increase prices to the government, and depreciate public credit. House *Ex. Doc.* No. 111, 39th Cong., 2d sess., pp. 15–16 (Ltr, Ingalls to McDowell, 7 Nov 1866).

THE OLD FERRY ON THE COLORADO RIVER AT FORT YUMA

the roads leading to them were hard to travel. The most expensive posts of his Division, he advised, were in Arizona where most of the troops were stationed. Only a limited amount of forage could be obtained there, so that forage and Quartermaster stores were shipped by water from San Francisco, via the Gulf of California to the Colorado River, and from there by river steamer to Fort Yuma, a distance of 2,210 miles. Including overland transportation of 308 miles from Yuma to Tucson, it cost by contract almost 21 cents per pound to send stores from San Francisco to Tucson.[79]

Meigs was well aware that reduction of transportation costs was the key to economy in his Department. To ascertain what changes should be made in routes and modes of supply at western posts, he sent Bvt. Maj. Gen. Rufus Ingalls on a tour of inspection in 1866 from Fort Leavenworth through Colorado, Utah, Montana, Idaho, and Oregon, and back by way of the Gulf of California, the Colorado River, and Denver.[80]

[79] RG 92, Personal Narrative Rpts, F.Y. 1867, pp. 6, 9 (Allen's Rpt, 17 Jan 1867).
[80] House Ex. Doc. No. 111, 39th Cong., 2d sess., p. 2 (AAG to Ingalls, 4 May 1866).

STAGECOACH STATION, FT. KEARNY, NEBR.

Ingalls, whose pre-Civil War service had made him thoroughly familiar
with the western frontier, proposed no change in the flow of supplies
from east to west for posts in New Mexico and Colorado Territory, and
for those on the North and South Platte, the Laramie, and upper Missouri
Rivers. Changes had already been made on the Pacific Coast, he
reported, and with General Allen taking over as chief quartermaster he
would effect others. Ingalls' principal suggestions were to supply the
posts in Utah from the west instead of the east, and to utilize to a greater
extent the Colorado and Columbia Rivers as supply lines.[81] Though the
Department, impressed with his findings, decided to determine which
supply routes were preferable by comparing rates offered in bids from
freighters of both the Pacific Coast and Missouri, improvement of transportation in the Military Division of the Pacific was left to Chief
Quartermaster Allen.[82]

---

[81] *Ibid.*, pp. 2–25 (Ingalls' Rpt, 14 Dec 1866).
[82] RG 92, OQMG Letter Book, vol. 95, pp. 25–27 (Actg QMG Rucker to Allen, 18 Jan
1867).

Freighting Supplies

In 1866, western posts were as dependent on wagon transportation for the delivery of their supplies as they had been before the war.   There were some very costly routes on the Pacific Coast and in Arizona, and military stores were carried over these routes, and to a certain extent over supply lines in Texas, in government wagon trains.[83]   Most western posts on the Plains, however, received their supplies in wagons that were privately owned by freighting companies.   When necessary, quartermasters routed military personnel on the overland routes across the Plains by stagecoach at so much per man per mile.   But so high were the rates demanded by the companies that held a monopoly of this business that the chief of the transportation branch in the office of the Quartermaster General at Washington recommended such transportation be used as sparingly as possible.[84]

Long before the Civil War, the Quartermaster's Department had determined that the cheapest and most satisfactory means of transporting military stores to the posts on the Plains was by contract.   Freighting supplies to those posts in 1866 was performed almost entirely by contractors.   Under contracts awarded annually to the lowest bidders, they transported military stores at rates fixed at so much per 100 pounds per 100 miles, the rates being adjusted to the season of the year, that is, lower for the summer than for the winter months.   Since the Department was firmly committed to the use of private transportation as an economy measure, it was not long before military supplies destined for posts in the Military Division of the Pacific and in Texas were also being sent under contract.   Distance and difficult routes caused rates to be much higher in the Military Division of the Pacific than on the supply lines of the Plains or in Texas.[85]

This trend toward contracting for the transportation of supplies by no means eliminated the need for government-owned wagons.   It was possible to reduce the number of such wagons and teams at posts and depots and thereby reduce expenditures for maintenance, but a certain amount of government transportation had to be retained to meet emergencies, such as might be created by the failure of a contractor to fulfill his obligations, or by an unexpected movement of troops, or by the loss of supplies at a post through fire.   In addition, the posts had to maintain

---

[83] (1) House *Ex. Doc.* No. 1, 39th Cong., 2d sess., p. 58 (QMG's Rpt, 1866). *Annual Report of the Quartermaster General, 1868*, pp. 53–54 (Rpt of Bvt. Lt. Col. J. C. G. Lee, 15 Aug 1868).

[84] House *Ex. Doc.* No. 1, 39th Cong., 2d sess., p. 158 (Rpt, Col. Alexander Bliss, 1 Oct 1866, appended to QMG's Rpt, 1866).

[85] See, *Annual Report of the Quartermaster General, 1868*, pp. 12–13, for examples, of contracts made and rates allowed.

BULL TRAIN BRINGING WOOD TO FT. RENO, OKLA.

a designated amount of wagon transportation organic to the military units assigned to the post. Such transportation accompanied the troops on military expeditions. In Arizona, New Mexico, and the Rocky Mountains, much of this transportation was done by pack mules, but because the troops were not skillful in the management of pack trains, such transportation was very costly.[86]

Transportation by Transcontinental Railroads

The freighters were soon to be toppled from their dominant position by the advance of the transcontinental railroad lines. During fiscal year 1866, their wagon trains carried almost 81,500,000 pounds, or 40,750 tons of military stores at a cost of more than $3,250,000.[87] Before the close of the next fiscal year, the Quartermaster's Department, for the first time, was able to make use of the Union Pacific Railroad to forward its supplies. It shipped military stores as far as Fort Sedgwick, Colorado Territory, on the Omaha branch of the line, and to Fort Harker, Kansas, on the branch from Kansas City, at a saving of 389 and 215 miles of wagon transportation, respectively.[88] During fiscal year 1868, the freighters' share of military transportation was reduced to some 22,645 tons while the Union Pacific Railroad carried 18,605 tons.[89]

The completion of the Union Pacific Railroad in 1868, the construction of other transcontinental lines in later years, and the extension of the system of railroads in Texas, forced a reduction in rates for wagon transportation, but the railroads did not entirely supersede the wagon

[86] *Annual Report of the Quartermaster General, 1870,* p. 12.
[87] House *Ex. Doc.* No. 1, 39th Cong., 2d sess., p. 158 (Rpt of Col. Alexander Bliss, 1 Oct 1866, appended to QMG's Rpt, 1866).
[88] House *Ex. Doc.* No. 1, 40th Cong., 2d sess., p. 533 (QMG's Rpt, 1867).
[89] *Annual Report of the Quartermaster General, 1868,* pp. 26, 28.

trains.[90]   Wagons and stagecoaches were still needed "to be the pioneer in advance of the railroad" as new regions were developed and new posts established, and wagon transportation continued to be required for the supply of posts located on lines lateral to the railroads.[91]   Transportation of military supplies in the West remained a costly business, with transportation after 1867 continuing to be divided between the wagon trains and the railroad lines.   On the eve of the Spanish-American War, the wagon trains carried some 32,647 tons of freight and the railroads over 48,745 tons.   The stagecoach lines also were still participating in Quartermaster transportation to the extent of carrying 967 passengers and a little over a quarter of a ton of stores during the fiscal year ending 30 June 1897.[92]

Although, in general, western transportation expenditures remained high, the extension and use of the Union Pacific Railroad did diminish costs along its line and to most of the older posts in the Missouri country. If this was gratifying to the Quartermaster's Department, the Quartermaster officer in charge of transportation in the Washington office must have rued the day he got involved in the settlement of accounts of the federally subsidized transcontinental lines.   Until 1873, the Department paid in cash to the Pacific roads one-half of what they earned in transporting troops and supplies.   The other half, charged against the Department's appropriation for the transportation of the Army, the Treasury retained to be used in payment of the interest on the bonds issued by the United States in the railroads' favor as required by the acts of 1862 and 1864 which subsidized construction of the roads.[93]

Influenced by reaction against government liberality to the roads, rumors of corruption, and the revelations of the notorious Credit Mobilier affair, Congress enacted legislation in 1873 which directed the Secretary of the Treasury to withhold the whole of the roads' earnings for such government service.[94]   Despite litigation and further congressional debate, this application of earnings continued to be enforced until 1878 in the Pacific railroad accounts adjusted in the Quartermaster General's office and the Treasury Department.   Fearful that the government might never realize the principal of the subsidy bonds, Congress at that time provided for the establishment of a sinking fund to liquidate the debts of the Union Pacific and Central Pacific Railroads to the United States,

---

[90] For the impact of the Union Pacific Railroad on wagon rates see, *ibid., 1879,* p. 12.

[91] House *Ex. Doc.* No. 1, 39th Cong., 2d sess., p. 158 (Bliss Rpt, 1 Oct 1866, appended to QMG's Rpt, 1866).

[92] *Annual Report of the Quartermaster General, 1897,* p. 38.

[93] (1) *Ibid., 1868,* p. 6; *ibid., 1873,* p. 74.   (2) 12 *Stat.* 489–98 (Jul 1, 1862); 13 *Stat.* 356–65 (Jul 2, 1864).

[94] 18 *Stat.* 508 (Mar 3, 1873).

one-half of the compensation they earned for military transportation being carried to the credit of the sinking fund and the other half applied to the interest on the bonds issued in their behalf by the United States.[95]

More work was involved in the adjustment of these railroad accounts than could be accomplished by the limited clerical force of the Quartermaster General's office, and large numbers of unsettled accounts accumulated in the office. Their number was further increased as the Pacific railroad lines were extended and consolidated, bringing thousands of miles of new railroad under the operation of the Pacific railroad laws. Much of this new mileage was constructed without government aid and the railroad companies sought compensation for transportation carried over the unsubsidized portions of their roads. The Supreme Court having found in favor of the Central Pacific Railroad in its suit against the government in 1866, the Quartermaster's Department thereafter had to settle accounts for transportation over the unsubsidized portions of the road, drawing upon its appropriation for Army transportation. That fund was exhausted even before the order embodying the Court's findings reached the office, and it could not make settlement until Congress passed a deficiency appropriation bill.[96]

Congressional legislation, court rulings, and directives from the offices of the Secretary of War and Secretary of the Treasury were so numerous that settlement of transportation accounts became increasingly complicated in the postwar years. Legislation dealing with the land-grant railroads added to the difficulties of the Quartermaster's Department. Early in the war, Meigs had ruled that the Department would pay to land-grant railroads 66⅔ percent of the military tariff rates being paid to other railroads. The 33⅓ percent deducted was for the value to the United States of the conditions attached to the land grants which provided that the railroads should remain public highways for the use of the government, free from toll or other charges upon the transportation of any property or troops of the United States. This rebate continued to be applied to all military transportation on the land-grant railroads until 1874, when Congress ordered all payments to such roads discontinued. They were directed to the courts for a decision as to whether they were legally entitled to payment and for recovery by suit of the amounts that might be legally due them.[97]

Of the 49 land-grant railroads to which the prohibitory payment law applied, only 9 were clearly bound to transport troops and supplies free of cost to the government. Two of the roads brought suit and the courts

[95] 20 *Stat.* 58 (May 7, 1878).
[96] *Annual Report of the Quartermaster General, 1887*, pp. 156–57.
[97] 18 *Stat.* 74 (Jun 16, 1874); p. 133 (Jun 22, 1874); p. 453 (Mar 3, 1875).

sustained the position Meigs had taken during the war.[98]   Although the
Supreme Court found in favor of the roads, the law forbidding payment
remained on the statute books.   Despite the fact that failure to change
the law or make payments created dissatisfaction, all but one of the land-
grant railroads continued to serve the Department.

Meigs repeatedly urged Congress to repeal the prohibitory payment
laws, to fix a certain rate of compensation for the services of the land-
grant railroads to the government, and to authorize his Department to
make payments from the regular Army transportation appropriation as
had been done before 1874.   Yet 6 years after the passage of the first
prohibitory law, only one appropriation had been made to settle the
accounts due the roads.[99]   During that time, the indebtedness of the
Quartermaster's Department to the roads had steadily increased, and the
$300,000 appropriated by Congress to settle the arrears, on the basis of
50 percent of the tariff rates for like transportation performed for the
public at large, was insufficient.   Congress had fixed the rates of compensation, but it was the mid-1880's before settlement was put on a
regular basis through the passage of annual special appropriations for
the purpose.

Burdened with the problems of transportation expenditures and
settlement of accounts, one Quartermaster officer, charged with these
responsibilities in the office of the Quartermaster General, had enough
imagination and foresight to suggest the desirability of training a "transport corps."   Reporting to the Quartermaster General in 1884, Lt. Col.
C. G. Sawtelle wrote:

The history of all wars, modern and ancient, proves that army is the
weakest whose transportation facilities are the most inefficient. A well
equipped and organized transportation service is a necessary adjunct to every
army in the field, and its absence, or even its presence with ignorant or
inexperienced officers in charge, has resulted in more disasters and defeats
and unsuccessful marches and campaigns than perhaps any other cause.[100]

He suggested that it might be expedient and proper to institute measures
for instructing officers in the organization and direction of the "transport"
of the army, including the equipment, construction, and operation of
railroads in time of war.   For this purpose, he argued, the curriculum
might be expanded at the Artillery School at Fort Monroe, Va., and at
the school of application at Fort Leavenworth, Kans.   He conceded that
the scattered condition and the exceedingly small size of the Army probably did not permit the organization of such a corps, an essential part of

[98] *Annual Report of the Quartermaster General, 1877*, pp. 11, 111–15.
[99] *Ibid., 1880*, p. 105.
[100] *Annual Report of the Quartermaster General, 1884*, p. 143.

European armies, but in case of war, he believed, "our country would be found sadly deficient in this most important requisite to successful military operations."[101]   The Spanish-American War proved him a true prophet.

Distribution Difficulties

Although in the long run, the shift from wagon routes to transcontinental railroad lines resulted in more rapid and certain delivery of supplies to the small companies of troops scattered at posts throughout the West, that obviously was not the situation in 1886.   Quartermaster distribution of supplies then was greatly hampered by the constant forays of the Indians and embarrassed, in consequence, by the nonfulfillment of contracts by freighters.   The Army was in no position to control the Indians.   All the posts on the Plains were undergarrisoned because, in the closing months of 1866, the volunteers had to be mustered out of service before they could be replaced by regular troops enlisted under legislation passed by Congress but enacted too late to permit the men to be sent to remote frontier posts.[102]   Since frequent troop movements occurred and district commanders often changed the destination for supplies ordered, quartermasters also experienced considerable confusion in forwarding them.   The result was that several posts were left short of supplies and additional requisitions had to be sent forward late in the season when winter storms delayed and sometimes prevented delivery.[103]

The sufferings endured at remote, inaccessible posts were as intense as any experienced at Valley Forge.   Take the situation that developed at Fort Phil Kearny in the unprecedently severe winter of 1866–67.   Located in the mountainous regions of Wyoming, on a fork of the Powder River, 233 miles from Fort Laramie, Fort Phil Kearny was in process of construction as a post on the wagon road that was being opened from Fort Laramie to Virginia City, Mont.   Garrisoned by five companies of the 18th Infantry, it was harassed by the Sioux and Cheyenne, who were determined to resist construction of the wagon road through their only remaining hunting grounds.   On 31 December 1866, the post lost by massacre a party of 76 men, 3 officers, and 2 civilians, going to the relief of a wagon train sent out to obtain timber.

---

[101] *Ibid.*, pp. 142–143.

[102] House *Ex. Doc.* No. 1, 40th Cong., 2d sess., p. 31 (Rpt, Lt. Gen. W. T. Sherman, 1 Oct 1867, appended to SW Rpt, 1867).

[103] RG 92, Personal Narrative Rpts, F.Y. 1867, pp. 137–50 (Rpt, Chief QM J. L. Donaldson, Mil. Div. of Missouri, 1 Jul 1867); pp. 151–59 (Rpt, Chief QM L. C. Easton, Dept. of Missouri, 31 Jul 1867); pp. 587–95 (Rpt, Chief QM William Myers, Dept. of the Platte, 23 Aug 1867).

GUARDING THE SUPPLY TRAIN

At that time, Bvt. Brig. Gen. George B. Dandy had been relieved as post quartermaster as Fort Laramie and was en route to assume the same duties at Fort Phil Kearny.   He arrived at the fort on 27 December to find the garrison shut up in the stockade in a demoralized condition from fear and half frozen from lack of fuel.   There were only a few tons of hay and very little corn on hand to feed the mules of the wagon trains and the horses of the 2d Cavalry company that had recently arrived.   To prevent them from starving to death, Dandy sent most of them to Fort Laramie, but many of them died on the road from starvation and cold. He retained only enough animals to haul timber for fuel from a distance of 6½ miles.   By mid-January the supply of hay was exhausted, and he was trying to keep the animals alive on three to four pounds per day of cornmeal and hominy that he obtained from the commissary.   The animals were reduced to such extremity that they ate their harness and the tongues and bodies of the wagons.   Too thin and weak to work, the animals finally had to be turned loose to care for themselves.

Then, in order to obtain the necessary daily supply of timber for fuel, the men had to pack it on their backs through the snowdrifts.

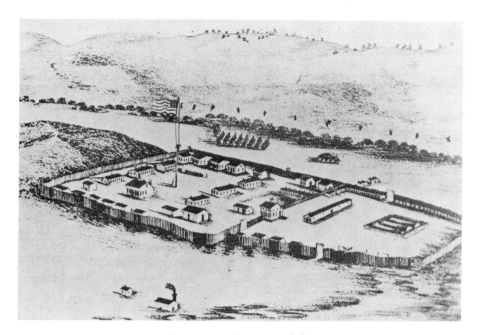

FORT PHIL KEARNY, 1867

In consequence, the hospital was soon filled with frostbitten patients. Supplies, estimated for a garrison of five companies that had swelled to eleven, were exhausted long before fresh shipments could be expected. One-third of the whole force was in the hospital with scurvy, reduced as it was to a daily fare of bacon and hard bread, the only rations available. The soldiers' quarters were badly ventilated and so insufficient that some of the companies lived in tents during that severe winter. Having been sent to Fort Phil Kearny in the dead of winter, it was impossible for Quartermaster Dandy to do anything except share the general hardships and await the arrival of succor.[104]

The degree of suffering endured at Fort Phil Kearny was not duplicated elsewhere, but other posts also ran short of commissary supplies. For months during that winter, it was impossible to keep communications open with such remote forts as C. F. Smith, on the Big Horn River in southern Montana, Buford at the junction of the Bruneau and Snake Rivers in southwestern Idaho, and Berthhold on the Missouri River in North Dakota. All were located in the country of the unfriendly Sioux. Even after the coming of the transcontinental railroads improved trans-

[104] *Ibid.*, F.Y. 1867, pp. 117–133 (Dandy's Rpt, 30 Jun 1867).

portation, life at the frontier posts remained rugged. Though few in numbers, the troops were called upon not only to fight the Indians, but also to get in their supply of fuel and forage and to construct their quarters from whatever material was nearest at hand—timber, stone, adobe, or sod.

Quarters at Western Posts

Inspection of post quarters in 1866 brought forth some well-merited criticism. Bvt. Brig. Gen. J. F. Rusling wrote Meigs that sod should be used as a "dernier resort, and sod or dirt were vile," so bad and disagreeable in fact that no troops should be required to shelter under them. "Dirt, dampness, disease, vermin, all infest such structures," he reported, "and the United States Government, I take it, means better than that by the faithful troops that serve it." [105] Sod had been used at Fort Sedgwick, Colo., and when General Sherman, commanding the Military Division of the Mississippi, visited there in the summer of 1866 the quarters looked like hovels. "Surely," he wrote, "had the southern planters put their negroes in such hovels, a sample would, ere this, have been carried to Boston and exhibited as illustrative of the cruelty and inhumanity of the man-masters." [106] At Fort Yuma, Ariz., the buildings were of adobe, roofed with zinc, "the worst roofing that could have been used in that infernal climate," Rusling informed Meigs.[107] Quarters provided for the troops in Arizona were generally condemned by the assistant inspector general of the Military Division of the Pacific, who thought the troops were suffering unnecessarily, for they were exposed to weather "as the negro of the south or the peasant of Ireland has never been." [108] To this criticism, the commanding general of the Department of California, General McDowell, rejoined: "I know nothing of the huts in Ireland; but I have seen plenty of negro cabins that were very comfortable as compared with a tent, and this is the comparison to make." [109] He thought the inspector's opinion should be received with some allowance.

Believing that it was true economy to make the soldier comfortable since that improved his health, efficiency, and morale and prevented desertion, Meigs wished to offer better barrack accommodations than in

---

[105] RG 92, Rusling, Reports of Inspections in QMD, I, 3 (Denver Rpt, 12 Sep 1866).

[106] House *Ex. Doc.* No. 23, 39th Cong., 2d sess., p. 7 (Sherman to Gen. J. A. Rawlins, 24 Aug 1866).

[107] RG 92, Rusling, Reports of Inspections in QMD, II, 54–56 (San Francisco Rpt, 16 May 1867).

[108] House *Ex. Doc.* No. 1, 40th Cong., 2d sess., p. 85 (Inclosure to General Halleck's Rpt, 18 Sep 1867, appended to SW's Rpt, 1867).

[109] *Ibid.*, pp. 94–95.

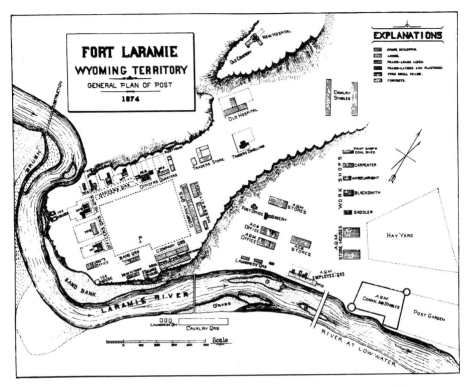

GENERAL PLAN OF FORT LARAMIE, WYOMING TERRITORY, 1874

the past, to make quarters, reading rooms, and mess rooms "more attractive than the sutler's shop and the groggery." [110] When he suggested, however, that Sherman reconsider the advisability of erecting a permanent garrison at Fort Sedgwick, Colo., that most expensive post on the Plains, he became involved in an exchange of views over staff and line responsibilities, a clash of viewpoints that arose with increasing frequency in the postwar years.[111] General Sherman, convinced that Fort Sedgwick would have to be retained as a military post, was equally certain that, in all matters relating to the shelter of troops on the Plains, a large degree of discretion should be left with the commanding general.[112]

Meigs agreed with Sherman's interpretation of his authority, and supposed that he intended to, and in fact did, exercise supervision and control over Quartermaster operations in his command. He reminded

[110] RG 92, OQMG Letter Book, vol. 92, pp. 370–71 (Meigs to Sherman, 9 Jul 1866).
[111] *Ibid.*, pp. 302–03 (Meigs to Sherman, 28 Jun 1866).
[112] See RG 92, QMD, Register of Letters Received, 3 Jul 1866.

Sherman that in the course of the war there had been few complaints that Quartermaster officers failed to obey orders of military commanders or failed to cooperate zealously and successfully with them and under their instructions, and he assured him that no such case would be permitted to arise in the future. On the other hand, the Secretary of War and the bureau chiefs under him were responsible for Army expenditures and Meigs added, "we do not meet this responsibility by saying to each General commanding a Division we have such appropriations spend them as you will." A general supervision and regulation had to be retained at Washington, Meigs insisted, to enable these officers to know what is done, to regulate expenditures, and to answer the questions of Congress and the Executive.[113]

Reasonableness got Meigs nowhere. By order of the Secretary of War, acting on a recommendation of Lieutenant General Grant, General in Chief, Meigs was directed to place $1 million in the hands of Sherman's chief quartermaster, to be spent, in such amounts in sheltering the troops on the Plains and within the Military Division Sherman commanded, as he might direct.[114] Thereafter, Meigs did not "feel at liberty to give orders" on sheltering the troops in the Military Division of the Mississippi, though he sent information along to Chief Quartermaster Easton, and later advised Assistant Quartermaster General Donaldson, when he was sent to relieve Easton, that he was "to exercise nearer control of the operations and expenditures" of the Quartermaster's Department in that division.[115] The grant of the so-called sheltering fund proved an exception to the system of keeping application of appropriations for barracks and quarters under the direct personal control of the Secretary of War, though other unsuccessful efforts were made by commanding officers to obtain approval of a system under which there would be assigned to each departmental commander the amount of money that could be spared for construction purposes.[116]

Except for hospitals, for which after 1870 the Surgeon General made separate estimates and obtained appropriations, the Quartermaster's Department built most barracks, quarters, storehouses, and other military buildings from funds annually appropriated by Congress for "construction of temporary huts and stables," and for repairing buildings at estab-

---

[113] RG 92, OQMG Letter Book, vol. 92, pp. 366–70 (Meigs to Sherman, 9 Jul 1866).

[114] *Ibid.*, pp. 388–89 (Meigs to Easton, 12 Jul 1866).

[115] *Ibid.*, pp. 469–98 (Meigs to Easton, 25 Jul 1866); vol. 94, p. 337 (QMG to Donaldson, 1 Dec 1866).

[116] See, for example, RG 92, OQMG Letter Book, 1873–A, General and Misc., pp. 496–98 (Indorsement, Meigs to AG, 24 Jul 1873).

lished posts.[117]   This legislation was in accord with War Department views on construction.   Since most western military posts were themselves temporary, the War Department considered it advisable to keep the troops in cantonments, occupying quarters they themselves constructed from local materials.[118]   Only by special authorization of the War Department could contracts be made to purchase material for the erection of temporary posts in the West.   No permanent buildings could be constructed, except by order of the Secretary of War, and such authority was also necessary to make any alterations.   To construct permanent buildings, the Quartermaster's Department had to submit detailed estimates to Congress, which enacted special appropriations for the project.   Such had been the law since 1859, until Congress put a limit of $20,000 on the cost of a permanent building in 1872.   Congress later also provided that no expenditures exceeding $500 could be made on any building without the approval of the Secretary of War and only upon detailed estimates prepared by the Quartermaster's Department.[119]

While the Quartermaster's Department, utilizing funds provided for the incidental expenses of the Army, could and did hire and pay skilled artisans and laborers to a limited extent to construct and repair buildings, principally in the East, most construction work at western posts had to be done by the troops.   Since the Department's staff was too small to permit assigning an experienced quartermaster to each western post where construction was under way, much of it was under the direction of inexperienced officers.   Inexperience proved costly.   Some of the first sites selected for the construction of new military posts on the Texas frontier, for example, had to be abandoned for lack of water or timber after considerable expenditures had been made by the Quartermaster's Department to forward workmen and materials.[120]

Obviously, the buildings provided under these conditions were of the rudest construction, providing unwholesome and uncomfortable quarters for officers and men.   Assistant Surgeon John S. Billings, reporting on barracks and health, charged that the statement made that "we have the best-fed and worst-housed Army in the world" seemed more nearly correct than such generalizations usually were.[121]   Dark, cheerless, noisome, and

[117] (1) RG 92, OQMG Letter Book, vol. 106, pp. 592–93 (Meigs to Surgeon General, 17 Oct 1870).   (2) RG 92, OQMG Letter Book, 1878–A, General and Misc., p. 746 (Meigs to SW, 29 Jun 1878).

[118] (1) RG 92, OQMG Letter Book, vol. 90, p. 36 (Actg QMG Rucker to Donaldson, 16 Apr 1867).   (2) *War Department General Orders, 1867*, GO 76, 15 Aug 1867.

[119] (1) *War Department General Orders, 1868*, GO 95, 23 Nov 1868.   (2) 11 *Stat.* 432 (Mar 3, 1859); 17 *Stat.* 128 (May 28, 1872); 24 *Stat.* 97–98 (Jun 30, 1886).

[120] *Annual Report of the Quartermaster General, 1868*, pp. 10, 54–56; 58–63.

[121] John S. Billings, *A Report on Barracks and Hospitals with Descriptions of Military Posts* (Washington, 1870), p. XXXIII.   Hereafter briefly cited as Billings, *Report on Barracks.*

overcrowded, Army barracks produced a mortality rate from disease in the period 1867–70 that was 50 percent greater than it should have been, Billings reported. Army regulations established some rather flexible standards for air space for each man. In 1863, they called for 225 square feet of room north of 38° north, and 256 square feet south of that latitude. Setting the average height of rooms at 10 feet, that gave each soldier 375 and 426 cubic feet, respectively. But this provision was qualified by the authorization that when the number of officers and men made it necessary, the commanding officer could reduce the amount of quarters pro rata. Practically speaking, there were no regulations. At Fort Griffin, a frontier post in Texas, the barracks consisted of 4 rows of small frame huts, 10 to a row, each hut measuring 13 by 8½ by 6 feet, giving 660 cubic feet of air space to each hut. Each row of huts was supposed to accommodate one company, but even if the company strength was only 60, each shanty would be occupied by 6 men, giving each man only 110 cubic feet of air space.[122] Other posts offered accommodations that were no better than those at Fort Griffin.

One-half of the Army posts in 1870 had barracks that were built with a central aisle, each side of which was lined with a row of double bunks, usually placed in two tiers, though those at Fort Buford in Dakota Territory had three tiers. Their use had long since been discontinued in European armies, and Billings thought it was imperative to put an end to this evil in the American Army. When Meigs inspected the frontier posts of Texas in the winter of 1869–70 and saw the rough board, vermin-infested bunks in which the men slept, he was horrified and determined to have iron beds manufactured and sent as soon as possible.[123] There had been agitation for the introduction of iron bedsteads more than a decade before 1861, but lack of funds and then war had deferred action. Meigs attacked the problem with renewed vigor, and 25 years after the subject had first been broached, he could report that nearly all military posts had been supplied with single iron bedsteads.[124]

A majority of the posts lacked proper bathing facilities. At Fort Buford, a basin of water out of doors was the only facility. Even the Missouri River at that point was too rapid and dangerous to permit the men to make use of it in the summer.[125] In the existing state of appropriations, construction of bathhouses could not be permitted. The Secretary of War regularly rejected all plans and estimates for them,

[122] *Ibid.*, p. 194.
[123] RG 92, OQMG Letter Book, vol. 105, pp. 205–06 (Meigs to Acting QMG McFerran, 11 Jan 1870).
[124] *Annual Report of the Quartermaster General, 1873*, p. 25.
[125] Billings, *Report on Barracks*, p. 402.

holding that the troops could provide for their own needs without expense to the government.[126]

When dusk fell, the barracks became a gloomy place, lit by the flickering light from an occasional candle, as they had been since the days of the Revolution. Under regulations, the Subsistence Department in the post-Civil War period furnished 1 pound and 4 ounces of candles to every 100 rations.[127] On order of the Secretary of War, a board of officers convened in the summer of 1878 to report upon lighting barracks with lamps fed with mineral oil, or as it was later called, kerosene. As a result of that report, the Secretary authorized a trial of such lamps at certain military posts. Supply responsibility for lamps and mineral oil was transferred from the Subsistence to the Quartermaster's Department in the spring of 1881.[128] The Department estimated that the new method of lighting would cost the government about $2,500 per year more than the old, but since the lamp would give the light of 16 candles, the morale of the troops would be much improved.[129]

As improvements began to be made for the comfort of the soldier, the War Department also tried to furnish a better means for the use of his leisure hours than was offered by the grog shop. Immediately after the Civil War, Congress had provided for the establishment of schools at posts, garrisons, or permanent camps to instruct the enlisted men in "the common English branches of education, and especially in the history of the United States." [130] When no suitable room or buildings could be set apart for educational and religious purposes, the Secretary of War directed the Quartermaster's Department to construct such buildings, the plans and detailed estimates of cost being forwarded by the commanding officer, through the Quartermaster General, for the approval of the Secretary.[131] As General Grant interpreted the law, however, all posts west of the Mississippi were considered temporary and not entitled to the benefit of the act.[132]

For the next dozen years, little was accomplished under this law, but early in 1878, by order of the Secretary of War, a board of officers, including the Quartermaster General, met to consider steps for carrying out the law. The board recommended that post funds be used for this purpose and that a more liberal application also be made of Quarter-

[126] RG 92, OQMG Letter Book, 1875–A, General and Misc., p. 363 (Meigs to SW, 30 Mar 1875); *ibid.*, 1877–A, pp. 473–74 (Meigs to SW, 17 Jul 1877).
[127] *Revised U.S. Army Regulations of 1861*, p. 244.
[128] *Headquarters of the Army General Orders, 1881*, GO 50, 24 May 1881.
[129] *Annual Report of the Quartermaster General, 1881*, pp. 12–13.
[130] 14 *Stat.* 336 (Jul 22, 1886).
[131] *War Department General Orders, 1886*, GO 80, 24 Sep 1866.
[132] RG 92, OQMG Letter Book, vol. 99, p. 293 (Acting QMG Rucker to AG, 10 Apr 1868).

master appropriations.   In consequence, the Quartermaster's Department furnished an increasing number of posts with buildings to be used for schools, chapels, reading rooms, and libraries.[133]   Approval of another recommendation of the board resulted in the Quartermaster's Department procuring and forwarding to the post libraries such periodicals and newspapers as the Department's appropriation for incidental expenses permitted it to purchase.

Fully convinced that it was "cheaper to amuse soldiers than punish them for faults resulting from ennui and want of interesting employment for leisure hours," Meigs, as a member of the board, had approved of bowling alleys for the troops.   Quartermaster funds were not available for such purposes, but the troops might build their own bowling alleys, and Meigs was so much interested in their welfare that he prepared drawings of a billiard table that he requested the editor of *Builder and Woodworker* to publish.   This was a journal known to the Army, and publication of his drawings in it would provide "do-it-yourself" plans for the soldiers, enabling them also to build their own billiard tables.[134]

This effort to ameliorate the life of the soldier came at a time when officers of the Army were urging a change in policy that would lead to the abandonment of temporary posts in the West in favor of large permanent garrisons where troops might be concentrated.   By the 1880's, transcontinental railroads crossed the continent, settlement had spread across the country, and the Indians were under greater control.   The transition period following the Civil War, when troops lived in holes in the ground, in houses made of green cottonwood logs infested by vermin, and in temporary shanties, was coming to an end.   Sherman, then serving as Commanding General of the Army, appealed to Congress for generous treatment, for decent quarters, and for repeal of the law permitting construction of only temporary shelters on the frontier.   To overcome local pride which might obstruct any movement to abandon specific posts, Sherman recommended the appointment of boards of officers to review the problems of coastal defense and inland posts and determine which should be maintained and which posts might be disposed of by sale. If the money thus obtained could be used to build durable barracks on permanent sites, economy, he argued, would be promoted.   Such construction would bring Army barracks in line with what was happening

---

[133] (1) *War Department General Orders, 1878*, GO 24, 18 May 1878. (2) RG 92, OQMG Letter Book, 1880–A, General and Misc., p. 339 (Meigs to Officer in Charge of Education of the Army, 6 Apr 1880); *ibid.*, 1881–E, pp. 2508–10 (Same to same, 2 Nov 1881).

[134] RG 92, OQMG Letter Book, 1881–B, pp. 703–04 (Meigs to F. T. Hodgdon, 18 Feb 1881); *ibid.*, 1881–C, 1266–67 (Meigs to Capt. Arthur McArthur, 14 Mar 1881).

all over the United States, "where old log cabins are giving place to the more lasting brick houses of the farmer and mechanic." [135]

The law on building temporary huts was not altered, and Congress continued parsimonious in dealing with the general appropriations for Army expenses. While the Quartermaster General found that he could not persuade the Committee on Appropriations to increase the annual funds for barracks and quarters, still by playing on local interests and enlisting the influence of senators and members of the House of Representatives, the Army obtained a number of special appropriations, generally for $100,000, for the construction of specific new posts beginning in the late 1870's.[136] The trend toward concentration in permanent garrisons began, and Congress authorized the President to designate and place under the control of the Secretary of the Interior the lands of any military reservation that became useless for military purposes.

General appropriations for barracks and quarters, however, continued to be inadequate, usually ranging from $650,000 to $750,000. Since the buildings at many posts were the outgrowth of temporary quarters, poorly constructed to begin with and unsatisfactory even after they were enlarged and altered, they required constant repairs to keep them inhabitable. The annual drain for their maintenance left only a small part of the appropriation available for the erection of new buildings that the Quartermaster's Department sought to construct of stone, brick, or other durable material, according to plans carefully drawn and including the most approved sanitary requirements. Until the end of this period, Quartermasters General continued to appeal for adequate appropriations.[137]

Surplus Supplies and Procurement

Neither transportation problems nor construction projects wholly absorbed the attention of the Quartermaster's Department in the post-Civil War years. The broad field of procurement and its problems also demanded consideration. When the Civil War ended, the large wartime procurement of Quartermaster supplies ground to a halt as quickly as Meigs could send out orders. Obviously, with the Volunteer army promptly demobilized and the maximum strength of the Regular Army fixed for many years at about 25,000 men, the surpluses of Quartermaster supplies on hand at the depots obviated the necessity for procuring many

---

[135] *Annual Report of the Secretary of War, 1881,* I, 35–36 (Sherman's Rpt, 3 Nov 1881, appended); see also *ibid., 1877,* I, 63 (Pope's Rpt, 15 Sep 1877, appended).

[136] RG 92, OQMG Letter Book, 1879–D, General and Misc., p. 2315 (Meigs to General of the Army, 21 Oct 1879).

[137] See *Annual Report of the Quartermaster General, 1890,* p. 4; *1893,* p. 10; *1894,* p. 6.

items for some years to come.   This was not true for such perishables as forage and fuel, but economy dictated that, at every post where it was possible, these supplies were to be provided by troop labor.   On the other hand, the Quartermaster's Department did not have to procure clothing and equipage.   Clothing stocks required no replenishment for 5 years, and the textile supply was so large that the first cloth was not procured until 1877.[138]   With the restoration of peace, many supplies were obtained by requisition on the general depots.

Return to Contract Procedure

War had necessitated many open-market purchases, but peace led Meigs to emphasize anew that supplies unobtainable at depots were to be procured by contracts awarded to the lowest bidders.   It was Quartermaster policy to purchase supplies locally at the places where they were needed, provided they could be obtained at as reasonable rates as elsewhere, taking into account the cost of transportation.   This policy particularly applied to forage, lumber, and other products of the country in which the posts and depots were located.   As settlement moved westward, the Subsistence Department followed the same policy.   Increasingly, commissaries directed their efforts toward obtaining supplies, such as fresh beef, flour, and other commodities, from producers near the points of consumption.[139]   Although the Subsistence Department encouraged such local procurement, the main purchasing depots for subsistence continued to be at New York, Baltimore, Boston, Louisville, St. Louis, Chicago, and New Orleans, to which San Francisco and Portland, Ore., were added in the 1870's as production on the Pacific Coast made subsistence supplies available there.   As far as such Quartermaster stores as hardware and other manufactured articles were concerned, they still could be obtained cheaper at St. Louis or Chicago than at any western post or depot.[140]

To promote a more economical administration of the procurement of supplies, the War Department changed its contract procedure in the fall of 1867, largely through Meigs' efforts, to give greater uniformity and system.   In the past, the subordinate officers of the Quartermaster's Department, on duty at the various posts and depots where stores were consumed, made the contracts for Quartermaster supplies.   Under the

[138] *Annual Report of the Quartermaster General, 1871,* p. 10; *ibid., 1877,* p. 25.
[139] RG 192, CGS, Letters to SW, 1866–72, pp. 99; 232 (Annual Rpts. CG of Subsistence, 19 Oct 1868; 20 Oct 1869).
[140] RG 92, OQMG Letter Book, vol. 96, pp. 69–70 (Acting QMG Rucker to Donaldson, 12 Apr 1867); *ibid.,* vol. 99, p. 205 (Same to Easton, 25 Mar 1868).

new regulation, all contracts for Subsistence and Quartermaster supplies and services for the troops within any geographical command, except those for clothing and equipage, were made on the basis of advertisements and proposals received by the chief quartermasters and chief commissaries of the military departments or districts and submitted by them to the commanding generals, upon whom rested the responsibility of making the awards as well as causing the advertisements to be made.[141]   Thus, Quartermaster and Commissary officers executed the details of contracting for supplies, but commanders made the final decisions, on the information collected by the staff officers.   When larger quantities of supplies were needed to stock general depots, or transportation contracts were made over routes affecting more than one general command, chief quartermasters and chief commissaries transmitted all related contract papers to the chief of the bureau concerned for his decision under the general supervision of the Secretary of War.

Although Meigs believed that, under the law, the Secretary of War ultimately had to be responsible for all administration in regard to contracts and expenditures of the appropriations of the Army, he nevertheless had always endeavored to give control over the awarding of contracts, on which their operation might absolutely depend for success, to the generals commanding troops or military divisions and departments. Meigs maintained that he found this practice conducive to efficiency, economy, and harmony of administration.[142]

Conflict Over Contract Control

Harmony was not noticeably promoted, however, in the persistent conflict between staff and line that was as apparent in the fields of contracts and expenditures as it was in construction.   Ignoring the control he exercised over contracts and staff officers in his department, Brig. Gen. John Pope, commanding the Department of the Missouri, made a sweeping denunciation of the over-concentration of every detail of Army administration in Washington and of the supply staffs that "absolutely control the supplies of the Army to the smallest article, and regulate the manner of its transportation and delivery to the Army."   He charged that many of the staff officers, although holding commissions in the Army, had never served a day with troops, "and are as ignorant practically of the condition, the circumstances, and the surroundings of the Army, and of the country in which the largest part of it is serving, as they are of such

[141] *War Department General Orders, 1867*, GO 97, 12 Nov 1867.
[142] RG 92, OQMG Letter Book, 1879–C, General and Misc., p. 1597 (Meigs to Col. Rufus Saxton, 30 Apr 1879); *ibid.*, 1879-B, pp. 1024–28 (Meigs to AG, 21 May 1879).

military service in the Chinese Empire." Pope did not hesitate to declare that concentration of Army administration in Washington had reached a point "where every sort of fraud is made possible." [143] For his part, the Commissary General of Subsistence found that parts of the general order on contract procedure had been so construed by some division and department commanders as to relieve him of a portion of the duties assigned to him by law. [144] The order remained in effect, however, until 1879 when a board of officers made changes in the control of contracts that relieved commanding generals of all responsibility, thereby fanning anew the staff-line controversy and causing General Schofield to "attack the Staff as encroachers upon Military Command." [145] Meigs considered the changes injudicious and informed the General of the Army that haste had resulted in publishing the new order before it had been submitted to the heads of bureaus and the General of the Army for criticism and revision. Through Meigs' efforts, control and responsibility in making contracts for supplies within their proper commands were restored to the commanding generals. Great care was taken, however, to restate the responsibilities of the Secretary of War as well as the relations of staff officers to their commanders. Meigs hoped that this revision would tend to end the "constant and annoying disagreement between line and staff." [146]

To the commanding officer, the problem of expenditures was simple. The Secretary of War made his recommendations for the War Department appropriations. When made, the appropriations ought to be turned over to the proper bonded officers of the Army to be expended for the purposes for which they were made, under the direct orders of the General of the Army and his subordinates in command. Thus, every dollar would be spent precisely for the purpose for which it was asked, and, according to General Pope, estimates would decrease surprisingly. [147] To the supply chief, the problem was complicated by several factors. The annual estimates of the Quartermaster's Department were based

[143] Pope's letter, addressed to Judge M. F. Force, 13 March 1876, at the time Alphonso Taft was appointed Secretary of War, is reproduced in the Burnside Report. Senate *Report* No. 555, 45th Cong., 3d sess., pp. 116–19. (2) His letter, also published in the *North American Review* and the *Army and Navy Journal*, brought prompt reaction from both Meigs and Commissary General R. Macfeely. RG 92, OQMG Letter Book, 1878-B, General and Misc., pp. 1276–81 (Meigs to SW, 8 May 1878). RG 192, CGS, Letters to SW, 1873–79, pp. 350–55 (Macfeely to SW, 28 May 1878).

[144] RG 192, CGS, Letters to SW, 1873–79, pp. 202–11 (Macfeely to SW, 8 Nov 1876).

[145] (1) *War Department General Orders, 1879*, GO 10, 3 Mar 1879. (2) RG 92, OQMG Letter Book, 1879-C, General and Misc., pp. 1604–05 (Meigs to Sherman, 1 Jun 1879).

[146] (1) *War Department General Orders, 1878; 1880*, GO 72, 14 Jul 1879; GO 40, 22 May 1880. (2) RG 92, OQMG Letter Book, 1880-A, General and Misc., pp. 506–08 (Meigs to McDowell, 23 Apr 1880).

[147] Senate *Report* No. 555, 45th Cong., 3d sess., p. 119.

upon experience of the actual requirements of the service during past years. They were made out in the fall of the year and attempted to declare, in anticipation, the wants of the military service for the whole of the year, which did not begin until 10 months after they were presented and that ended nearly 2 years after their presentation. Submitted to the Secretary of War, these estimates were sometimes reduced by him before transmittal to Congress, whose members, in the interests of enforcing economy, might still further reduce them in the appropriation bill they passed.

Restrictive Legislation Governing Expenditures

Not only were supply operations restricted by inadequate appropriations but they were also hampered by the rigidity of the legislation governing expenditures. Since the Quartermaster's Department had first been established as a bureau in Washington in 1818, it had been possible to transfer moneys appropriated for one branch of expenditures to another within the same department.[148] In 1868, however, Congress repealed that law and provided that funds could be used only for the purpose for which they had been appropriated.[149] This restriction often caused great embarrassment to quartermasters. Their funds came to them from the Secretary of War upon the basis of monthly estimates, transmitted through department and division headquarters where they were revised by commanding officers with the advice of their chief quartermasters, then forwarded to Washington for examination in the office of the Quartermaster General, and finally submitted for the Secretary's approval, attention being called to any apparently excessive expenditures.[150] Since the exigencies of the service were constantly changing, a quartermaster might find, for example, that, having requested and received funds to erect temporary shelter for troops, he really needed transportation money because the troops were on the move and not going into quarters. Yet, under the law, he could not use sheltering funds for transportation purposes, nor could he resort to the use of credit because the law forbade any expenditure beyond the appropriation.

As the fiscal year drew to a close, some officers of the Department would have expended all the funds in their hands belonging to specific appropriations, while others would still have a surplus. This necessitated transfers of funds from one class of officers to another, who often were

---

[148] The law had been on the statute books since 1809. 2 *Stat.* 535–36 (Mar 3, 1809).
[149] 15 *Stat.* 36 (Feb 12, 1868).
[150] RG 92, OQMG Letter Book, 1872–A, General and Misc., pp. 87–90 (Meigs to SW, 25 Jan 1873).

stationed far apart. Such transfers would be made until all accounts were paid or the appropriation was exhausted. Unfortunately, delays in the payment of accounts occurred under this system that tended to increase the expenses of the Department.

Other restrictions that Congress placed on the use of appropriations that were intended to promote economy resulted only in inconvenience and increased supply costs. In 1870, Congress enacted legislation that made appropriations applicable only to the service of the fiscal year for which they were appropriated.[151] To end transportation contracts on 30 June, for example, in the midst of the season of active troop movements, of river navigation, and of transportation on the Plains, was both inconvenient and costly. If, as sometimes happened, appropriations were not made until the fiscal year began, new contracts could not be made and put into operation until the greater part of the transportation season had ended. In consequence, the Department often had to resort to temporary and irregular arrangements that entailed higher costs. The Subsistence Department, confronted with the necessity of supplying distant posts that required early preparations, unsuccessfully sought to have a clause inserted in Army appropriations bills providing that $300,000 of the money appropriated for that Department might be applied by the Commissary General of Subsistence before 1 July to the purchase of supplies required for advance shipments to posts on the upper Missouri and to the distant posts in Texas and Arizona.[152]

Previously, money appropriated for any fiscal year had been available until expended and the work of supplying the Army had gone on without interruption. Under the act of 1870, all appropriations ceased to be available except for payment of services already rendered, or for settlement of contracts previously made, and the work of the Quartermaster's Department was liable to be seriously delayed and embarrassed during the interval needed to advertise, execute, and put in operation contracts for the new fiscal year.

The act of 1870 had other effects that complicated operations because under the law, officers were required to keep separate accounts for each appropriation. In the past, quartermasters had estimated for the amount of funds they would need, the money being sent to them in a lump sum and used to pay all proper expenses until exhausted. When they submitted their accounts to the Quartermaster General and the Treasury Department, the latter analyzed them and entered on the Treasury books the amounts chargeable against the several appropriations noted on the vouchers. In 1836, there had been only four appropriations

[151] 16 *Stat.* 251 (Jul 12, 1870).
[152] RG 192, CGS, Letters to SW, 1873–79, p. 103 (10 Oct 1874).

for the Department but by 1870 there were nine, with some quarter-masters drawing from all of them and therefore required to keep nine separate accounts.[153]   Meigs complained that

the necessity of keeping, whenever possible, in the hands of each disbursing-officer, or subject to his draft, a considerable balance of each and every appropriation which he is likely to use, instead of a general balance applicable to all, increases the amount of money lying idle, locked up in the depositories, and subject to draft by disbursing officers, and thus increases the remittances to them and lowers the balances in the Treasury available for remittance to the posts where actually needed.[154]

A bill to simplify the accounts of disbursing officers was urgently needed. A committee prepared such a bill but no legislation resulted, and, year after year, the Quartermaster General urged the need for relief, not only for the disbursing officers but also for those in the Washington office who examined accounts and returns.[155]

One more illustration will suffice to show the difficulties under which the supply bureaus operated.   In 1872, Congress provided that the proceeds of sales of old material, condemned stores, or other public property of any kind had to be covered into the Treasury as miscellaneous receipts and could be made available for use of the Department only under a new appropriation.[156]   Even the proceeds of property sold to other Departments and bureaus were not exempt from this provision.   The loss of the proceeds from such sales had the effect of reducing the appropriation, since supplies disposed of by sale could not be replaced by purchases made with funds derived from such sales as had been the practice in the past. Thus, in one fiscal year, the Quartermaster's Department lost about $1 million from the sale of old property.

The Subsistence Department was at a particular disadvantage under this law, for it handled extremely perishable supplies, yet the sale of any damaged subsistence to prevent loss to the government resulted in loss to the Department's appropriation.   Subsistence stores might be placed at a post to meet the needs of a garrison for 6 months, but, at the end of half that time, the garrison might move to a distant point, leaving a 3 months' subsistence supply.   Because the supplies were not needed

---

[153] The nine appropriations disbursed by the Department were regular supplies, incidental expenses, cavalry and artillery horses; barracks and quarters; transportation of the army, clothing and equipage, stores, erection and repairs of hospitals, and national cemeteries.

[154] RG 92, OQMG Letter Book, 1873–A, General and Misc., pp. 87–90 (Meigs to SW, 25 Jan 1873).

[155] (1) House *Report* No. 87, 42nd Cong., 3d sess., pp. 16–18. (2) *Annual Reports of the Quartermaster General, 1874*, pp. 6–7. (3) RG 92, OQMG Letter Book, 1880-E, General and Misc., pp. 2702–03 (QMG to SW, 14 Dec 1880)

[156] 17 *Stat.* 83 (May 8, 1872).

at the post and it would cost more to transport them than to buy fresh stores, the supplies would be sold, the proceeds going into the Treasury and being diverted from the appropriation. Called upon to succor starving Indians and replace supplies lost by emigrants or needed by railroad and land-surveying parties, the Subsistence Department sold supplies, or, in the case of the Indians, charged the value of those issues to the Indian Department. In these cases, too, the proceeds of sales were lost to the Department. Both the Quartermaster General and the Commissary General urged the Secretary of War to seek repeal of the law. In 1875, it was amended, but only to the extent of excepting subsistence sales from the provision requiring that the proceeds of all sales of public property be covered into the Treasury.[157]

Despite administrative difficulties created by legislation and assertions by some line officers that they could provide for the troops more efficiently and cheaper, the Quartermaster's Department did not fail in its supply responsibilities, not even when fiscal year 1877 closed on 30 June without congressional action on an appropriation bill for the next year.[158] Most supplies required for the Army were purchased under contract, the amount increasing as the surplus stocks of the Civil War were used up or deteriorated with the years to the point where they were condemned and sold.

Resort to Government Manufacture

Surplus stocks and the economy motive led to efforts to supply at least some of the items needed by the troops through government manufacture. In May 1873, the Chief of Ordnance suggested that his Department, having on hand a large stock of good and valuable material unused in its shops, could supply such wagons as the Quartermaster's Department needed. With the approval of the Secretary of War, a board, consisting of officers from the two departments, took under consideration the problem of revision of specifications as well as the transfer of responsibility for supplying Army wagons, ambulances, and their equipment from the Quartermaster's Department to the Ordnance Department.[159] Meigs saw some need for improvement of Army wagons, particularly the introduc-

---

[157] (1) RG 192, CGS, Letters to SW, 1873–79, p. 102 (10 Oct 1874). (2) 18 *Stat.* 410 Mar 3, 1875).
[158] (1) The appropriation act for fiscal year 1878 was not passed until November 1877. 20 *Stat.* 1 ff. Provision for the previous year had been delayed until 24 July 1876. 19 *Stat.* 97. (2) RG 92, OQMG Letter Book, 1876-B, General and Misc., pp. 1268–70 (Meigs to SW, 30 Jun 1876).
[159] (1) RG 92, OQMG Letter Book, 1873–A, General and Misc., pp. 289–90 (Meigs to SW, 26 May 1873). (2) RG 107, SW, Letters Sent, vol. 93, p. 677 (Special Order, 2 Jun 1873).

tion of metal hubs, but he rejected as administratively unsound the proposed transfer of responsibility and was unalterably opposed to government manufacture of articles readily provided by the facilities of private enterprise at reasonable rates.[160]   The Secretary made no transfer, and, since supplies of wagons on hand were ample for Army needs, no purchases were required so that the possibility of manufacture by the Ordnance Department was dropped.

In the summer of 1875, the stock of wagons had fallen so low that the Secretary of War authorized a supply of 200 to meet current demands and any sudden requirements.   At that time, Meigs was in Europe on a special assignment to study the organization of the military staffs of the European armies.   Bvt. Maj. Gen. Rufus Ingalls was serving as Acting Quartermaster General.   He obviously did not share Meigs' opposition to government manufacture because he proposed to have the Department produce the wagons.[161]   The Department erected shops for the manufacture of Army wagons on land leased near the Jeffersonville Depot, purchased material, and produced 109 wagons, at an average cost of $129.50 each.   When Meigs returned, he promptly closed the wagon factory, stored the material, and made a contract for the delivery of 50 wagons at $92.50 each.[162]

If Meigs' prudence had scotched government production of wagons at a Quartermaster depot, government manufacture of Quartermaster items soon was being advocated elsewhere, despite his fears that such a course would arouse the hostility of workers and private factory owners. In 1874, Congress had authorized the establishment of a military prison at Fort Leavenworth.[163]   It specifically provided for the production of Army shoes by prison labor.   In 1877, the Secretary of War directed that if the Quartermaster's Department found it practicable to manufacture at the prison not only shoes and boots but also other articles that it furnished to the Army, it was to provide all the necessary materials and tools, employ and pay civilian instructors and inspectors, and be responsible for the shipment of the manufactured items.[164]   The rapid develop-

---

[160] RG 92, OQMG Letter Book, 1873-A, General and Misc., pp. 432–39 (Meigs to Recorder of Board, 11 Jul 1873); ibid., 1873–B, General and Misc., pp. 991–96 (Meigs to SW, 22 Aug 1873).

[161] Ibid., 1875–A, General and Misc., pp. 446–47 (Ingalls to DQMG Saxton, 13 Jul 1875).

[162] (1) Ibid., 1876–B, pp. 1050–51 (Meigs to Lt. Col. J. A. Ekin, 23 May 1876); ibid., 1876-A, pp. 482–84 (Meigs to SW, 9 Aug 1876). (2) Annual Report of the Quartermaster General, 1876, p. 19.

[163] Originally authorized to be established at Rock Island, Ill., in 1873, the prison was transferred to Fort Leavenworth in 1874. 17 Stat. 582 (Mar 3, 1873); 18 Stat. 48 (May 21, 1874).

[164] War Department General Orders, 1877, GO 12, 19 Feb 1877.

ment of shoe manufacturing at the prison, followed shortly by a proposal
to produce barrack chairs there upon their being authorized for issue to
posts, again aroused Meigs' apprehensions.[165]   The latter were not shared
by Congress.   In 1879, it enacted legislation authorizing the Secretary
of War to cause such Army supplies as could be economically and properly manufactured at Leavenworth to be produced at the prison.[166]
Meigs did not change his views on government manufacture and remained
unconvinced of its economy, but, under this sanction, manufactures at
Fort Leavenworth were expanded to include not only shoes, boots, and
chairs, but also harness, kettles, pans, and other articles described as
"stove furniture."[167]

Introduction and Production of New Clothing

The large surplus stocks of clothing on hand at Quartermaster depots
precluded the possibility of introducing any changes in the uniforms of
the soldier in the immediate postwar years, though a demand for a new
uniform began to be made by 1869.   Moreover, older soldiers were convinced that the clothing issued to them before the war had been better
made than the garments they received in the postwar years.   Meigs,
however, thought their complaint was "a good deal like our grandfathers'
lament over the want of the fine peaches they had in their remote
youth."[168]   By 1872, depletion as well as deterioration of clothing stocks
permitted a change in the uniform to be ordered and, by the fall of the
following year, nearly all the troops had been supplied with the new
uniform.[169]

By that time, the old knapsacks, made of painted cloth, had also
become unfit for use by chemical decomposition, which turned black
paint soft and sticky.   Since new equipment would have to be procured,
Meigs recommended that it be improved.   The Ordnance Department
was already making a large part of the leather equipment of the soldier,

---

[165] RG 92, OQMG Letter Book, 1878-A, General and Misc., pp. 141–42 (Meigs to SW,
18 Jan 1878); *ibid.*, 1878-B, pp. 871–74 (Same to same, 11 Mar 1878).

[166] 20 *Stat.* 389 (Mar 3, 1879).

[167] *Annual Report of the Quartermaster General, 1880*, p. 111; *ibid., 1885*, p. 168.

[168] (1) RG 92, OQMG Letter Book, vol. 102, pp. 171–75 (Meigs to Bvt. Brig. Gen. John
H. Palmer, 24 Apr 1869).   (2) Not only the quality but the suitability of Army clothing
was questioned.   The hat was criticized as affording no warmth in winter and giving no
protection from the sun in summer, and the uniform coats were held to be so wadded and
tight-fitting as to render excessive muscular action almost impracticable.   RG 92, OQMG
Consolidated Correspondence File, Box 1171 (Lt. Col. Alfred A. Woodhull, "A Medical Report upon the Uniform and Clothing of the Soldiers of the United States Army," 15 April
1868).   Hereafter briefly cited as Woodhull Rpt.

[169] (1) *Annual Report of the Quartermaster General, 1872*, p. 12, *ibid., 1873*, p. 55.
(2) See *War Department General Orders*, GO 92, 26 Oct 1872, for a description.

7TH U.S. CAVALRY, 1867

and Meigs suggested that knapsacks, haversacks, and canteens also be furnished by that Department. This transfer was accomplished at the close of 1871.[170]

The production of the new clothing followed procedures that had been practiced for more than half a century.[171] Manufacturing operations at the Philadelphia Depot had been suspended at the close of the war and resumed only to a limited extent until the new uniform was adopted. The depot's production was supplemented by manufacturing operations at the Jeffersonville Depot and at San Francisco.[172] According to the Quartermaster General, the clothing was now so well cut and made that there was no need for company tailors to remake garments as they had been accustomed to do in the past. Nevertheless, requisitions for larger sizes than were needed by the soldiers continued to be made in order to permit the remaking of garments to their measurements. The effect was to exhaust the supply of larger garments, leaving an improper distribution of sizes on hand at the depots.[173]

During the Civil War, garments had been made in four sizes. This number was increased to five in the postwar period, but the distribution of sizes still fell far short of that provided by commercial houses. Determined to provide the soldier with better fitting garments, the Department attacked the problem in two ways. On the one hand, it permitted the issue of unmade garments—overcoats, dress coats, blouses, and trousers—charging them at actual cost to the soldier, and, on the recommendation of the Quartermaster General, an additional $5 was credited to each recruit's clothing money to pay for the expense of altering or fitting his clothing. On the other hand, the Department restudied the problem of sizes and, as a result, increased the number of sizes from five to twelve for trousers and to six for blouses.[174] The increased distribution of sizes made possible a better fitting of garments, but unmade clothing could still be requisitioned throughout this period. In 1893, the Quartermaster General condemned this practice; it produced unmilitary effects. In one company, he charged, "both close-fitting and loose blouses and coats" might be seen, while individual tastes in trousers ran "the gamut

---

[170] (1) *Annual Report of the Quartermaster General, 1872*, pp. 10–11. (2) *War Department General Orders, 1871*, GO 75, 26 Dec 1871.

[171] See *supra*, pp. 253, 348, 350.

[172] Clothing production at San Francisco developed after 1877. That development was in accordance with the law requiring preference to be given to the products of the Pacific Coast in purchasing supplies to be used by the troops on the Coast. (1) *Annual Report of the Quartermaster General, 1877*, pp. 23–24; *ibid., 1878*, pp. 17, 79. (2) 14 *Stat.* 92 (Jul 13, 1866).

[173] *Annual Report of the Quartermaster General, 1877*, p. 24.

[174] (1) *Ibid., 1883*, p. 57; *ibid., 1884*, p. 318. (2) *War Department General Orders, 1883*, GO 62, 4 Aug 1863; GO 66, 25 Sep 1883.

from the skin-tight variety, with swelling "hoodlum' or 'bowery' bottoms, to those of exaggerated, sailor-like proportions." [175]

In the postwar years, the troops made demands for seasonal clothing. Lt. Col. Alfred A. Woodhull, an assistant surgeon of the Medical Department, pointed out in 1868 that "the system of proportioning the clothing to the actual temperature is practised by every community except the military." As a practical solution to the problem, he recommended adoption of a loose-fitting outer uniform and use of the layering principle, practiced by both the Chinese and Maine lumbermen, to permit an increase or decrease of undergarments according to the season. [176] The layering principle in Army clothing found no application until World War II.

Special winter clothing to protect men standing guard at posts on the wind-swept western plains was a necessity. Without an appropriation for clothing, however, Meigs could only suggest that the troops should equip themselves with suitable protective garments, such as buffalo overcoats and overshoes and wool-lined, buckskin mittens by purchasing them out of company funds. Such had been the practice in prewar years, the garments being retained as company property and used as a common stock when the men went on guard duty. [177] As soon as funds became available, the Department proposed to provide cold-weather garments. Overshoes and mittens were issued and charged to the soldiers at cost price. Buffalo overcoats were provided only when their need was certified by the commander of the military department, and usually throughout this period they remained the property of the government. When the scarcity of buffaloes made such overcoats prohibitive in price, the Department substituted blanket-lined canvas coats. [178]

The Department approached the issue of summer clothing with more reluctance. Summer cotton uniforms had been issued to the troops until 1850 when, largely on the basis of experiments conducted by medical officers of the French army in Africa, a board of American officers had recommended and won approval for the use of a woolen uniform exclusively. The postwar request for a summer uniform found no support among Quartermaster officers or from the Surgeon General of the Army, who insisted that the use of light woolen fabrics was most conducive to the preservation of health in warm climates. [179]

---

[175] *Annual Report of the Quartermaster General, 1893,* p. 5.

[176] RG 92, OQMG Consolidated Correspondence File, Box 1171 (Woodhull Rpt.).

[177] RG 92, OQMG Letter Book, vol. 106, p. 474 (Meigs to Sherman, 23 Sep 1870).

[178] (1) *War Department General Orders, 1871,* GO 9, 8 Feb 1871. (2) *Annual Report of the Quartermaster General, 1884,* p. 21.

[179] (1) RG 92, OQMG Letter Book, vol. 89, pp. 106–07 (Meigs to Perry, 11 Jan 1866), vol. 91, pp. 227–29 (Perry to Meigs, 18 Apr 1866). (2) *Annual Report of the Quartermaster General, 1886,* p. 192.

FATIGUE WEAR IN THE 1880's

Requests for a summer uniform continued to be made and, in 1879, a board of officers approved adoption of such a uniform. Meigs disapproved of the recommendation on the basis of the increased costs that would result, and the General of the Army also disapproved. Meigs preferred that in hot weather the commanding officers of posts be authorized to allow their officers and men to use the uniform blue flannel sack coat with white pants and straw hats that they could buy from local traders. This was a practice that had prevailed for many years.[180] After 20 years of requests, a few garments, made of cotton duck, were sent for experimental issue to troops in Texas in May 1886. They gave so much satisfaction that the Quartermaster General recommended and the Secretary of War approved their issue to all troops in Texas. Authority was subsequently granted to supply such clothing to troops in the Departments of Arizona and Missouri.[181] Issue of a summer uniform to all the troops was not accomplished before the Spanish-American War.

When Samuel B. Holabird became Quartermaster General in the summer of 1883, one of the first acts of his administration was to devise a suit of canvas clothing, similar to the working clothes worn by miners in the western states, to be worn by soldiers on fatigue duty. Such duty was very hard on uniform clothing, and while the clothing allowance of

[180] (1) *War Department General Orders, 1879,* GO 76, 23 Jul 1879. (2) Even in 1868, the practice of wearing light straw hats in warm weather was so common that a medical report on Army clothing recommended that formal authority be granted for the use of such hats. RG 92, OQMG Consolidated Correspondence File, Box 1171 (Woodhull Rpt.).
[181] *Annual Report of the Quartermaster General, 1888,* pp. 17; 236 ff.

some posts was ample, at others it was inadequate because of the nature of the extra work required. Using shelter tents in storage, Holabird had the material dyed a dark brown and fashioned into fatigue coats and trousers. The adoption of these garments, issued without cost to all enlisted men on fatigue and extra duty, met a long felt want in the Army.[182]   However slowly changes were made, the Department gradually moved in the direction of providing more comfortable clothing, adapted to particular needs.

Ration Changes

Improvements in the provision and preparation of rations added to the soldier's well-being but were effected only after persistent demands and much delay.   Construction of the transcontinental railroads made it unnecessary to place and keep at western posts such large quantities of rations as had been required when supply had depended on the arrival of wagon trains, dispatched only at special seasons of the year.   More frequent deliveries by railroads provided fresher supplies that were more palatable to the troops.[183]   During the first few years after the war, this was about the only observable improvement.   No changes were made in the ration issued to the troops, though the Commissary General suggested that it could probably be improved by the introduction of a greater variety of components.   He later proposed that the problem be brought before a board of officers then preparing a system of regulations for the Army.[184]

The provision of bread for the Army often provoked criticism, usually from officers of the Medical Department who maintained that the ration was insufficient in amount. It was not the size of the ration that was at fault so much as the way in which the flour was converted into bread. The Subsistence Department issued only flour—18 ounces daily to the soldier as a component of his ration; it was made into soft bread by the post bakery over which the Department exercised no control. For his flour, the soldier received 18 ounces of bread, but his flour would have yielded more bread and a considerable saving could thus be made on the flour ration.   It was estimated that each soldier lost about 1 percent per day in flour.[185]   Under regulations, any food saved from the ration could be sold, the proceeds to be used for the purchase of other subsistence items at original cost from local producers or from the Subsistence Department.   Thus, in effect, the savings could be used to intro-

---

[182] *Ibid., 1884*, pp. 21, 309–10.

[183] RG 192, CGS, Letters to SW, 1866–1872, p. 99 (Annual Rpt, 19 Oct 1867); pp. 517–20 (Ltr, 5 Jun 1871).

[184] *Ibid.*, pp. 369–80 (Annual Rpt. 20 Oct 1869); pp. 533–34 (Ltr, 8 Aug 1871).

[185] *Ibid.*, 1882–84, p. 4 (Ltr, 19 Dec 1882).

duce greater variety into the established ration through the purchase of dairy products, seasonings, and fresh fruits and vegetables.

The Commissary General of Subsistence was convinced that no better system could be devised for feeding the troops, "none that would be more elastic, more economical, or better suited to our service and the necessities of our soldiers." [186] What was needed, he urged, was a modification of regulations to prevent the post bakery from being converted into a money-making machine to support bands, libraries, schools, gymnasiums, and chapels at posts. Funds obtained from ration savings were being diverted to the support of such projects instead of being used to introduce greater variety in the soldier's diet. In effect, the soldier was not getting the whole of the ration allowed him.[187] As long as such desirable post projects had to be obtained without funds from Congress, funds from ration savings would continue to be diverted to such purposes.

During most of the years between the Civil War and the Spanish-American War, the Subsistence Department considered the ration allowance ample and made few changes.[188] Greater variety was introduced by a growing list of substitute items that could be furnished in lieu of the standard issue. Thus, mutton or dried, pickled, or fresh fish could be issued instead of fresh beef in 1879. Canned fresh or corned beef, first used as part of the travel ration in 1878, was added to the regular ration as a substitute item 10 years later.[189]

The ration did not provide for the issue of potatoes, onions, or fresh vegetables because of their extremely perishable nature and the impracticability of furnishing them at all seasons. In any case, they could be cultivated in post gardens or purchased from local producers with the funds obtained under the ration savings system. By 1890, however, the

[186] *Ibid.*, 1880–81, pp. 614–15 (Ltr, 1 Jun 1881).

[187] (1) *Ibid.* See also *ibid.*, 1866–72, p. 370 (Annual Rpt, 20 Oct 1869); p. 533 (Ltr, 8 Aug 1871); *ibid.*, 1882–42, pp. 3–5 (Ltr, 19 Dec 1882). (2) The extent to which the soldier was affected is well illustrated in the returns of subsistence stores from David's Island, N.Y., where the savings were extremely large in 1883. For the first 3 months of that year, the money value of the savings purchased by the Subsistence Department amounted to $1,932.48, or more than 44 percent of the money value of the same articles issued in that period at the recruiting depot on David's Island by the Department. In other words, nearly one-half of the subsistence issued, excluding beef, was sold as savings instead of being consumed by the men. *Ibid.*, 1882–84, pp. 156–57 (Ltr, 19 Apr 1883).

[188] The impression that the soldier was liberally supplied was generally accepted, but Maj. T. A. McParlin, assistant surgeon at Fort Leavenworth, was of another opinion. Making a comparison of the American and British ration in 1875, he concluded that the American ration was lower in energy value and especially deficient in fresh vegetables and milk. His tabulation of the nutritive value of various diets caused him to place the Army ration only slightly ahead of the famine diet of the Lancashire laborers in 1862. Samuel C. Prescott, "A Survey of Rationing and Subsistence in the United States Army, 1775 to 1940," chap. IV, pp. 19–24. This is a manuscript prepared for the National Defense Research Committee, OSRD, in 1944. On file in QM Historian's Office.

[189] (1) *War Department General Orders, 1879*, GO 6, 7 Feb 1879; GO 16, 10 Mar 1879. (2) RG 192, CGS, Letters to SW, 1886–88, pp. 599–600 (Macfeely to SW, 19 Jan 1888).

general demand for their inclusion in the ration induced the Commissary General of Subsistence to recommend that they be added. By law, one pound of vegetables was added to the ration, the proportion of fresh potatoes, onions, cabbage, beets, turnips, carrots, and squash, or of canned tomatoes being determined by the Secretary of War.[190] With increased knowledge of nutrition, greater attention was at last beginning to be paid to a well balanced diet for the troops.

The finest rations in the world could be spoilt by poor cooks. To improve the quality of the food served, the Subsistence Department published and distributed to the Army pamphlets on bread-making and on Army cooking.[191] Any long-range improvement, however, depended on getting better cooks. To encourage this objective, an Army board on cooking proposed that extra compensation be allowed to company cooks. Neither this proposal nor the repeated recommendations of the Commissary General for the enlistment of cooks and bakers for the Army produced any result.[192]

On the other hand, the Quartermaster's Department was successful in introducing a system of common mess halls for enlisted men in place of the former method of messing by companies. Tried first at the recruiting depot at David's Island in 1888, the experiment proved so successful that common mess halls were adopted at a number of the larger posts by 1893. Their use had the advantage of providing better cooking than in the company mess, pleasanter service of the food, and withal greater economy in preparation. Then the Quartermaster General joined the Commissary General in recommending that Congress provide for the employment of trained cooks so that better and more scientific cooking might be introduced in the consolidated mess in order to promote the health and well being of the soldier.[193] Training for cooks was not provided, however, until schools for cooks and bakers were established in 1905.

Administrative Developments

Administration of the responsibilities for transportation, construction, and the procurement of forage, horses and mules, clothing and equipment, and general supplies had to be carried out by a dwindling

[190] (1) RG 192, CGS, Letters To SW, 1889–90, pp. 265–66 (Ltr, 24 Jan 1890). (2) 26 Stat. 158 (Act of June 16, 1890). (3) War Department General Orders, 1890, GO 78, 25 Jul 1890.
[191] (1) RG 92, OQMG Consolidated Correspondence File, Box 773 (Macfeely to Surgeon General of the Army, 11 Dec 1877); (Rpt of Board on Army Cooking, 3 Feb 1879). (2) RG 192, CGS, Letters to SW, 1880–81, p. 470 (Macfeely to WD Chief Clerk, 19 Jan 1881).
[192] (1) RG 92, OQMG Consolidated Correspondence File, Box 773 (Board Rpt. 3 Feb 1879): (2) RG 192, CGS, Letters to SW, 1889–90, p. 283 (Macfeely to SW, 5 Feb 1890).
[193] Annual Report of the Quartermaster General, 1888, pp. 5–6; 1889, p. 23; 1893, pp. 10–11.

staff of Quartermaster officers.[194]   Reduction of the Army to a peacetime basis following the Civil War necessarily led to a consideration of the proper organization of all the supporting supply bureaus.[195]   The War Department originally began planning for a permanent Army of 100,000 men, and Meigs solicited the advice of his officers on how to reorganize his Department to adapt its personnel to the needs of such an Army. The War Department reduced its proposed strength figures in the next few months, and when Meigs submitted his recommendations in December 1865, his proposed organization was to serve a minimum force of 50,000 men capable, by filling up companies to the maximum, of an increase to 82,600 men.   Since the services of Volunteer officers would be lost, Meigs recommended an increase in the number of regular officers in the Department from 67, as then provided by law, to 89.   Even with that number, he pointed out that the Department would still require the services of officers detailed from the line to serve as acting assistant quartermasters at the many posts that would have to be established on the frontier.   Meigs proposed that such officers be allowed an additional compensation of $10 a month.   Under the war-tested provisions of the reorganization act of 1864, the Department had been able to meet every demand made upon it, and Meigs therefore also recommended that the act be continued in force, except so far as certain provisions became obsolete by the disbandment of the Volunteer army.[196]

The legislation enacted by Congress in the summer of 1866 differed considerably from the proposals made by Meigs.   Congress continued the provisions of the act of 1864 in force only until 1 January 1867.

[194] Among other duties, not enlarged upon, were the settlement of Civil War claims, a tedious, time-consuming responsibility that lasted for many years, and the carrying out of an increasing number of relief projects that called for the issue and distribution of surplus food, clothing, bedding, and tentage to victims of fire, flood, earthquake, tornadoes, yellow fever epidemics, and the ravages of grasshoppers. Most of these relief measures were the result of congressional action. For example, in 1866, Congress authorized the issue of condemned clothing and surplus camp and garrison equipage, bedding, and hospital furniture to families made homeless by fire in Portland, Maine.   In 1874 it provided for the issue of Army clothing to persons on the western frontier made destitute by the ravages of grasshoppers during the previous summer. (1) 14 *Stat.* 364 (July 14, 1866); 18 *Stat.* 314 (Feb 10, 1874). (2) See also *Annual Report of the Quartermaster General, 1876,* p. 20; *1880,* p. 20; *1884,* p. 22; *1887,* pp. 17–18.

[195] Although in July 1866, Congress had provided for a minimum strength of 54,302 rank and file, susceptible of increase to 75,382 men, the reported strength of the Army on 30 September 1866 was only 37,545. Three years later, Congress ordered a sharp decrease and by 1876 the authorized strength had been brought down to 27,500 men. For the next 22 years, the actual number of enlisted men in the Army was around 25,000. (1) 14 *Stat.* 332–33 (Jul 28, 1866); 15 *Stat.* 318 (Mar 3, 1869); 19 *Stat.* 97 (Jul 24, 1876). (2) House *Ex. Doc.* No. 1, 39th Cong., 2d sess., p. 2 (AG Rpt, 20 Oct 1866). (3) *Annual Report of the General of the Army, 1876,* p. 20.

[196] (1) RG 92, OQMG Letter Book, vol. 87, pp. 122–23 (Meigs to AQMG Thomas *et al.,* 9 Oct 1865). (2) House *Report* No. 33, 40th Cong., 3d sess., pp. 29–30 (Ltr, Meigs to Grant, 18 Dec 1865).

It not only authorized fewer officers for the Department than Meigs had requested but also provided for a further gradual diminution of the existing staff by directing that vacancies in the grades of captain and major were not to be filled until the strength of the Department was reduced to 59 officers and 16 military storekeepers.[197]

About 10 years later, Congress further reduced the Department's staff to 57 officers. At that time, it also provided that no more appointments were to be made in the grade of military storekeeper, that grade ceasing to exist as soon as it became vacant by reason of the resignation or death of the incumbents.[198] The number of military storekeepers steadily decreased after 1875 until by 1890 there was only one left. His retirement was not due until 1905, when the grade of military storekeeper would cease to exist.

In the post-Civil War years, most of the Quartermaster officers were once again assigned as quartermasters in charge of depots or as chief quartermasters of military departments. Few in number, these quartermasters could not discharge all assigned functions, and their efforts had to be supplemented by those of line officers detailed for duty as acting assistant quartermasters at posts. An economy-minded Congress that authorized the use of troop labor to provide shelter, fuel, and forage for the Army was unlikely to see the need for compensating such line officers for the heavy responsibilities they were called upon to discharge. Though not bonded, they disbursed large sums of money; they erected barracks and storehouses; they provided transportation for supplies and troops; and they had charge of stables and public animals. Repeatedly, the Quartermaster General renewed the recommendation for compensation that he first made in December 1865, but Congress continued to ignore his plea.[199]

Since troop movements were frequent, line officers doing duty as acting assistant quartermasters were changed often. In fiscal year 1870, for example, the average number of them serving in that capacity was 150, but the total number for the year was 433.[200] Such turnover among

[197] In addition to the brigadier general heading the Department, Meigs had called for a staff of 8 colonels, 16 lieutenant colonels, and 64 majors, or a total of 89 officers and 16 military storekeepers. Instead, Congress had provided 6 colonels, 10 lieutenant colonels, 15 majors, and 44 captains, or a total of 76 officers, including the Quartermaster General, and 16 military storekeepers. By allowing vacancies to go unfilled until the number of majors was reduced to 12 and the captains to 30, the final authorized strength of the Department was fixed at 59 officers. 14 *Stat.* 334 (Jul 28, 1866).

[198] In addition to the Quartermaster General, the authorized staff of the Department after 1875 consisted of 4 colonels, 8 lieutenant colonels, 14 majors, and 30 captains, holding the positions, respectively, of assistant quartermaster general, deputy quartermaster general, quartermaster, and assistant quartermaster. 18 *Stat.* 338–39 (Mar 3, 1875).

[199] See *Annual Report of the Quartermaster General, 1869*, p. 5; *1870*, p. 4; *1873*, p. 9; *1879*, p. 4.

[200] *Ibid., 1870*, p. 4.

acting assistant quartermasters was characteristic for the whole of this period.   Greater economy in the maintenance of Quartermaster property would undoubtedly result, Meigs felt, if the employment of acting assistant quartermasters could be placed on a more permanent basis, but that decision rested with commanders of military departments and districts, and no change in the policy governing assignment was made.[201] To aid the burdened acting assistant quartermasters, Meigs began, in 1873, to recommend the enlistment of post quartermaster sergeants. Such noncommissioned officers, by remaining at posts in charge of property when the garrison changed, he argued, would preserve knowledge and responsibility so often lost through the frequent change of acting assistant quartermasters.   It was the summer of 1884, however, before Congress authorized the appointment of post quartermaster sergeants, limiting the number of 80.[202]

The legislation reorganizing the Quartermaster's Department in 1866 had an immediate effect upon the organization of the Quartermaster General's office in Washington.   Failure to prolong the life of the reorganization act of 1864 beyond January 1867 terminated the divisional organization of the office of the Quartermaster General that had been established under the act.   The workload of the former nine divisions had decreased with the close of the war and consolidation of duties had begun to take place in the fall of 1866, but the final dissolution of the divisional organization was not ordered until 19 August 1867.[203]   In lieu of divisions, branches were designated.   In 1868, for example, there were five branches, each under an officer.   These included branches for transportation, clothing and equipage, inspection, national cemeteries, and regular supplies, the last a catchall that included not only regular supplies but also all business relating to barracks and quarters, purchase of animals, and investigation of war claims.   Changes were made in the office organization from time to time, and the number of branches tended to increase.   Since only four officers were usually assigned to assist the Quartermaster General, it became customary to place a number of branches under the supervision of one officer.   Thus, in 1890, Deputy Quartermaster General M. I. Ludington had under his supervision the following branches: inspection, fiscal, money and property accounts, clothing and equipage returns, barracks and quarters, and care and maintenance of national cemeteries.[204]   Not until 1895 did a divisional organization of the office again emerge.   Then, four divisions, each with

[201] RG 92, OQMG Letter Book, 1873–B, General and Misc., pp. 1003–04 (Meigs to Lt. M. L. Courtney, 25 Aug 1873).
[202] 23 *Stat.* 109 (Jul 5, 1884).
[203] *Annual Report of the Quartermaster General, 1868,* p. 20.
[204] *Ibid., 1890,* pp. 6–7.

subordinate branches were established—Supply and Transportation, Construction and Repair; Correspondence and Examining, which included all matters relating to finance, returns, money and property accounts, and inspection; and Mail and Records, which also included separate branches for claims and national cemeteries.

Organizational developments in the Subsistence Department followed much the same pattern as that in the Quartermaster's Department. Following the Civil War, Congress reduced its authorized staff. In 1866, it had a total of 28 officers in addition to the Commissary General of Subsistence. Congress decreased that number to 25 in 1874 and to 21 in 1895.[205] Except for three officers assigned to the Washington office, the others were designated as purchasing commissaries at depots or chief commissaries of military departments. The efforts of this small staff had been supplemented during the war by the appointment of numerous assistant commissaries of subsistence, but the expiration of the law authorizing such officers, coupled with the necessity for their services, led to the continued detailing of line officers to serve in the anomalous position of acting assistant commissaries.[206] The Commissary General of Subsistence tried, without success, to have the position of assistant commissary restored and also worked to have commissary sergeants appointed.[207] Congress authorized the appointment of commissary sergeants who were to be responsible for receiving and preserving subsistence supplies at posts in 1873, the Secretary of War being directed to appoint one commissary sergeant at each military post or place of deposit for subsistence stores.[208] This then remained the organization of the Subsistence Department until the Spanish-American War.

Staff and Line Controversy

Throughout much of this period, Congress devoted attention to the problem of Army and War Department organization. In the course of committee investigations, much information was elicited and many views were expressed on the controversy between staff and line that involved the General of the Army, the Secretary of War, commanding generals of military departments, and the chiefs of the staff bureaus. Stemming from

[205] (1) 14 *Stat.* 334 (Jul 28, 1866); 18 *Stat.* 244 (Jun 23, 1874); 28 *Stat.* 656 (Feb 12, 1895). (2) The distribution of officers in 1895 included, besides the Commissary General, 2 colonels and 3 lieutenant colonels, each assigned as an assistant commissary general; and 8 majors and 8 captains, assigned as commissaries.
[206] House *Ex. Doc.* No. 1, 40th Cong., 2d sess., p. 581 (CGS's Rpt, 1867).
[207] (1) *Ibid.,* p. 582. (2) RG 192, CGS, Letters to SW, 1866–72, p. 237 (Annual Rpt, 1868); p. 370 (Annual Rpt, 1869).
[208] 17 *Stat.* 485 (Mar 3, 1873).

lack of clearly defined lines of command, the conflict assumed large proportions after the Civil War, though evidence of disagreement is apparent as early as 1821. Insofar as the supply bureaus were concerned, the basic point at issue was control. Staff officers recognized only the orders of the Secretary of War, and it was charged that "should he be a civilian, unaccustomed to military routine, they are more likely to control his action than to be controlled by it." [209] The viewpoint of the commanding general was well stated by Maj. Gen. George G. Meade. "The staff corps, being constituent parts of the Army, should in all purely military matters, be under the orders of the general commanding the Army, this officer being himself under the orders of the Secretary of War, as representing the President." [210] The problem of control, however, was not resolved in the period 1865 to 1898.

Proposed Consolidation of Supply Bureaus

Still pursuing economy, congressional committees were convinced that objective could be promoted by consolidating some of the supply bureaus, in particular, by merging the Subsistence, Pay, and Quartermaster's Department into one supply agency. The practicability of such consolidation was generally conceded in 1869, but whether it would promote efficiency or economy was questioned. When the proposal was first examined, there were some supply officers who favored consolidation, among others, Bvt. Maj. Gen. Rufus Ingalls.[211] As Congress investigated and studied the problem of War Department organization again and again, the viewpoint of those who had favored consolidation changed to opposition.[212] The view of the Army was well summarized by General Meade, who had had a fair opportunity, as he noted, to observe the workings of the existing system, both in time of war and peace.

It has always worked well. I doubt if any army is better supplied or has its wants more promptly attended to than ours; and, when consideration is given to this fact, it would seem to me the part of prudence is to let well enough alone, and not hazard experiments, which, even if successful, could attain no better result than all admit is now attained.[213]

Content to look to the past rather than the future, veteran officers of the Civil War saw no need for change and the consolidation proposal was

[209] House *Report* No. 33, 40th Cong., 3d sess., p. 2.
[210] House *Report* No. 74, 42d Cong., 3d sess., p. 16.
[211] House *Report* No. 33, 40th Cong., 3d sess., pp. 117–120.
[212] House *Misc. Doc.* No. 56, 45th Cong., 2d sess., pp. 55–56 (Ingalls testifying, 12 Jan 1878).
[213] Senate *Report* No. 555, 45th Cong., 3d sess., p. 468.

dropped, not to be revived until the Spanish-American War emphasized anew the inadequacies of organization.

Retirement of Meigs

Throughout the prolonged period of investigation, Meigs continued to fill the position of Quartermaster General, but in view of the proposals to change the retirement system and the eagerness of his subordinates for promotion, he might well have felt uneasy about his tenure.   Efforts to make compulsory the system of retirement adopted in 1862, authorizing the President, *in his discretion*, to place on the retired list officers of 62 years of age or who may have served 45 years, aroused his ire.   In 1861, the 45-year old Meigs advised Seward that he would find the Army and Navy "clogged at the head with men, excellent patriotic men, men who were soldiers and sailors forty years ago, but who now merely keep active men out of the places in which they could serve the country."   Sixteen years later he could see no justification for revising the retirement system to permit the promotion of younger men.   A bill to make retirement compulsory at 62 was under consideration in the Senate in 1877 and Meigs, then himself approaching that age, cried out: "Is it to the interest of the country to put competent men out of position to put able-bodied men on the retired, the pension list and forbid them to serve, forbid the country to make any use of knowledge and experience they have gained." [214]

When Meigs became 62 in 1878 and it was generally believed that the War Department intended to retire from active service those officers who were eligible for retirement, the efforts of those seeking to become his successor were intensified.   In 1866, Congress had provided that the Quartermaster General was to be appointed by selection from the officers of the Department, thus putting a premium on seniority.[215]   The three senior officers of the Department, ranked in order of their seniority, were Robert Allen, Daniel H. Rucker, and Rufus Ingalls.   Both Allen and Rucker were older than Meigs, and Ingalls, with the support of Grant and other generals of the Army of the Potomac that he had so ably served as Chief Quartermaster, campaigned actively for the post.[216]

Meigs did not retire but rumors of his impending retirement con-

---

[214] (1) RG 92, OQMG Letter Book, 1877-B, General and Misc., p. 1514 (To Senator J. D. Cameron, 1 Nov 1877). (2) *OR*, ser. I, vol. I, 368 (Meigs to Seward, 6 Apr 1861).

[215] 14 *Stat*. 336 (Jul 28, 1866).

[216] (1) See RG 94, AGO, Appointment, Commission and Personnel (ACP) file on Ingalls (Grant to President, 27 April 1877); (John B. Gray to President, 31 July 1879); Hancock to President, 13 March 1879). (2) Allen never sought the position. He died 4 years after Meigs retired.

tinued to circulate, and Lt. Gen. P. H. Sheridan backed the appointment of his father-in-law, Bvt. Maj. Gen. D. H. Rucker. "It would be a gracious act on the part of the President," he suggested, to give such recognition to Rucker, who would then retire.   Rucker, whose real rank was that of colonel, appreciated Sheridan's efforts, but naturally he preferred to retire after his appointment as Quartermaster General had been confirmed, particularly since his sole means of support would be his retirement pay.[217]

On 6 Februray 1882, aged 65 and after 46 years in the service of his country, 21 of them as Quartermaster General, Meigs was retired from active duty.   Appreciating the motives that led Rucker to seek the office, Meigs recommended that he be appointed.   On 13 February, Rucker was appointed Quartermaster General, assuming the duties of the office a week later.   At the same time, he applied for retirement, his request being granted on 23 February.   Ingalls who had been seeking the office for several years was appointed Rucker's successor and accepted the position even before official confirmation of his appointment had been received by the War Department from the Senate and before his commission was issued.   "Shall his commission be antedated to the 10th and his acceptance be regarded as of that date," the Adjutant General queried. His commission was so dated, with rank from 23 February 1882.   Ingalls served as Quartermaster General until 1 July 1883, when he requested retirement under the law of 30 June 1882.   It amended earlier legislation by providing for retirement of an officer at his request after 40 years' service and automatically placed him on the retired list when he became 64 years old.[218]

This law insured a far more rapid succession of Quartermasters General than had been possible in the years when there had been no retirement lists or even later when retirement had been at the discretion of the President.   During the next 15 years, four men, all veterans of the Civil War, served successively as Quartermaster General—Samuel B. Holabird, 1 July 1883 to 16 June 1890; Richard N. Batchelder, 26 June 1890 to 27 July 1896; Charles G. Sawtelle, 19 August 1896 to 16 February 1897; and George H. Weeks, 16 February 1897 to 3 February 1898.

[217] RG 92, AGO, ACP file on Rucker (Ltr, Sheridan to President, 5 Jul 1880); (Telegram, Sheridan to Sherman, 18 Jun 1880); (SW to President, 22 Jun 1880); (Rucker to Sheridan, 23 Jun 1880).
[218] (1) RG 94, AGO, ACP file on Ingalls.   (2) 22 *Stat.* 118 (Jun 30, 1882).

CHAPTER XII

The Spanish-American War

Background of Unpreparedness

When the United States went to war with Spain in 1898, the country was wholly unprepared; the lessons of 1861 had been completely obscured by the subsequent victories of the Union Army. That Army was the most powerful military force in the world in the spring of 1865, but whatever bright expectations it then entertained for the future were quickly dissipated by the rapid demobilization of its strength and the indifference of the public and its representatives in Congress to the needs of the Army in the post-Civil War years. The Army resigned itself to the minor glories of Indian fighting and routine garrison life.

On the eve of the Spanish-American War, the Regular Army numbered 2,143 officers and 26,040 enlisted men, stationed at some 80 posts, most of which were located in the West.[1] This fragmentation of the troop strength made it difficult to keep even two companies of infantry together long enough to give them systematic instruction. In consequence, although all of the general officers and most of the field officers were veterans of the Civil War, junior officers in the lower grades gained no experience in handling large bodies of men. Supply officers were equally handicapped because they had no opportunity to solve the complex problems involved in the logistical support of large units. Their duties were confined to the routine supply of minuscule garrisons that were stationed either at frontier posts or at coastal fortifications guarding the major harbors.[2]

Although the Regular Army was small, the War Department en-

---

[1] This was the strength as of 1 April 1898. Senate *Doc.* No. 221, 56th Cong., 1st sess., "Report of the Commission Appointed by the President to Investigate the Conduct of the War Department in the War with Spain," (8 vols., Washington, 1900), I, 113. This commission was headed by Maj. Gen. Grenville M. Dodge, and its report will hereafter be briefly cited as Dodge Commission *Report*.

[2] Whatever skills and techniques had been developed by the Civil War quartermasters in supplying large bodies of troops were lost to the Department upon their retirement or death. Of the 57 officers in the Department on 1 April 1898, only 5 had seen service as quartermasters during the Civil War, and 4 of them had filled posts of minor importance during the last year of the war.

countered no problem in the procurement of manpower in 1898. Public feeling, already aroused by reports of the situation in Cuba, was brought to a high pitch by the sinking of the battleship *Maine*. In consequence, when McKinley yielded to pressure and Congress, on 25 April, formally declared that a state of war had existed since 21 April, there was no lack of men willing to take up arms.[3] On 22 April, Congress had authorized the President to call for volunteers, and his proclamation the following day brought response from 125,000.[4] In a little more than a month, they were mustered into service. By that time, an additional force of 75,000 volunteers were being called for on 25 May. In the meantime, on 26 April, Congress authorized an increase of the Regular Army to about 61,000, and, on 11 May, provided for 16 regiments consisting of engineers, cavalry, and volunteer infantry, especially accustomed to tropical climates and called immunes.[5] By August, the Regular Army numbered 58,688 officers and men and the Volunteer Army, 216,029, making a total strength of 274,717.[6]

As in the past, two supply bureaus, the Subsistence and Quartermaster's Departments, continued to be responsible for subsisting, clothing, and equipping this force that mushroomed in the short time of 3½ months. In the course of the post-Civil War years, these bureaus, too, had suffered a diminution of strength, so much so that they had relied heavily upon officers detailed from the line to carry out their work. On the eve of the Spanish-American War, the Subsistence Department had an authorized strength of only 22 officers, including the Commissary General of Subsistence.[7] There was a total of 57 officers in the Quartermaster's Department. In addition to officers detailed to assist in performing supply duties, each Department also made use of the services of post sergeants. There were 96 commissary sergeants and 80 quartermaster sergeants.

Both Departments were under the direction of newly designated chiefs, competent men with long years of experience in their respective departments who, nevertheless, would still need time to familiarize themselves with the heavy responsibilities they were assuming. On 3 February 1898, 12 days before the battleship *Maine* was blown up in the harbor of Havana, Brig. Gen. Marshall I. Ludington, the last of the Civil War quartermasters to become Quartermaster General, was appointed to the

---

[3] 30 *Stat.* 364.

[4] *Ibid.*, pp. 361–63.

[5] *Ibid.*, pp. 364–66; 405.

[6] *War Department Annual Reports, 1898,* I, 257, 260.

[7] *Ibid.*, I, 549 (Rpt of Commissary General, 17 Oct 1898).

post.[8]   A week after the formal declaration of war, Commissary General William H. Nash retired, to be succeeded, on 3 May, by Brig. Gen. Charles P. Eagan.[9]   Promotion on a basis of seniority from within the Departments to the top position had resulted in a rapid turnover of chiefs in the past decade and obviously could not be conducive to the formulation, let alone the development, of any program of improvement. To weakened leadership was added restricted strength authorizations in the Departments, which made experienced quartermasters and commissaries unavailable in the numbers required for war.   Both the Subsistence and the Quartermaster's Departments were physically unprepared to satisfy such demands from the field and, as in past wars, had to make extensive use of inexperienced personnel.

When it increased the military establishment in April, Congress also provided for an expanded supply organization for the support of tactical units in the field.   As in the Civil War, the Army was organized by corps, divisions, and brigades.   Congress authorized a chief quartermaster and a chief commissary of subsistence, with the rank of lieutenant colonel, for each army corps; a chief quartermaster and a chief commissary of subsistence, with the rank of major, for each division; and an assistant quartermaster and a commissary of subsistence, with the rank of captain, for each brigade.[10]   Under this law, 7 corps quartermasters, 22 division quartermasters, and 65 brigade quartermasters were appointed, along with 28 chief commissaries of subsistence, 7 with the rank of lieutenant colonel and 21 with that of major, and 69 commissaries with the rank of captain.[11]

Legislation was also necessary to increase the efficiency of the supporting depot and military departmental organization as well as of the office arrangements in Washington.   In 1898, the country was divided for administrative purposes into eight military departments, each of which required a chief quartermaster and a chief commissary of subsistence on

[8] Ludington had been seeking this honor since the summer of 1896 when Quartermaster General Richard N. Batchelder retired, but his aspirations had been denied by the appointment first of Charles G. Sawtelle, who served only 6 months, and then by that of George H. Weeks, who retired within a year.

[9] General Nash had served as Commissary General only 12 days, an honor accorded him as senior officer of the Department. This honor had rotated with amazing rapidity since General Robert Macfeely resigned in 1898. Including Nash, 7 men served as Commissary General between 1890 and the beginning of the Spanish-American War, of whom 3 retired in 1898. William H. Bell, having been appointed in November 1897, retired 2 months later, to be succeeded by Samuel Cushing who served 3 months. He, in turn, was followed by Nash, whose service ended in 12 days.

[10] 30 *Stat.* 361 (Apr 22, 1898).

[11] (1) *Annual Report of the Quartermaster General, 1898*, p. 155.   (2) *War Department Annual Reports, 1898*, I, 555–60 (Rpt of Commissary General).

the staff of the commanding general. In addition, officers were needed for the increased number of supply depots and to carry the rapidly expanding workload of the offices of the Quartermaster General and of the Commissary General of Subsistence. At the end of May, Ludington, recalling Meigs' efforts in the Civil War, drafted a bill similar to that enacted by Congress in 1864. He requested the authorization of additional temporary personnel and proposed to expand his existing office organization from four to eight divisions.[12] To compensate officers for the immense volume of work that would be imposed on those appointed to take charge of the office divisions as well as of the great supply depots, Ludington recommended that Congress grant them a temporary increase in rank.[13]

In July, Congress enacted legislation along the lines suggested by Ludington, making it applicable to both the Subsistence and Quartermaster's Departments. To the Subsistence Department, Congress temporarily added 8 majors and 12 captains; in the Quartermaster's Department, the additional officers included 2 colonels, 2 lieutenant colonels, 3 majors, and 20 captains. In both Departments, Congress granted additional temporary rank, next above that then held but not above colonel, to officers assigned to the important supply depots as well as to those assigned as assistants to the chiefs of the respective departments. In the Quartermaster's Department, such temporary rank was also to be given to the quartermaster acting on the staff of the Commanding General of the Army and to no more than four special inspectors.[14] The latter, like those of the Civil War, were to be under the control of the Quartermaster General to be used by him to make inquiries and secure information on the state of the Department. Unlike the Civil War measure, the act of July 7, 1898, did not enumerate and describe the divisional organization of the office of the Quartermaster General but simply authorized the Secretary of War to make such distribution of duties as he deemed in the best interests of the service. Ludington's proposed reorganization was immediately put into effect.[15] Profiting from past experience, the Quar-

---

[12] The proposed division of duties in the office of the Quartermaster General was as follows: the first division was to handle all matters relating to funds, estimates, returns, and money accounts; the second was to deal with water and rail transportation; the third was to have charge of clothing and equipage; the fourth was to supervise wagon transportation, animals, and forage; the fifth division was to handle construction; the sixth was to take charge of sewerage, lighting, heating, and ground rentals; the seventh was to be responsible for all personnel matters; and the eighth division was to handle all claims and supervise the operation of the national cemeteries.

[13] RG 92, OQMG Document File, 1800–1914, Case 117402 (Ludington to SW, 30 May 1898).

[14] 30 *Stat.* 714–15 (Jul 7, 1898).

[15] RG 92, OQMG Document File, 1800–1914, Case 117402 (Ludington to SW, 8 Jul 1898; Ludington to AG, 7 Aug 1898).

termaster General effected a more prompt reorganization than had occurred during the Civil War.

The number of additional officers authorized by Congress was not actually as large as appeared on the surface. Under the legislation enacted in April 22 and July 7, 121 positions were added to the Quartermaster's Department. Of these, 78 were filled by appointments from civil life and 21 by appointment of officers from the line. Inasmuch as 22 regular officers of the Department were commissioned in the Volunteer service and one accepted a Volunteer commission in the Judge Advocate General's Department, the actual number of Volunteer and Regular officers available for service in the Department during the war was 155.[16] The total number of officers in the Subsistence Department in the war period was 129.[17] Congress also added one military storekeeper to the Quartermaster's Department and increased the number of post quartermaster sergeants by an additional 25.[18]

The lack of an adequately trained Army that could be supported in the field by a sufficient number of experienced supply officers was only one facet of the general unpreparedness of the country in April 1898. In characteristic fashion, the McKinley administration had failed to coordinate its foreign and military policies; it declared war and then got ready to wage war. Russell A. Alger, Secretary of War, thereupon found that the government machinery was altogether inadequate to meet the emergency. "It had, during thirty years, been called upon only to plan for and meet the requirements of the regular army in time of peace, and naturally enough had become quite fixed in the narrow grooves of peace." [19] Obviously, even the most effective staff organization would have been hard pressed under wartime demands, but while the admittedly weak organization was responsible for much of the disorder that ensued, Congress, through its indifference to the problem of national defense, shared in that responsibility.

---

[16] Dodge Commission *Report*, I, 437 (QMG's Rpt to Commission, 14 Oct 1898). The number of officers in the Department in any given month of the war varied for appointments were made throughout the war. Thus, of the 121 Volunteer officers, 60 were appointed in May, 28 in June, 26 in July, and 7 in August. Of the appointees, 23 qualified in May, 49 in June, 31 in July, 14 in August, and 4 in September.

[17] General Eagon reported that 20 officers were added under the act of July 7 and 101 under the act of April 22, of whom 9 never qualified under their commissions. Since 5 regular Subsistence officers were commissioned in the Volunteer service, the total added to the Department was 129. *Ibid.*, 1, 545–46 (Eagan's Rpt to Commission, 6 Oct 1898).

[18] 30 *Stat.* 571; 728 (Jul 1 and 8, 1898).

[19] Russell A. Alger, *The Spanish-American War* (New York, 1901), p. 7.

Clothing and Equipping the Troops

The supply bureaus were as ill prepared to respond to any sudden demand for large quantities of supplies as they were to provide guidance by experienced personnel. The Quartermaster's Department had little or no reserve stock on hand at its general depots; appropriations had neither encouraged nor permitted the accumulation of reserves, and, in fact, it was only with the strictest economy that the Department had been able to procure clothing and equipage to which the Regular Army was entitled. When the war began, such factors were ignored while enterprising journalists denounced the ludicrous supply operations of a Department that sent American soldiers, clothed in woolen uniforms, to fight in a tropical climate. But no time was allowed for preparations, and haste and inexperience accounted for most of the shortcomings. Supply operations in 1898, however, were singularly free of the corruption and fraud that had maked those of 1861. Indefinite charges of fraud and collusion in awarding war contracts were made in the press, but the commission, later appointed by the President to investigate the conduct of the War Department and popularly known as the Dodge Commission, found no evidence to substantiate the charges. Those who made them invariably failed to appear before the Commission, though invited to do so.[20]

When Quartermaster General Ludington became aware in March of the probability of trouble with Spain, he conferred with the Secretary of War on the need for making preparations. Lack of funds and restrictive legislation controlling expenditures seriously hampered his efforts to take action. Since the crisis developed in the last quarter of the fiscal year, his appropriated funds were running low. As of 1 April, he had a balance of slightly more than $2,500,000 that he could use for preparatory measures and to that amount he was limited. Under laws enacted by Congress in the post-Civil War years and still in effect, the Department's expenditures could not exceed its appropriation for the fiscal year, and it could enter into no contracts calling for the future payments of money in excess of that appropriation. Generally, no contract could be made unless it was authorized by law or was under an appropriation that was adequate to its fulfillment. Contracts for clothing, subsistence, forage, fuel, quarters, and transportation were exceptions to this last restriction, but none could be made that exceeded "the necessities of the current year."[21] As in the past, the Quartermaster's Department generally had to make contracts by advertising for bids and awarding the contracts to

---

[20] Dodge Commission *Report,* I, 138–40 (Rpt to President, 9 Feb 1899).
[21] See *ante,* pp. 495–96.

the lowest bidders, though emergencies did permit open-market purchases. However, when Congress appropriated funds for the next fiscal year in March 1898, 5 weeks before the war began, it limited such open-market purchases to no more than $200 and required that each such purchase be immediately reported to the Secretary of War.[22]

On 9 March, Congress appropriated $50 million for national defense, but, under the narrow interpretation given to the law by an Administration determined to prevent any disturbance to its peace efforts, not a dollar was made available for any other purpose.[23] Of this fund, the Quartermaster's Department was allotted $500,000 for the specific purpose of transporting ordnance to the seacoast for the fortifications there.[24] None of this money could be used for the accumulation of Quartermaster supplies for offensive war. Not until about 20 April was another allotment of $1 million made from that fund to the Department. Even though Ludington anticipated trouble, there was little that he could do legally to prepare for it. Given the limitations imposed by Congress and the attitude of the McKinley administration on preparations, it is doubtful whether a more aggressive officer would have undertaken to stretch the law to the extent necessary to put the Quartermaster's Department in readiness to clothe, equip, and transport the thousands of volunteers soon to be under arms. The Commission Investigating the Conduct of the War nevertheless later suggested that "possibly someone else would have gone into the market earlier, anticipating approval of his acts in case war was declared and the Army increased tenfold."[25] As soon as war was inevitable and Congress made funds available, the Department worked energetically to meet the demands made upon it.

In the meantime, Ludington did initiate certain actions to improve the supply situation. When he became Quartermaster General in February, he found that clothing stocks were low, and his first efforts were directed toward building them up. As in the past, Army clothing and tentage were still being manufactured at the depots, principally at Philadelphia, but clothing was also produced at Jeffersonville and San Francisco. In March, Ludington instructed the depot quartermasters

---

[22] 30 *Stat.* 322 (Mar 15, 1898).

[23] (1) 30 *Stat.* 274. (2) Alger later attributed this restrictive interpretation of the law to McKinley, but there is no evidence that the Secretary of War exerted himself to alter this view or to urge the necessity of placing the Army in readiness for any demands. that might be made upon it. Alger, *The Spanish-American War*, pp. 8–9.

[24] About $10 million went to the Ordnance Department and $5,500,000 to the Engineers for fortification purposes. The Medical Department received $20,000 and the Signal Corps $225,400.

[25] Dodge Commission *Report*, I, 127 (Commission to President, 9 Feb 1899). There is no evidence that any other supply bureau chief operated along the lines suggested by the Commission.

to push production.   Clearly, government manufacture alone would not suffice for wartime needs, and, on 26 March, he directed the depot officers at New York, Philadelphia, St. Louis, and Chicago to explore market conditions and gather information on what tentage and clothing items were available for immediate purchase and how rapidly additional supplies could be produced.   Within his limited means, he authorized the purchase of some material for clothing and tentage early in April.[26]

Preliminary procurement activity was confined to the Philadelphia Depot.   On 20 April, Ludington directed the depot quartermaster to advertise and invite proposals for such Army textiles as kersey and flannel and for blankets, forage caps, leggings, ponchos, summer underwear, and shoes.   He was also to invite proposals for the manufacture of a large number of blouses, flannel shirts, and trousers to be made from material that the depot had on hand.   By 25 April, the Quartermaster General further authorized him to invite proposals for more than $3 million of clothing and tentage.[27]   When war was formally declared, the Department also initiated purchases at New York, Chicago, St. Louis, Boston, and Baltimore that aggregated over $3 million.

Quartermaster attention was at first concentrated on clothing and equipping the troops to be sent on expeditions against Cuba and Puerto Rico.   When news arrived of Commodore Dewey's victory over the Spanish fleet at Manila, it became necessary to send troops to the Philippine Islands.   The first expedition sailed on 25 May.   In the course of dispatching other troops to Manila, the United States annexed the Hawaiian Islands on 7 July and placed them for military purposes under the Department of California.   The depot quartermaster at San Francisco clothed the troops for these expeditions, drawing upon the markets of San Francisco and Portland for his supplies as well as expanding the manufacturing operations of the depot itself.[28]

Supply of clothing and tentage generally was hampered by the fact that the required fabrics for their production, made according to Army specifications, were not available.   The Quartermaster's Department could find, for example, only a few thousand yards of kersey, specified for use in Army trousers, and there was practically no standard tent duck on the market.   To meet the immediate tentage requirements of the troops first mustered into service, the Department purchased all canvas of fair quality that it could obtain throughout the country.   Naturally, the life of such tentage was short and, in the rainy season, the troops

[26] *Ibid.*, I, 437–38 (QMG's Rpt to Commission, 14 Oct 1898).
[27] *Ibid.*, I, 438.
[28] RG 92, OQMG Document File, 1800–1914, Case 115533 (Rpt of Maj. O. F. Long, depot quartermaster, 25 Aug 1898).

suffered. Similarly, the Department had to substitute a lighter weight, dark blue fabric for the sky blue kersey used in the manufacture of trousers. It could get blue flannel for blouses, but the fabric was not dyed according to Army specifications which required the use of indigo. The result was that the blouses faded into various shades of blue, green, and purple. Deliveries of specification fabric did not begin to come in until a month after the Department made contracts.[29]

On 1 April 1898, the Quartermaster's Department was prepared to clothe and equip for 3 months the Army as then organized and an additional 8,000 to 10,000 men.[30] The regulation allowance of tentage for troops of the Regular Army was with the troops at the garrisons where they were stationed and they carried it with them into the field. Thus, there were about 28,000 shelter tents in the hands of the troops and another 10,000 at the depots, with an additional 6,500 due on contract as of 1 April.[31] A fair supply of camp kettles, entrenching tools, and other Quartermaster supplies were on hand; in fact, "a pretty good stock" of mess pans had been in storage since the Civil War.[32]

The Department was not prepared, however, to clothe and equip an Army that within a few months increased to more than 10 times the size of the peacetime force. The difficulties the Department encountered in shortages and production were matched by its inability to obtain firm requirement figures from the War Department. Before the war began, Ludington was told to make his arrangements for about 30,000 men. Then the number was changed to 80,000, but no one seemed to know what the strength of the Army to be called out might be. "There were so many changes," Ludington testified, and he received no official information until the President issued his proclamation, on 23 April, calling for 125,000 volunteers.[33] In little more than a month, they were at camps clamoring to be outfitted. More volunteers were raised, the size of the Regular Army was increased, and, by August, the Quartermaster's Department had to satisfy the demands of approximately 275,000 men.

---

[29] Dodge Commission *Report*, VII, 3140 (Ludington). Unless otherwise indicated, names cited in connection with the Dodge Commission Report will indicate the individual testifying.

[30] The Department had on hand at its depots and due on contract about 69,000 blankets, 28,000 blouses, 53,000 forage caps, 98,000 cotton flannel drawers, 28,000 campaign hats, 23,000 overcoats, 12,000 ponchos, 47,000 dark blue flannel shirts, 62,000 pairs of shoes, 305,000 pairs of cotton and 167,000 pairs of woolen socks, 35,000 pairs of trousers and 23,000 pairs for mounted soldiers, and 170,000 cotton and 84,000 woolen undershirts. See *ibid.,* I 453, for a table of the principal articles of clothing and equipage on hand and due in on contract.

[31] *Ibid.,* I, 437 (QMG's Rpt to Commission, 14 Oct 1898).

[32] *Ibid.,* VII, 3140 (Ludington).

[33] *Ibid.,* VII, 3147.

When the Regulars took the field, they were clothed in the regulation blue wool uniform. For years, troops serving on campaigns in Texas, Arizona, and the hot, arid plains of the Southwest had been unsuccessful in their efforts to obtain a summer uniform.[34] The clothing on hand at the depots ready for issue to the troops on 1 April consisted of the same heavy wool items, unsuitable for the tropical climate in which the Army was soon to be operating. Even if consideration had been given to the procurement of lightweight clothing, the time element did not permit its production. To meet objections, the Department first reduced the weight of the kersey for trousers from 22 to 16 ounces, then removed the lining from the blouse in May, and also furnished summer underwear.[35] Later, as an emergency makeshift, since no khaki cloth was produced in the United States, canvas suits, made of twilled or plain duck in khaki color, were manufactured. Quartermasters issued more than 5,000 suits of canvas clothing to the Fifth Army Corps at Tampa before it sailed, and canvas suits clothed the Rough Riders before they went to Tampa. The Department furnished canvas suits to all troops going to Puerto Rico, and it later shipped sufficient quantities of this uniform to Cuba to equip all the troops there but various factors delayed issue.[36] The Quartermaster General doubted that this clothing afforded as much protection as the woolen uniform, and apparently it proved as hot. At Manila, Chief Quartermaster James W. Pope met the need for lightweight clothing by purchasing khaki and white summer uniforms locally, but sufficient time had been allowed before the expedition left San Francisco to equip each man with a supply of Nankeen underclothing, light cotton socks, gingham shirts, and a white drill suit in addition to the regular wool uniform.[37]

The Department was much criticized for its failure to furnish sufficient clothing at the camps where the troops were assembling. The Chief Quartermaster at Chickamauga testified that clothing could not be furnished as fast as it was wanted in May. Most regiments were inadequately supplied with underwear and shoes. Maj. Gen. Nelson A. Miles, Commanding General of the Army, reported that several of the volunteer regiments came to Tampa without uniforms or blankets. Much of this clothing deficiency arose out of the fact that many of the states, in filling the quotas for the first call for volunteers, held their men in camp for

---

[34] See *ante*, pp. 503–04.

[35] Dodge Commission *Report*, VI, 2648 (Col. William S. Patten, chief of Clothing and Equipage Division).

[36] (1) *Ibid.*, I, 442–43 (QMG's Rpt to Commission, 14 Oct 1898). (2) See infra, p. 527.

[37] (1) Dodge Commission *Report*, I, 443. (2) RG 92, OQMG Document File, 1800–1914, Case 115533 (Pope Rpt, 16 Nov 1898).

several weeks before they were mustered into the federal service.   Clothing wore out during that time and, when the volunteers were turned over to the War Department, they were reported, in many cases, to be without proper clothing, barefoot, and with only the shirt worn when leaving home.   When the War Department made a second call for volunteers, a better cooperation existed between it and the state officers. The Quartermaster's Department delivered supplies in advance to muster points and encountered no great difficulties in equipping troops enlisted under that call.[38]   The Quartermaster General asserted that he made every effort to relieve deficiencies by telegraphing authority to purchase at point of muster such articles as shoes, drawers, stockings, shirts, and even tents, if procurable.[39]

When Col. William S. Patten took charge of the Clothing and Equipage Division in the office of the Quartermaster General on 15 May, he found a situation in reference to clothing requisitions that he could only describe as "a mess."   Troops were being mustered in and concentrated at camps in Georgia, Alabama, and Florida, and, on orders of the War Department, "they piled their requisitions" into the Washington office.   The only solution was to ship supplies in bulk to the various points of concentration as fast as they became available without waiting for requisitions to arrive or be examined.   He simply judged what kind and quantity of supplies were likely to be needed, and the Quartermaster General urged depot quartermasters to inform the office when the supply of any particular articles ran low.   There was no "red tape," the Colonel testified, so far as the office of the Quartermaster General was concerned.[40]

The Department made a good procurement record, much better, in fact, than in a similar period of unpreparedness at the opening of the Civil War.   As in 1861, it had to purchase whatever was available on the market to meet immediate needs, and though much of the clothing fell below Army standards, still there was no use of shoddy.   Industrialization had progressed enormously in the past 30 years and production was now more rapid than in 1861.   Col. Amos S. Kimball, depot quartermaster at New York, proudly reported that "100,000 uniforms, consisting of blouses and trousers, were manufactured and ready for delivery in less

---

[38] (1) *Annual Report of the Quartermaster General, 1898*, p. 77. (2) RG 92, OQMG Document File, 1800–1914, Case 115533 (Patten to QMG, 16 Aug 1898).

[39] (1) Dodge Commission *Report*, I, 435–36 (QMG's Rpt to Commission, 14 Oct 1898). (2) The acting Chief Quartermaster of the 7th Corps, for example, reported that he purchased underclothing, shoes, and some blankets at Jacksonville, Fla., for the regiments that arrived short of clothing, but uniforms could not be supplied in that manner, and it was 10 days to 2 weeks before they were received. *Ibid.*, III, 338 (Capt. C. B. Baker).

[40] *Ibid.*, VI, 2647; I, 439 (QMG's Rpt to Commission, 14 Oct 1898).

EQUIPMENT OF SOLDIER IN 1898

than 2 weeks." [41]   Within a period of 3½ months, the Department fully
equipped an Army of 275,000 and was in a position to maintain its stock
of supplies.   The short duration of the war, however, left the Department
with a considerable surplus on hand.

Quartermasters purchased and contracted for clothing and equipage
at the principal depots of Philadelphia, Jeffersonville, New York, St. Louis,
San Francisco, Chicago, and Boston, and at purchasing offices in Cincinnati, Detroit, Baltimore, New Orleans, St. Paul, and Washington.
Though the Department purchased most of the clothing, it manufactured
considerable quantities at the Philadelphia, Jeffersonville, and San Francisco depots.   The St. Louis depot also produced a small quantity of
trousers.   The same system, introduced a hundred years earlier, was still
being followed at the Philadelphia Depot.   Cut garments, prepared in a
cutting department that was expanded so that its output was more than
3,000 garments a day, were given out to seamstresses living in the area.

[41] RG 92, OQMG Document File, 1800–1914, Case 115533 (Kimball to QMG, 1 Sep
1898).

Their number increased from 1,100 before the war to between 4,000 and 5,000 in the war months.[42]

The demand for tentage was so large because so many troops in both active campaign and camps were sick that issues far exceeded regulation allowances and much tentage was required for ordinary hospital purposes. The peacetime practice of manufacturing all Army tents at the Philadelphia Depot had to be supplemented by procurement under contract. Tents were manufactured wherever material could be obtained and skilled workmen were available. For example, under special arrangements with the Post Office Department, its Mail Bag Repair Shop manufactured some 10,000 common and conical tents from fabric supplied by the Philadelphia Depot.[43] Government production of tents—conical, common, hospital, wall tents and shelter halves—was pushed at the Philadelphia Depot, where the introduction of electric sewing machines, operated by women, greatly expedited their manufacture.[44] Of the tents obtained during the months of the war, the principal purchasing depots procured over 172,000 and the Philadelphia Depot manufactured over 199,000.[45]

Despite the rapidity with which the Department procured clothing and equipage, there were delays in clothing the troops at the camps. Some of the delay was attributable to the inexperience of volunteer quartermasters who did not know the sizes of the men they were to clothe, the method of requisitioning supplies, nor the proper issue procedures. Most of the delay, however, resulted from the breakdown in transportation. Colonel Patten was shipping clothing as fast as it became available, and he assumed that the troops at Tampa, for example, were being well outfitted. Much to his surprise, he later learned that this was not true. When Major General Miles arrived at Tampa, he informed the Secretary of War that 15 cars, loaded with uniforms, had been sidetracked 25 miles away and remained there for weeks while the troops suffered for lack of clothing.[46] Similarly, though canvas suits were sent to General Shafter's troops in Cuba on 6 July and were on transports in the harbor, the difficulty of unloading supplies at Siboney and the lack of transportation from the coast prevented distribution until after the surrender of Santiago when issue was begun on 25 July.[47]

[42] *Ibid.,* 115533 (Col. John Furey to QMG, 3 Sep 1898).

[43] *Ibid.,* Case 133396 (Maj. T. E. True to QMG, 25 Aug 1898).

[44] *Ibid.,* Case, 133396 (Maj. G. S. Bingham to Philadelphia Depot QM, 14 Aug 1898).

[45] *Annual Report of the Quartermaster General, 1898,* pp. 75, 76.

[46] Dodge Commission *Report,* VI, 2647 (Patten); II, 888–89 (Ltr, Miles to SW, 4 Jun 1898).

[47] *Ibid.,* II, 949, 970 (Telegrams, Alger to Shafter, 4 Jul 1898; AG to Shafter, 7 Jul 1898); I, 129 (Commission to President, 9 Feb 1899).

Subsistence Problems

As the Quartermaster's Department made haste to clothe the troops as soon as war was declared, so the Subsistence Department quickly turned its attention to feeding them. Although it was known that American soldiers would be fighting in a tropical climate, investigators later uncovered no evidence to show that the Department gave serious study or consideration to modifying the components of the ration. There were no conferences between personnel of the Subsistence Department and the Commanding General of the Army or Maj. Gen. William R. Shafter, commanding the expedition to Cuba. Nor did the Department consult with the Surgeon General of the Army as to the proper foods to be used. Except for the inclusion after 1890 of a pound of vegetables, the garrison ration had changed little in the past hundred years, but by the use of a growing list of substitutive components, the ration, as fixed by law, was capable of giving greater variety and was also liberal in amount. The field ration still called for bacon, hard bread, coffee and sugar, beans, rice, or hominy, and when possible, potatoes, onions, and canned tomatoes. A travel ration, first introduced in 1878 and somewhat modified in subsequent years, gave the troops hard bread, canned fresh or corned beef, canned baked beans, and coffee and sugar. Commissaries issued this ration to soldiers traveling on cars, stages, transports, or otherwise than by marching, or when, for short periods, they were separated from cooking facilities.[48]

Subsistence officers gave some thought to the problem of supplying an army in Cuba with fresh bread and meat. Lt. Col. James F. Weston, who was to serve as Chief Commissary on the Shafter expedition and became Commissary General of Subsistence in 1900, gave consideration to the difficulties involved even before the Regulars were ordered to camps in the South.[49] Exploring the possibility of furnishing the troops with fresh bread in the field, he learned that a New York baking company could be induced, at a reasonable cost, to dismantle its ovens and machinery and set them up in Florida or Cuba, as the Army required, to turn out 100,000 loaves daily. The Acting Commissary General thought, however, that any army put into the field would have to use hard and not soft bread.[50]

---

[48] (1) *War Department Annual Reports, 1898*, I, 550–52 (Rpt of Commissary General, 17 Oct 1898). (2) *War Department General Orders, 1878*, GO 59 (1 Aug 1878). See also GO 73 (28 Sep 1881); GO 104 (28 Aug 1882); GO 3 (16 Jan 1883).

[49] Senate *Doc.* 270, 56th Cong., 1st sess., "Food Furnished by Subsistence Department to Troops in the Field," 3 vols., Washington, 1900), III, 2384–85 (Weston to Gen. S. T. Cushing, 24 Mar 1898). Hereafter briefly referred to as Court of Inquiry *Record.* See also Weston's testimony, *ibid.*, I, 151–52.

[50] *Ibid.*, III, 2386 (Osgood to Weston, 8 Apr 1898).

As early as December 1897, when the Subsistence Department sent a commissary to the Klondike, Commissary Weston had called attention to the possibilities of supplying fresh beef in cans. Canned fresh beef, or roast beef as it was designated commercially, was already a part of the travel ration and, with the threat of war, Weston centered his efforts on its use. He discussed the problem with the Armour Packing Company, tried cooking a hash or stew using canned beef, and later at Tampa, as Chief Commissary of the expedition to Cuba, he had similar experiments conducted by Capt. H. L. Riley, commanding Troop E, 3d Cavalry. Adding potatoes, onions, flour, and condiments—"just what a soldier has"—Colonel Weston informed the Commissary General that he could make the canned beef into a palatable stew. The canned meat was in fact stringy and tasteless, and, under exposure to tropical sun, became increasingly disagreeable in appearance. Yet it was the best product of its kind available under existing standards in the meat packing and canning industries. Weston therefore argued that canned beef could be furnished without loss; it would be healthful; and it offered a solution to a difficult problem that had to be met. Neither he nor any other commissary contemplated that the troops would be subsisted on canned beef for any extended period of time or that they would, through lack of cooking facilities, be compelled to eat it cold as it came from the can, without vegetables and condiments.[51] Yet that was the situation that developed on the transports and during the campaign in Cuba.

If the Subsistence Department engaged in no foresighted planning for subsisting troops in the tropics, it was not negligent in its procurement of rations. In anticipation of war, the Acting Commissary General of Subsistence, early in April, advised all chief commissaries of military departments and all purchasing commissaries to have at all posts travel rations sufficient for the wants of the full garrison if they were ordered to move. He also directed them to list the firms from whom components of the field and travel rations could be obtained at once, if wanted in large quantities. The posts had large supplies of rations on hand in the spring of 1898, and when the War Department moved the Regulars to Chickamauga Park, New Orleans, Mobile, and Tampa in mid-April, they took along 30 days' rations to prevent deterioration of subsistence stocks at the depleted garrisons. In addition, the Subsistence Department ordered all rations and stores for sale, over and above what were needed by the reduced garrisons left at the posts, shipped to the southern camps, if that course was economical. The effect was to place in the hands of regiments larger amounts of rations than they could properly care for,

---

[51] *Ibid.*, III, 2384–85 (Weston to Cushing, 24 Mar 1898); II, 1859–60 (Rpt, Court of Inquiry, 29 Apr 1899).

and General Shafter subsequently requested suspension of the order requiring troops to bring with them a 30-day supply of rations.[52]

In the meantime, early plans for operations against Cuba called for the dispatch of an expedition of 70,000 men, and the Secretary of War ordered the Subsistence Department to concentrate 90 days' supply of rations for that number of men at Tampa. Although neither this proposed expedition nor several others materialized, subsistence orders in preparation for them resulted in huge quantities of rations—from 6 million to 7 million rations—being sent to Tampa, adding materially to the storage problem that developed there.

Among the components purchased and sent to Tampa were 1 million pounds of canned roast beef. The purchasing commissary at Chicago made this first purchase on 11 May on orders from Colonel Weston, then serving in the Washington office. On the same day, he ordered an additional 2,100,000 pounds, of which 620,000 pounds were shipped to San Francisco for the Manila expedition. When General Eagan assumed the duties of Commissary General of Subsistence that month, he directed additional purchases to be made to the end of June in New York and Chicago, until 6,847,174 pounds of canned roast beef were acquired, including 350,000 pounds delivered by Armour and Company from stock shipped to Liverpool and brought back.[53] The Court of Inquiry later concluded that the amount of canned fresh beef procured by the Commissary General was "excessive, unnecessary, and not demanded by the emergencies of the existing situation." [54]

The Department was equally generous in its procurement of other components of the ration. The expeditionary force to Cuba, for example, carried with it 1,198,055 rations of potatoes, onions, and canned tomatoes. Subsequent shipments to the depot commissary in June and July added almost 2 million more.[55] The rate of spoilage was high, but even if it had run to 75 percent, the Court of Inquiry concluded that nearly 1 million rations of vegetables should have found their way to the troops. This was a quantity sufficient to allow issue of the full vegetable component of the ration to 16,000 men for 62 days.[56]

Investigation fully revealed that if the Department erred in procurement, it erred on the side of over-supply. Troops made no complaints of ration shortages at the camps in the southern states. Troops arriving at a camp with travel or field rations turned in their baked beans, hard

---

[52] Dodge Commission *Report*, II, 881 (Shafter to AG, 27 May 1898).
[53] Court of Inquiry *Record*, III, 1948–67 (Purchase orders).
[54] *Ibid.*, II, 1875 (Rpt, Court of Inquiry).
[55] *War Department Annual Reports, 1898*, I, 652 ff. (Rpt, CGS, 17 Oct 1898).
[56] Court of Inquiry *Record*, II, 1865–66 (Rpt, Court of Inquiry).

ISSUING BEEF AT TAMPA

bread, and bacon at the commissary depot in exchange for fresh meat and flour.[57] Regiments had the flour baked into bread either by local bakers—an arrangement that did not always prove satisfactory—or, if their baking ovens had been carried along, the regiments baked their own bread. Such a field bakery might turn out 800 loaves in 10 hours. Regiments that baked their own bread were usually able to save money for their company funds.[58]

The fresh meat issued to the troops in camp was refrigerated beef, supplied under contract and delivered by the packing companies in refrigerated cars. Regimental commissaries drew directly from the cars on orders of the depot commissaries deposited with the representatives of the packing companies.[59] This was the first war in which the Army was not supplied with beef on the hoof as the source of its fresh meat.

[57] Dodge Commission *Report,* IV, 1242–43 (Lt. Col. James N. Allison, Chief Commissary, Camp Alger).
[58] *Ibid.,* III, 166–67 (Brigade Commissary J. C. Baldridge); III, 333 (Lt. Col. O. E. Wood, Chief Commissary, Seventh Corps).
[59] *Ibid.,* I, 548 (CGS Reply, 6 Oct 1898); III, 167 (Capt. J. C. Baldridge).

SERVING DINNER AT TAMPA

When the troops embarked for Cuba, they were directed to supply themselves with 10 days' travel rations. Because canned corned beef was not available in any large quantity at Tampa, commissaries provided most of the troops with canned fresh beef. It had been a component of the travel ration for 20 years but was still generally unfamiliar to the troops because canned corned beef, popularly known as "salt horse," had been most widely used in the past. Delayed in sailing and lacking cooking facilities on board the transports, the soldiers subsisted on cold canned beef, baked beans, and coffee from 8 to 24 June, when the landing at Daiquiri was completed.

Under the stress of circumstances, canned roast beef then became a part of the field ration, though Army regulations did not authorize it. When the expedition landed, a commissary depot was established at Siboney, and, to facilitate issues, Colonel Weston testified, no formal requisitions were required for rations. Regimental commissaries had only to give the number of men for whom they were drawing and select what they wanted from the stock on hand.[60]   The latter included an abundance of bacon, some canned corned beef, and ample quantities of potatoes, onions, and canned tomatoes.   With complete freedom of choice and ample supplies on hand at the depot, many of the troops still received canned roast beef, despite the fact that on the prolonged voyage to Cuba tinned beef had become unpalatable and even distasteful to them.   No testimony taken later clarified the reason for this choice of rations, though it is possible that the inexperience of regimental commissaries may have had something to do with it.   In any case, the testimony was conclusive that the Army in Cuba was insufficiently subsisted from the landing to the surrender of Santiago, the insufficiency being directly traceable to the deficiency in transportation that permitted no more than the accumulation of 1 day's supplies in advance of Army needs at the front.[61]

Refrigerated fresh beef was not sent to Cuba until 21 July, the day after the port of Santiago was opened for navigation.   The expeditions to Puerto Rico and the Philippine Islands included refrigerated beef in the rations carried with them.   Transports, equipped with refrigerating apparatus, were furnished either by the government or by the packing company making the delivery.   Where such transports were not supplied, as was the case with some troops going to the Hawaiian and Philippine Islands, the Quartermaster's Department shipped beef cattle in pens on the transports for slaughter and use on the way.   On arrival at Manila, the troops temporarily obtained refrigerated beef from the Navy until the Chief Commissary could make a contract with Australian packers for furnishing a regular supply.

In Cuba, the soldiers at first received the refrigerated beef with great satisfaction.   Arrangements for issuing and transporting the beef to the camps, however, were inadequate and inefficient.   Carelessly handled and exposed to sun and rain en route to the regimental camps, a considerable portion of the refrigerated beef became tainted before it reached the troops and was either rejected or trimmed down before cooking. The prolonged use of canned beef by the troops in the field met with no favor anywhere, but the Court of Inquiry later found that their complaints were not sufficiently strong to reach corps and division commanders and their commissaries.

On 21 December 1898, the Commanding General of the Army, Maj. Gen. Nelson A. Miles, testifying before the Dodge Commission, created a sensation.   He charged that canned fresh beef was furnished the troops "under pretense of experiment" and was really beef pulp from

---

[60] Court of Inquiry *Record*, I, 156.
[61] *Ibid.*, II, 1863 (Rpt, Court of Inquiry, 29 Apr 1899).

which the beef extract of commerce had been boiled out.   He claimed
that its use caused sickness.   He went on to charge that the refrigerated
beef furnished the troops in Cuba and Puerto Rico, as well as at the
camps at Tampa, Chickamauga, and Jacksonville was "embalmed," or
treated with chemicals to preserve it.   In his judgment, he testified, the
use of such beef was one of the serious causes of so much sickness and
distress among the troops.[62]

These spectacular charges brought immediate demands from the
packing companies that they be given an opportunity to appear before
the Dodge Commission.[63]   The latter had been sitting nearly 3 months
before such charges were aired for the first time, and "stranger and more
inexcusable and more unsoldierly still," according to Secretary Alger,
during all those months, "with this pretended knowledge of facts which,
if they existed, should have been made known to the Secretary of War,
for the protection of the army, General Miles had never mentioned the
subject." [64]

Miles' insinuations of negligence, dishonesty, and even criminal
incompetency on the part of the Subsistence Department reflected the
lack of harmony between the Commanding General of the Army and
the supply bureaus and fully revealed the frayed relations existing with
the Secretary of War.   His charges goaded the Commissary General into
denying them in language that was vituperative and highly improper in
an officer.[65]   Intemperate though his reply was, General Eagan's statement and the testimony of many other witnesses convinced the Dodge
Commission that there was no foundation in fact for the charges and
insinuations made by General Miles.   The Court of Inquiry, convened
under War Department orders early in 1899 to investigate these allega-
tions, came to the same conclusion.[66]   Careful and prolonged investigation by two commissions proved General Miles' charges unwarranted and
untrue, but the legend that embalmed beef was furnished to the troops
in the Spanish-American War persists to this day.

---

[62] Dodge Commission *Report*, VII, 3255–3261.

[63] See for example, *ibid.*, VIII, 408–09 (Swift & Co. to Commission, 24 Dec 1898).

[64] Alger, *Spanish-American War*, p. 377.

[65] As a result, General Eagan was tried by court martial, found guilty, and recommended
to be dismissed from the service. President McKinley, however, commuted the sentence
to suspension from rank and duty for 6 years. General Eagan was reinstated in the service
late in 1900 and, at his own request, was immediately thereafter placed on the retired list.
AGO, General Orders and Circulars, 1899, GO 24, 7 Feb 1899.

[66] (1) Dodge Commission *Report*, I, 153 ff. (Rpt to President, 9 Feb 1899).   (2) Court
of Inquiry *Record*, II, 1855 ff. (Rpt of Court of Inquiry, 29 Apr 1899).

Procurement of Wagons, Ambulances, and Animals

The procurement of horses, mules, wagons, and ambulances to provide mobility for the Army in the field continued to be a function of the Quartermaster's Department. On 1 April 1898, the Department had no reserve of wagons or ambulances and, in fact, had bought none in the 9 months before the war started. Such wagons and ambulances as the Army did possess were in the hands of the Regular troops and were carried with them into the field when mobilization began—a total of 500 four-mule escort wagons, 592 six-mule Army wagons, and 96 Red Cross ambulances. On 1 April, the Army had 6,701 horses, of which 6,120 were cavalry horses, 500 artillery horses, and 81 draft and siege battery horses, and it also had 2,021 mules, 81 of which were pack animals.[67]

The startingly small amount of field transportation on hand on the eve of the war was the direct result of the policy of retrenchment that had been pursued in the post-Civil War years. By 1895, it was believed that the Army would never again need wagon trains, since the Indian troubles were over, and if it did, wagons could be hired from contractors. On War Department orders, the Army's fine trains were broken up. Quartermaster Thomas Cruse recalled their loss with regret.

Wagons that cost two hundred dollars were sold to farmers for fifteen—and their stock were unable to pull them! Harness went for two dollars which had cost forty. It was nothing less than a crime! Lack of those trains caused the Army endless trouble— and lives—when we got into camps, but the reformers and amateur economists had their way.[68]

To save money, the wagon transportation of even the small Regular Army had been sold off and it had no more than five pack trains.

In the interests of economy, Congress had also limited the purchase of draft animals to 5,000 in the appropriation act for 1889—a limitation that was reenacted in succeeding appropriation acts. As late as 15 March 1898, on the eve of the Spanish-American War, Congress provided that the number of horses purchased, added to those on hand, was not to exceed the number of enlisted men and Indian Scouts in the mounted service.[69] This restriction was not suspended until 7 June 1898.[70]

When the war began, Col. Crosby P. Miller, in charge of procurement of wagons and animals in the office of the Quartermaster General,

[67] (1) Dodge Commission *Report*, I, 466 (QMG's Rpt to Commission, 14 Oct 1898). (2) *Annual Report of the Quartermaster General, 1898*, p. 10.
[68] Thomas Cruse, *Apache Days and After* (Caldwell, Idaho, 1941), pp. 255–56.
[69] 25 *Stat.* 486 (Sep 22, 1888); 30 *Stat.* 323 (Mar 15 1898).
[70] 30 *Stat.* 433.

estimated that the Army needed about 5,000 wagons. His estimate was based on an allowance of 25 wagons to a regiment of infantry, 45 to the cavalry, and 5 to a light battery, making about 275 wagons for a division and about 750 to a corps.[71] The manufacturers of wagons were completely unable to meet such a demand. Captain Cruse attended a meeting on wagon transportation in the Secretary's office, on 3 April, at which General Alger asked that the Studebaker Company furnish 200 six-mule Army wagons and 1,000 escort wagons as soon as possible, "say—within two months." To this request Clem Studebaker replied:

I couldn't agree to turn out two hundred six-mulers in a year. When you people sold off all your big wagons, some two years ago, we used up all our stock. Now we have neither material nor machinery to make them.[72]

In anticipation of the needs that war would create, Ludington early in April called for information from all prominent wagon and harness manufacturers of the country on how rapidly and at what prices they could supply the Army in an emergency.[73] To get wagons made according to Army specifications would have taken 9 months. The best that the manufacturers could do was to produce from materials that they had on hand about 50 wagons a week.[74] When the war began, these replies became the basis for purchase action. By telegram, the Department obtained bids and promptly awarded contracts for the first wagons. In order to limit the various kinds of wagons obtained so that the problem of furnishing parts in the field might be controlled, the Department made no awards to companies that could supply only a small number of wagons.[75]

To Supply the transportation needed, the Department began by furnishing the regiments what they would actually require in camp— four wagons to each regiment and enough wagons for the depot quartermaster—an objective that it did not accomplish until well into July. It supplied troops ordered to Cuba first, while those left at the camps had to operate with reduced transportation. By far the larger number of wagons furnished were so-called farm wagons, drawn by four mules. The Department procured and issued 3,605 of this type by the end of August. It also purchased a few spring wagons, a small number of Army six-mule wagons, and some escort wagons. In all, the Department procured during the war 4,620 wagons, but not all were delivered before the

[71] Dodge Commission *Report,* VI, 2625.
[72] Cruse, *Apache Days and After,* p. 264.
[73] Dodge Commission *Report,* I, 439 (QMG's Rpt to Commission, 14 Oct 1898).
[74] *Ibid.,* VI, 2625 (Miller).
[75] *Ibid.,* I, 439 (QMG's Rpt to Commission, 14 Oct 1898); VI, 2626 (Miller).

war ended and the Department rejected some because they failed to meet the standards set.[76]

Relatively few of the thousands of wagons procured saw service in the field overseas. The failure of the Quartermaster's Department to provide a sufficient number of transports with adequate carrying capacity for the Cuban expedition had the effect of limiting the land transportation available for the Santiago campaign. Colonel Humphrey testified that he shipped from Port Tampa 114 wagons, 1,336 pack and draft mules, 578 government horses, and 381 privately owned horses.[77] In addition, Shafter's Army also had 84 wagons that were sent from Mobile. He took no more land transportation because the vessels were fully loaded.

Under the most favorable circumstances, this land transportation would have been barely enough for the Army; in the conditions existing in Cuba it proved painfully deficient. The road upon which the Army operated rapidly became impassable for wagon transportation. Wagons stalled in the mud or broke down, delaying the trips to the supply depots at Siboney and Daiquiri. So bad were the roads that the ability of a pack mule to carry a load was reduced 50 percent. Mules that ordinarily could carry 250 pounds became heavily loaded, Maj. Gen. A. R. Chaffee testified, when they had two boxes of crackers, weighing 100 pounds, on their backs.[78] Teamsters and packers as well as soldiers were disabled by fevers to such an extent that the efficiency of transportation was much impaired. Soldiers who could handle six-mule teams replaced the civilian teamsters; experienced packers, however, were not as easily found and, on occasion, pack trains were laid up for lack of packers.[79] To the effects of rain, impassable roads, and the decimated ranks of labor must be added the wholly unanticipated demands for rations, for Shafter was feeding about as many refugees as he had soldiers in his Army.[80] As a result, land transportation in Cuba was taxed to its utmost.

The Quartermaster's Department sent new Army wagons or animals with the first expeditions to the Philippine Islands. As more troops and supplies were landed and the siege of Manila began, the question of providing land transportation became increasingly important. To meet this need, Chief Quartermaster Pope resorted to hiring pony carts and even employed bull carts drawn by carabaos, a slow means of transportation but still the best, he found, for moving supplies. Scarcity of carts made hiring expensive and he bought ponies and teams, though the price

[76] Ibid., I, 439, 466; VI, 2626.
[77] Ibid., VII, 2642–43; 3677–78.
[78] Ibid., IV, 910.
[79] John D. Miley, In Cuba with Shafter (New York, 1911), pp. 87–88.
[80] Dodge Commission Report, VII, 3199 (Shafter).

A PACK TRAIN MOVING AMMUNITION TO THE FRONT

of a pony soared from $15 and $20 to $100 and $150 per animal. To eke
out the lack of animals and vehicles, he employed Chinese and natives
to pack in stores. Lieutenant Colonel Pope early advocated the use of
coolie labor for military purposes and though his suggestion of bringing
500 to 1,000 Chinese from Amoy and Hongkong was not approved, they
were increasingly employed in the field as the Filipino insurrection
began.[81]

Production of ambulances was more difficult than of wagons. As an
Army item, none could be immediately purchased on the market and only
two companies—the Studebaker Company and the Milburn Wagon Company at Toledo—manufactured Army ambulances. The regulation
allowance of ambulances was 3 to a regiment, making 27 to a division.
The Quartermaster's Department ordered production of 500 Rucker and
50 Red Cross ambulances, the contracts being divided between the two
companies. They came in so slowly that the Department had great
difficulty in meeting the requirements of the Surgeon General who
directed the distribution of ambulances to the Army.[82]

[81] RG 92, OQMG Document File, 1800–1914, Case 115533 (Pope Rpt, 16 Nov 1898);
Case 133396 (Pope Rpt, 11 Aug 1899).
[82] Dodge Commission *Report*, VI, 2627–28 (Miller).

The Department was at all times able to supply mules and harness more rapidly than wagons. Experienced, qualified Quartermaster officers purchased mules. They also procured mules for pack trains, fitted out the trains at Jefferson Barracks, and shipped them with packers to Tampa and Mobile.[83] Horses for the Cavalry and Artillery of the Regular Army had for some time been purchased by boards of regular officers appointed for the purpose. Capt. James B. Aleshire, later to become Quartermaster General, had been furnishing nearly all the horses required by the Army and he continued making purchases. To supply the Volunteer Cavalry, boards, usually consisting of one Volunteer officer and two Regulars, generally purchased horses in the states from which the regiment came, so far as practicable and economical. These boards kept alert to the formation of any combinations to force prices upward and by moving to other localities if they detected such efforts, they protected the interests of the government. The Department bought a total of 36,800 animals during the war, of which 16,618 were horses and 20,182 were mules. By the end of August 1898, it had issued 36,033 animals, of which 16,483 were horses and 19,550 were mules.[84]

Distribution Problem

The meagre transportation with the Regulars when they were mobilized at Tampa, Mobile, New Orleans, and Chickamauga Park, and the difficulty of providing volunteer regiments and depot quartermasters at the camps with wagons promptly had much to do with the transportation and distribution snarls that developed. Col. James C. G. Lee, chief quartermaster at Chickamauga Park, found the incoming regiments so poorly supplied with transportation that it was wholly inadequate for camping purposes. To haul baggage and supplies, he had to supplement such transportation with teams hired from citizens.[85] His experience was not unique. When Capt. James B. Bellinger arrived at Tampa in mid-May to take charge of the depot, he was confronted with an appalling situation. There were 1,000 cars of supplies on sidetracks in and about Tampa, and the depot had 5 government wagons and 12 hired civilian wagons to unload them. Freight was arriving at the rate of 50 cars a day and could be unloaded at the rate of only two or three.[86] Adequate wagon transportation was essential to relieve the railroad block by emptying freight cars, to make available for issue the quartermaster and com-

---

[83] Cruse, *Apache Days and After*, pp. 264–67.
[84] Dodge Commission *Report*, I, 466 (QMG's Rpt to Commission, 14 Oct 1898).
[85] RG 92, OQMG Document File, 1800–1914, Case 115533 (Lee to QMG, 11 Sep 1898).
[86] *Ibid.*, Case 115533 (Bellinger Rpt, 18 May–31 Aug 1898).

missary stores necessary for equipping and feeding the troops, and to furnish the regiments with transportation necessary for hauling supplies to their camps. The task was further complicated by the fact that all wagons procured by the Department were sent "knocked down" and had first to be assembled, and all harness had to be fitted to mules that were "green." [87] The arrival of a superintendent of wagon transportation about the end of May and the erection of shops to repair wagons and harness did much to relieve the inadequacies of wagon transportation at Tampa.

Vast quantities of freight were shipped to Camp George H. Thomas at Chickamauga Park, Ga., to Camp Alger at Dunn-Loring, Va., to Camp Meade in Pennsylvania, and to other camps at Anniston, Huntsville, Knoxville, Lexington, and other localities through the South. At Tampa, the amount shipped in proved overwhelming because the depot could not be expanded as rapidly as troops and supplies arrived. Not only were large numbers of Regulars concentrated immediately at Tampa, but early in May, in preparation for a movement on Cuba that failed to materialize, an army of 70,000 men was ordered there with 90 days' supplies for them and 30 days' rations for their animals.[88]

The distribution of supplies was not as easily accomplished as their procurement in 1898. As in earlier years, the emphasis in distribution was not on storage but on transportation. The major Quartermaster depots were primarily purchasing offices or manufacturing plants. They afforded only a minimum amount of storage space, but that was ample to care for the needs of an Army whose size was well below 30,000 in the years following the Civil War. The Quartermaster's Department needed no large facilities for storing reserve stocks during those years, since retrenchment policies and meagre appropriations had prevented the accumulation of reserve stocks sufficient for even the small Army of that day. When the war began, the Department procured supplies and sent them as rapidly as possible to the camps where the troops were concentrating and to the embarkation points for the expeditions to Cuba, Puerto Rico, and the Philippine Islands. Quartermasters rented local storerooms and sheds and erected temporary storehouses.

Developing Crisis in Railroad Transportation

Under the supervision of the office of the Quartermaster General, chief quartermasters of the military departments and of general depots

---

[87] Ibid.

[88] (1) Annual Report of Major General Commanding the Army, 1898, p. 9. (2) Dodge Commission Report, VII, 3241 (Miles).

made contracts with the railroad companies for the shipment of supplies. These contracts called for general freight rates set by the carload preferably, or by the 100 pounds, if the shipment involved was small, or by class.[89]   For the most part, the chief quartermasters secured advantageous rates, but there was no co-ordination of shipments made by individual quartermasters nor any advance notice of freight shipments to the depot quartermasters at the camps.   With each quartermaster advised to send supplies forward as fast as they became available, congestion was inevitable at the destination points where freight cars could not be unloaded as quickly as they arrived, despite the Quartermaster General's instructions to pay no demurrage charges.   Confusion was further heightened at reception points, where certain supplies might be urgently needed, by the fact that materials of different classes, belonging to different departments, were frequently packed in the same car so that to obtain smaller packages of medicines and medical supplies, for example, large packages of quartermaster or commissary stores had first to be removed.

The congestion became so bad at Tampa that it was impossible to get ordinary freight shipments through.   The Department thereupon shipped carloads of fast freight, but these too being sidetracked, it made carload shipments by express and by special trains of fast freight.   Even such shipments were delayed.   Captain Bellinger found a special fast freight trainload of clothing, lost for 10 days, on a siding some 18 miles from Tampa.[90]   No small part of the difficulties of the Medical Department, it was charged, was occasioned by the slowness with which the Department transported medical supplies.   Like clothing, receipt of medical supplies was also delayed, even when shipped by fast freight. Supplies, for example, sent from the St. Louis depot to Chickamauga on 17 May were not received by the end of the month.[91]

Depot Quartermaster Kimball at New York reported that in the haste to get subsistence stores placed at Tampa to accompany the expedition, the depot instructed concerns from whom the stores were bought to deliver direct to the shipping lines and turn in their shipping receipts immediately to the depot office, but dealers failed to do so.[92]   Large numbers of freight cars were shipped on railroad waybills that the quartermaster did not receive until days and weeks after the cars arrived.   He could not determine the contents of freight cars because bills of lading were not sent in advance of stores, and shipping invoices were missing or

[89] Dodge Commission *Report,* VI, 2609 (Col. Charles Bird, deputy chief of Transportation Division).

[90] RG 92, OQMG Document File, 1800–1914, Case 115533 (Bellinger Report).

[91] Dodge Commission *Report,* I, 174 (Rpt to President, 9 Feb 1899); III, 732 (Maj. C. M. Gandy, brigade surgeon); V, 2319 (Deputy Surgeon General J. Morris Brown).

[92] *Ibid.,* I, 523 (Ltr, Kimball to QMG, 3 Jun 1898).

delayed.   This situation was not corrected until 2 June, when Ludington directed all depot and chief quartermasters to forward bills of lading promptly.[93]

A board of officers originally selected Tampa as a satisfactory site from which to dispatch a small force to Cuba.   Tampa, however, served by only two lines of single-track railroad, one of which controlled communication with the port, 9 miles distant, was not suited for handling an army of 25,000 men and the large amount of supplies required for its effective operation.   Much of the transportation congestion at Tampa stemmed from the lack of any plan for organizing a base depot.   Tampa, for example, just grew until it outstripped its facilities and confusion became ever greater.   Troops arrived before supply officers had camp sites ready or supplies on hand.   When the flood of supplies came, the quartermaster had only a small number of wagons to transport them, few facilities in which to store them, and no means to tell what the supplies were or for whom they were intended.   At Tampa, Captain Bellinger took steps to bring the situation under control.   To reduce confusion in the future, he advised the Quartermaster General of the need to send car numbers on bills of lading.   To reduce existing congestion, the depot quartermaster obtained more wagons and hired men to open, inspect, and determine the contents of cars backed up on sidings in all directions in the Tampa area.   Since it was impractical in the existing congestion for the railroads to place cars, Captain Bellinger had wagons driven alongside the tracks wherever possible, and the cars unloaded.   Where the class of stores permitted, they were unloaded on the ground, covered with paulins, and placed under guard.[94]   By mid-June, Quartermaster Bellinger could report that freight cars were being unloaded at the rate of about 70 a day; that only 100 cars of the Florida Central and Peninsular line and 111 of the Plant system remained unloaded at Tampa.   There were also 50 at Port Tampa and several hundred cars on sidings north of Tampa still to be unloaded, but he expected to have the tracks completely cleared in another week.[95]

Not all of the congestion at Tampa could be attributed to the shortcomings of the Quartermaster's Department.   Captain Bellinger found himself in the midst of what he described as a "cold, calculated railroad fight" between the two railroads—the Florida Central and Peninsular line and the Plant line—serving Tampa.   The Plant line also controlled the 9 miles of communication between Tampa and Port Tampa.   The

[93] *Ibid.,* I, 523 (Teleg, Ludington to Depot QM at St. Louis *et al.,* 2 Jun 1898).
[94] RG 92, OQMG Document File, 1800–1914, Case 115533 (Bellinger Rpt, 18 May–31 Aug 1898).
[95] Dodge Commission *Report,* I, 524–25 (To QMG, 15 Jun 1898).

railroads had ample sidings, but congestion had filled them as far north as Columbia, S.C., or half the distance from Tampa to Washington.[96] Instead of supporting Quartermaster Bellinger's efforts to eliminate congestion, the two roads became locked in a fierce competitive struggle, the Plant line refusing to transfer cars for unloading to the Florida Central. Only through Bellinger's determined efforts was an interchange track built so that 25 to 30 cars could be transferred daily instead of the 3 to 4 previously permitted by the Plant System's control of the connecting switch for the two railroads.[97] The Plant line also continually ran passenger trains between Tampa and the port, carrying crowds of sightseers and tourists, and the line's regular freight, passenger, and express business between Tampa and Key West went on without interruption.[98] Such freight was insignificant in comparison with what the line carried for the Army but the railroads' attitude was nevertheless revealing.

Between 18 May and 31 August, the depot at Tampa handled 13,239 carloads of freight or 158,862 tons. In an even shorter space of time, it also handled an enormous number of cars used in transporting 66,000 troops with their baggage and over 15,000 animals.[99]

Although it was late June before freight car congestion at Tampa was relieved, there was little complaint of the way in which the Quartermaster's Department handled the transportation of troops by railroad. As was customary, post quartermasters made the arrangements with the railroads under War Department contract for transporting the Regulars in April. On 8 May, in anticipation of the movement of volunteer forces, the Quartermaster General prepared lists of those to be transported from each locality and sent them to the chief quartermasters of the military departments concerned. The latter consulted with the railroads and settled in advance as many of the preliminaries as possible.[100] As a result, the bids were all in before the movement of volunteer troops began, and the Department obtained advantageous rates, averaging 1⅓ cents per mile.[101] It provided better accommodations for the soldier than in the Civil War. It furnished tourist sleeper cars or Pullmans to troops traveling over 24 hours, three men occupying a section. When

---

[96] The Florida Central had a sidetrack capacity at Tampa, its terminus, of about 350 cars that it expanded to 530. The Plant System had a sidetrack capacity at Tampa of about 680 cars and at Port Tampa of 850 that it increased to 848 and 1,003, respectively. RG 92, OQMG Document File, 1800–1914, Case 115533 (Bellinger Rpt, 18 May–31 Aug 1898).

[97] (1) *Ibid.,* (Ltr, Bellinger to H. B. Plant, 3 Jun 1898; Plant to Bellinger, 4 Jun 1898, appended to Bellinger's Rpt). (2) Dodge Commission *Report,* VII, 3639–40 (Col. C. F. Humphrey, Chief Quartermaster of Shafter's Army).

[98] Miley, *In Cuba with Shafter,* pp. 24–25.

[99] RG 92, OQMG Document File, 1800–1914, Case 115533 (Bellinger Rpt).

[100] Dodge Commission *Report,* I, 440 (QMG's Rpt to Commission, 14 Oct 1898).

[101] *Ibid.,* VI, 2608–09 (Bird).

day coaches had to be used, Ludington expressly stipulated that each soldier was to have a double seat for himself.[102]   On the whole, there was little criticism of the railroad transportation provided for the troops, although there were some complaints voiced about the delays that occurred, particularly in transporting the sick to their homes from Montauk Point.[103]

Delays frequently occurred as a result of factors over which the quartermaster had no control.   The wild scramble for railroad transportation that ensued at Tampa, for example, when Shafter received orders to sail, took place despite the careful preparations made by Captain Bellinger and the traffic manager of the Plant line.   Orders to move to Port Tampa for embarkation came on 5 June.   Bellinger and the traffic manager worked out a schedule calling for the arrival of trains at Port Tampa at half-hour intervals.   The trains were to be ready at a given hour and the troops were notified to break camp.   They were to haul their baggage to the designated siding, ready to be placed on the train. Bellinger allowed an average of 7 to 8 boxcars per regiment for company and regimental baggage.   Some delay occurred because the railroad was unable to switch out the accumulation of freight cars and clear the track in time.   Far more delay was occasioned by the excessive amount of baggage in the hands of the troops and the time it took them to transfer it from camp to cars and unload it.   Bellinger recalled that one regiment of less than 700 men used 15 boxcars for its baggage.

In the midst of this operation, General Shafter issued orders on the evening of 7 June to rush the movement; he intended to sail at daybreak with such troops as were on board the transports.   To expedite the movement, Bellinger then arranged to have a train for each of the remaining regiments placed at designated points along the track and moved out as soon as loaded during the night.   This placed a heavy strain on railroad equipment, and it was agreed that, if necessary, boxcars would be used by the troops.   In the meantime, Bellinger sent a letter to each division, brigade, and regimental commander, advising of the arrangements and notifying him that a wagon train of 25 wagons would be sent to each regiment to assist in hauling their baggage to the railroad.   His careful arrangements nevertheless went awry.   A corps commander notified the different organizations that they would be loaded as soon as possible. This was construed as an order to break camp at once and, with some 7 or 8 regiments up all night, confusion reigned supreme.   When a wagon train appeared, it was at once seized by the nearest regiment. In the wild haste to reach the railroad and not be left, troops so overloaded

---

[102] *Ibid.,* I, 440.
[103] *Ibid.,* V, 2198–2200 (Kimball).

wagons that fresh teams gave out before they had gone half a mile through the heavy sand.   Regiments ordered to move early in the evening arrived at the railroad only by daybreak for lack of wagons that never reached them.   Despite this disregard for plans, all the troops reached Port Tampa by 11 A.M.   Some 17,000 troops were moved from Tampa to the port in about 40 hours.[104]

The Department was criticized much more severely for the kind of transport vessels it furnished for the troop movement to Cuba.   In the years since the Civil War, Quartermaster supply operations had involved little or no shipment of troops or supplies by water.   For more than half a century it had not been necessary to send any large body of troops by sea to invade a foreign country.   Whatever knowledge the Department's officers had acquired in the Mexican War and in the course of the Civil War was completely lost to the quartermasters of 1898.   So much was this true that the deputy chief of the Transportation Division of the office of the Quartermaster General could testify "that the Army had never done anything of this kind; we had never transported troops by sea; it was something new to the Army of the United States." [105]

Ocean Transportation

In anticipation of the demands that might be made upon the Department, Ludington, on 24 March, directed his depot quartermaster at New York to ascertain and report on the number and carrying capacity of vessels that could be chartered on short notice from shipping companies in the coast-line trade.   In forwarding the desired information, Colonel Kimball advised the Quartermaster General that the Navy had an absolute option on all ships of the most prominent steamship companies.[106] Scouting and other ships could be purchased for "national defense" by the Navy Department without violating the spirit of the act appropriating $50 million, but the Quartermaster's Department operated under limitations.   It lacked funds and, in any case, did not feel warranted in demanding vessels before they were absolutely neded nor, conditioned by the many years of retrenchment, did it feel justified in chartering and maintaining them at large expense in advance of their need.   As soon as troop movements were determined, the Quartermaster's Department called upon owners of vessels to supply as many ships as they could spare without

---

[104] RG 92, OQMG Document File, 1800–1914, Case 115533 (Bellinger Rpt).

[105] Dodge Commission *Report*, VI, 2612 (Bird).

[106] (1) *Ibid.*, I, 467 (Ltr, Ludington to Kimball, 24 Mar 1898 and reply 29 Mar 1898). (2) See also *ibid.*, V, 2191–92 (Kimball).

however crippling too severely their commercial interests.[107]   The Dodge
Commission was of the opinion that a sufficient number of ships should
have been furnished promptly, even if such action compelled the seizure
of every steamer on the Atlantic and Gulf coasts sailing under the
American flag.[108]

Until June 1898, the Supplies and Transportation Division of the
office of the Quartermaster General supplied all means of transportation.
Increasing demands for transportation led the Quartermaster General
to place all wagon and animal procurement in a separate division.   Rail
and water transportation continued to be under the direction of Col.
Charles Bird until 18 July when, by order of the Secretary of War, the
Quartermaster General established two branches in the Transportation
Division, one to direct all railroad transportation and the other to have
exclusive charge of the ocean transport service.   At the Secretary's suggestion, Col. Frank J. Hecker became chief of the Transportation Division, Colonel Bird remaining as deputy chief.   Hecker was a Detroit
banker and railroad executive whose services were enlisted by Secretary
Alger to expedite the procurement of transports and to whom, on 20 June,
he granted full authority to charter or purchase ships.   Under this
authority, Hecker began his operations at once as a civilian agent, but
by 8 July he was commissioned a colonel in the Volunteer service.[109]

Before 1 July, Colonel Bird had chartered for the Cuban operation
43 transports, having an aggregate tonnage of 104,201 tons, with a
carrying capacity of 23,622 men, including their arms, ammunition, equipment, and supplies.   He had also obtained 4 water boats, 3 steam lighters,
2 ocean tugs, and 3 deck barges for the same expedition.   In addition,
he had chartered 14 transports on the Pacific Coast, having an aggregate
tonnage of 41,152 tons, with a carrying capacity of 13,688 men, including
their complete equipment and supplies.[110]   Under Colonel Hecker's
direction, quartermasters chartered additional transports to carry troops
and supplies to Cuba, Puerto Rico, and the Philippine Islands.   Suitable
vessels still could not be chartered and, by order of the Secretary of War,
Colonel Hecker purchased 14 large steamships and had them hastily
fitted up to carry troops and supplies to Cuba and Puerto Rico.[111]
Although the Transportation Division had difficulty in procuring ships,
it did not repeat the errors of the Civil War.   It did not employ middlemen to charter or purchase ships; the Dodge Commission uncovered no

[107] *Ibid.*, I, 445 (QMG's Rpt to Commission, 14 Oct 1898).
[108] *Ibid.*, I, 135 (Rpt to President, 9 Feb 1899).
[109] (1) RG 92, OQMG Document File, 1800–1914, Case 156557 (Alger to Hecker, 20
Jun 1898).   (2) *Annual Report of the Quartermaster General, 1898*, pp. 54, 61.
[110] *Annual Report of the Quartermaster General, 1898*, pp. 58, 59.
[111] For an account of Hecker's activities, se Dodge Commission *Report*, VI, 2767 ff.

scandals; and quartermasters paid reasonable prices for the charter and purchase of vessels.

In obtaining ships, the Department was handicapped not only by its self-imposed limitation of the demands made on shipowners but also by congressional opposition to granting American registry to foreign ships. Consequently, the only vessels it could charter for the Shafter expedition were the American merchant vessels engaged in the coastal trade on the Atlantic and the Gulf. These, for the most part, were small ships constructed for carrying freight and not designed for the transportation of large bodies of men. The Department chartered them at prices based on so much per gross ton, the companies providing the officers and crew and also victualing the ship.[112] The Department provided only coal and water. It also experienced some difficulty in chartering transports on the Pacific Coast. Because most of the steamship companies there were engaged in trade with the Far East and South America, the services of their vessels could be obtained only upon their arrival at their home ports. Except for one vessel secured through the Navy Department, the Washington office chartered all transports used on the Pacific Coast. They were all ocean vessels that were in themselves superior to any obtained for the Cuban operation.

As soon as each vessel was chartered, it was fitted up, under the supervision of Quartermaster officers at New York and San Francisco, respectively, for the transportation of troops to Cuba and the Philippine Islands. The time allowed for this work was so short, particularly for the first transports sent to Port Tampa in May, that, in some instances, quartermasters put material on board and sent along ship carpenters to make alterations while the vessels were en route.[113] They built wooden bunks, added washing facilities and water-closets, but made no arrangements for cooking, except such as would permit the men to prepare hot coffee, since the troops were to carry travel rations. They added wind scoops and sails to furnish air between decks, and, as long as the hatchways could be kept open and there was no storm, plenty of ventilation could be provided to keep the men comfortable. The ships for the Cuban operation were not equipped for any extended voyage but were simply intended to carry men on a 36-hour run to Havana. When the far more distant Santiago became the destination of Shafter's army, complaints about unsatisfactory transports reached the department. Quarters, it

---

[112] Maj. John W. Summerhayes, who had charge of outfitting the chartered ships at New York, testified that on the first transports sent to Tampa the owners furnished the provisions, boarding the officers for $1.50 a day, and if the men wanted anything more than their travel rations, they had to pay 50 cents per day. *Ibid.,* VI, 2413.

[113] *Ibid.,* I, 470 (Ltr, Ludington to Kimball, 9 May 1898).

was reported, were crowded, poorly ventilated, and unsanitary. The ships were obviously ill suited for service as troop transports. To alleviate the discomfort and suffering experienced by the troops, the Department substituted hammocks for bunks and procured electric plants to provide light and run ventilating fans, but lack of time prevented the installation of some of them. It provided galleys for cooking and more comfortable accommodations generally on the vessels chartered for the 7,000-mile voyage of the troops to Manila.[114]

Limited in its choice of vessels and lacking time to make adequate changes to accommodate the troops comfortably, the Department undoubtedly selected the best transports available. It is utterly incomprehensible, however, that it should have failed to ascertain the correct carrying capacity of the ships sent to Port Tampa. Secretary Alger wrote that the British standard for estimating carrying capacity of ships was adopted by officers of the Quartermaster's Department who were assisted by an officer of the Navy, detailed for the purpose by Secretary Long. That method of assigning one man to each ton-and-a-half carrying capacity proved to be a too-generous estimate, since the ships chartered were not troop ships.[115] Colonel Kimball, in his report on ships in March, had also furnished gross tonnage figures as submitted by the shipowners.

The Department apparently had doubts about the reported carrying capacity of the vessels sent to Port Tampa because, early in May, it requested Maj. James W. Pope, then depot quartermaster at Tampa, and Col. Charles F. Humphrey, soon to become Chief Quartermaster of the Shafter expedition, to ascertain "the extreme carrying capacity of each of the ships" in order that the Department might determine whether sufficient ships had been sent to carry troops and supplies. Colonel Humphrey reported that a board of officers had examined the vessels and found that they could not be "loaded to carry the number certified by the agents at time of charter."[116] By the time Shafter's army was to sail, the original fleet assembled at Port Tampa had been increased to 38 vessels, including 2 water boats, 3 steam lighters, 1 collier, 1 tug, and 2 decked barges. Estimated to have a carrying capacity of 20,000 to 25,000 men, the fleet was actually able to transport less than 17,000 men, and most of the vessels were uncomfortably crowded, stuffy, and badly

---

[114] *Ibid.,* I, 446–47 (QMG's Rpt to Commission, 14 Oct 1898); I, 477 (Telegram, Ludington to Summerhayes and Kimball, 14 Jun 1898); VI, 2410 ff. (Summerhayes); VI, 2614 (Bird).

[115] Alger, *The Spanish-American War,* p. 75.

[116] Dodge Commission *Report,* I, 468 (Ltr, QMG to Humphrey, 2 May 1898; Ltr, Maj. Bird to Maj. Pope, 4 May 1898); I, 469 (Telegram and ltr, Humphrey to Ludington, 9 May 1898).

equipped.[117] Instead of the troops being on board for no more than 48 hours, the point of destination for the fleet involved a 6-day journey.

The confusion at Tampa when the troops broke camp to move to Port Tampa was duplicated at the embarkation on 7 June. It was heightened by the frantic efforts of the troops who, on hearing that the capacity of the ships had been overestimated, were determined not to be left behind. "Everybody was in feverish haste to go on board the transports," Lt. Col. John D. Miley, aide-de-camp to General Shafter, recalled; "often, before one regiment was completely embarked the next would arrive, impatient and chafing at any delay in giving them the assignment of a vessel." [118] At Port Tampa, there was only one long pier from which supplies and men could be placed on board the transports. It extended for about half a mile along a canal into which the ships had to be brought. There was no dock and the limited wharf facilities made loading a difficult operation. The railroad track was about 50 feet from and parallel to the canal. All boxes and packages had to be carried from the cars and across the sand on the backs of stevedores or trucked over improvised platforms. Nine vessels could lie for loading in the canal with two more at the slip and two at the pier built at the end of the narrow strip of land.[119] As soon as the ships were loaded, they were warped to the other side and out of the canal, stern first, by tugs, and anchored in the bay until the loading of all ships was completed.[120]

Chief Quartermaster Humphrey was in charge of the ocean transportation. He had never loaded ships before but he was assisted by a civilian shipmaster, Capt. James M. McKay, who for some 20 years had been engaged in trade between Florida and Cuba.[121] The loading of supplies had already been accomplished before the troops arrived. Statements made that property was loaded in a helter-skelter way, with ammunition separated from artillery guns and commissary, medical, and quartermaster stores intermingled, led the Dodge Commission to inquire into the method of loading. General Shafter had ordered rations and ammunition put on board each ship so that in the event it became detached, the ship could act separately.[122] That order was executed, but both Colonel Humphrey and Captain McKay stoutly maintained that stores were loaded in order and by themselves. Men on the wharf had

---

[117] (1) *Annual Report of the Quartermaster General, 1898*, p. 63. (2) Dodge Commission *Report*, IV, 987 (Maj. Gen. A. R. Chaffee).

[118] *In Cuba with Shafter*, p. 27.

[119] Dodge Commission *Report*, VII, 2668 (Capt. James M. McKay, ship captain and assistant to Colonel Humphrey).

[120] *Ibid.*, VII, 2640–41 (Humphrey).

[121] *Ibid.*, VI, 2655 (McKay); VII, 3209 (Shafter).

[122] *Ibid.*, VII, 3208 (Shafter).

checked them as they were put on board, and both the Commissary and Ordnance Departments had officers present looking after their own stores. It is to be noted that the Medical Department did not follow this practice, and regimental stores were not reported. Colonel Humphrey kept a tabulated report of everything which he submitted to General Shafter on 19 June, though captains of ships received no such lists.[123]

Though Captain McKay insisted that loading was orderly, sufficient testimony was given to indicate that medicines, stores, and hospital furniture were often put in the holds of transports under all sorts of freight, and that, because of lack of proper landing facilities and the difficulty of getting at the contents of ships, perhaps a third of the medical supplies taken aboard at Port Tampa were not put ashore until after the surrender of Santiago. Since the Quartermaster's Department was responsible for loading, shipping, and unloading medical stores, the Dodge Commission concluded that, to the extent that slow transportation and delivery failures accounted for lack of such supplies, the Department had to share the blame for the shortages of medical supplies that harassed the Army in Cuba.[124]

Loading the transports was complicated by the limited wharf facilities at Port Tampa and by the fact that full cargoes were not on hand. It frequently was necessary to bring transports into the canal to be loaded and, before loading was finished, send them into the harbor to be brought back later to complete the cargo. To obtain complete rations to be loaded on any one vessel, supply officers often had to go not only from car to car but also from one train to another in order to complete rations.[125] Colonel Humphrey averred that he loaded all supplies that came to him, but the number of transports was inadequate to carry everything. Because shipping space was unavailable, General Shafter ordered a fully equipped train of 40 ambulances to be left at Tampa; wagons, he decided, would have to serve the dual purposes of supply carriers and ambulances.[126]

Limited railroad facilities and inadequate harbor accommodations did not harass the quartermasters at San Francisco. Transportation facilities were in no way taxed by the mobilization and embarkation of troops for the Philippines. Nor was it necessary for the quartermasters to supervise the embarkation at once of any large body of men. Owing to the difficulty of obtaining transports, the Eighth Army Corps, comprising the forces of the Philippine expedition, was dispatched in seven

[123] *Ibid.*, VI, 2660–61 (McKay); VII, 3642 (Humphrey); pp. 3673–85 (Tabulated report).
[124] *Ibid.*, I, 174–75 (Rpt to President, 9 Feb 1899).
[125] *Ibid.*, VII, 3667 (Humphrey).
[126] *Ibid.*, VI, 3037 (Maj. B. F. Pope, chief surgeon); VII, 3194 (Shafter).

separate movements, beginning on 25 May and ending in October.[127] Only the troops of three of these expeditions reached Manila in time to take part in the assault and capture of that city.

Quartermaster Humphrey completed the loading of supplies for Shafter's expedition to Cuba on the morning of 6 June, when he reported to the general that he was ready to receive troops by noon. Loading of the troops did not begin until the following day because of the delay occasioned by the congestion on the railroad. When the troops did arrive, no schedule had been prepared in advance for assigning transports to troops and for informing regimental commanders of the assignment before they reached the port. Lt. Col. Joshua W. Jacobs, assistant to Colonel Humphrey and afterwards Chief Quartermaster of the Fifth Corps, testified that he never saw any specific program for troop embarkation, but Captain McKay was as certain that such a program had existed.[128] Colonel Humphrey pointed out, however, that if such a schedule had been made in advance it would have gone by the board, since troops did not arrive at their designated times. In general, Humphrey knew the ships that would be used by brigades and divisions. He was notified by telephone or telegraph when specific regiments or batteries broke camp and started to the port, and he was informed of the number of men in each organization. When a regiment arrived, Colonel Humphrey, for the first time, assigned the troops to a ship, fitting strength of regiments to capacity of ships.[129]

With some 10,000 men hastily embarking from a narrow pier with limited facilities for handling them, congestion and some confusion were inevitable. To Captain McKay, it seemed orderly enough but to Colonel Theodore Roosevelt of the Rough Riders, it was a "higglety-pigglety business." The intense excitement of that June morning came through as he testified how he and Colonel Wood, determined to get their men to Cuba, had hunted for Colonel Humphrey who allotted them the *Yucatan.*

The *Yucatan* was coming in at the dock, and by that time we found there was a great scramble for the transports, and Colonel Wood jumped in a boat and went out in midstream. I happened to find out by accident that the transport *Yucatan* had also been allotted to the Second Infantry and the Seventy-first New York, and I ran down to my men and left a guard on the *Yucatan,* holding the gangplank against the Second Infantry and the Seventy-first New York, and then letting aboard only the Second Infantry, as there was no room even for all of them.[130]

[127] *War Department Annual Reports, 1898,* I, pt. 2, pp. 268–69.
[128] Dodge Commission *Report,* V, 1842–43 (Jacobs); VI, 2657–59 (McKay).
[129] *Ibid.,* VII, 3640, 3651 (Humphrey).
[130] *Ibid.,* V, 2258.

EMBARKING THE TROOPS AT PORT TAMPA

This seizure and holding of a ship not only never occurred according to Captain McKay and Colonel Humphrey, but General Shafter insisted it would never have been permitted. "He would not have allowed such an act of insubordination as taking any of the boats; had they gotten onto the wrong ship, they would have gotten off very shortly." [131]

Despite all difficulties, supplies and troops—as many as General Shafter could risk taking—were on shipboard within a week and started out of the harbor on 8 June only to be recalled as a result of a false rumor that the Spanish fleet had been sighted. The expedition did not sail until 14 June, arriving 6 days later at Daiquiri, selected as the point of debarkation. If anything, quartermasters experienced more difficulty in landing the expeditionary force than in embarking it in the first place.

The Department was not remiss in its efforts to provide lighters; in anticipation of the need and without requisition, it had searched for suitable steam lighters as soon as the war began. Colonel Bird went from Boston to Galveston without locating more than four. General Ludington urged his quartermasters at Port Tampa, Mobile, Pensacola, and at other ports on the Gulf to help solve this problem.[132] The Department

---

[131] *Ibid.*, VII, 3209. See Maj. Gen. Leonard Woods' testimony supporting Shafter, VII, 3605–06. See also VI, 2659 (McKay); VII, 3651–52 (Humphrey).

[132] *Ibid.*, VI, 2615 (Bird); I, 502–04 (Ltrs, Ludington to Maj. Pope, 30 Apr, 4 May; to Maj. Pullman, 30 Apr; to Col. Humphrey, 7, 25 May 1898).

LANDING THE TROOPS AT DAIQUIRI

managed to furnish the expedition two light-draught steamers, the *Cumberland,* and the *Manteo* that carried stevedores to Cuba and could be run to the small wharf at Daiquiri and unloaded. It also provided two steam lighters, the *Laura* and the *Bessie,* a sea-going tug, the *Captain Sam,* and two decked barges. General Shafter counted on using the 153 lifeboats of the transports that had a carrying capacity of over 3,000 men, and he expected to have help from the Navy.[133] What appeared to be ample preparations for debarkation turned out to be sadly inadequate. En route to Cuba one of the decked barges was lost, the *Bessie* had to turn back for repairs, the steam-tug *Captain Sam* deserted, and only one steam lighter, the *Laura* reached Cuba. The Navy could not continue to spare boats for the landing of supplies.

Disembarking the troops—men with their blanket rolls, 3 days' rations, ammunition, and rifles—caused no particular trouble. Some were landed by the Navy, but many came ashore in the small boats of the expedition that, for the most part, the troops themselves manned. Landing supplies, however, posed difficulties. The harbor of Daiquiri was actually an open roadstead, only slightly sheltered. There was only

[133] *Ibid.,* VII, 3195 (Shafter); 3642, 2674 (Humphrey).

A Small Boat Landing Troops at Daiquiri

one place that a transport could anchor with safety and that was at the
pier of the iron company, but, since it was 80 feet from the water to the
top of the pier, it was useless.   There remained one small dock at which
all supplies had to be landed from vessels having a draught of less than
8 to 10 feet.   The expedition's lighterage had been sharply decreased
by losses, but the demands made upon what remained were decidedly
increased by the greater distance the supplies had to be lightered because
of the unwillingness of the transport captains to run the risk of bringing
their vessels close in to the rocky, precipitous shore.[134]

General Shafter called for more lighters and, in response, tugs with
barges in tow were dispatched by the Quartermaster's Department from
Mobile, New Orleans, and Key West, but all were lost in storms at sea.
The unsuccessful efforts of the Department to relieve the acute situation
at Daiquiri led it to enter into a contract with the New York firm of
D. Van Aken & Co.   The latter was to send an expedition of skilled
artisans and laborers with the necessary equipment for constructing

[134] *Ibid.*, VI, 2662–63 (McKay); II, 971, 974 (Telegram, Shafter to AG and reply, 7 Jul
1898).

lighters, barges, docks, and wharves, and for repairing railroads and engines.   By the time the expedition arrived on 23 July, Santiago had surrendered, and it was ordered to Puerto Rico where it was employed in unloading transports and performing other services needed by the troops serving under Maj. Gen. Nelson A. Miles.[135]

Unloading supplies at Manila was also beset with difficulties.   Chief Quartermaster Pope, arriving on board the *Newport* on 25 July, found a situation that he described as one of the most remarkable ever to confront a transportation officer.   The first expedition, consisting of three transports, had arrived, unloaded at Cavite, and departed.   The four transports of the second expedition had arrived on 16 July but were still unloading in the harbor when the third expedition anchored in the bay. The troops, investing the city of Manila, had established their camp, called Dewey, several miles north of the city and were also holding the town of Cavite.   These two places were separated by the bay and land communication was impossible, since the 12-mile long road around the bay was impassable.   The troops at Cavite and Camp Dewey had to be fed and clothed and communications had to be kept open, but the only means of transportation, the Chief Quartermaster reported, was one small rented launch belonging to the Department and two small steamers.   The latter were under the control of the Navy but allowed to tow cascos, loaded with rations and other supplies, across the bay at stated times. The casco was the native lighter, a heavy flat-bottomed boat, capable of holding from 50 to 100 tons of freight, covered with matting to protect the stores.   Since the water was so shallow that neither the steamers nor the launch could approach Camp Dewey, getting the cascos to shore without destroying the stores was a problem.   Lieutenant Colonel Pope emphatically recommended that in dispatching future expeditions every transport should be provided with a good high-powered launch, of light draft, for landing troops and supplies and for towing ships' boats in case of necessity.[136]

Criticism and Investigation

The shortcomings of the supply bureaus in clothing, equipping, subsisting, and transporting the Army might all have been promptly forgotten after the collapse of Spanish resistance if there had been no publication of the famous "Round Robin," a paper signed by Col. Theodore Roosevelt and the general officers of the Fifth Army Corps,

---

[135] For the report of the quartermaster of this expedition, see RG 92, OQMG Consolidated Correspondence File, Box 1065 (Rpt, Capt. W. P. Williams to Brig. Gen. J. C. Gilmore, 28 Sep 1898).

[136] RG 92, OQMG Document File, 1800–1914, Case 115533 (Rpt, 16 Nov 1898).

demanding that the troops, disabled by malarial fever, be sent home from Cuba.   Further revelations concerning the dirty, overcrowded transports that brought the sick to the camp at Montauk Point, the lack of fresh water, insufficient medicines, and want of medical care on shipboard, as well as the inadequate housing, transportation facilities, and supplies at the hastily erected Camp Wickoff itself aroused such a storm of criticism against the War Department and the supply bureaus that Secretary Alger called for a full investigation.   President McKinley appointed a commission, headed by Grenville M. Dodge, an army officer of Civil War fame and chief Engineer in the building of the Union Pacific Railroad, to examine into the conduct of the war.[137]

The Commission, after months of taking testimony in various cities throughout the country, submitted a report to the President on 9 February 1899.[138]   In reference to the Quartermaster's Department, it praised the zeal and industry of its officers in accomplishing "the herculean task" of obtaining and issuing within so short a period the immense quantity of materials required by the Army and, in particular, commended the effort that had been made to protect the interests of the government.   It was critical, however, of the lack of system exhibited in supplying the camps, the lack of administrative or executive ability shown in the failure to prevent congestion at Tampa, and the lack of foresight in preparing a fleet of transports.   In general, it attributed most of the shortcomings of supply to the scarcity of trained officers and the general unpreparedness. So intense, however, were the excited feelings of the country at the time the Commission sent its findings to President McKinley that the report was condemned as a "whitewash."   After a lapse of more than half a century, a cooler judgment must support the conclusions of the Dodge Commission.   It avoided making a scapegoat of Quartermaster General Ludington, Surgeon General M. Sternberg, Commissary General Eagan, and Secretary of War Alger for the unpreparedness that had handicapped operations.   Though the Commission threw out for consideration the suggestion that the Quartermaster's, Subsistence, and Pay Departments might be consolidated and a separate Transportation Division created, its findings produced no immediate reforms, but the lessons drawn from the war ultimately did result in far-reaching changes, not only in the Quartermaster's Department but also in the War Department as a whole.

[137] Dodge Commission *Report*, I, 237 (Ltr, Alger to President, 8 Sep 1898; McKinley to Commission, undated).
[138] For the report see *ibid.*, I, 107 ff.

CHAPTER XIII

Conversion of a Department into a Corps

Root's Reform Measures

The years between the close of the Spanish-American War and the declaration of war against Germany in 1917 were marked by significant developments in Quartermaster operations stemming from the shortcomings revealed in 1898 and the recommendations made for their improvement. These developments were effected against a background of long over-due reforms in Army and War Department organization. For the Quartermaster's Department, the administrative reforms meant the conversion of the Department, as it had existed since 1818, into the Quartermaster Corps of today.

Despite the pressure for reform built up by the barrage of criticism that struck the War Department in 1898 and the findings of the Commission Investigating the Conduct of the War, reforms were introduced only gradually. Elihu Root, who became Secretary of War on 1 August 1899, was the guiding force behind the reform measures, but President McKinley's appointment of him was dictated not by a desire to bring about reorganization of the War Department but by the need to obtain the services of a lawyer who could handle problems of colonial administration resulting from the acquisition of overseas possessions.[1] Much of the new Secretary's attention was devoted to these problems, but he also began a close study of the War Department which resulted in the initiation of a series of reforms designed to eliminate the confusion and inefficiency that had characterized War Department administration in the past.

Two of Root's proposals—the establishment of the General Staff and the short detail system—were fundamentally important to the supply departments in the changes they brought about. According to Newton D. Baker, who was Secretary of War during World War I, Root's creation of the General Staff was his outstanding contribution to national defense, for without it the country's participation in that war "would necessarily

---

[1] Philip C. Jessup, *Elihu Root* (2 vols., New York, 1838), I, 215.

have been a confused, ineffective, and discreditable episode." [2]   Persistent in his advocacy of this reform, Root slowly but steadily built support for the measure. [3]

The past record of friction between the Commanding General of the Army and the Secretary of War and the supply bureau chiefs was clear enough.   In theory, the Commanding General was the senior military adviser to the President and the Secretary of War, but in practice he had functioned chiefly as the field commander of the combat forces. He was responsible for the efficiency and discipline of the troops and for other purely line matters, but he had no direct supervision of the supply agencies that provided support for the field forces.   The Secretary of War held the purse strings and, to that extent, exercised control over the chiefs of the supply bureaus, but, for the most part, their actions were unco-ordinated, and no one in the War Department was responsible for long-range planning.

Under the zealous guidance and influence of Secretary Root, Congress enacted legislation in 1903 creating the position of Chief of Staff and the General Staff Corps. [4]   It abolished the separate office of Commanding General of the Army.   It gave authority to the Chief of Staff, under the direction of the President or of the Secretary of War, to supervise all troops of the line and the special staff and supply departments.   To assist the Chief of Staff, Congress established a General Staff Corps and made it responsible for mobilization and defense planning.

Legislation created the General Staff; interpretation and application of the law was another matter.   Obviously, the supply departments were not going to welcome General Staff supervision, and bringing them under the control of the new agency was not easily accomplished.   Difficulties in defining General Staff responsibilities and particularly in fixing relationships between the General Staff and the supply and administrative bureaus developed at once.   Opposition grew to such an extent that Congress included a limiting provision in the National Defense Act of 1916 to the effect that the General Staff was not to be "permitted to assume or engage in work of an administrative nature that pertained to established bureaus or offices of the War Department." [5]   Only the stand taken by Secretary of War Newton D. Baker in rejecting the opinion of the Judge Advocate General as to the meaning of the law saved the essential principles of the General Staff, but it did not restore in time

---

[2] *Ibid.,* I, 240.

[3] *Five Years of the War Department Following the War with Spain, 1899–1903, As Shown in the Annual Reports of the Secretary of War* (n.d., n.p.). p. 165 (Rpt, 27 Nov 1901); pp. 292 ff. (Rpt, 1 Dec 1902).   Hereafter briefly cited as *Five Years of the War Department.*

[4] 32 *Stat.* 830–31 (Feb 14, 1903).

[5] 39 *Stat.* 168 (Jun 3, 1916).

its power "to make it a vigorous director of war preparations before the outbreak of hostilities with Germany." [6] The objective of co-ordinating War Department activity was not gained in the years before World War I.

Impact of the Detail System

Even before he had achieved his purpose of establishing a General Staff Corps, Root had struck a blow against entrenched bureaucracy. In the course of his intensive study of organizational problems, the Secretary became impressed by the separation of line and staff that had resulted from detailing officers of the line to permanent staff positions in the Quartermaster's Department and in the other supply bureaus. Critics argued that such officers, appointed for life to staff positions after only a short period of service with troops during the early part of their careers, lost touch with the troops in the field and became ignorant of their needs. They attributed much of the maladministration of the supply services during the Spanish-American War to this policy.[7]

The pendulum was now allowed to swing to the other extreme. To correct the evils flowing from permanent tenure, Root proposed and Congress enacted legislation providing for a short detail system, under which officers of the line were to be detailed to serve in a staff position for a period of 4 years, after which they would again return to service with the troops.[8] This provision, however, applied immediately to future staff appointments. As long as there remained any officers holding permanent appointments in the Quartermaster's Department and in the other supply bureaus, they were to be promoted according to seniority. By the end of June 1901, three officers had been detailed from the line for duty in the Quartermaster's Department. The number increased to nine by the end of the next fiscal year.[9]

The new system received favorable endorsement from no bureau chief. It ran counter to the whole basic philosophy of the Quartermaster's Department. Since the days of Jesup, continuous training of quartermasters in time of peace to provide efficient staff officers in the event of war had been an objective. The Department was in full accord

---

[6] John D. Millett, "The Director of Supply Activities in the War Department; An Administrative Survey, I," *The American Political Science Review,* XXXVIII (April 1944), No. 2, p. 254.

[7] See, for example, Dodge Commission *Report,* VIII, 566–67 (Ltr, Chas. F. Benjamin to Capt. Evan P. Howell, 16 Jan 1899).

[8] (1) *Five Years of the War Department,* p. 64 (Rpt, 29 Nov 1899). (2) 31 *Stat.* 755 (Feb 2, 1901).

[9] *Annual Report of the Quartermaster General, 1901,* p. 26; *1902,* p. 25.

with the convictions expressed by a contributor to the *Army and Navy Journal*.

An Ingalls or a Rucker cannot be picked by chance or made to order; long years of training and superior business capacity are required for their making, while their functions in a great war are not less essential than those of the commanding general.[10]

Brig. Gen. Charles F. Humphrey, who became Quartermaster General when General Ludington retired in 1903, repeatedly criticized the effects of the new system on the efficiency of the Department. In his opinion, Quartermaster duties constituted a profession that could be learned only by close application and long experience. This, he contended, was an age of specialization in the commercial world and should be no less so as far as Quartermaster business was concerned.[11]

Humphrey's successor, Brig. Gen. James B. Aleshire, reported that in 1907 most of the important work of the department—major construction projects, operation of general depots, and supervision of the Army Transportation Service—were all being carried on under the direction of officers of the old force of the Department who held permanent assignments. Selection of field officers would ultimately be necessary, he conceded, but they would not have the technical knowledge necessary for efficient service. Bad as the situation was in peace, Aleshire predicted that it would be worse in war, when the Department would require officers of zeal, experience, and efficiency but would find it difficult to obtain them since the type required would seek duty with troops in the line.[12]

The short detail system had its defects and brought new problems. Line officers were reluctant to volunteer for detail to staff positions because considerable study was necessary to pass the examination for appointment, which, in any case, brought no increase in pay or rank. Moreover, many of their superior officers were not in sympathy with such appointments. They held that any duty that took a line officer from his branch of service was time wasted and was likely to decrease his efficiency.

When the Chief of Staff requested Quartermaster General Humphrey to submit suggestions for the reorganization of his Department in the spring of 1904, he promptly seized the opportunity to recommend adoption of a system of permanent appointment of commissioned officers in

---

[10] *Army and Navy Journal*, vol. 41, p. 886 (Ltr to editor, 23 Apr 1904). A lively debate on this topic was conducted in letters to the editor.

[11] (1) *Annual Report of the Quartermaster General, 1905*, pp. 59–60. (2) See also views of Quartermaster officers on the detail system, RG 92, OQMG Document File, 1800–1914, Case 201640 (Bd. of officers' minutes, 25 Mar, 22 Apr 1904). National Archives.

[12] *Annual Report of the Quartermaster General, 1908*, pp. 54–55.

the Department for all grades, including 30 of the 60 captains authorized for the Department.[13] Other supply chiefs made similar proposals. Critics decried the suggested restriction of the detail system to the junior grades in each staff department as the "edge of a wedge which later may be driven into the head destroying the whole structure" that Root had erected.[14] Humphrey enlarged on his proposed modification again the following year, but it was 1906 before any action was taken. Then, Congress provided for a partial abandonment of the short detail system but made it applicable only to the Ordnance Department.[15] This concession, however, encouraged the Quartermaster General and the other supply bureau chiefs to renew their attacks, and only the slowness of Congress to act prevented complete abandonment of the system before World War I.

Renewed Interest in a Service Corps

If the Quartermaster's Department showed only a tepid interest in the measures thus far sponsored by the Secretary of War, there was one reform that it had been advocating ever since the days of the Mexican War, when the idea of an enlisted service corps was first suggested by Deputy Quartermaster Thomas Cross and endorsed by Quartermaster General Jesup.[16] The Spanish-American War had served once again to emphasize the need for such a corps of reliable, experienced men. It would relieve the Quartermaster's Department from its dependence upon civilians who had no knowledge of army regulations, orders, or business methods.

Humphrey, who, as Chief Quartermaster with Shafter's Army, had painfully experienced the inadequacies of civilian help in Cuba, submitted a draft of a bill for creating a service corps to the Secretary of War soon after he became Quartermaster General. He reiterated his arguments in its behalf year after year during his service as chief of the Department.[17] By that time, the Commissary General of Subsistence, the Adjutant General's Office, and departmental commanders were all recommending the establishment of a service corps. The latter were particularly impressed with the need of such a corps as a means of

---

[13] RG 92, OQMG Document File, 1800–1914, Case 201640 (Humphrey to Chief of 3d Div, General Staff, 31 Aug 1904).

[14] *Army and Navy Journal*, vol. 41, pp. 1276–77 (6 Aug 1904).

[15] 34 *Stat.* 455 (Jun 25, 1906).

[16] See *ante*, pp. 243; 286–87.

[17] (1) RG 92, OQMG Document File, 1800–1914, Case 201640 (Humphrey to SW, 16 Feb 1904). (2) *Annual Report of the Quartermaster General, 1904*, p. 32; *1905*, pp. 62–63; *1906*, p. 49.

eliminating the detail of men from the line for extra duty, which weakened organizations and decreased the efficiency of the Army.[18] In 1906, the General Staff drafted another bill for creating a service corps. The Secretary of War sent it to Congress but no action was taken.[19] Like his predecessor, Quartermaster General Aleshire year after year recommended establishment of such a corps, but War Department efforts failed to secure the necessary legislation.[20]

Establishment of the Quartermaster Corps

In the meantime, the War Department sponsored another reform that had been recommended by the Dodge Commission and one that had been given much attention even earlier in the reorganization efforts of post-Civil War days.[21] Secretary Root satisfied himself that separate supply departments, acting independently of each other and responsible only to a civilian Secretary of War, constituted a bad arrangement that was productive of confusion, conflict, unnecessary expenditure of money, and increased paper work, and that they also made for difficulty in fixing responsibility. He therefore recommended the consolidation of the Commissary, Pay, and Quartermaster's Departments into one supply agency in the fall of 1901.[22]

This initial effort to secure legislation was unsuccessful but interest in the reform remained high. Consolidation of the supply bureaus offered many problems and various proposals were much debated in the next 10 years.[23] Late in 1911, a renewed legislative effort appeared to have a good chance of success. Congress proposed to incorporate for consideration in the coming Army appropriation bill various reform measures, including consolidation of the three supply bureaus and the establishment of a service corps.

Economy of operation had been stressed as one of the most important advantages to be derived from adoption of these reforms, but Secretary

---

[18] RG 92, OQMG Document File, 1800–1914, Case 309460 (Chief of Staff to SW, 16 Nov 1905).

[19] *Ibid.,* Case 309460 (Taft to Chairman, Senate Committee on Military Affairs, 27 Jan 1906).

[20] (1) *Annual Reports of the Quartermaster General, 1907,* pp. 51–53; *1908,* p. 59; *1909,* p. 92; *1910,* pp. 60–61. (2) *War Department Annual Reports, 1907,* I, 17; *1910,* I, 26.

[21] (1) Dodge Commission *Report,* I, 148. (2) See *ante,* pp. 512–13.

[22] *Five Years of the War Department,* p. 163 (Rpt, 27 Nov 1901).

[23] (1) The first drafted bill was circulated to the Commissary General of Subsistence and the Quartermaster General for their comments. RG 92, OQMG Document File, 1800–1914, Case 307782 (TAG to CGS, 15 Jan 1902); RG 94, AGO Document File, Case 441861 (Memo, TAG for Ludington, 25 Jan 1902). (2) For later proposals see, *ibid.,* Case 1584440 (Sharpe to SW, 26 Sep 1907); RG 92, OQMG Document File, 1800–1914, Case 307782 (Sharpe to SW, 31 Dec 1907; Aleshire memo for file, 4 Jan 1909).

of War Henry Stimson did not take a favorable view of congressional efforts in 1912 to use consolidation for the purpose of cutting down the number of officers in the Army.[24] He had good reason for his attitude. Among other agencies, the Quartermaster's Department had been handicapped by personnel shortages ever since 1898. As soon as the Spanish-American War ended, legislation had reduced the Department to its prewar Regular establishment of 57 officers. Congress discontinued the increased rank that had been conferred on certain Quartermaster officers during the war. It retained in existence the office of military storekeeper, created in 1898, only until its incumbent vacated it through retirement or death. The appointments of all volunteer quartermasters also came to an end, except that Congress did permit the President to continue in service or to appoint 30 volunteer quartermasters, with the rank of major, and 40 volunteer assistant quartermasters, with the rank of captain.[25] This legislation temporarily gave the Department a staff of 128 officers until early in 1901, when Congress authorized a total of 96 officers for the Department.[26]

With this staff, the Department had been expected to supply Quartermaster officers for executing the duties of the Department in the Philippines, Puerto Rico, Cuba, and later in the Canal Zone; to staff and administer the Army Transport Service; and to direct the activities of clothing, equipping, and sheltering an Army that was greatly expanded in size. Whereas for fiscal year 1898, omitting appropriations made for the conduct of the war, Congress provided almost $8 million for the regular service of the Quartermaster's Department, by fiscal year 1908 that amount had grown to nearly $36 million. Although the volume of the Department's work increased in proportion to the increase of appropriations, the number of its officers had not kept pace.

The legislation of 1901 very clearly had made inadequate provision for the Department. The result had been that officers of the line had to be detailed for duty in the Department as acting quartermasters. In 1905, 21 had been so detailed; by 1908, the number had grown to 79, of whom 45 were lieutenants, performing duties that by reason of their importance required "a ripe experience and mature judgment."[27] On

---

[24] RG 92, OQMG Document File, 1800–1914, Case 319603 Addtl. (Ltr, Stimson to Chairman, House Committee on Military Affairs, 4 Jan 1912).

[25] (1) 30 *Stat.* 977 (Mar 2, 1899). (2) The military storekeeper retired on 12 January 1901, thereby discontinuing that position.

[26] 31 *Stat.* 751 (Feb 2, 1901). The Department consisted of 6 assistant quartermasters general, with the rank of colonel; 9 deputy quartermasters general, with the rank of lieutenant colonel; 20 quartermasters, with the rank of major; and 60 quartermasters, with the rank of captain, under a Quartermaster General, with the rank of brigadier general.

[27] *Annual Report of the Quartermaster General, 1905*, p. 59; *1908*, p. 41.

the one hand, such detail evoked complaints from the line that its efficiency was being impaired, and, on the other, Quartermasters General maintained that the lack of a sufficient number of qualified officers hampered Quartermaster operations.   Repeated requests for additional personnel finally led Congress to authorize 30 more officers for the Department in 1911, but since Quartermaster General Aleshire 3 years earlier had shown a need for 216 officers, the authorized strength of 126 was still inadequate.[28]   With much justice, Stimson opposed efforts to reduce officer strength in effecting consolidation of the three supply departments because the Quartermaster's Department in 1912 was still drawing upon the line for officers to serve as acting quartermasters in addition to those regularly detailed to that staff.   The War Department once more reviewed the whole matter of the proposed reforms.[29]

On 24 August 1912, Congress enacted legislation that created the Quartermaster Corps by merging into one supply agency the former Subsistence, Pay, and Quartermaster's Department.[30]   The Head of the new organization was named Chief of the Quartermaster Corps of the Army, but brevity and familiarity with the former designation both suggested a reversion to the title of Quartermaster General of the Army, a change that Congress made in 1914.[31]   Major General Aleshire became the first chief of the Quartermaster Corps, and was succeeded on his retirement, in September 1916, by the former Commissary General of Subsistence, Maj. Gen. Henry G. Sharpe.   Under a plan worked out by Aleshire, the consolidation was put into effect in the United States by 1 November 1912 without delaying or interfering with the supply, service, and pay of the Army.   Consolidation was made effective in the Philippine Department on 1 January 1913.

The commissioned strength of the Corps, as fixed by the 1912 legislation, was set at 183 officers.   The three former supply bureaus had a total strength of 223 officers when the law was approved.   A reduction of 40 officers was thus required.   The authorized strength was to be gradually achieved by not filling vacancies in certain designated grades. By 1915, the commissioned strength of the Corps stood at 185.   The National Defense Act of 1916 reversed this downward trend by setting the commissioned strength at 369 officers.[32]

[28] 36 *Stat.* 1045, (Mar 3, 1911).   Under this act, the distribution of officers was as follows: 1 brigadier general, 8 colonels, 12 lieutenant colonels, 27 majors, and 78 captains.

[29] RG 92, OQMG Document File, 1800–1914, Case 319603 Addtl. (Statement, Chief of Staff to SW, 6 Jan 1912).

[30] 37 *Stat.* 591–93.

[31] (1) RG 92, OQMG Document File, 1800–1914, Case 487541 (SW to Chairman, House Committee on Military Affairs, 5 Dec 1913).   (2) 38 *Stat.* 356 (Apr 27, 1914).

[32] 39 *Stat.* 170 (Jun 3, 1916).   Under this law, the Corps consisted of the following officers: 1 Quartermaster General, with the rank of major general; 2 assistants with the

Creation of a Service Corps

The act of August 24, 1912, not only created the Quartermaster Corps by consolidating three supply bureaus but it also militarized the Corps by establishing a service corps of enlisted men to do for the Army the work of clerks, engineers, firemen, carpenters, blacksmiths, packers, teamsters, and laborers, work which civilians and soldiers detailed on extra duty had previously performed. The total enlisted strength was not to exceed 6,000 men. The Quartermaster Corps built up this service corps gradually through a system of examinations, the successful candidates replacing civilian employees and relieving enlisted men of the line of extra duty. By 30 June 1916, the service corps had a total of 5,379 enlisted men.[33]

The years 1898–1917 were marked by more fundamental administrative changes than had affected the Department since its establishment as a bureau in 1818. Of significance, too, is the fact that adjustments to these changes were in many cases still being made on the eve of the country's entrance into the war with Germany.

Development of the Army Transport Service

During these same years, many modifications and developments were also made in Quartermaster operations or in the way in which the functions assigned to the Department were carried out. Clearly some of these developments were a direct result of recommendations made by the Dodge Commission and of efforts on the part of the Quartermaster's Department to remedy shortcomings exposed by the Spansh-American War. In other cases, they represented new departures intended to produce greater efficiency in the Army. As in so many instances in the past, economy, too, was a motivating factor that frequently made itself felt.

The annexation of Hawaii and the acquisition of Cuba, Puerto Rico, Guam, and the Philippine Islands, as a result of the Spanish-American War, established the United States as a colonial power and brought new problems of occupation and colonial administration to the Army.[34] For

rank of brigadier general; 21 colonels; 24 lieutenant colonels; 68 majors, 180 captains; and 73 pay clerks then in active service who were appointed and commissioned second lieutenants in the Corps.

[33] *Annual Report of the Quartermaster General, 1916*, p. 4.

[34] Under the Teller resolution, the United States disclaimed any intent to exercise sovereignty or control over Cuba. The troops were withdrawn in 1902 but not before the Platt amendment had made provision for American intervention to preserve Cuban independence and to maintain a government capable of protecting life, property, and individual liberty.

the Quartermaster's Department, whose historic mission was the transportation of troops and supplies, the postwar Army responsibilities necessitated the development of an efficient transport service.

When the Spanish-American War ended, the Department had in service a sizable fleet of both government-owned and chartered vessels. As rapidly as the services of the chartered vessels could be relinquished, the Department sent such ships to their home ports for termination of their charters. By the end of fiscal year 1899, the Quartermaster's Department had no chartered vessels in service on the Atlantic Coast. It still used 15 chartered vessels on the Pacific Coast, which were engaged in transporting men and supplies required in the operations against the Filipino insurrectionists led by Aguinaldo.[35]

During the war, such vessels as the Department had purchased had been hastily fitted to transport troops to Cuba and Puerto Rico. Criticism had caused the Department to try to improve accommodations on these ships, but the demand for their services limited the alterations that could be made. As soon as the need for these ships decreased, the Department entered into contracts to refit the transports in order that more comfortable accommodations could be provided for officers and enlisted men. In 1899, the Department transferred most of these refitted ships to the Pacific where the need was greatest, though it also intended to provide a fleet of such transports for service on the Atlantic.[36]

Regulation of the transport service was as essential to its success as improvement of equipment. Even before the remodeled transports were ready for service, the Quartermaster General pointed out the necessity for formulating regulations to govern the organization and maintenance of the Army Transport Service. A board of officers, convened for this purpose after the war, conferred with Quartermaster officers and consulted the rules and regulations governing the conduct of service of well-established steamship lines, and particularly those used in the British transport service. From the latter, the board adopted a basic policy. In the maintenance of distant garrisons, it would be as advantageous to the American service, as it was to the British, to make provision for sending out families with troops. The drafted regulations, approved by the Secretary of War, were published on 16 November 1898.[37] Under these regulations, the Department established two home ports, one at New York City and the other at San Francisco. It placed each under the direction of a General Superintendent of the Army Transport Service,

[35] *Annual Report of the Quartermaster General, 1899*, pp. 10, 13.

[36] *Ibid.*, pp. 84–85 (Col. Chas. Bird to QMG, 13 Sep 1899).

[37] RG 94, AGO Document File, 1800–1914, Case 122525 (Maj. Gen. William Ludlow, Pres. of Board, to TAG, 26 Oct 1898).

who was aided by an assistant and other subordinate officers.   In addition, the War Department assigned a transport quartermaster, commissary, and surgeon to each vessel.

So improved were the accommodations offered by the Quartermaster's Department on Army transports and so smoothly did they operate under the regulations that the return of volunteer troops to San Francisco and the transportation of new levies to Manila in 1899 was accomplished "practically without loss of life, disease, or injury to health." [38]   This was in marked contrast to the difficulties that had beset the Quartermaster's Department in 1898.   With quiet satisfaction, ex-Secretary Alger wrote:

> The same Quartermaster-General who was severely criticized and abused in 1898 had since then transported half way round the globe a force over three times the size of the regular army in 1898, and is now transporting supplies of all kinds that distance for a force of 70,000, without accident, without complaint, and without, I venture to say, one-half of the anxiety, annoyance and labor it caused to send Shafter's army of 17,000 one-twelfth of that distance.[39]

The Department took in stride the dispatch of troops to China in 1900 at the time of the Boxer Rebellion when the United States and the European powers sent an international expedition to relieve the foreign legations besieged in Peking.   A Quartermaster officer recalled that American troops were landed in China in better condition, with more complete equipment of every class, and larger and better stores of all supplies than those of any other country.[40]   With equal ease, the Department handled the transportation demands made upon it for sending troops to Cuba in 1906 and to Vera Cruz in 1914.

Under Quartermaster direction, the Army Transport Service operated an ocean transport service, a harbor boat service, and an inter-island service in the Philippines during the years before World War I.   Beginning on 31 August 1898, the Quartermaster's Department established a regular line of Army transports that provided weekly service between New York and the islands of Cuba and Puerto Rico.   A similar bimonthly service was provided on the Pacific Coast between San Francisco and Manila.   Even before the Spanish-American War, the Department had owned 10 steam tugs, launches, and propellers, most of which were used for harbor service at New York.[41]   Under the Army Transport Service, the number of government-owned tugs, lighters, launches, and

---

[38] *Five Years of the War Department*, p. 26 (Rpt, 29 Nov 1899).

[39] Alger, *The Spanish-American War*, pp. 464–65.

[40] (1) Cruse, *Apache Days and After*, p. 288.   (2) RG 92, AGO Document File, 1800–1914. Case 1327399 (Aleshire to TAG, 11 Apr 1908).

[41] *Annual Report of the Quartermaster General, 1897*, p. 41.

miscellaneous small craft performing Quartermaster, Signal, and Artillery Corps work at harbors on the Atlantic, Pacific, and Gulf coasts increased until, on the eve of World War I, they numbered well over 200.[42]   The necessity of lightering military supplies from ship to depot at Manila had caused the Department, in 1898, to authorize the Chief Quartermaster to purchase a sufficient number of launches, tugs, and lighters for his requirements.   Ten years later, the Department was maintaining and operating at Manila and other ports in the Philippine Islands 56 launches and 160 lighters, cascoes, and other small boats.[43]   In addition, the Army Transport Service operated an inter-island boat service in the Philippines for the transportation of passengers and supplies between the various ports.[44]

Attack on Army Transport Service

The Army Transport Service had scarcely been established before it had to weather an attack on its continued existence.   In the spring of 1901, such interested organizations as the U.S. Export Association raised the question of whether the government should employ its own transports or patronize established lines of steamers.[45]   For reasons of economy, Secretary Root was inclined to agree with the arguments advanced by commercial lines.   They were particularly applicable in the case of the Army transport line carrying passengers and supplies to Cuba and Puerto Rico.   Reduction of the number of troops in these islands had decreased transportation needs to such an extent that Secretary Root was certain commercial lines could handle the limited amount of Army business more economically than government-owned transports.   He therefore discontinued the Army Transport Service to Cuba and Puerto Rico on 30 June 1901 after the Quartermaster's Department had made contracts with commercial lines.[46]   He also favored discontinuance of the transport service on the Pacific but deferred action until October of the following year when the Quartermaster's Department solicited bids from commercial lines.[47]

Neither Quartermaster General Ludington nor his successor, Brig. Gen. Charles F. Humphrey, agreed with the Secretary.   Ludington wrote feelingly of the futile efforts to secure suitable commercial ships for the

[42] Ibid., 1916, p. 42; 1917, p. 62.
[43] Ibid., 1908, p. 32.
[44] See Ibid., 1905, p. 55; 1913, p. 44; 1916, p. 43.
[45] RG 92, OQMG Document File, 1800–1914, Case 164216 (Pres. of Assoc. to Root, 8 Apr 1901).
[46] War Department Annual Reports, 1901, I, 16.
[47] Ibid., 1902, I, 49–50.

transportation of the armies during the war with Spain.   He deemed it a wise policy to retain a sufficient number of transports as part of the equipment of the Army so that the Department might be able to meet promptly any emergency demand for transportation.[48]   Humphrey, who had been serving as Chief Quartermaster at Manila before his appointment as Quartermaster General early in 1903, was as firmly convinced that the abandonment of the Army Transport Service would be a mistake. He argued that not only did the service afford comfortable, healthy accommodations for the troops, but it also allowed the Army to send the family of an enlisted man to the Philippines, thereby diminishing the hardships of foreign service.   In addition, it provided other services essential to the government, such as carriage of mail free of expense to the Post Office Department and safe transferral of large sums of currency and coin.   To clinch his argument in favor of retention of the Army Transport Service, he had prepared a detailed compilation of expenditures showing that this service cost less than similar service on commercial lines.[49]

The Secretary of War did not abolish the Army Transport Service. He did not restore transport service on the Atlantic but sailings between San Francisco and Manila were continued until 1917, though Secretary Root reduced the number from bimonthly to monthly departures in 1902.   The Department had to dispose of some vessels when the Secretary terminated service on the Atlantic, but on the eve of World War I the Army Transport Service still had 16 transports in operation.

Efforts to Improve Various Aspects of Railroad Transportation

Railroad congestion at Tampa in 1898 had led the Dodge Commission to conclude that a lack of executive or administrative ability, either on the part of the Quartermaster's Department or the railroad officials, had been responsibile for that condition.[50]   Obviously, it behooved the Department to scrutinize its methods of operation more closely with a view to their improvement.   The greater demands for water transportation following the Spanish-American War, however, caused the Department to defer consideration of the problems involved in the transportation of troops and supplies by rail until a later time.

Review and revision of the Department's method of settling accounts for railroad transportation was of immediate urgency.   The clerical work of preparing, verifying, and settling such accounts, involving free, land-

---

[48] *Annual Report of the Quartermaster General, 1902*, p. 16.
[49] *Ibid., 1903*, pp. 16–17.
[50] Dodge Commission *Report*, I, 147.

grant, or bond-aided railroads, was difficult and voluminous. The Quartermaster's Department handled not only Army transportation, but legislation also required it to provide transportation for the property and supplies of all other Executive Departments, and the Department prepared the accounts for such service in duplicate.[51]

For many years, railroad companies had been presenting their accounts to the quartermasters with whom they did business and who were located in the areas in which the railroads receiving payment operated, as for example, at New York, Chicago, Omaha, San Francisco, Seattle, and other cities. In the summer of 1900, a board of Quartermaster officers, working with representatives of the railroad companies, the War Department Auditor, and the Comptroller of the Treasury, made a report after spending considerable time seeking ways to improve the method of settlement. Among other things, the board recommended the establishment of a central office in Washington where all railroad accounts in the future would be paid.[52]

A lack of personnel to man such an office led the Department to defer action, but, in 1905, Quartermaster General Humphrey again raised the issue. He enlarged at length on the greater economy and efficiency that could be promoted by bringing into a central office the clerks then handling the settlement of accounts at all the different Quartermaster offices. Since all settlement was subject to revision by the Auditor for the War Department in Washington, much vexatious correspondence would be reduced and centralized operations, he declared, would eliminate much duplication of activity.[53] Humphrey's recommendation to the Secretary of War met with considerable opposition from western railroad companies, who feared that a Washington office would not lead to prompt settlement of their accounts.[54] Their opposition was seemingly strong enough to cause action again to be deferred.

Greater centralization was inevitable but the Department attacked the problem piecemeal a few years later. With the approval of the Secretary of War, it discontinued seven disbursing offices for the settlement of transportation accounts on 1 July 1910. This first reduction having demonstrated that further consolidation was in the best interests of the service, the Department closed three more offices the following year. By 1 July 1912, only four of the 15 disbursing offices that had

---

[51] 23 *Stat.* 111 (Jul 5, 1884).

[52] RG 92, OQMG Document File, 1800–1914, Case 140765 (Ludington to SW, 28 Jun 1900).

[53] *Annual Report of the Quartermaster General, 1905*, pp. 42–44.

[54] See RG 92, OQMG Document File, 1800–1914, Case 140765 for a number of such protests.

settled accounts in the past continued in operation—at Washington, Chicago, St. Louis, and San Francisco.[55]

Even as it simplified these transactions, the Quartermaster's Department gave attention to the problem of possible congestion in the handling of supplies and troops at future mobilization periods. Late in 1907, it solicited the views of depot quartermasters and railroad officials on the desirability of attaching distinctive cards to all freight cars carrying carload lots of Quartermaster supplies, the cards to indicate in large letters the destination of the contents, the consignor, the consignee, and, so far as practicable, the contents of the car. It proposed to use such cards in both peace and war. Depot quartermasters saw some value in the plan in time of war, but most railroads rejected the proposal because it violated a basic rule that they had adopted prohibiting the placing of any signs or cards on freight cars by anyone.[56]

The Office of the Quartermaster General made a renewed attack upon the problem in 1912 when it took up the question with the American Railway Master Car Builders' Association. It then limited the use of placards to such times as the country was threatened with war or was at war. It adopted a series of placards, each placard to give information on point of origin, consignee and destination, date shipped, consignor, and by color of a broad band in the center of the placard to give information on type of supplies. (Green, for example, indicated subsistence.) All railroads agreed that freight cars so placarded would be given right of way from point of origin to destination and that such cars would be placed in the fastest moving freight trains. They also agreed that such freight cars would be kept constantly moving to destination point, and, once there, would be discharged and released without the necessity of waiting for formal bills of lading and official papers, the placards themselves serving to identify all shipments.[57]

Beginning in 1911, the Office of the Quartermaster General gave increasing attention to the preparation of data useful in the transportation of troops and supplies in the event of a general mobilization. Thus, it prepared card indices showing the routing from all mobile army posts to the principal ports on the Atlantic, Pacific, and Gulf Coasts. It secured information on terminal facilities at points where troops might be concentrated. It gathered data on railroad equipment—number and

[55] *Annual Report of the Quartermaster General, 1911*, pp. 48–49; *1912*, pp. 46–47.

[56] RG 92 OQMG Document File, 1800–1914, Case 232872 (Ltr, OQMG to officer in charge, General Depot, 12 Dec 1907; ltr, Lt. Col. F. C. Hodgson to QMG, 14 Dec 1907; ltr, Commissioner, Truck Line Assoc., to Maj. J. S. Littell, 15 Jan 1908).

[57] (1) RG 165, War College Div. Document File, Case 9392–1 (Memo, Actg QMG for Chief of Staff, 26 Jan 1916). (2) *Annual Report of the Quartermaster General, 1916*, pp. 47–48.

types of locomotives, passenger cars, and freight cars.   It held conferences on rates and fares.   At the time of the Vera Cruz expedition in April 1914, the American Railway Association sent a representative to Washington to offer its assistance.   Subsequently, the Quartermaster Corps made tentative arrangements with a committee of that Association, whereby, if it became necessary to mobilize all the forces of the United States, the Association would establish a branch office in Washington with a corps of expert railroadmen to work under the instruction of the War Department and assist in the expeditious operation of troop and supply trains.[58]   The Quartermaster General was convinced that the government could count upon the wholehearted cooperation of the railroad officials in carrying out the provisions of the legislation enacted in 1906.   This legislation had provided that in time of war, or threatened war, the railroads, at the request of the President, would give preference and precedence over all other traffic to the transportation of troops and materials of war.[59]

When the outbreak of war in Europe induced various individuals to propose the establishment of a national board of transportation and to offer suggestions on the relation of railroads to national defense, the Quartermaster General countered that all practical preliminary arrangements had already been made.   He rejected, as undesirable, a suggestion that a transportation division be created in the General Staff in view of the fact that a division of the War Department charged with the duties of transportation was already in existence.[60]

A proposed congressional resolution of 7 December 1915 which looked toward government acquisition and called for action to coordinate lines of communication and transportation with national defense caused the Quartermaster General to comment that in his opinion the existing law of June 29, 1906, provided ample legislation.   All that was required to put that law into proper effect was the adoption of certain details. He proposed the enactment of a law that would give the Secretary of War authority to call officials of transportation lines to meet officers of the War Department in conference and that would permit him to grant a per diem allowance to the railroad officials.[61]

---

[58] RG 165, War College Div. Document File, Case 9201-2 (Ltr, Walter E. Emery to Pres. Wilson, 31 Jul 1915, and 2d ind., Actg QMG to TAG, 11 Aug 1915; Case 9201-8 (TAG to QMG, 20 Sep 1915, and 1st ind., Actg QMG to TAG, 25 Sep 1915); Case 9201-11 (Aleshire to TAG, 4 Feb 1916).

[59] 34 *Stat.* 587 (Jun 29, 1906).

[60] RG 165, War College Div. Document File, Case 9201-11 (Aleshire to TAG, 4 Feb 1916).

[61] *Ibid.,* Case 9201-14 (QMG to Chief of Staff, 19 Jan 1916).   The proposed action of the resolution was rejected by the War Department. *Ibid.,* (Ltr, SW to Chairman, Senate Military Affairs Committee, 5 Jan 1916).

The General Staff was by no means so certain that the existing legislation would suffice. The law prescribed no penalty for failure to give preference and precedence to, or to expedite, military traffic, and the War College Division, in making its report, was doubtful that the existing law would have relieved the congestion at Tampa in 1898. Its report went on to point out that it was a matter of common knowledge that, early in 1916, a large portion of the freight cars of the country were on side tracks and in railroad yards from the Atlantic seaboard back for hundreds of miles towards the interior, loaded with goods destined for Europe, because there were insufficient ships available to forward them. One railroad had ordered its agents to refuse transportation for export, since 8,000 loaded cars were on its side tracks as far from New York as Scranton, Pa. The War College Division found the measures taken by the Quartermaster Corps valuable in case of mobilization, but, again, it thought that they would be effectual only if the railroad officials at the time of mobilization were willing to comply with the Act of June 29, 1906.

Revelatory of the failure to resolve differences between the General Staff and the supply bureau, the report added that, in any case, the plans prepared by the Quartermaster General were part of the duty outlined for a transportation section of the General Staff. "Execution," the War College Division pronounced, "rather than preparation of such plans is a proper function of the Quartermaster Corps." While it approved the suggestion of conferring with railroad officials, the Division maintained that the War Department should be represented at such conferences by members of the General Staff, not by Quartermaster officers.[62]

For all its aspirations, the General Staff apparently evolved no plan for co-ordinating railroad service in the event of national necessity. For its part, the Quartermaster Corps believed that the "careful plan of cooperation" with the railroads, which it had adopted, and their assistance in the past and interest in this plan "demonstrated that the problem of rail congestion, which was the bugaboo of the mobilization of troops in 1898, has been entirely eliminated."[63] Both the Staff and the Quartermaster Corps overlooked the need for co-ordination among the various supply services, and no one gave a thought to the basic problem of adequate storage facilities to the rear to prevent congestion at port docks and progressively into the interior along railroad sidings, despite the fact that the nature of that problem had already been pointed up by shipment of goods to Europe in the winter of 1915–16.

---

[62] Ibid., Case 9201–14 (Memo, Chief, War College Div, for Chief of Staff, 4 Feb 1916).
[63] Annual Report of the Quartermaster General, 1916, p. 49.

Clothing Problems

The provision of suitable clothing for military personnel in the Tropics had first become a problem when Shafter's Army was sent to Cuba, but the continued presence of troops in the Philippines and Cuba after the war made the development and issue of such clothing of continuing urgency. Development of an appropriate service uniform for troops serving in the Tropics caused the greatest anxiety to the Department and engaged its attention throughout the years before the United States went to war with Germany.

After a year's experimentation by American manufacturers, the Quartermaster General concluded, in the fall of 1899, that they could produce khaki of quality, strength, and color equal to the English fabric and in sufficient quantities to meet Army needs. Meanwhile, to supply the 22 additional regiments being organized and equipped for service in the Philippines, the Department had to go into the English market and purchase sufficient cloth for the purpose.[64] The Quartermaster General proved to be too sanguine in his expectations; 2 years later the problem of a fast color was still being worked upon, and the demand for khaki clothing in the Philippines and Cuba was so great that the Department could make none available to state militia, and only in a few cases could it furnish such clothing to Regular troops at extreme southern posts in the United States.[65] Experimentation continued, and the Regulars in the United States wore the abundant supply of white bleached duck clothing left on hand in Quartermaster depots after the Spanish-American War.

The problem of developing a fast color for tropical clothing was complicated by the necessity of making all military clothing less conspicuous in the field in view of the improved range of the rifle. The Army conducted extensive tests from 1900 to 1902 to determine the visibility of different colors. After many disappointments, the Department finally succeeded in producing an olive-drab color that it believed met Army requirements for invisibility, fastness, and serviceability.[66] When the War Department appointed a board of officers to consider the uniforms and equipment of the Army, the Quartermaster's Department was able to submit perfected samples that led to the adoption of the olive-drab shade for overcoats and service winter uniforms at the same time that changes in the design of the uniform were also adopted.[67]

---

[64] *Ibid., 1899*, p. 95 (Rpt, Col. Wm. S. Patton to QMG, 1 Sep 1899).
[65] *Ibid., 1901*, p. 66 (Rpt, Chief of Clothing and Equipage Br to QMG, 15 Aug 1901).
[66] *Ibid., 1902*, p. 6.
[67] *AGO, General Orders and Circulars, 1902*, GO 81 (17 Jul 1902); GO 132 (31 Dec 1902).

The traditional blue uniform was retained only for dress purposes. Quartermaster General Humphrey reluctantly abandoned it as a service uniform. He acknowledged the advantages of the olive-drab uniform for active field service, but he undoubtedly voiced the sentiments of many veterans when he declared that for a uniform in time of peace the blue was in every respect preferable. Blue-clad men on parade presented a "far neater, more imposing, and more soldierly appearance than their companions in olive drab." [68] With some minor modifications adopted later, the new olive-drab service uniform consisted of the familiar breeches and sack coat worn by the troops in World War I.

Large stocks of clothing had been left on hand after the Spanish-American War and economy required that they should be absorbed by issue before the new uniform was made available to the troops. Nevertheless, adoption of the new uniform, early in 1902, led to a hasty promulgation of an order requiring officers to equip themselves with it by 1 January 1903, despite the fact that issue to enlisted men was to begin only after the available supply of old-style clothing became exhausted, and obviously it would take years to deplete that stock. [69] Inevitably, pressures built up to begin issue of the new uniform immediately. A too early effort was made to introduce the new uniform by equipping troops returning from the Philippines with it because they would have no woolen clothing. Since adherence to that policy would have equipped the Army long before all the blue clothing had been issued, the War Department discontinued the policy within a year. [70] In the meantime, efforts were made to induce the enlisted men to draw the old-style clothing by offering it at reduced prices, and subsequently such clothing could be drawn for wear when not on duty. By such means, the Quartermaster's Department gradually reduced stocks. Issue of the new uniform to all organizations began in the summer of 1906.

To the distress of the Department, khaki was retained for summer clothing when the new uniform was adopted in 1902. Quartermaster interest in securing adoption of the olive-drab shade for cotton clothing was heightened by the fact that the entire domestic output of khaki was controlled by one corporation which alone possessed the secret of dyeing gray cotton, the basis of the khaki, the necessary fast color. To relieve the situation, the Department recommended that the use of cotton khaki uniforms in the United States be discontinued, and that olive-drab,

[68] *Annual Report of the Quartermaster General, 1905*, p. 16.

[69] *AGO, General Orders and Circulars, 1902*, GO 81 (17 Jul 1902). The time by which officers were to supply themselves with the new uniform was later extended to 1 July 1903. *Ibid.*, GO 132 (31 Dec 1902).

[70] (1) *Ibid., 1902*, GO 122 (13 Jul 1904). (2) *Annual Report of the Quartermaster General, 1903*, p. 6.

unlined winter service uniforms be used for summer wear. It also suggested that since successful experiments had been made to produce a cotton fabric in an olive-green shade—a color that most nearly approached the olive-drab and was suitable for service wear in summer and in the Tropics—standards and specifications for that shade could be adopted and thereby also relieve the conditions surrounding the supply of khaki.[71] The Secretary of War took these proposals under consideration. In the meantime, the demands for khaki clothing outran the ability of the contractors to supply it. To satisfy the demands from the Philippine Division, the Quartermaster's Department authorized its chief quartermaster to purchase material and manufacture at Manila the khaki clothing required for use of the Philippine Scouts and Regular troops.[72]

Dissatisfaction with the existing situation led the Department to continue its experimentation to perfect a more suitable color and cloth for summer service uniforms. By 1909, it had developed an olive-drab cotton cloth which it claimed was softer, more pliable, cooler, and more comfortable to wear than the old khaki. It also claimed that the fabric had permanency of color.[73] An Army board subsequently disagreed with these findings, but the olive-drab summer uniform was adopted, though its issue did not begin until the summer of 1912, after the existing stocks of khaki clothing had, for the most part, been exhausted.

Complaints continued to be almost as numerous as in previous years, however, for permanency of color proved no more satisfactory in olive-drab than in khaki material. Because cotton service uniforms were considered unfit for use in campaigns, the War Department did not accumulate any in its reserve supply. The general dissatisfaction led the Quartermaster Corps to continue experimenting in the hope of developing a more suitable fabric made of a mixture of cotton and wool. Early in 1914, it again offered a proposal made 8 years earlier. It suggested that a uniform of mixed cotton and wool, or of wool might provide a more satisfactory field service outfit during all seasons of the year. The Corps solicited comments from the field. In consequence, although the olive-drab cotton service uniform was retained for use in the Tropics, its issue to troops in the United States, Alaska, and China was abolished. The War Department suspended the date of that action pending the outcome of Quartermaster experiments with the mixed cotton and wool fabric.[74]

These experiments were still in progress on the eve of World War I,

---

[71] *Annual Report of the Quartermaster General, 1906*, pp. 37–38.

[72] *Ibid., 1907*, p. 44.

[73] *Ibid., 1909*, p. 31.

[74] RG 165, War College Div. Document File, Case 6894–19, record card (OCS Memo for TAG, 2 Jan 1914; 3d ind., OCQMC to CofS, 25 Mar 1914; 4th ind., OCS, to Chief, QMC, 26 Mar 1914). *Ibid.*, Case 6894–32, record card (TAG to QMG, 24 Jul 1914).

but other problems also required attention.   American manufacturers were dependent on imported dyestuffs and the outbreak of war in 1914 immediately closed their source of supply.   The olive-drab shade, so carefully adopted by the Department for the service uniform, could not be obtained for use in 1917.   Domestic dye production was initiated, but the Quartermaster Corps also took steps to develop a satisfactory substitute fabric made of brown and gray mixed meltons that could be readily procured from various woolen mills.[75]

One of the lessons drawn from the Spanish-American War was the wisdom of having an adequate reserve of supplies on hand to meet emergency demands.   In submitting its report to the President, the Dodge Commission had recommended that the Quartermaster's Department should maintain at all times a 4-months' supply of all articles of clothing and equipment needed by an army of 100,000 men.[76]   The experiences of the war remained so vivid for Quartermaster officers that they constantly worked to build and maintain a reserve stock in the years before World War I.[77]   Interest in this problem was not restricted to the Quartermaster's Department.   In response to a question raised by the War College Board, then functioning in lieu of a General Staff not yet established, the Secretary of War directed the Board, in June 1903, to take under consideration a study covering the establishment of permanent general depots for reserve supplies of all classes of war materiel and to recommend regulations for the administration and inspection of such depots.[78]   The War College Board leisurely pursued its study during the next few years.

In 1905, Congress cut the appropriation for clothing and equipment by $750,000.   Quartermaster General Humphrey quickly pointed out that the number of troops to be supplied was practically the same as in 1904 and that the cost of supplies and materials was increasing.   Despite his comments, Congress did not recognize the need for more funds and, in the following year, it again appropriated only $4 million for clothing and equipment as it had in the previous year.   Humphrey warned the Secretary of War that a deficiency had been avoided only by curtailing much-needed purchases and by carrying a stock that was totally inadequate to meet emergencies.[79]

---

[75] *Annual Report of the Quartermaster General, 1915,* p. 22; *ibid., 1916,* p. 21.

[76] Dodge Commission *Report,* I, 148.

[77] Lt. Col. Thomas Cruse observed that, while he was stationed at Philadelphia as depot quartermaster from 1911 to 1915, building a reserve stock "became almost an obsession with me." *Apache Days and After,* p. 309.

[78] RG 165, War College Div. Document File, Case 6271 (Memo Rpt of Subcommttee of Third Div, undated).

[79] *Annual Report of the Quartermaster General, 1905,* p. 15; *1906,* p. 35.

Not only did Congress fail to heed the warning of the Quartermaster General, who was soon to retire, but it also further reduced the funds for clothing and equipment, appropriating only $3 million for fiscal year 1907. Since, by careful computation, over $5,500,000 would be needed, this appropriation, Quartermaster General Aleshire reported, was not only inadequate to meet the needs of the Army and supply the militia but also left no margin for preparing for an emergency. Decreasing appropriations and increasing costs meant that the limited working stock, accumulated in the years since the Spanish-American War, had become so reduced that practically no dependence could be placed upon it. The "hand-to-mouth" policy being pursued, Aleshire pointed out, was disadvantageous, uneconomical, and unsafe. He added that unless a reserve supply was built up, the Department, as in 1898, would be "severely and unjustly criticised for failing to accomplish the impossible" in any emergency.[80]

Aleshire's efforts won a modest increase in the appropriation for fiscal year 1908, and Congress made far larger sums available for reserve stocks in the next 2 years. With the backing of Maj. Gen. Leonard Wood as Chief of Staff, Aleshire took steps to put into effect a plan to build a reserve supply of clothing sufficient to uniform 85,000 men.[81]

In the fall of 1910, the War College Division of the General Staff submitted recommendations for the establishment of depots of supplies in the areas within which troops would be mobilized in the event of war.[82] With the Secretary of War's approval, the Chief of Staff implemented these recommendations to the extent of establishing only one of the proposed chain of general supply depots until the practicability of the scheme could be tested. Field Supply Depot No. 1 was ordered set up at Philadelphia, where military storehouses already in existence could be released for the purpose.[83] On the basis of lists prepared by the various supply bureaus, the General Staff drew up a standard list of field supplies to be kept on hand at this depot. The clothing reserve stocks already accumulated by the Quartermaster General formed a part of the stock directed to be placed in Field Supply Depot No. 1.[84] At a later date, other field supply depots were to be established at Atlanta, St. Louis, Omaha, San Francisco, and at, or in the vicinity of, Springfield, Mass.

By 30 June 1913, a considerable amount of the designated quantities

[80] Ibid., 1907, p. 37–38.
[81] Ibid., 1910, p. 46.
[82] RG 165, War College Div. Document File, Case 6271-9 (Memo, Chief, War College Div, for Secretary, General Staff Corps, 9 Nov 1910).
[83] Ibid., Case 6271-35 (Memo, Chief of Staff for TAG, 9 Feb 1911).
[84] (1) Ibid., Case 6271-52 (Memo, Brig. Gen. W. W. Wotherspoon for Secretary, General Staff Corps). (2) Annual Report of the Quartermaster General, 1911, pp. 20–22; 27.

of clothing and equipage was on hand at Field Supply Depot No. 1, but a year later large deficiencies existed in the reserve stocks. With the approval of the Secretary of War, the Quartermaster Corps used these reserve supplies to clothe and equip the troops sent to Vera Cruz and concentrated on the Mexican border.[85] The Quartermaster Corps was unable to rebuild its reserve stocks because not only did the War Department fail to include the estimates deemed necessary by the Quartermaster General, but, except for 1 year, Congress also further cut the amount or failed entirely to appropriate funds for the purpose.[86] It necessarily followed, too, that the proposed chain of field supply depots was never established.

Following the outbreak of revolution in Mexico in 1910, border troubles became steadily worse. When Mexicans, under the leadership of Francisco Villa, invaded American territory in March 1916, the President sent an expeditionary force under Brig. Gen. John J. Pershing in pursuit. In May and June, most of the organized militia of the states were called into active service and concentrated on the border. To clothe and equip these troops, the Quartermaster Corps utilized all supplies on hand. The reserve proved inadequate to meet the demands, and, under authority of the Secretary of War, the Corps made purchases at the general depots, either in open market or after inviting proposals upon short notice.[87]

On the eve of World War I, reserve stocks of clothing and equipage had been wiped out. Despite Aleshire's warnings, Congress made no

[85] *Annual Report of the Quartermaster General, 1914*, pp. 11, 21.

[86] In the 8-year period before World War I, the amounts estimated as necessary for reserve supplies by the clothing branch of the Quartermaster General's office, included in the estimate by the War Department, and actually appropriated by Congress were as follows:

Fiscal year	Amount estimated by clothing supply branch	Amount included in estimate	Amount appropriated by Congress
1909.........	$2,500,000.00	$2,500,000.00	$1,274,873.86
1910.........	1,549,615.61	1,549,615.61	1,549,615.61
1911.........	1,494,653.64	494,653.64	494,653.64
1912.........	332,041.76	332,041.76	332,041.76
1913.........	2,051,889.34	131,700.00	....
1914.........	1,596,893.79	596,893.79	244,958.79
1915.........	2,906,064.45	225,389.95	225,389.95
1916.........	225,000.00	200,000.00	....
Total......	12,656,158.59	6,030,294.75	4,121,533.61

Ibid., 1916, p. 20.

[87] *Ibid., 1916*, p. 20.

appropriations for their replacement in fiscal year 1916. Quartermaster Cruse later wrote:

> But we had been assured that the United States was not going into the war; therefore, we were told, the Army needed no unusual allowances. When we *did* go into the struggle there was not in stock sufficiency of ordinary articles to outfit our two regular divisions.[88]

Construction Demands

Other functions of the Quartermaster's Department were affected by the aftermath of the Spanish-American War. Colonial empire necessitated the maintenance of a larger Army than had existed before 1898. The continuing warfare in the Philippines emphasized the need for immediate action, but, initially, Congress enacted legislation early in 1899 that only temporarily increased the size of the Regular Army to no more than 65,000 enlisted men and authorized a force of volunteers not to exceed 35,000.[89] Since the volunteer force had to be discharged not later than 1 July 1901 and the Regular Army then reverted to its prewar strength, Secretary Root urged reorganization of the Army in the fall of 1900. In response to his recommendations, Congress made provision for an Army whose strength might be varied by the President, according to the exigencies of the time, from a minimum of approximately 60,000 to a maximum of 100,000.[90] During the next decade, however, the strength of the Army never approached the maximum, averaging only about 65,500.

This increase of the Army from its prewar strength of about 25,000 made immediate demands upon the Quartermaster's Department, for it required an increase in barracks, hospitals, and post accommodations. In order to secure a definite plan for the location and distribution of military posts needed for the proper accommodation, instruction, and training of the Army as reorganized by Congress, Secretary Root appointed a board of general officers in November 1901. He transmitted its report and recommendations to Congress the following May.[91]

The policy of the War Department, according to Secretary Root, was to increase the size of the posts in which the Army was quartered rather than to increase their number. This policy was dictated by a desire to promote "economy of administration" and, even more impor-

---

[88] Cruse, *Apache Days and After*, p. 309.

[89] 30 *Stat.* 979–80 (Mar 2, 1899).

[90] (1) 31 *Stat.* 748 ff. (Feb 2, 1901). (2) *Five Years of the War Department*, pp. 136–37 (Rpt, 20 Nov 1900).

[91] See House *Doc.* 618, 57th Cong., 1st sess., "Results of Preliminary Examinations and Surveys of Sites for Military Posts."

tant, to promote "efficiency of officers and men." Large posts made possible systematic study and practice in schools under the direction and influence of officers of high rank that would be impossible if troops and officers were scattered among small posts.[92]   Accustomed as Army officers were, however, to the system of scattered posts that had been erected as protection against the Indians, the recommendations of the board advanced no definite plan for concentrating troops in a few posts.   Of the 65 existing posts at which troops were stationed, the board recommended that 52 be permanently and 13 temporarily occupied.   The board also recommended the erection of 7 new regimental posts in contrast to earlier company posts.[93]   A decade later, Secretary of War Henry Stimson was to point out that Army Regulations then made no mention of the importance of combined maneuvers; that the "beautiful park" idea of post construction had been firmly fixed; and that "as a whole, the Army was not aware of its own shortcomings." [94]

Guided by the board's approved plan for a system of permanent posts, the Quartermaster's Department constructed and repaired, both in the United States and in the Philippine Islands, barracks, quarters, hospitals, storehouses, and miscellaneous buildings under the liberal appropriations made by Congress.   "It is safe to say," the Quartermaster General reported, "that a vastly greater amount of construction work was planned, undertaken, and contracted for during the fiscal year 1902–03 than during any previous year in the history of the Army." [95]

The Quartermaster General augmented the regular corps of architects and draftsmen employed in the Construction and Repair Division of his office by hiring a number of temporary employees.   So extensive did the construction work become that the Department also obtained the service of an experienced architect.   Placed in charge of the Department's force of architects and draftsmen, he was directed to revise drawings and specifications to improve the general appearance of buildings and, in the interest of economy, to eliminate unduly elaborate details of design and construction so that better buildings might be constructed at no increase in cost.[96]

The cost factor became increasingly important because as the work progressed the cost of all material and labor rose steadily.   Contracts awarded for construction from funds for fiscal year 1906, for example, showed a 12 percent increase over those for the previous year.   Between 1902 and 1905, construction costs advanced until they were 36 percent

[92] *Five Years of the War Department*, pp. 266–67 (Rpt, 1 Dec 1902).
[93] House *Doc.* No. 618, 57th Cong., 1st Sess., pp. 7–8.
[94] *War Department Annual Reports*, 1912, I, 164.
[95] *Annual Report of the Quartermaster General, 1903*, p. 21.
[96] *Ibid., 1905*, p. 9.

higher at the end of that period than at the beginning.[97]   The increased
costs of heavy timber, durable lumber, and high-grade flooring led to the
adoption of concrete and iron construction.   The introduction of extensive heating, water, and sewerage systems and the substitution of electric
or gas lighting for the former kerosene lamps added to construction costs
but provided modern, comfortable accommodations.   By 1910, the Quartermaster's Department had moved toward the concentration of all public
utilities at a post as a further means of introducing economy.[98]

The recommendations made in the report of the board of general
officers in May 1902 were applicable only to inland posts that accommodated the mobile Army.   Coastal fortifications were not included in
their review inasmuch as a general plan for the distribution and shelter
of the Coast Artillery Corps had been adopted by the Endicott Board in
1886 with the approval of the President and Congress.   The building of
coastal fortifications was not a responsibility of the Quartermaster's Department, but it paid for the construction of barracks, quarters, shops,
storehouses, and other miscellaneous buildings for the troops assigned to
these fortifications from Quartermaster appropriations and constructing
quartermasters directed the work.[99]

One effect of the Spanish-American War was to stimulate a more
rapid completion of the coastal fortification work that had been initiated
in a most leisurely manner in 1888.   The acquisition of colonial possessions as a result of the war also made necessary an extension of the work
of the Endicott Board.   The Secretary of War appointed a new board
to give consideration not only to building coastal defenses in Hawaii and
the Philippines but also to reviewing coastal fortifications of the United
States in the light of the effect upon them caused by changes in ordnance
and ship construction.   Subsequently, it also became necessary to protect
the Panama Canal.   The necessity for sheltering troops at all of these
places added to the burden of construction that the Quartermaster's
Department carried in the years before 1917.

In addition to the construction and repair of barracks, quarters,
hospitals, storehouses, and other buildings at interior posts and coastal
fortifications, the Quartermaster's Department also directed other construction for which Congress made provision.   Beginning in June 1902,
Congress appropriated funds for the construction, equipment, and maintenance of suitable buildings at military posts and stations to be used
as post exchanges; schools; libraries; reading, lunch, and amusement
rooms; and gymnasiums.   By 1905, the Department had expended

[97] *Ibid.*, p. 6.
[98] *Ibid., 1910*, p. 37.
[99] See, for example, statistical statements, *ibid., 1911*, pp. 75 ff; *1916*, pp. 91 ff.

$1,500,000 for these purposes.[100]   It furnished gymnastic apparatus to nearly every one of the completed post exchanges and to many of the minor posts, and it built bowling alleys at the most important posts. Secretary of War William H. Taft regarded athletic exercise as a necessity for the troops and hoped appropriations would continue to be made until every permanent military post had a fully equipped gymnasium, including a swimming pool.[101]   Congress must have been in agreement because appropriations for these purposes continued to be made during these years.

The permanent military posts constructed in that period were a far cry from the primitive frontier posts erected largely by troop labor in the years of Indian warfare.   Oddly enough, their location had remained unchanged, though the reasons for their erection at particular sites had long since ceased to have any meaning.   From the viewpoint of economy, Quartermasters General recommended abandonment of such posts as were no longer needed.   Secretaries of War were equally cost-minded but they were also concerned with increasing the efficiency of the Army by stationing troops at fewer posts in order to provide better opportunities for training.[102]   Proposals to abandon any military post, however, aroused local opposition which tended to prevent such action.

The necessity for reorganizing the Army upon a basis of larger tactical units and for rearranging garrisons with this in view grew increasingly important.   In the fall of 1911, Secretary of War Henry Stimson again attacked this fundamental problem.   He was highly critical of the scattered distribution of the Army.   Troops were stationed in 24 states and territories and at 49 posts, 31 of which had a capacity for less than a regiment each.   He emphasized the expense of garrisoning troops at obsolete posts that had "universally been constructed upon a plan which involves a maximum initial cost of construction and a maximum cost of maintenance in money and men." [103]

Cost arguments generally provoke congressional interest, and the House called upon Stimson to furnish additional information.[104]   The War College made a careful study which formed part of a broader report prepared by the General Staff on "The Organization of the Land Forces

[100] *Ibid., 1905*, p. 6.

[101] *War Department Annual Reports, 1905*, I, 39.

[102] (1) See, for example, *Annual Report of the Quartermaster General, 1905*, p. 7.   (2) *War Department Annual Reports, 1906*, I, 48; *1909*, I, 32–34.

[103] (1) *War Department Annual Reports, 1911*, I, 13–14.   (2) RG 165, War College Div. Document File, Case 6270–13 (Memo, Chief of Staff for QMG, 27 Dec 1911); Case 5270–16 (Aleshire to Chief of Staff, 12 Jan 1912).

[104] House Resolution 343, 62d Cong., 2d sess., reprinted in *War Department Annual Reports, 1912*, I, 156.

of the United States." [105]   One immediate consequence was that Congress
provided that no part of the funds appropriated for the Army was to be
expended for permanent improvements at any Army post which had been
or might in future be ordered abandoned by the President.[106]   A much
needed reform appeared to be in the making, but the Wilson administration shelved the Stimson plan when it came into office.   A thorough
rearrangement of posts did not result.   On the eve of World War I,
troops were still garrisoned at the same widely distributed posts, where
existing barrack accommodations had been built by constructing quartermasters to provide for a minimum strength of 65 for infantry companies.
Since the National Defense Act of 1916 raised the minimum strength to
100 and also provided additional units to regiments, the quartermasters
were confronted with the necessity of immediately extending barrack
accommodations for which funds had first to be acquired.[107]

Improvement in Rations

Stung by the criticism leveled against the Subsistence Department in
the Spanish-American War, the Acting Commissary General of Subsistence, Brig. Gen. John F. Weston, set out, as soon as opportunity permitted, to review and improve the rations furnished the Army.   Upon his
recommendation, the Secretary of War appointed a board of officers, on
20 December 1899, to consider and report upon the composition of the
ration for the use of troops in tropical climates.[108]

The high rate of sickness among the men serving in Cuba, Puerto
Rico, and the Philippines had focused attention on the problem of
properly feeding troops operating in tropical countries.   Many officers
had decided convictions as to what components constituted a suitable
tropical ration.   Some were highly critical of the large amount of meat
included and the high energy value of the ration generally.   Others
rejected the theory that eating large quantities of fresh meats had a
deleterious effect upon the health of the troops and insisted that the
natives of Cuba and Puerto Rico were also large meat eaters, when they
were able to procure it.[109]

[105] (1) *Ibid.*, I, 71–153; 157–76.   (2) RG 165, War College Div. Document File, Case
6270–25 (Memo, Chief of Staff for QMG, 9 Feb 1912).
[106] 37 *Stat.* 582 (Aug 24, 1912).
[107] *War Department Annual Reports, 1916*, I, 199.
[108] AGO, Hq of Army, Special Order No. 295 (20 Dec 1899).
[109] The controversy was productive of many papers published on the subject by medical
officers.   See, for example, *Journal of the Military Service Institution of the United States*,
vol. 24, pp. 375–97, an article by Maj. Louis L. Seamen, entitled "The U.S. Army Ration,
and its Adaptability for Use in Tropical Climates," vol. 26, pp. 309–46, "The Ideal Ration
for the American Army in the Tropics," by Capt. Edward L. Munson; vol. 28, pp. 83–95,

A wealth of letters, papers, and reports, including reports from three boards of officers convened, respectively, in Cuba, Puerto Rico, and the Philippines, were submitted to the board, which proposed changes in the ration to make it more suitable for use in the tropics.[110]   Careful study of all of the views expressed led the board to conclude that the components of the ration would have to be about the same in all climates—that is, a meat, bread, vegetable, fruit, seasoning, and a coffee and sugar component. The real problem was to find a ration that, by substitution among its various ingredients, would be suitable for all climates.

The Board prepared such a list of the kinds and quantities of substitutive articles composing the ration.   It did not reduce the meat ration, holding that the necessity for such reduction could best be determined in each case by the immediate commander on the ground.   Submitted to the Acting Commissary General for comment, he approved the list with some minor changes.[111]   The Surgeon General also endorsed its adoption. To put the findings of the board into effect, the War Department obtained legislative authority from Congress since the components of the ration had previously been fixed by law.   Early in 1901, Congress authorized the President to

prescribe the kinds and quantities of the component articles of the Army ration, and to direct the issue of substitutive equivalent articles in place of any such components whenever, in his opinion, economy and a due regard for the health and comfort of the troops may so require.[112]

This change permitted greater flexibility and allowed for more variety in the diet of the soldier.   The kinds and quantities of the standard components of the garrison ration and their substitutive equivalents were announced to the Army some 2 months later.   At the same time, the components and substitutive articles of the field ration and the travel ration were also set forth.[113]

In the meantime, the Acting Commissary General of Subsistence was also concerned with the problem of providing troops with a satisfactory emergency ration for use on active campaigns.   At his request, the Secretary of War appointed a board of officers in January 1899 to examine, test, and report on various emergency rations, including that which was

"The Soldier's Ration in the Tropics—Its Use and Its Abuse," by Maj. Louis L. Seaman; vol. 29, pp. 24–28, "Meat Ration in the Tropics," by Maj. P. R. Egan.

[110] For the gist of their recommendations, see board report, 13 March 1900, included in *Annual Report of the Acting Commissary General of Subsistence, 1900*, pp. 35–36.

[111] (1) The Acting Commissary General saw no reason, for example, for increasing the amount of canned salmon from 16 to 18 ounces, and he recommended retention of cornmeal as a substitutive component since so many men came from the southern states where it was customarily used. (2) For the board's list see *ibid.*, p. 37.

[112] 31 *Stat.* 758 (Feb 2, 1901).

[113] *War Department General Orders, 1901*, GO 56, 23 April 1901.

then in existence.[114] The board recommended no change, but in the opinion of Acting Commissary General Weston, the existing emergency ration was one in name only because it failed to meet the essential military requirements for such a ration—that it be small in volume, so packaged as to be easily transported in the pockets or haversacks of the troops, and composed of components that could be eaten, if necessary, without being cooked. He recommended that the whole problem of emergency rations be placed before the board of officers then considering the tropical ration.[115]

The board examined and tested samples of emergency rations but since none proved satisfactory, it determined to develop its own. Drawing upon their knowledge of the "pinole" used by the Indians of the Southwest and the Mexicans, the officers of the board formulated a meat and bread component made from parched and ground grain and powdered beef, compressed into cakes weighing 4 ounces each, that could be eaten dry or used to make a soup or porridge, salt and pepper being included in the package for extra seasoning. The ration also included a chocolate component that consisted of equal parts of pure chocolate and pure sugar, molded into cakes weighing 1⅓ ounces each. Each can of emergency ration was to contain 3 cakes of the meat and bread component, 3 cakes of the chocolate component, ¾ of an ounce of fine salt, and 1 gram of red pepper. The board requested authority to have 2,000 of these rations produced and tested in the field.[116] The tests proving satisfactory, the board recommended adoption and issue of this ration as the Army's emergency ration.

The ration was not adopted, though it was widely used in the Philippines. Its use was not wholly successful, however, and the Subsistence Department continued experimentation. After that Department was merged with the Quartermaster's Department in 1912, food experts of the Department of Agriculture were called upon to work with officers of the Medical Department and the Quartermaster Corps to perfect a satisfactory emergency ration. Their efforts were not successful, and the emergency ration used in World War I, somewhat refined and reduced in weight from 16 to 12 ounces, was essentially the same as that formulated by the board of officers in 1900.[117]

---

[114] (1) AGO, Hq of Army, Special Order No. 17, 21 Jan 1899. (2) The existing emergency ration had been adopted on 5 December 1896. (See War Department GO No. 49). It called for 10 ounces of bacon, 16 ounces of hard bread, 4 ounces of pea meal or an equivalent component for making soup, 2 ounces of roasted and ground coffee or ½ ounce of tea, 4 grains of saccharin, 0.64 ounces salt, 0.04 ounces of pepper, and ½ ounce of tobacco.

[115] *War Department Annual Reports, 1901,* I, 487 (Ltr, Weston to TAG, 5 Jan 1900).

[116] *Ibid.,* I, 497 (Pres. of Board to Commissary General, 3 Aug 1900).

[117] Compare the formula and specifications of 1900 and 1918. See *Annual Report of*

Improving the variety, quality, or quantity of the rations issued to the troops made little difference if the food was not properly prepared. Brig. Gen. Charles P. Eagan had attributed much of the sickness prevalent during the Spanish-American War to the lack of trained cooks.[118] As early as 1876, Commissary General Robert Macfeely had suggested that the efficiency of the Army would be increased and desertions decreased if cooks and bakers were enlisted and rewarded with extra pay.   For the next 22 years, he and his successors had called attention to this deficiency and had also urged the need for a school to train such personnel.[119] As soon as Eagan was appointed Commissary General on 3 May 1898, he had drafted a bill to enlist cooks.   Congress had authorized their enlistment on 7 July 1898, but too late to procure them for active operations in the war.[120]

In the fall of 1900, Acting Commissary General Weston renewed the recommendation, often made in the past, for the establishment of one or more schools for the training of cooks and bakers.[121]   The Secretary of War did not approve his proposal.   The General Staff, to whom a similar suggestion was later submitted, believed it would be best to rely, as in the past, upon recruiting officers securing suitable cooks from among men who professed to have some culinary skill.[122]

The persistent efforts of General Weston, who became Commissary General in December 1900, finally bore fruit in 1905.   The War Department established a training school for cooks and bakers at Fort Riley, Kansas, under the direction of the commandant of the School of Application for Cavalry and Field Artillery.[123]   It later established other schools at Washington Barracks, D.C., at the Presidio, San Francisco, and at Fort Sam Houston, Texas.   The Subsistence Department issued a manual for Army bakers in 1910 and also made available a new revised edition of the manual for Army cooks, published in 1896.

Trained cooks and bakers required improved equipment to enable them to prepare better food for the Army.   Before the Subsistence Department could initiate any program of experimentation to improve utensils and equipment, the issue of control of such equipment as garrison and field bake ovens, kitchen and mess hall furniture, and individual mess

---

the Commissary General, 1901, p. 70, and Annual Report of the Quartermaster General, 1919, pp. 70–71.
    [118] Dodge Commission Report, I, 550–51 (Eagan Reply to Commission's inquiries, 6 Oct 1898).
    [119] Ibid., I, 558–61 (Eagan memo for Investigtaing Committee, 6 Oct 1898).
    [120] 30 Stat. 721.
    [121] Annual Report of the Commissary General of Subsistence, 1900, p. 49.
    [122] See Army and Navy Journal, vol. 41, p. 453 (2 Jan 1904).
    [123] War Department General Orders, 1905, GO 2 (4 Jan 1905); GO 63 (24 Apr 1905).

equipment had to be settled.   Testimony before the Dodge Commission
had elicited the fact that three supply departments had to cooperate in
getting food to the troops in the field.   The Subsistence Department
bought rations, the Quartermaster's Deparment transported and distributed them, and the Ordnance Department provided the knives, forks,
spoons, canteens, tin cups, and haversacks that comprised the field mess
kits.   The Quartermaster's Department was also responsible for building,
altering, and repairing bake ovens constructed in bake houses at garrisoned posts and in the field, and furnished the utensils used in them.[124]
That Department also authorized the Subsistence Department to purchase
portable bake ovens for use in the field.

The Acting Commissary General was of the opinion that his Department ought not only to be charged with responsibility for providing food
but should also be given the authority to provide equipment used in the
preparation of food in order that responsibility for any failure to furnish
proper rations could be definitely fixed.   He hoped that the Secretary
of War, under authority granted him, would transfer responsibility for
such equipment from the Quartermaster's Department to the Subsistence
Department.   This, he urged, was in line with the views of the Dodge
Commission that held "there should be a division of the labor now
devolving upon the Quartermaster's Department." [125]

The transfer of responsibility was not made immediately.   To
bring it about, the Secretary of War had to recommend changes in the
wording of the Army appropriation bill, since the designation of the
supply agency procuring equipment was determined by the specific appropriations made in that bill.   The Commissary General persisted in his
efforts to recover the responsibility he had once had and, by 1906, when
the Subsistence Department had a training school for bakers in operation
at Fort Riley, he won the backing of the Chief of Staff.   Though Congress
failed to act in that year, it transferred responsibility for bake ovens and
equipment to the Department on 10 June 1907.[126]

Under the direction of Brig. Gen. Henry G. Sharpe, who succeeded
Weston as Commissary General, the Subsistence Department initiated a
program of experimentation to perfect a knock-down field oven and a
field range suited to the needs of the Army.[127]   By 1910, the Army

---

[124] At the request of the Commissary General, responsibility for the construction of
bake ovens had been transferred to the Quartermaster General in 1894 to eliminate the
necessity of having two contractors, one to erect the building and the other to build the
brick oven and chimney, and to eliminate the delays that arrangement caused.   *War Department General Orders, 1894*, GO 40, 29 Aug 1894.

[125] (1) *Annual Report of the Acting Commissary General of Subsistence, 1900*, pp. 47–
48.   (2) Dodge Commission *Report*, I, 148 (Rpt to President, 9 Feb 1899).

[126] *War Department General Orders, 1907*, GO 66 (27 Mar 1907); GO 128 (10 Jun 1907).

[127] *Annual Report of the Commissary General of Subsistence, 1908*, p. 10.

adopted two new types of field ovens and field ranges.   Other developmental work went forward after the Subsistence Deparement was merged with the Quartermaster's Department in 1912, but, under the impact of war in Europe, interest was centered primarily upon the perfection of a satisfactory rolling field kitchen.[128]   Until 1917, the effects of the Spanish-American War continued to make themselves felt in the changes introduced in rations and equipment, and in the training of cooks and bakers.

Economy Measures

Efforts to improve the operations of the supply bureaus on the basis of the recommendations made by the Dodge Commission represented one line of development during the years 1898 to 1917.   Not all the changes and introduction of new procedures in Quartermaster operations resulted from the impact of the Spanish-American War.   All, however, were intended to promote the efficiency of the Army and, as so often occurred in the past, all were much affected by the need to economize.   Colonial possessions and their defense proved expensive.

The first steps taken to promote economy came as soon as conditions in the Philippines permitted a reduction of expense.   To determine what retrenchment measures might be undertaken, the Secretary of War sent the Quartermaster General, the Commissary General of Subsistence, and the chiefs of other supply and administrative bureaus on a tour of the Philippines in the summer of 1901.   Actions taken as a result of recommendations made by General Ludington and General Weston included the release of rented storage space, the construction and consolidation of warehouses at Manila, the abandonment of outlying subsistence depots, the reduction in the number of sales stores, and the greater use of native fodder as forage.   The War Department policy of concentrating troops at fewer posts also greatly decreased transportation costs.[129]

The economy drive made itself felt in most Quartermaster activities. Its effects on construction and transportation have been noted.   In the latter field, economy accounted in part for the transfer of some of the Army's transport business to commercial lines.   In the construction program, economy dictated the use of lumber that conformed to commercial sizes and the procurement of commercial-type plumbing fixtures.   It also brought about a revision of plans for barracks, quarters, and other build-

---

[128] RG 165, War College Div. Document File, Case 8330–3 (Memo, Chief of War College Div. for Chief of Staff, 11 Feb 1914 and 1st ind., Aleshire to Chief of Staff, 19 Feb 1914). See also Case 8330–10 (Memo, Chief, War College Div. for Chief of Staff, 9 Dec 1915); Case 8330–17 (Same for same, 18 Aug 1916).

[129] (1) *Annual Report of the Commissary General of Subsistence, 1902*, p. 16.   (2) *Annual Report of the Quartermaster General, 1902*, pp. 24–25.

ings that reduced costs. In general, during these years, the Quartermaster's Department pursued a policy of adapting its specifications for supplies and materials that were not distinctively military to similar commercial articles of high standards. The effect was to widen competition under ordinary conditions and to decrease costs. To reduce clothing manufacturing costs, the Department substituted a straight standing collar for the standing falling collar of the service coat, replaced bellows pockets with patch pockets, and eliminated cuffs from sleeves. It also used woolen fabrics in lieu of the more expensive worsteds previously demanded in specifications. By 1910, Quartermaster General Aleshire reported with satisfaction that much progress had been made in the elimination from clothing specifications of the distinctive features that had existed between government and ordinary commercial practice. Only the special colors and forms of the cut of articles of outer uniforms, as prescribed by regulations, remained to distinguished garments worn by the soldier from similar well-made articles found in the commercial trade.[130] While such measures promoted economy, they did not necessarily produce the most satisfactory uniform for field service.

Decentralization of Procurement

The economies effected in the purchase of supplies by the Quartermaster's Department were brought about at the same time that it made marked progress in decentralizing procurement to the field in order to promote efficiency in operations. Although Quartermaster General Humphrey had made some suggestions in 1903 for decentralizing the business methods of the Department, it was his successor, Brig. Gen. James B. Aleshire, who put into effect a thoroughly decentralized system that radically changed Quartermaster methods of operation.

Aleshire had long given thought to the system of supply and, about a month after he became Quartermaster General in 1907, he placed before the Secretary of War his plan for decentralizing operations.[131] Briefly, his plan provided that designated depots of the Department furnish supplies upon requisitions approved by military department commanders within the limit of funds allotted to their chief quartermasters from the appropriations and subject to such instructions regulating this method of supply as were recommended by the Quartermaster General. The system was based on the principle that Congress had placed to the credit of the Quartermaster's Department in the United States Treasury certain

---

[130] *Annual Report of the Quartermaster General, 1910,* pp. 17–18.
[131] RG 94, AGO Document File, 1800-1914, Case 1273468 (Aleshire to Taft, 10 Aug 1907).

sums of money that it appropriated for designated purposes. As the agent of Congress, and under the direction of the Secretary of War, the Quartermaster's Department expended these funds in accordance with law and regulations. For this purpose, it apportioned to each chief quartermaster, or quartermaster in charge of an independent station, public work, or other project, a sum sufficient for the ordinary administrative needs of his territorial department or work. In turn, the chief quartermaster allotted to post quartermasters sufficient credits to meet their needs.

Aleshire thought of the Quartermaster general supply depots as wholesale houses from which supplies might be ordered within a limit of cost established by the apportionment and allotment of funds made. When it was to the advantage of the Government, supplies might also be purchased at department headquarters or in the vicinity of posts.

Under this system, Aleshire placed the whole business of procuring supplies on a money-value basis and operated it in accordance with the principle of banking methods. A post quartermaster ordered through his chief quartermaster supplies from a depot which were not to exceed the credit he had for his post. The depot filled the order, sent an invoice showing cost, and received a draft on the Quartermaster General or a credit transfer from him for the value. When the depot quartermaster had to replenish his stock, the Quartermaster General cashed the drafts by placing money to his credit.

Aleshire argued that the system had many advantages. It placed on departmental commanders and their chief quartermasters the responsibility for the proper and economical supply of their commands and thus insured a proper equipment of troops for field service at all times. It gave chief quartermasters and other quartermasters a limited degree of independence of action and experience in meeting supply responsibilities in peace that they would be required to meet in time of war. It relieved the office of the Quartermaster General of many details and gave elasticity to the whole Department. Since allotments of funds could not be exceeded, the system would have the effect of enforcing greater economy in isssues, better care and protection of supplies obtained, and would also tend to prevent deficiencies in appropriations. Moreover, Aleshire believed the system would obviate the accumulation of surplus stores at posts in the military departments and would lessen losses through deterioration of stocks remaining too long in storage.

The arguments in behalf of the system struck Secretary Taft as sound and he approved Aleshire's plan on 15 August 1907. There was delay in inaugurating the system, for no data had been kept in the Washington office or at the depots, on the basis of which Aleshire could allot funds to the chief quartermasters.[132]   The compiling of this information was a time-consuming task and the new system did not go into effect until 1 July 1908.[133]

Aleshire by no means intended to limit his system solely to the procurement of supplies but also proposed to use the same principles and methods in the procurement of necessary Quartermaster services.   The system as it applied to services also went into effect on 1 July 1908.[134] Aleshire pursued his policy of decentralization further by ridding his office of some of the details and correspondence pertaining to certain classes of employees.   This he did by placing their selection from lists of eligibles furnished by local Civil Service Commissioners in the hands of chief quartermasters, depot quartermasters, and quartermasters of independent stations.[135]   In the course of preparing instructions for placing the system of decentralization in operation for the procurement of supplies and of services, Aleshire came to the conclusion that it could also be extended to the Army Transport Service.   He turned the problem of working out the details of its application over to Col. J. B. Bellinger, then General Superintendent of the Army Transport Service at San Francisco.[136]

The introduction of these radical changes was not effected without difficulties.   On the one hand, misinformation about the system caused local communities to fear the loss of depot business, and Aleshire had to reassure Congressmen and their constituents that such would not be the effect of decentralization.[137]   On the other hand, the instructions for putting the system into effect that seemed crystal clear to Aleshire struck his chief quartermasters and their clerks as murky.   There were complaints of the additional work imposed on chief quartermasters and post quartermasters by the system and demands for more clerical help.   There was, in fact, more or less confusion in putting the system into operation. The Quartermaster General sent out his chief clerk to explain the system. He observed that old clerks, "do not take hold of the matter, have no

[132] RG 92, Letter Books of General J. B. Aleshire, I, 265 (Aleshire to Col. J. G. Harbord, 10 Sep 1907).

[133] War Department General Orders and Circulars, 1908, GO 18 (24 Jan 1908).

[134] Ibid., GO 73 (8 May 1908).

[135] This scheme was promulgated in Circular No. 26, Q.M.G.O., 1907.

[136] (1) RG 92, Letter Books of General J. B. Aleshire, IV, 421–23 (Aleshire to Bellinger, 29 Jun 1908).   (2) Instructions governing the procurement of supplies are found in Circular No. 1, Q.M.G.O., 1908 and for the procurement of services in Circular No. 11, Q.M.G.O., 1908.

[137] RG 92, OQMG Document File, 1800–1914, Case 239012 (Aleshire to Hon. S. Sherley, 13 Mar 1908).   (2) RG 92, Letter Books of General J. B. Aleshire, III, 440–41 (To Charles A. L. Reed, 20 Mar 1908), IV, 178–79 (To Hon. C. W. Fulton), IV, 180–82 (To Hon. Jonathan Bourne, 2 May 1908).

interest in it, and will not study the circulars and understand the requirements." The office of the chief quartermaster and depot quartermaster at Omaha lagged behind all others in putting the system into satisfactory operation. Aleshire attributed their difficulties to the preponderance of elderly clerks employed there. Of seven clerks employed in the chief quartermaster's office, two were 70 and the other five were 59, 64, 74, and 75, respectively. Under Civil Service rules, the Department could only rid itself of the aged or the inefficient clerks by demoting them and thus making vacancies in the higher positions for efficient younger clerks. It is understandable why the Quartermaster's Department and the War Department were warm supporters of Civil Service retirement plans.[138]

A revision in 1909 of the original circulars setting forth instructions governing procurement of supplies and services greatly simplified procedures and produced satisfactory results.[139] The Chief of Staff commended the Quartermaster General for so successfully working out the complicated details of this decentralization scheme.[140] When, 3 years later, the Quartermaster's, Subsistence, and Pay Departments were consolidated to form the Quartermaster Corps, Aleshire requested that the policy of decentralization, which had been so successful in the Quartermaster's Department since 1908, be approved as the policy of the newly created Corps. The Secretary of War agreed to this request.[141] This was the system of decentralization under which the Quartermaster Corps was operating when the United States went to war with Germany in 1917.

Establishment of the Remount Service

In the midst of decentralizing Quartermaster operations to the field, General Aleshire persuasively advocated another reform that he had long cherished to increase the efficiency of the Army. This was the establishment of a remount service for the Army. For many years, horses and mules for the use of the Army had been purchased by the Quartermaster's Department under contract after advertising for bids. Procurement under the contract system had many disadvantages. It resulted in delays, necessitated deliveries at large horse markets where the animals easily became infected with diseases, and provided no opportunity for judging the character and disposition of animals accepted and shipped to the troops.

---

[138] RG 92, Letter Books of General J. B. Aleshire, VII, 338–42 (To Col. George Ruhlen, 9 Jul 1909), V, 478–79 and VI, 136–37 (To Maj. D. E. McCarthy, 26 Dec 1908 and 1 Feb 1909).

[139] Circulars No. 6 and No. 7, 1909.

[140] *War Department Annual Reports, 1909*, I, 205 (Rpt, Chief of Staff, 1 Dec 1909).

[141] RG 92, 0QMG Document File, 1800–1914, Case 381685 (Aleshire to SW, 4 Sep 1912).

Prompted by a desire to give local horse raisers in the vicinity of Army posts an opportunity to sell directly to the Government, Congress, in 1905, also provided for open-market purchase of animals at military posts, when needed, at prices not to exceed a maximum fixed by the Secretary of War.[142] Unfortunately, local horse raisers and farmers were not appreciably encouraged by this provision.

Aleshire's views on the methods to be pursued in purchasing animals for the Army had first been offered in February 1907 when, as a major on duty in the office of the Quartermaster General, he presented a paper before the General Staff and Army War College on his proposed reform.[143] Five months later he was appointed Quartermaster General and, in submitting an annual report covering the operations of his predecessor during the previous fiscal year, he took the opportunity to reiterate his views.[144]

Aleshire proposed that three or more remount depots be organized, located, and equipped. To each depot, he suggested assigning a remount district, each depot and district to be under the charge of an officer of the Quartermaster's Department, preferably one detailed from the Cavalry or Field Artillery and especially suited for this duty. These depot officers would be responsible for all animals, supplies, property, and funds. They would supervise the care and handling of the horses, and, when directed by proper authority, would purchase young horses, conforming to specifications, within the remount district assigned to their depots. The depots and their commanding officers would be under the general supervision of a Remount Division that Aleshire proposed to establish in the office of the Quartermaster General. Aleshire was certain that a remount service would prove more economical than the contract system, and that the Army would be supplied with young, sound, well-broken animals.

To demonstrate the superiority of this method and to justify its extension to the procurement of all remounts and draft and pack animals, Aleshire called for a practical test. He hoped to obtain the use of the abandoned Fort Reno military reservation in Oklahoma in order to put the plan on trial, and he worked diligently to enlist the support of Cavalry officers for the remount service.[145]

Congress authorized the establishment of a remount service in May 1908, and the War Department turned over to the Quartermaster's

---

[142] 33 *Stat* 836 (Mar 2, 1905).

[143] This paper was subsequently published in the *Journal of the United States Cavalry Association*, XVIII, No. 66 (October 1907), pp. 279–326).

[144] *Annual Report of the Quartermaster General, 1907*, pp. 33-36.

[145] RG 92, Letter Books of General J. B. Aleshire, II and III, *passim*.

Department the Fort Reno reservation for use as a remount depot.[146] Within 3 years, the Department established additional remount depots at Fort Keogh, Mont., and at Front Royal, Va. It added two auxiliary remount depots in March 1916 at El Paso and Fort Sam Houston, Tex., to maintain in good condition the animals belonging to the forces operating along the Mexican border.[147] A Remount Branch, first set up in the Supplies Division of the office of the Quartermaster General late in April 1912, and subsequently transferred to the Transportation Division, supervised the remount depots.[148]

The Remount Service promptly proved its superiority over the old method of procuring remounts that had resulted in the purchase of older horses either under contract or in open market. The new system encountered difficulty, however, in purchasing young horses for Cavalry purposes because such animals were no longer being bred as extensively as in former years. Draft horses and mules were proving more profitable to the farmer. Conferences between representatives of the War Department and the Department of Agriculture resulted in the formulation of a plan for encouraging the breeding of horses suitable for the Cavalry, the plan to be executed by the Department of Agriculture.[149] Put into operation by 1912, the plan had the effect of steadily improving the type, breeding, and appearance of young horses purchased by the Quartermaster Corps.

Development of Motor Transportation

The Quartermaster's Department initiated reform in the method of procuring animals at a time when development of motor vehicles was already raising the question, in European if not in American armies, of whether the day of animal-drawn transports was not over. Foreign armies had already given much attention to testing various types of motor cars, but Quartermaster General Ludington rejected a proposal to build a car for the United States Army in 1900. He considered that the condition of the average roads traversed in military operations, unpaved and often deep with mud, made them entirely unsuitable for automobile use. The necessity for sudden, hurried movement under all conditions of weather and in every description of country, with varying amounts and

---

[146] (1) 35 *Stat.* 119 (May 11, 1908). (2) *War Department General Orders, 1908,* GO 59 (18 Apr 1908).

[147] (1) *War Department General Orders,* GO 80, 29 Apr 1909; GO 117, 30 Aug 1911. (2) *Annual Report of the Quartermaster General, 1916,* p. 62.

[148] RG 92, OQMG Document File, 1800–1914, Case 365930.

[149] RG 92, OQMG Document File, 1800–1914, Case 293506 (Capt. Kirby Walker to the QMG, 18 Jan 1910).

weights of cargo "enjoins the Army from using any method of transportation which is in any degree experimental, or untried and unproven."[150]

The views expressed in 1900 were still entertained by his successor in 1907.[151]   Even as a means of Army passenger transportation in cities, it was the policy of the Quartermaster's Department to reject requests for automobiles.[152]   Lack of funds to purchase both animal-drawn transportation and automobiles made experimentation impossible even if the Department had been enthusiastic about the possibilities of motor transport.   Quartermasters and other officers, however, continued to exhibit an interest in the subject, and, by 1910, the General Staff, while regretting that lack of funds made inadvisable the trial of motor vehicles for the transportation of troops, had nevertheless come to the conclusion that the adoption of some form of traction vehicle for transporting supplies in the field was a pressing necessity.[153]

Officers of the Quartermaster's Department were equally convinced of the need at that time, and they carefully went into the question of the efficiency and economy of motor trucks as compared with animal-drawn transportation.   They found the ordinary commercial truck to be far more economical and efficient than the animal-drawn wagon when used in cities and on macadam roads, and the Department purchased commercial trucks for that purpose.   But the same truck was not suitable as a means of transportation for the Army in the field.   In 1911, the Department began a developmental and testing program designed to produce a truck to meet Army requirements.[154]

This first test did not prove conclusive.   Lack of funds again hampered the pursuit of any special test program, but the Quartermaster Corps purchased motor trucks for use at various quartermaster installations, and quartermasters made careful reports of the efficiency, stability, and economy of their operation.   Although the commanding general of the Southern Department thought it was a mistake to wait until a satisfactory type of motor transportation for field service was developed, the

---

[150] RG 92, OQMG Document File, 1800–1914, Case 109744 A (Ltr, John Brisben Walker to Elihu Root, 1900 and 1st ind., Ludington, 31 May 1900).

[151] *Annual Report of the Quartermaster General, 1907,* p. 32.

[152] (1) RG 92, OQMG Document File, 1800–1914, Case 224689 (Ltr, Purchasing Commissary, N.Y. to TAG, 6 Oct 1908, and 2d ind., Aleshire, 12 Oct 1908). (2) *Ibid.,* Case 228564. Quartermaster General Humphrey had bought automobiles for use in Havana, at San Francisco, and for the constructing quartermasters at Walter Reed Hospital in Washington in 1906 only to have the Treasury rule that he had no authority for such purchases under the Appropriation Act, and they were charged against his account.

[153] *Ibid.,* Case 228564 (Memo, Lt. Col. D. A. Frederick, for Acting Chief of Staff, 7 Jun 1910).

[154] *Ibid.,* Case 320076 (Aleshire to Chief of Staff, 2 Nov 1911): (Memo, Capt. A. E. Williams for QMG, 3 Nov 1911).

Quartermaster Corps pursued its developmental program, limited by the funds it was able to save from the appropriation for Army transportation for the purpose.[155]   The first specifications of the Quartermaster Corps for trucks were written in 1913 after extensive correspondence with manufacturers and with the Society of Automobile Engineers.   As the developmental program continued, the Corps revised these specifications and brought them up to date annually.

In 1916, Pershing's expedition into Mexico afforded an opportunity for testing the work done so far by the Corps and for determining the value of motor transportation.   Any lingering doubts as to its superiority over animal-drawn transportation were forever settled.   The first call for two motor-truck companies came from the Southern Department on 11 March 1916.   Each company was to consist of 27 motor trucks of 1½ tons capacity, equipped with the necessary personnel for their operation.   With the approval of the Secretary of War, the Quartermaster Corps purchased the trucks, hired the necessary personnel at the factories manufacturing the trucks, and dispatched trucks and operators by special-train service to Columbus, New Mex., within 5 days.   By 30 June 1916, the Corps had purchased, for use on the Mexican border, 588 motor trucks, 57 motor tank trucks, 10 motor machine-shop trucks, 6 motor wrecking trucks, 75 automobiles, 61 motorcycles, and 8 tractors for repairing roads, as well as other miscellaneous road machinery, repair parts, and equipment.[156]

The operation and maintenance, under emergency conditions, of this varied motor equipment—there were 13 different types of trucks alone made by 8 manufacturers—created a host of new problems that ranged from the establishment of repair shops to the supply of spare parts and the procurement of competent personnel.   The practical experience gained, though acquired by only a few officers, was of much value, for within a few months after the final withdrawal of the Army from Mexico the United States entered World War I.

Summary

The Quartermaster's Department had been given no opportunity to redeem and consign to oblivion, by outstanding supply achievements later in the conflict, the poor showing that it had made when the Spanish-American War began.   Unlike the Civil War, that war was of too short duration to permit the Department to overcome the drag of unprepared-

---

[155] RG 92, OQMG Personal File—Gen. J. B. Aleshire, Box 2 (Ltr, Brig. Gen Tasker Bliss to Inspector General E. A. Garlington, 10 Dec 1913); (Ltr, Aleshire to Bliss, 26 Jan 1914).
[156] *Annual Report of the Quartermaster General, 1916*, p. 56.

ness and inexperience before it ended.   But if, in consequence, supply shortcomings were not forgotten, that fact was conducive to creating a favorable atmosphere for reform and it enabled Secretary of War Elihu Root to effect some fundamental administrative changes before the crest of the reform wave spent itself in 1904.   Consolidation of three of the supply bureaus into one Quartermaster Corps and its militarization were made possible only after persistent efforts and because Root's initial reforms had eliminated the fear of even greater bureaucracy.   Though it took the crisis of 1898 to stimulate action, most of the administrative reforms and some of the operational changes made in the Subsistence and Quartermaster's Departments, as, for example, the creation of the remount service and the establishment of Army schools for cooks and bakers, had been advocated for many years.

The initial drive for increasing the efficiency of the Army and the War Department soon gave way to the more familiar leisurely pace that had characterized prewar reform efforts.   As was customary in other postwar periods, developments in the years 1898–1917 were hampered by the need to economize.   No sense of urgency drove the Quartermaster Corps after war broke out in Europe in 1914.   It was persuaded, as was the War Department and the public generally, that the country was not going to become involved in World War I.   A newly consolidated Corps, under the leadership of a Quartermaster General—Maj. Gen. Henry G. Sharpe—who had been appointed on 16 September 1916 and whose career had been predominately that of a Subsistence officer, was called upon to support a war, the supply demands for which were far greater than those of the Spanish-American War and for which the Corps was as unprepared in 1917 as it had been in 1898.

CHAPTER XIV

Supply in the Zone of Interior
1917-1918

The effectiveness of the reforms initiated after the Spanish-American War, designed to promote a more efficient War Department organization and to co-ordinate its activities through the creation of a General Staff, was tested in 1917 and found wanting. "The whole General Staff and War Department organization, generally, fell like a house of cards," Maj. Gen. Johnson Hagood later wrote, "and a new organization had to be created during the process of the war." [1]

War Department Organization in April 1917

On 6 April 1917, Newton D. Baker was Secretary of War. Congress had provided for an Assistant Secretary of War in 1890, but not until Benedict Crowell took over that office in November 1917 did it acquire much significance. The Secretary's chief military advisor was the Chief of Staff. In the 14 years since Congress had created the office of Chief of Staff and established a General Staff Corps to assist the Chief, little had been accomplished to develop an effective instrument for co-ordinating the supply activities of the War Department. The act of 1903 had placed the supply bureaus under the supervisory control of the Chief of Staff, but in 1917 these bureaus were still operating as semi-independent, decentralized, and unco-ordinated agencies. Though the channel of communication between supply chiefs and the Secretary of War was through the Office of the Chief of Staff, for all practical purposes, the chiefs of the five supply bureaus, as well as the heads of six other administrative bureaus, reported directly to the Secretary of War. Even in peacetime, this outmoded organization was burdensome to the Secretary of War, but in war it made it impossible for him to keep abreast of the expanding operations of each bureau. [2]

Lack of co-ordination was the basis for most of the supply difficulties

---

[1] *The Services of Supply* (Boston, 1927), p. 27. General Hagood served for 7 years in the War Department before the war and acted as Chief of Staff, Services of Supply, American Expeditionary Forces, during World War I.

[2] *Investigation of the War Department*: Hearings before the Committee on Military Affairs, Senate, 65th Cong., 2d sess., Pt. 3, p. 1741 (Baker). Hereafter briefly cited as *W.D. Investigation Hearings*.

encountered at the beginning of the war, but the failure of the Chief of Staff to promote co-ordination resulted in large measure from the lack of support given to the General Staff Corps. Not only were the bureaus unenthusiastic about Staff supervision, but, according to a critic of General Staff organization early in 1916, the Army at large was "no more than lukewarm in its support." Moreover, he detected a distinct spirit of hostility developing in Congress.[3] Only 4 years earlier, Congress had reduced the number of General Staff officers from 45 to 36. When Congress passed the National Defense Act in 1916, it authorized a gradual increase in their number to 55, to be accomplished through five annual increments, but it defeated any real benefit to be derived from the increase by providing that no more than half of the officers of the General Staff were to be located in Washington at one time. In April 1917, there were only 19 in that city, the rest being stationed at various departmental headquarters.[4]

The small number of General Staff officers doomed to failure Staff efforts to plan for war and to co-ordinate War Department supply activities. Not only were there no war plans, but, as soon as the war began, the availability of General Staff officers for such work was further decreased because many of them were promoted, placed in command of divisions, and ordered out of Washington.[5] Even the Chief of Staff was in no position to influence developments. So lightly was the post regarded that the President sent Maj. Gen. Hugh L. Scott, Chief of Staff, to Russia in May as a member of the United States Mission, and detached his successor, Gen. Tasker H. Bliss, for other work abroad in October 1917. An Acting Chief of Staff functioned during the absence of the Chief of Staff. Between 6 April and 31 December 1917, the office was rotated among three officers no less than six times, only one incumbent serving as long as 2 successive months.[6] Under these circumstances, it

---

[3] RG 120, War Department Historical Files, Box 152 (Historical Rpt, "Summary History of the General Staff," quoting Maj. R. H. Van Deman).

[4] (1) 39 *Stat.* 167. (2) General Peyton C. March, *The Nation at War* (New York, 1932), pp. 45–46.

[5] *War Expenditures:* Hearings before the Select Committee on Expenditures in the War Department, House, 66th Cong., 2d sess., Ser. 4, Pt. 57, p. 3071 (Samuel T. Ansell, Esq.). Hereafter briefly refered to as *War Expenditures Hearings.*

[6] The services of these officers were as follows:

Date	Chief of Staff	Acting Chief of Staff
Apr 6– May 15, 1917	Maj. Gen. Hugh H. Scott	
May 15– Aug 8, 1917	Absent with U.S. Commission to Russia	Gen. Tasker H. Bliss
Aug 8– Sep 22, 1917	Maj. Gen. Hugh L. Scott *	
Sep 23– Oct 29, 1917	Gen. Tasker H. Bliss	
Oct 29– Dec 16, 1917	Absent in France	Maj. Gen. John Biddle
Dec 16– Jan 9, 1918	Gen. Tasker H. Bliss **	
Jan 9– Mar 3, 1918	Absent in France	Maj. Gen. John Biddle
Mar 4– May 19, 1918	Absent in France	Gen. Peyton C. March
May 20– end of war	Gen. Peyton C. March	

is not surprising that there was no co-ordination of supply bureau operations. The lack of co-ordination, in fact, permitted developments that broke down such single-agency control of some functions as had existed before 1917.

OQMG Organization in April 1917

In April 1917, the Quartermaster Corps was one of five supply bureaus under the general direction of the Chief of Staff. At that time, Maj. Gen. Henry G. Sharpe had been Quartermaster General for 7 months. Sharpe, a most competent commissary, had served for 29 years in the Subsistence Department, becoming Commissary General of Subsistence in 1905, a post he held until Congress merged the Subsistence Department with the Pay and Quartermaster's Departments in 1912. A student of supply, Sharpe had for many years worked to achieve the establishment of a supply corps. He was a dedicated officer, whose devotion and loyalty to the service Secretary of War Baker fully appreciated. General Sharpe was not, however, a man of forceful character. He lacked the aggressiveness required in the crisis of 1917 to combat the inroads upon his authority that were made both from within and outside the War Department.

The expanded organization of the Office of the Quartermaster General, created to meet the demands of the Spanish-American War, had gradually contracted after 1898 until by 1911 only five divisions remained. Except for changes at the Branch level, necessitated by the absorption of the Subsistence and Pay Departments in 1912, those five divisions— Administrative, Finance and Accounting, Supplies, Construction and Repair, and Transportation—were still in existence on 6 April 1917 when the United States declared war against Germany.[7] Similar divisional organizations were maintained at the general depots of the Corps and in the offices of the chief quartermasters of the four military departments into which the United States was divided for administrative purposes.[8]

---

* Maj. Gen. Hugh L. Scott retired on 22 September 1917.

** Gen. Tasker H. Bliss retired on 31 December 1917, but, by direction of the President, he was continued on active duty as Chief of Staff until 19 May 1918.

Table prepared from information submitted by the Adjutant General to the Hon. Royal C. Johnson, 13 December 1919. See *War Expenditures Hearings*, 66th Cong., 2d sess., Ser. 4, Pt. 25, p. 1308.

[7] (1) *Annual Report of the Quartermaster General, 1911*, pp. 4–6; *1919*, p. 10. (2) General Sharpe disclosed that, after consultation with a firm of New York efficiency experts, the Office had been organized to handle efficiently the work that devolved upon it by law. RG 92, AGO 201 file on Sharpe (Ltr, Sharpe to Senator Frelinghuysen, 26 Feb 1919).

[8] These departments were, under War Department order, in process of being reorganized into six departments by 1 May 1917. War Department GO 38, 2 Apr 1917.

The names of the five divisions of the Office of the Quartermaster General were indicative of the broad duties imposed on the Corps. As in the past, it was still charged with providing the means of transportation needed in the movement of troops and supplies. It had also, since 1885, become responsible for handling the freight shipped by all executive departments of the government. The Corps continued to furnish all animals used by the Army as well as forage and wagons. It provided subsistence, clothing, camp and garrison equipage, and articles authorized to be kept for sale to the troops. It constructed barracks, quarters, storehouses, and other buildings needed by the Army; it repaired roads and bridges and built docks, and wharves for military purposes. It supplied, distributed, and accounted for funds for the payment of military personnel. The Corps had charge of all national cemeteries in the country. In addition to these specific functions, the Corps was also responsible generally for attending to all matters connected with military operations that were not expressly assigned to some other bureau of the War Department.

To execute these diverse functions, the Quartermaster Corps, on 6 April 1917, had 205 officers. In the National Defense Act of 1916, Congress had provided for an increase of 183 officers to the existing Quartermaster staff of 113, the additional officers to be added in annual increments over the next 5 years. In the existing emergency, the President, by Executive Order, authorized the immediate addition of all increments, but, on the outbreak of war, the Corps was still 91 officers short of its authorized strength.[9] Of the 205 officers the Corps did have, 55 were on permanent assignment and 150 were detailed from the line. As soon as the war began, the Corps was badly crippled, for the War Department reassigned 66 of the detailed officers and sent them back to the line.[10]

Anticipating that development, Quartermaster General Sharpe had expected in any emergency to draw trained personnel from the Officers' Reserve Corps. The National Defense Act of 1916 had authorized the establishment of such a Corps, and many of the most efficient and valuable clerks in the Office of the Quartermaster General had taken the examinations and qualified for commissions in the Quartermaster section of the Officers' Reserve Corps. In May 1917, Sharpe requested The Adjutant General to call such Reserve officers to active duty in the Washington office, where their experience could be put to work to expedite the increasing business of the Corps. The Acting Chief of Staff disapproved

[9] (1) 39 *Stat.* 170. (2) Henry G. Sharpe, *The Quartermaster Corps* (New York, 1921), p. 26.

[10] *War Expenditures Hearings,* 66th Cong., 2d sess., Ser. 4, Pt. 43, p. 2268 (Sharpe).

his application on the basis of a recommendation made by The Adjutant General who feared its effects upon his own office. It was then decided that any Civil Service employee or enlisted man, given a commission as a Reserve officer and called to active duty, would have to be sent to some other station than the one at which he was located when called into service. The effect was to deprive the Office of the Quartermaster General at a critical time of much needed, valuable, experienced assistance. These men, through long years of training and thorough knowledge of the workings of the Office, were most familiar with the laws, decisions, and precedents regulating the Corps and, as a result, were best qualified to prepare tables of requirements and draw up estimates for Congress. The very men whose services were denied to Sharpe were later ordered back to Washington and assigned to duty in the Office after he had been relieved as Quartermaster General.[11]

Establishment of the Council of National Defense

Realizing that the Quartermaster Corps lacked sufficient trained personnel to handle its rapidly expanding wartime business, Quartermaster General Sharpe eagerly sought the aid of experts available within the organization of the Council of National Defense.[12] This Council, composed of the Secretaries of War, Navy, Agriculture, Interior, Commerce, and Labor, had been created as a result of a rider to the Army Appropriation Bill passed by Congress on August 29, 1916. This legislation gave recognition to the problems of industrial mobilization and economic control. It charged the Council with the "co-ordination of industries and resources for the national security and welfare" and with the "creation of relations which will render possible in time of need the immediate concentration and utilization of the resources of the Nation." Though created in the summer of 1916, the Council was not fully organized until 3 March 1917.[13]

The Council itself dealt only with top policy questions. The actual work of planning was done by the Advisory Commission created 11 October 1916. The Commission consisted of seven men, appointed by the Council of National Defense, with the approval of the President. Each man represented a certain line of industry or activity, and each headed

[11] (1) Sharpe, *The Quartermaster Corps*, pp. 19, 36–39. (2) *Army Reorganization:* Hearings before House Committee on Military Affairs, 66th Cong., 1st sess., Pt. 14, pp. 650–51. Hereafter briefly referred to as *Army Reorganization Hearings*. (3) *War Expenditures Hearings*, 66th Cong., Ser. I, Pt. 6, pp. 519–20 (Goethals).

[12] *War Expenditures Hearings*, 66th Cong., 2d sess., Ser. 4, Pt. 43, p. 2259.

[13] (1) 39 *Stat.* 649. (2) *First Annual Report, Council of National Defense, 1917* (Washington, 1917), p. 6.

a committee in his special field that would permit bringing together experts who could advise the government.[14]   Of these, the Committee on Supplies, dealing with cotton goods, woolen goods, leather and shoes, played a major role in Quartermaster operations in 1917.[15]   It soon became apparent to the Council and the Advisory Commission that wartime requirements would necessitate a program of co-ordination, and, by resolution of the Council on 31 March 1917, a General Munitions Board was created to co-ordinate purchases made by the War and Navy Departments, to assist in the acquisition of raw materials, and to establish precedence of orders between the War and Navy Departments and between the military and industrial needs of the country.[16]   Because the authority and scope of action of the General Munitions Board were only vaguely defined and the centralization of authority sought by the Advisory Commission was not achieved, the Council of National Defense soon took further action.   In July, it transformed the General Munitions Board into the War Industries Board.   Presidential action in March of the following year brought about a complete reorganization of the War Industries Board and a greater extension of its powers.[17]   The relations between the Quartermaster Corps and the Council of National Defense and its committees and boards will become more apparent as some of the Corps' major wartime supply operations are analyzed.

---

[14] Following are the names of the seven men, their positions, and the committee each headed:

Daniel Willard (President, Baltimore & Ohio Railroad), Committee on transportation and communication

Howard E. Coffin (Vice-president, Hudson Motor Co.), Committee on munitions and manufacturing (including standardization) and industrial relations

Julius Rosenwald (President, Sears, Roebuck & Co.), Committee on Supplies

Bernard Baruch (Banker), Committee on raw materials, minerals, and metals

Dr. Hollis Godfrey (President, Drexel Institute), Committee on engineering and education

Samuel Compers (President, American Federation of Labor), Committee on labor, including conservation of health and welfare of workers

Dr. Franklin Martin (Secretary, General American College of Surgeons, Chicago), Committee on medicine and surgery, including general sanitation.

[15] The Committee on Supplies was created by resolution of the Advisory Commission of the Council of National Defense on 12 February 1917 to cooperate in an advisory capacity with the purchasing officers of the War and Navy Departments in securing their requirements of clothing, equipment, and subsistence, and in co-ordinating the buying by these departments of these supplies. *Fist Annual Report, Council of National Defense, 1917*, p. 65.

[16] Representatives of the supply bureaus of the War and Navy Departments were appointed to the General Munitions Board along with appointees from the committees on raw materials, manufacture, supplies, and medicine of the Advisory Commission. *Ibid.*, pp. 20–21.

[17] Grosvenor B. Clarkson, *Industrial America in the World War* (New York, 1923), pp. 35–36; 48–50.

Sheltering the Troops

In April 1917, as in 1898, the Quartermaster Corps was unprepared to cope with the demands made upon it. Although other supply bureaus were equally unprepared, the Corps' position was more critical since it immediately had to transport, clothe, feed, and shelter an expanding Army. Woefully understaffed and lacking funds, the Corps entered upon a 9-month period of frantic endeavor, made more difficult by the failure of the Chief of Staff's Office to sustain the authority and functions of the Quartermaster General. Relieving General Sharpe of some of his duties was intended to speed achievement of some of the intended objectives and incidentally ease his burden, but since such transfers always involved the loss of experienced personnel, the effect upon his Office was demoralizing. It led him to protest that divided authority and parceling out his vital functions were likely to result in serious consequences for which he would nevertheless be held responsible.[18]

Providing shelter for the troops called into service was one such function removed from his control. Ever since the period of the Mexican border trouble, the Office of the Quartermaster General had been studying the problem of housing troops in the field. Its Construction and Repair Division had designed and prepared plans for a series of temporary buildings and had also prepared schedules of the necessary materials to be used in their erection. In response to an inquiry from the Secretary of War in March, the Quartermaster General reported that his Office had available working drawings and blueprints for the construction of temporary cantonment buildings to shelter troops at regimental, brigade, or division training points. Blueprints, he reported, had been forwarded and more would be sent immediately to the various department commanders. He also indicated that his Office had under way some tentative negotiation with a number of large concerns that manufactured ready-made structures in the expectation that utilization of such resources would make possible the erection of temporary shelters for practically any number of troops on very short notice.[19]

Receiving no further instructions even after war had been declared, Quartermaster General Sharpe pressed for a policy decision in April. Numerous requisitions for funds to provide shelter for National Guard troops were pouring into his Office. Would such troops remain in tentage with temporary kitchens and mess shelter of frame construction,

---

[18] RG 120, War Department Historical Files, Box 143 (Memo, Sharpe for Chief of Staff, 17 Sep 1917).

[19] *Ibid.*, Box 143 (Ltr, TAG to QMG, 21 Mar 1917 and 1st ind., Sharpe to TAG, 21 Mar 1917).

similar to those that had been constructed on the Mexican border, or, he queried, would they be housed in temporary buildings such as were provided for maneuver camps? To expedite any construction program, he pointed out, the Corps would also have to be advised immediately concerning the location of, and the number of troops to be cared for at, the various mobilization camps for the National Guard, the Regular Army, and any other troops that might be raised.[20] It was 7 May 1917, however, before the War Department directed the commanding generals of the several military departments to select sites for the construction of cantonments for the training of the mobilized National Guard and the National Army.[21]

Early in April, it became apparent to the General Munitions Board of the Council of National Defense that the construction of cantonments, additions to Government arsenals, and expansion of other manufacturing concerns engaged in the production of war materials and supplies was a vital part of the preparation for carrying on the war. A group of civilian experts, formed into the Committee on Emergency Construction, began a study of the problems involved.[22] Because of the magnitude of the work and the limited time available, the Committee recommended that an experienced and capable officer be charged solely with the construction of cantonments. The General Munitions Board proposed to make office room available for him and his staff and to furnish him with adequate civilian assistance.[23]

The Secretary of War approved of these recommendations and ordered Col. I. W. Littell, Chief of the Construction and Repair Division in the Quartermaster General's Office, placed in charge of cantonment construction. A separate division, to be known as the Cantonment Division, was established in the Office, absorbing most of the limited personnel of the Construction and Repair Division. The latter division continued in charge of construction and repair work at permanent posts

[20] RG 92, AGO Document File, Case 2570158 (Sharpe to TAG, 9 Apr 1917); Case 2599172 (Memo, Sharpe for Chief of Staff, 13 Apr 1917).

[21] (1) *War Department Annual Reports, 1917*, I, 25. (2) The National Army Plan, developed by the War College Division of the General Staff and the Army War College, was a long-range program that was eventually adapted and made to serve as the basis for the Selective Service Act of May 18, 1917. The distinction drawn between Regular Army, National Guard, and draftees under the Act was later abolished by designating all three as the "United States Army." *War Department General Orders, 1918*, GO 73, 7 Aug 1918. (3) For development of the plan, see Marvin A. Kreidberg and Merton G. Henry, *History of Military Mobilization in the United States Army, 1775–1945* (Department of the Army Pamphlet No. 20–212, Washington, 1955).

[22] *First Annual Report, Council of National Defense, 1917*, pp. 23–24.

[23] (1) RG 120, History of Construction, Book I (Exhibits), pp. 11–12 (Committee on Emergency Construction to W. A. Starrett, 10 May 1917). (2) RG 92, AGO Document File, Case 2597942 (Memo, Maj. P. E. Pierce for Acting Chief of Staff, 16 May 1917).

and stations.   Because the Cantonment Division operated directly under the Secretary of War, the Quartermaster Corps was relieved of all responsibility for cantonment construction, except the preparation of estimates required by that Division.[24]

The task confronting the Cantonment Division was enormous.   In April 1917, there were sufficient barracks only for sheltering the Regular Army.   Additional housing had to be provided for the increments to the Regular Army, for the expanded National Guard, and for the men drafted into the National Army.   Early in May, War Department plans called for the construction of 32 cantonments, but insufficient funds and shortages of supplies, labor, and transportation compelled a revision of these plans.   Late in May, the General Staff decided that cantonments would be constructed only for 16 divisions of the National Army by 1 September.   The National Guard would be mobilized in camps that, for the most part, would be under canvas, with only certain divisional storehouses and quarters for special uses constructed of wood.   For climatic reasons, it located these National Guard camps in the southern states.[25]

The Committee on Emergency Construction, acting in an advisory capacity, assisted Colonel Littell in building up an organization adequate for the task, in obtaining the services of qualified men to direct the work of the Division, and in selecting responsible contractors to carry out the construction.   On the advice of the Committee, and in the interest of economy, the Cantonment Division abandoned the one-story barrack used in Quartermaster plans in favor of a two-story barrack.   Working through the various subcommittees of the Council of National Defense, the Cantonment Division obtained construction materials and equipment.

If the camps were to be ready by 1 September, speed was essential. Some sites were not selected, however, until June.   Because work had to begin even before completed plans and specifications could be made available for use in submitting competitive estimates, the ordinary method of advertising for bids and awarding contracts to the lowest bidders could not be followed.   Since no form of government contract met this situation, the Council of National Defense developed a new one.   This contract provided that work should be done on a cost-plus basis with a graded

[24] (1) RG 120, History of Construction, Book I (Exhibits), p. 32 (Ltr, Sharpe to Chief of Staff, 17 May 1917); p. 33 (Memo, Littell for Chief of Staff, 18 May 1917). (2) RG 92, OQMG General Correspondence File, 1917–1922, Box 7997 (TAG to Col. I. W. Littell, 19 May 1917).

[25] RG 92, OQMG General Correspondence File, 1917–1922, Box 7997 (Memo, Chief, War College Div., for Chief of Staff, — May 1917; Memo, Acting Chief of Staff, Gen. T. H. Bliss, for TAG, 29 May 1917; Ltr, Committee on Emergency Construction to Col. I. W. Littell, 25 May 1917).

scale of percentages decreasing from 10 percent to 6 percent on the cost of the work as the total cost of work increased.[26]   The use of this type of contract was much criticized and condemned later, but General Littell testified that no contractor received as high as 6 percent, the actual amount varying between 2 and 3 percent.   A minority report of the Committee on War Expenditures held the cost-plus system justifiable, inevitable, and unavoidable.[27]

By October 1917, the Cantonment Division had, for the most part, completed the initial construction of cantonments.   Attention was then turned to other types of construction—the building of munitions plants, proving grounds, aviation fields, port terminals, and interior depots. Before the war, the Quartermaster Corps had been responsible for all such construction, but in the absence of any co-ordinating influence in 1917, various supply bureaus had been permitted to obtain funds for construction purposes in appropriation and deficiency bills.[28]   Competition for materials had inevitably resulted.   To restore centralized control, the Secretary of War on 5 October 1917, directed the Cantonment Division to assume responsibility for all construction made necessary in the United States by the emergency, whether provided for by existing or pending appropriations.[29]

The Ordnance Department and the Corps of Engineers agreed to the transfer of work, but it required a considerable number of conferences to resolve difficulties with the Signal Corps.[30]   So far as the Quartermaster Corps was concerned, the Secretary's order resulted in the transfer of what remained of the prewar Construction and Repair Division to the Cantonment Division as a branch of that organization, along with its personnel and records.[31]   To this time, the Quartermaster General had regarded the Cantonment Division as an organizational unit of his Office, but that division had shown an increasing degree of independence.   Its chief did not even consult the Quartermaster General on the reorganization required by the new responsibilities resulting from the Secretary's order of 5 October.   The Quartermaster General was critical of these

---

[26] *W.D. Investigation Hearings*, 65th Cong., 2d sess., Pt. 2, p. 2323 (Littell).

[27] *War Expenditures Hearings*, 66th Cong., Ser. I, vol. 3, p. 414.

[28] The Signal Corps, for example, had been granted funds to construct, maintain, and repair barracks, quarters, stables, storehouses, magazines, administrative buildings, hangars, sheds, shops, garages, and other permanent buildings necessary for the shelter of aviation troops, public animals, stores and equipment.   40 *Stat.* 43 (May 12, 1917).

[29] RG 92, OQMG General Correspondence File, 1917–1922, Box 7997 (Ltr, TAG to QMG, 5 Oct 1917).

[30] *Ibid.*, Box 7997 (Ltr, Maj. W. A. Starrett to Maj. W. W. Taylor, 8 Dec 1917).

[31] OQMG Office Order No. 106, 10 Oct 1917.

developments and considered unnecessary the additional authority requested by the Cantonment Division to execute its expanded duties.[32]

The Secretary made additional changes after he reassigned Sharpe to other duties. He placed the Cantonment Division under the Chief of Staff to function as part of the Operations Division on 9 February 1918. In the following month the Cantonment Division was renamed the Construction Division.[33] Although the Construction Division was entirely separated from the Office of the Quartermaster General by this directive, there still were many matters that, by reason of existing conditions, continued to be handled through that Office. Thus, the Office of the Quartermaster General hired most of the civilians employed by the Construction Division; officers commissioned in the Quartermaster Corps were assigned to the Construction Division; and the Quartermaster Corps accounted for all funds expended by the Construction Division and all property it used in connection with its construction work. As a result of these ties, the impression was created that there was no separation and, in consequence, confusion and an unwillingness to cooperate fully were fostered. To clarify this situation, the chief of the Construction Division proposed that an Executive Order be issued converting the Division into a separate bureau of the War Department to handle all construction.[34] That objective, however, was not attained in 1918.

Loss of Transportation Function

For all practical purposes, the Quartermaster General had lost his responsibility for construction in May 1917. Before the summer was over, a War Department order relieved him of still another function, namely, the responsibility for transporting troops and supplies overseas. To carry out this duty, the Corps had, since the Spanish-American War, maintained an Army Transport Service. A General Superintendent and his assistants directed the whole of the Army Transport Service at the home ports of the vessels, and the Water Transportation Branch in the Transportation Division of the Office of the Quartermaster General provided general supervision.

In April 1917, the Army Transport Service had only 16 vessels. All but four of the troop transports were in service in the Pacific, and the four that comprised the Atlantic fleet were primarily engaged in the

---

[32] RG 92, OQMG General Correspondence File, 1917–1922, Box 7997 (2d ind., QMG to TAG, 20 Dec 1917).

[33] War Department GO 14.

[34] RG 120, History of Construction, Book II (Exhibits), pp. 185–88 (Memo, Brig. Gen. R. C. Marshall, Jr., for ASW, 2 Aug 1918).

Canal Zone.[35] Although the Service did not own many ships, it could, under the direction of the Quartermaster General, charter commercial vessels and refit them for service. In preparation for demands for additional ships, the Water Transportation Branch maintained a record on various commercial vessels of American registry, giving their tonnage, capacity, and general suitability for transport use. Major General Sharpe later insisted that even if the Army Transport Service owned only a few ships, it had "the nucleus of an organization" that needed only the necessary orders and financial support to permit it to expand readily to any extent demanded.[36]

Before the declaration of war, the Quartermaster General instructed the Chief of the Transportation Division to communicate with the chairman of the Shipping Board and impress upon him the necessity for making ships available as transports. Col. J. M. Carson, Depot Quartermaster at New York City and, after 8 May 1917, also General Superintendent, Army Transport Service, recommended more specific action. As early as December 1916, he urged that plans be prepared, if they did not already exist, to enable the Army to take possession of the German and Austrian ships interned at New York harbor since August 1914 and to seize the docks at Hoboken where they were berthed. Many of these vessels were passenger ships, admirably adapted for use as troop transports. The Quartermaster General replied that he would take steps to do this as soon as it became necessary, but representatives of the Treasury Department immediately seized the vessels when war was declared. The Shipping Board subsequently took over their operation, and weeks of valuable time were lost before the question of their use by the Army was favorably settled.[37]

The docks at Hoboken were not included in the seizure of the German ships. Colonel Carson again urged the importance of obtaining them, but not until he personally presented the matter to the Quartermaster General and the Secretary of War on 15 April did he receive instructions the following day to take possession of the docks. Despite the colonel's energetic measures to clear the docks of property belonging to the steamship companies that owned them, it was mid-May before they were ready for transports. Approximately a week later on 21 May, he received orders to prepare to send the first convoy of American troops to France. With the cooperation of the steamship companies whose vessels were to be used, and with the assistance of the shipyards and of

---

[35] *Annual Report of the Quartermaster General, 1917,* pp. 55–58.

[36] Sharpe, *The Quartermaster Corps,* p. 352.

[37] (1) *Ibid.,* pp. 356–58. (2) RG 92, OQMG Historical Files, Box 50 (Ltr, Lt. Col. F. P. Jackson to Brig. Gen. J. M. Carson, 3 May 1919, and appended report from Carson).

the Naval officers of the New York Navy Yard in fitting out the ships, he dispatched the expedition on 14 June 1917.

Since there was no embarkation camp at which the troops could be held until they could board transports, Colonel Carson had to communicate with the posts from which they were being drawn and regulate the arrival of the troops so that they could march directly from the train to the designated ship. Without adequate co-ordination, the possibilities for things to go wrong were innumerable, and the need for such control was clearly evident to one observer.

Slowly and confusedly the troopships were here being prepared for sea. Slowly and more confusedly supplies and troops were being brought. Evidently the first convoy of this expedition has been hurriedly ordered. Lack of system, lack of direction, cohesion, and organization were evident upon all hands and in everything. Supplies and troops were loaded in confusion and disorder. Men were sent to ships unprepared to receive them. Supplies were piled in pell-mell. Many had to be unloaded. Some ships received too many troops, some too few, and had to be changed. Men came expecting to go aboard to live and had to stay ashore or on a lighter and live as best they could. Troops intended to be put aboard ships to live had to be held for a couple of days in railroad freight yards, blocked in by freight trains, and most dirty and uncomfortable.[38]

Because the docks offered inadequate storage space for all the freight that was to accompany the expedition, Colonel Carson also had to attempt to regulate the arrival of supplies and equipment. Although the tonnage for the expedition was limited, the War Department had established no priority lists for shipments nor did it exercise any co-ordination. Each supply bureau shipped the supplies that would be required by its representatives in France, one bureau alone shipping about 12,000 tons of freight to New York to be forwarded with the expedition.[39] Though the Quartermaster Corps was supposedly responsible for the transportation of supplies and troops, its control, in the existing state of unco-ordinated action, had been undermined by the action of the various supply bureaus in securing appropriations for making shipment of their own materials. They had created traffic sections that handled the shipment of their supplies by railroad, sending the finished products to the ports as rapidly as they were procured. At the ports, where available tonnage was scant and where port officers had to consider the immediate needs of the American Expeditionary Forces as well as the necessity for a balanced lading of the vessels, much of this material could not be

---

[38] Robert L. Bullard, *Personalities and Reminiscences of the War* (New York, 1925), pp. 26–27.

[39] (1) Sharpe, *The Quartermaster Corps*, pp. 360–61. (2) RG 92, OQMG Historical Files, Box 50 (Carson Report).

forwarded. Within a short time, Army freight cluttered the docks at the ports and, with no storage space available there, remained in freight cars that clogged the rails so far inland that by December freight transportation almost came to a halt.

Colonel Carson's experience in preparing for the first convoy convinced him that as Depot Quartermaster and General Superintendent he did not have sufficient authority to handle satisfactorily the military details of embarkation. A port commander was obviously necessary, and pending the appointment of such an officer, he suggested that he be so designated. Quartermaster General Sharpe approved, but the Chief of Staff did not assign this duty to Colonel Carson. Instead, he instructed the Commanding General of the Eastern Department to exercise the functions of a commander of the port of embarkation until a line officer could be designated for such duty. He directed General Superintendent Carson to report to the commanding general for instructions.[40]

Shortly after the first convoy sailed, Colonel Carson received orders to send a second division abroad as soon as possible. To insure proper supervision and co-ordination, Quartermaster General Sharpe recommended, on 20 June 1917, that ports of embarkation be established at New York, Newport News, and such other ports as might be necessary. He proposed that the New York port be designated for the transportation of troops and general supplies and the Newport News port for the shipment of animals, forage, and heavy ordnance. He recommended that a commanding officer be assigned to each port of embarkation who would be under the orders of the Secretary of War and would have authority to communicate directly with the chiefs of the supply bureaus. He further recommended the establishment of a concentration camp at the New York port and a depot to accommodate 10,000 animals at the Newport News port. He proposed that bureau chiefs furnish timely information of contemplated shipments to the port commander who would decide on the priority of all shipments.[41]

The Secretary of War approved of the proposals. Approximately 5 weeks later, on the recommendation of the General Staff, co-ordination was carried much further than Sharpe had envisaged. A section to take charge of the embarkation of troops and supplies for transatlantic transportation and to exercise direct control under the Secretary of War was

---

[40] (1) RG 94, AGO Document File, Case 2612095 (Memo, Chief, War College Div. for Chief of Staff, 5 Jun 1917). (2) RG 92, OQMG Historical Files, Box 56 (Memo, Acting Chief of Staff for TAG, 6 Jun 1917, exhibit in Appendix III, p. 5 for "History of Purchase Storage & Traffic Division").

[41] RG 120, War Department Historical Files, Box 162-A (Memo, Chief of War College Div. for Chief of Staff, 5 Jul 1917, copy in "History of Purchase, Storage & Traffic Division," Appendix IV, pp. 15–16).

established in the Office of the Chief of Staff.   This section, co-ordinating and supervising all troop movements to Europe and all shipments of supplies from points of origin to ports of embarkation and controlling the employment of all Army transports used in the transatlantic service as well as all supplementary commercial shipping, was placed under the direction of Brig. Gen. F. J. Kernan, temporarily detailed as Chief of the Embarkation Service.   Col. Chauncey B. Baker, who had been serving as chief of the Transportation Division in the Quartermaster General's Office, was detailed as his principal assistant.[42]   The effect of this order was to relieve the Quartermaster Corps of all responsibility for overseas transportation of troops and supplies.   The Transportation Division still retained its prewar responsibility for railroad and motor transportation.

Centralized Control of Subsistence Procurement

War had brought the loss of two of the basic functions of the Corps for the duration of the conflict.   Its impact was to be felt in other changes, particularly in the shift from a system of decentralized procurement to one of centralized control.   Quartermaster purchase of food for the Army was an entirely decentralized function before the war.   Depot quartermasters bought all subsistence, basing their purchases on requirements figured by departmental quartermasters and procuring from dealers in the immediate vicinity of the posts to be supplied.   The system had been efficient in providing the small prewar Army with high quality food at relatively low prices.

Sharpe did not anticipate any need for change in this system, and, at the outbreak of war, he instructed the officers of the 13 Quartermaster depots to provide subsistence supplies for the various organizations assigned to the different camps and cantonments under their jurisdiction. Shortly thereafter, the War Department issued instructions to the camps and cantonments which required them to lay in a 3 months' supply of food—1 month's supply at camp, 1 month's supply en route, and 1 month's supply on requisition.   Quartermasters at the camps bought all perishable stores, and depot quartermasters procured all other subsistence.[43]   The large purchases required for the rapidly expanding Army and procured by quartermasters competing against each other materially affected prices. Moreover, the prices they paid varied greatly and the subsistence stores they purchased were not uniform in quality.   At times, there was a

[42] (1) War Department GO 102, 4 Aug 1917. (2) Sharpe, *The Quartermaster Corps*, pp. 364–67 (Memo, TAG for QMG, 27 Jul 1917).

[43] RG 120, War Department Historical Files, Box 153 (Memorandum, Lt. Col. Wm. R. Grove, 24 Dec 1917, sub: Method of Handling Subsistence During 1917).

congestion of purchase orders in certain areas, particularly in the New York area where the quartermaster of the New York Depot was filling practically all overseas shipments of subsistence.   Competition between the armed services further disturbed market conditions, while purchases by Allied governments added to the abnormal demand.

By the summer of 1917, it was apparent that certain food commodities would be scarce.   The Council of National Defense undertook to provide the requirements of the Army and Navy without unduly influencing the price paid by civilians.   Working through the National Canners' Association, it made arrangements to secure military requirements of such articles as canned peas, corn, beans, tomatoes, and fruits by allotment to all the canners of the country.[44]

When the U.S. Food Administration was organized in August, it continued to make such allotments.   On 8 October 1917, by proclamation of the President, 20 of the principal items of food supply were placed under the control of the Food Administration.   They were in such great demand that it was believed that supply would not be sufficient and that control of their sale and distribution would be necessary.   Depending upon actual or prospective shortages, the Food Administration later brought other food items under its control.   In order to co-ordinate all purchases of food products intended for military purposes, a Food Purchase Board was organized in December at the suggestion of the Food Administrator.   The Board was composed of members representing the Quartermaster General, the Paymaster General of the Navy, the Food Administration, and the Federal Trade Commission.   Thereafter, when an actual or prospective shortage existed for foods that were to be purchased, the Food Purchase Board took charge, recommending the method of procurement and the prices to be paid, the latter being determined after an investigation of costs by the Federal Trade Commission.

Under the plan of control finally developed, the Office of the Quartermaster General obtained articles on the allocated purchase list by requesting the Food Administration to allocate the quantity required. The Food Administration allotted the amount to the producers of the commodity in question, dividing the business among them in proportion to their capacity.   When informed that the allotment had been made, the Office of the Quartermaster General directed procurement through the proper general supply depot in whose area the designated industry was located, under terms and at prices decided upon by the Food Purchase Board.   The Office procured under this control plan flour, sugar, all canned vegetables, canned and evaporated fruits, salmon, sardines, canned

---

[44] First Annual Report, Council of National Defense, 1917, p. 67.

milk, and fresh beef.   The products so handled totaled about 40 percent of all food requirements for the Army.[45]

Before the end of 1917, the Office of the Quartermaster General developed a plan for the control of practically all the remaining items of subsistence it procured.   During the first 9 months of the war, subsistence procurement remained in the hands of the depot quartermasters.   There was no shortage of rations and the absence of criticism is evidence that they performed satisfactorily despite all obstacles.   Centralized control was a necessity, however, and led to the establishment of a Subsistence Division in the Office of the Quartermaster General on 2 January 1918. On the previous day, the Office put into effect a control plan that covered 33 principal subsistence items.   Under that plan, depot quartermasters, and later zone supply officers, solicited bids and reported them to the Subsistence Division.   Quartermaster officers in the Division compared the bids with current market prices and accepted the most advantageous bid, the purchase being completed by the local supply officer.   In effect, the plan provided centralized control with decentralized purchase.   The Division gradually extended the list of controlled items until, by the time the armistice was signed, it included almost all subsistence items not allotted through the Food Administration.[46]

Developments in Procurement of Textiles and Clothing

In April 1917, Sharpe also relied upon the existing decentralized Quartermaster procurement system to obtain the textiles, clothing, and equipment needed by the troops of the Regular Army and the National Guard, both raised to their authorized maximum war strength, and by the forces of the National Army to be called to the colors, a total of approximately 1,500,000 men by September.[47]   Although it is doubtful that the Quartermaster General, or most Army officers, then appreciated the problems of industrial mobilization confronting a democracy at war, Sharpe knew that the Corps would need the cooperation of the business community in making large purchases.   In February 1917, he proposed that boards of award be established at Quartermaster purchasing depots, to be composed of depot officers and one or more competent businessmen,

---

[45] (1) *America's Munitions, 1917–18: Report of Benedict Crowell* (Washington, 1919), pp. 440–41.   (2) RG 120, War Department Historical Files, Box 147 (Rpt, "History of the Subsistence Division," pp. 10–13.

[46] (1) Sharpe, *The Quartermaster Corps*, pp. 93–96.   (2) RG 120, War Department Historical Files, Box 147 (Rpt, "History of the Subsistence Division," pp. 13–15).

[47] (1) *War Department Annual Reports, 1917*, I, 12.   (2) RG 120, War Department Historical Files, Box 143 (1st ind., TAG to QMG, 23 May 1917, to ltr, TAG to CG, Eastern Department, 22 May 1917).

the latter to be designated by the Council of National Defense. These businessmen were not to be connected with any firm that would be likely to submit proposals on Quartermaster items of supply, but, by reason of their qualifications and expert knowledge, they could serve in an advisory capacity to the depot purchasing officer on the board of award, which would examine bids, make awards, and enter into contracts.[48]

The Council of National Defense adopted a resolution along somewhat different lines that Secretary of War Baker communicated to the president of the Chamber of Commerce of the United States. It requested that the latter appoint a small committee in each of the cities in which the Quartermaster Corps had a purchasing depot, to the end that advice and assistance could be furnished the local quartermaster in case it became necessary when unusually large purchases had to be made on short notice.[49]

The president of the U.S. Chamber of Commerce hurriedly organized such advisory committees at six major purchasing depots at Boston, New York, Philadelphia, Chicago, St. Louis, and San Francisco, where bids were to be opened early in March.[50] Later, he provided advisory committees at other depots. The service of these committees varied. At some depots, quartermasters never called upon them; at others, notably at New York and San Francisco, the depot quartermasters relied heavily on their assistance. The advisory committees sought to eliminate middlemen, to put the quartermasters in touch with reputable manufacturers, and to resolve difficulties caused by government specifications. Their primary importance was in bringing about contact between government and industry and in selling government business to manufacturers who generally lacked confidence in the government's business methods which they viewed as bad. As purchase of Quartermaster supplies gradually became centralized in Washington through the efforts of the Council of National Defense, the depot quartermasters' power in the placement of contracts decreased and the necessity for advisory committees also declined.

The Quartermaster Corps was greatly handicapped in meeting any emergency demands for clothing and equipment because it lacked sufficient trained personnel; it had no funds; and it had no stock of reserve clothing on hand—that had been exhausted when the National Guard was called into service on the Mexican border in June 1916. When, on 3 March 1917, the Secretary of War directed the Quartermaster Gen-

[48] RG 120, War Department Historical Files, Box 143 (Memo, Sharpe for SW, 4 Feb 1917).
[49] RG 92, OQMG Historical Files, Box 3 (Historical Rpt, "Problem in Industrial Mobilization," prepared by H. Phelps Putnam).
[50] War Expenditures Hearings, 66th Cong., 2d sess., Ser. 4, Pt. 43, p. 2259 (Sharpe).

eral to procure, without delay and to the extent of existing appropriations, the clothing and equipment needed to equip at war strength all existing National Guard organizations, Quartermaster General Sharpe could only reply that there was no existing appropriation for the procurement of clothing and other Quartermaster supplies.[51]   During the fall of 1916, the clothing appropriation had become exhausted and deficiencies had been created in order to support the National Guard and Regular Army of 250,000 men, stationed principally on the Mexican border.

Sharpe expected a new appropriation bill to pass on 4 March 1917, and, in anticipation, he directed his quartermasters to advertise for bids on sufficient quantities of textiles, clothing, and equipment to provide during fiscal year 1918 for the Regular Army which was estimated at 160,000 men.   Congress, however, adjourned without enacting such legislation; it did not pass the Army Appropriation Act until 15 June 1917. With the Secretary of War's sanction, the Corps therefore had to make arrangements for entering into contracts with the successful bidders before Congress appropriated funds in order that the manufacturers could produce the articles of clothing and have them ready for delivery promptly by 1 July, or the beginning of the next fiscal year.[52]

The contracts provided clothing only for the then existing Regular Army strength of approximately 160,000 men, but later in March, as the likelihood of war became more evident, Sharpe obtained authority from the Secretary of War to increase the amounts of these contracts to cover 500,000 men.   Early in April, before Congress assembled in special session, the Secretary authorized Sharpe to make purchases for an additional 500,000 men.[53]   Late in May, the Secretary extended this authority to include still another 500,000 men.   Though such action helped alleviate the existing situation, the effect, in general, of Congress' delay in passing the appropriation bill was to retard materially the procurement of supplies.

The extent to which the Quartermaster Corps could make preparation to clothe and equip troops was based on what it estimated to be the capacity of the country's mills to produce cloth.   On 13 March 1917, Sharpe informed the Chief of Staff that, assuming funds were available, clothing and equipment for 1,000,000 men could, under existing conditions, be procured within 10 months, or by December 1917, although

[51] RG 94, AGO Document File, Case 2545048 (TAG to QMG *et al.*, 3 Mar 1917, and 1st ind., Sharpe to TAG, 3 Mar 1917).

[52] *W.D. Investigation Hearings*, 65th Cong., 2d sess., Pt. 2, pp. 469–70; 870–73 (Sharpe).

[53] (1) RG 94, AGO Document File, Case 2555459 (TAG to QMG, 21 Mar 1917, and 1st ind., Sharpe to TAG, 21 Mar 1917). (2) RG 120, War Department Historical Files, Box 143 (Memo, Sharpe for Chief of Staff, 3 and 4 Apr 1917). (3) Frederick Palmer, *Newton D. Baker* (2 vols., New York, 1911), I, 118–19; 247.

the Corps might have to purchase some blankets that did not conform to specifications.[54]   Shortly thereafter, the Chief of Staff called into Federal service a number of National Guard organizations, having an estimated strength of 68,000 men.   Actually, the men numbered 89,000, but Sharpe was prepared to clothe and equip them immediately.   Referring more specifically to his previous time estimate, he noted that it would take 4 months, or until the end of July, to complete the equipment of the Regular Army and the National Guard, both raised to war strength and totalling approximately 500,000 men.   To equip another 500,000 men would take an additional 5 months.[55]   Thus, Sharpe again emphasized that it would be the end of December before the Corps could clothe and equip 1,000,000 men—a fact that he endeavored to impress anew on the Chief of Staff in the course of a personal conference.[56]   Inasmuch as the Committee on Supplies later took action to increase production by encouraging nonessential industries, such as carpet factories, to convert their plants to the manufacture of Army fabrics—in this instance to the production of melton for Army overcoats—-the Quartermaster Corps actually provided clothing for 1,640,502 men by the end of December 1917.[57] By 11 November 1918, it had clothed more than 3,500,000 men.

Supply was not accomplished without crisis.   By mid-July 1917, the Chief of the Supplies Division reported that between unanticipated demands and delinquencies, the clothing supply situation was such that if the entire National Guard was called out on 1 September, according to War Department plans, a part of that force would have to train in citizens' clothes.   He therefore recommended that the assembling of the National Army be deferred a month.   The bulk of the supplies for equipping these troops was being turned out in factories in the East during August and could not be shipped to reach distant points by 1 September.[58]

By using cotton clothing at all cantonments in the South, the Quartermaster General had hoped to provide the first increment of the National Army with sufficient woolen clothing to prevent suffering.   But War Department orders to furnish woolen clothing to certain other troops caused him to doubt that the first troops of the National Army could be provided with more than one cotton coat and pair of breeches, two suits of cotton underwear, one pair of shoes and cotton stockings, a hat, and

---

[54] RG 120, War Department Historical Files, Box 143 (Sharpe to Chief of Staff, 13 Mar 1917).

[55] *Ibid.*, Box 143 (Sharpe Memo, 2 Apr 1917).

[56] His estimate of the time required to clothe and equip 1,000,000 men was reiterated on 19 April 1917. *Ibid.*, Box 143 (Sharpe to TAG).

[57] *W.D. Investigation Hearings*, 65th Cong., 2d sess., Pt. 2, p. 599 (Sharpe).

[58] *Ibid.*, pp. 493–97 (Memo, Sharpe for Brig. Gen. A. L. Smith, 15 Jul 1917; Memos, Smith for QMG, 18 and 24 Jul 1917).

two blankets per man. Sharpe made it clear that the impossibility of equipping the entire United States Army with woolen clothing by 5 September was "a fact and not a theory." [59]

Much of the difficulty experienced by the Corps in supplying sufficient clothing during the first phase of supply, extending from 6 April to 31 December, stemmed from the failure of the General Staff in preparing troop schedules to consult with the Quartermaster General as to whether supplies were on hand to meet those schedules. This first supply period covered a time when "there was no policy and yet many policies." Although providing clothing and equipment for the Army is predicated upon Army strength, yet in those months the War Department failed to approve and furnish to the Quartermaster Corps and the other supply bureaus any reliable strength program on which to base supply requirements. Even when projects were approved, the War Department failed, in many instances, to inform the Quartermaster General's Office of them in time to be of any use.[60]

Calculation of requirements was further upset by a shift in operational plans. When the original plan for raising the Army was under discussion, the President had no intention of sending any troops abroad until 1918. The Corps based its program of clothing procurement on this premise. Early in May, however, the President, in response to Allied pleas, decided to ship troops abroad at once. Such troops not only had to be provided with woolen uniforms and underclothing but also with a 6 months' reserve of woolen clothing. Within a few months, Maj. Gen. John J. Pershing, commanding the American Expeditionary Forces, called for enormous quantities of woolen clothing. Using Quartermaster allowance tables, based on actual issues on the Mexican border in 1916 which had provided a 4 months' allowance for 25,000 men, Pershing requisitioned the same quantity for that number of men per month.

In addition to the supply demands created by initial issue and maintenance of reserve stocks for the Expeditionary Forces, the War Department also organized and sent to Europe large numbers of technical troops, none of whom had been included in the original estimate made by the Quartermaster General. In fact, there was scarcely a day, Sharpe commented, that a requisition did not come to his Office for outfitting some technical troops for overseas duty, the dispatch of whom had not previously been contemplated. Furthermore, large numbers of men in training camps had also to be clothed though they, too, had not been included in the original plan. The cumulative effect was to decrease the supplies intended for the troops called into the camps, which were also opened

---

[59] *Ibid.*, pp. 500–502 (Memo for Chief of Staff, 25 Aug 1917).
[60] *Army Reorganization Hearings,* 66th Cong., 1st sess., I, 1091 (Colonel Daly).

earlier than the Quartermaster General had recommended. The War Department, Sharpe complained, could never appreciate the impact upon supply of calling out troops earlier than planned.[61]

In making its initial clothing contracts in March, the Quartermaster Corps followed the established procedure of advertising for proposals and awarding contracts to the lowest bidders. On the day following the declaration of war, Sharpe requested authority to purchase by negotiation as was provided by law whenever an emergency existed.[62] On 8 April 1917, a meeting was held in the Secretary of War's office, attended by all the bureau chiefs and by members of the Council of National Defense and the Advisory Commission. Those attending thoroughly explored the problem of how purchases were to be made. They emphasized the dangers of competition between the various procurement agencies of the government, and Commission members advised that advertising for the tremendous quantities of supplies required would greatly disturb industry and would inevitably stimulate the market, causing inflation of prices.[63]

As a result, Secretary Baker published an order which changed the method of purchase.[64] The order directed that for the duration of the emergency, contracts for all supply and equipment of the Army and for fortification and other works of defense could be made without advertising for bids. It further directed that, when possible, supply bureaus were to inform the General Munitions Board of contemplated orders for supplies so that the Board might assist in placing the orders and co-ordinating purchases for the War Department with those for the Navy and other government departments. When time did not permit a supply bureau to consult the Board, the order directed the bureau to contract for supplies without reference to the Board.

In consequence of this directive, the Quartermaster Corps, to all intents and purposes, temporarily lost control of its purchasing power. The Committee on Supplies, an advisory agency, "practically preempted the Quartermaster General's functions of purchase by lodging control in the hands of a civilian." [65] The Secretary of War approved a certain list of articles, prepared by the Council of National Defense, which were

---

[61](1) *W.D. Investigation Hearings*, 65th Cong., 2d sess., Pt. 2, pp. 494–95 (Memo, Acting Secretary, General Staff, for QMG, 20 Jul 1917; Memo, Sharpe for Chief of Staff, 21 Jul 1917); p. 505 (Memo, Sharpe for Chief of Staff, 11 Sep 1917). (2) RG 120, War Department Historical Files, Box 143 (Memo, Sharpe for Chief of Staff, 8 Sep 1917; Memo, Sharpe for Secretary of War, 17 Sep 1917).

[62] *W.D. Investigation Hearings*, 65th Cong., 2d sess., Pt. 2, p. 477 (Sharpe to SW, 7 Apr 1917). Approval was granted by 1st indorsement on 9 April 1917.

[63] (1) *War Expenditures Hearings*, 66th Cong., 2d sess., Ser. 4, Pt. 43, p. 2250 (Sharpe). (2) *First Annual Report, Council of National Defense, 1917*, pp. 65–66.

[64] *W.D. Investigation Hearings*, 65th Cong., 2d sess., Pt. 2, p. 517 (Order, 12 Apr 1917).

[65] J. Franklin Crowell, *Government War Contracts* (New York, 1920), p. 58.

to be purchased exclusively through the Council. The list included woolens, cottons, knit goods, leather, and shoes.[66] In placing contracts for these supplies, the Office of the Quartermaster General, under the Secretary's directive, followed a procedure whereby it estimated yardage required for the items of clothing wanted and then applied to the Committee on Supplies for information which would indicate where, with whom, and at what price the Corps should make the necessary contracts.[67] At first, Col. H. J. Hirsch, the purchasing quartermaster at the Philadelphia Depot, executed such contracts, but this arrangement soon proved too cumbersome and he and his assistants were moved in November into the office of the Committee on Supplies in Washington, where, according to the vice-chairman of that Committee, "he was attached to us to sign and validate the contracts" and "generally O.K'd everything that we O.K'd." [68]

In Sharpe's opinion, there never was a loss of Quartermaster responsibility. Technically, as long as a Quartermaster officer met with the Committee and signed the contract, the Committee on Supplies did not purchase cloth. In any case, Sharpe fully approved of the Secretary's order of 12 April. Calling upon the Council of National Defense to assist in the procurement program, he maintained, was "one of the most prudent steps" taken by the War Department. The Council had to induce manufacturers to undertake government business because they were not eager to enter into contracts, and the Quartermaster Corps, Sharpe testified, had insufficient personnel for the task.[69]

Rejecting the charge that General Sharpe became "a rubber stamp," *The New York Times* summed up public reaction to the hearings being conducted on War Department operations by the Senate Committee on Military Affairs when it editorialized:

> Evidently he relied too much upon the Committee detailed to help him. It knew more about business than he did, but the fact did not release General Sharpe from the obligation to supervise its transactions, in fact to regulate them.[70]

The job, the editor concluded, was too big for him. For his part, Secretary Baker doubted whether any one man, given the unprecedented situation that faced the country in 1917, could have taken the Quartermaster Corps and expanded it to meet all the supply needs of the Army.[71] This

[66] *Annual Report of the Quartermaster General,* 1917, p. 23.

[67] *Ibid.*

[68] *War Expenditures Hearings,* 66th Cong., 2d sess., Ser. 1, Pt. 4, p. 415. Compare Sharpe's views of this function. *Ibid.,* Ser. 4, Pt. 43, pp. 2242–43.

[69] *W.D. Investigation Hearings,* 65th Cong., 2d sess., Pt. 2, pp. 595–96; 631.

[70] December 23, 1917.

[71] RG 94, AGO 201 file on Sharpe (Ltr, Baker to Maj. Gen. James Harbord, 11 Sep 1922).

was a war unlike any in which the country had ever been engaged. It was a war of matériel which called for vast amounts of supplies and for organization of the nation's resources for military purposes.

Although the hearings proved disadvantageous to the Quartermaster General, the intent of Congress was to investigate the operations of the Council of National Defense. In contrast to the policy of separation of government and business which Sharpe had advocated in his proposal calling for the establishment of boards of businessmen to assist depot purchasing officers, the Council of National Defense pursued an opposite policy for guiding industrial mobilization, under which its committees, such as the Committee on Supplies, apparently acted as government agents or advisors and, at the same time, as representatives of industry.[72]

This blending of government agent and business representative gave rise to a considerable amount of criticism. Among the more serious charges made were that the Council "absorbed constitutional functions belonging to regular departments of the government;" that it lodged the power to negotiate contracts and fix prices in advisory commodity or trade committees and consequently only a nominal responsibility remained with the legally liable contracting officers of the government; and that it evolved a plan of operation under which "representatives of interested industries acted on committees which both sold and bought from the government in the same act."[73] The lack of co-ordination in the prewar supply bureau system, however, had afforded the Council both the occasion and the opportunity "to assume the role of a coordinating agency under executive authority."[74]

The contract procedures followed by the Committee on Supplies particularly aroused congressional ire. In placing contracts, that Committee made use of two types. For woolens, cottons, and knit goods, it allocated awards among the mills according to capacity. The allocation method had to be used, the Committee argued, wherever demand exceeded capacity, and profits in the civilian market, in consequence of scarcity, were more lucrative than in government work.[75] In effect, the allocated award was a cost-plus contract. The Committee took into consideration all labor and material costs, overhead expenses, and plant investment in arriving at actual cost, and allowed a 10 percent profit, which it considered reasonable when manufacturers were "working for

[72] W.D. Investigation Hearings, 65th Cong., 2d sess., Pt. 3, pp. 1851–54 (Walter S. Gifford, Director, Council of National Defense).

[73] Crowell, Government War Contracts, p. 61.

[74] Ibid., p. 60.

[75] War Expenditures Hearings, 66th Cong., 2d sess., Ser. I, Pt. 4, pp. 415–16 (Charles Eisenman).

the Government on one thing." [76]   The other form of contract used by the Committee on Supplies was based on competitive bidding.   Because there were enough shoe manufacturers to fill Army requirements and only the number of lasts had to be increased to meet Army demands for shoes, the Committee on Supplies used competitive bidding in awarding contracts for shoes and leather. [77]

Defenders of the Council admitted that the form of organization was never ideal but pleaded, in justification, that there had been no time "to quibble over technicalities of precedents."   The administrative machinery was effective, they maintained, and there was no abuse of the trust the Council imposed in the men it chose to operate it. [78]   The Committee on Supplies handled contracts aggregating approximately $800 million in the 9 months of its existence. [79]   Its work ended when the War Department reorganization in 1918 provided for co-ordination of the supply bureaus.   The Clothing and Equipment Division, first established in the Office of the Quartermaster General on 18 January 1918 and later transferred to the Office of the Director of Purchase in the General Staff, abandoned the allocation method and contracted on a competitive basis for textiles, clothing, and equipment.

Wool Supply

In the course of procuring textiles in 1917, the Committee on Supplies soon decided that it would be desirable to control the supply of wool. There was no actual shortage of wool even though the limited domestic supply was inadequate to meet domestic requirements and though war had deprived the United States of its prewar sources of supply in Australia and New Zealand.   The wool market of South America was still available to it, but it was the submarine threat to shipping that posed the danger of a wool shortage and made conservation desirable.

The possibility of shortage and the certainty of rising prices led the Boston Wool Trade Association, even before war was declared, to offer the government its entire stock of wools, wool tops, and noils at prices prevailing on 2 April 1917.   The Association telegraphed its patriotic resolution to the President on 5 April and the Assistant Secretary of War acknowledged receipt of the message. [80]   Information of the resolution

[76] *Ibid.,* p. 418.

[77] *Ibid.,* p. 422.

[78] (1) *Ibid.,* Ser. I, Pt. 4, p. 373 (Grosvenor B. Clarkson).   (2) *W.D. Investigation Hearings,* 65th Cong., 2d sess., Pt. 3, pp. 1851–54 (Walter S. Gifford).

[79] *War Expenditures Hearings,* 66th Cong., 2d sess., Ser. 1, Pt. 4, p. 412 (Charles Eisenman).

[80] *W.D. Investigation Hearings,* 65th Cong., 2d sess., Pt. 2, pp. 1008–09 (OQMG Memo, 27 Dec 1917).

was passed along to the Quartermaster General, but Sharpe took no action because the Secretary of War had indicated that the matter had been referred to the General Munitions Board. In any case, it was Sharpe's understanding that, under the law appropriating funds for the purchase of clothing, the Corps could not use any part of the funds to buy wool or any other raw materials as such action would practically be a speculative transaction. It was the duty of the Corps to purchase only the manufactured article and in the past it had never purchased wool.[81] The Advisory Commission's Committee on Raw Materials took the offer of the Boston Trade Association under consideration but did not act, because the Committee learned that it, too, had no authority to purchase. The Secretary and Treasurer of the National Association of Wool Manufacturers later charged that the government lost millions of dollars by its failure to accept that offer.[82]

Wool prices began to rise sharply in the ensuing weeks and the vice-chairman of the Committee on Supplies "was very keen" on buying wool in order to assure a supply, to stabilize the market, and to save the government money.[83] When, in June, the Council of National Defense indicated that it would be necessary to control the wool supply of the country, Sharpe consulted with the accounting officials of the Treasury Department who now construed the language of the act appropriating funds for the Army for fiscal year 1918 to permit the purchase of all materials necessary in the manufacture of Army clothing and equipage, a reversal of the interpretation formerly entertained.[84]

Although Sharpe received authority to purchase wool in June, further delays occurred in working out procedures. The Navy Deparement, the Council of National Defense, and the Department of Commerce were all concerned with the problem of wool supply. By 1 August, Sharpe established a wool purchasing office at Boston in compliance with the advice of the Council of National Defense. The quartermaster in charge of this office acted as the disbursing officer and assumed accountability for the wool purchased by the Committee on Wool Supply of the Council of National Defense.[85] The committee bought only a little over 600 million pounds of wool before the end of the year, and none was sold or allotted to dealers or manufacturers until February 1918.[86] In 1918,

[81] *Ibid.*, 1009; 1013 (Sharpe); *Ibid.*, Pt. 3, p. 1463 (Col. John P. Wood).

[82] *Ibid.*, Pt. 3, pp. 1411–12 (Winthrop L. Martin).

[83] *Ibid.*, Pt. 3, pp. 1277–78.

[84] *Ibid.*, Pt. 2, p. 1013 (Memo, Maj. H. M. Lord for QMG, 6 Jun 1917).

[85] *Ibid.*, pp. 1014–15 (Memo, Lt. Col. H. M. Lord for QMG, 1 Aug 1917; QMG to Depot Quartermaster, 1 Aug 1917); pp. 1018–24 (Memo, Sharpe for SW, 11 Sep 1917, inclosing regulations governing wool purchase).

[86] RG 92, OQMG Historical Files, Box 43 (Historical Record of the Office of the Wool Purchasing Quartermaster, 1 Aug 1917 to 30 Apr 1919).

the Office of the Quartermaster General took over complete control of the wool market.

Production of Clothing

Once the Committee on Supplies had obtained the required amount of cotton and woolen fabrics, the Quartermaster Corps handled their conversion into coats, trousers, shirts, and overcoats. It either contracted with clothing manufacturers to whom it allocated the cloth, deducting the cost of the fabric from the contract price, or the Corps produced these garments in its own depot factory facilities. Unlike earlier war periods, the Corps did not immediately expand its depot factory facilities. Undoubtedly, this resulted from a basic policy adopted by a board of officers late in 1915. The board, which included the Quartermaster General, was of the opinion that "the Government ought not to establish a monopoly in the production of any of its war material, and ought not to manufacture its own war material to the exclusion of patronage of private manufacturers capable of aiding it." Government-owned factories were to be operated only "for the purpose of establishing standards, of understanding costs of production, of insuring that attention shall be given to improvement, and of qualifying its officers in all respects as experts with respect to the material needed." [87]

In time, the limited factory operation, that had been continuously maintained at the Philadelphia Quartermaster Depot since the days of Callender Irvine, expanded until in 1918 that factory was rapidly becoming the largest clothing manufacturing plant in the United States. It employed 3,000 workers in its shop to make trousers and woolen coats, and in addition, as in earlier war periods, it had on its payrolls 2,000 outside seamstresses who produced in their homes denim jumpers and trousers, white clothing, and olive-drab shirts. A shirt factory at the Jeffersonville Depot expanded its operations until it employed a sewing force of 20,000 women. Shirts had been made in the depot area since 1872, bundles of cut-out garments being issued to women who sewed the shirts in their homes. The Corps also established a uniform factory at the Jeffersonville Depot in February 1918. It reached a productive capacity of 750 woolen coats and 1,500 pairs of woolen trousers per day.[88]

Despite all efforts, serious shortages of clothing developed in the fall of 1917. The situation became especially acute at camps located in the southern part of the country where troops, clothed in cotton uniforms,

[87] RG 165, War College Div. Document File, Case 9432–7 (Chief of Staff to SW, 10 Dec 1915).

[88] *America's Munitions, 1917–1918: Report of Benedict Crowell*, pp. 486–87.

U.S. ARMY UNIFORMS, 1918

Shortages and Investigation

were exposed to the onslaught of an early and particularly severe winter.
To the lack of overcoats, blouses, and other essential items of woolen clothing, critics attributed an epidemic of pneumonia that swept through the
camps. Rumors began to spread of a failure in the supply program
generally, and apprehensions for the success of the war effort mounted,

particularly in view of the congestion developing at the ports and in the country's railway system.   The whole situation led to an extensive investigation of the war effort by the Senate Military Affairs Committee, beginning 12 December 1917.

That investigation lasted until 29 March 1918.   Testimony was taken from the Secretary of War, the bureau chiefs whose supply preparations were in question, members of the Advisory Commission, the Committee on Supplies, and from others whose evidence might help clarify the problem.   So far as the Quartermaster Corps was concerned, the investigating committee centered much of its attention on the shortage of clothing while other supply activities during the first 9 months of the war went unnoticed in the absence of criticism.

Sharpe and other Quartermaster officers, then and later, vigorously rejected charges made by Maj. Gen. George W. Goethals and others that the Quartermaster Corps was inefficient and that conditions within it were chaotic.[89]   The amount of supplies procured by Quartermaster officers contradicted the sweeping generalization of inefficiency leveled against them and the Corps generally.   Mistakes had been made, but even in the procurement of clothing Quartermaster officers by the close of 1917 were beginning to surmount the difficulties that had been encountered.   By the time General Goethals became Acting Quartermaster General in December 1917, the Corps was meeting the demands of initial supply.   More troops had been clothed than Sharpe had thought possible in April, and contracts for additional supplies of clothing had been made. Under Quartermaster officers, the bulk of such procurement was also accomplished before the Clothing and Equipage Division was absorbed in the General Staff on the eve of the Armistice and, in fact, a large proportion of all the articles procured was obtained before that Division was established in January 1918.[90]

Though overlooked in the furor over clothing shortages, the Corps procured ample stocks of subsistence during the opening months of the war and also made provisions for the better preparation of rations served the troops.   It established 16 additional schools for bakers and cooks, one at each of the National Army cantonments, to provide trained bakers, mess sergeants, and cooks for the new organizations created in the National Army, a development for which Sharpe was responsible and that was in marked contrast to the lack of attention given to the preparation of food in past wars.   The Corps also immediately procured automobiles

---

[89] (1) *War Expenditures Hearings*, 66th Cong., 2d sess., Ser. 4, Pt. 43, pp. 2273–74; 2280–81. (2) RG 94, AGO 201 file on Sharpe (Ltr, Sharpe to Senator Frelinghuysen, 26 Feb 1919).

[90] See data on manufactures, *Annual Report of the Quartermaster General, 1919*, p. 57.

and motor trucks, animals, harness, forage, and wagons, although a force of men had to cut down trees and season the wood in especially built kilns before the wagons could be manufactured.[91]

Quartermaster operations were not restricted solely to procurement activities in 1917. The Corps established and operated a Remount Service and provided for the construction of a number of remount depots. It made plans for, and by January 1918, had opened a Quartermaster Training School at Jacksonville, Fla., that functioned as a reception, replacement, activation, and unit training center to provide the personnel sent abroad. The Corps also took steps to renovate and repair clothing, shoes, and equipage, and laid the foundation for later salvage and reclamation operations. Within the limitations imposed upon it, the Corps under Sharpe met in 1917, as effectively as it could, the needs of the expanding Army and was accomplishing far more than the public was made aware of in the course of the congressional investigation.

War Department Reform Measures

That investigation, however, convinced the committee that a more effectual supply organization was needed in the War Department. As a solution, Congress proposed to create a Ministry of Munitions, a bill for that purpose being debated while the hearings were in progress. The Administration was adamantly opposed to this solution, preferring to bring about reorganization by giving the President blanket authority to make such readjustments as he deemed necessary in the existing agencies. This view finally won favorable support and led to the passage of the Overman Act of May 20, 1918, under which Congress gave the President power to co-ordinate and consolidate the executive bureaus, agencies, and offices as the emergency demanded for purposes of economy and greater efficiency of operation.[92]

Even before the hearings of the investigating committee began, the War Department had been trying to improve its supervision of supply. Shortly after testimony began to be taken, the Department inaugurated measures to improve supply operations and forestall the establishment of a Ministry of Munitions. On 20 December 1917, Secretary Baker established a War Council to oversee and co-ordinate all matters of supply in the field armies.[93] The Council was "a temporary expedient to bridge over the time required for the reorganization of the General Staff" by making available the services of a group of experienced officers. In

---

[91] *Annual Report of the Quartermaster General, 1917*, pp. 75–76.
[92] 40 *Stat.* 556–57.
[93] War Department GO No. 160.

addition to the Secretary of War, the Assistant Secretary, and the Chief of Staff, the Council included the Judge Advocate General, the Chief of Coast Artillery, the Chief of Ordnance, and the Quartermaster General. Creation of the War Council afforded the Secretary of War an opportunity to replace, without humiliation, some of the bureau chiefs because, under his order, the administrative duties of a bureau chief serving on the Council were delegated to an acting chief. As soon as Sharpe was detailed to the War Council, the War Department recalled to active duty the famed engineer who built the Panama Canal, Maj. Gen. George W. Goethals, U.S. Army, retired, and assigned him as Acting Quartermaster General on 19 December 1917. Goethals assumed charge of the office on 26 December.[94]

The War Council was of short duration. When Gen. Peyton C. March arrived in Washington to serve first as Acting and then as Chief of Staff, he objected vigorously to its continuation. On his recommendation, the Secretary abolished the War Council early in June 1918.[95] At that point, the War Department relieved General Sharpe from duty with the Council and assigned him to the command of the Southeastern Department.[96] He did not resume his duties as Quartermaster General and, for the rest of the war period, the post was filled by an Acting Quartermaster General.

OQMG Expansion Under Sharpe

During the first 9 months of the war, there had been relatively little reorganization in the Office of the Quartermaster General.[97] Such changes as Sharpe had introduced in the fall of 1917 were limited to creating new branches and divisions to handle expanding Quartermaster business. Thus, he set up a Fuels and Forage Branch and a Conservation Branch in the Supplies Division and established a Motor Branch, responsi-

---

[94] Benedict Crowell and Robert F. Wilson, *The Armies of Industry* (2 vols., New Haven, 1921), I, 12. (2) War Department GO No. 159.

[95] March, *The Nation at War*, pp. 48–49.

[96] (1) War Department GO 54, 3 June 1918. (2) Sharpe's new assignment ended his career as a supply officer. Viewing events from the perspective of the postwar years, Baker wrote Sharpe in 1921 that "I wish I could have had a clearer and more helpful view of some of the tremendous difficulties with which you were beset." He felt the Army owed Sharpe an immeasurable debt, and by way of setting the record straight he recommended that Sharpe be given the Distinguished Service Medal for his outstanding success in subsisting the troops in the war. The award was made but on the basis of Sharpe's service in the Southeastern Department, and he declined to accept it. RG 94, AGO 201 file (Ltr, Baker to Sharpe, 29 Aug 1921; ltr, Baker to Harbord, 11 Sep 1922; ltr, Sharpe to Pershing, 23 Feb 1923). By that time Sharpe was out of the service; he retired in February 1920.

[97] See Chart No. 1, Organization of the Office of the Quartermaster General As of April 6, 1917.

ble for purchase of motor-propelled vehicles, in the Transportation Division. Expanding remount activities led him to create a separate Remount Division on 3 October and the mounting storage problem resulted in the establishment of a Warehousing Division on 16 October 1917.

This last development represented a belated appreciation of the need for storage planning. Neither the Quartermaster Corps nor the War Department generally had understood the need for storage facilities. Beyond providing for the building of such facilities at the Army cantonments, little had been done. The Corps used existing commercial facilities exclusively for handling overseas shipments. In part, Quartermaster failure to plan for storage construction was explained by the lack of funds available for such projects. On 1 November 1917, the Corps' storage space totaled less than 3 million square feet, and by that time freight cars were being used as warehouses through lack of storage space in which to unload them, either at the depots or at the ports of embarkation. More than five times that amount became available by the end of the war.[98]

A lecture on modern commercial warehousing techniques, given at the Army War College in August 1917 by O. D. Street, General Manager of Distribution for the Western Electric Co., stimulated Quartermaster General Sharpe to action. When he established the Warehousing Division in October, he borrowed the services of Street and some members of his staff to organize that division. In two detailed reports to the Quartermaster General, Street laid the foundation for a successful storage and distribution program for handling supplies shipped within the country and abroad.[99] Much of what he recommended, Sharpe's successor, Acting Quartermaster General Goethals, carried into effect. In his dual capacity as chief of the Corps and as Director of Storage and Traffic and later as Director of Purchase, Storage and Traffic in the General Staff, Goethals supervised and co-ordinated the storage system of all the supply bureaus and also formulated plans and directed the construction of additional storage facilities.[100]

Reorganization Under Goethals

In the winter of 1917–18, the War Department initiated a series of organizational changes in both the General Staff and the Office of the Quartermaster General in an effort to perfect a workable supply system

---

[98] RG 120, War Department Historical Files, Box 165-I (Historical Rpt, "Administrative History of the Office of Director of Storage," pp. 46, 130).

[99] *Ibid.*, Box 144 (Street to Sharpe, 16 Nov 1917 and 21 Dec 1917).

[100] *Annual Report of the Chief of Staff, 1919*, pp. 170 ff.

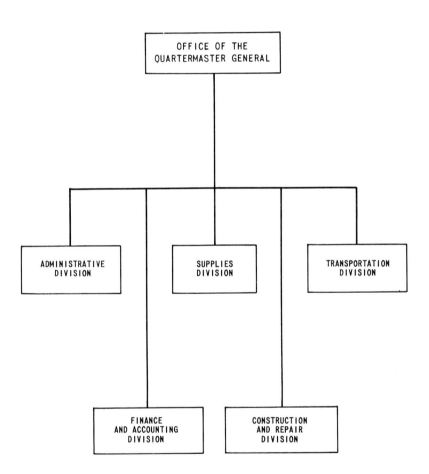

Chart I

ORGANIZATION OF THE OFFICE OF THE QUARTERMASTER GENERAL
AS OF APRIL 6, 1917

and provide the necessary co-ordination between the Staff and supply bureaus.   In relieving the Quartermaster Corps of responsibility for water transportation and construction, the War Department had been moving in the direction of making the Corps primarily a procuring and distributing agency.   That trend was accelerated when General Goethals took charge because he viewed the Corps as a large purchasing organization which he proceeded to staff with civilians who he thought would be better able to handle the job than military men.[101]   In so doing, he satisfied some of the objections that had been raised.

To silence criticism of procurement procedures, Goethals promptly took from the Council of National Defense the purchases it had been making for the Quartermaster Corps.[102]   He had the Philadelphia contracting office, which had been moved to Washington in the fall of 1917 and established in the office of the Committee on Supplies, transferred to the Office of the Quartermaster General.   He incorporated it in the Supplies and Equipment Division which was shortly redesignated the Clothing and Equipage Division.

No less than three reorganizations of the Office of the Quartermaster General occurred during the first 6 months of 1918, and changes were almost constantly being made between reorganizations.   Needless to say, the series of rapid reorganizations produced considerable confusion. Despite the fluidity of organization in 1918, the Corps supplied the troops, at least in the zone of interior, for the shortage of shipping did not permit shipment overseas of any large amounts of supplies until the last 5 months of the war.   Whether personnel and organizational units were reshuffled in the Office of the Quartermaster General or transferred later to the Office of the Director of Purchases and Storage in the General Staff, they maintained continuity of operations.

Goethals initiated the first tentative reorganization of the Office on 26 January 1918, dividing the organization into operating divisions and service bureaus, the latter including General Administration, Personnel and Planning, and Quartermaster Supply Control.   The operating divisions were Supply and Equipment, Remount, and such former branches as Fuel and Forage, Motors, Subsistence, and Conservation (later Reclamation), were raised to the status of divisions.   A supplementary order in February restored the Warehousing Division, which had been inadvertently omitted.[103]

Even before this reorganization took place, Goethals had brought to

---

[101] *War Expenditures Hearings*, 66th Cong., Ser. 1, Pt. 6, p. 520.
[102] *Ibid.*, pp. 518–19.
[103] (1) *Annual Report of the Quartermaster General, 1919*, pp. 14–15.   (2) See Chart No. 2, Organization, January 26, 1918.

the attention of the Chief of Staff the supply difficulties that were being experienced as a result of the failure to control traffic and to co-ordinate inland traffic service.   Inland traffic was supposedly under Quartermaster control but actually was being directed by each supply bureau while responsibility for the transport service was then vested in the Embarkation Service.[104]   In consequence, the Secretary of War established in the Office of the Chief of Staff a Storage and Traffic Service, transferring to it the Embarkation Service.   At the same time and only 9 days after his appointment as Acting Quartermaster General, the Secretary also designated Goethals as Director of the Storage and Traffic Service, with authority to supervise and control the transportation of troops and supplies, both by land and sea, and to make provision for the necessary storage facilities on the seaboard and at interior points.[105]   About 2 weeks later, the Secretary of War established a Purchase and Supply Service in the Office of the Chief of Staff to supervise and co-ordinate the purchase programs of the supply bureaus.[106]

In the first important wartime reorganization of the General Staff that occurred on 9 February 1918, these two services became two of the five divisions into which the General Staff was divided.[107]   Within little more than a month, the operations of these two divisions, having given rise to a great deal of duplication and complication, the divisions were consolidated to form the Purchase, Storage and Traffic Division of the General Staff.   The Secretary appointed Acting Quartermaster General Goethals as Director of that division.[108]   General March had decided to put him in charge of all the supply of the Army, relieving him of his Quartermaster duties as soon as the Chief of Staff could bring back from France Brig. Gen. Robert E. Wood, whom the Secretary appointed Acting Quartermaster General on 9 May 1918.[109]

When the Purchase, Storage and Traffic Division was formed in April, a second reorganization of the Office of the Quartermaster General occurred.[110]   Primarily, it was concerned with developing executive control and decreasing the number of division chiefs reporting to Acting Quartermaster General Goethals, thereby easing the heavy burden he was carrying in the interim before General Wood relieved him of Quartermaster responsibilities.   One of the civilians whom Goethals had brought

[104] *War Expenditures Hearings*, 66th Cong., Ser. 1, Pt. 6, p. 518 (Geothals).

[105] War Department GO 167, 27 Dec 1917.

[106] War Department GO 5, 11 Jan 1918.

[107] War Department GO 14.   The other three divisions were War Plans, Executive, and Operations.

[108] War Department GO 36, 16 Apr 1918.

[109] (1) War Department GO 46.   (2) March, *The Nation at War*, pp. 187–88.

[110] See chart, *Annual Report of the Quartermaster General, 1919*, facing p. 16.

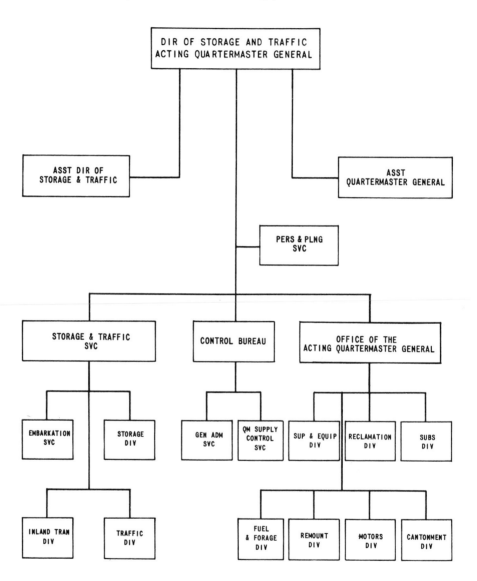

Chart 2
ORGANIZATION, JANUARY 26, 1918
Showing Relation of Control and Operation under the Director of
Storage and Traffic and the Acting Quartermaster General

to Washington was Robert J. Thorne, former president of Montgomery, Ward & Co. On 8 March 1918, Goethals had assigned Thorne as Assistant to the Acting Quartermaster General, with control of such matters as might, from time to time, be delegated to him.[111] Under the new reorganization in April, lines of authority for all divisions went to the Acting Quartermaster General through Thorne's office and his influence was felt throughout the organization. In addition to Thorne, Goethals appointed a second Assistant to the Acting Quartermaster General and gave him authority over the Remount and Reclamation Divisions. In the weeks following the announcement of this reorganization, the Acting Quartermaster General appointed two more Assistants.

By June 1918 still a third rearrangement of the Office organization was made necessary by the establishment of new commodity units within the Office and by the appointment of these additional Assistants, one of whom became responsible for all financial activities of the Corps. Expanding business had split the Supplies and Equipment Division into three commodity divisions—Clothing and Equipage, Hardware and Metals, and Vehicles and Harness. Changes were also made in the Subsistence Division, which in line with its past experience had tended to become a complete unit in itself, handling all subsistence problems from requisitions through purchase, inspection, storage, and distribution. Beginning in May with the removal from the Subsistence Division of the purchase responsibility for bakery equipment, that division became increasingly a commodity purchasing division like others in the Office.[112] The divisions were still grouped under assistants, with Thorne acting both as general Assistant to Acting Quartermaster General Wood and assistant in charge of specific divisions.[113] This was the final reorganization of the Office of the Quartermaster General before its absorption into the Purchase and Storage Division of the General Staff.

The reason this absorption could take place without disrupting the Army supply program was that one man directed the development of the Office of the Quartermaster General along such lines as to make it the basis for consolidation of supply functions. Goethals, as Acting Quartermaster General and as Director, first, of Storage and Traffic and, then, of

[111] War Department GO 24.

[112] See RG 120, War Department Historical Files, Box 147 (Rpt, "History of the Subsistence Division").

[113] (1) The divisions under Thorne were Supply Control, Clothing and Equipage, Hardware and Metals, Vehicles and Harness, Subsistence, and Depot. A second assistant had charge of the Conservation and Reclamation, Fuel and Forage, and Remount Divisions; a third, Motor Transport Service; and a fourth, Finance and Accounts; while an Executive Office had charge of the Administrative, Personnel, and Methods Control Divisions. (2) See Chart No. 3, Third Reorganization of the Office of the Quartermaster General, June 1918.

Purchase, Storage and Traffic in the General Staff, pursued the same policy line at both the Quartermaster and the Staff level.

Goethals had long advocated consolidating Army purchases of standard items in one supply bureau, leaving purchase of special technical supplies to the respective bureaus using them. When he first took charge of the Quartermaster Corps, he found so much competition for supplies among the supply bureaus and between the services that he was convinced that the appointment of a minister of munitions would be most advisable. Since the Administration was opposed to that course of action, he concluded that the only alternative was for the War Department to bring about such co-ordination and consolidation of purchases as would eliminate competition.[114] This view found little support among supply bureau chiefs who feared that any sweeping reorganization of existing procurement machinery would disorganize the bureaus to such an extent as to interfere with the effective support that they claimed they were giving to the American Expeditionary Forces. Among the bureau chiefs, Goethals, found only one—the Chief of Ordnance—willing to agree to a consolidation of purchases.[115]

The new Chief of Staff, however, warmly supported Goethals. General March later wrote:

> Experience had shown that the interior organization of the various bureaus was such as to render an effective supervision of their activities by the General Staff, as contemplated by General Orders, No. 14, impossible. As the result of a careful consideration of the matter I became convinced that a consolidation of procurement, except of certain specialized equipment, of storage, of finance, and of transportation, together with a positive and direct central control of these activities by the General Staff, was essential to the elimination of the unsatisfactory conditions existing and to the rapid, efficient, and economical utilization of the resources of the country to the development of the Army program as a whole.[116]

Until the passage of the Overman Act, in May 1918, made transfer of functions possible, Goethals was hampered by the existing inflexibility. The first 5 months of 1918 were a period of "supervisory charge of purchases with a view to consolidation" that did not work very satisfactorily.[117]

Changes in Field Organization

In the meantime, reorganization in the Office of the Quartermaster General during these months was being paralleled by changes in the

---

[114] War Expenditures Hearings, 66th Cong., Ser. 1, Pt. 6, p. 522 (Goethals).
[115] Ibid., p. 523.
[116] Annual Report of the Chief of Staff, U.S. Army, 1919, p. 20.
[117] War Expenditures Hearings, 66th Cong., Ser. 1, Pt. 6, pp. 523–24.

Chart 3
THIRD REORGANIZATION OF THE OFFICE OF THE QUARTERMASTER GENERAL
JUNE 1918

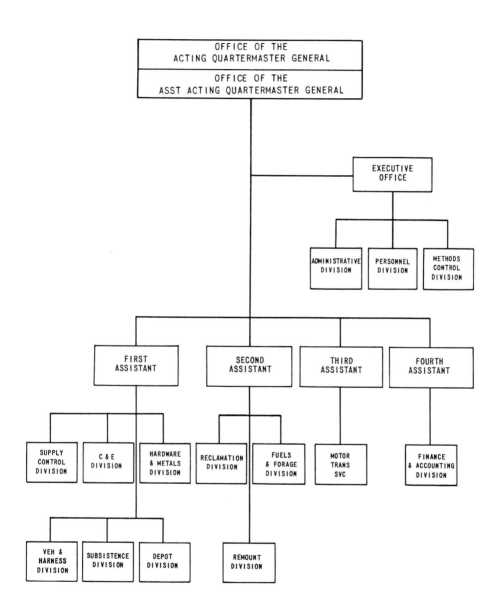

Quartermaster field organization. It will be recalled that at the outbreak of the war, departmental quartermasters were assigned to the staffs of the commanding officers of the military departments, who consolidated estimates and forwarded requisitions to depot quartermasters. The latter procured and stored supplies, issuing them on requisition. Since particular depots handled the procurement of designated supplies—for example, clothing and equipage at Philadelphia and wagons and harness at Jeffersonville—a kind of "centralized decentralization" characterized the existing system.[118] Post and camp quartermasters supplied troop units in the field, usually by requisitioning through departmental quartermasters on the depots, or, in case of emergency, by making direct purchase.

By exempting supply of divisional camps from departmental control in the fall of 1917, the importance of the departmental quartermaster had been diminished in favor of the depot quartermaster, and the supply channel not only for the camps but also for remount depots and animals embarkation depots ran directly from the Quartermaster General to the point of issue.[119] As control of purchases and distribution became centralized in Washington, the authority of the depot quartermasters, in turn, was diminished. Their main function became that of storing supplies, which were procured in Washington, and issuing them to the National Army cantonments and to the National Guard camps that were attached to their particular supply depots for Quartermaster supplies.

The managers of supply soon learned, however, that centralizing the control of purchases in Washington was likely to leave undeveloped many areas of resources and production in the country. They resolved that problem by developing the zone system because it was apparent that under the direction of the various divisions of the Office of the Quartermaster General, the quartermasters of the existing 13 general supply depots could procure, produce, inspect, manufacture, store, and distribute Quartermaster supplies. Control continued to be exercised by the various central divisions of the Office of the Quartermaster General located either at Washington or at some other point suitable for transacting the business. The Acting Quartermaster General assigned to each general supply depot a certain "zone of jurisdiction" in which it carried out its activities of procurement, production, inspection, manufacture, and storage. Within his zone, each depot quartermaster ascertained production facilities, recommended to the proper division of the Quartermaster General's Office the employment of qualified producers, kept informed of market conditions, and was prepared to make recommendations for purchase

---

[118] *Annual Report of the Quartermaster General, 1919*, p. 9.
[119] *Ibid.*, p. 13.

when shortage of any article existed and supply was obtainable in his zone.   On the basis of this information, the division in the Washington office placed purchase orders and allocated them properly throughout the industries of the country.[120]

Early in June 1918, Acting Quartermaster General Wood amended these instructions to exclude from the zone system the Remount purchasing zones and such zones of operation as the Motor Transport Service established.   He also excluded from the zone system the procurement or inspection of wool, cotton, and other "commodities in their unfabricated state." [121]   These instructions with their amendment formed the basis for the new zone system, the concept of which remained essentially the same, although many changes and revisions were later made in the system.

A Consolidated Service of Supply

In Washington, a Staff study of the supply problem looked not only toward consolidating the procurement activities of the supply bureaus and standardizing their methods, but also toward assuming, on the basis of the Overman Act, direct control of, and responsibility for, the supply program.   The outcome was the formulation of a tentative plan for a consolidated service of supply that Goethals presented to the Chief of Staff for approval in the summer of 1918.[122]   Even this plan did not contemplate merging all procurement activities.   Briefly, Goethals proposed a central agency for the procurement of all standard articles of Army supply, leaving in the bureaus the purchase, production, and inspection of highly technical material.   He also called for the centralized administration of rail and water transportation, embarkation, and all distribution, including storage.   The Chief of Staff approved the plan in principle on 26 August and gave authority to outline the successive organizational changes that would be involved.[123]

The basic consideration in instituting changes was the maintenance of an uninterrupted flow of supplies, and the shift to Staff control was brought about only on the basis of preparation and gradual change. A first step toward consolidation had been taken even before this plan

---

[120] RG 92, OQMG Correspondence File, 1917–22, Box 238 (Acting QMG Wood to all Divisions and General Supply Depots, 13 May 1918).

[121] *Ibid.*, Box 5073 (Acting QMG Wood to all Divisions and General Supply Depots, 4 Jun 1918).

[122] RG 120, War Department Historical Files, Box 144 (Memo, Goethals for Chief of Staff, 18 Jul 1918).

[123] For copy of the March memorandum, 26 August 1918, see RG 120, History of Construction, Book I (Exhibits), p. 121.

was formulated or approved.   As soon as the Overman bill became law
on 20 May 1918, the War Department instituted a system of interbureau
procurement.   In anticipation of the law's passage, Goethals, as Director
of the Purchase, Storage and Traffic Division, issued a circular early in
May setting forth a uniform procedure to be followed by all supply
bureaus under the interbureau procurement system.

Briefly, each supply bureau was to continue to be responsible for
the determination of requirements, design, and specifications and for the
issue of the articles it had heretofore handled, but for those of its supplies,
the procurement of which under this system was assigned to another
bureau, the issuing bureau had to requisition on the procuring bureau.
Although Goethals established the procedures for this system in May, the
supply bureaus put through only a few orders under it before the end
of July 1918.[124]   The Purchase, Storage and Traffic Division effected
consolidation of procurement by groups of articles, making these assignments in supply circulars that it issued.   The Division pursued a general
policy of consolidating purchase of particular items of supply in the supply
bureau that was already purchasing the major part of those items.   Under
the workings of the interbureau procurement system, the Quartermaster
Corps became the most important War Department purchasing agency.
The procurement divisions within the Office of the Quartermaster General, which expanded to handle the consolidated purchases assigned to
them, became the nucleus around which were developed the procurement
divisions of the Purchase and Storage Division of the General Staff.

Along with the increase of procurement responsibility, through
consolidating within the Quartermaster Corps the purchase of a large
number of articles, went the removal of such functions as were extraneous
to making it primarily a purchase and distribution service.   This development, it will be recalled, had begun early in the war, when the War
Department transferred responsibility for camp construction from the
Corps in May, and for all repair work in October 1917.   This initial
removal was followed by the loss of control over the transportation of
troops and supplies overseas, when the War Department established the
Embarkation Service in August 1917.   The War Department did not,
however, transfer the Water Transportation Branch of the Quartermaster
General's Office, formerly responsible for administering the Army Transport Service, to the Staff until 22 April 1918, when the Purchase, Storage
and Traffic Division absorbed it.[125]   Quartermaster control over rail
transportation was lost on 10 January 1918 at the time the War Depart-

---

[124] *Annual Report of the Quartermaster General, 1919*, p. 19.
[125] *Ibid., 1918*, p. 7.

ment placed the Inland Transportation Service under the charge of Goethals as Director of Storage and Traffic.

In this piecemeal loss of the transportation function, the Corps retained responsibility for motor transportation. This function was of recent growth but, except for a few motor vehicles used for special purposes, the Corps had complete responsibility for motor transportation before the war. With the outbreak of war and the grant of special appropriations, each supply bureau began to purchase its own motor vehicles without regard to the advantages that would accrue from limiting procurement to a few models. The usual difficulties of competition for supplies and complications from lack of standardization ensued. In order to bring supply of motor transportation under a single control, the War Department organized a Motor Transport Service as part of the Office of the Quartermaster General on 18 April 1918. Its purpose was to consolidate the purchase, procurement, maintenance, and repair of all motor-propelled vehicles for the Army, except tanks, caterpillars, and artillery tractors.[126] The Acting Quartermaster General placed the Service under the direction of a third Assistant.

About 4 months later, the War Department reorganized the Service as a separate agency and redesignated it the Motor Transport Corps, thereby removing all responsibility for motor vehicles from the Quartermaster Corps.[127] Insofar as purchase responsibility was concerned, however, this proved a temporary arrangement. Within 3 weeks, the War Department returned responsibility for the procurement of motor-propelled vehicles and spare parts to the Corps and the Acting Quartermaster General established a Motor and Vehicles Division in his Office. The War Department's action was in line with the general principle of consolidating purchase responsibility in one agency.[128]

Placing responsibility for all financial activities of the Corps, including pay of the Army, under the direction of a fourth Assistant to the Acting Quartermaster General in the June 1918 reorganization of the Office, paved the way for the removal of this function. The necessity for standardizing and co-ordinating fiscal and accounting methods of the several supply bureaus led to the appointment of a Director of Finance as assistant to the Director of Purchase, Storage and Traffic. He was made responsible for and had authority over the preparation of estimates, disbursements, money accounts, property accounts, finance reports, and

---

[126] War Department GO 38, 18 Apr 1918.

[127] War Department GO 75, 15 Aug 1918.

[128] (1) *War Expenditures Hearings,* 66th Cong., 2d sess., Ser. 4, vol. 3, pp. 3157–58 (March). (2) RG 120, War Department Historical Files, Box 165–F, PS&T Supply Cir. No. 87 (5 Sep 1919).

pay and mileage of the Army.   The War Department thereupon removed all such activities from the Quartermaster Corps in October 1918 and from the other supply bureaus during the next 2 months.   The former Assistant in charge of Quartermaster financial activities became the Director of Finance.[129]

By that time, an almost complete removal of functions from the Office of the Quartermaster General had occurred.   On 12 September 1918, the War Department also appointed Acting Quartermaster General Wood Director of Purchase and Storage in the Purchase, Storage and Traffic Division.[130]   About 2 weeks earlier, the Acting Quartermaster General had been directed to report to the Director of Purchase, Storage and Traffic, and the Corps had been given responsibility for and authority over storage, distribution, and issue of all Army supplies within the United States.[131]   In the September directive, that authority was revoked and given to General Wood as Director of Purchase and Storage and not as Acting Quartermaster General.   On 18 September, the War Department removed all divisions responsible for storage and distribution of Quartermaster supplies from the control of the Quartermaster General and ordered them to report to the Director of Storage in the office of the Director of Purchase and Storage.   This marked the beginning of the consolidation of storage.   Since the 13 general supply depots of the Quartermaster Corps contained about 70 to 80 percent of the storage space occupied by all the supply bureaus, it was feasible and convenient, in effecting consolidation of storage, to attach to the Quartermaster system the storage methods and functions of the other supply bureaus.   By the time the armistice was signed, the storage units of three of the other supply bureaus had also been transferred to the Director of Storage.[132]

The War Department also placed under Director Wood's control the former Conservation and Reclamation Division of the Office of the Quartermaster General, renamed the Salvage Division.   Conservation and reclamation activities in 1917–18 marked the first organized effort to lessen the waste entailed in war.   Profiting from the experience of Great Britain and France, Sharpe had established a Conservation Branch in his Office on 5 October 1917.   It became a separate division less than a month later.   Beginning with the conservation of food and kitchen waste,

---

[129] (1) RG 92, OQMG Historical Files, Box 7 (Digest of PS&T Supply Circulars—No. 98, 11 Oct 1918).   (2) *War Expenditures Hearings,* 66th Cong., 1st sess., Ser. 1, Pt. 1, p. 184 (Ltr, ACofS, Director of PS&T, to Committee on Military Affairs, 12 Jun 1919).

[130] (1) RG 92, OQMG Historical Files, Box 7 (Digest of PS&T Supply Circulars—No. 91, 12 Sep 1918; No. 109, 4 Nov 1918).   (2) See Chart No. 4, Organization of Office Director Purchase and Storage, November 1918.

[131] PS&T Div. Supply Cir. No. 80, 27 Aug 1918.

[132] *Annual Report of the Chief of Staff, 1919,* p. 179.

Chart 4
ORGANIZATION OF OFFICE DIRECTOR PURCHASE AND STORAGE
AS OF NOVEMBER 1918

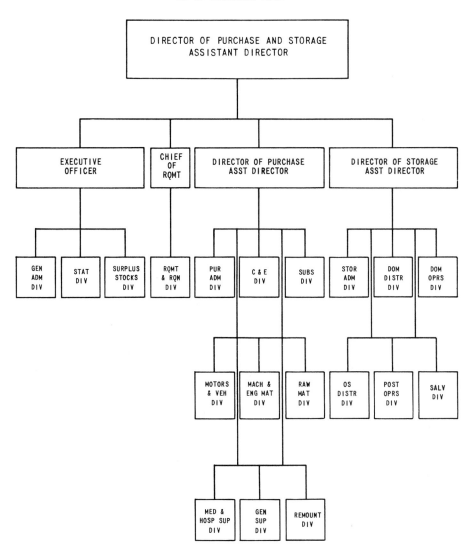

the division's activities had expanded to include the repair of shoes, clothing, and equipment, and the operation of laundries and dry-cleaning facilities.[133]

On 18 September, the War Department removed all Quartermaster procurement divisions from the control of the Quartermaster General and ordered them to report to the Director of Purchase of the office of the Director of Purchase and Storage, though the actual absorption did not take place until October. During that month, the War Department also transferred the procurement units of the other supply bureaus. The Purchase, Storage and Traffic Division formally confirmed the transfer of Quartermaster procurement, storage, and distribution functions on 6 November, only 5 days before the armistice brought an end to hostilities.[134] At Goethals' insistence, the reorganization of the Army supply system was carried through to completion after the armistice. Although the Purchase, Storage and Traffic Division did not make consolidated purchases before the war ended, its absorption of the supply bureaus' procurement function set a precedent for centralization.[135]

In November 1918, the only functions remaining in the Office of the Quartermaster General were the control of personnel, the operation of the Remount Service, and the maintenance of national cemeteries. After the signing of the armistice altered the situation, the Director of Purchases and Storage took into his office both the remount and cemeterial services, and control of Quartermaster personnel became a part of the Purchase, Storage and Traffic Division. Except for the name and the classification of personnel, no vestige remained of the Quartermaster Corps in Washington or in the field in the zone of interior, where the Director of the Purchase, Storage and Traffic Division used the Quartermaster system of supply zones as the basis for consolidating the storage and distribution activities of the other supply bureaus. The Corps' organization was not destroyed, but it was used as the basis for a new Staff organization, the Purchase and Storage Division, that absorbed the supply operations of all the supply bureaus.[136]

[133] RG 120, War Department Historical Files, Box 145 (Rpt, "Functions and Operations of the Salvage Service").

[134] *War Expenditures Hearings*, 66th Cong., Ser. 1, Pt. 1, p. 146 (PS&T Supply Cir. No. 110).

[135] *Ibid.*, Ser. 1, Pt. 6, pp. 523; 528–29 (Goethals).

[136] RG 92, OQMG Historical Files (H. Phelps Putnam, "Short Sketch of the Organization History of the Quartermaster Corps and the Purchase and Storage Division," p. 36).

CHAPTER XV

Quartermaster Theater Operations, 1917-1918

Among the staff officers accompanying Maj. Gen. (later General of the Armies) John J. Pershing when he sailed from New York on 28 May 1917 was Col. Daniel E. McCarthy, Chief Quartermaster of the American Expeditionary Forces (A.E.F.). His formal designation to the post had been announced only 2 days earlier.[1] In the initial organization of the Headquarters of the A.E.F., the Chief Quartermaster was one of 15 chiefs constituting Pershing's administrative and technical staff.

Administrative Developments

Development of a satisfactory general staff system to meet the needs of modern war was one of several pressing problems that demanded General Pershing's immediate attention. "It required no genius," he later wrote, "to see that coordination and direction of the combat branches and the numerous services of large forces could be secured only through the medium of a well-constituted general staff, and I determined to construct it on the sound basis of actual experience in war of our own and other armies."[2]

General Pershing originally established his Headquarters at Paris, removing it to Chaumont early in September 1917.[3] Based on comprehensive study of the staff organizations of the French and British armies, Pershing divided the organization of Headquarters, A.E.F., into the General Staff and the Administrative and Technical Staff. The General Staff included a Chief of Staff and his assistants, a secretary to the General Staff, and five sections—Administrative Policy, Intelligence, Operations, Training Policy, and Co-ordination. The Administrative and Technical Staff was composed of the Adjutant General, Inspector General, Judge Advocate, Chief Quartermaster, Chief Surgeon, Chief Engineer Officer,

---

[1] *U.S. Army in the World War, 1917–19* (17 vols., Washington, 1948), XVI, 1 (Hq AEF GO 1, 26 May 1917).
[2] John J. Pershing, *My Experiences in the World War* (2 vols., New York, 1931), I, 103.
[3] *Ibid.*, I, 128, 129, 163.

General Purchasing Agent, Chief of Gas Service, Director General of Transportation, Commanding General of the Line of Communications, Chief of Red Cross, and Provost Marshal General.[4] In the absence of any directive to the contrary, each chief of the Administrative and Technical Staff felt free to communicate directly with the Commanding General of the A.E.F. or his Chief of Staff.[5] Adding the five chiefs of the General Staff sections, 20 heads of departments and staff bureaus had access to General Pershing. Like Secretary Baker, he was in danger of being overwhelmed in administrative detail.

The arrival of the first American contingent in France also required the establishment of an organization to provide logistical support for it and the divisions that would soon be following. According to Field Service Regulations published before the war, the commanding general of the field forces controlled the theater of operations, and General Pershing decided that these regulations, at least initially, would furnish the best basis on which to erect his supply organization for the A.E.F. In conformity with these regulations, he divided the theater of operations into a forward or combat zone and a rear zone, called in 1917 the Zone of the Line of Communications. For administrative purposes, this Line of Communications was sub-divided into several sections—one advance section, one intermediate section, and eventually eight base sections, with a ninth added after the armistice. These base sections were grouped around the major port areas of France and England. Each base included at least one important port for receiving and forwarding munitions, equipment, and other supplies shipped from the United States.[6] Beyond these sections lay the intermediate section in which the great storage depots came to be located. The advance section took in the area between the intermediate section and the forward zone or zone of operations. In this section, General Pershing established the billeting and training areas for the first divisions of the A.E.F.[7]

A commanding officer was in charge of each of these sections, and all of these officers were under the jurisdiction of the Commanding General, Line of Communications. The latter was responsible for the care and storage of all supplies, material, and equipment, as well as for the construction, maintenance, and repair of all agencies necessary to accomplish this purpose. The Commanding General, Line of Communications, was further responsible for the distribution of supplies among the several depots in accordance with approved plans for military

---

[4] *U.S. Army in the World War, 1917–19*, XVI, 13 ff. (Hq AEF GO 8, 5 Jul 1917).
[5] See James G. Harbord, *The American Army in France* (Boston, 1936), p. 212.
[6] General Johnson Hagood, *The Services of Supply* (New York, 1927), p. 44.
[7] See Map of France Showing QMC AEF Activities.

operations.   Separate and apart from the control over supply exercised by the Commanding General, Line of Communications, were two other phases of supply.   One of these was the procurement of supplies, material, equipment, and plants necessary for the support of the American troops in France, responsibility for which rested with the Chiefs of the Supply Departments, A.E.F., and the other was the transportation of supplies, responsibility for which Pershing vested in a Director General of Transportation in September 1917.[8]   The General Staff exercised general supervision over the whole supply organization at Headquarters, usually through the Co-ordination Section.

A chief quartermaster as well as a representative from each of the other supply departments served on the staff of the Commanding General, Line of Communications.   Similarly, the staff of the commanding officer in each geographical section included a section quartermaster and other representatives of the supply departments.   The Chief Quartermaster at General Headquarters did not deal directly with his subordinates in the sections but operated through the chief quartermaster, Line of Communications, whose office duplicated that of the Chief Quartermaster, A.E.F.   A troublesome deficiency in the existing arrangements, however, was the failure to differentiate between the responsibilities of the bureau chiefs, A.E.F., and the bureau chiefs, Line of Communications.   Possibly conducive to even more difficulty was the independence of the Director General of Transportation who was responsible solely to the Commander-in-Chief.[9]

This initial organization proved increasingly unworkable, and, early in February 1918, the Chief of Staff, at General Pershing's direction, convened a board of officers, with Col. Johnson Hagood designated as senior member, to consider the problem and to reorganize the entire A.E.F. Staff.[10]   Analysis of the existing organization indicated the immediate necessity for providing a single and direct line of responsibility for all matters of supply in order that the demands of any emergency might be met without hesitation or uncertainty.   The board's recommendations were embodied in a directive on 16 February, the detailed interpretative construction of it being communicated in another directive approximately 5 weeks later.[11]

The Line of Communications was redesignated the Services of Supply, and all the technical and supply staff, which previously had

[8] U.S. Army in the World War, 1917–19, XVI, 136 (Hq AEF GO 73, 12 Dec 1917).

[9] Hagood, The Services of Supply, pp. 78–82.

[10] Ibid., pp. 134–35.

[11] U.S. Army in the World War, 1917–19, XVI, 216–26 (Hq AEF GO 31, 16 Feb 1918); pp. 249–57 (Hq AEF GO 44, 23 Mar 1918).

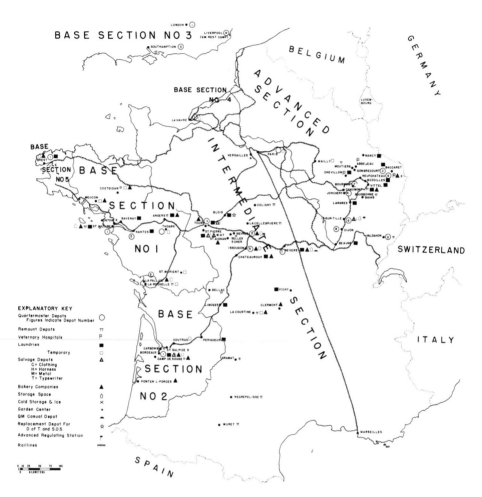

MAP OF FRANCE SHOWING QMC AEF ACTIVITIES
Prepared in Office Chief QM, AEF, May 27, 1918

MAP 7

formed part of General Pershing's Staff at Chaumont, were removed to Tours to report to the Commanding General, Services of Supply, for co-ordination of their functions of procurement, distribution, transportation, and construction, and to act as his staff.   Thereafter, the Chief Quartermaster served in a dual capacity as Chief Quartermaster, A.E.F., and as Chief Quartermaster on the staff of the Commanding General, Services of Supply.

In the course of this reorganization, the chiefs of the General Staff sections became designated as Assistant Chief of Staff, G–1, G–2, G–3, G–4, and G–5.   The G–4 section had supervision of all supply departments, and, little by little as the war went on, G–4 at General Headquarters "took over the function of direct and complete responsibility to General Pershing for supply," proposing on the eve of the armistice to relegate the Commanding General, Services of Supply, to the role of subordinate of the Assistant Chief of Staff, G–4.   The cessation of hostilities halted this development without settling the principles involved.[12]

When Colonel McCarthy arrived in Paris in June 1917, he opened his office in three small rooms.   The rapid increase of business and the arrival of additional Quartermaster officers and clerks soon made removal to larger quarters necessary, and he leased hotels and other large buildings for the purpose.   Colonel McCarthy organized his office along the lines of a departmental quartermaster's office.[13]   Becoming incapacitated by illness, he had to relinquish his post early in August and return to the United States.   Col. (later Brig. Gen.) Harry L. Rogers succeeded him as Chief Quartermaster on 13 August 1917, serving for the duration of the war.[14]

Shortly after Colonel Rogers took charge, the Office of the Chief Quartermaster consisted of four divisions—Administrative, Finance and Accounting, Supplies, and Transportation.[15]   This was much the same organization as existed in the Office of the Quartermaster General at Washington.   An organizational unit to handle construction was unnecessary.   At the suggestion of Quartermaster General Sharpe, the War Department made the Engineer Corps responsible for constructing barracks

---

[12] Hagood, *The Services of Supply,* pp. 321–29.

[13] RG 120, AEF SOS Historical Files, Box 129 (Rpt, Col. D. E. McCarthy to TAG, 6 Mar 1920).

[14] (1) *U.S. Army in the World War, 1917–19,* XVI, 53 (Hq AEF GO 21).   (2) Colonel Rogers had been relieved from duty late in June 1917 as Departmental Quartermaster, Southern Department, with headquarters at Fort Sam Houston, Texas.   Reporting to General Pershing on 23 July, he was assigned to inspection work.   He was on duty in connection with the re-location of Headquarters at Chaumont when Pershing appointed him Chief Quartermaster.

[15] RG 92, OQMG, Gen. H. L. Rogers Private File, Box 24 (CQM Office Memo, 17 Aug 1917).

to house personnel of the Expeditionary Forces. Under existing regulations, it already had responsibility for all other types of construction in the theater of operations. This action eliminated the need for two similar organizations abroad.[16]

Under the original organization of General Headquarters, A.E.F., the Quartermaster Corps was responsible for transporting personnel and supplies, providing Quartermaster transportation, and repairing all vehicles of all services and organizations, except military vehicles. It was also responsible for clothing, Quartermaster equipment, subsistence, fuel, forage, lights, water, camp sites, quarters and offices and their equipment, pay of personnel and general disbursements, laundries and baths, remounts, claims, salvage, Quartermaster workshops and storehouses, cold storage and refrigerating plants, labor, Quartermaster personnel, and cemeteries and burials.[17]

By 14 September, the Chief Quartermaster had lost responsibility for railroad transportation, a separate Transportation Department under a Director General of Transportation having been established as one of the technical services of the Headquarters, A.E.F.[18] Three months later, the Chief Quartermaster also lost control of the Army Transport Service in Europe, supervision of it being placed under the Director General of Transportation on 18 December 1917.[19] The Quartermaster Corps still retained responsibility for motor transportation and "its efficient operation," although it was organized as the Motor Transport Service on 8 December. About 2 months later, Headquarters, A.E.F., also removed that responsibility from the Quartermaster Corps, transferring it to the Service of Utilities when the Line of Communications was reorganized as the Services of Supply in February 1918.[20] The actual transfer did not take place, however, until Headquarters, Services of Supply, was established at Tours the following month.

As in the zone of interior, so in the theater of operations it was found advisable, General Pershing wrote, to give relief to the Quartermaster Corps by eliminating from its responsibilities such traditional functions as construction and transportation, leaving the Corps free to develop its operations as a supply service.[21] To supply proper was added the func-

16 (1) Sharpe, *The Quartermaster Corps*, pp. 297–300 (QMG to TAG, 26 May 1917; 1st ind., TAG to QMG, 16 Jun 1917). (2) RG 165, War College Div. Doc. File, Case 10083-2 (Memo, Chief of War College Div for Chief of Staff, 5 Jun 1917).

17 *U.S. Army in the World War, 1917–19*, XVI, 20–21 (Hq AEF GO 8, 5 Jul 1917).

18 *Ibid.*, XVI, 74–75 (Hq AEF GO 37).

19 *Ibid.*, XVI, 146 (Hq AEF GO 78).

20 *Ibid.*, XVI, 130 (Hq AEF GO 70, 8 Dec 1917); 216 (Hq AEF GO 31, 16 Feb 1918).

20 *Ibid.*, XVI, 130 (Hq AEF GO 70, 8 Dec 1917); 216 (Hq AEF GO 31, 16 Feb 1918).

21 *Final Report of Gen. John J. Pershing* (Washington, 1920), p. 73.

tion of salvage, a responsibility that had been left largely undeveloped in the Army to that time but which, in 1917, was early recognized as vital in conserving overseas resources.   Although the main emphasis in the theater as in the zone of interior was on developing a supply service, the Corps also retained certain other responsibilities, such as pay of the Army and graves registration, which were not supply functions.

In the Staff reorganization of February 1918, the Chief Quartermaster was charged with responsibility for the pay of personnel and general disbursements; for Quartermaster material, including clothing, subsistence, fuel, and forage; for the transportation of water beyond water points; remount service; laundries, baths, and disinfection of clothing; salvage service; cold storage and refrigeration; Quartermaster shops, depots, and storehouses; graves registration service; and inspection of Quartermaster activities.[22]   Any decrease in duties occasioned by removal of functions from the Corps caused no reduction in its workload because assignment of new duties more than balanced transfers.   In February 1918, Headquarters, A.E.F. made the Corps responsible for operation of a garden service.   The following month, it assigned the Corps the duty of establishing sales stores in each sector occupied by the A.E.F. and directed the Chief Quartermaster to provide rolling sales stores for accommodating the troops at the front.[23]   The Corps became responsible for administering a depot that handled the effects of the deceased members of the A.E.F.   It also organized railroad supply units, paid the Octroi dues to French towns, and operated a baggage service.[24]

When the Office of the Chief Quartermaster was transferred from Chaumont to Tours in March 1918, its work expanded rapidly.   For administrative purposes, the Chief Quartermaster reorganized the office to include a Deputy Chief Quartermaster, who acted in his place during his frequent absences on inspection and other duties.   Besides this officer, the new organization usually included two principal assistants to the Chief Quartermaster, who were assigned important duties as occasion required.   The Chief Quartermaster also established an Inspection Service under one officer who had a varying number of traveling inspectors reporting to him on supply problems, finance, and the condition of the remount and other services.   In addition to the Inspection Service, the

[22] U.S. Army in the World War, 1917–19, XVI, 223 (Hq AEF GO 31, 16 Feb 1918).

[23] Ibid., XVI, 233, 238, 241–42 (Hq AEF GO 34, 25 Feb 1918; GO 37, 7 Mar 1918).

[24] Octroi was a form of municipal tax or duty, which, under a law dating back to the beginning of municipal government in France, the communes were authorized to levy on certain articles destined for local consumption. Among these were foods, fuels, gasoline, lubrication oils, fodder, building materials, and engineering supplies. Through Quartermaster negotiation, these levies were at first reduced to a flat rate and later most towns removed the tax entirely.

work of the office was organized into six divisions and three other services, each under a chief. The divisions included Administrative, Supplies, Personnel, Finance, Accounting, and Construction and Repair.[25] The other services were Remount, Salvage, and Graves Registration.[26]

It will be recalled that in each section of the Line of Communications an officer of the Quartermaster Corps, designated a section quartermaster, was responsible originally to the Chief Quartermaster, Line of Communications, and, after the February 1918 reorganization, to the Chief Quartermaster, Services of Supply, for supervising the depots and other activities of the Corps that were located in his geographical section. Similarly, in each of the armies, corps, and divisions in which the troops were organized, a Quartermaster officer served as a member of the technical staff of the commanding officer of each of these military organizations. These quartermasters functioned under G–4 of the General Staff in the case of armies and corps, and under G–1 in the case of divisions. Regiments had regimental supply officers on the staffs of their regimental commanders.

The connecting link between the armies and the services in the rear was the regulating station under the control of a regulating officer. The regulating station was a large railyard where cars from the supply depots and from the rear were received and made up into trains for the divisions.[27] Upon the regulating officer, who was originally a member of the Co-ordination Section of the General Staff, and, after reorganization, a member of the Staff's G–4 section, fell the responsibility for maintaining a steady flow of supply. While all the supply services clamored to have their shipments rushed through, the regulating officer, acting under special or secret instructions, declared priorities in the supply of things the Army needed most. He exercised the necessary control "to get to the armies at the proper time those things most urgently needed to defeat the enemy and to place embargoes on things which can be dispensed with

---

[25] In the absence of responsibility for construction, the inclusion of a Construction and Repair Division raises questions. The Corps did engage in a limited amount of such work. It was responsible, for example, for designing the cold-storage plant at Gievres and for furnishing the material and equipment for it, though the actual construction of the plant was carried out by Quartermaster personnel under Engineer supervision. The Construction and Repair Division appears to have been something of a "catch-all," for among its duties were drafting and illustrating for the Corps; designing equipment, chevrons, and other insignia; map-making; and drawing up organization charts. RG 92, OQMG Historical Files, Box 75 (Historical Report of Chief Quartermaster, A.E.F., 1917–19, p. 35). Hereafter briefly cited as CQM Report.

[26] *Ibid.*, pp. 33–35.

[27] *U.S. Army in the World War, 1917–19*, XVI, 137 (Hq AEF GO 73, 12 Dec 1917); p. 252 (Hq AEF GO 44, 23 Mar 1918).

for the time being." [28]   The Chief Quartermaster and the chiefs of the other supply services fulfilled their responsibilities when they delivered to the regulating officer the supplies called for by him, and Quartermaster control of its supplies ceased at the regulating station.

Quartermaster Units and Personnel Strength

To execute the varied functions assigned to it, the Quartermaster Corps needed a large force of officers and enlisted men.   When General Pershing sailed for France, Quartermaster personnel accompanying him consisted of 16 officers, 10 enlisted men, and 12 field clerks.   The number of officers and enlisted men increased slowly, and, during most of the war, lack of trained personnel seriously handicapped the Corps. [29]   A month after Colonel Rogers became Chief Quartermaster, two commissioned officers and one clerk did the work of the Supplies Division in his office. There were only 143 Quartermaster officers in the A.E.F. on 21 September 1917, of whom only 32 were officers of the Regular Army.   The entire Quartermaster personnel—commissioned, enlisted, and civilian—in France on 6 October 1917 had increased to less than 2,500.   On recommendation of his Chief Quartermaster, General Pershing cabled Washington that this number was entirely inadequate properly to handle supplies for the troops already in France. [30]

Obviously, Quartermaster enlisted personnel did not keep pace with demands any more than the Corps' officer personnel did.   Congress had authorized the establishment of Quartermaster units in 1912, but, when the United States entered the war, provision had been made for only four types—truck, wagon, pack, and bakery companies.   The War Department subsequently transferred the truck companies to the Motor Transport Corps when it separated that organization from the Quartermaster Corps.   By the end of the war, the Quartermaster Corps in the A.E.F. employed 26 distinct types of units.   In addition to the authorized units, the A.E.F. used six other types of Quartermaster organizations, for which tables of organization had been prepared but not submitted for approval. [31]

Nearly as many Quartermaster Corps organizations arrived in France

[28] RG 120, AEF Gen Hq Proceedings of Board of Officers, 1917–19, Box 2206 (Memo, Brig. Gen. Geo. Van Horn Mosely, ACS, G-4, for TAG, 3 Jun 1919).

[29] RG 92, OQMG, Gen. H. L. Rogers Private File, Box 3 (Memo, Col. W. R. Grove for Acting QMG, n.d. but circa May 1918).

[30] RG 92, OQMG Historical Files, Box 75 (CQM Report, p. 23).

[31] RG 92, OQMG, Gen. H. L. Rogers Private File, Box 11 (Memo, Col. John S. Chambers for Chief Quartermaster, 2 Jan 1919).

during the period from July to September 1918 as had arrived during all the other months of the war. The Personnel Division of the Chief Quartermaster's Office was constantly plagued by its inability to obtain authorized personnel from the United States according to approved schedule. In consequence, units had to be hastily organized in France from inexperienced personnel at the Corps' disposal. Of the 706 units in France on 15 December 1918, 262 or 37 percent were organized in the A.E.F.[32] By 11 November 1918, Quartermaster Corps personnel in the A.E.F. numbered 4,665 officers and 90,066 enlisted men.[33]

Initial Supply Preparations

Despite personnel shortages, the Quartermaster Corps fulfilled its responsibilities so satisfactorily that, at the end of the war, Pershing reported that "no army was ever better provided for" than the A.E.F.[34] Preparations began before any troops reached France. Two days after Pershing sent for Colonel McCarthy, the latter was at the Office of the Quartermaster General and, in the 11 days before the *Baltic* sailed, he and his four assistants raced against time to prepare requisitions for clothing, subsistence, harness, tools, tarpaulins, gasoline, ranges, tents, stationery, and all the other multifarious necessities required to support the first convoy being sent to France. Requisitions called for a 6-months' supply for these troops and also provided such additional supplies as would be needed by Headquarters and the depots, remount stations, veterinary hospitals, and other facilties that Quartermaster officers would be establishing soon after their arrival. Colonel McCarthy assumed that some articles could be obtained abroad, but only actual investigation by Quartermaster officers after arrival could determine what supplies would be available and in what quantities.

Preliminary preparations included consultations with Quartermaster General Sharpe and his assistants. The Chief Quartermaster and his staff also held conferences with British officers on duty in the Office in order to supplement information obtained from military observers' reports as to what troops would need in the way of rations and clothing when operating under the new methods of warfare, such as trench fighting. Before departing, Colonel McCarthy requested Quartermaster General Sharpe to send as soon as possible the nucleus of an organization for

---

[32] *Ibid.*
[33] RG 92, OQMG Historical Files, Box 75 (CQM Report, p. 3).
[34] *Final Report of Gen. John J. Pershing,* p. 73.

handling the transport service, as well as clerks, warehousemen, wheel-wrights, blacksmiths, tailors, shoemakers, and mechanics.[35]

On board the steamship *Baltic,* he wasted no time. His staff held classes for the benefit of the reserve quartermasters to instruct them in their duties and responsibilities. While en route, General Pershing appointed Colonel McCarthy on 31 May to serve as senior member of a board of officers detailed to consider the advantages and disadvantages of such ports as the French might indicate for use as possible bases for the A.E.F., and to examine the rail facilities leading to the Western Front.[36] The board made a study of the various harbors in the southwestern part of France that would likely be assigned for American use. The *Baltic* docked at Liverpool on 8 June, and 2 days later Colonel McCarthy and the other officers of the board arrived at Boulogne, the first of the A.E.F. to reach France. Ten days later, the board submitted its report, recommending that the ports of St. Nazaire, La Pallice, and Bassens be turned over to the American forces for permanent use. These were the only available ports on the west coast of France capable of accommodating vessels of more than moderate draft. The board further proposed that three other ports—Nantes, Bordeaux, and Pauillac—be designated for emergency use since they were capable of handling light-draft shipping. It recommended acceptance of the French plan of establishing instruction camps and bases of supplies in the interior and of using the ports as reshipping points. The board also recommended that steps be taken immediately for the construction of wharves, storehouses, and camps; that personnel and material be sent to France without delay to be used in building and operating refrigerating plants, slaughter houses, and artesian wells; that laborers be brought to France as enlisted personnel; and that a general officer of the line, with sufficient staff, be detailed as commander for the service of the rear.[37]

Selection of the ports was determined not only by availability but also by the fact that "the main railroad routes from these ports toward northeastern France were not included in the service of the rear" for either the French or British armies as were the railroad lines farther north.[38] In consequence, they were available for the transportation of supplies for the American Army. Double-track railway lines from St. Nazaire and Bordeaux joined at Bourges and continued on through

[35] RG 120, AEF SOS Historical Files, Box 129 (Rpt, Col. D. E. McCarthy to TAG, 6 Mar 1920).

[36] *Organization of the Services of Supply* (Monograph No. 7, prepared in Historical Br, War Plans Div, General Staff, June 1921, Washington, 1921), p. 116 (TAG to Col. D. E. McCarthy, 31 May 1917).

[37] *Ibid.,* pp. 117–21 (Board's Rpt, 20 Jun 1917).

[38] Pershing, *My Experiences in the World War,* I, 83.

Nevers and Dijon to Neufchâteau where other radiating lines extended toward the Lorraine sector. In the event that another port and rail line became necessary to supplement the support afforded via these ports and railroads, the A.E.F. could also make use of the port of Marseilles and the railroad leading north from it.

These considerations were of the utmost importance because they helped determine the sector of the front where the A.E.F. would be most effective in fighting as a unit—and General Pershing was determined to maintain the identity of the American troops as a separate fighting unit rather than permit their incorporation in French and British units. With the British committed to operations covering the channel ports and the French concerned about the safety of Paris, the battlefront from the Argonne Forest to the Vosges Mountains, Pershing later wrote, afforded a clear-cut opportunity for the "decisive use of our army." [39] Availability of the western ports and the railroads leading to northeastern France led to an early tentative understanding between Pershing and Gen. Philippe Pétain, Commander-in-Chief of the French Armies, as to the general area of A.E.F. activities and the location of the Line of Communications.

Depot System

In accordance with the recommendations made by the board of officers on ports, Pershing sent Quartermaster officers to St. Nazaire to establish a base and make provision for the first convoy arriving there on 26 June 1917. Within a few weeks, St. Nazaire was throbbing with Quartermaster activities. From the first medium-sized storeroom on the docks, taken over from the French on 26 June, storage space grew until, on 11 November 1918, the Quartermaster Corps occupied seven buildings with a total covered storage space of 162,317 square feet. About a year after the first convoy arrived at St. Nazaire, ships were unloading an average of 212,585 cargo tons a month at the port, 63.5 percent of which consisted of Quartermaster supplies.[40]

St. Nazaire was the beginning of the gigantic supply structure built on the Line of Communications for the storage and distribution of the matériel and supplies needed to support the A.E.F. The Quartermaster Corps established general depots in the base, intermediate, and advance areas of the Line of Communications.

Base depots, such as the depot established at Montoir, 4 miles from St. Nazaire, or the depot built at St. Sulpice, near Bordeaux on the main

---

[39] *Ibid.*, I, 83.

[40] RG 92, OQMG, Gen. H. L. Rogers Private File, Box 27 (Historical Rpt, Lt. Col. E. K. Coulter, The Quartermaster Corps, AEF, pp. 10, 95–96).

line of the Paris-Orleans railroad, served the dual purpose of temporary storage and reserve storage depots. Primarily, base depots provided temporary storage for supplies that had to be unloaded quickly from the ships arriving in the port to prevent congestion and to reduce turnabout time for them, thereby making their tonnage available for more extended use in the transportation crisis of 1917. Since railroad facilities from the ports were also inadequate, quartermasters could not in any case send supplies directly to the interior from cars loaded at shipside. Base depot facilities not only provided temporary storage but also afforded an opportunity for sorting and classifying supplies that become disorganized in the hasty unloading of ships, thereby making possible regular balanced shipments to the intermediate and advance storage depots. One of the regular daily shipments out of the Quartermaster depot at St. Sulpice, for example, was 250,000 rations, forwarded to the great regulating station at Is-sur-Tille. By 11 November 1918, the St. Sulpice depot consisted of 57 buildings, representing 1,439,300 square feet of covered storage space. In addition, the Corps also had 900,000 square feet of open storage space.[41] As supply activities expanded, the Corps established other Quartermaster depots in the various base sections, while the Engineers constructed warehouses, additional docking facilities to increase capability of unloading steamships at the ports, and rail trackage and yards.[42]

Based on the assumption that the A.E.F. would operate on the northeastern frontier of France and in Alsace-Lorraine, the development of an adequate supply system called for the establishment of centrally located depots in the intermediate section of the Line of Communications, where accumulated reserves could be held in readiness and from which stock levels at the advance depots could be filled. The initial thrust forward of the Line of Communications was marked by the opening of offices at

[41] RG 92, OQMG Historical Files, Box 75 (CQM Report, p. 205).

[42] As of 11 November 1918, Quartermaster depots in the base sections were as follows:

Base Section 1—Headquarters and Depot No. 1, St. Nazaire; Depot No. 2, Nantes; Depot No. 3, Thouars; Depot No. 4, Montoir; Depot No. 5, Les Sables d'Olonne.

Base Section 2—Headquarters and Depot No. 1, Bordeaux; Depot No. 2, La Pallice (subsequently transferred to Base Section 7); Depot No. 3, St. Sulpice; Depot No. 4, Coutras.

Base Section 3—Headquarters and Depot No. 1, London; Depot No. 2, Liverpool; Depot No. 3, Southampton.

Base Section 4—Headquarters and Depot No. 1, Le Harve; Depot No. 2, Rouen; Depot No. 3, Calais.

Base Section 5—Headquarters and Depot No. 1, Brest.

Base Section 6—Headquarters and Depot No. 1, Marseille; Depot No. 2, Miramas.

Base Section 7—Headquarters and Depot No. 1, La Rochelle; Depot No. 2, La Pallice; Depot No. 3, Rochefort.

Base Section 8—Headquarters, Padua; Depot No. 1, Villa Franca di Verona (subsequently removed to Alessandria).

Nevers in July 1917. Quartermaster operations began when 51 enlisted men of the Quartermaster Corps arrived at Nevers from St. Nazaire on 8 July to establish a depot that for a time operated both as an advance and intermediate depot. When Headquarters, A.E.F. authorized the Intermediate Section on 13 August, Nevers became Headquarters and Depot No. 1 for the Intermediate Section. Nevers was selected as a depot point because it was centrally located whichever way the front might move. Its location and the fact that it was also a division point on the French railway system were important considerations in the work of transferring supplies from the base ports. It was planned to make Nevers the main intermediate supply base, but the needs of the expanding A.E.F. outgrew the possibilities of the Nevers Depot, the necessary expansion of which was precluded by the lack of available space for adding new warehouses and railroad sidings. In consequence, General Headquarters later established the main intermediate depot at Gievres early in 1918.

Until that time, the depot at Nevers received and handled all supplies sent forward from the bases. It was the principal distributing point in France. The shift to the use of the Gievres depot was gradual. Even in July and August 1918, the depot at Nevers received no less than 6,000 carloads of supplies each month and distributed an average of 200 carloads daily. As the depot at Gievres grew, the amount of matériel handled at Nevers diminished, and it was designated as the depot for supplying office equipment and stationery for the entire A.E.F. In the early months of its existence, the Quartermaster depot at Nevers had the distinction of being used as a training center for inexperienced Quartermaster personnel. Newly arrived Quartermaster officers and enlisted men alike were put through a short course of training and then dispatched to other projects. Thus, the Chief Quartermaster took detachments of officers and enlisted men from the depot personnel at Nevers to aid in establishing the Quartermaster depots at Dijon and Bordeaux.[43]

The intermediate depot established at Gievres was a reserve storage depot for all the supply services, each of which had its own section. The Quartermaster section became the largest Quartermaster depot of the A.E.F. The commanding officer of the Gievres depot, as a member of G–4, co-ordinated the construction, warehousing labor, and the apportionment of freight cars at the depot. Built near the town of Gievres on a tract of land that stretched between the Paris-Orleans Railroad and the Selles-Villefranche highway in the Tours district, the depot was centrally located and had unlimited possibilities for growing to serve the

---

[43] (1) RG 92, OQMG, Gen. H. L. Rogers Private File, Box 28 (Historical Rpt, Quartermaster Depot No. 1, Intermediate Section). (2) See also, RG 92, OQMG Historical Files, Box 75 (CQM Report, p. 137 ff.).

purposes of the A.E.F. The Quartermaster section expanded rapidly. On 20 March 1918, Quartermaster personnel included a depot quartermaster, a field clerk, about 40 enlisted men of the Corps, and a labor battalion. The depot quartermaster operated only eight Quartermaster warehouses. Eight months later, when the war ended, the number of warehouses had expanded to 107, and Quartermaster personnel on duty had increased to 147 commissioned officers, one field clerk, and 7,412 enlisted men.

The storage of subsistence occupied about half the total space of the depot. The Corps used 17 warehouses for storing clothing and about as many for the storage of miscellaneous property. It stored in the open, under tarpaulins, supplies, such as escort wagons, water carts, and rolling kitchens, which were shipped directly from the base ports and assembled at the depot by a large staff of exports. The refrigerating plant erected at Gievres was one of the largest of its kind in the world. Designed by Quartermaster officers, the refrigerating plant was built by Quartermaster personnel under the supervision of the Engineers Corps from material furnished by the Quartermaster Corps. The ice box was large enough to hold at one time 18 million pounds of fresh beef. In addition to the large amounts of clothing, rations, and other supplies that the Corps handled at Gievres, it stored huge quantities of coal and wood there. It operated four gasoline storage tanks, each with a capacity of 500,000 gallons, and also stored a large stock of lubricating oils at the Gievres depot.

Operation of the Quartermaster depot, with its numerous warehouses, hundreds of cars, and miles of railroad tracks, required efficient checking devices and controls. Quartermasters handled as many as 667 cars in one day, loading 410 and unloading 257. One single order had called for the shipment of as much as 4,596 tons of foodstuffs and tobacco. To fill this largest order received at the depot, the depot quartermaster had 457 cars loaded, sealed, and ready for shipment 19½ working hours after he received the order. Gievres supplied as many as 800,000 men at one time. It supplied all the divisions of the American Army fighting beside the French at Chateau-Thierry, the American divisions in the St. Mihiel drive, and, until the armistice was signed, the American troops fighting in the Argonne and north of Verdun.[44] The Corps established other Quartermaster depots in the intermediate section at Montierchaume and Issoudun, but they were not on as large a scale as the depot at Gievres.

The last supply link on the Line of Communications was the depot

44 (1) RG 92, OQMG, Gen. H. L. Rogers Private File, Box 28 (Historical Rpt, Gievres, Intermediate Quartermaster Depot No. 2). (2) RG 92, OQMG Historical Files, Box 75 (CQM Report, p. 147 ff.).

established in the Advance Section. By October 1917, the organization of the Line of Communications had developed to such an extent that it became necessary to take steps to organize the Advance Section. The establishment at Neufchâteau of Headquarters, Advance Section, Line of Communications, was officially announced on 14 December 1917.[45]

The largest and only permanent advance depot was built at Is-sur-Tille for the use of all the supply services. The Quartermaster Depot at Is-sur-Tille was opened on 7 December. One week later supplies began arriving, although the warehouses were not yet completed and stocks had to be stored in the open under tarpaulins. Starting with 2 warehouses, the Quartermaster Depot expanded until it had in operation, at the time of the armistice, 9 clothing warehouses; 8 subsistence warehouses; 8 miscellaneous property warehouses; 12 steel hangars, used to cover forage and rations; and 6 combination warehouses and shops.

Shipments from the Advance Quartermaster Depot to the combat units passed through the Regulating Station located at Is-sur-Tille. Peak operations for the Quartermaster Depot were reached in September 1918 when it forwarded 464 carloads of supplies to troops on the firing line and supplied 1,036,785 men, including certain French troops.[46]

The Corps established a number of other Quartermaster advance depots, all but one of which were of minor importance.[47] The depot established at Dijon, on 23 July 1917, was known as the Bread and Meat Depot because, at least until the spring of 1918, it supplied practically all troops beyond that point with fresh bread and was the distribution point for fresh beef issued to troops in the Advance Section. Such beef distribution eventually proved unsatisfactory because Dijon was located too far behind the regulating station at Is-sur-Tille to permit shipments of beef to arrive regularly for inclusion in the balanced rations that were loaded there and sent to the front. In consequence, fresh beef began to be shipped directly to Is-sur-Tille from the depot at Gievres. After the Corps placed a mechanical bakery in operation at Is-sur-Tille, practically all bread for the Advance Section was furnished from that point.[48]

Supply of Petroleum Products

The storage and distribution of the bulk of Quartermaster supplies were handled through the depot system established on the Line of Com-

[45] U.S. Army in the World War, 1917–19, XVI, 142 (Hq AEF GO 75).

[46] RG 92, OQMG Historical Files, Box 75 (CQM Report, p. 113).

[47] Other depots were established at Gondrecourt, La Valdahon, Jonchery, Neufchâteau, and Bourmont.

[48] RG 92, OQMG Historical Files, Box 75 (CQM Report, pp. 129–31).

LOADING CAR WITH SACKED BREAD, DIJON

munications, but the handling of gasoline, for which the Chief Quarter-master, A.E.F., was made solely responsible, posed special problems. The French supplied their armies by using 50-liter bidons, or cans, that were filled at bases and shipped forward by rail and truck. Such a system afforded high mobility but required innumerable cans and tended to congest transportation facilities. This tendency alone made it advisable for the A.E.F. to reduce the use of cans to a minimum and to adopt the American system of bulk distribution, that is, the use of tank storage, railway tank cars between storage points, and motor tank truck distribution for local use.

Obtaining the necessary equipment was difficult. The Office of the Chief Quartermaster selected Bordeaux and Pallice as the main practical ports for receipt of gasoline piped into storage tanks from tank steamers. It used existing installations of the French refiners and erected additional storage facilities. The Gasoline and Oil Branch in the Office of the Chief Quartermaster, A.E.F., directed operations. The Branch chief hired six French railway tank cars and ordered 2,950 tank cars from the United States. None of the latter had arrived by April 1918, and the British

Government came to the assistance of the A.E.F. by agreeing to rent 50 railway tank cars to the Branch for the duration of the war. By the time the armistice was signed, 549 tank cars had been delivered from the United States. Pending the arrival of storage tanks from the United States, the Gasoline and Oil Branch had a considerable number of small capacity storage tanks constructed in France and put into immediate use. Wherever consumption justified it, the Branch installed storage tanks and pumps in the base and intermediate areas.

Until late in June 1918, however, General Headquarters refused to allow delivery of bulk gasoline in the Advance Section and would not permit it to be forwarded even in tank cars. At the time of the Chateau-Thierry push, the shortage of packaged gasoline prevented the French from adequately supplying the American divisions that had been thrown into combat. Headquarters, A.E.F., ordered the Chief Quartermaster to arrange for immediate delivery of 650,000 gallons per month to the Paris Group. With cans unobtainable, the Gasoline and Oil Branch could guarantee delivery only if it was permitted to forward bulk gasoline. General Headquarters acquiesced and the Branch at once erected gasoline depots. It successfully filled requirements from these depots in bulk, with motor tank wagon delivery to units. Thereafter, General Headquarters allowed the Branch to place portable bulk storage at any designated locations in the Advance area.

Deliveries of motor gasoline showed a tremendous increase after June 1918. Over 48½ million gallons were delivered between January and December 1918, and more than three-fourths of that amount was delivered in the last 6 months of the year. Deliveries in 1918 also included approximately 5 million gallons of aviation gasoline and about 1½ million gallons of kerosene as well as 4 million gallons of lubricating oil, and almost 2½ million pounds of grease.[49]

Other Quartermaster Activities on the Line of Communications

In addition to its depot operations on the Line of Communications, the Quartermaster Corps was engaged in numerous other activities that were scattered throughout the geographical areas of that Line. In Base Section 1, for example, of which St. Nazaire was the Headquarters, the Corps operated six field bakeries, a gasoline and oil distribution station, and two coal storage yards. It had under cultivation two gardens, three bulk production farms, and a seedling nursey. It also maintained in

---

[49] (1) RG 92, OQMG, Gen. H. L. Rogers Private File, Box 5 (Rpt, Gasoline and Oil Branch of the Supplies Division, undated). (2) *Ibid.*, Box 8 (Brief History of the Operations of the Gasoline and Oil Branch, 16 Jan 1919).

that Section a remount depot, a salvage depot, and an Effects Depot that received and arranged for the disposition of all personal property, effects, and records of American soldiers at the time of their death, capture, or disappearance while serving with the A.E.F.[50]

The scope and variety of Quartermaster activities in the Intermediate Section were greater than in any other section.   Not only did they include all activities, except the operation of an Effects Depot, to be found in Base Section 1, but within the Intermediate Section the Quartermaster Corps also opened and operated factories that produced candy, hard bread, and macaroni for the A.E.F.[51]   A large assortment of metal products was likewise manufactured under Quartermaster supervision.   Within its boundaries was located the major salvage depot at St. Pierre-des-Corps.[52]

The Corps also conducted numerous Quartermaster activities in the Advance Section.   At Is-sur-Tille, the Quartermaster Corps maintained three salvage sheds, a degreasing plant, a fuel and forage yard, two coal docks, an electric light plant, a carpenter shop, a tin shop, a paint shop, a box mill, a saw mill, and a sales commissary that did a business of approximately $100,000 a month.   At Is-sur-Tille, the Corps established a mechanical bakery.   This development marked an almost revolutionary change in the method of providing bread for the Army.   In lieu of assigning bakery companies to operate field bakeries with the divisions of the Army, the Corps erected a large mechanical bakery in the rear of the regulating station, from which bread was supplied to the troops at the front.   Adoption of this plan was based on Allied experience, and, by obtaining the necessary machinery on a replacement basis from the British, the Corps facilitated the early operation of the mechanical bakery. This plant, when in full operation, had the advantage of using less fuel and less personnel—7 bakery companies of 101 men each—to produce the same amount of bread that 27 companies turned out in field bakeries. The Corps did not complete the mechanical bakery until 1 December 1918, but from August, 11 bakery companies, using such parts of the bakery equipment as were available and improvising others, provided 580,000 pounds of field bread per day.[53]

Storage for Combat Units

Storage on the Line of Communications was but one part of A.E.F. requirements.   Provision had also to be made for storage in the combat

[50] For a detailed description of these activities, see RG 92, OQMG, Gen. H. L. Rogers Private File, Box 28 (Historical Rpt, Base Section One).

[51] *Infra*, p. 670.

[52] *Infra*, p. 676.

[53] RG 92, OQMG, Gen. H. L. Rogers Private File, Box 7 (Memo, Col. L. L. Deitrick, Bakery Br, to Supplies Div, 14 Dec 1918).

units.[54] Placing supplies in the hands of combat troops involved certain basic considerations. Among these were regularity and promptness in the receipt of supplies as a necessary means of maintaining troop morale and efficiency. But it was essential that the paperwork needed to obtain supplies be held to a minimum and that the delivery of supplies to organizations be placed, as much as possible, on an automatic basis. Only the authorized standard reserve of supplies could be placed in the hands of the troops if their mobility was to be preserved. Moreover, undue accumulations of supplies at the front had to be avoided to minimize the danger of their destruction or capture.[55]

Storage in combat units developed into two kinds—railhead stockages and stockages known as an army park or depot. The railhead was the point on the railroad at which supplies were discharged. The place at which the trains of a division received its supplies was called the refilling point, but it was possible for railhead and refilling point to be one and the same place. Railhead storage was not a responsibility of the Quartermaster Corps but was placed under the authority of the regulating officer.

In the early months of A.E.F. participation in the war, it was generally believed that all supplies could be delivered to divisions at their railheads. Experience soon demonstrated the impossibility of utilizing for all supplies this method of delivery for an army of nearly a million men, operating in a limited area with its railroad transportation under French control. Railheads were fully occupied in handling only rations and forage. Since freight cars were limited in number and had to be quickly released, the only alternative to prevent the development of congestion was the establishment of parks and dumps. As soon as commanders determined the military objective and stabilized operations to the point where it was possible to establish a supply park, such a facility was provided to supply the Army. Quartermasters drew supplies for a Quartermaster army park principally from the Quartermaster intermediate depot at Gievres and the Quartermaster advance depot at Is-sur-Tille. The first such army park was established near Melun during the operations of the Paris Group about Chateau-Thierry. It was a small park that was set up essentially for emergency reserve purposes only and all the supply services utilized it.

Of far more importance was the Quartermaster Army Park at Fleury, established on 3 October 1918 to insure the proper supply of all Class 2

---

[54] The volume of records and the difficulty of using them prevents any detailed analysis of front-line storage operations within the scope of this brief treatment.

[55] *Final Report of Gen. John J. Pershing*, p. 64.

and 3 supplies, that is clothing and equipment, to the First Army, numbering about a million men, when it began its Argonne-Meuse operations.   With the troops engaged in active fighting, suffering heavy casualties, exposed to gas attack, and requiring large renewals of clothing and equipment, the Quartermaster Park at Fleury became a depot of general issue.   The Chief Quartermaster of the First Army had direct control of the park.   Divisions, corps, and all elements of the First Army submitted their requisitions by messenger, telephone, or telegraph to the Chief Quartermaster of that Army, whose office checked them immediately.   He ordered issues made at once from the park to the using organizations with a minimum of formalities.[56]

Parks or dumps at division or corps levels were indefinite in form and rather haphazard affairs.   In evaluating Quartermaster storage operations in the combat units, Maj. C. W. Halsey, of G–4, General Headquarters, A.E.F., observed that "combat operations of the American armies, as army organizations, were not of long enough duration to develop any very complete experience in army stockage practice." [57]

Introduction of Automatic Supply

Storage operations constituted only one part of the overall Quartermaster responsibility for providing logistical support to the A.E.F.   The Corps was also responsible for furnishing the troops with clothing, personal and organizational equipment, rations, forage, fuel, and animals.   Its efforts to procure supplies during the months of the war carried it into the field of production.

Quartermaster supply operations began as soon as the first Headquarters of the A.E.F. was opened in Paris.[58]   The main dependence of the A.E.F. for supplies was necessarily on the resources of the United States since there was a shortage of almost all supplies in Europe.   Inasmuch as tonnage was the crux of the whole supply problem, however, it

---

[56] (1) RG 92, OQMG Historical Files, Box 75 (CQM Report, pp. 498–99). (2) *U.S. Army in the World War, 1917–19*, XIV, 172 (Undated Rpt, Gen Hq A.E.F., 4th Section). (3) *Ibid.*, XVI, 249–56 (Hq AEF GO 44, 23 Mar 1918) provides details on requisitions and methods of supply. (4) "Operations of the Quartermaster Corps, U.S. Army During the World War: Notes on Army, Corps and Division Quartermaster Activities in the A.E.F." (Monograph No. 9, Quartermaster Corps School, Philadelphia, Pa.), p. 9 ff. (Extract, Chief QM, First Army to CG, First Army, 10 Dec 1918).

[57] *U.S. Army in the World War, 1917–19*, XIV, 173.

[58] As a matter of fact, the first Quartermaster purchase abroad was made as soon as the Commander-in-Chief's party arrived in London. Considering the volume of A.E.F. records, no one should be surprised that the first Quartermaster purchase was a few boxes of carbon paper to carry on the necessary clerical work at Headquarters, the shortage having developed while General Pershing's party was en route on the *Baltic*.

was vital to supplement the resources of the United States with whatever supplies could be obtained in Europe.

As far as possible, procurement of supplies from the United States was placed on an automatic basis. Adoption of a system of automatic supply had been proposed by Chief Quartermaster McCarthy in May 1917. Quartermaster General Sharpe, who had not approved of this proposal, recommended the use of requisitions submitted monthly or oftener, if necessary, direct to the Depot Quartermaster at New York as a means of avoiding unnecessary accumulation of supplies in France.[59] Subsequently, General Pershing recommended adoption of the system of automatic supply of standard items and the gradual accumulation of a 90-day reserve. Despite Sharpe's dissent, the Secretary of War approved.[60] The 90-day reserve was distributed so as to provide 45, 30, and 15 days of supply, respectively, in the base, intermediate, and advance sections. When the danger to shipping from submarine attack decreased, the 90-day reserve was reduced to 45 days of supply.[61]

There were exceptions to the general rule of automatic supply. Requisitions for material that was a regular item of troop supply and emergency requisitions for quantities of regular items above the standing calls constituted special requests for supplies and were designated "exceptional supply." Forage, for example, always had to be carried as exceptional supply because the Corps purchased a large proportion of the animals used by the A.E.F. in France and Spain. Without knowing the number of animals on hand in the A.E.F. and the quantity of hay that the French government provided, the Office of the Quartermaster General in Washington was unable to compute forage requirements on an automatic basis.[62]

Local Procurement

Adoption of the policy of purchasing supplies in Europe was dictated by the acute shortage of shipping in 1917. That shortage was such that during the first 7 months of its existence, the A.E.F. was almost entirely dependent on France for its logistical support. Less than 500,000 of the approximately 5 million tons of supplies needed during those months

[59] RG 120, AEF SOS Historical Files, Box 129 (Rpt, Col. D. E. McCarthy to TAG, 6 Mar 1920, Appendix F).

[60] (1) *U.S. Army in the World War, 1917–19*, XV, 10–11 (Pershing cable, 7 Sep 1917). (2) RG 165, War College Div. Doc. File, Case 7702–15 (Memo, Sharpe for Chief, War College Div, 4 Oct 1917; Memo, Chief of Staff for TAG, 18 Oct 1917).

[61] *Final Report of Gen. John J. Pershing*, p. 11.

[62] RG 92, OQMG, Gen. H. L. Rogers Private File, Box 6 (Memo, Lt. A. B. Rosenkrans for Col. Crusan, 6 Dec 1918).

were shipped from the United States.[63]   Only such supplies as could not be procured abroad were sent in order that the space thus saved could be used for the transportation of troops.   From the beginning of the war until 31 December 1918, the A.E.F. required approximately 18 million ship tons of material.   Of this amount, 10 million tons were obtained in Europe and about 8 million tons were shipped from the United States. Over half of the amount purchased in Europe represented Quartermaster supplies.[64]

When purchase of supplies in Europe was initiated in June to supply the limited wants of the first Expeditionary Forces, each supply service handled procurement independently, with the same competitive results as occurred in the United States.   By August, General Pershing established a General Purchasing Board to co-ordinate the purchase operations of the supply departments, the Red Cross, and the YMCA.   He appointed Charles G. Dawes as General Purchasing Agent.[65]   General Headquarters supervised the Board until it was placed under the control of the Commanding General, Services of Supply.   The Board had no authority to make purchases, but it exercised the power of control and veto of purchases.   Before purchase orders could be placed by the Quartermaster Corps or any other supply service, they had to be submitted to the General Purchasing Agent for approval.   The latter was also responsible for locating supplies in Europe.

Dawes continued, in 1918, to maintain that military necessity required purchases in Europe and to urge that the insufficient tonnage available be used for transporting articles of "first necessity unobtainable here."   The Chief Quartermaster, A.E.F., fully agreed with him.   By the summer of 1918, however, manufacturers in the United States questioned that policy, and the War Industries Board sent a mission overseas to look into the question of foreign purchases in general and shoe procurement in England in particular—a development indicative of a trend toward buying American goods that, had the war continued for many more months, would have become more pronounced, particularly so as the shipping crisis passed.[66]

[63] RG 92, OQMG Historical Files, Box 75 (CQM Report, p. 42).

[64] Charles G. Dawes, *A Journal of the Great War* (2 vols., New York, 1921), II, 33, 34.

[65] (1) Pershing, *My Experiences in the World War*, I, 148–49. (2) Dawes, *A Journal of the Great War*, I, 19–21. (3) *U.S. Army in the World War, 1917–19*, XVI, 57 (Hq AEF GO 23, 20 Aug 1917); p. 64 (Hq AEF GO 28, 30 Aug 1917).

[66] (1) RG 92, OQMG Records, Report of Maj. Roy A. Shaw, 24 Sep 1918. (2) The purchase of shoes in England brought protests from the American shoe manufacturers who maintained there were ample facilities for the production in the United States of shoes of superior wearing quality. Moreover, it was claimed that it required five times the space to transport the same quantity of hides as leather as was necessary for the finished product, shoes.

Chief Quartermaster McCarthy delegated responsibility for the pro-curement of Quartermaster supplies to Lt. Col. Harry E. Wilkins, one of the four assistants who accompanied him to Paris. The latter was designated Chief Purchasing Officer of the Quartermaster Corps. His office, originally organized in Paris, continued to be maintained in that city and remained under the jurisdiction of the Chief Quartermaster, A.E.F., when General Headquarters moved to Chaumont and later when the supply services were transferred to the Headquarters, Services of Supply, at Tours. When Pershing established the General Purchasing Board, the Chief Purchasing Officer of the Corps became the representa-tive of the Chief Quartermaster, A.E.F., on that board. Its membership also included representatives from the other supply services.

The small office of the Chief Purchasing Officer of the Corps ex-panded until it became a great business organization, with agents not only in France but also in the principal cities of Great Britain, Italy, Switzerland, and Spain. These purchasing agents reported to, and worked through, the representatives of the General Purchasing Board also stationed in these cities. The Chief Purchasing Officer organized his Paris office into divisions. The principal one was the Purchasing Division composed of five commodity branches, one manufacturing branch, and one branch that handled the delivery and transportation of supplies purchased. In addition, the organization included a Subsistence Manufacturing Division, an Accounting and Auditing Division, a Person-nel Division, and a Chief Clerk in charge of all records and files.[67]

In the beginning, each supply service bought its own items of supply although under the co-ordinating control of the General Purchasing Agent. In time, under the leadership of a Quartermaster officer, Lt. Col. N. D. Jay, who served as Assistant General Purchasing Agent, the Gen-eral Purchasing Board developed a system of purchase by category in order to bring about a more effective control of purchases, prevent competition between the supply services, and withal secure the ad-vantages to be obtained from large transactions. A directive of the Commanding General, Services of Supply, established categories of sup-plies used by more than one supply service, and it authorized the General Purchasing Agent to designate the particular service that would purchase such supplies for all the supply departments.[68] Under these categories, the Quartermaster Corps purchased all textiles and clothing except special aviator's and gas-protective clothing, all insignia, blankets, mattresses and bedding, tentage, tarpaulins, jute and burlap, kitchen utensils, lamps,

---

[67] RG 92, OQMG, Gen. H. L. Rogers Private File, Box 28 (Historical Rpt, Chief Pur-chasing Officer, Q.M.C., A.E.F., p. 12).
[68] Dawes, *A Journal of the Great War*, II, 17, 59.

refrigerating machinery, tanks, horseshoes, agricultural implements, office fixtures and supplies, coal, oil, gasoline, paints, printing plant supplies, and hides and leather.   In addition, the Corps bought its own supplies which were not handled by other services, as, for example, salvage machinery.[69]

Clothing, textiles, and subsistence were the principal supplies purchased by the Chief Purchasing Officer.   Most purchases of clothing and textiles were contracted for in the usual manner.   The shortage of blankets caused the Chief Purchasing Officer to buy commercial blankets of all kinds in the fall of 1917.   On 14 October 1917, the War Department approved the Chief Quartermaster's request for authority to purchase 200,000 blankets in Spain.   Three days later, it also authorized him to contract with the British Government for 200,000 uniforms.   Early in December, Pershing complained to the War Department by cable that the failure of the Quartermaster Corps to land supplies of winter clothing long requested had produced a serious situation.[70]   The Corps had shipped considerable quantities of clothing, but, obviously, the rate at which clothing wore out surpassed any past experience on which it based a replacement factor.   In December 1917, the War Department advised the Chief Quartermaster to limit his purchases of Spanish textiles to quantities required only for emergency needs because large contracts were being filled in the United States.   A month later, however, it requested him to report what additional amounts of clothing could be purchased in Europe.[71]   Among the articles of clothing purchased in England during the war were 1,000,000 overseas caps, 278,000 wool coats, over 2,000,000 pairs of wool drawers, 1,150,000 pairs of gloves, 237,000 flannel shirts, almost 2,000,000 pairs of field shoes, and nearly 4,500,000 pairs of wool stockings.   The Chief Purchasing Officer also bought smaller quantities of these and other articles of clothing in Spain and France, while he purchased thousands of yards of textiles in all three countries.[72]

Clothing and textiles could be procured by regular purchase, but certain other supplies had to be purchased only on terms that called for replacement either of the supplies themselves or of the raw materials used in their production.   Such arrangements were particularly likely to be necessary in purchasing subsistence.   Thus, the shortage of shipping in the winter and spring of 1918 resulted in the delivery of insufficient stocks

[69] RG 92, OQMG Historical Files, Box 75 (CQM Report, p. 50).

[70] RG 92, OQMG, Gen. H. L. Rogers Private File, Box 7 (Cable No. 360-S, 11 Dec 1917).

[71] (1) *Ibid.* (Cable No. 632, 12 Jan 1918).   (2)RG 120, War Department Historical Files, Box 143 (Ltr, Acting Chief of Staff to CG, AEF, 13 Dec 1917).

[72] For a statement showing the deliveries of clothing, textiles, and insignia purchased in Europe during the war, see RG 92, OQMG, Gen. H. L. Rogers Private File, Box 7.

of fresh beef for the Army. When various organizations of the A.E.F. purchased fresh beef locally, the French government notified the A.E.F. that it expected the return of an equal amount of beef for all that had been purchased. Similarly, in the summer of 1918, the Purchasing Division, Office of the Chief Purchasing Officer, obtained 20,000 pounds of rice from the French Intendence on a replacement basis.[73] The purchase of metal products generally entailed the replacement of an equivalent tonnage of bulk metals because, by the end of 1917, Germany controlled the area of France that produced more than 80 percent of its iron and steel, and French war industries were themselves dependent on outside sources for their raw material.

Production Activities

The purchases of supplies carried the Chief Purchasing Officer of the Corps into the field of production. As the A.E.F. expanded, it became evident that the resources of France would have to be developed to the utmost to provide adequately for the American troops. Because of their bulk and the consequent saving in ship's tonnage, the Chief Purchasing Officer selected for procurement in France three items of subsistence supply—macaroni, hard bread, and candy. None of these items was available on the market because of the shortage of raw materials, and most factories equipped for their production were already operating under military control by the French government. Through the efforts of the Purchasing Division, the French government turned over to the Quartermaster Corps a number of factories, complete with operating personnel. In the case of macaroni production, the Corps furnished the flour and provided the necessary personnel to supervise manufacture, inspection, and shipment of the product. Most of these developments occurred between July and November 1918. In that period, 20 French factories turned out hard bread for the American forces and 13 candy factories operated to supply the wants of the Expeditionary Forces. The Corps furnished sugar and cocoa beans for the manufacture of candy, supplied coke and coal for operating the factories, and, in many instances, provided wooden boxes, paper, nails, and cartons for packing purposes. By such means supply caught up with demand.[74]

The Quartermaster Corps also carried on production that utilized its own personnel and materials in plants that it either erected or leased. The sheet metal and hollow ware shops near Bourges were one example. In February 1918, the Quartermaster Corps faced an acute shortage of

---

[73] RG 92, OQMG Historical Files, Box 75 (CQM Report, pp. 53, 68).
[74] *Ibid.*, pp. 53–57.

pans, coffee boilers, and galvanized iron cans, which formed an important part of the equipment of field kitchens. The coffee boilers and pans had to be made in graduated sizes in order that they might be nested and stored in the field ranges. Since articles of the correct dimensions could not be procured in France, the Chief Purchasing Officer made arrangements whereby the Corps virtually took over the operation of a French factory, supplying fuel and raw material and applying American methods of factory management. The Corps retained French management and employees, but it directed the supervision, inspection, and warehousing of materials, and, in rush periods, it detailed American soldiers to work in the factory. The Corps contracted for the entire output of metal articles, which were made according to Army specifications. When the Quartermaster Corps terminated contracts in January 1919, total production had aggregated 204,601 finished articles, and it was estimated that these products had saved ocean tonnage space amounting to 123,136 cubic feet.[75]

The Coffee Roasting Plant, established at Corbeil-Essenes near Paris and operated under the direction of the Chief Purchasing Officer, furnishes another example of Quartermaster manufacturing operations. To save space on transports, the Chief Purchasing Officer bought practically the entire European supply of green coffee in 1917—some 16 million pounds. Not until the European stock of green coffee had been exhausted in the fall of 1918 did it become necessary to make regular shipments from the United States, and by that time the height of the tonnage crisis was over. To roast and grind the coffee, the Corps installed the latest equipment in the plant. That plant became the largest in Europe, with an initial capacity of 500,000 rations a day which increased to 1,500,000 rations a day by the time the armistice was signed. When operations ceased, the Corps employed 300 French civilians in addition to 3 officers and 215 enlisted men of the Corps.[76]

Establishment of the Garden Service

The exploitation of French resources took other forms that were directed by the Supplies Division, Office of the Chief Quartermaster, A.E.F., rather than by the Chief Purchasing Officer. In December 1917, the Chief Quartermaster learned that both the French and British armies had been cultivating vegetable gardens near the front lines and at camps located in training areas. He deemed it expedient to take over French

[75] RG 92, OQMG, Gen. H. L. Rogers Private File, Box 28 (Historical Rpt, Chief Purchasing Officer, pp. 28–30).

[76] RG 92, OQMG Historical Files, Box 75 (CQM Report, pp. 58–67).

military gardens established in those sectors in which American troops replaced French soldiers so that the work already begun would not be lost. The French had built up a remarkable system of kitchen gardens, pursuing a method whereby ready-grown vegetable seedlings were furnished to the troops cultivating gardens. Such local production had the advantage of insuring prompt delivery of fresh vegetables and at the same time saving ocean, rail, and motor transportation.

On the basis of an investigation and report on the French system, the Chief Quartermaster established a Garden Service Branch in the Supplies Division of his Office. It furnished technical direction, land, tools, seeds, and seedlings. The Branch set up its technical headquarters at Versailles where the French were operating their seedling nursery. By directive, General Headquarters ordered each division commander to appoint a garden officer and establish a garden in each divisional training area and at each permanent post and camp.[77] The Garden Service Branch acquired about 3,000 acres of land, of which it placed about half under cultivation by the time the war ended. Some 157 officers were in charge of the different gardens. Although the armistice intervened before the Garden Service reached large proportions, it had drawn up extensive plans for 1919, and its actual accomplishments were considerable. The final reports received from all garden officers about 15 November 1918 indicated that the Service had produced approximately 10 million pounds of vegetables in these gardens at a cost (not including the labor of enlisted men) of about one-third the prevailing market prices.[78]

Wood and Coal Procurement

The Fuel Branch of the Supplies Division in the Office of the Chief Quartermaster directed the procurement of coal and wood, the supply of which involved different problems. Obtaining sufficient wood for fuel purposes was complicated by the fear of the French authorities that A.E.F. needs would encroach on those of its civilian population and, even more important, that satisfying these needs might deplete a natural resource of France difficult to replace. Procurement required tactful handling.

In October 1917, the Chief Quartermaster procured a large number of "coupes" or wood lots near the regulating station at Is-sur-Tille through which the troops would have to be supplied. He employed a large force

---

[77] U.S. Army in the World War, 1917–19, XVI, 233 (Hq AEF GO 34, 25 Feb 1918).
[78] (1) RG 165, War College Div. Doc. File, Case 10184–16 (Chief Quartermaster, AEF, to QMG, 6 Aug 1918). (2) RG 92, OQMG, Gen. H. L. Rogers Private File, Box 5 (Rpt on Garden Service).

of expert Spanish woodcutters under contract on a piecework basis. They cut about 75,000 cords.   This development so alarmed the French that a conference was arranged and an agreement worked out whereby 10 percent of the wood cut by the A.E.F. in the coupes was to be sold to the civilian population.   The Chief Quartermaster developed a close co-operation between his office and the French Forestry Service with the result that the Corps accumulated a fairly large supply of ready-cut wood.

In the winter of 1918–19, the Corps estimated that no less than 400,000 cords of wood would be needed for the combat troops alone. To meet this requirement, the Chief Quartermaster organized a battalion of labor troops that grew from 9,500 to 11,000 men.   Working under the direction of a competent forestry officer and following closely in the wake of the advancing armies, this organization, known as the Fuel Wood Project Advance Section, produced in 3 months one-third of the supply required for the winter maintenance of a troop program that called for 4,500,000 men.[79]

On the basis of a report on coal submitted to Chief Quartermaster McCarthy in June, he made arrangements whereby France provided 100 tons a day for 90 days.   This agreement called for a ton-for-ton return of the coal at the earliest possible moment.   In view of the existing shortage of shipping and French objections to receipt of anthracite coal from the United States, the Fuel Branch in the Office of the Chief Quartermaster began negotiations for a regular coal supply from England and for ships with which to transport it to France.   The Purchasing Agent for Great Britain, representing the Chief Purchasing Officer, entered into the negotiations and became convinced that procedures followed by the British Admiralty in obtaining its supply would have to be applied to fill A.E.F. coal requirements in Great Britain. The outcome was that, during the war, coal was purchased entirely in England on estimates prepared by the Fuel Branch.   These were forwarded via the Paris office to the Purchasing Agent for Great Britain in London.   He transmitted them to Harris & Dixon, Ltd., which acted as sole agent of the A.E.F. for the procurement of coal in Great Britain, obtaining the allotment of tonnage from the British coal controller. Harris & Dixon, Ltd., presented a permit to the British Coal Exportation Committee and shipments followed.[80]   The importation of British coal began in October 1917.   The shipments during that month reached

---

[79] RG 92, OQMG, Gen. H. L. Rogers Private File, Box 5 (Memo, Lt. Col. F. T. Hill for Maj. E. K. Coulter, 26 Nov 1918). See also *ibid.,* (Rpt, Maj. W. E. Mannear to Maj. Gen. H. L. Rogers, 29 Mar 1919).

[80] *Ibid.,* Box 5 (Memo, Lt. Col. D. B. Wentz for Chief QM, 29 Nov 1918; memo, Lt. Col. F. T. Hill for Maj. E. K. Coulter, 26 Nov 1918).

28,336 tons. By October 1918, the total amount of coal shipped from Great Britain for the A.E.F. during the intervening 12 months was over one million tons.[81]

Growth of Salvage Operations

The shipping crisis of 1917 and the need to save tonnage had other results than the purchase and production abroad of supplies. It stimulated the growth of salvage operations, a novel and striking development of the war. Though repairs, particularly of wagons and harness, had been undertaken in earlier wars, never before had the Quartermaster Corps made a systematic attempt to salvage the enormous waste of war. Contributing to this development was a War Department order, effective 15 July 1917, that abolished the fixed clothing allowance for the soldier. That order set his allowance for the duration of the war as the quantity of clothing necessary and adequate for the service upon which he was engaged. The directive ordered clothing that was worn or damaged through fair wear and tear to be turned in to the Quartermaster Corps for replacement. In addition, all articles of clothing, equipage, and other supplies abandoned on the march, in camp, or picked up on the field of battle were eventually to be turned in to the salvage depots for renovation, repair, and, if practicable, for re-issue.[82]

At the direction of Colonel McCarthy, Quartermaster officers had investigated British and French methods of salvage savings as soon as headquarters had been established in Paris.[83] It is doubtful that, in the summer of 1917, the Corps had envisaged the extent to which salvage operations would grow. Initially, the Corps directed its efforts to making repairs. The wear and tear on clothing and shoes in the training areas led to the development of a repair program as a means of extending the life of these articles and thereby reducing the amount of tonnage required for Class 1 supplies. General Headquarters directed the Corps to organize shops for the repair of clothing and to provide each supply company with half-soling machines for the repair of shoes.[84] This method of shoe repair by small shops operated by supply companies prove ineffective, and, within less than a month, General Headquarters directed the Chief Quartermaster to establish shoe repair shops on a scale suitable for handling all the repair work necessary in the Army.[85]

---

[81] RG 92, OQMG Historical Files, Box 75 (CQM Report, p. 88).

[82] (1) *War Department General Orders, 1917*, GO 89, 11 Jul 1917. (2) *U.S. Army in the World War, 1917–19*, XVI, 49 (Hq AEF GO 16, 19 Jul 1917).

[83] RG 120, AEF SOS Historical Files, G-4, Box 129 (Rpt, Col. D. E. McCarthy to TAG, 6 Mar 1920).

[84] *U.S. Army in the World War, 1917–19*, XVI, 56 (Hq AEF GO 23, 20 Aug 1917).

[85] *Ibid.,* XVI, 77 (Hq AEF GO 38, 17 Sep 1917).

The rapid accumulation of clothing and equipment requiring repairs in the fall of 1917 caused Chief Quartermaster Rogers to initiate a further study of the problem. In consequence, Headquarters, A.E.F., established a Salvage Service, attaching it to the Quartermaster Corps.[86] It had become obvious that salvage operations would have to be developed as a centralized, well-controlled activity. As set up, the Salvage Service collected and repaired all Quartermaster articles as well as those that were common to several departments and therefore required similar equipment and labor for their repair. This partial centralization of salvage operations prevented unnecessary duplication of repair facilities. Salvage operations for those articles pertaining only to one department were handled by the supply department having responsibility for the article.

General Headquarters designated an officer as Chief of Salvage Service, Line of Communications, and assigned him as assistant to the Chief Quartermaster, Line of Communications. It also detailed one officer for each army to serve as Chief of the Army Salvage Service and assistant to the Chief Quartermaster of the army. He had direct control of all Salvage Service personnel in the army area.

Salvage operations extended from base depots to front-line trenches. Salvage squads collected abandoned material from battlefields. Pioneer Infantry and Labor Battalions of the Corps assisted them in this work, and, following heavy offensives, commanders also detailed line troops to help recover abandoned material. Salvage squads deposited such material at dumps and salvage officers then had it transported to railheads where the material was sorted into classes. Salvage officers had serviceable articles delivered at once to supply officers for immediate re-issue to troops. They shipped unserviceable articles to the rear. Those of a highly technical nature, they sent to the depot of the appropriate supply service for repair. Those articles in general use throughout the Army and all unserviceable Quartermaster items, they shipped to Quartermaster salvage depots.

Both shops and depots repaired unserviceable material. Shops served local troops and were located at certain base ports and troop centers. In most instances, articles of clothing repaired at shops were returned to their original wearers. Depots handled the unserviceable material recovered at the front, as well as large amounts of clothing and other material sent from training areas. At the salvage depots, clothing was disinfected, laundered, repaired, and then sent to general supply depots for re-issue.

[86] (1) *Ibid.*, XVI, 168–71 (Hq AEF GO 10, 16 Jan 1918). (2) RG 92, OQMG Historical Files, Box 75 (CQM Report, pp. 26–27).

SACK AND TENT DEPARTMENT, SALVAGE DEPOT, ST. PIERRE-DES-CORPS

The first Salvage Service depot established was opened, on 13 January 1918, at St. Pierre-des-Corps, a suburb of Tours. Salvage operations expanded so rapidly that 11 months later the Salvage Service was operating 4 depots, 20 shops, 66 laundries, and 77 disinfectors.[87] It employed a large number of refugees at the salvage depots. By the time the armistice was signed, salvage work at St. Pierre-des-Corps was being done by 730 men and 5,300 women under the direction of 26 officers and 45 enlisted men.[88]

Salvage savings were impressive. During the month of September 1918, the Salvage Service depots and shops reclaimed for re-issue more than 2,600,000 articles of clothing and equipment valued at over $7,250,000. This was in addition to the large amount of servicable material collected on the battlefield during that month, valued at $8 million and turned over to supply officers for immediate re-issue.[89] The

[87] RG 92, OQMG Historical Files, Box 75 (CQM Report, p. 297).
[88] *Ibid.*, p. 311.
[89] *Ibid.*, p. 310.

HARNESS DEPARTMENT, SALVAGE DEPOT, ST. PIERRE-DES-CORPS

Salvage Service made additional savings by using the waste products of the kitchens. It sold or converted these waste products into soap for laundries and hospitals, into dubbin for waterproofing shoes, and into fertilizer, glycerine, and other products of commercial value. The disposal by sale of articles that could not be repaired and of waste products that could not be converted to Army use added other savings.

Laundry Operations

The development of salvage service facilities included such extensive laundry operations for sterilizing garments that all laundry functions eventually came under the control of the Salvage Service. Under authorization of General Headquarters, the Quartermaster Corps provided and operated laundries to do such laundry work without charge as was essential for troops in the zone of the advance and for patients and operating personnel in hospitals.[90]   No laundry work, however, was performed for troops not serving in the zone of the advance.

At no time during the war were adequate laundry facilities available for combat troops.   By cable in November 1917, Pershing had requested that one mobile laundry be furnished each division embarking for France. Only four mobile laundry units arrived at Bordeaux between 5 July and 22 August 1918; ten more arrived at Marseille in November after the armistice was signed.   The Chief of the Salvage Service criticized the inadequate facilities provided for washing the clothes of men who were actually in the front lines when, at the same time, newspaper accounts were extolling the amout of work turned out by mobile laundries that had been erected in the various training camps in the United States.[91] Insufficient facilities for laundering clothes resulted in an extensive amount of lice infestation among the troops.   Inspection reports showed that until the armistice was signed, 90 percent of the troops at the front were in verminous condition.[92]

Baths and Disinfesting Plants

Hot baths for the men, disinfestation of their uniforms, and issue of clean underclothing were the basic essentials in controlling this problem.   By directive, in the spring of 1918, the Quartermaster Corps assumed responsibility for establishing bathing and disinfecting plants for troops operating in the zone of the advance.[93]   Except during 2 months after the close of the war, when this responsibility was vested in a separate division of the Office of the Chief Quartermaster, A.E.F., it was a branch function of the Salvage Service.

Quartermaster Corps personnel in the field operated portable bathing units and mobile delousers, both horse-drawn and steam-driven.   After the armistice, the Corps systematically built stationary bathing and disinfecting plants at base ports and in embarkation areas.   All disinfecting activities were carried on through the Quartermaster Corps.   A large part of the personnel performing the work, however, belonged to the Medical Department but was attached to the Corps.   Some 2 weeks after the armistice, General Headquarters detailed Col. H. L. Gilchrist of the Medical Department for duty under the direction of the Chief Quartermaster and placed him in charge of all delousing activities in the Army.

---

[90] *U.S. Army in the World War, 1917–19,* XVI, 175 (Hq AEF GO 13, 21 Jan 1918).
[91] RG 92, OQMG, Gen. H. L. Rogers Private File, Box 24 (Memo, Col. T. B. Hacker for Col. A. M. Davis, 4 Dec 1918).
[92] RG 92, OQMG Historical Files, Box 75 (CQM Report, p. 383).
[93] Hq SOS Bulletin 12, 20 May 1918.

At the same time, it also attached to the Quartermaster Corps the equipment and personnel of the degassing service of the Chemical Warfare Service. Used to provide hot baths for men who had been subjected to mustard gas, this service was no longer needed after 11 November 1918. Since the demustardization process was similar to that of bathing and delousing, the equipment and personnel of the degassing service could be usefully employed in the Quartermaster program.[94] So effectively had the process of bathing and delousing been carried out that, 6 weeks after Colonel Gilchrist's assignment, the lice-infestation dropped from 90 percent to less than 3 percent.[95]

Wagons and Harness

The developments analyzed in reference to procurement, storage, and distribution emphasize the reshaping of the Corps in the theater into a supply agency. These developments were in harmony with those that had also made the Corps in the zone of the interior primarily a supply agency. World War I marked the last exercise of that broad responsibility for the transportation of men and supplies that had been the basic function of the Quartermaster General since 1775. In the complexities of modern war, Army transportation became too large an enterprise to remain a sub-service of a supply agency. Both rail and water transportation for the A.E.F. in France were placed under the control of a Director General of Transportation before the end of 1917. Responsibility for the motor transport service was also removed from the Corps early in 1918.[96] Such responsibility for transportation as remained with the Chief Quartermaster, A.E.F., during the war was limited to the provision of vehicles and animal transportation used by the combat units. The Animal Drawn Transportation Branch in the Chief Quartermaster's office provided all vehicles and harness; the Remount Service purchased all public animals used in the A.E.F.

At the beginning of the war, vehicles and harness were supposed to arrive with organizations as troop property. But since some organizations came unequipped and other combat organizations were, in some cases, detailed for duty in the Services of Supply, a policy was soon established of pooling all vehicles and harness on arrival at the base ports. These

---

[94] *U.S. Army in the World War, 1917–19*, XVI, 547 (Hq AEF GO 216, 26 Nov 1918).

[95] RG 92, OQMG Historical Files, Box 75 (CQM Report, p. 388).

[96] See *supra*, p. 650.

MOVING SUPPLIES TO THE FRONT, 1 OCTOBER 1918

pooled supplies were held at the disposition of the Animal Drawn Transportation Branch to insure distribution on the priority basis desired.[97]

Requisitioned quantities of vehicles and harness failed to arrive on time, and the Branch had to purchase a considerable amount of such supplies from the French and British.[98]   Deliveries from these sources were slow, undoubtedly made more so by the inadequacies of railroad transportation.   Even more difficulty was experienced in obtaining a stock of spare parts for the repair of vehicles.   It was usually necessary, in the early months of the war, to obtain parts by taking them from completed vehicles.   In consequence, depots were top heavy with the less expendable items, a condition that was being rapidly improved by the

[97] RG 92, OQMG, Gen. H. L. Rogers Private File, Box 5 (History of the Animal Drawn Transportation Branch, 6 Dec 1918).

[98] From the French, the Branch purchased 2,000 chariots de parc, 4,039 ration or tool carts, 430 water carts, 190 medical wagons, 3,399 fourgon wagons, and 164,119 single sets of harness. Purchases from the British consisted of 2,090 general service wagons, 1,320 water carts, and 826 single sets of harness. *Ibid.*

time the Quartermaster Corps was successful in meeting the demands made upon it for vehicles.

Remount Service

Far more difficult was the task of the Remount Service in providing horses and mules for the A.E.F.   Pershing called supply of animals during the height of operations "one of the biggest, if not the biggest problem" in the A.E.F.[99]   The shortage of animals was a serious problem throughout the war.

Of the 243,360 animals received by the Army during the war, only 67,725 were sent from the United States.[100]   The supply of animals in the United States was ample but shipping space was not.   The first animals to reach France, in July 1917, arrived in the same convoy with the troops to which they were to be assigned, but the shipment of animals with troops was later discontinued.   The shortage of shipping and a French supply offer led Pershing to recommend that no more animals be shipped from the United States.   The inability of the French government to carry out its offer of 7,000 animals a month, however, resulted in a resumption of shipment from the United States in November 1917. Animals continued to be sent until April 1918 when priority of shipping had to be given to troops, food, supplies, and munitions.   Shipment of animals from the United States was not resumed until September 1918 and then the number fell far short of what was required.

In the meantime, the shortage of animals grew increasingly critical. By the end of August 1918, it amounted to 72,000 animals.   In an effort to bring some measure of relief, it was proposed to motorize a number of units, especially artillery brigades, and to reduce the animal allowance to each combat division from 6,719 to 3,803.   Even when put into effect, this proposal would by no means have eliminated the shortage.   On three separate occasions during 1918, the French army came to the aid of the A.E.F. by turning over animals directly to American combat troops so that the full effect of American arms might be felt.   One such occasion occurred in the fall of 1918 when, after the St. Mihiel salient had been wiped out, Marshal Foch ordered 13,000 animals turned over to the

---

[99] RG 92, OQMG, Gen. H. L. Rogers Private File, Box 76 (Pershing to Chief, Remount Service, 29 Mar 1919).

[100] Of these 67,725 animals, 5,938 were cavalry horses, 32,835 were draft horses, 28,399 were draft mules, and 533 were pack mules. "Operations of the Quartermaster Corps, U.S. Army During the World War: Report of Remount Service, A.E.F." (Monograph No. 5, undated, prepared by Quartermaster Corps School, Philadelphia, Pa.), pp. 1, 94.

U.S. Army to enable it to swing around and immediately begin the Argonne offensive.[101]

The British government also furnished animals for the A.E.F. It offered to equip the divisions that were to train in the British area and by agreement supplied ten divisions. To reduce the animal shortage, the Quartermaster Corps also developed a plan to procure horses and mules in Spain. It made purchases despite the German influence brought to bear to prevent sales and the difficulties encountered in obtaining transportation for the animals to France. Of the 243,360 animals received by the A.E.F. in France, the Corps purchased 135,914 from the French, 21,259 from the British, and 18,462 from the Spanish.[102]

Though the Remount Service in the A.E.F. was not officially established until September 1917, remount work began from the time Chief Quartermaster McCarthy opened his office in Paris.[103] In June, one officer and clerk had charge of remount work, but, by 31 December 1918, personnel of the Remount Service had increased until it numbered 493 officers and 14,596 enlisted men. Their duties included not only the purchase of animals and the administration of Remount depots, but also the care, conditioning, training, and maintenance of animals. For this purpose, the Service had Remount squadrons on duty with the three Armies as well as Army, corps, and division Remount officers. Despite the handicaps under which the Remount Service operated—lack of proper installations, insufficient personnel, inadequate transportation facilities, and other hampering restrictions—its operations were effective enough to win Pershing's commendation.[104]

Clothing Changes

Supply operations constituted a major part of Quartermaster activities in the theater, but no account of such activities would be complete without illustrating the effects that the impact of war—that is, the changed methods of warfare and the employment of new instruments of defense and attack—had upon the most important Quartermaster items of supply furnished the soldier. These were his clothing and his rations.

The uniform that clothed the American soldier in 1917 had been developed to meet the needs of a peacetime Army, but it was found to be unsatisfactory in many respects for wartime operations. No one article of that uniform was more completely unsuited to the needs of the

---

[101] (1) *Ibid.,* p. 23.   (2) RG 92, OQMG Historical Files, Box 75 (CQM Report, pp. 345–46). (3) *Final Report of Gen. John J. Pershing,* pp. 70–71.

[102] RG 92, OQMG Historical Files, Box 75 (CQM Report, p. 354).

[103] *U.S. Army in the World War, 1917–19,* XVI, 78 (Hq AEF GO 39, 18 Sep 1917).

[104] RG 92, OQMG, Gen. H. L. Rogers Private File, Box 76 (Pershing to Col. Frank S. Armstrong, 29 Mar 1919).

troops engaged in trench warfare than the campaign hat that had been designed to afford protection against the sun on western plains.   As early as June 1917, the Chief Quartermaster recommended the adoption of a soft cap.   He contracted for and French firms produced large quantities of overseas caps, the material being furnished by the Quartermaster Corps.[105]

Early in the war, General Headquarters appointed a board of Quartermaster officers to make recommendations, based on British and French experience, on the type of winter clothing that the troops would need.[106] In consequence, Headquarters authorized rubber boots and arctic overshoes for issue to the troops and sale to officers.   It added to the authorized list of clothing lined leather gloves and one-fingered mittens.[107]   The peacetime shoe that had been recommended by the Munson Board in 1912 gave way to a sturdier field shoe, but it was 12 April 1918 before the War Department adopted a specification for the production of the so-called "Pershing" hobnail boot, a heavier shoe with flesh-out upper leather and a more waterproof construction designed to suit the demands of trench warfare.   General Headquarters also eliminated canvas leggings in favor of woolen spiral puttees in an effort to combat the problem of mud and cleanliness.

When it was found that the weight of the fabric used in the uniform that clothed the troops in the winter of 1917–18 afforded inadequate protection, the War Department approved the recommendations of Chief Quartermaster Rogers to substitute 20 oz. for 16 oz. melton used in the uniform and 32 oz. for 30 oz. melton used in the overcoats.   It also authorized an increase in the weight of flannel shirting and of woolen underclothing.[108]

Rations

Trench warfare and the extensive use of toxic gases soon developed the necessity for providing food that was protected against spoilage by gas and dampness.   The reserve ration, established in prewar days and still carried by the soldier in combat operations in 1917, called for 12 oz. bacon, 16 oz. hard bread, 1.12 oz. coffee, 3.2 oz. sugar, and 0.16 oz. salt.[109] For troops operating in front-line trenches, this ration was unsatisfactory, since cooking was impracticable.

[105] RG 120, AEF Gen Hq, AG File, Folder 414 (1st ind. Col. D. E. McCarthy, 30 Jun 1917 on Rpt, Lt. Col. C. E. Stanton to Col. McCarthy, 29 Jun 1917).

[106] Hq AEF Special Orders No. 23, 1 Jul 1917.

[107] *U.S. Army in the World War, 1917–19*, XVI, 76 (Hq AEF GO 38, 17 Sep 1917).

[108] (1) RG 120, AEF Gen Hq, AG File, Folder 414-A (Memo, Rogers for Chief of Staff, 12 Jan 1918).   (2) RG 165, War College Div. Doc. File, Case 6773–172 (Memo, Acting Chief of Staff for TAG, 6 Feb 1918).

[109] *U.S. Army in the World War, 1917–19*, XVI, 60 (Hq AEF GO 18, 28 Jul 1917).

The Subsistence Branch of the Chief Quartermaster's Office proposed changes that the War Department subsequently approved. The revised reserve ration called for food to be packed in ration-sized amounts. In lieu of bacon, the reserve ration provided for 16 oz. of canned meat (corned beef, fresh roast beef, or corned beef hash) put up in a 1-pound can, or an equivalent amount of canned salmon or sardines, and 16 oz. of hard bread to be packed in two half-pound cans. The ration included the same amount of sugar, salt, and coffee as previously allowed but substituted soluble coffee for the roasted and ground coffee issued in the past. Utilizing solidified alcohol, the soldier in an advanced position, where the use of fire was prohibited could prepare a cup of coffee.[110] The troops at all times carried a supply of 2 days' reserve rations. Whenever they had consumed these rations, the supply officer replaced them, sending a requisition to the division quartermaster through G–1.

The smaller tins of the individual reserve ration were also assembled and shipped in 25-ration units that were hermetically sealed in galvanized iron containers. These were known as special reserve rations and were supplied in addition to the reserve rations carried by the men. The iron containers were kept in the trenches and used only when other food could not be supplied. The special reserve ration was considered part of the sector equipment and was left in the trenches when a division was relieved. By cable in October 1917, General Pershing ordered the shipment of 2 million reserve rations packed in iron containers. Shipment was to be made at the rate of 100,000 per month. Other orders followed, but not until the early fall of 1918 did the supply of special reserve rations equal the demand. The supply of soluble coffee was never sufficient.[111]

The garrison ration, issued to all troops of the A.E.F. wherever transportation permitted, was not materially changed in its basic components. Working with personnel from the Chief Surgeon's Office, the Chief Quartermaster made some modifications to get the best ration possible for the troops. He introduced a considerable number of substitutive articles, and, in an effort to economize on transportation, the Quartermaster Corps included boneless beef and dehydrated vegetables. Dehydrated vegetables were no more popular with the soldiers of World War I than they had been with those of the Civil War despite the improvements that had been made in their production. General Rogers added tobacco

---

[110] (1) RG 92, OQMG, Gen. H. L. Rogers Private File, Box 6 (Memorandum Statement covering the Organization and Operation of the Subsistence Br, 14 Dec 1918). (2) RG 165, War College Div. Doc. File, Case 9164–12 (Memo, Acting Chief, War College Div, for Chief of Staff, 9 Nov 1917).

[111] RG 92, OQMG, Gen. H. L. Rogers Private File, Box 5 (Memorandum Statement Covering the Organization and Operation of the Subsistence Br, 14 Dec 1918).

UNLOADING STORES OF "CANNED WILLIE" AND "HARDTACK"

to the ration in the summer of 1918 and also provided for the issue of a half pound of candy every 10 days. The issue of both tobacco and candy was much appreciated by the troops in France.[112]

When American troops gained their first experience in trench warfare in October 1917, a need immediately arose for containers in which hot food as well as drinking water could be carried to the men in the trenches from rolling kitchens that had to be kept several miles to the rear. This immediate need was met by using ordinary milk cans of $2\frac{1}{2}$- and 5-gallan capacity. When filled, the can was carried on a pole by two men, or by one man using either a Yukon pack or a Canadian tumpline. Both of these items, used by the British forces, had originated with the Indians and trappers of Alaska and Canada. The Yukon pack

---

[112] (1) For the components of the various rations issued to the A.E.F.—garrison, field, reserve, special reserve, and travel ration—see *U.S. Army in the World War, 1917–19*, XVI, 479–82. (2) *Army Reorganization:* Hearings before the Committee on Military Affairs, 66th Cong., 1st sess., I, 1081–82 (Rogers' testimony).

CARRYING FOOD TO MEN IN TRENCHES

was a strapped bag that permitted a man to carry provisions on his back. The tumpline was a single strap worn across the forehead or breast to assist in carrying a pack upon the back. The Chief Quartermaster, A.E.F., purchased a sufficient supply of Yukon packs and tumplines from the British Expeditionary Forces.[113]

Experience demonstrated that a Thermos-type container was needed to carry hot food to men under fire. The French were using such a 5-gallon container called the "Marmite Norvegienne." The Chief Quartermaster took steps to manufacture the marmites in France for the American Army, but demand exceeded the ability to supply in Europe, and production had to be started in the United States. Each division of

[113] (1) RG 92, OQMG, Gen. H. L. Rogers Private File, Box 76 (Memos, Chief of Staff for CQM, 2 Nov 1917 and 14 Jan 1918). (2) For description and use of the Yukon pack and tumpline, see RG 165, War College Div. Doc. File, Case 7776–5 (Memo, Acting Chief of Staff for TAG, 7 Jan 1918).

the A.E.F. had to be supplied with 1,070 marmites, 200 Yukon packs, and 100 tumplines.[114]

This equipment met the need but did not prove satisfactory, and, early in March 1918, Maj. Gen. R. L. Bullard, commanding the First Division, submitted recommendations to the Commander-in-Chief that called for the development of a 5-gallon marmite can, shaped and fitted with proper shoulder straps to permit it to be carried on a man's back. Adoption of such a can, he argued, would reduce the size of carrying parties, make it easier to get through trenches, and would permit free use of hands to assist the carrier in finding his way through trenches at night. The Corps developed and tested sample Bullard marmites and placed extensive orders for their manufacture, but the armistice stopped operations before any considerable number were turned out.[115] Developmental work had to be carried on in reference to other equipment but this one example suffices to illustrate the problem confronting the Quartermaster Corps.

Summary

In summary, the impact of war made itself felt in modifications of supplies and equipment, in changed Quartermaster functions and operations, and, in consequence, in changes in organization itself. The temporary loss of the functions of transportation and construction in 1917 foreshadowed their permanent loss in 1941. On the other hand, the demands of war led to the evolution of a new function, salvage. From something of "a novelty in military activities," the Salvage Service became "an economic necessity in the repair and avoidable prevention of the waste of war." [116] For the first time in war, the Corps took the field as a militarized organization, bringing to life a concept that had been urged by Quartermaster officers as early as the Mexican War. The number and types of units multiplied rapidly and contributed much to promoting the greater effectiveness of the Corps in war. In consequence, General Hagood could report that "in the matter of supply the operation of the Quartermaster Department in the Great War was not only far superior to anything that we had in any previous war, but, as a rule, throughout the A.E.F. the service was more efficient and more satisfactory to the individual than it had been at home in time of peace." [117]

---

[114] RG 92, OQMG, Gen. H. L. Rogers Private File, Box 76 (Memo, CQM for Capt. Weed, 5 Apr 1920).

[115] *Ibid.*

[116] Harbord, *The American Army in France,* p. 500.

[117] Hagood, *The Services of Supply,* p. 342.

CHAPTER XVI

An Interlude of Peace

The armistice signed on 11 November 1918 halted combat operations, but, while Quartermaster operations both in the zone of the interior and in the A.E.F. were diverted from wartime supply to demobilization, peace did not diminish the Corps' activities. One of these activities, the program for the care of the dead, assumed larger proportions after the armistice than during the months of combat and continued to be of major importance for more than a decade after the war had ended.

Graves Registration Service

Graves registration activities were not new in 1917. They had originated in the Civil War when for the first time the government had assumed the obligation of identifying, when possible, and burying in registered graves the remains of all who died in that war and had created a national cemeterial system for the realization of that purpose.[1] A fundamental principle—the return of remains to their native soil—emerged out of that war. When troops were sent overseas during later wars, that principle was extended to include areas outside the continental limits of the United States. First used in the Spanish-American War, the precedent continued to be applicable to those who died in overseas garrisons in the years preceding World War I and had a far broader application in that war.[2]

If the activities were not new, the organization of the Graves Registration Service into units according to definite Tables of Organization was accomplished for the first time in the history of the Army in 1917. Such organization was made possible only because the Corps itself had been militarized in 1912. The first recommendation made by Quartermaster General Sharpe to the Secretary of War on 31 May 1917, however,

---

[1] See *ante* pp. 464–66.

[2] In 1898, Congress by special appropriation had provided funds enabling the Secretary of War, in his discretion, to cause the remains of those killed in action or who died at military camps or at places outside the United States to be brought home. At the request of next to kin, the remains of servicemen could be buried in national cemeteries or returned to their homes for private burial. (1) 30 *Stat.* 730, Act of Jul 8, 1898. (2) *Annual Report of the Quartermaster General, 1898,* pp. 23–24.

had called for the organization of a burial corps of civilians. Approximately a month later, at the direction of the Chief of Staff, a board of Quartermaster officers was convened to formulate plans for a militarized formation. It was 7 August 1917 before the Chief of Staff and the Secretary of War approved these plans for the organization of graves registration units. Each unit was to consist of two commissioned officers and 50 enlisted men, suitably graded.[3]

At the request of General Sharpe, Chaplain Charles C. Pierce, U.S.A., retired, who had organized and conducted graves registration work in the Philippine Islands after the Spanish-American War, undertook similar activities in 1917. He was recalled to active duty on 31 May 1917 and commissioned a major (later colonel) in the Quartermaster Corps.[4] Major Pierce participated in the planning for the Graves Registration Service, recruited men for the four authorized units, and made arrangements for their preparatory training. When, on 2 August, General Pershing cabled for a general superintendent for all American cemeteries to be established in Europe, the War Department appointed Major Pierce to that post and also named him chief of the Graves Registration Service on 27 September 1917. He and the First Graves Registration unit, however, did not reach France until 31 October.[5]

The delay in planning for and dispatching units of the Graves Registration Service had permitted a separate line of development to be followed in the A.E.F. In France, the Chief Quartermaster had promptly gathered information on Allied experience in caring for their dead, and, on 29 August, Headquarters, A.E.F., had established its organization, known as the Burial Department, under the direction of the Chief Quartermaster.[6] After Major Pierce arrived in France, he prepared regulations for merging the Graves Registration Service and the A.E.F. Burial Department.

Some difficulties had to be resolved, since the original plan had made provision for the Graves Registration Service to bury the dead. General Pershing maintained that the "dead at the front must necessarily be

---

[3] (1) *War Department General Orders, 1917*, GO 104, 7 Aug 1917. (2) RG 94, AGO General Correspondence File, Box 672, File 322.052 GRS (Memo, Capt. H. R. Lemly for QMG, 20 Jul 1917).

[4] (1) RG 94, AGO, 1242 ACP 80 (Special Orders 125, 31 May 1917). (2) Chaplain Pierce had established and directed the U.S. Army Morgue and Office of Identification at Manila. For more details on this activity, see, Edward Steere, *The Graves Registration Service in World War II*, QMC HISTORICAL STUDIES No. 21 (GPO, 1951), pp. 10–11.

[5] (1) RG 92, OQMG General Correspondence File, 1917–22, Box 4909, File 320 GRS (Capt. H. R. Lemly to Administration Div, 9 Aug 1917). (2) *Ibid.*, (Cable, Pershing to TAG, 2 Aug 1917). (3) *Ibid.*, (Pierce to Capt. Lemley, 21 Nov 1917). (4) RG 92, OQMG Historical Records, Box 75 (Historical Report, Chief QM, 1917–19, p. 415).

[6] *U.S. Army in the World War, 1917–19*, XVI, 62 (Hq AEF GO 27, 29 Aug 1917).

buried by units themselves." [7]   In any case, the personnel strength of the Graves Registration Service was barely sufficient to locate and register the graves after the burials had been made.   Regulations therefore continued to place responsibility for burials on burial officers and on details of enlisted men selected by commanding officers of the divisions and corps.   Regulations required the burial officers to report all burials and grave locations to the chief of the Graves Registration Service for the purpose of recording and taking charge of burial places.

The Commanding General also objected to the proposed shipment of caskets and burial equipment as "impracticable."   Quartermaster General Sharpe, on 31 May 1917, had taken a similar view, recommending that "the bodies of our soldiers who die in Europe be interred there and no attempt made to bring them back until after the close of hostilities." [8] Any program for the return of the dead was therefore deferred.   In uniting the Graves Registration Service and the A.E.F. Burial Department, Major Pierce also combined the methods of operation evolved by the British and French governments earlier in the war with those that the Army had used in the Philippines.   Headquarters published governing regulations for the Service on 15 February 1918. [9]

These regulations made the Graves Registration Service responsible for deploying units and groups along the line of battle.   When hostilities began in any given sector, such units and groups could immediately start their work of identifying bodies and marking graves.   Under battlefield conditions, burial details frequently had to make hurried interments in undesirable locations.   Nor was there any surety that, in the midst of an advance or heavy fighting, instructions would be so perfectly executed that identities would be preserved.   Graves Registration units, following closely after the combat troops, registered and verified the temporary markings of graves, searched for bodies that had been inadequately interred, as well as those that had been overlooked, and re-interred and concentrated them in properly located cemeteries.   In addition to this basic function, the Graves Registration Service also kept accurate and complete records on the location and identification of graves of all officers and soldiers of the A.E.F. and all civilians attached to it; located and acquired all necessary cemeteries for American use; maintained and controlled the cemeteries; and compiled a registry of all burials.

The Graves Registration units began their work in March 1918.

[7] (1) RG 92, OQMG General Correspondence File, 1917–22, Box 4909, File 320 GRS (Cable, Pershing to Chief of Staff, 31 Dec 1917). (2) *Ibid.,* (Pierce to Lemly, 21 Nov 1917).

[8] RG 94, AGO General Correspondence File, Box 672, File 322.052 GRS (Memo, Capt. H. R. Lemly for QMG, 20 Jul 1917).

[9] *U.S. Army in the World War, 1917–19,* XVI, 211–13 (Hq AEF GO 30, 15 Feb 1918).

At that time, the Service consisted of 4 units, a total of 8 officers and 200 men. When the armistice was signed, there were 18 units, of which 5 were provisional units that had been organized in France, comprising a maximum strength of 49 officers and 872 men.[10] The Graves Registration Service also employed large numbers of labor troops and clerical personnel.

After the armistice, the work of concentration and maintenance became of primary importance. There were more than 2,300 military cemeteries under the control of the Graves Registration Service.[11] They were scattered all over France, from the historic battlefields of Chateau-Thierry and the Argonne to the base ports on the Atlantic Coast. In addition, there were burial grounds in England, Italy, and Belgium, some in Germany, and even a few in the Murmansk region on the shores of the Arctic Ocean in northern Russia.

Of the 70,000 burials in France, approximately 15,000 were in isolated graves. In compliance with the wishes of the French Government to assemble in large cemeteries as many isolated burials as possible, and until the ultimate policy of the United States was announced, General Headquarters, A.E.F., instructed the Graves Registration Service on 13 November 1918 to begin a recheck of all graves in France. The Graves Registration Service accordingly made concentrations in central cemeteries that were established in the forward areas where American troops had fought, though it undertook no concentrations in the rear areas and base sections.[12] The first and largest of these was the Argonne Cemetery at Romagne. In all, the Graves Registration established 15 such concentration cemeteries in the battle areas.

The Service had by no means completed the work of recovery and concentration of remains by the summer of 1919, but, with the intent of putting this phase of the operation on a maintenance basis, the Commanding General, SOS, directed the Graves Registration Service to complete its activities in the Advance Section by 1 July. The work of the graves registration companies thus came to an end. Colonel Pierce and his staff returned to Washington, where the office of the Chief of the Graves Registration Service was established as a branch of the General Administrative Division and subsequently, by consolidation with the Cemeterial Branch in 1920, it emerged as a separate Cemeterial Division in the Office of the Quartermaster General.[13]

[10] RG 92, OQMG Historical Records, Box 75 (Historical Rpt, CQM, 1917–19, p. 416).

[11] *Ibid.,* p. 418.

[12] "The Work of the American Graves Registration Service," Documentary Supplement, Doc. 3 (Memo, Office of Chief, GRS, for CG, SOS, AEF, 24 Jul 1919). Typescript study on file, Office, QM Historian.

[13] RG 92, OQMG General Correspondence File, 1917–22, Box 233 (Memo, Col. W. C. Jones

Program for the Return of the Dead

Based on past precedent, the War Department was committed to the policy of bringing home its soldier dead from Europe, though not before the end of the war. It was 6 October 1919 before the War Department formally announced its policy in a letter to the Quartermaster General. By that directive, all remains of American soldiers in Great Britain, Belgium, and Italy were to be returned to the United States unless the nearest relatives made a request for their permanent burial in the military cemeteries located in those countries. On the other hand, no remains of American soldiers were to be left in Germany, Luxemburg, and north Russia, regardless of requests made. All remains in France—and most were located there—were to be returned, but only on specific request of the nearest relatives.[14]

The possibility that such a policy would be pursued had resulted in a considerable amount of public discussion and even controversy after the armistice. The War Department resolved this problem by permitting the nearest next of kin of each dead soldier to decide, on the basis of a questionnaire sent out by The Adjutant General's office, whether the body should remain in one of the overseas military cemeteries or be returned to the United States for burial.[15] The Quartermaster General recognized that a special organization would be needed to handle the specific problems of exhumation, shipment, and concentration of remaining bodies. On 24 October 1919, he submitted a tentative plan of organization that, with some slight modifications, met with approval by the Secretary of War.[16] In short, it reconstituted the Graves Registration Service, Q.M.C., in Europe, and charged it with responsibility for the disinterment abroad and the repatriation of the dead. The plan also provided for the establishment by the Corps of an office at Hoboken, responsible for the shipment and transportation of the dead. The entire operation remained under the direct supervision of the Cemeterial Division of the Office of the Quartermaster General.

Despite the announcement of policy and the establishment of the necessary administrative organization in 1919, the repatriation program did not begin until the following year. Lengthy discussions were entailed in making arrangements with the governments of the countries in which

for QMG, Director of P&S, 7 Feb 1920; sub: Report on Graves Registration Service); (P&S Notice 43, 26 Feb 1920, sub: Organization of Cemeterial Division).

[14] *Annual Report of the Quartermaster General, 1920*, p. 59.

[15] RG 92, AGO Records, File 319.12 (Annual Report of the Quartermaster General, 1921, p. 45).

[16] "History of the American Graves Registration Service, Q.M.C., in Europe," I, 56–57. (3-volume, typescript study on file in Office, QM Historian).

the dead were temporarily buried.   France did not authorize removals from the Zone of the Armies, where most of the remains were located, until 15 September 1920.[17] After October, the work moved forward without interruption.

By the end of fiscal year 1922, most of the dead, whose return had been authorized by next of kin, had been brought to the United States. The repatriation program was officially ended with the arrival at New York of the transport *Cambria* on 30 March 1922.[18] For many years after that date, however, bodies continued to be shipped to the United States as search located them and the process of identification reduced the number of unknowns.   In all, more than 46,000 remains were returned for burial in the United States.[19]

To honor all American soldiers who gave their lives in the war and in recognition of the unidentified dead, the body of one unknown soldier was selected with fitting ceremony from among those in France, returned to the United States, and buried with extraordinary honors in the Arlington National Cemetery on 11 November 1921.[20] A decade later, after much careful planning, the Tomb of the Unknown Soldier was completed.

Establishment of Overseas Military Cemeteries

The work of concentration after the armistice had reduced the number of burial places from 2,300 to approximately 700.   The cost of maintaining even that number would have been excessive, so the War Department decided that, after shipment of the bodies authorized for return to the United States had been accomplished, those that remained would be interred in a few permanent military cemeteries, designed as memorials to those who gave their lives for their country.[21]   A considerable amount of preliminary planning eventually led to a decision to establish eight permanent cemeteries, of which six were to be in France, one in England, and one in Belgium.[22]   More than 30,000 American

[17] RG 94, AGO Records, File 319.12 (Annual Report of the Quartermaster General, 1921, p. 45).

[18] RG 92, OQMG General Correspondence File, 1917–22, File 293.1 (Europe, I) (Memo, QMG for SW, 9 Mar 1922).

[19] RG 94, AGO Records, File 319.12 (Annual Report of the Quartermaster General, 1924, p. 27; 1925, p. 31).

[20] (1) *Ibid.*, 1922, p. 22. (2) 42 *Stat.* 211 (Public Resolution, Nov 4, 1921). (2) "Arlington National Cemetery," *The Quartermaster Review*, (May–June 1937), pp. 33; 66.

[21] "The Work of the American Graves Registration Service," Documentary Supplement, Doc. 15 (Rpt, Chief, American Graves Registration Service, QMC, in Europe, to TQMG, 4 Feb 1926).

[22] The cemeteries are Brookwood in England, Flanders Field in Belgium, and Aisne-Marne, Meuse-Argonne, Oise-Aisne, Somme, St. Mihiel, and Suresnes in France.

soldiers, representing about 40 percent of those who lost their lives in the war, were buried in these cemeteries.

Under congressional authorization, the American Graves Registration Service, Q.M.C., in Europe, purchased the necessary real estate for establishing the cemeteries or acquired rights of burial in perpetuity.[23] Construction quartermasters, under the supervision of the Graves Registration Service, carried out all construction work and improvements. Placing grave markers in the cemeteries was handled as a separate project. The proposed use of marble slab-type markers for graves in the national cemeteries aroused opposition from those who were impressed by the simple white wooden crosses and the Star of David that had been erected as temporary markers in the overseas cemeteries. The Secretary of War bowed to the sentiment that favored their retention and, on 17 December 1924, approved adoption of these two types of headstones for the military cemeteries. By the end of fiscal year 1929, the Service had erected headstones at all graves.[24]

In 1923, Congress established the American Battle Monuments Commission, an organization entirely independent of the War Department. It made the Commission responsible for the erection of war memorials and for the beautification of the military cemeteries in Europe.[25] The more economy-minded Graves Registration Service disapproved of the Commission's elaborate plans. Under the terms of the law, the entire care and responsibility of the grounds, as well as of the monuments and memorials erected, were to revert to the Quartermaster Corps when the duties of the Commission terminated. As the work of the Commission neared completion in 1932, and the Corps prepared to assume this responsibility, the President, by Executive Order, directed that, effective 21 May 1932, the maintenance of memorials and the administration of the overseas military cemeteries were to be transferred to the American Battle Monuments Commission.[26] Though the question of re-transfer of responsibility to the Corps was raised later, no action was taken and Quartermaster responsibility for the miiltary cemeteries in Europe terminated in 1934.

Pilgrimage of the Gold Star Mothers

The Graves Registration Service managed one other important project, namely, the pilgrimages of the Gold Star Mothers to the overseas

[23] 42 *Stat.* 490 (Act of Apr 1, 1922); 42 *Stat.* 1162 (Act of Jan 22, 1923).

[24] RG 94, AGO Records, File 319.12 (Annual Report of The Quartermaster General, 1929, p. 60).

[25] 42 *Stat.* 1509 (Act of Mar 4, 1923).

[26] Executive Order 6614 (Feb 26, 1934) as amended by Executive Order 6690 (Apr 25, 1934).

military cemeteries. Though such a project had been advocated in the
midst of the controversy over permanent burial abroad or repatriation,
it was 1929 before Congress enacted legislation authorizing the Secretary
of War to arrange for pilgrimages to the European cemeteries "by mothers
and widows of members of the military and naval forces of the United
States who died in the service at any time between April 5, 1917 and
July 1, 1921, and whose remains are now interred in such cemeteries." [27]
These pilgrimages, paid for by the United States, were to be made at
such times as the Secretary of War designated between May 1, 1930, and
October 31, 1933. By subsequent amendment, Congress extended eligi-
bility for pilgrimages to mothers and widows of men who had died and
were buried at sea, or who died at sea or overseas and whose places of
burial were unknown.[28]

The Secretary of War delegated all responsibility for planning and
managing the pilgrimages to The Quartermaster General.[29] The cemeterial Division in the Office of The Quartermaster General retained
responsibility for supervising and co-ordinating all activities connected
with the pilgrimages. It determined the number of mothers and widows
entitled to make the pilgrimage and the costs of the undertaking. It
submitted estimates for funds to Congress. The Quartermaster General
decentralized operation of the plan to offices established in New York
and Paris. Quartermasters at a New York port of embarkation were
charged with all details relative to meeting the mothers and widows on
arrival in New York, and with providing suitable accommodations during
their sojourn in New York and en route to and from Europe. The Chief,
American Graves Registration Service in Europe, handled all matters
connected with the pilgrimage, from the arrival of the mothers and
widows at the port of debarkation in Europe until their departure for the
United States.[30]

The Office of The Quartermaster General determined that 17,389
women were entitled to the benefits of the legislation enacted by Congress.
Of this number, 3,653 made pilgrimages during the calendar year 1930,
the largest number for any year of the project.[31] The following year,
only 1,784 indicated their intention of going. Before the project ended
with the arrival in New York, on 24 August 1933, of the steamship

[27] 45 *Stat.* 1508 (Act, Mar 2, 1929).

[28] 46 *Stat.* 334 (Act, May 15, 1930).

[29] By general order, the title of the chief of the Quartermaster Corps was changed to
read The Quartermaster General after 31 January 1924. *War Department General Orders,*
GO 2.

[30] RG 94, AGO Records, file 319.1 (Annual Report of The Quartermaster General, Fiscal
Year 1930, pp. 15–17).

[31] *Ibid.,* Fiscal Year 1931, p. 36.

Washington, carrying the last of the Gold Star Mothers, a total of 6,693 had visited the European cemeteries.   With the closing of the New York and Paris offices on 31 October 1933, Quartermaster Corps responsibility for the pilgrimages came to an end.

Quartermaster Re-embarkation Duties

Long before the Corps relinquished its responsibility for maintaining military cemeteries overseas, Quartermaster activities in demobilizing men and supplies in the A.E.F. came to an end.   The joyous celebration that marked the signing of the armistice brought only a temporary interruption in the wartime pace of Quartermaster operations in the A.E.F. The thoughts of the soldiers quickly turned to home, and whereas since June 1917 the stream of men and supplies had moved from base ports to the front, the current after November had to be reversed.   The War Department assigned most of the duties in connection with the reembarkation of the troops to the Quartermaster Corps.   These included reclothing and re-equipping the troops, providing them with bathing and delousing facilities at embarkation centers, caring for and feeding them at the great embarkation camps, looking after their baggage, paying them, and, just before they marched aboard the transports, exchanging their francs for dollars.

Brest, Bordeaux, and St. Nazaire were converted from ports of debarkation to ports of embarkation, and nearly all American troops returning to the United States passed through one of these three ports. Embarkation camps were built near these three bases to take care of Army units smaller than a division.   The outfitting, equipping, and inspecting of divisions took place at Le Mans.   Designated as an embarkation center on 14 December 1918, Le Mans functioned as such until late in the spring of 1919.   By that time, the majority of the 2 million soldiers in the A.E.F. had started home, and the remainder, mostly in the Army of Occupation, could be cared for in the embarkation camps at the base ports.   Embarkation operations ceased at Bordeaux on 30 June, and at St. Nazaire on 26 July 1919.   Brest continued operations until the last American departed for home.   Between 11 November 1918 and the first week of October 1919, 1,063,936 American soldiers sailed from Brest.   At the end of August, General Pershing had embarked with the First Division, and, by October 1919, the A.E.F. had ceased to exist.   The few remaining troops were designated simply as the American Forces in France.[32]

---

[32] For details on how Quartermaster duties in reference to embarkation were carried out, see RG 120, W.D. Historical Files, Box 165-I ("Brief History of QM and Purchase and Storage Demobilization Activities").

Disposal of War Matériel

The cessation of hostilities also posed other problems. On 11 November 1918, the Quartermaster Corps, as well as the other supply services of the A.E.F., had on hand many months' supply of reserve stocks of all kinds of war matériel. In addition, the Corps had innumerable contracts outstanding for all types of supplies, deliveries of which were to be made months ahead to support the campaigns of the spring and summer of 1919 that had been projected before the armistice. Shipments from the United States of supplies that were surplus were stopped at once. Three days after the armistice, Headquarters, SOS, issued an order authorizing the cancellation of contracts, the termination of the purchase of supplies, and the cessation of construction work.[33]

Since practically all Quartermaster material obtained in Europe had been bought by the Chief Purchasing Office, Q.M.C., A.E.F., its disposal was, logically also made his responsibility. In addition to his other duties, he was designated as Chief Sales Officer, Q.M.C., A.E.F. When, on 17 December 1918, Headquarters, SOS, appointed a General Sales Agent to have charge of all sales of surplus Army stocks in Europe, the Chief Sales Officer, Q.M.C., became the Corps' representative on the General Sales Board. Brig. Gen. C. R. Krauthoff of the Quartermaster Corps was appointed General Sales Agent.[34]

Supplementing the work of the General Sales Board, but in no way superseding or interfering with the regular Army organization, was the U.S. Liquidation Commission, created by the War Department on 11February 1919. Established as the central agency to facilitate disposition of all claims against the United States and to dispose of all property belonging to the United States that was acquired in connection with the war and outside the territorial limits of the United States, the Liquidation Commission began work in Europe early in March 1919.[35] Both the General Sales Agent and the Liquidation Commission acted in advisory capacities, co-ordinating the work of disposing of surplus stocks and liquidating accounts.

Long before the General Sales Board was organized, the Quartermaster Corps began disposing of surplus articles. Quartermasters at once inventoried warehouse stocks after 11 November, and, except for a small amount of new blankets and clothing which were returned to the

[33] (1) Hq SOS GO 54, 14 Nov 1918. (2) RG 92, OQMG Historical Records, Box 75 (Historical Rpt, CQM, AEF, 1917–19, p. 529).
[34] RG 92, OQMG Historical Records, Box 75 (Historical Rpt, CQM, AEF, 1917–19, p. 535).
[35] (1) WD GO 24, 11 Feb 1919. (2) March, *The Nation at War*, p. 178.

United States, the Corps disposed of practically all surplus Quartermaster supplies in Europe. Since the populations of the wartorn countries of Europe were in dire need of relief, disposal of food stocks, clothing, and other materials presented no problem. The Corps made many of its early sales to relief commissions, among them the American Relief Commission for Belgium and Northern France, headed by Herbert Hoover. It made such sales from list prices plus the cost of transportation. Of the $1,500 million estimated as the value of all supplies in the A.E.F. available for sale, over one-third, or $600 million, of this amount represented the value of Quartermaster stores.[36]

Throughout the spring and early summer of 1919, the Corps continued to make piecemeal sales to European governments, although at the same time the U.S. Liquidation Commission was negotiating with the French government to dispose of, by bulk sale, all remaining Army supplies and installations in France. The latter included Quartermaster refrigerating plants, coffee-roasting plants, and the mechanical bakery at Is-sur-Tille, as well as numerous warehouses and shops. Bulk sale to the French government on reasonable credit was desirable because of the existing world shortage of cash and credit, the impossibility of selling surplus material in France without the payment of duty to and supervision by the French government, the certainty of deterioration, and the opposition that would be aroused by retention of troops in France to guard and handle surplus material. Under the agreement worked out, the French government also assumed all liability for property requisitioned for the A.E.F. and for restoring such property to its original condition.[37] By this agreement, the greater part of the surplus property in France, which was estimated to have cost about $1,125 million, was sold to the French government for $400 million. Sale of surplus property to various other purchasers accounted for almost another $100 million.[38]

In consequence of the agreement, all the great depots and installations of the A.E.F. in France were turned over to the French government in the late summer and fall of 1919. Except for the activities of the Graves Registration Service, Q.M.C., in Europe, and support of the Army of Occupation in Germany, Quartermaster operations overseas came to an end. The last of the Corps, as an organization of the A.E.F. and of the American Forces in France, left that country on 10 January 1920.[39]

---

[36] RG 92, OQMG Historical Records, Box 75 (Historical Rpt, CQM, AEF, 1917–19, p. 539).
[37] *Ibid.*, pp. 550–54.
[38] *Report of the Chief of Staff, 1919* (Washington, 1919), p. 236.
[39] RG 120, W.D. Historical Files, Box 165-I ("Brief History of QM and Purchase and Storage Demobilization Activities," pp. 53–54).

Industrial Demobilization

In the United States, similar problems of troop demobilization, contract termination, and disposal of surplus war matériel confronted the Secretary of War. The War Department was still in the process of reorganization, and, at the time the armistice was signed, the complete absorption of the divisions of the Office of the Quartermaster General in the Purchase and Storage Division of the Purchase, Storage and Traffic Division was being accomplished.[40] Preoccupied with problems of reorganization and the acceleration of production necessary for winning the war, the Purchase, Storage and Traffic Division had drafted no long-range plans and had made no preparations for easing the impact of demobilization on the economy of the country. The United States was as unprepared for industrial demobilization in November 1918 as it had been for mobilization in April 1917. The need for such planning was a lesson subsequently drawn from the economic dislocation that followed World War I.

When the war ended, the Office of the Director of Purchase and Storage had an immense quantity of supplies on hand, and a still greater amount either in production or obligated for by contract. These supplies included raw materials, machinery, precision instruments, and medical and hospital supplies, since the Purchase and Storage Division had absorbed most of the supply operations of all the supply bureaus. Its director also served as the Acting Quartermaster General.

The sudden capitulation of the enemy and at a time when the United States was preparing for a major military effort in 1919 resulted in enormous quantities of supplies being on hand or due in about the time of the armistice. Industrial production was then reaching its peak.[41] In anticipation of campaigns projected, the supply agencies had to execute contracts far enough ahead to allow sufficient lead time for the manufacture of the war matériel that would be needed by the troops. As the Chief of Staff later explained to the House War Expenditures Committee:

Eight months ahead of the armistice, on November 11, 1918, we were working on a program which contemplated laying down in March 1919, an army of 80 divisions in France and 18 at home which was about a million more than we had on November 11, when we cut off and stopped it. But the buying going on in September, October, and November was not all for these months but for the months ahead, for the spring campaign; so on the day when the armistice was signed, and when I shut down everything in the United States, the storehouses all along the seacoast were filled with supplies of foodstuffs making for the seacoast to go across the water, and food products in

---

[40] See *ante,* p. 644.
[41] Bernard Baruch, *American Industry in the War* (Washington, 1921), pp. 6–7.

the course of delivery all the way along back. When the armistice was signed we stopped trains and held trains filled with food products a long time, until we could get storage for them, and we encouraged contractors to store stuff and hold it for us until we could dispose of it. We had a three months' supply on November 11, which was based not on the strength of the army at that date, but based on the spring drive of the next year. We were buying supplies and laying in supplies, not for an army of more than 3,000,000 men, but for an army of more than 5,000,000 men.[42]

When hostilities ceased, the War Department immediately suspended existing contracts for the procurement of supplies and took all possible steps to reduce war expenditures. The personnel of the commodity divisions of the Office of the Director of Purchase and Storage, who had been pushing procurement at top speed, now turned to the termination of contracts and the making of settlements and adjustments. At the end of World War I, undelivered balances on contracts that involved some 30,000 contracts and that totaled about $4 billion were canceled.[43]

Policies guiding termination established that all articles completed under a contract were to be paid for on the terms provided in the contract; and for all uncompleted products, the contractor was to be reimbursed for his expenditures and paid for the use of his capital and services.[44] The War Department set up the machinery for handling contract termination after the armistice. Zone supply officers in the 14 procurement zones into which the country was divided became responsible for terminating contracts and negotiating settlements. Local boards of review were established, on 16 November 1918, in each zone to examine and tentatively approve the settlements made by the zone supply officers. These boards had final authority to approve all settlements of contracts that were terminated without cost to the government. They had to refer all other settlements to the Claims Board in the Office of the Director of Purchase and to the War Department Claims Board for final approval.[45] The War Department established the Claims Board, on 20 January 1919, to supervise and co-ordinate the work of the various War Department agencies engaged in the settlement of claims resulting from contract termination and to authorize and approve such settlements. Subsequently, when Congress passed the Dent Act, which conferred full authority on the Secretary of War to adjust all contracts, the War Department Claims Board was made the agency for carrying out the law.[46]

[42] *Congressional Record*, July 29, 1919, p. 3546.

[43] Erna Risch, *Demobilization Planning and Operation in the Quartermaster Corps*, QMC HISTORICAL STUDIES No. 19 (Washington, 1948), p. 27.

[44] (1) *Report of the Chief of Staff, 1919*, pp. 197–98. (2) March, *The Nation at War*, p. 180.

[45] *Annual Report of the Quartermaster General, 1919*, pp. 150–51.

[46] (1) *War Department Circulars, 1919*, Cir 26, 20 Jan 1919. (2) *War Department General Orders and Bulletins, 1919*, GO 33, 3 Mar 1919. (3) 40 *Stat.* 1272–75 (Mar 2, 1919).

Surplus Disposal in the Zone of Interior

The end of hostilities posed an immediate storage problem because cancellation of overseas requirements and the accumulation of stocks from incomplete contracts greatly in excess of requirements resulted in serious congestion at storage points. Pending disposition of surplus stocks, stores not only were accumulated in general supply depots, but supplies that had been ordered shipped or were in transit to ports of embarkation for the supply of troops overseas were also diverted to the three Army reserve depots of Schenectady, New Cumberland, and Columbus. Construction of these depots was nearing completion at the time the armistice was signed.[47] It was estimated that, on 11 November 1918, there were approximately 600,000 tons of such supplies on the docks and about 400,000 tons were moving toward the seaboard, all routed to the overseas forces.[48]

The accumulation of huge quantities of supplies on hand, resulting from large amounts that were turned in as camps were abandoned in the United States, shipped from overseas, and accepted before contracts could be terminated necessitated a sharp increase in storage space for the protection of the supplies until they could be disposed of as surplus. In December 1918, the total warehousing space under control of the Storage Service was approximately 64,617,110 square feet. One year later, the space still being used for supplies in the possession of the government had increased to approximately 76,278,446 square feet, owned by the government, and to 300,262,472 square feet of leased space, 290,776,828 square feet of which were open storage.[49]

The necessity to dispose of accumulated surplus supplies was recognized before the war ended, and Congress authorized disposal, on July 9, 1918, but the problem did not become urgent until after the armistice.[50] Then, a Surplus Property Division was set up, on 30 November 1918, in the Office of the Director of Purchase and Storage and given jurisdiction over all surplus property except salvage—that is, waste material valuable only for scrap or junk. Originally, all sales of surplus property involving a cost price in excess of $5,000 for such supplies had to be approved by the Director of Purchase, Storage and Traffic. That amount was later raised to $100,000 and, with the appointment of a Director of Sales early in January 1919, his approval had to be obtained for sales in excess of that figure. The surplus property was then sold at auction or to the highest

---

[47] *Annual Report of the Quartermaster General, 1919,* pp. 161–62.
[48] RG 120, W.D. Historical Files, Box 165-I ("Brief History of QM and Purchase and Storage Demobilization Activities," p. 236).
[49] *Ibid.,* p. 241.
[50] 40 *Stat.* 850.

bidder on sealed proposals.   Sales to government departments or Allied governments were an exception to this general method.   In such sales, the price was not to be less than the invoice price, including the cost of inspection and transportation.[51]

In view of the large quantities of supplies held by the War Department, the existing shortages, and the restrictions that had been imposed during the war, the public eagerly sought the release of surplus material, particularly foodstuffs.   Before any large-scale disposal program could be initiated, however, supply officers had to determine what stocks were on hand.   An inventory of all supplies in the zone supply depots, Army reserve depots, port terminals, and posts was begun on 31 December 1918 and completed 4 months later.   In addition, before supplies could be declared surplus to Army needs, the Chief of Staff had to take into account certain determining factors.   In November 1918, he had to consider the possibility that the armistice might be short-lived and that military operations might be resumed.   The Chief of Staff therefore instructed the supply departments to provide for a margin of safety, and he called upon them to retain supplies necessary for the troops still in the A.E.F. and for initially equipping a complete army of 1,500,000 men.   He viewed this order only as a temporary measure to enable the supply departments to cancel contracts and dispose of surplus stores.   At the same time, he also wanted to retain an adequate reserve of nonperishable supplies for the Army, the National Guard, and the Reserve Officers' Training Corps to avoid a repetition of the serious lack of material that had existed at the outbreak of World War I.

Varying troop strength figures in the months after the armistice further complicated the disposal program.   The total number of men to be rationed and supplied was materially reduced, on the one hand, by the unanticipated rapidity of demobilization and, on the other, by the decrease in the authorized size of the permanent peacetime Army. In the absence of action by Congress, General March, in January 1919, called upon the supply departments to provide the full amount of supplies required to support a peacetime Army of 500,000 men.   By June, however, Congress had reduced the number to 300,000.[52]   The effect was to compel a downward revision of requirements and to release additional supplies as surplus to Army needs.

The delay in releasing surplus material evoked considerable criticism of the War Department.   In answer, the Secretary of War offered a

[51] (1) *Annual Report of the Quartermaster General, 1919*, pp. 122–23.   (2) *Report of the Chief of Staff, 1919*, pp. 201–02.

[52] (1) *Report of the Chief of Staff, 1919*, p. 234.   (2) Report No. 171, *War Expenditures Hearings*, 66th Cong., Ser. I, vol. 3, pp. (10), (11).

plausible explanation based on the aforementioned considerations that had to be taken into account, and this slowed the declaration of materials as surplus.[53]   His explanation was less satisfying to others later who thought he leaned "too far toward the side of the producers and the commercial distributors" and overlooked the interests of the consumers.[54] The Graham Committee investigating war expenditures was particularly disturbed by an agreement made by the Acting Quartermaster General with the canners' association which called for withholding from the market, during the 1919 season, 200 million cans of vegetables that were surplus to Army needs.   Under pressure, the agreement had later to be abandoned, though it was not abrogated until 23 May 1919.[55]

Congress later directed the Secretary of War to provide for direct purchase of surplus supplies by the public.   In consequence, a plan for sale and distribution of surplus supplies through the parcel post system was developed, under which orders were received, consolidated, and forwarded by the local postmaster to the general supply depot in the area of which the post office was located along with the funds to pay for the supplies.   The latter were shipped to the postmaster who made the distribution.

The Post Office Department, however, was not equipped to handle the tremendous volume of business involved, and about 6 weeks after the plan began to operate, distribution through a system of Army retail stores replaced the parcel post system.   Between 3 August and 24 September 1919, when the War Department abandoned use of the parcel post system, it sold approximately $12 million worth of surplus supplies, three-fourths of the amount being subsistence.   Zone supply officers supervised the operation of 26 retail stores, established in principal cities throughout the country on 25 September 1919.   By 1 November, the number of stores had increased to 77.   They remained in operation until late in February 1920.   Thereafter, the Quartermaster General closed them, one by one, whenever overhead operating expenses exceeded 10 percent of receipts or when he lacked supplies to replenish stocks. The Quartermaster General reported that over $35 million worth of surplus supplies had been disposed of through the retail stores by 30 June 1920.[56]

[53] Ltr, SW to Hon. H. D. Flood, Appendix to Minority Report, Report No. 171, *War Expenditures Hearings*, 66th Cong., Ser. 1, vol. 3.

[54] Crowell, *Government War Contracts*, p. 295.

[55] (1) See majority and minority reports of the Select Committee on Expenditures in the War Department, Report No. 171, *War Expenditures Hearings*, 66th Cong., Ser. I, vol. 3. (2) See also *ibid.*, Ser. 5, vol. 1, pp. 43–58, 81.

[56] (1) *Annual Report of the Quartermaster General, 1920*, p. 50.   (2) RG 120, W.D. Historical Files, Box 165-I ("Brief History of QM and Purchase and Storage Demobilization Activities," pp. 248–50).

In terms of general sale of surplus material, the Surplus Property Division, from the time of its establishment on 30 November 1918 to 30 June 1920, sold surplus property amounting to $382,247,081. This property had originally cost the government $488,485,476, the percentage of recovery being 83.23 percent. As of 30 June 1920, the Division still had about $200 million worth of surplus property on hand, and the disposal program continued to be active for a long time after the war.[57]

Zone of Interior Salvage Operations

The Director of Purchase and Storage delegated responsibility for the sale and disposal of all unserviceable government material, accumulated in the process of demobilizing the wartime Army and dismantling camps established during the war, to the Salvage Division in his Office. Between 1 December 1918 and 31 December 1919, the sale, by public auction or under sealed proposals, of unserviceable property amounted to more than $11 million. The Division did not sell all waste; in the process of classification, it reclaimed large quantities of unserviceable property and returned such supplies to organizations for further use. In this same period, unserviceable property to the value of almost $3 million was so recovered and used.[58] In 1920, surplus disposal and salvage operations again became responsibilities of the Quartermaster General, and sale of waste materials, disposal of surplus property, and the settlement of claims arising out of cancellation of contracts absorbed a considerable share of the Corps' efforts for years to come.

Salvage operations in the zone of the interior during the war, as in the A.E.F. overseas, had also included the operation of laundry facilities and repair shops for clothing, shoes, and canvas items. The War Department had adopted a general policy of establishing repair shops and laundries of sufficient capacity to meet requirements at each camp, cantonment, or permanent post where a considerable number of troops were in training. When the war began, the government had owned 14 small steam laundries, located at posts throughout the country and servicing a few hundred men. The war had brought increased demands for laundry work that could not be satisfied through the use of commercial laundries. On 8 August 1918, the Secretary of War had authorized the expenditure of more than $5 million for the construction of laundries to service from 30,000 to 40,000 men in each of 20 camps and posts. Five days later, he had also authorized the construction of repair shops, warehouses, and

---

[57] *Annual Report of the Quartermaster General, 1920,* p. 49.
[58] RG 120, W.D. Historical Files, Box 165-I ("Brief History of QM and Purchase and Storage Demobilization Activities," p. 270).

other necessary facilities for salvage purposes at each of the National Army cantonments and National Guard camps. He had further authorized the establishment of dry cleaning plants at Atlanta, Fort Sam Houston, El Paso, and Alcatraz.[59]   This construction work had been well under way at all points and, in some instances, the facilities had been completed and were in full operation by the time the armistice was signed.

With the end of the war, the Salvage Division curtailed repair activities at the camps and centered such work at base salvage plants to promote co-ordination, reduce expenses, and permit the personnel at camps to concentrate on getting unserviceable and surplus property ready for disposal. The function of disposal overshadowed all other activities of the Salvage Division at that time. Although the Division sharply reduced the amount of repair work, it did introduce improved methods of operation in the winter of 1918–19.   It also proposed, and the Secretary of War approved, the provision of free laundry service to the troops beginning with fiscal year 1920. Such free service was to replace the flat $1 per month rate charged each soldier during the war.[60]

Such activity, however, was of limited duration. As the troops were demobilized and camps were dismantled and abandoned, the War Department, on 1 October 1921, ordered the repair of shoes, clothing, and hats, and the dry cleaning of clothing at government expense for the enlisted man discontinued.[61] The Quartermaster General transferred various repair shops to post exchanges, which employed civilian shoemakers, tailors, and hatters. The enlisted man thereafter paid for such repair work at regular rates established by the post exchanges.[62] Free laundry service also came to an end on 1 October 1921. After that date, the enlisted man paid $2 per month for laundry service, with no limitation on the number or kind of pieces he sent to the laundry. In the years of peace that followed, the equipment of Army laundries, first procured during World War I, became old and obsolescent, and, by 1935, The Quartermaster General was making efforts to obtain funds to provide up-to-date equipment.[63] Adequate maintenance and even expansion of the laundries was greatly handicapped by the meager funds granted by Congress for this purpose during the postwar years. On the eve of

[59] (1) RG 120, W.D. Historical Files, Box 145, file 7–46.1 ("Functions and Operations of the Salvage Service," pp. 10–13). (2) *Report of the Quartermaster General, 1919*, p. 117.

[60] RG 120, W.D. Historical Files, Box 145, file 7–46.1 ("Functions and Operations of the Salvage Service," p. 92).

[61] *War Department Circulars, 1921*, Cir. 245, 16 Sep 1921.

[62] RG 94, AGO Records, file 319.12 (Annual Report of the Quartermaster General, 1922, p. 11).

[63] *Ibid.*, (Annual Report of The Quartermaster General, 1935, p. 6).

World War II, there were only 33 Quartermaster fixed laundries, 29 of which were in the United States and 4 in its overseas possessions.

Postwar Reorganization

Demobilization in 1918 generated many problems, the most important of which undoubtedly were those relating to the strength of the peacetime Army to be maintained and the organization to be provided for the Army and the War Department. Both had been reorganized during the war as a result of emergency legislation and under the pressure of war conditions. When hostilities ended and the wartime Army began to disintegrate, a decision had to be made on the size of the force to be maintained. The War Department, too, needed to be put on a permanent peacetime basis, its organization taking cognizance of the lessons learned during the war.

Immediately following the armistice, the General Staff began a study of the problem that culminated in a number of recommendations. Based on this study, the Secretary of War submitted to Congress a bill for reorganizing and increasing the efficiency of the Army.[64] Hearings on the proposed reorganization were held by both the Senate and House Committees on Military Affairs from August 1919 through January 1920.

Of interest to the supply services were those provisions of the bill which vested authority in the President to make such distribution of the duties, powers, functions, records, and personnel of previously existing departments, bureaus, and offices as he might deem necessary for the efficiency of the service, and those provisions that strengthened the General Staff in its control of the entire Military Establishment, including the supply bureaus. Of additional and specific interest to the Quartermaster Corps were the proposals to retain separate agencies to handle the functions of finance and motor, rail, and water transportation—functions that before the war had been the responsibility of the Corps.

Maj. Gen. Harry L. Rogers presented the views of the Quartermaster Corps in reference to reorganization. While serving as Chief Quartermaster of the A.E.F., he had been appointed Quartermaster General in the summer of 1918, with the rank of major general dating from 22 July, but he had remained on duty overseas. Subsequently, demobilization activities in the A.E.F. had kept him in France until February 1919, at which time he assumed his duties as Quartermaster General and also

---

64 (1) For the bill, S. 2715, see *Reorganization of the Army: Hearings* before the Subcommittee of the Committee on Military Affairs, U.S. Senate, 66th Cong., 1st sess., p. 16 ff. Hereafter briefly cited as *Reorganization of the Army*. (2) For the formulation of the bill, see the testimony of General March, *ibid.*, p. 84.

became Director of Purchase and Storage. Testifying before the Senate Committee on Military Affairs in the fall of that year, he argued vigorously against perpetuating those separate agencies that had been created from the Quartermaster Corps. They were only productive of unnecessary expense and overhead, and he further charged that separation had materially impaired efficiency of operations. He favored a single large supply organization that would handle supplies common to all branches of the service. He also objected to General Staff operation, believing its function should be only supervisory in character.[65] It would be difficult to assess the influence of the general's argument, but when Congress passed the National Defense Act, on June 4, 1920, it restored the functions of transportation and construction to the Corps. The prewar responsibility of the Corps for paying military personnel, however, continued to be vested in a separate Finance Department.

It fell to General Rogers to re-establish the Quartermaster Corps under the new legislation. By War Department directive, the transfers of the records and of the enlisted and civilian personnel of the Transportation Service, Motor Transport Corps, Construction Division, and Real Estate Service were made effective on 15 July 1920.[66] On the same date, all commissioned personnel of these activities were detailed temporarily for duty with the Corps. All field duties of the transferred agencies were assumed by quartermasters, that title being once more restored to use.

Under the National Defense Act of 1920, Congress abolished the Purchase and Storage Service and substituted for it the title of Quartermaster Corps. As reorganized under the law, the Office of the Quartermaster General consisted of three divisions and five services. The latter included Control, Supply, Construction, Transportation, and Remount; the divisions were General Administrative, Personnel, and Cemeterial.[67] As the scope of activities decreased in the postwar years, organizational changes took place that reduced the number of divisions and services in the Office. Within a decade, the Office had returned to its prewar organization which consisted of four divisions—Administrative, Supply, Transportation, and Construction—each having subordinate branches and sections.[68] This organization continued to exist until World War II brought a proliferation of divisions to take charge of the rapidly expanding business of the Corps.[69]

[65] *Ibid.*, pp. 544–50.

[66] (1) *War Department General Orders, 1920*, GO 42, 14 Jul 1920. (2) RG 92, OQMG General Correspondence, 1917–22, Box 237 (Telegram, QMG to depot officers, 14 Jul 1920).

[67] OQMG Cir 11, 28 Jul 1920.

[68] OQMG 00 22, 2 Jun 1930.

[69] Erna Risch, *The Quartermaster Corps: Organization, Supply, and Services* in U.S. ARMY IN WORLD WAR II (Washington, 1953), I, 11 ff.

Congress, in the National Defense Act of 1920, fixed the size of the peacetime Army at not more than 280,000 men. This number was considerably less than the War Department had originally proposed but was more than double the size of the Army in 1917. In 1920, when the country generally seemed satisfied to return to "its traditional diplomacy of isolation from Europe," and men were inclined to accept as accomplished fact that war had been ended for all time, many leaders considered a large army unnecessary. The need for economy further enhanced their desire to relieve the people of the burdens of war in peacetime by pursuing what Senator John S. Williams of Mississippi called "our traditional policy of conserving the financial resources of the people during times of peace" and only when war came requiring them to submit to the immense strains then necessary.[70]

Such considerations operated against establishing and maintaining the force authorized by Congress in 1920. During the next 20 years an Army of 280,000 men was never achieved. In fact, 7 months after Congress passed the National Defense Act, it reduced the size of the Army to 175,000 men.[71] In 1922, it cut the maximum authorized strength of the Regular Army still further to 12,000 officers and 125,000 enlisted men.[72] Even this strength could not be attained because Congress failed to appropriate sufficient funds for support. The Secretary of War, therefore, directed that the enlisted strength of the Regular Army be maintained at an average of 118,500 men for fiscal year 1923.[73] Budgetary economies kept the Army at about this size until 1936 when Congress passed the War Department Appropriation Act for that year making sufficient funds available to permit an increase of enlisted strength to 165,000 men. It was 1938 before it made any increase in the number of officers.[74]

As the size of the Army decreased, the proportion of officers and enlisted men allotted to the Quartermaster Corps also declined. In the National Defense Act of 1920, Congress authorized a commissioned strength, including the Quartermaster General, of 1,054 officers for the Corps and a maximum enlisted strength of 8,000 men. Until 1936, the average enlisted strength of the Corps never exceeded 7,600, and the shortage of personnel was such that men had to be detailed from the line to perform Quartermaster Corps duties. Not only was there a decrease in the number of enlisted men required, but, by 1928, there was also a

---

[70] Fred Greene, "The Military View of American National Policy, 1904–40," *American Historical Review*, LXVI, No. 2, p. 358.

[71] 41 *Stat.* 1098 (Feb. 7, 1921).

[72] 42 *Stat.* 721–24 (Act, Jun 30, 1922).

[73] *Annual Report of the Secretary of War, 1923*, p. 125.

[74] 49 *Stat.* 1282 (Act, May 15, 1936); 52 *Stat.* 216–17 (Act, Apr 13, 1938).

material decrease in the higher enlisted grades and a corresponding increase in the lowest grade. It became so difficult to secure and keep men qualified to perform the specialized duties of the Corps that civilians had to be hired to do the work.[75] During this 20-year period, the Corps never attained its allotted commissioned strength. Its actual commissioned strength hovered around 700 officers. Since quite a few of these officers were detached for other than Quartermaster Corps duties, the shortage of officer personnel was acute. Repeatedly, The Quartermaster General warned that the procurement of sufficient commissioned personnel to bring the Corps to its authorized strength was a primary requirement.[76] When the German Army invaded Poland in 1939, the Quartermaster Corps consisted of 718 officers and 10,545 enlisted men.[77]

If lack of funds kept both Army and the Quartermaster Corps understrength, the status of Quartermaster officers was improved, for the National Defense Act provided that officers above the grade of captain, who since 1903 had been detailed from other branches of the Army, were thereafter to be permanently commissioned in the Quartermaster Corps. When the reorganization of the Army and the War Department was under consideration in 1919, the question of permanent appointments as opposed to the detail system was once more reviewed. In the course of his testimony, Quartermaster General Rogers insisted that experience during the war and even earlier, in operations on the Mexican border, had amply demonstrated the need for permanently assigned specialists.[78] Congress incorporated his views in the Act, and the concept of career supply officers won acceptance.

Congress also made provision for a 4-year tour of duty for appointees to the post of Quartermaster General. General Rogers' opposition to the General Staff prevented his reassignment for a second tour of duty as Quartermaster General. General Pershing, then Chief of Staff, opposed his reappointment, and in 1922 Maj. Gen. William H. Hart succeeded him. He, in turn, was followed, in the intervening years before World War II, by Maj. Gen. B. Franklin Cheatham, Maj. Gen. John L. DeWitt, Maj. Gen. Louis H. Bash, and Maj. Gen. Henry Gibbins.[79] Except for General DeWitt, all of these officers had long years of training and experi-

[75] RG 94, AGO Records, file 319.12 (Annual Report of The Quartermaster General, 1928, p. 2).

[76] *Ibid.*, (See Annual Reports of The Quartermaster General, 1931, p. 1; 1937, p. 1).

[77] *Annual Report of the Secretary of War, 1940*, App. B, Table D.

[78] (1) *Reorganization of the Army*, pp. 546–47. (2) Compare General Pershing's views, *ibid.*, pp. 1439–40.

[79] General Hart served from 28 August 1922 to 2 January 1926; General Cheatham, from 3 January 1926 to 17 January 1930; General DeWitt, from 3 February 1930 to 2 February 1934; General Bash, from 3 February 1934 to 31 March 1936; and General Gibbins, from 1 April 1936 to 31 March 1940.

ence in the work of the Corps.   It was well-established practice to select The Quartermaster General from among the senior officers of the Corps.[80]

Impact of Retrenchment

These Quartermasters General guided the operations of the Corps during the 20 years that followed its reorganization in 1920.   For at least a decade and a half, lack of funds, shortage of personnel, and public indifference to Army needs hampered operations.   Considerations of economy that influenced the size of Army appropriations immediately after the war were reinforced by the prolonged economic depression that followed the stock market crash in 1929.   The latter brought further cuts in War Department budgets.   In the midst of the ensuing retrenchment, the Secretary of War noted that successive reductions in military appropriations had been absorbed by "continuing in service obsolete and inefficient equipment, and where absolutely necessary, by suspending technical research and development work." [81]

Pursuit of such a policy, which permitted the War Department "to maintain the structural framework of trained personnel indispensable to orderly mobilization in emergency," was inevitable in view of the huge surpluses of clothing and equipment in existence at the end of World War I.   Much of this equipment was already obsolescent at the end of the war, but its existence precluded requests for funds to purchase new items. The War Department was aware of the risks involved, but, even as it inaugurated a policy of modernization and development of new types of equipment for future procurement, it announced in 1922 its policy of requiring the use of equipment on hand until the wartime supply became exhausted.[82]

Maintenance of wartime equipment grew increasingly expensive and efforts to improve the appearance of wartime clothing proved ineffective. By 1930, the Corps was attempting to replace obsolete equipment and to develop clothing suited to Army requirements.   Lack of funds continued to hamper such efforts.   It was not until New Deal measures were inaugurated in the 1930's to combat depression and unemployment that relief and emergency funds became available to arrest "the deterioration of the Army's matériel condition." [83]

---

[80] The exception to this practice, General DeWitt, was an Infantry officer who before World War I had been detailed to the Corps for two brief periods.   His supply experience, however, was broadened by the services he performed during the war and by his staff assignments after the war.

[81] *Annual Report of the Secretary of War, 1933*, pp. 18–19.

[82] Risch, *The Quartermaster Corps: Organization, Supply, and Services*, I, 52.

[83] R. Elbertson Smith, *The Army and Economic Mobilization* in U.S. ARMY IN WORLD WAR II (Washington, 1959,) p. 125.

Officer, Drum Major, Bandsman, Private and First Sergeant in special parade uniforms

16TH U.S. INFANTRY, 1930
(Note that the first sergeant's insignia should carry only two arcs.)

Postwar Construction Program

This general trend of development followed in the two decades after 1920 is fully reflected in Quartermaster activities. When Congress returned responsibility for construction, including repairs, operation of utilities, and handling of real estate, to the Quartermaster Corps in 1920, retrenchment was the order of the day. A 42-percent reduction in appropriations for construction in 1922, as compared to 1921, reveals the extent of the retrenchment that the Corps had to make. Congress also cut the costs of maintenance and repairs by more than $5 million in 1922, as compared with the preceding year.[84] This period of retrenchment lasted through 1925. The War Department had given considerable thought to the problem of sheltering the troops, but not until March 1926 could it initiate an Army housing program to replace with proper permanent buildings the temporary structures erected during the war, many of which were still in use. At that time, Congress enacted legislation that authorized the Secretary of War to dispose of 43 military reservations or portions of them. The act further provided that the net proceeds derived from the sale of such properties, including proceeds from the sale of surplus buildings, were to be credited to a Military Post Construction Fund, to remain available until expended for permanent construction at military posts as directed by Congress.[85] This legislation marked a distinct departure from the policy established in 1884, which had required the transfer to the Department of the Interior of military reservations no longer needed by the War Department.[86] Their subsequent disposal had in no way redounded to the benefit of the Army.

The Army housing program as projected was to cover a 10-year period and involve a total expenditure of approximately $148 million. A modest beginning was made in the program during fiscal year 1927, a little more than $7 million being appropriated that year for the construction of hospitals, barracks, and quarters.[87] The Corps gave careful attention to post lay-out plans, applying modern methods of city planning for grouping buildings to produce a harmonious arrangement and to insure economy in the building of roads, sewer and water systems, and other utilities.[88]

---

[84] RG 94, AGO Records, file 319.12 (Annual Report of the Quartermaster General, 1922, pp. 14–15).

[85] 44 *Stat.* 203–07 (Act, Mar 12, 1926).

[86] 23 *Stat.* 103 (Act, Jul 5, 1884).

[87] For a listing of the projects, see RG 94, AGO Records, file 319.12 (Annual Report of The Quartermaster General, 1927, pp. 67–68).

[88] See an article by the City Planning Adviser to the War Department, George B. Ford, "New Army Posts for Old," *The Quartermaster Review,* IX (Nov–Dec 1929), pp. 19–22.

In addition to providing funds for housing, Congress made money available, by fiscal year 1929, for 49 miscellaneous construction projects, the costs of which amounted to more than $16 million. These projects ranged from construction of magazines, shops, warehouses, and similar facilities to restoration of the Lee Mansion and construction of the Tomb of the Unknown Soldier. These appropriated funds also covered the purchase of furniture for officers', warrant officers', and noncommissioned officers' quarters and for officers' messes.[89]

So far as the Army housing program was concerned, the depression years of the Thirties served to expedite the work, since the program fitted in admirably with the efforts to relieve distress and unemployment by constructing public works. When, in November 1929, the President issued instructions to expedite public work construction, the Corps had more than $22,500,000 still available from existing appropriations for its construction program. Ordinarily, the preparation of plans and specifications, the soliciting of bids, and the execution of contracts involving such a large sum would have taken from 12 to 15 months. By concentrating all efforts on the job, the Construction Service, in 7 months, placed under contract construction work totaling more than $19,500,000. The War Department afforded further relief to the economy of the country by instructing all field commanders to begin repair and maintenance work immediately in the various corps areas, for which the Quartermaster Corps released and allotted to them more than $2,500,000.[90]

During these years, a large amount of non-military construction was assigned to the Corps and directed by its Construction Service. This work included marking battlefields and other places of national fame, erecting tombs and monuments, and restoring colonial forts and historic buildings.[91]

By the time the first decade of the housing program was nearing an end, approximately $150 million had been allotted for construction purposes. Considerable improvement had been made, but the maintenance costs for World War I housing still in use were running excessively high, and the Secretary of War was urging further appropriations.[92]

[89] A specific listing of these projects is to be found in, Brig. Gen. William E. Horton, "The Work of the Construction Service, Quartermaster Corps," *The Quartermaster Review*, VIII (Sep–Oct 1928), pp. 6–8.

[90] RG 94, AGO Records, file 319.12 (Annual Report of The Quartermaster General, 1930, pp. 54–55).

[91] The restoration of Old Fort Niagara and Fort McHenry and the erection of an ornamental gateway to indicate an approach to the old fort on Roanoke Island were the first white child, Virginia Dare, was born in 1589 are three examples of this kind of work.

[92] (1) RG 94, AGO Records, file 319.12 (Annual Report of The Quartermaster General, 1935, p. 12). (2) *Annual Reports of the Secretary of War, 1936*, p. 39; *1937*, pp. 35–36.

From 1935 to 1940, the funds provided by Congress were supplemented by allotments from the Public Works Administration. At the close of fiscal year 1939, the Secretary of War referred to the "marked betterment in housing facilties," but the Chief of Staff considered that the crowded housing conditions had been only partially alleviated, since the increase in the size of the Army more than offset the construction provided.

General Malin Craig, Chief of Staff, was of the opinion that full use was not being made of the technical skill and experience of the Corps of Engineers. He believed that responsibility for any new construction ought to be vested in that Corps in order to distribute the construction workload and to free the Quartermaster Corps for its task of supplying and maintaining troops in the field and in garrison. With this purpose in view, he had a study prepared for submission to the Secretary of War in 1939 that presaged the ultimate transfer of construction to the Corps of Engineers in World War II.[93]

Army Transport Service

Quartermaster transportation of men and supplies and the development and procurement of suitable equipment showed the effects of budgetary economies common to the War Department generally. The transportation of men and supplies had been a primary Quartermaster function since 1775, but the restoration of that responsibility to the Corps in 1920 proved to be only temporary; it was permanently separated from the Corps early in World War II.[94] When the Corps reassumed responsibility for transportation in the summer of 1920, the separate agencies had initiated arrangements to settle claims and dispose of surplus equipment that the Corps carried to completion. So far as the Army Transport Service was concerned, it became the policy of the Quartermaster General to restore it to its prewar basis. The Corps tried to dispose of all surplus floating equipment, including Army transports as well as harbor boats and Coast Artillery vessels, by sale or transfer to other Departments. A prompt release of chartered vessels had been started as soon as the return of the A.E.F. made this feasible, and, by 30 June 1921, all such vessels had been returned to their owners.[95]

The Army's wartime transport requirements had led the U.S. Shipping Board to submit a plan to Congress as a basis for obtaining the

[93] (1) *Annual Reports of the Secretary of War, 1939*, pp. 1, 31–32. (2) A volume of the U.S. ARMY IN WORLD WAR II series in preparation by Leonore Fine and Jesse A. Remington, "The Corps of Engineers: Military Construction in the United States," provides greater detail of these wartime developments.

[94] Risch, *The Quartermaster Corps: Organization, Supply, and Services*, I, 16–22.

[95] RG 94, AGO Records, file 319.12 (Annual Report of the Quartermaster General, 1921, p. 181).

necessary appropriations for construction purposes. Actually, the war ended before the intended troop transports were ever completed. At that point, the War Department requested that only 6 of the originally proposed 70 B class transports be completed at the Hog Island yards for its use. These were vessels suitable for combined troop and cargo purposes. It also wanted 5 of the vessels being built at Camden shipyards, the speed and design of which made them especially suitable for permanent transports on the long Pacific Ocean runs.[96] In the early 1920's, the Corps substituted the Hog Island B type transports for the old transports that it had purchased in the Spanish-American War. It also replaced old harbor boats by recently constructed vessels. The Corps anticipated that completion of this replacement program would furnish the Army Transport Service with practically a new fleet.

At the time the Corps resumed responsibility for the Army Transport Service, 16 of the Army-owned transports were assigned to active operations, the rest being out of commission, awaiting sale or other disposition. In the course of the following years, the ever-present need to economize reduced the number of transports in active operation. A decade after the armistice, the Army Transport Service was operating 7 passenger transports and 2 freight transports on regular schedules to the insular possessions of the United States. It also had in operation one cable ship.[97] These vessels were then in satisfactory condition, but their upkeep was becoming of much concern to the Corps. The limitation on funds prevented the accomplishment of even essential repair work and the need to economize became a decisive factor in still further reducing transport service. The Corps undertook to improve the condition of the ships by introducing newer safety devices and improving ventilation and other facilities but progress was slow. By 1932, only 6 transports were in operation, 2 of which were freight transports. This remained the size of the Army Transport Service until the emergency period and the outbreak of World War II brought sudden expansion in equipment, personnel, and funds.[98]

Rail and Motor Transportation

The postwar years brought no new developments in Army use of railroad transportation but the War Department did profit from the

---

[96] For details, see *Annual Report of the Chief of Transportation Service, 1919* (Washington, 1919), pp. 134–39.

[97] RG 94, AGO Records, file 319.12 (Annual Report of The Quartermaster General, 1928, p. 34).

[98] Chester Wardlow, *The Transportation Corps: Responsibilities, Organization, and Operations* in U.S. ARMY IN WORLD WAR II (Washington, 1951), pp. 28–42.

experience gained in World War I. That war had clearly demonstrated the need for centralized control of inland transportation and traffic operation, and the War Department retained such control in the years of peace that followed the armistice. The designation of the Quartermaster General as Traffic Manager for the War Department and his authorization to exercise jurisdiction over all transportation activities of the Army, including rates, routings, and methods of shipment, underscored the change. The War Department also specifically directed all bureaus and branches to use no funds or personnel for the maintenance of traffic sections, a development in the early months of World War I that had been productive of confusion and congestion in traffic.[99] The Corps' attention was primarily centered on the development of closer relations with the railroad carriers, and the maintenance of a troop movement bureau in the Office of The Quartermaster General by the American Railway Association, which represented practically all the carriers of the United States, contributed much to this objective.[100]

When Congress returned responsibility for motor transport to the Quartermaster Corps in the summer of 1920, reduction of personnel and disposal equipment had already been largely accomplished in the 20 months since the armistice. Vehicles that would be needed by the Army had been designated for retention before the disposal program was initiated. Although the Corps was responsible for procuring all Army vehicles, except those used in combat, its procurement of new vehicles during the 1920's was inconsequential by reason of the large amount of wartime equipment on hand. As of 30 June 1929, the Corps had purchased only 763 new vehicles, of which 709 were passenger cars and 54 were trucks and other miscellaneous vehicles acquired for experimental purposes. Of the 17,305 vehicles of various types and makes that the Corps had on hand, 16,542 had been purchased during the war.[101]

Not all of them were in operation. On 30 June 1930, Tables of Allowances called for 13,514 motor vehicles, but lack of funds for operation, maintenance, and replacements made possible the authorized operation of only 8,366 during that fiscal year. Lack of funds for the procurement of gasoline further reduced the number to 7,496.[102] With limited funds available for purchase, the Quartermaster Corps could make little progress in determining the extent to which animal transport might, with safety, be replaced by modern motor vehicles.

99 *War Department General Orders, 1923,* GO 21, 5 Jun 1923.

100 (1) RG 94, AGO Records, file 319.12 (Annual Reports of The Quartermaster General, 1922–37, *passim*). See *ante,* p. 572 for early proposals for a troop movement bureau.

101 RG 94, AGO Records, file 319.12 Annual Report of The Quartermaster General, 1929, p. 38).

102 *Ibid.,* (Annual Report of The Quartermaster General, 1930, p. 63).

The Corps also possessed an extensive stock of spare parts for the wartime vehicles. Accordingly, during the Twenties, it developed and operated a system of spare parts distribution to service such vehicles. It did not expand the system to include servicing any of the new motor vehicles acquired later. Since the Corps was procuring relatively few of them, it decided not to stock parts for this equipment.[103] As the years passed, maintenance of war-purchased vehicles became increasingly costly. More and more, the using services complained of unsatisfactory equipment, and The Quartermaster General reported to the Secretary of War that such a result was to be expected. Maximum motor transportation efficiency for the Army, he explained, could not be accomplished with models and types of vehicles purchased during 1917–18 for war purposes.[104] Not until Congress passed the War Department Appropriation Act for fiscal year 1935, forbidding the use after 1 January 1935 of funds to repair vehicles purchased before 1 January 1920, could the Corps begin to eliminate such vehicles from further operation.[105]

During the postwar years, the Quartermaster Corps worked closely with the automotive industry to develop vehicles suitable for military purposes. Quartermaster officers attended most of the important transportation conferences, at which they offered suggestions and recommendations of value to the commercial transport interests. At Holabird Quartermaster Depot, the Corps experimented and developed designs and inventions that were adopted by the automotive industry. Within the limits of available funds, the Corps conducted a program for the development of motor vehicles suited to military purposes, but, obviously shortages of funds (during fiscal years 1933 and 1934 no funds were appropriated for the purpose) made impossible any adequate program of development and testing.[106]

Wartime experience had emphasized one fact that the Corps never lost sight of in the postwar years. Wartime procurement of nearly 275,000 motor vehicles, of over 200 different makes, had driven home the necessity for centralized control of motor-vehicle procurement in order to keep within reasonable limits the number of different types of such vehicles. Only by standardization could the Corps hope to supply spare parts efficiently for the maintenance and repair of the motor fleet. The problem of standardization had long been under study by Quartermaster officers. When, in the spring of 1931, Congress appropriated funds for

[103] OQMG Cir 1–10, 12 Dec 1928, par. 16; *ibid.*, 18 May 1933, par. 19.

[104] RG 94, AGO Records, file 319.12 (Annual Report of The Quartermaster General, 1932, p. 80).

[105] 48 *Stat.* 623 (Act, Apr 26, 1934).

[106] RG 94, AGO Records, file 319.12 (Annual Report of The Quartermaster General, 1934, p. 15).

the purchase of badly needed motor transport in the Army, the funds to be made available for immediate expenditure as an unemployment relief measure, The Quartermaster General unveiled a procurement plan that would promote standardization.   This was to be accomplished by "writing into specifications performance requirements, quality and sturdiness of materials and design plus outside dimensions that will make units interchangeable in various types of vehicles." [107]

Under this plan, the Corps purchased the first substantial number of trucks procured since the war.   They represented six types, ranging from 1½- to 6-ton capacity.   Since the sizes and types could not be procured within the price stipulated in the appropriation act, the Corps, with War Department approval, purchased units and assemblies for chassis of all the authorized types and assembled the vehicles at the Holabird Depot. This action provoked vigorous criticism from some representatives of the automotive industry.   Coupled with departmental competition and genuine disagreement on how best to attain standardization, it led to an extended discussion of the procurement and standardization policy recommended by The Quartermaster General.   The War Department settled one phase of the disagreement in September 1933 when it directed that, as a general rule, motor vehicles would be supplied as complete vehicles by the automotive industry.[108]

Attack upon the policy of standardization and interchangeability then came from the Comptroller General, who questioned the legality under procurement law of the policy of writing specifications in such detail that stipulations practically eliminated competition and made award certain for a particular product.[109]   As long as the Corps could not write specifications to obtain uniformity of design, materials, or external dimensions, and had to accept the lowest bid from a responsible bidder, standardization could not be achieved.   Only legislative action could resolve the conflict between procurement law and standardization efforts.   The viewpoint of the Comptroller General found its way into Army Regulations.[110]

---

[107] (1) *Ibid.*, (Annual Report of The Quartermaster General, 1931, pp. 57–58).   (2) See also Col. Edgar S. Stayer, "The Year's Advancement in Military Motor Transport," *The Quartermaster Review*, XII (Jul–Aug 1932), pp. 33–37.

[108] *War Department General Orders, 1933*, GO 9, 11 Sep 1933.

[109] *Decisions of the Comptroller General of the United States*, vol. 13, (Jul. 1, 1933, to Jun. 30, 1934), pp. 184–91; 477.

[110] AR 850–15, Sec. I, par. 3d (1939) states: "The procurement of motor vehicles other than combat vehicles will be limited to models produced commercially by two or more competing companies and available at reasonable prices, and with the minimum deviation from standard commercial chassis necessary to conform to approved military characteristics set up for the using arm or service to which the vehicle is allocated.   The parts and unit assemblies so used will be standard production in the automotive industry."

The Quartermaster Corps undertook no large-scale replacement of obsolete motor equipment in the postwar years. Instead, limited funds compelled the Corps to follow a piecemeal procurement of motor vehicles of manufacturers' standard commercial production which resulted in the acquisition of a motor fleet of different makes and models (over 300). It also led to the virtual abandonment of Quartermaster distribution of parts and units. Available funds did not permit the purchase of stocks of units and parts for so many makes and models of motor vehicles as were purchased after the war. It therefore became necessary to decentralize such procurement and to buy locally the units and parts needed for repair purposes.[111]

The Quartermaster General continued to stress the need for standardization in order to make maintenance in a wartime theater feasible. In the summer of 1939, the War Department, acting on recommendations of the Quartermaster Technical Committee, modified its position to the extent of directing that all military requirements for general-purpose tactical motor transportation be met by five chassis types. In order to insure maximum standardization, it directed that procurement of the largest possible number of vehicles be accomplished on a once-a-year basis. The War Department further directed that maximum interchangeability of major parts and unit assemblies be obtained within the industry applicable to standard chassis and capable of meeting essential performance requirements of the arms and services.[112]

This action made possible further progress toward standardization. The only remaining obstacle was adherence to the practice of procuring on a competitive basis. Legislation permitting the abandonment of the formal advertising method was passed on 2 July 1940. It authorized the Secretary of War to enter into contracts "with or without advertising." [113] Though passage of the law did not bring to an end the long struggle over standardization, it did remove one of the principal obstacles to acquiring uniform vehicles. By that time, however, the country was well into the emergency period and would soon be at war.

Industrial Mobilization and Procurement Planning

Other than the purchase of food, forage, and fuel, which accounted for the larger part of Quartermaster expenditures during most of these

---

[111] RG 94, AGO Records, file 319.12 (Annual Report of The Quartermaster General, 1935, p. 8; 1937, pp. 11–12).

[112] Vernon Carstensen, "Motor Transport Under The Quartermaster General, 1903–1942," pp. 70–71 (Historical MSS on file in Office, QM Historian). This study provides a far more detailed analysis of the standardization problem than is presented in this chapter.

[113] 54 *Stat.* 712.

years, Quartermaster procurement of supplies was minimal in amount. This was a natural consequence of having on hand huge surpluses of clothing and equipment that obviated the need for procurement. The development of policies governing procurement was, to some extent, shaped by the need to economize. No account of this development would be complete, however, without some brief reference to industrial mobilization and procurement planning during these years. Such planning was an innovation in Quartermaster activities, a direct legacy of the war that Congress incorporated into the defense system.

Under the National Defense Act of 1920, the Assistant Secretary of War was charged with making "adequate provision for mobilization of matériel and industrial organizations essential to war-time needs." Since the law also made the General Staff responsible for "the mobilization of the manhood of the Nation and its material resources in an emergency," a conflict of authority was raised that had to be resolved by evolving a workable division of responsibility.[114]

About a year later, an Army board, headed by Maj. Gen. James G. Harbord, Deputy Chief of Staff, was appointed to resolve the conflict. Its recommendations, later embodied in a general order, provided for General Staff determination of the supply requirements of the Army and vested responsibility for fulfilling these requirements in the Assistant Secretary of War.[115] In carrying out their respective functions, the General Staff and the Assistant Secretary of War had to rely on the Quartermaster General and the chiefs of the other supply bureaus, who were responsible for most of the essential elements of military supply as analyzed by the Harbord board. Preparation of specifications and detailed drawings of the matériel to be obtained; inspection, test, and acceptance for adoption of types; and storage and issue were elements that involved only the military relationship of the supply branches with the General Staff. Purchase, production, and inspection of facilities were elements of military supply that placed the supply bureaus under the control and supervision of the Assistant Secretary of War.[116]

In the broader planning field, the development of strategic war plans and plans for the mobilization of manpower remained a duty of the General Staff. General Staff divisions did much preliminary work before

---

[114] 41 *Stat.* 763–64 (Jun 4, 1920).

[115] (1) *Hearings* before the Committee on Military Affairs, HR, 69th Cong., 2d sess., "Historical Documents Relating to the Reorganization Plans of the War Department and to the Present National Defense Act," (Washington, 1928), pp. 580–83. (2) *War Department General Orders, 1921*, GO 41, 16 Aug 1921.

[116] The so-called Harbord decision provided only a temporary arrangement; procurement matters later required further clarification which was finally obtained in an Army Regulation 5–5, issued on 16 July 1932.

a basic War Department Mobilization Plan was published in 1923.   Its
publication resulted in the preparation of annexes and unit plans by all
lower command and staff echelons, among which was the Quartermaster
annex to the General Mobilization Plan.   In the course of the next
decade, during which the plan was repeatedly revised, Quartermaster
planning efforts were directed toward the preparation of studies of war
reserves; tables of organization and of basic allowances; regulations governing transportation, shelter, and supply of troops during mobilization;
and Quartermaster unit plans and requirements for specialists and their
training.   War Department manpower planning culminated in the
Protective Mobilization Plan of 1937.   When actual mobilization began
in the summer of 1940, the revised Protective Mobilization Plans proved
useful as a guide, though the planners had failed to provide an adequate
force for meeting the demands made by World War II.   They had also
assumed that mobilization would be sudden on the outbreak of war
rather than relatively slow during many months of nominal peace.[117]

While the General Staff projected plans for the mobilization of manpower, the Assistant Secretary of War was responsible for two closely
interrelated functions—procurement planning and industrial mobilization planning.   The latter was the broader function that could be carried
forward only on the basis of well-developed procurement plans.   Concerned with formulating policies intended to facilitate the transition of
the country's economy from a peacetime to a wartime footing, the Office
of the Assistant Secretary of War performed industrial mobilization
planning.[118]

On the other hand, the Assistant Secretary's direction of procurement
planning was largely supervisory in character.   Within the framework
of policies enunciated by his office, he relied on the Quartermaster Corps
and the other supply services to develop detailed procurement plans.
Much of the early planning of the Corps was concerned with working
out plans for the conversion of each Quartermaster article of supply into
terms of raw or finished material required, and with investigating the
resources of the country in materials and manufacturing facilities.[119]   In
accordance with the requirements established in the Industrial Mobiliza-

---

[117] (1) For a fuller discussion of mobilization planning, see Marvin A. Kreidberg and
Merton G. Henry, *History of Military Mobilization in the United States Army, 1775–1945*
(DA Pamphlet No. 20–212, GPO, 1955), pp. 377–492. (2) References to Quartermaster
participation in this planning are to be found in RG 94, AGO Records, file 319.12 (Annual
Reports of The Quartermaster General, 1924–37, *passim*).

[118] For exhaustive analysis of such planning, see Harold W. Thatcher, *Planning for
Industrial Mobilization, 1920–40*, QMC HISTORICAL STUDIES No. 4 (n.p., August 1943).

[119] RG 94, AGO Records, file 319.12 (Annual Reports of The Quartermaster General,
1921–37, *passim*).

tion Plan, the Quartermaster planners drafted plans for an integrated program of wartime procurement that would avoid the difficulties experienced during World War I. These plans, calling for decentralization of procurement operations, soon centered the latter in procurement districts that were more or less coterminous with the nine corps areas into which the country was divided for military purposes. Procurement planners in the districts surveyed the production facilities within their districts that were capable of furnishing the clothing, equipment, and other supplies needed by the troops to be mobilized in their corps areas.

On the basis of their findings, the Quartermaster planners specifically allocated to these industrial facilities the needs of the Corps, executing production schedules with the plants that were earmarked for the use of the Corps. On the day of mobilization (M Day) and during the following war period, contracts were to be negotiated with the allocated facilities in accordance with the war procurement plans that were kept up to date by periodic revisions. The peacetime method of formal advertising for bids in contracting for supplies was to be abandoned, and, on M Day, planning activities were to be absorbed by current procurement operations.[120] The transition from a state of limited emergency, proclaimed by the President in 1939, to war in 1941 was so gradual that no M Day was recognized and, in consequence, the provisions of the procurement plans and Industrial Mobilization Plan were not implemented according to schedule. Nonetheless, such planning provided a greater degree of industrial and military preparedness in 1941 than had existed in 1917.

Procurement Policy

In the course of these years, procurement policy governing daily operations followed a line of development that was not identical with that taken by the procurement planners for future emergencies. Unlike the decentralized procurement shaped by the planners, the concept of centralized control guided daily operations. It will be recalled that when General Aleshire became Quartermaster General in 1907, he had introduced a decentralized system of procurement, but that designated classes of supplies had been handled by certain depots, as, for example, the Philadelphia Depot, which, since its establishment, had been a center for the procurement of clothing and equipage and which also manufactured such supplies at its factory. Under the impact of war, this system,

---

[120] For a comprehensive account of the development of Quartermaster procurement plans, see Thomas M. Pitkin and Herbert R. Rifkind, *Procurement Planning in the Quartermaster Corps, 1920–40*, QMC HISTORICAL STUDIES No. 1 (n.p., March 1943).

described as "a sort of decentralized centralization," had given way to greater and more effective centralization of control and operations. Progress in that direction had been furthered by the passage of the Overman Act on May 20, 1918. That law permitted greater consolidation of Army purchasing through the establishment of an interbureau procurement system, whereby all articles bought mainly by one supply bureau were centralized for purchase in that agency.[121] Centralizing contracting first in the commodity divisions of the Office of the Quartermaster General and later in the Purchase and Storage Division in Washington, as well as in a few field procurement offices, had not proved conducive to an effective use of the country's resources in 1918. To remedy that situation by a wider distribution of contracts and by building on the existing Quartermaster depot system, the War Department had established a zone system, under which it divided the country into procurement and distribution zones and designated the depot quartermasters as zone supply officers responsible for supply activities in their zones.[122]

The value of centralized control of procurement had been fully demonstrated during the war, and Quartermaster General Rogers and his successors retained it as the policy of the Office. The War Department inactivated a number of wartime depots following the armistice and abandoned the zone system in favor of the former depot system. Once again, the Quartermaster Corps resumed, in 1920, the practice of centralizing purchase of specific articles in designiated depots and, during the next two decades, extended and refined it. In addition, the Corps introduced decentralized procurement for such supplies as could be more economically obtained at depots, posts, camps, and stations.[123]

Not all of the advantages growing out of the Overman Act were lost. The National Defense Act of 1920 provided that the Quartermaster General was to be responsible for the purchase and procurement for the Army of all supplies of standard manufacture and of all supplies common to two or more branches. Special or technical articles used or issued exclusively by a supply department were to be procured by that department. The War Department implemented this provision of the law on 25 September 1920.[124] Interbranch procurement, however, made little or no progress in the next 10 years. In 1931, the Assistant Secretary of War appointed a board of officers to study supply tables of the War Department branches in order to eliminate dual procurement of articles

---

[121] See *ante*, pp. 628, 639.

[122] *Annual Report of the Quartermaster General, 1919*, p. 31.

[123] RG 94, AGO Records, file 319.12 (Annual Report of The Quartermaster General, 1931, p. 57).

[124] *War Department General Orders, 1920*, GO 61.

of common use in the Army.[125]   Other boards continued the work but the goal had by no means been achieved by 1940.

The need for economy in Quartermaster supply operations led to efforts to improve procurement methods by eliminating wasteful practices and duplication of work.   This development was further stimulated by the impact of the depression that began in 1929, and was reflected in Quartermaster participation in consolidated contracts and the system of interdepartmental procurement.   Having participated on an experimental basis in some lubricating oil contracts annually entered into by the Navy Department, the Corps, in 1930, extended this practice to cover Quartermaster requirements for lubricating oils for almost every purpose. Such consolidated contracts had the advantage of giving the Corps uniform and satisfactory grades of oil at less cost, reducing paper work required in advertising for bids, and eliminating the need for Quartermaster testing, since the Navy Department provided exhaustive tests of the products.[126]

The Corps soon also obtained the gasoline it required through contracts negotiated by the Navy Department.   In the 1930's, additional legislation and executive direction broadened the application of the system of interdepartmental procurement.   As a result, the Corps also made purchases under the General Schedule of Supplies of the Treasury Department and purchased from the Federal Prison Industries, Inc., such articles as brooms, brushes, automobile tags, steel furniture, and other items it procured for the Army.[127]

In summary, it became Quartermaster Corps policy throughout the years between World War I and II to fill the larger part of Army requirements for Quartermaster supplies by direct procurement from manufacturers and producers, letting contracts by formal advertising until 2 July 1940 when that method was abandoned.   It obtained some supplies by participation in consolidated contracts made by other governmental agencies and by purchase from other such agencies.   The Corps also manufactured some articles in factories that it operated at its depots as it had been doing since the days of the Mexican War.

Quartermaster procurement of supplies and services, however, was not accomplished without criticism, particularly during the depression years.   Then, the sale to the Corps and other government agencies of prison products, produced in competition with private enterprise, aroused

----

[125] RG 94, AGO Records, file 319.12 (Annual Report of The Quartermaster General, 1932, p. 32; 1933, p. 23).

[126] *Ibid.,* (Annual Report of The Quartermaster General, 1930, pp. 32–33).

[127] (1) 47 *Stat.* 1517 (Mar 3, 1933); 46 *Stat.* 392 (May 27, 1930). (2) *General Orders and Bulletins, 1928–33,* Bulletin 15 (Ex. Order 6166, 10 Jun 1933).

opposition among various manufacturing interests who protested the practice. Similarly, the operation of Quartermaster repair shops and laundries, and the manufacture of products at government-owned factories, particularly the production of clothing by the factory at the Philadelphia Depot, brought so many complaints that a congressional committee investigated such operations and services. The net effect was to curtail though not to eliminate, government competition with private enterprise.[128]

Research

The Corps has always been interested in and responsible, in cooperation with the using arms, for the development of Quartermaster items of supply. The development and completion of the best types of equipment and armament in time of peace was an announced basic policy of the War Department following World War I, even if actual procurement had to be deferred to a future time.[129] To implement this policy, the War Department directed the chiefs of the branches of the Army to make annual surveys of adopted types of equipment and armament with which their troops were provided in order to determine if such types were abreast of current developments and satisfactory for an emergency. These annual surveys and the reports of deficiencies based on them were a primary stimulant to improvement of design. Those portions of the surveys that pointed out inadequacies in Quartermaster items of issue were forwarded to The Quartermaster General for action. The Corps thereupon took steps to improve the existing design of the articles or to develop new ones. It sought their adoption as standardized items of issue, and it prepared and held in readiness specifications governing their procurement.[130]

While this policy and its implementation had the virtue of introducing an element of systemization into developmental work, the Corps evolved no integrated program of research. Only as the annual surveys reported deficiencies in clothing and equipment did the Corps take steps to improve items individually. It did not stress the relationship of items of equipment to each other, except in the field of motor transport items. The Office of The Quartermaster General made efforts to co-ordinate Quartermaster research within the Corps and with other supply services.

---

[128] For a fuller treatment of this development and of procurement in general, see Harry B. Yoshpe and Marion V. Massen, *Procurement Policies and Procedures in the Quartermaster Corps During World War II*, QMC HISTORICAL STUDIES No. 17 (Washington, 1947), pp. 12–18.

[129] Risch, *Quartermaster Corps: Organization, Supply, and Services*, I, 52.

[130] See AR 850–25, 15 Dec 1924.

The establishment of a Quartermaster Corps Technical Committee early in 1922 on instructions of the Secretary of War furthered co-ordination. This Committee served as an advisory board on equipment problems and was responsible for effecting complete co-ordination among all interested branches of the Army during development of types of equipment for which the Corps had responsibility.[131]

Obviously, the huge stocks of surplus supplies on hand after the war hindered the development of new items, despite expressed War Department policy to the contrary. An even more restrictive factor during these 20 years was the inadequacy of funds for research purposes.[132] World War II critics of this prewar research program dismissed its accomplishments as negligible. They charged that the Army started World War II using the same kind of equipment with which it had ended the previous war. Others added that the situation was much worse, since items developed as a result of field experience in 1917 and 1918 were modified in peacetime to make them more suitable for garrison life. This was undoubtedly true of the evolution of the Army uniform.[133] On the other hand, the Quartermaster Corps developed in these years the basic uniform fabrics used throughout World War II.[134]

As interest in preparation for national defense revived in the decade of the Thirties, the Corps did accomplish much that was of value. In 1936, for example, the Corps established a Subsistence Research Laboratory at Chicago. It was responsible for the development of the D ration, an emergency ration of the survival type, and of the C ration, a combat-type ration designed to provide a soldier with three nutritionally balanced, satisfying meals a day, independent of central messing facilities.[135]

The modernization of standard equipment for which the Corps was responsible progressed steadily, though slowly. The Corps developed a few new pieces of equipment, the most notable of which were the jeep and other multiple-wheel-drive vehicles. Though at this late date it is impossible to determine whether more could have been accomplished and at a faster pace, within the limits imposed by stringent budgets, a

---

[131] OQMG 00 10, 24 Jan 1922. This order officially established the Committee, but its minutes actually date from 10 October 1921.

[132] See Mark S. Watson, *Chief of Staff: Prewar Plans and Preparations* in U.S. ARMY IN WORLD WAR II (Washington, 1950), pp. 32, 42, 47–49.

[133] See Erna Risch and Thomas M. Pitkin, *Clothing the Soldier of World War II*, QMC HISTORICAL STUDIES No. 16, (Washington, 1946), pp. 30 ff.

[134] These included 18-ounce serge for enlisted mens' uniforms, 32-ounce melton for overcoats, elastique for officers' uniforms, and herringbone twill for work clothes.

[135] (1) See Harold W. Thatcher, *The Development of Special Rations for the Army*, QMC HISTORICAL STUDIES No. 6 (Washington, 1944), *passim*, for more details on prewar developments in this field. (2) See also Walter Porges, "The Subsistence Research Laboratory" (CQMD Historical Studies No. 1, 1 May 1943). On file in Office, QM Historian.

certain amount of essential preparatory groundwork was laid in the decade of the Thirties that permitted the development of a more scientific research program later.

Quartermaster Support of Non-Military Projects

In 1933, the Quartermaster Corps was afforded an opportunity to test the effectiveness to meet emergencies of the organization that it had developed after World War I. In this test, the Corps functioned not in support of a military mobilization but of a non-military project. This was by no means an unusual assignment. Participation in relief measures had long ago become an accepted though little publicized facet of Quartermaster Corps activities. As early as 1838, a Quartermaster officer had been directed to relieve the distress of Charleston, S.C., citizens, whose homes had been destroyed by fire, by furnishing them with accommodations in the barracks and quarters of the forts in the harbor.[136] In the ensuing 95 years, the Corps supplied sufferers in tornadoes, cyclones, hurricanes, yellow fever epidemics, earthquakes, fires, and floods with tents, cots, blankets, bed sacks, and clothing. Floods were almost a yearly event in the Mississippi Valley.[137] Most of such supplies the Corps furnished on a loan basis, since this was government property for which it was accountable. Frequently, the articles supplied were not returned and their value became a total loss to the Army's clothing appropriation. Upon occasion, Congress provided funds and authorized purchase of tentage for relief purposes.[138]

Some of these disasters reached major proportions. Such were the Mississippi Valley floods of 1913 and 1927. In the 1927 flood, the Corps expended supplies valued at almost $3 million, and The Quartermaster General warned that the loss of tentage in particular would be seriously felt in event of a similar disaster in the next year or in an emergency requiring mobilization.[139] Still another major disaster in which the Corps furnished a large measure of relief was the earthquake and fire that swept through San Francisco in 1906. To meet the continuing needs in that city, Congress appropriated funds and made provision for reimbursing the Corps for the supplies it had issued, the value of which was almost

---

[136] RG 92, OQMG Letter Book, No. 26, p. 247 (Ltr, Actg QMG to Asst. QM Engle, 9 May 1838).

[137] See, for example, RG 94, AGO Records, file 319.12 (Annual Reports of the Quartermaster General, 1881, p. 20; 1882, p. 7; 1884, p. 22).

[138] See, for example, 26 Stat. 33 (Act, Mar 31, 1890); 30 Stat. 216 (Joint Resolution, Mar 24, 1897).

[139] RG 94, AGO Records, file 319.12 (Annual Report of The Quartermaster General, 1927, pp. 48–50; 54).

$700,000.[140] The relief policy was so well established by the 1930's that when the needs of the unemployed in the depression years surpassed the ability of charitable organizations to meet them, the Corps loaned cots and bedding to accredited charitable organizations for the use of the unemployed.[141]

When Franklin D. Roosevelt became President, he made a major effort to relieve unemployment. In response to his suggestion, Congress, in March 1933, enacted legislation establishing the Civilian Conservation Corps.[142] That Corps enrolled young men to work on forestry, flood control, prevention of soil erosion, and similar projects, the work to be under the technical supervision of the Departments of Agriculture and Interior. The War Department was charged with many important functions in support of the Civilian Conservation Corps, in the execution of which the Secretary of War assigned to the Quartermaster Corps the task of supplying the men with food, clothing, equipment, and shelter, and of transporting them to and from their work camps.

Enrollment began on 6 April without causing any supply difficulties, but, on 12 May, the President directed that the entire quota of men—about 300,000—were to be at work by 1 July. Since this force was almost three times the strength of the Regular Army within the continental limits of the United States, this acceleration of enrollment required a supply effort closely paralleling that needed in a major military mobilization. In consequence, it provided a fair test of the effectiveness of the Quartermaster Corps' supply machinery.[143]

The Quartermaster Corps clothed and equipped the men without any delay, since it still had on hand from World War I large stocks of Army clothing, tentage, and other equipage. Their availability greatly reduced the requirements that had to be filled by purchase. Distinctive articles of the uniform, however, had to be altered before issue in order to make them suitable for civilian wear. The Quartermaster Corps accomplished most of the alterations, as well as the production of large quantities of denim clothing and tentage at the Philadelphia Depot's

[140] (1) *Ibid.*, (Annual Report of the Quartermaster General, 1906, pp. 40–42). (2) For Quartermaster activity in this disaster see reports in RG 92, OQMG Document File, 1800–1915, Boxes 5338, 5339.

[141] RG 94, AGO Records, file 319.12 (Annual Reports of The Quartermaster General, 1932, pp. 47–48; 1933, p. 30).

[142] 48 *Stat.* 22–23 (Act, Mar 31, 1933).

[143] (1) A full report on Quartermaster support of the Civilian Conservation Corps is to be found in RG 94, AGO Records, file 319.12 (Annual Report of The Quartermaster General, 1933, pp. 69–76). Additional data is in sections of subsequent Annual Reports for 1934 through 1937. (2) See also Capt. Francis V. Fitz Gerald, "The President Prescribes–The Organization and Supply of the C.C.C.," *The Quartermaster Review*, XIII (Jul–Aug 1933), pp. 7–18.

clothing factory, the laboring force of which was more than doubled to do the work. The Quartermaster General decentralized purchases of all classes of supplies to the depots, directing depot quartermasters to circulate purchase information as widely as possible among prospective bidders, including those at facilities listed in procurement plans. Once the Civilian Conservation Corps completed initial mobilization, the Philadelphia Depot purchased all clothing and equipage to avoid competition among the depots, but it continued to make awards of contracts in all parts of the country.

To subsist the men of the Civilian Conservation Corps, The Quartermaster General provided the same ration furnished Regular Army personnel. The camps procured perishables locally, except that in some cases Quartermaster supply depots purchased meats on monthly contracts. Subsistence supply functioned smoothly, but difficulties had to be solved in transporting rations to work camps remote from markets.

The Quartermaster Corps provided tentage for shelter both at conditioning camps and at work projects. Corps area commanders were responsible for the construction of temporary buildings and the installation of utilities at work projects, with Quartermaster personnel providing technical advice and assistance.

Transportation was a serious problem. Since most of the men came from congested centers in the East and a large number of work projects were located in the Far West, The Quartermaster General reported that "a transcontinental movement of almost unparalleled proportions in peace time" had to be undertaken. The corps area commander handled movements within his corps area unless they involved the use of sleeping car equipment. In such cases, the Office of The Quartermaster General made the arrangements. It also handled all movements from one corps area to another. The American Railway Association and the Pullman Company assigned some of their personnel to the Office to assist in transportation. The carriers also placed some of their personnel on duty at each corps area headquarters. In consequence of these arrangements and the cooperation of the railroads, the Quartermaster Corps accomplished the movement of Civilian Conservation Corps personnel without incident.

By the time the first work camps—some 1,470—were completed, the task of the Quartermaster Corps in supporting the Civilian Conservation Corps had become routine and subsequent expansions of the program posed no problems. The demands made on the Quartermaster Corps necessitated no changes in organization, and, so smoothly did supply operations function, that Quartermaster officers were convinced the Corps was not only properly organized but sufficiently flexible to meet every emergency in the future.

Impact of the Emergency

Six years later, war began in Europe. The small but potentially expandable Quartermaster Corps at once felt its impact. To house the growing Army, and to clothe, equip, and subsist it, the Corps' organization in the field and at Washington was expanded. That expansion could be orderly because of the extended period of the emergency which lasted from the presidential proclamation of limited emergency in September 1939 to the attack on Pearl Harbor on 7 December 1941. During these months, Quartermaster preparations were accelerated and when war came not only was the Army better prepared but the Quartermaster Corps also was in better position to support it than it had been in any previous war.

CHAPTER XVII

In Retrospect

The Quartermaster supply function undoubtedly is as old as the first army that took the field, but the term "Quartermaster" appears not to have come into general usage in Europe until the rise of standing armies in the 16th century. The derivation of the term is traced to the German "Quartier-Meister" or the Dutch "Kwartiermeester." It was late in the 17th century, however, before the title "Quarter-Master-General" was introduced in the British Army. Beginning in 1686, one or more British Quarter-Masters-General were appointed. Service in the colonial wars familiarized American colonists with British army organization and led the Continental Congress to establish the post of Quartermaster General in Washington's Army in 1775.

For 43 years after the Continental Congress authorized the appointment of the first Quartermaster General, that officer functioned as the principal staff officer of the commanding general of the forces that took the field, but his existence was wholly dependent on a state of war. When the country was at peace, his office ceased to exist. No matter how small an Army was maintained in peacetime, the troops still had to be transported to their destinations, provided with quarters, and furnished with rations, clothing, equipment, and ammunition. In the absence of a Quartermaster General, such supply duties devolved upon the Secretary of War. Even more compelling than the need to relieve the Secretary of such responsibilities was the necessity to provide the military establishment in time of peace with an organization that would make it efficient in time of war. That fact was forcibly demonstrated during the War of 1812.

In the years following that war, persistent efforts eventually resulted in a reorganization of the staff departments in 1818. A fundamental change was then introduced in the concept of the Quartermaster General of the Army. Secretary of War John C. Calhoun sought and obtained legislation creating staff bureaus in Washington, and the Quartermaster General became a bureau chief residing at the capital. His tenure was no longer limited to a war period and, in the absence of pension and retirement systems, his assignment was for life. It was not until 1882 that provision was made for mandatory retirement. After Maj. Gen.

Montgomery C. Meigs retired in that year, the Secretaries of War generally followed the principle of seniority in selecting the Quartermasters General who succeeded him.

The term "bureau chief" is apt to evoke an image of an officer who headed a subdivision of the War Department and executed the various responsibilities assigned to him through a large number of subordinates, both military and civilian, functioning in assigned areas of a compartmentalized agency. Nothing could be farther from the actuality in 1818 and for many years thereafter. When Quartermaster General Thomas S. Jesup set up his office in one or two rooms of the War Department building in 1818, he viewed it as "properly a Military One" and insisted on being permitted to select officers from the Army who were sufficiently qualified as clerks to handle all clerical duties and who, at the same time, were sufficiently versed in the details of military service to make them useful and efficient. His ulterior motive was to make his office a school of instruction, in which young officers would have an opportunity to educate themselves for the various duties of the staff. As originally established, therfore, Maj. Trueman Cross, who acted as assistant to the Quartermaster General, headed the office staff. It also included two other officers and a sergeant but no professional clerks because Jesup opposed employing them on the grounds that they would be of little assistance to him beyond casting accounts and copying letters.

As Quartermaster duties increased and the number of officers available to assist him in Washington dwindled to two officers and sometimes to one, Jesup's views on clerical help necessarily changed. By 1824, he employed two civilian clerks. To keep the office records current, the War Department also detailed three sergeants for duty as extra clerks. In emergencies, Congress authorized the temporary hire of extra civilian clerks, but, in the pre-Civil War years, the permanent clerical staff did not exceed six men. Perched on three-legged stools before high desks, reminiscent of Scrooge's mercantile establishment so vividly described by Charles Dickens, these clerks kept the large letter books of the office in longhand, recorded contracts and claims, and carefully maintained the ledgers of property and monetary accountability, each clerk being assigned certain responsibilities. The same chief clerk and most of his assistants served throughout the years before the Civil War. As in the case of the military personnel, the civilian clerk, in the absence of a retirement system, served at his post until death removed him.

Not until the Civil War increased the work of the office tremendously did the Quartermaster General establish a divisional organization of duties, largely along commodity lines. A Quartermaster officer and his assistants who were served by an increasingly large clerical staff directed the work of each division. After the Civil War, the office force expanded during subsequent war years and contracted in periods of retrenchment but, although the number of divisions dwindled to as few as four by 1898, the divisional organization was thereafter retained.

The Civil War marked the first time that female clerks were hired in the office of the Quartermaster General. Retrenchment after the war did not eliminate them; in fact, there was considerable pressure to continue employing those most in need. General Meigs had viewed the advent of the female clerk with alarm. His sympathies, however, were touched by their appeals, and he was instrumental in getting Congress to enact a special law during the war to allow a certain number of female copyists to be employed in the office. But when the Secretary of War referred more and more needy female applicants to him in the postwar years, he tartly informed the latter that the limit of employment in his office had been reached. He was glad, he wrote the Secretary in 1877, that the office "has been able to offer a refuge to so many widows and relations of deceased officers," but he quickly added that under the revised statutes a woman had the right to aspire to any clerkship for which she was competent in any bureau. If the law was therefore enforced in all War Department offices, he pointed out, the Secretary would be able to extend employment to more female applicants and thus spare himself the pain of refusing them. The female clerk and copyist remained. The general use of the typewriter before the close of the 19th century assured her continuing employment, for, when Meigs first experimented with the use of the Sholes and Glidden typewriter in 1874, he found that women were better and more rapid copyists than men with "this instrument."

The shift from chief staff officer of the commanding general to bureau chief, heading an office in Washington, had an impact that was not immediately apparent. Concerned with problems of property accountability, funds control, and the preparation and defense of estimates for appropriations, the Quartermaster General, as well as other bureau chiefs, reported directly to the Secretary of War rather than to the Commanding General of the Army. In time, they developed a close and influential relationship with Congress. That influence aroused suspicions that the interests of the staff were being promoted at the expense of those of the line. A general feeling developed, too, that the needs of the line were not even known to the staff officer. That attitude furthered the resentment against staff removal from line control and laid the basis for the staff and line controversy, involving the Commanding General of the Army, the Secretary of War, and the staff bureaus, that grew to large proportions after the Civil War. The fundamental problem of control was not tackled until Elihu Root as Secretary of War

pushed through legislation in 1903 that abolished the separate office of
Commanding General of the Army, established the position of Chief
of Staff, and brought the supply departments under the latter's supervision. The long-range objective of this reform, however, was not
achieved before World War I.

In addition to this shift in basic control, two other developments,
attributable to the reform spirit engendered by the Spanish-American
War, brought changes affecting Quartermaster personnel. One of these
was the introduction of the detail system. For 85 years the Department
had adhered to the Jesup concept of developing a body of officers trained
and experienced in the conduct of the Department's business. Pursuit
of that policy had been eminently successful; it had produced Quartermasters of the caliber of Ingalls, Allen, and Rucker. At Root's insistence,
Congress had discarded that concept in favor of the idea that line officers
could be detailed for 4-year tours of duty in the Quartermaster's Department to execute its functions. This rotation, proponents of the detail
system argued, would permit the line officer to acquire an insight into
supply operations, would provide the staff bureaus with a better knowledge of the needs of the Army, and, it was anticipated, would resolve the
line and staff controversy. The change was to be effected gradually, but
ultimately it would end the separation of line and staff, to which critics
attributed much of the maladministration of the supply services during
the Spanish-American War. At a time when the commercial world was
increasingly emphasizing specialization, it was abandoned in the Quartermaster's Department, though not without protest from succeeding Quartermasters General. This sweeping change proved temporary in character. Congress modified it in 1920 to the extent of permanently
commissioning in the Corps officers above the grade of captain, who, since
1903, had been detailed from other branches of the Army. It thereby
re-established a career for supply officers.

Militarization of the Corps had been a reform advocated by Quartermaster officers since the time of the Mexican War. It was finally achieved
in 1912. Before that time, the Department had employed many civilians
to do the work of clerks, blacksmiths, packers, teamsters, engineers, firemen, carpenters, and laborers. Quartermasters frequently experienced
difficulty in controlling such civilian workers. Failure of such workers
to carry out instructions could conceivably hamper operations. When
civilians were not available for the tasks to be performed or funds did
not permit their hire, commanders detailed soldiers on extra duty for the
purpose. Opposed by commanding officers, this practice was a solution
that worked a hardship on the Army, particularly during active operations, when Army strength might be diminished at a time of greatest

need. For the first time, Congress authorized the establishment of a service corps of enlisted men in 1912 which demonstrated its usefulness a few years later in World War I. Though only truck, wagon, pack, and bakery companies existed in 1917, before the war ended the War Department had authorized, and the Quartermaster Corps in the A.E.F. had used, 26 different types of units.

Along with these trends came modifications in the responsibilities assigned to the Quartermaster General. These changes transformed the organization from a transportation agency to a supply department responsible for the procurement, distribution, maintenance, and salvage of supplies. Although the Quartermaster General in 1775 had a basic responsibility for quartering the troops, his primary function was the transportation of men and supplies. Procurement was limited to the purchase of tentage and the means to enable the troops to erect huts for winter quarters. The Quartermaster General also procured the boats, when necessary, and the wagons, animals, and forage needed to keep supply lines moving and to permit the Army to take the field.

Transportation and construction continued to be the major functions of the Quartermaster's Department throughout the 19th century. In 1862, when railroads began to play an increasingly important role in wartime operations, Thomas A. Scott, an experienced railroadman then serving as Assistant Secretary of War, suggested the establishment of a separate transportation agency. Neither that proposal nor a similar recommendation made by the Dodge Commission in 1899 received consideration. The increasing complexities of modern war ultimately brought a reassignment of Quartermaster responsibilities and the establishment not only of separate Transportation and Motor Transport Services but also a separate construction agency during World War I. Though these arrangements proved temporary, the precedent set was to be followed in World War II and responsibility for transportation and construction were to be permanently removed from the Corps.

In the meantime, the Department had been acquiring other responsibilities over the years that permitted it to emerge as the chief supply agency of the Army in the decades before World War II. The first changes were gradual, but World War I brought a drastic reorientation of the Corps' responsibilities. Despite the Secretary of War's opposition, the Department had become completely responsible for the procurement, distribution, and issue of clothing in 1842. The Civil War resulted in additional responsibilities in the care of the dead and the maintenance of national cemeteries. When Congress merged the Subsistence and Pay Departments with the Quartermaster's Department in 1912, it transferred the responsibilities of those two agencies to the newly created Quartermaster Corps. By that date, the Corps had broad responsibilities in several fields of Army supply.

In 1918, the Corps' headquarters and field organization provided the basis on which to build the staff structure called the Purchase and Storage Division, which absorbed the supply operations of all the supply bureaus. Although this proved to be only a temporary arrangement that Congress abolished in the National Defense Act of 1920, the provisions of that law reserved to the Corps a major role in interbranch procurement by providing that the Quartermaster General was to be charged with the purchase and procurement for the Army of "all supplies of standard manufacture and of all supplies common to two or more branches." Congress exempted from the centralized procurement responsibility vested in the Quartermaster General only those technical or special articles used or issued specifically by one supply department. Despite the temporary return to the Corps of the responsibility for transportation and construction, the emphasis was predominantly on its function as a supply agency.

Most of the major changes that altered the organization, functions, and personnel of the Corps occurred in the first decades of the 20th century. These, the later history of the Corps would disclose, were but a prelude to even more fundamental modifications which were to come in the wake of revolutionary military developments that in 1939 were still hidden in the future.

The history of the Corps reveals that its operations followed a cyclical pattern that was common to all supply services. Wartime expansion was inevitably succeeded by peacetime retrenchment. In the years of peace, the Quartermaster General was unable to prepare ahead of time for future emergencies. Only too often the funds at his disposal were barely sufficient to cover current operating expenses. Stringent economies had frequently to be practiced to enable the Department to stay within appropriated funds.

Not all unpreparedness, however, can be attributed to lack of funds. Quartermaster officers tended to become imbued with the same apathy toward military preparedness that infected the civilian population and which influenced Congress and the Executive branch of government alike throughout the 19th century. For approximately 9 of the 100 years of that century, the country was engaged in war. The brief years of war in contrast to the long years of tranquility could not dim the bright image of peace that the people of the United States charished. Protected by a broad expanse of water and sheltered by the British navy that patrolled it, they felt no menace to their way of life. Turning their attention to the conquest of a continent, they enjoyed the advantages of low defense costs and could afford the luxury of a small Army, only large enough to provide police action against the Indians who obstructed the westward movement.

The opening decades of the 20th century saw no change in the civilian attitude. Quartermaster officers, shaken by their experience in the Spanish-American War, did make a concerted effort to build up reserve stocks of supplies. These supplies were depleted, however, when the Quartermaster General had to equip the organized militia of the states, called into active service and concentrated on the Mexican border when the President sent Pershing and the punitive expedition in pursuit of Villa. The Quartermaster Corps was left as unprepared to meet the demands made upon it in 1917 as it had been in earlier wars. The attractiveness of the slogan "the war to end wars" and a willingness to believe that victory in World War I meant its achievement, only added to the prevailing public indifference to the state of the Army after 1918.

When any war broke out, the Quartermaster General was at once called upon to transport, shelter, clothe, equip, and subsist immediately a rapidly mushrooming force. Congress then loosened the purse strings and placed ample funds at the disposal of the supply bureau, but haste made for waste. Money could not buy the time required to manufacture and produce the supplies so urgently needed and therefore substitute articles, usually inferior to the standard items obtained in the past, had to be accepted. Quartermasters promptly became the targets for criticism, much of which they did not merit, and congressional investigating committees sought the reason for supply failures. As the war progressed, the initial confusion and shortages were always overcome. Galvanized into action, the quartermasters often achieved amazing results, supported by the tremendous production efforts of the country. The costs, however, were high.

With the end of a war, Congress and the War Department gave first consideration to reducing costs. This meant demobilizing the Army, getting the volunteers and draftees back to their normal civilian pursuits, and reducing the size of the Regular Army that had been expanded in wartime. The country's lavish support of war measures and its tremendous production effort resulted in the receipt of large quantities of supplies, contracted for months earlier but which could not be used by the reduced number of peacetime troops. Demobilization also meant the prompt release of rented storage facilities and the disposal of surplus supplies, usually at a fraction of their original cost. Military appropriations became smaller; retrenchment was again the controlling objective. To ease the rigorous economies imposed on the Army, reserves of wartime supplies being held at depots were used until exhaustion of such stocks compelled the Quartermaster General to seek larger appropriations for the support of the Army. By that time, the supply bureau had slipped into the state of unpreparedness that preceded every war. The competent supply organization developed for the support of war was replaced by the small staff needed for peacetime operations, and supply lessons learned painfully under pressure sometimes appeared to be completely lost to quartermasters removed by decades of peace from the demands of war.

In the Revolutionary War, Maj. Gen. Nathanael Greene, forced to assume the duties of Quartermaster General against his inclinations, complained that no one ever heard of a quartermaster. Certainly the annals of military history support his assertion. Glory is deservedly the combat soldier's reward, but the historical record does not reveal him as overly generous in sharing credit for victory with the supply officer without whose work that goal could not be reached. Only rarely is the effort of the Quartermaster officer praised. An abundant and steady flow of supplies is taken for granted by the troops, usually without any awareness of the problems involved in its maintenance. Let supplies or transportation be delayed, however, and denunciations of the quartermaster at once fill the mail pouches. If encomiums were few for Quartermaster officers, they may take quiet satisfaction in the fact that in the history of the Corps no military operation of the U.S. Army failed for want of supplies. Despite difficulties and occasional failures, they gave unstinted support to the line in the doldrums of peace as well as in the spirited stimulation of war.

BRIGADIER GENERAL THOMAS S. JESUP
FATHER OF THE CORPS
8 MAY 1818–10 JUNE 1860

Col. (Maj. Gen.) Thomas Mifflin
14 Aug 1775–16 May 1776
28 Sep 1776–7 Nov 1777

Col. Stephen Moylan
5 Jun–27 Sep 1776

Maj. Gen. Nathanael Greene
2 Mar 1778–26 Jul 1780

Col. Timothy Pickering
5 Aug 1780–25 Jul 1785

Samuel Hodgdon
4 Mar 1791–19 Apr 1792

James O'Hara
19 Apr 1792–30 May 1796

John Wilkins, Jr.
1 Jun 1796–16 Mar 1802

Brig Gen. Morgan Lewis
4 Apr 1812–2 Mar 1813

Brig. Gen. Robert Swartwout
21 Mar 1813–29 Apr 1816

Col. George Gibson
29 Apr 1816–14 Apr 1818

Brig. Gen. Joseph E. Johnston
28 Jun 1860–22 Apr 1861

Brig. Gen. Montgomery C. Meigs
15 May 1861–6 Feb 1882

* No picture of Col. James Mullaney (29 Apr 1816–14 Apr 1818) has been found.

Brig. Gen. Daniel H. Rucker
13–23 Feb 1882

Brig. Gen. Rufus Ingalls
23 Feb 1882–1 Jul 1883

Brig. Gen. Samuel B. Holabird
1 Jul 1883–16 Jun 1890

Brig. Gen. Richard N. Batchelder
26 Jun 1890–27 Jul 1896

Brig. Gen. Charles G. Sawtelle
19 Aug 1896–16 Feb 1897

Brig. Gen. George H. Weeks
16 Feb 1897–3 Feb 1898

Brig. Gen. Marshall I. Ludington
3 Feb 1898–13 Apr 1903

Brig. Gen. Charles F. Humphrey
12 Apr 1903–1 Jul 1907

Maj. Gen. James B. Aleshire
1 Jul 1907–12 Sep 1916

Maj. Gen. Henry G. Sharpe
13 Sep 1916–12 Jul 1918

Maj. Gen. Harry L. Rogers
22 Jul 1918–27 Aug 1922

Maj. Gen. William H. Hart
28 Aug 1922–2 Jan 1926

Maj. Gen. B. Franklin Cheatham
3 Jan 1926–17 Jan 1930

Maj. Gen. John L. DeWitt
3 Feb 1930–2 Feb 1934

Maj. Gen. Louis H. Bash
3 Feb 1934–31 Mar 1936

Maj. Gen. Henry Gibbins
1 Apr 1936–31 Mar 1940

BIBLIOGRAPHICAL NOTE

National Archives

Record Group No. 11. Papers of the Continental Congress.

This is a voluminous collection of many items, much of them relating to supply in the Revolutionary War. Of these, the following are particularly useful:

Reports of the Board of War. 6 vols. Item No. 147.

Letters of the Board of War. 2 vols. Item No. 148.

Letters and Reports of the Secretary at War. 7 vols. Items No. 149–151.

Letters of Maj. Gen. Nathanael Greene. 7 vols. Items No. 155, 173.

Letters of Thomas Mifflin and others. 1 vol. Item No. 161.

Letters of Ephraim Blaine and others. 1 vol. Item No. 165.

Reports of Committees. 12 vols. Items No. 21–22, 27, 29, 31, 34.

Record Group No. 92. Records of the Office of the Quartermaster General.

The basic archival material used in this volume is found in this record group. The number is applied to all Quartermaster documents as well as to those of some other agencies that were later absorbed by the Quartermaster's Department. It is a voluminous collection of hundreds of bound volumes and boxes of documents from which the history of Quartermaster supply operations must be laboriously dredged, for there is no inventory of these records. The following major collections of correspondence are of primary importance:

Letter Books. In the first period of record keeping, 1820–1889, outgoing correspondence was copied in letter books—some 107 volumes to 1870. After that date the letters were copied in books of the respective responsible divisions in the Office and a set called Letter Book, General and Miscellaneous, was also maintained.

Clothing Book, Letters Sent. 33 vols. The outgoing correspondence relative to clothing was copied in these books for the period 1827–1870, when the Clothing and Equipage Division began to maintain its books of outgoing correspondence.

Letters Received. The incoming correspondence for the period 1820–1889 is filed in 208 boxes and indexed in registers.

Register of Letters Received. 142 vols. For the period 1820–1889, all incoming correspondence was entered in Registers of Letters Received, each letter being given a symbol to permit location. The letters frequently are not found in the designated location and, in consequence, the Registers themselves remain valuable, for they give the date, sender's name, and the purport of the letters received.

OQMG Consolidated Correspondence File, 1794-1915. 1,275 boxes. In time, letters received pertaining to a common subject were consolidated for convenience of use and filed under subject heads. In later years both incoming and outgoing correspondence were filed together on some subjects.

OQMG Document File, 1890–1914. 8,607 boxes. In 1890 the "book period" of record keeping gave way to the "record card period." Information formerly entered in the Register of Letters Received and briefs of Letters Sent were copied on record cards, the incoming and outgoing correspondence being filed together to form the Document File.

OQMG General Correspondence File, 1917–1922. 4,042 ft. This is the third period of record keeping in which incoming papers and copies of outgoing correspondence were placed in one file and classified by subject according to the War Department decimal classification scheme.

There are other volumes in this record group that are informative for wartime supply operations, especially in the field. For the Mexican War the following are useful:

Official Letters from Col. Henry Whiting, AQMG, with Gen. Taylor's Army in Mexico, 1846–47. 2 vols.

Official Letters to Col Henry Whiting, 1846–47. 5 vols.

Official Letters to Maj. D. D. Tompkins, QM at New Orleans. 9 vols.

Official Letters from Maj. D. D. Tompkins. 6 vols.

Letter Books of Maj. Geo. H. Crosman, QM at Philadelphia, 1845–46. 4 vols.

For the Civil War period, the following should not be overlooked:

Letters of Brig. Gen. Stewart Van Vliet to QMG, 26 May 1846—7 Aug 1865. 1 vol.

Letters Issued, AQMG Office, Louisville, 18 Feb–16 June 1862. 1 vol.

Rusling, Reports of Inspections in QMD. 2 vols. These are important not only for the Civil War but for the post-Civil War period, and particularly for conditions in the West.

Annual Reports from QM Officers, 1863. 5 vols.

Personal Narrative Reports of Officers, QMD, for Fiscal Years 1864–1868. 12 vols. Filed alphabetically by name of the officer and copied in volumes, these reports are extremely important for they spell out the operations in which the officers were engaged in the field and at depots. Though the reports were not instituted before the last year of the war, the officers generally give a background of their activities that frequently carry the narrative back to 1861.

For the World War I period, the following collections are of major importance in this record group:

OQMG Historical File. 63 boxes. During World War I a Historical Branch was set up in the OQMG. It collected documents relating to supply operations in the zone of interior under the OQMG and under the Purchase and Storage Division of the General Staff. Along with the documents there are filed drafts of historical reports prepared in the Branch.

General H. L. Rogers' Private File. 77 boxes. This is a valuable collection of documents and historical reports recording the activities of the QMC in the A.E.F. It includes the Report of the Chief Quartermaster, A.E.F., as well as material pertaining to the Purchase and Storage Division when Rogers served as chief.

Report of Maj. Roy A. Shaw to Acting QMG. 10 Sections. This is a report of an inspection visit made to England and France in the summer of 1918 and covers such subjects as requirements for QM supplies in the AEF, overseas shipments, stocks, packaging, QM salvage, foreign purchases of QM supplies.

The following miscellaneous volumes and boxes of material provide useful information for supply operations:

OQMG Estimates and Reports, 1835–1848. 3 vols.

OQMG Register of Contracts, 1818–60. 12 vols.

OQMG Decision Book, 1842–1870. 10 vols.

Annual Reports from QM Officers to QMG, 1863–1878. 37 boxes.

Letter Book, Western River Transportation. 1 vol.

Charter Parties and Names of Crews of Vessels, 1847. These are copies entered in bound volumes.

Vessels Engaged in Mexican War and on Western Rivers During the Civil War.

Letters Received from Heads of Departments and Bureaus, 1863–1870. 12 boxes and 24 volumes.

Reports of QMG to SW and Heads of Departments. 8 vols.

Letter Books of General J. B. Aleshire. These are valuable for the pre-World War I years when General Aleshire served as QMG.

Letters from Maj. Gen. Thomas S. Jesup, 1828–1846. 1 box.

Included in this record group are the records of the Schuylkill Arsenal, a large collection of documents consisting of letter books, orders on the military storekeeper, inspection books, reports on employees, seamstress books, and other miscellaneous records that cover the period 1846 to 1916. They are particularly valuable for tracing developments at the Clothing Establishment and the Philadelphia Depot.   Among the more important volumes are the following:

Letter Books, 1842–1846. 8 vols. Letters sent to the QMG and others from the Purchasing Office of the Office of Clothing and Equipage, Philadelphia.

The Quartermaster General Letter Books, 1856–1860.   15 vols.

Letters Sent, 1861, by AQMG Chas. Thomas.   2 vols.

Crosman Letter Books, 1862–1865.   5 vols.

Record Group No. 92.   Records of the Office of the Commissary General of Purchases.

Entered under the record group number for Quartermaster records is a vast collection loosely referred to as the records of the Office of the Commissary General of Purchases.   They are, in fact, a grand melange of records of some seven supply agencies that operated in Philadelphia, which, in the course of transfer of records between Washington and Philadelphia before their final deposit at the National Archives, became interspersed in addition with records from quartermasters and commissaries stationed in the field and at departmental headquarters.   The seven supply agencies at Philadelphia were the Office of the Purveyor of Public Supplies, the Office of the Superintendent of Military Stores, the Office of the Commissary General of Purchases, the Office of the Military Storekeeper, the Office of the Military Agent which later became the Office of the Quartermaster Office, the Clothing Establishment, and the Office of Army Clothing and Equipage that was established after the Quartermaster's Department absorbed the remaining functions of the Commissary General of Purchases in 1842.   The volumes are so intermingled that all distinction between the records of the different offices is lost and there is no arrangement by office.   At some time in the past, 561 of the 600 bound volumes were given numbered tags in the order in which they were shelved so that a volume can be located by tagged number.   Unfortunately, the unnumbered volumes are not so readily located.   A partial inventory, restricted to bound volumes originating in the Philadelphia offices, was prepared by James R. Masterson and provides a useful guide. Among the volumes of correspondence particularly useful for this study are the following:

Letters Sent, Commissary General of Purchases, 1812–1850.   18 vols.

Letters Sent, Purveyor of Public Supplies, 1800–1812.   8 vols.

Letters Sent, Office of the Military Storekeeper, 1801–1857.   10 vols.

Letters Sent, William Linnard, 1802–1847.   11 vols.   Linnard served first as military agent and then as Quartermaster Officer at Philadelphia.

The so-called miscellaneous collection, not inventoried by Masterson, includes a vast array of ledger books, abstracts of orders, issues, receipts and other supply documents. Among the more important volumes are the following:

Letter Book of Capt. A. R. Hetzel, 1835–37. 1 vol. Tag No. 074.

Letters Sent by R. F. Loper, Transport Agent, 1847. Tag No. 076.

Letter Book, Capt. I. R. Irwin, at Port La Vaca, 22 Jun 1846–31 Mar 1847. Tag No. 078.

Letter Book, 18 Apr–27 June 1847, Capt. A. R. Hetzel, Vera Cruz Depot. Tag No. 085.

Letter Book of Capt. James M. Hill, Brazos Santiago, 1 Oct–31 Dec 1846. Tag No. 088; 1 Jan–31 Mar 1847. Tag No. 089; 1 Oct 1845–30 Sep 1846. Tag No. 090.

Letter Book, Capt. W. M. D. McKissack, Santa Fe, 1 Jun 1846–16 Oct 1848. Tag No. 091.

Letters Sent, Bvt. Maj. Chas. McClure, Chief Commissary, New Mexico, 1868–1870. Tag. No. 145, 147.

Contracts. List giving names of contractors, quantities, prices, 1812–1837. Tag No. 256.

Letter Book, William Linnard, 1823–25. Untagged.

Included in this record are many loose papers that provide detailed information on early supply operations. They are referred to as:

Coxe and Irvine Papers. They are boxed in 113 cardboard containers and 27 metal trays. They are papers of the offices of Tench Coxe, Purveyor of Public Supplies, and Callendar Irvine, Commissary General of Purchases.

Record Group No. 93. Revolutionary War Records.

In this record group the most important volumes for Quartermaster history are the following:

Letter Books of Col. Timothy Pickering. Vols. 82–88; 123–126.

Letter Book of Samuel Hodgdon, 30 Dec 1782–10 Dec 1783. Vol. 93.

Record Group No. 94. Records of the Adjutant General's Office.

A guide to the use of these records is provided in a "Preliminary Inventory," No. 17, compiled by Lucille H. Pendell and Elizabeth Bethel. Since the AGO handled records, orders, and correspondence of the Army, documents that could not be located in QM files frequently were found in this record group, which was therefore used for supplementary purposes. As in the case of QM correspondence, that of the AGO also follows the "book period," the "record card period," and the "decimal classification period." Records used from this collection include the following:

Letters Sent, 1800–1889. 95 vols.

Letters Received, 1805–1889. 620 ft.

Registers of Letters Received, 1814–1889. 133 vols.

AGO Document File, 1890–1917. 2,967 ft.

Decimal Correspondence File, 1917–1925.   790 ft.

Records of the Appointment, Commission, and Personal Branch.   In this ACP file is to be found information on the military service of QM officers—for the period 1863–1894.   Before that date such information is found in Letters Received, and after that date in 201 files.

Orders and Circulars, 1797–1910.   2,082 vols.   This is one of the most complete collections of orders and circulars for these years.   The first volume contains the orders of General James Wilkinson, 1787–1809.

In its capacity as custodian of Army records, the AGO also maintained other groups of records in addition to those emanating from its Office and divisions.   Of these, the most important for Quartermaster operations are the very fragmentary Post-Revolutionary War Manuscripts and Post-Revolutionary War Papers for the period 1784–1815.   These appear to be arbitrarily divided into two record group numbers: 94 and 98.   Included in RG No. 94 are:

QM Accounts and Returns, 1792–1811.

Letter Book of Samuel Hodgdon, 26 Aug 1799–22 Oct 1800.

Orderly and Company Book, 1795–1813.

St. Clair Papers.

Record Group No. 98.   Post-Revolutionary War Records.

Journal of Quartermaster General James O'Hara.   This is the most important volume for QM history in this record group.

Record Group No. 107.   Records of the Office of the Secretary of War.

A preliminary checklist has been compiled by Lucille H. Pendall for this large collection of records.   To develop the relationship between the Quartermaster's Department and the Office of the Secretary of War and to analyze the role of the Secretary of War in supply operations, the following records are useful:

Letters Sent, 1800–1889.   151 vols.   A general chronological arrangement is followed.   For the years 1800–1870, the volumes are designated Military Books; for the period 1871–1889, Letters Sent.

Letters Received, 1800–1889.   212 ft.

Registers of Letters Received.   227 vols.   Keyed by symbol to the Letters Received, these registers are valuable, for the abstracts provide the correspondent's name, date, and purpose of the letter—the only information sometimes available for missing letters received.

Letters Sent to the QMG and the Purchasing Department, 18 Nov 1814–23 May 1815.   1 vol.

Registers of Letters Received from the QMG and Purchasing Department, Oct 1814–June 1815.   1 vol.

Reports to Congress, 3 Feb 1803–31 Dec 1870.   11 vols.   Copies of letters, submitting reports to Congress in reply to resolutions of Congress. These often include copies of the reports.

Contracts, 1 May 1799–7 Nov 1810. 2 vols. These are copies of articles of agreement and contracts between the Secretary and contractors and other persons for rations, quarters, and other supplies.

Record Group No. 120. Records of the American Expeditionary Forces.

This is a voluminous record collection that includes not only the documents of the A.E.F. but also those of the War Department for the war period. The following collections were used:

AEF SOS Historical Files. 79 ft.

These files are a general historical file for the period 1917–1923, and include reports, statistics, lists, orders, bulletins, memoranda, related correspondence, and similar materials assembled for the preparation of histories of SOS operations. Drafts of historical monographs and reports are also filed in this collection. Among the records are those of the QMC in the AEF, which was made a part of the SOS in 1918. These records include the general correspondence of the chief quartermaster as well as the correspondence of the Supplies, Remount, and Salvage Divisions of his office.

War Department Historical Files, 1917–1923. 50 ft. These are the records of the wartime organization and operation of the War Department. The files were created and assembled by the Historical Section, established by the Secretary of War in January 1918, in the War College Division of the General Staff. They include documents as well as prepared drafts of historical monographs and reports. They are particularly valuable for development of relationships between the Purchase, Storage and Traffic Division and the QMC.

History of the Construction Division, 1919. 18 vols. This is a narrative history of construction during the war that was prepared by Gen. R. C. Marshall, supported with appendices, exhibits, reports, memoranda, blueprints.

Records of the Motor Transport Corps.

Record Group No. 165. Records of the War College Division, General Staff.

Document File, 1903–1919. 211 ft. The records of this file are kept in accordance with the "record card period," the cards being used to locate pertinent documents under subject heads. The file is valuable for tracing relationships between the Staff and QMC in the pre-World War I period and for such planning developments as occurred in reference to clothing, reserve depots, and QM supply operations generally.

Record Group No. 192. Records of the Commissary General of Subsistence.

There is a wealth of material on Army subsistence in these records. The following proved valuable:

Letters Sent to the Secretary of War, 1840–1889. 10 vols.

Letters Sent to the Secretary of War, 1884–1893. 12 vols. These are letter press copy books of letters sent to the Secretary.

Letters Sent, 1818–1889. 132 vols.

Letters Received, 1818–1889.

Registers of Letters Received, 1818–1889. 80 vols. Letters received during the first years of the bureau are missing, but abstracts are found in the Registers.

Correspondence Record Cards. For the years 1890–94, only bound volumes of record cards providing abstracts of incoming and outgoing correspondence are available.

Correspondence File, 1894–1912. Copies of letters sent and letters received are filed together.

Lists of Proposals for Subsistence Contracts, 1819–1841. 5 vols.

Registers of Contracts, 1819–1907. 31 vols. These give such data as names of contracting parties, dates and places of contracts, period covered, costs. Copies of the contracts so listed before 1891 and all related correspondence were destroyed in that year by authority of Congress.

Manuscript Collections

Abeel, James. Letter Book of Col. James Abeel, Deputy Quartermaster General, 10 May 1778–10 Sep 1778. Manuscript Div., Library of Congress.

Account Book of Purveyor's Office, 1802. Manuscript Collection, New York Public Library.

Blaine, Ephraim. Papers of Ephraim Blaine. 5 vols. Manuscript Div., Library of Congress.

Brown, Maj. Gen. Jacob. Official Letter Book No. 1, 12 April 1814 to 23 December 1815; No. 2, 1 Jan 1816 to 5 Feb 1828. Manuscript Div., Library of Congress.

Dearborn, Gen. Henry. Letters and Orders of General Dearborn, 1812–13. 2 vols. New York Historical Society.

Duer, William. Papers on Revolutionary affairs, army supplies, and land operations. New York Historical Society. Two bound volumes of papers and many boxes of letters arranged chronologically.

Greene, Maj. Gen. Nathanael. Letters to and from Major General Nathanael Greene, 1778–1780. 12 vols. American Philosophical Society Library.

Hay, Udny. Papers and Correspondence of Undy Hay, Deputy Quartermaster General, Revolutionary War, 1776–1792. New York Historical Society.

Hodgdon, Samuel. Instructions and Correspondence of Samuel Hodgdon, 1794–1800. Manuscript Div., Library of Congress.

Hughes, Hugh. Letter books of correspondence with deputies and other officers, 1776–1782, of Hugh Hughes, Quartermaster General of New York, Revolutionary War. 19 vols. New York Historical Society.

Irvine, Brig. Gen. William. William Irvine Papers. Pennsylvania Historical Society.

Jesup, Maj. Gen. Thomas S. Jesup Papers. Manuscript Div., Library of Congress.

Meigs, Maj. Gen. Montgomery C. Meigs Papers. Manuscript Div., Library of Congress.

Morris, Robert. Robert Morris Papers, 1768–1803. Manuscript Collection, New York Public Library.

Morris, Robert. Papers of Robert Morris, including the financier's Official Diary, 3 vols., and his Official Letter Books, volumes A through E; his personal correspondence, 1777–1781. Manuscript Div., Library of Congress.

Piatt, John H. John H. Piatt Letter Book, 9 Jul 1812–7 Jan 1814. Manuscript Div., Library of Congress.

Stanton, Edwin M. Stanton Papers. Manuscript Div., Library of Congress.

Stewart, Charles. Correspondence of Charles Stewart, 1777–1782. Manuscript Div., Library of Congress.

Swartwout, Robert. Swartwout Papers. Manuscript Collection, New York Public Library.

U.S. Army. Miscellaneous records, principally quartermaster general and supply accounts and returns, 1795–1848. 26 vols., and loose papers. Manuscript Div., Library of Congress.

U.S. Army. Reports on the Reduction of the Army, 1821. Manuscript Div., Library of Congress.

Washington, George. Washington Papers. Manuscript Div., Library of Congress.

Wayne, Anthony. Wayne Papers. Pennsylvania Historical Society.

Wilkinson, James. Wilkinson Papers. Chicago Historical Society.

Printed Primary Sources

Alger, Russell A. *The Spanish-American War.* New York, 1901.

American State Papers. Washington, 1832–61. 38 vols.
    Class II   *Indian Affairs.* 2 vols.
    Class III   *Finance.* 5 vols.
    Class V   *Military Affairs.* 7 vols.
    Class X   *Miscellaneous.* 2 vols.

Aylett, William. "Correspondence of Col. William Aylett, Commissary General of Virginia," *Tyler's Quarterly Historical and Genealogical Magazine,* I (1919–20), 87–110; 145–161.

Ballagh, James C. (ed.). *The Letters of Richard Henry Lee.* New York, 1911. 2 vols.

Bandel, Eugene. *Frontier Life in the Army, 1855–61.* Ralph P. Bieber (ed.). Glendale, Calif., 1932.

Baruch, Bernard. *American Industry in the War.* Washington, 1921.

Basler, Roy P. (ed.). *The Collected Works of Abraham Lincoln.* Rutgers University Press, 1953. 8 vols.

Bassett, John S. (ed.). *Correspondence of Andrew Jackson.* Washington, 1926. 2 vols.

Billings, John D. *Hardtack and Coffee.* Boston, 1888.

Birkbeck, Morris. *Notes on a Journey in America.* London, 1818.

Buhoup, Jonathan W. *Narrative of the Central Division.* Pittsburgh, 1847.

Bullard, Robert L. *Personalities and Reminiscences of the War.* New York, 1925.

Burnett, Edmund C. (ed.). *Letters of Members of the Continental Congress.* Washington, 1921–36. 7 vols.

Butterfield, Consul W. (ed.). *Journal of Capt. Jonathan Heart.* Albany, 1885.

———. *Washington-Irvine Correspondence.* Madison, Wis., 1882.

Calendar of Virginia State Papers. Richmond, 1875–93. 11 vols.

Carter, Clarence E. (ed.). *The Territorial Papers of the United States.* Washington, 1934–. 24 vols.

Clarkson, Grosvenor B. *Industrial America in the World War.* New York, 1923.

Commager, Henry S. (ed.). *The Blue and the Gray.* New York, 1950. 2 vols.

Cooke, Lt. Col. Philip St. George. *Journal of the March of the Mormon Battalion of Infantry Volunteers* in Senate *Executive Document* No. 2, 31st Cong., Special Sess.

Crowell, Benedict. *America's Munitions, 1917–18: Report of Benedict Crowell.* Washington, 1919.

Cruikshank, Maj. E. (ed.). *Documentary History of the Campaign on the Niagara Frontier in 1812*. Welland, Ont., 1896–1907. 8 vols. in 4.

Cruse, Thomas. *Apache Days and After*. Caldwell, Idaho, 1941.

Dana, Charles A. *Recollections of the Civil War*. New York, 1902.

Darlington, Mary C. *Fort Pitt and Letters from the Frontier*. Pittsburgh, 1892.

Darnell, Elias. *A Journal Containing an Accurate and Interesting Account of . . . Those Heroic Kentucky Volunteers and Regulars, Commanded by General Winchester*. Philadelphia, 1854.

Davis, Capt. John. "The Yorktown Campaign: Journal of Captain John Davis, of the Pennsylvania Line," *Pennsylvania Magazine of History and Biography*, V (1881), 290–310.

Dawes, Charles G. *A Journal of the Great War*. New York, 1921. 2 vols.

Denny, Maj. Ebenezer. "Military Journal of Major Ebenezer Denny," *Publications of the Historical Society of Pennsylvania*, VII, 207–409.

Dodge, Nathaniel S. *Hints on Army Transportation*. Albany, 1863.

Drake, Francis S. *Life and Correspondence of Major-General Henry Knox*. Boston, 1873.

Essarey, Logan (ed.). "Messages and Letters of William Henry Harrison," *Indiana Historical Collections*, IX, Indianapolis, 1922.

First Annual Report, Council of National Defense, 1917. Washington, 1917.

Fitzpatrick, John C. (ed.). *The Diaries of George Washington, 1748–99*. New York, 1925. 4 vols.

——. *The Writings of Washington*. Washington, 1931–39. 30 vols.

Force, Peter (ed.). *American Archives*. Washington, 1837-53. 4th and 5th series. 9 vols.

Ford, Worthington C. (ed). *Correspondence and Journals of Samuel Blachley Webb*. New York, 1893–94. 3 vols.

—— and Others (eds.). *Journals of the Continental Congress, 1774–1789*. Washington, 1904–37. 34 vols.

Furber, George C. *The Twelve Months Volunteer*. Cincinnati, 1850.

Gibson, George Rutledge. *Journal of a Soldier Under Kearny and Doniphan, 1846–47*. Ralph P. Bieber (ed.). Glendale, Calif., 1935.

Grant, Ulysses S. *Personal Memoirs of U. S. Grant*. New York, 1885–86. 2 vols.

Graydon, Alexander. *Memoirs of a Life*. Harrisburgh, 1811.

Hagood, Maj. Gen. Johnson. *The Services of Supply*. Boston, 1927.

Hammond, Isaac W. (ed.). *Diary and Orderly Book of Sergeant Jonathan Burton*. Concord, N.H., 1885.

Hammond, Otis G. (ed.). *Letters and Papers of Major-General John Sullivan*. New Hampshire Historical Society *Collections*, XIII–XIV. Concord, N.H., 1931. 2 vols.

Harbord, James G. *The American Army in France*. Boston, 1936.

Haupt, Gen. Herman. *Reminiscences of General Herman Haupt*. Milwaukee, Wis., 1901.

Heath, Maj. Gen. William. "Heath Papers," Massachusetts Historical Society *Collections*, ser. v, vol. IV; ser. 7, vols. IV–V.

Henry, Capt. William Seaton. *Campaign Sketches of the War With Mexico*. New York, 1848.

Hiltzheimer, Jacob. "Extracts from the Diary of Jacob Hiltzheimer, 1768–1798," *Pennsylvania Magazine of History and Biography*, XVI (1892), 93–102, 160–177, 412–22.

Hitchcock, Maj. Gen. Ethan Allen. *Fifty Years in Camp and Field*. W. A. Croffut (ed.). New York, 1909.

Hitchcock, Henry. *Marching with Sherman*. New Haven, 1927.

Hughes, John T. *Doniphan's Expedition*. Cincinnati, 1850.

Johnson, Robert U., and Clarence C. Buel (eds.). *Battles and Leaders of the Civil War*. New York, 1884–88. 4 vols.

Kenly, John R. *Memoirs of a Maryland Volunteer*. Philadelphia, 1873.

Lee, Richard H. *Memoir of the Life of Richard Henry Lee*. Philadelphia, 1825. 2 vols.

Leib, Charles. *Nine Months in the Quartermaster's Department: The Chances for Making a Million*. Cincinnati, 1862.

Lodge, Henry C. (ed.). *Works of Alexander Hamilton*. New York, 1904. 12 vols.

Lowe, Percival. *Five Years a Dragoon, 1848–54*. Kansas City, 1926.

McAfee, Robert B. *History of the Late War in the Western Country*. Lexington, 1816.

McCallum, Bvt. Brig. Gen. D. C. *Reports of Bvt. Brig. Gen. D. C. McCallum and the Provost Marshal General*. Washington, 1866. 2 parts.

McMichael, Lt. James. "Diary of Lieutenant James McMichael of the Pennsylvania Line, 1776–78," *Pennsylvania Magazine of History and Biography*, XVI (1892), 129–59.

Majors, Alexander. *Seventy Years on the Frontier*. Col. Prentiss Ingraham (ed.). Chicago, 1893.

March, General Peyton C. *The Nation at War*. New York, 1932.

Matthews, William and Dixon Wecter. *Our Soldiers Speak, 1775–1918*. Boston, 1943.

Meade, George Gordon (ed.). *The Life and Letters of George Gordon Meade*. New York, 1913. 2 vols.

Mearns, David C. (ed.). *Lincoln Papers*. New York, 1948. 2 vols.

Meigs, Gen. M. C. "Documents. General J. C. Meigs on the Conduct of the Civil War," *The American Historical Review*, XXVI (Jan 1921), pp. 285–303.

Miles, Gen. Nelson A. *Personal Recollections and Observations*. New York, 1896.

Miley, John D. *In Cuba with Shafter*. New York, 1911.

Moylan, Stephen. "Selections from the Correspondence of Col. Stephen Moylan, of the Continental Cavalry," *Pennsylvania Magazine of History and Biography*, vol. 37 (1911), pp. 341–61.

Myers, William Starr (ed.). *The Mexican War Diary of George B. McClellan*. Princeton, 1917.

Page, Charles A. *Letters of a War Correspondent*. Boston, 1899.

Parker, Lt. Robert. "Journal of Lieutenant Robert Parker, of the Second Continental Artillery, 1779," *Pennsylvania Magazine of History and Biography*, XXVII, 404–29; XXVIII, 12–25.

Parsons, Bvt. Maj. Gen. Lewis B. *Report to the War Department*. St. Louis, 1867.

Pennsylvania Archives. Ser. 1, 12 vols. Philadelphia, 1852–56.

Pershing, John J. *My Experiences in the World War*. New York, 1931, 2 vols.

Reed, William B. *Life and Correspondence of Joseph Reed*. Philadelphia, 1847. 2 vols.

Richardson, James D. (comp.). *A Compilation of the Messages and Reports of the Presidents, 1789–1904*. Washington, 1896–1904. 10 vols.

Richardson, William H. *Journal of William H. Richardson*. New York, 1848. 3d edition.

Rusling, James F. *Men and Things I Saw in Civil War Days*. New York, 1899.

St. Clair, Maj. Gen. Arthur. *A Narrative of the Manner in which the Campaign Against the Indians, in the Year One Thousand Seven Hundred and Ninety-One, Was Conducted, Under the Command of Major General St. Clair . . .* Philadelphia, 1812.

Sargent, Winthrop. "Winthrop Sargent's Diary While with General Arthur St. Clair's Expedition Against the Indians," *Ohio Archaeological and Historical Quarterly*, vol. 33 (July 1924), No. 3, pp. 237–73.

Scribner, B. F. *Camp Life of a Volunteer*. Philadelphia, 1847.

Seymour, William. "Journal of the Southern Expedition, 1780–83, by William Seymour, Sergeant-Major of the Delaware Regiment," *Pennsylvania Magazine of History and Biography*, VII (1883), 286–98, 377–94.

Sharpe, Henry G. *The Quartermaster Corps in the Year 1917 in the World War*. New York, 1921.

Sherman, William T. *Personal Memoirs of Gen. W. T. Sherman*. New York, 1891. 4th ed., revised. 2 vols.

Smith, William Henry (ed.). *The St. Clair Papers: The Life and Public Services of Arthur St. Clair*. Cincinnati, 1882. 2 vols.

Symonds, H. C. *Report of a Commissary of Subsistence, 1861–65*. Sing Sing, N.Y., 1888.

Temple, William Grenville, U.S.N. *Memoir of the Landing of the United States Troops at Vera Cruz in 1847*. Philadelphia, 1896.

Thacher, James. *A Military Journal During the American Revolutionary War*. Boston, 1827.

Thian, Ralph P. *Legislative History of the General Staff of the Army of the United States.* Washington, 1901.

Trobriand, Regis de. *Four Years with the Army of the Potomac.* Boston, 1889.

Underwood, Thomas Taylor. *Journal of Thomas Taylor Underwood.* Cincinnati, 1945.

Waldo, Albigence. "Valley Forge, 1777–78: Diary of Surgeon Albigence Waldo, of the Continental Line," *Pennsylvania Magazine of History and Biography,* XXI (1897), 299–323.

The War of the Rebellion: A Compilation of the Official Records of the Union and Confederate Armies. Washington, 1880–1901. 130 vols.

Wilkinson, Gen. James. *Memoirs of My Own Times.* Philadelphia, 1816. 3 vols.

Wilson, Frazer E. (ed.). *Journal of Capt. Daniel Bradley.* Greenville, Ohio, 1935.

Winchester, Brig. Gen. James. "Papers and Orderly Book of Brigadier General James Winchester," *Michigan Pioneer and Historical Society Historical Collections,* XXXI, 253–312.

Young, Sergeant William. "Journal of Sergeant William Young. Written during the Jersey Campaign in the Winter of 1776–1777," *Pennsylvania Magazine of History and Biography,* VIII (1884), 255–78.

U.S. Army in the World War, 1917–19. Washington, 1948. 17 vols.

Printed Military Sources

Annual Reports.   Annual Reports of the Secretary of War, the Commissary General of Purchases, the Commissary General of Subsistence, and the Quartermaster General were a valuable source of information, particularly those which carried appended reports of subordinate officers and other documentary material.   These reports are located as follows:

American State Papers, Class V *Military Affairs.*   The annual reports the period 1822 to 1838 are printed in these volumes.

Senate *Executive Documents,* and House *Executive Documents.* 25th–36th Congress.   The annual reports are printed in either the Senate or House *Executive Documents* for the years 1839–1860.

Annual Reports.   For the years 1861 through 1920, the annual reports of the Secretary of War, including subordinate offices, were printed and published in Washington each year.   The annual reports of the Quartermaster General were also printed and published separately in Washington.   A bound compilation of the Civil War reports of the Quartermaster General 1861–65, is particularly informative and useful.

Record Group No. 94.   AGO file 319.12.   National Archives. Though annual reports were prepared by the Quartermaster General for the years 1921 through 1938, they were not printed for reasons of economy.   They are available at the National Archives and are noted here to complete the record of location.

General Orders, Circulars, Bulletins.   Generally, the instructions primarily of the War Department, Adjutant General's Office, and Quartermaster General's Office are used in this volume.   Those printed and compiled and bound, normally on a yearly basis, after about 1860 are readily available.   Orders were printed for many years before that date, but few collections of them exist outside of the National Archives.

Laws.   The following collections of military laws are useful:

Callahan, John F.   *The Military Laws of the United States.*   Baltimore, 1858.
Cross, Col. Trueman.   *Military Laws of the United States.*   Washington, 1838.
Hetzel, Capt. Abner R.   *Military Laws of the United States.*   Washington, 1846.   3d edition.

Registers.   The following provide the military service record of officers:

Cullum, Bvt. Maj. Gen. George W.   *Biographical Register of Officers and Graduates of the Military Academy at West Point, N.Y., From Its Establishment, in 1802 to 1890.*   New York, 1891.   3 vols.   3d ed., revised.   Supplemental volumes 4 through 9 cover the period 1890–1950.
Hamersly, Thomas H. D.   *Complete Regular Army Register of the United States for One Hundred Years, 1779–1879.*   Washington, 1880.
Heitman, Francis B.   *Historical Register of Officers of th Continental Army During the War of the Revolution, April, 1775, to December, 1783.*   Washington, 1914.   Revised and enlarged edition.
————.   *Historical Register and Dictionary of the United States Army, 1789–1903.*   Washington, 1903.   2 vols.

Regulations.   The following early regulations for the Army, published periodically were useful:

General Regulations for the Army.   Washington, 1821, 1825, 1835, 1841.
Revised Regulations for the Army of the United States, 1861.

Legislative Sources

Annals of Congress, 1789–1824.   Washington, 1825–37.   42 vols.
Journal of the Executive Proceedings of the Senate of the United States, 1789–1901. Washington, 1828–1909.   32 vols.
Hearings:
Army Reorganization.   Hearings before the Committee on Military Affairs, House of Representatives, 66th Cong., 1st and 2d sessions.   Washington, 1920.
Historical Documents Relating to the Reorganization Plans of the War Department and to the Present National Defense Act.   Hearings before the Committee on Military Affairs, House of Representatives, 69th Cong., 2d session.   Washington, 1927.
Investigation of the War Department.   Hearings before the Committee on Military Affairs, Senate, 65th Cong., 2d session.   Washington, 1918.   8 parts.
Reorganization of the Army.   Hearings before the Subcommittee of the Committee on Military Affairs, Senate, 66th Cong., 1st and 2d sessions.   Washington, 1919.
Staff Service of the Army, General Service Corps, Consolidation of Certain Branches. Hearings held before the Committee on Military Affairs, House of Representatives, 62d Cong., Washington, 1911.
War Expenditures.   Hearings held before the Select Committee on Expenditures in the War Department, House of Representatives, 66th Cong., 2d session.
House *Executive Documents:*
No. 119, 29th Cong., 2d sess.   "Correspondence with General Taylor."
No. 60, 30th Cong., 1st sess.   "Messages of the President of the United States, with the Correspondence Therewith Communicated between the Secretary of War and Other Officers of the Government, on the Subject of the Mexican War."   Washington, 1848.
No. 91, 33d Cong., 2d sess.   "Report upon the Cost of Transporting Troops and

Supplies to California, Oregon, New Mexico, Etc. by Maj. Gen. Thomas S. Jesup, QMG."

No. 17, 34th Cong., 1st sess., s.n. 851. "Army Contracts, 1855."

No. 33, 35th Cong., 1st sess., s.n. 955 "Estimate for Utah Expedition."

No. 50, 35th Cong., 2d sess., s.n. 1006 "Army Contracts, 1858."

No. 58, 35th Cong., 1st sess., s.n. 955 "Army Contracts, 1857."

No. 58, 35th Cong., 2d sess., s.n. 1006 "Army Contracts, 1857."

No. 71, 35th Cong., 1st sess., s.n. 956. "Utah Expedition."

No. 99, 35th Cong., 1st sess., s.n. 958. "Contracts, Utah Expedition."

No. 23, 39th Cong., 2d sess., s.n. 1288. "Inspection Reports, 1866."

No. 111, 39th Cong., 2d sess., s.n. 1293. "Ingalls Inspection Report, 1866."

No. 377, 40th Cong., 2d sess., s.n. 1346. "Vessels Bought, Sold, and Chartered by the U.S. since April 1861."

No. 618, 57th Cong., 1st sess. "Results of Preliminary Examinations and Surveys of Sites for Military Posts."

House *Miscellaneous Document*

No. 56, 45th Cong., 2d sess. "Reorganization of the Army," Report of a Subcommittee of the Committee on Military Affairs. Washington, 1878.

House *Reports:*

No. 78, 36th Cong., 2d sess., s.n. 1105 "Abstracted Indian Trust Bonds."

No. 2, 37th Cong., 2d sess., s.n. 1142 and 1143. "Government Contracts."

No. 33, 40th Cong., 3d sess., s.n. 1388. "Army Organization, 1869."

No. 74, 42d Cong., 3d sess., s.n. 1576. "Army Staff Organization."

No. 87, 42d Cong., 3d sess., s.n. 1576. "Expenditures in the War Department."

House *Report of Committee*

No. 108, 37th Cong., 3d sess., Report of the Joint Committee on the Conduct of the War. Washington, 1863. 3 parts.

Senate *Executive Documents:*

No. 62, 34th Cong., 3d sess., s.n. 881. "Purchase, Importation, and Use of Camels and Dromedaries to be Employed for Military Purposes, 1857."

No. 37, 37th Cong., 2d sess., s.n. 1122. "Vessels Purchased or Chartered Since April 1861."

No. 221, 56th Cong., 1st sess. "Report of the Commission Appointed by the President to Investigate the Conduct of the War With Spain." Washington, 1900. 8 vols.

No. 270, 56th Cong., 1st sess. "Food Furnished by Subsistence Department to Troops in the Field." Washington, 1900. 3 vols.

Senate *Reports of Committees*

No. 71, 37th Cong., 3d sess., s.n. 1151. Report of the Joint Committee on the Conduct of the War.

No. 75, 37th Cong., 3d sess., s.n. 1151. Report in Part. The select committee of the Senate appointed to inquire into the chartering of transport vessels for the Banks expedition.

No. 84, 37th Cong., 3d sess., s.n. 1151. Report of select committee on transportation for the Banks expedition.

No. 555, 45th Cong., 3d sess "Reorganization of the Army, 1878."

U.S. Statutes at Large.

Secondary Works

Bancroft, Hubert H. *History of Utah.* San Francisco, 1890.

Beers, Henry P. *The Western Military Frontier, 1815–1846.* Philadelphia, 1935.

Billings, John S. *A Report on Barracks and Hospitals with Descriptions of Military Posts.* Washington, 1870.

Bolton, Charles K. *The Private Soldier Under Washington.* New York, 1902.

Burnett, Edmund C. *The Continental Congress.* New York, 1941.

Carrington, Henry B. *Battles of the American Revolution, 1775–1781.* New York, 1904. 6th ed. revised.

Clark, Victor S. *History of Manufactures in the United States, 1607–1860*. Washington, 1916.

Conkling, Roscoe P., and Margaret B. Conkling. *The Butterfield Overland Mail, 1857–69* Glendale, Calif., 1947. 2 vols.

Crowell, Benedict, and Robert F. Wilson. *The Armies of Industry*. New Haven, 1921. 2 vols.

Crowell, Benedict. *The Road to France*. New Haven, 1921. 2 vols.

Crowell, J. Franklin. *Government War Contracts*. New York, 1920.

Curtis, Edward E. *The Organization of the British Army in the American Revolution*. New Haven, 1926.

Davis, Joseph S. *Essays in the Earlier History of American Corporations*. Harvard Economic Studies, XVI. Cambridge, 1917.

Duane, William. *Military Dictionary*. Philadelphia, 1810.

Dunbar, Seymour. *A History of Travel in America*. New York, 1937.

East, Robert A. *Business Enterprise in the American Revolutionary Era*. Columbia University Press, 1938.

Fortescue, Sir John W. *A History of the British Army*. London, 1899–1930. 13 vols.

Frantz, Joe B. *Gail Borden, Dairyman to a Nation*. Norman, 1951.

Freeman, Douglas S. *George Washington*. New York, 1948–52. 6 vols.

French, Allen. *The First Year of the American Revolution*. New York, 1934.

Ganoe, William A. *The History of the United States Army*. New York, 1924.

Gosnell, H. Allen. *Guns on the Western Waters*. Louisiana State University Press, 1949.

Gras, N. S. B., and Henrietta M. Larson. *Casebook in American Business History*. New York, 1939.

Greene, Francis V. *The Revolutionary War and the Military Policy of the United States*. New York, 1911.

Greene, George W. *The Life of Nathanael Greene*. New York, 1871. 3 vols.

Hatch, Louis C. *The Administration of the American Revolutionary Army*. Harvard Historical Studies, X. New York, 1904.

Henry, Robert S. *This Fascinating Railroad Business*. New York, 1942.

——. *The Story of the Mexican War*. New York, 1950.

Hittle, James D. *The Military Staff: Its History and Development*. Harrisburg, Pa., 1944.

Holdcamper, Forrest R. (ed.) *Merchant Steam Vessels of the United States, 1807–1868*. The Steamship Historical Society of America, *Publication* No. 6. Mystic, Conn., 1952.

Hungerford, Edward. *The Story of the Baltimore and Ohio Railroad, 1827–1927*. New York, 1928. 2 vols.

Hunter, Louis C. *Steamboats on the Western Rivers*. Cambridge, 1949.

Jacobs, James R. *The Beginning of the U.S. Army, 1783–1812*. Princeton, 1947.

James, Marquis. *The Life of Andrew Jackson*. New York, 1940.

Jessup, Philip C. *Elihu Root*. New York, 1938. 2 vols.

Johnson, Victor L. *The Administration of the American Commissariat During the Revolutionary War*. Philadelphia, 1941.

Johnston, Henry P. *The Yorktown Campaign and the Surrender of Cornwallis, 1781*. New York, 1881.

Kamm, Samuel R. *The Civil War Career of Thomas A. Scott*. Philadelphia, 1940.

Kapp, Friedrich. *The Life of John Kalb*. New York, 1884.

Freidberg, Marvin A., and Merton G. Henry. *History of Military Mobilization in the United States Army, 1775–1945*. Department of the Army Pamphlet No. 20–212. Washington, 1955.

Lewis, Lloyd. *Sherman Fighting Prophet*. New York, 1932.

Martin, I. J. Griffin. *Stephen Moylan*. Philadelphia, 1909.

Meneely, A. Howard. *The War Department, 1861*. New York, 1928.

Nevins, Allen. *Fremont the West's Greatest Adventurer*. New York, 1928.

Palmer, Frederick. *Newton D. Baker*. New York, 1911. 2 vols.

Pelzer, Louis. *Marches of the Dragoons in the Mississippi Valley*. Iowa City, 1917.

Perkins, Jacob R. *Trails, Rails and War, The Life of General, G. M. Dodge.* Indianapolis, 1929.

Phisterer, Frederick. *Statistical Record of the Armies of the United States.* New York, 1901.

Pickering, Octavious, and Charles W. Upham. *The Life of Timothy Pickering.* Boston, 1867–73. 4 vols.

Pitkin, Thomas M., and Herbert R. Rifkind. *Procurement Planning in the Quartermaster Corps, 1920–40.* QMC HISTORICAL STUDIES No. 1, n.p., 1943.

Plum, William R. *The Military Telegraphy During the Civil War in the United States.* Chicago, 1882. 2 vols.

Risch, Erna, and Thomas M. Pitkin. *Clothing the Soldier of World War II.* QMC HISTORICAL STUDIES No. 16. Washington, 1946.

Risch, Erna. *Demobilization Planning and Operation in the Quartermaster Corps.* QMC HISTORICAL STUDIES No. 19. Washington, 1948.

———. *The Quartermaster Corps: Organization, Supply, and Services,* I. U.S. ARMY IN WORLD WAR II. Washington, 1953.

——— and C. L. Kieffer, *The Quartermaster Corps; Organization, Supply, and Services,* II. U.S. ARMY IN WORLD WAR II. Washington, 1955.

Sanders, Jennings B. *Evolution of Executive Departments of the Continental Congress, 1774–1789.* Chapel Hill, 1935.

Settle, Raymond W., and Mary Lund Settle. *Empire on Wheels.* Stanford University Press, 1940.

Shannon, Fred A. *The Organization and Administration of the Union Army, 1861–1865.* Cleveland, 1928. 2 vols.

Sharpe, Henry G. *The Art of Supplying Armies in the Field as Exemplified During the Civil War.* n.p., n.d.

Simes, Thomas. *The Military Guide for Young Officers.* Philadelphia, 1776. 2 vols.

Smith, Justin H. *The War with Mexico.* New York, 1919. 2 vols.

Smith, R. Elbertson. *The Army and Economic Mobilization.* U.S. ARMY IN WORLD WAR II. Washington, 1959.

Spaulding, Oliver I. *The United States Army in War and Peace.* New York, 1937.

Sprague, John T. *The Origin, Progress, and Conclusion of the Florida War.* New York, 1848.

Steere, Edward. *The Graves Registration Service in World War II.* QMC HISTORICAL STUDIES No. 21. Washington, 1951.

Steiner, Bernard C. *The Life and Correspondence of James McHenry.* Cleveland, 1907.

Stille, Charles J. *Major General Anthony Wayne and the Pennsylvania Line in the Continental Army.* Philadelphia, 1893.

Sumners, Festus P. *The Baltimore and Ohio in the Civil War.* New York, 1939.

Thatcher, Harold W. *The Development of Special Rations for the Army.* QMC HISTORICAL STUDIES No. 6. Washington, 1944.

———. *Planning for Industrial Mobilization, 1920–40.* QMC HISTORICAL STUDIES No. 4. n.p., 1943.

Thayer, Theodore. *Nathanael Greene Strategist of the American Revolution.* New York, 1960.

Turner, George E. *Victory Rode the Rails.* Indianapolis, 1953.

Upton, Emory. *The Military Policy of the United States.* Washington, 1912. 3d edition.

Wardlow, Chester. *The Transportation Corps: Responsibilities, Organization, and Operations.* U.S. ARMY IN WORLD WAR II. Washington, 1951.

Watson, Mark S. *Chief of Staff: Prewar Plans and Preparations.* U.S. ARMY IN WORLD WAR II. Washington, 1950.

Weber, Thomas. *The Northern Railroads in the Civil War, 1861–1865.* New York, 1952.

Weigley, Russell F. *Quartermaster General of the Union Army.* New York, 1959.

Williams, Kenneth P. *Lincoln Finds a General.* New York, 1949–56. 4 vols.

Yoshpe, Harry B., and Marion V. Massen. *Procurement Policies and Procedures in the Quartermaster Corps During World War II.* QMC HISTORICAL STUDIES No. 17. Washington, 1947.

Magazine Articles

Aleshire, James B. "Remounts," *Journal of the United States Cavalry Association*, XVIII, No. 66 (Oct 1907), 279–326.

"Arlington National Cemetery," *The Quartermaster Review*, XVI (May–June 1937), 29–33, 66–68.

Barnes, Will C. "Camels on Safari," *The Quartermaster Review*, XVI (Jan–Feb 1937), 7–13, 68–72.

Brown, M. L. "Asa Whitney and His Pacific Railroad Publicity Campaign," *Mississippi Valley Historical Review*, XX (Sep 1933), 209–24.

Burnett, Edmund C. "Continental Congress and Agricultural Supplies," *Agricultural History*, II, No. 3 (Jul 1928), 111–28.

Cometti, Elizabeth. "The Civil Servants of the Revolutionary Period," *Pennsylvania Magazine of History and Biography*, vol. 75, pp. 159–69.

Curtis, Edward E. "The Provisioning of the British Army in the Revolution," *The Magazine of History, with Notes and Queries*, XVIII, 232–241.

Egan, Maj. P. R. "Mat Ration in the Tropics," *Journal of the Military Service Institution of the United States*, vol. 29, pp. 24–28.

Fitzpatrick, John C. "Bread and the Superintendent of Bakers of the Continental Army," *DAR Magazine*, LVI, No. 9 (Sep 1922), 513–20.

Fitz Gerald, Capt. Francis V. "The President Prescribes—The Organization and Supply of the C.C.C.," *The Quartermaster Review*, XIII (Jul–Aug 1933), 7–18.

Ford, George B. "New Army Posts for Old," *The Quartermaster Review*, IX (Nov–Dec 1929), 9–22.

Greene, Fred. "The Military View of American National Policy, 1904–40," *American Historical Review*, LXVI, No. 2 (Jan 1961), 354–77.

Hart, Charles H. "Colonel Robert Lettis Hooper, Deputy Quartermaster General in the Continental Army and Vice President of New Jersey," *Pennsylvania Magazine of History and Biography*, XXXVI (1912), 60–91.

Horton, Brig. Gen. William E. "The Work of the Construction Service, Quartermaster Corps," *The Quartermaster Review*, VIII (Sep–Oct 1928), 6–9.

Jameson, J. Franklin. "Correspondence of John C. Calhoun," American Historical Association, *Annual Report for 1899*, II, 93–1204.

——. "Papers of Maj. Gen. Nathanael Greene," Rhode Island Historical Society *Publications*, vol. 3, No. 3, pp. 159–67.

King, John. "John Plumbe, Originator of the Pacific Railroad," *Annals of Iowa*, vol. VI, 3d ser. (Jan 1904), 289–96.

Knopf, Richard C. "Wayne's Western Campaign: The Wayne-Knox Correspondence, 1793–94," *Pennsylvania Magazine of History and Biography*, vol, 78, No. 3 (Jul 1954), 298–341.

Ludwig, Christopher. "Christopher Ludwig, Baker-General in the Army of the United States During the Revolutionary War," *Pennsylvania Magazine of History and Biography*, XVI (April 1892), 343–48.

McKee, Marguerite M. "Service of Supply in the War of 1812," *The Quartermaster Review*, VI (Jan–Feb 1927), 6–19; (Mar–Apr 1927), 45–55.

Millett, Lt. Col. John D. "The Direction of Supply Activities in the War Department: An Administrative Survey," *The American Political Science Review*, XXXVIII (April 1944), 249–65; (June 1944), 475–98.

Munson, Capt. Edward L. "The Ideal Ration for the American Army in the Tropics," *Journal of the Military Service Institution of the United States*, vol. 26, pp. 309–46.

Nelson, Harold L. "Military Roads for War and Peace, 1781–1836," *Military Affairs*, XIX, No. 1 (Spring, 1955), 1–14.

Parker, Theodore R. "William J. Kountz, Superintendent of River Transportation Under McClellan, 1861–62," *The Western Pennsylvania Historical Magazine*, XXI, 237–54.

Robinson, C. W. "The Life of Judge Augustus Porter," *Publications* of the Buffalo Historical Society, VII (1904), 229–75.

Seaman, Maj. Louis L. "The Soldier's Ration in the Tropics—Its Use and Its Abuse," *Journal of the Military Service Institution of the United States*, vol. 28, pp. 83–95.

———. "The U.S. Army Ration and Its Adaptability for Use in Tropical Climates," *Journal of the Military Service Institution of the United States*, vol. 24, pp. 375–97.

Stayer, Col. Edgar S. "The Year's Advancement in Military Motor Transport," *The Quartermaster Review*, XII (Jul–Aug 1932), 33–37.

Tomes, Robert. "The Fortunes of War," *Harper's New Monthly Magazine*, XXIX (June 1864), 227–31.

Trumbull, J. Hammond. "A Business Firm of the Revolution, Barnabas Deane & Co., *Magazine of American History with Notes and Queries*, XII (1884), 17–28.

Williams, Samuel. "Two Western Campaigns in the War of 1812," Ohio Valley Historical Series *Miscellanies*, VII (1871), No. 2, 9–53.

Wright, Col. John W. "Some Notes on the Continental Army," *William and Mary College Quarterly Historical Magazine*,. XI, second series, No. 2 (Apr 1931), pp. 81–105 and No. 3 (July 1931), pp. 185–209; XII, second series, No. 2 (April 1932), pp. 79–103.

Wymans, Walker D. "Freighting: A Big Business on the Santa Fe Trail," *The Kansas Historical Quarterly*, vol. 1. (Nov 1931), No. 1, pp. 17–27.

———. "The Military Phase of Santa Fe Freighting, 1846–1865," *The Kansas Historical Quarterly*, vol. 1 (Nov 1932), No. 5, pp. 415–428.

Index

☆US GOVERNMENT PRINTING OFFICE : 1989 O - 247-883 : QL 3